THE ENCYCLOPEDIA OF

TAXATION & TAX POLICY

SECOND EDITION

Edited by

Joseph J. Cordes
Robert D. Ebel
AND
Jane G. Gravelle

Also of interest from Urban Institute Press:

Contemporary U.S. Tax Policy
by C. Eugene Steuerle

Local Tax Policy: A Federalist Perspective
by David Brunori

Property-Tax Exemption for Charities
edited by Evelyn Brody

Tax Justice: The Ongoing Debate
edited by Joseph J. Thorndike and Dennis J. Ventry Jr.

State Tax Policy: A Political Perspective
by David Brunori

SECOND
EDITION

THE ENCYCLOPEDIA OF

TAXATION & TAX POLICY

THE URBAN INSTITUTE PRESS
Washington, D.C.

THE URBAN INSTITUTE PRESS
2100 M Street, N.W.
Washington, D.C. 20037

Library of Congress Cataloging-in-Publication Data

The encyclopedia of taxation and tax policy / Joseph J. Cordes, Robert D. Ebel, and Jane G. Gravelle, editors.— 2nd ed.
    p. cm.
 Includes bibliographical references and index.
 ISBN 0-87766-752-7 (alk. paper)
 1. Taxation—Encyclopedias. I. Cordes, Joseph J. II. Ebel, Robert D. III. Gravelle, Jane. IV. Urban Institute.
 HJ2305.E53 2005
 336.2'003—dc22

                                                    2005020901

ISBN 0-87766-752-7 (paper, alk. paper)

Printed in the United States of America

10 09 08 07 06 05   1 2 3 4 5

THE URBAN INSTITUTE is a nonprofit, non-partisan policy research and educational organization established in Washington, D.C., in 1968. Its staff investigates the social, economic, and governance problems confronting the nation and evaluates the public and private means to alleviate them. The Institute disseminates its research findings through publications, its web site, the media, seminars, and forums.

Through work that ranges from broad conceptual studies to administrative and technical assistance, Institute researchers contribute to the stock of knowledge available to guide decisionmaking in the public interest.

Conclusions or opinions expressed in Institute publications are those of the authors and do not necessarily reflect the views of officers or trustees of the Institute, advisory groups, or any organizations that provide financial support to the Institute. In addition, the conclusions or opinions expressed by the authors do not necessarily reflect the views of the authors' emloyers, agencies, or organizations.

Contents

Foreword

Taxes are a mirror of a people's values and priorities. They provide invaluable insights into how individuals relate to one another, to their government, and to their broader society. Who pays taxes, how much, on what basis, and for what services are central questions that help define a nation's concept of fairness.

The editors of *The Encyclopedia of Taxation and Tax Policy* are acutely aware of the role taxes play in society, in the economy, and in governance. As they note in the preface, taxes combine the best of human motives—paying for needed services that people acting privately have little incentive to offer—with what some would call the worst attribute of social organization—using the power of governments to commandeer part of individuals' income for collective pursuits.

The first edition of the *Encyclopedia* was a formidable undertaking, one that responded to a need first identified by members of the National Tax Association for an authoritative, comprehensive, readable guide to key issues of public finance. That volume was nearly five years in the making. While digitization speeded up the production of this second edition, it nevertheless was a complex, time-consuming undertaking involving 236 contributions from all areas of tax scholarship and practice.

The editors have structured this book to encompass both broad tax issues, such as ability to pay, tax evasion, and fairness in taxation, and narrow ones, such as the inverse elasticity rule, seigniorage, and capital import neutrality. The entries' concise definitions, knowledgeable and clearly written essays, and references to other information sources should appeal not only to specialists seeking out the thinking of other experts, but to general readers as well. Dry as the topic may seem, the entries are not devoid of humor, such as the observation that some farm owners seeking to offset high nonfarm income may be more engaged in "farming the tax code" than the land.

Making the complex understandable was the editors' goal in compiling the *Encyclopedia*. Some entries correct popular misconceptions. For example, the mortgage interest deduction is by no means the principal tax benefit of owning a home (untaxed imputed rent is). Others shed light on the complexities of estimating the impacts of much debated aspects of the tax code. For example, it is extremely difficult to compute the average size of the marriage penalty because we know little about how much partners' would earn and thus the taxes they would pay if they were not part of the same tax-filing unit. Still others translate for the informed generalist arcane terms experts use with abandon. For example, the entry defining sumptuary taxes notes that this type of excise tax, which is designed to discourage the consumption of specific commodities or services, is more familiarly known as a sin tax.

The *Encyclopedia* is an important element on the Urban Institute Press's distinguished list of books on federal and state taxation and tax policy. As a growing deficit gnaws away at policymakers' tax and spending options, tax issues have become more important to policymakers and the public. The insights and understanding this *Encyclopedia* and the other Urban Institute tax books can bring to the debate over tax policy are needed now more than ever.

William Gorham   Robert Reischauer
President Emeritus   President
The Urban Institute   The Urban Institute

Preface to the
Second Edition

Taxes are what we pay for civilized society.

U.S. Supreme Court Associate Justice Oliver Wendell Holmes Jr.
Compania General de Tabacos de Filipinas v. Collector of Internal Revenue
275 US 87, 100 (1927)

Far-reaching economic developments have forced policymakers, analysts, and the public they serve to revisit basic questions on the structure and level of the public's finances and government's role in determining both. These developments range from marketplace globalization and the accompanying difficulty of taxing mobile factors of production, a continuing shift to an economy based on services and communications instead of bricks-and-mortar manufacturing, a growth in e-commerce and electronic technology that can either erode or broaden tax bases and simplify or complicate tax administration, and an aging population that demands public expenditures but is less readily taxable by many conventional means.

Also at play are less sweeping and often arcane changes that nevertheless carry huge implications for taxes. For instance, the growing sophistication of tax planning can lead to both legitimate tax avoidance and illegal evasion. The advent of electronic money has caused a corresponding decline in the paper trails that allow transactions to be followed—for good or ill. And as taxes and the tax system grow more complex, policy changes are often legislated piecemeal, with little regard for the system as a whole or for their long-term effects.

Fortunately, these changes in the tax environment have been accompanied by dramatic advances in the knowledge of public finance economics. In the past 25 years, the frontiers of public finance theory have been expanded, and the literature on how to finance the public sector and how taxes work and affect behavior has burgeoned. Frameworks for public-sector decision-making have evolved (e.g., public choice theory, cost-benefit analysis, optimal taxation), and so have the tools (from sophisticated spreadsheet models and dynamic scoring techniques to the development and maturity of mathematical and statistical microsimulation techniques). Meanwhile, new fields are appearing. Although students of public finance have long examined state and local finances along with federal finances, not until the early 1960s did the knowledge base on fiscal decentralization and intergovernmental relations develop in earnest, and not until the 1990s did much of the new thinking about models for multitiered assignment of taxing powers, intergovernmental grants, and local public goods emerge.

Why does it all matter? From the scholastic writings of St. Thomas Aquinas (c. 1225–1274), who tried to resolve the issue of what makes a "just price," to those of the 19th century classical economists, particularly Smith, Malthus, Ricardo, and Marshall, who called their discipline "political economy," a core question has been what could be done to make public and private institutions responsive to people's needs and society as a whole better off.

In sum, the issues of taxation and tax policy combine the best human motives—paying for needed services that people acting privately have little or no incentive to offer—and, for some, the worst social organization—using government's power to commandeer part of one's income for collective pursuits. These motives and misgivings energize but also cloud broad debates on such issues as the "proper" criteria for distributing the tax payment responsibility, the structure of fiscal relationships among governments, and the art of forecasting and monitoring tax flows. They even permeate questions about details—for example, inventory accounting, trust fund finance, apportionment of multistate and multinational business income, the fair and efficient treatment of various business sectors, and tax shelters.

But whether the topics are as broad as the principles of just taxation or as narrow as the mechanisms of a tax credit for low-income housing, what pulls it all together and makes it important is that a system of taxation is more than a compendium of dry tax law and economic data. It is also an expression of community relationships among individuals and between the people and their governments.

Research on the first edition of this book began ten years ago when the National Tax Association (NTA)—a unique organization that represents a cross section of tax practitioners and administrators, policymakers, business executives, and academics—identified a major gap in the economic policy knowledge base: despite a wealth of scholarly literature, textbooks, and digital information, there was no "knowledge central"—no single source of rigorously peer reviewed but highly readable information on the key issues of public finance.

This gap prompted the best tax scholars and practitioners to put together the *Encyclopedia on Taxation and Tax Policy*. The goal is to provide a reference book on tax and tax-related public sector issues in a format that generalists and seasoned experts alike can use to get a quick and reliable introduction to a topic and specialists can rely on for the best thinking of other experts. For some, this volume will serve as a quick one-stop source for definitions, concepts, and topic overviews. However, others may want to read the book cover to cover to get an overview of the discipline and a sense of how various tax issues relate to one another.

The essays in this book cover the full range of U.S. tax issues. Entries included cover

(i)   fundamental economic concepts and behavior (e.g., tax incidence, effects of taxes on labor supply, savings, portfolio choice);

(ii)   more specialized economic and tax concepts (e.g., capital export neutrality, cost of capital, and tax illusion);

(iii)   each type of tax levied (e.g., income, sales, property) and taxes levied in other countries or under consideration in the United States (e.g., a national value-added tax) and on nontax revenues;

(iv)   important features of current taxes (e.g., deductions for charitable contributions, taxation of multinational corporations, circuit breakers);

(v)   tax measurement and accounting (revenue estimating and forecasting, basis, depreciation, deferral);

(vi)   tax administration and related topics (e.g., tax evasion, intergovernmental cooperation, economic substance doctrine, property tax assessment);

(vii)   techniques and tools of tax analysis (e.g., generational accounting, general equilibrium models, progressivity measures);

(viii) institutions (nature and role of congressional committees, federal and state tax offices, and public interest groups); and

(ix)   important related public finance issues (budgets and budget processes, federalism).

Selecting the authors for each of the essays in this book was easy: the membership of the National Tax Association comprises the nation's top experts in public-sector economics. By drawing largely on NTA members, who combine a historical understanding of public financing with an up-to-date, "hands-on" perspective, the editors identified the best authors, who, in turn, helped compile the list of essay topics.

It was a pleasure to work with all the contributors to the *Encyclopedia*. All met their deadlines and gave priority to both updating their essays and preparing the 45 new entries, so revision went quickly. We are especially grateful to contributors who stepped in to update essays when the original authors could not and to those who amended entries at the last minute as new evidence came in and laws were revised. Further help and advice was also received from Gerald Bair, Joan Casey, Victor Chen, Wayne Eggert, William Fox, William Gorham, Steve Maguire, Frederick Giertz, Jennifer Gravelle, Sonya Hoo, Anya Arax Manjarrez, Sandy Navin, Theresa Plummer, Betty Smith, Eugene Steuerle, Emil Sunley, Frederick Stocker, and the members of the NTA's Board of Directors. A very special thanks goes our colleagues at the Urban Institute Press, who combined long hours of expert work with good judgment in order to make this second edition suitable for publication: Will Bradbury, Kathleen Courrier, and Scott Forrey.

The Editors Joseph J. Cordes
           Robert D. Ebel
           Jane G. Gravelle

Ability to pay

Richard A. Musgrave
Harvard University and University of California at Santa Cruz

One of two widely held principles of fair taxation.

Dating back to Adam Smith, this principle calls for people to contribute to the cost of government in line with their ability to pay. Accomplishing this requires that tax burdens be assigned so that individuals with a higher ability to contribute will pay more. Thus, tax liabilities are to be distributed so as to equalize burdens across taxpayers whose capacities differ. The principle is appealing, and a further discussion of its merits and of how equal burdens are to be defined is given elsewhere. Here, some major problems of implementing ability-to-pay taxation are noted.

To begin with, an index has to be chosen to measure taxable capacity or ability to pay. Two centuries ago, property and wealth measured ability to pay; income has since replaced property and wealth as the best indicator. Recently, support has increased for using consumption as a measure.

Because ability to pay relates to the taxpaying capacity of individuals, ability-to-pay taxation requires a direct and personal form of taxation. The personal income tax meets this condition, but indirect consumption taxes, such as the sales or value-added tax, do not. This limitation, however, does not apply to an expenditure tax, assessed on the taxpayer's total consumption. Therefore, an expenditure tax would permit the use of exemptions and progressive rates as under the income tax.

Cross-references: benefit principle; consumption taxation; fairness in taxation; tax equity analysis.

Adjusted current earnings

Mark B. Booth
Congressional Budget Office

A broad measure of a corporation's income used to calculate federal income tax liability from the alternative minimum tax.

In the Tax Reform Act of 1986, Congress designed the alternative minimum tax (AMT) system for corporations. This Act created a broader measure of the federal income tax base and included an adjustment based on adjusted current earnings (ACE). Congress defined ACE to conform closely to earnings and profits as described in the Internal Revenue Code. From 1987 to 1989, Congress temporarily placed in effect a similar adjustment based on the company's book income rather than ACE, after which the adjustment was based on ACE. Congress instituted the AMT system with the adjustments for ACE or book income to ensure that corporate taxpayers with significant economic income could not substantially reduce or eliminate their income tax through tax-preferred exclusions, deductions, or credits.

Since the inception of ACE, its contribution to the alternative minimum tax has changed largely because of legislative changes. From 1991 to 1993, ACE contributed roughly half of the broader tax base under the AMT system compared with the regular tax system. Tax law changes enacted in the Omnibus Budget Reconciliation Act of 1993 substantially reduced the importance of ACE. However, the Taxpayer Relief Act of 1997 changed the AMT tax base to conform more closely to the regular tax before the ACE adjustment, thus increasing the importance of the ACE adjustment.

Computing ACE

Corporations calculate ACE after making specific AMT adjustments to the regular income tax base for certain excluded income and allowed deductions. Corporations first make these specific adjustments—most important to depreciation of capital assets—to compute an interim measure of their AMT base called preadjustment alternative minimum taxable income (AMTI). To compute ACE, they then make three further modifications, the "adjustment based on ACE": (1) to include income, such as tax-exempt income, that is required in calculating earnings and profits but not required in calculating preadjustment AMTI; (2) to exclude deductions, such as the dividends-received deduction, that are allowed in calculating preadjustment AMTI but not in calculating earnings and profits; (3) to include other income or exclude other deductions as specified separately, such as for depreciation, that are unrelated to earnings and profits.

After computing ACE, corporations calculate their (post-adjustment) AMTI by adding an amount equal to 75 percent of the difference between ACE and the preadjustment AMTI to the preadjustment AMTI. In effect, the income included and deductions disallowed by the adjustment for ACE are taxed at only 75 percent of the 20 percent tax rate applied to the full AMT base. In contrast, the specific adjustments made to calculate the preadjustment AMTI are, in effect, taxed at the full 20 percent rate.

A corporation's adjustment based on ACE may be negative in certain years—reducing preadjustment AMTI—if past positive adjustments were a result of timing effects. For example, if some of a corporation's depreciation is delayed but not permanently disallowed, the ACE adjustment could become negative when the depreciation is allowed. Permanent adjustments for ACE, such as those resulting from tax-exempt income or the dividends-received deduction, do not cause this timing effect. In any given year, the adjustment based on ACE may reduce preadjustment AMTI only to the extent that the adjustments in previous years had increased preadjustment AMTI (net of previous reductions).

Depreciation rules

Analysts estimate that depreciation was the most important adjustment based on ACE until the tax law changed in 1993. (We cannot know with certainty the magnitude of the various adjustments because corporations do not report them separately on their income tax returns.) In general, for an asset placed in service after 1989, but before 1994, ACE requires that depreciation be calculated using the straight-line method over the asset's useful lifetime. For equipment investment, this depreciation method compares unfavorably with calculating preadjustment AMTI, which allows firms to accelerate depreciation at a rate not to exceed one and one-half times the straight-line rate (the 150 percent declining balance method). For assets placed in service from 1981 through 1989, ACE requires that the remaining basis be depreciated under the straight-line method, rather than allowing some acceleration as under the depreciation system used to calculate preadjustment AMTI. (These calculations are further complicated, in some cases, by the required use of the depreciation lifetime used for book purposes.)

The Omnibus Budget Reconciliation Act of 1993 repealed the separate depreciation calculation for ACE, effective for property placed in service after December 31, 1993. Many people had criticized the depreciation adjustment for ACE because it further complicated corporate tax accounting. The adjustment for ACE has become much less significant since 1993, as corporations have replaced old property with new property that does not require any adjustment. From 1991 to 1993, the adjustment based on ACE averaged about 5 percent of total receipts less total deductions of corporations. For each year from 1995 through 2000, the adjustment measured about 1 percent of total receipts less total deductions.

The Taxpayer Relief Act of 1997 conformed AMTI depreciation recovery periods to regular depreciation periods. (Differences remained in the rates of depreciation allowed under the two systems.) The change to AMTI recovery periods made ACE relatively more important in the AMT base, but firms became less likely to fall under the AMT. In 2000, for the first time since 1991, more of the AMT base was generated by the adjustment based on ACE than by the AMTI adjustment for depreciation.

Other components

The other components of the adjustment based on ACE have remained generally unchanged since 1986 and remain in effect. These include adjustments for depletion allowances, intangible drilling costs, construction period carrying charges, long-term contracts, installment sales, asset bases following ownership changes, and inventories that use the last in, first out (LIFO) accounting method. The adjustments based on earnings and profits, such as for tax-exempt income and the dividends-received deduction, also have been unchanged.

ADDITIONAL READINGS

Gerardi, G. Geraldine, Hudson Milner, and Gerald Silverstein. "The Effects of the Corporate Alternative Minimum Tax: Additional Results from Panel Data for 1987–1991." In *National Tax Association—Tax Institute of America, Proceedings of the Eighty-Sixth Annual Conference, 1993,* edited by Frederick Stocker (40–49). Columbus, OH: National Tax Association, 1994.

Lathrope, Daniel J. *The Alternative Minimum Tax: Compliance and Planning with Analysis.* Boston: Warren, Gorham, and Lamont of the RIA Group, 1994, Supplements 1995–2004.

Lyon, Andrew B. *Cracking the Code: Making Sense of the Corporate Alternative Minimum Tax.* Washington, DC: The Brookings Institution, 1997.

U.S. Department of the Treasury. *Statistics of Income, Corporation Income Tax Returns.* Washington, DC: U.S. Department of the Treasury, Internal Revenue Service, various years.

Cross-references: alternative minimum tax, corporate; basis; earnings and profits.

Adjusted gross income
Susan C. Nelson and Julie-Anne Cronin
U.S. Department of the Treasury

A measure of an individual taxpayer's net income used in calculating personal income taxes.

Section 62 of the Internal Revenue Code defines adjusted gross income (AGI) as gross income from all sources not specifically excluded, minus certain deductions. Because AGI is a creature of the tax code, its components have changed over the years with tax law changes.

AGI can be understood in part by comparison with other measures of income. AGI primarily measures money income, not comprehensive income, and it does not include many forms of money income that are part of comprehensive income. From the perspective of the economy as a whole, AGI is similar to personal income in the National Income and Product Accounts (NIPA) but differs from it primarily in the same ways it differs from comprehensive income. In terms of the income tax system, AGI is the broadest measure of income, but, compared with taxable income (the income to which tax rates are applied), AGI does not reflect the personal differences that affect individuals' ability to pay taxes.

Components of AGI

The major sources of income in AGI in 2004 included wages and salaries; taxable interest and dividends; alimony received; business income from partnerships, Subchapter S corporations, sole proprietorships, and farms; rents and royalties; capital gains; taxable pension and Individual Retirement Account (IRA) distributions; unemployment compensation; and some Social Security benefits. The deductions taken in AGI include trade and business expenses, expenses attributable to rents and royalties, and certain losses from the sale or exchange of property. The Form 1040, on which individuals calculate their income tax, refers to other allowable deductions as "adjustments to income" or as "statutory adjustments." For 2004, these adjustments included primarily educator expenses, qualified education and student loan interest expenses, alimony payments, moving expenses, certain savings for retirement (such as contributions to Keogh plans for the self-employed and to IRAs for employees and their spouses), Medical Savings Account and Health Savings Account contributions, one-half of the self-employment tax, and a health insurance deduction for the self-employed.

Recent changes in the definition of AGI

Tax law amendments have changed the definition of AGI in the past 15 years. The most recent income adjustments were for health- and education-related provisions. Legislation in 1996 and 2004 introduced adjustments for contributions to Medical Savings Accounts and Health Savings Accounts. The Tax Reform Act of 1997 and the Economic Growth and Tax Relief Reconciliation Act of 2001 added adjustments for student loan interest, educator expenses, and for certain higher education expenses.

The most significant revisions, expanding the definition of AGI, came in the Tax Reform Act of 1986 (TRA86). Among these revisions were the full inclusion of long-term capital gains (previously, 40 percent was included in the AGI, and before 1979, 50 percent had been included). TRA86 also imposed limits on "passive losses" that would be allowed in calculating AGI. It changed moving expenses and unreimbursed employee business expenses from income "adjustments" to itemized deductions. (Starting in 1994,

moving expenses were again allowed as an adjustment to income instead of as an itemized deduction.) It eliminated the adjustment to income for a married couple with a second earner and the exemption for the first $400 of dividends received. Working to narrow the definition of AGI, TRA86 also allowed self-employed individuals a deduction for up to 25 percent of their health insurance premiums.

Other legislation has made more modest changes in the definition of AGI. Legislation in 1991 added the adjustment to income for one-half of an individual's self-employment tax. In 1984, half of Social Security benefits were for the first time included in the AGI for taxpayers with other income of $25,000 ($32,000 for married couples), and in 1994 the share was increased to 85 percent for individuals with other income of $34,000 ($44,000 if married). Similarly, in 1979 unemployment compensation was initially added to AGI for persons with other income of $20,000 ($25,000 for couples), and in 1987 for all taxpayers regardless of other income. The Economic Recovery Tax Act of 1981 (ERTA) and TRA86 both substantially revised the depreciation schedules, with ERTA liberalizing the deductions and TRA86 tightening them. Consequently, a given amount of business profits (as measured for the company's records) contributed less to AGI in the early 1980s than it did after 1986. Recent tax revisions have added deductions for self-employed individuals' health insurance and education deductions, and have restored some of the deduction for IRAs that had been curtailed in 1986.

Comparison with comprehensive income, personal income, and taxable income

AGI can be compared conceptually and quantitatively to other frequently used measures of income. Comprehensive income, or the Haig-Simons definition of income as consumption plus changes in net worth, is a broader concept of income than AGI.

Haig-Simons is a comprehensive measure of income ("economic income") defined as the increase in an individual's power to consume (sum of consumption plus net wealth). AGI excludes most forms of non-money income as well as some types of money income. Components of comprehensive income not in AGI include imputed rent on owner-occupied housing, unrealized capital gains, and in-kind fringe benefits of employees. Including any of these in income for tax purposes would entail substantial valuation problems. Sources of money income that are missing from AGI include welfare payments, interest on state and local government bonds, employer-provided contributions for health and pension plans, and income on savings through life insurance. These forms of income are excluded more for policy than for administrability reasons.

Personal income in the NIPA is also broader, on balance, than AGI (it amounted to $8.4 trillion in 2000, compared with $6.3 trillion of AGI), but AGI includes $1.6 trillion in sources of income that are missing from personal income. The largest of these is net capital gains ($574 billion), followed by taxable private pensions ($413 billion) and personal contributions to Social Security and related programs ($358 billion). Personal income includes the following major items that are not in AGI: nontaxable transfer payments ($946 billion), employer-provided fringe benefits ($541 billion), investment income of life insurance or private pension funds ($470 billion), imputed rental and personal interest income ($350 billion), and differences in accounting treatment between NIPA and tax regulations ($107 billion). In addition, there is a $792 billion discrepancy, or gap, between AGI as reported to the Internal Revenue Service and AGI as the NIPA would calculate it. Some of the gap represents noncompliance with the tax code (Park 2002).

For tax purposes, AGI represents a broad measure of net income; however, in most respects it does not reflect differences in personal circumstances that the public wants to take into account before levying taxes. Such differences include family size, marital circumstances, or particularly large expenditures for purposes that the public either wants to encourage (such as charitable contributions or home ownership) or views as appropriate adjustments to a measure of ability to pay (such as state and local income taxes, extraordinary medical expenses, or extraordinary casualty losses). More specifically, in 2001 AGI ($6.2 trillion) exceeded taxable income ($4.3 trillion) by the amount of personal exemptions ($728 billion) plus the amount of either itemized deductions ($885 billion) or the standard deduction ($482 billion) (Internal Revenue Service, Individual Income Tax Returns 2001, 31).

ADDITIONAL READINGS

Internal Revenue Service. *Statistics of Income Bulletin* (various years). Washington, DC: Internal Revenue Service.

Park, Thae S. "Comparison of BEA Estimates of Personal Income and IRS Estimates of Adjusted Gross Income." *Survey of Current Business* (November 2002): 13–21.

Pechman, Joseph A. *Federal Tax Policy.* Washington, DC: The Brookings Institution, 1987.

Cross-references: charitable deductions; family, tax treatment of; health expenditures, tax treatment of; income tax, federal; individual retirement accounts; interest deductibility; itemized deductions; Social Security benefits, federal taxation.

Airport and Airway Trust Fund

Joseph J. Cordes
George Washington University

A trust fund established in 1970, financed by aviation excise taxes and dedicated to funding public investments in the air transport system.

The Airport and Airway Trust Fund was established on July 1, 1970, by the Airport and Airway Revenue Act of 1970.

The 1970 act created new aviation user taxes that were to be deposited into the trust fund. These taxes, and interest earned on the deposits, were to be used to meet specified airport and airway obligations in the United States. Authorized expenditures from the trust fund include monies spent on such things as qualified airport planning and construction, safety measures, and related departmental administrative expenses.

The original act that created the trust fund was amended in 1973, 1976, and 1979 to authorize spending for additional items of aviation-related expenditure. These included increased funding for safety and security equipment costs, snow-removal and noise-suppression equipment, construction of physical barriers and landscaping to reduce the effects of airport noise on areas adjacent to public airports, airport terminal development (i.e., public, non-revenue-producing areas including baggage facilities and passenger-moving equipment), and specified amounts for maintenance of airway facilities.

The Omnibus Budget Reconciliation Act of 1990 increased the aviation taxes that finance the trust fund by 25 percent. Aviation user taxes failed to be reenacted as part of the 1995 budget impasse between the president and Congress, but were renewed in the Taxpayer's Relief Act of 1997, which extended aviation-related excise taxes until September 30, 1997. In 2000, The Wendall H. Ford Aviation Investment and Reform Act for the 21st Century (AIR-21) extended the expenditure authority of the trust fund and most significantly ensured that all Airport Trust Fund revenues would be spent on aviation programs.

In 2002 the Airport Trust Fund financed 100 percent of Federal Aviation Administration (FAA) spending for airport improvement, facilities and equipment, and research, engineering and development. Trust fund revenues also covered more than $0.80 of every $1.00 in the FAA budget for operations and maintenance. Overall, the Airport Trust Fund supports more than 90 percent of the FAA budget, with the remainder of FAA funding coming from the Treasury General Fund.

The most important and visible aviation-related excise tax is the Air Passenger Ticket Tax, which equals 7.5 percent of the fare on all domestic airline tickets, plus a charge per domestic flight segment, which in 2002 equaled $3.00 and was indexed for inflation to the Consumer Price Index (CPI) starting in January 2003. In addition, a tax on international departures and international arrivals was initially set at $12.00 in 1997 and was indexed for inflation to the CPI starting in 1999. In 2002 the Air Passenger Ticket Tax and the International Departure/Arrival tax together accounted for about $7.5 billion of a total of $9.1 billion in aviation excise tax revenue. Excise taxes on airline cargo and aviation fuels raised the remaining aviation tax revenues.

In the 1990s all users of U.S. airways and airports expressed concern—also raised by beneficiaries of other federal trust funds—that Congress was reluctant to authorize the full spending of trust fund revenues because trust fund surpluses contributed to reducing the federal budget deficit. There have also been debates about whether the current mix and form of taxes that finance the trust fund allocate the costs of funding public aviation infrastructure fairly among the different users. General and business aviation users of airports believe that the taxes they pay into the trust fund represent a fair share of the benefits they receive from public investments in aviation infrastructure, but commercial users believe that the trust fund subsidizes general and business aviation users because it is largely financed by the tax on passengers of commercial airlines.

ADDITIONAL READINGS

Erin, Henry. "Excise Taxes and the Airport and Airway Trust Fund." *Statistics of Income Bulletin* 23, no. 3 (Winter 2003–2004): 44–51.

U.S. General Accounting Office. *Airport and Airway Trust Fund: Effects of the Trust Fund Taxes' Lapsing on FAA's Budget.* Washington, DC: U.S. General Accounting Office, 1996.

Cross-references: benefit principle; excise taxes; fairness in taxation; user charges, federal.

Alcoholic beverage taxes, federal

Thomas F. Pogue
University of Iowa

Federal alcoholic beverage taxes are of decreasing importance as sources of revenue and in their impact on individuals' consumption decisions.

In fiscal year 2004, alcoholic beverage taxes accounted for less than 0.5 percent of federal revenues, down from over 5 percent in 1950. And they absorb a small and diminishing share of consumers' budgets—less than 0.2 percent of Americans' total consumption spending in 2004.

The taxes are fixed dollar amounts per unit of beverage—in 2004, $13.50 per proof-gallon of distilled spirits; $18 per 31-gallon barrel of beer; $1.07 per gallon of table wine. At these rates, the alcohol in distilled spirits is taxed most heavily, at $0.21 per ounce; alcohol in beer and wine is taxed at $0.10 and $0.07 per ounce, respectively.

Tax rates have been adjusted only infrequently. From 1951 to 2004, the tax on distilled spirits was increased twice (1985 and 1991), and the taxes on beer and table wine were increased once (1991). Since the last tax increase in 1991, inflation has eroded the taxes' real value, which is defined as the purchasing power that consumers lose because of the taxes. From 1991 through 2004, inflation, measured by the consumer price index, reduced the real value of alcohol taxes by 39 percent. The decrease in real value since 1951 has been even greater. To maintain the 1951 levels, the tax on distilled spirits would have to be $76 in 2004 instead of $13.50, the tax on beer would have to be $65 instead of $18, and the tax on wine would have to be $1.24 instead of $1.07.

Congress could have prevented such erosion by indexing the taxes so that they automatically increase enough to offset inflation, or it could have stated the taxes as a percentage of selling price. But it has chosen to do neither.

Taxes on alcoholic beverages are commonly regarded as less fair than broad-based income and consumption taxes because they depend on individuals purchasing alcoholic beverages—something that is not closely related to either individuals' ability to pay taxes or the benefits they receive from government. The taxes are not horizontally equitable because persons with the same income purchase different amounts of the beverages and therefore bear different tax burdens (see *horizontal equity*). Indeed, about 30 percent of all families escape the taxes because they do not buy alcoholic beverages. The taxes are also regressive, absorbing a larger percentage of the income of low-income persons than of middle- and high-income persons (see *progressivity*). The significance of this regressivity is diminished, however, by the fact that about one-half of the poorest one-fifth of families do not purchase alcoholic beverages. Further, alcohol taxes are less regressive when related to lifetime income rather than income for any single year.

In addition to generating revenue, the taxes make alcoholic beverages more expensive, causing consumers to shift some of their purchases to other products. Studies have shown that alcohol abusers, as well as individuals who drink moderately, reduce their consumption of alcohol when beverage prices rise in response to either taxes or other factors. Drinking by young and underage people appears to be especially sensitive to alcohol prices. For a review of studies of the effects of prices and taxes on alcohol consumption, see National Institute on Alcohol Abuse and Alcoholism (2000, 341–54).

The potential for reducing abusive consumption is the main rationale for taxing alcoholic beverages more heavily than most other products. Individuals who drink excessively not only harm themselves by impairing their health and decreasing their productivity and income, they also impose *external* costs on others. External costs include the loss of life and property due to alcohol-related accidents, as well as a share of the medical and other costs of alcoholism. Harwood (2000) estimates the 1998 level of these costs at $185 billion.

The prices on which alcohol abusers base their consumption decisions do not include external costs. Abusers therefore underestimate the costs that their consumption of alcohol imposes on society at large. And they consume more than they would be willing to pay for if they had to pay prices that reflect external costs. The result is an inefficiently high level of production and consumption of alcoholic beverages.

Alcoholic beverage taxes counter the effects of this under-pricing. Higher taxes lead to higher alcohol prices that lead in turn to decreases in abusive consumption and external costs. Taxes can, in principle, be set high enough to push market prices to levels that fully reflect external costs. However, combined federal, state, and local taxes are currently well below this level. Pogue and Sgontz (1989) placed external costs at more than $0.74 per ounce of alcohol consumed, stated in the 2004 purchasing power of dollars. Estimates by Miller and Blincoe (1994) are even higher, about $1.70 per ounce of alcohol consumed just for the external cost of alcohol-related crashes. Even if these estimates are off by half, they imply that external costs are large relative to the taxes on alcoholic beverages. Further, federal taxes are much weaker deterrents to abusive consumption today than they have been in the past because of the decrease, noted above, in the real value of the taxes on beer and distilled spirits.

Following Cook and Moore (1994), a growing number of studies advocate increasing alcoholic beverage taxes to reduce abusive consumption and the related external costs. To maintain their effectiveness, the taxes should, of course, be indexed so that their real values do not fall with inflation. To avoid tax competition among states, taxes aimed at reducing external costs should be levied by the federal government. And, because external costs depend on the amount of alcohol consumed, equal taxes should apply to beverages with equal alcohol content, which is presently not the case.

Taxes on beer and distilled spirits could be tripled without exceeding their highest post-prohibition real values, reached in 1951. Although smaller increases would not restore the taxes to these peak values, they would nevertheless generate a significant amount of revenue. For example, the Congressional Budget Office (2003, 231) estimates that increasing all federal taxes on alcoholic beverages to the equivalent of $0.25 per ounce of alcohol would increase revenue by $4 to $5 billion annually over the 2004 to 2008 fiscal years. And, unlike an increase in the income tax, increases in alcoholic beverage taxes would generate revenue without reducing incentives to supply labor and save. These considerations have led the National Advisory Council on Alcohol Abuse and Alcoholism to recommend that both federal and state governments increase alcohol taxes and adjust them for inflation using the Consumer Price Index.

Proposals to increase taxes on alcohol, whether to reduce external costs, increase revenue, or both, commonly meet with several objections. First, as noted above, the taxes are widely perceived as unfair because they are based on purchases of alcoholic beverages rather than ability to pay. Second, they penalize the many individuals who do not consume excessively in order to limit abusive consumption by a few. There is thus a trade-off of costs; external costs are decreased, but only by imposing higher costs (higher tax burdens) on moderate drinkers. The tax rate that minimizes the sum of these two categories of cost is termed the *optimal* tax. Studies that have estimated the optimal tax conclude that it is considerably larger than current taxes. The need for this trade-off of costs would, of course, be eliminated if it

were possible to tax only abusive consumption, but that is not feasible. Third, because higher federal taxes would reduce alcohol consumption, state and local governments would also have to increase their tax rates on alcoholic beverages or suffer revenue losses. Finally, although higher taxes may reduce external costs, they may not be the least costly and disruptive means of doing so. Opponents of alcoholic beverage taxes advocate other measures—educating the public, especially youths, about the dangers of alcohol abuse; treating abusers; controlling access by minors; and increasing penalties for driving while under the influence of alcohol. Alcoholic beverage taxes are seen as appropriate for financing these measures but not for financing general government.

In sum, increasing and maintaining the real values of federal alcoholic beverage taxes would entail several difficult trade-offs. It would reduce abuse and external costs but penalize those who consume moderately. It would generate revenue and do so without curtailing work and saving incentives. But the resulting distribution of tax burdens would be less fair than if the revenues were obtained with the personal or corporate income taxes. Because individuals evaluate these trade-offs differently, there is no consensus on the question of whether federal alcoholic beverage taxes should be increased or allowed to erode with inflation, as they have during the past four decades.

ADDITIONAL READINGS

Cook, Philip J., and Michael J. Moore. "This Tax's for You: The Case for Higher Beer Taxes." *National Tax Journal* 47, no. 3 (September 1994): 559–73.

Harwood, Henrick J. "Updating Estimates of the Economic Costs of Alcohol Abuse in the United States: Estimates, Update Methods, and Data." Report prepared by the Lewin Group for the National Institute on Alcohol Abuse and Alcoholism, December 2000.

Joint Committee of the States to Study Alcoholic Beverage Laws. *Impact on Alcoholic Beverage Control of Taxation and Mark-up.* Cleveland: Joint Committee of the States to Study Alcoholic Beverage Laws, 1953.

Leung, Siu Fai, and Charles E. Phelps. "The Demand for Alcoholic Beverages." In *Economic Research on the Prevention of Alcohol-Related Problems,* edited by Gregory Bloss and Michael Hilton (1–31). Bethesda, MD: National Institutes of Health, 1993.

Manning, Willard G., Emmett B. Keeler, Joseph P. Newhouse, Elizabeth M. Sloss, and Jeffrey Wasserman. "The Taxes of Sin: Do Smokers and Drinkers Pay Their Way?" *Journal of the American Medical Association* 261, no. 11 (March 1989): 1604–9.

Miller, Ted R., and Lawrence J. Blincoe. "Incidence and Cost of Alcohol-Involved Crashes in the U.S." *Accident Analysis and Prevention* 25, no. 5 (1994): 583–91.

National Institute on Alcohol Abuse and Alcoholism. *10th Special Report to the U.S. Congress on Alcohol and Health.* Washington, DC: U.S. Government Printing Office, 2000.

Pogue, Thomas F., and Larry G. Sgontz. "Taxing to Control Social Costs: The Case of Alcohol." *American Economic Review* 79, no. 1 (March 1989): 235–43.

U.S. Congress, Congressional Budget Office. *Budget Options.* Washington, DC: U.S. Government Printing Office, 2003.

Cross-references: consumption taxation; excise taxes; horizontal equity; progressivity, measures of.

Allocation rules, multinational corporations

Barbara Rollinson
Horst and Frisch, Incorporated

Margie Rollinson
Ernst & Young LLP

Rules that determine how multinational corporations must divide expenses between domestic source and foreign source income for tax purposes.

Overview

Multinational corporations often incur expenses in one country that support operations in another country. In order to determine how much tax is owed to any one country, it is necessary to determine how to treat these expenses. Some of them may be readily traceable to income earned in a single country; however, some expenses may support income that is earned in more than one place. For example, a corporation with operations in the United States and Canada may undertake research and development (R&D) in the United States that leads to a new product that is produced and sold in both the United States and Canada. As another example, a U.S. corporation may decide to expand its operations in the United States and in the rest of the world and finance this worldwide expansion by borrowing (and thus incurring interest expense) in the United States. In both of these cases, expenses incurred in the United States support the production of both U.S. and foreign source income; therefore, both U.S. and foreign source income should bear a portion of the expenses.

In the absence of specific rules about how to treat these expenses, companies would have an incentive to claim them in countries in which they faced the highest marginal income tax rates. Therefore, higher tax countries have an incentive to prevent taxpayers from assigning all of these expenses to their high-tax income. Like so many tax issues affecting multinational corporations, countries recognize that unless they make an effort to resolve differential tax treatment of these types of expenses, double deduction or no deduction anywhere may result. Bilateral income tax treaties usually provide that when a corporation organized in one country has branch operations in another country, each country recognizes that there are situations in which expenses included in one country benefit operations in the other and thus should be allowed as a deduction in the other country. In addition, tax treaties usually contain provisions for resolving cases of double taxation, including cases caused by differential treatment by the tax authorities in each country that leads to no deduction of an item of expense in either country.

U.S. rules

The Internal Revenue Code provides expense allocation rules for situations in which a foreign branch, or other types of foreign operations, is involved. In general, the goal is to match the expenses with the income these expenses generate. If the income is deemed to arise within (or without) the United States, then the expense will also be allocated against income from sources within (or without) the United States. If the income is deemed to arise partly from within and partly from without, then the expense will be apportioned between income from sources within and without the United States.

This overall goal of matching income and expenses is achieved in different ways for different types of expenses. In the case of expenses that are readily traceable to an item of income earned in a specific country, the expenses are matched with and offset against that item of income. When the expenses are linked to more than one item of income, a ratable part of these expenses is allocated to and reduces each type of income. The treatment of this latter type of expense is the subject of extensive rules in the U.S. Internal Revenue Code and its regulations. In keeping with the general rule of matching income and expense, most of these expenses may be allocated in proportion to the income they generate. For example, general and administrative expenses usually may be allocated based on the gross income. For two types of expenses, interest and R&D, the goal is the same, but, because of the nature of the expenses and their potential importance, the approach is somewhat more refined.

Interest expense

Interest expense is allocated based on the theory that money is fungible. In other words, if a company incurs debt to finance an expansion at one of its plants, the debt can be considered as supporting the maintenance of cash on hand during the expansion of other existing assets. Thus, a dollar of borrowing can be viewed as supporting all the company's assets. To implement this theory, generally, a company must classify each of its assets based on the type of income the asset produces and then allocate the interest expense based on the tax basis value of the assets. (The minor exceptions to this general rule are for interest expense associated with special transactions, such as certain types of nonrecourse debt and integrated financial transactions. In addition, a company may elect to use the fair market value of assets to apportion interest, and more recently, may also use a modified tax basis.)

A multinational corporation that has assets and incurs interest expense in U.S. and foreign subsidiaries must determine which assets and what interest expense are allocated. Before the Tax Reform Act of 1986, each separately incorporated entity allocated its own interest expense based on its own assets. This practice allowed companies to isolate their debt in subsidiaries with no foreign assets, and thus no interest would be classified as foreign. Since the Tax Reform Act of 1986, however, the U.S. Internal Revenue Code has generally required a group of affiliated U.S. corporations to allocate interest expense as if all the members were a single corporation. Thus, the assets of any U.S. company that is at least 80 percent owned by a common parent and any interest expense incurred by those same companies are allocated using affiliated group apportionment ratios. For this purpose, until recently, foreign corporations were not included in the affiliated group. This so-called "water's edge" fungibility means that if a U.S. company owns 100 percent of a Canadian company, the value of its stock in the Canadian company will be included in the U.S. company's assets, but the underlying assets held by the Canadian company and the interest expense the Canadian company incurs will not be included. Some have argued that water's edge fungibility should be replaced with "worldwide" fungibility. Under worldwide fungibility, assets and interest expense of both U.S. and foreign subsidiaries that are part of a worldwide group would be taken into account. In fact, this approach was adopted in tax legislation enacted in 2004. A practical difficulty with implementing worldwide fungibility under the current scheme of asset-based allocation is that U.S. multinationals would be forced to require their foreign subsidiaries to classify their assets for U.S. tax purposes.

Research and development

Fashioning a general rule to determine how to allocate R&D "properly" has proved to be a more difficult undertaking. R&D expenses incurred in a given year are currently deductible, yet they frequently generate future income. In addition, R&D may not relate to all of the taxpayer's income because it may support only certain product categories. However, requiring companies to provide special analysis showing how R&D should be allocated would be an expensive and imprecise undertaking. Thus special regulations provide general rules for allocating R&D. R&D is divided up based on the standard industry classification to which it relates. Because R&D is assumed to be most valuable in the country in which it is undertaken, a certain percentage of this R&D is allocated exclusively to the country in which most of it is undertaken, and the remainder is allocated in proportion to domestic and foreign sales of the corporation in those same standard industry classifications.

Determining the appropriate percentage for the exclusion apportionment fraction has proved quite controversial. For a number of years, Congress passed special legislation that set temporary amounts for this percentage. The current exclusive apportionment percentage of 50 percent found in the regulations is supported by a 1995 Treasury study that reiterates the diversity of "proper" percentages depending on the type of R&D and the company's business structure.

The regulations also offer the option of dividing R&D expenses based on the relative amounts of gross income within and without the United States. If this method is selected, 25 percent of the R&D expenses are allocated exclusively to the location in which most of the R&D is undertaken. In addition, this option is limited by a "floor" that provides that the allocations to foreign source income must be at least 50 percent of those that would have been allocated to foreign source income under the sales method. The reason for this backstop is that comparing gross income with sales is something of a mismatch since the definition of foreign gross income includes, for example, dividends from a foreign corporation; thus, foreign gross income may be much closer to a net concept than domestic gross income.

Impact of U.S. allocation rules on multinational corporations

U.S. corporations are taxed on their worldwide income and allowed a foreign tax credit for foreign taxes paid up to the amount of tax that would have been paid in the United States. U.S. allocation rules, which classify some expenses incurred in the United States as foreign sources, do not affect the deductibility of an item of expense for U.S. tax purposes. Instead, these rules affect the calculation of a U.S. corporation's foreign tax credit limitation. An increase (decrease) in expenses classified as foreign decreases (increases) a corporation's foreign tax credit limitation. For corporations whose foreign operations are largely in low-tax locations or that earn types of income that are lightly taxed abroad, the allocation rules have little practical impact because these corporations are still able to credit all foreign taxes paid. Conversely, for corporations operating predominantly in locations with tax rates higher than those found in the United States, these rules operate to restrict the foreign tax credits allowed by the corporation.

ADDITIONAL READINGS

Hufbauer, Gray Clyde. "U.S. Taxation of International Income." Washington, DC: Institute for International Economics, 1992.

Organization for Economic Cooperation and Development. "Model Double Taxation Convention on Income and Capital." Paris: Organisation for Economic Cooperation and Development, 1995.

U.S. Department of the Treasury. "The Impact of the Section 861-8 Regulation on U.S. Research and Development." Washington, DC: U.S. Department of the Treasury, 1983.

———. "The Relationship between U.S. Research and Development and Foreign Income." Washington, DC: U.S. Department of the Treasury, 1995.

U.S. Internal Revenue Code. Sections 861, 862, and 864 and the regulations under each of these sections.

Cross-references: foreign tax credit; multinational corporations, taxation.

Alternative minimum tax, corporate

Andrew B. Lyon

PricewaterhouseCoopers LLP

A complex tax (either federal or state) designed to increase the income tax on businesses that the legislature believes pay too little relative to "standard" rules of taxation.

Minimum taxes are intended to increase tax payments from taxpayers who, under the rules of the regular tax system, are believed to pay too little tax relative to a more standard measure of their income. The U.S. federal income tax has both a personal and a corporate alternative minimum tax (AMT). Standard rules of business income taxation call for the recognition of income as it accrues, that is, at its receipt or when all events have occurred that fix the right to receive the income, whichever comes first. Deductions are permitted only when definite liabilities have been incurred. These standard rules are strongly influenced by (but differ somewhat from) both financial accounting practices and economic principles of income measurement. (Note that both standard rules and regular tax rules depart from economic measures of income by not allowing a deduction for the opportunity cost of equity-financed capital. The standard rules, as embodied in the AMT, additionally depart from economic principles by making little or no attempt to adjust measured income for the effects of inflation. The regular tax system gives some consideration for inflation through accelerated depreciation for equipment and valuation rules for inventory.)

Rules of the regular tax system make many departures from the standard rules, in a manner that generally results in a lower measure of income. The motives for these departures—or tax preferences—may include an aim for simplicity, an incentive for certain activities, political influence, or better accounting for other economic factors, such as inflation.

Corporate and individual minimum taxes were first put into the U.S. tax code in 1969. Initially, the minimum tax functioned much like an excise tax on specified tax preferences in excess of some fixed amount. As part of the Tax Reform Act of 1986, the corporate minimum tax was significantly modified to cover a broader range of preferences and is now called the alternative minimum tax. It is an *alternative* tax because the rules for this minimum tax constitute a complete, alternative set of rules to the regular tax system. It is a *minimum* tax because a corporation must pay the larger of its AMT or its regular tax liabilities.

AMT calculation

The AMT has its own rules for the measurement of income and deductions, and it has separate tax rates. While closely following the rules of the regular system, the AMT has a broader definition of income and a less generous set of deductions. Further, most business tax credits, such as the credit for research and experimentation, cannot be used to reduce tax payments under the AMT.

Given the larger measure of taxable net income under the AMT, practically all corporations would pay AMT were it not for the fact that the tax rate under the AMT is lower than the maximum tax rate under the regular tax system. The tax rate under the AMT is 20 percent, while the top tax rate under the regular tax system is 35 percent. Because the regular tax rate is 75 percent higher than the AMT rate, a firm's income must be at least 75 percent greater under the AMT before it must make payments under this system. It might at first appear that such a significant percentage change in net income would require that the AMT use tremendously different measures of includable income or allowable deductions relative to the regular tax system. But for the typical manufacturing firm, gross receipts and deductions are 10 to 20 times larger than its net income. A 5 to 10 percent change in includable receipts or allowable deductions is sufficient to create an AMT liability.

The starting point for the determination of income for AMT purposes is the corporation's regular taxable income. Regular taxable income is modified by a series of additional computations, termed *adjustments* and *preferences*. Adjustments can either increase or decrease taxable income, whereas preferences are calculated on a property-by-property basis and only enter to the extent that they are positive. Adjustments include a portion of accelerated depreciation on buildings and equipment, amortization of pollution control facilities, mining exploration and development expenses, income reported under the completed contract method of accounting, and installment sales income.

Preferences include percentage depletion, intangible drilling costs, bad debt deductions of financial institutions, and interest on certain bonds that would otherwise be tax exempt. Between 1987 and 1989, an additional preference was one-half the amount by which a corporation's book income (with certain modifications) exceeded its taxable income for AMT purposes. This preference was enacted as an explicitly temporary measure and was replaced in 1990 with an alternative measure of income, adjusted current earnings. Since 1990, 75 percent of the difference between adjusted current earnings and the firm's taxable income for AMT purposes is included in income.

AMT is calculated by applying the 20 percent tax rate to the AMT measure of income. The resulting amount of tax may be reduced by foreign tax credits, although the credits are calculated using AMT rules. (Under current law, net operating losses may not reduce tentative minimum tax by more than 90 percent. Until recently, this rule also applied to foreign tax credits, but this limit was repealed by the 2004 corporate tax legislation.) After subtracting foreign tax credits, the tentative minimum tax is compared to the firm's regular tax liability before all credits except the foreign tax credit. If the tentative minimum tax is larger, the firm pays the excess as AMT, in addition to its regular tax liability. If the firm's regular tax liability exceeds its tentative minimum tax, it may further reduce its regular tax by allowable business credits, but generally not below its tentative minimum tax. For firms with large amounts of business credits, such as the credit for research and experimentation, the AMT may serve to increase the firm's tax liability by delaying the use of these credits even if the firm pays no AMT.

A major element of the increase in tax liability under the AMT involves differences in the timing of deductions. Because firms may switch between the AMT and the regular tax, a system of credits for taxes paid under the AMT and adjustments to the basis of depreciated property is needed to prevent the AMT from collecting taxes in excess of the value of the timing preference. The tax credit for AMT payments can only be used to offset future regular tax liability. Further, it may not be used to reduce regular tax payments below the tentative minimum tax (the same floor that limits the use of most business tax credits). A firm that pays AMT and eventually claims all of its AMT credits will have the same total tax liability over this period as it would have had in the absence of the AMT. Because the AMT credits are taken at a later date than the firm's AMT payments, however, the AMT has accelerated the tax payments. The cost to the firm of this acceleration is the forgone earnings on these funds. If a firm must wait a long time before claiming its AMT credits, this cost may be

a sizable fraction of the AMT payment. Calculations indicate that firms undertaking investment in equipment while temporarily subject to the AMT generally face a higher cost of capital than firms on the regular tax (Lyon 1990). Interestingly, firms that are presently on the regular tax and are anticipating a short period of AMT liability in the future may face increased investment incentives as a result of the tax.

AMT revenues

As shown in the table, between 1987 and 2001, AMT revenues ranged from a high of $8.1 billion (1990) to a low of $1.8 billion (2001), corresponding to between 8.4 percent and 1.1 percent of total corporate income tax receipts after credits. AMT credits claimed over this period were about 60 percent of the AMT paid. Between 1995 and 2001, AMT credits claimed have exceeded payments of AMT, resulting in a negative net direct contribution to corporate tax revenues. Additional tax revenue is raised indirectly from the AMT from its limitation on general business credits.

Firms paying AMT represented only 1 to 2 percent of all corporations. AMT incidence was much more likely, however, for larger firms. Since 1987, approximately 20 to 40 percent of all corporate assets have been held by firms paying AMT (or firms that had credit use denied due to AMT) (Lyon 1997; Carlson 2001). Beginning in 1998, smaller corporations have been exempted from the AMT.

TABLE 1. Alternative Minimum Tax: 1987–2001

Year	Total AMT ($ billions)	AMT credits ($ billions)	Net AMT, after credits ($ billions)[a]	Total AMT as % of total corporate income tax, after credits	Net AMT as % of total corporate income tax, after credits	Minimum tax credit balance ($ billions)[b]
1987	2.2	—	2.2	2.5	2.5	2.2
1988	3.4	0.5	2.9	3.5	3.0	5.1
1989	3.5	0.8	2.7	3.6	2.8	7.8
1990	8.1	0.7	7.4	8.4	7.7	15.2
1991	5.3	1.5	3.8	5.7	4.1	19.0
1992	4.9	2.3	2.6	4.8	2.5	21.6
1993	4.9	3.1	1.8	4.1	1.5	23.4
1994	4.5	3.3	1.2	3.3	0.9	24.6
1995	4.3	4.8	−0.5	2.7	−0.3	24.1
1996	3.8	4.7	−0.9	2.2	−0.5	23.2
1997	3.9	4.1	−0.2	2.1	−0.1	23.0
1998	3.3	3.4	−0.1	1.8	−0.1	22.9
1999	3.0	3.4	−0.4	1.6	−0.2	22.5
2000	3.9	5.2	−1.3	1.9	−0.6	21.2
2001	1.8	3.3	−1.5	1.1	−0.9	19.7

Source: IRS, Statistics of Income, 1987–2001. Data for 2001 are preliminary.
a. Net AMT does not include general business credits not allowed due to AMT.
b. Credit balance shown is calculated as the difference between AMT paid and AMT credits claimed. It excludes unallowed nonconventional source fuel credits and unallowed qualified electric fuel credits. Including these credits, the credit balance at the end of 2001 was $24.9 billion.

Recent legislation has reduced the incidence of the AMT to some degree. Effective for investments in 1999, equipment is depreciated over the same recovery periods for AMT and regular tax purposes, although the method of recovery for most equipment under the regular tax (double declining balance) remains more accelerated than under the AMT (150 percent declining balance). Moreover, temporary "bonus depreciation" provisions for equipment, in effect for 2001 to 2004, applied under the AMT and no depreciation adjustments were required for such property.

Why an AMT?

The existence of the minimum tax appears to be an inconsistency in the formulation of tax law. One part of the tax system gives special deductions, exclusions, and incentives, and another part of the tax system takes them away (Graetz and Sunley 1988). Why, then, a minimum tax?

Some analysts believe the minimum tax is an appropriate "second-best" method to reduce the magnitude of deviations from economic measures of income if political constraints prevent their direct elimination. Corporations for which income measured under the minimum tax differs greatly from income measured under the regular tax are likely to pay minimum tax. Taxable income under the minimum tax, however, is not the same as economic income.

Further, because a firm undertaking a tax-preferred activity can still avoid the minimum tax if the firm additionally undertakes other activities without such preferences, tax-preferred activities will still attract investment. If one desires, for reasons of efficiency, to limit the amount of the economy's resources devoted to a given tax-preferred activity, the minimum tax will not be as effective as a direct reduction in the tax preference for that activity.

Others argue that the minimum tax does just what it is supposed to do. It allows tax policy to meet two social objectives: providing tax incentives to encourage particular activities and ensuring, for reasons of fairness, that corporations with positive incomes pay at least some tax. Of course, corporate taxes are ultimately borne by people, and the fact that a given corporation pays a low rate of tax may not have implications for equity among individuals.

If the fairness concern is that individuals who earn income from certain corporate activities pay too little tax on this income, this directly conflicts with the assumed objective of encouraging the activity through a tax preference.

ADDITIONAL READINGS

Avi-Yonah, Reuven. "The Case for Retaining the Corporate AMT." *SMU Law Review* 56 (Winter 2003): 333–42.

Carlson, Curtis. "Who Pays the Corporate Alternative Minimum Tax? Results from Corporate Panel Data for 1987–1998." In *Proceedings of the Ninety-Fourth Annual Conference on Taxation*, edited by Sally Wallace (349–56). Washington, DC: National Tax Association, 2001.

Chorvat, Terence R., and Michael S. Knoll. "The Case for Repealing the Corporate Alternative Minimum Tax." *SMU Law Review* 56 (Winter 2003): 305–32.

Graetz, Michael J., and Emil M. Sunley. "Minimum Taxes and Comprehensive Tax Reform." In *Uneasy Compromise: Problems of a Hybrid Income-Consumption Tax*, edited by Henry J. Aaron, Harvey Galper, and Joseph Pechman (285–419). Washington, DC: The Brookings Institution, 1988.

Lyon, Andrew B. *Cracking the Code: Making Sense of the Corporate Alternative Minimum Tax*. Washington, DC: The Brookings Institution, 1997.

———. "Investment Incentives under the Alternative Minimum Tax." *National Tax Journal* 43 (December 1990): 451–65.

Cross-references: adjusted current earnings; alternative minimum tax, personal; capital cost recovery; cost of capital; income tax, corporate, federal; taxable income, corporate.

Alternative minimum tax, personal

David Weiner
Congressional Budget Office

An additional tax paid by some individuals that can result from the use of certain tax preferences. (See also alternative minimum tax, corporate.*)*

The personal alternative minimum tax (AMT) requires individuals to calculate their income tax a second way, differently from the regular income tax. Separate tax rates and definitions of taxable income apply in both of these tax systems. The AMT limits the use of certain tax preferences, or exceptions to a comprehensive measure of income. A taxpayer's final liability is the greater of the tax liabilities calculated under the regular tax system and the AMT system. The AMT is defined as the amount by which the tax calculated under the broader AMT base, the tentative minimum tax, exceeds regular tax liability. The AMT can also increase taxes by limiting the use of certain tax credits. The tax base under the AMT is broader than that under the regular tax, and the top marginal tax rates are lower than under the regular tax. While few taxpayers currently pay the AMT (as of 2004), the number of taxpayers it affects and the dollars collected from it are expected to grow unless it is reformed to mitigate the effects of inflation and scheduled reductions in the regular income tax.

History of the AMT

The AMT has its origins in the "add-on" minimum tax, which was first introduced into the tax system in 1969. Unlike the dual tax systems of the AMT, the minimum tax was a separate tax in which a flat 10 percent rate was applied to certain tax preferences in excess of an exempted amount of $30,000. A taxpayer's total liability was the sum of the regular tax and the minimum tax. The minimum tax was introduced to collect taxes from wealthy individuals who paid little or no tax because they took advantage of tax preferences to reduce their taxable income. The minimum tax was strengthened in 1976 when the exemption amount was changed to the greater of $10,000 or half the taxes paid under the regular tax. The rate was also increased to 15 percent. The Revenue Act of 1978 introduced the AMT into the tax system, which already had the minimum tax. The preferences for certain itemized deductions and excluded capital gains were moved from the minimum tax to the AMT. By using the AMT rather than the minimum tax, taxpayers only paid additional tax on capital gains income if their AMT exceeded their regular tax liability. Congress anticipated that "capital formation will be facilitated and every individual will pay at least a reasonable amount of tax with respect to large capital gains." The AMT exempted the first $20,000 from tax and had a graduated rate schedule of 10, 20, and 25 percent.

In 1982, Congress repealed the minimum tax and expanded the AMT. Most preference items under the minimum tax were moved to the AMT. The exemption was increased to $30,000 for a single taxpayer and $40,000 for taxpayers filing jointly. A flat rate of 20 percent was applied to alternative minimum taxable income after the exemption was deducted. The next major revision to the AMT occurred with the Tax Reform Act of 1986. Additional preference items were added to expand the AMT base. One of the largest preference items—the excluded portion of long-term capital gains—was eliminated from the regular tax (and thus as a preference under the AMT). The AMT rate was raised to 21 percent, and the AMT exemption was phased out for high-income taxpayers. For each dollar that the alternative minimum taxable income exceeded a specified threshold, the exemption amount was reduced by 25 cents. For taxpayers with large amounts of income, the exemption was completely eliminated. Finally, AMT generated in the current year could in some circumstances be taken as a credit against regular tax liability in future years. In 1990 Congress raised the top marginal income tax rate to 31 percent and the AMT rate to 24 percent. The top marginal income tax rate was increased again in 1993, and a graduated rate schedule of 26 and 28 percent was introduced to the AMT. The

exemption amounts were increased to $45,000 for married individuals and $33,750 for unmarried individuals.

The AMT can limit the use of certain tax credits if those credits reduce tax liability below the liability calculated under the AMT. Beginning in tax year 1998, Congress eliminated the AMT's impact on certain personal tax credits (e.g., child credit, earned income credit, education credits, dependent care credit). As of 2004, the use of all personal credits against the AMT had not been extended permanently.

In 2001, in conjunction with reductions in regular tax rates, Congress raised the AMT exemption amounts. For tax years 2001 and 2002, the exemption amount was raised to $49,000 for married individuals and $35,750 for unmarried individuals. For tax years 2003 and 2004, the amounts were raised to $58,000 for married individuals and $40,250 for unmarried individuals. As of July 2004, the exemption amounts are scheduled to go back down to their pre-2001 levels beginning in tax year 2005.

Growing impact of the AMT

Two factors are expected to increase the number of taxpayers the AMT affects and the amount of revenue it generates. First, inflation causes an increasing number of taxpayers to be affected by the AMT because the parameters of the regular tax are indexed for inflation and the parameters of the AMT are unindexed. If a taxpayer's income grew only at the rate of inflation, indexing parameters under the regular tax prevents tax rates from rising (see inflation indexation of income taxes). However, because AMT parameters are unindexed, inflation causes a taxpayer's tax rate under the AMT to rise over time. Therefore, taxes under the AMT will grow more quickly than under the regular tax, and more and more taxpayers will become subject to the AMT.

Reductions under the regular income tax can also cause more taxpayers to be affected by the AMT, unless the AMT parameters are adjusted to reduce this effect. The Economic Growth and Tax Relief Reconciliation Act of 2001 along with the Jobs Growth and Tax Relief Reconciliation Act of 2003 enacted a series of tax reductions that will be phased in over 10 years through 2010. As of 2004, these tax reductions are scheduled to expire after 2010. Both of these acts raised the AMT exemption level but neither extended the higher levels permanently.

The combination of inflation and the phased-in tax reductions is expected to increase the number of returns the AMT affects from fewer than 5 million in 2002 to about 30 million in 2010. The amount of additional revenue the AMT generates is expected to grow from under $10 billion in 2002 to about $90 billion by 2010. These estimates are based on the laws scheduled to be in effect in 2010 (as of 2004) and assume that the AMT parameters remain at their currently scheduled pre-2001 levels in 2010. Under current law, the tax cuts enacted in 2001 and 2003 are scheduled to expire at the end of 2010, reducing the impact of the AMT

TABLE 1. AMT Statistics for Selected Years

	Tax year			
	1983	1988	1994	2001
Returns with AMT liability	265	114	369	1,120
AMT returns as a percentage of all returns	0.3%	0.1%	0.4%	1.1%
Total AMT liability	$2.5	$1.0	$2.2	$6.8
AMT liability as a percentage of total liability	0.9%	0.2%	0.4%	0.8%

Source: Statistics of Income, Internal Revenue Service (Washington, DC: U.S. Government Printing Office, various years).
Notes: Numbers of returns are in thousands. Dollar amounts are in billions.

beyond that year. However, even if the tax cuts are not extended, inflation will continue to drive more and more taxpayers onto the AMT as long as the AMT parameters remain unindexed.

Tax preferences

Tax preferences are exceptions to a comprehensive measure of income under an ideal income tax. The items considered tax preferences for purposes of the AMT have changed over time. These preferences are items that can be excluded from regular taxable income or deductions allowed under the regular tax that would not be allowed under a comprehensive income tax. Not all tax preferences are included in the AMT, and the list has changed over time. The preferences described below are among those included under the tax law in effect in 2004.

The use of exemptions and deductions is limited under the AMT. While the AMT has its own exemption level, it does not allow deductions for personal exemptions or the standard deductions allowed under the regular tax. Some itemized deductions, including miscellaneous itemized deductions and deductions for taxes paid, are completely disallowed. Others are more limited. For example, medical deductions are allowed only to the extent that they exceed 10 percent of adjusted gross income, compared with 7.5 percent under the regular tax. Deductions for investment interest and home mortgage interest are subject to separate rules under the AMT, which can reduce the size of the deduction compared with the regular tax. The itemized deductions allowed under the minimum tax are not, however, subject to the itemized deduction limitation that applies to higher-income individuals under the regular tax.

Many of the other preferences under the AMT are associated with the timing of income and deductions for investors in noncorporate businesses. Deductions for depreciation of equipment, oil depletion allowances, allowances for intangible drilling costs, or mining exploration and development costs are allowed at a slower rate under the AMT than under the regular tax. The difference between deductions allowed under the regular tax and the AMT is included in the alternative minimum taxable income.

Other examples of timing preferences include deductions associated with a financial institution's bad debt, deductions for newspaper circulation expenses, deductions for research and experimentation expenses, and the use of the "percentage-of-completion" or the "installment" methods of accounting. It is these timing preferences that generate credits that can be taken against future regular tax liability.

The AMT has grown beyond its original intent

The minimum tax and the AMT were originally designed to ensure that wealthy individuals pay some income tax. These individuals would not be able to avoid paying income taxes through the use of certain tax preferences or tax shelters. Aside from a general sense of fairness, it has been argued that overall confidence and compliance with the tax system could be undermined if nonwealthy taxpayers feel that wealthy taxpayers pay little or no income tax. The AMT improved on the design of the original minimum tax by taxing only excessive use of tax preferences and not the use of any one preference.

Largely because it is unindexed, the AMT has gone beyond its original intent and now affects taxpayers other than those wealthier taxpayers who pay no income tax. As currently structured, most taxpayers affected by the AMT are subject to it because they have large families, take the standard deduction, or live in jurisdictions with higher taxes. While the AMT still limits the use of certain preference items not available to many taxpayers, the preference items putting most taxpayers on the AMT are the basic parameters of the regular tax—the standard deduction, the personal exemption, and the lowest marginal tax rate brackets.

The AMT has been partially successful in ensuring that wealthy taxpayers pay some income tax. In 2001 nearly 1,100 tax filers with AGI over $500,000 paid some income tax because of the AMT. However, nearly 900 filers in that range paid no federal income tax despite the presence of the AMT. In general, the reach of the AMT does not currently extend to lower-income taxpayers or the highest-income taxpayers. Of the more than one million returns paying AMT in 2001, over 80 percent reported adjusted gross incomes between $75,000 and $500,000. The AMT exemption prevents most lower-income taxpayers from being affected. Most of the highest-income taxpayers do not pay AMT because more of their income is taxed at the top marginal rates under the regular income tax; this makes their regular tax liability higher than that calculated under the AMT, which has lower marginal rates.

The AMT does limit the advantage of certain tax preferences for some taxpayers and does subject some wealthier filers to tax, but it is not without cost. A growing number of taxpayers have become subject to the AMT, and many taxpayers beyond those affected must do the calculations for the AMT. These additional calculations add significantly to the complexity of the tax system, requiring more time for preparing tax returns and making the income tax less transparent for those affected.

Several options have been suggested for reducing the growing impact of the AMT. The options include indexing the basic AMT parameters for inflation and eliminating some of the preference items affecting most taxpayers (e.g., the personal exemption, standard deduction, or state tax deductions). Some proponents of reform have proposed the complete repeal of the AMT. Under current law, the AMT is expected to generate a significant amount of revenue; therefore, repeal or reform could be costly. To the extent that AMT reform requires an increase in other taxes, the benefits of reform should be weighed against the impact of policies that offset the revenue losses.

ADDITIONAL READINGS

Burman, Leonard E., William G. Gale, Jeffrey Rohaly, and Benjamin H. Harris. "The Individual AMT: Problems and Potential Solutions." *National Tax Journal* 55, no. 3 (September 2002): 555–96.

Feenberg, Daniel R., and James M. Poterba. "The Alternative Minimum Tax and Effective Marginal Tax Rates." *National Tax Journal* 57, no. 2 (June 2004): 407–27.

Harvey, Robert P., and Jerry Tempalski. "The Individual AMT: Why It Matters." *National Tax Journal* 50 (September 1997): 453–74.

Rebelein, Robert, and Jerry Tempalski. "Who Pays the Individual AMT." OTA Working Paper No. 87. Washington, DC: U.S. Treasury Department, 2000.

U.S. Congressional Budget Office. *The Alternative Minimum Tax.* Washington, DC: U.S. Congressional Budget Office, 2004.

Cross-reference: income tax, federal.

Apportionment

Robert P. Strauss

Carnegie-Mellon University

Involves the division of a business's multijurisdictional taxable economic activities among taxing jurisdictions.

Apportionment of a tax base can be contrasted to allocation of a tax base and harmonization of jurisdictions' taxes. Allocation involves the attribution of certain types of business receipts of a multistate business, usually investment income (dividends, interest, and royalty income), to one taxing jurisdiction. Harmonization denotes the extent to which taxing jurisdictions recognize, for their own tax purposes, taxes imposed by other jurisdictions on the same taxpayer. State corporate income taxes often do not allow the deduction of other states' corporate income taxes in determining businesswide taxable income. Apportionment entails the proportionate attribution of multistate business activity to each of the states with the authority to tax the multistate activity.

The current state business tax apportionment laws reflect the historical evolution of the realities of U.S. businesses and the revenue needs of the states. When markets were local or regional in character, geographic attribution of the profits due to the sale of tangible and intangible personal property was unnecessary. Indeed, business taxation in colonial times typically involved the imposition of a local real property tax and the collection of various fees related to the privilege of doing business in the area. As the corporate form became more popular during the Industrial Revolution as a means of raising capital and insulating investors from some business risks, the states devised various incorporation fees, often based on the extent of capitalization. These fees were variously called franchise or capital stock taxes, and they persist to this day, although the limitations on the amount per firm that can be collected lighten their burden and typically eliminate them from serious state tax planning considerations. It should be noted that a series of U.S.

Supreme Court cases in the 19th century generally supported a state's right to impose a tax for the privilege of doing business and also supported as permissible measurement of the privilege to include net income.

Before the voluntary development in 1957 among the states of a model business tax statute with extensive apportionment rules, the Uniform Division of Income for Tax Purposes Act (UDITPA), business taxpayers typically reported state income on the basis of accounting records of their establishments in the state. Such separate accounting of an establishment's revenues, expenses, and profits and losses, however, has largely been replaced by the proportionate attribution of business income to states in which the business has sufficient activity, on the basis of such state-specific factors as payroll, property, and sales. The first two factors may be viewed as supporting attribution on the basis of the origin of the activity of a multijurisdictional business, while the last factor (sales) may be viewed as supporting attribution on the basis of access to markets in which one does business, or the destination of the activity of a business.

The general purpose of apportionment is to avoid, reduce, or eliminate the risk of multiple taxation of multistate business activity. The extent to which any state may tax an interstate business is regulated by the Commerce, Due Process, and Equal Protection clauses of the U.S. Constitution and attending case law and, in the case of state corporate income taxes, by a specific federal statute that defines when a multistate business may be initially subjected to a state corporate income tax.

Public Law (PL) 86-272 provides specific guidelines for determining the taxability under state corporate income tax of businesses engaged in the interstate sale of tangible personal property. Under PL 86-272, taxability or *nexus* in a state is not established if a business merely solicits orders for the sale of tangible personal property into the state in question. Solicitation by nonemployees of the business (for example, contract sales representatives), the displaying of goods in a state by business employees, and the shipment of the business's goods by business employees in a business-owned vehicle into a state are protected activities under PL 86-272 and presumptively do not constitute nexus. Maintenance of an office (owned or rented), ownership of other real property, ownership of inventory, solicitation of orders by employees with the authority to accept them, purchasing, or frequent installation by business employees in the state, on the other hand, are not protected activities and are sufficient to constitute nexus (taxability) in the state in question.

State taxation of other aspects of interstate business (e.g., the sale of intangible personal property) is not protected by federal statute but has been limited by a series of Supreme Court decisions. UDITPA distinguishes between income to be apportioned among taxing states and income, primarily from investments, to be entirely allocated to the state of a corporation's commercial domicile. Under the Act, income taxable in State A is determined by averaging the payroll, property, and sales (on a destination basis) fractions of such activities attributable to State A as compared with all states in which the business is taxable, and multiplying this percentage by the businesswide taxable income:

$$Taxable\ Income_A = \frac{1}{3}\left(\frac{Payroll_A}{Payroll} + \frac{Property_A}{Property} + \frac{Sales_A}{Sales}\right) Taxable\ Income$$

A variety of complications arise and are dealt with in the Act to implement this equation. For example, real property is measured at cost (as contrasted with market), while rental property is included in the property factor by capitalizing it, usually at 12.5 percent; compensation of executives is sited to the commercial domicile of the corporation, and specific rules are suggested to deal with employees who work in multiple jurisdictions. Difficult issues arise in the treatment of the location of factors in states without an income tax, and the treatment of sales to tax-exempt organizations and governments. Administrative considerations, technological change, and the nature of particular service industries (especially telecommunications, banking, and transportation) have led to the development of industry-specific apportionment rules. The Multistate Tax Commission (MTC), a voluntary organization of states, continues to refine and detail this basic formula, which member states subsequently adopt through amendments to their business tax statutes and through adoption of MTC regulations. The apportionment equation presumes that the business's income is known; however, in the case of multitiered corporations, the nature of the filing unit, as defined by state tax law, interacts with the apportionment formula in affecting the state-by-state business tax liability.

The states vary considerably as to whether they permit or require a corporation to file on a consolidated, combined, unitary, or separate basis. A consolidated corporate filing unit for federal income tax purposes includes all domestic subsidiaries owned 80 percent or more by the parent corporation (typically a holding company). Were this consolidated entity subjected to state corporate income taxation, the denominators in the equation would reflect the property, payroll, and sales of the consolidated corporation, and the income would reflect the income of the aggregation of these subsidiaries. However, since PL 86-272 limits application of a state corporate income tax to only those parts of a corporation with substantial contact, businesses typically resist such an inclusive definition of the filing unit for a state's corporate income tax. Combined reporting involves the aggregation of only those subsidiaries that are taxable in a state; in some states, the aggregation prohibits offsetting positive income in some subsidiaries with negative income in others. Issues arise as to whether the aggregation is *before* or *after* apportionment to each specific state.

Application of a state unitary filing requirement entails identifying and aggregating those parts of a multistate corporation that have various economic links with each other (operational interdependence, functional integration, centralized management and span of control, purchasing policy, etc.), and one of which has sufficient contact in the state under PL 86-272 to permit state taxation. States have applied unitary filing requirements to the worldwide activities of domestic- and foreign-headquartered corporations.

California has been the most innovative and aggressive in the application of the unitary principle of business taxation, and was upheld in two important Supreme Court cases dealing with the unitary taxation of a domestically headquartered company and an internationally headquartered company, respectively, *Container Corporation of America v. California Franchise Tax Board* in 1983, and *Barclays Bank v. California Franchise Tax Board* in 1994.

While the equation above is the most common apportionment rule embodied in state corporate income tax statutes, the U.S. Supreme Court has been quite permissive in finding that variants of it do not represent an undue burden on interstate commerce. A number of states have tried to emphasize the sales factor more heavily than the other factors in the equation to raise further revenues from out-of-state firms, and have provided optional formulas (one, two, or three factors in the equation) to tax local firms more favorably.

The U.S. Supreme Court has afforded the states considerable latitude in adopting variants of the above formula that weight each measure of business activity equally. While a majority of the states with some form of corporate net income tax initially adopted the three-factor formula with coefficients of one-third on each of the measures of business activity, over time they have favored weighting the sales factor (on a destination basis) more heavily than one-third in the hope of shifting the tax incidence to out-of-state firms. As of 2004, only 13 states rely on the equally weighted formula shown above, while 29 states utilize apportionment formulae that place a weight of more than one-third on sales, and 4 apportion *solely* on the basis of sales.

ADDITIONAL READINGS

Anand, Bharat N., and Richard Sansing. "The Weighting Game: Formula Apportionment as an Instrument of Public Policy." *National Tax Journal* 53, no. 2 (June 2000): 183–200.

Edmiston, Kelly D. "Strategic Apportionment of the State Corporate Income Tax: An Applied General Equilibrium Analysis." *National Tax Journal* 55, no. 2 (June 2002): 239–62.

Goolsbee, Austan, and Ed Maydew. "Coveting Thy Neighbor's Manufacturing: The Dilemma of State Income Apportionment." *Journal of Public Economics* 75, no. 1 (January 2000): 125–43.

Gordon, Roger. "A Critical Look at Formula Apportionment." In *Final Report of the Minnesota Tax Study Commission*, edited by Robert D. Ebel and Therese J. McGuire. Boston: Butterworths, 1986.

Hellerstein, Jerome R., and Walter Hellerstein. *State Taxation, Vol 1. Corporate Income and Franchise Taxes.* 3rd ed. Boston: Warren, Gorham, and Lamont, 1998.

Schoettle, Ferdinand P. *State and Local Taxation: The Law and Policy of Multi-Jurisdictional Taxation.* Newark, NJ: LexisNexis, 2004.

Cross-references: income tax, corporate, state, and local; Multistate Tax Commission; state formula apportionment.

Automatic stabilizers

Robert M. Coen
Northwestern University

Built-in features of the fiscal system that tend to reduce fluctuations in economic activity.

Just as shock absorbers on an automobile smooth out road bumps without action on the part of the driver, automatic stabilizers cushion the economy to external shocks without explicit action on the part of government authorities. The principal examples of automatic stabilizers are the income tax and unemployment benefits. A negative macroeconomic shock, such as a decline in foreign demand for a nation's exports, causes output and employment in export industries to contract. As workers in the export sector experience declines in their incomes, they will be inclined to reduce consumption spending, thereby spreading the initial shock to other parts of the economy and magnifying its effect. Automatic stabilizers limit these repercussions by sustaining disposable income when pretax, pretransfer income declines. For example, if wages are subject to a marginal tax rate of 20 percent, a worker whose wage income declines by $1,000 will suffer only an $800 loss in disposable income because tax liability falls by $200. An unemployed worker whose wage income falls to zero will nonetheless have positive disposable income equal to unemployment benefits received. Under a positive macroeconomic shock, automatic stabilizers act to restrain the growth of disposable income and spending when pretax income rises.

Automatic stabilizers can reduce economic fluctuations, but they cannot eliminate them because they do not fully replace lost income. Furthermore, they cannot reverse a cumulative decline in output or restrain a cumulative increase. Discretionary fiscal actions may also be needed to increase stability, just as the driver of a car may increase the smoothness of the ride by reducing speed or steering to avoid potholes. However, discretionary stabilization policy requires that authorities forecast the need for policy changes and then implement the changes. Because of lags in data collection, forecasting errors, and lengthy legislative processes, discretionary actions may be ineffective or even destabilizing. By contrast, an income tax collected via withholding at the source operates as a stabilizer automatically and immediately whenever income changes. Unemployment benefits are not quite as automatic, since unemployed workers must file claims to receive them.

Intermediate between passive reliance on automatic stabilizers and active use of discretionary policies are stabilization policy rules, sometimes referred to as feedback rules or formula flexibility. An example would be a rule stipulating that tax rates are to be reduced during recessions and increased during booms. Such a rule eliminates the implementation lags that beset discretionary policies, but not recognition lags, because information still needs to be collected and analyzed to determine the state of the economy. Automatic stabilizers have the distinct advantage of eliminating both recognition and implementation lags.

Effectiveness of automatic stabilizers

The power of automatic stabilizers depends principally on the extent to which taxes change when income changes—that is, on the marginal tax rate. (Transfers such as unemployment benefits may be thought of as negative taxes, such that the larger the fraction of lost earnings replaced by unemployment benefits, the higher the marginal tax rate.) The marginal tax rate can be expressed as the product of the average tax rate, t, and the revenue elasticity of the tax system, E. While t might be set to finance a desired ratio of public expenditures to output, E depends on the design of the fiscal system. For example, a progressive income tax has an $E > 1$ and provides greater built-in stability than a flat-rate income tax, for which $E = 1$. Any fiscal system for which E is positive provides some degree of built-in stability.

Musgrave and Miller (1948) proposed an index of built-in stability that measures the percentage of national output (gross domestic product, or GDP) change prevented by the cushioning effect of the fiscal system. In a static, Keynesian macroeconomic model, the index takes the form $\alpha = \beta Et / (1 - \beta + \beta Et)$, where β is the marginal propensity to spend out of disposable income, $0 < \beta < 1$. If E is zero, there is no built-in stability and α is zero. For reasonable values of $E = 1.1$, $t = 0.3$, and $\beta = 0.6$, the tax system would reduce by 33 percent the decline in GDP resulting from a decline in exogenous demand, relative to a situation in which E is zero. Kiefer (1980) surveys estimates of α for the federal income tax and the fiscal system as a whole.

Greater stability of the U.S. economy after 1945 may be attributed in part to a higher ratio of federal receipts to GDP, since for a given value of E, α increases as t increases. On the other hand, built-in stability is reduced by tax reforms that are intended to reduce excess tax burdens by cutting marginal tax rates and indexing personal exemptions and tax brackets to inflation, while leaving t unchanged. Also, shifts in tax sources away from taxes with high Es (personal and corporate income taxes) to those with smaller Es (sales, excise, payroll, property, and estate taxes) tend to reduce built-in stability.

The Musgrave-Miller index has several deficiencies. Automatic stabilizers tend to create budget deficits during recessions that must be financed by borrowing or monetary expansion. Increased government borrowing may raise interest rates and thereby reduce investment spending, negating part of the cushioning effect of the stabilizers. The index does not distinguish between real and nominal changes in income or between demand and supply shocks, and it does not consider effectiveness in moderating fluctuations in the price level as well as output. In a dynamic economy with lagged responses of spending to income or production to demand, a sensible goal for stabilization policy may not be to reduce the effect of a shock on the level of GDP, but rather to minimize the variance of GDP around its full-employment level. The variance depends in complex ways on the lags, as well as on the nature of recurring stochastic shocks to the economy, and full-employment GDP may itself be affected by automatic stabilizers. Depending on the economic structure, an income tax may be either stabilizing or destabilizing (Johansen 1974). Nonetheless, the major insights provided by the index remain valid in a variety of settings.

Rational-expectations macroeconomic models have shown that activist stabilization policies are likely to be ineffective, but they support a modest role for automatic stabilizers that serve to decentralize changes in taxes on the basis of information that becomes known to central authorities only with lags (McCallum and Whitaker 1979). If households are forward-looking and believe that government will make up for any reduction in current taxes by raising future taxes, leaving unchanged the present value of taxes, then private spending may be unaffected by a recession-induced decline in current taxes. However, if consumers cannot fully differentiate between idiosyncratic income shocks and those that are common to all workers, or they are credit-constrained, there will be imperfect capitalization of future taxes, and the reduction in consumption due to a common income shock may be smaller the higher the marginal income tax rate (Christiano 1984; Auerbach and Feenberg 2000). Also, a higher income tax rate reduces the variance of after-tax income and therefore reduces precautionary saving and increases current spending (Cohen and Follette 2000).

Implications for budget analysis and policy

If at the onset of a recession the government's budget is balanced, it will go into deficit during the recession, as automatic stabilizers do their job. A policy rule or constitutional amendment that requires an annually balanced budget would therefore undermine automatic stabilizers. To adhere to such a policy, tax sources with very small Es would have to be adopted, or discretionary changes in tax rates and expenditure programs would have to be enacted to offset the fiscal impacts of automatic stabilizers, but these are likely to be destabilizing, requiring that tax rates be increased in

recessions. An alternative budget policy that allows automatic stabilizers to operate would set the average tax rate to achieve a balanced budget *when the economy is operating at high employment,* permitting deficits to be run in recessions and surpluses in booms (Friedman 1948). Because state and local governments are usually required to maintain balanced budgets, their fiscal systems cannot contribute much to built-in stability.

Because of automatic stabilizers, the conventionally measured budget deficit is often an inaccurate gauge of discretionary fiscal policy. A rise in the official deficit does not necessarily indicate active pursuit of expansionary fiscal programs; it may simply reflect the operation of built-in stabilizers. To assess discretionary fiscal policy, the impact of the state of the economy on budget receipts and expenditures must be removed, resulting in a cyclically adjusted measure referred to as the high-employment, standardized-employment, or structural deficit (Brown 1956; Council of Economic Advisers 1962, 78–82). Estimates of the standardized deficit by the Congressional Budget Office indicate that in the recession year 2003, when GDP was 2 percent below its full-employment level, automatic stabilizers increased the federal deficit by $62 billion, or 20 percent (U.S. Congress 2004, 139).

ADDITIONAL READINGS

Auerbach, Alan J., and Daniel Feenberg. "The Significance of Federal Taxes as Automatic Stabilizers." *Journal of Economics Perspectives*, 14 (Summer 2000): 37–56.

Brown, E. Cary. "Fiscal Policy in the Thirties: A Reappraisal." *American Economic Review* 46 (December 1956): 857–79.

Christiano, Lawrence J. "A Reexamination of the Theory of Automatic Stabilizers." In *Monetary and Fiscal Policies and Their Applications*, edited by Karl Brunner and Allen Meltzer (147–206). Amsterdam: North-Holland, 1984.

Cohen, Darrel, and Glenn Follette. "The Automatic Fiscal Stabilizers: Quietly Doing Their Thing." *Economic Policy Review* 6, no. 1 (April 2000): 35–68.

Council of Economic Advisers. *Annual Report.* Washington, DC: U.S. Government Printing Office, 1962.

Friedman, Milton. "A Monetary and Fiscal Framework for Economic Stability." *American Economic Review* 38 (June 1948): 245–64.

Johansen, Leif. "Some Aspects of Automatic Stabilizers." In *Public Finance and Stabilization Policy*, edited by Warren L. Smith and John M. Culbertson (175–202). Amsterdam: North-Holland, 1974.

Kiefer, Donald W. "The Automatic Stabilization Effects of the Federal Tax Structure." In *The Business Cycle and Public Policy, 1929–80.* U.S. Congress, Joint Economic Committee. Washington, DC: U.S. Government Printing Office, 1980.

McCallum, Bennett T., and John K. Whitaker. "The Effectiveness of Fiscal Feedback Rules and Automatic Stabilizers under Rational Expectations." *Journal of Monetary Economics* 5 (1979): 171–86.

Musgrave, Richard A., and M. H. Miller. "Built-In Flexibility." *American Economic Review* 38 (March 1948): 122–28.

U.S. Congress. Congressional Budget Office. *The Economic and Budget Outlook: Fiscal Years 2005 to 2014.* Washington, DC: U.S. Government Printing Office, 2004.

Cross-references: rainy day funds; revenue elasticity (tax elasticity).

Average effective tax rate

Richard Sansing

Dartmouth College, Tuck School of Business

The ratio of a taxpayer's nominal income tax liability to income.

The average effective tax rate is a widely used, albeit theoretically dubious, measure of corporate income tax burdens. Corporate effective tax rates have also been used in studies examining the relation between tax burdens and firm size, as part of the debate over whether large firms face higher political costs. The appropriate way to measure both the ratio's numerator and denominator continues to be debated, even though the usefulness of the average effective tax rate for decisionmaking purposes has not been established.

Many attribute the increases in nominal corporate tax burdens in the Tax Reform Act of 1986 (TRA86) to the low average corporate effective tax rates calculated and publicized by lobbying groups such as Citizens for Tax Justice. Subsequent research documents an increase in corporate effective tax rates in the years following the enactment of TRA86.

Financial accountants define the corporate average effective tax rate as *income tax expense for financial reporting purposes divided by pretax accounting income.* Income tax expense is pretax accounting income less "permanent differences" between pretax financial accounting income and taxable income, multiplied by the statutory tax rate. Interest income from state and municipal bonds that is exempt from tax is an example of a permanent difference. A firm facing a 35 percent tax rate with $100 of pretax financial accounting income that includes $20 of tax-exempt interest income would report an income tax expense of $28 = ($100 – $20) × 0.35, and would have an effective tax rate of 28 percent.

Others define the effective tax rate differently, including only the current portion of the income tax expense in the numerator. This approach excludes the deferred income tax expense, which is the product of the statutory tax rate and the difference between accounting income and taxable income due to temporary differences in the definitions of accounting and taxable income—for example, differences in the calculation of depreciation. Continuing the above example, suppose a corporation with a pretax financial accounting income of $100 and $20 of tax-exempt interest income reports a depreciation expense of $85 for tax purposes but only $65 for book purposes. The firm's income tax expense of $28 consists of a current income tax liability of $21 = [$100 – $20 – ($85 – $65)] × 0.35 and a deferred tax liability of $7. With only the current portion of the federal income tax expense in the numerator, the average effective tax rate is 21 percent instead of 28 percent.

The exclusion of deferred taxes from the numerator is a matter of considerable controversy because it compares a cash basis numerator to an accrual basis denominator. Some argue that deferred income tax expense should be included in the numerator to provide a consistent comparison, while others argue for the inclusion of the present value of deferred taxes to reflect the fact that these taxes may not actually be paid for many years.

Another problem in interpreting an effective tax rate with only the current portion of tax expense in the numerator is that the tax rate depends on the change in firm size. Suppose assets are depreciated faster for tax purposes than book purposes. If the corporation just replaces assets as they wear out, this difference will not cause the effective tax rate to differ from the statutory tax rate; higher depreciation on new assets will offset lower depreciation on old assets. The firm must be growing for the book-tax difference to cause the effective tax rate to decrease below the statutory tax rate. If the firm is shrinking, the book-tax difference will cause the effective tax rate to exceed the statutory tax rate.

Finally, even the current portion of the income tax expense may not equal the actual income taxes paid; the two can differ because the tax savings associated with the exercise of stock options are treated as a contribution to equity capital instead of a reduction in tax expense. In addition, the subsidiaries included in consolidated financial statements often differ from those included in consolidated tax returns because the consolidation rules for tax and financial reporting differ.

Although most of the debate over corporate effective tax rates has focused on the numerator, the appropriate denominator is also open to question. Fullerton (1984) defines the denominator as "correctly measured corporate income." However, financial accounting income is not, and does not purport to be, equivalent to economic income. Economic income is not well defined if markets are either imperfect or incomplete. In practice, the accounting principle of conservatism tends to understate income. For example, asset appreciation is not recognized until a sale occurs, and most research and development expenditures are expensed when incurred. The effective tax rate measure will fail to reflect such tax-preferred investments, because it reflects the difference between taxable income and financial accounting income, not the difference between taxable income and economic income.

The average effective tax rate omits the implicit taxes on tax-favored investments. Demand for tax-favored investments forces investors to bear an implicit tax in the form of a lower pretax rate of return than they could obtain from an investment with a less favorable tax treatment. In addition, the effective tax rate only reflects a taxpayer's nominal tax burden; it reveals nothing about which individuals bear the real economic burden of the tax.

Differences regarding the definition of pretax financial accounting income and taxable income imply that the numerator and denominator may have different signs. A firm with a current tax liability of $10 and a pretax financial accounting loss of $100 has an effective tax rate of –10 percent, as does a firm with pretax financial accounting income of $100 receiving a $10 refund (due to a carryback of a current tax loss). That firms in two very different situations have the same effective tax rates casts doubt on the meaning of the measure.

Other issues related to the measurement of effective tax rates include whether to compare domestic taxes to domestic income or worldwide taxes to worldwide income, and whether to include non-income taxes and/or shareholder-level taxes in the numerator.

The debate over effective tax rates reflects the absence of a theoretical foundation regarding their use. This stems from a more basic problem: the decision context in which the effective tax rate measure is to be used is rarely, if ever, specified. Because the various measures cannot be compared under a fineness criterion, one measure can only be judged superior to another if it leads to a better decision on the part of the user of the information, which requires the specification of a user and a decision context. Arguments over which measure is better in the absence of a specific decision context cannot be resolved.

ADDITIONAL READINGS

Beaver, William, and Joel Demski. "The Nature of Income Measurement." *The Accounting Review* 54 (1979): 38–46.

Birnbaum, Jeffrey, and Alan Murray. *Showdown at Gucci Gulch.* New York: Random House, 1987.

Christensen, Kevin, Robert Cline, and Tom Neubig. "Total Corporate Taxation: Hidden, Above-the-Line, Non-Income Taxes." *Tax Notes* 93 (December 3, 2001): 1333–40.

Citizens for Tax Justice. *Corporate Taxpayers and Corporate Freeloaders.* Arlington, VA: Tax Analysts, 1985.

Clowery, Grant, Ed Outslay, and James Wheeler. "The Debate on Computing Corporate Effective Tax Rates—An Accounting View." *Tax Notes* 30 (March 10, 1986): 991–97.

Dunbar, Amy, and Richard Sansing. "Measuring Corporate Tax Preferences." *Journal of the American Taxation Association* 24 (Fall 2002): 1–17.

Dworin, Lowell. "On Estimating Corporate Tax Liabilities from Financial Statements." *Tax Notes* 29 (December 2, 1985): 965–71.

Egger, John. "Citizens for Tax Justice's Latest Misrepresentation of Corporate Tax Burdens." *Tax Notes* 29 (December 2, 1985): 956–63.

Fullerton, Don. "The Use of Effective Tax Rates in Tax Policy." *National Tax Journal* 39 (1986): 285–93.

———. "Which Effective Tax Rate?" *National Tax Journal* 37 (1984): 23–42.

Guenther, David, and Richard Sansing. "Valuation of the Firm in the Presence of Temporary Book-Tax Differences: The Role of Deferred Tax Assets and Liabilities." *The Accounting Review* 75 (January 2000): 1–12.

———. "The Valuation Relevance of Reversing Deferred Tax Liabilities." *The Accounting Review* 79 (April 2004): 439–53.

Gupta, Sanjay, and Kaye Newberry. "Corporate Average Effective Tax Rates after the Tax Reform Act of 1986." *Tax Notes* 55 (May 4, 1992): 689–702.

———. "Determinants of the Variability in Corporate Effective Tax Rates: Evidence from Longitudinal Data." *Journal of Accounting and Public Policy* 16 (Spring 1997): 1–34.

Hanlon, Michelle. "What Can We Infer about a Firm's Taxable Income from Its Financial Statements?" *National Tax Journal* 56 (December 2003): 831–63.

Hanlon, Michelle, and Terry Shevlin. "The Accounting for the Tax Benefits of Employee Stock Options and Implications for Research." *Accounting Horizons* 16 (March 2002): 1–16.

Manzon, Gil B. Jr., and George A. Plesko. "The Relation between Financial and Tax Reporting Measures of Income." *Tax Law Review* 55, no. 2 (2002): 175–214.

Omer, Thomas C., Karen H. Malloy, and David A. Ziebart. "Measurement of Effective Corporate Income Tax Rates Using Financial Statement Information." *Journal of the American Taxation Association* 13 (Spring 1991): 57–72.

Plesko, George A. "An Evaluation of Alternative Measures of Corporate Tax Rates." *Journal of Accounting and Economics* 35 (June 2003): 201–26.

Cross-references: tax; tax illusion; tax price.

B

Banks, state taxation of

William F. Fox
University of Tennessee

The structure of state bank taxes across the United States has been driven by judicially imposed restrictions on the ability of states to tax national banks and by congressional legislation (see Symons 1984). These limitations on state taxation arose because, in times past, nationally chartered banks were regarded as instrumentalities of the U.S. government. The banks issued currency, served as fiscal agents, and acted as depositories of public monies. State-chartered banks could be taxed with any structure, but given the restrictions on the taxation of national banks, states limited their taxation of state-chartered banks to what was permissible for national banks. The major reason was so that state banks would not be placed at a competitive disadvantage. Moreover, state banks could avoid the higher taxes by applying for and receiving a national charter.

In *McCulloch v. Maryland,* the U.S. Supreme Court saw Congress as having the power to permit any form of state taxation of national banks that it deemed appropriate. Congress has acted on several occasions to authorize states to impose taxes on national banks. The most recent legislation became effective in 1976 and represents two significant steps in federal tax policy for national banks. First, states are permitted to impose any type of tax on banks without the necessity of obtaining further congressional approval, as long as the tax does not discriminate against national banks. Second, whether a tax discriminates against national banks is measured by comparing the tax on national banks with the tax on state banks, rather than with that on nonbanking corporations. Thus, the only limitation in existing legislation is that a state must tax national banks in the same manner as it taxes banks chartered in the state.

Current bank tax structure

A combination of shifting federal legislation, historical developments that led states initially to impose dissimilar tax structures, and unique characteristics of the banking industry has resulted in differences between many states' tax structures for banks and other corporations. Defining the differences between banks and other corporations is becoming increasingly difficult as federal legislation has significantly expanded the financial services that banks can offer and blurred the differences between banks and other corporations. Bank taxes are usually structured using some combination of corporate income, franchise, and share taxes. Base definitions for the corporate income tax are often a variant of the federal corporate income base definition, but the specific characteristics differ by state. The base for share taxes is the value of banking shares, deposits, or some other indicator of intangible personal property. The importance of share taxes comes from the history of federal legislation. Share taxes were the only permissible form for taxing national banks until 1926, when Congress first permitted states to adopt an income-based franchise tax. Franchise taxes are levied with either a corporate income tax or a share tax base. Thus, state taxes have either income or intangible property as the tax base, and the franchise tax is a legal distinction, rather than a conceptually different tax base. However, the legal distinction is important because court rulings indicate that the income from federal securities can only be taxed using a nondiscriminatory franchise or other nonproperty tax. Thus, states imposing a corporate income tax on banks cannot tax the interest from federal securities. At least twenty-three states use their franchise tax to tax the interest from federal securities.

Currently, 23 states impose a corporate income tax on banks, 23 have a franchise tax, and 5 use share taxes. These state totals include at least five states that levy more than one form of taxation and others that use one structure as a minimum for the other. Banks are taxed with the Single Business Tax in Michigan and the Business and Occupations Tax in Washington. Nevada and Wyoming have no statewide tax on banking.

Tax rates on income (using either an income-based or a franchise-based tax) range from 12.5 percent in the District of Columbia to 0 percent in 15 states (local rates are also imposed in some states such as New York). Rates on intangible assets (using either a share tax or a franchise tax) are more difficult to compare because of the widely different bases. The Business and Occupations tax in Washington (which is actually levied on receipts) has the highest rate, and 32 states are lowest with a 0 percent tax rate. Ernst & Young (2004) recently estimated that banks and credit institutions pay approximately 4.5 percent of all taxes on businesses, and a similar percentage of total corporate income taxes.

Income for multistate corporations is normally apportioned across states using either separate accounting or formulary apportionment. A common means for formulary apportionment of nonbanking corporations is a three-factor formula based on the percentage of the firm's sales, payrolls, and property located in the state. Traditionally, the three factors were equally weighted, but most states have moved to greater weight on the sales factor. Historically, state tax structures have given less consideration to apportionment of bank income than to income earned in other industries because banks were presumed to earn their income in a single state. There is an increasing tendency to allow apportionment of income, but a number of states, such as Mississippi, continue to allocate income earned from intangibles.

Changing environment and tax structure

The environment in which banks operate has changed radically in the past 20 years. Development of interstate banking, branchless banking, loan securitization, and diversification of allowable bank functions are four sources of this transformation. First, state-level expansions of interstate banking powers have permitted accelerated interstate banking and nearly every state allows some form of interstate banking. Federal legislation has been an important element in the changing bank environment, as a number of federal actions, including the Garn–St. Germain Act and the International Banking Act of 1978, have expedited interstate banking.

Second, technological advances in the collection, storage, and transmission of information have been facilitated by branchless banking. For example, computer technology has allowed "electronic banking" to be operationally and economically feasible through automated teller machines, electronic funds transfer systems, and many other means.

Third, securitization of loan activity is perhaps the single most important way financial institutions are able to engage in cross-state activity. Securitization is not a new phenomenon, dating back at least to the activities of the Federal National Mortgage Association (Fannie Mae) in the 1930s, but it has accelerated as a result of standardization of mortgage contracts and development of computer technology that has permitted securitization of nonmortgage loans.

Finally, the Gramm-Leach-Bliley Act of 1999 (GLB) significantly diversified the set of financial services that banks and their affiliates can offer. The Act establishes financial holding companies and financial subsidiaries that can deliver a wide array of financial services including securities underwriting, insurance underwriting, and equity investment activities (see Lazarus and Clark 2002).

The changes in the banking industry have invalidated the traditional assumption that firms operate within a single state and initially encouraged a number of states to reform their tax structures. Indiana, Minnesota, New York, Tennessee, and West Virginia were among the states to undertake reforms a decade or more ago, but few states have enacted changes of this magnitude during recent years. New York has acted more recently to change its legislation in light of the GLB Act.

The reforms were targeted at three major issues. First, states attempted to define financial institutions for tax purposes, though the GLB Act may have created problems that states have yet to address. Historically, states have often defined banks based on a regulatory definition, such as whether the firm takes deposits and makes loans. States that modified their definition of financial institutions often defined these institutions as firms that are in substantial competition with banks (West Virginia) or moneyed capital (California), or are doing the business of a financial institution (Tennessee).

Second, efforts were made to rationalize the geographic distribution of taxation on a financial institution's income. The motivation has been a desire to tax income generated by financial institutions with multistate presence. Formulary apportionment has been used in all states making changes. A driving force in the formula's structure in each state has been a decision regarding whether financial institutions should be taxed on a destination or origination basis. Minnesota and Tennessee developed formulas patterned on destination principles, and New York followed origination principles. Indiana adopted a dual tax structure that used origination-based rules for domiciled financial institutions (with a credit for taxes paid in other states) and destination rules for nondomiciled financial institutions.

Important considerations in revised formulas have been the number of factors, the specific factors to be used, and how the situs of the factors are to be established. The number of factors has varied from the one-factor receipts-based formula used in Tennessee to three-factor formulas adopted in states such as New York. Much consideration of the specific factors has centered on the property factor and the role, if any, for intangible property. Origination-based formulas tend to establish situs where the financial institution is located, destination-based formulas where the market is located.

Third, nexus was redefined in some states because branchless banking and loan securitization activities of financial institutions can only be taxed on a destination basis with a broader definition of nexus than that which has traditionally been used. Minnesota and Tennessee defined nexus to exist for financial institutions that have either a physical presence in the state or regularly solicit business in the state. Many banks initially complied with the legislation, but both states have seen legal challenges to the nexus standard in recent years. In Tennessee, the court has recently ruled that some degree of physical presence was necessary (*J. C. Penney v. Johnson*).

ADDITIONAL READINGS

Ernst & Young LLP. "State and Local Taxes Paid by the Financial Services Industry." Washington, DC: Quantitative Economics and Statistics Group, 2004.

Lazarus, Laura A., and Scott A. Clark. "Financial Services Modernization: Effect of the Gramm-Leach-Bliley Act on State Taxation of Financial Institutions through New York Analysis." *State and Local Tax Lawyer* 7 (2002).

Symons, Edward L., Jr. "State Taxation of Banks: Federal Limitations." *The Banking Journal* 99, no. 9 (October 1984): 814–41.

Tannenwald, Robert, and Ranjana G. Madhusdhan. "State Taxation of Bank Income with Unlimited Interstate Banking." In *Proceedings of the Eighty-Eighth Annual Conference on Taxation, 1995,* edited by Robert D. Ebel (271–76). Columbus, OH: National Tax Association, 1996.

Cross-references: apportionment; income tax, corporate, state and local.

Basis

Joseph J. Cordes
George Washington University

The amount a taxpayer uses to determine the cost of acquiring an asset, and which is used to determine the asset's capital gain or loss.

The basis of an asset is a key element in computing a taxpayer's capital gain or loss upon the sale of that asset. In the simplest case, when shares of corporate stock were all acquired at the same time, the basis would be the purchase price of the stock plus any brokerage fee. For example, if 100 shares of corporate stock were purchased at $20 per share (including brokerage fees) and later sold for $30 per share (net of broker commissions), the capital gain would be the difference between the $2,000 purchase price of the stock, which is its basis, and the $3,000 received from the sale.

Determining the basis of physical assets, such as real estate property, is more complicated because one must take into account any improvements made by the owner, as well as any depreciation claimed on the asset. Thus, a landlord who buys a house as a rental-income property would increase the basis by the amount of any improvements made on the house, and decrease the basis by the amount of any depreciation deductions claimed. For example, if the property were initially purchased for $50,000, and the landlord subsequently made $5,000 worth of improvements and claimed a total of $20,000 in depreciation, the *adjusted basis* of the property would be $35,000 = ($50,000 + $5,000 − $20,000). In both cases, the basis is adjusted to properly measure the change in the taxpayer's wealth attributable to the asset. If the cost of improvements was not added to the initial purchase price, the capital gain (loss) triggered by the sale would overstate (understate) the taxpayer's true gain (loss) because the sales price of the asset would presumably include the value of the improvements made. Similarly, failure to subtract depreciation deductions from the basis would cause the capital gain (loss) registered upon sale to understate (overstate) the owner's gain (loss) by the amount of tax deductions for depreciation that the owner had already been able to claim over the asset's life.

Some administrative complications in determining the basis are encountered by increasing numbers of taxpayers who acquire shares of stock in a company, or in a mutual fund, over a period of time, as occurs, for example, when dividends are automatically reinvested. When the time comes to sell the shares in the company or fund, what basis should be used to determine the taxpayer's capital gain or loss? If the shareholders have kept good records as to when different shares of stock were acquired, they can give written instructions that the sale is to consist of stock purchased at specific dates. In this case, the basis is determined by the purchase price of shares acquired on those dates. If the taxpayers cannot identify when particular shares of stock were purchased, they must normally use a first in, first out rule under which the basis is determined by using the price per share paid for the earliest purchase. Taxpayers with shares in a mutual fund can, however, use the average cost of shares acquired as their basis.

When assets are transferred between parties rather than sold, numerous rules apply to determine the basis. One such rule that affects individual taxpayers is the provision for determining basis when, for example, a parent makes a gift of an asset to a child. In this case, the basis of the asset is *carried over* from its original owner to the recipient of the gift. Assets transferred by inheritance qualify for a *stepped-up* basis. In this case, the heir's basis is the fair market value of the inherited asset at the time of the original owner's death. In effect, the stepped-up basis at death wipes out any taxes that would have been owed on capital gains.

One recurring issue in defining the basis of capital assets has to do with the proper treatment of inflation. Because the tax basis is stated in dollars of the year it was purchased, while the sale price is stated in the inflated dollars of more recent years, simply subtracting the basis from the asset's sales price will overstate the taxpayer's real capital gain when the asset is sold. The most direct way of addressing this problem is to index the basis to take inflation into account. Several administrative proposals have been made to adjust the basis for inflation, but none has been implemented to date.

ADDITIONAL READINGS

U.S. Congress. Congressional Budget Office. *Indexing Capital Gains.* Washington, DC: U.S. Government Printing Office, 1990.
Federal Tax Handbook. Paramus, NJ: Prentice Hall, 1990.

Cross-references: capital gains taxation; corporate reorganizations; depreciation recapture; inflation indexation of income taxes.

Basis adjustment

Joseph J. Cordes
George Washington University

A reduction in the basis, used to determine tax deductions for depreciation of physical assets.

Depreciation deductions for physical assets are determined by applying a schedule to the acquisition cost, or depreciable basis, of the asset. A basis adjustment reduces the amount of the asset that can be depreciated by the amount of any tax credits that the taxpayer receives in connection with purchase of the asset. For example, if a piece of equipment costs $1,000, and the firm is eligible to receive an investment tax credit equal to 10 percent of the cost of the investment, the after-tax cost of making the investment to the taxpayer would be $900. In such cases, it can be argued that the amount of capital cost recovery should be based on the taxpayer's out-of-pocket outlay of $900 rather than the purchase price of $1,000. A way of achieving this result would be to adjust—reduce—the depreciable basis of the asset by the amount of the credit claimed.

A basis adjustment was required for the original investment tax credit adopted in 1962 but was dropped in 1964. A half basis adjustment was enacted in 1982 and remained in force until 1986, when the investment credit was abolished. One reason for adjusting the depreciable basis when an asset qualifies for an investment tax credit is that it reduces the advantage that the credit gives to assets of shorter durabilities. Since the present value of depreciation deductions is larger for short-lived assets, adjusting the basis has the effect of reducing the economic value of the investment credit relatively more for short-lived than for long-lived assets. This partially offsets the fact that the investment credit reduces the user cost of shorter-lived assets relatively more than it does the user cost of longer-lived assets.

ADDITIONAL READING

Gravelle, Jane G. *The Economic Effects of Taxing Capital Income.* Cambridge, MA: MIT Press, 1994.

Cross-references: cost of capital; investment tax credits.

Benefit principle

Joseph J. Cordes
George Washington University

Along with the ability-to-pay principle, one of the two major approaches for considering the fairness of taxation.

The benefit principle, which dates to the 17th century, holds that people should pay taxes according to the benefits they receive from government programs. This requires that public expenditures be financed by taxes that place a heavier burden on taxpayers who derive greater benefits from those expenditures. The merits of the benefit principle are discussed further under *fairness in taxation.* This entry briefly summarizes the main advantages and limitations of using the benefit principle to judge the fairness of particular taxes. The most attractive feature of the benefit principle is that it puts the government-taxpayer relationship and the relationship between consumers and producers in the marketplace on equal footing. Under this view, governments provide goods and services that are of value to taxpayers, and taxes, although compulsory, become analogous to prices that people should pay for these services. Just as it is fair for consumers to "pay for what they get" in the marketplace, so too it is fair for them to pay taxes according to how much they benefit from government spending.

More recently, taxing according to benefits received has also been seen as a way of confronting taxpayers with the true cost of government goods and services. It is hoped that this will lead taxpayers to make better-informed decisions about the size and scope of government. Taxpayers are more likely to demand more government services if they believe that these services are "free" than if they must pay the costs in the form of benefit taxes or user charges. There are, however, some factors that limit the applicability of the benefit principle in gauging the fairness of financing government. One is that it is very hard to accurately measure the benefits that people receive from a wide range of goods and services. For example, how would one measure the individual benefits from the peace of mind that people get from having their borders defended, or from government programs that improve the environment? In some cases, these problems can be overcome by using tax bases that bear some relation to benefits received. For example, federal and state gasoline taxes enjoy wide support as benefit-based taxes because people believe that how much one benefits from federal and state highways bears some relationship to the amount of gasoline that one buys. Similarly, many economists believe that government goods and services are reflected in residential property values such that property taxes are often seen as a local benefit tax.

At the same time, taxes are compulsory, not voluntary, and the benefit principle does not account for a taxpayer's ability to pay. In several cases, application of the benefit principle and application of the ability-to-pay principle can cause the same tax to be viewed differently. For example, gasoline taxes are often seen as regressive taxes because consumers generally pay a lower share of their income in such taxes as their income rises. But, from the standpoint of the benefit principle, gasoline taxes are seen as providing a rough kind of tax fairness by distributing the burden of paying for public roads according to how much people drive.

ADDITIONAL READING

Musgrave, Richard A. *The Theory of Public Finance,* ch. 4. New York: McGraw-Hill, 1959.

Cross-references: ability to pay; Airport and Airway Trust Fund; fairness in taxation; fuel taxes, federal; property tax, real property, residential; tax price; Tiebout model; user charges, federal.

Border tax adjustments

Charles Vehorn
International Monetary Fund

International tax arrangements on goods traded between countries to avoid double taxation or nontaxation.

The tax treatment of goods shipped from one country to another would create serious economic distortions if some goods were taxed in both countries while others escaped taxation in both countries. Border tax adjustments make economic distortions in the prices of traded goods less likely to occur. These adjustments can follow either the destination principle or the origin principle (both principles are discussed more fully in subsequent entries). The destination principle, which is the most common international practice, provides for taxation only by the importing country. This country sets the tax rate, levies the tax, and retains the revenue for itself. Any tax paid by the exporter on inputs is refunded by the exporting country. The origin principle provides for taxation only by the exporting country. Any production that originates in the country, whether consumed at home or exported abroad, is taxable, whereas imports are exempt.

Type of taxes involved

Border tax adjustments are made for indirect taxes such as the sales tax—at either the retail level or intermediate level—the value-added tax (VAT), a cascading turnover tax, excise taxes, or state monopolies. Although some would argue that border tax adjustments should be made for direct taxes as well, General Agreement on Tariffs and Trade rules apply the origin principle to such taxes (income taxes, payroll taxes, Social Security charges, and property taxes) and make them ineligible for adjustments. Thus, this entry focuses only on indirect taxes.

The mechanism of adjustment varies depending on the type of tax. Messere (1994) has described the method of adjustment for selected consumption taxes (see table 1). For example, under a VAT, an exporter normally would receive a refund

for taxes paid on inputs by claiming a credit (as documented by the purchase invoice and verified at the border) on the VAT return. In VAT terminology, exported goods are zero-rated (see *value-added tax, national,* for further discussion). The importer, on the other hand, pays the domestic rate of VAT on all imports, at the time of either importation or subsequent domestic sales. Trade between two countries following the destination principle ensures that exports and imports will be subject to the VAT only once, by the importing country. Cases of double taxation or nontaxation are avoided.

Complications arise if a country attempts to make border tax adjustments for "taxes occultes" (hidden taxes). Taxes occultes can be defined as consumption taxes on (1) auxiliary materials used in the transportation or production of goods (e.g., energy, fuel, lubricants, packing, stationery); (2) durable capital equipment (e.g., machinery, buildings, vehicles); and (3) services (e.g., transportation, advertising) (OECD 1968). These hidden taxes were far more troublesome in cascading tax systems of the 1960s and earlier than in more current systems using the VAT. Excise taxes on gasoline also represented a source of taxes occultes. Since these taxes were hidden, it became virtually impossible to make a precise border tax adjustment, so most adjustments were based on averaging, and disputes concerning over- or undercompensation emerged. As more countries moved to the VAT, the concerns about adjustments for hidden taxes lessened (Messere 1979). But as countries adopt environmental taxes, similar complications affecting competitiveness could emerge (Ismer and Neuhoff 2004; Zhang and Baranzini 2004).

TABLE 1. Border Tax Adjustment Mechanism under Different Types of General Consumption Taxes

Type of tax	Method of adjustment	Amount of refund
Exports		
Manufacture and wholesale sales tax	Exporter does not usually pay tax, but sometimes tax already paid is refunded	Usually none, but if tax is paid then actual amount is refunded
Retail sales tax (RST)	Exporter does not pay tax	None
Value-added tax (VAT)	Exporter does not normally pay tax, but any tax paid on inputs is refunded	Actual amount of tax paid is refunded[a]
Cascading tax	Tax already paid by exporter is refunded	Estimated tax paid on similar domestic products sold in home market
Imports		
Manufacture and wholesale sales tax	Domestic rate of tax charged, sometimes at time of importation and sometimes on subsequent domestic sales	Same as tax charged on similar domestic products
Retail sales tax (RST)	Same as in manufacture and wholesale sales tax, but more often charged later on subsequent domestic sales	Same as tax charged on similar domestic products
Value-added tax (VAT)	Same as in manufacture and wholesale sales tax	Same as tax charged on similar domestic products
Cascading tax	Tax paid at time of importation	Estimated tax paid on similar domestic products sold in the home market

Source: Messere (1994).
a. This is according to the transparent VAT system originally preferred by the EC commission under which exporters pay VAT on their inputs and get it refunded when goods are exported; importers pay VAT at the time of importation. Some countries with a VAT have adopted the RST model. Currently all EC countries use the model under the deferred payment method applying to intracommunity trade.

If trading partners were to do nothing when goods crossed their borders, the tax consequences would vary depending on the type of tax in each country. If, for example, the exporting country imposed a retail sales tax and the importing country a manufacturer sales tax, then a consumer good could escape taxation by both countries. If, on the other hand, an exporting country imposed a manufacturer sales tax and the importing country a retail sales tax, then double taxation could occur (Messere 1994).

Arguments for and against

Most of the arguments either for or against border tax adjustments depend on assumptions about tax shifting. If the tax is fully shifted forward (i.e., fully reflected in the price to consumers), neutrality is maintained between a domestic good and a similar imported good, and international trade is not affected by refunding taxes paid to exporters. If the tax is partially shifted forward, imports may be inhibited and exports enhanced (OECD 1968).

The two main arguments in favor of border tax adjustments following the destination principle could be characterized as the "benefits to consumers argument" and the "competition argument." If consumers bear the tax burden and receive the benefit from government spending, consumption taxes should be collected in the country where consumers reside rather than where producers reside. The second argument points out that, in the absence of rebates and equalizing import taxes, firms in countries with high consumption tax rates cannot compete with firms in countries with low consumption tax rates unless taxes are adjusted at the border.

One argument against border tax adjustments notes that it may not be appropriate to seek neutrality on the revenue side of a government's budget while ignoring neutrality on the expenditure side. Differences in certain government expenditures (such as infrastructure) may reduce business costs disproportionately, giving certain firms in one country an advantage over similar firms in other countries. Some have generalized this argument by stating that trade between countries can be affected by various nonfiscal factors (minimum wage laws, social welfare programs, natural resources). So why single out adjustments for distortions from taxation without making adjustments for other distorting factors? The response to this argument is that the tax factor is inherently different from these other factors. If the government did nothing with respect to border tax adjustments, it would in fact be applying the origin principle.

Current policy issues

European Community

The European Community (EC), in moving toward a single market, must focus on the tax implications of intracommunity trade. As a first step, all members had to substitute a VAT for turnover taxes and follow the destination principle. In 1987, the EC Commission proposed a VAT clearinghouse system to facilitate removal of border controls. Under this proposed system, the destination principle would be maintained. However, exporters would collect VAT from importers and importers would claim credit for the VAT they paid to exporting countries. The exporting country would then be required to report the amount of tax collected on exports to a clearinghouse, which would calculate net flows to ensure that the country of destination received the correct amount of revenue (Kopits 1992). One important drawback to the clearinghouse system is that it can only be successful to the extent that each member country correctly reports the tax collected by exporters and the tax credit claimed by importers, while at the same time ensuring that any fraud is quickly detected.

Instead of the clearinghouse, however, the EC adopted a transitional regime that began on January 1, 1993. This system was to be in effect for at least four years and extended automatically thereafter until a definitive system had been developed. Under the transitional regime, exports to VAT payers in another country continue to be zero-rated. The importer is formally liable for the VAT on the imports, but is also allowed to take a credit for these purchases against the VAT collected on sales. The transitional regime relies heavily on information sharing, maintains the destination principle, avoids use of an administratively complicated clearinghouse mechanism, and protects the importer from any prefinancing costs of the VAT (Hill and Rushton 1993).

Former Soviet Union countries

The problem faced by countries in the former Soviet Union (FSU) in the early 1990s was identical to that faced by EC countries. How should trade between FSU countries be treated under the VAT? Almost all FSU countries initially followed the VAT model adopted by the Russian Federation in 1991. In that original VAT law, imports were not taxed, regardless of whether the goods were from FSU countries or countries other than the FSU. Exports to countries outside the FSU were zero-rated. Exports to FSU countries were apparently subject to VAT, but with certain restrictions that allowed a credit for imports, so a modified origin principle prevailed. At the end of 1992 the Russian Federation changed its VAT law, appearing to reflect the destination principle. Exports were zero-rated and all imports were subject to the VAT. However, another provision in the law allowed trade between FSU countries to be regulated by international agreements, including an agreement between most FSU countries that exports, rather than imports, would be subject to VAT (Sunley and Summers 1995). More recently, FSU countries in general have enacted new tax laws stipulating use of the destination principle for all trade, except trade in the energy sector.

ADDITIONAL READINGS

Hill, Roderick, and Michael Rushton. "Harmonizing Provincial Sales Taxes with the GST: The Problem of Interprovincial Trade." *International VAT Monitor* (October 1993): 21–32.

Ismer, Roland, and Karsten Neuhoff. "Border Tax Adjustments: A Feasible Way to Address Nonparticipation in Emission Trading." Working Paper no. 36. Cambridge, MA: The Cambridge–MIT Institute, 2004.

Kopits, George. "Overview." In *Tax Harmonization in the European Community: Policy Issues and Analysis,* edited by George Kopits. Washington, DC: International Monetary Fund, 1992.

Messere, Ken. "A Defense of Present Border Tax Adjustment Practices." *National Tax Journal* 32 (December 1979): 481–92.

———. "The International Consumption Tax Rules." *Bulletin for International Fiscal Documentation* 48 (December 1994): 665–80.

Organization for Economic Cooperation and Development. *Border Tax Adjustments and Tax Structures in OECD Member Countries.* Paris: OECD, 1968.

Sunley, Emil M., and Victoria P. Summers. "An Analysis of Value-Added Taxes in Russia and Other Countries of the Former Soviet Union." *Tax Notes International* 10 (June 19, 1995): 2049–72.

Zhang, Zhong Xiang, and Andrea Baranzini. "What Do We Know about Carbon Taxes? An Inquiry into Their Impacts on Competitiveness and Distribution of Income." *Energy Policy* 32 (2004): 507–18.

Cross-references: consumption taxation; destination principle; origin principle; value-added tax, national.

Budget-balance requirement

Ronald Snell
National Conference of State Legislatures

Most states have legislation mandating that expenditures not exceed revenues.

Requirements that states balance their budgets are often said to be a major difference between state and federal budgeting. State officials certainly take seriously an obligation to balance the budget, and in the debate over a federal balanced budget in the early and mid-1990s, much of the discussion centered on those states with balanced budgets. This entry is concerned with the nature, definition, and enforcement of state balanced-budget requirements.

Nature of state balanced-budget requirements

All states except Vermont have a legal requirement to balance their budget. Some are constitutional, some are statutory, and some have been derived by judicial decision from constitutional provisions about state indebtedness that do not, on their face, call for a balanced budget. The Government Accountability Office has commented that "some balanced budget requirements are based on interpretations of state constitutions and statutes rather than on an explicit statement that the state must have a balanced budget."

The requirements vary in stringency from state to state. In some states, the requirement is that the introduced budget be balanced or that the enacted budget be balanced. In others, policymakers are required to ensure that expenditures in a fiscal year stay within the cash available for that fiscal year. Yet other states may carry unavoidable deficits into the next fiscal year for resolution.

There are three general kinds of state balanced budget requirements:

1. The governor's proposed budget must be balanced (43 states and Puerto Rico).
2. The budget the legislature passes must be balanced (39 states and Puerto Rico).
3. The budget must be balanced at the end of a fiscal year or biennium, such that no deficit be carried forward (37 states and Puerto Rico).

Such provisions can be either constitutional or statutory but are more rigorous if they are constitutional since they are not subject to legislative amendment. Some states have two or all three of the possible balanced-budget requirements, and a few have only a statutory requirement that the governor submit a balanced budget. Weighing such considerations, 36 states have rigorous balanced-budget requirements, 4 have weak requirements, and the other 10 fall in between those categories.

What has to be balanced?

State balanced-budget requirements in practice refer to operating budgets, not capital budgets. Operating budgets include annual expenditures—such items as salaries and wages, aid to local governments, health and welfare benefits, and other expenditures that are repeated from year to year. State capital expenditures, mainly for land, highways, and buildings, are largely financed by debt. Court decisions and referendums on borrowing have led to the exclusion of expenditures funded by long-term debt from calculations of whether a budget is balanced.

In practice, the following kinds of state revenues and expenditures also have little impact on state balanced budgets:

- Almost all federal reimbursements or grants to a state are committed to specific purposes, and the governor and legislature have little discretion over the use of most federal funds.
- Transportation trust fund money raised from state motor fuel taxes is usually earmarked for highways and other transportation purposes.
- Some tax collections may be diverted to local governments or other specified purposes without appropriations.
- Some states allow agencies or programs to collect and spend fees, charges, or tuition without annual or biennial appropriations.

In each of these cases, it is practically impossible for revenues and expenditures to get out of balance, since expenditures are controlled by available funds. Thus it is not surprising that "balancing the budget" tends to focus on the general fund, even though general-fund expenditures compose only 50 to 60 percent of total state spending.

Enforcement of balanced-budget requirements

State requirements to balance the budget do not impose legal penalties for failure to do so. There are, however, two sorts of enforcement mechanisms. Prohibitions against carrying deficits into the next fiscal year and restrictions on the issuance of state debt help to enforce balanced-budget provisions by making it difficult to finance a deficit. In many states, governors or joint legislative–executive commissions can revise the budget after it has been enacted to bring it into balance.

Unlike the federal government, states are not able to issue debt routinely. Issues of general obligation debt require at least the approval of the legislature and, in many states, voter approval. The issue of revenue bonds requires legislation to create an agency to issue the bonds and the creation of a revenue stream to repay the debt. These practices place the issuance of debt fully into public view. However, it is extremely rare for a state government to borrow long-term funds to cover operating expenses. While Louisiana did in 1988 and Connecticut did in 1991, there do not appear to be any other examples of this practice from recent years.

A legislature and a governor can jointly revise a budget at any time. But most legislatures are not in session throughout the year, and some legislatures meet for only a few months every other year. Requiring legislative consent for every change in a budget would impose delays or the costs of special sessions. Therefore, many state constitutions allow governors or special commissions to revise budgets after they have been enacted to bring expenditures into line with revenues.

Thirty-six states allow governors some degree of authority to reduce spending when it is necessary to maintain a balanced budget, even if enacted budgets call for specific amounts of expenditure. Some states prohibit executive budget revisions, and many restrict the amounts and nature of such reductions. Some states have, in addition, joint legislative and executive boards or commissions that are constitutionally permitted to make budget revisions—for example, to deal with unforeseen revenue shortfalls, emergencies, or unanticipated federal funds.

Practice

State balanced-budget rules are not as rigid as those recommended for the federal government in the early 1990s, which would have forbidden total expenditures above total revenues in any year, as well as new borrowing. By this standard, states routinely run deficits because they borrow to finance capital expenditures. But this does not violate state balanced-budget requirements. Nor does rolling deficits in operating funds forward from one fiscal year to the next, if a state constitution permits the practice.

Fiscal stress, however, can induce governors and legislators to adopt expedients so they can observe the letter, if not the spirit, of balanced-budget requirements. Among these are selling state assets, postponing payments to vendors, reducing payments to pension funds, borrowing from one state fund to finance expenditures from another, and using "creative" accounting. Such expedients reflect the stress that can arise between legal demands for a balanced budget and political demands for the continuation of state programs with-

out tax increases. The fact that such expedients tend to be limited to times of fiscal stress is in itself a measure of how seriously state elected officials take their responsibility to produce balanced budgets.

ADDITIONAL READINGS

Advisory Commission on Intergovernmental Relations [ACIR]. *Fiscal Discipline in the Federal System: National Reform and the Experience of the States.* Washington, DC: ACIR, 1987.

Briffault, Richard. *Balancing Acts: The Reality behind State Balanced Budget Requirements.* New York: Twentieth Century Fund Press, 1996.

National Association of State Budget Officers. "Budget Processes in the States." Washington, DC: National Association of State Budget Officers, 2002.

Snell, Ronald K. *State Balanced Budget Requirements: Provisions and Practice.* Denver: National Conference of State Legislatures, 1996.

Cross-references: budgeting, state; budget policy, state and local; budget processes, state.

Budgeting, state
Ronald Snell
National Conference of State Legislatures

There is a similarity of state practices regarding the budgeting framework and administrative process.

The state budget process is central to the administration of state government. In addition to allocating resources, budgets set policy, review and evaluate policy, and lay the foundation for future planning and program review. This discussion is concerned with the elements of state budget processes that are found in most states.

State practices are fairly similar. Important structural differences include the nature of a state's requirement to balance the budget; an annual or biennial budget cycle; the governor's authority to revise the enacted budget; and whether earmarked or federal funds are subject to the appropriations process. The most important political difference among states is the balance between legislative and executive authority in composing the budget. Governors' line-item vetoes are one element in the legislative/executive balance, but tradition and partisanship are equally decisive.

The framework of budgeting—the fiscal period

Budgets are for a specific period of time: a fiscal year or a biennium. Although 21 states enact budgets on a biennial schedule, only North Dakota, Oregon, and Wyoming enact true biennial budgets. Elsewhere, biennial states enact separate budgets for two fiscal years at once. The relative advantages of annual and biennial budgets have been debated at length, and states occasionally change from one to the other. Nebraska shifted to biennial budgeting in 1987, Connecticut did so in 1991, and Arizona did so in 1999. No state has moved in the other direction in the past decade. The current state and federal interest in biennial budgeting is motivated by the hopes of saving time and political energy, and of having more opportunity for program evaluation and review. The overall experience of states, however, is that neither budget cycle has overwhelming advantages or disadvantages.

Fiscal years begin on July 1 for all but four states. July 1 is the date on which the federal fiscal year began until the federal government changed to October 1 in 1974. Alabama and Michigan adopted the federal practice. New York begins its fiscal year April 1 and Texas on September 1. The advantage of a fiscal year that begins in or after the middle of a calendar year lies in the legislative calendar. State legislatures that are not in session year-round convene in January or February, and a July beginning for the new fiscal year allows time to enact a budget.

The framework of budgeting— balanced-budget requirements

State balanced-budget requirements give revenue forecasting even more importance for states than for the federal government, which can routinely borrow to maintain programmed expenditures. States are less able to do so. State long-term, general-obligation borrowing requires at least legislative approval and may take a vote of the people. Constitutional and statutory restraints on state borrowing put teeth into balanced-budget provisions. Balanced-budget provisions themselves do not require all states to make sure a year's expenditures are less than the year's resources. Thirty-eight states are constitutionally prohibited from carrying over a deficit from one fiscal year (or biennium) to the next—the most rigorous antideficit provision. In other states, the requirement is that a governor submit a balanced budget, or that the budget enacted by the legislature be in balance.

Most states, in most years, balance their operating budgets. Capital expenditures are not necessarily included in determining whether a budget is balanced, and some other obligations may be omitted. Recessions or unforeseen fiscal problems can force state governments to take extreme measures to comply with the letter of the law, such as shifting resources among state accounts ("internal borrowing"), counting the sales of assets or the proceeds of borrowing as revenues, deferring vendor payments or contributions to retirement funds, or sophistry in accounting. Such measures are sometimes attacked as evidence of bad faith on the part of governors and legislators. However, the real issue is the tension between demands for a balanced budget and demands that spending for state programs be sustained.

The budgeting process—the executive budget

All states follow the model of executive budgeting. Executive budget offices and staff draft a proposed budget to submit to the legislature. As a rule, executive budget proposals are comprehensive—they include all sources of funding and expenditures, with the possible exceptions of state authorities and enterprises that generate their own revenue. The governor's budget also includes proposals for the budgets of other elected state officials—many states elect officials such as the treasurer, the attorney general, the auditor, and the superintendent of public schools, who may have substantial budgets to administer.

In most states, the proposed executive budget dominates the legislative budgeting process. In some states it is adopted with relatively few changes, and in most it establishes the agenda of budget discussion and negotiation. In most states, the executive budget is the only comprehensive planning document the state produces. Strong legislative budget processes dominate in a few states—Arizona, Colorado, and Texas, for example—and in those the executive budget may be largely disregarded.

The budgeting process—executive and legislative coordination

Whether the executive or legislative branch dominates the budget process, there is generally far more cooperation between the legislative and executive branches than is typical for Congress and the president. The agenda-setting role of the executive budget in many states is one reason. Another is the executive line-item veto in the 41 states where it exists. A final reason is the political expectation that a state will enact a balanced budget before the beginning of its fiscal year, an expectation that is almost always met. Late budgets and vetoes are most likely when a state is experiencing serious fiscal difficulties. Otherwise, executive and legislative negotiations are intended to resolve budget disagreements and avoid vetoes and late budgets. Governors used line-item vetoes in only 5 of the 41 states that permitted them in 1993 (Snell 1995).

Postenactment budget revisions

Although budgets become effective only after legislative enactment and executive approval, many states allow budget revisions to be made without involving the entire legislature. Most legislatures are not in session throughout the year, and some legislatures meet for only a few months every other year. Requiring legislative consent for every change in a budget would impose delays or the costs of special sessions. Therefore, 36 states allow governors some degree of authority to reduce spending when it is necessary to maintain a balanced budget, even if enacted budgets call for specific amounts of expenditure.

Some states prohibit executive budget revisions. Many states restrict the amounts and nature of such revisions. Some states have, in addition, joint legislative and executive boards or commissions that are constitutionally permitted to make budget revisions—for example, to deal with unforeseen revenue shortfalls, emergencies, or unanticipated federal funds.

Thus, state constitutions do not necessarily require as strict a separation of legislative and executive authority as the federal constitution does for the federal government. Governors and legislatures may make significant midyear changes in a budget, as needed. Additional appropriations or appropriations for new purposes are called *supplemental* appropriations. Legislatures that convene at the beginning of a calendar year usually find a list of proposed supplementals awaiting their consideration, with its length and amount depending on the problems that have arisen to that point in the fiscal year and on the revenue available for use.

Administration of the budget

Budget administration is the responsibility of the executive branch, although the legislative and judicial branches protect their independence by maintaining control of their budgets. Other elected executive branch officials administer their budgets, and they and the judiciary occasionally clash with governors when governors see a need for government-wide budget cuts (legislators are less likely to disagree with governors on this point, for political reasons).

Budget administration is usually centralized in a budget or accounting office, which releases funds to agencies on a schedule (the allotment process). Such offices are usually responsible for monitoring revenues and expenditures, and issuing monthly reports at least for internal use, but increasingly for public information. Such central budget offices may include or coordinate their work with state purchasing offices and personnel departments. The current trend is to decentralize purchasing and personnel management to agencies as much as possible. Financial auditing may be the responsibility of an executive official. Performance auditing and program review, however, are often the responsibility of a legislative agency (44 legislatures have one) and are closely tied to legislative budget oversight.

ADDITIONAL READINGS

Axelrod, Donald. *Budgeting for Modern Government,* 2d ed. New York: St. Martin's Press, 1995.

Clynch, Edward J., and Thomas P. Lauth, editors. *Governors, Legislatures, and Budgets: Diversity across the American States.* New York: Greenwood Press, 1991.

Eckl, Corina L. *Legislative Authority over the Enacted Budget.* Denver: National Conference of State Legislatures, 1992.

Grooters, Jen. *Legislative Budget Procedures in the 50 States.* Denver: National Conference of State Legislatures, 1998.

National Association of State Budget Officers. *Budget Processes in the States.* Washington, DC: National Association of State Budget Officers, 2002.

National Conference of State Legislatures. *State Strategies to Manage Budget Shortfalls.* Denver: National Conference of State Legislatures, 1996.

Rosenthal, Alan. *Governors and Legislatures: Contending Powers.* Washington, DC: Congressional Quarterly Press, 1990.

Snell, Ronald K. *Fundamentals of Sound State Budgeting Practices.* Denver: National Conference of State Legislatures, 1995.

Cross-references: budget-balance requirement; budget policy, state and local; budget processes, state.

Budget policy, state and local

Jeffrey I. Chapman
Arizona State University

The environment of state and local budget policy delineated by changing size and composition, unsettled issues, and cries for reform.

The importance of the state and local sector has greatly increased since 1960. From 1960 to 2000, for example, the share of spending by state and local governments in total government spending rose from 33 to 44 percent, and the share of general revenue collected by state and local governments rose from just over 33 percent to more than 49 percent of revenue collected by all levels of government (Economic Report of the President 2005, table B-82).

Changing composition of state and local expenditures

There have been some significant changes in the composition of state and local expenditures over the past several decades. Table 1 illustrates dramatic changes in three categories of state expenditures: public welfare and corrections expenditures have more than doubled, while expenditures on highways have fallen by about two-thirds. Note that these percentages have been stable since 1990. As table 2 shows, for local governments there have been fewer dramatic expenditure changes, with only highway expenditures falling by about 50 percent. Conversely, what is notable is that so many expenditure categories have not changed over the 30 years. Tables 3 and 4 show that the composition of state and local revenues has remained quite stable. Table 3 shows only a few categories of revenue sources that have changed much since 1960. In particular, the total amount of taxes, as a percentage of total revenues, has decreased because the decline in sales taxes and other taxes has offset the increase in income taxes. Charges have nearly doubled to offset this tax decline. This has probably resulted in increased efficiency if the charges have been accurately set. However, it has also probably increased regressivity.

Table 4 shows roughly similar results for local governments. Total taxes have declined as a percentage of total revenues; however, in this case, the decline has occurred because of the fall in property taxes. Again, this decline has been offset by the increase in charges and miscellaneous revenue sources. It should be noted that local governments receive about 8 percent of their total revenues from utilities, whereas the state receives about 1 percent.

Budget issues today

Any analysis of state and local budgeting must address several policy issues, among them: (1) a lack of any theory of budgeting; (2) budget and fiscal stress, including tax and expenditure

TABLE 1. State Direct Expenditures: Percentage Distribution (Fiscal Years)

	1960	1970	1980	1990	1994	2001	2003
Higher education	16	22	20	18	17	20	18
Public welfare	12	19	24	27	32	32	34
Health and hospitals	11	10	11	10	10	9	9
Corrections	2	2	3	5	5	5	5
Highways	34	22	13	11	11	10	9
Interest on debt	3	3	5	6	5	4	4
Other	22	22	24	23	21	21	21

Source: Government Finances, selected years; http://www.census.gov.

TABLE 2. Local Direct Expenditures: Percentage Distribution (Fiscal Years)

	1960	1970	1980	1990	1994	2001	2003
Local education	44	44	41	40	40	42	41
Public welfare	6	8	6	5	5	4	4
Health and hospitals	6	6	7	8	9	8	8
Police and fire	8	7	8	8	8	8	8
Highways	10	6	6	5	5	4	4
Interest on debt	3	4	4	5	5	5	4
Other	23	25	28	29	28	29	31

Source: Government Finances, selected years; http://www.census.gov.

TABLE 3. State Revenue Sources: Percentage Distribution (Percent of General Fund)

	1960	1970	1980	1990	1994	2001	2003
Intergovernmental	21	24	23	22	24	26	28
Total taxes	55	53	48	47	44	47	42
Property	2	1	1	1	1	1	1
Personal income	7	10	13	15	14	18	14
Sales	32	30	23	23	22	22	21
Other	14	11	11	8	7	7	6
Charges and misc.	8	10	12	15	14	16	16
Other	3	5	8	1	1	1	1
Insurance contracts	13	11	15	15	17	10	13

Source: Government Finances, selected years; http://www.census.gov.

TABLE 4. Local Direct Revenue Sources: Percentage Distribution (Fiscal Years)

	1960	1970	1980	1990	1994	2001	2003
Intergovernmental	27	34	39	33	34	35	37
Total taxes	49	43	33	35	35	33	34
Property	43	36	25	26	26	24	25
Personal income	1	2	2	2	2	2	2
Sales	4	4	5	5	5	6	6
Other	2	1	1	2	2	2	2
Charges and misc.	13	14	18	20	20	21	20
Utility	10	7	9	9	9	9	8
Other	2	2	2	3	3	2	1

Source: Government Finances, selected years; http://www.census.gov.

limits; (3) budgetary structures; (4) operating versus capital budgets; and (5) increasing interaction between state and local budgets.

Lack of budgetary theory

Currently, there is no unified budgeting theory for state and local government. However, there are some potential candidates for a beginning discussion. For example, the models of principal-agent relationships (Eisenhardt 1989), which are concerned with controlling both measurable and nonmeasurable outputs, might be a useful starting point. Alternatively, controlling the levels of taxes and expenditures might be addressed through a Tiebout analysis (Dowding et al. 1994). Finally, since the budget itself is a political document, some elements of game theory might be appropriate in its analysis.

Budgets, tax and expenditure limits, and fiscal stress

The focus of state and local tax and expenditure limits is on the budget. Since it is the document that reflects the outcome of the public decisionmaking process, it becomes the document controlled by these constraints. To the extent that budgets are politically constrained, fiscal stress is likely. The budget will not realize forecasted revenues and will not be able to allocate resources to all claimants.

Budgetary structures

Much discussion concerning budgets revolves around the types of approaches that can be used to facilitate the budget as either a control, management, or planning device (Lee, Johnson, and Joyce 2004). A line-item budget—in which the budget is concerned with inputs such as number of employees and their salaries, the amount of capital, and the amount of materials and supplies—is principally a control device. The budget can be performance based, in which performance measures are developed by the jurisdiction and then adequate funding is established to ensure meeting those benchmarks. For example, the desired number of minutes for an ambulance to arrive at an emergency scene is determined and then financed. Decisions are made at the performance level, and these budgets are used for management decisions. The third type of budget is planning oriented. In this type, the mission of a particular agency is defined and then budget decisions are made to support this mission. A subcomponent of this type of budget is the modified zero-based budget that asks each agency manager to predict what would happen if specified increments or decrements of the budget were to occur. Although zero-based budgeting was not absolutely successful at the national level, some state and local jurisdictions have successfully used a modified form. Another subcomponent of this type of budget is the entrepreneurial budget, in which decisions are decentralized to make each manager accountable for results (Cothran 1993). It should be noted that underlying

all of these budgets is the simple line-item form, which must always be followed, regardless of any other sophisticated methodology. This makes the other budget formats more expensive than the line-item form.

Operating versus capital budgets

The operating budget of a jurisdiction is designed to control, manage, or plan the jurisdiction's current activities. The capital budget is designed as a plan for obtaining and financing long-term capital assets, usually accumulated through the issuance of debt. Although most state and local jurisdictions have moved to a separation of operating and capital budgets, there still may be confusion over the appropriate use of each. This is especially true when the operating budget contains payments for such debt-like instruments as certificates of participation, which are not technically debt. Further confusion occurs when earmarked fund accounting appears in the operating budget, yet the funds are used to finance long-run capital projects. Although there are formal accounting rules designed to force the reporting of these transactions correctly and consistently (Government Finance Officers Association 2003), many jurisdictions do not follow the full Governmental Accounting Financial Reporting standards.

Intergovernmental budget relationships

Over time, the relationships between state and local budgets have become more complex. Local governments are now closely tied to state budgets and state controls. On the expenditure side, this tie relates to state-mandated services financed by the local government, while on the revenue side, it relates to state subventions and tax sharing with the local governments. Some states, when their revenues fall, may take some of these revenues back from the local governments. This "shift-and-shaft" federalism can cause fiscal stress at the local level while the state solves its budgetary problems. A side effect of this activity is the disengagement of the state and local budget cycles, since the mandates and revenue shifts are sometimes decided after the local budget is adopted.

Budget reforms

Recommending budget reforms has always been a popular subject (for examples, see Schick 1990 or the California Citizens Budget Commission 1995). In particular, two sets of reforms seem to be consistent among all recommendations.

One is that the budget should become a useful source of information for public decisionmaking. The other is that budgets should be comprehensive, using standardized data formats, written in plain English, accompanied by a narrative summarizing the actions taken, and understandable by both elected officials and the citizens.

The budget should also be an honest reflection of decisions undertaken. An explicit discussion of tax expenditures, the use of special funds, and a statement of fiscal condition should be an integral part of the budget document. In addition, a presentation of current expenditures, the baseline trend—including cost-of-living allowances and caseload increases—and budget expenditures should be presented, so that actual changes can be determined. State and local governments do not have the luxury of the continuous deficit finance that the national government has utilized over the past several decades. These governments can be exceedingly stretched between constituent demands for fewer taxes and more service entitlements. Because of this, the issues that face state and local budgets tend to carry more emotional weight than those at the national level, and consequently it is far more difficult to reach consensus.

ADDITIONAL READINGS

California Citizens Budget Commission. *Reforming California's Budget Process* (preliminary report). Los Angeles: Center for Governmental Studies, 1995.

Cothran, Dan A. "Entrepreneurial Budgeting: An Emerging Reform?" *Public Administration Review* 53, no. 5 (September/October 1993): 445–54.

Dowding, Keith, Peter John, and Stephen Biggs. "Tiebout: A Survey of the Empirical Literature." *Urban Studies* 31, no. 4/5 (1994): 767–97.

Economic Report of the President. Washington, DC: United States Government Printing Office, 2005.

Eisenhardt, Kathleen M. "Agency Theory: An Assessment and Review." *Academy of Management and Review* 14 (1) (1989): 57–74.

Government Finance Officers Association. *Governmental Accounting, Auditing and Financial Reporting.* Chicago: Government Finance Officers Association, 2003.

Lee, Robert D., Jr., Ronald W. Johnson, and Philip G. Joyce. *Public Budgeting Systems,* 7th ed. Sudbury, MA: Jones and Bartlett, 2004.

Schick, Alan. *The Capacity to Budget.* Washington, DC: Urban Institute Press, 1990.

Tyler, Charlie, and Jennifer Willard. "Public Budgeting in America: A Twentieth Century Retrospective." *Journal of Public Budgeting, Accounting and Financial Management* 9, no. 2 (Summer 1997): 189–219.

Cross-references: budget-balance requirement; budgeting, state; budget processes, state.

Budget process, federal

Al Davis
formerly, House Budget Committee

Updated by
Philip Joyce
George Washington University

Annual procedures whereby the president submits a budget for congressional review and disposition.

The U.S. government has an annual budget cycle. The cycle normally begins when the president submits the budget to Congress early in the calendar year. The president's budget translates many of his political priorities into a plan of action. Then Congress responds. At a minimum, Congress must pass annual appropriations bills or one or more "continuing resolutions" that may substitute for appropriations bills. In many years, Congress does more. It passes legislation that changes the permanent laws affecting revenues and spending, such as Medicare. The congressional budget process is used to coordinate budget-related congressional action.

Time horizon

In the 1970s, presidential and congressional budgets typically covered one year. During the 1980s, the budget time horizon grew longer. Five-year congressional budgets became the norm and are now required by law. Even longer projections have sometimes been made. For example, the budget resolution approved in 1996 covered a seven-year period. The new congressional majority wanted to balance the budget and it took seven years to show that the plan could achieve balance, relying as it did on savings to grow from cutting the rate of growth of spending.

A longer budget horizon promotes better planning and discourages gimmicks that create only onetime savings or onetime revenue gains. A longer horizon also discourages spending initiatives or tax cuts that are small for many years but balloon in later years. However, over a longer time period, technical estimating limitations become more severe. Moreover, the policies assumed in a very long-range budget may not be sustainable because the current Congress cannot tie the hands of future Congresses. This fact is particularly salient in the case of appropriations because they are made annually and do not become part of permanent law.

Economic assumptions

Underlying any federal government budget is a set of economic assumptions. For example, a president may decide that his program will be "good for the economy," and he may assume in his budget that economic growth will be higher, or inflation or unemployment lower, than in recent years. His assumptions may be more optimistic than the consensus of private economic forecasters. Congress is likewise free to decide on its own economic assumptions for the congressional budget resolution. The levels of revenues, entitlement spending, and deficits in the budget are quite sensitive to the underlying economic assumptions. Optimistic assumptions can bring budgets closer to balance and minimize the size of spending cuts or revenue increases needed to bring the budget into balance. Presidential budgeting during the late 1980s was criticized for using "rosy scenario" economic assumptions to make it look as if the president's program would achieve a balanced budget.

The power of economic assumptions can be illustrated: in early 1997, the Congressional Budget Office (CBO) estimated that if interest rates became 1 percentage point lower than the CBO had projected through the year 2002, with no change in inflation, the budget deficit would be lower by $48 billion in 2002. In 1997, the congressional budget resolution assumed a deficit reduction of $34 billion in the year 2002 to come mainly from a reduction in interest rates. This reduction, in turn, was to come from law changes to reduce budget deficits. (Lower interest rates reduce the cost of federal debt service.) As a result, the congressional budget did not have to recommend law changes that by themselves would balance the budget. Once policies were recommended to move the budget close to balance, the assumption was that a dividend from lower debt service costs would bring the budget the rest of the way into balance.

So-called technical assumptions, such as those about patterns of medical service use, are also very important in making budget projections. Typically, the congressional budget process relies on the CBO to make these assumptions.

Economic and technical assumptions can change over time. These changes can greatly alter perceptions about budgetary problems and influence the federal government's response. For example, in January 2001, CBO projected a fiscal year 2005 surplus of $433 billion and cumulative surpluses of $5.6 trillion between 2002 and 2011. This represented a substantial improvement in the budget outlook since even a year earlier (when the 2005 surplus was only projected at $268 billion, and the cumulative 10-year surpluses were estimated at approximately $3 trillion). This substantial improvement in the forecasted outlook was driven entirely by changes in economic and technical assumptions; no significant budget legislation had been enacted during 2000. The 2001 surplus forecast, however, helped to pave the way for the Bush tax cuts that were enacted during 2001. By January 2003, a deficit of $73 billion was forecast for fiscal year 2005. While a significant portion of this change resulted from policy changes (the Bush tax cut and spending for the war on terrorism), as much as half of it resulted from changes in the economy or in technical assumptions.

When the federal budget was far out of balance, the major limiting factors on congressional budget action were the difficulty in reaching agreement and lawmakers' tolerance for painful cuts in spending or painful increases in taxes. If the federal budget comes to balance, the budget agenda may become more sensitive to small changes in budgetary projections. For example, if a $20 billion deficit is projected, Congress might want to eliminate the deficit. If a $20 billion surplus is projected, Congress might want to cut taxes or increase spending. Such swings in policy could occur, even though they would be driven by statistically tiny errors in budgetary projections, given that total spending and revenues currently exceed $2,000 billion.

President's budget

The president's budget is not just a set of highlights and suggestions, or a presentation of the president's political preferences—although it is surely that. The president's budget is normally presented in great "line-item" detail. Large documents are printed and backed up with detailed supporting materials from the government agencies. Because of the president's prominence as a nationwide elected official, his ability to marshal the resources of the executive branch, and, in comparison, Congress's representation of so many varied points of view, the president's budget is often the point of departure for subsequent congressional decisions.

Congressional budget

The present congressional budget process was implemented in the Congressional Budget Act of 1974. That legislation was partly a congressional response to concerns over President Nixon's unilateral and aggressive withholding of authority to spend. The new budget act created a new, less one-sided mechanism. The legislation was also a response to the criticism that Congress lacked a mechanism for coordinating the response of its numerous committees to the president's budget, or for coordinating an alternative budget. The drafters of that legislation did not wish to take away more power than necessary from the then-standing committees of Congress. When they created the new budget committees, they did not eliminate other committees, nor did they intend that the budget committees become creators of "line-item" authorization law changes or appropriations bills. The mission of the budget committees and the budget resolution is to provide guidelines and targets for the money-related actions of other committees. The budget resolution allows Congress to speak with one voice to its various committees.

The original budget act included a variety of procedural rules, and since its passage, the Senate has added its own special procedural rules, which are too extensive to discuss in this entry. The act also established the CBO, which produces baseline budget projections, studies related to the budget, and estimates of the budget effects of proposed legislation, except for changes in revenues, which are generally estimated by the Joint Committee on Taxation. The CBO is independent of the executive branch and is separate from the much smaller staffs of the House and Senate budget committees.

The congressional budget takes the form of a resolution that is voted on by the House and the Senate, first separately and then in response to a conference committee recommendation. The final budget resolution is not submitted to the president for his approval or veto. The congressional document is normally quite different in character from the president's budget.

Content of a budget resolution

The report accompanying the budget resolution includes a statement of underlying economic assumptions. These are recommended by the budget committees and need not be identical to the president's, or the same as the advisory assumptions normally suggested by the CBO.

The congressional budget resolution presents total spending, total revenues, the recommended change in revenues, the budget deficit (or surplus), and the implied level of federal debt that is subject to statutory limit. (If that level of debt is higher than the amount authorized by current law,

Congress must later vote to raise the "debt ceiling," even though it has already voted on a budget that will create higher debt. This must-pass debt legislation often becomes a vehicle for legislative riders, one of which was the original Gramm-Rudman-Hollings (GRH) law discussed further on.) In the budget resolution, spending is broken down among 20 budget "functions" covering such categories as defense, international affairs, agriculture, transportation, Medicare, other health services, and net interest. The "functions" include many government programs and do not track one-for-one with congressional committee jurisdictions.

Officially, the amounts in the budget resolution no longer include the Social Security trust funds, which are expected to run surpluses for many years. Nevertheless, committee report language typically provides projections for the budget including Social Security, and the budget has been discussed in terms of the total, including Social Security. For example, when the 1997 budget resolution was presented as a plan for balancing the budget, that balance was achieved only with Social Security Trust Fund surpluses included. The official numbers in the budget resolution continued to show deficits because they did not include Social Security surpluses.

The report on a budget resolution also includes committee "allocations" (i.e., ceilings) and a revenue floor, and it may include "reconciliation instructions." Allocations and the floor on revenues are enforced through points of order in the House and Senate. Most often, it takes 60 votes in the 100-member Senate to waive a point of order against considering legislation that would cause spending to exceed a budget allocation or revenues to be cut below the floor. In the House, the "rule" controlling amendments and debate may waive points of order, and the rule is subject to a majority vote.

One allocation is made to the Appropriations Committee. Appropriations are made each year for fixed dollar amounts. This one allocation covers a great deal of spending. For example, for fiscal year 1997, spending determined by appropriations was about $550 billion, one-third of total spending including Social Security. For a "budget year" (e.g., for calendar year 1997, the "budget year" was the coming fiscal year, 1998), this allocation is enforceable by a point of order. In the more than 20 years since the process began, total appropriations have been held quite closely to the allocation in the budget resolution.

Because there is only one budget resolution allocation for all appropriations, program-by-program assumptions that the budget committees may have used may not be very influential. On the other hand, if a major issue, such as a division of funds between defense and nondefense, were to be articulated and fully debated, the assumption associated with that decision might greatly influence the subsequent appropriations process.

The rest of the budget comprises revenues and "mandatory" spending. Mandatory spending includes "entitlements," which are created by laws that entitle certain classes of people to benefits. The largest entitlements are Social Security ($470 billion in 2003) and Medicare ($274 billion). Mandatory spending also includes obligatory spending, such as interest on the federal debt ($153 billion in 2003) and payments arising from court decisions. Typically, neither tax law nor underlying authorizations specify numerical amounts; rather, they set the terms and conditions under which individuals pay taxes and receive benefits such as Social Security. Unlike spending subject to appropriations, revenues and mandatory spending will be whatever results from the underlying law. For this reason, revenues and mandatory spending are more difficult to predict, and they are more difficult to control than spending subject to appropriations.

While detailed appropriations are the responsibility of a single committee in the House and Senate, responsibility for revenues and mandatory spending is spread among many committees. The report on a budget resolution creates allocations for each of the authorizing committees. These allocations cover the total amount of mandatory spending contemplated in the budget resolution. Because the authorizing committees have different program responsibilities, the program implications of these multiple allocations may be clearer than for the single allocation provided for annual appropriations. For example, if the Committee on Ways and Means has a spending allocation that is significantly below the current law level, Congress probably knows whether Medicare reductions are likely and, if so, the broad outlines of the probable changes.

Although there are points of order against considering legislation that would cause spending to exceed an allocation, or revenues to fall below the floor, points of order are powerless to reduce spending that would occur under existing law or to raise revenues. For this reason, management of mandatory spending, unlike appropriations, also takes place through "reconciliation instructions" to the various authorizing committees. These instructions do not have to be included in a budget resolution, but they frequently have been included since budget deficits became a concern. Reconciliation instructions are numerical targets stretching over several years. Recently, the time span has been five years or more.

From 1981 through 1993, the instructions were to reduce mandatory spending and/or raise revenues. After 1995, however, the new congressional majority began to include instructions for major tax cuts. Tax cuts were ultimately enacted in 1997, 2001, and 2002.

Historically, Congress has usually come quite close to meeting the reconciliation targets, although in one year a reconciliation effort was abandoned, and once, during the mid-1980s, reconciliation action was not completed until early in the next session of Congress. In 1995, reconciliation was not completed because the president vetoed the implementing legislation. In 1996, Congress completed action on only one of three reconciliation bills that were planned in the budget resolution.

Level of detail in a budget resolution

Much less detail is reported in budget resolutions than in the president's budget. This is not to say that the numbers in a budget resolution are arbitrary. To win a majority of votes for budget resolutions, the budget committees, congressional leadership, committee chairs, and others must reach understandings about the assumptions behind the budget resolution's numbers. Budget committee reports may or may not be specific about these understandings.

Reconciliation amounts are usually net numbers, and committees have frequently included both pluses and minuses in their reconciliation recommendations. For example, the tax-writing committees might have been reconciled to raise $50 billion in added revenue over several years. Such an instruction would not normally preclude tax cuts when they are paid for with other changes. For example, a committee might include $60 billion of added revenues and $10 billion of tax cuts to arrive at the net increase of $50 billion. A committee might even pay for tax cuts with spending reductions rather than tax increases.

Misunderstandings about the congressional budget process

The congressional budget process is sometimes misunderstood. As explained above, the congressional budget resolution frequently lacks the kind of detail that some observers desire. There may not be an up-or-down vote on a budget resolution that reflects the president's budget submission. There is no one up-or-down vote that sends an entire congressional budget to the president for his signature (or veto). The budget resolution is not sent to the president.

A vote on a House-Senate conference agreement on the budget resolution is not the end of budget-related votes. After this vote, there are votes on up to 13 separate appropriations bills (House, Senate, and conference agreements). There may also be votes on interim appropriations measures called "continuing resolutions." Finally, there are often votes on a reconciliation bill.

Gramm-Rudman-Hollings fixed deficit targets

In 1985, budget law took a new turn when the Gramm-Rudman-Hollings (GRH) law was enacted. This law pushed budget statutes beyond establishing institutions and procedures. It required that budget deficits be brought down to specified amounts. The budget was to be balanced in 1991 (a later amendment to the Gramm-Rudman Hollings law delayed the target date for a balanced budget to 1993). If Congress did not enact legislation sufficient to do so, automatic spending cuts would be triggered. This automatic mechanism did not include tax increases. The manner in which spending would be cut was specified by formula, and some programs were exempted—for example, Social Security. GRH did not achieve its original aims; in fact, the actual deficit for fiscal year 1993 (the year in which GRH projected a balanced budget) was $255 billion.

In 1990, the 1985 GRH law was replaced by the Budget Enforcement Act (BEA). Before 1990, Congress had delayed and revised the targets. In 1990, Congress passed major deficit-reduction legislation and changed the law to emphasize prevention of future legislation that would increase budget deficits. The pursuit of further deficit reduction then became, once again, a matter of judgment, rather than law.

"Pay as you go" and caps

The BEA established a two-part control mechanism. Spending subject to appropriation was made subject to a separate series of annual limits, or caps on both budget authority and outlays. If this spending exceeded the cap in any year, there would be an automatic cut in programs subject to appropriation.

The second part of the mechanism was called "pay as you go." Pay as you go covered the rest of the budget: mandatory spending and revenues. In simplified terms, if the cumulative effect of mandatory spending and revenue legislation is to raise the budget deficit in any one year, then "sequestration" is triggered. Mandatory spending programs like Medicaid and farm price supports are cut across the board, except that Medicare can be cut by no more than 4 percent, and numerous programs, such as Social Security and unemployment compensation, are exempt. There is no automatic increase in revenues. In 1993, as part of another deficit-reduction bill, the caps and pay-as-you-go mechanisms were extended. In 1997, the mechanisms were again extended as part of another deficit-reduction bill.

Constitutional amendment to balance the budget

In the early 1990s, a major budget process issue became a proposed constitutional amendment to require a balanced budget. In the Senate, in both 1995 and 1996, that amendment fell a few votes short of the necessary two-thirds needed to send it to the states for possible ratification. However, since 1997, the constitutional amendment has seemed less urgent to supporters because of the passage of legislation that reduced program spending enough to balance the budget.

Line-item veto

In 1996, Congress passed a law (the Line Item Veto Act of 1996) to give the president the power to react to enacted legislation by canceling funding for items drawing upon appropriations, to cancel new items of mandatory spending, or to cancel "limited tax benefits," if the president found that such cancellations would reduce budget deficits. After cancellations by a president, the burden is on Congress to enact legislation overturning the cancellations. The law provides for expedited congressional procedures to make it less difficult than normal for Congress to work its will in this matter. In 1997, the president canceled a number of items that were included in appropriations bills, one item of added direct spending from a budget reconciliation bill, and two "limited tax benefits" from a tax bill. In June 1998, the Supreme Court declared the new law to be unconstitutional.

Current budget projections

The federal budget, which had been in deficit continually between fiscal year 1969 to fiscal year 1997, experienced surpluses in each year from fiscal year 1998 ($69 billion, or 1.1 percent of GDP) to fiscal year 2001 ($127 billion, or 1.4 percent of GDP). Starting in fiscal year 2002, however, a dramatic turnaround occurred. In fact, the government experienced a fiscal year 2002 deficit of $158 billion, a dramatic $285 billion turnaround in one year. For fiscal year 2003, the deficit ballooned again to $375 billion, and the forecast is for a deficit approaching $500 billion for fiscal year 2004. This reversal in fiscal fortunes resulted from a number of factors, including the aforementioned tax cut, the wars on terrorism and Iraq, and deterioration in the economy in the early 2000s. While there have been calls for additional fiscal discipline, no specific disciplinary measures have been enacted.

ADDITIONAL READINGS

Congressional Budget Office, *The Budget and Economic Outlook.* Washington, DC: U.S. Government Printing Office, annual.

Council of Economic Advisers. *Annual Report of the Council of Economic Advisers and Economic Report of the President.* Washington, DC: U.S. Government Printing Office, annual.

Office of Management and Budget. *Budget of the United States Government.* Washington, DC: U.S. Government Printing Office, annual.

Cross-references: revenue estimating, federal; revenue forecasting, federal; Social Security Trust Fund.

Budget processes, state

Bruce A. Wallin

Northeastern University

Annual procedures whereby state governors submit budgets for legislative review and disposition.

While state governments in the United States are often noted for their diverse approaches to politics and policies, their general budget processes are very similar.

In almost every state, proposed budgets are put together in the executive branch. Most state fiscal years run from July 1 to June 30, and governors begin the process in July or August by having their budget offices send out instructions for budget requests to the various departments and agencies. These instructions usually give each spending unit a rough idea of what they might expect in continued, expanded, or (rarely) reduced resources. By the fall, agency requests are received by the budget office and reviewed, often with an eye toward cutting expenditures seen as unnecessary. Hearings on the budget requests may be conducted within the executive branch and might include representatives of the governor, budget officials, and department heads, who may wish to appeal the decisions of the budget office. The governor then prepares a final budget proposal, which includes projected revenues and appropriations, and a budget message (Rosenthal 1990).

Governors customarily submit proposed budgets to their state legislatures in late January or early February. Most commonly, the budget is referred to one committee in each house, usually called the "appropriations" committee. This is very different from (and far more efficient than) budgeting at the federal level, where each house has a budget committee, many authorization committees, and an appropriations committee, which in itself is divided into many subcommittees. After committee hearings, debates, markup sessions (where bills are gone over and changed line by line), and votes, the budget bill is sent to the floor of the whole chamber, where it may be amended and is ultimately voted on.

Budget bills usually originate in the lower house, mirroring the practice for revenue bills at the federal level, following the philosophy that all revenue actions should be initiated in the chamber closest to the people in terms of number of constituents per representative and frequency of elections. A similar process then occurs in the Senate, with committee work preceding debate and final action on the Senate floor. In most cases, a budget that passes a state senate will differ in some manner from the budget that passes the house, and a conference committee will be appointed by legislative leaders to work out a compromise. That compromise must then be approved by both houses of the state legislature.

The budget bill is then sent to the governor. Governors may sign the bill, veto the entire bill (which almost never occurs), or in most states sign it with a line-item veto, allowing the governor to strike portions of the bill that he or she dislikes. Any vetoes then return to the state legislature for override attempts, usually requiring two-thirds of the state legislature. Some evidence suggests that while the item veto is thought of only as a tool of fiscal restraint, it is frequently used to alter policy (Gosling 1986). Item vetoes are rarely overridden.

It is important to note that significant variations in state budget processes do exist (NCSL 1995). In 20 states, the budget is a biennial one, enacted every two years instead of annually. The argument for biennial budgeting is that it is more efficient, allowing the legislature to spend time on other important policy issues, time that would otherwise be consumed by the budget process. Evidence on the effect of biennial budgeting on state policy is unclear because there is no agreement on how to identify "good policy." In another variation, 14 states have joint budget committees, with representatives of both houses of the state legislature receiving the budget from the governor. The existence of a joint budget committee may make the legislative process more efficient.

In a few states (Arkansas, California, and Rhode Island), a super-majority of legislators is needed to pass a budget. The goal of super-majority approval is fiscal discipline, the argument being that it will be more difficult to get, say, two-thirds of a state legislature to agree to a budget with unnecessary spending.

Finally, variations exist in the veto powers of governors. Governors in 43 states have the power of line-item veto, meaning that they can veto portions of a budget passed by the legislature. But in 26 states, governors may also veto language in an appropriations bill, giving them more power (Council of State Governments 2003). In addition, provisions for override vary by state. Giving the governor the most power is an override that calls for two-thirds of *elected* legislators to override; less restrictive is the provision for override by two-thirds *present* at the time of the vote.

The roles of the main participants in the state budget process are fairly typical in all states. The governor may be viewed as budget balancer for two reasons. First, the governor is the one individual in the process who represents the entire state, and a balanced budget is a common denominator for most citizens, at least in principle. Second, submitting a budget in balance gives the governor power over the legislature in determining the ultimate shape of the budget. Facing a proposed budget in balance, a legislature desiring tax cuts would have to find expenditure reductions to finance them, while a legislature seeking to increase spending over a governor's request would have to find the added revenues to finance it. It is usually easier to accept the broad parameters of the governor's budget.

State legislators can generally be characterized as spenders or tax-cutters, as they seek to please their constituents by bringing benefits back to their districts, or use the budget to reward special interests who may have provided the rationales for budget items, and perhaps gained access by means of campaign contributions. Department or agency heads are also generally spenders, since in the public sector, size of budget is a measure of success, a substitute for profit in the private sector. Most individuals who head agencies also believe in their mission and are therefore likely to want to spend more and have a clientele of their own to serve.

The governor has much more power in the state budgeting process than the president does in federal budgeting. First, governors usually submit a budget in balance, which as already noted makes it more difficult for the legislature to change it. Second, governors have an informational advantage over state legislators, as the imbalance of staff resources at the state level tilts much more strongly toward the executive than it does at the federal level. Third, in many states, the job of state legislator is a part-time one, or at least allows legislators to pursue other professional activities, giving the governor the advantages of time and focus. Fourth, the line-item veto gives a governor more power than the president, who must veto an entire bill.

It is also important to note that many states allow the budget to be revised after it has been enacted, often without involvement of the legislature, which may be out of session. Most often, governors are given the power to reduce, but not add to, spending. Many legislatures also are allowed to enact supplemental appropriations to respond to needs that present themselves during the fiscal year.

State budgeting for the most part continues to be "traditional" or "line-item" budgeting, with incrementalism the prevailing decision system employed. As a consequence, most of the emphasis of state budgeting is placed on analyzing the change in inputs from the previous year's budget (Rosenthal 1990, 136). While producing stability and making it easier to compromise, incrementalism results in some programs outliving their usefulness or at least growing beyond need. Comprehensive reform measures have for the most part been unsuccessful, including zero-based budgeting and planning, programming, and budgeting systems (NCSL 1995). Zero-based budgeting sought to have programs analyzed from top to bottom, with varying output levels estimated for various levels of resources. Planning, programming, and budgeting systems sought to move from line-item budgeting to the presentation of budgets in program packages, with multiyear planning and performance measures. Both reforms often fail as a result of calculation problems, as well as political and organizational resistance. More successful reforms to state budgeting have included better revenue estimating, often involving joint legislative-executive committees, and multiyear forecasting of revenues and expenditures. Performance budgeting has increasingly found its way into state budgeting, especially on the executive side.

Budgeting at the state level is greatly affected by legal, political, economic, and demographic variables (Gold 1995). Legally, almost all states are either statutorily or constitutionally required to balance their budgets. Most states also have limits on how much they can borrow, usually expressed as a percentage of appropriations. Twenty-one states face constitutional or statutory tax and/or expenditure limitations (TELs), most a product of the tax revolt kicked off by California's Proposition 13 in 1978 (Advisory Commission on Intergovernmental Relations 1991). For example, taxes are often limited to a percentage of the tax base, and expenditure growth may be tied to inflation plus population growth. These TELs usually require a super-majority override by the legislature or public override by referendum. Political variables include tax competition—the fear that taxpayers will flee a state if its tax burden is much higher than that of a neighboring state.

Many exogenous variables have an important impact on state budgeting. Most important is the economy. A drop in economic performance reduces revenues while simultaneously causing increased expenditures for welfare and unemployment programs. Important demographic variables include the number of school-age children, as education spending is one of the two largest expenditure commitments of states; the number of youth in the 16–24 high-crime cohort, which has a great impact on correctional spending; and the number of elderly, which affects state budgets most directly through increased Medicaid expenditures, especially those funneled to nursing homes. Finally, federal policies also have an impact on state budgets, through increases or decreases in federal aid, changes in federal tax policy, or the imposition of federal mandates, especially those that are unfunded. While Congress passed a law limiting the use of unfunded mandates, it was not made retroactive and includes several loopholes.

In sum, because of balanced-budget requirements, limits on revenue increases for fear of taxpayer flight, and built-in expenditure pressures based on inflation and increasing population served, state budgeting is revenue constrained. Surges in revenue will allow states to embark on additional spending or to pursue tax cuts. But in the absence of such revenue windfalls, state budgeting is for the most part highly routinized, with incremental decisions made by actors constrained by their environment.

ADDITIONAL READINGS

Advisory Commission on Intergovernmental Relations [ACIR]. *Significant Features of Fiscal Federalism 1991,* vol. 1. Washington, DC: ACIR, February 1991.

Council of State Governments. *Book of the States,* vol 35. Lexington, KY: Council of State Governments, 2003.

Gold, Steven D. *The Fiscal Crisis of the States.* Washington, DC: Georgetown University Press, 1995.

Gosling, James J. "Wisconsin Item-Veto Lessons." *Public Administration Review* 46 (July–August 1986): 292–300.

National Conference of State Legislatures. *Fundamentals of Sound State Budgeting Practices.* Denver: National Conference of State Legislatures, May 1995.

———. *Legislative Budget Procedures: A Guide to Appropriations and Budget Processes in the States, Commonwealths, and Territories.* Denver: National Conference of State Legislatures, 2004.

Rosenthal, Alan. *Governors and Legislatures: Contending Powers.* Washington, DC: Congressional Quarterly Press, 1990.

Cross-references: budget-balance requirement; budgeting, state; budget policy, state and local.

Business location, taxation and

William T. Bogart
York College

Updated by
Nathan B. Anderson
University of Michigan

The relationship between government fiscal and regulatory policy and firm site choice and investment decisions.

The effect of government policy on a firm's site selection and investment decisions is a familiar question to government officials and academics alike. Although this entry focuses on a business's decision to locate in various regions or states in the United States, the concepts are applicable to international location problems as well. There has long been a consensus among academics that government fiscal policy plays almost no role in interregional location decisions and at best a supporting role in intraregional or intrametropolitan location de-

cisions. This consensus has been challenged in recent years, but there is still no broad support in the academic literature for the proliferation of state and local government programs designed to affect firm location decisions. Because taxes raise revenue to finance government services, and since government regulations can have effects similar to taxes, the broad sweep of government activity is considered here, rather than the more narrow focus of taxes.

Theory of business location

In order to understand the relationship between taxation and business location, it is necessary to consider the general theory of business location. Economic theory typically assumes that firms make decisions in an attempt to maximize profits (revenues minus costs). Both revenues and costs can vary with the firm's location. One component of costs is the expense of the local public sector. Local taxes add to the cost of doing business, while local government services can reduce the cost of doing business either directly (e.g., infrastructure) or indirectly (e.g., good schools are a source of skilled workers). The level of local taxes can also affect the relative advantage of the nonprofit corporate form.

Two conditions must be met for government policy to affect a firm's location decision. The first is that some aspect of government policy must vary over space. If every government levies the same taxes, provides the same public services, and administers the same regulations, then a firm's location decision will be made entirely on the basis of factors other than government policy. The second condition is that the increase in profits resulting from government policy in one location relative to the other exceeds any loss in profits resulting from the location choice. For example, if a company stands to save $2 million in taxes by moving from one place to another at a cost of $4 million in lost profits, it will not make the move. Economists investigating the variation in taxes relative to other factors have typically found that the other factors (e.g., labor costs, access to markets) dominate the firm's decision at the intermetropolitan or interregional level. However, once a firm has decided to locate in a particular metropolitan area, intergovernmental differences can play a significant role. One ongoing controversy is the incidence of taxes levied on businesses. If the taxes are completely shifted, then nominal differences in taxes at various locations are irrelevant for a firm's decisions.

How taxes affect business location

There are two ways that taxes and government spending affect business location decisions. The first is directly through increasing (in the case of taxes) or decreasing (in the case of public services) the cost of doing business. The second is indirectly through the effects of government policy on output markets or factor markets.

The level and mix of state and local government taxes varies greatly in the United States. This would seem to be prima facie evidence for taxes as an important factor in business location decisions. There are two ameliorating factors that should be noted, though. First, state and local taxes are deductible from income for the purposes of computing federal taxes owed. This reduces the variability among states, as high state taxes are partially compensated for in part by lower federal taxes. Second, the taxes may be capitalized into asset values, especially land, so that the economic incidence of the tax is not on the firm facing the nominal incidence of the taxes.

Since states differ in the emphasis of their tax systems on various factors of production, the relative attractiveness of a location will depend on the type of firm—for example, labor-intensive versus capital-intensive firms. Two important topics for analysis are therefore the relative mobility of production factors and the possibility of substituting among production factors. Wasylenko and McGuire (1985) demonstrate that location determinants vary by industry, and the effect of taxes will therefore also vary by industry.

It is also important to identify the appropriate tax rate to be used in the analysis: marginal or average. For a firm considering an incremental expansion, the marginal effective tax rate is the most relevant. For a firm considering relocation, the average effective tax rate is the most important.

In addition to its direct effect on a firm's profits, government policy also has indirect effects. For example, if the public school system is excellent, a firm might face a labor market with a large supply of qualified workers. Regulatory policy at the local level (for example in the form of zoning laws and building codes), workers' compensation schemes and unemployment insurance at the state level, and environmental policy at the federal level can also affect a company's cost of doing business. Because federal laws apply everywhere in the country, it might at first seem surprising to find them making a difference among locations. Recently, though, there has been concern that Superfund and related legislation and regulation have created a disadvantage for "brownfield" locations (industrial sites) relative to "greenfield" locations (undeveloped or agricultural sites). Because brownfields are typically located in the older parts of metropolitan areas, especially central cities, the environmental legislation has added another reason for companies to avoid locating in central cities in favor of surrounding areas. Central cities typically have higher taxes than their suburbs, making it difficult to precisely identify the reason for a given location decision. The nature of the environmental liability and the incentive to pursue "deep pockets" also reduce the efficacy of central cities' programs designed to make themselves more attractive relative to the suburbs.

Evidence

Two methods are used to identify the effect of government policy on firm location. The first is to survey businesses on the importance of government policy in their location decisions, the second to statistically test the relationship between measurable aspects of government policy and business location decisions. Both of these methods have drawbacks. The survey method suffers from a sample selection bias in two respects. The first, and more serious, is that only businesses that have both chosen to locate in a particular area and survived until the survey date will be included. The second is the typical survey problem of nonresponse. The other main problem facing the survey method is the difficulty in identifying the marginal effect of a particular government policy, holding all other relevant variables equal.

The statistical methods also have some problems. One is sample selection bias, because the places where development incentives are used do not represent a random sample. A second statistical problem in evaluating the effectiveness of economic development programs is that they are usually small relative to the local economy, making their impact more difficult to identify. The third problem, related to the other two, is distinguishing the independent effect of the program in question from unobservable local characteristics. Papke (1993) summarizes the statistical problems and demonstrates the state of the art in addressing them. There had been a long-standing consensus among academics using both methodologies that government policy had either no effect or only a small effect on firms' location decisions. This general finding had four basic explanations: (1) that taxes did not vary much across locations, (2) that the variation in taxes was exceeded by the variation in other factors, such as labor costs or access to markets, (3) that the taxes could be shifted, and were therefore irrelevant for the firm's location decision, and (4) that high taxes were accompanied by high levels of desirable public services.

The consensus that government policy has little effect has been challenged in recent years. Bogart (1998) outlines three conditions in which taxes would be important for firm location decisions. First, taxes would be more important for intrametropolitan location decisions, in which the labor force is held constant and transportation costs are also roughly equal across locations. Second, taxes would be important in deciding among locations that have equivalent public services. Third, taxes would be more important to those firms that face an elastic demand for their product that prevents them from shifting the tax to their consumers. Recent empirical evidence provides some support for the theoretical arguments presented above. The most comprehensive surveys of the empirical literature are found in Bartik (1991) and Wasylenko (1997). Newman and Sullivan (1988) provide an excellent introduction to the econometric literature. Table 1 summarizes the econometric evidence. There are two principal conclusions. One is that taxes are a more important determinant of intrametropolitan business location decisions than of intermetropolitan business location decisions. The second is that econometric analysis that controls for specific community characteristics is more likely to find that taxes are important.

TABLE 1. Summary of Econometric Studies of Tax Effects on Business Location

Type of study	Percentage of studies with at least one statistically significant negative tax effect	Mean elasticity of business activity with respect to taxes (range)	Median elasticity
Interarea studies	70 (57 studies)	−0.25 (s.e. = 0.05) [−1.40 to 0.76] (48 studies)	−0.15
Interarea studies with controls or "fixed effects"	92 (12 studies)	−0.44 (s.e. = 0.11) [−1.02 to 0.00] (11 studies)	−0.35
Interarea studies with public service controls	80 (30 studies)	−0.33 (s.e. = 0.09) [−1.40 to 0.76] (25 studies)	−0.27
Intra-area studies	57 (14 studies)	−1.48 (s.e. = 0.54) [−4.43 to 0.62] (9 studies)	−1.59
Intra-area studies using specific community data	70 (10 studies)	−1.91 (s.e. = 0.60) [−4.43 to 0.62] (7 studies)	−1.95

Source: Adapted from table 2.3 in Bartik (1991).
Note: s.e. = standard error.

A related question is whether government policies designed to promote business location are self-financing—that is, whether the additional tax revenues provided by the business exceed the cost of providing the incentive. Of course, to the extent that incentives do not affect business location decisions, they clearly are not self-financing. Bartik (2003) discusses estimates of the cost of incentives and suggests they may come at a relatively large cost. However, by comparing "winners" and "losers" in the firm site selection process, Greenstone and Moretti (2003) are able to show that "winning" localities (i.e., localities where large plants locate) seem to benefit in the form of increased property values and labor earnings while experiencing no deterioration in their government's financial position. Courant (1994) provides a thoughtful critique of the economic literature, suggesting that research needs to focus on the contribution of tax incentives to the quality of life in an area.

Government policy

Despite the long-held academic consensus on the ineffectiveness of state and local government economic development programs, such programs have a long history and remain very popular. Bartik (1994) summarizes state and local government programs in the 1980s and 1990s, distinguishing among so-called "first-wave" (attraction of branch plants), "second-wave" (providing free government services to new and small businesses), and "third-wave" (providing government services through quasi-market organizations) development policies. Although local governments remain involved in local economic development policies, Bartik (2003) discusses how other groups (e.g., private firms, citizen advisory boards) also play a prominent role.

There are two possible reasons that these programs have continued to spread despite lukewarm academic endorsement. One is that the government officials anticipated the recent academic findings in support of these policies. The other is that government officials find themselves in a "prisoners' dilemma" with respect to offering incentives, whereby they are offering incentives rather than relying on their own mer-

its because of the threat of other governments luring businesses away. Bogart (1998) provides an excellent review of this literature and the related concepts.

ADDITIONAL READINGS

Bartik, Timothy. *Who Benefits from State and Local Economic Development Policies?* Kalamazoo, MI: Upjohn Institute for Employment Research, 1991.

———. "What Should the Federal Government Be Doing About Urban Economic Development?" Staff Working Paper 94-25. Kalamazoo, MI: Upjohn Institute for Employment Research, 1994.

———. "Local Economic Development Policies." Staff Working Paper 03-91. Kalamazoo, MI: Upjohn Institute for Employment Research, 2003.

Bogart, William T. *The Economics of Cities and Suburbs.* Upper Saddle River, NJ: Prentice-Hall, 1998.

Courant, Paul N. "How Would You Know a Good Economic Development Policy If You Tripped Over One? Hint: Don't Just Count Jobs." *National Tax Journal* 47, no. 4 (1994): 863–81.

Eisinger, Peter K. "State Economic Development in the 1990s." Working Paper 18. Madison, WI: The Robert M. LaFollette Institute of Public Affairs, 1993.

Greenstone, Michael, and Enrico Moretti. "Bidding For Industrial Plants: Does Winning a 'Million Dollar Plant' Increase Welfare?" NBER Working Paper no. 9844. Cambridge, MA: National Bureau of Economic Research, 2003.

Mark, Stephen T., Therese J. McGuire, and Leslie E. Papke. "The Influence of Tax on Employment and Population Growth: Evidence form the Washington, D.C., Metropolitan Area." *National Tax Journal* 53 (2000): 105–23.

Newman, Robert J., and Dennis Sullivan. "Econometric Analysis of Business Tax Impacts on Industrial Location: What Do We Know, and How Do We Know It?" *Journal of Urban Economics* 23 (1988): 215–34.

Papke, Leslie. "What Do We Know about Enterprise Zones?" In *Tax Policy and the Economy,* edited by James Poterba (37–72). Cambridge, MA: MIT Press, 1993.

Wassmer, Robert. "The Use and Abuse of Economic Development Incentives in a Metropolitan Area." *Proceedings of the Eighty-Sixth Annual Conference, National Tax Association* (1993): 146–57.

Wasylenko, Michael. "Taxation and Economic Development: The State of the Economic Literature." *New England Economic Review* (March/April 1997): 37–52.

Wasylenko, Michael, and Therese McGuire. "Jobs and Taxes: The Effect of Business Climate on States' Employment Growth Rates." *National Tax Journal* 38 (1985): 497–511.

Cross-references: commuter taxes; enterprise zones; tax abatement programs; tax competition.

Capital cost recovery

James Mackie
Department of the Treasury

Income tax features intended to allow businesses to recover the costs associated with the depreciation in value of tangible assets that are used to produce income.

Income tax regulations generally do not allow a deduction for the cost of a new asset when purchased. Instead, they spread out the deduction over a period roughly consistent with the asset's useful economic lifetime. The amount allowed as an annual deduction reflects (however roughly) the reduction in the value of the capital asset each year. It is called depreciation, or capital cost recovery.

Depreciation and measurement of economic income

Depreciation defined

Let's begin with an income tax based on the idealized concept of economic income. Economic income is a measure of the change in a household's real economic well-being that has occurred over some accounting period, typically taken to be a year. It is defined as the household's change in wealth, measured before consumption purchases. Changes, up or down, in the (market) value of its capital assets, including buildings and machines, are part of a household's overall change in wealth and are included in economic income. When assets fall in value from year to year, they are said to depreciate, and this depreciation must be allowed as a deduction when measuring and taxing economic income.

Depreciation versus current cash outlays or expenses

A distinguishing feature of capital is its durability. A capital asset has value beyond the end of the year in which it is purchased. Consequently, it is inappropriate to deduct the full cost of a new capital asset in the year in which it is purchased because that cost does not represent a change in wealth. In fact, the initial purchase of a capital asset, such as a machine, has no effect on economic income. When a businessman purchases a machine, he simply exchanges one asset, money, for another asset of equal worth, the machine.

Rather than the initial purchase price, it is the change in the value of the machine over the year that affects economic income. Because the machine is durable, any fall in value typically will be much less than the full price paid for the machine. The decline in value is likely to continue for many years after the machine is purchased and should reduce income in each of these years.

While the machine's value may rise over the course of a year, there are many reasons to expect that typically a machine's value will fall over time. For one thing, it might physically wear out as it is used to produce output. Alternatively, new and superior types of machines might become available, thereby reducing the market value of this now obsolete machine. However motivated, the fall in the value of the machine—its depreciation—should be allowed as a deduction in computing the businessman's taxable income. Of course, if the machine rises in value, this appreciation should be taxable.

Inflation, real changes in asset values, and depreciation

Inflation can lead to changes in asset values that do not reflect changes in economic well-being. For example, suppose that over the course of a year the general price level doubles. Then, if a businessman's assets also double in value, he is no better off in terms of the real (inflation-adjusted) purchasing power of his assets than he was at the beginning of the year. Only if the value of his assets more than doubles will he be better off. Consequently, purely nominal growth in asset values should not trigger tax liability; the tax system should adjust—index—for inflation.

In indexing for inflation, values are measured at a consistent price level—for example, in end-of-year prices. If the general price level doubles, then measuring the real change in asset values requires first doubling all beginning-of-year asset values. This implies that depreciation allowances that are appropriate without inflation need to be increased proportionately with the increase in the general price level. Otherwise, depreciation allowances will decline in real value over time, causing overtaxation. The following example illustrates this point.

Suppose that at the beginning of the year, the businessman has an asset worth $100. The asset wears out at a rate of 10 percent per year, and its relative price does not change. If there is no inflation, then at the end of the year the asset is worth $90, so $10 is the proper depreciation allowance. In contrast, suppose there is 50 percent general price inflation. Then at the end of the year, the asset is worth $90 × (1 + the inflation rate) = $135. But the $35 nominal increase in value is due only to inflation in the general level of prices; it does not represent real purchasing power. Far from rising in value, measured in constant (year-end) prices, the asset has declined in value, or depreciated, from $150 ($100 × [1 + the inflation rate]) to $135, or by $15. To account for the 50 percent inflation rate, the depreciation deduction allowed under the tax law must increase from $10 (no inflation) to $15. If the depreciation system were not indexed for inflation, the taxpayer would owe tax on $5 of purely nominal income and so would be overtaxed relative to the standard set by economic income. Proper income measurement requires a 50 percent increase in the depreciation allowance, exactly equal to the increase in the price level. In the next year, without inflation in either year, the depreciation allowance would be $9 (10 percent of $90). With a 50 percent inflation rate in both year one and year two, however, the proper depreciation allowance would be $20.25, reflecting the change in the value of the asset, measured in end-of-year-two prices. Hence, to index the second year's no-inflation depreciation allowance of $9 requires multiplying by a factor of 2.25, which equals (1 + the inflation rate in year one) × (1 + the inflation rate in year two) and represents the total increase in the general price level over the two-year period since the asset's original purchase.

Depreciation in practice

Deviations from the standard provided by measuring and taxing economic income are common in real world tax systems. These deviations can often be interpreted as attempts to meet other criteria or to compromise between competing objectives.

Administrative concerns and depreciation as changes in market value

Simplicity and ease of administration are important features of the tax system. Unfortunately, they conflict with a desire to measure and tax economic income. The measurement of depreciation as changes in market values is often one casualty of the conflict between accurate income measurement on the one hand, and simplicity and administrability on the other. Typically, income tax systems provide for depreciation allowances without reference to actual or estimated changes in the market value of the assets. For example, tax systems often allow a constant fraction of an asset's initial purchase price as a depreciation deduction (so-called straight-line depreciation). Although these schedular depreciation deductions are unlikely to match real economic depreciation, schedular deductions are simpler than would be a system based on actual or estimated changes in market values.

Administrative concerns and indexation for inflation

Another common casualty of the conflict between income measurement and simplicity/administrability is indexation of depreciation allowances (as well as many other components of the tax system) for inflation. Practical proposals to index depreciation for inflation are often criticized as unworkably complex and subject to taxpayer abuse and manipulation. In addition, indexing depreciation allowances, while leaving other features of the tax code unchanged, might not improve the overall capital income tax system.

Accelerated depreciation as an investment incentive

Another conflict in tax design arises out of the inconsistency between the desire to tax income, perhaps because of a belief that it represents an equitable tax base, and the desire to encourage efficient amounts of saving and investing. Since saving/investing is done out of after-tax income, and then the return earned on the amounts saved and invested also is taxed, an income tax overtaxes future consumption relative to current consumption. It is common to refer to this problem as one of overtaxing, hence discouraging, saving and investment. Because it reduces the tax burden on investment, accelerated depreciation can be seen as a compromise between the goals of measuring and taxing economic income on the one hand and providing an adequate incentive to save and invest on the other.

Depreciation allowances that are pushed forward in time, relative to those that "ought" to be allowed (e.g., based on changes in the economic value of assets over time), are referred to as accelerated depreciation allowances. The extreme example of accelerated depreciation is immediate expensing of capital outlays, under which the full cost of an investment is deducted in the year it is purchased.

Accelerated depreciation allowances are more valuable to a taxpayer because they allow him to receive the cash flow from depreciation earlier in the investment's life. Because of the time value of money, an earlier deduction is worth more to the taxpayer than one or a series of deductions occurring later in time; it has a larger (discounted) present value. One of the important components in the cost of capital is the present value of the cash flow from depreciation. By increasing this present value, accelerated depreciation reduces the cost of capital and the associated effective tax rate, providing an investment incentive.

The benefit from accelerated depreciation also can be understood by analogy to an interest-free loan. In the early years of an asset's life, accelerated depreciation gives the taxpayer larger depreciation allowances than those implied by, say, economic income accounting. During each of these early years, the government in effect loans the taxpayer an amount equal to the difference between the tax reduction based on accelerated depreciation and that implied by economic depreciation. But in later years, this pattern reverses as allowed depreciation deductions eventually fall below economic depreciation. During these years, the taxpayer repays the loan, but without interest. Accelerated depreciation thus provides the taxpayer with an interest-free source of investment funds.

Depreciation in relation to tax neutrality

While accelerated depreciation might help reduce distortions in the consume/save choice, it can create distortions in the allocation of investment funds across projects. Accelerated depreciation is almost certain to give some assets lower effective tax rates than others and so violate the tax neutrality standard. Neutrality, the uniform taxation of all investments, is a commonly accepted tax policy goal. It is rooted in a concept of economic efficiency that defines an allocation of investment as efficient if it is impossible to increase output by shifting funds from one investment project to another. Efficiency thus requires that all investments have the same pretax return, which means they must also have the same effective tax rate. A tax based strictly on economic income meets the neutrality criterion—it imposes an effective tax rate equal to the statutory tax rate on all investments.

Starting from a system that measures and taxes economic income, a shift to accelerated depreciation is almost certain to violate tax neutrality. For one thing, accelerated depreciation is likely to offer a tax reduction only for so-called depreciable assets (e.g., machinery and buildings). Other assets (e.g., inventories and land) typically are not depreciated and so will not receive a tax reduction. For another, if past practice is any indication, only some depreciable assets will qualify for accelerated depreciation, and even among those that do qualify, the degree of acceleration probably will vary from asset to asset. Assets that do not qualify for accelerated depreciation or that qualify only for limited acceleration will have a higher effective tax cost than do assets that fully qualify, thereby violating the neutrality standard.

Accelerated depreciation in lieu of indexing depreciation for inflation

As discussed, inflation can cause overtaxation of investment income when depreciation is not indexed. This overtaxation can be reduced by offering accelerated depreciation allowances. Thus, accelerated depreciation can be justified as a simple way to adjust for inflation. The adjustment provided by accelerated depreciation is rather crude, however, as it is unlikely to be set properly for every asset at any one inflation rate, or to be changed as the inflation rate changes over time.

ADDITIONAL READINGS

Feldstein, Martin S. "The Welfare Cost of Capital Income Taxation." *Journal of Political Economy* 86, no. 2 (April 1978): 29–51.

Gravelle, Jane G. "The Capital Cost Recovery System and the Corporate Income Tax." Report No. 79-230. Washington, DC: Congressional Research Service, 1979.

Hulten, Charles R., and Frank C. Wykoff. "The Measurement of Economic Depreciation." In *Depreciation, Inflation and the Taxation of Income from Capital,* edited by Charles R. Hulten. Washington, DC: Urban Institute Press, 1981.

Rosen, Harvey S. "The Personal Income Tax." In *Public Finance,* 3rd ed., ch. 16. Boston: Richard D. Irwin, 1992.

U.S. Department of the Treasury. *Report to the Congress on Depreciation Recovery Periods and Methods.* Washington, DC: Office of Tax Policy, U.S. Department of the Treasury, 2000.

———. "What Is to Be the Tax Base?" and "A Model Comprehensive Income Tax." In *Blueprints for Basic Tax Reform,* ch. 2 and 3. Washington, DC: U.S. Government Printing Office, 1977.

Cross-references: cost of capital; income tax, corporate, federal; income tax, federal; marginal effective tax rate; taxable income, corporate.

Capital export neutrality

Peggy B. Musgrave
University of California, Santa Cruz

A term introduced and developed in the 1960s to describe a situation in which the overall burden of taxation on capital owned by resident entities of a given country is the same whether that capital is invested abroad or at home.

In tax terms, capital export neutrality requires the same proportionate tax wedge between the before- and after-tax rates of return wherever the capital owned by the resident entities of a given country is invested. If this condition is met, the tax system neither encourages nor discourages capital export, and the investor's choice of investing in the domestic economy or in foreign economies will not be influenced by tax considerations. Capital export neutrality is to be distinguished from capital import neutrality, which requires equal tax treatment for all capital invested *within* a given country, regardless of the nationality of its ownership (see "capital import neutrality" entry).

The economic significance of capital export neutrality is that it promotes international efficiency in the allocation of capital. In the absence of tax inducements or barriers to international capital flows, capital will tend to be invested where returns are the highest, rather than where there are tax advantages to be had or disadvantages to be avoided. Since maximization of world output and income requires that investment be located where it is the most productive, capital export neutrality is consistent with the world production efficiency criterion. These considerations bear on efficiency distortions that arise from differential taxation of capital income in the international setting only, leaving aside the distorting impact of capital income taxation that may arise even in the closed economy.

Capital export neutrality requires that investments made at home and abroad be taxed at the same *effective* rate of tax, allowing for differences in tax-base definition as well as in statutory rates of tax. This is not readily achieved because the total tax burden on foreign investment income may involve taxation in both the host or source country (where the income is earned) and the home or residence country (where the income is received). Without some adjustment, full double taxation of foreign-source income would therefore present a severe barrier to investments made abroad.

There are three measures that the country of residence may take to alleviate this tax penalty: (a) exempt foreign-source income from its tax, (b) allow the foreign tax to be deducted from foreign income before application of its tax, and (c) allow the foreign tax to be credited against its tax that is applied to foreign income (gross of foreign tax).

Regarding (a), unless the rates of tax in residence and source countries are equal, capital export neutrality will not prevail, with the tax differentials resulting in either tax penalties or tax incentives for investing abroad. To minimize this distortion, the members of the European Union are moving to a system of source taxation—that is, exemption by the country of residence—but with rates of tax contained within a narrow band so as to reduce differentials. With respect to (b), tax differentials are moderated but not eliminated by the deduction method, which therefore does not meet the standard of capital export neutrality, although consistent with the narrower interests of the residence country. In the case of (c), a full credit for the foreign tax with a refund if the former exceeds the latter does secure an equal tax treatment of investment at home and abroad. Thus, since the source country taxes first, the country of residence has the capability of achieving capital export neutrality by taxing global income accompanied by the neutralizing mechanism of a full foreign tax credit.

Following this principle, the United States, along with several other industrialized countries, applies its federal corporation tax to the global (domestic and foreign) income of resident corporations with a credit for foreign tax. The credit is, however, provided only to the limit of the residence tax on the same income. While this offers a large degree of capital export neutrality, it may fall short of a complete solution in other ways:

1. In theory, the concept should be extended to require equalization of net fiscal burdens, allowing for those government expenditure benefits that reduce the costs of production and raise the rate of return to capital. Since it is generally assumed that such expenditure benefits are not closely related to the level of corporate income tax, the concept of capital export neutrality is in practice applied to taxes in isolation.
2. Because the tax burden on capital income involves both corporate and individual income taxes, both should be allowed for in a fully neutral treatment. But to allow for both becomes highly complex if corporate and individual income taxes are subject to varying degrees of integration from country to country (Sato and Bird 1975). However, since most decisions to invest abroad are made at the corporate level, it has been customary to examine the conditions for capital export neutrality as they apply to the corporate income tax alone.
3. The requirement that effective rates be equalized for investments made at home and abroad rests on the usual assumptions that the burden of the corporate tax falls on corporate profits. If shifting occurs, the conditions for capital export neutrality have to be adjusted accordingly (Musgrave 1969, 111–15).
4. Capital export neutrality obtained through residence taxation of global income calls for foreign profits of domestic corporations to be taxed concurrently, whether earned in a foreign incorporated subsidiary or in a foreign branch. To avoid taxing foreign incorporated subsidiaries directly, the United States defers its tax on profits of the foreign incorporated subsidiary until distributed as dividends. This practice of deferral is inconsistent with capital export neutrality (Hines 1994).

ADDITIONAL READINGS

Gordon, Roger H., and James R. Hines Jr. "International Taxation." In *Handbook of Public Economics,* vol. 4, edited by Alan J. Auerbach and Martin Feldstein. Amsterdam: North Holland, 2002.

Grubert, Harry, and John Mutti. "Taxing Multinationals in a World with Portfolio Flows and R & D: Is Capital Export Neutrality Obsolete?" *International Tax and Public Finance* 2, no. 3 (1995): 439–57.

Hines, James R., Jr. "Credit and Deferral as International Investment Incentives." *Journal of Public Economics* 55, no. 2 (1994): 323–47.

Musgrave, Peggy B. *United States Taxation of Foreign Investment Income: Issues and Arguments.* Cambridge, MA: International Tax Program, Harvard Law School, 1969.

———. "Sovereignty, Entitlement, and Cooperation in International Taxation." *Brooklyn Journal of International Law* 26, no. 4 (2001): 1335.

Musgrave, Richard A. "Criteria for Foreign Tax Credit." In *Taxation and Operations Abroad,* edited by Russell Baker. Princeton, NJ: Tax Institute Symposium, 1960.

Sato, Mitsuo, and Richard M. Bird. "International Aspects of the Taxation of Corporations and Shareholders." *Staff Papers,* July 22, 1975. Washington, DC: International Monetary Fund.

Cross-references: capital import neutrality; national neutrality.

Capital gains taxation

Gerald E. Auten
U.S. Treasury Department

Capital gains are the changes in value of capital assets such as corporate stock, real estate, or a business interest.

Under a pure net accretion (Haig-Simons) approach to income taxes, real capital gains would be taxed each year as they accrue and real capital losses would be deducted. Capital gains are generally taxed only when "realized" by sale or exchange, however, because estimating the values of many assets would be difficult, taxing income that had not been realized could be viewed as unfair, and paying taxes on accruals could force the liquidation of assets. Taxation upon realization, however, leads to other problems that require policy compromises.

Current law

Since 1987, realized capital gains have been fully included in adjusted gross income. In general, long-term gains in the 10 and 15 percent tax brackets are currently taxed at a 5 percent rate (a 0 percent rate in 2008) and those in higher tax brackets are taxed at 15 percent. Assets held at least 12 months are eligible for taxation as long-term gains. Depreciation on real estate is "recaptured" by taxing it at ordinary rates subject to a maximum rate of 25 percent, and gains on collectibles are taxed at ordinary rates subject to a maximum rate of 28 percent.

Capital losses can be used to offset capital gains, and a maximum of $3,000 of capital losses can be used to offset other taxable income. A limit on deducting capital losses is needed to prevent taxpayers from offsetting taxes on other income by recognizing capital losses but not capital gains. Unused capital losses can be carried forward to future years.

Since 1997, taxpayers have been able to exclude up to $250,000 ($500,000 on joint returns) of gains on principal residences. The taxpayer must have owned and occupied the house as a principal residence for at least two of the previous five years. The exclusion can be used multiple times, but only once in any two-year period. Previously, taxpayers were allowed tax-free rollover of gains into a replacement residence of equal or greater value, and a one-time exclusion of up to $125,000 for taxpayers age 55 and over. The previous system had been criticized for being complex, creating incentives to buy ever-larger residences, and generating little tax revenue. The exclusion provides significant simplification, but has led to problems such as attempts to convert capital gains on rental properties into excludable gains.

When appreciated assets are transferred by bequest, the basis is generally stepped up to the value of the assets on the date of death. Thus, accrued gains on assets held at death are not taxed under the income tax, although they may be subject to the estate tax. Step-up is currently scheduled to be repealed if the estate tax is repealed. Part of the rationale for step-up in basis was that the gains were subject to the estate tax, and thus repeal of step-up can be seen as ensuring that the gains are eventually subject to some form of tax.

Since 1993, gains from the sale of certain original-issue small business stock held for five years have been eligible for a 50 percent exclusion. The maximum rate under the provision is 14 percent (50 percent of tax rates up to 28 percent). Eligible corporations must have less than $50 million of assets (including the proceeds of the stock issue) and meet various other complex requirements. A rollover provision for gains on small business was introduced in 1997.

The capital gains of C corporations are fully taxed at the regular corporate rates, and capital losses can only be used to offset capital gains.

History of capital gains taxation in the United States

Capital gains have been taxed from the beginning of the income tax, but the rates and other provisions have changed frequently. From 1913 to 1921, capital gains were taxed at ordinary rates, initially up to a top rate of 7 percent. Because of

concern that the high income tax rates during World War I reduced capital gains tax revenues, from 1922 to 1934 taxpayers were allowed an alternative tax rate of 12.5 percent on capital gains on assets held at least two years. From 1934 to 1941, taxpayers could exclude percentages of gains that varied with the holding period. For example, in 1934 and 1935, 20, 40, 60, and 70 percent of gains were excluded on assets held 1, 2, 5, and 10 years, respectively. Beginning in 1942, taxpayers could exclude 50 percent of capital gains on assets held at least six months or elect a 25 percent alternative tax rate if their ordinary tax rate exceeded 50 percent. The 1969 and 1976 Tax Reform Acts substantially increased capital gains tax rates. The 1969 Act imposed a 10 percent minimum tax, excluded gains, and limited the alternative rate to $50,000 of gains. The 1976 Act further increased capital gains tax rates by increasing the minimum tax to 15 percent. In 1977 and 1978, the maximum tax rate on capital gains reached 39.875 percent with the minimum tax and 49.875 percent including interaction with the maximum tax. In 1978, Congress reduced capital gains tax rates by eliminating the minimum tax on excluded gains and increasing the exclusion to 60 percent, thereby reducing the maximum rate to 28 percent. The 1981 income tax rate reductions further lowered capital gains rates to a maximum of 20 percent.

The Tax Reform Act of 1986 repealed the exclusion of long-term gains, raising the maximum rate to 28 percent (33 percent for taxpayers subject to certain phaseouts). When the top ordinary tax rates were increased by the 1990 and 1993 Budget Acts, an alternative tax rate of 28 percent was provided. Effective tax rates exceeded 28 percent for many high-income taxpayers, however, because of interactions with other tax provisions. The Taxpayer Relief Act of 1997 reduced capital gains tax rates and introduced a separate rate schedule for long-term gains. Beginning May 7, 1997, long-term gains in the 15 percent tax bracket were taxed at a 10 percent rate, and gains in higher tax brackets were taxed at 20 percent. Beginning in 2001, capital gains in the 15 percent bracket on assets held at least five years were taxed at 8 percent. Capital gains in the 28 percent and higher brackets on assets purchased in 2001 or later and held for at least five years were to be eligible for an 18 percent rate. The multiple rates introduced in 1997 have been criticized for their complexity. The Jobs and Growth Tax Relief Reconciliation Act of 2003 reduced tax rates on capital gains and dividends to 5 and 15 percent for gains realized on or after May 6, 2003, and before 2009 as described above.

Economic issues in capital gains taxation

Inflation

Taxing nominal gains raises the effective tax rate on real capital gains and can impose a tax in cases of real economic losses. Several studies have shown that a large percentage of reported capital gains reflect the effects of inflation, and that capital gains of lower- and middle-income taxpayers commonly represent not only nominal gains but real economic losses. Indexing the cost or basis of assets for changes in the price level has frequently been proposed to correct for inflation.

Deferral

From the standpoint of economic accretion, the deferral of capital gains taxes until realization reduces the present value of the tax, thereby reducing the effective tax rate below the statutory tax rate. The combination of deferral and inflation can produce effective tax rates higher or lower than statutory rates.

Lock-in effects

Because capital gains are taxed only when realized, high capital gains tax rates discourage the realization of capital gains and encourage the realization of capital losses. Investors induced to hold appreciated assets because of capital gains tax when they would otherwise sell are said to be "locked in." Lock-in effects impose efficiency losses when investors are induced to hold suboptimal portfolios with inappropriate risk or diversification, or to forego investment opportunities offering higher expected pre-tax returns. Investors with appreciated property may also incur unnecessary transactions costs to avoid capital gains taxes if they obtain cash from their investment by using it as security for a loan, or reduce their risk by selling short an equivalent asset (selling short against the box). The lock-in effect is greater for long-held, highly appreciated assets and is increased by the step-up in basis at death.

Behavior responses and revenues

Behavioral responses associated with capital gains tax rates are complex. In the absence of tax law changes, transitory fluctuations in income may induce taxpayers to accelerate or defer realizations of gains. Similarly, taxpayers may time realizations to take advantage of differential tax rates on short- and long-term gains. Statutory changes in tax rates are likely to result in both short-run and long-run responses. There may be a large short-run response to lower capital gains rates if taxpayers initially react by unlocking significant amounts of accumulated gains (such as the 50 percent increase in long-term gains after the 1978 capital gains tax reduction). The long-run response to a rate cut, which is generally thought to be smaller, may include higher realizations from more rapid turnover, from sales of more highly appreciated assets, and from sales of assets that would otherwise be held for life, transferred using a tax-free like-kind exchange or given to charity. The fact that realizations were a low percentage of GDP when tax rates were high in the 1970s, late 1980s, and early 1990s, and a much higher percentage of GDP when capital gains rates were low in the mid-1980s and late 1990s, is sometimes cited as evidence of the long-term response (see the accompanying table on realized gains). However, it is difficult to disentangle the effects of tax rates from the effects of economic and market factors.

Anticipated tax rate changes also affect behavior. An anticipated increase in capital gains tax rates may induce taxpayers to accelerate realizations of capital gains. For example, in 1986, realized capital gains doubled as taxpayers accelerated asset sales ahead of the increase in capital gains tax rates effective in 1987. Taxpayers may also defer realizations in anticipation of a reduction in capital gains tax rates.

Empirical studies have provided widely ranging estimates of the responsiveness of capital gains because of differences in the data and the apparent sensitivity to the assumptions inherent in the different methodologies. In a seminal study that played a role in the 1978 capital gains tax cut, Feldstein, Slemrod, and Yitzhaki (1980) estimated an elasticity of realizations of corporate stock gains for a cross-section sample of wealthy taxpayers of about −3.8 and concluded that reducing rates from 1970s levels would increase revenues. Auten and Clotfelter (1982) used panel data to separate permanent and transitory responses, and estimated transitory elasticities generally larger than −1.0, and permanent elasticities generally averaging about −0.5, implying that rate reductions might lead to increased revenues in the short run but lower revenues in the long run. Burman and Randolph (1994) reported a large transitory response (−6.4) and a small permanent response (−0.2). Auerbach and Siegel (2000) further illustrate the sensitivity of results to alternative models as they reported a permanent elasticity of −1.7 and a transitory elasticity of −4.4 for a model including the future tax rate. Time series studies generally report elasticities between −0.5 and −0.9, implying that realization responses only partly offset the effects of tax rate changes. Time series results have sometimes been interpreted as being more indicative of longer run taxpayer responses to changes in tax rates because tax rates vary over time primarily due to legislated changes. Other recent research (Ivkovic, Poterba, and Weisbenner 2004) has examined brokerage firm data on trading by individual investors and found evidence of lock-in effects and other tax-motivated trading.

Whether the long-run response to lower capital gains rates is large enough to offset the lower rate has been debated for over 70 years and is likely to remain controversial.

Savings and investment effects

Capital gains tax rates may affect the savings rate through the after-tax rate of return, but this effect is generally believed to be small. Capital gains tax rates may affect the quantity of investment through the cost of capital, and the allocation of investment through effects on the relative returns to risk-taking. Preferential tax rates for capital gains may increase the proportion of higher risk investment such as in startup or venture capital businesses.

An income tax with a flat rate and full deduction of losses could increase the incentives for risky investment by reducing the expected variance of after-tax returns. A tax with

TABLE 1. Realized Capital Gains and Taxes Paid on Capital Gains, 1976–2001

Year	Total positive realized capital gains ($billions)	Taxes paid on capital gains ($billions)	Effective tax rate on capital gains (%)	Gains as percent of gross domestic product	Maximum tax rate on long-term gains (%)
1976	39.5	6.6	16.8	2.2	39.9
1977	45.3	8.2	18.2	2.2	39.9
1978	50.5	9.1	18.0	2.2	39.9
1979	73.4	11.8	16.0	2.9	28.0
1980	74.1	12.5	16.8	2.7	28.0
1981	80.9	12.9	15.9	2.6	28.0/20.0
1982	90.2	12.9	14.3	2.8	20.0
1983	122.8	18.7	15.2	3.5	20.0
1984	140.5	21.5	15.3	3.6	20.0
1985	172.0	26.5	15.4	4.1	20.0
1986	327.7	52.9	16.1	7.4	20.0
1987	148.4	33.7	22.7	3.2	28.0
1988	162.6	38.9	23.9	3.2	28.0
1989	154.0	35.3	22.9	2.8	28.0
1990	123.8	27.8	22.5	2.2	28.0
1991	111.6	24.9	22.3	1.9	28.9
1992	126.7	29.0	22.9	2.0	28.9
1993	152.3	36.1	23.7	2.3	29.2
1994	152.7	36.2	23.7	2.2	29.2
1995	180.1	44.3	24.6	2.5	29.2
1996	260.7	66.4	25.5	3.3	29.2
1997	364.8	79.3	21.7	4.4	29.2/21.2
1998	455.2	89.1	19.6	5.2	21.2
1999	552.6	111.8	20.2	6.0	21.2
2000	644.3	127.3	19.8	6.6	21.2
2001	349.4	65.7	18.8	3.5	21.2

Source: Office of Tax Analysis, U.S. Treasury Department

Notes: Realized gains include positive amounts of both short- and long-term capital gains. The maximum rate includes the effects of the 3 percent phaseout of itemized deductions for high-income taxpayers (computed for 1994–97 as 29.188 = 28 + [0.03 × 39.6]). Taxpayers in the income range over which personal exemptions are phased out or subject to certain other phaseout provisions could pay higher effective tax rates. In 1988 through 1990, taxpayers in the so-called "bubble" tax bracket paid a 33 percent tax rate on capital gains.

progressive tax rates and limited deduction of losses, however, is more likely to discourage risky investments.

Income conversion

Preferential tax rates for capital gains induce taxpayers to attempt to convert ordinary income into capital gains taxed at a lower rate. Executive compensation may be shifted from salaries to capital gains. Many tax shelters prior to the 1986 act were based on investments that produced operating losses from the deduction of expenses at ordinary tax rates and the deferred taxation of capital gains at preferential rates.

Distribution of tax burden

The income distribution effects of raising or lowering capital gains tax rates has been an important issue affecting debates about capital gains rate changes. Capital gains are more highly concentrated among high-income households than other forms

of income and therefore it is argued that capital gains rate cuts would be regressive.

Equity and efficiency

Tax equity implies that capital gains income should be taxed at the same rates as other income. However, if the responsiveness to tax rates is greater for capital gains than for other forms of income, the excess burden of the income tax is reduced by providing lower rates for capital gains than for other income. In addition, the capital gains tax on corporate stock can be viewed as an aspect of the double taxation of corporate income that can raise both equity and efficiency concerns.

ADDITIONAL READINGS

Auerbach, Alan, and Jonathan Siegel. "Capital Gains Realizations of the Rich and Sophisticated." *American Economic Review* 90 (May 2000): 276–82.

Auten, Gerald, and Charles Clotfelter. "Permanent vs. Transitory Effects and the Realization of Capital Gains." *Quarterly Journal of Economics* 97 (November 1982): 613–32.

Auten, Gerald, and Joseph Cordes. "Cutting Capital Gains Taxes." *Journal of Economic Perspectives* 5 (Spring 1991): 181–92.

Burman, Leonard, and William Randolph. "Measuring Permanent Responses to Capital-Gains Tax Changes in Panel Data." *American Economic Review* 84 (September 1994): 794–809.

Congressional Budget Office. *How Capital Gains Tax Rates Affect Revenues: The Historical Evidence.* Washington, DC: Congressional Budget Office, 1988.

———. *Perspectives on the Ownership of Capital Assets and the Realization of Capital Gains.* Washington, DC: Congressional Budget Office, 1997.

Eichner, Mathew, and Todd Sinai. "Capital Gains Tax Realizations and Tax Rates: New Evidence from Time Series." *National Tax Journal* 53 (September 2000): 663–81.

Feldstein, Martin, Joel Slemrod, and Shlomo Yitzhaki. "The Effects of Taxation on the Selling of Corporate Stock and the Realization of Capital Gains." *Quarterly Journal of Economics* 94 (June 1980): 777–91.

Gompers, Paul, and Josh Lerner. "The Venture Capital Revolution." *Journal of Economic Perspectives* 15 (Spring 2000): 145–68.

Gravelle, Jane G., 1994. *The Economic Effects of Taxing Capital Income.* Chapter 6. (MIT Press: Cambridge and London).

Ivkovic, Zoran, James Poterba, and Scott Weisbenner. "Tax Motivated Trading by Individual Investors." National Bureau of Economic Research [NBER] Working Paper 10275. Cambridge, MA: NBER, 2004.

U.S. Congress, Joint Committee on Taxation. *Proposals and Issues Relating to the Taxation of Capital Gains and Losses (JCS-10-90).* Washington, DC: Joint Committee on Taxation, March 23, 1990.

U.S. Treasury Department, Office of Tax Analysis. *Report to Congress on the Capital Gains Tax Reductions of 1978.* Washington, DC: U.S. Government Printing Office, 1985.

Zodrow, G. "Economic Analyses of Capital Gains Taxation: Realizations, Revenues, Efficiency and Equity." *Tax Law Review* 48, no. 3 (1993): 419–527.

Cross-references: elasticity, demand and supply; income tax, corporate, federal; income tax, federal; portfolio choice.

Capital import neutrality

Peggy B. Musgrave

University of California, Santa Cruz

A condition in which the same effective tax rate applies to all capital income earned within a given country, regardless of the investor's country of residence.

Capital import neutrality, to take an example, would require that capital income earned on investments in France to be taxed at the same rate regardless of whether the investments were made by entities residing in the United States, Germany, or France (Musgrave 1960; Musgrave 1969, 119–20). Capital import neutrality is met when an international tax system is based entirely on the source principle. Thus, in the example given above, only France, the country of source, would be entitled to tax capital income arising in France. Each country of residence would in effect provide exemption from its own tax for foreign-source income accruing to its investors. This contrasts with capital export neutrality in which capital income accruing to resident entities of a given country is taxed at the same rate wherever that income is earned, whether at home

or abroad. This is accomplished by having the country of residence permit foreign tax to be credited against its own tax (see *capital export neutrality*).

Unfortunately, it is difficult to meet both standards at the same time. Only if effective tax rates were the same in all countries could capital import and export neutrality be met simultaneously. But once tax rates differ, the two criteria are in conflict, and tax policy with respect to foreign investment has to choose between the two.

Opinions differ as to which of these two concepts should be given priority. The case for capital export neutrality rests on the proposition that, in order to secure worldwide efficiency in capital allocation, the choice of location should not be affected by tax considerations. This is accomplished under a system of residency taxation combined with foreign tax credit. In contrast, capital import neutrality, which is secured under a system of taxation solely by country of source of income, leaves capital open to tax differentials between countries of residence and source. Capital is thus attracted to low-tax countries, and the international allocation of capital is distorted by tax differentials. That distortion will be larger the greater are tax differentials, including, in particular, the presence of tax havens. Even though U.S. investors in France would pay the same tax rate as U.K. investors in France, they would each have to pay different taxes depending on whether they invest at home or abroad. Only if all tax rates were the same would this not be the case.

Proponents of capital import neutrality hold that firms, when competing in foreign markets, should not be handicapped (as they would be under capital export neutrality) because their residence lies in a higher-tax country (Vogel 1988). This competitive disadvantage is debatable (Shoup 1974, 36–38), but the question is whether it should be viewed as causing inefficient allocation. Different rates of corporate tax among countries reflect differences in domestic tax policy that may give rise to differing rates of capital formation. Once taken, be it wise or unwise, that policy choice should bear equally on the choice between domestic and foreign investment. There would seem to be no reason to counteract its overall effect by favoring foreign versus domestic investment. It should also be noted that capital import neutrality may be met at the expense of horizontal equity in taxation, which requires that all those entities residing in a given country be subject to the same tax treatment by that country.

While economists mostly support the superior efficiency case for capital export neutrality, this occurs at a cost. A source-based system is much simpler to administer and comply with than a residence-based system, particularly if combined with the foreign tax credit. The choice of economic efficiency is thus bought at the cost of additional administrative complexity. This may well be why some countries apply a "territorial" or source-based tax system, a system that meets capital import neutrality but leaves the distribution of capital flows open to tax rate differentials. This is a defect that may be remedied by a move towards rate equalization, a policy being followed by the European Union. Furthermore, a reduction in rate differentials is helpful not only in approaching capital import neutrality, but also in achieving capital export neutrality (see *capital export neutrality*). However this is at the cost of some loss of independence in tax policy.

In concluding, it may be noted that the case for capital import neutrality in taxation may be strengthened if allowance is made for the offsetting effects of public expenditure benefits, in which case source taxation and capital import neutrality may cause less interference with capital export neutrality (Gandenberger 1983).

ADDITIONAL READINGS

Gandenberger, Otto. "Kapitalexportneutralität versus Kapitalimportneutralität" *Aufsätze zur Wirtschaftspolitik.* Forschungsinstitut für Wirtschaftspolitik an der Universität Mainz, 1983.

Musgrave, Peggy B. *United States Taxation of Foreign Investment Income: Issues and Arguments.* Cambridge, MA: International Tax Program, Harvard Law School, 1969.

Musgrave, Richard A. "Criteria for Foreign Tax Credit." In *Taxation and Operations Abroad,* edited by Russell Baker. Princeton: Tax Institute Symposium, 1960.

Shoup, Carl S. "Taxation of Multinational Corporations." In *The Impact of Multinational Corporations on Development and International Relations.* Technical Papers: Taxation. New York: United Nations, 1974.

Vogel, Klaus. "The Search for Compatible Tax Systems." In *Tax Policy in the Twenty-First Century,* edited by Herbert Stein. New York: John Wiley, 1988.

Cross-references: capital export neutrality; national neutrality.

Charitable deductions

William C. Randolph
Department of the Treasury

Preferential tax treatment of expenditures or gifts to organizations that the law qualifies as having a socially beneficial characteristic and for which the donor is not motivated by direct benefit when making the contribution.

Since 1917, individual federal taxpayers have been allowed to deduct gifts to charitable and certain other nonprofit organizations. Such organizations (hereafter called "charitable") were already exempt from the income tax. A charitable deduction extended the benefits of exemption to individual taxpayers, so that income donated to charitable organizations was exempted from all levels of income taxation.

The deduction was intended to subsidize the activities of private organizations that provide viable alternatives to direct government programs. The 1917 law increased tax rates, and the deduction was introduced to alleviate congressional concern that the higher tax rates would discourage private charity (Wallace and Fisher 1977). To control the revenue loss, total charitable deductions were limited to 15 percent of taxable income. Corporations were first allowed a deduction in 1935.

Under the current federal income tax, individuals who itemize deductions can deduct contributions to certain organizations operated for religious, charitable, scientific, literary, or educational purposes. The list also includes domestic government entities, fraternal societies, organizations that prevent cruelty to children or animals, and several other types of socially beneficial organizations. Organizations must be operated in a nonprofit form and are subject to other restrictions.

Types of deductible contributions include cash, financial assets, and other noncash property such as real estate, clothing, and artwork. In general, the law limits gifts of cash or other non–capital gains assets to no more than 50 percent of the (slightly modified) adjusted gross income. Contributions of capital gains property are generally limited to 30 percent of adjusted gross income. Both individuals and corporations can carry forward contributions that exceed the limits and use them as deductions in later years.

A donation of appreciated capital gains property can be deducted at its full current market value. The capital gains portion is, in effect, deducted twice. It is implicitly deducted once against itself because the capital gains will never be taxed. It is also explicitly part of the itemized deduction, so that other income is shielded from taxation.

In 2002, individual deductions totaled $136.4 billion. In 2000, corporate deductions totaled $10.7 billion. For fiscal year 2004, the Joint Committee on Taxation estimates the tax expenditure at $27.9 billion for deductions by individuals and $1.8 billion for deductions by corporations.

The deduction subsidizes giving by lowering the price that people must pay privately to support charitable organizations. A charitable contribution of one dollar that is deducted from taxable income lowers the donor's tax bill and thus decreases the resources available for the donor's other consumption, the price, by less than a dollar. For example, if a donor's marginal tax rate is 30 percent, a deductible one-dollar cash gift to charity will reduce the donor's taxes by 30 cents, so the price of the gift to the donor will only be 70 cents.

This price reduction affects giving in two ways, which economists refer to as income and substitution effects. The income effect results because the reduced price effectively makes more income available for all consumption. If people normally give more as income rises, the income effect of the price reduction will induce people to increase giving. The substitution effect arises because the reduced price makes giving cheaper relative to other commodities, which will induce people to give more. Empirical studies indicate that both the income and substitution effects cause people to increase charitable giving (Clotfelter 1985).

Many policy justifications have been offered for the charitable deduction. Some argue that an ideal income tax should not treat gifts to charity as part of an individual's income (Andrews 1972). Under this view, an income tax should reallocate resources that would have been used for private consumption and use them for public consumption. Because charitable giving is not used for the giver's private consumption, it would not be fair to include it in the tax base.

Some argue that private charitable activity is superior to direct government activity (Belknap 1977). For example, private social and religious organizations provide some services that substitute for government programs, such as providing food or shelter for the poor. The tax deduction and tax exemption subsidize those organizations while avoiding the direct participation of government, which might be more intrusive and also risk violating the constitutional principle of separation of church and state.

A similar argument can be made for encouraging donations to private educational institutions. Not only might the tax deduction be less intrusive than direct government spending, but private institutions sometimes approach education differently from public institutions. Competing approaches can encourage pluralism and increase innovation. Another justification for the deduction and the exemption is that private charitable organizations may provide social goods more efficiently than the government. Because taxes are mandatory and the burden of taxation and governance is spread among many people, individuals can have little incentive to increase government efficiency. In the private nonprofit sector, however, competition among organizations for donations creates an incentive for the organizations to operate efficiently.

Popular policy justifications can often be reduced to descriptions of the many socially desirable activities of charitable organizations. To an extent, this justification is simply an individual expression of taste for more of a good thing. It is natural for such people to argue for a subsidy that encourages others, whose tastes may differ, to give more. Even if tastes did not differ, however, some charitable activities would be supplied inadequately if there were no subsidy. This is because the activities may create additional social benefits, external to those experienced by a donor. A person who donates money to help the poor, for example, receives private satisfaction from the act of generosity, but other people, aside from the poor, also benefit from a reduction in poverty. The donor does not account for this external benefit, however, but decides how much to give by comparing the private cost of a contribution with the private satisfaction received. Consideration of the additional external benefits would warrant a larger donation. All potential donors could be made better off as a group if they were either compelled through taxes or encouraged by subsidy to give more.

Examples of subsidized activities with external benefits abound. Education and religion can improve moral conduct, decrease crime, and increase civic responsibility. Education can decrease poverty. Education and scientific research increase general knowledge and speed the rate of technological progress, which can improve the standard of living. In each case, benefits extend to people beyond those who provide voluntary financial support or benefit directly from the activities.

Economic efficiency of the tax subsidy provided by the charitable deduction can be evaluated by comparing costs with benefits. The cost of a deductible charitable contribution is shared with other taxpayers. The after-tax cost is borne privately by the donor, but the amount by which the deduction reduces taxes is an additional social cost shared with other taxpayers. Cost-sharing occurs, whether it means that tax must be increased or government spending decreased to make up for the tax revenue forgone as a result of the deduction. The amount of external benefit provided by the subsidy increases with the satisfaction that other potential donors experience if the subsidy increases giving, measured by the extent by which the amount of charity would have been inadequate without a subsidy, and the degree to which the subsidy actually does increase giving.

External benefits can be difficult to measure and probably vary greatly among subsidized activities. For example, people probably benefit by different amounts from poverty reduction and scientific innovation. Further, many subsidized organizations provide a mix of public services that have external social benefits with social goods that could be provided adequately to organization members through the use of membership fees. A subsidized increase in such services would provide no external benefits. Finally, even if a charitable activity has external benefits, the tax subsidy only increases the external benefits to the extent that it increases giving.

Substantial empirical research suggests that the subsidy does increase giving (Clotfelter 1985), although the estimated size of the effect is not very robust in more recent evidence (Steinberg 1990). Some published evidence suggests that the subsidy increases certain types of charitable giving more than others. For example, Schiff (1990) found that giving to support elementary education is more sensitive to the subsidy than giving to health and medical charities. This evidence suggests that the most efficient policy might subsidize different types of charity at different rates. Randolph (1995) suggests that studies have generally overstated the degree to which the subsidy increases giving, which weakens, somewhat, its economic policy justification. Joulfaian and Rider (2004) and Auten, Sieg, and Clotfelter (2002) provide more recent additions to this empirical inquiry.

Economists often argue that a deduction is not the best device for providing a subsidy. An efficient subsidy would vary with the amount of external benefits, whereas the tax subsidy rate provided by a charitable deduction varies only with the giver's tax rate. A deduction thus provides larger subsidies to charitable organizations favored by higher-income taxpayers because they face higher marginal tax rates. The deduction also currently provides no subsidy for gifts by people who do not itemize deductions. Some argue that a tax credit would be a fairer and more efficient form of subsidy because the subsidy rate would not depend as much on the giver's level of income (Hochman and Rodgers 1977).

ADDITIONAL READINGS

Andrews, William D. "Personal Deductions and the Ideal Income Tax." *Harvard Law Review* 86 (December 1972): 309–85.
Auten, Gerald E., Holger Sieg, and Charles T. Clotfelter. "Charitable Giving, Income, and Taxes: An Analysis of Panel Data." *American Economic Review* 92, no. 1 (March 2002): 371–82.

Belknap, Chauncey. "The Federal Income Tax Exemption of Charitable Organizations: Its History and Underlying Policy." In *Research Papers Sponsored by the Commission on Private Philanthropy and Public Needs,* vol. 4. U.S. Department of the Treasury (1977): 2025–43.

Clotfelter, Charles T. *Federal Tax Policy and Charitable Giving.* Chicago: University of Chicago Press, 1985.

Hochman, Harold M., and James D. Rodgers. "The Optimal Tax Treatment of Charitable Contributions." *National Tax Journal* 30, no. 1 (March 1977): 1–18.

Joulfaian, David, and Mark Rider. "Errors-In-Variables and Estimated Income and Price Elasticities of Charitable Giving." *National Tax Journal* 57, no. 1 (March 2004): 25–43.

Randolph, William C. "Dynamic Income, Progressive Taxes, and the Timing of Charitable Contributions." *Journal of Political Economy* 103, no. 4 (August 1995): 709–38.

Schiff, Jerald. *Charitable Giving and Government Policy: An Economic Analysis.* New York: Greenwood Press, 1990.

Steinberg, Richard. "Taxes and Giving: New Findings." *Voluntas* 1, no. 2 (November 1990): 61–79.

Wallace, John A., and Robert W. Fisher. "The Charitable Deduction under Section 170 of the Internal Revenue Code." In *Research Papers Sponsored by the Commission on Private Philanthropy and Public Needs,* vol. 4. U.S. Department of the Treasury (1977): 2131–61.

Yetman, Michelle H., and Robert J. Yetman. "The Effect of Nonprofits' Taxable Activities on the Supply of Private Donations." *National Tax Journal* 56, no. 1 (March 2003): 243–58.

Cross-references: adjusted gross income; itemized deductions; Joint Committee on Taxation, U.S. Congress; nonprofit organizations, federal tax treatment.

Child care credit

Amy E. Dunbar

University of Connecticut Department of Accounting

A nonrefundable credit based on employment-related expenses of household-type services for the care of children under age 13, a disabled spouse, or other dependent.

The Internal Revenue Code provides tax benefits in the form of a credit or exclusion for child care expenses incurred by tax-payers deemed to be gainfully employed. The credit was enacted in the Tax Reform Act of 1976 by repealing Section 214, which allowed an itemized deduction for child care expenses, and replacing it with Section 44A (redesignated as Section 21 by the Tax Reform Act of 1984). The Section 129 dependent care exclusion for assistance from employers was enacted by the Economic Recovery Tax Act of 1981 and subjected to a $5,000 cap by the Tax Reform Act of 1986.

Both the credit and the exclusion are subject to earned income ceilings that limit the qualified child care expenses in any taxable year to an amount not in excess of the earned income of the employee, or if the employee is married, the lower of the employee's earned income or the earned income of his or her spouse. Thus, these benefits generally are not available to one-earner couples. (Spouses who are full-time students or incapable of caring for themselves are deemed to earn a monthly amount equivalent to $1/12$ of the maximum child care expenses.)

Congress has made several changes to Sec. 21, effective 1982, 1989, and 2003, as shown in table 1. From 1976 to 1981, a credit of 20 percent of qualified child care expenses was allowed with a maximum credit of $400 for each of the taxpayer's first two dependents. The 20 percent credit was the same for all taxpayers. In an effort to make the credit more progressive, Congress enacted a sliding scale credit in 1982. From 1982 to 1988, the credit was 30 percent of qualified expenses for taxpayers with incomes of $10,000 or less. The credit is reduced by 1 percent for each $2,000 or fraction thereof of income above $10,000. For taxpayers with adjusted gross income (AGI) above $28,000, the credit rate is 20 percent. The Family Support Act of 1988 increased the allowable expense limit to $2,400 from $2,000 for one child and to $4,800 from $4,000 for two or more children. Expenses, however, only qualified if the child was under age 13 (rather than 15 before 1989). In addition, eligible expenses were reduced, dollar for dollar, by the amount of expenses excludable from the taxpayer's income under the dependent care exclusion. The Economic Growth and Tax Relief Reconciliation Act of 2001 increased both the rate and the allowable

TABLE 1. Determination of Child Care Tax Credit

	1976–81			1982–88		1989–2002			2003–10	
	One child	Two or more children		One child	Two or more children	One child	Two or more children		One child	Two or more children
Maximum expenses	$2,000	$4,000		$2,000	$4,000	$2,400	$4,800		$3,000	$6,000
Credit rate	20%	20%								
			AGI ≤ $10,000	30%	30%	30%	30%	AGI ≤ $15,000	35%	35%
			$10,001–$28,000	Credit reduced by 1% for every $2,000 increment of AGI				$15,001–$43,000	Credit reduced by 1% for every $2,000 increment of AGI	
			AGI > $28,000	20%	20%	20%	20%	AGI > 43,000	20%	20%
Maximum credit	$400	$800		$600	$1,200	$720	$1,440		$1,050	$2,100
Minimum credit	$400	$800		$400	$800	$480	$960		$600	$1,200

Note: AGI = adjusted gross income.

expenses, as shown in table 1, for the years 2003 through 2010. In 2011, the child care credit will be determined under the rules in effect for 2002.

Table 2 reports the total child care credits and total credits claimed in selected years on all returns filed as reported by Publication 1304, "Individual Income Tax Returns." The child care credit represents a large portion of the total credits claimed, increasing from 1979 to 1988. In 1989, the net effect of the Family Support Act of 1988 reduced the total child care credits claimed. ("Total credits" as reported in Publication 1304 do not include the earned income credit that was refunded or offset against taxes other than income taxes. For example, in 1988, individual taxpayers paid approximately $413 billion in income tax after credits and received $12 billion in credits, including $5 billion of earned income credit, of which $4 billion was child care credit. The large increase in "total credits" in 1999 is due to the Sec. 24 child tax credit.)

Empirical research

Prior research has focused primarily on the issue of child care credit progressivity because Congress has addressed such progressivity several times. (Whether the child care credit should be evaluated based on progressivity concerns is addressed by Steuerle 1998.) The 1976 conversion of a deduction to a credit and the 1982 change to a sliding scale credit were intended to increase the credit's progressivity. In the Revenue Reconciliation Act of 1989 debates, Congress again addressed the perceived regressivity of the credit, but no changes to the credit were enacted at that time.

Using tax return data, Dunbar and Nordhauser's (1991) examined the progressivity of the child care credit by considering the impact of the credit on the income distribution using the Kakwani and Suits indices. A comparison of the Kakwani and Suits tax indices is provided in Formby, Seaks, and Smith (1984). (See *progressivity, measures of*). They concluded that the child care credit contributes to the overall progressivity of the federal income tax. The tax law change in 1982 increased the progressivity of the child care credit, although the lower deciles continue to reflect regressivity. Many taxpayers are in the lower deciles because they are in one-earner families. If such taxpayers are married, they are generally precluded from claiming the credit.

Altshuler and Schwartz (1996) also use tax return data to examine the progressivity of the credit, but they use a lifecycle approach. They compute the Suits index using both annual and "time-exposure" income to measure ability to pay.

They conclude that the credit is progressively distributed, but replacing the annual with time-exposure income increases the proportion of the credit received by lower-income taxpayers.

Gentry and Hagy (1996) examine the distributional effects of both the credit and the exclusion using both the 1989 National Child Care Survey and tax return data. They provide a discussion of the rationales for tax treatment of child care, providing equity and efficiency arguments for and against tax provisions for child care. They note that previous literature focused primarily on the vertical equity, while their research also captures some horizontal equity concerns. They find that among families that use tax relief for child care expenses, the benefits average 1.24 percent of family income. Benefits as a percentage of income vary systematically over the income distribution. Despite being regressive at low income levels (mainly due to the credit being non-refundable), tax relief is progressively distributed over most of the income distribution with the ratio of benefits to income falling above the bottom quintile of the income distribution. The benefits of tax relief also vary among families with the same income depending on a family's structure and its labor market and child care choices.

Using data from the 1986 National Longitudinal Surveys of Labor Market Experience of Youth, Averett, Peters, and Waldman (1997) focus on the effect of the credit on labor supply. They examine the effects of the credit on the labor supply decisions of married women with young children, finding that the elasticity of labor supply is close to 1. Their policy simulations show that the credit substantially increases labor supply.

Prior research generally finds that the tax expenditure for the child care credit is distributed progressively and does increase the labor supply. If Congress wishes to increase the progressivity of the credit, the credit could be increased further for low-income taxpayers (which was done effective 2003) or the credit for high-income taxpayers could be phased out.

ADDITIONAL READINGS

Altshuler, Rosanne, and Amy Ellen Schwartz. "On the Progressivity of the Child Care Tax Credit: Snapshot versus Time-Exposure Incidence." *National Tax Journal* 49 (1996): 55–71.

Averett, Susan L., Elizabeth Peters, and Donald M. Waldman. "Tax Credits, Labor Supply, and Child Care." *The Review of Economics and Statistics* 79 (1997): 125–35.

Dunbar, Amy, and Susan Nordhauser. "Is The Child Care Credit Progressive?" *National Tax Journal* 44 (1991): 519–28.

Formby, John P., Terry G. Seaks, and W. James Smith. "Difficulties in the Measurement of Tax Progressivity: The Case of North America." *Public Finance* 39 (1984): 297–313.

TABLE 2. Total Credits Claimed on All Returns and Credits Claimed on Returns ($ 1,000s)

	1979	1982	1985	1988	1990	1995	1999	2001
Child tax credit	793,143	1,501,453	3,127,702	3,812,849	2,549,004	2,517,962	2,675,147	2,721,061
Total credits	6,780,186	7,854,493	10,248,044	7,047,140	6,831,187	10,040,198	35,892,344	45,631,198

Gentry, William M., and Allison P. Hagy. "The Distributional Effects of the Tax Treatment of Child Care Expenses." *In Empirical Foundations of Household Taxation,* edited by Martin Feldstein and James M. Poterba (99–128). Chicago: University of Chicago Press, 1996.

Kakwani, Nanok C. "Measurement of Tax Progressivity: An International Comparison." *Economic Journal* 87 (1976): 71–80.

Steuerle, C. Eugene. "Systematic Thinking About Subsidies for Child Care." *Tax Notes* 78 (1998): 749.

Suits, Daniel. B. "Measurement of Tax Progressivity." *American Economic Review* (September 1977): 747–52.

Cross-references: family, tax treatment of; income tax, federal.

Child tax credit

Gregg A. Esenwein
Congressional Research Service, Library of Congress

A refundable income tax credit for dependent children under the age of 17.

For tax year 2004, families with incomes below certain levels and with qualifying children were allowed a credit against their federal income tax of $1,000 for each qualifying child. To qualify for the credit, the child must be an individual for whom the taxpayer can claim a dependency exemption. The child must be under the age of 17 at the close of the calendar year in which the taxable year of the taxpayer begins.

For families with one or two qualifying children, the credit is refundable to the extent of 10 percent of a taxpayer's earned income in excess of $10,750. (This earned income threshold is indexed annually for inflation.) For families with three or more children, the child tax credit is refundable to the extent that the taxpayer's Social Security taxes exceed the taxpayer's earned income tax credit or to the extent of 10 percent of their earned income in excess of $10,750, whichever is larger.

The child tax credit is phased out for taxpayers whose adjusted gross incomes (AGIs) exceed certain thresholds. For married taxpayers filing joint returns, the phaseout begins at AGI levels in excess of $110,000; for married couples filing separately, the phaseout begins at AGI levels in excess of $55,000; and for single individuals filing as either heads of households or as singles, the phaseout begins at AGI levels in excess of $75,000. These phaseout thresholds are not indexed for inflation.

The child tax credit is allowed in full against a taxpayer's alternative minimum tax.

Legislative history

The child tax credit was enacted as part of the Taxpayer Relief Act of 1997. Congress established the child tax credit to address concerns that the tax structure did not adequately reflect a family's reduced ability to pay taxes as family size increased. The decline (prior to its indexation) in the real value of the personal exemption over time was cited as evidence of the tax system's failure to reflect a family's ability to pay.

Initially, for tax year 1998, families with qualifying children were allowed a credit against their federal income tax of $400 for each qualifying child. For tax years after 1998, the credit increased to $500 per qualifying child. For families with three or more children, the child tax credit was refundable.

The Economic Growth and Tax Relief Reconciliation Act of 2001 (EGTRRA) made several major changes to the child tax credit. The child tax credit was increased to $1,000, with the increase scheduled to phase in between 2001 and 2010. For calendar years 2001 through 2004, the credit was $600. In calendar years 2005 to 2008, the credit is scheduled to be $700; for calendar year 2009, $800; and for calendar year 2010, $1,000.

The 2001 Act also extended the refundability of the child tax credit to families with fewer than three children. For tax years 2001 through 2004, the credit was made refundable to the extent of 10 percent of a taxpayer's earned income in excess of $10,000. Refundability was scheduled to increase to 15 percent for 2005 and later years. The refundability threshold is indexed for inflation. The 2001 Act permanently allowed the child tax credit to offset alternative minimum tax liability. All of the provisions of the 2001 Act, however, are scheduled to sunset at the end of 2010.

The Jobs Growth and Tax Relief Reconciliation Act of 2003 (JGTRRA) increased the child tax credit to $1,000 for tax years 2003 and 2004. The JGTRRA provisions expire after 2004 and, absent congressional action, the child tax credit is scheduled to revert to $700 in 2005. It will then increase to $1,000 via the phase-in schedule originally established under EGTRRA.

Analysis

Economic theory does not provide an answer to the question of how the costs of child rearing should be accounted for under an income tax. Proponents of an increased child tax credit argue that the current credit is not large enough to offset the costs of raising a child. In this view, children should be considered an investment in the future, and as such, the costs associated with child rearing should be deducted, as are other investment costs. Critics argue, however, that the federal income tax was never intended to provide offsets for the full financial responsibility of raising children. Indeed, some argue that the decision to have children represents a choice of how to consume one's income, and therefore the costs of raising children should not be a consideration when assessing income taxes.

Historically, the federal income tax has differentiated among families of different size through the combined use of personal exemptions, dependent care credits, standard deductions, and the earned income tax credit. These provisions were modified over time so that families of differing size would not be subject to federal income tax if their incomes fell below the federal poverty level.

The child tax credit represents a departure from past policy practices because it is not designed primarily as a means of differentiating between families of different size at or near the poverty threshold, but rather is designed to provide general tax reductions to middle- and upper-income taxpayers with dependent children under the age of 17. Poverty-level families with incomes below the refundability threshold receive no tax benefits from the child tax credit.

Empirical evidence from the Congressional Budget Office suggests that for families with children (except those families in the highest income quintile), the overall federal tax burden fell between 1979 and 2000. The 2001 and 2003 Acts (with their reductions in marginal income tax rates, reductions in taxes on capital gains/dividend income, and marriage penalty tax relief), continued the trend of reducing federal taxes on families, especially high-income families filing joint returns.

Cross-references: child care credit; families, tax treatment of; income tax, federal.

Circuit breaker

John E. Anderson
University of Nebraska

A mechanism that provides a state income tax credit for selected taxpayers with high local property tax burdens.

A circuit breaker is a targeted means of providing property tax relief. The term *circuit breaker* is adapted from the common home electrical device that trips when an electrical circuit is overloaded. In similar fashion, a property tax circuit breaker is designed to trip, providing relief, when a taxpayer is overloaded with property tax burden.

The credit mechanism is defined by specifying two parameters. First, we must define what is meant by being overburdened with property taxes. Circuit breakers do that by specifying a threshold proportion of income taken by the property tax beyond which the taxpayer is presumed to be overburdened. Second, the size of the tax credit must be specified as some share of the property tax in excess of the threshold proportion of income. Note that the circuit breaker mechanism presumes an ability to pay that is reflected by the taxpayer's income. When the property tax is high relative to income, the taxpayer is overburdened and deserves relief.

The general form of a circuit breaker credit mechanism can be described as a credit (C) for which a taxpayer qualifies when property tax liability (P) exceeds some threshold proportion (b) of income (Y). The credit is specified as a fraction (a) of the property tax in excess of the proportion of income bY.

$C = a[P - bY]$, if $P > bY$,

$C = 0$ otherwise.

For example, a state can specify the circuit breaker as providing a 50 percent credit for property taxes paid in excess of 5 percent of income. In that case $a = 0.50$ and $b = 0.05$. If a taxpayer's property tax bill exceeds 5 percent of income, the taxpayer qualifies for the credit. If the property tax bill is less than 5 percent of income, the taxpayer does not qualify and receives no credit. The credit is then 50 percent of the property tax liability in excess of 5 percent of income: $C = 0.5[P - 0.5Y]$. Table 1 lists the credit amount for several hypothetical taxpayers with income Y and property tax liability P.

A taxpayer with an income of $20,000 first qualifies for the credit when property taxes exceed $1,000 (5 percent of income). Hence, a taxpayer with an income of $20,000 and property tax liability of $1,500 would qualify for a credit of $250 (50 percent of the difference between $1,500 and $1,000). The credit then reduces the effective property tax from $1,500 to $1,250. If the property tax were to rise to $2,000, the credit would increase to $500, reducing the net property tax liability to $1,500.

Similarly, a taxpayer with an income of $40,000 first qualifies for the credit when property tax liability exceeds $2,000 (5 percent of $40,000). A taxpayer with this income and a property tax bill of $3,800 would qualify for a credit of $900 (50 percent of the difference between $3,800 and $2,000), reducing the property tax bill to $2,900.

Both homeowners and renters can be included in a circuit breaker program. In the case of renters, a share of the rent paid to the landlord is assumed to be allocated to paying the property tax. That share of the rent is counted as property tax payment to local governments. The circuit breaker then applies as in the case of a homeowner.

The state can specify a maximum credit to be earned. For example, the credit ceiling could be $1,000. Regardless of the taxpayer's property tax liability in relation to income, a credit of no more than $1,000 would be provided. The state can also specify several different sets of parameters a and b in the general formula above. For example, the credit could be more generous for the elderly, with $a = 1.0$ and $b = 0.03$. In that case, an elderly taxpayer would qualify for the credit when the property tax liability first exceeds 3 percent of income,

TABLE 1. Circuit Breaker Examples

Income Y	Property tax P	Credit C	Net property tax after credit P–C
20,000	1,000	0	1,000
20,000	1,500	250	1,250
20,000	2,000	500	1,500
40,000	2,000	0	2,000
40,000	3,800	900	2,900

and the credit would be a full 100 percent of the property tax in excess of 3 percent of income.

A primary advantage of this form of property tax relief is that state resources are targeted specifically to those taxpayers most in need of it. If the state has $100 million it can spend on providing local property tax relief, that sum will be more effectively used when it is targeted to specific taxpayers than if it is spread across all property owners. Alternative mechanisms of providing property tax relief, such as a homestead exemption, spread the relief across all homesteads. The state's resources are not targeted to those most in need. Of course, defining an overburdened taxpayer is a problem. While a person whose property tax bill exceeds 5 percent of income may indeed be overburdened with local property tax, that person may simply have chosen to spend an extremely large share of income on housing. While housing expenditures generally fall as a share of income as income rises, there are certainly exceptions. Circuit breaker mechanisms define need in terms of property tax relative to income. In order to eliminate relief to very high income taxpayers or to those with exceptionally large housing expenditures, a phaseout mechanism for high-income taxpayers or a cap on the credit can be applied.

A fully refundable credit makes the state's income tax more progressive, regardless of the tax rate structure. With a fully refundable property tax credit, a taxpayer without income tax liability can file a return, claim the credit for property taxes, and receive a check from the state. Some states have a single flat income tax rate, yet have progressive income tax systems because of their reliance on a circuit breaker mechanism. For convenience of property tax payment, the credit is sometimes frontloaded. That is, the state credit is received before the property tax bill is due the local government.

Because the circuit breaker mechanism provides *state* income tax relief for *local* property taxes paid, the state government is making an indirect commitment to fund local government activity. The precise workings of a given state's circuit breaker mechanism should therefore be considered in tandem with that state's method of distributing state resources to local governments. Revenue-sharing formulas, aid distribution formulas, grants, and equalization mechanisms are all methods that states use to facilitate local government provision of public goods and services.

Thirty-five states and the District of Columbia in the United States have adopted circuit breaker programs. The parameters of the circuit breakers vary widely from state to state. In some cases, the circuit breaker provides a small amount of aggregate property tax relief to a narrowly targeted group of taxpayers. In other cases, hundreds of millions of dollars of property tax relief are provided to large numbers of taxpayers. Homeowners, renters, the elderly, and the disabled are all provided property tax relief in varying degrees by the circuit breaker mechanism. Details on each state's circuit breaker mechanism are provided in Baer (2003). For a thorough review of the role of circuit breakers in providing property tax relief, see Gold (1979).

Two states, Michigan and Wisconsin, use the circuit breaker mechanism to provide property tax relief for agricultural property owners. While most states provide preferential treatment for agricultural property through use value assessment or a classified property tax system, these two states have chosen to employ a circuit breaker mechanism on the state income tax. Farmers whose property taxes are high relative to their income receive a credit on the state income tax for some portion of the property tax they pay to local governments.

Incentive effects of circuit breakers are a potential concern. If, on the margin, a taxpayer pays only 50 percent of the property tax, the price of local public goods, such as education, is significantly reduced. The taxpayer may then be more likely to vote for additional local public goods, increasing demand for those goods and putting upward pressure on property tax rates. While in theory this potential effect is worth consideration, in practice the demand for local public goods is known to be quite inelastic (unresponsive to price). Besides, only a fraction of the taxpayers receive the benefit of the circuit breaker credit. The others face the full price of local public goods, not subsidized by the credit. Thus, the effect of the circuit breaker is not likely to raise property tax rates.

Capitalization of the circuit breaker tax relief is also worth consideration. To the extent that the circuit breaker reduces the property tax, we would expect the market value of property to reflect the reduced tax liability. Tax relief can be expected to be at least partially capitalized into higher property values.

ADDITIONAL READINGS

Baer, David. *State Programs and Practices for Reducing Property Taxes (2003–04).* Washington, DC: American Association of Retired Persons (AARP), 2003.

Gold, Steven D. *Property Tax Relief.* Lexington, MA: D.C. Heath, Lexington Books, 1979.

Sjoquist, David L. "Taxation of Real Property." In *Taxation and Economic Development: A Blueprint for Ohio Tax Reform,* edited by Roy Bahl. Columbus, OH: Battelle Press, 1995.

Cross-references: homestead exemption and credit programs; property tax, real property, residential.

Classification

Joan M. Youngman
Lincoln Institute of Land Policy

Differential property taxation according to property use.

Classified property tax systems impose different effective tax rates on specified types or classes of property. Today almost all such systems are the result of legislative or constitutional enactments, but in the past it was not uncommon for local assessors informally to adjust valuations in order to benefit homeowner and other favored groups.

The most common classifications distinguish residential, commercial, industrial, and agricultural property. Effective tax rates for each classification may be varied through the valuation process if assessed values of different classes represent different percentages of full market value. Another method is to apply different tax rates to similarly derived assessed values. Mathematically these two approaches can yield identical results, but the former, which alters the percentage of market value on which different classes are assessed, offers the appearance of uniformity through a single nominal tax rate. This was the method utilized for unauthorized de facto classification in the past. Partial exemptions for particular types of property, such as homestead exemptions for owner-occupied primary residences, can be considered another type of classification. By extension, complete exemption of various categories, such as schools or houses of worship, may be analyzed as a form of classification as well. Differential taxation of land and buildings, such as is found in a number of Pennsylvania cities, uses classification in recognition of the distinct economic characteristics of structures and unimproved land (Oates and Schwab 1997).

Almost all states assess agricultural property not on the basis of market value, but according to a formula or assigned value intended to reflect some measure of income expected from agricultural use. This "current-use assessment" seeks to avoid burdening farmers with taxes that reflect sale value for nonagricultural purposes. There is substantial controversy as to the impact of these subsidies on farmland preservation and urban development (e.g., Anderson and Griffing 2000).

Classification in its broadest aspect at one time offered a remedy for the most serious inequities of the original general property tax, which from colonial times had attempted to tax equally all property, including intangibles, moveable personal property, and real estate. As intangible property such as securities and bank accounts grew in importance, and moveable tangible property could not be readily identified for assessment purposes, the tax came to be seen as an unfair burden on real estate, borne primarily by agricultural landholders whose property could not escape taxation. By the 20th century, this purported uniformity had broken down so far as to make its repeal a major tax reform goal (e.g., Van Sickle 1927). The initial classification and differential treatment of real property, tangible personal property, and intangible property achieved this objective. Special treatment of other types of property, from business inventories to public utilities, was a natural extension of this approach.

Nonneutrality and favoritism are the greatest potential drawbacks to classification. The land portion of the tax will not be affected by actions of the current owner if assessments are based on market value at highest and best use. This neutrality ends if property use determines the effective tax rate. Politically, uniformity requirements were designed in part to counter pressure for special treatment of influential property owners. "Uniformity provisions not only limited the way that the tax burdens could be distributed, but discouraged tax increases by

making it more difficult to target politically weak groups" (Fisher 1996, 51; see also Newhouse 1984). Whether economic development suffers when businesses pay higher effective tax rates than residential and agricultural property owners is the subject of continuing debate (e.g., Dye, McGuire, and Merriman 2001).

Many de facto fractional assessment classification systems developed over long periods without legislative sanction, usually assessing residential property at a lower percentage of full value than commercial and industrial property. However, without an accurate market-value base and without legislation specifying effective tax rates, such systems were often little more than records of past assessments, updated only on sale. Classification thus shared some elements of the "Welcome, Stranger" approach of reassessment upon sale that was found unconstitutional in *Allegheny Pittsburgh Coal Company v. Webster County* (United States Supreme Court 1989).

A series of state court cases in the 1960s and 1970s provided the first sustained legal challenge to long-standing but unauthorized systems of classification and fractional assessment. The influential 1975 *Hellerstein* decision by the New York Court of Appeals noted that

> The vast majority of States require assessors, either by statute or constitutional prescription, to assess at full value, true value, market value or some equivalent standard. . . . Where full value is required, the standard has been almost universally disregarded. . . . For nearly 200 years our statutes have required assessments to be made at full value and for nearly 200 years assessments have been made on a percentage basis throughout the State. The practice has time on its side and nothing else. It has been tolerated by the Legislature, criticized by the commentators and found by our own court to involve a flagrant violation of the statute. Nevertheless the practice has become so widespread and been so consistently followed that it has acquired an aura of assumed legality. (New York Court of Appeals 1975, 37 N.Y. 2d 10–13)

State court decisions overruling such "extra-legal" fractional assessments were frequently followed by statutes or constitutional amendments explicitly permitting classification. Although this led to nonuniform effective tax rates, the specification of assessment methods and tax classes represented a major reform. At present, all states provide special treatment or exemption for personal property, nearly all mandate current-use assessment of qualifying agricultural land, and many allow classification of business and residential property (International Association of Assessing Officers 2000, 44–48).

ADDITIONAL READINGS

Anderson, John E. "Preferential Assessments: Impacts and Alternatives." In *The Property Tax, Land Use and Land Use Regulation,* edited by Dick Netzer (62–87). Northampton: Edward Elgar Publishing, Inc., 2003.

Anderson, John E., and Marion F. Griffing. "Use-Value Assessment Tax Expenditures in Urban Areas." *Journal of Urban Economics* 48 (2000): 443–52.

Dye, Richard F., Therese J. McGuire, and David Merriman. "The Impact of Property Taxes and Property Tax Classification on Business Activity in the Chicago Metropolitan Area." *Journal of Regional Science* 41 (2001): 757–78.

Fisher, Glenn W. *The Worst Tax? A History of the Property Tax in America.* Lawrence: University Press of Kansas, 1996.

International Association of Assessing Officers. *Property Tax Policies and Administrative Practices in Canada and the United States.* Chicago: International Association of Assessing Officers, 2000.

Newhouse, Wade J. *Constitutional Uniformity and Equality in State Taxation.* Buffalo: William S. Hein and Company, Inc., 1984.

New York Court of Appeals. *Hellerstein v. Assessor of Islip.* 37 N.Y.2d 1, 332 N.E.2d 279, 371 N.Y.S.2d 388 (1975).

Oates, Wallace E., and Robert M. Schwab. "The Impact of Urban Land Taxation: The Pittsburgh Experience." *National Tax Journal* 50 (1997): 1–21.

United States Supreme Court. *Allegheny Pittsburgh Coal Company v. Webster County.* 488 U.S. 336 (1989).

Van Sickle, J. V. "Classification of Land for Taxation." *Quarterly Journal of Economics* 42, no. 1 (1927): 94–116.

Cross-references: property tax assessment; property tax, farm; property tax, real property, business; property tax, real property, residential.

College savings plans

Raquel Meyer Alexander
University of North Carolina–Wilmington

LeAnn Luna
University of Tennessee

Tax treatment of higher education expenses.

During the last several years, two tax-advantaged education savings vehicles have emerged: (1) The Coverdell Education Savings Account (Coverdell) and (2) Internal Revenue Code (IRC) §529 Plans. For federal income tax purposes, both Coverdell and IRC §529 plans provide for nondeductible contributions, tax-free accumulation of earnings, and tax-free withdrawals for qualified higher education expenses such as tuition, fees, supplies, and limited amounts of room and board. Coverdell accounts also allow tax-free distributions when used for private primary and secondary schools' tuition and fees. All nonqualifying distributions are subject to both an income tax (at ordinary rates) and a 10 percent penalty on the earnings portion of the distribution.

Coverdell Education Savings Accounts

The Coverdell Education Savings Accounts are a product of 1997 federal legislation (IRC §530). Previously called the "Education IRA," Coverdell accounts limit annual contributions to $2,000 per year per beneficiary under age 18. Parents control the investments with options similar to an ordinary IRA or taxable account. The account beneficiary or the parent may be the owner, but only the beneficiary may withdraw funds. If the named beneficiary does not attend college, or does not need the funds because of scholarships or grants re-

ceived, the account may be rolled over without penalty to another family member.

Coverdells have a relatively small annual contribution limit of $2,000 and are subject to income phaseouts. Coverdell contributions may be made by anyone (e.g., parents, grandparents, or friends). However, the $2,000 annual contribution limit is per beneficiary. The contributor's income phaseouts apply to adjusted gross income between $95,000 and $110,000 for single taxpayers and between $190,000 and $220,000 for married taxpayers filing jointly.

Section 529 plans

The IRC §529 Plans were first introduced by Michigan in 1986 and were codified in 1997. The prepaid tuition plan was the first type of IRC §529 plan. Prepaid tuition plans lock in tuition costs at certain institutions through the purchase of tuition credits. In most cases, the tuition credits can only be used at in-state public institutions, and the cost varies by institution. Prepaid tuition accounts earn little or no income. Therefore, benefits only accrue if the beneficiary is able to attend the institution chosen (sometimes decades) in advance. These plans have fallen out of favor since 2001 when the tax benefits of §529 college savings plans (529 plans) increased.

Under the Economic Growth and Tax Relief Reconciliation Act of 2001 (PL 107-16), qualified withdrawals from 529 plans became tax-exempt for federal income tax purposes. Currently all 50 states and the District of Columbia have at least one 529 plan. In addition, approximately 200 private colleges and universities recently formed a private 529 plan that offers prepaid tuition credits to the participating institutions as well as a small investment return if funds are used at other schools. As noted above, both 529 plans and Coverdell accounts are controlled by the contributor, grow tax-free, and allow tax-free distributions for education expenses. However, several important differences between 529 plans and Coverdell accounts exist.

Contribution limitations

For higher-income taxpayers, or those that wish to set aside large amounts, 529 plans are superior. Section 529 plans have no contributor income limitations, and the contribution amount far exceeds the Coverdell's $2,000 annual contribution per beneficiary. Contribution limits are established by each plan and can be made until the account balance reaches a certain threshold—currently ranging from $205,175 in Louisiana to $305,000 in Hawaii, South Dakota, and New Jersey.

Financial aid

For financial aid purposes, 529 plan assets are attributed to the contributor while Coverdell assets are attributed to the owner (either parent or student). This distinction can be quite important for financial aid purposes, as approximately 5 percent of the parents' nonretirement assets are considered available for college funding, compared with about 35 percent of the student's assets. Qualified distributions from either plan are not considered the student's or parent's income, and thus, do not affect financial aid eligibility. However, the same expenses cannot be used to receive more than one tax benefit (i.e., an expense can be used for the Hope or Lifetime learning credits or as a qualified distribution for Coverdells or 529 plans).

Estate and gift tax treatment

Section 529 plans have unique estate and gift planning features that present planning opportunities. Recall that 529 plans allow contributors to direct the account, make withdrawals, and change beneficiaries. Coverdell contributions cannot be refunded or transferred to another beneficiary, and upon majority, beneficiaries may withdraw the funds for any purpose. For estate tax purposes, 529 plans are excluded from the contributor's estate while Coverdells are included in the owner's estate (either the parent or the student). For gift tax purposes, 529 plan contributions are considered gifts of a present interest and, as such, are eligible for the annual gift tax exclusion of $11,000 per year per donor per beneficiary. Under a special provision, §529 contributors can elect to make five years' worth of contributions in a single year (without making any contributions or other gifts in the next four years), thereby increasing the annual tax-free contribution limit for that year to $55,000. Married couples may give $110,000 without gift tax consequences.

State income tax treatment

The state tax treatment of 529 plans differs from that of Coverdells. First, 24 states and the District of Columbia allow for income tax deductions for all or a portion of a contribution to their own state-sponsored 529 plan. Eight states provide other incentives such as contribution matching, income tax credits or in-state tuition for out-of-state program participants. The state benefits are frequently a function of the contributor's tax filing status and/or the number of beneficiaries. No state allows deductions for contributions to an out-of-state plan. Coverdell contributions are not tax deductible for state tax purposes. The tax treatment of 529 plan distributions also varies by state. All states except Alabama do not tax qualified distributions from in-state plans. Four states currently tax residents on qualified distributions from out-of-state plans. (For a more complete discussion of plan differences, see http://www.savingforcollege.com.) All qualified Coverdell distributions are tax-free for state income tax purposes.

Investment choices and related fees

Investment choices for 529 plans are much more restrictive than those of Coverdells because the particular state 529 plan parents choose dictates the investment options. For example, investors in the New Hampshire 529 plan may only choose among select Fidelity funds. In many cases, 529 plan investment options are limited to age-based portfolios that become more conservative as the beneficiary approaches college age. Other states allow for more choices, such as a conservative, moderate, or aggressive asset allocation.

The fund performance and related fees and expenses vary widely from state to state. For example, some plan fees exceed 2 percent per year while others are less than 1 percent. Some plans charge a front-end load of up to 6 percent and others may be purchased directly, commission free. Congress, the Securities and Exchange Commission (SEC), and National Association of Securities Dealers (NASD) are each independently investigating whether advisors ignore state income tax benefits or low-fee funds and instead direct clients to higher fee funds, which results in lower expected investment returns (House Committee on Financial Services 2004). Dynarski (2004) finds that 529 plan fees are higher on average than the fees for retail mutual funds, IRAs, or Coverdells. Alexander and Luna (2004) find some evidence that investors are choosing plans with higher plan fees and not choosing plans with favorable state tax consequences.

ADDITIONAL READINGS

Alexander, Raquel Meyer, and LeAnn Luna. "State-Sponsored §529 College Savings Plans: The Influence of Tax and Nontax Factors on Investors' Choices." University of North Carolina–Wilmington working paper (2004).
Dynarski, Susan. "Who Benefits from the Education Saving Incentives? Income, Educational Expectations, and the Value of the 529 and Coverdell." *National Tax Journal* 58, no. 2 (June 2004): 359–83.
U.S. House Committee on Financial Services. "Investing for the Future: 529 State Tuition Savings Plans." 108th Congress, 2nd session, June 2, 2004. Washington, DC: U.S. House Committee on Financial Services.

Cross-references: education tax credits, higher education, federal; individual retirement accounts.

Commuter taxes

Robert W. Wassmer
California State University, Sacramento

Employment-based taxation designed to charge for public services that accrue to persons who work, but do not reside, in a jurisdiction.

The term *commuter taxes* usually refers to an employee-, income-, or payroll-based tax that is paid by an individual to the jurisdiction where they work but do not reside. This can occur if residence is in one state and employment in another. The burden of this interstate situation has been nearly eliminated by most states allowing a credit, or income exemption, for income taxes paid to other states. Commuter taxes are considered here to be an intrastate issue that arises where local jurisdictions can levy local income taxes. A tax of this type is most likely to occur within a metropolitan area and be placed on a suburban resident who commutes to central city employment.

This entry presents the history of commuter taxes in the United States, statistics on their use, recent proposals for greater use, the motivation behind their adoption, and an economic evaluation of their desirability and impact.

History

The first local tax on labor income was adopted by Philadelphia in 1938 in response to increased expenditure needs and declining property values brought on by the Great Depression. Toledo next adopted a payroll tax in 1946. Adoptions followed in St. Louis in 1948 and later in other cities in Ohio and Pennsylvania. In the 1960s and 1970s, cities adopted local income taxes for the additional reasons of providing property tax relief and collecting revenue from central city workers who were increasingly living in surrounding suburbs. In 1962, Detroit adopted a local tax whose base was federal adjusted gross income, and residents were taxed at only half the rate of nonresidents. New York City adopted a similar tax in 1966. In 1999, the New York State Legislature repealed New York City's 0.45 percent commuter tax that had previously raised $350 million annually.

Statistics

Gessing (2003) notes that local commuter taxes of some sort were used in the following 12 states in 2003: Alabama, California, Delaware, Illinois, Indiana, Kentucky, Michigan, Missouri, New Jersey, New York, Ohio, and Pennsylvania. In Alabama and Colorado, cities and counties impose occupational license fees on individuals that are not residents. In Michigan, cities can impose a nonresidential income tax of 0.5 percent. Kansas City and St. Louis in Missouri levy a 1 percent commuter tax. The state of Ohio allows all cities and villages to charge a commuter tax of up to 1 percent without voter approval, and up to 2 percent with voter approval. Most Ohio cities levy the 2 percent rate. In Pennsylvania, all cities, townships, and school districts can impose a 1 percent tax on income earned within their borders. Home rule municipalities can levy an additional 1 percent, while under separate provisions, the cities of Philadelphia, Pittsburgh, and Scranton can charge a higher commuter tax. At just over 3.9 percent, the city of Philadelphia imposes the highest commuter tax rate in the United States. In the last 30 years, Philadelphia has lost over a half million residents. Inman (2003) attributes over 40 percent of this population loss to increases in the city's wage tax rate.

Recent proposals

In 2003, New York City's mayor proposed applying the city's progressive wage tax at a maximum rate of 2.75 percent to nonresidents who commute into the city. It was estimated that this proposal would raise over $1 billion in revenue.

In the same year, the Washington, D.C., City Council supported the institution of a progressive commuter tax ranging from 0.5 to 2 percent. Strauss (1998) has completed a study on the desirability of instituting a commuter tax in Washington, D.C., and concluded that a tax between 0.5 and 1 percent on commuter wages could be justified in that city.

In addition, proposals for up to a 1 percent tax on nonresident city workers have been floated in Atlanta, Baltimore, Indianapolis, and Pittsburgh. Some recent proposals have attempted to soften the burden of such a tax by allowing a nonresident to pay only the amount of commuter tax that has not already been paid as another residential wage tax. For example, if Pittsburgh enacts a 1 percent commuter wage tax and a suburban resident who works in the city already pays 0.5 percent to the city he or she resides in, Pittsburgh could only collect the remaining 0.5 percent.

Motivation

Local jurisdictions usually impose an income tax on nonresidents based on three general arguments. The first is that a local income tax, of any sort, provides needed revenue diversification. Diversification has been sought after many states imposed local limits on property taxation. Local income taxes allow cities and counties to meet these property tax limits and also yield a lower rate of taxation on the alternate base of local sales (see Brunori 2003). This is important because the burden (or hurt) imposed by any tax more than doubles when the rate of taxation doubles. Diversification through the adoption of a local income tax, like portfolio diversification, also provides greater total revenue stability.

A second justification for commuter taxes is that when people commute from an area of residence to a different area of employment, the benefits of locally provided services spill over jurisdictional boundaries. City services that benefit both residents and commuters (such as streets, sanitation, public safety, and cultural amenities) are likely to be underprovided if only residents are asked to pay for them. Ladd and Yinger (1989) found that, for large U.S. cities, a 10 percent difference in employment per capita (i.e., more commuters) results on average in a 2.9 percent greater city expenditure on all general services, and a 3.9 percent increase in police and fire expenditure.

Considering the concept of benefit taxation, it is also appropriate to ask commuters to pay taxes to their jurisdiction of employment in proportion to the benefits they derive from the services it provides. If commuters derive fewer benefits than residents, it is also reasonable to set the nonresidential income tax rate lower than the resident rate. Counterarguments to this motivation for commuter taxes include cries of "taxation without representation," and claims that if local business taxes are shifted forward and/or backward, commuters already pay for city services in the form of higher prices for goods and services purchased within the city and/or lower wages.

The third, and probably least noble motivation given for the imposition of a commuter tax is that it allows a jurisdiction to export taxes to nonresidents for the sole purpose of lower local residential or business tax rates, or greater local expenditure. Because both actions benefit local elected officials in the short term, there is a strong political motivation to pursue such exporting. Alternatively, the exportation of a city commuter tax may be justified on the equity basis of "ability to pay." The argument given is that through little direct fault of its own, a central city often contains the poorest population and the harshest atmosphere in which to provide local services in a metropolitan area. Normal levels of local government service in a central city would hence require highly regressive taxes. Central city tax exporting reduces the need for this form of taxation and has been argued to be socially optimal. The taxation of commuters at a level greater than benefits received from local services may also discourage affluent residents who are employed in the central city from moving to the suburbs.

Evaluation

Local commuter income taxes can be evaluated on the criteria of public perception, simplicity, equity, and efficiency. In a public opinion survey conducted by the Advisory Commission on Intergovernmental Relations (ACIR) in 1987, people were asked which form of revenue should their local government use to meet additional costs. Property taxation and income taxation finished equally behind the choices in preferred order of user charges, sales taxation, and no new taxes. Even though local income taxation is federally deductible, the public may still dislike its further use because of the heavy reliance on income taxation by both states and the federal government.

But the local income tax deserves praise for its simplicity. The existence of state and federal income taxes solves many administrative problems. Simplicity also lies in the broad base and low rates that characterize most local income tax systems in the United States. Equivalent tax rates on a comprehensive tax base also verify that the local income tax meets the standard measure of horizontal equity. The near elimination of double taxation through usually allowing only one type of jurisdiction in a state to levy local income taxes, and basing local income taxation on either place of residence or employment, also enhances the local income tax's fairness.

Except for cases in which the pretax outcome is deemed undesirable, a tax is considered more efficient the less it does to alter market outcomes. Economic outcomes are altered in the presence of a commuter tax dependent on who ultimately pays the tax. A fundamental finding of public economics is that who the law says pays the tax has very little to do with who really bears its burden. An employee, even though legally responsible for payment of a commuter tax, could demand higher wages and hence shift his or her tax payment partially (or completely) back onto the employer. Conversely, an employer asked to make local payroll taxes could shift them forward onto employees by paying lower wages.

The more employment is concentrated in a metropolitan area's central city that levies a commuter tax, the greater the likelihood for the tax to be paid by commuters in the form of lower after-tax wages. This is due to the difficulty that workers in a metropolitan area face in trying to escape the commuter tax by finding work in the suburbs. The greater the employment opportunities available in suburban cities that do not levy a commuter tax, the more likely these taxes are paid by business in a central city where the tax is levied. Central city business bears the burden of the commuter tax in the forms of a lower profit, or a lower return on immobile inputs (such as land or buildings). This situation puts central city business at a disadvantage and in the long run it could cause relocation to the suburbs.

With respect to this issue, Ladd and Yinger (1989) examine 78 of the largest U.S. cities in 1982 and concluded that the export potential of a commuter income tax is approximately 2.5 times that of the local property tax, and six times greater than a local sales tax. Because many of these large cities continue to face fiscal problems, Ladd and Yinger strongly recommend its greater use. But as Gessing (2003) notes, they do not consider that if employers pay part of the commuter tax, then its imposition may drive business to the suburbs and possibly make the long-term fiscal crisis of central cities even worse. As evidence, Grieson (1980) found that the 1976 increase in the Philadelphia income tax rate from 3.31 to 4.31 percent caused a long-term decline of 10 percent in the city's 1975 employment level. Stull and Stull (1991) also found that an additional percentage point added to a city's local income tax in the Philadelphia metropolitan area would cause the average home value in the city where the increase occurred to fall by approximately 4 percent.

So far, there is little empirical evidence to support the contention that an expansion of commuter taxes in the United States is justified based on commuter exploitation of central cities. After accounting for the benefits that San Francisco bestowed upon suburban commuters, and the revenue that commuters provided the city through the forward and backward shifting of existing business taxes other than a commuter tax, Smith (1972) concluded that nonresident workers pay more than their fair share in central city taxes. Greene, Neenan, and Scott (1974) looked at the net benefit flow from Washington, D.C., to its suburbs and also found that, if the dollar cost of service is counted, suburban residents are paying at least their fair share. Alternatively, if a welfare measure based on what suburban residents would actually be willing to pay for central city services was used, suburbia would gain a net flow of benefits. Even under this finding, Greene and colleagues note that commuters are already paying their fair share of indirect taxes to the central city and a commuter tax would not charge the appropriate suburban residents for the net flow of benefits they receive.

After looking over these studies and others, Bradford and Oates (1974) concluded that suburban exploitation appears to be of "minor quantitative importance"; nevertheless, they do recommend further study. Finally, Shields and Shideler (2003) have recently found that an additional nonresident user of streets, public safety, and parks/libraries in a "workplace" community respectively increase the average expenditure on these items in large U.S. cities by $21, $54, and $23. This offers some evidence in support of the positive impact that nonresident commuters have on local expenditure and a justification for commuter taxes. But Shields and Shideler note that employers may already be adequately paying through other local business taxes imposed upon them.

ADDITIONAL READINGS

Advisory Commission on Intergovernmental Relations [ACIR]. *Changing Public Attitudes on Government and Taxes.* Washington, DC: ACIR, 1987.

———. *Local Revenue Diversification: Local Income Taxes.* SR-10. Washington, DC: ACIR, 1988.

———. *Significant Features of Fiscal Federalism.* M-180. Washington, DC: ACIR, 1992.

Aronson, J. Richard, and John L. Hilley. *Financing State and Local Governments.* 4th ed. Washington, DC: The Brookings Institution, 1986.

Bradford, David F., and Wallace E. Oates. "Suburban Exploitation of Central Cities and Government Structure." In *Redistribution through Public Choice,* edited by Harold M. Hochman and George E. Peterson. Washington, DC: The Urban Institute, 1974.

Break, George F. *Financing Government in a Federal System.* Washington, DC: The Brookings Institution, 1980.

Brunori, David. *Local Tax Policy: A Federalist Perspective.* Washington, DC: Urban Institute Press, 2003.

Fisher, Ronald C. *State and Local Public Finance,* 2d ed. Chicago: Irwin, 1996.

Gessing, Paul. *Commuter Taxes: Milking Outsiders for All They're Worth.* Alexandria, VA: National Taxpayers Union, 2003.

Greene, Kenneth V., William B. Neenan, and Claudia D. Scott. *Fiscal Interactions in a Metropolitan Area.* Lexington, MA: Lexington Books, 1974.

Grieson, Ronald E. "Theoretical Analysis and Empirical Measurements of the Effects of the Philadelphia Income Tax." *Journal of Urban Economics* 8 (1980): 123–37.

Inman, Robert P. "Should Philadelphia's Suburbs Help Their Central City?" Federal Reserve Bank of Philadelphia *Business Review* Q2 (2003): 25–36. http://www.phil.frb.org/files/br/brq203ri.pdf.

Ladd, Helen F., and John Yinger. *America's Ailing Cities: Fiscal Health and the Design of Urban Policy.* Baltimore: Johns Hopkins Press, 1989.

Shields, Martin, and David Shideler. "Do Commuters Free-ride? Estimating the Impacts of Interjurisdictional Commuting on Local Public Good Expenditures." *Journal of Regional Analysis and Policy* 33 (2003): 27–42.

Smith, R. Stafford. *Local Income Taxes: Economic Effects and Equity.* Berkeley, CA: Institute of Governmental Studies, 1972.

Strauss, Robert P. "The District of Columbia's Individual Income Tax: Structure, Characteristics, and Policy Alternatives." In *Taxing Simply, Taxing Fairly.* Washington, DC: Tax Revision Commission, 1998.

Stull, William J., and Judith C. Stull. "Capitalization of Local Income Taxes." *Journal of Urban Economics* 29 (1991): 182–90.

Cross-references: residence principle; fiscal federalism; tax reform, state; origin principle; destination principle.

Congressional Budget Office
Phillip Joyce
George Washington University

Legislative branch agency responsible for forecasting the budget baseline, estimating the costs of spending programs, and preparing budget-related scenarios.

The United States Congress established the Congressional Budget Office (CBO) in 1974 to provide the legislative branch with an independent source of information on the budget and the economy. CBO was created at the height of budgetary conflict between the Congress and President Nixon, particularly concerning the impoundment of (refusal to spend) appropriated funds. The Congress passed the Congressional Budget and Impoundment Control Act of 1974 (the Budget Act) in an effort to reassert the congressional "power of the purse."

The Budget Act made a number of changes designed to enable the Congress to engage in overall fiscal policy. Specifically, the Act required enactment of a congressional budget resolution, created new Budget Committees in each house to produce and enforce the budget resolution, prohibited unilateral presidential impoundment, and established CBO to support the Congress in economic and budgetary matters.

The functions of CBO today are very much as they were at its creation, and include the following:

- Producing a budget baseline (covering at least five years, and sometimes as many as ten) that projects the trajectory of the federal budget (revenues, spending, and the surplus or deficit) under current law;
- Supporting Congress in enacting and enforcing the budget resolution through producing the baseline, tracking legislation to determine compliance with the budget resolution (so-called "scorekeeping"), and estimating the budgetary effects of changes in law required under the reconciliation process;
- Producing estimates of the five-year cost to the federal government of any spending legislation reported out of a congressional committee (and beginning in 1996, the cost of certain bills to state and local governments); and
- Producing longer-term studies of economic and budgetary issues being considered by the Congress, as requested.

CBO is organized along product lines. The budget baseline and cost estimating work is all done in the Budget Analysis Division (BAD), which is the single largest CBO division. BAD's work is informed by work done in other divisions, particularly by the economic forecasts developed in the Macroeconomic Analysis Division (MAD). CBO's policy analysis work is done by the program divisions, which deal with issues ranging from national security to health and human services, to natural resources and commerce.

One of the program divisions—the Tax Analysis Division (TAD)—studies tax policy issues. The Budget Act was noticeably vague concerning CBO's role in tax analysis. Cost estimates for revenue bills were done prior to the Act by the Congressional Joint Committee on Taxation (JCT). The drafters of the Budget Act, which included the tax writing committees (who control the JCT), were loath to cede that power to CBO. Therefore the cost estimating power continued to reside with JCT. CBO's role in tax policy, therefore, has leaned more toward the production of baseline estimates and policy analyses.

The Congressional Budget Act provided for fixed terms for the director of CBO, beginning in January 1975, and commencing every four years after that point. Formally, the CBO director is appointed jointly by a letter signed by the Speaker of the House and the president pro tempore of the Senate. Informally, the Budget Committees in each house typically make recommendations concerning filling vacancies. There have been six appointed directors in CBO's 30-year history:

Alice M. Rivlin, 1975–83
Rudolph G. Penner, 1983–87
Robert D. Reischauer, 1989–95
June O'Neill, 1995–99
Daniel L. Crippen, 1999–2003
Douglas Holtz-Eakin, 2003–

In addition, at two times in CBO's history acting directors have led the agency. From March 1987 until March 1989, Edward M. Gramlich, and then James L. Blum, led the agency when Congress was unable to agree on a replacement for Penner. In early 2003, Barry Anderson served as acting director for a short period before the selection of Holtz-Eakin.

The Congressional Budget Act states that directors are selected without regard to political affiliation, and that the agency is to do its work in a nonpartisan manner. A strong culture of nonpartisanship has been developed in the organization, established by Director Rivlin and reinforced by each of her successors. There has typically been very little turnover accompanying changes in directors. CBO reports attempt to present the facts and carefully avoid making policy recommendations or pronouncements

Given the intense political environment in which tax policy is made, it is not surprising that CBO's role in tax policy has made some waves. These controversies have tended to surround three areas. First, because CBO is required to produce baseline revenue estimates, and because these estimates are frequently wrong, it has opened the agency up to criticism. Forecasting revenues is an inherently uncertain enterprise; compounding that uncertainty has been the pressure to produce these estimates for five to ten years into the future. At several points in CBO's history, the agency has been criticized for either being too optimistic or too pessimistic in forecasting revenues. For example, in the late 1990s, Republicans took the agency to task for underestimating revenues; the critics believed that these underestimates had held down the size of desired tax cuts.

Second, throughout the 1980s, but reaching a crescendo in the mid-to-late-1990s, was a criticism of the CBO on the grounds that its economic models relied on a methodology that used "static" rather than "dynamic" assumptions. This line of argument held that CBO did not adequately take into account the positive economic effects of tax cuts, and thus overstated their cost. In fact, pressure was put on the last four CBO directors to engage in more "dynamic" scoring. CBO has resisted that effort, arguing that its models had appropriately accounted for behavioral effects associated with tax changes.

Third, beginning in the 1980s, CBO began to provide periodic reports that evaluated the distributional effect of taxes. These reports presented data on the effect of federal taxes on different income groups. Initially, these were not used for policymaking, but over time Democratic members of Congress, in particular, used them to gauge the "fairness" of various tax proposals. The so-called budget "summit" at Andrews Air Force base in 1990 reportedly relied extensively on these data. Republicans criticized these data—then and later—as feeding into a Democratic "class warfare" political strategy.

CBO now has an established role as a source of nonpartisan economic and budgetary advice, not only for the Congress, but for the news media and the public as well. It has unquestionably contributed to the resurgence of the Congress in the budget process, and could be viewed as the only unqualified success story associated with the 1974 Budget Act.

ADDITIONAL READINGS

Congressional Budget Office. *The Budget and Economic Outlook, Fiscal Years 2005–2014.* Washington, DC: Congressional Budget Office, 2004.
———. *Effective Federal Tax Rates, 1979–2001.* Washington, DC: Congressional Budget Office, 2004.
Kates, Nancy D. *Starting from Scratch: Alice Rivlin and the Congressional Budget Office.* Cambridge, MA: John F. Kennedy School of Government, Harvard University, 1989.
Meyers, Roy T. "Congressional Budget Office." In *International Encyclopedia of Public Policy and Administration,* edited by Jay Shafritz (486–92). Boulder, CO: Westview Press, 1997.

Cross-references: Finance Committee, U.S. Senate; Joint Committee on Taxation, U.S Congress; Ways and Means Committee.

Consumption taxation

Gilbert E. Metcalf
Tufts University

Taxation based on consumption, as opposed to some other measure of ability to pay, most notably income.

To understand the different ways in which consumption taxes can be implemented, it is useful to begin with the Haig-Simons definition of income: income (Y) equals consumption (C) plus changes in wealth (W), or $Y = C + \Delta W$. First, note that the key difference between income and consumption taxation is the inclusion or exclusion of W in the tax base. Changes in wealth—or savings—are not taxed by consumption taxes but are taxed by income taxes. Second, note that this relationship suggests that consumption can be taxed directly (e.g., via a sales or excise tax) or indirectly by imposing an income tax with deductions for increases to savings (and inclusion of withdrawals from savings in the tax base). A national sales tax on all goods and services would be one way to implement a consumption tax, while an income tax with IRA treatment of all savings would be a way to implement the consumption tax indirectly. The expenditure tax proposed by Kaldor (1955) is an example of this indirect approach. Recently, it has been revived as a component of the Nunn-Domenici USA Tax Plan.

Value-added taxes (VATs) provide a third method of implementing consumption taxes. Value added in production is the difference between the sale price of produced goods and services and the cost of goods and services used in production. A VAT can be viewed as a type of national sales tax where the tax is collected in increments at each stage of production and distribution. A key feature of a consumption-style VAT is that investments by the firm are deducted (expensed) rather than depreciated. The effective tax rate on investment equals zero if a firm can expense its investment. While taxes are paid on the returns to that investment (i.e., on the value of goods and services generated by the investment), those taxes can be viewed as the government's share of the return because of its equity stake in the investment following the tax deduction resulting from expensing.

As described above, all financial transactions are ignored when calculating value added. All cash proceeds into the firm (stock sales, proceeds from borrowing) are ignored, as is all cash out (dividends, interest, debt repayment). This approach is often characterized as the R (for real transactions) base approach, a terminology credited to Meade (Institute for Fiscal Studies 1973). Alternatively, one can include all financial transactions ($R + F$ base). Thus, all cash proceeds are included as taxable income, and all cash outflows are deducted. So long as the same tax rate applies to all transactions, these two approaches generate the same tax consequences to a firm. The present discounted value of taxes paid on proceeds from borrowing, for example, should just equal the present discounted value of taxes saved by deducting principal and interest on that debt. The $R + F$ approach is better suited for use in taxing financial services where value added is difficult to disentangle from financial activities (borrowing and lending).

As an accounting identity, value added is allocated to workers (wages) and capital owners (dividends and retained earnings). However, as noted above, investment expensing means that the taxes on value added allocated to capital owners are offset by the reduction in taxes due to expensing. In other words, the only capital owners who will incur the burden of a consumption tax are those who own capital before a consumption tax is implemented (ignoring transitional rules). This gives rise to the distinction between "old" and "new" capital and is an important issue in tax reforms.

It is often claimed that a consumption tax is a combination of a wage tax plus this lump sum tax on old capital. There are (at least) two important observations to make about this claim.

First, if a future observer sees that individuals file tax returns paying taxes on their wage income only, that observer will not be able to say if this is a "wage" or a "consumption" tax. To distinguish between the two forms of taxation, the observer would need to know what happened to old capital at the time of the reform. If a wage tax has been enacted along with a levy on existing capital, then the observer would be looking at a consumption tax. In other words, the distinction between a wage tax and a consumption tax based on treatment of old capital may mislead an observer. We would enact what looks like a consumption tax, but what really is a wage tax, by forgiving the tax on old capital and vice versa.

Second, the claim would suggest that in the absence of old capital, wage and consumption taxes are equivalent. But consider an entrepreneur who thinks up a great idea after the new law has been enacted and sells it for $1 million. (Or perhaps he finds oil on a previously worthless piece of property and sells it for $1 million.) All consumption financed by this $1 million would escape taxation under a wage tax. A personal cash flow tax would tax all cash coming to an individual, with a deduction for any savings (into qualified accounts); in this case, the consumption financed by proceeds from the sale of the idea would be taxed. In certain cases, the U.S. Treasury staff's blueprints could be provided for a tax prepayment option in which additions to savings are not deducted; nor are the principal and return from that savings taxable (when withdrawn for consumption) (U.S. Treasury Department 1977). While tax prepayment is a useful—perhaps essential—option for certain assets (houses, jewelry, etc.), it could not be used for taxing returns such as our entrepreneur receives. In this context, the tax prepayment approach would be identical to a wage tax.

Variations on these approaches to taxing consumption abound; generally, the focus on how one implements a consumption tax follows from administrative and distributional concerns about windfall gains and losses in the transition from some existing tax system to the consumption tax system. One popular variant is the Hall-Rabushka flat tax, which is a two-part tax. The business tax is essentially a VAT with a deduction allowed for compensation to workers. The second tax is a personal tax on compensation at the same tax rate. Described this way, shifting the labor tax component from the business tax to a personal tax has no economic effect. The motivation for shifting the labor tax component is to allow a generous personal exemption to effect greater tax progressivity. A slight variant on the Hall-Rabushka flat tax is Bradford's (1987) X-tax (see *X-tax*). It differs in having a progressive rate structure on the personal tax, the top rate of which equals the business tax rate.

An important unresolved question is whether bequests and gifts should be included in the base of a consumption tax when the tax is explicitly levied on consumption. Clearly, the receipt of gifts should not trigger a consumption tax liability. One might argue that the gift of a bequest (or other monetary gift) should be treated as consumption (and hence taxed) because the bequest generates consumption benefits for the donor. An altruistic motive (e.g., Blinder 1974) might justify the consumption benefits of the gift. However, the donor of a gift derives utility from his or her ability to increase the bequest recipient's utility. Because the consumption tax reduces the purchasing power of the gift, the donor now receives less utility from a given bequest. In effect, the donor has been taxed on the gift, and explicit inclusion of the bequest in the consumption tax would constitute double taxation. Under a strategic bequest motive (e.g., Bernheim et al. 1985), the gift can be viewed as a payment for services from the recipient. Because these services (visits, home care, affection) are likely to be untaxed, the consumption tax should properly tax bequests. The Meade Commission's approach to taxing bequests was to propose a separate wealth tax to "encourage dispersion in the ownership of wealth" (Institute for Fiscal Studies 1973, 518).

Historical antecedents

The intellectual arguments for consumption taxation can be traced back to Thomas Hobbes. Writing some 350 years ago, he argued that "The Equality of Imposition consisteth rather in the Equality of that which is consumed, than of the riches of the persons that consume the same" (Hobbes 1651, 387). His argument was based on the logic that the state provides protection for the enjoyment of life and that taxes are the price of that protection. Because consumption is the material manifestation of the enjoyment of life, so should consumption be the base of taxation. Or as Hobbes put it, "For what reason is there, that he which laboureth much, and sparing the fruits of his labour, consumeth little, should be more charged, than he that living idlely getteth little, and spendeth all he gets: seeing the one hath no more protection from the Commonwealth than the other?"

More recently, Kaldor (1955) argued for an expenditure tax as a surtax to coexist with the current income tax in the United Kingdom. More recently still, the Meade Commission (Institute for Fiscal Studies 1973) in the United Kingdom and the U.S. Treasury Department (1977) have made forceful cases for consumption taxation. Despite these proposals, no country has shifted its tax system wholly to a consumption base. However, there has been a shift in the mix from income toward consumption taxation in a number of ways in the last 20 years. First, the European Community (EC) passed two directives in 1967 that mandated all EC members to implement VATs. As a result, the mix of consumption and income taxes has shifted to the point where consumption taxes (VATs, excise taxes, etc.) constitute between 15 and 25 percent of tax revenues for EC countries (see Metcalf 1995). Second, there has been a tremendous growth in defined contribution pension programs and other tax-deferred savings programs in the United States and other industrialized countries. Current estimates are that roughly 50 percent of personal savings in the United States receive consumption tax treatment (Gale 1995).

Rationale for consumption taxation

There are three major reasons that many economists have advocated a shift from income to consumption taxation: simplicity, efficiency, and fairness. The essential argument for simplicity is that income is difficult, if not impossible, to measure accurately, while the measurement of consumption is relatively straightforward. Most of the complexity in the current income tax system arises from the need to measure income. Two oft-cited examples are depreciation and capital gains. A consumption tax of any of these forms would eliminate these problems. Capital expenditures are expensed (deducted) under a consumption tax and capital gains are ignored. On the other hand, efforts to achieve distributional goals can add complexity to a consumption tax. For example, every VAT in place in Europe and other industrialized countries has exemptions and multiple rates, which add considerable complexity to the tax code. Transitional concerns are also likely to add complexity. For example, most serious consumption tax plans in the United States have gone to great lengths to preserve basis in existing assets and to prevent the taxation of withdrawals from savings accumulated before tax reform.

The major case for efficiency is that a consumption tax eliminates the intertemporal consumption distortion by ending the tax on savings. Moreover, reducing the effective tax on capital encourages economic growth through greater rates of investment. With respect to the effect of consumption taxation on savings, the intertemporal distortion depends importantly on the rate of return subject to taxation. As Bradford (1995) has shown, a consumption tax only exempts the risk-free return from taxation. Given that the risk-free return is a small component of the total return on savings, the efficiency gains from a consumption tax vis-à-vis an income tax may be modest. Moreover, while a consumption tax may reduce intertemporal distortions, there still remains a distortion between the consumption of purchased goods and nonpurchased goods—most notably leisure. In addition, when comparing income and consumption taxes, a higher tax rate would be required to raise the same amount of revenue with the consumption tax versus the income tax, given the nontaxation of savings.

Finally, some economists have argued for a shift to consumption taxation based on fairness. Hobbes employed a benefits principle to justify consumption taxation. More recently, Kaldor (1955) argued that the difficulties associated with taxing income are so great that a shift to an expenditure tax would in fact raise more revenue from the very wealthy than income tax does—a view at sharp variance with conventional wisdom.

The common perception is that a consumption tax would be highly regressive compared with an income tax. This follows from the fact that the savings rate relative to income rises with income. Whether a consumption tax need be more regressive than an income tax depends on (1) the degree of progressivity of the income tax being replaced, (2) the structure of the consumption tax being contemplated, and (3) the way in which progressivity is measured. Ignoring the first point here, there are several comments to be made. First, progressive elements can be built into a consumption tax: progressive rate structure and personal exemptions, to name two. Second, conventional measures of progressivity in the tax code use annual income to measure economic well-being. This approach biases measures of tax progressivity in a downward direction. If people are making consumption decisions on the basis of lifetime income, then consumption income ratios will be very high for "low" income individuals and very low for "high" income individuals who might have the same lifetime income. Not all economists are convinced by the lifetime income analysis, however. A revenue-neutral tax shift from income to consumption taxation would undoubtedly result in high-income taxpayers receiving a tax cut. This fact creates substantial political difficulties for the enactment of a consumption tax. It should be noted, however, that much of the objection here is really an objection to the ending of the double taxation of capital income that occurs under the current income tax system. The same problem would arise in a shift to an integrated income tax system.

Conclusion

In practice, consumption is inherently easier to measure than income, and the dynamic efficiency gains from encouraging savings and investment could be large. However, that argument is weakened by the difficulties associated with transitioning from the current income tax system to a proposed consumption tax system. In addition, concerns about the fairness of moving from an income to a consumption tax base loom large in the tax reform debate.

To date, the transitional difficulties have stood as a major obstacle to wholesale change. However, there has been piecemeal change, and the current U.S. tax system is a hybrid of an income tax and consumption tax system that has gradually shifted from a predominant reliance on income as the tax base toward a greater reliance on consumption as the tax base. In so doing, we have come (perhaps unconsciously) to the result Kaldor proposed 50 years ago:

> However inadequate the system of income taxation may be in relation to the objectives which it seeks to attain, it is inconceivable that, within any foreseeable period, it should be wholly abandoned in favor of an alternative system based on personal expenditure. The most that can be hoped for therefore is to introduce a spending tax that can be operated side by side with the income tax, and that would take some of the weight off the income tax without imposing an excessive administrative burden. (Kaldor 1955, 224)

ADDITIONAL READINGS

Bernheim, B. Douglas, Andrei Shleifer, and Lawrence H. Summers. "The Strategic Bequest Motive." *Journal of Political Economy* 93 (1985): 1045–76.

Blinder, Alan. *Toward an Economic Theory of Income Distribution.* Cambridge, MA: MIT Press, 1974.

Bradford, David. "On the Incidence of Consumption Taxes." In *The Consumption Tax: A Better Alternative?* edited by Charles Walker and Mark Bloomfield. Cambridge, MA: Ballinger, 1987.

———. "Consumption Taxes: Some Fundamental Transition Issues." In *Frontiers of Tax Reform,* edited by Michael J. Boskin. Stanford: Hoover Institution Press, 1995.

Brashares, Edith. "Replacing the Federal Income Tax with a Consumption Tax." In *Handbook on Taxation,* edited by W. Bartley Hildreth and James A. Richardson (549–78). New York: Marcel Dekker, 1999.

Gale, William. "Reinventing the Federal Tax System." *The Brookings Review* (Fall 1995).

Gordon, Roger, Laura Kalambokidis, Jeffrey Rohaly, and Joel Slemrod. "Toward a Consumption Tax and Beyond." *American Economic Review* 94, no. 2 (May 2004): 161–65.

Hobbes, Thomas. *Leviathan.* New York: Penguin Books, 1651 (Penguin edition published in 1968).

Institute for Fiscal Studies. *The Structure and Reform of Direct Taxation: Report of a Committee Chaired by Professor James E. Meade.* London: George Allen and Unwin, 1973.

Jack, William. "The Treatment of Financial Services Under a Broad-Based Consumption Tax." *National Tax Journal* 53, no. 4 (December 2000): 841–52.

Kaldor, Nicolas. *An Expenditure Tax.* London: George Allen and Unwin, 1955.

Metcalf, Gilbert. "Value Added Taxation: A Tax Whose Time Has Come?" *Journal of Economic Perspectives* 9 (1995): 121–40.

Musgrave, Peggy B. "Consumption Tax Proposals in the International Setting." In *Tax Conversations: A Guide to the Key Issues in the Tax Reform Debate,* edited by Richard Krever (447–70). Boston: Kluwer Law International, 1997.

Organisation for Economic Co-Operation and Development (OECD). *Consumption Tax Trends: VAT/GST, Excise and Environmental Taxes.* Paris: OECD, 2001.

Rousslang, Donald J. "Should Financial Services Be Taxed under a Consumption Tax? Probably." *National Tax Journal* 55, no. 2 (June 2002): 281–91.

Toder, Eric J. "Consumption Tax Proposals in the United States." In *Tax Conversations: A Guide to the Key Issues in the Tax Reform Debate,* edited by Richard Krever (159–86). Boston: Kluwer Law International, 1997.

U.S. Treasury Department. *Blueprints for Basic Tax Reform.* Washington, DC: U.S. Government Printing Office, 1977.

Cross-references: expensing; expenditure tax; fairness in taxation; flat tax; life cycle model; progressivity, measures of; retail sales tax, national; retail sales tax, state; value-added tax, national; value-added tax, state; X-tax.

Corporate reorganizations
David Reishus
Lexecon

Tax treatment of corporate mergers, acquisitions, and reorganizations.

Corporate transactions that transfer ownership of corporate business assets—mergers, acquisitions, reorganizations, and the like—constitute one of the most complex areas in tax policy and practice. Corporate transactions may generate tax consequences at the corporate or shareholder level or both. Economically similar transfers of ownership in corporate assets can be accomplished through a myriad of legal forms. These transfers pose fundamental questions in corporate income tax policy: how broad is the corporate tax base, when is income recognized, and how should distributions from corporations be taxed to individuals?

Tax treatment of corporate transactions

Taxation of corporate transactions generally follows one of two paradigms. The first is a purchase and sale of assets. The second is a tax-free reorganization in which corporate enterprises change form but retain their ongoing tax characteristics. The following outline characterizes U.S. rules, although these principles are applied widely; Scholes et al. (2002) provide an economic interpretation of relevant U.S. tax law. In practice, however, there are additional options and constraints beyond those outlined here.

The exchange of stock for cash or other types of property is treated as a sale. The selling shareholder recognizes and is taxed on a capital gain (or loss) to the extent the sale price exceeds (is less than) the selling shareholder's basis in the stock. The buyer obtains a basis in the stock equal to the purchase price. There is no tax effect at the corporate level. Purchasing all of the stock in a corporation for cash is the simplest mechanism from a tax perspective for transferring ownership of corporate assets. An exchange of stock in one corporation for stock and securities in another corporation can often be structured as a tax-free reorganization. As a result of the transaction, the assets of the first corporation come under control of another corporation's shareholders. Properly structured, the exchange of stock will not trigger tax to any party. The transferring shareholders have the same bases in the second company's stock as they previously held in their original stock.

At the corporate level, the two paradigms also apply. Following a tax-free reorganization, the tax attributes of a corporation—asset bases, accounting methods, net operating loss carryforwards, foreign tax credit carryforwards—remain essentially intact. The assets of the corporation are not treated as having been sold, and no recognition of gain occurs. The use of the acquired attributes by the new corporation, however, may be restricted to deter trading in tax attributes.

Alternatively, a corporation sells all its assets. This sale triggers gain or loss, along with any applicable recapture, and thus generates corporate tax liability to the selling corporation. The buyer obtains a new basis in the assets. The new owner depreciates and amortizes the assets, depending on their characteristics, using these new bases. If the proceeds of the sale of substantially all of the assets are then distributed to the shareholders of the selling corporation, the liquidating distribution from the selling corporation is treated as a sale of the shareholders' stock, rather than as a dividend.

The elusive search for neutrality

Application of the two alternative paradigms to economically similar transactions highlights problems of consistency and neutrality. For example, the tax consequences at both the corporate and shareholder levels can be dramatically different depending on whether the selling shareholder receives cash or stock, even if the received stock is widely traded, highly liquid, and easily used as collateral.

Nonlinearities in the corporate tax system may inherently provide an incentive to merge. For example, if tax losses do not fully offset profits in an economic sense, two separate corporations, one with losses and one with gains, may pay more tax than if they merge and combine their tax attributes. In an attempt to limit mergers as a means of trading in losses or other tax attributes, complex rules have been developed to limit their use after a merger. The shuffling of corporate identities in mergers highlights conflicting principles regarding the tax base for corporate profits. Are profits of the whole corporate sector, each corporation, or historical lines of business the appropriate target of the corporate tax? Like other portions of the corporate income tax, merger tax rules display aspects of each of these possibilities.

To the extent that a corporate transaction does not meet the requirements for tax-free treatment, a sale occurs and tax liability is triggered. A corporation selling assets immediately recognizes gain (or loss). The tax due on a corporation's sale serves as a disincentive to its acquisition, just as taxation on realization of capital gains tends to "lock in" gains and discourage sales of appreciated property. The buyer obtains a step-up (or step-down) in the bases of the assets that—depending on the details of the transaction and depreciation schedules, recapture rules, goodwill amortization, ordinary income and capital gains tax rates, and other factors—may compensate over time for the immediate tax consequences to the seller. The balance in current U.S. tax law usually tips so that the immediate adverse tax consequences to the selling corporation exceed the ultimate benefits to the buyer, thus discouraging corporate asset sales.

The use of debt, particularly in leveraged buyouts, has also been identified as a tax incentive for corporate mergers (Bulow et al. 1990). To the extent that interest deductibility encourages the use of debt, this incentive is widespread and not limited to corporate mergers. While the use of debt in corporate mergers has been a focus of concern, there is little agreement on whether interest deductibility provides the incentive to merge or not.

The treatment of cash in acquisitions poses problems for the integrity of the classic two-tier corporate tax regime. In general, cash earned by corporations that is distributed to shareholders is treated as a dividend and taxable in full as ordinary income to individual shareholders. To the extent that the double taxation of dividends traps assets in corporate form, acquisitions of corporate assets may be encouraged relative to new investments (King 1989). Moreover, in a cash acquisition, selling shareholders only pay tax (at capital gains rates) to the extent that the proceeds exceed basis in their stock. Thus, cash that leaves the corporate sector via an acquisition may bear less tax than that paid out as dividends. As such, the tax system further encourages cash acquisitions as a means of moving equity beyond the reach of the corporate income tax (Joint Committee on Taxation 1989). The amount of cash leaving the corporate sector via acquisition is large; in 1985, during the mid-1980s merger boom, $70 billion left the corporate sector via cash acquisitions, exceeding the level of cash dividends in that year (Bagwell and Shoven 1989). Differential individual income and capital gains tax rates along with basis recovery exacerbate this distortion. Solutions to this problem are complex and may generate nonneutralities and perceived inequities of their own (Warren 1993). Corporate tax integration, as implemented in a number of countries, reduces the tax wedge between dividends and distributions via cash acquisitions. As most implementations of corporate tax integration require tracking of dividends and previously taxed income and the characterization of corporate distributions, corporate tax integration alone does not resolve the complexities in taxing corporate transactions.

Do taxes affect corporate mergers?

Several studies have measured the impact of specific tax provisions on the incentive for mergers. The ability to accelerate the use of net operating loss carryforwards and the potential benefits from asset step-ups have little impact on the aggregate level of corporate acquisition activity, even though in specific instances they, and other minor rules, are important. Auerbach and Reishus (1988) find these tax provisions have little effect on the probability of merger. Hayn (1989) finds modest impact of these provisions on the premium obtained in an acquisition. Scholes and Wolfson (1990) find that anticipated changes in tax rules influence the timing of a transaction.

Hayn (1989) and others find that the form a merger takes, whether a taxable cash acquisition or a tax-free reorganization, is strongly influenced by tax factors. The type of tax benefits available at the corporate level affects whether cash or stock is used and thus the corresponding tax treatment. In general, qualifying as a tax-free reorganization for those desiring that status increases the likelihood of merger completion. Buyers may use cash for nontax reasons, such as in limiting exposure to the seller's legal liability or in responding to a tender offer. When cash is used, the immediate tax charge may discourage acquisitions.

Leveraged buyouts, acquisitions involving large increases in debt, have been the object of specific study. Kaplan (1989) and Schipper and Smith (1991) both found large savings in taxes after these transactions, most of which were a result of increased interest deductions. Thus, to the extent the acquisition is necessary to obtain such a highly leveraged corporate structure, interest deductibility encourages leveraged buyouts.

Foreign direct investment may occur through direct investment in assets or through the acquisition of existing corporations. Home country treatment of foreign taxes can interact with the tax treatment of existing corporations relative to investment in new physical capital; this interaction can encourage or discourage acquisition as a form of direct foreign investment. Auerbach and Hassett (1993) find little evidence

of this predicted effect resulting from the Tax Reform Act of 1986. Utilizing differences in state tax rates, Swenson (2001) finds that higher state tax rates leads to higher levels of direct foreign investment through acquisition, the opposite of the effect on other forms of direct investment.

In summary, current evidence suggests that tax factors have only a modest impact, with exceptions in particular cases, on the aggregate level of corporate mergers and the choice of merger partners. Taxation does influence the form of a merger, whether cash or stock, and thus its tax status, which may indirectly influence economic outcomes. Interest deductibility may encourage mergers, to the extent that the acquisition is necessary to achieve the high leverage.

ADDITIONAL READINGS

Auerbach, Alan J., and Kevin Hassett. "Taxation and Foreign Direct Investment in the United States: A Reconsideration of the Evidence." In *Studies in International Taxation,* edited by Alberto Giovannini, R. Glenn Hubbard, and Joel Slemrod. Chicago: University of Chicago Press, 1993.

Auerbach, Alan J., and David Reishus. "The Effect of Taxation on the Merger Decision." In *Corporate Takeovers: Causes and Consequences,* edited by Alan J. Auerbach. Chicago: University of Chicago Press, 1988.

Bagwell, Laurie Simon, and John B. Shoven. "Cash Distributions to Shareholders." *The Journal of Economic Perspectives* 3, no. 3 (Summer 1989): 129–40.

Bulow, Jeremy I., Lawrence H. Summers, and Victoria P. Summers. "Distinguishing Debt from Equity in the Junk Bond Era." In *Debt, Taxes, and Corporate Restructuring,* edited by John B. Shoven and Joel Waldfogel. Washington, DC: The Brookings Institution, 1990.

Hayn, Carla. "Tax Attributes as Determinants of Shareholder Gains in Corporate Acquisitions." *Journal of Financial Economics* 23 (June 1989): 121–53.

Joint Committee on Taxation. *Federal Income Tax Aspects of Corporate Financial Structures.* Washington, DC: Joint Committee on Taxation, January 18, 1989.

Kaplan, Steven. "Management Buyouts: Evidence on Taxes as a Source of Value." *The Journal of Finance* 44, no. 3 (July 1989): 611–32.

King, Mervyn. "Economic Growth and the Life-Cycle of Firms." *European Economic Review* 33 (1989): 325–34.

Schipper, Katherine, and Abbie Smith. "Effects of Management Buyouts on Corporate Interest and Depreciation Tax Deductions." *The Journal of Law and Economics* 34, no. 2 (pt. 1) (October 1991): 295–341.

Scholes, Myron S., and Mark A. Wolfson. "The Effects of Changes in Tax Laws on Corporate Reorganization Activity." *Journal of Business* 64 (1990): S141–64.

Scholes, Myron S., Mark A Wolfson, Merle M. Erickson, Edward L. Maydew, and Terrence J. Shevlin. *Taxes and Business Strategy: A Planning Approach.* Upper Saddle River, NJ: Prentice Hall, 2002.

Swenson, Deborah L. "Transaction Type and the Effect of Taxes on the Distribution of Foreign Direct Investment in the United States." In *International Taxation and Multinational Activity,* edited by James R. Hines Jr. Chicago: University of Chicago Press, 2001.

Warren, Alvin C. *Reporter's Study of Corporate Tax Integration.* Philadelphia: American Law Institute, Federal Income Tax Project, 1993.

Cross-references: income tax, corporate, federal; integration, corporate tax.

Cost of capital

Jane G. Gravelle

Congressional Research Service, Library of Congress

The amount that must be paid for the use of capital, either real or financial, usually measured as an annual percentage rate.

The term "cost of capital" is often used differently by economists, financial commentators, and businessmen, although it refers in general to the amount that must be paid for the use of capital, either real or financial. The financial press sometimes seems to equate the cost of capital with the interest rate. Businessmen may mean the required return the firm must earn (the hurdle rate) to undertake a given investment project.

Following Jorgenson's (1963) work, which crystallized the concept, economists generally use the term to mean the implicit rent that is paid in a given period for the use of capital goods (e.g., machinery). This measure is also called the "user cost of capital" or the "rental price of capital." As used by economists, the cost of capital is the price of capital, just as the wage rate is the price of labor. Cost-of-capital measures are derived from a discounted cash flow method, where the present value of the stream of expected earnings sums to the cost of the asset.

To illuminate the differences between uses of the "cost of capital" term, consider how the measure is altered by the introduction of depreciation, risk, inflation, and taxes.

First however, there are circumstances under which all uses of the cost of capital would be the same—when there is a uniform level of risk and thus a single type of financial asset (e.g., only bonds), and there is no depreciation, no taxes, and no inflation. In this case, the cost of capital is the rate of interest, denoted i. If the interest rate is 6 percent, the cost of capital is 6 percent, or 6 cents per dollar of capital.

Introducing depreciation

Suppose the capital in question is a machine, whose value falls by a certain percentage each period as the machine gets older and experiences wear, tear, and obsolescence. If the firm were renting this machine from a lessor, its rent would include not only interest on the use of capital but also an amount to compensate the lessor for the deterioration in value of the machine. Suppose the machine loses 10 percent of its value each year. In that case, the cost of capital for the machine is the sum of the interest paid (i) and the depreciation rate (d), or $i + d$. If the interest rate is 6 percent and the depreciation rate is 10 percent, the cost of capital is 16 percent, or 16 cents per dollar of capital.

The user cost of capital, inclusive of depreciation, therefore varies across different types of assets. It is larger for machinery, which depreciates more quickly, than for structures.

Introducing risk—debt versus equity finance

The cost of capital will not be represented properly by using the interest rate if there are different forms of financial investments. Equity investments generally earn higher rates of return than debt investments, presumably owing to the greater riskiness of equity investments. Typically, the cost-of-capital measure is adjusted to incorporate that risk by providing a weighted average of debt and equity. For example, if a firm borrows f percent of its capital, pays an interest rate of i, and has a required equity return of E, then the cost of capital will be: $fi + (1 - f)E + d$.

Introducing inflation

The interest rate, or the equity return, in the cost-of-capital formula should be the real rather than the nominal return. The nominal interest rate during an inflationary period is composed of two parts: the real return and the inflation premium necessary to retain the real value of the asset. For example, if the interest rate is 6 percent and the inflation rate is 4 percent, the real interest rate is only 2 percent. When a firm repays the nominal principal in cheaper dollars, that repayment plus the inflation premium is just enough to maintain the real value of the principal.

Introducing taxes

Hall and Jorgenson (1967) incorporated taxes into the cost of capital; economists have since further refined this measure. If there were no inflation, and if taxable income were measured correctly, the cost of capital to a firm would be the interest rate, if debt-financed. The firm pays no tax on interest because although the profits of its investments are taxed, they are fully offset by the deductibility of the interest. However, the firm must pay a tax on the equity return to stockholders or other equity owners; thus, if E represents the rate of profit after the tax required by equity interests, the cost of capital for equity finance is $E/(1 - u)$, where u is the firm's tax rate. With depreciation, and a mixture of debt and equity finance, the cost of capital is $fi + (1 - f)E/(1 - u) + d$.

When inflation is present, but tax depreciation is measured correctly (i.e., reflects true economic decline but is restated in nominal dollars each period), the cost of the debt-financed investment, net of depreciation, is $i(1 - u) - p/(1 - u)$, where i is the nominal interest rate and p is the inflation rate. Note that this value is smaller than the real interest rate ($i - p$) with no tax. This is because the firm can deduct nominal interest. Thus, the firm's after-tax real cost of borrowing is $i(1 - u) - p$, smaller than the $(i - p)/(1 - u)$ cost if the inflation premium were not deductible. This real cost is grossed up by the tax rate if economic income is otherwise correctly measured.

In general, tax depreciation is measured according to tax accounting rules that neither adjust for inflation nor reflect the true pattern of economic depreciation. In this case, the cost of capital is $(R + d)(1 - uz - k)/(1 - u)$, where z is the present value of tax depreciation deductions per unit of investment, k is any investment credit allowed, and R is the weighted after-tax discount rate of the firm, where $R = f[i(1 - u) - p] + [1 - f]E$. E is assumed to be the real rate of profit. The value of z may be larger than economic depreciation $[d/(R + d)]$ because tax depreciation is accelerated, but this effect is offset by the fact that depreciation deductions are not normally indexed for inflation (and thus would be discounted at the nominal discount rate, $R + p$, making the value of z smaller).

For many applications, there is an additional, crucial measure: the pretax rate of return, or the net cost of capital. This measure is taken by calculating the cost of capital and then subtracting the depreciation rate. The measure that is left is the pretax rate of return, subsequently denoted as r.

Applications of the cost-of-capital measure

The cost-of-capital measure is used in several ways: in summarizing the often complex features of the tax code into a single measure of effective tax rate, in assessing the effects of tax changes on the allocation and size of the capital stock, and in measuring the efficiency consequences of tax policy.

Effective tax rates

The cost-of-capital measure can be used to construct effective marginal tax rates. One measure is the *firm level* effective tax rate, which shows the effects of features such as investment credits and tax depreciation. This measure of effective tax rate is derived by subtracting the firm's after-tax rate of return from the pretax rate of return, and dividing by the pretax rate of return, or $(r - R)/r$. It thus shows what fraction of the internal pretax rate of return, r, is paid in taxes. If economic income is equal to taxable income (in a present-value sense), the effective tax rate will be the firm's statutory marginal tax rate.

Effective tax rates typically vary across assets. To aggregate these measures, the pretax returns on different assets should be weighted by the contribution of the asset to the total capital stock to obtain an overall pretax return, and hence an overall effective tax rate.

Another measure of effective tax rate is the *total* effective tax rate. To measure this tax burden, one must measure the real after-tax rate of return to investors. This return would be a weighted average of the after-tax real interest rate, or $i(1 - t) - p$, where t is the tax rate of the bondholder. The equity rate in the corporate sector will be $E(1 - v)$, where v is the real effective personal-level tax burden (arising from dividend and capital gains taxation).

There is some disagreement as to how to weight and measure different tax rates. For example, v, in a traditional model, represents the sum of the effective personal-level taxes on corporate stock: taxes on dividends and effective real tax burdens on capital gains. Some proponents of the "new view" of

dividends distinguish between equity investment obtained through new stock issues and investment of retained earnings, arguing that the dividend tax is not an effective burden on this latter (and dominant) source of equity finance. Another issue is whether the ratio of debt-to-equity finance at the margin is the same as the ratio on average, and how risk might be treated in measuring tax rates.

Effects of tax changes on the cost of capital and investment

The cost-of-capital measure is important, given its role as a measure of the price of capital inputs, in estimating the effects of tax policy changes on the size and allocation of the capital stock. One issue is the extent to which changes in tax liability alter interest rates or equity returns. To hold rates of return (either the firm's after-tax rate, or the individual investor's after-tax rate of return) constant will lead to a different result than if, say, the capital stock is held constant. Thus, assessment of the effects of tax changes on the cost of capital and on investment will depend not only on how investment responds to changes in price but also on whether the estimate takes into account feedbacks from the economy as a whole.

It is important to distinguish between the gross cost of capital (inclusive of depreciation) and pretax return (which is sometimes referred to as the net cost of capital). The percentage change in the price of capital appropriate for assessing changes in investment demand should be measured as a fraction of the gross (depreciation-inclusive) cost; this effect will be smaller than the percentage change in pretax return for assets that depreciate.

Another application of the cost-of-capital measure is in calculations of the efficiency effects of a tax change. In general, a tax system results in the most efficient allocation of capital if the pretax returns are equal across all assets. The cost-of-capital concept is necessary to derive the pretax return; this measure, in turn, provides input for assessing whether a tax change leads to more or less economic efficiency.

Magnitude of the cost of capital

Most estimates of the firm's discount rate (R) range in the neighborhood of 4 to 6 percent for a corporate firm. The cost of capital after all taxes (i.e., after personal taxes) would be slightly lower. Overall effective tax rates in the U.S. economy as of 2003 have been estimated at around 30 percent (including owner-occupied housing), suggesting an overall pretax rate of return of around 7 percent. All of these rates of return are net of any inflation premium. The depreciation rate averages about 15 percent for equipment, 2 to 3 percent for structures, and about 3 percent overall, including land and inventories that do not depreciate. Gravelle (1994) contains data on effective tax rates and the magnitude of the measures used to compute the cost of capital. Updated data can be found in Brazell and Mackie (2000) and Gravelle (2001, 2004).

ADDITIONAL READINGS

Brazell, David W., and James B. Mackie III. "Depreciation Lives and Methods: Current Issues in the U.S. Capital Cost Recovery System." *National Tax Journal* 53 (September 2000): 531–62.

Gravelle, Jane G. *The Economic Effects of Taxing Capital Income.* Cambridge, MA: MIT Press, 1994.

———. "Whither Tax Depreciation?" *National Tax Journal* 54 (September 2001): 513–26.

———. "The Corporate Tax: Where Has It Been and Where Is It Going?" *National Tax Journal* 57 (December 2004): 903–23.

Hall, Robert E., and Dale W. Jorgenson. "Tax Policy and Investment Behavior." *American Economic Review* 58 (June 1967): 391–414.

Jorgenson, Dale W. "Capital Theory and Investment Behavior." *American Economic Review* 54 (May 1963): 247–59.

Cross-references: capital cost recovery; deferral of tax; marginal effective tax rate.

Cross-border shopping

Donald Bruce and William Fox
University of Tennessee

Inability to enforce destination-based taxation has resulted in significant cross-border shopping in response to tax differentials. Recent research indicates that governments react at least in part by following their neighbors' tax rate changes.

Given our global system of largely open economies and varying commodity tax rates, it comes as no surprise that purchasers can often reduce their commodity tax burden by crossing a border into another jurisdiction in order to take advantage of a lower commodity tax rate. Early research focused on direct cross-border shopping, where the purchaser physically crosses the border to make the purchase. Bootlegging or smuggling is similar to direct cross-border shopping, in that a third party crosses the border, purchases a large number of taxable items at the lower tax rate, and then resells them in the high-tax jurisdiction.

Cross-border shopping has taken on a much broader meaning in recent years with the advent of mail order and electronic commerce. In the words of Austan Goolsbee (2000), these technologies have created a "world without borders." Essentially, purchasers can cross-border shop by simply visiting a remote vendor's web site or calling their catalog order hotline.

Commodity tax institutions and cross-border shopping

Consider the simple case of an open economy with two taxing jurisdictions, or states, where the commodity tax rate in the purchaser's state of residence is higher than the commodity tax rate in the second state. Assuming that the marginal cost of obtaining a taxable commodity is the same in both jurisdictions, cross-border shopping is expected to occur when the tax savings exceed the transportation costs involved in crossing the border to make the purchase. Mail order and electronic commerce have the capacity to dramatically increase cross-border shopping since the technologies can potentially reduce transportation costs to zero—except for shipping and handling charges that are better seen as a pricing strategy than as transportation costs—and the effective tax rate in the low-tax jurisdiction may be equal to zero.

Most state commodity taxes are legally structured as destination-based taxes in the United States, in that the tax liability is determined according to the rules in the jurisdiction where the purchaser intends to use or enjoy the commodity. Local sales taxes, on the other hand, are often levied on an origination basis, though the proposed Streamlined Sales Tax Agreement requires that local taxes be imposed on a destination basis. This provision has created political difficulties in some states. Destination-based taxation obviously removes any benefit to cross-border shopping. In an open economy, however, destination-based commodity taxes are notoriously difficult to enforce. Indeed, consumer sales taxes as they are currently levied in the United States are effectively based on the tax rate in the jurisdiction in which the sale is made. The seller is typically legally required to assume that the purchaser is a resident of that jurisdiction when the buyer takes possession of the good at the time of purchase.

In the case of catalog or Internet sales in the United States, however, the tax is typically based on the purchaser's home jurisdiction since possession is not taken in the purchasing state. Further, if the remote vendor does not have nexus (normally interpreted as some form of physical presence) in the purchaser's home state, the vendor cannot be required by the home state's tax authority to collect and remit the sales tax on behalf of the purchaser. In this case (and others where the tax is not paid in the purchasing jurisdiction), however, the purchaser is still obligated to pay the equivalent use tax to his home state through a voluntary remittance program. Voluntary remittance by individuals is very low, even though 19 states allow for compliance through individual income tax returns. Voluntary remittance of tax due on business purchases is much better, but is still very poor on the standards of state tax compliance (see Gutmann and Woodwell 2003).

State-level use taxes (levied in every sales taxing state) and restrictions on the importation of large quantities of selective sales taxable commodities are intended to turn the commodity tax system into a destination-based tax. These attempts have largely failed for three reasons. First, the use taxes are confusing and often misunderstood, resulting in notoriously low compliance. Second, third party information on out of state purchases is normally very limited. Third, bootlegging or smuggling activities continue to sidestep import restrictions, and the large tax differentials that exist between states create strong incentives for them to continue. For example, state cigarette tax rates currently vary from 2.5 cents per pack in Virginia to $2.05 per pack in New Jersey.

Theoretical and empirical research on cross-border shopping

Research on cross-border shopping in the 1970s and 1980s consisted mainly of empirical analyses of purchasers' responses to tax differentials. The research was grounded in a consumption function, where the relative price was the tax-inclusive price in the neighboring jurisdiction divided by the tax-inclusive price in the home jurisdiction. These studies almost always found that an increase in the home state's tax rate reduced the home state's sales tax base, suggesting that cross-border shopping was responding to tax rates, often with elastic responses (see Fox 1986; Walsh and Jones 1988).

Recent research has turned to how governments respond to cross-border shopping. Theoretical research has explored tax rate competition between bordering governments when destination-based taxation cannot be enforced. Mintz and Tulkens (1986) employed a welfare maximization model and determined that tax rates can respond either positively or negatively to neighbor-jurisdiction tax rates depending on how much citizens value local public services. Kanbur and Keen (1993) devised a revenue maximization model that focused on differences in jurisdiction size (e.g., small versus large governments). They found reaction functions to be generally positive, meaning that a jurisdiction's tax rate is projected to increase as tax rates in neighboring jurisdictions increase. They concluded that optimizing behavior leads smaller governments to undercut larger governments. Both of these studies showed that the reaction functions can be discontinuous in certain situations. Theory also indicates that lower transportation costs give governments less capacity to differentiate rates from neighbors because of the increased ease of cross-border shopping. This finding suggests that electronic commerce will result in lower and more similar commodity tax rates unless states are able to enforce the taxes on a destination basis.

Much of the recent empirical work has sought to test the tax competition propositions in the theoretical work, and specifically how home states or jurisdictions respond to rate increases in other states or jurisdictions. For example, Luna (2004) and Rork (2003) both provided empirical evidence that commodity tax rates in the home jurisdiction respond positively to those in neighboring jurisdictions. Luna (2004) also found that increases in the local sales tax rate relative to rates in neighboring jurisdictions reduce the domestic sales tax base, echoing the earlier studies in suggesting the presence of increased cross-border shopping as relative tax rates diverge.

A case study of cross-border shopping

Cross-border shopping not only influences tax policy at the margin, but has affected overall tax structures. Bosnia and Herzegovina was formed in 1996 with two entities and one autonomous city (Brcko), each of which had widely different commodity tax rates and bases (Fox 2003). Political leaders in each place quickly learned that vendors were importing and selling in ways that took advantage of differences in the tax structures. For example, for a time the sales tax was collected at retail in one entity and at import in the other. This created the incentive for vendors to avoid the tax by importing into the area that taxed at retail and selling in the area that taxed at import. Both vendors and consumers would also cross into the lowest-tax entity and bring goods home.

The lost tax revenues (particularly on commodities such as oil) and economic activity were a significant concern and led the political leaders to discuss the creation of what amounted to border controls between the entities. The result was a decision to harmonize the tax structures and to create a system of destination-based taxation. The reformed commodity tax structure is in place and appears to significantly lessen any potential for tax-induced cross-border shopping, though the incentives for tax competition (particularly from Brcko) remain in place.

ADDITIONAL READINGS

Fox, William F. "Tax Structure and the Location of Economic Activity along State Borders." *National Tax Journal* 39, no. 4 (1986): 387–402.

———. "Destination Based Indirect Taxation: The Case of Bosnia and Herzegovina." *European Journal of Law and Economics* 16, no. 1 (2003): 5–22.

Goolsbee, Austan. "In a World without Borders: The Impact of Taxes on Internet Commerce." *Quarterly Journal of Economics* 115, no. 2 (2000): 561–76.

Gutmann, Don, and Stan Woodwell. "Department of Revenue Compliance Study." Olympia, WA: Washington Department of Revenue, 2003. http://dor.wa.gov/Docs/Reports/Compliance_Study/compliance_study_2003.pdf.

Kanbur, Ravi, and Michael Keen. "Jeux Sons Frontieres: Tax Competition and Tax Coordination when Countries Differ in Size." *American Economic Review* 83 (1993): 877–92.

Luna, LeAnn. "Local Sales Tax Competition and the Effect on County Governments' Tax Rates and Tax Bases." *Journal of the American Taxation Association* 26, no. 1 (2004): 43–62.

Mintz, Jack, and Henry Tulkens. "Commodity Tax Competition between Member States of a Federation: Equilibrium and Efficiency." *Journal of Public Economics* 29 (1986): 133–72.

Rork, Jonathan C. "Coveting Thy Neighbors' Taxation." *National Tax Journal* 56, no. 4 (2003): 775–87.

Ferris, J. Stephen. "The Determinants of Cross Border Shopping: Implications for Tax Revenues and Institutional Change." *National Tax Journal* 53, no. 4 (December 2000): 801–24.

Walsh, Michael J., and Jonathan D. Jones. "More Evidence on the 'Border Tax' Effect: The Case of West Virginia 1979–84." *National Tax Journal* 41, no. 2 (1988): 261–66.

D

Deferral of tax

Emil M. Sunley
International Monetary Fund

A tax strategy or plan whereby income may be deferred or postponed for some period of time.

The concept of tax deferral relates to the timing of tax payments. Taxpayers prefer to pay taxes tomorrow, next year, five years from now, or in the hereafter, rather than today. This is because a dollar today is worth more than a dollar in the future. Tax deferral is sometimes suggested to be unimportant because it involves "only postponing" a tax payment that will eventually have to be made. But as Surrey (1971) points out, deferral of taxes is analogous to the government making interest-free, nonrecourse loans without collateral. Moreover, taxes deferred are taxes partly forgiven, and taxes deferred forever are taxes forgiven.

Just as taxpayers prefer to pay taxes later, the government prefers to receive tax payments now instead of in the future. If the government receives a dollar of taxes today, it can be invested to earn interest, or it can be used to reduce the amount of borrowing the government otherwise would have to do, thus saving interest payments on the avoided debt.

Many tax incentives or preferences take the form of tax deferrals. Examples from the U.S. income tax include accelerated depreciation, the deferral of income from controlled foreign corporations, the deferral of interest on U.S. Series EE savings bonds, and the deferral of capital gains until the gains are realized. Sophisticated tax planning often involves a mastery of tax rules in order to minimize taxes by deferring them to the future.

The value of tax deferral

According to Andrews (1991), the value of tax deferral can be measured in four ways: interest on the deferred tax, present value of the deferred tax, increase in the after-tax rate of return, and the effective tax rate on the investment.

Possibly the simplest way to measure the value of deferring taxes is to compute the interest earned by investing the funds that would not be available if the taxpayer had to pay the taxes currently. Suppose a taxpayer defers paying $1,000 of tax and invests the funds, earning a 10 percent after-tax return. If he defers the tax one year, he earns $100. If he defers the tax two years, he earns $210 ($100 each year plus an additional $10 by investing the $100 earned the first year for one year). If he defers 10 years, he earns $1,594 ($100 a year compounded at 10 percent).

A second way of measuring the value of deferring tax is to compute the present discounted value of the deferred tax. The taxpayer's discount rate is crucial to understanding this way of measuring the value of deferral. The discount rate is essentially the after-tax rate of return that the taxpayer can earn on invested funds. If a taxpayer can defer paying $1,000 of tax for one year and her discount rate is 10 percent (i.e., she can earn a 10 percent after-tax return), then she needs to set aside $909.09 today to have $1,000 a year from now when the tax must be paid ($1,000 = $909.09 × 1.1). Thus, the present discounted value of paying $1,000 in tax a year from now is $909.09, assuming the taxpayer's discount rate is 10 percent. Thus, deferring tax one year is equivalent to paying only 90.9 percent of the tax liability. If $1,000 of taxes can be deferred 10 years, the present value is only $385.54, again assuming a 10 percent discount rate. Thus, deferring the tax 10 years is equivalent to paying only 38.6 percent of the tax liability.

These first two methods—interest earned and present discounted value—are closely related. The first approach looks at how much will be available in, say, 10 years if taxes are deferred, while the second approach looks at how much would have to be set aside today to pay the taxes in the future. To see this, recall that if $1,000 of taxes can be deferred for 10 years, the taxpayer can earn $1,594 over the 10-year period. At the end of 10 years, he will have $2,594 available—the initial $1,000 plus the $1,594 of after-tax earnings. The present discounted value of $2,594 10 years from now and discounted at 10 percent is $1,000 (i.e., $2,594 × .3855 = $1,000). Or put another way, if a taxpayer has a tax liability of $2,594 10 years hence, he needs to set aside $1,000 today, assuming he can earn 10 percent after taxes on these funds.

The third method of measuring the value of deferral looks at the after-tax rate of return. If a taxpayer in the 28 percent tax bracket puts his money in a savings account paying 10 percent, he has to pay tax each year on the earnings, and thus his after-tax rate of return is 7.2 percent. Suppose the tax rules allow a taxpayer to defer paying tax for five years. If the taxpayer invests $1,000 in the savings account, his account will grow to $1,610.51 at the end of five years. He will then have to pay taxes of $170.94 (28 percent on the $610.51 of interest earnings), leaving $1,439.57 after tax. His after-tax rate of return is 7.56 percent because $1,000 invested at 7.56 percent per year compounded will grow to $1,439.57 in five years. Thus, deferring tax for five years in this example increases the after-tax rate of return from 7.2 to 7.56 percent.

A final method of measuring deferral is the effective tax rate. This method is closely related to the after-tax rate of return because the effective tax rate on an investment is defined as the percentage reduction in the rate of return resulting from taxes (i.e., the difference between the before-tax and after-tax rates of return divided by the before-tax rate of return expressed as a percentage). In the savings account example, when the taxpayer defers taxes for five years, the before-tax rate of return is 10 percent and the after-tax rate of return is 7.56 percent. Thus, taxes reduce the rate of return by 24.4 percent (from 10 to 7.56 percent). When interest income is taxed currently, the after-tax rate of return is 7.2 percent, giving an effective tax rate of 28 percent, which is just equal to the nominal tax rate.

For a taxpayer in any given tax bracket, deferral is worth more the longer the period of deferral and the higher the rate of return that can be earned on invested funds (and thus the higher the taxpayer's discount rate). Table 1 measures the value of deferral by computing the effective tax rate for a taxpayer in the 28 percent tax bracket, assuming various periods of deferral and various before-tax rates of return. Lower effective tax rates indicate that deferral is more valuable. As shown in table 1, if the before-tax rate of return is 10 percent, the effective tax rate is 28 percent if there is no deferral, 24.4 percent if deferral is for 5 years, 20.6 percent if deferral is for 10 years, and 12.8 percent if deferral is for 25 years. Similarly, if the period of deferral is 10 years, the effective tax rate is 23.9 percent if the before-tax rate of return is 5 percent, but it falls to 15.8 percent if the before-tax rate of return is 20 percent. Deferral is also worth more the higher the taxpayer's marginal tax rate because the amount of taxes that can be deferred on a given amount of income varies directly with the taxpayer's marginal tax rate.

Tax deferral is often combined with other incentives or preferences. For example, employer contributions to a pension plan are excluded from the employee's income in the years the contribution is made, and the income earned on the funds in the pension plan is not taxable when earned. Instead, the taxes on both the employer contribution and the earnings are deferred until the employee receives a pension or other distribution from the plan. There may be an additional benefit from this treatment because many taxpayers are in lower tax brackets after retirement.

Examples of U.S. tax deferral preferences

Capital gains are taxed only when realized. This is clearly a practical solution because of the difficulty of valuing assets each year. But this practical solution provides a significant tax benefit. A person who invests in a savings account is taxed each year on the interest earnings whether or not the funds are withdrawn from the account. In contrast, a person who invests in non-dividend-paying stock only pays tax on any gain (or recognizes a loss) when the stock is sold. This tax deferral reduces the effective tax rate on appreciating assets. In addition to deferral, the gain may never be taxed because under U.S. law, if appreciated stock passes at death to an heir, the unrealized capital gains at the time of death are not taxed.

The most important investment incentive in the United States and many other countries is accelerated depreciation. The tax law allows the cost of depreciable assets to be recovered more rapidly than the actual decline in the value of the assets—that is, economic depreciation. Accelerated depreciation is a deferral preference because the total amount of depreciation allowed over the life of the asset is unaffected. By being able to claim depreciation deductions earlier, the taxpayer can defer taxes to a later year. Because it is difficult to measure the actual decline in the value of assets, it is difficult to know just how much tax deferral is permitted under various depreciation rules. Companies, however, generally take slower depreciation for book or financial purposes, which may indicate that companies believe the depreciation allowed for tax purposes to be accelerated relative to the actual decline in the value of the assets. In fact, the tax savings resulting from the difference between book and tax depreciation becomes the deferred tax item on the liability side of the company's balance sheet.

Before the Tax Reform Act of 1986, accelerated depreciation on real estate and machinery and equipment was one of the key elements of tax shelters. These tax-favored investments produced artificial losses that sheltered other income from taxation.

Immediate write-off or expensing (sometimes called instantaneous depreciation) is an extreme form of accelerated depreciation. Although only allowed in the United States for a limited amount of depreciable assets, for research and experimentation expenditures, and for certain exploration and development costs of oil and mineral properties, it would be a normal rule under a cash-flow tax. As Brown (1948) showed, expensing results in the after-tax rate of return on the investment being the same as the before-tax rate of return, implying a zero effective tax rate on the investment.

TABLE 1. Effective Tax Rates for Different Tax Deferral Periods and Discount Rates (Nominal tax rate = 28 percent)

Discount rate (percent)	Period of deferral (years)			
	0	5	10	25
5	28.0	26.1	23.9	18.4
10	28.0	24.4	20.6	12.8
20	28.0	21.6	15.8	7.8

Source: Author's calculations.

The income of foreign corporations controlled by U.S. shareholders is generally not subject to U.S. taxation as earned, except for certain tax haven income. The foreign income becomes taxable only when the shareholders receive dividends. This permits U.S. companies to defer tax on their foreign income until it is distributed.

A final example is the deferral of tax on interest income earned on U.S. Series EE savings bonds. Interest on these bonds is only taxable when the bonds are redeemed, unless the investor elects to pay tax currently—and few do. These bonds can be quite attractive investments for individuals who expect to hold them until retirement, when they will be in a lower tax bracket.

ADDITIONAL READINGS

Andrews, William D. *Basic Federal Income Taxation,* pp. 256–64. Boston: Little, Brown and Company, 1991.

Brown, E. Cary. "Business-Income Taxation and Investment Incentives." In *Income, Employment, and Public Policy: Essays in Honor of Alvin H. Hansen.* New York: W. W. Norton & Co., 1948.

Surrey, Stanley S. "The Tax Reform Act of 1969—Tax Deferral and Tax Shelters." Boston College Industrial and Commercial Law Review 12 (February 1971): 307–18.

Cross-references: capital cost recovery; capital gains taxation; cost of capital; expensing; marginal effective tax rate; multinational corporations, taxation.

Delaware holding company

David Brunori

Tax Analysts and George Washington University

A term used to describe tax planning techniques to minimize state corporate taxes.

Delaware holding company is a term of art used to describe a variety of tax planning techniques designed to minimize state corporate tax burdens. The term originated with the use of Delaware investment companies authorized under 30 Delaware Code Section 1902, which provides an exemption from corporate income taxes for companies that merely hold intangible assets. Delaware holding companies are also known as Delaware investment companies and passive investment companies. Most of the techniques that give rise to substantial tax savings can be accomplished in any low or no tax state. Indeed, far more holding companies have been created in Nevada (reportedly over 100,000), which has no corporate tax, than in Delaware (reportedly about 8,000).

The most common method of minimizing taxes through a Delaware holding company is the creation of a passive investment subsidiary in state with low or no corporate tax. Nonbusiness or passive income is usually allocated to the state in which the income-producing asset is located, rather than subject to the apportionment formulas in the various states in which the corporation does business.

In the typical scenario, a corporation will establish a subsidiary in Delaware or another state that does not tax corporate income or passive income. As part of the transaction, the parent company transfers valuable intangible assets such as trademarks, patents, or copyrights to the subsidiary. The parent company then leases the intangible asset back and pays the subsidiary. For example, the XYZ Company may transfer its valuable trade name "XYZ" to a subsidiary located in Delaware. XYZ will then lease the name back and pay the subsidiary a percentage of its total profits.

Typically, the parent corporation would deduct the payments to the subsidiary from its taxable income in all states in which it pays corporate taxes. Assuming that all of the statutory requirements are met, the subsidiary would incur little or no corporate tax on the payments received from the parent. If the payments to the subsidiary are set high enough, the parent corporation can avoid virtually all state corporate income tax liability. The creation of passive investment companies also allows many corporations to avoid or minimize state taxes based on the value of capital stock or net worth employed in the state.

The Delaware holding company can also be used to sell unwanted appreciated assets without paying taxes. The parent corporation contributes the unwanted assets to the holding company. The holding company will then sell the assets to an unrelated party. Assuming the assets are the type permitted to be held by a Delaware holding company, neither the parent nor the subsidiary would pay tax on gain realized from the sale.

The use of Delaware holding companies has been the subject of heated and prolonged debate amongst political leaders and policy analysts. Many public finance experts believe that the availability of the technique has contributed to a significant decline in corporate tax revenue. Multinational corporations are known to have sheltered billions of dollars in profits by establishing subsidiaries that own intangible assets. For example, according to the Multistate Tax Commission, corporate tax minimization efforts have resulted in over $12 billion in lost revenue in 2001 alone.

Delaware holding companies are criticized because, for most corporations, they serve exclusively as a vehicle for minimizing taxes. In the vast majority of cases, the holding companies have no regular employees, own no property other than intangibles, and conduct no business other than leasing intangibles to related parties for tax purposes. As has been widely reported, hundreds of holding companies are often located at one address in Delaware or Nevada. Defenders of Delaware holding companies note the planning techniques utilized to minimize taxes are legal and that the states should continue to recognize the separate existence of business organizations. Defenders also argue that if the subsidiary has no physical presence in a state, the state cannot impose taxes on the subsidiary.

As a result of mounting revenue losses, some states have taken steps to deter the use of Delaware holding companies.

Eight states have enacted legislation that essentially denies deductions from gross income for royalties and other payments for intangibles made to related companies.

The use of combined reporting also prevents corporations from sheltering corporate income by using Delaware holding companies. When states require combined reporting, all related corporations that are operated as a single business are treated as one taxpayer for apportionment purposes. With combined reporting, the Delaware holding company profits are included in the combined report and apportioned to the state where the income is earned. Seventeen states require corporate taxpayers to use combined reporting. In these states, corporations cannot use Delaware holding companies to minimize corporate tax burdens.

Depletion, cost and percentage

Jane G. Gravelle
Congressional Research Service, Library of Congress

Deductions to reflect the using up of mineral deposits.

Depletion deductions are allowed to recover investment costs in a mineral reserve, which becomes depleted as minerals are extracted. These investment costs include the costs of acquiring mineral properties (purchase of lease bonuses) and exploration costs. There are two depletion methods—cost and percentage. Cost depletion allows recovery of costs at the same estimated rate as the mineral is extracted; it is an appropriate method for recovering costs (although its value is reduced by inflation). Percentage depletion allows an arbitrary deduction of a percentage of gross sales and, in some cases, may be many times the original cost. Percentage depletion is limited to independent producers of oil and gas and then allowed only for limited quantities (up to 1,000 barrels of oil a day or the gas equivalent); it is allowed at a 15 percent rate. Marginal (stripper) wells receive special benefits. Percentage depletion is allowed at a variety of different rates for other minerals. Despite the limits on percentage depletion for oil and gas, the subsidy value of percentage depletion is largest for these fuels: $0.6 billion, compared with $0.3 billion for other fuels (primarily coal) and $2 billion for nonfuel minerals.

Percentage depletion originated with oil and gas and was a substitute for discovery value depletion, enacted in 1918 and allowing recovery of market value rather than cost. For many years, percentage depletion for oil and gas was one of the most hotly debated tax subsidies. In later years, percentage depletion was justified on the grounds of maintaining a domestic oil and gas capacity for national defense in the face of low-cost foreign production. The provision was repealed for major producers when prices rose dramatically in the 1970s. The provisions for other minerals, which were enacted after those for oil and gas, and justified in part to provide parity, were retained.

The oil and gas production industry retains important tax subsidies, but they are in the form of the ability to expense or rapidly recover a large fraction of the cost of finding mineral deposits.

ADDITIONAL READING

U.S. Congress, Senate, Committee on the Budget. *Tax Expenditures*. Washington, D.C., December 2002.
U.S. Joint Committee on Taxation, U.S. House Committee on Ways and Means, and the Senate Committee on Taxation. "Estimates of Federal Tax Expenditures for Fiscal Years 2005–2009." Washington, DC: U.S. Joint Committee on Taxation, 2005.

Cross-references: capital cost recovery; expensing; inflation indexation of income taxes.

Depository institutions, federal taxation of

Edith Brashares
Horst and Frisch Incorporated

Special tax provisions that deviate from those of the general corporate income tax are provided to certain institutions that derive income from lending.

While most providers of financial services are taxed under the general corporate income tax rules (see *corporate income tax, federal*), some are subject to special tax provisions. In particular, a distinction is made between depository institutions that derive most of their income from lending activities in which funds are taken from depositors and lent to borrowers, and "nondepository" institutions that do not take deposits, but instead borrow to finance or securitize loans. Nondepository institutions are neither given special tax treatment nor as regulated as depository institutions. In general, bank holding companies are considered nondepository institutions and can engage in nonbanking activities.

Unlike the other depository institutions, credit unions are exempt from federal income tax. (Internal Revenue Code section 501(c)1 exempts federally chartered credit unions, while 501(c)14 exempts state-chartered credit unions from paying federal income taxes.) Credit unions are not-for-profit, have a mutual organization structure in that the owners and depositors are one and the same, and distribute earnings back to members. Membership is limited to those sharing a "common bond," such as the same profession. Repeal of this tax exemption, for at least some credit unions, was proposed in 1971, 1973, 1978, 1985, and 1992 (see American Bankers Association 1989 for further discussion).

The remaining depository institutions, thrifts and banks, are subject to federal income tax. Thrifts include domestic building and loan associations, savings and loan associations, mutual savings banks, and cooperative nonprofit mutual banks. While most consumers today would consider thrifts and banks as interchangeable, there are differences that have historic roots. In general, thrifts had a primary objective of taking deposits from individuals and using the funds to provide home mortgages, while banks used deposits from both individuals and businesses to finance commercial and industrial, as well as consumer, loans. These operating differences were reflected in distinctions in tax treatment, though the tax differences have narrowed as thrift and bank activities have become similar.

Special tax treatment of depository institutions has generally reflected the fact that their primary income derives from taking deposits and lending. Depository institutions are subject to special rules with respect to bad debts, gains and losses on debt obligations, and insolvent institutions' priorities for payments. Because depository institutions can deduct interest expense to purchase and carry bonds, unlike other taxpayers, who are more restricted, banks and thrifts are subject to special rules with respect to tax-exempt bonds. Other special provisions include interest exclusion on some obligations, net operating loss, alternative minimum tax treatment, and provisions that apply to thrifts (see Rook 1989 and U.S. Department of the Treasury 2001 for more details).

Starting in 1997, depository institutions could potentially elect to be taxed as a Subchapter S corporation (see *Subchapter S corporations*). Unlike Subchapter C corporations, S corporations do not pay federal income tax at the entity level, but instead the income is allocated to shareholders and taxed at the shareholder level. In addition to the general eligibility restrictions, Subchapter S depository institutions cannot use the reserve method for accounting for bad debts. This means Subchapter C depository institutions converting to S status must recapture into income existing bad debt reserves before converting (see U.S. Department of the Treasury 2001).

Bad debts

Taxpayers, other than certain depository institutions, are required to use the specific charge-off method to account for bad debts. Essentially, a deduction for a bad debt is allowed when a loan becomes partially or totally worthless. Large banks and thrifts with assets of $500 million or more are required to use the specific charge-off method. Treasury regulations allow banks and thrifts to treat debts as worthless for tax purposes when they are charged off for regulatory purposes (conclusive presumption). This generally allows the losses to be recognized sooner.

Small banks and thrifts can use the reserve method for accounting for bad debts, but are limited to using the experience and fill-up methods for determining reserve deductions. For growing institutions, the reserve method generally accelerates future loss deductions and is equivalent to an interest-free loan from the government equal to the tax rate times the reserve amount. Under the experience method, the reserve is based on the six-year moving average of charge-offs less recoveries (net charge-offs) during the year as a percentage of

the amount of loans outstanding at the end of the year. The deduction for bad debts is then the amount by which this percentage times the amount of loans at the end of the year exceeds outstanding reserves adjusted for net charge-offs. The fill-up method allows a deduction for the difference between base year reserves (1987) and current reserves (determined after the reduction for current year losses). This method was very popular before the base year was fixed in 1986, particularly for thrifts.

The Tax Reform Act of 1986 repealed the bad debt reserve method by large banks as well as nondepository institutions. In addition, as a result of the Tax Reform Act of 1969, small banks were no longer eligible to use the percentage of eligible loan reserve method for determining reserves after 1988. Under this method, a bank's allowable reserve equaled a specific percentage of its eligible loans. The bad debt reserve deduction was the change in allowable reserves plus net charge-offs. (See Neubig and Sullivan 1987 for a discussion of the effects of the 1986 act on banks.)

Depository institutions that no longer qualify for reserve treatment are required to recapture (include in income) all or part of bad debt reserves. Recapture is intended to prevent the duplication of deductions—first as a reserve addition and then when the loan is charged off.

Currently, when a small bank or thrift becomes large, reserve recapture is done using either the four-year spread or the cutoff method. Under the four-year spread approach, 10 percent of reserves are recaptured into income in the first year, 20 percent in the second, 30 percent in the third, and 40 percent in the fourth. However, if the institution has a large net operating loss deduction that is expiring, it can choose instead to recapture more in the first year, two-ninths of the residual in the second, three-ninths in the third, and four-ninths in the fourth year. Under the cutoff approach, the reserve associated with a stock of loans outstanding at the time of recapture cannot be added to. The amount of the reserve is then adjusted for net charge-offs, while the amount of the associated stock of loans is adjusted for charge-offs and loan collections. If adjusted reserves exceed adjusted loans, then the difference is recaptured and the reserve balance is decreased by this amount. If adjusted reserves are less than or equal to the adjusted loans, then none of the reserve is recaptured. The cutoff method can effectively delay when the recapture occurs. These two recapture methods were also allowed in 1986 when the reserve method was repealed for large banks.

When reserve recapture was necessary for thrifts in 1996, the recapture regime was different, reflecting the regulatory problems with recapturing pre-1988 reserves and the additional special assessment thrifts paid to capitalize the deposit insurance fund. In general, the amount of post-1987 reserves recaptured was included ratably over six years. Large thrifts recaptured the excess of total reserves over pre-1988 reserves (excluding supplemental reserves). Small thrifts also excluded post-1987 experience-based reserves from recapture because they could continue to use experience-based reserves. Post-1987 experience reserves were to be recaptured later under rules applicable to banks if a thrift became a large depository institution. (This approach forgave tax on pre-1988 reserves of former thrifts so that small thrifts were treated on a par with larger thrifts. However, small banks that become large banks were liable for recapture of their post-1987 experience-based reserves.) For the first two years following the tax law change, though, thrifts satisfying a residential loan requirement could suspend recapture. The loan requirement was that the principal amount of residential loans the taxpayer made during the year had to meet or exceed the average of the principal amount of residential loans the taxpayer made during the six most recent taxable years beginning before January 1, 1996. (See Brashares and Koch 1997 for details on the 1996 tax law changes and prior tax treatment of thrifts.)

Before the tax changes in 1996, whereby thrifts were treated the same as banks, thrifts received preferential bad debt treatment in exchange for satisfying certain criteria. Thrifts had to have a thrift charter and satisfy the qualified thrift asset test. In general, thrifts could choose the most advantageous approach each year for determining additions to reserves for (qualifying) residential loans: (1) percentage of taxable income, (2) experience, or (3) fill-up. While reserves were adjusted each year for the amount of net charge-offs, the reserve addition under the percentage of taxable income method was the amount by which 8 percent of taxable income (determined without regard to the bad debt deduction) exceeded the addition to reserves for nonresidential (nonqualifying) loans. However, the deduction could not exceed the amount needed to increase reserves to 6 percent of qualifying loans. (In addition, total reserves plus surplus could not exceed 12 percent of deposits.) Unlike the experience method, the amount of the deduction was unrelated to bad debt experience and could result in reserve growth without relation to loan losses. Before 1986, the percentage allowed was higher and essentially enabled thrifts to pay little tax by having large additions to reserves. (When thrifts were first taxed in 1952, the rate was 100 percent. The rate was lowered to 60 percent in 1969, 40 percent in 1976, and 8 percent in 1986.)

Gains and losses as ordinary income

For both banks and thrifts, gains and losses realized on the sale or exchange of a debt obligation are treated as ordinary, instead of a capital gain or loss, if the debt obligation was acquired after July 11, 1969. This restriction limited tax avoidance when capital gains received significant preferential treatment. (See *capital gains taxation*.) An obligation obtained before this time has the gain or loss allocated ratably between long-term capital gain or loss from before July 12, 1969, and the ordinary income or loss after July 11, 1969. The capital gain portion is limited to the net gain recognized on all sales or exchanges of debt obligations for the year.

Insolvent depository institutions

Given the overriding concern with insuring depositors against losses from the insolvency of the institution, it is not surprising that insolvent institutions receive special treatment with respect to tax payment. Taxes cannot be collected, except employment taxes, when the collection would diminish an institution's assets necessary for payment of its depositors.

Interest expense and exclusion

To discourage interest rate arbitrage using tax-exempt bonds (see *tax-exempt bonds*), the interest expense deduction is effectively denied for purchasing and carrying most tax-exempt bonds acquired after August 7, 1986. The disallowed interest expense is the average adjusted tax bases of tax-exempt obligations acquired after August 7, 1986, over the average adjusted tax bases of all assets times the total interest expense. Tax-exempt bonds acquired before August 8, 1986, but after 1982, limit interest disallowance to 20 percent. Before 1983, there was no disallowance. The 20 percent disallowance continues to apply to certain small-issue bonds, particularly those where the issuer anticipates issuing no more than $10 million of obligations in a year.

Before repeal in 1996, depository and other financial institutions were encouraged to make loans to employee stock ownership plans (ESOPs) by excluding 50 percent of the interest on certain securities acquisition loans made after July 18, 1984. (See *employee stock ownership plans*.) The 1989 tax law changes added restrictions, such as the ESOP being obliged to own 50 percent or more of the stock after the acquisition.

Net operating losses

Like other taxpayers, a bank can carry a net operating loss back 2 years or forward 20 years. However, the loss attributable to a bank's bad debt deduction could be carried back 10 years or forward 5 years if the bank used the specific charge-off method, and the net operating loss was for a taxable year beginning after 1986 and before 1994. For losses attributable to tax years beginning after 1975 and before 1987, unlike other taxpayers, all banks were entitled to a 10-year carryback and a 5-year carryforward period. The longer carryback was granted to offset the effect of phasing down the percentage of eligible loans reserve method. Similarly, for losses in tax years between 1981 and 1986, thrifts were entitled to a 10-year carryback and a 5-year carryforward before 1987.

Alternative minimum tax

Unlike the other corporate alternative minimum tax provisions, the preference for bad debt reserves affected only depository institutions. (See *alternative minimum tax, corporate*.) The preference, repealed in 1996, was for the excess of the bad debt deduction over the experience reserve deduction and primarily affected thrifts.

Special thrift provisions

While most corporations are not entitled to deduct dividends that they pay, thrifts can deduct "dividends" that are more accurately described as interest paid to depositors. The key requirement is that the depositor can withdraw the paid or credited dividend amount on demand. Similarly, banks and other nonmutual corporations that receive dividends from mutual savings banks or savings and loans associations must treat the dividends as interest and not eligible for the dividends-received deduction.

As with other taxpayers, the tax treatment of distributions to shareholders that are not redemptions or liquidations comes first from earnings and profits in the taxable year. The next sources, by rank, are somewhat unique to thrifts. These sources are earnings and profits accumulated in tax years beginning after December 31, 1952 (when thrifts became taxable), pre-1988 reserve for losses on qualifying loans to the extent that additions to this reserve exceed those that would have been allowed under the experience method, and supplemental reserves for losses on loans. For redemption and liquidation distributions, the first source is pre-1988 reserves for qualifying loans followed by supplemental reserves, earnings and profits for the taxable year, and earnings and profits accumulated in taxable years beginning after December 31, 1952.

Federal Savings and Loan Insurance Company (FSLIC) payments reimbursing losses as part of 1988 and 1989 transactions are exempt from tax. Tax law in 1993 clarified that FSLIC assistance was compensation for losses and disallowed a loss deduction. Net operating losses as a result of these loss deductions were limited.

ADDITIONAL READINGS

American Bankers Association. "The Credit Union Industry: Trends, Structure, and Competitiveness." Prepared under the Direction of the Secura Group. Washington, DC: American Bankers Association, November 10, 1989.

Brashares, Edith, and Cathleen Koch. "Changing the Tax Treatment of Thrifts: The Importance of the Rules of the Game." Mimeograph. Paper presented at the American Economic Association Annual Meetings, New Orleans, January 1997.

Neubig, Thomas S., and Martin A. Sullivan. "The Effect of the Tax Reform Act of 1986 on Commercial Banks." In *Office of Tax Analysis, Department of the Treasury, Compendium of Tax Research, 1987* (279–305). Washington, DC: U.S. Government Printing Office, 1987.

Rook, Lance W. *Federal Income Taxation of Banks and Financial Institutions.* 6th ed. Boston: Warren, Gorham, and Lamont, 1989.

U.S. Department of the Treasury. "Comparing Credit Unions with Other Depository Institutions." Washington, DC: U.S. Department of the Treasury, January 2001.

Cross-references: banks, state taxation of; income tax, corporate, federal; Subchapter S corporations; tax-exempt bonds.

Depreciation recapture

Joseph J. Cordes
George Washington University

Larry Ozanne
Congressional Budget Office

Leonard E. Burman
The Urban Institute

A provision in tax law that is intended to limit the ability of taxpayers to convert otherwise fully taxable income into tax-preferred capital gains.

Accelerated depreciation can become a means of converting ordinary income into preferentially taxed capital gains. For example, consider a partnership that buys construction equipment and leases the equipment to firms with contracts for various construction projects. Suppose the partners buy a tractor for $100,000 in the middle of one year, lease for that year and the next three, and then sell it. Economists have estimated that, with normal wear and tear, construction tractors depreciate, or fall in value, at the rate of 16.31 percent per year. Assuming this tractor followed the normal pattern and that prices were stable over the four years, it would sell for about $54,000. During the four years, the partners would have been able to depreciate the tractor for tax purposes under the 200 percent declining balance method with a useful life of five years. By the time of the sale, according to IRS's standard depreciation tables, the partners could have claimed $83,000 of depreciation deductions, leaving an adjusted basis in the tractor of $17,000. Without recapture, the partners would have a taxable capital gain on the sale of $37,000 ($54,000–$17,000), which under current rates would be taxed at 15 percent. The $37,000 capital gain in this example, however, is entirely a result of accelerated depreciation deductions. It really is rental income previously earned from the tractor that was deferred because tax depreciation was accelerated relative to economic depreciation. Had tax depreciation equaled economic depreciation, the partners would have reported $37,000 more rental income over the four years they owned the tractor and that income would have been taxed at their ordinary rate of, say, 35 percent. Thus, accelerated depreciation would allow investors to convert ordinary income, which is taxed at a rate of up to 35 percent, into capital gains, which are taxed at rates of up to 15 percent.

Recapture rules remove this opportunity to convert ordinary income to capital gain. They require that capital gain from a sale be taxed as ordinary income, up to the amount of depreciation deductions already claimed. In the example here, all $37,000 of gain would be recaptured as ordinary income. No gain from the sale of the tractor would be taxed as a capital gain unless the sale price exceeded the $100,000 purchase price.

Currently, all depreciation on equipment is recaptured at ordinary rates, while depreciation on structures is recaptured at ordinary rates up to a maximum rate of 25 percent. Recapture also applies to expensed investment, such as allowed under section 179 of the tax code or the so-called "bonus depreciation" enacted in 2002 and 2003 and set to expire at the end of 2004.

Although the concept of requiring that accelerated depreciation be recaptured is simple in principle, the regulations governing recapture are among the more complex elements of tax law. Furthermore, the recapture rules are imprecise because of problems in the measurement of economic depreciation for any particular asset sale. In the above example, had the prices of tractors been rising 5 percent per year while other prices remained stable, the sale price of the tractor would have been $10,000 higher. This extra amount could reasonably be treated as a capital gain and taxed at 15 percent. Or if all prices had been rising at 5 percent per year, the $10,000 would not have been income at all but inflation that logically should not be taxed. In either case, recapture rules would tax it as ordinary income.

Nonetheless, tax experts recognize the necessity of recapture to avoid creating incentives for tax shelters and the accompanying incentives for investors to engage in tax arbitrage, such as those that existed in the early 1980s. These incentives are strongest, and hence the need for a strong and workable recapture provision is greatest, when the tax code allows highly accelerated depreciation while simultaneously taxing capital gains at preferential rates. Tax changes that were enacted in 1986 reduced the effective need for recapture rules considerably by aligning tax depreciation more closely with the economic depreciation of assets and by taxing capital gains at the same rate as other income. Subsequent changes have increased the role of recapture provisions. Changes in law have reintroduced a preferential tax rate for capital gains, while the slowing of inflation has widened the gap between tax and economic depreciation, particularly for equipment.

Note that the benefits of converting ordinary income to capital gains do not exist under the corporate income tax. Under that tax, capital gains are taxed at the same rate as ordinary profits.

ADDITIONAL READINGS

Brazell, David W., and James B. Mackie III. "Depreciation Lives and Methods: Current Issues in the U.S. Capital Cost Recovery System." *National Tax Journal* 53, no. 3 (September 2000): 531–62.

Gravelle, Jane G. "Whither Tax Depreciation?" *National Tax Journal* 54, no. 3 (September 2001): 513–26.

Cross-references: basis; capital cost recovery; capital gains taxation; tax arbitrage; tax shelters.

Destination principle

George Carlson
Deloitte & Touche LLP

In designing general business (e.g., value added) and transaction (e.g., sales) taxes, a choice is made between taxing goods where they are produced ("origin") or where they are purchased or consumed ("destination"). In an open economy, and for a tax that is not uniform across all commodities, the choice may strongly affect tax productivity, equity, and efficiency.

Under the destination principle of taxation, goods and services are taxed where they are purchased or consumed, rather than where they are produced or originate. Destination-basis treatment can be contrasted with the origin principle, under which goods and services are taxed where they are produced.

Consider the case of a sales or value-added tax that is levied by Jurisdiction B. With respect to goods and services that are produced in Jurisdiction A (the origin), but sold in Jurisdiction B (the destination), the destination principle is implemented if Jurisdiction B applies what are popularly known as "border tax adjustments" to imports and exports. Specifically, in implementing the destination principle, Jurisdiction B should apply the tax to goods imported from Jurisdiction A and rebate or "forgive" the tax on exports from Jurisdiction B. (Domestically produced and consumed goods and services are, of course, taxed by Jurisdiction B as well.) The effect of these so-called destination principle border tax adjustments is to ensure that all goods sold in Jurisdiction B (the destination jurisdiction) are taxed, regardless of where they are produced or originate. Similarly, goods or services produced in Jurisdiction B but exported and sold elsewhere, say to Jurisdiction A, are not taxed by Jurisdiction B under the destination principle. (Those goods would be taxed by Jurisdiction A, if Jurisdiction A chose to apply the destination principle.)

International tax and trading rules, established by the General Agreement on Tariffs and Trade, allow destination principle border tax adjustments to be applied to taxes on products (also known as indirect taxes), such as excise, sales, or value-added taxes, but not to direct taxes, such as income and social insurance taxes. Thus, under these international rules, indirect taxes can be imposed at the border on imports and rebated on exports, but no explicit adjustments can be made for direct taxes with respect to either imports or exports. In countries with federal systems of government, such as the United States and Canada, subnational governmental entities may also be able to levy taxes. If so, the movement of goods and services among these subnational units of government requires a choice between the destination and origin principles. In the United States, for example, states tend to follow a destination principle method of taxation by applying their sales taxes to the "use" as well as sales of commodities.

The primary effect of the destination principle is to tax consumption, rather than production. All goods and services sold in the destination jurisdiction are taxed, provided they are not specifically exempted from the tax base. Many jurisdictions, for example, choose to exempt food and medicine and other "necessities" from taxation for reasons of fairness and equity. These exemptions reflect policy decisions that are separate and distinct from the decision to apply the destination or origin principle. But provided a good or service is generally subject to taxation, the destination principle demands that the tax be levied no matter where the good or service was produced. Only the destination of the sale of the good or service is relevant in determining tax liability. Because the destination of a service (e.g., financial advice) can be less certain than that of a good (e.g., an automobile), it may be more difficult to apply the destination principle to some services than to goods.

A completely general tax that is applied uniformly to either the consumption or production of all goods will not affect the allocation of resources in an economy. In an open economy, this implies that the choice of either origin or destination principle border tax adjustments is irrelevant to resource allocation. In particular, assuming a comprehensive tax applying at the same rate to all products, the choice of either the destination principle or the origin principle will not affect the distribution of resources, or the direction or extent of trade between two countries. There is a monetary difference between the two principles in that a general tax imposed under the origin principle will initially worsen the country's trade balance, causing an offsetting devaluation in its currency, whereas a general tax imposed under the destination principle will have no trade balance repercussions. This is another way of saying that currency depreciation and destination principle border tax adjustments produce the same results. Finally, there is a fiscal difference in that taxes on imports are collected by the destination jurisdiction and the destination jurisdiction collects no taxes on exports.

The choice between the destination and origin principle, however, will have resource allocation and trade balance effects for a tax that does not apply uniformly to all commodities. Since a tax that is treated under the destination principle taxes goods (or services) where they are consumed, a nonuniform tax imposed on the destination basis will alter consumption patterns. In particular, application of the destination principle will decrease consumption and increase net exports of any commodity that is taxed more heavily than average and will increase consumption and decrease net exports of any commodity taxed more lightly than average.

ADDITIONAL READING

Carlson, George N., G. C. Hufbauer, and K. B. Krauss. "Destination Principle Border Tax Adjustments for the Corporate Income and Social Security Taxes." Office of Tax Analysis paper no. 20. Washington, DC: Office of Tax Analysis, 1976.

Cross-references: border tax adjustments; capital export neutrality; consumption taxation; origin principle; residence principle; telecommunications and electronic commerce, state taxation of; value-added tax, national; value-added tax, state.

Dividends, double taxation of

Joseph J. Cordes
George Washington University

Taxation that comes about in the U.S. tax system because corporate profits are taxed once by the corporate income tax and then again when these profits are distributed to shareholders.

Income corporations earn in the United States is currently subject to two levels of tax. Corporate profits are subject to the corporate income tax. When these profits are distributed to the shareholders who own the corporations, these distributions are also included in the shareholders' taxable income.

The consequence of this system is that the return on equity investments in corporate activities is taxed twice. For example, if the statutory corporate tax rate is 34 percent and the personal tax rate is 33 percent, one dollar of corporate earnings is first reduced by 34 cents in corporate profits taxes, which leaves the corporation with 66 cents that can either be kept as retained earnings or paid out in dividends. If the 66 cents is paid out in dividends, this amount would be included in a shareholders' taxable income and would be subject to the personal tax of 33 percent, leaving the shareholder with 44 cents. This situation may be contrasted with a dollar that is earned by, for example, a business that is not incorporated. In that case, one dollar of earnings would be subject only to the personal income tax, and the owners of the unincorporated business would get to keep 66 cents.

Double taxation of corporate earnings has long been considered a nettlesome problem of the U.S. tax system, and it is believed to affect business behavior in several ways. One that has received particular attention is the corporation's decision as to how much of its after-tax earnings to retain and how much to pay out to shareholders in dividends. Another is the corporation's decision about how to finance its investments.

Retained earnings versus dividend payout

One way corporations can reduce the sting of the double tax is to retain earnings rather than pay them out in dividends. If the retained earnings are invested wisely by the corporation, each dollar of retained earnings should increase the value of the firm, which raises its share price. Such price appreciation translates into a capital gain for shareholders; and although capital gains are ultimately subject to tax, they are taxed more lightly than dividends, mainly because of tax deferral. Although retained earnings are neither good nor bad in and of themselves, economists believe that the decision to retain earnings or pay them out should be based on nontax considerations.

Equity versus debt finance

Double taxation also makes equity finance "more costly" to the corporation than debt finance. This is because corporations are allowed to deduct interest payments on corporate taxes as a business expense but are not allowed to take a tax deduction for the costs of equity finance. As a consequence, the returns from corporate investments that are ultimately paid out to bondholders are subject to only one level of tax. In effect, this means that, in order to pay bondholders their required return after tax, one dollar of investment financed by debt needs to earn a lower overall rate of return than does one dollar of investment financed by equity because the dollar financed by debt is subject only to the personal income tax, while the investment dollar financed by equity is subject to both the corporate and personal income taxes.

Policy implications

Double taxation of corporate equity has given rise to calls for integrating the corporate and personal income taxes. This is discussed in more detail in the entry *integration, corporate tax*. The tax system also has features that are designed to attenuate the effects of double taxation, including the tax treatment given to Subchapter S corporations. In 2003, the administration proposed to eliminate the tax on dividends by establishing excludable dividend amounts that would limit benefits to current dividends on income that had been subject to the corporate tax. This approach was needed to prevent firms from paying out previously accumulated earnings and also disallowed the passthrough of preferences. Concerns about complexity and about undermining existing corporate tax incentives led to an alternate proposal to reduce the tax rate on dividends and capital gains to a maximum of 15 percent. This provision is effective through 2008, but may be extended.

ADDITIONAL READINGS

Auerbach, Alan J., and Kevin A. Hassett. "On the Marginal Source of Investment Funds." *Journal of Public Economics* 87, no. 1 (January 2003): 205–32.

Cross-references: dividends-received deduction; income tax, corporate, federal; income tax, federal; integration, corporate tax; Subchapter S corporation.

Dividends-received deduction

George A. Plesko
MIT Sloan School of Management

A deduction corporations may take in some cases for dividends received from another corporation.

The dividends-received deduction (DRD) has been present in some form since the establishment of the corporate income tax in 1909. The rationale for the DRD is to eliminate the possibility of taxing corporate income more than twice—the traditional U.S. approach to corporate income. In the absence of a DRD, intercorporate dividends would be taxed at least three times: first as income to a corporation, then as income to the corporation receiving the distribution, and then again when the income is distributed to the individual shareholders. To the extent there is additional intercorporate ownership, this income could be subject to additional layers of corporate taxation.

The DRD is generally governed by sections 243–246 of the Internal Revenue Code, which define the types of eligible dividends and the holding period requirements (currently 45 days). Allowable deductions vary depending on the type of stock (preferred versus common) and the type of company paying the dividend (public utility, small business, or foreign). Initially, the DRD was equal to 100 percent of all dividends received, but the deduction level has changed, or been restricted, several times since its inception, frequently since 1986. From 1913 to 1917, the DRD was eliminated, but it was reinstated at 100 percent in 1918. The DRD remained at 100 percent until 1937, when it was reduced to 90 percent and later further reduced to 85 percent. In 1965, a two-tier DRD was established, with the allowable exclusion based upon the amount of ownership. If the companies were members of an affiliated group (80 percent or more ownership), the DRD was 100 percent. Dividends from nonaffiliated companies were classified as "portfolio dividends" and subject to an 85 percent deduction. The Tax Reform Act of 1986 reduced the DRD to 80 percent for portfolio dividends. As part of the Omnibus Budget Reconciliation Act of 1987, the DRD for portfolio dividends received or accrued after December 31, 1987, was reduced to 70 percent in the case of ownership of less than 20 percent of the corporation. This ownership-dependent three-tiered level of DRD continues today.

Although interest payments are tax-favored to a corporation, the existence of the DRD creates opportunities for corporations to issue dividend-paying stock that closely resembles debt but has a lower yield. Jassy (1986), for example, has shown how the DRD creates arbitrage opportunities for firms with net operating losses. Since the DRD affects the relative pricing of debt and preferred stock, it gives all firms an opportunity to substitute preferred shares for debt at a potentially lower cost to the firm, and with different financial reporting effects.

ADDITIONAL READINGS

Engel, Ellen, Merle Erickson, and Edward L. Maydew. "Debt-Equity Hybrid Securities." *Journal of Accounting Research* 37, no. 2 (1999): 249–74.

Erickson, Merle, and Edward L. Maydew. "Implicit Taxes in High Dividend Yield Stocks." *Accounting Review* 73, no. 4 (1998): 435–58.

Frischmann, Peter J., Paul D. Kimmel, and Terry D. Warfield. "Innovation in Preferred Stock: Current Developments and Implications for Financial Reporting." *Accounting Horizons* 13, no. 3 (1999): 201–18.

Grubert, Harry. "Enacting Dividend Exemption and Tax Revenue." *National Tax Journal* 54, no. 4 (December 2001): 811–27.

Jassy, Everett L. "Issuances of Floating Rate Preferred Stock by Special Purpose Subsidiaries of Loss Corporations." *Tax Lawyer* 39, no. 3 (1986): 519–62.

Lind, Stephen A., Stephen Schwarz, Daniel J. Lathrope, and Joshua D. Rosenberg. *Fundamentals of Corporate Taxation.* Mineola, NY: Foundation Press, 1987.

Schaffer, D.C. "The Income Tax on Intercorporate Dividends." *Tax Lawyer* 33, no. 1 (1979): 161–82.

Cross-references: dividends, double taxation of; income tax, corporate, federal; integration, corporate tax.

Dynamic revenue estimating

John Diamond

Baker Institute for Public Policy, Rice University

Pamela Moomau

Joint Committee on Taxation, U.S. Congress

Incorporating the effects of policy-induced changes in total economic activity into estimates of the effects of the policy on government budget receipts.

The "revenue estimate" of a proposal to change tax law is the official estimate of the proposal's likely effects on federal government receipts. The budget effects of both revenue and expenditure proposals are estimated as part of the budget process; this entry focuses on dynamic revenue estimating of tax legislation. The Office of Tax Analysis (OTA) in the Department of the Treasury produces executive branch revenue estimates. The staff of the Joint Committee on Taxation (JCT) is responsible for estimating the revenue effects of changes to the Internal Revenue Code for Congressional purposes. The JCT uses baseline economic projections and present law receipts forecasts produced by the Congressional Budget Office (CBO). (See *revenue forecasting, federal* and *revenue estimating, federal.*)

At the federal level, the official revenue estimate of a tax bill can play an important role in the legislative process. (See *budget process, federal.*) Consequently, many public finance economists and members of Congress have become interested in the methodology used for estimating the revenue effects of specific tax proposals. Much of the interest centers on the extent to which revenue estimates account for the potential impact of tax proposals on taxpayer behavior. This interest is mainly driven by the concern that failure to include behavioral responses could produce estimates that are biased against proposals that encourage growth. The inclusion of behavioral responses in revenue estimates is often referred to as "dynamic revenue estimating." However, the connotation of "dynamic revenue estimating" has evolved in recent years to refer specifically to the inclusion of economic growth effects in revenue estimates.

Behavioral assumptions in conventional revenue estimates

Because government budgets use current dollar, cash flow accounting, revenue estimates predict changes in current dollar, cash receipts during the budget period. Tax legislation can affect government receipts directly by changing tax rates, or by changing the definition of income or transactions that are subject to taxation. These types of direct effects are the "static" part of a revenue estimate.

In many cases, tax law changes provide incentives for taxpayers to change their behavior to minimize their tax burden. For example, taxpayers might delay their receipt of income to take advantage of a future decrease in tax rates. If a tax proposal changes the relative treatment of different forms of compensation, taxpayers may shift their forms of compensation to reduce their tax liability. Accelerated depreciation allowances for certain types of investment may encourage more investment in the tax-favored property. In response to an increase in an excise tax on a product, consumers decrease their taxed purchases of the product. While purely static estimates do not take such responses into account, the conventional revenue estimates produced by OTA and JCT do.

All of these behaviors can occur without substantially affecting the total volume of economic activity, or gross national product (GNP), and are sometimes referred to as "microeconomic" behavioral effects. "Macroeconomic" behavioral effects are those that change the total level of economic activity, or GNP. Such effects include an increase in people's willingness to work, an increase in the aggregate level of domestic investment, and changes in the total demand for goods and services. The term "dynamic revenue estimating" generally refers to estimates that incorporate the macroeconomic effects of proposed legislation on the size of the tax base. Conventional revenue estimates do not incorporate effects of macroeconomic behavioral responses on the tax base.

Current state of dynamic revenue estimating

A form of dynamic revenue estimating of recently passed tax legislation is routinely done after the fact by both OTA and CBO, as they incorporate the effects of any legislation that has been enacted into law into semiannual updates of their baseline forecasts for present law receipts. In addition, revenue estimates in the president's budget proposal each year are produced using an economic baseline that incorporates the broad outlines of the tax policy included in the president's budget.

Beginning in 2003, the House of Representatives instituted a rule, House Rule XIII.3.(h)(2), that effectively requires that JCT either provide a supplementary macroeconomic analysis, including dynamic revenue effects, for any tax bill or resolution reported out of the Ways and Means Committee to the House Floor, or that JCT explain why such an analysis would not be "calculable." Accordingly, JCT prepares either a full-scale macroeconomic analysis, including an analysis of the range of possible dynamic revenue effects, or more limited statements regarding the potential macroeconomic effects or lack thereof for bills reported out of the Ways and Means Committee. In 2003 and 2004, CBO has produced dynamic estimates of the president's budget proposals (including both spending and tax provisions) for fiscal years 2004 and 2005, respectively. (See *dynamic scoring.*) There are, however, practical difficulties in producing dynamic revenue estimates for every tax proposal Congress considers.

Two approaches have been suggested to implement dynamic revenue estimating of tax provisions; each has strengths and weaknesses. The first method uses complex computer simulations of the economy to estimate the dynamic effects of tax policy changes. This approach requires detailed modeling of the sources of taxable income (wages, interest, dividends, capital gains, and corporate income) and the relation of taxable income to total income in the economy. It also requires that the models be calibrated so that behavioral responses in the model match empirically estimated responses, and that simulations of the economy under present law produce a reasonable approximation of current economic conditions. The benefit of this approach is that these models are based on economic theory. Such models can include a wide variety of behavioral responses and are capable of examining both individual and corporate tax issues. In addition, some of these models include a monetary sector, and most of them include a government sector so that responses of monetary and government budget policies to tax policy changes can be incorporated in the analysis. However, the complexity of building large-scale models makes it difficult to use this approach for multiple versions of tax proposals in a timely manner that is consistent with the legislative process. The types of economic interactions accounted for differs significantly among the various models currently available. Thus, estimating agencies often use several models to show the range of estimates across modeling structures. For example, see JCT (2003) and CBO (2003). JCT (2003) also provides a detailed list of the issues related to dynamic scoring.

The second approach applies statistically estimated measures of the responsiveness of individual or firm behavior to the applicable tax base for each tax proposal. The assumed responsiveness of taxpayers to each type of proposal is measured from historical data. The appeal of this method is that it is fairly easy to implement in a timely manner, once a reasonable set of response parameters has been estimated. One frequently cited application is the use of an estimated elasticity of taxable income to changes in marginal tax rates on individual income. However, this approach is applicable in only a small subset of tax proposals that Congress considers. For example, this approach would not be useful in determining the effects of changes in the definition of taxable income, deductible expenses, tax credits, the corporate tax rate, and depreciation schedules. Behavioral response parameters comparable to the "taxable income elasticity" for most changes in tax policy other than individual income tax rates have not yet been estimated. This approach often has the additional disadvantage that it does not account for possible interactions between multiple tax provisions within the same tax bill. Finally, this approach ignores several factors that are important in determining the macroeconomic effects of changes in tax policy, such as monetary policy, changes in personal saving

and investment in the long run, and whether changes in tax policy are assumed to be financed with reductions in spending, new government debt issues, or increases in other taxes.

The inability of economists to reach a consensus on the magnitude (and possibly the sign) of certain behavioral responses hampers both of these approaches. The JCT and CBO currently use the first approach, using computer simulation models for macroeconomic analysis.

ADDITIONAL READINGS

Congressional Budget Office. "How CBO Analyzed the Macroeconomic Effects of the President's Budget." Washington, DC: Congressional Budget Office, July 2003.

Joint Committee on Taxation, U.S. Congress. "Overview of Work of the Staff of the Joint Committee on Taxation to Model the Macroeconomic Effects of Proposed Tax Legislation to Comply with House Rule II.i.(h)(2), 2003." JCX-105-03. Washington, DC: Joint Committee on Taxation, December 2003.

Cross-references: budget process, federal; dynamic scoring; revenue estimating, federal; revenue forecasting, federal.

Dynamic scoring

Douglas Holtz-Eakin
Congressional Budget Office

Incorporating macroeconomic feedbacks into estimates of the budgetary impacts of legislation.

Dynamic scoring is one approach to projecting the budgetary impact of legislation. For virtually every bill reported out of committee, the Congressional Budget Office (CBO) provides Congress with an estimate of the legislation's budgetary impact. Those estimates serve as the bill's official "score" in the congressional budget process and consist of a projection of the bill's year-by-year effects on revenues or outlays (excluding interest). Although CBO prepares all estimates of spending proposals, it reports the revenue estimates of the Joint Committee on Taxation (JCT) for most tax legislation. (CBO is required to use JCT's revenue estimates for most tax legislation. In general, JCT estimates the revenue effects of legislation that changes the Internal Revenue Code. CBO estimates the revenue effects of other bills.) Both CBO and JCT also provide numerous informal estimates of proposals earlier in the legislative process to assist policymakers in bill writing.

Baseline versus budget cost estimates

The formal and informal cost estimates complement CBO's semiannual 10-year projections of outlays and revenues. The latter constitute the budget baseline—the budgetary implications of current law for outlays and receipts. The CBO baseline is constructed by developing a projection of the economy that includes overall economic output, the composition of purchases, the composition of incomes, and measures of inflation, interest rates, and other prices. This projection incorporates the impact of current-law policy on the economic decisions of households, firms, and overall economic performance.

Static versus dynamic scoring

Estimates of the budgetary impact of legislation also incorporate a wide array of behavioral responses that affect how much the bill might cost or yield. Under static scoring, those responses comprise four categories of taxpayer reaction. First, the estimates include changes related to the timing of economic activity. For example, a cost estimate of an increase in capital gains taxes takes into account the fact that taxpayers will advance their realizations of gains prior to the effective date of the new, higher tax rate. Second, the estimates include shifts in the composition of economic activity. For example, an estimate of the cost of an expansion of government-provided health insurance includes private-sector responses shifting labor compensation between nontaxable fringe benefits and taxable wages. Third, estimates include any effects on supply and demand. Hence, a cost estimate of an increase in gasoline taxes reflects decreased gasoline consumption as consumers react to the higher price. Finally, estimates include interactions with other provisions of law. Consequently, cost estimates of more rapid depreciation allowances for capital take into account not only the lower income tax receipts that result but also how the reduction in taxable proprietorship income decreases the payroll tax liabilities of the self-employed.

For every piece of legislation, however, the budgetary impacts are estimated using the same, unchanging baseline projections of overall gross domestic product (GDP) and its aggregate income components. Specifically, the estimates do not include the effects of legislation on the supply of labor or on saving (and hence on overall economic growth); they do not include effects on income that might result from the influence outlays and taxes may have on technological progress; they do not include the increases or decreases in output that are caused by the way subsidies or taxes reallocate resources among various activities; they do not include the effects on national saving and other incentive effects that result from the government's financing of the budget change; and they do not include the income and employment effects that arise from the impact of fiscal policy on aggregate spending in the economy in a recession.

In contrast, dynamic scoring would include those macroeconomic feedback effects in formal cost estimates. Thus, the issue of dynamic scoring has a fairly narrow scope both in terms of the types of responses to be considered and the types of budgetary documents that would be affected. At present, neither the CBO nor the JCT conducts dynamic scoring of formal budget estimates. However, these macroeconomic effects are part of the CBO's baseline projections of income, outlays, and revenues. Information on the likely macroeconomic effects of legislation is routinely provided to Congress in the agency's publications. For example, the CBO's "The Budget

and Economic Outlook: An Update," published in August 2001, provided estimates of the likely macroeconomic impact of the Economic Growth and Tax Relief Reconciliation Act of 2001 (EGTRRA) and recent analyses of the impact of the president's budget proposals have included dynamic feedbacks (Congressional Budget Office 2001, 2003, 2004).

Advantages to dynamic scoring

There are important advantages to dynamic scoring. The inclusion of macroeconomic effects allow the budget to better reflect what would actually happen if the legislation was enacted. Improved accuracy is especially significant when legislators seek to offset one budgetary change (e.g., a tax cut) with another (e.g., reduced outlays). Macroeconomic feedbacks affect the magnitude of the offset and therefore sometimes influence the size of the initiative.

Dynamic scoring also helps policymakers compare the relative policy merits of alternative proposals. Proposals with identical static budget costs may have very different economic impacts. For example, not all tax reductions have salutary effects on incentives. Dynamic scoring's explicit consideration of macroeconomic feedbacks can help highlight important policy differences in otherwise comparable proposals.

Issues in the conduct of dynamic scoring

Implementing dynamic scoring as part of formal budget estimates also raises difficult issues. A practical concern is that cost estimates are produced in a short time frame. Cost estimates are part of the legislative process. Thus, they must be produced in time to be useful to legislators in a way that does not hinder the budget process. In this regard, the current practice of leaving macroeconomic effects out of cost estimates has practical benefits. It significantly speeds the process of generating estimates; it imparts a degree of consistency across estimates; and it helps the legislative process by separating revenue and spending measures.

Full dynamic scoring requires using existing approaches to compute the budget changes relevant to decisions about saving, labor supply, and other behaviors. These computations can be used as inputs into macroeconomic models to generate estimates of macroeconomic income and inflation changes. Finally, budget models can then be used to estimate the budgetary impacts of the legislation. In some cases, the procedure involves multiple iterations through these steps. Of course, as the CBO and JCT build a body of modeling expertise, the need for additional iterations may diminish.

Moreover, without a fixed baseline, coordination across cost estimates becomes more difficult and budget scores depend upon the order in which estimates are produced. Currently, because macroeconomic effects are not now included, every cost estimate is based on the same baseline projections of income, interest rates, the price level, and other macroeconomic variables that affect outlays, and receipts are the same for every proposal until the baseline is revised (typically twice a year). If cost estimates were fully dynamic, an enacted proposal would imply new levels of incomes, prices, outlays, and revenues for the baseline; and every other proposal's cost estimate would change. Cost estimates that vary during the course of a session of Congress could significantly burden lawmakers by creating moving targets for financing.

However, adopting conventions that limit the reach of dynamic scoring could reduce both of these problems. Dynamic scoring could be confined to "significant" proposals. (Since 2003, a House of Representatives rule has required the JCT to conduct a dynamic revenue estimate of Ways and Means legislation whenever the effects would be large enough to be "calculable.") But choosing a threshold (e.g., large in absolute impacts or large in percentage impacts?) for deciding what is "significant" raises a host of additional issues.

One issue is that dynamic scoring that includes demand effects requires projections of the future of monetary policy. Projecting the effect of tax changes on demand, income, and prices is complicated by the possible responses of the Federal Reserve. The central bank takes fiscal policy into account along with other factors in determining monetary policy. Thus, a fiscal stimulus might induce the Federal Reserve to undertake a smaller monetary stimulus in which case a tax cut or spending increase might generate little or no incremental effect on demand. Depending on the assumption made about the Federal Reserve's policy, the estimated demand-side effects of a tax change would be very different.

A clear means of dealing with the difficulties raised by demand effects is to produce cost estimates without them. That strategy eliminates the difficulty of trying to judge the Federal Reserve's reaction and focuses dynamic scoring on the supply-side impact on the economy's long-run capacity to produce.

Dynamic scoring also requires projections of future fiscal policy to ensure long-run balance. Over the long term, the federal budget must balance. (More precisely, the ratio of public debt to GDP must stabilize. Any imbalance that satisfies this restriction may be tolerated.) When spending is increased or a tax cut is enacted, any budget loss must be offset by reducing government spending or increasing taxes in the future. The precise choice of financing methods will affect not only the size but possibly the direction of the dynamic budget impact (for example, see Congressional Budget Office 2004).

In contrast to modeling assumptions in dynamic scoring, the financing assumption requires the CBO or JCT to make assumptions about the future acts of Congress. The assumptions adopted may raise the perception of policy advocacy on the part of the budget estimators.

Conclusion

Dynamic scoring of legislation would expand the range of economic behaviors incorporated into estimates of budgetary impacts. Increasing the use of dynamic scoring would potentially increase the accuracy of specific estimates and would enhance legislators' ability to evaluate the policy merits of proposed legislation. However, dynamic scoring would also create a number of problems affecting the timeliness and consistency of the estimation and budget process.

There are steps that can be taken to lessen these concerns. Dynamic estimates might be limited to proposals of a certain size; the estimates could exclude effects on aggregate demand; and the Congress could provide clearer direction about the financing assumptions to be used.

ADDITIONAL READINGS

Congressional Budget Office. "The Budget and Economic Outlook: An Update." Washington, DC: Congressional Budget Office, 2001.
———. "An Analysis of the President's Budgetary Proposals for Fiscal Year 2004." Washington, DC: Congressional Budget Office, 2003.
———. "How CBO Analyzed the Macroeconomic Effects of the President's Budget." Washington, DC: Congressional Budget Office, July 2003.
———. "An Analysis of the President's Budgetary Proposals for Fiscal Year 2005." Washington, DC: Congressional Budget Office, 2004.
———. "Budget and Economic Outlook: Fiscal Years 2006 to 2015." Washington, DC: Congressional Budget Office, 2005.

Cross-references: budget process, federal; budget process, state; dynamic revenue estimating; revenue estimating, federal; revenue estimating, state.

Earmarking of taxes

Frederick Stocker
Ohio State University

Updated by
Steven Maguire
Congressional Research Service

In contrast to the practice of combining all revenues in a general fund and allocating them to expenditures through a budgeting process, earmarking reserves revenues from certain sources for particular expenses.

Earmarking refers to the practice of dedicating a specific stream of tax revenue to a specific expenditure purpose. The most common contemporary example is the dedication of highway revenues (gas taxes, motor vehicle registration fees) to the construction and maintenance of streets and highways.

Earmarking is important in state and local fiscal systems. In 1993, 24 percent of state tax revenue came from earmarked sources, a share that remained more or less stable for a decade but was far below the 51 percent share for 1954. The earmarked share exceeded 50 percent in five states and was less than 10 percent in eight (National Conference of State Legislatures 1995).

State taxes most often earmarked are excise taxes on motor fuel, tobacco, alcoholic beverages, and insurance. Among broad-based taxes, the most significant are state general sales taxes and corporate income taxes, although typically only a small portion of revenue from these sources is earmarked. By state program area, earmarking is most extensive in connection with highways and local government assistance.

Earmarking provisions are sometimes contained in state constitutions, sometimes in the statutes. The former are obviously more restrictive and more durable.

At the federal level, examples of earmarking are found in the Old Age, Survivors, Disability, and Health Insurance programs, where payroll taxes are set aside in trust funds. The Highway Trust Fund and the Airport and Airway Trust Fund are other major examples.

Generally, public finance and public administration experts disapprove of earmarking on the grounds that it rigidifies the public budget, depriving elected officials of the freedom to allocate funds among competing expenditure programs in ac-

cordance with currently perceived needs. It causes some parts of the budget to be overfunded relative to what elected representatives would otherwise have appropriated, and other parts to be underfunded.

Also, earmarking is criticized for removing part of the public budget from the same legislative scrutiny and oversight given to general fund expenditures. It is for these same reasons that proponents of certain government programs often favor earmarking as a guarantee that their function will receive continued funding, regardless of shifting legislative priorities. Earmarking revenues for a popular cause (e.g., education) to help pass an otherwise unpopular general tax increase is also a common practice.

Many faces of earmarking

Earmarking is not a single, clearly defined phenomenon; rather, it covers many different fiscal practices and institutional arrangements. At one extreme, earmarking can be thought of as essentially what happens in private market exchange, where proceeds from the sale of privately produced goods are "earmarked" to finance production costs. In the public sector, a common form of earmarking occurs in such enterprises as water and sewer systems, transit systems, and the like, where user revenues are dedicated to production of an essentially private good.

Similarly, special districts (transit districts, airport districts) illustrate a form of earmarking in that their revenues, most commonly user charges but sometimes including general tax levies, are set aside for support of the special purposes of the district.

Although rarely referred to as "earmarking," clearly all revenue received by school districts is dedicated to education purposes.

Special levies of units of general government (a state, county, or city) can also be said to be earmarked to their designated purpose. An example is a county property tax levy for children's services. Earmarking is a central feature of "tax increment financing," whereby taxes a business pays are used to pay the costs that the government incurs in providing it with facilities and services (e.g., job training).

All bond issues involve earmarking, most clearly in the case of revenue bonds (where debt service is met from a specified revenue stream) but also with general obligation debt, where a portion of general tax revenues is pledged to meet interest and principal. This is perhaps the least controversial form of earmarking.

While these examples indicate the pervasive nature of earmarking, most debate has focused on earmarking revenues for services that demonstrate a high degree of publicness and for which the quid pro quo is far from clear. We find a continuum ranging from situations in which benefit taxes are feasible and acceptable (the gas tax applied to highway expenditures), through taxes where there is a less clear but still plausible connection with the designated purpose (setting aside hunting and fishing license revenues for outdoor recreation programs and facilities), to those where there is no logical connection at all (earmarking lottery profits for education or for social services to the elderly).

The benefits basis of earmarking

Earmarking finds its strongest equity rationale in the benefits connection, where it extends the quid-pro-quo concept (the accepted basis for private market transactions) into the tax-financed sector. Dedication of highway user tax revenues for highway purposes represents the benefit principle at its best (notwithstanding the tenuous relationship between taxes paid and benefits received by different categories of highway users). The equity rationale for earmarking general taxes finds its limit in the fact that there are very few services or facilities for which there is a corresponding "earmarkable" tax.

Earmarking and the allocation of resources

The conventional indictment of earmarking is that it *presumptively* distorts budget allocations in a less efficient direction by constraining decisions of the legislature. This indictment, however, is not always pertinent because earmarking often does not apply to *marginal* dollars. If revenues from the earmarked source are less than the legislature would have appropriated in any case, earmarking does not increase the total funding, except perhaps temporarily. Its role is purely cosmetic. The classic example is the earmarking of lottery profits for education. Research has also shown that earmarked tax increases or new taxes do not necessarily increase public spending on the targeted budget item. In most cases, earmarked taxes substitute for some other tax.

While earmarking may not increase total funds for the targeted function, it may nevertheless weaken opposition to particular revenue measures that otherwise would fail. Earmarking profits from (taxes on) gambling clearly aids legalization of such activities. The time-honored practice of selling a new tax by earmarking the money for education is a familiar if transparent stratagem for softening taxpayer resistance. To the extent that this ruse succeeds, the earmarked function presumably shares in the additional funds to at least the same extent that it would in any revenue gain from nonearmarked sources.

From the standpoint of economic efficiency, such uses of earmarking are criticized as "little more than fraud," leading to a counterefficient tendency to overtax and overspend (Oakland 1985). This criticism presumes (1) that earmarking does in fact increase political support for the tax increase and (2) that increased revenues produce an inefficient overexpansion in the public budget rather than a correction of some (yet to be explained) tendency to underfinance the public sector.

Earmarking has been defended as a strategy for "unbundling" items in the public budget. If public expenditures were financed through a system in which citizens voted directly on a series of tax/expenditure issues, the "package deal" that characterizes government general fund budgets could be avoided (Buchanan 1963). Voters would be given wider scope for public choice, and the resulting budget allocations would, arguably, more accurately reflect citizen preferences. This thesis argues the advisability of presenting voters a number of discrete programs or projects, each accompanied by a tax, rather than an omnibus package.

In recent years, this view has gained acceptance, perhaps reflecting growing skepticism by the public that their elected representatives are capable of spending tax money wisely, where it does the most good. General tax levies have had less success in the legislatures and at the polls than those earmarked for specifically designated purposes. If this trend continues, earmarking will become more prevalent in state/local fiscal systems.

Underlying the earmarking question is the perennial conflict between rules and discretion in public-sector decisionmaking. Constitutional and, to a lesser extent, statutory earmarking provides a rule constraint on legislative action or direct democracy. The absence of such constraints leaves revenue allocation to discretionary choice. Conflicting preferences in this matter are likely to continue.

ADDITIONAL READINGS

Bird, Richard M., and Joosung Jun. "Earmarking in Theory and Korean Practice." A paper prepared for the Asian Excise Tax Conference. Singapore: International Tax and Investment Center and Centre for Commercial Law Studies, National University of Singapore, 2000.

Borg, Mary O., and Paul M. Mason. "The Budgetary Incidence of a Lottery to Support Education." *National Tax Journal* 41 (March 1998): 75–85.

Buchanan, James M. "The Economics of Earmarked Taxes." *Journal of Political Economy* 71 (October 1963): 457–69.

Ebel, Robert D. "Earmarking of Taxes." In *A Fiscal Agenda for Nevada,* edited by Robert D. Ebel. Reno: University of Nevada Press, 1990.

Jung, Changhoon. "The Effect of Local Earmarking on Capital Spending in Georgia Counties." *State and Local Government Review* 34, no. 1 (Winter 2002): 29–37.

National Conference of State Legislatures. *Earmarking of State Taxes.* Denver, 1995.

Oakland, William H. "Earmarking and Decentralization." In *Proceedings of the Seventy-Seventh Annual Conference* (274–77). Columbus, OH: National Tax Association, 1985.

Cross-references: benefit principle; budget processes, state; user charges, federal.

Earned income tax credit

Jonathan Barry Forman

University of Oklahoma College of Law

A refundable income tax credit for low-income working taxpayers.

The earned income tax credit (EITC) was originally enacted in 1975, and over the years it has grown to be one of the principal antipoverty programs in the federal budget. The credit underwent significant expansions in 1990 and 1993. In 2003, some 19 million taxpayers were expected to claim more than $34 billion of earned income credits, with an average credit per taxpayer of $1,784 per year (U.S. Congress 2004). In 2004, some families will be entitled to claim an earned income credit of up to $4,300 per year (IRS 2003).

Unlike most other tax credits for individuals, the earned income credit is refundable. That is, if the earned income credit exceeds the taxpayer's tax liability, the Internal Revenue Service (IRS) will refund the difference. In 2003, of the roughly $34 billion of earned income credits claimed, almost $31 billion was attributable to the portion of the credit that exceeds taxpayers' tax liabilities (U.S. Congress 2004).

The statute provides that a taxpayer's earned income credit will equal a specified percentage of the taxpayer's earned income up to a maximum dollar amount (U.S. Code, Title 26, Section 32). The maximum credit amount is available to taxpayers over a certain income range and is phased out as a taxpayer's income increases beyond a specified phaseout floor. The IRS publishes tables each year to help taxpayers and their employers determine the proper amount of credit.

Six separate schedules apply, depending on how many qualifying children the taxpayer has and the marital status of the taxpayer. For 2004, a family with two or more qualifying children is entitled to claim an earned income credit of up to $4,300 (IRS 2003). The credit is computed as 40 percent of the first $10,750 of earned income. For married couples filing joint returns, the maximum credit is reduced by 21.06 percent of earned income (or adjusted gross income, if greater) in excess of $15,040 and is entirely phased out at $35,458 of income. For heads of household, the maximum credit phases out over the range from $14,040 to $34,458.

Similarly, a family with one child is entitled to an earned income credit of up to $2,604. The credit is computed as 34 percent of the first $7,660 of earned income. For married couples filing joint returns, the maximum credit is reduced by 15.98 percent of earned income (or adjusted gross income, if greater) in excess of $15,040 and is entirely phased out at $31,338 of income. For heads of household, the maximum credit phases out over the range from $14,040 to $30,338.

Childless individuals between the ages of 25 and 65 are entitled to an earned tax income credit of up to $390. The credit is computed as 7.65 percent of the first $5,100 of earned income. For married couples filing joint returns, the maximum

credit is reduced by 7.65 percent of earned income (or adjusted gross income, if greater) in excess of $7,390 and is entirely phased out at $12,490 of income. For heads of household and single individuals, the maximum credit phases out over the range from $6,390 to $11,490.

These maximum earned income credit amounts will expand even beyond 2004, as the applicable earned income and phaseout amounts are indexed for inflation.

To be a "qualifying child" within the meaning of the earned income credit, an individual must satisfy three tests: relationship, residency, and age. The relationship test is satisfied if the child is the taxpayer's child, stepchild, or a descendant of a child or of a sibling or stepsibling. The residency test is satisfied if the child has lived with the taxpayer at least one-half of the taxable year, in a household located in the United States. The age test is satisfied if the child is (1) under age 19, (2) a full-time student under age 24, or (3) permanently and totally disabled. Also, to be eligible for the credit, childless taxpayers must be at least age 25 but under age 65. One result is that many low-income workers, even those who pay taxes, may be left out of the EITC.

The earned income credit is available to both employees and independent contractors, as the term "earned income" is defined to include wages, salaries, tips, and other employee compensation, and the net earnings from self-employment. To claim the credit, a taxpayer must file IRS Form 1040 or Form 1040A. Taxpayers with children must also fill out Schedule EIC to claim the credit.

Taxpayers with children may elect to receive advance payment of a portion of their earned income credit in their paychecks throughout the year. To receive the credit in advance, a taxpayer must fill out IRS Form W-5, the Earned Income Credit Advance Payment Certificate, and give it to his or her employer. The employer then includes a portion of the employee's advance earned income credit amount along with wages, and the remainder of the credit is refunded only after the taxpayer files an income tax return. The IRS publishes tables to help employers determine the proper amount of advance payment. For example, an employee earning between $147 and $270 a week in 2004 gets a $30 per week paycheck increase by electing to receive advance payment of the credit. In practice, this option is rarely used, in part because it leads to added complexity since the taxpayer must also still file the EITC form; the General Accounting Office reports that fewer than 1 percent of those eligible for the EITC elect advance payment.

History of the credit

The earned income credit grew out of the welfare reform efforts of the early 1970s (Forman 1988). The credit was originally added to the Internal Revenue Code by the Tax Reduction Act of 1975. Over the years, the credit has been expanded, and it is now one of the principal antipoverty programs in the federal budget for working families.

As originally adopted in 1975, the earned income credit was intended to offset the Social Security taxes of low-income workers with children and to provide those taxpayers with an increased incentive to work. An eligible taxpayer could claim a refundable credit equal to 10 percent of the taxpayer's earned income for the taxable year, which did not exceed $4,000 (a maximum credit of $400). That $400 maximum credit was reduced $1 for each $10 of income in excess of $4,000. Thus, the credit was completely phased out at an income level of $8,000. As enacted, the original earned income credit was available to taxpayers only for calendar year 1975.

Subsequent revenue acts extended the credit, and the Revenue Act of 1978 made it a permanent part of the Internal Revenue Code. The Deficit Reduction Act of 1984 increased the maximum amount of the earned income credit and renumbered it to its current location in the Internal Revenue Code (U.S. Code, Title 26, Section 32). The Tax Reform Act of 1986 expanded the credit significantly, and it has been indexed for inflation since 1987.

The Omnibus Budget Reconciliation Act of 1990 also expanded the credit and added a supplemental credit amount for families with two or more children. The Omnibus Budget Reconciliation Act of 1993 expanded the credit even further and made a small credit available to certain childless workers (up to $390 in 2004). The Taxpayer Relief Act of 1997 added provisions to improve compliance, and the Economic Growth and Tax Relief and Reconciliation Act of 2001 made changes to provide marriage penalty relief and promote simplification. By 2003, more than 19 million families were expected to claim over $34 billion of earned income credits, with an average credit per family of $1,784 (U.S. Congress 2004).

Analysis

The earned income credit is an income transfer program that provides significant financial assistance to low-income workers, especially those with children. Unlike increasing the minimum wage, the expansion of the earned income credit over the past two decades has provided benefits targeted to help the working poor. Also, unlike most other welfare programs or a negative income tax, the earned income credit provides significant work incentives to low-income workers (Forman 1988).

The earned income credit is not without its problems. For example, the General Accounting Office has estimated that only about 75 percent of households eligible for the credit actually claimed it in 1999 (U.S. General Accounting Office 2001). Households with one or two qualifying children had the highest participation rates—96 and 93 percent, respectively. But only 62.5 percent of eligible households with three or more children claimed the credit in 1999, and only 44.7 percent of eligible childless households claimed it. While these are still relatively high participation rates when compared with

other transfer programs such as food stamps and Temporary Assistance for Needy Families (TANF), it still means that some 4.3 million eligible households failed to claim the credit in 1999. Moreover, remarkably few taxpayers elect to receive their credits by means of the advance payment mechanism.

Compliance with the earned income credit is also a problem. For example, IRS audit data for 1999 show earned income credit overclaim rates estimated to be between 27 and 32 percent of dollars claimed or between $8.5 billion and $9.9 billion (U.S. General Accounting Office 2003). Compliance with the advance payment rules is also problematic. For example, an estimated 49 percent of the individuals who filed income tax returns in 1989 and who had definitely received the advance payment failed to report that receipt on their return, and an estimated 45 percent of those who had received advance payment of the credit failed to even file returns (U.S. General Accounting Office 1992).

Finally, the earned income credit has also been implicated in some perverse disincentives for work and marriage. While the credit unequivocally increases the incentive to work in the phase in range of the credit (up to $10,750 of earnings for workers with two children in 2004), the combination of income and Social Security taxes and the phaseout of the credit may discourage work by an even greater number of relatively low-income workers falling in the applicable phaseout ranges (e.g., from $15,040 to $35,458 of earnings for married workers with two or more children in 2004) (Eissa 1996). Lowering the phaseout rate could reduce this work disincentive, but it would also stretch out the phaseout range, which in turn would subject more taxpayers to the lowered phaseout rate.

Worse still is the earned income credit's impact on marriage. For example, in 2004, if a single father with two children and $15,000 of earnings marries a single mother with two children and $15,000 of earnings, the couple will face a huge marriage penalty. Before the marriage, each could claim a refundable earned income credit of $4,098 (in 2004). After the marriage, the couple would only be able to claim a single earned income credit of just $1,149. So far, however, the empirical research has not been able to find much impact of the earned income credit's marriage penalties and bonuses on marriage and divorce (Dickert-Conlin and Houser 2002).

Given the concerns about participation, compliance, and disincentives for work and marriage, it seems likely that Congress will reconsider the credit's operation in coming years. One option would be to replace the current earned income credit with an exemption from Social Security taxes for the first $10,000 of wages, and to supplement the exemption with a refundable family allowance tax credit based upon the number of children in the family (Yin et al. 1994). This approach would reduce marginal tax rates and their disincentive effects on low-income workers. Moreover, a Social Security tax exemption would reach 100 percent of low-income workers, and it would be less complicated than first collecting Social Security taxes and then using the earned income credit to refund them.

ADDITIONAL READINGS

Dickert-Conlin, Stacy, and Scott Houser. "EITC and Marriage." *National Tax Journal* 55, no. 1 (March 2002): 25–40.

Eissa, Nada. "Tax Reforms and Labor Supply." In *Tax Policy and the Economy 10,* edited by James Poterba (119–51). Cambridge, MA: MIT Press, 1996.

Forman, Jonathan Barry. "Improving the Earned Income Credit: Transition to a Wage Subsidy Credit for the Working Poor." *Florida State University Law Review* 16, no. 1 (1988): 41–101.

Internal Revenue Service. "Revenue Procedure 2003-85." *Internal Revenue Bulletin 2003-49* (2003): 1184–90.

U.S. Code, Title 26, Section 32.

U.S. Congress, House of Representatives, Committee on Ways and Means. *2004 Green Book: Background Material and Data on Programs within the Jurisdiction of the Committee on Ways and Means.* Washington, DC: U.S. Government Printing Office, 2004. http://waysandmeans.house.gov/Documents.asp?section=813.

U.S. General Accounting Office. "Earned Income Tax Credit: Advance Payment Option Is Not Widely Known or Understood by the Public." GAO/GGD-92-26. Washington, DC: U.S. General Accounting Office, 1992.

———. "Earned Income Tax Credit Participation." GAO-02-290R. Washington, DC: U.S. General Accounting Office, 2001.

———. "Earned Income Tax Credit: Qualifying Child Certification Test Appears Justified, but Evaluation Plan Is Incomplete." GAO-03-794. Washington, DC: U.S. General Accounting Office, September 2003.

Ventry, Dennis J., et al. "Special Issue: The Earned Income Tax Credit." *National Tax Journal* 53, no. 4 (December 2000): 973–1265.

Yin, George K., John Karl Scholz, Jonathan Barry Forman, and Mark J. Mazur. "Improving the Delivery of Benefits to the Working Poor: Proposals to Reform the Earned Income Tax Credit Program." *American Journal of Tax Policy* 11, no. 2 (1994): 225–98.

Cross-references: budget process, federal; fairness in taxation; labor supply, taxes and; progressivity, measures of; tax equity analysis.

Earnings and profits

Mark B. Booth
Congressional Budget Office

A tax accounting concept to identify corporate distributions to shareholders as either ordinary income or capital.

When a corporation distributes cash or other property to a shareholder, it must, for tax purposes, classify the distribution as either a dividend or a return of capital. To classify distributions, corporations must compute a measure from the Internal Revenue Code called "earnings and profits" (E&P), which represents either a flow of annual income, called "current E&P," or a cumulative amount of income, called "accumulated E&P," measured as accruing from the beginning of the federal income tax in 1913. The classification has important federal tax consequences for shareholders. Individuals, for example, generally pay tax at ordinary income tax rates on dividends, pay no tax on a return of capital that is less than their invested basis, and pay tax at a limited rate on capital gains. The classification has less importance for tax years 2003 through 2008 as a result of the Jobs and Growth Tax Relief Reconciliation Act of 2003. That legislation temporarily set the tax rate on qualifying div-

idends at the same limited rate that applies to most capital gains. E&P has several other applications in the federal tax code unrelated to classifying dividends, such as determining a part of the base of the alternative minimum tax for corporations (see *adjusted current earnings*), but those applications are much more limited in scope and are not discussed in detail here.

The tax code limits dividends to that being paid out of a corporation's current or accumulated E&P. No limit applies, for example, if a corporation has a positive balance of accumulated E&P or a positive amount of current E&P in the year of distribution (both as measured before deducting distributions), and its annual distributions do not exceed either measure: those annual distributions are considered dividends for tax purposes. The limit to the amount of distributions that must be considered dividends is called the "E&P limitation," and it has changed little since 1936. In determining the classification of a distribution, a corporation first compares the value of the distribution with its current E&P. If none or only a portion of the distribution is considered a dividend under that test, the corporation then compares the distribution with accumulated E&P to determine if a greater portion qualifies as a dividend. If only a portion of a corporation's total distributions are dividends, certain rules are applied to allocate the distribution types and amounts to specific shareholders based on factors including the chronological order of distribution and the E&P limit exceeded.

The computation

A corporation generally computes its current E&P the way it computes its taxable income; however, it may not use the tax-preferred treatment of certain income and expenses that the tax code does allow for when calculating taxable income. It also must make other adjustments to its taxable income. These changes make current E&P correspond more closely to economic income than taxable income. Accumulated E&P is computed by adding up all the annual amounts of current E&P, be they positive or negative (loss).

Accelerated depreciation generates the most significant difference between current E&P and taxable income. When calculating current E&P, a corporation must depreciate its assets using a straight-line method. In addition, tax-exempt interest income, such as from municipal bonds or life insurance contracts, must be included in E&P. Also, when calculating current E&P, corporations may not account for income using the preferential completed contract or installment sales methods of accounting, and those in the extractive industries may not use the preferential treatment of costs termed "percentage depletion." Additional differences include the treatment of charitable contributions and capital losses. Federal income taxes and distributions themselves are also deducted to determine current E&P.

The E&P limitation defines dividends as being paid out of a corporation's economic income earned either during the year of distribution or over the entire period since 1913. If a distribution exceeds the E&P limitation, the excess is considered a return of capital that the shareholder contributed to the corporation. The shareholder is not subject to tax, up to the amount of the shareholder's invested basis in the corporation. If the distribution also exceeds the basis of the shareholder's investment, then the excess is taxed as a capital gain to the shareholder.

Criticisms of E&P and the limitation

The measure of E&P is criticized as being too complex and costly for corporations to compute. Corporate reorganizations in particular add to the complexity.

The E&P limitation is also imprecise when applied to specific distributions. Corporations—especially large, publicly traded ones—often experience rapid turnover of their shareholders, and the annual and cumulative measures of E&P do not track the transactions between corporations and specific shareholders well. For example, a shareholder may purchase stock in a corporation that recorded large losses in E&P in the first year of ownership, but at least a portion of any distribution that year would still be a taxable dividend if the corporation had remaining accumulated E&P; so too would a distribution in subsequent years, regardless of accumulated E&P, if the corporation then recorded even small current gains.

Possible reforms

Requiring corporations to allocate specific distributions to the earnings and investments of specific shareholders would impose an administrative burden that is generally considered to be prohibitively expensive. Short of that reform, it is not clear that incremental changes to the E&P limitation would significantly improve its precision. To reduce the complexity of the federal tax code, several groups and individual analysts over the years have endorsed the complete elimination of the measure of E&P and the E&P limitation. One alternative would be to tax all (nonliquidating) distributions as dividends, but that treatment would treat true returns of capital as taxable income to shareholders. Another alternative would be to rely on state law defining dividend distributions, but that treatment might be difficult to enforce and could encourage tax avoidance strategies because federal income tax rates are much higher than those of the states.

If policymakers eliminated or reformed the use of E&P, other applications of E&P in the tax code would also need to be addressed, including the alternative minimum tax and foreign tax credit.

ADDITIONAL READINGS

American Bar Association, Section on Taxation, Earnings, and Profits Work Group. "Elimination of 'Earnings and Profits' from the Internal Revenue Code." *Tax Lawyer* (Winter 1986): 285–330.

Blum, Walter J. "The Earnings and Profits Limitation on Dividend Income: A Reappraisal." *Taxes* (February 1975): 68–87.

Schwartz, Stephen, and Daniel J. Lathrope. *Corporate and Partnership Taxation,* 4th ed. Eagan, MN: Thomson West, 2003.

U.S. Department of the Treasury. "Integration of the Individual and Corporate Tax Systems." Washington, DC: U.S. Government Printing Office, January 1992.

Cross-references: adjusted current earnings; alternative minimum tax, corporate.

Economic substance doctrine

Joseph Bankman
Stanford Law School

A doctrine that allows the government to disregard the tax consequences of transactions that have no significant nontax purpose or effect.

The income tax might be thought of as a set of interrelated but quite specific rules. The use of rules rather than standards provides certainty that both business and individual taxpayers value. In general, even a rule that produces an unintended and undesirable result remains good law until it is withdrawn or amended. In some cases, however, where the unintended result of a rule is to form the basis for a tax shelter—a transaction unrelated to the taxpayer's business that is designed to produce a tax (but not economic) loss—the government may challenge the transaction under the judge-made economic substance doctrine. The government may also rely on a number of closely related doctrines, such as the business purpose doctrine, described more fully in Bankman (2000). That doctrine, briefly stated, allows the government to disregard the tax consequences of transactions that have no significant nontax purpose or effect. Thus, the economic substance doctrine limits the loss to the fisc from a badly designed rule. It does not attack the rule per se, but attacks tax-motivated transactions designed to exploit the rule.

A good example of the use and limitation of the economic substance doctrine can be found in a recent case, *ACM v. Commissioner* (157 F.3d 231, 3rd Cir. 1998). The facts of that case, simplified here for expositional purposes, were as follows: In 1998, Colgate-Palmolive formed a partnership, the partners of which included itself, a wholly owned subsidiary, and a foreign bank not subject to U.S. tax. The partnership bought $250 million of publicly traded Citicorp debt, and sold the debt a few months later for $225 million cash and a contingent installment payment due in a later year with a fair market value of $25 million. The sale generated no significant gain or loss for financial reporting purposes. Treasury regulations then in effect established a default rule in which the basis, or cost, of property sold in a contingent sale was allocated equally to each payment. The result was that only $125 million of the partnership's $250 million basis for the property was allocated to the first payment of $225 million, producing a gain of $100 million in the year of sale; the remaining $125 million of the partnership's basis for the property was allocated to the later payment of $25 million, producing a loss of $100 million in that later year. The partnership agreement allocated all the gain and loss to the foreign bank not subject to U.S. tax. However, after absorbing the $100 million gain, the bank sold its interest back to the partnership, leaving Colgate and its subsidiary to recognize the $100 million loss on the back end. Colgate used this loss to shelter gain recognized on the sale of a subsidiary.

The drafters of the regulation realized that, in any given year, the equal-recovery-of-cost rule might produce a mismatch between economic gain and tax gain, and included a provision that allowed a taxpayer to petition out of the rule in those situations. Unfortunately, however, the drafters of the regulation neglected to provide the government any means of voiding the equal-recovery-of-cost rule.

All aspects of the transaction were structured ahead of time by Merrill Lynch, which also provided that the foreign taxpayer absorb the income. Colgate paid Merrill Lynch approximately $2 million in fees and incurred another $2 million of transaction costs to engineer the deal. Evidence introduced at the trial showed that Merrill Lynch had structured nearly identical transactions for 10 other domestic corporations.

The government argued that the transaction lacked economic substance because its only significant motivation or effect was to help Colgate avoid paying tax, and the court agreed.

Ambiguities in the doctrine

The economic substance doctrine is far from perfect. It contains a number of structural ambiguities that make the doctrine difficult to apply in many cases. First, the doctrine does not specify what imbues a transaction with economic substance. Profit equal to the riskless rate of return? The amount of profit on the same investment made in a manner that does not avoid taxes? The amount of profit realized on an alternative tax-favored investment?

Second, as suggested by the last question, the doctrine co-exists uneasily with the fact that tax advantages are embedded in asset prices and reduce before-tax return. An investment explicitly granted a tax break by Congress (such as an investment in low-income housing, which is eligible for a tax credit) may be expected to offer a low, or even negative, before-tax rate of return. The purpose of the tax break is to motivate investment. As a consequence, the presence of tax motivation cannot be grounds for denying the tax benefit, and hence the economic substance doctrine cannot apply in this sort of case. More broadly, the doctrine must be read to provide an exception for any set of transactions that are consistent with legislative intent. In many cases, litigation under the doctrine requires determination of the legislative intent behind the rule on which the transaction is based.

Third, the doctrine does not specify the scope of the transaction that must have economic substance. Taxpayers may be expected to tie the suspect transaction to other transactions, and

argue that the linked transactions together have economic substance. In *ACM*, for example, Colgate argued that the temporary investment in Citicorp debt, which gave rise to the tax loss, was tied to a later investment by the same partnership in Colgate debt, and that the tied investments together had economic substance.

Other approaches

The ambiguities stated above, as well as other ambiguities, have led some critics to urge that the doctrine be abandoned in favor of a strict literalist approach to the law. The remedy for bad rules, it is argued, is to write better rules. The difficulty with this position is that the current law contains tens of thousands of separate rules, many of which are decades old. Some of these rules worked well enough when they were drafted, but today are fodder for tax shelters. Other rules were badly drafted even then, and now wait to be discovered by the tax shelter community. It would not be economically feasible (or even possible) to locate all the faulty rules. It is possible, of course, to rewrite each faulty rule once it serves as the basis for a tax shelter, so that the life of the tax shelter is short, and indeed the government routinely does so. But that process will not safeguard the fisc. At equilibrium, there will always be one or more extant tax shelters. If the taxpayer's literalist reading of the statute is accepted and the economic substance doctrine or other similar doctrines are thrown out, then these shelters will work, and the revenue loss will be enormous. A single class of shelter could eliminate most of the corporate tax base in a matter of months. Major tax reform (e.g., moving to a cash flow tax or a mark-to-market system) would give the system a clean start and reduce the possibilities for shelter. However, that sort of reform is nowhere on the horizon, and even under the most coherent tax system, rules will be miswritten and generate new shelter opportunities.

Others have urged that the economic substance doctrine be dropped in favor of antiabuse doctrines of more limited scope. In fact, such doctrines already play an important role in the tax law. Unfortunately, within their limited domain, these doctrines are prey to some of the same ambiguities that plague the economic substance doctrine (see Bankman 2004).

Another possibility would be to replace the economic substance doctrine with a more explicit intent or purpose-based interpretive theory. The government would then no longer have to fight the application of badly written rules only when they were used in stand-alone transactions without economic substance. It could instead attack the misuse of the rule even when tied to normal business operations. This, however, would deviate far from a rule-based system and for that reason is not viewed as a serious policy option.

Current and future utility of the doctrine

Notwithstanding its flaws, the economic substance doctrine has worked out surprisingly well. Courts have relied upon the doctrine to deny billions of dollars in shelter losses, and the presence of those cases has helped convince taxpayers to settle other cases, also involving billions of dollars of tax losses. The reason the doctrine has worked so well is that the cases litigated thus far have involved shelters with no connection to the taxpayer's ordinary business, and no meaningful investment of any kind. As a result, the shelters have offered no real possibility of economic profit aside from avoiding tax, particularly once the promoter fees and transaction costs are taken into account. In addition, taxpayers have made the courts' task easier by leaving paper trails showing a lack of business motivation.

Unfortunately, tomorrow's shelters are unlikely to present such an easy case. To understand how sensitive the economic substance doctrine is to changes in shelter design, it might be useful to again consider the shelter in *ACM,* in which Colgate sought to offset a gain realized on the sale of a subsidiary by buying and then selling Citicorp debt, and structuring that latter sale to take advantage of a badly written regulation. If Colgate had held the debt for a year before selling it, it would have realized interest income in excess of the fees and transaction costs. This would have raised the "how much profit?" ambiguity in the doctrine described above, and made the successful application of the doctrine to that transaction less likely. Indeed, Colgate could have avoided the application of the doctrine entirely had it been able to structure the earlier sale of the subsidiary in the same way it structured the sale of the Citicorp debt. The subsidiary sale had an economic motive, so the fact that the sale was made to take advantage of a faulty regulation would have been irrelevant.

It is presumably costly to put business risk in a tax shelter, or to integrate aggressive tax planning in ordinary business operations—otherwise we would see that mix in today's tax shelters. But faced with the string of government court victories against the current generation of shelters, and with billions of dollars of taxes at stake, we may expect many taxpayers to incur that cost.

There is another cloud hanging over the economic substance doctrine. Support for literal interpretation of statutes and regulations has increased dramatically within the tax field. This mirrors a general trend in law (Bankman 2001). The trend is particularly pronounced in recent judicial appointments. The economic substance doctrine, of course, is used to deny benefits realized under a literal interpretation of a governing statute or rule. No court has yet rejected the doctrine, although some courts have found the doctrine inapposite to the case presented, and other courts have found the transactions in question to have passed muster under the doctrine. However, faced with increasingly hard cases, one or more courts may reject the doctrine as overly vague and without statutory support. We may expect, in that case, to see an immediate explosion in tax shelter use.

ADDITIONAL READINGS

Bankman, Joseph. "The Economic Substance Doctrine." *U.S.C. Law Review* 74, no. 5 (2000): 5–30.

———. "The Business Purpose Doctrine and the Sociology of Tax." *S.M.U. Law Review* 45, no. 1 (2001): 149–57.

———. "The Tax Shelter Battle." In *The Crisis in Tax Administration,* edited by Henry Aaron and Joel Slemrod (9–37). Washington, DC: The Brookings Institution, 2004.

Cross-references: nexus; tax.

Education financing, state and local

Sheila Murray
The RAND Corporation

Yas Nakib
George Washington University

Kim Rueben
The Urban Institute and Public Policy Institute of California

The financing of primary and secondary education, focusing on the roles courts have played in changing funding sources.

The financing of primary and secondary schooling in the United States is almost exclusively the responsibility of state and local governments. This reliance on state and local revenue can be traced to the 10th Amendment of the U.S. Constitution, which reserves for the states all functions not expressly granted to the federal government. As such, education became a state responsibility and each state has established a system of state and local finance in which local school districts have significant responsibility for raising school funds and deciding how those funds are spent. Local control of key educational decisions led to significant differences in education spending among districts within and across states. These disparities have come under legal scrutiny, and, over the past three decades, this has led to an increasing role of state governments in school finance.

A short history of school finance reform

In the 1960s, critics began to formulate legal challenges to the system of local funding for public schools. There was broad agreement on the source of the problem: local control of key educational decisions had led to significant differences in education spending among districts within states. An early strategy argued that the educational needs of all children must be met and that meeting those needs might require the state to spend more on educating low-achieving, low-income students than on students from affluent, well-educated families. The courts were unsympathetic to this line of argument. The courts concluded that a "needs-based" theory left too many questions unanswered. For example, the Virginia Supreme Court wrote in *Burris v. Wilkerson,* "The courts have neither the knowledge, nor the means, nor the power to tailor the public monies to fit the varying needs of the students throughout the state."

A strategy that did prove to be successful in state courts argued that poor school districts had little property wealth that they could tax (Coons, Clune, and Sugarman 1970; Minorini and Sugarman 1999). The 1971 *Serrano v. Priest* case in California was the first using the Coons et al. principle to be decided for the plaintiffs when the California State Supreme Court declared the state school funding program to be unconstitutional. The basis of this ruling became known as the "fiscal neutrality" standard. In 1973, in *San Antonio Independent School District v. Rodriguez,* the United States Supreme Court rejected an attempt to establish a similar standard; state funding programs, it argued, violated the "equal protection" clause guaranteed by the U.S. Constitution.

Following this ruling, school finance reforms have been pursued on a state-by-state basis, with some states carrying out school finance reform via litigation while others change state aid formulas through legislation. While most reforms involved redistributing funds between districts, some states simply decided to increase funding for all districts.

These efforts have increased the role of the state in education finance. Murray, Evans, and Schwab (1998) considered the effect of court-mandated school finance reform on the level and distribution of per pupil spending in the United States between 1970 and 1990. They found that court-mandated reform decreased within-state inequality significantly by raising spending at the bottom of the distribution while leaving spending at the top unchanged. Court-mandated finance reform often leads states to increase spending for education through higher taxes. (California, which seems to have leveled its education spending, is a notable exception.)

Since the 1990s, many of the challenges to state finance systems have focused on ensuring that all students in a state have equitable access to adequate educational opportunities as required by state education clauses (Minorini and Sugarman 1999). The argument is that some districts do not provide students with an adequate education and that it is the state's responsibility to see that they receive the funding to allow them to do so. The remedy might require some districts to spend more (perhaps significantly more) than other districts, depending on their student population. For example, in districts with many students from low-income families and families where English is not the first language spoken, an "adequate education" may cost more money, and the state is required to ensure that these needs are met. These new adequacy cases are a rebirth of the "needs-based" claims of the late 1960s.

An adequacy claim places more emphasis on outcomes than a "wealth-neutrality" or "spending-equalization" claim. But there is a second important strand to this emerging adequacy stance: adequacy typically emphasizes absolute, rather than relative, standards of performance. In the past, debates over equity focused on comparisons among children and districts and on how well they fared relative to each other. Adequacy demands setting an absolute standard rather than defining equity in terms of the relative spending across systems.

Structure and operations of current finance systems

This section describes the financing programs that raise and allocate resources from state (and federal) governments to districts and schools.

Sources of revenue

Historically, local schools were financed almost exclusively by the property tax. In 1920, more than 83 percent of school revenues came from the local property tax. Early in the 20th century, states increased their role in directly financing local public education. This state support, commonly known as "state aid," was first used as a tool to help enforce state mandates, such as the length of the school year or minimum teacher qualifications. Early state aid was distributed on a per capita, per student, or per teacher basis rather than as a function of a district's ability to pay or the cost of educating different types of children.

Toward the end of the 20th century, the state share of spending per pupil has, on average, surpassed the local share of spending per pupil. For example, in 1970, local districts were responsible for about 53 percent of K–12 revenues, while the state share was less than 40 percent. By 1999, however, states provided roughly half of all resources for K–12 education, leaving the federal share at approximately 7 percent (NCES, various years).

To finance increased state aid, states have used a variety of tax and revenue-raising instruments, including income tax, sales taxes (especially sin taxes on cigarettes and alcohol), lotteries, and fees. The local property tax has remained by far the dominant tax for local school districts. However, combined with state aid, reliance on the property tax is declining for school districts and other local governments. For example, in 1977, state and local governments derived 21 percent of their revenues from the property tax. By 2002, that percentage had fallen to 17 percent (Murray and Rueben 2005).

Allocation of state aid to local school districts

State funding is typically distributed as basic aid and categorical funding. Basic aid is revenue used to provide basic education support, typically on a per-pupil basis, sometimes taking into account differences in the costs faced by districts. Every state has a different system of financing schools, but several common formulas are used to distribute basic state aid. Four basic types of formulas are described below: flat grants, foundation programs, power equalization programs, and full state funding. Categorical aid is targeted to a particular purpose, rather than being general aid. Examples of categorical aid include subsidization of student transportation; directed funds for particular groups, such as disabled students or students from disadvantaged backgrounds; and support for particular curricular areas, such as vocational or foreign language education. Most federal aid to schools is categorical in nature (Murray 1995). Readers interested in a more thorough treatment should consult Monk (1990), Odden and Picus (2004), and U.S. Department of Education (2001).

Flat grants provide a specified number of units of state support for each unit of quantifiable need. "Need" in flat grants typically takes the form of average daily attendance or school district enrollment and is independent of the receiving school district's fiscal capacity. Still, flat grants based on pupil counts do work to equalize school spending as they help one dimension of fiscal capacity: the need, as measured by the number of pupils. Indeed, as the size of a population-based flat grant increases (as a percentage of education spending), the state approaches equalization of tax burdens and educational spending. The extreme case of a flat grant is full state funding (present in Hawaii), in which the state's grant fully covers the costs of providing public schools.

Flat grants may also take the form of *matching grants,* in which the grant is linked to a particular investment by the receiving district. Interestingly, many early programs of state aid took the form of matching grants that worked *against* equalization, as grants tended to be linked to teacher counts, and wealthier districts were more likely to have higher teacher counts per pupil.

Foundation programs and district power equalization (DPE) programs are two types of equalization grants that provide more assistance to "poorer" districts. Foundation grants establish the minimum level of funding, while DPE programs are designed to give districts equal capacity to raise funds yet keep the ability to decide on the appropriate level of spending.

Foundation programs, unlike flat grants, attempt to establish an inverse relationship between state aid and fiscal capacity—that is, state aid is higher for districts with less ability to raise funds locally. The basic formula for a foundation aid program has two components. First, the state sets a "foundation level"—the level of spending intended to guarantee a minimum acceptable level of education provision. This foundation may simply be a function of enrollment or attendance, or may take into account cost differences from district to district. From this foundation, the state subtracts some common tax rate times the total value of the school district's tax base. This subtracted portion of the formula is the share of the foundation level of school provision that the state expects the school districts to cover; it then uses state aid to lift all districts to the foundation level. In addition, foundation grants allow for optional local tax levies so that school districts desiring to spend above the foundation level may do so. As with flat grants, foundation grants are imperfect. Critics of foundation grants often argue that foundation levels may be set too low, that the foundation program is too inflexible (as the foundation level must frequently be reset to keep up with inflation or changes in costs), and that foundation grants do not achieve equalization because the optional tax levies can enable wealthier districts to outspend poorer districts.

DPE programs, or guaranteed tax-based programs, allow all districts to act "as if" they all had the same tax base per student. Specifically, under DPE programs, the state chooses a guaranteed tax base per student, V. If district j sets a tax rate t_j and has a tax base V_j, it will raise $t_j V_j$ from local sources, receive state aid of $t_j(V - V_j)$, and thus spend $t_j V$ on education. In such a program, higher spending per pupil requires a higher tax rate. Thus, differences in education spending per pupil might remain, but spending differences would result from varying tax rates, reflecting local school districts preferences, and not from the unequal distribution of the local tax base (Evans et al. 1997).

Under a full state-funding program, the state sets tax bases and rates, and distributes aid on the basis of educational need, not on a district's ability to raise revenues (Evans et al. 1997).

Most states have adopted a combination of foundation and power equalization programs (U.S. Department of Education 2001). In general, political considerations preclude a state from adopting a pure form of one of the above programs. In order to attain legislative passage, states sometimes incorporate "hold harmless" clauses, which allow a district to choose between the funds due to it under the new formula and those that would accrue under the prior formula, whichever is greater. Other compromises may include provisions for guaranteeing a district a minimum amount of state funding even if not entitled under the existing formula. Some states have adopted a combination of foundation and power equalization programs. U.S. Department of Education (2001) provides a useful classification of the basic form of each state's support programs.

Federal aid for education

The federal role in K–12 public schooling funding is through the compensatory programs detailed in the Elementary and Secondary Education Act (ESEA). Each of the federal education programs has different priorities and provisions governing the allocation of funds among states, school districts, and other agencies. Each reauthorization of ESEA has modified the purposes of the individual programs slightly. The 2001 reauthorization of the ESEA, named the No Child Left Behind (NCLB) Act (PL 107-110), authorized eight programs:

Title I—Improving the Academic Achievement of the Disadvantaged

Title II—Preparing, Training, and Recruiting High Quality Teachers and Principals

Title III—Language Instruction for Limited English Proficient and Immigrant Students

Title IV—21st Century Schools

Title V—Promoting Informed Parental Choice and Innovative Programs

Title VI—Flexibility and Accountability

Title VII—Indian, Native Hawaiian, and Alaska Native Education

Title VIII—Impact Aid Programs

The U.S. Department of Education typically allocates funds to states through statutory formulas; the states then allocate funds to school districts either through formulas or competitive grants. The number of school-age children from low-income families is the primary factor in the formula for most of the compensatory programs, and federal funds, historically, were to be used specifically for programs for eligible students. The largest program is the Title I program; in 2004, appropriations for part A of the Title I program were over $12 billion.

The NCLB Act and enactment of the 1994 reauthorization of the ESEA brought important changes to the federal role. The Title I program was redesigned to provide more flexible support through waivers for high-poverty schools (schools with more than 50 percent of students participating in the free and reduced-price lunch programs) to operate schoolwide Title I programs. Schools operating schoolwide programs are not required to track Title I expenditures separately and are encouraged to combine Title I funds with other federal, state, and local resources to improve the overall quality of instruction. The NCLB reauthorization also mandated increased accountability and required schools to meet specific standards in order to maintain funding eligibility.

Does money matter? Do school finance reforms make a difference?

There are at least two ways to approach the question of the impact of school finance reforms. The first is to argue that if finance reform changed the level or distribution of resources, we can answer this question by looking at evidence on the link between resources and student outcomes. A second approach is to examine specifically if student outcomes have improved or equalized following school finance reform.

The debate over whether the level of education spending impacts outcomes is long, contentious, and ongoing. Hanushek (1986, 1162; 1997) summarizes the existing "education production function" literature by stating, "There appears to be no strong or systematic relationship between school expenditures and student performance." However, recent work, including Ladd and Ferguson (1996), shows that properly specified econometric models find that additional resources generate better outcomes. Others have argued that measures other than test scores should be considered. Card and Krueger (1992a, b) provide important direct evidence that increases in education spending raise the rate of return to education. However, Betts (1995), using data from the National Longitudinal Survey of Youth, finds no evidence that increases in spending raise wages. Given the state of this literature, it is not surprising that trying to untangle the connections between spending and outcomes is difficult.

While evidence generally shows that school finance reforms have narrowed the spending discrepancies within states and to an extent across states (Murray et al. 1998), the evidence of how student outcomes have changed following these reforms is also murky. Downes (1992) looked at the

California experience following *Serrano v. Priest* and finds that greater equality in spending was not accompanied by greater equality in measured student performance. Using nationwide individual student data, Downes and Figlio (1997) find that court-mandated school-finance reforms do not result in significant changes in either the mean level or the distribution of student performance on standardized tests. They do find, however, that legislative reforms that are not a result of a court decision lead to higher test scores in general; the estimated effect was particularly large in initially low-spending districts. Hoxby (2001) finds little evidence that school finance has a significant effect on the high school dropout rate. Finally, Card and Payne (1998) focus on the impact of finance reform on SAT scores. They conclude that the evidence points to a modest equalizing effect of school-finance reforms on the test score outcomes for children from different family backgrounds (though they would agree that the evidence is not decisive).

So, despite recent advancement in this field, the primary conclusion to draw from literature relating school spending to outcomes is that the effect of spending is not yet completely understood.

ADDITIONAL READINGS

Betts, Julian. "Does School Quality Matter? Evidence from the National Longitudinal Survey of Youth." *Review of Economics and Statistics* 77, no. 2 (May 1995): 231–50.

Blanchard, Lloyd A., and William D. Duncombe. "Tax Policy and Public School Finance." In *Handbook on Taxation,* edited by W. Bartley Hildreth and James A. Richardson (345–400). New York: Marcel Dekker, 1999.

Card, David, and Alan B. Krueger. "Does School Quality Matter? Returns to Education and the Characteristics of Public Schools in the United States." *Journal of Political Economy* 100 (February 1992a): 1–40.

———. "School Quality and Black-White Relative Earnings." *Quarterly Journal of Economics* 107 (February 1992b): 151–200.

Card, David, and A. Abigail Payne. "School Finance Reform, the Distribution of School Spending, and the Distribution of SAT Scores." Working Paper No. 6766. Cambridge, MA: National Bureau of Economic Research, 1998.

Cohen, Cecilia, and Frank Johnson. *Revenues and Expenditures for Public Elementary and Secondary Education: School Year 2001–02.* NCES 2004-341. Washington, DC: U.S Department of Education, National Center for Education Statistics, 2004.

Coons, John E., William H. Clune, and Stephen D. Sugarman. *Private Wealth and Public Education.* Cambridge, MA: Harvard University Press, 1970.

Downes, Thomas A. "Evaluating the Impact of School Finance Reform on the Provision of Education: The California Case." *National Tax Journal* 45, no. 4 (December 1992): 405–19.

Downes, Thomas A., and David N. Figlio. "School Finance Reforms, Tax Limits, and Student Performance: Do Reforms Level-Up or Dumb Down?" Medford, MA: Tufts University, 1997.

Evans, William N., Sheila E. Murray, and Robert M. Schwab, "Toward Increased Centralization in Public School Finance." In *Intergovernmental Fiscal Relations,* edited by Ronald C. Fisher. Boston: Kluwer Academic Publishers, 1997.

Ferguson, Ronald. "Paying for Public Education: New Evidence on How and Why Money Matters." *Harvard Journal of Education* 28 (1991): 465.

Grogger, Jeff. "School Expenditures and Post-schooling Earnings: Evidence from High School and Beyond." *Review of Economics and Statistics* 78 (November 1996): 628–37.

Hanushek, Eric A. "The Economics of Schooling." *Journal of Economic Literature* 24 (September 1986): 1141–77.

————. "Assessing the Effects of School Resources on Student Performance: An Update." *Educational Evaluation and Policy Analysis* 19, no. 2 (Summer 1997): 141–64.

Hoxby, Caroline M. "All School Finance Equalizations Are Not Created Equal." *Quarterly Journal of Economics.* 116, no. 4 (2001): 1149–1525.

Husted, Thomas A., and Lawrence W. Kenny. "Evidence from the States on the Political and Market Determinants of Efficiency in Education." Gainesville: University of Florida, 1996.

Ladd, Helen F., and Ronald F. Ferguson. "How and Why Money Matters: An Analysis of Alabama Schools." In *Holding Schools Accountable: Performance-Based Reform in Education,* edited by Helen F. Ladd (265–98). Washington, DC: Brookings Institution Press, 1996.

Minorini, Paul, and Stephen Sugarman. "School Finance Litigation in the Name of Educational Equity: Its Evolution, Impact, and Future." In *Equity and Adequacy in School Finance,* edited by Helen F. Ladd and Rosemary Chalk. Washington, DC: National Academy Press, 1999.

Monk, David H. *Educational Finance: An Economic Approach.* New York: McGraw-Hill, 1990.

Murray, Sheila E. "The Structure of Education Finance for K–12 Public Education." Working paper. Santa Monica, CA: The RAND Corporation, 1995.

Murray, Sheila E., and Kim Rueben. "School Finance and the Insurance Value of the Property Tax or How We Stopped Worrying and Learned to Love the Property Tax." Santa Monica, CA: The RAND Corporation, 2005.

Murray, Sheila E., William N. Evans, and Robert M. Schwab. "Education Finance Reform and the Distribution of Education Resources." *American Economic Review* 88 (September 1998): 789–812.

National Center for Education Statistics (NCES). *Digest of Education Statistics.* Washington, DC: NCES, various years.

Odden, Alan, and Lawrence Picus. *School Finance: A Policy Perspective,* 3rd ed. New York: McGraw-Hill, 2004.

Rubenstein, Ross, and Lawrence O. Picus. "Politics, the Courts, and the Economy: Implications for the Future of School Financing." In *State and Local Finances Under Pressure,* edited by David L. Sjoquist (60–93). Northhampton, MA: Edward Elgar, 2003.

U.S. Department of Education, National Center for Education Statistics. *Public School Programs of the United States and Canada: 1989–99.* NCES 2001-309. Washington, DC: US Department of Education, 2001.

Cross-references: tax and revenue capacity; tax limitations; Tiebout model.

Education tax credits, higher education, federal

Dennis Zimmerman
Congressional Budget Office

Tax credits created in 1997 for postsecondary education.

The Taxpayer Relief Act of 1997 created two tax credits for postsecondary education expenses. One, the Hope Scholarship Credit, can be claimed for each student in the family (including the taxpayer, the spouse, or dependents) for two taxable years for expenses incurred attending a qualified education program. Each student's credit is equal to 100 percent of the first $1,000 of qualified tuition and fees and 50 percent of the next $1,000 (amounts are indexed). Tuition and fees financed with scholarships, veterans' education assistance, and other income not included in gross income for tax purposes do not qualify (with the exception of gifts and inheritances).

The other, the Lifetime Learning Credit, provides a 20 percent credit for the first $10,000 of qualified tuition and fees that

taxpayers pay for themselves, their spouse, or their dependents. The credit is available for any number of years and for any level of postsecondary education.

Both credits are phased out for single taxpayers with a modified adjusted gross income over $40,000 ($80,000 for joint-return taxpayers). Those income limits are indexed. Neither credit is refundable, and the sum of these and other credits is limited to the excess of the taxpayer's regular income tax liability over the minimum tax.

Rationales for the credits

Federal subsidy of higher education has three potential economic justifications: a capital market failure; external benefits; and nonneutral federal income tax treatment of physical versus human capital. Subsidies that correct these problems are said to provide taxpayers with "social benefits."

Capital market failure

Many students find themselves unable to finance their postsecondary education from earnings and personal or family savings. Student mobility and a lack of property to pledge as loan collateral require that commercial lenders charge high interest rates on loans for postsecondary education to reflect their high risk of default. As a result, students often find themselves unable to afford postsecondary loans from the financial sector. By definition, this financial constraint bears more heavily on lower-income groups than on higher-income groups and leads to inequality of opportunity. It is also inefficient because these students, on average, might be expected to earn a rate of return on postsecondary education loans that is higher than the rate of return earned on the alternative loans made by the financial sector.

This "failure" of the capital market is attributable to the legal restriction against pledging an individual's future labor supply as loan collateral—that is, against indentured servitude. The federal government pursues an alternative strategy to correct this market failure—it provides a guarantee to absorb most of the financial sector's default risk associated with postsecondary loans to students. This financial support is provided through the Federal Family Education Loan Program and the Direct Loan Program. These programs guaranteed approximately $46 billion of loans for postsecondary education in fiscal year 2003. This guarantee is an entitlement, and it equalizes some of the financing cost for most students' education investment. When combined with Pell grant programs for lower-income students, this entitlement appears to correct some of the capital market failure and improve the equality of opportunity.

External benefits

Some benefits from postsecondary education may accrue not to the individual being educated, but rather to the members of society at large. These external benefits are not valued by individuals, causing them to invest less than is optimal for society (even assuming no capital market imperfections). External benefits are variously described as taking the form of better citizenship and increased productivity generated by knowledge.

Public subsidies to postsecondary education that are at least partially motivated by external benefits are considerable. The state and local sector is by far the major contributor, financing about 43 percent of education costs for all students at public institutions in 1999–2000. The federal government provided additional billions of dollars of interest subsidies through the student loan program over and above the value of the guarantee being provided, several billion dollars in work-study grants, and a variety of other assistance programs. Thus, federal and state and local subsidies to higher education that are designed to increase external benefits total tens of billions of dollars per year.

Nonneutral taxation of human capital

A third potential justification sometimes advanced for providing subsidies to human capital investment is the possibility that investment in human capital is more heavily taxed than is investment in physical capital. Some believe this to be true because individuals are not allowed to recover education expenses, such as tuition costs, over their lifetime. But forgone earnings, scholarships, and government grants represent a larger share of an individual's human capital investment than do most students' direct outlays, such as tuition, and these investments are effectively deducted when incurred because they are never included in income in the first place.

The effective marginal tax rate on physical capital investment is estimated to be about 33 percent. Using reasonable assumptions about marginal tax rates for an individual as a student and as a recipient of his education investment returns, the timing of these returns over a 40-year period, and the share of investment expensed, the tax on human capital investment is 25 percent, actually lower than the tax on physical capital.

Summary

The return from investment in human capital receives more favorable treatment from the federal income tax than does the return from investment in physical capital. Thus, nonneutral income taxation cannot be used to justify subsidy of postsecondary education. The existence of a capital market failure and the presence of external benefits from higher education investments do provide justifications for public subsidy of higher education. However, the federal student loan program and Pell grants have partially corrected the capital market failure, and tens of billions of dollars of annual state and local and federal subsidies have probably gone a long way toward compensating for the existence of external benefits. At a minimum, additional subsidies such as the tax credit should be carefully targeted to those students still suffering from lack of access to capital or otherwise underinvesting in their own education.

Effect of tax credit

Potential students induced to enroll in higher education by these credits cause investment in education to increase. But the overall effectiveness of the tax credit depends upon whether the cost of the marginal investment dollar of those already investing in higher education is reduced. For those whose tuition and fees exceed qualified tuition and fees, the credit applies to the last dollar of tuition and fees, and the student's price is reduced by 50 percent with the Hope Credit and by 20 percent with the Lifetime Learning Credit. The portion of the credit (and the federal revenue loss) that appears either as an increase in the quantity of education or as higher tuition depends upon the structure of the demand and supply schedules for higher education.

It is clear from the structure of these tax credits that tuition and fee payments will exceed qualified tuition and fees for a large number of students who are eligible for these credits. These students experience an income effect and a subsidy to participation but no marginal price effect. Moreover, because the subsidy is channeled through the tax system, students and families with lower income and little or no tax liability receive little or no benefit, even though these students are likely to have a larger participation response. The middle- and upper-middle-class students who receive tax benefits are likely to be relatively unresponsive to price changes, particularly with respect to participation. Thus, many of these families enjoy a windfall gain and the federal taxpayer gets no offsetting social benefits in the form of increased investment.

ADDITIONAL READINGS

Congressional Budget Office. "Private and Public Contributions to Financing College Education." Washington, DC: Congressional Budget Office, January 2004.

Gravelle, Jane, and Dennis Zimmerman. "Tax Subsidies for Higher Education: An Analysis of the Administration's Proposal." Congressional Research Service Report 97-581 E, May 30, 1997.

Kane, Thomas J. "Beyond Tax Relief: Long-Term Challenges in Financing Higher Education." *National Tax Journal* (June 1997): 335–49.

Long, Bridget Terry. "The Impact of Federal Tax Credits for Higher Education Expenses." National Bureau of Economic Research working paper no. 9553. Cambridge, MA: National Bureau of Economic Research, 2000.

McPherson, Michael, and Morton Owen Schapiro. *Keeping College Affordable.* Washington, DC: The Brookings Institution, 1991.

Orszag, Peter R., and Thomas J. Kane. "Financing Public Higher Education: Short-Term and Long-Term Challenges." *Ford Policy Forum* (April 2004): 33–39.

Cross-references: child care credit; education financing, state and local; income tax, federal.

Elasticity, demand and supply

David N. Hyman
North Carolina State University

Two measures of the sensitivity of buyers and sellers to price changes that play an important role in evaluating the effects of taxes.

Demand elasticity measures the responsiveness of quantities demanded of an item relative to changes in its price. *Supply elasticity* gauges the responsiveness of quantities supplied of an item relative to changes in its price. Demand elasticity is usually called price elasticity of demand to distinguish it from measures of the sensitivity of amounts bought to changes in economic variables other than the item's price. Similarly, supply elasticity is commonly referred to as price elasticity of supply.

Price elasticity of demand is calculated by dividing the percentage change in the quantity demanded of an item by the percentage change in the price that caused it, other things being equal. The following formula can be used to calculate price elasticity of demand for small changes in price:

$$\text{Price elasticity of demand} = \frac{dQ/Q}{dP/P}$$

where Q is the initial quantity demanded, dQ is the change in quantity demanded caused by the change in price dP, and P is the initial price of the item.

Because the demand for a good is likely to fall as its price rises, the price elasticity of demand will be a negative number indicating the percentage change in the quantity demanded of an item resulting from a 1 percent change in its price. Price elasticity of demand is equal to the inverse of the negative slope of a demand curve (dQ/dP) multiplied by the ratio of the initial price of the item to its quantity demanded.

The absolute value of the price elasticity of demand can range from zero to infinity. When this value is between 0 and 1, demand is said to be inelastic; when it is greater than 1, demand is said to be elastic. The demand for an item is said to be of unitary elasticity if the absolute value of its price elasticity of demand is exactly equal to 1.

Knowledge of the price elasticity of demand helps businesses forecast changes in revenue due to changes in market prices. Revenue is the price multiplied by the quantity of an item purchased in a market. If demand is inelastic, a price increase will result in an increase in revenue because the effects of a given percentage increase in price on revenue will not be offset by a larger percentage decline in quantity demanded. When demand is elastic, an increase in price will cause revenue to decline because the positive effect of the higher price on revenue will be swamped by the negative effect of a larger percentage decline in quantity demanded. The same logic can be used to forecast the effects of price declines on total revenue and expenditures on an item.

Supply elasticity is calculated in the same way as price elasticity of demand: by dividing the percentage change in the quantity supplied by the percentage change in the price that caused that change in quantity. Because supply curves generally exhibit a positive slope, price elasticity of supply is a positive number. Supply is said to be inelastic when the price elasticity of supply is between 0 and 1. Supply is said to be elastic when its price elasticity exceeds 1.

Estimates of price elasticities of demand and supply are useful in forecasting the loss in efficiency in the use of privately owned resources in response to taxes. The excess burden of a tax is the cost of distortions in choices that result from that tax and is measured as the loss in net benefits from wasteful resource use over and above the dollar amount of tax paid. The excess burden of a tax depends on the willingness of buyers and sellers to adjust their behavior in response to tax-induced price changes.

Taxes on goods or services traded in markets (including productive resources such as labor, capital, and land) inevitably affect the demand and supply of these items and therefore their market prices. The price changes, the responsiveness of buyers and sellers to tax-induced price increases, and therefore the excess burden of a tax depend on the taxed items' price elasticities of demand and supply.

Other things being equal, the more elastic the demand for a taxed good or service, the greater the buyers' response to a tax-induced price increase and the greater the excess burden of a tax placed on its sale. Similarly, the excess burden of a tax will also vary with the taxed item's price elasticity of supply. The higher the price elasticity of supply of a good or service, the greater the excess burden of a tax on its sale.

To minimize the excess tax burden, it would be best to tax goods and services whose demand or supply is highly inelastic. For example, because the overall supply of land in a nation is usually perfectly inelastic, a tax on land results in no excess burden. Similarly, the excess tax burden on goods with few good substitutes (such as certain drugs or basic foodstuffs) would also be very low because there would be little change in the quantities of these items demanded in response to any tax-induced price increases.

The price elasticity of demand and supply of a taxed good or service will also influence the incidence of the tax between the good's buyers and sellers. When demand is highly inelastic, buyers will not respond to a tax-induced price increase by substantially reducing the quantity demanded. A tax increases the cost of selling each unit of a product and therefore usually decreases the willingness of sellers to supply given quantities. If a taxed item's price elasticity of demand were zero, the sellers could raise the price by the tax per unit and not cause a decrease in quantity demanded.

If the elasticity of demand for an item is not zero, an attempt by sellers to raise the product's price by the full amount of the tax will cause a surplus on the market because buyers will want to buy less at a price that includes the full tax. In this case, the new market equilibrium price will be somewhere between the initial price and the sum of that price and the tax per unit, with the tax being shared by the buyers and sellers. Buyers would pay a higher price than before, and sellers would receive a lower net price after paying the tax per unit. In general, other things being equal, the more inelastic the demand for a taxed item, the greater the share of the tax paid by buyers in terms of a price increase.

The incidence of a tax between buyers and sellers is also affected by the price elasticity of supply. If sellers are to succeed in shifting a portion of a tax on a good or service they offer for sale in markets, they must make the good scarcer in the market. The price elasticity of supply indicates the willingness and ability of sellers to reduce quantities supplied in response to a tax. For example, the price elasticity of supply of labor of prime-aged males in the workforce has been estimated to be zero. This implies that a tax on labor services (as results from an income or payroll tax) will not cause these workers to reduce the number of hours they work. Because workers do not respond to the tax by working fewer hours, labor is not made scarcer, and its price (wages or salaries) cannot rise in the marketplace. Under these circumstances, the entire tax on labor income must be borne by workers, who will not shift any of the cost of the tax to the buyers (the employers) in the market. In general, the more inelastic the supply of a taxed good or service, the greater the incidence of that tax on the sellers in the market.

In the long run, supply is generally more elastic than it is in the short run. An industry of constant costs is one whose long-run supply curve is a flat line that is infinitely elastic at all points. In such industries, the minimum possible average cost of producing a product is constant and does not vary in the long run with the number of firms in the industry. Many industries in the United States have perfectly elastic supply curves in the long run. Firms in these industries will incur losses as a result of a tax on the sale of their product. Firms that fail will leave the industry, and as this occurs, market supply will decrease and market price will rise. Price will continue to rise until it equals the minimum possible average cost of production plus the tax, so that the net price received by sellers equals their minimum possible cost. In cases where supply is perfectly elastic in the long run, a tax will be shifted forward fully to buyers.

Cross-references: excess burden; incidence of taxes; inverse elasticity rule; labor supply, taxes and.

Elasticity of substitution between labor and capital

Robert S. Chirinko
Emory University and CESifo

A property of the production function that affects the response of capital formation to relative prices and tax rates.

The elasticity of substitution between labor and capital (referred to in the literature and in this entry as σ) measures the extent to which the optimizing firm substitutes capital for labor in production. John Hicks (1946) defined it as the percentage change in the capital/labor ratio with respect to a percentage change in the price of labor relative to the price of capital. The value of σ has a substantial impact on the way in which tax policies affect resource allocation and factor incomes through variations in relative factor prices. This entry reviews the development of σ in production analysis, the econometric issues with estimating this production function parameter, and the impact of alternative values of σ on tax policy evaluations.

The production function most frequently used in economic analysis was developed by Charles Cobb and Paul Douglas, who were searching for a formal structure to explain the observed graphical relations among aggregates of output, labor, and capital for U.S. manufacturing. The Cobb-Douglas production function has two key properties: constant returns to scale and a value of σ that is constant and equal to 1.0. An important implication of the Cobb-Douglas assumptions is that factor shares are constant, determined exclusively by fixed production characteristics. Observing that this property was violated, Arrow et al. (1961) introduced a constant elasticity of substitution (CES) production function that determines factor shares as the product of relative factor prices and fixed production characteristics. The CES production function allows for a wide range of substitution possibilities between labor and capital. When σ equals 0, there is no possibility of substitution between factors, the production function is Leontief, and the isoquants are right-angled. At the other extreme, if substitution between factors are extremely large, σ tends toward infinity, and isoquants become straight-lines. The Cobb-Douglas value of σ equal to 1.0 is a special case of the CES production function. (See Chung [1994] for a formal analysis of CES and Cobb-Douglas production functions.)

When production is characterized by the CES function, σ equals the price elasticity of the capital stock, where output is held fixed (thus highlighting substitution effects) and the relevant price of capital is the Jorgensonian cost of capital. (This equality does not hold for all production functions, such as the translog; see chapter 9 in Berndt [1991] for further discussion.) The cost of capital framework translates legislated tax policies into an economically meaningful price variable, and σ is thus critical in determining how much taxes affect real outcomes.

Estimating σ has been an active area of research for many decades, though a consensus value has remained elusive. Estimates of σ can be differentiated by whether capital stock or investment flow data are the dependent variable and whether time-series or panel data are used (see Chirinko [2002, table 1] for further details and a range of estimates). Here we focus on business fixed capital. Econometric specifications using capital stock data follow directly from the first-order condition linking the stock of capital to the flow of output and price of capital relative to the price of output. A difficulty with this approach is the assumption that the firm is at its long-run equilibrium, which is unlikely to be accurate for most observations. Another class of studies models investment spending (equal to the change in the capital stock plus depreciation) and its adjustment to the long-run equilibrium defined by the first-order condition. Parameter estimates from investment equations may be biased because adjustment dynamics are difficult to specify and such an approach emphasizes transitory variation. Moreover, since most empirical studies using either capital stock or investment flow data are based on aggregate or industry time series, parameter estimates may be further biased by simultaneity, capital market frictions, or firm heterogeneity. These problems are better addressed with microdata that vary in both the time series and cross-section dimensions. While some recent studies with panel data have narrowed the range of estimates of σ, substantial differences remain about its value and hence the appropriateness of the frequently used Cobb-Douglas assumption.

Simulation studies highlight the importance of alternative values of σ in tax policy evaluation. In the MPS macroeconometric model, for example, Chirinko and Eisner (1983) assess the impact of increasing the investment tax credit in full model simulations. When the σ for equipment capital is lowered from the Cobb-Douglas value of 1.00 to 0.19 (the latter estimate is based on modifications to the key estimated equation), incremental equipment investment spending is 60 percent lower in the first two years after the investment stimulus and 40 percent lower after five years. The net effect of σ on the budgetary impact of a tax stimulus is ambiguous— a larger σ raises budgetary costs as more investment receives the subsidy, but the additional capital lowers budgetary costs due to more output and tax revenues.

General-equilibrium models that focus on steady-state behavior show a similar sensitivity to σ. Harberger (1959) quantifies the welfare improvements that would follow from replacing the existing corporate income tax with a "neutral" capital tax (i.e., equalizing capital income taxation on all firms in both the corporate and noncorporate sectors). The distortions from the existing corporate tax aggregated across industries amount to 1.66 percent of total capital income when σ equals 0.5. This figure rises markedly to 2.48 percent if σ equals 1.0. Using a more elaborate simulation model, Engen, Gravelle, and Smetters (1997) show that when a comprehensive income tax is replaced by a consumption tax, the increase in steady-state net output is 3.80, 6.80, and 9.50 percent higher than the distorted benchmark for σ equal to 0.50, 1.00, or 1.50, respectively. (See Chirinko [2002, table 2] for additional studies.) While it is a bit risky to offer generalizations about economies with a multitude of taxes and substitution possibilities, the larger σ is, the larger the impact of distortionary taxation and the larger the scope for ameliorative public policies.

The importance of σ in affecting real allocations and the uncertainty concerning its precise value suggest that tax policy analysis must be undertaken with a range of values of this critical parameter.

ADDITIONAL READINGS

Arrow, Kenneth J., Hollis B. Chenery, Bagicha S. Minhas, and Robert Solow. "Capital-Labor Substitution and Economic Efficiency." *The Review of Economics and Statistics* 43 (August 1961): 225–50.

Berndt, Ernst R. *The Practice of Econometrics: Classic and Contemporary Reading.* Massachusetts: Addison-Wesley, 1991.

Chirinko, Robert S. "Corporate Taxation, Capital Formation, and the Substitution Elasticity between Labor and Capital." *National Tax Journal* 55 (June 2002): 339–55.

Chirinko, Robert S., and Robert Eisner. "Tax Policy and Investment in Major U.S. Macroeconomic Econometric Models." *Journal of Public Economics* 20 (March 1983): 139–66.

Chung, Jae Wan. *Utility and Production Functions: Theory and Applications.* Oxford: Blackwell Publishers, 1994.

Engen, Eric, Jane Gravelle, and Kent Smetters. "Dynamic Tax Models: Why They Do The Things They Do." *National Tax Journal* 50 (September 1997): 657–82.

Harberger, Arnold C. "The Corporation Income Tax: An Empirical Assessment." In *Tax Revision Compendium,* vol. 1 (231–50). Washington, DC: House Committee on Ways and Means, 1959.

Hicks, John R. *Value and Capital,* 2nd ed. Oxford: Clarendon Publishers, 1946.

Cross-reference: cost of capital.

Electronic tax filing, state

Harley Duncan
Federation of State Tax Administrators

State-led innovations in the use of computer technology to simplify tax administration and compliance.

Over the course of the past 10 years, states have made significant efforts to encourage taxpayers to file their tax returns electronically rather than on paper. They have developed a variety of vehicles for the electronic filing of both individual income tax returns and various types of business tax returns (e.g., sales and use tax, income tax withholding, and other business taxes.) In addition, several states recently have mandated electronic filing for certain taxpayers to decrease paper filings and relieve budget shortages.

Electronic filing (e-filing) provides a fast, accurate, and secure method of filing tax returns that can be beneficial for both taxpayers and tax administration agencies. It provides substantial advantages to state tax agencies because it eliminates the need for manually handling paper returns and capturing the data from paper returns. This eliminates errors in data transcription, makes the data available more quickly for compliance and customer service purposes, and reduces agency costs. E-file is also beneficial to taxpayers because it reduces the administrative burden of filing and allows the tax authority to produce any refund due the taxpayer more quickly.

Individual income taxes

The greatest strides in e-filing have been made with individual income tax returns, where the largest efficiency and customer service (faster refunds) gains are to be had. The various types of individual income tax e-filing programs available include the following:

Federal and state electronic filing. This program allows taxpayers to e-file their federal *and* state tax returns in one transmission to the Internal Revenue Service (IRS). The IRS then forwards the state data to the appropriate state tax agency for processing. Federal and state returns are filed by tax practitioners who provide return preparation services to individuals or directly by individuals who use approved computer software that directs the return to an approved intermediary for forwarding to the IRS (called online filing). The practitioners and filing intermediaries often assess a fee to the taxpayer for the electronic filing, but as e-filing has matured, the fees have generally been reduced or absorbed into the tax preparation or software costs. Thirty-seven states plus the District of Columbia participate in the Fed/State Electronic Filing Program. The other five states with a personal income tax (California, Maine, Massachusetts, Minnesota, and New York) have a similar program, except that they receive the electronic returns directly from the tax practitioner or filing intermediary rather than through the IRS. The vast majority of e-filed income tax returns are received from practitioners or through the online filing program.

Direct Internet filing. To address issues of the costs associated with electronic filing and to leverage the increased use of Internet technology by individuals, a number of states have developed web-based tax-filing applications that allow a taxpayer to access a state web site directly and file the state individual income tax return for free. Twenty-six states had a free direct filing program for individual income taxes in 2004. Access to the state Internet filing sites is available from the Federation of Tax Administrators web site at http://www.taxadmin.org.

Telefile. The first approach to e-filing was a "telefile" application in which a Touch-Tone telephone key pad is used to enter the data for filing a simple income tax return, employing interactive voice response capabilities. In 2004, about 25 states deployed a telefile application, including eight that had partnered with the IRS on a Fed/State telefile return where both the state and federal returns were completed in a single phone call. The data from the call is transmitted initially to the IRS and subsequently to the state. Participation in telefile programs has declined steadily over the past several years, due largely to competing alternatives (software and direct Internet filing). From 2003 to 2004, at least four states dropped their telefile programs due to high costs.

2-D barcode returns. Millions of tax returns that are prepared by practitioners or individuals using computer software and that could be electronically filed are not due to a combination of cost and taxpayer or tax preparer preference. Instead, they are printed to paper and mailed to the tax authority. Some states have begun requiring that computer-produced returns that are printed contain a two-dimensional barcode that contains all the data on the return. This enables the tax administration agency to scan the bar code once the return is open (much like products are scanned at a grocery store) and immediately capture all the data on the return and to process it from that point forward as if it were an electronic return. Barcodes are estimated to reduce the time associated with manually entering data from a paper return by 90 percent. Nineteen states accepted 2-D barcoded returns for the 2004 filing season.

Electronic filing mandates. Since 2002, an increasing number of states have mandated the electronic filing of tax returns by certain taxpayers, largely to allow the tax agency to achieve budget savings and to allow staff resources to focus on customer service and compliance activities rather than return processing.

Mandates generally apply to practitioners who filed a certain number of returns during the prior tax-filing season. For example, all practitioners who filed over 200 returns in the previous year are required to file all returns electronically in the coming year, unless the tax administration agency grants an exception. Seven states implemented mandates for the 2004 tax-filing season, and at least three states will implement mandates for the 2005 filing season. The following states have mandated the electronic filing of personal income tax returns (effective for the 2004 filing season unless otherwise noted): Alabama (2005 filing season), California, Connecticut (2005 filing season), Massachusetts, Michigan, Minnesota, Oklahoma, Rhode Island, Virginia (2005 filing season), and Wisconsin. (In Massachusetts and Rhode Island, the requirement is to file electronically or to produce returns that contain a scannable 2-D bar code.)

2004 filing season results

Based on reports from 37 of the 42 income tax jurisdictions, through August 2004, the state income tax filings looked like this:

- A total of 98.2 million returns of all types had been filed, with 56.7 million being filed on paper, 39.4 million being filed electronically, and 2.1 million being filed via telefile.
- Electronic returns increased by 25 percent (about 8 million returns) from the same point in the 2003 filing season.
- Electronic filing increased by 3.1 million returns in California alone (86 percent), where an electronic-filing mandate was instituted for the 2004 filing season.
- Telefile returns dropped by 21 percent in 2004.
- Direct Internet-filed returns increased to 1.5 million returns—a 45 percent increase over 2003.
- Paper income tax returns dropped by 10 percent in 2004.
- States received 9.4 million returns with a scannable bar code in 2004, up from 7.5 million such returns in 2003.

Business taxes

Most states have developed one or more applications for the electronic filing of various business tax returns, including motor fuel tax returns (35 states), sales and use tax returns (30 states), and income tax withholding (21 states). (See http://www.taxadmin.org/fta/edi/ecsnaps.html for a brief summary of state programs.) States use a variety of technologies in these programs, including the following:

- Electronic data interchange (EDI) or similar structured computer-to-computer data transfer programs for returns containing large volumes of information, such as motor fuel returns and sales and use tax returns;
- Web-based applications that allow the taxpayer to access a state-developed web site to enter and transmit tax return data, usually used for sales and use tax returns and withholding returns; and
- Telefile or interactive voice response programs for entering returns with limited information, such as withholding returns or sales tax returns with no sales for the reporting period.

Encouraging voluntary use of the business tax filing programs has proven to be difficult. This is partially due to the fact that for larger, multistate businesses, filing electronically with each individual state does not reduce the administrative burden much. Also, business tax e-filing does not have the attraction of a quicker tax refund that individual income tax returns have. Some states have begun to mandate electronic filing for certain business taxpayers, including Alabama, Florida, Massachusetts, Minnesota, Missouri, Oklahoma, Tennessee, Texas, and Wisconsin.

Cross-references: budget process, state; income tax, state; tax reform, state.

Employee stock ownership plan

Gerald Mayer
Congressional Research Service, Library of Congress

Updated by
Jane Gravelle
Congressional Research Service, Library of Congress

An employee benefit plan that is required to invest primarily in the stock of the sponsoring employer.

The employee stock ownership plan (ESOP) is a defined contribution plan. Unlike a defined benefit plan, where an employer agrees to pay employees a given amount of retirement benefits, under a defined contribution plan, an employer agrees to make contributions to accounts set up for each employee. An ESOP qualifies under the tax code as either a stock-bonus plan or a combination stock-bonus plan/pension plan (also called a money-purchase pension plan). An ESOP may be combined with other kinds of employee benefit plans, such as a profit-sharing plan or a 401(k) plan.

Unlike other pension plans, ESOPs must invest most of their funds in the stock of the sponsoring employer. ESOPs are also unique among employee benefit plans in their ability to borrow money to buy stock. An ESOP that has borrowed money to buy stock is a leveraged ESOP; an ESOP that acquires stock through direct employer contributions of cash or stock is a nonleveraged ESOP.

Although employers are not required to provide a pension plan for their employees, private employers that do provide such plans must meet the legal requirements of the Employee Retirement Income Security Act of 1974 (ERISA). Like other defined contribution plans, ESOPs qualify for certain tax benefits. In particular, employers may deduct contributions to an ESOP as a business expense. (For tax years beginning after December 31, 1997, this provision does not apply to contributions made by an S corporation to repay an ESOP loan.) Employees are not taxed on employer contributions to the ESOP or on the earnings on invested funds until they are distributed.

ESOPs also qualify for special tax benefits. Contributions to a leveraged ESOP are subject to less restrictive limits than contributions to other qualified employee benefit plans. For loans made before the enactment of the Small Business Job Protection Act of 1996, which became law on August 20, 1996, qualified lenders may exclude more than 50 percent of the interest earned on an ESOP loan from their gross income if the ESOP owns more than 50 percent of the company's stock. An employer may deduct dividends paid on stock held by an ESOP if the dividends are paid to plan participants or if the dividends are used to repay a loan that was used to buy the stock. A stockholder in a closely held company may defer recognition of the gain from the sale of stock to an ESOP if, after the sale, the ESOP owns at least 30 percent of the company's stock and the seller reinvests the proceeds from the stock's sale in a U.S. company. For tax years beginning after December 31, 1997, the last two provisions do not apply to stock in an S corporation.

To qualify for the above tax benefits, an ESOP must meet the minimum requirements established in the Internal Revenue Code. Many of these requirements are general ones that apply to all qualified employee benefit plans. Other requirements apply specifically to ESOPs. In particular, ESOP participants must be allowed voting rights on stock allocated to their accounts. In the case of publicly traded stock, full voting rights must be passed through to participants. For stock in closely held companies, voting rights must be passed through on all major corporate issues. For lenders to qualify for the 50 percent interest exclusion on ESOP loans, full voting rights must be passed through to participants on stock acquired with the loan. Closely held companies must give employees the right to sell distributions of stock to the employer (a put option) at a share price determined by an independent appraiser. An ESOP must also allow participants who are approaching retirement to diversify the investment of funds in their accounts.

ESOPs have multiple objectives. ESOPs are created to broaden stock ownership. As a kind of defined contribution plan, ESOPs are also designed to provide employees with a source of retirement income. Finally, ESOPs are intended to provide employers with a tax-favored means of financing. In contrast to conventional debt financing, both the interest and the principal on an ESOP loan are tax deductible. The 50 percent interest exclusion may allow lenders to charge below-market interest rates on ESOP loans.

The effectiveness of ESOPs in broadening stock ownership depends largely on the effect of pension plans on private saving. Evidence suggests that private pension plans tend to have a positive effect on the net rate of private saving. Therefore, ESOPs probably have some effect on the distribution of stock ownership. Because ESOPs are required to invest primarily in the stock of the sponsoring employer, the effectiveness of ESOPs in providing employees with retirement income depends, to a large extent, on the profitability of the sponsoring employer. Some evidence suggests that, when combined with employee participation in decisionmaking, ESOPs may improve worker productivity. Congress has questioned the effectiveness of ESOPs as a tax-favored source of finance and has repealed the 50 percent interest exclusion for ESOP loans. However, in 2001, a significant benefit was added when corporations were allowed to deduct dividends on stock in retirement plans.

ADDITIONAL READINGS

Blasi, Joseph R. *Employee Ownership: Revolution or Ripoff?* Cambridge, MA: Ballinger, 1988.

Blinder, Alan S., ed. *Paying for Productivity: A Look at the Evidence.* Washington, DC: The Brookings Institution, 1990.

Conte, Michael A., and Helen H. Lawrence. "Trends in ESOPs." In *Trends in Pensions 1992*, edited by John A. Turner and Daniel J. Beller (135–48). Washington, DC: U.S. Government Printing Office, 1992.

Mayer, Gerald. *Employee Stock Ownership Plans: Background and Policy Issues.* Washington, DC: Library of Congress, Congressional Research Service, 1994.

U.S. General Accounting Office. *Employee Stock Ownership Plans: Benefits and Costs of ESOP Tax Incentives for Broadening Stock Ownership.* PEMD-87-8. Washington, D.C., December 29, 1986.

———. *Employee Stock Ownership Plans: Little Evidence of Effects on Corporate Performance.* PEMD-88-1. Washington, D.C., October 29, 1987.

Young, Karen M., ed. *The Expanding Role of ESOPs in Public Companies.* New York: Quorum Books, 1990.

Cross-references: pensions, tax treatment; profit-sharing plans.

Energy taxes

Geraldine Gerardi
U.S. Department of the Treasury

Eric Toder
The Urban Institute

Excise taxes imposed on energy products or on final energy consumption.

Over the past thirty years, there has been considerable discussion of new or additional taxes on energy. This interest was first sparked by the 1973–74 oil embargo and the subsequent concern over forging a national energy policy. Both the reasons for considering energy taxes and the specific tax bases considered have varied over time, however, and interest in energy taxes has waned in recent years.

Taxes on energy have been considered for four major reasons: (1) to reduce adverse effects attributable to energy consumption, such as dependence on imported oil and global warming, (2) to capture windfall gains to domestic producers from decontrol and higher world oil prices, (3) to fund particular programs, and (4) to raise revenue to reduce large projected budget deficits.

Congress has addressed some of these concerns over the past three decades. For example, in 1980 Congress enacted the Crude Oil Windfall Profit Tax to capture some of the gains to domestic producers from the removal of oil price controls that were in place in the 1970s. The tax raised less revenue than anticipated because oil prices declined in 1982, and it was repealed in 1988. Temporary taxes have also been imposed on crude oil and imported refined petroleum products to finance the cleanup of oil spills and hazardous substances under the Superfund program, and on motor fuels to finance the cleanup of leaking underground storage tanks. (Excise taxes on transportation fuels that are used to fund certain mass transit and highway construction and maintenance programs, aviation services and airport improvements, and the costs of water transportation have been in place for some time.) In 1993, the Clinton administration proposed a broad-based tax on the energy content of fuels, but Congress rejected the tax and enacted a modest increase in existing motor fuel taxes as part of a deficit reduction package. Since the Clinton proposal failed, there have been no major initiatives to impose broad-based energy taxes in the United States.

In addition to the energy taxes imposed and increased in recent years, environmental groups have discussed a tax on the carbon content of fossil fuels to address environmental concerns, in particular the effect of carbon emissions generated from the combustion of fossil fuels on the potential for global warming. Carbon taxes or energy-related environmental taxes have been discussed in many countries and have been implemented in some (including Denmark, Finland, the Netherlands, Norway, and Sweden). Energy taxes could help achieve goals for reduced growth in carbon emissions, such as those agreed to in the Kyoto protocol, but there has been no significant movement in that direction to date.

Reasons for taxing energy

Tax experts normally favor taxes that are neutral and do not affect spending or investment patterns. Such a system is equitable and conducive to economic efficiency because it lets relative prices reflect true resource costs. Taxes on energy consumption are often justified, however, on the grounds that market prices do not reflect the full social costs of producing and consuming energy. Among the reasons advanced for energy taxes are several types of market imperfections.

Dependence on imported oil

The United States is heavily dependent on imported oil. But much of the world's oil supply comes from politically turbulent regions and the market price of oil may fail to reflect the potential insecurity of oil supplies. Imports currently account for over one-half of U.S. oil consumption. Taxes that reduce energy consumption or increase domestic production and encourage investment in conservation and alternative energy production, by reducing U.S. dependence on oil, could lower the economic cost of any future oil supply interruption. It is not clear, however, that energy taxes are the best way to protect against disruption of supply. Providing for government stockpiles or subsidizing private stockpiles are other options, and the United States has invested in a strategic oil reserve. U.S. vulnerability to oil price shocks has also been lessened (compared with the 1970s when two such shocks occurred) by the reduced market power of OPEC, increased worldwide competition in production, and the removal of domestic price controls, which inhibited the economy's ability to adjust to higher world oil prices.

Conservation of nonrenewable resources

A second reason advanced for energy taxation is to reduce the depletion of nonrenewable resources. The fact that some resources are becoming scarcer or more expensive to extract does not provide a compelling reason to reduce energy extraction if capital markets are functioning properly. Federal income tax incentives that favor extraction, such as the expensing of intangible drilling costs, may encourage overproduction. A concern that resources are being used up too rapidly would suggest that these provisions be reviewed.

Underpricing of energy: regulation and environmental costs

A past rationale for energy taxes was to offset regulatory policies that controlled energy prices, but these regulations are no longer in place. Another reason that energy may be underpriced is that market prices for energy fail to take into account the damage to the environment from energy production and use. These environmental costs vary by type of fuel and use and the extent to which they are internalized to producers and consumers by existing environmental regulations. Recent proposals to tax the carbon content of fossil fuels reflect concerns about the effect of greenhouse gas emissions on global warming.

Unattractiveness of alternative revenue-raising options

When deficit reduction was a high priority, some analysts supported energy taxes because, as consumption taxes, they do not reduce after-tax returns, and therefore do not discourage saving and capital formation. Others object to energy taxes because they are regressive, burdening lower-income households more than higher-income households. However, energy taxes appear less regressive when distributed according to estimated lifetime income and when the indirect effects of taxing the energy used to produce energy-intensive goods are taken into account. Proponents of energy taxes also claim that revenues could be "recycled" in ways that benefit low-income households.

Some proponents of using carbon taxes to combat global warming point to a "double dividend" from such taxes—they reduce the long-term environmental damage from high fossil fuel consumption, and, at the same time, the revenues could be used to reduce other taxes (such as income or payroll taxes) that adversely affect labor supply and saving. This argument is logically flawed, however, because it ignores two adverse effects of energy taxes. First, by raising the price of goods relative to wages, energy taxes adversely affect labor supply in a manner similar to taxes on wages. Second, energy taxes, by distorting the relative price of goods and inputs, reduce the efficiency of current production. Still, if an energy tax does significantly reduce environmental damage, it could result in a net long-run efficiency gain, even if there is no "double dividend."

Types of energy taxes

These are several types of energy taxes and the choice of a particular tax should reflect the policy objective.

Oil import fee

An oil import fee is the most direct way to reduce imports because it discourages consumption of imported oil and encourages production of both domestic oil and alternative fuels. An oil import fee should be imposed on both crude oil and refined petroleum products, but, in practice, it is difficult to apply the tax to all products with oil content. Failure to apply the tax to oil-intensive produce (such as petrochemicals) would increase imports of these products, with adverse effects for domestic producers. An oil import fee would differentially affect the prices of alternative consumer products and industries, increase state and local severance taxes, and increase the profits of domestic oil and gas producers as well as producers of competing fuels, whose prices would also rise.

Taxing oil imports from all countries could create political problems for the United States. However, exempting imports from certain countries, such as Canada and Mexico, would reduce the tax base. Moreover, nonexempt countries could avoid the tax by channeling imports through exempt countries.

Oil excise tax

Compared with an import fee, an oil excise tax would raise more revenue, but would be a less efficient way of reducing imports because it would not increase domestic production incentives. It would have effects similar to an oil import fee on consumer products and on the incentive to import oil-intensive products. It would not benefit domestic oil producers or encourage domestic production, but would benefit producers of alternative fuels and encourage the production of alternative fuels.

Broad energy taxes

Broad energy taxes are less effective than oil import or excise taxes in reducing dependence on oil imports because they do not encourage domestic production of oil or production of other taxed fuels. Broad energy taxes are more appropriate, however, for promoting general conservation or environmental improvements. A tax justified on the grounds of depletion of nonrenewable resources should cover most, but not all, energy sources. A broad energy tax would affect industries and uses more equally than an oil excise tax.

A broad energy tax could be imposed in several ways. The base could be the BTU content of the fuel, the carbon content of fuel, or the value of the energy at some point in the production or sale. A tax on value (or ad valorem tax) could be imposed on producers or consumers; however, the relative impact of the taxes on final prices would vary depending on point of production. These broadly based taxes would include, in addition to oil, the other fossil fuels (natural gas and coal) and other types of energy, such as hydroelectric, nuclear, and geothermal). Unless specifically excluded, such taxes would include renewable and nonpolluting energy sources, where the rationale for taxation is unclear.

The main objective of a carbon tax is to reduce global warming attributable to carbon emissions. A carbon tax would be applied according to the carbon content of the fuel (although such a tax would not be the same as a tax on carbon emissions, which depends on the efficiency with which the fuel is burned). A carbon tax would also have differential price effects among alternative fuels. The tax burden as a percentage of mine price (at the mine mouth or well head) would be substantially higher for coal than for oil and gas.

Energy consumption taxes

Taxes on energy consumption are not well defined. Energy is not an end in itself, but a means of obtaining some other final product. For example, heat in one's home can be obtained by burning fossil fuel directly, by burning wood, by insulation or use of machinery to store solar power, or by moving to a warmer climate. In practice, taxes on energy consumption are imposed on selected items of consumer expenditure and industrial purchases used for transportation, heating and cooling, and power generation. The tax base could include motor fuels, electric power, oil and gas purchased directly, and oil, gas, and coal burned by factories. The tax could be collected from intermediate sources or from the final consumer. A tax on the final consumer would be very complicated to collect. This tax could be designed to add the same percentage to the cost of all energy, making it more even among uses taxes on selected fuels, but making its objective unclear.

Motor fuel taxes

Motor fuels taxes are already imposed at both the federal and state levels. Traditionally, motor fuel revenues are allocated to trust funds. For example, the gasoline excise tax is allocated to the highway trust fund; taxes on jet fuel into the airport and airways trust fund, and so forth. Beginning in 1991, a portion of the motor fuels excise tax was allocated to the general fund and used for deficit reduction. In 1993, taxes on gasoline and other fuels were increased as a deficit reduction measure, and the revenue from the tax increase was allocated to the general fund. In 1997, however, the general fund tax was transferred to the highway trust fund.

The most important of the motor fuel taxes is the gasoline tax, which is currently imposed by the federal government at 18.4 cents per gallon; 0.1 cent per gallon is retained in the leaking underground storage tank trust fund. Imposing taxes on gasoline that are not used for highway construction can be justified on the grounds of pollution and congestion effects, and a gasoline tax is easier to administer and creates fewer competitive concerns for industries than do other energy taxes. Motor fuels taxes may not, however, be the best way to correct for the costs of driving. For example, driving in rural areas does not produce the same external costs as driving in urban areas does.

An alternative way of reducing gasoline consumption is to tax vehicles with low fuel efficiency. Currently, the United States imposes excise taxes on the sale of some new cars with above-average fuel consumption. The size of this "gas-guzzler" tax ranges from $1,000 to $7,700. Although the gas-guzzler tax discourages the purchase of certain fuel-inefficient cars, it does not promote other methods of fuel saving, such as carpooling or using more public transportation.

Conclusion

Energy taxes differ in form and can be used to promote various objectives. Current taxes in the United States are used primarily to fund transportation programs and are justified as user taxes. Proposals for broadly based energy taxes have had alternative rationales. In the 1970s and 1980s, some people favored taxes on oil imports or on all oil consumption to reduce dependence on oil imports, although these taxes would have had many uneven effects and administrative complexities. Others cited a variety of energy conservation and environmental considerations to support broad-based energy taxes, such as taxes on the energy content of fuels (BTU tax) or on the sales of energy products. In 1993, the Clinton administration proposed a BTU tax, but Congress rejected the proposal in favor of a modest increase in motor fuels taxes. In recent years, environmental considerations have led to interest in a carbon tax to reduce the potential for global warming from greenhouse gas emissions. As of 2004, however, it appears highly unlikely that the United States will enact any form of broad-based energy tax in the near future.

ADDITIONAL READINGS

Bovenberg, A. Lans, and Lawrence H. Goulder. "Costs of Environmentally Motivated Taxes in the Presence of Other Taxes: General Equilibrium Analyses." *National Tax Journal* 50 (March 1997): 59–87.

Bull, Nicholas, Kevin A. Hassett, and Gilbert E. Metcalf. "Who Pays Broad-Based Energy Taxes? Computing Lifetime and Regional Incidence." *The Energy Journal* 15 (1994): 145–64.

Gerardi, Geraldine, and Eric Toder. "The Economic Effects of Alternative Energy Taxes." *National Tax Journal* 37 (September 1984): 289–301.

Goulder, Lawrence H. "Environmental Taxation and the Double Dividend: A Reader's Guide." *International Tax and Public Finance* 2 (1995): 157–83.

Organization for Economic Cooperation and Development (OECD). *Environmental Taxes in OECD Countries.* Paris: OECD, 1995.

———. *Environmentally Related Taxes in OECD Countries: Issues and Strategies.* Paris: OECD, 2001.

Poterba, James. "Tax Policy to Combat Global Warming: On Designing a Carbon Tax." In *Global Warming: Economic Policy Responses,* edited by Rudigen Dornbusch and James M. Poterba (71–97). Cambridge, MA: MIT Press, 1991.

Cross-references: excise taxes; fuel taxes, federal; user charges, federal.

Enterprise zones

Leslie E. Papke
Michigan State University

Geographic areas targeted for economic development assistance.

Enterprise zone programs are geographically targeted tax, expenditure, and regulatory inducements used by state and local governments since the early 1980s and by the federal government since 1993. While the programs differ in their specifics, they all provide development incentives, including tax preferences to capital and labor, in an attempt to induce private investment location or expansion to depressed areas and to enhance employment opportunities for the residents therein. Most enterprise zones are designated in urban areas, but occasionally rural areas are selected.

Typically, state and local zone programs provide larger tax credits for business investment than for employment incentives. Investment incentives include the exemption of business-related purchases from state sales and use taxes, investment tax credits, and corporate income or unemployment tax rebates. Labor subsidies include employer tax credits for all new hires or zone-resident new hires, employee income tax credits, and job-training tax credits. Some programs assist firms financially with investment funds or industrial development bonds.

Enterprise zones have been criticized as ineffective and inefficient in stimulating new economic activity. This criticism is part of a long-standing debate on the effects of intersite tax differentials on the location of capital investment. It is argued that if tax-induced investment only represents relocation from another state, then tax competition is a zero-sum game for the country as a whole. In addition, the preferential treatment of certain types of investment or employment within enterprise zones may induce decisions that would not be economically sound in the absence of the tax incentives.

Often, however, redistribution of economic activity within a state may be a desirable goal. If investment is relocated from local labor markets with low unemployment to local labor markets with higher unemployment, the incentives may generate efficiency gains for the economy as underutilized resources are tapped. Efficiency gains may also result if reductions in unemployment produce positive externalities, such as reductions in social unrest.

In addition to encouraging existing businesses to locate in particular geographic areas, the incentives may induce the creation of new businesses that would not otherwise have been started. Such new businesses could produce taxable profits and incomes that would reduce the revenue cost of the incentives.

A partial equilibrium model can predict the theoretical effects of enterprise zone incentives offered to firms in those zones. If the zones are small relative to the rest of the economy, the effect on zone wages and employment will depend on the supply elasticity of factors to the zone and on the demand elasticity for zone output. For plausible parameter values, a labor subsidy or an equal-cost subsidy to both zone capital and zone resident labor will raise zone wages. A capital subsidy alone may actually reduce zone wages. Employment effects are likely to be small if labor is inelastically supplied.

If the zones are relatively large and spillovers into the rest of the economy are considered, the effects are more difficult to predict. The net employment effects for the nation of a federal enterprise zone program depend on features of both zone and nonzone sectors of the economy: the relative sizes of the two sectors, the elasticity of factor substitution in the two sectors, the elasticity of zone and nonzone product substitution in consumption, and the aggregate supply elasticities of production factors. The greater the number of areas designated as enterprise zones, the smaller the effects on zone wages. If capital is relatively fixed in the aggregate, as many empirical studies suggest, the net effect will be to relocate productive facilities inside the zone.

An empirical evaluation of an enterprise zone program frequently measures the amount of investment undertaken after the designation, the increase in the number of firms in the zone, and the change in zone employment. Cost-effectiveness is measured by direct spending and forgone revenue per job created (or, if the goal of the program is zone-resident employment, cost per zone-resident job). Of course, it is difficult to determine which jobs may be relocations from another area or which jobs would have been created in the absence of the zone program. These measures provide a rough accounting of the initial level of public investment required per zone job created, but they are not a full cost-benefit accounting of the program because they do not account for second round feedback effects (such as zone employee removal from welfare and income tax payments).

Two key methodological issues in empirical evaluations are (1) to separate the effects of zone designation from jobs and investments arising from other factors—for example, general upswings in the economy; (2) the evaluation must account for the depressed economic characteristics that led to the initial zone designation. Survey or case study methodologies provide useful information on zone participation, but they cannot isolate zone effects.

Econometric analysis is better suited to analyzing the effects of zone programs. If zone sites are randomly selected, the effect of the program can be measured by comparing the performance of the experimental and control groups. Usually, however, enterprise zone designation is based on economic performance, so the data are nonexperimental. This sample selection problem can be addressed with a variety of econometric techniques.

Econometric analysis of a zone's success faces a practical difficulty because conventional economic data are not available by zone. In most states, zones do not coincide with census tracts or taxing jurisdictions. As a result, zone areas cannot be pinpointed in standard data collections. ZIP Code–level data is available from the Census, but outcome measures are 10 years apart. Despite these difficulties, a number of studies have analyzed the federal program in Britain, the state and local enterprise zone initiatives in the United States, and the federal Empowerment Zone initiative.

In 1981, the United Kingdom began to designate areas as enterprise zones. The zones were small relative to U.S. zones, ranging in size from 100 to 900 acres, and consisted of vacant, unoccupied, or deteriorating industrial land within an economically declining community. In contrast to the state zones in the United States, British zone boundaries excluded both existing business and residential areas. The U.K. program focused almost exclusively on industrial development—community development was not a specific goal of the program. After a series of evaluations concluded that relocations were the source of activity in the zones, the British government is allowing the zones to expire.

In contrast to the United Kingdom, eligibility for state and local zone programs in the United States depends upon zone population characteristics. These include comparative unemployment rates, population levels and trends, poverty status, median incomes, and percentage of welfare recipients. Since the early 1980s, more than 40 states have enacted enterprise zone programs as part of their economic development policies. They differ widely in purpose, coverage, and incentive provisions. For example, while Michigan has only one zone, Louisiana has more than 800.

The state of Indiana had one of the first enterprise zone programs and its incentives provisions are both typical and idiosyncratic. In 1984, Indiana began to designate zones for a 10-year duration, subject to renewal. To qualify for consid-

eration and possible designation, the area had to have an unemployment rate at least 1.5 times the average statewide unemployment rate, and a resident household poverty rate at least 25 percent above the federal poverty level. Its resident population had to be between 2,000 and 8,000 persons and its geographic area between 0.75 and 3 square miles, all with a continuous boundary.

The two largest tax incentives included in the Indiana enterprise zone program were (1) a tax credit against local property tax liability equal to 100 percent of the property tax imposed on all inventories located in the zone, and (2) a tax credit for employers hiring zone residents equal to 10 percent of wages, with a ceiling of $1,500 per qualified employee.

Indiana's employment tax credit, which targets the hiring of zone residents, is typical of other enterprise zone programs. Also like other programs, the value of the tax preferences was tilted heavily toward capital investment. But the inventory tax credit was an unusual mechanism for increasing investment because most states do not include inventories in a business's tangible personal property tax base and would instead typically provide incentives for investment in machinery or equipment rather than inventories. In fact, tax restructuring changes in Indiana enacted in 2002 have eliminated this primary zone incentive.

Econometric evaluations of the Indiana and New Jersey programs find mixed effects on investment and employment. Indiana zones are estimated to have greater inventory growth and fewer unemployment claims than they would have in the absence of the zone designation. However, inventory investment appears to come at the cost of a drop in depreciable property. Moreover, despite the reduction in unemployment rates in the zones, a comparison of incomes from the 1980 and 1990 Census suggests that zone residents are not appreciably better off with the Indiana zone program.

Similar econometric analysis of the New Jersey enterprise zone program finds no positive effects on either business investment or employment. Multi-state econometric analyses that combine data from many states—thereby assuming zone programs have similar effects in every state—typically find no positive zone effects on business activity or employment.

While zone incentives typically target businesses, in urban markets increased activity may affect local housing markets. Several state programs have been evaluated for these indirect effects on urban housing markets but have found no positive effects on the value of residential property, rents, and vacancies.

Cost-per-job estimates from zone programs are rare. The available ones are not that different from earlier U.S. experiences with job subsidies such as the JOBS program of the late 1960s and early 1970s and the Urban Development Action Grant Program in the late 1970s. However, costs per zone-resident job are considerably higher. For example, in Indiana, calculations indicate that the annual cost of an Indiana zone job in 1990 was $4,564, compared with $31,113 per zone-resident job.

A further consideration is the distribution of the cost of the zone program between state and local governments. For example, in Indiana, local governments may bear the brunt of the cost of a state enterprise zone program if tax incentives are provided against local taxes without state reimbursement.

The 1993 federal program (contained in the Omnibus Budget Reconciliation Act of 1993) called for the creation of 95 enterprise communities (65 urban, 30 rural) and nine empowerment zones (six urban, three rural). The designations were to take place in 1994–95 and to last up to 10 years. Selected areas needed to demonstrate pervasive poverty, unemployment, and general distress, and applicants had to outline a plan of action that included local business and community interests.

Both enterprise communities and empowerment zones were to receive tax-exempt facility bonds, $3 million in Department of Heath and Human Services Social Service Block Grants, and priority for funds from many existing federal programs. Empowerment zones received additional benefits. The block grant amount was increased to $100 million and substantial employer tax benefits were added. Qualified employers receive a 20 percent employer tax credit for wages paid to qualified zone employees up to $15,000. Firms in empowerment zones may increase their Section 179 expensing by up to $20,000, to a total of $37,500 for qualified zone property.

The residence-based approach of the income tax credit differs significantly from another federal program designed to increase employment of the disadvantaged. The Targeted Jobs Tax Credit provides firms with a similar-sized subsidy for wages paid to targeted individuals—primarily welfare recipients and poor youth. Research has demonstrated that providing a subsidy based on individual characteristics may create a stigma that actually reduces the probability of being hired. Residence-based eligibility may eliminate this problem and encourage individuals who become employed to continue to live in the zone.

Over the 1990s, the number of empowerment zones under federal law expanded, and some revisions were made in the benefits. Special benefits were also enacted for the District of Columbia. Recent research examines the economic characteristics of depressed areas that were chosen in the three rounds of the federal Empowerment Zone designations that took place between 1993 and 2000, and finds that sites designated as empowerment zones in subsequent rounds were less depressed than earlier sites.

ADDITIONAL READINGS

Anderson, John E., and Robert W. Wassmer. "Bidding for Business: The Efficacy of Local Economic Development Incentives in a Metropolitan Area." Kalamazoo, MI: W. E. Upjohn Institute for Employment Research, 2000.

Bartik, Timothy J. *Who Benefits from State and Local Economic Development Policies.* Kalamazoo, MI: W. E. Upjohn Institute for Employment Research, 1991.

Bishop, John, and Mark Montgomery. "Does the Targeted Jobs Tax Credit Create Jobs at Subsidized Firms?" *Industrial Relations* (Fall 1993): 289–306.

Boarnet, Marlon G., and William T. Bogart, "Enterprise Zones and Employment: Evidence from New Jersey." *Journal of Urban Economics* 40 (1996): 198–215.

Bogart, William T. "Book Review: State Enterprise Zone Programs: Have They Worked?" *National Tax Journal* 56, no. 2 (June 2003): 439–42.

Bondonio, Danielle, and John Engberg. "Enterprise Zones and Local Employment: Evidence from the States' Programs." *Regional Science and Urban Economics* 30 (2000): 519–49.

Brintnall, Michael, and R. Green. "Comparing State Enterprise Zone Programs: Variations in Structure and Coverage." *Economic Development Quarterly* 2, no. 1 (1988): 50–68.

Connecticut Department of Economic Development. *Enterprise Zones: The Connecticut Experiment.* Hartford, CT: Connecticut Department of Economic Development, 1985.

Cordes, Joseph, and Nancy A. Gardner. "Enterprise Zones and Property Values: What We Know (Or Maybe Don't)." In *Proceedings of the Ninety-Fourth Annual Conference on Taxation* (279–87). Washington, DC: National Tax Association, 2001.

Dowall, David E. "An Evaluation of California's Enterprise Zone Programs." *Economic Development Quarterly* 10 (1996): 352–68.

Engberg, John, and Robert Greenbaum. "State Enterprise Zones and Local Housing Markets." *Journal of Housing Research* 10, no. 2 (1999): 163–87.

Erickson, Rodney A., and Susan W. Friedman. "Comparative Dimensions of State Enterprise Zone Policies." In *Enterprise Zones: New Directions in Economic Development,* edited by Roy E. Green (155–76). Newbury Park, CA: Sage Publications, 1991.

Friedlander, Daniel, David H. Greenberg, and Philip K. Robins. "Evaluating Government Training Programs for the Economically Disadvantaged." *Journal of Economic Literature* 35 (1997): 1809–55.

Gravelle, Jane G. "Enterprise Zones: The Design of Tax Incentives." CRS Report for Congress 92-476 S. Washington, DC: Congressional Research Service, Library of Congress, June 3, 1992.

Greenbaum, Robert T., and John B. Engberg. "The Impact of State Enterprise Zones on Urban Manufacturing Establishments." *Journal of Policy Analysis and Management* 23, no. 2 (2004): 315–39.

Ladd, Helen F. "Spatially Targeted Economic Development Strategies: Do They Work?" *Cityscape* 1(1): 193–211.

Papke, James A. *The Role of Market Based Public Policy in Economic Development and Urban Revitalization: A Retrospective Analysis and Appraisal of the Indiana Enterprise Zone Program—Year Three Report.* West Lafayette, IN: Center for Tax Policy Studies, Purdue University, 1990.

Papke, Leslie E. "What Do We Know about Enterprise Zones?" In *Tax Policy and the Economy* 7, edited by James M. Poterba (37–72). Cambridge, MA: MIT Press, 1993.

———. "Tax Policy and Urban Development: Evidence from the Indiana Enterprise Zone Program." *Journal of Public Economics* 54, no. 1 (1994): 37–49.

———. "The Indiana Enterprise Zone Revisited: Effects on Capital Investment and Land Values." *National Tax Association Proceedings of the Ninety-Third Annual Conference on Taxation,* edited by Sally Wallace (83–87). Washington, DC: National Tax Association, 2001.

Peters, Alan H., and Peter S. Fisher. "State Enterprise Zone Programs: Have They Worked?" Kalamazoo, MI: W. E. Upjohn Institute for Employment Research, 2002.

Rubin, Barry M., and Craig M. Richards. "A Transatlantic Comparison of Enterprise Zone Impacts: The British and American Experience." *Economic Development Quarterly* 6, no. 4 (1992): 431–43.

Rubin, Barry M., and Margaret G. Wilder. "Urban Enterprise Zones: Employment Impacts and Fiscal Incentives." *Journal of the American Planning Association* 55, no. 4 (1989): 418–31.

U.S. Department of Housing and Urban Development. "An Impact Evaluation of the Urban Development Action Grant Program." Washington, DC: Office of Policy Development and Research, 1982.

———. "State Enterprise Zone Update: Summaries of the State Enterprise Zone Programs." Washington, DC: U.S. Department of Housing and Urban Development, 1992.

U.S. General Accounting Office. "Enterprise Zones: Lessons from the Maryland Experience." GAO/PEMD-89-2. Washington, DC: U.S. General Accounting Office, 1988.

Wilder, Margaret G., and Barry M. Rubin. "Rhetoric versus Reality: A Review of Studies on State Enterprise Zone Programs." *Journal of the American Planning Association* 62 (1996): 473–91.

Cross-references: budget policy, state and local; business location, taxation and; fiscal disparities; tax competition; tax-exempt bonds; zoning, property taxes, and exactions.

Environmental taxes, federal

Thomas A. Barthold

Joint Committee on Taxation, U.S. Congress

Taxes levied on goods or services whose consumption or production is thought to affect the environment.

Policymakers may implement environmental policy through the use of taxes or subsidies that affect market prices or rates of return, thereby altering the environmental consequences of private market outcomes.

Federal tax policy has long had environmental consequences, although it is only over the past 30 years that tax policy has been used as an environmental policy tool. Many existing tax provisions with environmental ramifications were not motivated by environmental concerns. For example, income tax provisions passed to assist the timber industry in the 1920s permitted expensing (rather than capitalization) of the costs of reforestation and planting. Combined with preferential capital gains treatment for harvested timber, these income tax provisions may have encouraged a more rapid harvest of domestic timberland. Similarly, Congress first enacted the federal motor fuels tax in 1932, but it is only recently that this tax began to be discussed as an environmental tax, aimed at addressing the externalities caused by automobile use.

Efforts at environmental tax policy began after the 1973 oil embargo, although at that time, policy focused on energy conservation rather than pollution reduction. In the Energy Tax Act of 1978, Congress enacted the gas-guzzler excise tax, which varied with the Environmental Protection Agency's (EPA's) fuel economy rating of automobiles and provided tax credits for residential energy conservation expenditures. While the gas-guzzler excise tax remains in force today, Congress repealed residential energy credits in 1986.

After 1980, the use of tax policy to deal with environmental problems accelerated, as policymakers displayed a much greater interest in so-called "market solutions" to environmental control than in direct regulation. Better-known examples include the excise taxes on petroleum and hazardous chemicals, enacted in 1980 to fund the EPA's hazardous waste site cleanup program (Superfund). In 1989, in the aftermath of the *Exxon Valdez* oil spill, Congress imposed an additional excise tax on petroleum and petroleum products to fund the Oil Spill Liability Trust Fund. In the same year, Congress imposed an excise tax on the manufacture of ozone-depleting chemicals. In 1992, Congress enacted income tax deductions for the purchase of "clean fuel" vehicles and tax credits for the production of electricity from wind.

Since the mid-1990s, the implementation of environmental taxes has waned at the federal level. In 1993, Congress rejected President Clinton's proposal for a modified BTU (energy) tax. The Superfund taxes were allowed to expire in 1995, and the Oil Spill Liability Trust Fund tax was allowed to expire in 1994. Nevertheless, at present, more than 50 federal tax code provisions may be classified as environmental, and Congress has continued to examine proposals to provide tax subsidies to energy-conserving or pollution-reducing technologies.

Federal environmental tax policy generally falls into one of five categories: benefit taxes, taxes as insurance premiums, Pigouvian taxes (see below), liability taxes, or windfall profits taxes. First, Congress has assessed some taxes as user fees to fund specific direct-expenditure programs. This is sometimes called the benefit principle of taxation; those who benefit should pay the taxes, which approximate user charges. While the use of excise taxes imposed on highway motor fuels to fund expenditures from the Highway Trust Fund for the construction and repair of highways is the best-known example, the sport-fishing-equipment excise tax and the excise tax on motorboat fuels fund programs to ensure the survival of other fish species threatened by sport fishing.

Second, a tax may be assessed on an industry or group of consumers to fund an insurance pool against potential environmental risks arising from the taxed product. The tax is levied as an insurance premium in a mandated scheme of risk pooling. For example, the Oil Spill Liability Trust Fund tax imposed a tax of $0.05 per barrel of domestic and imported oil. While the primary liability for damage from an oil spill remains with the owner of the oil, the tax funded a trust fund that may be drawn upon to meet unrecovered claims that arise from an oil spill upon the high seas or from ruptured domestic pipelines. The tax and trust fund represent a social insurance scheme with risks spread across all consumers of petroleum.

Third, the federal government has used the tax code to deliver Pigouvian subsidies or impose Pigouvian taxes, named after British economist Arthur C. Pigou, on polluters. The premise of such a tax (or subsidy) is that when an externality causes marginal social costs (or marginal social benefits) to diverge from private marginal costs (or private marginal benefits), the market outcome may not produce an efficient level of output. Pigou was the first to propose that a tax equal to the difference between marginal social cost and private marginal cost would lead the market to an efficient outcome. The tax internalizes the externality into private costs. Examples of Pigouvian subsidies are the (short-lived) residential energy credits, which were premised on the belief that private market prices did not reflect the full social benefit of energy conservation. Examples of Pigouvian taxes are the gas-guzzler excise tax and the excise tax on ozone-depleting chemicals.

Fourth, Congress has funded specific environmental programs by imposing environmental taxes on taxpayers deemed to be liable for past environmental damage, rather than on taxpayers perceived to benefit from the expenditure program. Such taxes cannot be interpreted as Pigouvian if they are not related to current externalities. Nor can such taxes be seen as insurance premiums if the primary expenditure purpose is to remedy past environmental damage. Examples of such "liability" taxes are the expired Superfund excise taxes on petroleum and chemicals and the leaking underground storage tank tax imposed on fuels. These taxes fund trust funds, expenditures from which remedy past environmental damage.

The final category is that of windfall profits taxes. Regulatory control of supply may cause prices to rise beyond those that would prevail in a free market, creating high returns on the permitted sales. Alternatively, removal of previously existing price controls may cause prices to rise beyond those previously prevailing, creating high returns on existing sales. Economists refer to these increased profits as "inframarginal" or "windfall," meaning that they are profits on the level of the producers' economic activity that would have occurred without the change in regulatory policy. The most obvious example is the Crude Oil Windfall Profit Tax passed by Congress in 1980 in response to the deregulation of oil prices. This tax was repealed in 1988. Some have suggested that the tax on ozone-depleting chemicals is a windfall profits tax because production of and trade in these chemicals are governed by an international agreement.

Many taxes fall into more than one of these five categories. For example, motor fuels taxes may have both a benefit component and a Pigouvian component. In addition, environmental taxes often deviate from what economic theory dictates. The taxes assessed as user fees only inexactly measure benefits; for example, not all motorboats are used for fishing. The taxes assessed as insurance premiums reflect imperfect pricing of risks; the Oil Spill Liability Trust Fund tax was imposed at the same rate regardless of whether the importer employs harder-to-rupture double-hulled or single-hulled tankers. The Pigouvian taxes imperfectly measure marginal social cost or benefit. The residential energy credits were inframarginal for all those taxpayers who were planning to invest in home insulation, even without the tax break.

Depending on their incidence, liability taxes may inexactly recoup damages from parties held responsible for past environmental damage. For example, the burden may fall on the current owners of enterprises rather than those who were the owners at the time the damage occurred. In practice, it may not be possible to identify the inframarginal units of production on which to impose a windfall profits tax.

The environmental taxes enacted probably deviate from theoretical precepts for several reasons. There are practical problems of design. It may be difficult to identify the tax base. Congress must also weigh the costs of administration and compliance against the benefits of a "perfect" environmental tax. In addition, other policy concerns such as economic de-velopment or defense needs may lead to compromises with environmental policy concerns.

The existing federal "environmental tax" provisions vary in their budgetary importance. The Office of Management and Budget (OMB) projected that federal motor fuels taxes would yield revenues in excess of $35.5 billion in 2004. The narrower scope of other tax provisions limits their budgetary effect. For example, OMB projects the leaking underground storage tank tax to raise only $188 million in 2004. The Joint Committee on Taxation estimates the deduction for "clean fuel" vehicles will reduce revenues by approximately $200 million in 2004. While small relative to the federal budget, such figures might be substantial relative to the affected industry. In addition, if the intent of a tax is Pigouvian, a small revenue yield might reflect that the tax has successfully altered behavior.

ADDITIONAL READINGS

Barthold, Thomas A. "Issues in the Design of Environmental Excise Taxes." *Journal of Economic Perspectives* 8 (Winter 1994): 133–51.

Cropper, Maureen L., and Wallace E. Oates. "Environmental Economics: A Survey." *Journal of Economic Literature* 30 (June 1992): 675–740.

Pigou, Arthur C. *The Economics of Welfare,* 4th ed. London: MacMillan and Company, 1932.

U.S. Congress, House Committee on Ways and Means. *Hearings* Serial 101-98. Washington, DC: House Committee on Ways and Means, March 6, 7, and 14, 1990.

U.S. Congress, Joint Committee on Taxation. *Present Law and Background Relating to Federal Environmental Tax Policy.* Washington, DC: Joint Committee on Taxation, 1990.

Cross-references: benefit principle; energy taxes; environmental taxes, state; excise taxes; fuel taxes, federal; Highway Trust Fund, federal.

Environmental taxes, state

Robert A. Bohm
University of Tennessee at Knoxville

Michael P. Kelsay
University of Missouri–Kansas City

The states' tax and fee responses to activities judged environmentally harmful.

In general terms, an environmental tax can be thought of as a user charge on the environment. Using this definition, any activity that has a negative environmental impact creates an obligation to pay the tax. At a minimum, revenue from the tax should be adequate to fund cleanup efforts. At best, the tax may provide incentives to reduce or eliminate the environmental problems altogether. Institutionally, environmental taxes are often called fees or charges, indicating that the revenue is designated for special purposes and is deposited into a restricted account. When the word tax is used, common practice suggests that the revenue is deposited in the general fund. In this entry, these terms are used interchangeably to indicate a revenue instrument with an environmental base.

Environmental taxes take many forms at the state level. Some may be thought of as direct environmental taxes; the link between these taxes and recognizable environmental issues is readily apparent. Into this group fall generation or emission fees, disposal fees, and permit fees. A second group may be termed indirect environmental taxes. Here, the link to the environmental problem at hand may be rather remote. Into this group fall the so-called predisposal or advance disposal fees, as well as taxes on productive inputs and products that generate environmental costs when used. Indirect environmental taxes used by state governments are invariably thinly disguised product excise taxes.

Both direct and indirect environmental taxes may entail attempts to reflect differentially higher costs of treatment or higher risks associated with specific waste streams and activities with environmental impacts. For example, Missouri levied a disposal charge on all solid waste disposed of in the state and imposed a predisposal tax on the sale of automotive tires before the law expired January 1, 2004. Revenue from the disposal charge as applied to automotive tires has funded a substantial portion of cleanup and remediation of illegal tire dumps. The tire predisposal fee was intended to reflect the higher costs inherent in the disposal of tires in landfills and the need for scrap tire reduction technologies. Alternatively, California charges higher rates for large-quantity generators of medical waste and differentiates its hazardous waste disposal fee based upon the characteristics of the waste stream and the method of treatment.

State environmental taxes are levied over and above existing costs, charges, fees, or taxes in all but a few cases. Municipal solid waste services, for example, may be provided by local governments and funded by user charges, through general revenue, or by private companies. State solid waste taxes or fees represent a surcharge added to the direct cost of this service. Environmentally based levies on products such as tires and motor fuels are likewise additional charges. The exception to this rule is a case in which the state government itself is involved as primary provider of the service—solid waste services in Delaware and the District of Columbia, for example.

State environmental taxes in 2002

Table 1 summarizes the major state environmental taxes in use in the 50 states and the District of Columbia, based on surveys completed in 1995 and 2002. In addition to a generic name for each type of tax, the table shows the number of states using the tax in both years and the range of rate and base definitions in 2002. Permit fees, such as those used to fund state air quality programs and the National Pollution Discharge Elimination System, are not included in this summary.

Table 1 describes two generation fees. The hazardous waste generation fee is the most frequently employed environmental tax, used in 42 states in 2002 (down from 44 in 1995). This is a two-part tax that, in most cases, combines an annual fee per facility with a volume fee per ton generated. The volume fee varies depending on whether an on-site or off-site method of treatment, storage, or disposal is used. Six states impose a low-level radioactive waste fee (down from seven in 1995). Typically, this tax is based on both waste volume and a radioactivity charge.

Missouri and Maine present two interesting examples of the hazardous waste generation fee. In Missouri, the generator pays an annual fee of $1.00 per ton generated up to a maximum levy of $10,000.00. In addition, the generator managing hazardous waste by on-site storage or off-site storage that is not in conjunction with incineration, resource recovery, treatment, or other similar management method shall pay a tax determined by the following formula: $22.93 + ($.084015 \times$ number of tons generated). No generator pays more than $84,132.00 annually for this type of hazardous waste.

Alternatively, a generator utilizing an alternative management technique shall pay a tax determined by the following formula: $(\$11.47 + [\$.042008 \times$ number of tons generated$]) \times (.90785 \times$ number of tons generated). In this case, no generator shall pay more than $42,066.00 annually.

In Maine, the following fees apply: large quantity generators pay $40.00 per ton for waste generated and disposed of on site in a licensed facility; $100.00 per ton for waste stored from 90 to 180 days; and $40.00 per ton or $30.00 per ton for

TABLE 1. **State Environmental Taxation in the United States** (2002 and 1995)

Tax	States using tax in 2002 (1995)	Tax rate and tax base in 2002
Hazardous waste generator fee	42 (44)	From $300.00 to $200,000.00 annual fee per facility plus from $1.00 to $360.00 per ton generated
Hazardous waste disposal fee	41 (43)	From $1.00 to $214.00 per ton
Underground storage tank fee	38 (38)	From $10.00 to $30,000.00 annual fee per tank, plus $0.006 to $0.02 per gallon stored
Solid waste disposal fee	39 (36)	From $0.10 to $44.75 per ton
Waste tire fee	37 (28)	From $0.25 to $2.00 per tire
Motor fuels fee	16 (14)	From $0.002 to $0.16 per gallon
Low-level radioactive waste generator fee	6 (7)	From $3.00 to $13.00 per cubic foot
Coastal/inland spill fee	6 (6)	From $0.20 to $0.80 per gallon of imported pollutant
Water quality fee	4 (4)	From $0.02 to $0.59 per gallon of solvent, oil, ammonia, or petroleum product

waste transported off-site to a licensed facility for reuse, reclamation, or recycling. (The latter fees increase to $360.00 per ton and $270.00 per ton, respectively, if there is noncompliance with state waste reduction goals.) In addition, hazardous waste that is transported off a federally declared Superfund site may not exceed $200,000.00 per site in any calendar year. If hazardous waste is transported into Maine from out of state, the fees above are doubled.

In 2002, 41 states employed a hazardous waste disposal fee (down from 43 in 1995) and 39 levied a solid waste disposal fee (up from 36 in 1995). These taxes are in the form of surcharges, with widely varying rates between states. In addition, the rate may vary significantly within states. For example, in California, the rate per ton varies depending on waste category, volume, and disposal method.

In 38 states, the need for revenue to fund underground storage tax programs has led to the enactment of underground storage tank fees. Like the hazardous waste generator fee, this tax is often in two parts, an annual fee per tank and a rate per gallon used for environmental purposes.

Two product excise taxes are commonly used for environmental purposes. The tire predisposal tax is in place in 37 states (up from 28 in 1995). With the exception of North Carolina's ad valorem approach, the disposal calculation method used in the District of Columbia, and five states imposing a fee at the time of title transfer, states levy this tax on a per tire basis, with the rate ranging from $0.25 to $2.00 per passenger tire in 2002.

A motor fuel tax, which provides funds for environmental purposes related to fuel use, is in place in 16 states (up from 14 in 1995). In some instances, funds from this tax are directed toward underground storage tank programs; other uses include oil collection programs.

Two final taxes are the coastal/inland pollutant spill fee (six states in 2002 and 1995) and the water-quality fee on imported pollutants (four states in 2002 and 1995). The water quality fee, used to fund water cleanup programs, is levied on selected polluting liquids.

In general, the number of states using environmental taxes has remained remarkably stable from 1995 to 2002. With the exception of a slight increase in the highest rate levied on solid waste disposal (from $42.00 per ton to $44.75 per ton), the range of rates in use has not changed at all.

Environmental tax policy issues

To date, state environmental taxes have been levied on narrow bases with limited revenue goals. The jury remains out on the use of environmental taxes as more broadly defined tax instruments (Bohm et al. 1998). Likewise, little can be said about the incidence of these taxes. While a presumption of regressivity is common and may be correct, a firm conclusion cannot be documented.

Two factors dominate the policy discussion surrounding the enactment of state environmental taxes. First, the need to provide revenue to fund expanding state environmental programs is paramount. The second factor is a desire to provide incentives to reduce waste generation or encourage reuse and recycling. Economists have long argued for generation fees—that is, direct taxes on environmental emissions—as the best way to achieve the latter goal. Historically, these have been considered difficult to administer and politically impractical. However, as table 1 shows, states are venturing into this territory, as better emission monitoring has become more commonplace and the pursuit of environmental quality has risen on the political agenda.

Disposal fees and product excise taxes have long been the most popular forms of environmental taxation. With easy-to-measure or familiar tax bases, they represent certain sources of revenue. Disposal fees paid directly by generators are equivalent to generation fees. In most cases, however, disposal of environmental waste is institutionally separate from generation, and the tax must be shifted to the generator to achieve the same incentive effect as an emission fee. Still, disposal and product excise taxes do raise the cost of undesirable environmental practices, and these costs will be transmitted through the economy and alter behavior, albeit imperfectly. Furthermore, as has already happened in several states, these costs can be accentuated by means of differentially higher rates for particularly noxious waste or distasteful behavior.

Recent analysis indicates that hazardous waste taxes at the state level reduce the amount of waste generated by manufacturing facilities and that taxes on land disposal decrease the use of this waste management method (Sigman 2003).

ADDITIONAL READINGS

Anderson, Mikael. *Governance by Green Taxes.* New York: Manchester University Press, 1994.

Barthold, Thomas A. "Issues in the Design of Environmental Excise Taxes." *Journal of Economic Perspectives* (Winter 1994): 133–51.

Bohm, Robert A., and Michael P. Kelsay. "State and Local Government Initiatives to Tax Solid and Hazardous Waste." In *State Taxation of Business: Issues and Policy Options,* edited by Tom Pogue. Westport, CT: Praeger, 1992.

Bohm, Robert A., Chashong Ge, Milton Russell, Jinnan Wang, and Jintian Yang. "Environmental Taxes: China's Bold Initiative." *Environment* 40, no. 7 (September 1998): 10–19.

Bovenberg, A. Lans, and Lawrence H. Goulder. "Optimal Environmental Taxation in the Presence of Other Taxes: General-Equilibrium Analysis." *American Economic Review* (September 1996): 985–1000.

Carlin, Alan. *The United States' Experience with Economic Incentives to Control Environmental Pollution.* Washington, DC: U.S. Environmental Protection Agency, 1992.

Horner, J. Andrew. "Harnessing the Tax Code for Environmental Protection: A Survey of State Initiatives." *State Tax Notes* 14, no. 16 (April 1998): special supplement.

Kelsay, Michael P. *An Industrial and Commercial Waste Characterization and Life-Cycle Cost Analysis of Production Inputs and Disposal Options in the State of Missouri.* Kansas City: University of Missouri–Kansas City, 2001.

Levinson, Arik. *NIMBY Taxes Matter: State Taxes and Interstate Hazardous Waste Shipments.* Working paper no. 6314. Cambridge, MA: National Bureau of Economic Research, 1997.

Oates, Wallace. "Green Tax: Can We Protect the Environment and Improve the Tax System at the Same Time?" *Southern Economic Journal* (April 1995): 915–22.

Organization for Economic Cooperation and Development. *Environment and Taxation: The Case of the Netherlands, Sweden, and the United States.* Paris: Organization for Economic Cooperation and Development, 1994.

Pigou, Arthur C. *The Economics of Welfare,* 4th ed. London: Macmillan and Company, 1932.

Sigman, Hilary. "Taxing Hazardous Waste: The U.S. Experience." *Public Finance and Management* 3, no. 1 (2003): 12–33.

Cross-references: environmental taxes, federal; severance tax, state.

Estate and gift tax, federal

David Joulfaian
U.S. Department of the Treasury

The federal tax treatment of wealth transferred in contemplation of, or at the time of, death.

The estate and gift tax is the only wealth tax levied by the federal government. The estate tax was first enacted in 1916 and applied to the wealth of decedents with estates in excess of $50,000. It has undergone numerous changes, especially in 1976, 1981, and 1997. Significant temporary changes were introduced in 2001 and are set to expire in 2011.

The gift tax was enacted in 1924, repealed in 1926, and reenacted in 1932 in an attempt to reduce estate tax avoidance via the initiation of inter vivos gifts. In 1976, the gift tax was integrated with the estate tax under the unified transfer tax and a common tax rate schedule. Cumulative transfers, inter vivos gifts, and testamentary bequests below $1 million in 2011 are exempt from taxation. Both estate and gift taxes are complemented by a generation-skipping transfer tax (GSTT) with a flat rate of 55 percent for cumulative transfers in excess of $1 million per donor in 2011.

Purpose of the tax

The enactment of the estate and gift tax, and its evolving structure over the decades, serve a number of legislative objectives. First and foremost, estate and gift taxes were enacted for their revenue yield. In 2003, these taxes yielded about $22 billion and accounted for about 1.2 percent of federal government receipts. Although the estate tax is levied on only the wealthiest 2 percent of decedents' estates, the significance of this revenue source should not be understated.

A second objective is for these taxes to act as a backstop to the income tax by reducing the erosion of its base. Much of the capital income that escapes the income tax passes through the estate tax. Under the personal income tax, accrued capital gains are taxed only when realized, and interest income from state and local bonds, as well as proceeds from life insurance policies, among others, are tax-exempt. In contrast, all assets owned by decedents are likely to be included in their gross estates.

A third objective is to reduce wealth concentration. By taxing the wealthiest estates, the estate and gift taxes are expected to reduce the size of bequests, thus reducing the wealth accumulated over generations. This is also accomplished by subjecting capital income that has escaped the personal income tax to estate taxation.

Another objective is to tax each generation's wealth. Wealth transfers to grandchildren are taxed under the estate and gift taxes. However, because of the emphasis on taxing each generation, an additional tax—the GSTT—is also levied on these transfers. The rationale for the GSTT is that a tax should be levied on wealth transfers to children, coupled with another tax when they, in turn, transfer wealth to their children.

To minimize state objections to the enactment of death taxes by the federal government, the estate tax provides a tax credit for state death taxes, thereby keeping the state tax base intact. Effectively, the federal estate tax acts to minimize interstate competition for the wealthy, as the state death tax credit virtually offsets taxes levied by states on the wealthiest of estates.

The tax base

The estate tax is levied on wealth held at death. This includes real estate, cash, stocks, bonds, businesses, pensions, and life insurance policies owned by the decedent, which form the gross estate. Estates may value these assets at their market value on the date of death or six months from that date. Similar property is also taxed under the gift tax when transferred during life. Cumulative lifetime gifts are added back to the taxable estate.

Exclusions

The gift tax provides for an annual exclusion of $11,000 per donee, indexed for inflation. The estate tax provides for an exclusion of up to $750,000 for real property used on farms or in businesses, indexed for inflation. The exclusion is based on the difference between the market value of a property and the capitalized income from its use in business. Proceeds from life insurance policies on the life of the decedent but owned by others are also excluded from the estate. The GSTT provides an exemption of $1 million per donor, indexed for inflation, for transfers in 2011 and beyond.

Deductions

The following statutory deductions are allowed:

1. *Marital deduction.* All transfers of property between spouses, either through inter vivos gifts or bequests, are deductible from the estate and gift tax base.
2. *Charitable bequest deduction.* All money donated to charitable organizations are deductible from the gross estate.
3. *Debts.* The gross estate is reduced by the amount of debts held at death. These debts include mortgages and outstanding medical expenses.

4. *Other expenses.* These consist mostly of funeral expenses and expenses involving the settlement of the decedent's estate, such as attorney and executor commissions. They, too, are deductible from the estate tax base.

Rate structure

The tax rate schedule in effect in 2011 ranges from 18 percent on the first $10,000 of the combined taxable gifts and estates to 55 percent for the excess over $3 million. Generation-skipping transfers are taxed at a flat rate of 55 percent, in addition to the estate and gift taxes.

Tax credits

Several tax credits are available under the estate and gift tax. The largest of these is the unified credit.

Through 1997, the value of the unified credit was fixed at $192,800—equivalent to an exemption of $600,000—for combined estate and gift taxes. In 2011, the credit is set at $345,800, which will exempt the first $1 million from taxation.

The second largest credit is that for state death taxes. This credit is limited to a maximum of 16 percent of the federal taxable estate. State gift taxes do not benefit from a similar credit. The estate tax also provides for a credit for previously paid death taxes in order to minimize double taxation. In computing the heir's estate tax, the credit is set equal to the parent's estate tax on bequeathed wealth phased out over 10 years from the parent's date of death. The credit is not available for the estates of heirs dying more than 10 years after the parent's date of death.

Tax deferral

Estates with farmers and closely held businesses may defer a fraction of the estate tax. This fraction is equal to the share of such assets in the estate, provided that it is in excess of 35 percent. The tax is deferred for a period of 15 years from the date of death, with the principal payable over the last 10 years. The benefit of this deferral is also available to estates that are subject to severe liquidity constraints, at the discretion of the Internal Revenue Service Commissioner.

Temporary provisions

Under temporary legislation enacted in 2001, the reach of estate and gift taxes is curtailed through 2009, with the estate tax, including the GSTT, completely repealed in 2010. However, in 2011, the estate tax is reinstated to reflect the law as enacted in 1997. More specifically, the maximum estate, GSTT, and gift tax rates are reduced to 45 percent by 2009, and the size of exempted estate is expanded to $3.5 million under the estate tax and GSTT.

Income distribution

The potential effect on income and wealth distribution is an important consideration when levying estate and gift taxes. These taxes are levied on wealth and typically apply to the top wealth holders. The revenue obtained from the estate and gift taxes, when redistributed, could reduce the concentration of wealth in the hands of a few people. More important, if the tax were designed to stimulate inter vivos gifts and bequests to a wider number of recipients, then it could be thought of as a tool to discourage concentrations of wealth.

However, there are some instances in which the estate and gift tax could cause greater inequality. If the estate tax, for instance, were to reduce savings, it would lead to lower levels of capital and lower the real rate of return to labor. Lowering labor income may exacerbate existing inequalities between those who receive income from capital and those who receive income from labor.

Another possible scenario occurs when wealth is transferred by donors who are better off than the recipients. If such transfers are reduced by the estate and gift tax, then the level of inequality increases under the tax.

Behavioral effects

Estate taxes have incentive effects for both donors and heirs. Higher estate taxes may reduce the work effort and savings of parents motivated to leave large bequests to their children. This substitution effect is the result of the tax raising the price of bequests. An offsetting effect is the income effect, whereby parents may have to increase their work efforts and savings to cover the higher taxes. There is some empirical evidence that suggests that high tax rates may have adverse effects on wealth accumulation.

Estate taxes also affect the heirs' work effort and savings. Recent evidence suggests that large inheritances may speed up the retirement decision. Even for those who remain in the labor force, one may also observe a reduction in labor supply. However, labor supply effects are generally small. Similarly, consumption is also observed to rise in the aftermath of inheritance. But, again, these effects are small.

Taxes may also affect the timing of transfers between parents and children. Differences in the tax treatment of lifetime gifts and bequests may create incentives for parents to accelerate, or alternatively postpone, intergenerational transfers. Similarly, taxes may alter the division of bequests. High tax rates, for instance, may stimulate giving to charity at the expense of bequests to children.

ADDITIONAL READINGS

Bakija, Jon, William Gale, and Joel Slemrod. "Charitable Bequests and Taxes on Inheritance and Estates: Aggregate Evidence from across States and Time." *American Economic Review* 93, no. 2 (May 2003): 366–70.

Bernheim, B. Douglas. "Does the Estate Tax Raise Revenue?" In *Tax Policy and the Economy* 1, edited by Lawrence H. Summers. Cambridge, MA: MIT Press, 1987.

Cooper, George. "A Voluntary Tax? New Perspectives on Sophisticated Estate Tax Avoidance." Washington, DC: The Brookings Institution, 1979.

Davies, James B., and Peter Kuhn. "Intergenerational Transfers and the Distribution of Income and Wealth." In *Modeling the Accumulation and Distribution of Wealth,* edited by Denis Kessler and Andre Masson. New York: Oxford University Press, 1988.

Gale, William G., and James R. Hines Jr. *Rethinking Estate and Gift Taxation.* Washington, DC: Brookings Institution Press, 2001.

Holtz-Eakin, Douglas, David Joulfaian, and Harvey Rosen. "The Carnegie Conjecture: Some Empirical Evidence." *Quarterly Journal of Economics* (1993): 413–36.

Joulfaian, David. "A Quarter Century of Estate Tax Reforms." *National Tax Journal* 53, no. 3 (September 2000): 343–60.

———. "Taxing Wealth Transfers and Its Behavioral Consequences." *National Tax Journal* 53, no. 4 (December 2000): 933–57.

———. "Charitable Giving in Life and at Death." In *Rethinking Estate and Gift Taxation,* edited by James R. Hines and William G. Gale Jr. (350–75). Washington, DC: Brookings Institution Press, 2001.

———. "Gift Taxes and Lifetime Transfers: Time Series Evidence." *Journal of Public Economics* 88, nos. 9–10 (August 2004): 1917–29.

Joulfaian, David, and Gerald Auten. "Bequest Taxes and Capital Gains Realizations." *Journal of Public Economics* 81, no. 2 (2001): 213–29.

Joulfaian, David, and Kathleen McGarry. "Estate and Gift Tax Incentives and Inter Vivos Giving." *National Tax Journal* 57, no. 2 (June 2004): 429–44.

Joulfaian, David, and Mark O. Wilhelm. "Inheritance and Labor Supply." *Journal of Human Resources* (1994): 1205–34.

Kopczuk, Wojciech, and Joel Slemrod. "Estate Tax on Wealth Accumulation and Avoidance Behavior of Donors." In *Rethinking Estate and Gift Taxation,* edited by William G. Gale, James R. Hines Jr., and Joel Slemrod. Washington, DC: Brookings Institution Press, 2001.

Kotlikoff, Lawrence, and Lawrence Summers, "The Role of Intergenerational Transfers in Aggregate Capital Accumulation." *Journal of Political Economy* (1981): 706–32.

McGarry, Kathleen. "Inter Vivos Transfers or Bequests? Estate Taxes and the Timing of Parental Giving." *Tax Policy and the Economy* 14 (2000): 93–121.

Page, Benjamin R. "Bequest Taxes, Inter Vivos Gifts, and the Bequest Motive." *Journal of Public Economics* 87 (2003): 1219–29.

Pechman, Joseph A. *Federal Tax Policy,* 4th ed. Washington, DC: Brookings Institution Press, 1987.

Poterba, James. "The Estate Tax and After-Tax Investment Returns." NBER Working Paper no. 6337. Cambridge, MA: National Bureau of Economic Research, 1997.

———. "Estate and Gift Taxes and Incentives for Inter Vivos Giving in the United States." *Journal of Public Economics* 79 (2001): 237–64.

Stiglitz, Joseph E. "Notes on Estate Taxes, Redistribution, and the Concept of Balanced Growth Path Incidence." *Journal of Political Economy* 8 (1978): 5137–50.

Cross-references: fairness in taxation; family, tax treatment of; wealth taxation.

Estate, inheritance, and gift tax, state

Joel Michael
Research Department, Minnesota House of Representatives

State taxation of transfers of property made in contemplation or upon the death of the transferor.

States have long imposed taxes on inheritances or estates of decedents to raise revenues. A number of these state taxes, in fact, predate the 1916 enactment of the federal estate tax. With allowance in the 1920s of the credit for state death taxes against the federal estate tax, all states eventually enacted taxes to take advantage of the federal credit. As a dollar-for-dollar offset against the federal tax, the credit is as much a federal intergovernmental aid program to the states as it is a tax feature. By enacting a pickup estate tax, a state can effectively redirect money from the federal treasury to the state without affecting the net tax obligations of its taxpayers. Legislation enacted by Congress in 2001 temporarily repealed the credit (for 2005 though 2010), introducing a new era of state estate and inheritance taxation. So far, over half of all states have repealed or allowed their estate taxes to expire in response to the repeal. But these taxes will spring back into effect in 2011, if the federal credit becomes effective again.

Structure of the taxes

It is useful to divide the state taxes into two categories: pickup taxes and stand-alone taxes. All states impose pickup taxes. A minority imposes stand-alone taxes in addition to pickup taxes.

Pickup taxes. Pure pickup taxes (sometimes called soak-up taxes) are designed to equal exactly the credit under the federal estate tax for state death taxes. The tax base for pickup taxes is identical to the federal tax; rates range from 0.8 percent to 16 percent of the adjusted taxable estate. Because the credit reduces the federal estate tax dollar for dollar, a pickup tax imposes no additional tax liability on the estate or its heirs. As a result, the incidence and behavioral effects of a pickup tax are identical to those under the federal estate tax.

Stand-alone taxes. Estates must pay stand-alone taxes to the extent they are higher than the pickup tax. States impose stand-alone taxes either as estate taxes or inheritance taxes. Estate taxes follow the general structure of the federal estate tax, i.e., exemptions and rates apply to the overall estate. By contrast, inheritance taxes (sometime called succession taxes) vary their tax liability (exemption amounts, rate schedules, and so forth) based on the status of the recipient of transfers from the estate. Typically transfers to surviving spouses and minor children are subject to lower effective rates than transfers to adult children, more distant relatives, or unrelated individuals. Inheritance taxes are the more common structure for state stand-alone taxes.

Most stand-alone taxes now affect mainly estates that are below or modestly above the exemption levels of the federal estate tax and a pickup tax. They mainly extend the reach of tax to more estates and may increase the tax for average-size estates subject to federal tax; only rarely do they increase the tax burden on the largest estates. Put another way, most rates under stand-alone taxes are now below the top 16 percent rate allowed under the federal credit. However, in the recent past, a number of states imposed tax rates significantly higher than the federal credit rates.

A few states supplement their stand-alone taxes with state gift taxes that apply to inter vivos gifts. It should be noted, though, that an estate tax that follows the federal definitions of the tax base includes lifetime gifts above the exemption amount, since the federal tax is "unified"—that is, inter vivos gifts are added to the estate to determine the total tax base. Imposing a gift tax allows a state to tax gifts made by residents who move out of state before they die (but before making the gift) or whose total estates turn out to be less than the effective exemption amounts when they die.

Revenues

State estate and inheritance taxes raised about $6.7 billion in state revenues for fiscal year 2003, or about 1.2 percent of all state tax revenues. Annual revenue flows tend to be volatile, particularly in smaller states. A small number of estates pay the tax, and effective rates rise significantly as the taxable value of an estate increases. Small variations in the number of deaths of affluent individuals and the aggressiveness (or the lack) of their estate planning can significantly affect annual revenues for a state.

Tax competition and state taxes

Interstate tax competition has long characterized state estate and inheritance taxation as states compete to be more attractive domiciles for affluent individuals who provide tax revenues in excess of the consumption of public services. The initial scrimmages in this competition began in the early 20th century. For example, Florida and Nevada adopted constitutional prohibitions on inheritance and estate taxes in the 1920s on the assumption that this would make them more attractive domiciles for the affluent. The federal credit for state death taxes was enacted partially as a way to reduce this competition, as well as to respond to concerns that federal tax effectively preempted a traditional state revenue source.

Over the past four decades, most states repealed their stand-alone taxes and came to rely exclusively on pickup estate taxes. By the turn of century, about three-quarters of the states relied exclusively on pickup taxes (recall that from a taxpayer's perspective pickup taxes are effectively the equivalent of no tax). Available empirical evidence suggests that this remarkable pattern was strongly affected, if not directly caused, by interstate competition. The timing of states' reduction or elimination of stand-alone taxes closely follows regional patterns. States with stand-alone taxes are clustered in the Midwest and Mid-Atlantic.

Temporary repeal of the federal credit

In 2001, Congress temporarily repealed the credit for state death taxes. The credit was reduced in three annual steps (2002–04) and repealed in its entirety for deaths in 2005 through 2010. (The credit was replaced by a deduction, providing a partial offset for payment of state taxes for estates still subject to federal tax.) States have responded to the federal change in a manner consistent with past patterns.

Most of the states that imposed only pickup taxes have continued to do so, allowing their estate taxes to expire. In most instances, this occurred without state legislative action because many state pickup tax laws automatically incorporate changes in federal law. However, a few states have acted to do so, repealing their estate taxes.

The 2001 federal legislation has caused 13 pure pickup states and the District of Columbia to "decouple" from federal law and to begin again imposing stand-alone taxes (as of fall 2004), more than doubling the number of states with stand-alone taxes. These taxes typically equal the amount of the credit under some version of prior federal law. Most states have imposed these taxes by enacting legislative changes, although in some states this happened automatically because the state tax was tied to the federal credit as of a date before the 2001 changes. States that have decoupled are clustered in the Midwest, Mid-Atlantic, New England, and the Pacific Northwest, following past regional patterns for stand-alone taxes. The impact of repeal of the federal credit is still relatively new and it remains to be seen if more states will adopt stand-alone taxes to preserve revenues.

Economic effects of the taxes

The basic economic and behavioral effects of the state taxes mirror those under the federal estate tax. The one exception is the issue of whether stand-alone taxes affect migration behavior (or at least the rearranging of affairs to change legal domiciles) by those likely to be subject to the tax. The research done on this question has reached mixed results. Two of the more sophisticated recent papers reached contrasting conclusions. One study (Bakija and Slemrod 2004) relying on federal estate tax return data found that stand-alone state taxes had a statistically significant, but modest, effect on the number of federal estate tax returns. By contrast, a recent analysis of census migration data of a broader population found no relationship between stand-alone taxes and elderly migration (Conway and Rork 2004b). How state taxation affects migration or domicile shifting by the affluent will loom as a larger policy issue, if Congress makes repeal of the credit for state death taxes permanent.

ADDITIONAL READINGS

Bakija, Jon, and Joel Slemrod. "Do the Rich Flee from High State Taxes? Evidence from Federal Estate Tax Returns." NBER Working Paper 10645. Cambridge, MA: National Bureau of Economic Research (NBER), July 2004.

Burman, Leonard E., and William G. Gale. "The Estate Tax Is Down, But Not Out." *Tax Policy Issues and Options Policy Brief* no. 2. Washington, DC: Tax Policy Center, December 2001.

Burman, Leonard E., William G. Gale, and Jeff Rohaly. "The Distribution of the Estate Tax and Reform Options." Washington, DC: The Urban Institute, December 2004.

Conway, Karen Smith, and Jonathon C. Rork. "Diagnosis Murder: The Death of State Death Taxes," *Economic Inquiry* 42 (2004a): 537–59.

———. "State 'Death' Taxes and Elderly Migration: The Chicken or the Egg?" Working Paper. University of New Hampshire, April 2004b.

Gale, William G., Matthew Hall, and Peter Orszag. "Future Income Tax Cuts From the 2001 Tax Legislation." *Tax Notes* 98, no. 8 (February 17, 2003): 1141.

Michael, Joel. "State Responses to EGTRRA Estate Tax Changes." *Tax Notes* 103 (May 24, 2004): 1023–38.

Cross-reference: estate and gift tax, federal.

Excess burden

Harry Watson
George Washington University

Excess burden, also called efficiency cost or dead weight loss, occurs when a tax interferes with a taxpayer's economic decisions and efficient choice but generates no additional benefit to the tax collection agency.

It might appear that taxation is simply a transfer of resources from taxpayers to the government and that, apart from the costs of complying with or administering a tax, the only burden of taxation is the financial inconvenience felt by taxpayers. Unfortunately, the burden borne by taxpayers is seldom limited to their direct tax payments—that is, their direct burden. With almost all taxes there is an additional—excess—burden that is not related to any explicit tax liability. Unlike direct burden, which is determined by tax statutes, excess burden is determined by the way in which a tax code alters the decisions taxpayers make, so that it lacks the transparency of direct burden. As will be shown, this lack of transparency in no way lessens the potential adverse effects of the excess burden.

Excess burden arises when taxpayers are induced to make substitutions in order to ameliorate the impact of a tax. As most taxes alter relative prices or rates of return, such substitutions are a reasonable response on the part of taxpayers. For example, the introduction of an excise tax may induce consumers to substitute some untaxed good for the now more expensive taxed good, and the introduction of a payroll tax may induce firms to substitute capital for labor. These substitutions suggest that taxpayers are making choices that, in the absence of taxation, would be considered inferior. These inferior choices are the source of excess burden.

The cost of these substitutions for consumers is easily illustrated by the outcome of levying an excise tax on gasoline that is so high that no one buys any gasoline. As no revenue is collected, it is clear that there is no direct tax burden, but this does not mean that consumers do not suffer; most consumers would find relying exclusively on alternative forms of transportation to be quite burdensome. This cost to consumers is the excess burden of the tax, and most consumers would find it to be substantial. If the excise tax were then lowered enough so that some consumers were willing to buy gasoline, the excess burden would be reduced but not eliminated. Even with a lower excise tax, the pattern of automobile usage would differ from that observed in a no-tax world because consumers will have given up some of the benefits of using an automobile. This loss in benefits, which arises because the cost of driving has risen relative to the cost of other forms of transportation, represents the excess burden that remains with a lower excise tax.

Substitution effects are also costly for producers, as can be seen in the introduction of an income tax that discriminates between two different types of capital. Because the income tax reduces the resources available to the firm, the amounts of both types of capital used by the firm will decline. In addition, the differential tax treatment of capital will induce the firm to substitute capital with a lower after-tax cost for capital with a higher after-tax cost, resulting in a mix of capital that would not be found in a no-tax world. The tax-induced distortion in the mix of capital lowers the firm's productivity, and output falls relative to the level that would have been produced had the income tax reduced the resources available to the firm but not discriminated between different types of capital. In this case, the tax-induced loss in productivity represents excess burden.

As these illustrations suggest, substitution effects, and the excess burden they create, arise when taxation alters relative prices or rates of return. Therefore, to determine whether a tax creates excess burden, it is only necessary to ask whether the tax alters any ratio of prices or rate of return. Using this criterion, all tax systems that are in use, including personal and corporate income taxes, commodity taxes, and wealth taxes, produce excess burden.

If a tax is not to create any excess burden, it must be designed so that taxpayers will find that making substitutions yields no benefits. Because the range of substitution possibilities is so great, this is equivalent to requiring that the tax base be unaffected by any taxpayer decisions, a situation that is referred to as lump-sum taxation. Thus, a tax for which liability is only a function of age or gender would be a lump-sum tax. While lump-sum taxes are attractive because they minimize excess burden, they can be quite regressive because their very nature precludes any link between a taxpayer's economic circumstances and tax liability (see *lump-sum tax*).

Some insights into the factors that determine the magnitude of excess burden can be gained by considering a simple ad valorem excise tax. An approximation for the excess burden of this tax is given by

$$\left[\frac{\tau^2}{2}\right]\left[\frac{\varepsilon\eta}{\varepsilon + \eta}\right][PQ]$$

where τ is the ad valorem excise tax rate; P and Q are the market price and output levels, respectively; ε is the elasticity of demand; and η is the elasticity of supply. As excess burden depends on the square of the tax rate, it will increase more than proportionately as the tax rate increases. The above expression means that a 1 percent increase in the tax rate produces a 2 percent increase in excess burden, which suggests that even small increases in tax rates can produce significant increases in excess burden. Increases in either elasticity, which reflect a greater willingness of consumers or producers to make substitutions, also exacerbate excess burden. Conversely, if consumers or producers do not respond at all to the price changes, so that either ε or η is zero, excess burden is zero.

To appreciate the magnitude of excess burden, it is useful to divide the measure above by an approximation of the revenue this excise tax would raise, τPQ. In this case, the ratio of excess burden to revenue raised (the direct burden) is approximately

$$\left[\frac{\tau}{2}\right]\left[\frac{\varepsilon\eta}{\varepsilon + \eta}\right]$$

It is easy to find circumstances in which this ratio can be surprisingly large. For example, if the product is produced by a constant cost-competitive industry, so that η is very large, and if ε is 2, then this ratio is just τ. Thus, for a tax rate of 25 percent, excess burden is 25 percent of the tax revenue collected. Put differently, for this excise tax, each dollar the government collects costs the private sector an additional $0.25, a substantial charge for simply transferring resources from one sector of the economy to another.

Although most taxes are considerably more complicated than excise taxes, it is possible to derive similar excess burden expressions for these taxes. Given the simple nature of these expressions, it may appear that calculating the excess burden of any tax would be a straightforward exercise. In theory, this conclusion is correct; expressions that provide exact measures of excess burden (which are somewhat more complicated than the approximate expression presented earlier) have been available for a number of years. In practice, the determination of excess burden is problematic because elasticity values, such as ε and η in the case of an excise tax, are not easily obtained.

To appreciate the difficulties in implementing measures of excess burden, it is useful to consider the case of income taxation. An income tax may affect many relative prices, such as the price of current consumption relative to future consumption (savings) and the price of leisure relative to the price of other forms of consumption. As with excise taxation, how taxpayers respond to these relative price changes—as reflected in the elasticity of savings with respect to changes in after-tax interest rates and the elasticity of labor supply with respect to after-tax labor income—plays a critical role in determining the excess burden. Unfortunately, a paucity of data, combined with methodological disagreements, has produced a wide range of estimates for these elasticity values. Because excess burden increases as both these elasticities increase, using estimated elasticities that are close to zero implies that the excess burden of income taxation is insignificant, whereas using estimated elasticities that are large suggests that the excess burden of income taxation is a serious problem.

ADDITIONAL READINGS

Auerbach, Alan. "The Theory of Excess Burden and Optimal Taxation." In *Handbook of Public Economics,* edited by Alan Auerbach and Martin Feldstein. New York: North Holland, 1985.
Rosen, Harvey. *Public Finance,* 7th ed., ch. 13. Boston, MA: McGraw-Hill, 2004.
Stiglitz, Joseph E. *Economics of the Public Sector,* 3rd ed. New York: W. W. Norton & Co., 1999.

Cross-references: elasticities, supply and demand; excise taxes; head tax; income tax; lump sum tax; saving, taxes and; tax.

Excess profits tax

John Hakken
Deloitte & Touche LLP

A high-rate tax levied either on business profits that exceed a normal or fair rate of return on invested capital or on the sales price of a commodity in excess of its normal price.

Seeking to control the private gains from certain extraordinary government interventions in the economy, Congress has levied two different and quite distinct types of tax on "excess" profits. It enacted an "income-tax" type of excess profits tax on businesses as a temporary measure to control wartime profits during World War I, World War II, and the Korean War. Decades later, in 1980, when oil prices that had been regulated in response to the Arab oil embargo were decontrolled, it enacted an "excise tax" type of excess profits tax on domestic oil production to limit the profits that oil companies would reap from higher oil prices. Nine years later, after the production of ozone-depleting chemicals was restricted by the Montreal Protocol, the Senate adopted another "excise-tax" type of excess profits tax on the domestic production of these chemicals to limit the profits that chemical producers could reap by curtailing their production and raising their prices. Instead, however, Congress eventually enacted an ordinary excise tax on these chemicals.

The income-tax type

Each excess profits tax that Congress enacted during wartime had a slightly different tax base, but all the tax bases shared the same basic formula. Under that formula, a normal or fair amount of profit was determined for a consolidated group of businesses, and this amount was subtracted from the actual profits of the consolidated group, after certain conforming adjustments to actual profits had been made. The "normal" or "fair" amount of profit was generally calculated from some combination of the following: (1) actual profit during the prewar period, (2) the amount of invested capital during the prewar period, and (3) the change in the amount of invested capital since the prewar period. Whenever a business could show that extenuating circumstances had distorted its calculated normal profit, adjustments, alternative calculations, or other remedies were generally available.

Congress enacted two different excess profits taxes during World War I. The War Act of 1917 levied an excess profits tax on both corporations and noncorporate businesses at graduated rates, from 20 to 60 percent. The normal return of each business was based on its average return on invested capital during the prewar period of 1911 through 1913, but it was restricted to between 7 and 9 percent. The normal profit for the tax year was then calculated by multiplying the business's average amount of invested capital during the tax year by its normal return on invested capital. The War Act of 1918 increased the top rate of the first excess profits tax to 65 percent and levied a second excess profits tax—called a war profits tax—only on corporations, at graduated rates up to 80 percent. Corporations had to pay either the excess profits tax or the war profits tax, whichever was larger. The normal profit during the tax year under the war profits tax was generally calculated by taking the actual average annual profit during the prewar period and adding 10 percent of the change in invested capital since the prewar period. Under both taxes, invested capital was valued on a historical basis and consisted of (1) paid-in cash, (2) business assets contributed by owners, and (3) retained earnings.

In light of the subsequent development of the excess profits tax, certain features of the World War I taxes are particularly noteworthy. The excess profits tax enacted in 1917, for example, is notable for being the only excess profits tax levied on noncorporate businesses. Apparently, the commingling of noncorporate business assets and personal assets, along with the unlimited liability of noncorporate business owners, blurred the concept of invested capital enough to make its application to noncorporate businesses impractical. During World War II and the Korean War, Congress relied on steeply graduated income tax rates and income surtaxes to limit the profits of noncorporate businesses. A second notable feature of both World War I taxes is the way tax relief was granted. Because the tax rates were high and the measurement of excess profits was ad hoc, the tax commissioner was given broad discretion to grant businesses relief from the excess profits taxes whenever they appeared to be unduly burdensome. However, because the discretion was so broad and the basis for it so vague, the commissioner was flooded with relief requests. Therefore, subsequent excess profits taxes codified many relief provisions, stipulating the conditions for relief and enumerating the terms of that relief. The third notable feature is the difference in the way normal profits were computed under the two taxes. The excess profits tax enacted in 1917 required a business to reconstruct historically the entire amount of capital invested in it, so that a normal or fair rate of return could be applied to that amount (valued on a historical basis). The tax enacted in 1918 only required a business to adjust its prewar income for subsequent changes in invested capital, which made accounting for prewar investments unnecessary. Because the accounting was so much easier, subsequent excess profits taxes always offered businesses the option of computing normal profits by adjusting prewar income.

Between the two world wars, economists and lawyers thoroughly examined the theoretical underpinnings of the excess profits tax. Distinctions were drawn between (1) excess profits taxes that compared current profits with prior profits during a base period, and (2) excess profits taxes that compared current profits with profits that offered a hypothetical fair return on investment. Distinctions were also drawn between excess profits taxes that determined the excess profits of each business as a special case based on its profit history, and excess profits taxes that determined excess profits by universal rules, so that businesses with the same amount of income and the same amount of invested capital owed the same amount of excess profits tax regardless of their profit history.

In 1940, Congress levied an excess profits tax on corporations with graduated tax rates from 25 to 50 percent. After the United States entered World War II, and as its involvement grew, the tax on excess profits was raised three times, until the statutory rate reached a flat 95 percent during 1944 and 1945. Under the excess profits tax during World War II, corporations could compute their normal profit in one of two ways. Under the invested-capital method, the normal profit of a corporation equaled 8 percent of the first $5 million of invested capital, plus 6 percent of the next $5 million of invested capital, plus 5 percent of the remaining invested capital. The World War I definition of invested capital was expanded to include additional intangible assets and 50 percent of borrowed capital. (To make current profit conform to this concept of normal profit, 50 percent of the interest deduction was added back to income.) Under the earned-income method, normal profit equaled 95 percent of a corporation's "average" income during the 1936–1939 base period, plus 8 percent of any net addition to equity capital since the base period, minus 6 percent of any net reduction in equity capital since the base period. Excess profits were determined by deducting computed normal profits from actual profits after adjustments. Normal profits that could not be deducted during the current tax year could be carried forward or backward for two years. In addition, 10 percent of a corporation's excess profits tax payments were creditable against corporate income tax liabilities after the war.

In terms of the development of the excess profits tax, the ways in which the World War II tax attempted to adjust the calculation of excess profits for differences in investment risk are noteworthy. First, because a larger capital base allowed a corporation to reduce risk through diversification of its investments, the invested-capital method lowered the normal return on larger amounts of corporate capital. Second, because debt increased the risk to equity, the invested-capital method allowed a corporation to treat part of its borrowed capital as invested capital. Assuming that the corporation could borrow at an interest rate below the normal profit allowed on invested capital, the inclusion of borrowed capital effectively raised the normal profit rate allowed on leveraged corporate equity.

Third, because corporations that were engaged in riskier business activities typically earned a higher average rate of return on their investment, the earned-income method did not place a ceiling on the normal rate of return. Fourth, because a corporation might not have earned a normal return during the base period as a result of risk, corporations were sometimes allowed to construct an "average" base period income from the typical incomes of similar businesses.

The excess profits tax that Congress levied during the Korean War was similar in most respects to the one levied during World War II. The tax rate, however, was only 30 percent, and the amount of excess profits tax could not exceed a ceiling of 20 percent of corporate income. Smaller corporations had a lower ceiling.

The excise-tax type

The Crude Oil Windfall Profit Tax of 1980 imposed an excise tax on the domestic production of oil. The tax base for each barrel of domestic oil production was determined on a property basis and generally equaled the difference between the wellhead price of oil and the base price (adjusted for inflation), multiplied by one minus the state severance tax rate. In no case, however, could the annual tax base for a property exceed 90 percent of the property's annual net oil income. For most domestic oil production (defined as tier 1 oil), the base price equaled the highest controlled price for oil produced from the property during May 1979 (which averaged $13 per barrel) less $0.21. For "stripper oil" production from low-volume wells (defined as tier 2 oil), the base price equaled $15.20 per barrel. This base price was then adjusted for differences in the quality and production location of the oil. For the production of newly discovered oil, heavy oil, and incremental oil from chemical injectants (defined as tier 3 oil), the base price equaled $16.55 per barrel. It, too, was adjusted for quality and location. The tax rates initially varied from 70 percent on the production of tier 1 oil down to 30 percent on the production of tier 3 oil. Independent oil producers were eligible for reduced tax rates on up to 1,000 barrels per day of tier 1 and tier 2 oil production. Subsequent amendments gradually lowered the tax rate on newly discovered oil to 15 percent and eliminated the tax on stripper oil from independent producers. As enacted, the windfall profits tax was scheduled to be phased out over 33 months beginning in 1988, once $227.3 billion in net revenue had been collected, but no later than 1991. When oil prices plunged in 1986, revenues from the windfall profits tax evaporated, prompting Congress to repeal the tax in 1988.

Despite the immense compliance burden involved in calculating the net income separately for each oil-producing property, oil producers used the net income limitation extensively to cut their tax liability under the windfall profits tax. The net income limitation proved most effective in cutting the tax on tier 1 oil because, for many properties, the tier 1 base price was only slightly above the average cost of producing a barrel of oil. Interestingly, the net income limitation was more effective in cutting the tax owed by oil producers when the price of oil was high rather than low because each additional dollar in price, which normally added a dollar to the tax base, added only $0.90 to the tax base when the net income limitation was applied.

The excise tax on the production of ozone-depleting chemicals that the Senate (but ultimately not the full Congress) adopted in 1989 was closely related in concept to the windfall profits tax on the production of crude oil. The chemicals production tax would have imposed what amounted to a 100 percent tax on the manufacturer's sales price in excess of a base price based on 1987 sales. Moreover, the base price would have been adjusted for increases in production costs caused by inflation. Unlike the windfall profits tax on oil, the chemicals tax also would have imposed a minimum tax of $0.60 per pound on both the production and importation of ozone-depleting chemicals to encourage the use of less harmful alternatives.

Effects on economic efficiency

In theory, a tax on pure economic profit does not reduce economic efficiency because it does not change the allocation of economic resources. In other words, if an excess profits tax could be levied on pure economic profit, it would not change economic behavior. Anecdotal evidence strongly suggests, however, that past excess profits taxes did affect economic behavior. For example, the excess profits tax during World War II apparently encouraged manufacturers to advertise heavily to promote brand recognition that would benefit them after the war. With an effective excess profits tax rate of 85.5 percent, the after-tax cost of a dollar of advertising was only 14.5 cents. Likewise, the windfall profits tax on oil apparently encouraged some oil producers to adopt chemical recovery methods prematurely in order to get oil reclassified from tier 1 to tier 3, thereby reducing the tax by more than $5 per barrel on some production. Given the strong incentives from the high tax rates, the loss of economic efficiency under past excess profits taxes might have been substantial. In enacting such taxes, Congress had to balance the possible substantial loss of economic efficiency against the need to limit the redistributional consequences of government policies designed to redirect economic resources by regulating or deregulating industries or by engaging in war.

ADDITIONAL READINGS

Buehler, Alfred G. "The Taxation of Corporate Excess Profits in Peace and War Times." *Law and Contemporary Problems* 7 (Spring 1940): 291–300.

Chung, Edward. "Crude Oil Windfall Profit Tax, 1985." *Statistics of Income Bulletin* 6 (Fall 1986): 85–94.

Congressional Budget Office. *The Windfall Profits Tax: A Comparative Analysis of Two Bills.* Washington, DC: U.S. Government Printing Office, November 1979.

Keith, E. Gorden, and E. Cary Brown. "The Impact and Burden of Wartime Corporation Taxes." *Law and Contemporary Problems* 10 (Winter 1943): 121–32.

Peterson, C. Rudolf. "The Statutory Evolution of the Excess Profits Tax." *Law and Contemporary Problems* 10 (Winter 1943): 3–27.

Prentice-Hall. *Federal Excess Profits Tax.* New York: Prentice-Hall, 1954.

Shoup, Carl. "The Taxation of Excess Profits." Parts I, II, and III. *Political Science Quarterly* 55 (December 1940): 535–55; 56 (March 1941): 84–106; 56 (June 1941): 226–49.

———. "The Concept of Excess Profits under the Revenue Acts of 1940–42." *Law and Contemporary Problems* 10 (Winter 1943): 28–42.

Cross-references: energy taxes; environmental taxes, federal; income tax, corporate, federal.

Excise taxes

J. Fred Giertz

Institute of Government and Public Affairs, University of Illinois at Urbana-Champaign

Taxes levied on the manufacture, sale, or consumption of a single good or service or on a relatively narrow range of goods or services.

Excise taxes are an example of what have been traditionally called indirect taxes: taxes that are imposed on a transaction rather than directly on a person or corporation. Excise taxes are narrow-based taxes, as compared with broad-based taxes on consumption such as a general sales tax, a value-added tax, or an expenditure tax. Excise taxes can be collected at various stages, including the point of production, the wholesale level, or the retail level. They are also known as selective sales taxes or differential commodity taxes.

Excise taxes are levied on either a unit or ad valorem basis. For unit (also known as specific) excises, the tax is denominated in terms of money per physical unit produced or sold. Examples include the federal government taxes of 18.4 cents per gallon of gasoline, $13.50 per gallon of distilled spirits, and $3.10 per domestic flight segment for passenger airline travel. Ad valorem excises are based on a percentage of the value of the product or service sold. The 7.5 percent federal tax on the cost of domestic airline passenger tickets (in addition to the unit tax mentioned above) and the 3 percent tax on the cost of telephone services are examples of ad valorem taxes.

Rationale for excises

The use of excise taxes is explained or justified by a variety of rationales. Often more than one rationale will explain a particular tax. There are obviously alternative instruments, including other types of taxes, for achieving the same goals that excise taxes achieve.

Excises are sometimes employed simply to raise revenue because they are easy to administer. In the past (and continuing today in some less-developed countries), excise taxes were applied only to products produced in sectors of the economy with well-developed markets. Broader-based taxes, such as the income and general sales taxes, are difficult to administer when most of the economic activity takes place outside a structured market setting.

Excise taxes may also be employed to achieve particular redistributive results. Excise taxes are sometimes used as a means of implementing an ability-to-pay approach to taxation. So-called luxury taxes are an example of this approach. In the past, the United States levied excise taxes on so-called luxury items purchased by individuals—items such as expensive passenger vehicles, boats, aircraft, furs, and jewelry. By taxing items consumed disproportionately by higher-income individuals, excise taxes can be progressive. There are questions, however, concerning horizontal equity because not all people at the same income level have similar expenditure patterns for luxury items. Hotel occupancy taxes are another variant of this motive, where the intent is to shift the burden to nonresidents of a jurisdiction. Windfall profits taxes such as the excise on domestic oil in the 1970s also have a redistributive intent.

Excises are also levied on goods or services that are considered harmful or undesirable in an attempt to discourage consumption or punish the consumer. Taxes based on this rationale are labeled sumptuary excises. Examples include taxes on alcoholic beverages, tobacco products, and wagering. Because many goods and services taxed by sumptuary excises have relatively inelastic demands, these taxes may have only a limited impact on curtailing consumption. This presents an added benefit, however, for the government because it provides a relatively stable source of tax revenue. Sumptuary taxes are often popular politically because many citizens do not engage in the taxed activities, whereas purchasers of the taxed items do so voluntarily. Such taxes may have negative consequences from the standpoint of vertical equity because sumptuary excises are often highly regressive.

Excises may also be imposed as a technique for dealing with negative externalities. Taxes on "gas-guzzling" automobiles and gasoline can be explained as a kind of Pigouvian (corrective) tax to reduce the divergence of the private and social costs of pollution and congestion. Such taxes are usually an imperfect technique for internalizing externalities because an efficient Pigouvian tax should be related to the marginal damage caused by an activity, which is not necessarily proportional to the level of consumption.

While the goal of Pigouvian taxes is to correct for resource misallocation, liability taxes may also be levied on negative externalities to generate funds to mitigate the damages these activities create. The Superfund tax on pollution damage and leaking underground storage taxes are examples of liability taxes.

Excises may be used for border adjustment purposes if foreign firms are avoiding certain costs imposed on domestic firms. For example, if domestic producers are taxed to generate funds to deal with the negative consequences of the good they are producing, a border adjustment tax on the same good produced by foreign producers would "level the playing field." Excise taxes are also occasionally employed for regulatory purposes. An extreme example of this is an excise tax that some states have imposed on gambling devices that are, in fact, illegal.

Finally, excise taxes may be employed as a means of implementing a benefits-received approach to taxation. Gasoline taxes are an example. Gasoline usage is closely related to highway travel, thereby providing a link between taxes paid and benefits received from roadways. This link is further strengthened by earmarking where the revenues collected from an excise tax are designated for use in providing government services related to the activity. Examples include the earmarking of motor fuel taxes for highways and taxes on airline tickets for air traffic control and facilities expansion.

Economic impacts

The economic impacts of excise taxes are usually investigated using a partial equilibrium approach because excises apply to only one product or, at most, a narrow range of goods or services. An analysis of the incidence of an excise tax in a competitive industry is usually divided between its impacts in the short run and the long run. In the short run, an excise tax increases the price of the product, albeit by less than the full amount of the tax, and the price burden is shared by both the producers and the consumers. The exact effect depends on the elasticities of demand and supply for the product. The increase in price resulting from the tax will be greater as the elasticity of supply increases and the elasticity of demand falls. The impact on quantity will be greater as both the elasticity of demand and the elasticity of supply increase.

In regard to sharing the price burden, the more inelastic the demand is, the larger the share of the tax borne by consumers. The more inelastic the supply is, the larger the share borne by producers. In the limiting cases, consumers will bear the full price burden if demand is completely inelastic, whereas producers will bear the full price burden if supply is completely inelastic.

In the long run, the price will increase by more than it does in the short run because firms will exit the industry due to losses created by the tax. In constant cost competitive industries, the price will increase by the full amount of the tax; in increasing cost industries, by less than the amount of the tax; and in decreasing cost industries, by more than the amount of the tax. (A constant cost industry is one in which industry costs are unaffected by the exit or entry of firms. An increasing cost industry is one in which the costs of all firms in the industry increase with the entry of new firms. In a decreasing cost industry, the costs of all firms fall with the entry of new firms.)

In general, nothing can be said about the progressivity or regressivity of excise taxes because the answer depends on the consumption pattern by income class of each product that is taxed. As noted above, some excise taxes are highly regressive, such as those on tobacco and alcohol, while others, such as those targeting luxuries, may be progressive.

In regard to the welfare effects of excise taxes, excess burdens or deadweight losses generally result from the selective taxation of a small number of products. Such taxes distort consumer choices by driving a wedge between marginal cost and price. The more elastic the demand for a product, the greater will be the excess burden of an excise because such a tax will have a relatively large impact on the quantity consumed. In addition, the excess burden of an excise tax increases roughly with the square of the tax rate—doubling the tax rate quadruples the welfare loss. This result argues for the use of a broad-based tax on a wide range of commodities rather than a high tax rate on a small number of goods.

It also follows from this that tax optimality can be achieved with a general set of selective excise taxes (given the amount of revenue to be collected) by setting excise tax rates for various products inversely to their elasticity of demand. While such a plan may be efficient in the sense that it minimizes excess burdens, it may have negative equity (distributional) consequences by taxing goods with inelastic demands (such as necessities) very heavily.

From the standpoint of efficiency, a general tax on all consumption at a uniform rate will generally dominate a partial system of taxation using excises. Such a tax does not distort consumer choices at the margin as excise taxes do. However, the general tax on consumption needs to be truly broad-based, with all goods (including leisure) part of the tax base. Such a broad base is extremely difficult to achieve.

Use of excise taxes

Historically, excise taxes have played an important role in the tax systems of most governments. They have declined in relative importance, however, in the last hundred years because of the increased reliance on broad-based taxes such as income, general sales, and value-added taxes. Today, less-developed countries rely somewhat more heavily on excises than more highly developed countries.

In the United States, excise taxes are used by all levels of government, with states relying most heavily on this source of revenue. At the federal level in 2003, various excises (not including customs duties) amounted to $68 billion, or 3.7 percent of federal revenues. At the state level, excises accounted for $79 billion in revenues in 2001, or 10.6 percent of own-source state revenues. Local governments collected $18 billion, or 3.1 percent of own-source revenues from excises.

Among the large number of federal government excises are taxes on various fuels, tires for highway use, truck trailers, "gas-guzzling" automobiles, air transportation, telecommunications services, wagering, alcohol, tobacco, and firearms. States generally apply excise taxes to a narrower range of items including motor fuels, alcohol, tobacco, and wagering. Excises on highway fuels constitute the single largest category in terms of revenue for both the federal and state and local governments.

Some local governments, especially municipalities, tax a similar range of activities, although usually at a lower rate than the state.

ADDITIONAL READINGS

Bowman, John H. "Excise Taxation." In *Handbook on Taxation,* edited by W. Bartley Hildreth and James A. Richardson (549–78). New York: Marcel Dekker, 1999.

Cnossen, Sijbren, ed. *Theory and Practice of Excise Taxation.* Oxford: Oxford University Press, 2005.

Davie, Bruce F. "Tax Expenditures in the Federal Excise Tax System." *National Tax Journal* 47, no. 1 (March 1994): 39–42.

Keeler, Theodore E., Teh-Wei Hu, Willard G. Manning, and Hai-Yen Sung. "State Tobacco Taxation, Education and Smoking: Controlling for the Effects of Omitted Variables." *National Tax Journal* 54, no. 1 (March 2001): 83–102.

Oldenski, Lindsay. "Searching for Structure in the Federal Excise Tax System." *National Tax Journal* 57, no. 3 (September 2004): 613–37.

Poterba, James. "Lifetime Incidence and the Distributional Burden of Excise Taxes." *American Economic Review* 79, no. 2 (May 1989): 325–30.

Young, Douglas J., and Agnieszka Bieli'nska-Kwapisz. "Alcohol Taxes and Beverage Prices." *National Tax Journal* 55, no. 1 (March 2002): 57–73.

Cross-references: ability to pay; benefit principle; border tax adjustments, earmarking of taxes; elasticity, demand and supply; energy taxes; excess burden; fuel taxes, federal; incidence of taxes; luxury taxes; optimal taxation; progressivity, measures of; tobacco taxes.

Expenditure tax

J. Fred Giertz

Institute of Government and Public Affairs, University of Illinois at Urbana-Champaign

Seth H. Giertz

Congressional Budget Office

A broad-based (non-transactions-based) tax on annual consumption that may make use of exemptions, deductions, and graduated rates.

An expenditure tax is a broad-based consumption tax that uses annual consumption as the starting point for tax calculations. Similar taxes are also labeled as cash-flow taxes or consumed-income taxes. Unlike most widely used consumption-based taxes such as general sales taxes and the value-added taxes, an expenditure tax does not attempt to measure consumption transaction by transaction because that would be impractical. Rather, consumption is measured as the difference between income and savings over a year. Because the base is total annual consumption, an expenditure tax can make use of devices such as exemptions, deductions, and graduated marginal tax rates that are generally not available for transaction-based consumption taxes to adjust for ability to pay or to create incentives.

While the idea of an expenditure tax has been considered for more than 50 years, a full-blown expenditure tax has seldom been employed aside from a limited tax in Ceylon and India in the 1950s and 1960s. It has also been discussed as an instrument for suppressing domestic consumption during wartime. Despite the general lack of use, many elements of expenditure taxation have made inroads into the structure of the income tax where certain types of savings are excluded from the income tax base.

The base of an expenditure tax can be related to the traditional Haig-Simons (accretion) definition of income. Under the Haig-Simons approach, income is defined as the amount that can be consumed in a year without diminishing wealth; that is, income equals consumption plus changes in wealth. Rearranging, this relationship becomes consumption equals income less savings. This clearly shows that the exclusion of savings from taxation is the key difference between an income and consumption tax base.

Using this approach, the base for an expenditure tax can be determined in much the same way as the existing income tax base is derived. The only difference is that an expenditure base allows the unlimited availability of tax-qualified savings or investment vehicles, such as existing IRA, 401(k), 403(b), and 457 accounts. This is the basis for another version of expenditure taxation: the household portion of the unlimited savings allowance (USA) tax. (Note that various college savings plans, such as 529 accounts, and medical savings plans depart from the expenditure tax rationale because the distributions are generally tax-advantaged along with the contributions.) Currently, these types of tax deferral instruments are subject to contribution limits and withdrawal limitations and penalties (for both early and late withdrawals). Under a comprehensive expenditure tax, these restrictions would be eliminated. Any type of savings would automatically be excluded from the tax base, and withdrawals would be considered consumption and thus part of the tax base.

One important criticism of most consumption taxes is that they are difficult to tailor to ability to pay. Since most consumption taxes are transaction-based, it is nearly impossible to make such taxes explicitly progressive because the same rates generally apply to all purchases regardless of the purchaser's economic capacity. Attempts to address this problem, such as the exclusion of food from the base of the general sales tax, are blunt instruments that make imperfect adjustments. Since an expenditure tax is based on annual consumption, all of the devices available for an income tax to adjust for ability to pay and to incentivize activities can also be used with an expenditure tax, including exemptions, deductions, credits, and graduated marginal rates.

It should be noted that expenditure tax rates cannot be directly compared to income tax rates. Usually, income tax rates are "tax-inclusive rates" that apply to both the tax and the residual after the tax, while consumption tax rates are "tax-exclusive rates" that apply only to the after-tax residual. For example, a marginal income tax rate of 100 percent is confiscatory, while marginal expenditure tax rates can equal or exceed 100 percent. A 100 percent expenditure tax-exclusive rate is roughly comparable to a 50 percent income tax-inclusive rate. With a 50 percent marginal income tax rate, a taxpayer earning an extra dollar of income would have 50 cents remaining after taxes to spend for consumption. With a 100 percent marginal expenditure tax rate, one dollar of extra income would allow the taxpayer to spend 50 cents for consumption and pay 50 cents in taxes on the purchase. Generally, for the same revenue generated, an expenditure tax rate will be higher than the rate for an income tax. The difference between the two will be small at low marginal rates and will increase as the tax rates rise.

Some problems encountered with the income tax base would be less severe under an expenditure tax. For example, capital gains would only be taxed when realized and not reinvested. Only the dividend portion of corporate profits would be taxed, assuming the shareholder does not reinvest the profits. If gifts and bequests were considered consumption for the donor, there would be no reason for death taxes. If the expenditure tax structure were indexed for inflation, it would automatically deal with the problem of taxing inflationary returns to capital. Other problems, however, would remain, such as the difficulty of taxing housing consumption for owner-occupied homes, which would require the imputation of rent.

The rationale for an expenditure tax obviously relates directly to the standard discussion of whether income or consumption is the appropriate base for ability to pay. The normative aspect, going back at least to Hobbes, asks whether it is fairer to tax on the basis of what is produced (income) or what is used up of society's resources (consumption). There are also efficiency issues dealing with excess burdens and the empirical question of the impact an expenditure tax has on savings, investment, and ultimately, on the economic growth of a consumption *versus* an income tax base. The only unique aspect of this debate relating to expenditure taxation is the ability of an expenditure tax to target taxpayers' ability to pay more effectively than other consumption taxes.

The adoption of an expenditure tax involves the well-known problem of moving from an income to a consumption base. This transition is difficult because taxpayers who have accumulated wealth under an income tax system would be taxed under the consumption tax when the proceeds of their wealth are used, resulting in double taxation. For an expenditure tax, the transition could be managed by providing an exemption from the expenditure tax for existing wealth that has been previously taxed. This would require the use of transitional tax-advantaged accounts.

Although the replacement of the income tax with an expenditure tax has been discussed in the United States and the United Kingdom, it is unlikely that a comprehensive expenditure tax will be adopted soon in any country. However, the trend toward expanding savings exclusions under the income tax is likely to continue, making the income tax actually a hybrid tax that combines a consumption and income base. In fact, there have been proposals for an explicit dual system under which taxpayers would have both an expenditure and an income tax base, with possibly different rates applying to each base. This would institutionalize the existing de facto hybrid that exists under the current income tax with exclusions for various types of savings.

ADDITIONAL READINGS

Bradford, David. "Consumption Taxes: Some Fundamental Transition Issues." In *Frontiers of Tax Reform,* edited by Michael J. Boskin. Stanford, CA: Hoover Institution Press, 1996.

Kaldor, Nicholas. *An Expenditure Tax.* London: George Allen and Unwin, 1955.

Office of Tax Policy, U.S. Department of the Treasury. *Blueprints for Basic Tax Report.* Washington, DC: Office of Tax Policy, 1977. http://www. ustreas.gov/offices/tax-policy/library/blueprints/.

Prest, A. R. "The Structure and Reform of Direct Taxation." *The Economic Journal* 89, no. 354 (June 1979): 243–60.

Seidman, Laurence S. *The USA Tax: A Progressive Consumption Tax.* Cambridge, MA: MIT Press, 1997.

Cross-references: Ability to pay; consumption taxation; income tax, corporate, federal; income tax, corporate, state and local; flat tax; inflation indexation of income taxes; retail sales tax; value-added tax, national; value-added tax, state.

Expensing

Raquel Meyer Alexander
University of North Carolina at Wilmington

System that allows a taxpayer to deduct—expense—the costs of acquiring a depreciable capital asset as soon as these costs are incurred, rather than take a stream of depreciation deductions over the useful life of the asset.

Schemes that allow business firms to write off assets faster than true economic depreciation are referred to as accelerated depreciation. At the extreme of accelerated depreciation, the firm expenses—that is, deducts from taxable income the assets' full cost of acquisition. The result can be a dramatic reduction in tax liability (Rosen 2005).

The financial effects of allowing investment costs to be expensed are illustrated in table 1 below. In this example, the asset is assumed to have a purchase price of $8,000 and to provide a stream of economic returns of $3,800 in the first year, $3,000 in the second year, and $2,000 in the third year. At the end of the third year, the asset is assumed to have exhausted its useful economic life, providing no further return and having no scrap or salvage value.

If the tax rate is assumed to be 50 percent and the investment is expensed for tax purposes, the government receives the stream of tax payments shown in column 2 and the investor realizes the stream of after-tax cash flows shown in column 3. In the year in which the asset is acquired, its full cost is deducted in computing taxable income, reducing the investor's tax liability by $4,000. In effect, the government provides the investor with a tax rebate equal to the tax rate multiplied by the cost of the asset. In subsequent years, no further deductions are taken, and the full amounts of the cash flows produced by the asset are taxed.

Using standard techniques for evaluating investments, it is easily shown that with expensing, the asset has an after-tax return of 5.5 percent, the same as the before-tax return. In this case, the marginal effective tax rate on the investment is zero.

This occurs because expensing reduces after-tax returns and costs by the same proportion, determined by the tax rate. If the tax rate is 50 percent, the result under expensing is financially equivalent to one in which the government becomes a 50 percent partner in the investment. Through the tax system, the government shares 50 percent of the initial costs of the investment by allowing a deduction to be taken immediately, and then shares in 50 percent of the investment's proceeds. In other words, through the tax system, the investor keeps only 50 percent of the investment's returns, but also bears only 50 percent of the costs. As a result, per dollar invested, the investor earns the same return from the investment after taxes as before taxes.

The Internal Revenue Code (IRC) includes two provisions that allow certain taxpayers to immediately expense qualified purchases rather than take depreciation deductions over the asset's life. Under IRC §179, taxpayers may elect to immediately expense up to $100,000 of qualified purchases. IRC §168(k) allows taxpayers to immediately expense 30 or 50 percent of the cost of new property placed into service ("bonus depreciation").

IRC §179

IRC §179 allows taxpayers (other than estates and trusts) to deduct immediately the cost of qualifying depreciable property. To stimulate the economy in the short run, the Jobs and Growth Relief Reconciliation Act of 2003 (PL 108-27) increased the maximum deduction to $100,000 annually for tax years beginning in 2003. The §179 inflation-adjusted expense increases to $102,000 in 2004. In 2006, the maximum deduction reverts to $25,000. This deduction is applicable for purchases of new or used tangible depreciable property acquired for trade or business use. Only for tax years ending 2003, 2004, and 2005 does off-the-shelf computer software qualify for §179 purposes. Most states conform to the federal income tax treatment, although the enactment dates vary; California and Michigan do not allow the §179 expense election.

The §179 expense is subject to an investment limitation and a taxable income limitation. The investment limitation is calculated first and reduces the amount of §179 expense when the cost of qualifying property placed in service in the tax year exceeds $200,000 on a dollar-for-dollar basis. For tax years 2003

through 2005, this threshold is increased to $400,000 but reverts to $200,000 thereafter. The inflation-adjusted investment limit is $410,000 for 2004. For example, taxpayers who place $450,000 of qualified property into service in 2004 must reduce the §179 expense by $40,000, the amount by which the qualified purchases exceed the $410,000 threshold. Because of this investment limitation, §179 favors small businesses. The second limitation, based on the taxable income, disallows deductions that exceed the taxable income derived by the taxpayer from business income. Thus, taxpayers must have at least $102,000 of taxable business income to take the maximum §179 deduction in 2004. Any amount disallowed because of the income limitation may be carried forward indefinitely.

Bonus depreciation

Bonus depreciation was created by the Job Creation and Worker Assistance Act of 2002 (PL 107-147) and provides an additional first-year 30 percent depreciation allowance for qualified property purchased after September 10, 2001, and before May 5, 2006. Under the Jobs and Growth Tax Relief Reconciliation Act of 2003, bonus depreciation increases to 50 percent for purchases after May 5, 2003, and before January 1, 2005. Taxpayers may elect by property class to claim the 30 percent bonus rather than the 50 percent bonus depreciation. Currently, only 12 states allow bonus depreciation for state income tax purposes, and the remaining states that impose a general corporate income tax vary in their treatment. Qualified property for bonus depreciation includes the following categories: off-the-shelf software, water utility property, qualified leasehold improvements, and property accounted for under the modified accelerated cost recovery system (MACRS) that is no more than 20 years old.

Some taxpayers may not qualify for both the §179 deduction and the bonus depreciation due to property types, investment limitations, or income limitations. For taxpayers eligible for both, the §179 deduction is taken first. Bonus depreciation is then calculated for the property as reduced by the §179 allowance. Any remaining depreciable basis may be deducted through the MACRS.

Example

A new five-year property was purchased in January 2004 for $250,000. The taxpayer makes no other purchases during the year. Assume the taxpayer expenses $102,000 under §179. The depreciable basis is reduced to $148,000 ($250,000 − 102,000), and bonus depreciation would be $74,000 ($148,000 × 50 percent). Regular MACRS depreciation is based upon the unrecovered basis of $74,000 ($148,000 − $74,000).

Policy implications

Because expensing exempts the normal or competitive return on capital assets from taxation, the method of capital

TABLE 1. Expensing an $8,000 Investment Cost

	Pretax cash flows (1)	Tax liability with expensing (1) × 50% (2)	After-tax cash flow (1) minus (2) (3)
Initial outlay	$8,000	$4,000	$4,000
Year 1	$3,800	$1,900	$1,900
Year 2	$3,000	$1,500	$1,500
Year 3	$2,000	$1,000	$1,000
Internal rate of return	5.5%	n.a.	5.5%

Notes: Tax rate is assumed to be 50 percent.
n.a. = not applicable.

TABLE 2. **Depreciation on a Five-Year Property**

Recovery year	§179 expense	Bonus depreciation	MACRS depreciation
2004	$102,000	$74,000	$14,800 ($74,000 × 20%)
2005	—	—	$23,680 ($74,000 × 32%)
2006	—	—	$14,208 ($74,000 × 19.2%)
2007	—	—	$8,525 ($74,000 × 11.52%)
2008	—	—	$8,525 ($74,000 × 11.52%)
2009	—	—	$4,262 ($74,000 × 5.76%)

Note: MACRS = modified accelerated cost recovery system

cost recovery is appropriate if the objective is to tax consumption instead of income. Thus, recent proposals for replacing the income tax with a consumption-based flat tax have allowed outlays for new capital to be expensed. Similarly, a consumption value-added tax would allow outlays for new capital to be deducted when computing taxable value added.

If, however, the objective is to tax income instead of consumption, the appropriate method is to require the taxpayer to spread out deductions for the cost of the asset, based on the rate at which the asset depreciates in value over its useful lifetime (its economic depreciation). Under an income tax, allowing expensing of assets thus becomes a form of tax preference or tax expenditure because it allows the competitive investment return of assets to go untaxed. In this case, opportunities for tax arbitrage can arise if taxpayers are allowed to expense the cost of assets, while at the same time deducting the interest on the debt incurred to acquire these assets.

The economic effects of the two expensing provisions of the IRC are disputed. Supporters of the §179 expense expansion and bonus depreciation believe that because these provisions lower the cost of capital and increase cash flow, capital formation and employment rates would increase and provide a short run stimulus to the economy (Guether 2003). Further, more small business owners would benefit from the expanded expensing incentives as the §179 investment limitation increases. Finally, accounting would be simplified as businesses could maintain fewer tax depreciation records (Guether 2003).

Opponents note that equipment investment incentives lead to substituting capital for labor and may result in increased national productivity without employment growth (Guether 2003). Opponents also stress that during times of slow economic growth, temporary incentives are more effective than permanent ones. Business executives will accelerate capital acquisitions only if they believe that the §179 expansion and bonus deprecation will expire. So long as doubt exists, the incentives' efficacy as economic stimuli is unclear. If made permanent, the economic inefficiencies introduced by favoring investments in equipment relative to structures would increase (Gravelle 2003). In addition, the credibility of other "temporary" measures will be questioned and thereby undermine future fiscal policy (Gravelle 2003).

ADDITIONAL READING

Gravelle, Jane G. "Effects of the 1981 Depreciation Revision on the Taxation of Income from Business Capital." *National Tax Journal* 35 (March 1982).

———. "Capital Income Tax Revisions and Effective Tax Rates." CRS Report RL32099. Washington, DC: Congressional Research Service, 2003.

Guether, Gary. "Small Business Expensing Allowance under the Jobs and Growth Tax Relief Reconciliation Act of 2003: Changes and Likely Economic Effects." CRS Report RL31852. Washington, DC: Congressional Research Service, 2003.

Holtz-Eakin, Douglas. "Should Small Businesses Be Tax Favored?" *National Tax Journal* 48 (September 1995): 387–95.

Rosen, Harvey. *Public Finance,* 7th ed. New York: McGraw-Hill, 2005.

Cross-references: capital cost recovery; consumption taxation; flat tax; marginal effective tax rate; tax arbitrage; tax expenditures; value-added tax, national; value-added tax, state.

Export tax subsidies
David Brumbaugh
Congressional Research Service, Library of Congress

The U.S. tax system contains two separate tax benefits for exports: the extraterritorial income (ETI) exclusion, and the export source rule. The ETI exclusion permits firms to exempt between 15 and 30 percent of income from tax. The export source rule permits firms with sufficient foreign tax credits to exempt up to 50 percent of export income from tax.

The ETI provisions were enacted in 2000 but are the statutory descendants of two previous export tax benefits: the Domestic International Sales Corporation (DISC) provisions, enacted in 1971, and the Foreign Sales Corporation (FSC) benefit, which replaced DISC in 1984. Each benefit was intended to stimulate U.S. exports; the initial DISC provisions were designed to counter the incentive for overseas rather than domestic investment posed by the tax code's deferral of income earned through foreign subsidiaries. The evolution of the export benefit from DISC to FSC to ETI follows the path of a long-simmering dispute between the United States and the European Union (EU); it marks successive attempts by the United States to design an export tax benefit immune to challenges mounted by the EU, first under the terms of the General Agreement on Tariffs and Trade (GATT) and later under the World Trade Organization (WTO) agreements (GATT's successor).

The DISC/FSC/ETI dispute began soon after DISC's enactment, with European countries complaining that DISC violated GATT's prohibition against export subsidies. The United States attempted to solve the dispute by replacing DISC with a redesigned benefit, FSC. After a period of quiescence, the EU complained that FSC, too, violated international agreements banning export subsidies—in this case, the WTO agreements. The WTO subsequently ruled that FSC was, indeed, an export subsidy. Although the United States again attempted a redesigned tax benefit by enacting ETI, the WTO ruled against the U.S. export benefit and authorized the EU to impose retaliatory tariffs against imports from the United States. The EU began to phase in its tariffs in March 2004. In the meantime, the U.S. Congress is considering several bills that would simply repeal ETI rather than redesign it. (The legislation would also provide a tax benefit for U.S. production in general to offset some of the effects of ETI's repeal.)

The initial DISC provisions worked by granting a tax exemption to specially defined subsidiary corporations (DISCs) that were required to be incorporated in the United States and to be intensively engaged in exporting. Firms obtained the associated tax benefit by channeling their export sales through their DISC subsidiaries. The magnitude of the tax benefit depended on how much export income a parent exporter could allocate to its tax-exempt DISC for tax purposes; the more income that could be thus allocated, the larger the tax benefit. Under specially provided transfer pricing rules that generally departed from "arm's length" pricing (the price a firm would charge an unrelated entity), firms could allocate income to receive a tax exemption for 15 to 30 percent of export income.

A GATT panel in 1976 ruled that DISC was an impermissible export subsidy, but also found that as long as "arm's length" transfer pricing was used to allocate income, countries could use "territorial" tax systems for international taxation without necessarily violating GATT. (Under a territorial tax system, a home country does not tax income earned outside its own borders.) In view of this ruling, the FSC provisions that were adopted in 1984 attempted to achieve GATT legality by incorporating aspects of a territorial tax system into the U.S. export benefit. In general, a firm still obtained the tax benefit by selling exports through a tax-favored subsidiary (in this case, an FSC). Under FSC, however, the subsidiary FSC was required to be incorporated outside U.S. borders. As with DISC, the size of the tax benefit depended on the allocation of income between the parent exporter and its subsidiary FSC; as with DISC, special transfer pricing rules (which departed from the arm's length standard) resulted in an export benefit that could range between 15 and 30 percent of export income.

The EU began complaint proceedings against FSC in 1997, and a succession of WTO panels generally agreed that FSC was an export subsidy and was thus impermissible under the WTO agreements. The ETI provisions were again framed with an eye toward incorporating elements of a territorial system into the U.S. export tax benefit. With ETI, however, a firm need not sell its exports through a tax-favored subsidiary corporation. Instead, the ETI provisions simply provide that "extraterritorial income" is not subject to U.S. tax. The provisions defined extraterritorial income as income from property sold outside the United States, thus including both exports and goods produced by overseas operations within its scope. The provisions also held, however, that no more than 50 percent of exports could be attributable to foreign production. Thus, while the ETI provisions included within their

tax benefit an exemption for income from foreign production, the availability of that benefit was contingent on exporting. In effect, the ETI benefit applied to a firm's exports and a matching amount (if any) of its foreign-produced goods. The ETI provisions also set forth several percentages and rules that have the effect of limiting the exemption to between 15 and 30 percent of qualified income, thus providing a tax benefit of the same magnitude as FSC and DISC before it.

The export source rule

As an alternative to ETI, firms can use the export source rule to exempt up to 50 percent of export income from taxes; the rule can thus potentially produce a tax benefit larger than that of ETI. Because of its statutory mechanics, however, the source rule's benefit can only be used by firms with overseas operations—the rule works by permitting firms to use foreign tax credits to shield part of their export income from taxes, and thus requires a firm to have foreign income on which it has paid foreign taxes.

The foreign tax credit is the basic U.S. mechanism for alleviating double taxation of foreign-source income in cases of overlapping U.S. and foreign tax jurisdictions. Under its provisions, firms are permitted to credit foreign taxes they pay against U.S. taxes on a dollar-for-dollar basis. However, the tax code limits foreign taxes to offsetting taxes on foreign rather than domestic income. Foreign taxes that exceed U.S. taxes on foreign income are not creditable in the year they are paid and become "excess credits" in tax parlance.

It is the foreign tax credit's limitation and excess credits that help create the source rule's tax benefit. If a firm has excess credits from existing foreign-source income, any additional income that can be attributed to foreign sources is either partly or fully shielded from U.S. taxes by the excess credits. In the context of exporting, if an exporting firm has foreign operations that have produced excess foreign tax credits, any export income that can be attributed to foreign sources is shielded by the credits and, in effect, exempted from U.S. tax.

The tax code and associated regulations apply different source rules to different broad categories of exports. The rule for exporting inventory that is both produced and sold by an exporter generates the largest potential benefit; rules for other property—for example, personal property—do not confer the same potential benefit. The benefit works as follows: Regulations issued under Internal Revenue Code Section 863 permit income from the production and sale of inventory to be sourced under a "fifty-fifty split" rule. Fifty percent of the income is sourced where the property that was used to produce or sell the inventory is located; the remaining 50 percent is sourced under the so-called "title passage" rule—that is, where the property's title changes hands. Because the location of the title passage is quite flexible, a firm can assign half of its export income to foreign sources under the fifty-fifty split rule. The half allocated on the basis of property is generally allocated to the United States; the half allocated under the title passage rule can be allocated abroad. A firm with excess credits that both produces and sells its exports can thus exempt 50 percent of its export income from taxes. (For a more detailed explanation of how the source rule works, see U.S. Department of the Treasury 1993.)

The export source regulations were originally issued by the Treasury Department in 1922; they were drafted in response to a congressional mandate in the Revenue Act of 1921, which directed the secretary of the treasury to prescribe rules for determining the source of income when property is produced in one location and sold in another. The rules were thus not promulgated as an explicit means of stimulating exports. More recently, however, policymakers have become aware of the rule's impact. Before the Tax Reform Act of 1986, the fifty-fifty split could apply to personal property as well as inventory. However, following the principle that income should be sourced where the economic activity that generated it occurs, the 1986 act required that income from exports of personal property be sourced in the United States rather than abroad. At the same time, Congress permitted the fifty-fifty split and its consequent exemption to continue in the case of inventory, citing concern that repeal would "create difficulties for U.S. businesses competing abroad" (U.S. Congress, Joint Committee on Taxation 1987). And beginning in 1987, the congressional Joint Committee on Taxation began listing what it termed "the inventory property sales source rule exception" in its annual compilation of tax expenditures. The source rule for inventory has thus become a consciously provided tax benefit for export production.

Economics of export tax subsidies

While both the export source rule and the FSC/ETI provisions were enacted as export incentives, economic theory indicates neither provision has an impact on the U.S. balance of trade. While both benefits likely increase exports, exchange rate adjustments ensure that they increase imports by a like amount; the tax benefits are thus powerless to alter the trade balance. Indeed, under the current system of flexible exchange rates, any autonomous change in exports will trigger adjustments that neutralize any impact on the trade balance. Underlying the exchange rate adjustments is the more basic reason for a subsidy's inability to alter the trade balance: a trade deficit reflects an economy's aggregate decision to use more in the current period than it produces and to finance the difference by importing capital. It follows that the trade balance can change only if capital flows change; a trade deficit can decline only if capital imports also fall. Indeed, even if exchange rates were not flexible, this relationship implies that some alternative adjustment mechanism (for example, prices) would ultimately ensure a neutral effect on the trade balance.

This is not to say that neither the export source rule nor ETI increases exports—only that any increase in exports is matched by an increase in imports. The tax benefits for export income do pose an incentive for firms to increase their exports; each reduces the pretax rate of return required to make export investment attractive and thus increases export investment and export supply. How much exports actually expand depends on the elasticities of supply and demand for both U.S. exports and, given the accompanying exchange rate adjustments, U.S. imports. Based on Internal Revenue Service Statistics of Income data showing how often the source rule benefit is used and on empirical estimates of elasticities, Rousslang (1994) estimated that if the rule had not been in effect in 1990, U.S. exports would have been $518 million lower—less than 0.2 percent of total U.S. merchandise exports in 1990. A 2000 Congressional Research Service Report estimated that FSC increased exports by 0.2 to 0.4 percent. Both provisions thus likely have a small impact on exports.

Economic theory indicates that export subsidies reduce the economic welfare of the subsidizing country—in this case the United States. The welfare loss has two sources: reduced economic efficiency and worsened terms of trade. The efficiency loss occurs because the subsidy induces the United States to trade more than it would if it simply exploited its comparative advantage in various products. In exporting and importing more than it would without the rule, the United States forgoes production of some import-competing goods in favor of export goods that it makes less efficiently. The resulting welfare loss is a "deadweight" loss that is not matched by a welfare gain elsewhere; overtrading on the part of the United States is necessarily matched by an inefficient level of trade on the part of its trading partners.

The second welfare loss is a transfer of economic welfare from the United States to its trading partners. The source rule expands exports because U.S. producers pass on part of its subsidy to foreign consumers in the form of lower prices—a transfer from U.S. taxpayers to foreign consumers.

ADDITIONAL READINGS

Funk, William M. "The Thirty-Years Tax War." *Tax Notes* 93 (October 8, 2001): 271–81.

Rousslang, Donald J. "The Sales Source Rules for U.S. Exports: How Much Do They Cost?" *Tax Notes International* 8 (February 21, 1994): 527–35.

Rousslang, Donald J., and Stephen P. Tokarick. "The Trade and Welfare Consequences of U.S. Export-Enhancing Tax Provisions." *IMF Staff Papers* 41 (December 1994): 675–86.

U.S. Congress, Joint Committee on Taxation. "General Explanation of the Tax Reform Act of 1986." Washington, DC: U.S. Government Printing Office, 1987.

U.S. Department of the Treasury. "Report to the Congress on the Sales Source Rules." Washington, DC: U.S. Department of the Treasury, 1993.

Cross-reference: multinational corporations, taxation of.

Extenders

Jane G. Gravelle
Congressional Research Service, Library of Congress

A term referring to federal income tax provisions that are enacted on a temporary basis but are continually extended.

The Internal Revenue Code contains numerous temporary tax provisions granting benefits. Many of these provisions have been extended many times, and are viewed as, effectively, permanent provisions. Provisions may be enacted as temporary for a variety of reasons, but they have become popular devices for decreasing the budgetary cost of tax benefits, an effect that gained prominence as the budget process required estimates over five years (in the House) and ten years (in the Senate) horizons. Of the approximately two-dozen or so traditional extender provisions, only one was allowed to expire (a deduction for group legal services). Only a few, such as the low-income housing tax credit, have been made permanent.

One of the earliest temporary provisions was the targeted jobs tax credit, enacted in 1978 and aimed at hiring welfare recipients. It was subsequently replaced by the work opportunity tax credit and the welfare to work tax credit; both of which expired in 2003 but may be extended. Perhaps the most important of the "traditional extenders" is the research and experimentation tax credit, which was originally enacted in 1981 and has been extended nine times, in many cases retroactively. The credit expired in mid-2004 and if extended, which seems likely, will be extended retroactively. Other temporary provisions include energy and environmental tax benefits, geographically targeted tax benefits, and medical savings accounts.

Temporary provisions, in terms of revenue effect, were substantially increased in recent years by the tax cuts enacted from 2001 to 2003. In order to conform to a budgetary rule in the Senate that would otherwise have required a supermajority, the 2001 tax cut will sunset in 2010. Many provisions of the 2001 tax cut were phased in (again for budgetary reasons) and a significant part of the 2003 tax cut was a speedup of the phase-in, which itself expired. While the outcome of the 2001 tax cuts remains somewhat uncertain, the majority certainly intended to make these provisions permanent. Partial expensing (bonus depreciation), the most important provision enacted in 2002 as an economic stimulus, was intended as a temporary provision. Its rate was increased in 2003 but the expiration date (2005) was not altered. Although extending partial expensing has not been discussed, it remains a possibility. Another temporary provision enacted in 2003, lower rates for dividends and capital gains, was also intended by the majority party as a permanent provision.

The costs of the individual rate cuts in the 2001 and 2003 tax cuts are about ten times the size of the other, mostly pre-existing, extenders. According to the Congressional Budget Office (2004), the cost of extending the former is $306 billion in 2014, while the cost of the other extenders (outside of bonus depreciation) is $34 billion.

While there may be some merit to enacting provisions on a temporary basis to allow an evaluation, the current practice of continually extending temporary provisions creates unnecessary uncertainty and misrepresents the budgetary cost of tax provisions.

ADDITIONAL READING

Congressional Budget Office. "The Budget and Economic Outlook: An Update." Washington, DC: Congressional Budget Office, September 2004.

Cross-reference: research and experimentation tax credit.

Fairness in taxation

Richard A. Musgrave

Harvard University and University of California at Santa Cruz

A fundamental requirement of a good tax system is that it distributes the burdens of paying taxes fairly among taxpayers.

Few would deny that the tax burden should be distributed in a fair and equitable fashion, but views differ on what that implies. As Adam Smith saw it, "the subjects of every state ought to contribute towards the support of government, as nearly as possible, in proportion to their respective abilities; that is, in proportion to the revenue which they respectively enjoy under the protection of the state" (Smith 1904, 2:310). With this statement, Smith combined two principles of equitable taxation, more commonly viewed as distinct rules: (1) that contributions should be in line with benefits received, and (2) that the burden should be distributed in line with ability to pay. The two approaches differ in rationale and in their vision of fair taxation.

Taxation as payment for benefits received

The benefit principle holds that people should pay for the public services they receive, just as they must pay for their private purchases in the market. If these payments are fair, so will be benefit taxation.

Setting tax prices

In short, the benefit view calls for taxes to be seen as prices paid for public services, similar to what the consumer pays for private goods purchased in the market. The principle is the same for both sectors, but differences arise in application.

Consumers who purchase in the market pay a uniform price per unit of the same product but are free to adjust the amount bought. In this way, they equate price with the marginal utility they derive from their last unit. Because they must bid for goods in order to obtain them, they thereby provide signals to suppliers to furnish the desired amount. In this way, a competitive market secures an efficient assignment of resources, in line with what consumers prefer.

In the case of public goods, such as defense or weather forecasts, individual consumers are not free to vary their purchases. The same level of service is made available to all. But the marginal benefits derived by individual consumers will differ. In order to equate marginal benefit and price, their appropriate tax prices should differ accordingly. Moreover, as public goods are paid for by taxation and become available free of direct charge, consumers need not reveal their preferences by bidding in the market. Government, therefore, has no easy way to assess the correct tax price. A political process of budget voting is needed, to decide what services are to be provided and what tax prices are to be charged. If this democratic process is functioning well, its outcome will approximate a provision of public services that efficiently meets consumer demand. Its tax prices will also yield a burden distribution that is fair—that is, a distribution similar to that which it would have obtained had it been possible to charge market prices.

In short, benefit taxation fits into a natural order where, as suggested by John Locke (1960, 328) and Adam Smith (1904, 1:123), the invisible hand of the market—simulated in the provision for public goods by a political process—yields a result that is both efficient and just. But that claim of fairness requires the further premise that the distribution of income, out of which market purchases are made and benefit taxes are paid, must also be just (Wicksell 1958, 108). That condition is met in a view of distributive justice, such as that held by Adam Smith, that grants entitlement to earnings. Fair taxation in this setting means benefit taxation. Taxation has no redistributive role.

Burden distribution

Such distributionally neutral taxation, however, does not call for a head tax, where each pays the same amount. High-income individuals under the benefit rule may be expected to place higher marginal values on a given provision of public goods, so that benefit taxes will rise with income. Whether they should rise at a slower, proportional, or faster rate depends on consumer demand. More specifically, the appropriate pattern will depend on what economists call the income and price elasticities of demand (Buchanan 1961, 227). Thus determined, the fair relation of tax to income will reflect consumer evaluations based on market-determined earnings, not (as in the ability-to-pay context) on what society considers to be a fair distribution of income. Herein benefit taxation basically differs from the ability-to-pay school of thought.

Taxation in line with ability to pay

As distinct from the benefit rule, the ability-to-pay principle focuses on the tax side of the picture only. The taxpayer incurs a loss, and taxation should spread that loss in a fair and equitable fashion. This calls for taxpayers to contribute in line with their ability to pay.

Choice of index

In order to implement ability-to-pay taxation, an index is needed by which to measure "ability." That index has traditionally been thought of in terms of income, with income seen to provide the best measure of economic capacity. It follows that those with equal income should pay the same, while those with higher incomes should pay more. The former, referred to as horizontal equity, follows readily from the rule that equals should be treated equally. But the latter, referred to as vertical equity, has remained controversial because it requires a determination of how much more higher-income taxpayers should pay.

Equal sacrifice rules

As John Stuart Mill (1921, 155) put it, "equality ought to be the rule in taxation as it ought to be in all affairs of government. Whatever sacrifice it requires should be made to bear as nearly as possible with the same pressure upon all." Taxation in line with ability to pay thus became taxation so as to equate the sacrifice incurred.

Based on the premise that the utility of the last dollar of income falls as income rises, high-income person A should pay more so as to incur a sacrifice equal to that of low-income person B. The rule of "equal sacrifice" was subsequently given various interpretations, calling for equal absolute, equal proportional, or equal marginal sacrifice. These rules all let the amount of tax rise with income, more so the more rapidly marginal utility falls as income rises. Whereas the tax-to-income relationship under benefit taxation depended on consumer demand for public goods, it now hinges on the rate at which the marginal utility of income declines as income rises. With equal absolute sacrifice, taxation will be regressive, proportional, or progressive, depending on whether the elasticity of the marginal utility-of-income schedule falls short of, equals, or exceeds unity. Under the equal marginal rule, taxation is most progressive, with taxes collected by equalizing incomes from the top down until the necessary revenue is obtained.

Least total sacrifice

There is no conclusive reason, as a matter of fairness, for preferring one of these rules over the others. But economists, following Edgeworth (1958, 119), opted for the principle of equal marginal sacrifice, with Pigou (1928, 59) enshrining it as the "ultimate principle of taxation." By equating the mar-

ginal sacrifices incurred across taxpayers, the resulting burden distribution also serves to minimize aggregate sacrifice and thereby meets the economist's goal of maximizing society's aggregate welfare. In the process, the quest for fairness in taxation was thus joined with the utilitarian goal of maximizing aggregate welfare.

The premise of entitlement to earnings underlying the fairness view of benefit taxation no longer holds when judging fairness according to least total sacrifice. With marginal income utility declining, equal marginal sacrifice calls for a high degree of progression. Indeed, as Bentham (1962, 305) concluded, the logic of welfare maximization calls for income equalization—that is, for taxation to be extended beyond what is needed for the finance of public services and into a tax-transfer scheme to equalize incomes.

This case for highly progressive taxation was then qualified in two respects. First, as already stressed by Bentham, detrimental effects of taxation must be allowed for. Security of expectations and of property, as he argued, are given priority and are essential to accumulation. The reasoning from declining marginal utility of income to income equalization thus follows only from the unrealistic assumption that total income is fixed and remains unaffected by taxation. As economists now put it, taxation imposes a "deadweight loss" that must be taken into consideration. As taxes are imposed, the taxpayer will respond by engaging less in the taxed activity. This interferes with efficient resource use and imposes an additional burden, a deadweight loss that the taxpayer suffers but that does not add to Treasury revenues. That loss adds to the taxpayer's sacrifice and thus must be allowed for. (See *optimal taxation.*) Because the deadweight loss rises rapidly with the marginal tax rate, the case for income equalization and progressive taxation has to be qualified considerably. A similar argument, focusing on the level of output, points to the "supply-side effects" of high marginal rates.

A further qualification was to discard a central assumption underlying the earlier utilitarian case for highly progressive taxation—that is, the premise of an observable and declining marginal utility-of-income function, similar for and comparable across all taxpayers. That concept was discarded some 50 years ago as unrealistic and replaced by the concept of a social welfare function. Based on the subjective view of individual members of society on how successive units of income should be valued, that function is to be arrived at via a democratic process. It thus expresses a consensus on how society views distributive justice and with it the fair distribution of the tax burden.

Impartiality

The goal of least total sacrifice, as noted earlier, was embraced as matching the utilitarian goal of maximizing aggregate welfare. But why should welfare maximization be the fair and equitable goal? Bentham (1948, 3), the guru of utilitarianism, laid down as his central proposition that individuals will seek to pursue their own happiness. From this he proceeded to the conclusion that therefore the interest of the community will be the sum of the interests of its members, so that government should seek to maximize that aggregate interest. But why should A, with superior endowment, agree, in pursuit of his or her own happiness, to a policy that requires him or her to pay higher taxes or make transfers to less-favored B, as would be needed to maximize aggregate welfare?

The goal of maximizing aggregate welfare, it appears, does not follow as a matter of self-interest. Its acceptance requires an ethical underpinning. Where in the context of benefit taxation, that foundation was provided by entitlement to earnings, the underlying tenet now calls on individual members of society to view distributive justice from an impartial perspective. They should view the desirable state of distribution from behind a veil, without knowing what their own position therein will be (Rawls 1972, 136). They should value the interest of others as their own.

Judging from that position, individuals may favor a more or less equal distribution (and hence more or less progressivity in taxation), depending on their dislike of inequality. Or, as economists like to put it, their choice will depend on their willingness to gamble on doing better with inequality, compared with playing it safe with a more equal distribution. Thus, self-interest again enters the picture, but only after the premise of impartiality has been accepted. A political process, as noted above, then serves to translate these individual preferences into a social welfare function, and, based on its weights, the tax burden is distributed so as to minimize the aggregate burden.

Corrective taxation

So far, we have discussed general rules of fair taxation, such as the benefit and ability-to-pay principles. It remains to note that a fairness case may also be made for certain types of selective taxation that serve to correct unfair situations.

Even where entitlement to earnings is taken as the general rule, not all earnings may be seen to constitute deserved rewards. Thus, Henry George urged taxation of land rent, reflecting the Lockean stricture that such earnings are undeserved because natural resources are held in common, and no effort is involved in reaping the rent from them. Ever since Aristotle and Thomas Aquinas called for taxation of usury interest, monopoly or excess profits have been viewed as undeserved, and hence appropriate sources of taxation. The fairness case here may be traced to the premise of a natural order in which only competitive earnings are seen as deserved. Indeed, that premise is needed if the invisible hand of the market is to be both efficient and just. Of more recent concern, a fairness case may also be made for the taxation of activities, such as smoking, that generate external costs and thereby burden others. Not only may most of these forms of selective taxation claim merit on grounds of fairness, they also are supported by the economist's quest for efficient taxation.

Conclusion

As noted at the outset, the benefit and ability-to-pay rules offer different views of fair and equitable taxation, reflecting their respective premises of distributive justice. Benefit taxation is fair in the context of an order that recognizes entitlement to earnings. People with higher incomes should pay more because they attach a higher monetary value to the public service. The ability-to-pay approach calls for a pattern of taxation that minimizes the aggregate loss and thus serves the goal of welfare maximization. People with higher incomes should pay more to meet that goal. Entitlement to earnings is disregarded, with the claim to fairness derived from an impartiality-based view of distributive justice. The expenditure side of the budget is not taken into account.

Although the two principles differ, they may also be combined. A person may accept entitlement to earnings as the general rule but accept distributional corrections for extreme inequality, especially at the lower end of the scale. This may well be the typical position, as suggested by actual patterns of effective tax rates, with low or even negative rates at the bottom, followed by rates that sharply rise toward the middle and flatten out in the higher ranges.

But even where fairness is seen purely in ability-to-pay rather than benefit terms, there still remains the task of securing an efficient provision of public goods. Here, the efficiency role of benefit taxation—linking tax and expenditure choices—is pivotal. Reconciliation between the two concerns is thus needed. In principle, although not readily matched in practice, this would be met by a two-part system that combines (1) a "distribution branch" of the budget that offers a tax transfer scheme to establish what is considered a fair state of distribution, with (2) a benefit tax–financed "allocation branch" that provides for an efficient level of public goods.

This entry deals with principles and norms of fair taxation; it is not a critique of tax practice. This requires no apology because norms have their impact, even in the "real world" of tax legislation. Their importance should not be underestimated, but they are only part of the picture. Tax politics and pressure groups also affect tax policy, and what appears on the books reflects the tension between these two sides of the picture.

ADDITIONAL READINGS

Bentham, Jeremy. *An Introduction to the Principles of Morals and Legislation.* New York: Hafner Press, 1948. First published in 1789, edited by L. Lafleur.

———. "Principles of the Civil Code." In *The Works of Jeremy Bentham,* vol. 1. New York: Russell, 1962. First published in 1802, edited by J. Bowring.

Edgeworth, F. Y. "The Pure Theory of Taxation." *Economic Journal Vol.* 7, No. 25. Reproduced in *Classics in the Theory of Public Finance,* edited by R. A. Musgrave and A. Peacock (119–136). London: Macmillan, 1958. First published in 1897.

Locke, John. *Two Treatises of Government.* London: Cambridge University Press, 1960. First published in 1689, edited by P. Laslett.

Mill, John Stuart. *Principles of Political Economy,* books 4 and 5. London: Longman's, 1921. First published in 1848, edited by D. Winch.

Musgrave, Richard A. *The Theory of Public Finance.* New York: McGraw-Hill, 1959.

Musgrave, Richard A., and Peggy B. Musgrave. *Public Finance in Theory and Practice,* 5th ed. New York: McGraw-Hill, 1989.

Pigou, Arthur C. *A Study in Public Finance.* London: Macmillan, 1928.

Rawls, John. *A Theory of Justice.* Cambridge, MA: Harvard University Press, 1972.

Smith. Adam. *The Wealth of Nations,* vols. 1 and 2. New York: Putnam's, 1904. First published in 1776, edited by E. Cannan.

Wicksell, Knut. "A New Principle of Just Taxation." In *Classics in the Theory of Public Finance,* edited by Richard A. Musgrave and Alan T. Peacock (72–118). New York: MacMillan, 1958. First published in 1896 in *Finanztheoretische Untersuchungen.*

Cross-references: ability to pay; benefit principle; environmental taxes, federal; environmental taxes, state; income tax, federal; tax equity analysis.

Family, tax treatment of

Louis Kaplow

Harvard Law School and National Bureau of Economic Research

One's income tax status is determined in part by one's family status (marital status and number of dependents).

Income tax treatment of married couples

Tax systems must allocate burdens among single individuals, married couples, and families with varying numbers of dependents. The U.S. federal income tax originally treated each taxpayer separately, as do many developed countries today, but it now treats married couples as a unit. This means, for example, that couples in which each spouse earns $25,000 pay the same tax as couples in which one spouse earns $50,000 and the other earns $0. With individual treatment, the latter couple would have a relatively higher tax burden because of the tax system's graduated rates: an individual with $50,000 of income pays more than twice the tax of a single individual with $25,000.

Aggregation of spouses' incomes is supported by those who believe that spouses typically share resources. In addition, enforcing separate taxation would be difficult. Couples could manipulate which spouse receives unearned income and incurs deductible expenses. Indeed, under the individual taxation regime, spouses in community property states were each taxed on half of their earned income, and some states adopted community property laws, apparently so that their residents could receive this benefit.

But aggregation is blamed for discouraging the work effort of second earners (typically wives) whose labor supply is particularly responsive to effective wage rates and thus to taxes. Under individual taxation, a second earner would be taxed at a lower rate on initial earnings. The primary reason the income tax discourages second earners, however, is its failure to tax the imputed income of spouses who work in the home: if one earns $10,000 in the market, this will not be enough

after taxes to pay $10,000 to hire someone to perform domestic work that one no longer has time to do. The child care credit is a partial remedy for some families, and a modest two-earner deduction previously existed. Larger earned income allowances and taxing the second (lower-earnings) worker's income at lower rates have been proposed.

In addition, the extent of actual sharing within the family has been questioned. If spouses largely retain control over their own earnings, it is argued that they should be taxed separately on those earnings. Unequal sharing, however, does not obviously favor a policy of heavier taxation of couples with unequal incomes. Part of any increased tax burden may be borne by the relatively poor spouse, whose poverty is greater the less equal the sharing.

Another feature of the current system is that it uses a separate rate schedule for married couples, which taxes them at higher rates than single individuals. Prior to the 2001 tax cut, a married couple with $50,000 of income would have paid more than twice the tax of a single individual with $25,000 of income. Thus, prospective spouses with equal earnings would face a marriage penalty. Despite this penalty, however, prospective spouses face a net subsidy if their earnings are sufficiently unequal. A single individual with income of $50,000 and another with income of $0 would pay less income tax if they married: the tax savings from income splitting (being taxed as if each spouse earned $25,000) exceeds the tax cost because of higher rates for married couples. The 2001 tax cut eliminated the marriage penalty for the vast majority of taxpayers by expanding the standard deduction and the size of the 15 percent rate bracket, although this action expanded the marriage subsidy. Very high income individuals may still face a penalty. The 2001 provisions are technically set to expire in 2010, although they will likely be made permanent.

The primary rationale for applying a higher rate schedule to married couples is that economies of scale in living arrangements increase their ability to pay. Although scale economies increase well-being, they also imply that married couples benefit more per dollar of disposable income. This factor favors lighter taxation if higher taxes on those with higher incomes are justified on the grounds that marginal dollars are less valuable to the wealthy. Thus, it is ambiguous whether economies of scale favor higher or lower tax burdens on married couples. Also, many think that single individuals, by finding roommates, are able to realize scale economies.

Income tax treatment of dependents

In addition to the different rates applied to married couples and single individuals, the income tax reflects family size by allowing an exemption, $3,050 in 2003, for each member, and a credit of $500 for each child under 17. (This credit is temporarily $1,000, a provision likely to be made permanent.) These per-person allowances do not fall as family size increases, which would be analogous to the typical treatment in welfare programs. And the size of these allowances does not increase with income; rather, allowances are phased out at high incomes.

If the family really is the unit of taxation, it may seem natural to treat dependents like spouses. For example, if a spouse reduces effective income by almost half, perhaps adding children should produce a similar result. France takes such an approach, while giving less weight to children than adults. The U.S. income tax makes a partial allowance of this sort by subjecting single individuals to a lower rate schedule if they have dependents.

Such an extension of the taxable unit from married couples to the entire family would significantly increase the tax benefits from having dependents for middle- and upper-income couples. The distributive rationale for this result is that, when children are present, adults need substantially more income before they reach any given living standard—say, before they are able to afford a summer home. In contrast, the constant exemption reflects a view of children as fixed costs, affecting parents' ability to pay no differently from leasing a sports car, which would have the same annual cost regardless of the purchaser's income.

More generous treatment of married couples and dependents is sometimes viewed as undesirable because it would favor the rich: a given exemption is worth more to those in higher tax brackets, and an increasing exemption would benefit them to an even greater extent. But determining proper taxation of married couples and families with dependents is distinct, in important respects, from deciding upon the degree of progressivity. After all, coherent redistribution is impossible unless one first decides to and from whom one is redistributing income and which units are properly characterized as rich and poor.

Most analysis of the proper treatment of families emphasizes the redistributive role of the income tax. If, instead, tax burdens depended in part on benefits received from the government, rather different principles would apply. For example, the receipt of many tax-funded benefits, like public education, increases with family size, suggesting that heavier burdens be placed on larger families—or at least reducing the force of arguments favoring more generous treatment.

Social security and other transfer programs

Tax treatment of the family depends on more than the federal income tax, or the states' income taxes, which are much smaller in magnitude and usually treat families similarly. Social Security taxes, as well as Social Security benefit formulas and welfare programs, significantly affect the disposable income of different types of families. For all taxpayers but the rich, Social Security taxes are a sizable fraction of their tax burden, and these taxes do not adjust for family size in the same way as income taxes; nor do benefit rules respond in the same manner. To illustrate, a second earner entering the labor force bears the full effective burden of Social Security taxes but initially receives no increase in future retirement benefits. Similarly, the effect of the income tax on the poor cannot be determined without accounting for Social Security taxes and

benefits and other transfer programs, including the earned income tax credit (EITC), which is formally part of the income tax. The marriage penalty from the EITC, for example, can be thousands of after-tax dollars for some lower-income couples. Also, welfare payments are more easily identified as having a positive effect on fertility than income tax exemptions, although exemptions play a role and would have a significant effect under some proposed alternatives.

Gifts and bequests

Taxation of the family also concerns gifts and bequests. Indeed, a large portion of all giving, other than to public charities, is to family members, so tax issues concerning gifts have an important effect on the treatment of families. The income tax excludes gifts and bequests from donees' income and does not permit donors any deduction. (By contrast, spouses are implicitly each taxed on half of combined income; this is equivalent to assuming that resources are shared, giving a gift deduction to the higher-income spouse, and taxing the gift to the lower-income spouse.)

A comprehensive view of income might include gifts in donees' income, as they clearly increase ability to pay. Donors would still be denied a deduction on the theory that they have benefited by giving the gift at least as much as by direct consumption. (Also, as a quid pro quo may be present, some so-called gifts are really payments for services.)

A view that the tax system should maximize social welfare might be more favorable to gifts. Gifts do increase ability to pay, which is relevant for redistributive purposes. But gifts also have the desirable feature of the same economic resources providing a double benefit, to both donor and donee. Thus, subsidizing gifts may enhance economic welfare.

The current system does not fully embrace either view. Existing income tax treatment of gifts is commonly rationalized on the grounds that taxing or subsidizing them would be difficult, particularly for myriad small gifts within the family. However, there is a gift and estate tax, separate from the income tax, levied on large gifts by the wealthy.

Gifts of property are also important in an income tax system because they result in future income from the property being taxed to the donee, often a child in a low tax bracket, rather than to the donor, who may be in the highest bracket. Rules concerning trusts and other assignments of income reduce this practice, but outright transfers of property, as well as some less complete transfers, have long been permitted to shift the tax burden on future income to the donee. (Also, unrealized appreciation on property transferred as a gift is taxed to the donee; if given as a bequest, unrealized appreciation is never taxed.) Under the Tax Reform Act of 1986, however, unearned income of children under 14 is taxed to their parents, which eliminates much of the tax benefit from such transfers. This provision can be seen as embodying a view that—at least with respect to transfers of property—the entire (immediate) family is the unit of taxation, rather than just the married couple.

Future research

Many rules affect the tax treatment of families, and no consensus exists about their proper form. Further illumination of these issues should be gained from analysis that unavoidably will become ever more complicated. Simple, intuitive appeals will be increasingly qualified or displaced by arguments that (1) give greater attention to the economics of the family, such as by analyzing decisions to marry, have children, and allocate resources among members (Becker 1991); (2) appeal directly to principles of distributive justice and economic welfare, as in the vast literature on optimal income taxation, rather than rely primarily on abstract ability-to-pay norms (Kaplow 1996); (3) integrate the effects of all major tax and transfer programs (Boskin and Puffert 1987); (4) adopt a lifetime perspective, often used in studies of tax incidence, because individuals spend parts of their lives in different family units; and (5) more closely examine other countries' tax systems, which vary greatly from that in the United States in their treatment of the family (Pechman and Engelhardt 1990).

ADDITIONAL READINGS

Alm, James, and M. V. Lee Badgett. "Wedding Bell Blues: The Income Tax Consequences of Legalizing Same-Sex Marriage." *National Tax Journal* 53, no. 2 (June 2000): 201–14.

Becker, Gary S. *A Treatise on the Family.* Cambridge, MA: Harvard University Press, 1991.

Boskin, Michael J., and Douglas J. Puffert. "Social Security and the American Family." In *Tax Policy and the Economy,* vol. 1, edited by Lawrence H. Summers (139–59). Cambridge, MA: MIT Press, 1987.

Eissa, Nada, and Hiliary Williamson-Hoynes. "Explaining the Fall and Rise in the Tax Cost of Marriage: The Effect of Tax Laws and Demographic Trends, 1984–1997." *National Tax Journal* 53, no. 3 (September 2000): 683–712.

Kaplow, Louis. "Optimal Distribution and the Family." *Scandinavian Journal of Economics* 98 (March 1996): 75–92.

Pechman, Joseph A., and Gary V. Engelhardt. "The Income Tax Treatment of the Family: An International Perspective." *National Tax Journal* 43 (March 1990): 1–22.

Cross-references: ability to pay; child care credit; earned income credit; estate and gift tax, federal; fairness in taxation; labor supply, taxes and; marriage penalty; optimal taxation; progressivity, measures of; Social Security benefits, federal taxation.

Finance Committee, U.S. Senate

J. D. Foster

Tax Foundation (currently Office of Management and Budget)

Updated by editors

One of the three key fiscal committees of the U.S. Congress (along with the House Committee on Ways and Means and the Joint Committee on Taxation).

The Senate Finance Committee may be the most powerful committee in the United States Senate because of the enormous range of vital issues over which it has jurisdiction. The committee has sole Senate committee jurisdiction over tax legislation, but its jurisdiction also includes Social Security, Medicare, and Medicaid programs, and it is responsible for all legislation dealing with the national debt.

While the committee's most important work is reporting legislation to the full Senate, every year it also holds scores of hearings on issues within its jurisdiction. The purpose of those hearings is threefold: to establish a public record for legislative action; to allow citizens and interested parties to express their opinions and ideas directly to the committee; and to educate the members and committee staff. The committee also holds hearings on important executive branch nominees, including those for secretary of the Treasury, administrator of the Social Security Administration, and administrator of the Health Care Financing Administration.

As with all congressional committees, the Senate Finance Committee has a chairman drawn from the majority party and a ranking member drawn from the minority party. In general, the chairman and the ranking member are the most senior members (those who have served the longest on the committee) from their respective parties. The exception occurs when the senior member prefers to chair another committee of the Senate or when the senior member is part of his or her party's Senate leadership.

The committee chairman has tremendous power. The chairman chooses when the committee will hold hearings and the subject of those hearings. The chairman also determines whether and when legislation is to be considered. Thus, a chairman can move legislation swiftly, with the necessary members' support, or, acting alone, can bury legislation indefinitely. Members can sidestep the committee by bringing legislation directly to the Senate floor and offering it as an amendment to other legislation. However, the prospects for success are always in doubt because of the lack of committee support and because of various floor rules, including germaneness requirements that limit whether the amendment is in order for debate.

Members are appointed to the committee by their party caucuses according to each party's rules. The committee currently has 21 members; the chairman and 10 members are from the majority. The committee maintains a relatively small staff, which is bifurcated into majority and minority staffs. The sizes of the staffs are limited by the available budget, which is divided between the majority and minority staffs. Each staff has a director and a complement of tax, Social Security, and health care experts.

The committee has five subcommittees, covering taxation and Internal Revenue Service oversight; international trade; long-term growth and debt reduction; Social Security and family policy; and health care. Each subcommittee has its own chairman and ranking member. These subcommittees hold hearings and initiate and report legislation to be considered by the committee as a whole. The primary purpose of the subcommittees is to allow members to develop expertise in legislative areas of particular interest to themselves and their constituents.

Frequently, the Senate majority and minority leaders have also been Finance Committee members, ensuring a close working relationship between Senate and committee leadership.

Cross-references: Congressional Budget Office; Joint Committee on Taxation, U.S. Congress; Office of Tax Policy; Ways and Means Committee.

Fiscal architecture

Sally Wallace
Georgia State University

Economic, demographic, and institutional factors that determine pressures on expenditures and revenue sources.

Economic, demographic, institutional, and technological changes are constantly occurring throughout the world. These forces define the "fiscal architecture" of countries—the pressures on expenditures and revenue sources facing government officials worldwide. The concentration of world population has moved from developed to developing economies, the distribution of income in most countries has become increasingly disparate, and some developing countries are witnessing unprecedented increases in the percentage of elderly—others in the young. Population and income growth, as well as changes in the age distribution, economic base, and other factors imply pressures for public expenditures that are different depending on the type of economic and demographic change occurring. At the same time, similar factors affect the capacity of traditional revenue sources.

In the short run, many of these changes are beyond a country's control, but they cannot be ignored in the development of an effective fiscal policy. In the long run, government policy may impact some of these economic and demographic trends. At the same time, the institutional factors that govern a country and the technological changes faced by all countries also affect fiscal policy—from short- and long-term budgeting decisions to antipoverty policies to intergovernmental fiscal relations. This is because the fiscal architecture of a country impacts its expenditure needs and revenue-producing potential, and establishes a framework for developing polices that make "fiscal sense" and provide practical options. Fiscal architecture analysis looks at the specific determinants of revenue capacity, expenditure needs, and policy options (that may be constrained by the overarching fiscal architecture).

There are many examples of how fiscal architecture affects policy debates. A simple example follows. A country in which property rights are not well established and will not be for years would be ill advised to count on a market-based property tax to generate stable revenues in the near future. The increasing globalization of markets for products and services in the past decade has magnified the importance of recognizing these parameters and the opportunities they provide for (and the limitations they place on) policymakers. Understanding how these trends may affect the growth in revenue collections and change the composition of client populations may enable policymakers to redesign expenditure programs and revenue instruments to stabilize a country's long-term finances.

It is easy to list the pieces of a country's fiscal architecture, but difficult to develop an exhaustive list. Some of the parts include the following:

- Demographic characteristics, including population growth, age distribution, health status of the population, household composition, fertility rates, and life expectancy.
- Economic characteristics, including the importance of particular sectors (manufacturing, agriculture, services) and changes in the importance of these sectors, concentration of natural resources, size and type of economy (small open economy or large open economy, for example).
- Institutions, including not only institutions of revenue administration, but also the many social systems that make tax polices work, such as a system of postal addresses for tax billing and collection; computerization for tracking tax payments and, when necessary, recording and monitoring tax liens; a telephone or web site where one can download tax forms and instructions and have questions answered; property rights and rights of different levels of government; and a judicial system for tax appeal and quality assurance.

The impact of these various facets of fiscal architecture on public finances is obvious, but the extent of their integration into budgeting, forecasting, and intergovernmental grant development is very limited outside of the developed countries.

The methodology for analyzing the impacts of fiscal architecture on governments is based on the relationship between these components and the revenue and expenditures of governments at all levels. Since public expenditures are driven by the needs of the population, or clients, a basic relationship between changes in public expenditures and changes in demographic factors can be expressed as follows:

$$\Delta \mathrm{EXP}_i = \Delta \mathrm{CPOP}_i \left(\mathrm{PXPS}_i \right) + \left(\mathrm{CPOP}_i \right) \Delta \mathrm{PXPS}_i$$

where EXP_i is the total expenditure on the ith spending category, CPOP_i is the client population of the ith spending category, and PXPS_i is the production expense of the ith spending category.

In this expression, the left hand side is the change in expenditure for a particular spending category, EXP_i, and the right hand side of the equation contains the components of the change in expenditures. These are changes in the client population (elderly for retirement programs, school-age children for school expenditures, etc.) and changes in the costs of production associated with the cost of inputs (wages, materials, etc.). Demographic changes can influence both components of the expenditure calculation. For example, consider a change in the age distribution of the population. If a population becomes increasingly elderly, this will increase the need for retirement and health-based expenditures. However, such a trend will also influence the direct cost of providing those services, as labor shortages may ensue.

An expression for the relationship between changes in public revenues and changes in demographic and economic factors may also be expressed as follows:[1]

$$\Delta \text{Rev}_i = \Delta \text{TXBASE}_i \left(\text{TXRATE}_i \right) + \Delta \text{TXRATE}_i \left(\text{TXBASE}_i \right)$$

where Rev_i is the revenue from source i, TXBASE_i is the base for tax source i, and TXRATE_i is the tax rate for source i.

In this case, the tax base is determined by the particular revenue source. For personal or individual income taxes, the revenue source is some measure of taxable income, for consumption taxes, it is a measure of consumption, etc. Economic and demographic changes directly influence these tax bases. In the case of a consumption-based revenue source, the size of the population affects the total potentially taxable consumption, and the age distribution affects the type of consumption made. Traditionally, a more elderly population consumes different goods than does a younger population. The breadth of a country's tax base determines how much revenues will fluctuate as a result of these demographic changes. The tax rate, while exogenous to these demographic and economic changes, is a policy variable that can be used to compensate for changes in the tax base.

A few concrete examples of the impact of fiscal architecture (and changes in fiscal architecture) on critical components of the public finance system may help illustrate the need to integrate this concept into fiscal analysis.

For example, many countries have had an increase in female-headed households. This affects consumption patterns, labor supply, and need for elderly care. How do these changes, in turn, affect governments? They may reduce value-added tax (VAT) collections if the increased consumption comes out of non-taxed goods, such as food, and they may pressure governments to provide more care for the elderly. To mitigate these impacts, governments could increase the VAT rate, expand the tax base, or perhaps increase the payroll tax to support health care for the elderly. In some countries, a policy option may be feasible, while in others it may not be feasible, due to overarching institutional constraints.

As another example, consider changes in the structure of the economy. Among countries, there has been a general movement away from agriculture and toward manufacturing and service sector production. What impacts might this change have on governments' budgets? Tax handles may change and the administration of taxes may be made more difficult by the fluid, nontransparent nature of service production. Such a

change might call for more indirect taxation versus direct taxation. At the same time, changes in the economic base could call for new demands for infrastructure such as roads and telecommunications. These examples provide a context for the concept of fiscal architecture and fiscal architecture analysis.

A more specific example is the interaction of aging and pressures on pension systems. For a pay-as-you-go pension system, the basic relationship between revenues and expenditures can be expressed as follows:

$$P_b B = t P_w w$$

where P_b is the number of pensioners, B is the benefit per pensioner, t is the payroll tax rate, P_w is the number of workers, and w is the average wage per worker.

Rearranging this expression yields the following relationship between the tax rate and benefits:

$$t = \left(P_b / P_w \right) \left(B / w \right)$$

The right hand side of the expression is the "age-dependency ratio," the ratio of pensioners to working population (P_b/P_w), multiplied by the "replacement ratio," the ratio of average benefits paid to wages that supply the financing for the pension system (B/w). As the population ages, the number of pensioners relative to the number of workers may increase, putting pressure on the tax rate needed to maintain a balance in the pension fund. Fiscal architecture analysis highlights these strains on public finances and also develops options for dealing with the stress on revenues and expenditures. For example, in Russia, the age-dependency ratio is expected to increase from 22.8 percent in 2000 to 35 percent in 2025. The policy options available to the government are to increase the tax rate to support pensions, increase the age for receipt of pensions (effectively decreasing the number of pensioners), or reduce the benefits. Are some of these options more feasible than others? Yes. In the short run, due to labor contracts, there is little chance of changing the age for receipt of pensions, but there is more room for negotiating lower benefit levels.

Table 1 briefly illustrates the methodology of fiscal architecture analysis. Fiscal architecture characteristics appear in the first column, examples of changes in these areas appear in the second column, and the impacts of those changes appear in the other columns. This table highlights the impacts on the revenue side of the budget and shows where stress may be realized for each major change in a country's fiscal architecture. For example, for countries with aging populations, we might expect the tax base for consumption goods and income taxes to narrow. These changes call for careful consideration of policy options. In some countries, an expansion of the VAT base to cover more nontaxable goods is possible; in other countries, it is off-limits for institutional or political reasons. Working through this matrix—and its companion expenditure matrix, not presented here (see Wallace 2003b)—yields a fiscal analysis that is more sensitive to short- and long-term impacts of

---

[1] This equation assumes a given population to pay the tax. Obviously, if the number of taxpayers increases or decreases, this will directly affect the level of collections. For example, if there is a large increase in the labor force participation, we should expect to see an increase in income tax collections. The equation also assumes a given (constant) level of enforcement effort.

TABLE 1. Illustration of Fiscal Architecture and Projections of Fiscal Pressures

Variable	Basic trend	VAT	Import duties	Corporate income tax	Individual income tax
Demographic					
Age distribution	Relative increase in the number of elderly	Increased consumption of nontaxable goods	Increased demand for imports	Reduced consumption of durable goods	Reduced taxable income
Economic					
Service sector growth (output composition)	Growth in the sector as a share of GDP	Slightly negative impact, though more ambiguous than for corporate income tax or individual income tax	Increased due to demand for more technology	Decreased due to decrease in tax handles	Decreased due to tax handles
Institutional					
State of public records and data	Large variation among countries	May limit policy choices for multiple revenue sources: for example, property tax (due to lack of cadastre and other records), and VAT invoice credit mechanisms. May call for simplified systems such as a presumptive tax.			

Note: VAT = value-added tax.

changes in fiscal architecture on government expenditures and revenues.

ADDITIONAL READINGS

Alm, James. "International Experience with Expenditure Norms." Georgia State University, Andrew Young School of Policy Studies Working Paper, August 1999.

Lotz, Joergen, and Elliott Morris. "Measuring Tax Effort in Developing Countries." *IMF Staff Papers* 14, no. 3 (November 1967): 478–99.

Tanzi, Vito, and George Tsibouris. "Fiscal Reform over Ten Years of Transition." Working paper no. 00/113. Washington, DC: International Monetary Fund, 2000.

Tanzi, Vito, and Anthony J. Pellechio. "The Reform of Tax Administration." Working paper no. 95/22. Washington, DC: International Monetary Fund, 1995.

Wallace, Sally. "Changing Times: Demographic and Economic Changes and State and Local Government Finances." In *State and Local Finances Under Pressure,* edited by David L. Sjoquist (30–58). Northhampton, MA: Edward Elgar, 2003a.

———. "Fiscal Architecture: A Framework for Analysis of Public Expenditure Needs and Revenue Capacity." Washington, DC: The World Bank Group, 2003b.

Cross-references: budget process, federal; budget process, state; consumption taxation; income tax, personal; income tax, corporate; property tax entries; retail sales tax, state and local; revenue forecasting; value-added tax entries.

Fiscal disparities

Helen F. Ladd
Duke University

Differences across subnational governments in their abilities to meet the public expenditure needs of their residents.

Fiscal disparities refer to the variation across subnational jurisdictions in their ability to raise revenue to meet the public expenditure needs of their residents. Fiscal disparities are a natural outcome of a federal system of government—that is, one in which certain fiscal responsibilities are assigned to the central or national level and others to lower levels of governments. In a unitary system of government, fiscal disparities would not arise.

In a federal system, fiscal disparities arise because the capacity to raise revenue to finance publicly provided services relative to the amount needed to provide a standard package of public services varies across jurisdictions. For example, a city with a large proportion of low-income residents will be disadvantaged relative to a city of wealthier residents, both because the residents' low income makes it difficult for the city to raise revenue for public services and because the concentration of poor people may require the jurisdiction to spend more per capita than other jurisdictions to provide a standard package of public services. The term *fiscal disparities* refers to these differences across subnational governmental units at any specific level of government. Thus, in the U.S. context, one can talk about the fiscal disparities across states at any point in time or among school districts, cities, or any other category of local government within a state or metropolitan area.

When fiscal disparities exist, one jurisdiction can provide a higher level of services at a given burden on its residents than another jurisdiction—or can provide a given level of services at a lower tax burden on its residents. Some observers view such disparities as an unfair consequence of a federal system of government—and one that higher levels of government should try to minimize through various forms of intergovernmental assistance. In addition, when there are fiscal disparities, some people may make inefficient decisions about where to live or work in their attempt to benefit from the fiscal advantages of the wealthier jurisdictions. Other observers discount the equity criticism on the grounds that if such disparities truly imposed burdens on the people living in the fiscally disadvantaged communities, those people would simply relocate to other jurisdictions with more favorable fiscal positions. Moreover, any attempt to offset the disparities could lead to inefficient levels of public services as taxpayer voters would no longer face the fiscal discipline of paying fully for all the services communities choose to provide (see *fiscal equalization*).

To determine the magnitude of fiscal disparities, one needs first to measure not only each jurisdiction's capacity to raise revenue but also the expenditure burdens placed on it. Failure to look at the spending side along with the revenue side could well give a misleading picture of a specific jurisdiction's fiscal condition and, consequently, of the disparities across jurisdictions. For example, based on the capacity side alone, a large city with an above-average capacity to raise revenue relative to the size of its population would appear to be in strong fiscal condition. However, once the large expenditure burdens placed on the city by its economically disadvantaged resident population and the large influx of daily commuters or shoppers are considered, the city's fiscal condition may not look so favorable.

Second, the measure of local fiscal condition should reflect the effects of factors outside the immediate control of local officials. In particular, one should not use actual revenues, tax rates, or spending levels as measures of expenditure need. This consideration is particularly important if the magnitude of a local government's adverse fiscal condition signals the need for more assistance from a higher level of government. Ideally, one would not want the local government to be able to manipulate the size of its claim on that assistance as it would be able to do if fiscal condition were measured using factors, such as tax levels or spending, over which local officials have some control.

Third, measuring fiscal condition, especially that of local governments, is complicated by the observation that expenditure responsibilities often differ among jurisdictions of the same type. This problem is particularly severe if one compares fiscal conditions across large cities in different states. However, it can also arise within a state as, for example, when some cities have responsibility for kindergarten through 12th grade (K–12) education and others do not, or when some cities, such as San Francisco, have responsibility for county services as well as standard municipal services while others, such as Los Angeles, have responsibility for municipal services alone.

In addition to the use of simple measures such as per capita income, the literature focuses on two major approaches to measuring the revenue-raising component of fiscal condition. The first is the representative tax (or revenue) system as developed initially for states by the U.S. Advisory Commission on Intergovernmental Relations (ACIR). According to this approach, a jurisdiction's per capita capacity to raise taxes (or revenue, if capacity includes nontax revenue such as user charges and fees) is measured as the weighted average of its potential per capita tax bases where the weights are the average tax rates for each tax (for the whole country if the comparison is across states and within the state if the comparison

is for local governments within a state). This approach answers the question of how much revenue a jurisdiction would raise if it were to tax all its potential tax bases at the average tax rate; however, it takes no account of the behavioral effects of tax rates on tax bases or of the implied burden on local residents. Its strengths are the ease with which it can be described and its links to tax bases and to how noneconomists think about capacity to raise revenue.

The second approach asks a somewhat different question. How much revenue per capita would the jurisdiction raise if it imposed a standard burden on local residents (where the standard burden is defined as the taxes borne by residents as a percentage of resident income), taking into account the ability of the jurisdiction to export tax burdens to nonresidents? This approach is conceptually more appealing to economists because of its closer link to the decisionmaking process they have modeled, but the need to estimate export ratios raises thorny implementation problems.

Similarly, there are two common approaches to measuring expenditure need. One is to adjust average per capita spending levels for workloads. Thus, for example, if one school district has more pupils relative to the population or more pupils with special needs than others, its expenditure need would be higher than that of other jurisdictions. An alternative approach is to use regression analysis to develop cost indices that measure the costs that arise in one jurisdiction because of its characteristics relative to the costs in the average jurisdiction. Relevant characteristics for a city might include, for example, housing density, the poverty rate, and the amount of commercial property in the city. This approach is richer than the workload approach in that it can accommodate differences in the costs of service provision as well as the differences in workloads.

For many years, the ACIR measured the revenue-raising capacity of U.S. states. Recognizing the limitations of population as a measure of expenditure need, the ACIR in more recent years has introduced a measure of expenditure need based on a modified version of the workload approach. With the demise of the ACIR, additional work on fiscal disparities across states is likely to be limited. At the local level, a variety of recent studies have attempted to measure fiscal disparities for specific types of local governments within a state (Ladd 1994).

Two types of fiscal disparities have received significant attention: those across school districts within states and those within metropolitan areas. Starting with the *Serrano v. Priest* case in 1971, court cases in states throughout the country have focused public attention on disparities in the ability of local school districts to provide kindergarten through 12th grade education for their students (see *education financing, state and local*). Within metropolitan areas, the suburbanization of jobs and households has left many central cities with declining tax bases and increasing concentrations of poor households. These changes have led to a significant deterioration in the fiscal condition of central cities, both absolutely and relative to their suburbs.

ADDITIONAL READINGS

Ladd, Helen F. "Measuring Disparities in the Fiscal Condition of Local Governments." In *Fiscal Equalization for State and Local Government Finance,* edited by John E. Anderson (21–54). Westport, CT: Praeger, 1994.

———. *The Challenge of Fiscal Disparities for State and Local Governments: The Selected Essays of Helen F. Ladd, 1999.* Cheltenham, U.K., and Northampton, MA: Elgar, 1999.

Tannenwald, Robert. "Interstate Fiscal Disparity in 1997." *New England Economic Review,* Third Quarter 2002, 17–33.

U.S. Advisory Commission on Intergovernmental Relations. "Measures of State and Local Fiscal Capacity and Tax Effort." Report M-16. Washington, DC: U.S. Advisory Commission on Intergovernmental Relations, 1962.

Cross-references: education financing, state and local; tax and revenue capacity; tax and revenue effort.

Fiscal equalization

Helen F. Ladd
Duke University

Policies to equalize the fiscal position of subnational governments.

Fiscal equalization refers to attempts by a higher level of government within a federal system of government to reduce fiscal disparities among lower-level jurisdictions. (See *fiscal disparities.*) For example, the national government might endeavor to offset fiscal disparities across states (in the United States) or provinces (in Canada), and states or provinces might try to reduce disparities across local governments such as counties, municipalities, or school districts. The higher level of government may achieve its ends through equalizing aid programs, through the redesign of fiscal institutions, or through tax-base sharing.

Fiscal equalization policies have been justified on both efficiency and equity grounds. The efficiency argument starts from the view that it is socially inefficient for mobile tax bases, such as business activity, to make location and investment decisions based on tax rate differentials that are not offset by corresponding differences in locally provided public services. By reducing those differences, an equalization program could potentially increase the efficiency of the location decisions of both firms and mobile households. However, to the extent that it props up inefficient governments, a program of fiscal equalization could potentially introduce new distortions. For example, assistance to poor communities or to communities with high costs of providing public services could inappropriately induce people to move to those communities (see Oakland 1994, 202). Whether or not it would do so depends on the cause of the disparities that the policy is intended to offset.

In general, the equity case for fiscal equalization tends to be stronger than the efficiency case. The most persuasive equity argument is categorical in that it applies to specific public services such as elementary and secondary education or public health. For example, the case for ensuring that all children have access at reasonable cost to an adequate level of education is quite compelling, given the importance of education to a child's future income and life chances. While many people would agree with this view for education, extending the logic to a range of other locally provided public services is more controversial and may vary across states or cultures.

A second equity rationale applies to differences in the revenue potential from natural resources across subnational jurisdictions. In principle, it may be desirable to use a policy of intergovernmental grants to spread the fiscal benefits of such natural resources to the state or the nation as a whole. However, as Oakland (1994, 205) notes, capitalization and other considerations may make it difficult to implement such a policy fairly.

Similarly, a case for fiscal equalization can be made when some jurisdictions include disproportionate numbers of dependent households or have other characteristics that raise the costs of providing a given package of public services. For example, a jurisdiction with a disproportionate share of low-income households is likely to have below-average capacity to raise revenue and above-average costs of providing a given level of public services to its residents. Consequently, to provide a given level of services to its residents, such a jurisdiction would require an above-average tax rate. This outcome would be undesirable for two reasons. First, by providing an incentive for middle- and upper-income households to leave the jurisdiction, the high tax rate would exacerbate the situation by increasing the concentration of poor households. Second, it would be unfair to the nonpoor households in those jurisdictions in that they would be bearing a burden that is more appropriately placed at a higher level of government (see *fiscal federalism*).

A final, related, objective for an equalizing grant program is to make more equal the distribution of households' real incomes. While tax and transfer programs can best ensure that low-income households have adequate ability to purchase private goods and services, grants to communities with disproportionate numbers of low-income households may also be needed to ensure their access at reasonable cost to collectively determined goods and services, such as clean water and education. While the possibility that grants may be capitalized into housing prices may offset some of the benefits of such programs, it does not completely eliminate the argument for equalizing grants of this type. To the extent that factors such as disability, poverty, or discrimination restrict the mobility of low-income households, housing prices will not fully reflect differences in service quality or tax rates. In addition, even with full mobility, the impact of grants on housing prices is unclear because of complicated general equilibrium effects (Ladd and Yinger 1994).

The most widely used and discussed tool of fiscal equalization is intergovernmental aid. However, other tools are sometimes available. Consider, for example, the case of subnational governments in the United States. Because the powers of U.S.

local governments are created by state constitutions and laws, state governments essentially define the rules under which local governments within each state operate. Consequently, states can achieve their equalization goals not only by directing additional funds to needy jurisdictions but also by shifting responsibilities for certain expenditure functions (such as welfare or the judicial system, whose benefits extend beyond the boundaries of specific local governments) to a higher level of government or by empowering local governments to use additional taxes, such as payroll or wage taxes, to capture revenue from wealthier nonresidents. In addition, a state or a metropolitan area could introduce some form of tax-base sharing among local jurisdictions. The tax-base sharing program in the Minneapolis–St. Paul metropolitan area best illustrates that approach in the United States. Forty percent of the property tax base for new commercial and industrial property is put in a pool, taxed at a uniform rate, and redistributed to the local governments based on an equalizing formula (Luce 1998).

The main analytical issue with respect to equalizing aid programs is how to design formulas for distributing the aid. Not surprisingly, the appropriate design depends on the objective of the program. Consider, first, programs oriented toward particular categories of public services such as kindergarten through 12th grade (K–12) education. If the goal of the program is to ensure a minimum or threshold level of education services in all school districts, then aid should be in the form of a foundation grant. With such a program, each school district would receive enough aid so that, along with the revenue it would raise locally by imposing a minimum school tax rate, it could provide the minimum level of services. Assuming the goal were stated in terms of service levels rather than spending levels, the formula would have to take into account not only differences in the wealth of the school districts but also the fact that some districts have greater proportions of expensive-to-educate children. If, more generally, the goal were to ease the burden of providing a standard package of public services, the aid should vary inversely with a local jurisdiction's capacity to raise revenue and directly with its costs of providing that standard package. In this case, no additional incentive would be given for the local jurisdiction to attain the basic level of services. A third goal—ensuring equal service for a given level of sacrifice—could be achieved with a district power–equalizing grant. Finally, a goal of ensuring equal outcomes across districts would require that the state make all spending decisions and that local districts be prohibited from supplementing the state funds with locally raised revenues.

Views toward fiscal equalization have varied over time in the United States. In the 1970s, the federal government introduced a general revenue–sharing program designed to offset some of the fiscal disparities both across states and among local governments within states. That program, which ended in 1986, represented the most explicit attempt by the federal government to equalize the fiscal position of U.S. subnational governments. Other federal countries, such as Canada and Germany, have been much more aggressive in attempting to equalize the revenue-raising capacities of their subnational governments. At the state level, interest in policies to reduce within-state disparities varies across states. Partly in response to pressures from the courts, which have ruled that many state systems of education finance lead to unconstitutional disparities in educational opportunities, the states have most actively developed programs of equalizing aid for local school districts (see *education financing, state and local*). For the many developing countries and former socialist countries moving to decentralize their governmental systems, the issue of fiscal equalization is now becoming increasingly relevant (see Shah 1994 and Bird, Ebel, and Wallich 1995).

ADDITIONAL READINGS

Anderson, John E., editor. *Fiscal Equalization for State and Local Government Finance.* Westport, CT: Praeger, 1994.

Bird, Richard M., and Andrey V. Tarasov. "Closing the Gap: Fiscal Imbalance and Intergovernmental Transfers in Developed Federations." *Environment and Planning C: Government and Policy* 22, no. 1 (2004): 77–102.

Bird, Richard M., Robert D. Ebel, and Christine I. Wallich, eds. *Decentralization of the Socialist State.* Washington, DC: World Bank, 1995.

Ladd, Helen F., and John Yinger. "The Case for Equalizing Aid." *National Tax Journal* 47, no. 1 (1994): 211–24.

Luce, Thomas. "Regional Tax Base Sharing: The Twin Cities Experience." In, *Local Government Tax and Land Use Policies in the United States: Understanding the Links,* edited by Helen F. Ladd (234–54). Cheltenham, U.K.: Edward Elgar, 1998.

Musgrave, Richard A., and Peter Mieszkowski. "Federalism, Grants, and Fiscal Equalization." In *Public Finance in a Democratic Society,* vol. 3, *The Foundations of Taxation and Expenditure,* edited by Richard A. Musgrave (255–83). Cheltenham, U.K., and Northampton, MA: Elgar, 2000.

Oakland, William H. "Fiscal Equalization: An Empty Box." *National Tax Journal* 47, no. 1 (1994): 199–210.

Rafuse, Robert W. *Representative Expenditures: Addressing the Neglected Dimension of Fiscal Capacity.* Washington, DC: Advisory Commission on Intergovernmental Relations, 1990.

Rye, C. Richard, and Bob Searle. "Expenditure Needs: Institutions and Data." In *Financing Decentralized Expenditures: An International Comparison of Grants,* edited by Ehtisham Ahmad. Cheltenham, U.K.: Edward Elgar, 1997.

Shah, Anwar. *The Reform of Intergovernmental Fiscal Relations in Developing and Emerging Market Economies.* Washington, DC: World Bank, 1994.

Cross-references: education financing, state and local; fiscal disparities; fiscal federalism; tax and revenue capacity; tax and revenue effort.

Fiscal federalism

Richard M. Bird
University of Toronto

The analysis of the problems that give rise to, and arise from, the existence of more than one level of government within the same geographical area.

As originally developed by Musgrave (1959) and Oates (1972), the theory of fiscal federalism concerns the division of public-sector functions and finances in a logical way among multiple layers of government (King 1984). Much of the literature of fiscal federalism consists of relatively unrelated treatments of such issues as the "decentralization theorem" (Oates 1991), models for the assignment of powers (McLure 1993), discussions of intergovernmental spillovers and intergovernmental grants (Break 1980), fiscal mobility and migration (Wildasin 1991), and vertical fiscal imbalance and dependence (Hunter 1977). Oates (1998) reprints many other classic papers on fiscal federalism. The theoretical discussion of local public goods that has taken place in the context of the Tiebout model (Wildasin 1986) is not strictly part of "fiscal federalism" as defined here because it is concerned only with governmental relations at the same jurisdictional level. A more general, and relevant, theoretical framework to approach some of these problems might be the theory of overlapping clubs (Cornes and Sandler 1996), but as yet this has been little developed (Casella and Frey 1992).

Initially, stabilization and distribution were considered to be essentially "central" functions, with the only role for "subcentral" (state and local) governments arising in the allocative sphere. From this perspective, the main analytical task of fiscal federalism is to define the appropriate functions and finances of local governments as efficiently as possible—that is, in such a way as to maximize community welfare (often represented, for analytical convenience, by the median voter theorem). In a territorial variant of the benefit principle, it was suggested at an early stage that each jurisdiction could be most efficiently mapped in terms of the spatial dimension of the services it provided. Thus, there would be "local public goods," "state public goods," and "national public goods," with the presumed beneficiaries of each financing their provision in an appropriate way (Olson 1969). In practice, the overlapping and multidimensional nature of most public-sector activities makes it difficult to apply this approach very rigorously, particularly because few lower-level governments have sufficient own-source revenues to finance the services logically assigned to them.

Given the greater interjurisdictional mobility of the base of the income tax relative to that of the consumption tax, and of the latter relative to that of the property tax (and the efficiency problems arising from tax exportation, when not precisely offset by benefit spillovers), most analysts suggest that the local public sector should be financed basically by user charges and "local" taxes, especially the property tax, and states by consumption taxes, with the income tax being left largely to the central (federal) government (Musgrave 1983). As Bird (2000) stresses, however, this division of revenues means that state and local governments are likely to end up with greater expenditure responsibilities than can be financed from their own revenues. An important element of fiscal federalism from the beginning has thus been recognition of the probable need for intergovernmental grants to close the revenue gap. Considerable attention has been devoted to the appropriate design of such grants (Wilde 1971; Ahmad 1997),

as well as to empirical analysis of their effects on local spending patterns (Gramlich 1977; Rubinfeld 1987).

The theory of fiscal federalism applies as well, or as badly, to local service units in a metropolitan area as to states in a federation. In principle, however, there are important analytical and policy differences, not only between local-metropolitan problems and federal-state problems but even between "tight" federations such as Germany and "loose" federations such as Canada—with the United States somewhere in between (Bird 1986). These differences arise in part from the differing nature and rigidity of the constraints political institutions impose. The question has attracted considerable attention in recent years, in part because of the emergence of nascent "federal" institutions in the European Union. However, fiscal federalism has had little to say about the dynamics of institutional change in emerging (or disintegrating) federations. Moreover, it offers little guidance in dealing with such important intergovernmental finance problems as the appropriate size and scope of operation of local and intermediate-level governments in developing countries (Bird and Vaillancourt 1998) as well as the "transitional" countries of the former Soviet bloc (Bird, Ebel, and Wallich 1995), where, for example, the potential impact on stabilization is a major concern (Gramlich 1987; Rodden, Litvack, and Eskeland 2003).

In contrast, much good work has been done within this analytical framework on some of the problems arising from the common metropolitan area situation of divided political jurisdictions within an economically integrated region. A structure that puts people's places of work and residence in separate political jurisdictions, while making the latter primarily responsible for the most important local expenditure, education, has obvious implications for both efficiency and distribution (Wildasin 1986), as has been much explored in the literature on education finance. There is still much to be done, however, to satisfactorily explain local redistributive policies (Tresch 1981)—through, for example, education—and their impact on migration and other important economic variables (Wildasin 1991; Fischel 2001).

Much has been written about the virtues of decentralized government, from both a political and an economic perspective (Tullock 1994), but most of these supposed virtues can, in the conventional fiscal federalism framework, be achieved as well by regionally based central officials as by locally elected politicians. Perhaps some answers lie in the "supply-side" theories of government (Breton 1996) that have been developed in the broad "public choice" framework (Mueller 1992), because there is considerable similarity between the assumptions underlying public choice theory and federalist theory (Ostrom 1971). As yet, however, little progress has been made with respect to articulating these arguments in either normative or positive terms in the conventional fiscal federalism analysis, other than as simple assertions.

Nonetheless, important lessons have emerged from the fiscal federalism literature (Inman and Rubinfeld 1997). In particular, considerable progress has been made with respect to the appropriate assignment of tasks and finances in multilevel governments, especially in the design and effects of intergovernmental grants (Wildasin 1997; Bird and Smart 2002). While there is considerable variation in detail from state to state—let alone across countries—on the whole the observed assignment of functions to local and state governments accords broadly with the dictates of theory, with local governments responsible for "place-specific" services such as streets, water and sewerage works, refuse disposal, and fire and police services. In addition, in the United States, local governments are also generally responsible for providing primary and secondary education, although as a rule with substantial fiscal assistance from state governments; in other countries, education is often provided primarily by intermediate-level (state) governments and sometimes even by central governments. A common pattern everywhere is for one level of government to be involved in delivering a certain service while other levels are involved to varying degrees in financing and regulating it (Ter-Minassian 1997). Work on understanding the desirability and effects of alternative institutional structures that provide particular services is expanding rapidly, but there is still much to be done.

Local governments rely heavily on property taxes for revenue, while state governments rely on a mixture of sales and income taxes, and the federal government relies mainly on income (and payroll) taxes. The division of revenues differs in other countries: although almost everywhere, local governments get property taxes and central governments most income taxes, in some countries local income taxes—like national sales taxes—are much more important than in the United States (Owens and Panella 1991). Such taxes are almost invariably "piggybacked" on national taxes—that is, they take the form of surcharges. Only Switzerland comes close to matching the diversity of the state and local income and sales taxes found in the United States. Most other countries, whether formally federal or not, have much more territorially uniform fiscal systems. Although there is clearly vertical competition between levels of government for revenue (Keen 1998), most attention has been paid in the literature to horizontal tax competition (Wilson and Wildasin 2004), perhaps because, as a rule, local governments have access only to those revenue sources that higher-level governments do not want.

Local governments almost invariably depend in part, and sometimes very heavily, upon transfers from upper-level governments to finance the services for which they are responsible. The appropriate level and design of such transfers has been an important concern in the fiscal federalism literature. Some argue, for example, that a system of unconditional fiscal equalization grants is an essential component of an efficient (and equitable) fiscal federal system (Boadway and Flatters 1982). Others assert that there is no place for such transfers (Oakland 1994). The theoretical literature suggests that the only clear efficiency case for intergovernmental payments is to compensate local governments for benefit spillovers to ensure that they provide the optimal amount of the public ser-

vice in question. In practice, however, virtually no examples of the open-ended conditional matching grants this theory calls for can be found in any country (Ahmad 1997). On the contrary, most countries (other than the United States) have some system of unconditional transfers intended to equalize fiscal capacity. Moreover, most conditional matching grants are limited in amount and probably best interpreted in a principal-agent framework (Ferris and Winkler 1991)—that is, as mandated functions paid for, in large part, by transfers, but with some local payment. The latter is to ensure that local fiscal effort is maintained and also that, at the margin, local politicians remain electorally accountable for their actions to their constituents, as well as to the granting authority.

At the policy level, the Advisory Commission on Intergovernmental Relations (ACIR) (1990) carried out pioneering studies on fiscal disparities (sometimes referred to as "horizontal imbalance"), fiscal capacity, and fiscal effort. Curiously, this work has had its greatest policy impact in other federal countries such as Canada, where since 1967, a version of the ACIR's "representative tax system" has formed the basis of the federal provincial equalization system—which itself was based in large part on a system developed in Australia in the 1930s (and since extended from revenue to expenditure equalization). Similar systems of federal-state transfers, often based on formulas and usually unconditional in nature, are characteristic of most federal countries (Shah 1994). Apart from the brief experience with a small "revenue-sharing" system in the 1970s (Juster 1977), the United States is unique among federal countries in that it has never had a system of federal-state equalization transfers—although there are, of course, many federal-state conditional transfers, as well as some experience with fiscal equalization at the state and local levels.

ADDITIONAL READINGS

Advisory Commission on Intergovernmental Relations. "1988 State Fiscal Capacity and Effort." Information Report M-170. Washington, DC: Advisory Commission on Intergovernmental Relations, 1990.

Ahmad, Ehtisham, ed. *Financing Decentralized Expenditures: An International Comparison of Grants.* Cheltenham, U.K.: Edward Elgar, 1997.

Bird, Richard M. *Federal Finance in Comparative Perspective.* Toronto: Canadian Tax Foundation, 1986.

———. "Rethinking Subnational Taxes: A New Look at Tax Assignment." *Tax Notes International* 20 (May 8, 2000): 2069–96.

Bird, Richard M., and Michael Smart. "Intergovernmental Fiscal Transfers: Lessons from International Experience." *World Development* 30, no. 6 (2002): 899–912.

Bird, Richard M., and Francois Vaillancourt, eds. *Fiscal Decentralization in Developing Countries.* Cambridge, U.K.: Cambridge University Press, 1998.

Bird, Richard M., Robert D. Ebel, and Christine I. Wallich, eds. *Decentralization of the Socialist State: Intergovernmental Finance in Transition Economies.* Washington, DC: World Bank, 1995.

Blindenbacher, Raoul J., and Arnold Koller, eds. *Federalism in a Changing World—Learning from Each Other.* Montreal: McGill-Queen's University Press, 2002.

Boadway, Robin, and Frank Flatters. "Efficiency and Equalization Payments in a Federal System of Government: A Synthesis and Extension of Recent Results." *Canadian Journal of Economics* 15 (1982): 613–33.

Break, George F. *Financing Government in a Federal System.* Washington, DC: The Brookings Institution, 1980.

Breton, Albert. *Competitive Governments: An Economic Theory of Politics and Public Finance.* Cambridge, U.K.: Cambridge University Press, 1996.

Casella, Alessandra, and Bruno Frey. "Federalism and Clubs: Towards an Economic Theory of Overlapping Political Jurisdictions." *European Economic Review* 36 (1992): 639–46.

Cornes, Richard, and Todd Sandler. *The Theory of Externalities, Public Goods, and Club Goods,* 2d ed. Cambridge, U.K.: Cambridge University Press, 1996.

Ferris, James M., and Donald R. Winkler. "Agency Theory and Intergovernmental Relationships." In *Public Finance with Several Levels of Government,* edited by Remy Prud'homme (155–66). The Hague/Koenigstein: Foundation Journal of Public Finance, 1991.

Fischel, William A. *The Homevoter Hypothesis.* Cambridge, MA: Harvard University Press, 2001.

Gramlich, Edward M. "Intergovernmental Grants: A Review of the Empirical Literature." In *The Political Economy of Fiscal Federalism,* edited by Wallace E. Oates (219–39). Lexington, MA: Lexington Press, 1977.

———. "Subnational Fiscal Policy." *Perspectives on Local Public Finance and Public Policy* 3 (1987): 3–27.

Hunter, J. S. H. *Federalism and Fiscal Balance.* Canberra: Australian National University Press, 1977.

Inman, Robert P., and Daniel L. Rubinfeld. "The Political Economy of Fiscal Federalism." In *Perspectives on Public Choice: A Handbook,* edited by Dennis C. Mueller (73–105). Cambridge, U.K.: Cambridge University Press, 1997.

Juster, F. Thomas, ed. *The Economic and Political Impact of General Revenue Sharing.* Ann Arbor, MI: Survey Research Center, Institute for Social Research, University of Michigan, 1977.

Keen, Michael. "Vertical Tax Externalities in the Theory of Fiscal Federalism." *International Monetary Fund Staff Papers* 45 (1998): 454–85.

King, David. *Fiscal Tiers: The Economics of Multi-Level Government.* London: George Allen and Unwin, 1984.

McLure, Charles E., Jr. *Vertical Fiscal Imbalance and the Assignment of Taxing Powers in Australia.* Stanford, CA: Hoover Institution, 1993.

Mueller, Dennis C. *Public Choice II.* Cambridge, U.K.: Cambridge University Press, 1992.

Musgrave, Richard A. *The Theory of Public Finance.* New York: McGraw Hill, 1959.

———. "Who Should Tax, Where, and What?" *Tax Assignment in Federal Countries,* edited by Charles E. McLure Jr. (2–19). Canberra: Australian National University Press, 1983.

Oakland, William. "Fiscal Equalization: An Empty Box?" *National Tax Journal* 44 (1994): 199–209.

Oates, Wallace E. *Fiscal Federalism.* New York: Harcourt Brace Jovanovich, 1972.

———. "The Theory of Fiscal Federalism: Revenue and Expenditure Issues—A Survey of Recent Theoretical and Empirical Research." *Public Finance with Several Levels of Government,* edited by Remy Prud'homme (1–18). The Hague/Koeningstein: Foundation Journal of Public Finance, 1991.

———, ed. *The Economics of Fiscal Federalism and Local Finance.* Cheltenham, U.K.: Edward Elgar, 1998.

Olson, Mancur. "The Principle of Fiscal Equivalence: The Division of Responsibilities among Different Levels of Government." *American Economic Review Papers and Proceedings* 59 (May 1969): 479–87.

Ostrom, Vincent. *The Political Theory of a Compound Republic.* Blacksburg, VA: Public Choice Society, 1971.

Owens, Jeffrey, and Giorgio Panella, eds. *Local Government: An International Perspective.* Amsterdam: North-Holland, 1991.

Rodden, Jonathan, Jennie Litvack, and Gunnar Eskeland, eds. *Fiscal Decentralization and Challenge of Hard Budget Constraints.* Cambridge, MA: MIT Press, 2003.

Rubinfeld, Daniel. "The Economics of the Local Public Sector." In *Handbook of Public Economics,* vol. 2, edited by Alan J. Auerbach and Martin Feldstein (571–645). Amsterdam: North-Holland, 1987.

Shah, Anwar. *The Reform of Intergovernmental Fiscal Relations in Developing and Emerging Market Economies.* Policy and Research Series 23. Washington, DC: World Bank, 1994.

Ter-Minassian, Teresa, ed. *Fiscal Federalism in Theory and Practice.* Washington, DC: International Monetary Fund, 1997.

Tresch, Richard W. *Public Finance: A Normative Theory.* Plano, Texas: Business Publications, 1981.

Tullock, Gordon. *The New Federalist.* Vancouver: Fraser Institute, 1994.

Wildasin, David E. *Urban Public Finance.* London: Harwood Academic Publishers, 1986.

———. "Income Redistribution in a Common Labor Market." *American Economic Review* 81 (1991): 757–74.

———. "The Institutions of Federalism: Toward an Analytical Framework." *National Tax Journal* 57, no. 2 (June 2004): 247–72.

———, ed. *Fiscal Aspects of Evolving Federations.* Cambridge, U.K.: Cambridge University Press, 1997.

Wilde, James E. "Grants-in-Aid: The Analytics of Design and Response." *National Tax Journal* 24 (1971): 143–55.

Wilson, John Douglas, and David E. Wildasin. "Capital Tax Competition: Bane or Boon?" *Journal of Public Economics* 88, no. 6 (2004): 1065–91.

Cross-references: benefit principle; education financing, state and local; fiscal disparities; fiscal equalization; median voter theorem; tax and revenue effort; tax exportation.

Flat tax

William G. Gale
The Brookings Institution

A proposal for fundamental tax reform that would replace the income tax system with a consumption tax, to be collected by levying a flat-rate tax on businesses and individuals.

The Hall-Rabushka proposal has served as the blueprint for several proposals to reform the federal tax system, including a proposal introduced by Representative Richard Armey (R-Texas) and Senator Richard Shelby (R-Alabama) and one offered by presidential candidate Steve Forbes (R) in the 1996 presidential primaries.

In comparison to the Hall-Rabushka proposal, the personal income tax in 1994 provided exemptions of $9,800 for a family of four, an earned income tax credit (EITC), and the choice of a $6,350 standard deduction or itemized deductions for mortgage interest, state and local income and property taxes, charity, and large health expenditures. Estimates indicate that in 1996, a family of four taking the standard deduction and the EITC, with all income from wages, would pay no federal income taxes on the first $23,700 of income, 15 percent on the next $31,000 or so, 28 percent on the next $53,000, and higher rates on additional income, reaching 39.6 percent on taxable income above $250,000.

Without the personal exemptions, the flat tax is equivalent to a value-added tax (VAT), but with taxes on wages remitted by households rather than businesses. That is, the flat tax is a consumption tax, even though it looks like a wage tax to households and a variant of a VAT to most businesses. Therefore, other than the exemptions, the economic effects of the flat tax are essentially the same as those of a VAT or a sales tax.

The family exemptions make the flat tax progressive for low-income households. But at the high end of the income distribution, the tax is regressive, just like sales taxes and VATs.

The Hall-Rabushka proposal could be amended in several ways. Princeton economist David Bradford has proposed an X-tax similar to Hall-Rabushka but with graduated tax rates on household wage income to raise progressivity. (The business tax would be set equal to the highest tax rate on wage income.) The flat tax could also be modified to retain the EITC, allow a deduction for charitable contributions, and provide a tax credit (a one-to-one reduction in taxes paid under the flat tax) for payroll taxes paid. The credit would be a huge boon to lower- and middle-income households because most now pay more in payroll taxes than in income taxes. These changes would, of course, require higher rates. But a tax system with these features might be able to retain the progressivity of the current tax system while also reaping most of the gains of the Hall-Rabushka proposal's broader base, generally lower rates, and simplified compliance. The question remains, though, of how large these gains would be.

Evaluating the effects of adopting a flat tax

Analysts find it hard to predict with precision the effects of minor tax changes, and heated debate continues about the effects of the major 1980s tax reforms. Hence, efforts to evaluate the effects of uprooting the entire tax system must be appropriately qualified. (The economic effects of the flat tax are addressed by a number of contributions in Aaron and Gale 1996 and Zodrow and Mieszkowski 2002.)

A central issue in tax reform is always who wins and who loses. Under the flat tax, low-income households would lose because they now pay no income tax and are eligible for a refundable EITC of up to $3,370. Although the flat tax is more progressive than a VAT, it is more regressive than the current system. A flat tax would provide huge gains for high-income households because their marginal tax rate would fall and because they consume less of their income than do low-income households. As a result, if a flat tax were to raise as much revenue as the current system, the tax burden for the middle class would have to rise. Consumption taxes are generally less regressive when viewed over longer periods of time because income changes from year to year, but they would raise tax burdens on lower- and middle-income households over any time frame. (For further discussion, see Gale, Houser, and Scholz 1996 and Gentry and Hubbard 1997).

Perceptions of fairness may also be difficult to retain when, under the flat tax, some wealthy individuals and large corporations remit no taxes to the government while middle-class workers pay a combined marginal tax rate above 30 percent on the flat tax, state income tax, and payroll taxes.

As for simplicity, the flat tax would likely slash compliance costs for many businesses and households. But for many, the tax system is not that complicated. And fundamental tax reform would not end the demands for special treatment that have so tangled the income tax. Ten years hence, we may find that what started as simplicity has once again become a confused jumble. Thus, some simplification is likely with tax reform, but it is by no means a certain or lasting outcome. Moreover, many simplification gains could be made through changes in the income tax.

A third concern is how reform would affect different sectors of the economy. Removing the mortgage interest deduction and the deductibility of state and local property taxes may have profound effects on housing prices and home ownership, but the results would depend on how interest rates adjust, the sorts of grandfathering rules introduced, and other factors. How and when health insurance benefits and coverage rates would adjust after the tax-favored treatment of employer-provided health benefits is eliminated is an open question.

Removing the deduction for charitable contributions would reduce overall giving and could affect its composition as well: wealthy donors, for whom the write-off is now worth the most, tend to favor hospitals and universities; low-income donors, religious institutions.

Effects on businesses and investment would be complicated. The flat tax would eliminate corporate income taxes, put all businesses on an equal tax footing, reduce the statutory tax rate applied to business income, and make investment write-offs more generous. But it would also remove the deductibility of interest payments and of state and local taxes, and this could induce dramatic changes. For example, Hall and Rabushka estimate that General Motors' annual tax liability could rise to $2.7 billion from $110 million, while Intel's would fall by 75 percent. The effects of a consumption tax on international economic transactions and on the financial sector are potentially far-reaching and need to be examined carefully.

Economic efficiency and growth

Ultimately, increased economic efficiency and growth must be one of the key selling points of a consumption tax. Without a significant gain in living standards, uprooting the entire tax system is probably not worth the risks, redistributions, and adjustment costs it would impose. Efficiency gains might arise from five sources: the change of the tax base from income to consumption; a more comprehensive tax base, which eliminates the differential tax treatment of various assets and forms of income; lower tax rates, which raise the rate of return to working, saving, and investing and reduce incentives to avoid or evade taxes; reduced compliance costs; and the taxation of previously existing assets during the transition to a consumption tax. All but the first and last are attainable under income tax reform.

Although estimates vary, a recent study suggests that a pure flat tax proposal with limited personal exemptions would raise economic output by between 2 and 4 percent over the first nine years and between 4 and 6 percent in the long run. But these results need to be interpreted carefully. First, many of the gains are also available through judicious reform of the income tax, in particular by making the taxation of capital income more uniform. Second, the estimates provided do not allow for child exemptions, as the Hall-Rabushka proposal and all of the recent flat tax proposals do. Allowing exemptions for children reduces the effects by about 2 percentage points (e.g., a gain of 0 to 2 percent over 10 years). Third, the estimates apply to a pure, well-designed consumption tax. Compromises in the design, such as including mortgage interest deductions or allowing a transition, reduce the gains or turn them into losses.

Allowing for transition relief alone is enough to eliminate the impact on growth in the long run. The estimates also show that, even for well-designed consumption taxes, efficiency losses are possible. (The estimates cited in this paragraph are taken from Altig et al. 2001 and private communications with Kent Smetters. For additional analysis of the growth effects of tax reform, see Engen, Gravelle, and Smetters 1997.)

A key element in raising growth and a major motivation for tax reform is increasing saving. Proponents of the flat tax typically point to two reasons why consumption taxes should spur saving. First, a revenue-neutral shift to a consumption tax should raise the after-tax rate of return on saving, while keeping total tax payments constant. Second, consumption taxes reallocate after-tax income toward high-saving households. Such reasoning is straightforward but incomplete. Saving is likely to rise only a little, if at all, for several reasons.

First, the current U.S. tax system is not a pure income tax; it is a hybrid between a consumption tax and an income tax. About half of private savings already receive consumption tax treatment. Funds placed in pensions, 401(k) plans, Keogh plans, and most individual retirement accounts (IRAs) are not taxed until they are withdrawn. The return on these investments, then, is the pretax rate of return. But introducing a consumption tax would reduce the pretax interest rate, so that the rate of return on these forms of saving would fall, which could reduce saving.

Second, pension coverage could fall. Under an income tax, pensions are a tax-preferred form of saving. But a consumption tax treats all saving equally, making it less likely that workers and employers would continue to accept the high regulatory and administrative costs of pensions. Therefore, if workers do not resave all of their reduced pension contributions, saving would fall.

Third, under a pure consumption tax, all capital at the time of the transition is (implicitly) taxed again when it is consumed. But transition rules likely to be added to a consumption tax to avoid this double taxation would reduce or eliminate the long-term effect on saving and growth, as noted above.

The transition: Can we get there from here?

Even if a consumption tax is the right system for an economy starting from scratch, it may not be the right way to reform an existing system. The main transition issue is the taxation of "old capital"—capital assets accumulated earlier out of after-tax income whose principal would not have been taxed again under the income tax. Although some transitional treatment of old capital is typically thought to be likely, not having a transition—that is, implicitly taxing old capital again under a consumption tax—is arguably consistent with the three main goals of tax reform: efficiency, equity, and simplicity.

Certainly, not having a transition is simplest. The transition rules could be very complex, and the transition period could stretch out for years.

Not having a transition is also more efficient. Because only current assets or future wages can finance future consumption, a consumption tax is a tax on future wages and current assets. A consumption tax that exempts old assets is just a tax on future wages. And the same studies that show that a consumption tax (which taxes all old capital assets) is more efficient than an income tax also show that a wage tax is less efficient than an income tax—because not taxing capital requires higher tax rates on wages to raise the same revenue and hence distorts people's work decisions more. So exempting old capital removes any presumption that tax reform would result in a more efficient system.

Surely, the strongest argument for exempting old capital from taxes is fairness. The assets have already been taxed once; is it fair to tax them again? The answer may not be as obvious as it seems. First, a onetime implicit tax on existing capital is very progressive. The distribution of such capital is more skewed toward wealthy households than is the distribution of overall wealth, which in turn is more skewed than the distribution of income. Second, within any age group, wealthy households do most of the saving. Because these households would benefit most from eliminating the double taxation on future saving under a consumption tax, it is reasonable that they pay for some of the costs. Third, older households tend to have more assets than younger ones, and taxing capital places heavier burdens on older generations. But those older households have received transfers through Social Security and Medicare that far outreach what they have put in. And the vast majority of income and wealth for most elderly households is in the form of future earnings (which have not yet been taxed), housing (which receives extraordinarily preferential treatment under the current tax system), pension income (which already receives consumption tax treatment), Social Security benefits (which are not taxed under the flat tax), and Medicare benefits (which are not and would not be taxed). Relatively few elderly households finance much of their living expenses by other assets, and those that do tend to be very well off.

Pros and cons of the flat tax

In principle, replacing the income tax with a consumption tax, such as the flat tax, offers the possibility of improving the efficiency, equity, and simplicity of the tax system. But these gains are uncertain and depend critically on the details of the reform. At least some of the gains could be made simply by modifying the existing system.

Idealized consumption taxes may always look better than actual income tax systems. Once in place, though, they would be subject to the same compromises and pressures as the income tax is. They could even lead to a system that is less efficient and less fair than the one we have.

ADDITIONAL READINGS

Aaron, Henry J., and William G. Gale, eds. *Economic Effects of Fundamental Tax Reform.* Washington, DC: Brookings Institution Press, 1996.

Altig, David, Alan J. Auerbach, Laurence J. Kotlikoff, Ken A. Smetters, and Jan Walliser. "Simulating Fundamental Tax Reform in the United States." *American Economic Review* 91, no. 3 (June 2001): 574–95.

Engen, Eric, Jane Gravelle, and Kent Smetters. "Dynamic Tax Models: Why They Do the Things They Do." *National Tax Journal* 50 (September 1997): 657–82.

Gale, William G., Scott Houser, and John Karl Scholz. "Distributional Effects of Fundamental Tax Reform." In *Economic Effects of Fundamental Tax Reform,* edited by Henry J. Aaron and William G. Gale (281–320). Washington, DC: Brookings Institution Press, 1996.

Gentry, William, and R. Glenn Hubbard. "Distributional Effects of Adopting a National Retail Sales Tax." In *Tax Policy and the Economy,* vol. 11, edited by James M. Poterba (1–47). Cambridge, MA: MIT Press, 1997.

Hall, Robert, and Alvin E. Rabushka. *The Flat Tax.* Stanford: Hoover Institution Press, 1995.

Zodrow, George R., and Peter Mieszkowski. *United States Tax Reform in the 21st Century.* Cambridge, U.K.: Cambridge University Press, 2002.

Cross-references: consumption taxation; tax reform, federal; value-added tax, national; value-added tax, state; X-tax.

Flypaper effect

Amy Ellen Schwartz
New York University

The "flypaper effect" is the persistent empirical finding that an intergovernmental grant stimulates more spending by the recipient government than an equal increase in local resources, in contradiction of the theoretical prediction that the effects should be the same.

Dubbed the flypaper effect by Arthur Okun, the empirical regularity that "money sticks where it hits" has been observed in a wide range of settings and circumstances. This finding is regarded as an anomaly because it contradicts a prediction from the classic expenditure theory of public finance.

Nonmatching or "lump sum" grants to lower level governments should be seen by residents as equivalent to a similarly sized increase in community income as long as grants have no "strings attached"; that is, there are no binding restrictions placed upon taxing or spending behavior. If grants are perceived in this manner, when a (nonmatching) grant subsidizes an activity, government spending on the subsidized activity is predicted to increase, but by less than the full amount of the grant because residents will substitute a portion of the resources provided by the grant for spending that would otherwise have been financed by the community's own resources. In the strongest terms, the theory predicts that the propensity to spend an additional dollar on public services should be the same whether the additional dollar comes from a grant or from an increase in resident incomes.

Studies of the reaction of state and local governments to grants, however, consistently have found that local governments increase their own spending on the subsidized public service by more than the amount predicted by classic expenditure theory, hence Okun's observation that grant money "sticks where it hits."

Empirical explanations

Much of the original work that found evidence for the flypaper effect relied upon cross-sectional data and straightforward econometric techniques, and it has been argued that the flypaper effect may be an artifact of either the data or the methods that have been used to examine state and local governments' response to government grants.

One explanation offered for the anomaly points to confusion in previous research about whether grants are, in fact, unconditional. If grants are miscategorized as unconditional while there are significant restrictions on spending or taxation, whether tacit or explicit, then the coefficient on grants will be biased toward finding a flypaper effect.

An alternative explanation is that the models of state or local demand for public services are misspecified because the distribution of the tax burden—and hence the distribution of the grant's benefits—is uneven within the recipient jurisdiction, such that the median voter is disproportionately enriched by the grant. Thus, the median voter chooses more spending than would otherwise be predicted.

A third explanation is that the coefficient on income is biased because variables capturing the population's characteristics (and correlated with income) are insufficient or omitted.

A fourth explanation is that previous estimates may have been biased because the definition of "unconditional grants" failed to account for the process by which government grants "become" unconditional. In some cases, estimates were based upon grants that had matching requirements for low spenders, becoming effectively unconditional for high spenders. Ignoring this process may lead to bias in the estimated impact of grants.

Although some recent studies that have attempted to deal with the above issues have yielded smaller or insignificant flypaper effects, the flypaper effect nonetheless continues to be found in newer studies that use better data and statistical methods. These results have prompted some scholars to examine whether there might be alternatives to the simple model of public expenditure determination that might be more consistent with the flypaper effect.

Theoretical explanations

The central assumptions of the simple expenditure model are that individuals are well informed about tax rates, grants, and expenditures and that government expenditure decisions reflect the preferences of the informed median voter. Thus, some explanations for the flypaper effect argue that either the voter is poorly informed or that the government perversely ignores the preferences of the median voter.

To be more specific, it may be that voters are unable to distinguish the true price effect of an unconditional grant and perceive the lower average cost afforded by intergovernmental grants to be lower marginal costs. Perceiving lower marginal costs of government services, they respond, rationally, by increasing demand.

At the same time, government officials, motivated by a demand for higher spending than the median voter, may conceal the grant (or some part of it) from the voters. Thus, voters are unaware of the additional revenues and do not respond by choosing decreases in other taxes.

Alternatively, the model may mistakenly ignore the role that interjurisdictional competition plays in expenditure determination. If additional intergovernmental aid triggers mimicry in expenditure behavior, then an apparent flypaper effect may appear.

Again, empirical evidence suggests that, while these explanations offer important insight, they are also not fully satisfying.

More recent theoretical and empirical work has considered the process by which grants are awarded from higher to lower level governments. While previous literature treated the grants as exogenously determined, often by formula, the argument is that grant amounts are, in fact, endogenous—that is, driven by politics. Thus, the "formulas" are written to achieve a predetermined distribution of resources or to target more (or less) to jurisdictions that are particularly deserving based upon criteria not specified in the formulas. The possibility of endogenous grants suggests changes in both the econometric methodology and in the theory of expenditure determination and, under some circumstances, can explain the flypaper effect.

Conclusion

While much attention has been paid to the question of whether and why "money sticks where it hits," no clear consensus has emerged in the academic literature. What seems likely is that no single explanation will be found for all of the apparent flypaper effects observed in the empirical literature.

ADDITIONAL READINGS

Gramlich, Edward M. "Intergovernmental Grants: A Review of the Empirical Literature." In *Political Economy of Fiscal Federalism,* edited by Wallace Oates (219–40). Lexington, MA: D.C. Heath, 1977.

Hines, James R., and Richard H. Thaler. "The Flypaper Effect." *Journal of Economic Perspectives* 9, no. 4 (Fall 1995): 217–26.

Knight, Brian. "Endogenous Federal Grant and Crowd-Out of State Government Spending: Theory and Evidence from the Federal Highway Aid Program." *American Economic Review* 92, no. 1 (2002): 71–92.

Cross-references: intergovernmental grants; median voter theorem; retail sales tax, national.

Foreign corporations, federal taxation of

Timothy J. Goodspeed
Hunter College—City University of New York

Federal taxation of corporations owned by foreigners but incorporated and operated in the United States.

Corporations owned by foreigners but incorporated and operated in the United States are generally subject to the same taxation rules applying to corporations owned by U.S. citizens. In fact, tax treaties generally contain a nondiscrimination provision that requires equal treatment of U.S. and foreign companies.

Unless one looks at U.S. taxes paid by foreign-controlled corporations, one might think that a reference to the federal corporate income tax and tax treaties would suffice for this entry. However, available data indicate a puzzling surprise: foreign-controlled corporations operating in the United States pay surprisingly little U.S. tax compared with U.S.-controlled companies operating in the United States. As Grubert, Goodspeed, and Swenson (1993) report, the ratio of U.S. taxable income to assets was 0.58 for foreign-controlled corporations and 2.14 for U.S.-controlled corporations for 1987; the difference persists when sales are used in the denominator rather than assets and when the smaller categories of nonfinancial, manufacturing, and wholesale industries are examined. The data from 1987 to 1995 detailed in Grubert (1997) show a similar picture. Although somewhat variable over time, the average taxable income to asset ratio for foreign-controlled companies was 0.62 over the period, while the average for U.S.-controlled companies was 2.28.

The lack of U.S. tax revenue from foreign-controlled companies relative to U.S.-controlled companies has created a considerable amount of attention. For instance, in his 1992 presidential campaign, Bill Clinton suggested that increased auditing by the Internal Revenue Service (IRS) of foreign corporations could raise $45 billion over a four-year period, and Congress continues to scrutinize the behavior of foreign-controlled U.S. companies. The controversy centers on the amount of revenue that foreign-controlled companies should be paying to the U.S. government as opposed to what they actually pay—that is, are foreign-controlled firms able to avoid (or evade) paying tax to the U.S. government, or is the lack of revenue a natural consequence of differences between U.S.- and foreign-controlled companies?

How much revenue is involved? As a first approximation, one might assume that foreign- and U.S.-controlled companies are alike. For reasons to be mentioned momentarily, foreign-controlled companies are somewhat different from U.S.-controlled companies, but suppose for the moment that they are the same. This is tantamount to assuming that the entire difference in tax revenues stems from tax avoidance or evasion on the part of foreign-controlled companies. Because economic theory suggests that equivalent firms should have equal rates of return, one might suppose that the foreign rate of return (for instance, the average 1987–95 return of 0.62) should approximate the U.S. return (for instance, the average 1987–95 figure of 2.28). The total assets of the 45,000 foreign-controlled companies operating in the United States in 1987 were $959 billion, and Hobbs (2003) indicates that in 1995, the 60,157 foreign-controlled companies' assets had risen to $2.762 trillion. Thus, one might expect taxable income of foreign-controlled companies of about $20.5 billion in 1987 and $63 billion in 1995 and taxes paid of about $7 billion in 1987 and $21.4 billion in 1995. Because foreign-controlled companies actually paid $4.5 billion in 1987 and $15 billion in 1995, one might suspect a 1987 shortfall of about $2.5 billion and a 1995 shortfall of about $6.4 billion. Even given our assumption that the entire revenue shortfall is a result of tax evasion, the 1992 Clinton estimates would appear to have been exaggerated.

It is important at this point to reflect on the assumption that the entire revenue shortfall is a result of tax evasion. Is this assumption justified or do foreign-controlled companies differ in certain fundamental ways from U.S.-controlled companies? What sorts of mechanisms might foreign-controlled firms engage in to evade paying U.S. tax?

The hypothesis put forward most often by members of Congress as a means of evading U.S. taxes is "transfer pricing." (For a detailed description, see *transfer pricing, federal.*) In brief, suppose a parent company sells an input to its foreign subsidiary that the subsidiary uses to manufacture a product; the "transfer price" is the price the parent charges its subsidiary for the input. The potential for abuse results because the price charged will influence both parent and subsidiary profits (and hence taxes). Multinational corporations may have an incentive to transfer profits through judicious use of the transfer price so that high profits appear in the low-tax country and low profits in the high-tax country. In an attempt to eliminate such manipulative pricing practices, the U.S. government requires that the price be at "arm's length" of the price that an unrelated party would charge.

An often heard claim is that foreign companies evade U.S. taxes by not using arm's-length prices. The implication is that more IRS audits of foreign-controlled companies could recover the lost revenue.

A different method to avoid U.S. tax is a technique known as "earnings stripping," in which loans are taken from related offshore companies. The large interest payments from these transactions are deducted from U.S. taxable income, consequently lowering U.S. taxes paid. It should be noted that this outcome would also result if foreign-controlled companies took more legitimate loans from unrelated parties.

Both abusive transfer pricing and earnings stripping are methods by which foreign-controlled companies evade U.S. tax; if these are the cause of low foreign taxable income, there is a role for the IRS in cracking down on these activities. However, several natural business reasons may differentiate foreign and domestically owned companies and thus account for the difference in taxable income. These reasons include (1) the fact that many foreign-controlled firms are recent acquisitions, (2) exchange rate issues, (3) high startup costs of foreign-controlled firms, and a (4) potentially lower cost of capital for foreign-controlled firms. After an acquisition, book assets are revalued; because many foreign-controlled firms are recent acquisitions, one would expect higher asset values and hence a lower rate of return for foreign relative to U.S.-controlled companies. Exchange rates may be important because foreign-controlled companies might tend to import proportionately more component parts. Thus, an unexpected fall in the dollar will increase costs and decrease profits in a higher proportion than to their U.S.-controlled counterparts. Startup costs may be important because foreign-controlled entities are likely to have large initial costs as they learn about the new foreign business environment; these large initial costs would presumably diminish over time. If foreign firms have a lower cost of capital than U.S.-controlled firms, they may be willing to absorb a permanently lower return.

The results of Grubert et al. (1993) and Grubert (1997) indicate that the revaluation of book assets after an acquisition, the maturation process of young foreign-controlled firms, and exchange rate consequences for wholesale companies are important factors in explaining the difference in the rate of return of foreign versus domestically controlled companies. Grubert et al. (1993) find that these natural business reasons account for about half of this difference and Grubert (1997) finds that they explain an even larger 75 percent of the difference. Earnings stripping did not appear to have a significant effect, although Mills and Newberry (2004) find some difference depending on where the foreign firm is based. These results suggest about one-quarter to one-half of the difference can be attributed to transfer pricing but also suggest that the ballpark revenue figures calculated previously should be cut by between three-quarters and one-half to $1–2 billion in 1987 and $4–7.5 billion in 1995.

Collins et al. (1997) and Mills and Newberry (2004) present some recent evidence. In addition to their findings on earnings stripping, Mills and Newberry (2004) find that foreign-controlled firms with low foreign tax rates have a lower ratio of taxable income to assets than foreign-controlled firms with high foreign tax rates. This suggests that foreign-controlled firms, like their U.S.-controlled counterparts, are minimizing their U.S. taxes. However, Collins et al. (1997) were unable to document transfer-price manipulation by foreign-controlled firms that have close to zero taxable income. Moreover, a crackdown on transfer pricing practices that is viewed as unfair by a particular country (e.g., Japan) may invite retaliatory action by that country. All of the revenue estimates thus far have ignored this possibility.

Finally, it is interesting to note that calculations based on data in Hobbs (2003) suggest that the difference in the ratio of taxable income to assets for foreign-controlled versus U.S.-controlled firms may be narrowing. For 2000 (the latest year available), the ratio is 1.61 for foreign-controlled corporations and 1.62 for all other corporations.

ADDITIONAL READINGS

Collins, Julie, Dean Kemsley, and Douglas Shackleford. "Transfer Pricing and the Persistent Zero Taxable Income of Foreign-Controlled U.S. Corporations." *Journal of the American Taxation Association* 19 (Supplement, 1997): 68–83.

Graetz, Michael J., and Paul W. Oosterhuis. "Structuring an Exemption System for Foreign Income of U.S. Corporations." *National Tax Journal* 54, no. 4 (December 2001): 771–86.

Grubert, Harry. "Another Look at the Low Taxable Income of Foreign-Controlled U.S. Corporations." U.S. Treasury OTA Paper 74. Washington, DC: Office of Tax Analysis, 1997.

Grubert, Harry, Timothy J. Goodspeed, and Deborah Swenson. "Explaining the Low Taxable Income of Foreign-Controlled Companies in the United States." In *Studies in International Taxation,* ch. 7, edited by Alberto Giovannini, R. Glenn Hubbard, and Joel Slemrod (237–70). Chicago: University of Chicago Press, 1993.

Hobbs, James R. "Foreign-Controlled Domestic Corporations, 2000." *Statistics of Income Bulletin* (Summer 2003): 87–131.

Mills, Lillian F., and Kaye J. Newberry. "Do Foreign Multinationals' Tax Incentives Influence Their U.S. Income Reporting and Debt Policy?" *National Tax Journal* 57, no. 1 (March 2004): 89–107.

Cross-references: income tax, federal; multinational corporations, taxation.

Foreign corporations, state taxation of

Ben Miller
California Franchise Tax Board

Updated by
Jane G. Gravelle
Congressional Research Service, Library of Congress

Taxation by the states of the income of foreign country corporations.

State taxation of the income of foreign country corporations is subject to constraints imposed by the Constitution of the United States, in limited areas by treaties entered into by the United States, and by state statutes. Such taxation could also be limited by federal statute, but at present there are no federal statutory limitations on state taxation of foreign corporation income.

A distinction needs to be drawn between the taxation of foreign corporations' income and consideration of those corporations' income and activities in a combined report under "unitary taxation." A foreign corporation engaged in a unitary business with domestic corporations may be included in a combined report that is used to determine the amount of income assigned to a state, regardless of whether the foreign corporation is itself doing business in the state. (See *Barclays Bank PLC v. Franchise Tax Board,* 129 L.Ed.2d 244, 512 U.S. 298 [1994] and *Container Corporation of America v. Franchise Tax Board,* 77 L.Ed.2d 545, 463 U.S. 159 [1983].) This is commonly referred to as worldwide combined reporting (WWCR). Under the jurisprudence of the U.S. Supreme Court, *consideration of income* in a combined report or for purposes of formulary apportionment does not constitute taxation of the foreign corporation. For purposes of this discussion, however, taxation of income will include consideration of income.

In most circumstances, states tax the income of foreign country corporations on the same basis as they tax the income of corporations organized within their own boundaries or in other U.S. states. (It should be noted that state statutes may be worded either to tax income directly or to impose a tax measured by income. Legal differences may arise from this semantic difference, but they have no application for the purposes of this discussion.) These methods vary between states. Some states, in assessing tax, consider only the results of a single entity, while others use combined or consolidated reporting. There are numerous variations in state practices with respect to combined and consolidated reporting.

For corporations doing business within and outside state boundaries, almost all states determine the income assignable to activities within their boundaries on the basis of an apportionment formula, or formulary accounting. The apportionment formula compares various activities of the business within and without the state to determine the percentage of the business conducted within the state. Under formulary accounting, the entire income is considered, and geographic assignment is made by applying the apportionment formula to the entire income. Some states, however, may use separate accounting to determine the income attributable to activities within their state, either because it constitutes allocable, or "nonbusiness," income under the Uniform Division of Income for Tax Purposes Act (UDITPA) or because they believe separate accounting fairly reflects the results of activities within their state. Some, but not all, states use formulary accounting to assign income arising from activities within the United States and separate accounting to determine what portion of the income is earned within and outside of the United States. With respect to foreign corporations, separate accounting is more likely to determine income from activities within the United States and, perhaps also, within the individual state.

Under the Constitution, a state may not tax a foreign corporation unless that corporation has sufficient activities within the state to establish a taxable "nexus." Traditionally, nexus has required an actual physical presence in a jurisdiction. A physical presence can arise if the corporation owns property in the state or has employees in the state. The physical contact must generally be both purposeful and regular. An agent may also create nexus. The determination of what kind of contact can create nexus is continually evolving. The current view is that physical contact with the state is unnecessary and that "economic presence" suffices. Under this view, all that is required is that the corporation purposefully, and with some regularity, makes use of the market the state presents. Nexus for consideration of activities that occur outside the boundaries of a state, and the results of those activities, is provided by the "unitary business principle." This principle requires that the activities outside the state bear some rational relationship to the activities conducted within the state. This rational relationship entails more than controlling ownership.

In general, tax conventions between the United States and other countries do not apply to taxes imposed by subnational jurisdictions. An exception to this rule developed in the mid-1970s with respect to nondiscrimination clauses. Tax conventions negotiated and approved since that time make the nondiscrimination clause applicable to subnational taxes. In 1975, an effort was made in the renegotiation of the tax convention with the United Kingdom to include a provision that would have prohibited states from including the activities of foreign-incorporated entities in a worldwide combined report. The U.S. Senate refused to ratify the tax convention with this provision, and it was withdrawn. The U.S. Senate and the United Kingdom subsequently approved the revised tax convention and agreed upon a protocol—the Third Protocol—to recognize this change. No subsequent efforts to include such a provision in a tax convention have been accepted by the United States.

Friendship, commerce, and navigation (FCN) treaties contain both general nondiscrimination provisions and general provisions regarding income taxation, which are applicable to both national and subnational (state) jurisdictions. (It is understood that the the U.S. Department of State's position is that the more specific tax conventions are controlling over the general FCN treaties.) It appears that the language of the FCN treaties is broad enough to encompass states' permitted use of the worldwide combined report method, but the issue is controversial. The California Supreme Court has interpreted the language of FCN treaties to allow for the use of worldwide combined reporting (see *Barclays Bank International, Ltd., v. Franchise Tax Board,* 2 Cal.4th 708 [1992]). This may be an issue that the U.S. Supreme Court will ultimately be called upon to consider.

The tax base to which state income tax statutes are applied varies greatly. Many states define the income base by reference to the Internal Revenue Code. For those states, the taxation of foreign corporations normally mirrors that of the Internal Revenue Service. Income determined under the Internal Revenue Code and U.S. tax conventions will be the base for state tax purposes. Rules of "permanent establishment" and "effectively connected" income may be applied in either a separate entity context or a combined report context, depending upon the state. In either event, the likelihood is that no consideration will be given to the activities and income of a foreign corporation that occur or are assigned outside of the United States for federal tax purposes.

Other states provide their own definitions of income. In those cases, the determination of income is made under individual state law and the state chooses whether it will conform to the Internal Revenue Code's definition of U.S. source income and expenses, effectively connected income, and other limitations on the taxation of foreign corporations. Some states, even though conforming to or adapting the Internal Revenue Code's definition of income, may nonetheless consider all of the income of a foreign corporation that is doing business within their boundaries and use an apportionment formula to determine how much of the overall income is taxable by the state. The state of New York is an example (see *Bass, Ratcliff & Gretton, Ltd., v. State Tax Commission,* 266 U.S. 271, 69 L.Ed 282 [1924], and *Reuters, Ltd., v. State Tax Commission,* 82 NY2d 112, 623 NI2d 1145 [1993]).

The U.S. Supreme Court in *Barclays Bank PLC v. Franchise Tax Board,* 129 L.Ed.2d 244, 512 U.S. 298 (1994), upheld the states' right to use worldwide combined reporting and consider the income of foreign-incorporated entities that are part of a unitary business, regardless of whether the foreign entities were directly engaged in business within the state. Since 1986, however, most states have adopted either an elective or a mandatory "water's edge" reporting requirement in which they consider only the income of U.S.-incorporated entities and the U.S. income, as determined under the Internal Revenue Code, of foreign incorporated entities that have a presence in the United States.

McLure and Hellerstein (2002) discuss the recent trend toward weighting apportionment formulas more heavily to sales, and suggest that sales-only apportionment may violate international trade rules by providing a prohibited export subsidy. The European Union's 2003 report on U.S. barriers to trade stated that mandatory worldwide unitary reporting would violate trade agreements, as does the lack of uniformity in allocation formulas. States, as with the federal government, are dealing with the growth in corporate tax shelters. Houghton, Hogroian, and Weinreb (2004) summarize states' activities in recent years to move toward combined reporting in some circumstances or to expand "water's edge" rules to combat tax planning using offshore entities.

ADDITIONAL READINGS

European Commission. *Report on United States Barriers to Trade and Investment.* Brussels: European Commission, December 2003.

Houghton, Kendall L., Ferdinand Hogroian, and Adam Weinreb. "Unitary/Combined Filings: Old Concept, New Focus." *State Tax Notes* (August 9, 2004): 457–71.

McLure, Charles E., Jr. *The State Corporation Income Tax.* Palo Alto, CA: Hoover Press, Stanford University, 1984.

McLure, Charles E., Jr., and Walter Hellerstein. "Does Sales-Only Apportionment Violate International Trade Rules?" *Tax Notes* (September 9, 2002): 1513–21.

Cross-references: apportionment; foreign corporations, federal taxation of; nexus; state formula apportionment.

Foreign tax credit

Donald J. Rousslang
U.S. Department of the Treasury

A credit that allows U.S. residents (individuals and companies) to subtract the foreign income taxes they pay from U.S. income tax due on income earned abroad.

The U.S. foreign tax credit is simple in concept. The United States employs a global tax system and, under the residence principle, taxes the income its residents earn abroad. This foreign source income generally is also subject to tax in the foreign country under the source principle. To avoid double taxation of the foreign source income, a credit is given for foreign income taxes. That is, the taxpayer is allowed to subtract the foreign income tax from the tentative U.S. tax on the income (the U.S. tax before any allowance for foreign income taxes) and is required to remit only the difference (the residual tax) to the U.S. Treasury. If the foreign income tax exceeds the tentative U.S. tax, the Treasury does not give a refund. Foreign taxes other than income taxes (such as property taxes, excise taxes, payroll taxes, or value-added taxes) are deducted from taxable foreign source income, rather than credited against the U.S. tax. All foreign income taxes can be credited against U.S. tax, including income taxes levied by local governments below the national level, such as by a province in Canada or a canton in Switzerland. In contrast, income taxes imposed by U.S. states cannot be credited against the federal income tax; instead, they are deducted in deriving the income subject to the federal tax.

Corporate foreign tax credit

Although foreign tax credit is available to individuals with foreign source income (including wages earned abroad), the great bulk of foreign tax credits goes to U.S. corporations with operations abroad. U.S. corporations earn foreign source income by operating branches abroad and by operating or investing in affiliates incorporated abroad. Foreign source income earned through a foreign branch is subject to U.S. tax in the tax year in which it was earned. The tentative U.S. tax is simply the U.S. tax rate times the income of the branch. A credit is given for foreign income taxes and for any foreign withholding taxes that are levied when the branch remits the income to its U.S. parent. Losses a foreign branch incurs can be deducted from the corporation's domestic income to reduce the corporation's U.S. income tax. However, if the branch becomes profitable in succeeding years, its income is treated as U.S. source income, and no foreign tax credit can be claimed on it until the U.S. Treasury recovers the reduction in tax revenue caused by the branch's initial losses.

If the foreign source income is earned through a foreign affiliate that is a separate company incorporated abroad, the income generally is subject to U.S. tax only when it is remitted as dividends to the U.S. parent corporation. The U.S. tax on unremitted earnings is thus deferred until the earnings are repatriated. This is advantageous to the corporation because of the benefits of deferring tax.

To be eligible for a foreign tax credit on the affiliate's income, the U.S. parent must own at least 10 percent of the affiliate. A foreign affiliate that is separately incorporated abroad and that is at least 10 percent owned by the U.S. parent is called a foreign subsidiary. A subsidiary distributes dividends to the U.S. parent from earnings and profits after foreign income taxes. To determine the tentative U.S. tax and the foreign tax credit for the dividends, it is necessary to construct the foreign source income from which the dividends were derived. The formula for the tentative U.S. tax (T_A) on the underlying foreign source income is

$$T_A = \frac{t_{US}D}{(1 - t_F)}$$

where D is dividends, t_{US} is the U.S. tax, and t_F is the foreign income tax rate used for calculating the foreign tax credit (foreign income taxes paid divided by the subsidiary's earnings and profits as measured using the U.S. definition of taxable income). From the tentative U.S. tax, the U.S. corporation subtracts the sum of the foreign income taxes paid on the income underlying the dividends plus the foreign withholding taxes on the dividends. If the difference is positive, the U.S. corporation owes a residual U.S. tax. If the difference is negative, the U.S. corporation is said to have excess foreign tax credits.

In general, the U.S. parent corporation is allowed to sum the foreign source income and foreign taxes from all of its foreign operations, both branches and subsidiaries, when calculating foreign tax credit and residual U.S. tax. To be lumped together, however, the foreign source income must be within the same category of income (or income "basket"), as defined by the Internal Revenue Code. The main income baskets are for passive income (primarily interest, dividends, royalties, rents, or annuities received by the subsidiary), financial services income (income earned in banking, insurance, or finance), shipping income (income earned in international shipping), and general limitation income (primarily income earned abroad in the active conduct of a trade or business other than financial services, shipping, or income in the passive basket). Income in each of these baskets is subject to a separate foreign tax credit limitation. The maximum foreign tax credit that can be claimed in any basket (the foreign tax credit limitation) is the tentative U.S. tax. Any excess credits can offset residual U.S. tax on foreign source income earned during the previous two years or the following five years, but credits that cannot be used within that period are lost.

The separate income baskets help discourage U.S. corporations from moving offshore highly mobile investments (such as international shipping, financial services, and portfolio loans) that can easily be located in low-tax countries. Subpart F of the

Internal Revenue Code denies deferral for income from such investments, but U.S. corporations might still have a tax incentive to locate these activities abroad if they were allowed to combine the income and foreign taxes from these investments with those from other, less mobile, business activities that often generate excess foreign tax credits. The separate income baskets remove this incentive.

The foreign tax credit offsets most of the U.S. tentative tax on foreign source income. For example, in 2000, total taxable income of U.S. corporations was about $174.6 billion. Foreign taxes on this income (income taxes and withholding taxes) amounted to $61.5 billion, of which $48.4 billion was creditable against the U.S. tax. The residual U.S. tax on the income was $12.7 billion.

Credits versus deductions for foreign taxes

Taxpayers prefer receiving a credit for foreign taxes rather than a deduction, even if the foreign tax rate exceeds the U.S. rate and they are unable to credit all of the foreign taxes they pay. A simple example shows why. Denote foreign source income as Y, the U.S. tax rate as t_{US}, and the foreign tax rate as t_F. With a deduction for foreign income taxes, the U.S. tax is $t_{US}(1-t_F)Y$, whereas with a credit the residual U.S. tax is $(t_{US} - t_F)Y$. From these formulas, we see that if foreign income taxes are deducted, the rate of U.S. tax on the income would equal $t_{US}(1-t_F)$, which always exceeds the rate of residual U.S. tax after the foreign tax credit, $(t_{US} - t_F)$. If t_F is greater than t_{US}, there is no residual U.S. tax after the credit, but a U.S. tax payment would be required if the foreign income taxes were deducted.

Foreign tax credit and economic efficiency

According to conventional wisdom, for a capital-exporting country (a country that invests more abroad than it receives as inward foreign investment), a deduction for foreign taxes promotes national neutrality and maximizes the domestic income, whereas a foreign tax credit promotes capital export neutrality and maximizes the global income. Early statements of the conventional wisdom can be found in Richman (1963), Musgrave (1969), and Feldstein and Hartman (1979). These early statements are based on an analysis that assumes, among other things, that capital is homogeneous and either flows into or out of a country. Today, it is widely recognized that most countries (including the United States) experience simultaneously both significant inflows and outflows of capital. However, more recent research provides no definitive grounds for rejecting the notion that a foreign tax credit is the best tax policy for maximizing global income.

ADDITIONAL READINGS

Feldstein, Martin. "Tax Rules and the Effect of Foreign Direct Investment on U.S. National Income." In *Taxing Multinational Corporations,* edited by Martin S. Feldstein, James R. Hines Jr., and R. Glenn Hubbard (13–20). Washington, DC: National Bureau of Economic Research, 1994.

Feldstein, Martin, and David Hartman. "The Optimal Taxation of Foreign Source Investment Income." *The Quarterly Journal of Economics* 93 (November 1979): 613–29.

Musgrave, Peggy B. *United States Taxation of Foreign Investment Income: Issues and Arguments.* Cambridge, MA: The Law School of Harvard University, 1969.

Richman (Musgrave), Peggy B. *Taxation of Foreign Investment Income: An Economic Analysis.* Baltimore: Johns Hopkins Press, 1963.

Rousslang, Donald J. "Deferral and the Optimal Taxation of International Investment Income." *National Tax Journal* (September 2000): 589–600.

Cross-references: capital export neutrality; deferral of tax; national neutrality.

Franchise/privilege tax, state

Matthew N. Murray
University of Tennessee

Defines and describes special levies on the privilege of doing business.

A franchise is a right or privilege officially granted by the state, and a franchise tax is a special levy on this privilege. The privilege may reflect the right to start a business, to expand a business, or to sustain business activities over time. In some instances, the franchise provides unique privileges beyond simply the opportunity to conduct business. One example is the monopoly franchise that grants exclusive access to markets, as with public utilities. Another example is the corporate franchise that treats the business entity as a legal person subject to limited liability. Because business privileges are granted by the state and supported directly or indirectly by public-sector activities, the franchise tax represents an early form of benefit taxation.

Many taxes under many different guises have sought to tax business privileges generally and the corporate privilege specifically. Examples include occupation and license taxes; capital stock taxes; property taxes; special levies on utilities, financial institutions, and insurance companies; intangibles taxes; severance taxes; excess profits taxes; taxes on entertainment; levies on nonprofit entities; taxes on motor vehicles; certain transactions taxes like the Arizona sales tax; and the corporate income tax. More narrowly, the franchise tax itself typically takes the form of onetime or recurrent taxes on the corporate business enterprise. The tax is either a flat annual fee or is based on some measure of asset values.

Historical evolution

The modern franchise tax has its roots in the 19th century as corporations evolved in the new American states and efforts were made to tax the *corporate* privilege. The states took the lead because they, not the federal government, chartered corporations. The base of the tax was usually some measure of capital stock or asset holdings, under the premise that unique privileges afforded through the franchise would be capitalized into the value of the enterprise. Initially, use of the franchise tax was confined to specific industries (such as financial institutions), and its application was through the property tax. For example, in 1805 Georgia implemented a capital stock tax on banks, although it was effectively a property tax extended to include personal property holdings. New York State's capital stock levy on insurance companies, introduced in 1828, was also structured as a property tax (Seligman 1897).

As corporations expanded their reach in the American economy, the taxation of businesses and corporations also expanded (see Seligman 1897). Pennsylvania laid the groundwork for the broad state taxation of all corporations in the mid-19th century, and by 1891 the Pennsylvania tax on corporations had evolved into a tax on capital stock. By the turn of the century, franchise taxes on corporate capital stock were common across the states.

In the early years of its application, the franchise tax was the subject of considerable controversy and litigation. Important court decisions handed down heavily influenced the structure of today's franchise tax. For example, the courts concluded that the tax is not a property tax because its base may bear little resemblance to actual property values. One implication of this conclusion has been that states may circumvent the uniformity provisions that must typically be extended to taxpayers under the general property tax. The courts also concluded that the franchise tax is a tax on privilege. In practice, this ruling has allowed states to tax domiciled firms' out-of-state capital without violating the interstate commerce clause of the U.S. Constitution.

Modern franchise tax

The modern franchise tax is an ambiguous and ill-defined concept. If one relies simply on nomenclature, 23 states in 2003 imposed a tax on corporations categorized under the rubric of "franchise tax" (Commerce Clearing House 2002). However, this classification leads to confusion and misinterpretation. For example, the broad-based corporate franchise taxes in California, Florida, and New York are not included in this count because the base of these taxes is, in practice, corporate income. For those 23 states with a "franchise tax," the tax may take the form of onetime or recurrent registration fees or, more commonly, taxes on capital stock. This omits the comparable onetime origination (or qualification) fees and annual (or biennial) registration fees that most states require.

In those instances where the franchise tax falls on some measure of capital stock, the base will include some combination of shares of outstanding stock, surplus, undivided profits, and indebtedness, together intended to capture the extent of privileges granted through the franchise. One unique feature of the tax is that the base may include federal securities otherwise afforded preferential treatment under the tax code, because the courts have ruled that the tax is a privilege tax and not a property tax.

Apportionment practices vary substantially across the states. Some states choose to apportion domestic capital of in-state firms, paralleling treatment under the corporate income tax, whereas other states tax the entire domestic capital stock of in-state firms. Foreign firms are treated somewhat differently and can be taxed only on their in-state capital stock.

The rate structure of franchise taxes on corporate capital varies substantially across the states, with most states imposing taxes in the range of $1 to $3 per $1,000 of capital (see Commerce Clearing House 2002). Differential rates for foreign and domestic capital are not uncommon. (Pennsylvania has a franchise tax on foreign capital and a separate capital stock tax on domestic capital.) There are complications in some states, as with Georgia's 24-band rate structure and the practice in Illinois of separately taxing the capital stock of new enterprises, additional stock issuances, and the outstanding stock of incumbent firms.

In most states, franchise taxes (including onetime and recurrent levies) provide only a modest contribution to overall collections. Data on the relative importance of these taxes can be found in the U.S. Census, which includes state franchise taxes under the umbrella of "license taxes" but does not offer a more detailed breakdown (see their description of tax categories at http://www.census.gov/govs/www/class_ch7_tax.html). License taxes in Delaware were nearly 23 percent of tax revenues in 2003. Texas comes in a distant second at 7.3 percent. Most states derive well under 1 percent of tax revenue from license taxes, and even less from franchise taxes.

ADDITIONAL READINGS

Commerce Clearing House, Inc. *State Tax Handbook 2003*. Chicago: Commerce Clearing House, Inc., 2002.

Seligman, Edwin R. A. *Essays in Taxation*. New York: The MacMillan Company, 1897.

Cross-references: income tax, corporate, state and local.

Fringe benefits

Robert W. Turner
Colgate University

A variety of forms of compensation that are not taxed.

For the purposes of tax policy, the most useful definition of fringe benefits is voluntary employer expenditures on noncash forms of compensation. If taxes were paid on comprehensive income, the form in which employees receive compensation would not affect their taxation. Indeed, the Internal Revenue Code (Section 61) defines gross income as including "all income from whatever source derived" and specifically notes that "compensation for services, including . . . fringe benefits" is part of gross income. However, many fringe benefits are excluded from taxable income. These exclusions have implications for efficiency and equity and are the largest tax expenditures in the U.S. tax system, totaling more than $150 billion.

History

The U.S. income tax has always excluded some forms of compensation from the individual income tax base, while employers have always been allowed to deduct the cost of fringe benefits as well as wages from their taxable incomes. Employer contributions for accident and health insurance plans were nontaxable in the original income tax in 1913, although there was some ambiguity about the tax status of fringe benefits until the Internal Revenue Code of 1954. Similarly, term life insurance premiums became tax-exempt in 1920 and deferred compensation plans received favorable tax status in 1921.

By the early 1980s, several other fringe benefits had received statutory exclusions: up to $5,000 of death benefits, parsonage allowances, certain benefits provided to members of the Armed Services, meals and lodging for the convenience of the employer, group legal services, commuting through van pools, dependent care assistance, and employee educational assistance. The statute governing van pooling expired in the mid-1980s. Many other miscellaneous fringe benefits had always been untaxed even without statutory provisions; the Tax Reform Act of 1984 formalized the exclusions of miscellaneous fringe benefits. Miscellaneous fringe benefits that meet one of the following criteria are untaxed: a no-additional-cost service, a qualified employee discount, a working-condition fringe, a de minimis fringe, a qualified transportation fringe, or a qualified moving expense reimbursement. Special rules were written for parking, eating, and on-site athletic facilities. The Tax Reform Act of 1986 allowed self-employed workers to deduct 25 percent of their health insurance premiums; this percentage rose to 100 by 2003.

Beginning in the 1970s, employers began providing fringe benefits in the form of cafeteria or flexible benefit plans whereby employees could choose from a menu of several compensation options, including cash and several fringe benefits. These fringe benefits were made nontaxable in 1978. A related approach is the flexible spending plan, or salary reduction arrangement, which allows employees to set aside pretax dollars to spend on certain expenses (mostly health and child care) not covered by existing benefit plans.

Most of the statutory fringe benefits receive tax preferences only if provided in a nondiscriminatory manner, dating back to 1942, when nondiscrimination rules governing pensions were instituted. Other important limits are the $50,000 limit on the amount of term life insurance that can be provided tax-free to employees, the various restrictions and funding rules for pension and stock plans initiated by the Employee Retirement Income Security Act of 1974, and nondiscrimination and qualification rules for health and life insurance plans.

Fringe benefits as a share of total compensation were quite low until the three decades after World War II, when there was a rapid expansion. This expansion was caused by an increase in the number of fringe benefits offered as well as increased employer contributions to the traditional benefit plans. Rapid growth of fringe benefits as a form of compensation stopped around 1980. Both coverage and generosity of fringe benefits plans, especially health insurance plans, have declined for the past couple of decades.

The tax advantage to employees of receiving fringe benefits depends on marginal tax rates. Because most fringe benefits are excluded from federal, state, and Social Security tax bases, the tax price of fringe benefits (that is, the amount of after-tax wages that would be given up for a dollar's worth of fringe benefits) is considerably less than $1. Since 1980, the tax price has risen slightly as federal and state marginal tax rates have fallen. Because higher-income taxpayers generally have higher marginal tax rates, they receive a greater advantage.

In some cases, other tax subsidies can reduce the tax benefit of receiving fringe benefits. For example, the Health Insurance Portability and Accountability Act of 1996 created medical savings accounts for self-employed workers and workers at small firms; these individuals can set up tax-deferred savings plans, reducing the tax advantages of employer-provided pensions.

Efficiency effects

Not taxing fringe benefits gives rise to a consumption inefficiency because the goods provided as fringe benefits are made cheaper by the tax code. In this respect, health insurance has received the most attention. Many economists believe that the tax preference encourages more comprehensive health insurance to be provided and contributes to rising health care costs as consumers are shielded from the direct costs of their medical care.

The tax preferences given to pensions and other deferred compensation plans may affect national saving, although the effect is ambiguous because the tax preferences (other things being equal) lead to a larger government budget deficit. In addition, pensions may affect other forms of private saving (for example, someone who expects to receive a pension may feel less need to save for retirement).

Tax preferences for fringe benefits may also have important effects in labor markets. Tax preferences reduce the cost of labor differentially across firms and individuals because tax benefits increase with higher marginal tax rates. This effect may differ across workers, and some firms have cost advantages over others. Moreover, if employee preferences for fringes vary with skill levels, firms that use the skills of workers with a stronger preference for fringe benefits disproportionately may have lower costs than firms using other skill levels.

Because fringe benefits are tied to jobs, when compensation is paid in the form of fringes, labor mobility may be reduced, although this has good as well as bad effects. Some fringe benefits, notably pensions, can also affect the timing of retirement as well as quitting behavior.

The labor market effects of not taxing fringe benefits depend greatly on whether employees sort themselves into firms based on their differing demands for fringe benefits. Because the nondiscrimination rules that accompany the tax breaks given to fringe benefits mean that employers cannot tailor their fringe benefit offerings to each of their employees' wishes, heterogeneous preferences for fringe benefits should lead to a sorting equilibrium where some firms offer generous fringe benefit packages and others offer few or no fringes. Some firms are also more likely to replace the part of their workforce that do not want fringes with independent contractors, leasing arrangements, and part-time workers in order to satisfy the nondiscrimination rules. If workers are not perfect substitutes for each other, this leads to production inefficiencies. Sorting also exacerbates the adverse selection problem accompanying some fringe benefits, such as health insurance, because less healthy workers tend to congregate in firms offering more generous health insurance packages.

The importance of the distortions caused by the tax preferences given to fringe benefits depends on three things: the incidence of the tax preferences, the extent of job sorting that takes place, and the size of the effect tax preferences have on the amount of fringe benefits offered. Investigation of all of these issues is hampered by data problems.

Economic theory strongly suggests that workers bear the incidence of fringe benefit costs, and thus the incidence of tax preferences as well. Many arguments made about fringe benefits, however, are clearly based on the presumption that employers bear the costs (and receive the tax benefits). Statistical evidence has been inconclusive, although more and more studies are finding significant trade-offs between wages and a variety of fringe benefits (consistent with employee incidence).

Empirical evidence regarding whether workers sort into jobs on the basis of fringe benefit offerings is meager. There seems to be support, though, for the hypothesis that some sorting occurs.

The relationship between tax incentives and the provision of fringe benefits has been the subject of many studies, although the data problems outlined earlier plague this research as well. There is evidence that tax subsidies have significant effects on firms' decisions of whether to offer particular fringe benefits, especially health insurance. The tax subsidy seems to matter more for small firms than for large firms, for which there are other compelling reasons (for example, risk pooling leading to lower insurance costs) for offering fringe benefits. Tax considerations can also explain differences across firms and across time in the extent to which employees pay part of the cost of health insurance plans. There is also agreement that the tax advantage from paying compensation through fringes rather than wages affects fringes' share in total compensation. The magnitude of this effect, however, is uncertain. The results of some studies imply that full taxation of fringe benefits would cut by half or more the share of compensation paid as fringes. Other studies find smaller effects, with the fringe share of compensation falling by less than 15 percent if benefits are taxed fully.

Should fringe benefits be taxed?

Tax preferences are usually justified on the grounds of economic efficiency, equity (horizontal and vertical), or administrative efficiency.

Tax preferences for fringe benefits may improve economic efficiency if private markets lead to an underprovision of the fringes as a result of market failures. Indeed, there has been definite congressional intent to encourage the private provision of many goods typically provided as fringe benefits. Economists, however, seem more concerned with the distortions tax preferences cause than with the market failures they might correct.

Horizontal equity received much attention in the 1980s in the debate about taxing fringe benefits. A common argument was that tax subsidies for fringes are horizontally inequitable because two workers with identical total compensation will pay different amounts of tax if one receives more compensation as wages and the other more fringe benefits. But the disparity may be more apparent than real if workers choose their mix of wages and fringes by sorting themselves among employers who provide different ranges of fringe benefits.

The impact on vertical equity also depends on the incidence of the tax preferences. If employers can appropriate the benefits, few would argue that vertical equity is improved. If employees receive the benefits, the issue is whether well-off taxpayers or poorer taxpayers receive more benefits. Because the tax savings resulting from the tax preferences increase with marginal tax rates, taxing fringe benefits may improve vertical equity. Evidence also suggests that well-paid employees are more likely to receive a higher fringe share of compensation than low-paid workers, although there is evidence that moderate-income workers receive a higher fraction of their compensation as health insurance than do high-income workers. Some research suggests that younger workers respond more to changes in the tax advantages of pensions than do older workers and that tax subsidies are more important for blue-collar workers than for white-collar workers.

There is also evidence that low-income workers respond more to tax incentives than do high-income workers, so taxing fringe benefits could lead low-income workers to receive fewer fringes while high-income workers continue to receive them. This might have important social consequences if fringe benefits provide goods that society values and that the government would provide if private markets did not.

One reason fringe benefits have been excluded from the tax base is concern over the administrative complexity for the government, employers, and employees of including the value of fringe benefits in taxable income. Part of this complexity is simply the paperwork; another important element is uncertainty about the benefits' proper valuation. While the employee's willingness to pay for the fringe benefit is theoretically the best measure of value, employer cost is administratively easier (although it may be difficult for firms to allocate their total costs to individual workers properly).

Proposals to tax fringe benefits

Three reforms of the tax treatment of fringe benefits have been proposed: limits on the amount of benefits that can be received tax-free, tax credits for some percentage of the fringes' value as a replacement for the tax exclusion of fringes, and employer-based taxes. All of these options would reduce the tax benefits from receiving compensation as fringes rather than wages.

Limits, or caps, on the amount of benefits that can be received tax-free would tend to improve efficiency and vertical equity by eliminating the tax benefits of fringes high-income taxpayers receive while retaining the tax benefits for middle- and lower-income workers who receive less compensation in the form of fringes. Because of the way life insurance and pension benefits are valued, these limits would especially affect older workers. Also, because the costs of providing identical fringe benefits may differ substantially by region and industry, a single limit for all taxpayers may not be optimal. If limits are placed on specific benefits, other benefits would likely be substituted. To avoid this response, a limit on the overall amount of compensation provided as tax-free benefits is an attractive option. Replacing the exclusion of fringe benefits with a tax credit could also improve efficiency and vertical equity. The credit would work better for fringes currently excluded entirely from the tax base than for fringes such as pensions, whose tax benefits are based on deferring taxation.

Taxing employers instead of workers would be administratively less costly while still reducing the tax benefits of fringe benefits.

Conclusion

Many economists and tax experts think that some form of taxation of fringe benefits is desirable. They believe that both efficiency and equity would be improved. Potentially large amounts of revenue could be raised, which could finance new government spending, lower other taxes, or reduce the government budget deficit. Public opposition is strong, however, and there is no indication that any reform will be enacted soon.

ADDITIONAL READINGS

Burman, Leonard E., and Amelia Gruber. "First, Do No Harm: Designing Tax Incentives for Health Insurance." *National Tax Journal* 54 (September 2001): 473–93.

Carrington, William J., Kristin McCue, and Brooks Pierce. "Nondiscrimination Rules and the Distribution of Fringe Benefits." *Journal of Labor Economics* 20, part 2 (April 2002): S5–33.

Finkelstein, Amy. "The Effect of Tax Subsidies to Employer-Provided Supplementary Health Insurance: Evidence from Canada." *Journal of Public Economics* 84 (June 2002): 305–39.

Gruber, Jonathan, and Robin McKnight. "Why Did Employee Health Insurance Contributions Rise?" *Journal of Health Economics* 22 (November 2003): 1085–1104.

Gruber, Jonathan, and James Poterba. "Fundamental Tax Reform and Employer-Provided Health Insurance." In *Economic Effects of Fundamental Tax Reform,* edited by Henry J. Aaron and William G. Gale (125–62). Washington, DC: Brookings Institution Press, 1996.

Kosters, Marvin H., and Eugene Steuerle. "The Effect of Fringe Benefit Tax Policies on Labor and Consumer Markets." *Proceedings of the Seventy-Fourth Annual Conference on Taxation.* Columbus, OH: National Tax Association, 1981, pp. 86–92.

Munnell, Alicia H. "It's Time to Tax Employee Benefits." *New England Economic Review* (July/August 1989): 49–63.

Pesando, James E., and John A. Turner. "Labor-Market Effects of Canadian and U.S. Pension Tax Policy." In *Employee Benefits and Labor Markets in Canada and the United States,* edited by William T. Alpert and Stephen A. Woodbury (475–95). Kalamazoo, MI: W. E. Upjohn Institute for Employment Research, 2000.

Reagan, Patricia B., and John A. Turner. "Did the Decline in Marginal Tax Rates during the 1980s Reduce Pension Coverage?" In *Employee Benefits and Labor Markets in Canada and the United States,* edited by William T. Alpert and Stephen A. Woodbury (475–95). Kalamazoo, MI: W. E. Upjohn Institute for Employment Research, 2000.

Royalty, Anne Beeson. "Tax Preferences for Fringe Benefits and Workers' Eligibility for Employer Health Insurance." *Journal of Public Economics* 75 (February 2000): 209–27.

Selden, Thomas M., and John Moeller. "Estimates of the Tax Subsidy for Employment-Related Health Insurance." *National Tax Journal* 53 (December 2000): 877–87.

Stabile, Mark. "The Role of Tax Subsidies in the Market for Health Insurance." *International Tax and Public Finance* 9 (January 2002): 33–50.

Turner, Robert W. "Fringe Benefits: Should We Milk This Sacred Cow?" *National Tax Journal* 42 (September 1989): 293–300.

Cross-references: employee stock ownership plan; health expenditures, tax treatment of; horizontal equity; pensions, tax treatment of; profit-sharing plans; vertical equity.

Fuel taxes, federal

Kenneth D. Simonson
Associated General Contractors of America

Taxes levied by the federal government on gasoline, diesel fuel, and a variety of special fuels.

The federal government imposes taxes on gasoline, diesel fuel, and a variety of special fuels. Although collections amount to less than 2 percent of total federal receipts, fuel taxes play a significant role in numerous policy debates.

Federal fuel taxes are divided at specified rates among general revenues and trust funds dedicated to highways, mass transit, aviation, environmental cleanup, and recreation. In addition, in every Congress, proposals are made to alter fuel taxes for such purposes as energy conservation, clean air, and funding intercity passenger rail. However, proposals to increase fuel taxes always draw substantial opposition, and fuel taxes account for a smaller share of federal receipts in 2004 than when they were first enacted in 1932.

History

Beginning with Oregon in 1919, every state enacted gasoline taxes ranging from 2 to 7 cents per gallon. The first federal fuel tax on highway fuels was adopted in June 1932, at a 1-cent-per-gallon rate, as a one-year tax to reduce the deficit. The tax brought in 8 percent of federal receipts in fiscal 1933. Temporary extensions were enacted eight times from 1933 to 1956, at rates of 1 to 2 cents per gallon.

The Federal Aid Highway Act of 1956 established the interstate highway system and also created the Highway Trust Fund as a way to ensure the system's financing. All fuel tax receipts, along with revenues from tire, truck and bus, and highway use taxes, were transferred to the trust fund. Fuel taxes were raised to 3 cents per gallon in 1956 and to 4 cents in 1959.

In 1982, the fuel tax was raised to 9 cents per gallon, of which 1 cent was placed in a new mass transit account within the Highway Trust Fund. In 1984, the diesel tax, which is paid mainly by trucks, was raised to 15 cents in exchange for reducing the maximum tax on heavy trucks. An additional tax of 0.1 cents per gallon, dedicated to the new Leaking Underground Storage Tank (LUST) Trust Fund, was added in 1986.

Use of fuel taxes for general revenues resumed in 1990 with the enactment of a deficit-reduction package that included a five-year, 5-cent-per-gallon tax, split equally between the general fund and the Highway Trust Fund. In the next round of budget legislation, in 1993, the 1990 tax was extended to 1999 and redirected, starting in October 1995, to the Highway Trust Fund. At the same time, a new, permanent, 4.3-cent general-fund tax was imposed. In 1997, all general-fund revenues were returned to the Highway Trust Fund and the LUST tax of 0.1 cent, which had expired at the end of 1995, was reinstated.

As of mid-2004, the tax is 18.4 cents per gallon for gasoline (24.4 cents per gallon for diesel fuel). Of that, 0.1 cents goes to the LUST Trust Fund and 2.86 cents in the Highway Trust Fund goes to the mass transit account. Numerous exemptions or reduced rates have been enacted for certain fuels (for instance, three lower rates for ethanol blends) and users (for instance, farm, state and local government, and bus users).

Nonhighway taxes

Several other users pay fuel taxes. A fuel tax on noncommercial aviation fuel goes into the Airport and Airway Trust Fund. The tax on fuel used by vessels in commercial waterway transportation is placed in an Inland Waterways Trust Fund. Taxes on motorboat fuels go into the Aquatic Resources Trust Fund and the Land and Water Conservation Fund. Taxes on gasoline used in small power-tool and recreational engines go into a wetlands restoration program. Taxes on domestic and imported crude oil and imported petroleum products go into the Hazardous Substance Superfund. Imported cargo, including crude oil and refined products, is taxed for the Harbor Maintenance Trust Fund.

Administration

The gasoline tax has always been collected at the producer or importer level. Collection of the diesel fuel tax has varied,

however. Diesel fuel is chemically identical to heating oil, which is tax-exempt. To avoid taxing residential and commercial heating oil users, the diesel tax has been imposed at the retail (truck stop) or wholesale-distributor level. Concerns about widespread evasion by vendors selling untaxed heating oil to taxable users led Congress, in 1993, to move the collection point for diesel fuel to the producer level and to require that untaxed fuel be dyed at the time it leaves the producer's terminal.

Historically, the Internal Revenue Service (IRS) did not devote many staff to excise tax administration. Since the early 1990s, however, the IRS has worked jointly with state fuel tax administrators and the Department of Justice to crack down on fuel tax evasion. Nevertheless, federal and state rules for reporting and paying fuel taxes and for claiming exemptions or refunds still differ, making the taxes relatively complex for both the government and the taxpayers.

Pros and cons

Fuel taxes provide a stable and predictable level of funds because highway fuel use changes little from year to year. Fuel taxes provide a simple, easily collected, although imprecise, measure of highway use. These attributes make fuel taxes popular as one source of highway funding. Fuel taxes for other trust funds also serve in varying degrees as user fees that collect revenue from those who benefit from the expenditures that the taxes finance.

Advocates of fuel taxes for other purposes cite a variety of arguments. Some point to the fact that fuel taxes are broadly spread: every consumer pays fuel taxes, explicitly when buying gasoline and implicitly as part of the cost of trucking goods. Some refer to the far higher rates of fuel tax in other industrialized countries as justification. Some say higher fuel taxes are warranted to pay the costs of importing and burning oil that are not reflected in the market price. These costs include defense outlays to ensure that the United States has secure sources of foreign oil, expenditures to fill and maintain the strategic petroleum reserve, and costs of air pollution. A related argument for higher fuel taxes is to encourage development of renewable, domestic, or less-polluting fuel sources.

On the other side, some criticize fuel taxes for distorting market prices and causing producers and consumers to allocate personal and business spending inefficiently. Some oppose the gasoline tax because it is regressive; that is, lower-income families spend a higher percentage of income on the tax than do wealthier families. The tax also falls unevenly by location, occupation, and family size. Specifically, rural families, individuals who must use a vehicle in their jobs, and large families tend to spend more on gasoline than other families at the same income level, creating horizontal inequities. Some say that taxing only fuel is not an efficient or fair way to achieve environmental or national defense goals, which they feel should be addressed through taxes on all oil, all energy, general revenue sources, or through nontax means.

ADDITIONAL READINGS

Furchtgott-Roth, Diana. "The Measurement of Regressivity: The Case of the Motor Fuels Tax." Discussion Paper no. 63. Washington, DC: American Petroleum Institute, December 1990.

Institute for Research on the Economics of Taxation. "The Impact, Shifting, and Incidence of an Increase in the Gasoline Excise Tax." Washington, DC: Institute for Research on the Economics of Taxation, July 25, 1991.

Noto, Nonna A., and Louis Alan Talley. "Excise Tax Financing of Federal Trust Funds." Report 93-6 E. Washington, DC: Congressional Research Service, January 1993.

Poterba, James M. "Lifetime Incidence and the Distributional Burden of Excise Taxes." *American Economics Association Papers and Proceedings* 79 (May 1989): 325–30.

Talley, Louis Alan. "Federal Excise Taxes on Gasoline and the Highway Trust Fund: A Short History." Report RL-30304. Washington, DC: Congressional Research Service, March 29, 2000.

U.S. Congress, Congressional Budget Office. *Federal Taxation of Tobacco, Alcoholic Beverages, and Motor Fuels.* Washington, DC: Congressional Budget Office, August 1990.

U.S. Congress, Joint Committee on Taxation. *Description of "The Highway Reauthorization Tax Act of 2004."* JCX-20-04. Washington, DC: Joint Committee on Taxation, March 15, 2004.

Cross-references: benefit principle; environmental taxes, federal; Highway Trust Fund, federal; user charges, federal.

Gaming taxation, state

Claude Louishomme
University of Nebraska at Kearney

Donald Phares
University of Missouri–St. Louis

State taxation of legalized gambling.

In the 1990s, casino gaming took on a nationwide presence. In 1988, legalized casino gaming existed only in Nevada and New Jersey. By 1996, 22 states had Native American casinos and 10 had non–Native American casinos. The geographical expansion of gaming has continued. This has been especially true of Native American casinos, which had spread to 28 states by 2002. Expansion has been driven by entrepreneurs looking for profits, changing attitudes toward gaming, economic downturns, and the search by states and localities for new revenues in an era of shrinking federal aid and growing citizen resistance to tax increases.

The enactment of the Indian Gaming Regulatory Act in 1988 marks a pivotal point in casino expansion. It was passed to bring economic development to Native American nations. But the success of Native American casinos was not lost on the states. Several quickly moved to tap this source of investment, jobs, and public revenue. South Dakota was first in 1989 when a citizen initiative authorized limited-stakes casinos in Deadwood. Colorado, Iowa, and Illinois followed. However, Iowa initiated a new approach in July 1989 with legislation legalizing riverboat casino gaming. In 1991, Iowa and Illinois became the first states to launch riverboat casinos in the 20th century. Thus, a new trend began as several states, through legislative action and statewide ballot initiatives, adopted laws authorizing the operation of riverboat casinos. As a result, casinos emerged in Mississippi in 1992, Louisiana in 1993, Missouri in 1994, and Indiana in 1995.

The removal of legal prohibitions against casino gambling in so many jurisdictions was a dramatic departure from the past. From 1931 to 1977, Nevada held a monopoly on legal casino gambling. This 46-year dominance ended in 1977 when New Jersey authorized the operation of casinos in Atlantic City. The opening of casinos in seven additional states between 1989 and 1995 dramatically altered the geography of the gaming industry. Those changes have continued as Michigan voters approved the development of three casinos in Detroit in 1997; the number of states with Native American casinos grew from 22 in 1998 to 28 in 2002.

Non–Native American casinos

By 2002, non–Native American casinos were operating in 11 states. Native American casinos do generate revenues and jobs for states. However, Native American casinos are significantly different legal entities from non–Native American casinos. As a condition of operation, each tribe negotiates a "compact" with state government that, among other things, stipulates an agreed-upon payment to the state. Nevertheless, Native American casinos are not taxed and are not required to report gaming statistics. For this entry data were compiled for the 11 states with non–Native American casinos.

Gaming taxes and fees

States assess a mixture of taxes and fees on casino operations and their patrons. In many instances, the casino's home locality assesses additional taxes and fees. This analysis focuses primarily on statewide characteristics. These include the gaming tax and fees, device fees, application and annual license renewal fees, and admissions fees.

Gaming tax rates

State gaming tax rates are assessed at a fixed, graduated, or combination fixed and graduated rate, increasing with revenue from casino operations. Gaming tax rates are assessed on either gross receipts (GR) or adjusted gross receipts (AGR). AGR is the amount of gaming revenue remaining after patrons' winnings are deducted from gross receipts. States with a fixed tax rate include Michigan (18 percent of AGR), Missouri (20 percent), New Jersey (8 percent) and South Dakota (8 percent).

States that tax on an adjustable scale are Colorado, Illinois, Indiana, Iowa, Mississippi, and Nevada. Louisiana uses a combination flat and graduated rate. Colorado taxes the first $2 million of AGR at 0.25 percent, $2 to $4 million at 2 percent, $4 to $5 million at 4 percent, $5 to $10 million at 11 percent, $10 to $15 million at 16 percent, and over $15 million at 20 percent. Iowa taxes are set at 5 percent on the first $1 million of AGR, 10 percent on the next $2 million, and 20 percent above this.

Two states have switched from a fixed tax rate to an adjustable tax schedule since the mid-1990s. Indiana formerly taxed riverboat casinos at 20 percent of AGR. In July 2002, a new law increased this rate to 22.5 percent for boats that did not adopt flexible scheduling. Indiana's flexible scheduling eliminated the requirement that riverboat casinos must cruise and allowed licensees to conduct dockside gaming. All of the operating casinos in Indiana chose flexible scheduling and are now taxed with a graduated rate of 15 percent on the first $25 million of AGR, 20 percent from $25 to $50 million, 25 percent from $50 to $75 million, 30 percent from $75 to $150 million with a top rate of 35 percent over $150 million. Illinois switched from a fixed rate of 20 percent of AGR to a graduated tax in 1998. Since then the legislature has increased the gaming tax twice, in 2002 and then again in 2003. The most recent tax schedule includes a rate of 15 percent on AGR up to $25 million, 27.5 percent on AGR from $25 to $37.5 million, 32.5 percent from $37.5 to $50 million, 45 percent from $75 to $100 million, and 50 percent on AGR from $100 to $250 million.

The state of Louisiana uses a combination of fixed and graduated tax rates. Louisiana land-based casinos pay either an annual tax of $60 million or 21.5 percent of gaming revenue. All riverboat casinos, except Bally's, are taxed at 21.5 percent. Bally's pays between 18.5 and 21.5 percent depending on gaming revenue.

Other taxes and fees

The 11 states with casino gaming, in addition to assessing a gaming tax, subject casinos to other taxes and fees, including device fees, annual licensing fees, and payment for enforcement expenses. The number of states with gaming device fees has declined since 1996 from five to four. Colorado eliminated its $75 fee per slot machine, blackjack table, and poker table in 1999. However, Central City, Black Hawk and Cripple Creek—three municipalities in Colorado with casinos—collect annual device fees ranging from $750 to $1,265. States with annual gaming device fees are Mississippi (slots and tables), Nevada (nonrestricted and restricted slots and games fees, quarterly license fees on slots and games, monthly percentage fees, and live entertainment tax), New Jersey ($500 per slot), and South Dakota ($2,000 per table game and slot).

Eight states have annual licensing fees: Colorado ($500 to $2,000), Illinois ($5,000), Iowa ($5 per passenger carrying capacity, including crew), Louisiana ($100,000 plus a franchise fee of 3 percent of net gaming proceeds), Michigan (each of the three casinos pay one-third of $25 million times the previous year's consumer price index), Mississippi ($5,000 plus graduated fee based on the number of games), and South Dakota ($100 to $250). Indiana charges a $5,000 annual fee after the five-year review of the initial license. The minimum application fee in New Jersey is $200,000. Approved licenses are good for four years. New Jersey's minimum renewal fee is $100,000. In addition, Iowa, Missouri, and New Jersey pass all enforcement costs directly to the casinos. In Missouri, for example, the average annual cost per venue is $568,000. New Jersey also has an additional 1.25 percent "alternative investment tax" on gross revenues. Casino operators who do not contribute to the alternative investment fund are assessed an additional 2.5 percent tax.

Admission fees

Four states charge an admissions fee to casino patrons, five have no fee, and two (Iowa and Louisiana) permit a local option. The four states with an admission fee are Illinois ($3 for casinos with less than 1 million admissions in the previous calendar year; $4 with admissions between 1 and 2.3 million; and $5 with more than 2.3 million admissions), Indiana ($3 a person), Iowa (direct reimbursement of regulatory expenses), and Missouri ($2 a person per two-hour cruise). States with no admission fees are Colorado, Michigan, Mississippi, Nevada, and South Dakota. Iowa and Louisiana allow local jurisdictions the option of charging a fee. In Iowa, the city or county in which a casino is located may adopt an admission fee not exceeding 50 cents per person. In Louisiana, local jurisdictions have the option of charging a fee that ranges from $2.50 to $3.50.

As is evident from this summary, states use a number of taxing instruments to derive revenues from casinos, but casinos seem more than willing to incur these costs as a condition of doing business. The primary goal of states in assessing these various taxes and fees is to generate revenue.

Gaming revenues

Gaming tax revenues

The gaming tax is the main source of gaming revenues. This is applied to house winnings, calculated either as GR or as AGR from all gaming activities. In 2003, gaming tax revenues totaled $3.6 billion; the four states with admissions fees collected an additional $247 million in 2003, for a total gaming revenue of almost $3.9 billion.

In 2003, the 11 states with casino gaming collected a total of $3.6 billion in gaming tax revenue; this was nearly double the $1.86 billion collected in 1996. Nevada topped the list with $722 million. Illinois was a close second with $660 million, and Indiana was third with $592 million. Louisiana followed with $394 million, New Jersey with $346 million, Mississippi with $329 million, Missouri with $261 million, and Iowa with $126 million. Only three states had less than $100 million in gaming tax revenues. These included Colorado ($97 million), Michigan ($91.5 million), and South Dakota ($5 million). Two of these states have limited gaming: Colorado limits casinos to three former mining towns (Central City, Cripple Creek, and Black Hawk) and has a maximum single bet on any slot or table game of $5. South Dakota's limited stakes casinos are only allowed in the town Deadwood with gaming activities limited to slot machines, blackjack, and poker; the maximum bet limit is $100 per game.

Admission fee revenues

The four states with admissions fees collected $247 million in 2003: Missouri, $102 million; Indiana, $79 million; Illinois, $60 million; and Iowa, $6 million. Admission fee revenues constituted a significant portion of gaming revenue for the state of Missouri. Admission fee revenues represented 28 percent of state gaming revenue. Changes in the tax structures and rates in Illinois and Indiana from a fixed to a graduated assessment have increased revenues collected from the gaming tax. Nevertheless, the admissions fee still generated 8 percent of total state gaming revenues.

Total gaming tax revenue

In 2003, total state gaming revenue from wagering tax, admission fees, and gaming devices tax was $3.88 billion. The success of states that only came to legalized casino gaming in the 1990s, to capitalize on a new source of revenue, is impressive. Although Nevada leads all states by generating 18.7 percent of total nationwide gaming revenues, Illinois was a close second with 18.5 percent and Indiana was third with 17.3 percent. Louisiana generated 10.2 percent and Missouri generated 9.4 percent of the total. New Jersey, the first state to legalize casinos after Nevada, came in sixth, collecting 8.9 percent of the total gaming revenues in 2003. Mississippi generated 8.5 percent, while Iowa, the state that ushered in the era of riverboat casinos, collected 3.4 percent. Even though Colorado only allows limited stakes gaming, it made a respectable showing with 2.5 percent, reflecting its much larger population draw. The three casinos in downtown Detroit generated only 2.4 percent of the gaming revenues, which partly reflects the strong competition these venues face from their more established competitors across Lake Erie in Ontario, Canada. South Dakota remained the smallest revenue generator, producing 0.28 percent of total gaming revenues.

State general revenues and gaming revenues

The above figures clearly demonstrate that gaming has contributed significant amounts of revenue to state coffers. However, to get a clearer picture of the relative contribution of casino gaming to state governments' fiscal health, we look at revenues generated by this industry in terms of total state revenues. We use data from the 2002 state government finances and calculate "own-source" revenue by netting out intergovernmental, liquor store, and insurance trust revenues. Gaming revenues represent approximately 14.5 percent of own-source revenues in Nevada, 5.2 percent in Mississippi, 4.8 percent in Indiana, 3.4 percent in Louisiana, and 3.1 percent in Missouri. In Illinois revenues generated by the gaming tax and admission fee represent approximately 2.5 percent of the states'

own-source revenues. Iowa, New Jersey, and Colorado generate 1.7 percent, 1.4 percent, and 1.2 percent of their own-source revenues form gaming, respectively. Michigan and South Dakota receive less than 1 percent. Thus, while a total of nearly $4 billion is raised, the fiscal impact of gaming is significant in only a few states. For all 11 states combined, it is 3.5 percent.

Uses of state gaming revenues

The 11 gaming states use their revenues in a wide variety of ways, too many to enumerate. At one extreme is Missouri, which constitutionally dedicates almost all gaming proceeds to education. At the other is Nevada, where most (93 percent) proceeds go to the general fund. South Dakota puts all proceeds into restoring the city of Deadwood, and New Jersey dedicates 90 percent to physical and mental health services. Iowa puts most (over 90 percent) in the state general fund. Louisiana puts slightly more than half in the general fund with the rest used for education, public safety, and compulsive gaming programs. Michigan deposits funds into a State Services Fee Fund, which the legislature then allocates for K–12 public education in Michigan and capital improvement, youth programs, and tax relief in the city of Detroit. Indiana distributes much of its revenue back to localities for a variety of purposes. Colorado sends 50 percent back to gaming localities and the state historical society, and the rest goes to general revenue, much of which supports local services or infrastructure. Mississippi uses much of its funds for infrastructure such as roads. Illinois puts much of its revenue toward education.

In addition to state gaming funds, localities make wide and varied use of their own gaming revenues or those they get from the state. Much local spending goes into equipment and infrastructure or support of local public safety.

Conclusion

Casino gaming has become available in many parts of the country. The phenomenon has swept the nation in less than two decades. Although momentum for the industry's further expansion may have slowed, states that allow casino gaming have attached taxes and fees to this industry and thus secured significant revenues, collectively some $4 billion in 2003. Gaming revenues are likely to continue to grow with new states and venues coming online and activity increasing at existing venues.

ADDITIONAL READINGS

Forrest, David, O. David Gulley, and Robert Simmons. "Elasticity of Demand for UK National Lottery Tickets." *National Tax Journal* 53, no. 4 (December 2000): 853–64.

Gold, Steven D. "Casinos Are No Panacea for Ailing State Budgets." In *Casino Development: How Would Casinos Affect New England's Economy? Special Report No. 2,* edited by Robert Tannenwald (67–73). Boston, MA: Federal Reserve Bank of Boston, 1995.

Goodman, Robert. *Legalized Gambling as a Strategy for Economic Development*. Northhampton, MA: United States Gambling Study, 1995.

Leven, Charles, Donald Phares, and Claude Louishomme. *The Economic Impact of Casino Gaming in Missouri*. St. Louis: Leven and Phares Associates, 1997.

Madhusudhan, Ranjana. "Betting on Casino Revenues: Lessons from State Experiences." *National Tax Journal* 49 (1996): 401–12.

Oster, Emily. "Are All Lotteries Regressive? Evidence from the Powerball." *National Tax Journal* 57, no. 2 (June 2004): 179–87.

Paton, David, Donald S. Siegel, and Leighton Vaughan Williams. "Taxation and the Demand for Gambling: New Evidence from the United Kingdom." *National Tax Journal* 57, no. 4 (December 2004): 847–61.

Phares, Donald, Charles Leven, and Claude Louishomme. "Gaming in the United States: Taxation, Revenues, and Economic Impact." In *Handbook of Taxation*, edited by W. Bartley Hildreth and James A. Richardson (263–82). New York: Marcel Dekker, 1999.

Rubenstein, Ross, and Benjamin Scafidi. "Who Pays and Who Benefits? Examining the Distributional Consequences of the Georgia Lottery for Education." *National Tax Journal* 55, no. 2 (June 2002): 223–38.

Cross-references: destination principle; earmarking of taxes; origin principle; retail sales tax; tax exportation.

GATT

John H. Mutti
Grinnell College

An acronym for the General Agreement on Tariffs and Trade, an international trade oversight organization since superceded by the World Trade Organization (WTO).

This organization was founded by a multilateral treaty signed in 1948 that established general rules to govern international trade. As a result of the eighth round of GATT negotiations concluded in 1994, the Uruguay Round, the World Trade Organization (WTO) has superseded the GATT. The WTO is an umbrella organization that oversees multilateral trade rules, negotiating procedures, and dispute resolution mechanisms in several areas, including trade in goods, trade in services (the General Agreement on Trade in Services, or GATS), investment measures, and protection of intellectual property. A noteworthy achievement of the GATT is the substantial reduction in tariffs from the very high levels reached in the 1930s. Although the agreement deals primarily with trade relations, tariffs are not the only tax instruments or government fiscal policies treated by the GATT, and several GATT provisions and procedures are applicable to traditional public finance issues.

A fundamental principle of the GATT is that trade barriers be applied on a most-favored-nation basis: The most favorable trade conditions offered to one country must be extended to all other signatories. The multilateral approach contrasts with the bilateral focus of international tax treaties. The most-favored-nation provision contributed to a more rapid reduction in trade barriers than would have occurred under strictly bilateral negotiations. The provision also gives a country the opportunity to free-ride on the concessions of other countries without making reciprocal concessions. A country that fails to make meaningful offers, however, is unlikely to find that other signatories address the items of greatest interest to it. Many countries that pursued inward-oriented or isolationist development strategies felt no urgency to join the GATT. For example, Mexico and Venezuela only acceded to the agreement in the 1980s and China in 2001. As of 2004, countries such as Russia and Saudi Arabia are not members.

Another key principle of the GATT is the standard of national treatment. Once foreign goods enter a country and clear customs, they must be treated no worse than goods produced domestically. This provision keeps discriminatory domestic taxes and regulations from protecting domestic producers; otherwise, such regulations could be used to offset tariff concessions.

A goal of the GATT has been to reduce tariffs and discourage restrictive trade practices. Countries commit to bind their tariffs at a given rate and typically negotiate gradual reductions. If a government raises a tariff above its bound level, other signatories may demand compensation through concessions on other goods, or be authorized to retaliate by raising their own tariffs. The GATT attempts to prohibit or limit the use of quotas or discriminatory border treatment. More generally, it seeks to move to a system of transparent and predictable rules and away from the arbitrary and inconsistent application of discretionary standards.

A noteworthy aspect of the Uruguay Round Agreement was that the various negotiated items were treated as a single package, and countries could not choose to accept some items and reject others. New items addressed included trade in services, intellectual property protection, and trade-related investment measures. The round also dealt with agriculture and textiles, two areas that had escaped much GATT discipline in the past. Implementation of the agreement, however, led to limited expansion of market access for many developing counties, and their dissatisfaction with this outcome became a major obstacle to overcome before the initiation of another round of negotiations in 2001 at Doha, Qatar.

An important GATT provision governs border tax adjustments that apply to products traded internationally. Production taxes on exports can be rebated, and production taxes that domestic producers face can be imposed on imports. Because value-added taxes are regarded as taxes on products, they qualify for this border tax adjustment, whereas corporate income taxes do not. Although this distinction may rest on an incomplete analysis of the differential incidence of these taxes, it remains the basis for border tax adjustments, and rebating corporate income taxes constitutes a prohibited export subsidy.

A particularly controversial example of this prohibited subsidy was the U.S. Domestic International Sales Corporation (DISC) legislation of 1971, which levied a lower corporate income tax on export income. Action in this case demonstrates several important aspects of dispute settlement in the GATT and the WTO.

The European Community and Canada challenged the DISC, and under GATT procedures, a panel of impartial experts was appointed to evaluate whether the practice violated GATT standards. Because GATT members had to adopt the panel's recommendations unanimously, prolonged delay was common. In this case, final adoption did not occur until 1981 and was significantly influenced by a confidential protocol reached in 1979. The DISC was repealed and replaced by a Foreign Sales Corporation (FSC) provision, which was not challenged further in the GATT.

With the creation of the WTO in 1995, new dispute resolution procedures established that any rejection of a panel recommendation had to be unanimous, a change that gave more teeth to such procedures. In 1999 the European Union challenged the FSC provisions. The panel held that the 1979 protocol was not relevant and ruled against the FSC. A subsequent modification of U.S. law and a further challenge by the European Union resulted in another ruling against U.S. practice. In 2002 an arbitration panel authorized retaliation of $4 billion against U.S. exports.

The prohibition against export subsidization also will force many developing countries that create export-processing zones to change their practices if these zones tax export income more favorably than income from domestic sales. Although this limitation does not apply to countries with per capita incomes less than $1,000, middle-income countries will be most affected.

In 2003 the Doha Round negotiations broke down. With some large countries ignoring WTO rulings or aggressively negotiating regional trade agreements, the multilateral trading system promoted by the GATT is being undermined.

ADDITIONAL READINGS

Jackson, John Howard. *The World Trading System,* 2nd ed. Cambridge, MA: MIT Press, 1997.

Hufbauer, Gary Clyde, and Joanna Shelton Erb. *Subsidies in International Trade.* Washington, DC: Institute for International Economics, 1984.

Cross-reference: border tax adjustments.

General-equilibrium models

Charles L. Ballard
Michigan State University

Models that explicitly incorporate the interactions among markets, making them well suited to studying the incidence and excess burden of taxes.

Until the early 1960s, most research on the economics of taxation used partial-equilibrium models (which look at a single market in isolation). A partial-equilibrium analysis usually begins by specifying a market supply curve and a market demand curve for the commodity in question. Once taxes are introduced, the equilibrium quantity and prices change. These changes can be used to assess the incidence of taxes as well as their efficiency effects.

In some cases, partial-equilibrium models pose few problems. For example, a tax on hubcaps would probably have minor general-equilibrium effects on other markets, such as those for steel, metalworkers, and automobiles. If the interactions with other markets are small, it may be acceptable to ignore them by using a partial-equilibrium analysis. However, many important tax policy questions of the last generation have dealt with taxes that have substantial effects on multiple markets.

The shortcomings of partial-equilibrium models have been recognized for years. Authors such as Harry Brown (1939) and Richard Musgrave (1959) emphasized that taxes affect factor incomes as well as product prices. In 1955, Paul Wells presented a general-equilibrium analysis in diagrammatic form. However, these contributions lacked the precise mathematical basis necessary for quantitative answers to general-equilibrium questions.

The Harberger model and its descendants

An article by Arnold Harberger (1962) was a landmark for its rigorous, quantitative, general-equilibrium analysis of a tax policy question. Harberger's study focused on the corporation income tax in the United States, using a model with two sectors (corporate and noncorporate) and two factors of production (capital and labor). Harberger built on the rich history of two-sector models in international trade (Johnson 1971). Practical considerations dictated the choice of the two-sector model: such a model yields systems of equations that become extremely cumbersome when more than two sectors are studied. Unfortunately, the two-sector assumption is a simplification that ignores many details of the real economy.

The Harberger model encompasses a timeframe long enough to allow capital stock to be reallocated from the corporate to the noncorporate sector. However, it does not allow researchers to study long-term capital accumulation. In addition, Harberger's model is based on techniques of differential calculus; therefore, the results are only strictly correct for small changes in tax rates.

Harberger's most important conclusion was that capital bears approximately 100 percent of the burden of the corporate tax. Capital in both the corporate and noncorporate sector bear the tax burden because the total stock of capital is reallocated until the two sectors' net-of-tax returns are equal. This can only occur if there is a decrease in the net-of-tax return to capital in the noncorporate sector. Clearly, this result could only come from a general-equilibrium analysis.

The Harberger framework was extended and applied in a number of ways. Charles McLure (1969) extended the model to include more than one region, and Peter Mieszkowski (1972) emphasized the general-equilibrium effects of the property tax on capital prices. Michael Boskin (1975) estimated the welfare cost of the nontaxation of household activity. These extensions and applications are summarized in McLure (1975).

Computational general-equilibrium models

The limitations of two-sector models clearly demonstrated the need for models that could easily incorporate large numbers of sectors. The models that met this need came in two different forms. Johansen (1960) developed one form in a model for Norway. The Johansen approach, based on input-output analysis, employs matrix algebra to solve a system of linearized equations. This approach achieved its greatest popularity in Australia with the ORANI model and its descendants (Dixon et al. 1982). The Australian research effort focused more on international trade and industrial policy issues than on taxation. However, tax-policy issues have also been addressed (Powell and Lawson 1990).

By the late 1960s, Scarf (1973) had developed an algorithm that calculates a general equilibrium for an economy with any number of producers and consumers. Scarf's model avoids the small-change assumption of the Harberger model, as well as the linearization assumption of Johansen-type models. Studies using the methods of Johansen or Scarf are called computational general equilibrium (CGE) analyses.

The first major application of Scarf's methods in the area of taxation was by Shoven and Whalley (1972). Subsequently, Shoven (1976) used a CGE model to reexamine the corporate tax. He found that, for two sectors, the CGE model gives results similar to those of Harberger. However, when Shoven extended the CGE calculations to include 12 sectors, the estimated efficiency cost of the corporation income tax increased by about 40 percent. This indicated that incorporating more sectors can have important effects on the results of a general-equilibrium simulation exercise. According to these CGE calculations, the ratio of excess burden to revenue for the corporation tax could be as great as 24 percent.

Even Shoven's calculations probably understate the efficiency cost of the corporate tax because, like Harberger's calculations, they ignore the dynamic effects on capital accumulation. In the late 1970s and 1980s, CGE modelers turned more of their attention to dynamic issues. Shoven, Whalley, and their colleagues constructed a 19-sector model of the U.S. economy and tax system. This model calculates dynamic sequences of equilibria, and thus allows researchers to study the effects of taxes on capital accumulation. Ballard, Fullerton, Shoven, and Whalley (1985) used this model (known as the BFSW model) to study the integration of the corporate and personal income taxes (as well as other tax-policy questions). The model yields the result that labor may bear a significant portion of the corporation tax in the long run. This is because the tax reduces the rate of capital accumulation, which, in the long run, reduces the capital/labor ratio and causes wages to be lower than they would otherwise have been.

Jorgenson and Yun (1990) also studied tax policies with a multisector, dynamic CGE model. They found that tax reforms could lead to substantial welfare gains. Some of the greatest potential gains come from indexing the income tax base and incorporating the income of household assets into the tax base. According to Jorgenson and Yun, some tax reform proposals are associated with long-term gains of more than 10 percent of national wealth. This contrasts with welfare gains of 1 or 2 percent of wealth in the BFSW model. A large part of the difference is explained by differences in the dynamic specification. Jorgenson and Yun use a consumer that does not die. This specification can lead to extremely large savings responses. Consequently, the gains from dynamic tax-policy changes tend to be overstated.

None of the studies mentioned so far consider the effects of tax policy changes on people of different ages. Auerbach and Kotlikoff (1987) assessed these effects using a general-equilibrium model. At any given time, the model includes 55 overlapping generations of life-cycle consumers. Over time, consumers grow old and die, and new consumers are born. Auerbach and Kotlikoff used their model to study a wide variety of tax policy issues, including deficit finance, generational accounting, and Social Security. One of their most important insights has to do with the gains from moving toward a consumption tax. Under certain conditions, the long-run gains can be very large. However, a significant part of the long-run gain is merely a transfer from those who are old at the time of the policy change. The elderly are harmed when we shift from an income tax to a consumption tax because the consumption tax punishes spending, which is more likely to occur near the end of life.

Altig et al. (2001) use an enhanced version of the Auerbach-Kotlikoff model to assess the effects of a variety of fundamental tax reforms. Altig et al. and Fullerton and Lim Rogers (1993) incorporate variation both across age groups and within age groups. This detail in the household sector allows these authors to pay more attention to distributional issues than is paid in many CGE studies.

The models Auerbach and Kotlikoff (1987) and Altig et al. (2001) use suffer from some of the problems mentioned above in relation to the work of Jorgenson and Yun (1990). Regardless of whether the model involves overlapping generations or infinite-horizon consumers, a broad class of widely used dynamic models can generate unrealistically large responses. One of the most important challenges facing CGE modelers is to improve the techniques of calibration so as to generate responses that are more in line with the results of econometric studies. For discussion of these issues, see Ballard (2000) and Engen, Gravelle, and Smetters (1997).

As computational techniques have improved, there has been rapid growth in the number of researchers who use CGE models. Because of the flexibility of the approach, virtually any topic can be studied. Fullerton (1982) investigated revenue elasticities and the "Laffer Curve." He found that broad-based taxes in the United States are very unlikely to produce perverse revenue effects, whereby increases in tax rates would lead to decreases in tax revenues. Ballard and Medema (1993),

Bovenberg and Goulder (1997), and Ballard, Goddeeris, and Kim (2005) have studied the effects of environmental taxes. General-equilibrium modelers have also studied the interaction between taxes and the financial system (Slemrod 1983; Galper et al. 1988), the effects of a switch to a value-added tax (Ballard, Scholz, and Shoven 1987), the marginal welfare costs for different capital taxes (Fullerton and Henderson 1989), the effects of taxes on the housing market (Goulder 1989), the excess burden of commodity taxes (Goulder and Williams 2003), and the efficiency and distributional effects of universal health-insurance coverage (Ballard and Goddeeris 1999).

In most of the studies mentioned above, little attention has been devoted to international issues. However, studies such as those of Whalley (1980), Goulder and Eichengreen (1989), and Ballard and Kang (2003) have focused on the interactions between the tax system and the international economy. Researchers have also applied CGE techniques to tax policy questions in a number of other countries, including Belgium (Dewatripont et al. 1991), Mexico (Serra-Puche 1984), the Philippines (Clarete and Whalley 1988), Sweden (Bergman and Lundgren 1990), and the United Kingdom (Piggott and Whalley 1985).

ADDITIONAL READINGS

Altig, David, Alan J. Auerbach, Laurence J. Kotlikoff, Kent A. Smetters, and Jan Walliser. "Simulating Fundamental Tax Reform in the United States." *American Economic Review* 91 (June 2001): 574–95.

Auerbach, Alan J., and Laurence J. Kotlikoff. *Dynamic Fiscal Policy.* Cambridge, U.K.: Cambridge University Press, 1987.

Ballard, Charles L. "How Many Hours Are in a Simulated Day? The Effects of Time Endowment on the Results of Tax-Policy Simulation Models." Unpublished paper, Michigan State University, 2000.

Ballard, Charles L., and John H. Goddeeris. "Financing Universal Health Care in the United States: A General Equilibrium Analysis of Efficiency and Distributional Effects." *National Tax Journal* 52 (March 1999): 31–52.

Ballard, Charles L., and Kiwon Kang. "International Ramifications of U.S. Tax-Policy Changes." *Journal of Policy Modeling* 25 (November 2003): 825–35.

Ballard, Charles L., and Steven G. Medema. "The Marginal Efficiency Effects of Taxes and Subsidies in the Presence of Externalities: A Computational General Equilibrium Approach." *Journal of Public Economics* 52 (September 1993): 199–216.

Ballard, Charles L., John H. Goddeeris, and Sang-Kyum Kim. "Non-Homothetic Preferences and the Non-Environmental Effects of Environmental Taxes." *International Tax and Public Finance* 12, no. 2 (2005): 115–30.

Ballard, Charles L., John Karl Scholz, and John B. Shoven. "The Value-Added Tax: A General Equilibrium Look at Its Efficiency and Incidence." In *The Effects of Taxation on Capital Formation,* edited by Martin Feldstein. Chicago: University of Chicago Press, 1987.

Ballard, Charles L., Don Fullerton, John B. Shoven, and John Whalley. *A General Equilibrium Model for Tax Policy Evaluation.* Chicago: University of Chicago Press, 1985.

Bergman, Lars, and Stefan Lundgren. "General Equilibrium Approaches to Energy Policy Analysis in Sweden." In *General Equilibrium Modeling and Economic Policy Analysis,* edited by Lars Bergman, Dale Jorgenson, and Ernö Zalai (351–82). Cambridge, MA: Basil Blackwell, Inc., 1990.

Boskin, Michael J. "Efficiency Aspects of the Differential Tax Treatment of Market and Household Economic Activity." *Journal of Public Economics* 4 (February 1975): 1–25.

Bovenberg, A. Lans, and Lawrence H. Goulder. "Costs of Environmentally Motivated Taxes in the Presence of Other Taxes: General-Equilibrium Analyses." *National Tax Journal* 50 (March 1997): 59–88.

Brown, Harry Gunnison. "The Incidence of a General Output or a General Sales Tax." *Journal of Political Economy* 47 (April 1939): 254–62.

Clarete, Ramon, and John Whalley. "Interactions between Trade Policies and Domestic Distortions in a Small Open Developing Country." *Journal of International Economics* 24 (May 1988): 345–58.

Dewatripont, C., Simon Erlich, Victor Ginsburgh, and Denise Van Regemorter. "The Effects on Unemployment of Reducing Social Security Contributions: A General Equilibrium Analysis for Belgium." In *Applied General Equilibrium Modeling,* edited by Henk Don, Theo van de Klundert, and Jarig van Sinderen (135–53). Dordrecht, Netherlands: Kluwer Academic Publishers, 1991.

Dixon, Peter B., Brian R. Parmenter, John Sutton, and D. P. Vincent. *ORANI: A Multisectoral Model of the Australian Economy.* Amsterdam: North-Holland Publishing Company, 1982.

Engen, Eric, Jane Gravelle, and Kent Smetters. "Dynamic Tax Models: Why They Do the Things They Do." *National Tax Journal* 50 (September 1997): 657–82.

Fullerton, Don. "On the Possibility of an Inverse Relationship between Tax Rates and Government Revenues." *Journal of Public Economics* 19 (October 1982): 3–22.

Fullerton, Don, and Yolanda K. Henderson. "The Marginal Excess Burden of Different Capital Tax Instruments." *Review of Economics and Statistics* 71 (August 1989): 435–42.

Fullerton, Don, and Diane Lim Rogers. *Who Bears the Lifetime Tax Burden?* Washington, DC: The Brookings Institution, 1993.

Galper, Harvey, Robert Lucke, and Eric Toder. "A General Equilibrium Analysis of Tax Reform." In *Uneasy Compromise: Problems of a Hybrid Income-Consumption Tax,* edited by Henry J. Aaron, Harvey Galper, and Joseph A. Pechman (59–108). Washington, DC: The Brookings Institution, 1988.

Goulder, Lawrence H. "Tax Policy, Housing Prices, and Housing Investment." *Regional Science and Urban Economics* 19 (May 1989): 281–304.

Goulder, Lawrence H., and Barry Eichengreen. "Savings Promotion, Investment Promotion, and International Competitiveness." In *Trade Policies for International Competitiveness,* edited by Rob Feenstra (5–44). Chicago: University of Chicago Press, 1989.

Goulder, Lawrence H., and Roberton C. Williams III. "The Substantial Bias from Ignoring General Equilibrium Effects in Estimating Excess Burden, and a Practical Solution." *Journal of Political Economy* 111 (August 2003): 898–927.

Harberger, Arnold C. "The Incidence of the Corporation Income Tax." *Journal of Political Economy* 70 (June 1962): 215–40.

Johansen, Leif. *A Multi-Sectoral Study of Economic Growth.* Amsterdam: North-Holland, 1960.

Johnson, Harry G. *The Two Sector Model of General Equilibrium.* Chicago: Aldine-Atherton Press, 1971.

Jorgenson, Dale W., and Kun-Young Yun. "Tax Reform and U.S. Economic Growth." *Journal of Political Economy* 98 (October 1990): S151–93.

McLure, Charles E., Jr. "The Inter-Regional Incidence of General Regional Taxes." *Public Finance* 24, no. 3 (1969): 457–83.

———. "General Equilibrium Incidence Analysis: The Harberger Model after Ten Years." *Journal of Public Economics* 4 (February 1975): 125–61.

Mieszkowski, Peter M. "The Property Tax: An Excise or a Profits Tax?" *Journal of Public Economics* 1 (April 1972): 73–96.

Musgrave, Richard A. *The Theory of Public Finance.* New York: McGraw-Hill, 1959.

Piggott, John R., and John Whalley. *U.K. Tax Policy and Applied General Equilibrium Analysis.* Cambridge, U.K.: Cambridge University Press, 1985.

Powell, Alan A., and Tony Lawson. "A Decade of Applied General Equilibrium Modeling for Policy Work." In *General Equilibrium Modeling and Economic Policy Analysis,* edited by Lars Bergman, Dale Jorgenson, and Ernö Zalai 241–90. Cambridge, MA: Basil Blackwell, Inc., 1990.

Scarf, Herbert E. (with the collaboration of Terje Hansen). *The Computation of Economic Equilibria.* New Haven, CT: Yale University Press, 1973.

Serra-Puche, Jaime. "A General Equilibrium Model for the Mexican Economy." In *Applied General Equilibrium Analysis,* edited by Herbert E. Scarf and John B. Shoven (447–82). Cambridge, U.K.: Cambridge University Press, 1984.

Shoven, John B. "The Incidence and Efficiency Effects of Taxes on Income from Capital." *Journal of Political Economy* 84 (December 1976): 1261–83.

Shoven, John B., and John Whalley. "A General Equilibrium Calculation of the Effects of Differential Taxation of Income from Capital in the U.S." *Journal of Public Economics* 1 (November 1972): 281–322.

Slemrod, Joel. "A General Equilibrium Model of Taxation with Endogenous Financial Behavior." In *Behavioral Simulation Methods in Tax Policy Analysis,* edited by Martin Feldstein (427–58). Chicago: University of Chicago Press, 1983.

Wells, Paul. "General Equilibrium Analysis of Excise Taxes." *American Economic Review* 45 (June 1955): 345–59.

Whalley, John. "Discriminating Features of Domestic Factor Tax Systems in a Goods Mobile–Factors Immobile Trade Model." *Journal of Political Economy* 88 (December 1980): 1177–1202.

Cross-references: cost of capital; excess burden; incidence of taxes; income tax, corporate, federal; integration, corporate tax.

Generational accounting

John Sturrock
Arlington, Virginia

Generational accounting estimates how fiscal policy distributes resources among the average members of current and future generations.

Because someone, sometime, must pay for all that government ever buys, current fiscal policy affects both current and future generations. If government does not pay for its purchases of goods and services with current taxes, it must raise future taxes to retire the ensuing debt or pay interest forever. If one generation pays less, another pays more. Sooner or later, someone pays.

Fundamentals of generational accounting

To measure who pays how much, Auerbach, Gokhale, and Kotlikoff (1991) propose a system they call generational accounting. The system estimates the real (inflation-adjusted) net amount that the average member of any generation pays to all levels of government—federal, state, and local. A generation is defined by sex and year of birth. For example, current males comprise newborn boys, 1-year-old boys, and so on; future females comprise girls born next year, the year after that, and so on.

Net amounts paid to government consist of net taxes—that is, taxes minus transfers. Transfers are government benefits (such as welfare, Medicare, or Social Security), which differ from government payments for purchases in that the recipients do not provide current goods or services. In effect, transfers constitute negative taxes. For example, if a person pays $10,000 in taxes in a given year and receives $4,000 in transfers, his or her net taxes equal $6,000. Generational accounting does not estimate who benefits from government purchases (payments to businesses and government workers to provide items such as defense, highways, or public education); the system calculates only who pays for purchases with their net taxes. To compare the net taxes of different generations on the same per capita basis, generational accounting usually expresses the results in terms of the net taxes each generation pays over its lifetime as a share of the income it earns over its lifetime.

Theoretical assumptions

The calculations depend on two standard concepts—present value and the zero-sum constraint. Present value measures how much a future payment or receipt is worth today, depending on a discount (compound interest) rate. For instance, if the discount rate is 10 percent, a payment of $110 next year is worth $100 today; a payment of $121 two years from now is also worth $100 today. To find the present value of a stream of payments over many years, the analyst finds the present value of the payment in each year, then adds those present values together to find their sum.

The zero-sum constraint specifies that someone pays—future generations must pay with interest for government purchases not paid for by previous generations. That idea may be expressed as an equation:

$$PVF_t = NDG_t + PVG_t - PVC_t$$

where PVF_t is the present value (in the base year t) of the net taxes of future generations, NDG_t is the current net debt of government, PVG_t is the present value of prospective government purchases, and PVC_t is the present value of the net taxes of current (living) generations. The zero-sum constraint does not specify that government cannot borrow more or that it must ever retire any of its debt, only that it cannot borrow forever to pay interest.

Empirical assumptions

The calculations of the elements of the zero-sum constraint depend on assumptions about the policy schedule for taxes and transfers. Taxes are broken into those that apply to payroll, labor income, capital income, home value, and other bases (mostly sales). Transfers are broken into Social Security, Medicare, Medicaid, Food Stamps, unemployment insurance, and other programs. The per capita schedule by age and sex for each tax or transfer is estimated from official survey data. For instance, the average 40-year-old woman pays about half as much in payroll taxes as the average 40-year-old man; the average 85-year-old man receives about three-quarters more in Medicare than the average 65-year-old man. Generational accounting assumes that such ratios remain fixed (although the calculations for Social Security include the scheduled changes in the normal retirement age).

The calculations for generational accounting also depend on demographic and economic projections. For a base population, the system uses the Social Security Administration's (SSA's) 75-year intermediate path. That population projection is extended through 2200 by assuming that the age- and sex-specific rates of fertility, mortality, and net immigration remain at their respective values in the last year of SSA's projection. After 2200, the age and sex distribution of the population is assumed to remain constant. Finally, the calculations depend on an assumed discount rate and on projected growth of effective labor productivity (output per work hour, adjusted for the age and sex of the worker). For example, a base calculation for 1998 set the real discount rate at 6 percent (about the historical real rate of return on equity) and assumed that productivity grew in the long run at 1.2 percent a year.

The solution for the zero-sum constraint

Given such assumptions, the system finds the value of each element of the equation for the zero-sum constraint. The current value of government debt is estimated as the algebraic sum of past deficits. For the present value of prospective government purchases, the system starts with a stream of total purchases taken from an official long-term projection by the Office of Management and Budget or the Congressional Budget Office. Real per capita purchases by age are extended beyond the official horizon by assuming that they grow at the same rate as productivity. Those per capita amounts, together with the projected population by age, determine the extended stream of total prospective purchases. The entire stream is then discounted to find its present value.

The same method applies to the present value of the net taxes of all current generations over their remaining lives. The system starts from an official projection of the total amount of each type of tax or transfer, finds the projected per capita amount by age and sex, extends the projection by assuming that the real per capita amount by age and sex grows beyond the official projection at the same rate as productivity, discounts the resulting per capita stream for each current generation, and adds the resulting present values over the members of all current generations—newborns through those age 90 or older.

Given the values of those three elements, the zero-sum constraint's equation determines the present value of future generations' net taxes. There is no way to say how future generations will share their overall burden. As an illustrative device, therefore, generational accounting assumes that future generations all pay net taxes at the same rate.

To compare everyone on the same lifetime basis, generational accounting calculates the effective rate at which each generation pays net taxes over its entire life—its lifetime net tax rate. That calculation requires estimates of each genera-

tion's lifetime net taxes, past as well as prospective. Estimates of past net taxes use survey data (as far back as they go) to break each total tax or transfer into per capita amounts by age and sex. Given a generation's past and prospective net taxes, its net tax rate is the present value at birth of its lifetime net taxes as a percentage of the present value at birth of its lifetime labor income.

Examples of the findings of generational accounting

As estimated for a base year of 1998, the lifetime net tax rates of successive U.S. generations have risen and then fallen over the century (table 1). The early rise largely paid for an increase in the share of government purchases; the later decline coincided with longer lifetimes and higher per capita transfers for health care and Social Security. Most striking, the estimates reveal the extent to which policy has been biased against the future. To keep government purchases on their scheduled path, future generations would have to pay lifetime net taxes at a rate 77 percent higher than current newborns will pay—46 percent versus 26 percent. Of course, such an estimate predicts not what will happen, only what would happen if the assumed policy schedule remained fixed for current generations.

Limitations and contributions of generational accounting

Like most empirical efforts, generational accounting rests on uncertain or arguable premises. The estimates can vary under alternative forecasts of population and productivity or under different assumptions about who effectively pays a given tax or receives a given transfer. Generational accounting also assumes that prospective incomes are fixed, thereby ignoring the channel through which current deficits impose costs on young and future generations by reducing current national saving and hence prospective pretax income.

TABLE 1. Lifetime Net Tax Rates

Year of birth	Net tax rate (%)
1900	23
1910	27
1920	28
1930	29
1940	30
1950	30
1960	30
1970	30
1980	28
1990	26
1998	26
Future	46

Source: Gokhale et al. 2000.
Note: Future generations are those born after the base year 1998.

Finally, the results depend heavily on the assumed discount rate. For example, given the other base assumptions in 1998, the estimated lifetime net tax rate of future generations exceeded that of current newborns by 130 percent under a 9 percent discount rate and by 53 percent under a 3 percent discount rate. The higher rate approximates the real rate of return on private capital; the lower rate approximates the real rate of interest on long-term federal debt. The two rates differ largely because capital market participants assign different premiums to the risk of holding those assets. Prospective net taxes are also uncertain, but there is no market in them from which to infer the cost of their risk. Even if there were, people of different ages and with different lifetime incomes need not assign their prospective taxes and transfers the same cost of risk and, thus, need not discount them at the same rate.

Despite such limitations, generational accounting demonstrates how fiscal policy affects various generations. Even when results are uncertain or approximate, they often reveal overall patterns and suggest issues for further analysis. The system offers valuable insights that should inform policymakers, explicitly representing future generations and framing issues on lifetime bases in terms of ultimate constraints.

ADDITIONAL READINGS

This entry is an abridged version of material from two sources:

Congressional Budget Office. *Who Pays and When? An Assessment of Generational Accounting.* Washington, DC: Congressional Budget Office, 1995.

Gokhale, Jagadeesh, Benjamin R. Page, Joan Potter, and John R. Sturrock. "Generational Accounts for the United States: An Update." *American Economic Review* 90, no. 2 (May 2000): 293–96.

Other references include the following:

Auerbach, Alan J., Jagadeesh Gokhale, and Laurence J. Kotlikoff. "Generational Accounts: A Meaningful Alternative to Deficit Accounting." In *Tax Policy and the Economy,* vol. 5, edited by David Bradford (55–110). Cambridge, MA: MIT Press, 1991.

Auerbach, Alan J., Laurence J. Kotlikoff, and Willi Leibfritz, eds. *Generational Accounting around the World.* Chicago: University of Chicago Press, 1999.

Kotlikoff, Laurence J. *Generational Accounting: Knowing Who Pays, and When, for What We Spend.* New York: The Free Press, 1992.

———. "Generational Policy." In *The Handbook of Public Economics,* vol. 4, edited by Alan J. Auerbach and Martin S. Feldstein (1873–1932). Amsterdam: Elsevier, 2002.

Cross-references: earmarking of taxes; Social Security benefits, federal taxation; Social Security Trust Fund.

Head tax

Joseph J. Cordes
George Washington University

A tax levied in a fixed amount on individuals or households without regard to economic or other circumstances of the household.

Head taxes are an example of a lump-sum tax. Because the amount of the tax is fixed, without regard to what the taxpayer does, it cannot affect the taxpayer's behavior (unless the taxpayer migrates from the jurisdiction that levies the head tax). Head taxes, or poll taxes as they are sometimes called, have mainly served as an intellectual benchmark against which to assess the incidence of other, more practical taxes. In 1990, however, the British government attempted to replace the residential property tax with a poll tax in the form of a flat rate community charge, levied on all adults in a jurisdiction. This tax proved to be enormously unpopular and played a significant role in the fall from power of then–Prime Minister Margaret Thatcher.

ADDITIONAL READING

Smith, Peter. "Lessons from the British Poll Tax Disaster." *National Tax Journal* 44, no. 4 (1991): 421–37.

Health expenditures, tax treatment of

Louise Sheiner
Federal Reserve Board of Governors

Federal tax treatment of health expenditures made by individuals and by businesses on behalf of employees.

The federal tax system provides favorable tax treatment to health expenditures in numerous ways, the most important being that employer-paid health insurance expenses are deductible for the employer and not included in employees' taxable wages; taxpayers with cafeteria plans may be able to deduct their share of premium payments and some out-of-pocket health expenses; and health expenditures exceeding 7.5 percent of adjusted gross income are deductible for taxpayers who itemize deductions.

This favorable tax treatment reduced income and payroll taxes by roughly $100 billion in 2003, making it one of the largest "tax expenditures" in the current income tax system (Joint Committee on Taxation 2003).

Efficiency effects

The largest and most important tax expenditure for health is the exclusion of employer-paid health insurance premiums. As has long been recognized, the tax treatment of employer-paid health insurance provides an incentive for workers to be compensated in the form of health insurance rather than in cash wages. A $1 increase in employer-paid health expenditures costs only $(1 - ti - t_p)/(1 + t_p)$, where ti is the income tax rate (federal plus net-of-federal state tax) and t_p is the payroll tax rate. So, for an employee facing a 20 percent marginal income tax rate and a 7.65 percent payroll tax rate, an additional $1 in employer-paid health insurance costs only 67 cents.

Analyzing this tax subsidy's effect is not straightforward. The current subsidy is not simply a subsidy for all health expenditures, but rather for health expenditures financed through employer-paid health insurance premiums. Monies employers spend on health insurance premiums are excludable from taxable income, but employee health expenses for the employee's share of the insurance premium, for coinsurance and deductibles, and for noninsured health expenses are generally not deductible from taxable income. This tax structure can lead to distortions in different dimensions, including how much health insurance to consume, how much health to insure, and whether to purchase insurance through an employer.

Effect on health expenses and health insurance

Feldstein and Friedman (1977) were among the first to analyze how this excludability of employer-paid health insurance premiums affects the structure of employer-paid health insurance. They found that the tax subsidy reduced coinsurance rates (increasing the share of health expenditures covered by insurance) by about 50 percent. Recent work (see Gruber 2001) also found that the tax subsidy raises health spending significantly, both by inducing employers to offer insurance and by increasing the amount of insured health spending. Jack and Sheiner (1997) compared the efficiency consequences of a health insurance subsidy with those of a broad subsidy to health care. On the one hand, limiting the subsidy to health insurance premiums leads consumers to purchase insurance that is more heavily weighted toward premiums—that is, with lower coinsurance and deductibles—thereby increasing health expenditures. On the other hand, providing a subsidy to out-of-pocket payments reduces the effectiveness of any *given* coinsurance and deductible at holding down health expenditures. However, for reasonable parameter estimates, Jack and Sheiner found that the first effect prevailed, and that a subsidy to health insurance alone leads to lower coinsurance rates and greater health expenditures than would a broader subsidy to all health expenditures. For example, in their model, the current subsidy reduces coinsurance rates by about 40 percent, whereas a tax system that also provided the same rate of subsidy to out-of-pocket health expenditures would reduce coinsurance rates by only about 25 percent. They calculated that these lower coinsurance rates increased health expenditures by 13 and 7 percent, respectively.

Effect of the tax subsidy on pooling

The current tax system provides favorable tax treatment only to health insurance purchased through an employer. This subsidy encourages workers to purchase their insurance through their employer, rather than individually or through other associations. Two questions arise: is employer-based health insurance a good thing, and, if so, would workers purchase insurance this way even without the tax preference? There are differing views as to whether an employer-based insurance system is advantageous (Burman and Rodgers 1992). On the one hand, if individuals choose where to work for reasons unrelated to health status, then employer-based insurance can avoid the adverse selection problems that plague the private insurance market. On the other hand, if the availability of health insurance influences job choice, then the link between health insurance and employment may distort the labor market. For example, workers with preexisting conditions or with a preference for a particular health insurance plan may be less likely to switch jobs, and workers may be less likely to work for small firms because these firms typically face higher health insurance costs.

It is questionable whether employment-based insurance can exist in the absence of some form of employer-based tax subsidy. If workers can get equally tax advantaged health insurance through an individual market, then workers in good health might choose to drop employer insurance or to work in places that do not offer it, subjecting the employer-based insurance market to the same selection problems as those in the individual insurance market. This is a potential problem with proposals to provide greater tax subsidies for the individual purchase of health insurance.

Can the tax treatment of health expenditures explain the high rate of medical inflation?

While the tax treatment of health insurance clearly increases health expenditures, it is not known whether the tax system affects the growth rate of medical expenditures. The major factor underlying medical expenditure growth is the adoption of new technology, and most standard models with exogenous technology growth imply that constant tax policy does not affect the growth rate of technology adoption. But, it is possible that tax policy affects the type of insurance coverage, and that insurance coverage affects take-up rates of technology (Pauly 1986). It is also possible that technology itself is endogenous, and that the level of health expenditures affects the growth rate. None of these issues has been examined empirically.

ADDITIONAL READINGS

Burman, Leonard, and Jack Rodgers. "Tax Preferences and Employment-Based Health Insurance." *National Tax Journal* 45, no. 3 (1992): 331–46.
Feldstein, Martin, and Bernard Friedman. "Tax Subsidies, the Rational Demand for Insurance, and the Health Care Crisis." *Journal of Public Economics* 7 (April 1977): 155–78.
Gruber, Jonathan. "Taxes and Health Insurance." National Bureau of Economic Research Working Paper No. 8657. Cambridge, MA: National Bureau of Economic Research, December 2001.
Jack, William, and Louise Sheiner. "Welfare-Improving Health Expenditure Subsidies." *American Economic Review* 87 (March 1997): 206–21.
Joint Committee on Taxation. "Estimates of Federal Tax Expenditures for Fiscal Years 2004–2008." JCS-8-03. Washington, DC: Joint Committee on Taxation, December 2003.
Pauly, Mark. "Taxation, Health Insurance, and Market Failure in the Medical Economy." *Journal of Economic Literature* 24 (June 1986): 629–75.

Cross-references: fringe benefits; income tax, federal.

Highway Trust Fund, federal

Kenneth D. Simonson
Associated General Contractors of America

Federal trust fund that finances highway construction and certain other federal spending on transportation.

The federal Highway Trust Fund was created in 1956 to segregate revenues and outlays for highway construction from the rest of the federal budget. In large part, the fund continues as originally enacted, although there have been significant changes in both receipts and expenditures.

History

Before 1956, the federal gasoline tax went into the general fund. Congress appropriated money for highway spending independently of the amount collected from any one tax.

The Federal-Aid Highway Act of 1956 set up the Highway Trust Fund to provide continuity in planning and spending on highways, with a secure source of funding. The trust fund was credited with receipts from taxes on motor fuels, tires, trucks, and buses. Expenditures from the fund were authorized for payments to states for construction of the interstate highway system and other federal-aid highways. The payments were made at specified matching rates, generally 90 percent federal funds for interstate highways and 50 percent for primary routes. Construction of the interstate system was expected to require 13 years, and taxes were authorized for 16 years, through June 30, 1972. The trust fund was also credited with interest on unspent receipts and was debited for refunds paid from the Treasury to nonhighway users of fuel and local transit systems. Later laws repeatedly extended the life of the fund and the taxes going into it.

The Surface Transportation Assistance Act of 1982 made the most sweeping changes in the trust fund since its inception. Congress acted on reports it had requested from the administration showing that projected revenues were insufficient to allow completion of the interstate system and other spending, and that heavy trucks were not paying an amount proportionate to the pavement damage they caused. Accordingly, the act restructured highway taxes: It more than doubled fuel taxes (from 4 to 9 cents per gallon for gasoline and diesel) and earmarked 1 cent from each for a new Mass Transit Account. The truck tax, which had been imposed at a rate of 10 percent of the manufacturer's cost, was changed to a 12 percent retail excise tax, imposed at time of first retail sale or long-term lease. The tax on tread rubber, tires, and inner tubes became a tax on heavy tires only. A highway-use tax for heavy vehicles was hiked from $240 to a range of $100 to $1,900, depending on gross weight.

On the spending side, the act designated outlays for mass transit capital grants from the Mass Transit Account and created the so-called Interstate 4R program allowing expenditures for reconstruction, resurfacing, restoration, and rehabilitation, as well as the anticipated completion of the interstate network.

Truck taxes were further modified in 1984 to cap the highway-use tax at $550. To make up the revenue, the diesel tax was increased to 15 cents per gallon. Additional extensions of taxes and spending, plus minor modifications to each, were enacted in 1987. Fuel taxes were increased again for both Highway Trust Fund and general fund purposes in 1990 and 1993.

The Intermodal Surface Transportation Efficiency Act of 1991 (ISTEA, popularly pronounced "ice-tea") significantly changed spending priorities. The act made what were intended to be final allocations for completing the interstate system and created a new national highway system, consisting of interstates and other roads of "primary federal interest," to be supported by lower federal contributions, generally 80 percent. Although the chief focus of trust fund spending continued to be state-selected outlays on major highways, the act gave metropolitan planning organizations a voice in choosing projects. Highway construction was de-emphasized in favor of transit, bikeway, preservation, intermodal, and "intelligent vehicle/highway systems" projects. In short, what was formerly a purely highway construction funding mechanism was diversified into funding other modes and goals such as air quality improvement and technology support.

In 1997, the Transportation Equity Act for the 21st Century (TEA-21) returned the remaining 4.3 cents per gallon of general fund revenue to the trust fund, bringing trust fund rates to 18.3 cents for gasoline and 24.3 cents for diesel; 2.86 cents of those amounts are credited to the Mass Transit Account. That act also introduced a concept called revenue aligned budget authority, which required adjusting spending if actual trust fund receipts exceeded or fell short of estimates made at the time of enactment, so that Congress could no longer accumulate trust fund surpluses to make the unified budget deficit appear smaller.

Although TEA-21 expired at the end of September 2003, as of mid-2004, Congress had been unable to agree on funding totals or formulas for distributing funds for fiscal years 2004–2009. Instead, spending in 2004 was governed by short-term extensions of TEA-21. In fiscal year 2004, Highway Trust Fund receipts total approximately $29 billion. Outlays total $33 billion.

Policy issues

The United States is exceptional, if not unique, in segregating fuel and other tax revenue for highway purposes. Support for the general principle of dedicating revenue collected from highway users is widespread at the federal and state level. Nevertheless, several issues arise as to how the revenue should be apportioned and how broadly it should be spent.

One issue concerns the interdependence of trust fund and overall federal spending. Even though highway outlays come from an earmarked source, there are several constraints on this spending beyond having a positive balance in the trust fund. The budget resolution adopted annually by Congress dictates total federal spending. The resolution caps "discretionary" spending, which includes transportation. Highway interests must compete with other transportation priorities, which in turn must win a share of the discretionary piece of the total budget.

The level of highway taxes is interrelated with both total federal receipts and highway spending. In most years, trust fund receipts closely match outlays. However, the bulk of receipts are derived from taxes on the number of gallons of fuel sold. Increasing fuel efficiency of both automobiles and trucks has meant that fuel tax receipts grow very slowly in the absence of tax rate increases, even though the number of vehicle miles of travel usually rises from year to year. At the same time, the costs of highway spending programs tend to rise in line with prices and wages, meaning that the number of highway projects financed by a given set of tax rates declines from year to year. Thus, highway-spending proponents would like to see increasing highway tax rates. But highway taxes must go through the same legislative process as other taxes. In practice, this has meant that, since 1990, highway taxes go up only as part of a large budget "reconciliation" bill that includes many tax and spending changes and that raises fuel taxes for mass transit and sometimes general fund, as well as highway, purposes.

A third issue concerns the mix of highway taxes. Legislation in 1982 attempted to charge automobiles, light trucks, and heavy trucks appropriate shares of the total tax burden. The 1982 allocation was based on methodology that was controversial at the time and became increasingly outdated as each vehicle type's proportions, miles traveled, and fuel economy changed. Yet a 1997 update by the Federal Highway Administration concluded that the mix of taxes in effect in 1996 did allocate tax burdens fairly equitably among vehicle types.

Furthermore, some critics argue that existing taxes fail to charge accurately for either pavement damage or congestion costs. They suggest that heavy trucks be charged a tax that varies with distance traveled and maximum weight per axle or overall, and that automobiles be charged for use of congested roads through tolls, possibly varying with time of day. Defenders of the current truck tax system say that a combination of fuel and tire taxes and a weight-based annual use tax approximates a tax on distance and vehicle weights without requiring the technology or extensive administrative burden required of true weight-distance taxes. Opponents of congestion pricing believe it is politically and, perhaps, technologically infeasible to collect tolls from all vehicles in crowded urban areas.

ADDITIONAL READINGS

Congressional Budget Office. *Innovative Financing of Highways: An Analysis of Proposals.* Washington, DC: Congressional Budget Office, 1998.

Small, Kenneth A., Clifford Winston, and Carol A. Evans. *Road Work: A New Highway Pricing and Investment Policy.* Washington, DC: The Brookings Institution, 1989.

Talley, Louis Alan. "Federal Excise Taxes on Gasoline and the Highway Trust Fund: A Short History." Washington, DC: U.S. Library of Congress, Congressional Research Service Report RL-30304, March 29, 2000.

U.S. Department of Transportation. *Federal Highway Administration. 1997 Federal Highway Cost Allocation Study.* Washington, DC: U.S. Department of Transportation, August 1997.

U.S. General Accounting Office. "Highway Trust Fund: Overview of Highway Trust Fund Financing." Testimony GAO-02-435T. Washington, DC: U.S. General Accounting Office, February 11, 2002.

U.S. House of Representatives, Committee on Transportation and Infrastructure. "Hearing on Long-term Outlook on Highway Trust Fund: Are Fuel Taxes a Viable Measure?" Staff memo. Washington, DC: Committee on Transportation and Infrastructure, July 16, 2002.

Cross-references: benefit principle; earmarking of taxes; user charges, federal.

Homeowner preferences, individual income tax

Jane G. Gravelle
Congressional Research Service, Library of Congress

Income tax provisions that favor investment in owner-occupied housing.

Housing is an important part of the capital stock, and owner-occupied housing receives favorable treatment. Two of the biggest tax expenditure items are the mortgage interest deduc-

tion (costing more than $40 billion per year in 1997) and the property tax deduction (costing about $16 billion). Although these tax subsidies attract considerable attention, the fundamental benefit is that imputed rent is not included in income; if it were, business deductions for interest and property tax (along with depreciation and maintenance) would be appropriate. As a result of these tax preferences, the return on investment in owner-occupied housing is subject to negligible income taxes. Families are encouraged to own, rather than rent, housing and to consume too much housing.

There is disagreement as to the magnitude of the efficiency loss (which has been estimated to range from 0.1 to 1.0 percent of output). There are some arguments in favor of benefits for housing. They include the difficulty of taxing imputed rent and the possibility of spillovers for home ownership. Such spillovers have not been measured and are unlikely to be of a magnitude that would justify the significant tax benefits. Disallowing deductions would be a way of offsetting the benefit from exclusion of imputed rent, which is difficult to administer, but these options are imperfect. Disallowing mortgage interest deductions would not affect equity investments, for example. Disallowing property tax deductions might induce the states and localities to shift their sources of revenue. The immense popularity of these provisions makes it unlikely that they would be altered.

ADDITIONAL READINGS

Berkovec, James, and Don Fullerton. "A General Equilibrium Model of Housing, Taxes, and Portfolio Choice." *Journal of Political Economy* 100 (April 1992): 390–429.

Glaeser, Edward L., and Jessie M. Shapiro. "The Benefits of the Home Mortgage Interest Deduction." In *Tax Policy and the Economy,* vol. 17, edited by James M. Poterba (37–82). Cambridge, MA: MIT Press, 2003.

Gravelle, Jane G. *The Economic Effects of Taxing Capital Income.* Cambridge, MA: MIT Press, 1994.

Cross-references: homestead exemption and credit programs; imputed income; income tax, federal; interest deductibility; itemized deductions; mortgage interest deduction.

Homestead exemption and credit programs

Scott Mackey
National Conference of State Legislatures

Updated by
Terri Sexton
California State University, Sacramento, and Center for State and Local Taxation, University of California, Davis

State and local programs that provide tax relief to owners of residential property.

Homestead exemption and credit programs are the most widely used form of property tax relief. All 50 states and the District of Columbia have homestead exemptions or credits available to at least one class of qualified homeowner.

Elderly homeowners, followed by veterans and the disabled, are the most common recipients of tax relief. Only four states (Louisiana, Nevada, Vermont, and Wisconsin) do not offer older Americans some type of relief. Thirty-five states provide relief to all homeowners, though this is sometimes subject to income or asset restrictions. This entry focuses on homestead exemption and credit programs broadly available either to older Americans as a class or to all homeowners.

History

Most homestead exemption programs were created during the Great Depression to give poor homesteaders property tax relief that would help them avoid foreclosure. The early homestead exemption programs were generally available to all homeowners. In 1957, New Jersey developed the first homestead exemption program targeted to older Americans. The 1960s and 1970s saw rapid growth in the number of states with targeted homestead exemption programs, with many of the new programs targeted to the elderly. However, since that time states have tended to make the programs available more broadly to all households, or to all low-income households (Gold 1979).

Types of programs

The most common form of property tax relief for homeowners is the "homestead exemption," which allows a portion of the assessed value of the person's principal residence to be exempt from tax. A "homestead credit" has a similar effect but specifies the relief in terms of a reduction in, or credit based on, the homeowner's property tax bill. Such programs are frequently means tested, meaning that only persons with incomes below a certain limit qualify for relief and the amount of relief may fall as income rises toward this limit. "Circuit breaker" relief programs tie the benefits to both income and property tax payments. These programs limit the proportion of household income that can be collected as property taxes and the excess taxes are waived, rebated, or credited against income tax obligations.

Tables 1, 2, and 3 summarize the key features of homestead exemption and credit programs available broadly to older Americans and to all households. States in table 1 offer homestead exemption and credit programs without regard to the taxpayer's income, while states in table 2 target programs to low-income taxpayers. Table 3 indicates the states that provide circuit breaker programs. All three tables compare the treatment of elderly and nonelderly homeowners.

How the programs work

Homestead exemption programs reduce property taxes on residential property by exempting a certain amount of a home's value from taxation. Homestead exemption programs are usually mandated by state law, with local governments either absorbing the revenue loss or shifting the tax burden to other property.

The exemption may apply to all property taxes levied against the homestead or be restricted to a subset, usually school levies. In 18 states, a fixed amount of the homestead value is exempt from the property tax, ranging from $1,000 in Oklahoma to $100,000 for school taxes in South Carolina. In other states, the exempt value is determined as a percentage of market value. Ohio exempts 12.5 percent of owner-occupied property while Montana exempts 31.4 percent, Utah 45 percent, and South Dakota provides a full exemption (100 percent) from state taxes. In Hawaii, the exemption depends on age. Homeowners less than 55 years old are allowed an exemption of $40,000, while the exemption for those age 55 to 59 is $60,000 and increases by $20,000 for every additional 5 years of age, up to age 70 and beyond when the exemption reaches the maximum of $120,000 (table 1).

Many states that target their homestead exemption programs to elderly homeowners or provide larger exemptions for the elderly impose household income limits. For example, elderly homeowners in Alabama qualify for a full exemption from local taxes if their annual income is below $7,500. Income caps vary from this $7,500 up to $100,000 in the District of Columbia. In some states, the value of the exemption or percentage of value exempt varies with income. In Washington, for example, elderly homeowners qualify for an exemption of 35 percent of assessed value up to $40,000 if income is less than $24,000, and the exemption is increased to 60 percent of assessed value up to $50,000 if income is less than $18,000. Elderly homeowners in North Dakota receive an exemption of 100 percent up to $2,000 if their income is less than $8,000, and the percentage and maximum decline as income increases, so that those with income between $12,500 and $14,000 receive only a 20 percent exemption up to $400.

The degree of property tax relief provided by homestead exemption programs varies tremendously from state to state. The tax reduction depends upon the dollar amount of the exemption provided and the assessment ratio used in determining the taxable value of the property. For example, in Louisiana, each homeowner receives a $7,500 homestead exemption, and California homeowners receive a $7,000 exemption. Louisiana's program is much more generous, however, because the state uses a 10 percent assessment ratio in determining the taxable value of the home. A $100,000 house in Louisiana has a taxable value of $10,000, so the $7,500 homestead exemption effectively exempts $75,000 in actual value from property taxes (a 75 percent reduction in taxes). In contrast, California's assessment ratio is 100 percent, so its homestead exemption is worth $7,000 in actual value (a 7 percent reduction in taxes).

Homestead credit programs are generally state-financed and may involve direct rebates to taxpayers or, like homestead exemptions, may reduce property tax bills directly.

TABLE 1. State Homestead Credit and Exemption Programs without Income Eligibility Guidelines, 2004

	Credit or exemption for	
State	Elderly homeowners	All homeowners
Alabama (state taxes)	Full exemption	$4,000
Alabama (county taxes)	$2,000 to $4,000 (L)	$2,000 to $4,000
Alaska	$150,000	$10,000 (L)
Arkansas	$300 tax credit	$300 tax credit
California	$7,000	$7,000
Colorado	50% up to $100,000	
Delaware (school)	50% of tax up to $500	
District of Columbia	$30,000	$30,000
Florida	$25,000	$25,000
Georgia	$8,000	$8,000
Hawaii	$40,000 to $120,000	$40,000
Idaho	50% up to $50,000	50% up to $50,000
Illinois	$5,500 ($7,000 Cook County)	$3,500 ($4,500 Cook County)
Indiana	50% up to $35,000	50% up to $35,000
	20% of tax	20% of tax
Iowa	$4,850	$4,850
Kansas (school)	$20,000	$20,000
Kentucky	$26,800 (2004$)	
Louisiana	$7,000 (AV), $75,000 (MV)	$7,000 (AV), $75,000 (MV)
Maine	$2,500 to $7,000	$2,500 to $7,000
Massachusetts	$2,000	
Minnesota (school)	83% of tax up to $390	83% of tax up to $390
Mississippi	$7,500	$7,500 up to $300 tax
Montana	31.4%	31.4%
New York (school)	$30,000	$30,000
Ohio	12.5% of tax	12.5% of tax
Oklahoma	$1,000 (AV)	$1,000 (AV)
	$7,407 to $9,091 (MV)	7,407 to $9,091 (MV)
Rhode Island	$18,000 to $58,000 (L)	$15,000 to $52,500 (L)
South Carolina (school)	$150,000	$100,000
South Dakota	Up to 55% tax	Up to 35% tax
South Dakota (state)	Full exemption	Full exemption
Texas (school)	$25,000	$15,000
Texas (local)	$3,000 (L)	$3,000 (L)
Utah	65% (MV)	45% (MV)
West Virginia	$20,000 (AV), $33,333 (MV)	

Sources: State constitutions and statutes as posted on state web sites.

Notes: L = local option; AV = assessed value; MV = market value.

Alabama: elderly exemption can increase to full exemption on county taxes if income < $7,500.

Florida: elderly exemption can increase to $50,000 if income < $22,096 (2004$).

Hawaii: age 55 to 59: $60,000; age 60 to 64: $80,000; age 65 to 69: $100,000; age 70+: $120,000.

Maine: $7,000 if value is less than $125,000; $5,000 if value is between $125,000 and $250,000; $2,500 if value is greater than $250,000.

Massachusetts: if net worth excluding home is less than $40,000.

New York: elderly exemption increases to $50,000 if income is less than $62,100.

Credit programs can be designed to have exactly the same effect as exemptions. California exempts $7,000 in value, which, given the 1 percent tax rate, results in the same tax savings as a $70 credit. Arkansas, Connecticut, Delaware, Indiana, Maine, Minnesota, Montana, New Jersey, Pennsylvania, South Dakota, and the District of Columbia have homestead credit programs. These programs rebate a certain percentage of taxes due or provide a fixed credit to qualifying homeowners. Arkansas uses the latter method, providing a $300 rebate for all homeowners. Minnesota provides all homeowners with a credit of 83 percent of the school tax bill up to $390.

TABLE 2. State Homestead Credit and Exemption Programs with Income Eligibility Guidelines, 2004

| State | Credit or exemption for | | Income cap ($) |
	Elderly homeowners	All homeowners	
Alabama (local)	$5,000		12,000
Alabama (local)	Full exemption		7,500
Connecticut	50% of tax up to $1,250		11,700
District of Columbia	50% of tax		100,000
Florida	$50,000		22,096 (2004$)
Georgia (school)	$10,000		10,000
Georgia (state and local)	$4,000		10,000
Indiana	Additional 50% AV up to $6,000		25,000
Maine	Full exemption up to $1,000 taxes		15,000
Massachusetts	$4,000 (or $500 credit)		15,000
Montana		30% of tax	23,097
Montana		50% of tax	16,168
Montana		80% of tax	9,239
Nebraska	$40,000 or 80% of county average		31,501
New Hampshire	$5,000		20,400
New Jersey	Up to $1,450 tax		49,082
New York (school)	$50,000		62,100
New York	50% of AV (L)		32,400
North Carolina	Max of 50% AV or $20,000		18,800
North Dakota	20%–100%		14,000
Ohio	Up to 75% or $5,200		24,700
Pennsylvania	$500 tax		15,000
South Dakota	Up to 55%		20,000
Tennessee	$18,000		12,710
Washington	35% up to $40,000		24,000
Washington	60% up to $50,000		18,000
West Virginia	$30,000		18,180

Sources: State constitutions and statutes as posted on state web sites.
Notes: L = local option; AV = assessed value; MV = market value.
All income caps specified are for married couples. Lower caps may apply for single persons.
Connecticut: if single, 40% of tax up to $1,000.
Florida: this includes the $25,000 general exemption for all households.
Massachusetts: age 70 or above.
North Dakota: percentage varies with income.
Ohio: percentage and cap vary with income.

As in the case of exemptions, eligibility for credits may depend on income or the amount of the credit may vary with income. In Pennsylvania, only elderly or disabled homeowners with incomes less than $15,000 are eligible to receive the $500 tax credit. Montana homeowners with incomes below $23,097 qualify for a credit of 30 percent of their property tax with the percentage increasing to 50 percent if income is less than $16,168 and 80 percent if income is less than $9,239.

Circuit breaker programs usually require homeowners to pay their property tax bills and file for the credit later, either receiving a direct rebate or a refundable credit against their state income tax obligations. Under the most general form of circuit breaker, if property taxes (T) exceed a threshold percentage (p) of income (Y), the credit equals a percentage (c) of the tax over the threshold, up to a specified credit limit:

$$Credit = c(T - pY)$$

As income increases, the threshold percentage (p) may increase; the portion of tax over the threshold that the taxpayer must pay (1 − c) may increase; and the maximum credit may decrease. Eight states (Maine, Maryland, Michigan, Minnesota, Montana, Vermont, Wisconsin, and Wyoming) currently have circuit breaker relief programs for all homeowners.

Both Michigan and Minnesota have what are often referred to as threshold programs. Michigan homeowners with household income less than or equal to $73,650 are granted an income tax credit equal to 60 percent (c = 0.60) of the amount

TABLE 3.   **State Circuit Breaker Programs**

State	Eligibility	Income cap ($)	Maximum credit
Arizona	Elderly	5,501	$502
California	Elderly	38,505 (2003$)	$472.60
Colorado	Elderly	14,700	$600
Connecticut	Elderly	28,900	$350
Hawaii	Age 55+	20,000	$500
Idaho	Elderly	21,580	$1,200
Illinois	Elderly	35,740	$700
Iowa	Elderly	17,589	Full refund
Kansas	Age 55+	25,000	$600
Maine	All	46,900	$1,000
Maryland	All		Full refund
Massachusetts	Age 70+	63,000	$790
Michigan	All	73,650	$1,200
Michigan	Elderly		$1,200
Minnesota	All	101,690 (2004$)	$1,560
Missouri	Elderly	27,000	$750
Montana	All	23,097	Up to 80% of tax
Montana	Elderly	45,000	$1,000
Oklahoma	Elderly	12,000	$200
Utah	Elderly	24,798 (2004$)	$661
Vermont	All	75,000	Full refund
Wisconsin	All	24,500	$1,160
Wyoming	All	½ median household income in county	½ prior year or median tax in county
Wyoming	Elderly		$600

Sources: State constitutions and statutes as posted on state web sites.

Notes: All income caps specified for married couples. Lower caps may apply for single persons.

Maryland: net worth, excluding home, must be less than or equal to $200,000.

Massachusetts: home value must be less than $425,000.

Minnesota: $83,390 (2004$) income limit if single up to $101,690 with five or more dependents.

by which their property tax exceeds 3.5 percent ($p = 0.035$) of their income up to a maximum credit of $1,200. Minnesota's circuit breaker program is somewhat more complicated. The threshold percentage (p) increases from 1 to 4 percent as income increases up to $83,390 ($101,690 with five or more dependents for 2004). In addition, the percentage of tax over the threshold credited to the homeowner decreases from 85 to 50 percent over the same income range. The maximum credit for 2004 is $1,560.

Some states have simpler programs. Connecticut's sliding scale program allows a credit or tax reduction of a straight percentage (c) of taxes that declines as income increases, ignoring the threshold ($p = 0$). Married homeowners with incomes below $11,700 are entitled to a 50 percent tax reduction up to a maximum of $1,250, while those with incomes between $23,600 and $28,900 qualify for only a 10 percent reduction up to $250. Both Maine and Massachusetts refund all taxes ($c = 1.0$) above a specified threshold, which is 4 percent of income ($p = 0.04$) in Maine and 10 percent ($p = 0.10$) in Massachusetts. The maximum credits are $1,000 and $790, re-

spectively. Table 3 summarizes some of the key features of circuit breaker programs currently in use.

Program design issues

In states without state-financed homestead exemption or credit programs, local governments can shift the tax burden from exempt property to nonexempt property such as business property, vacation and second homes, and homes and other property owned by taxpayers who do not qualify for homestead exemptions. This is particularly true in states with generous homestead exemptions that are available to the general population, like those in Florida, the District of Columbia, Idaho, and Louisiana.

A large amount of exempt property reduces the tax base and may result in higher tax rates than would be necessary if all property were taxable. For this reason, homestead exemption programs widely available to all homeowners may not provide the full amount of tax relief that they appear to provide. Large homestead exemptions that are available to all homeowners shift the tax burden from homeowners to businesses. Homestead credit programs may avoid tax shifts if they are state financed. For this reason, these programs are popular with local officials. However, some states have found that homestead credit programs may increase local spending and taxes because local officials can increase tax rates without the full burden being borne by local taxpayers.

State decisions to target or not to target property tax relief programs to specific categories of homeowners are based upon several factors. States that choose to provide benefits to all homeowners, without regard to income, are often using exemption and credit programs as part of a broader policy to shift taxes from the local to the state level or from residential property owners to businesses. Most of the states that provide more generous benefits to the elderly than to the general population require elderly homeowners to meet income criteria. Targeting programs in this manner allows states to provide tax relief to elderly homeowners on fixed incomes without providing relief to wealthy retirees. This reduces the revenue loss to local governments or the state.

Participation issues

With homestead exemption programs, participation is automatic because the exemption is built directly into the property tax bill received by the homeowner. In some states, however, homestead credit programs require qualifying homeowners to claim their credit, often on a separate form submitted with income tax forms. Some elderly homeowners are not required to file an income tax form and therefore may fail to claim their credit. State outreach programs are necessary to let qualifying homeowners know about the credit and how to apply for it; some states provide information about the credit with both income tax forms and property tax bills.

ADDITIONAL READINGS

Gold, Steven D. *Property Tax Relief.* Lexington, MA: D.C. Heath and Company, 1979.

Mackey, Scott. *State Tax Policy and Senior Citizens.* Denver: National Conference of State Legislatures, December 1994, 37–58.

Cross-references: circuit breaker; property tax, real property, residential.

Horizontal equity

Joseph J. Cordes
George Washington University

A principle used to judge the fairness of taxes, which holds that taxpayers who have the same income should pay the same amount in taxes.

The principle of horizontal equity is a basic yardstick used to gauge whether tax burdens are fairly distributed. On the one hand, the idea that tax policy should strive for horizontal equity is uncontroversial (Musgrave 1990). It protects taxpayers

against arbitrary discrimination and seems consistent with basic principles of equal worth. Some might also argue that horizontal equity comports with the principle of "equal protection under law" set forth in the United States Constitution.

On the other hand, some tax scholars maintain that horizontal equity is not really an independent principle of tax fairness, but instead is subordinate to vertical equity, which holds that people with different incomes should pay different amounts of tax (Kaplow 1989). As a matter of logic, a tax system that assigns different tax burdens to people with different incomes should assign the same tax burden to people with the same income. Viewed in this way, equal treatment of equals in taxation is not an end in itself, but rather a means to ensuring that tax burdens are distributed in a way that is vertically equitable.

As Musgrave (1990) notes, however, horizontal equity can lay claim to being an independent standard of tax equity because it is consistent with a number of different underlying conceptions of tax fairness, although application of the vertical equity standard will differ. For example, the benefit principle of taxation holds that tax burdens should be assigned according to the benefits that taxpayers receive from government goods and services. If one assumes that the benefits taxpayers receive from government spending vary with their income level, a case can be made that taxation according to the benefit principle would require taxpayers with the same income to pay the same amount of tax. Under the benefit principle, vertical equity would require taxpayers with different incomes to pay different amounts of tax. However, depending on how benefits vary with income, vertical equity can require that benefit tax burdens be distributed regressively, proportionately, or progressively, depending on whether benefits from public goods and services rise less than proportionately, proportionately, or more than proportionately as income increases.

Under the ability-to-pay principle, people with the same incomes have the same ability to pay, and thus should pay the same amount in taxes. In contrast to the benefit principle, however, regressive taxes would not be deemed fair under the ability-to-pay principle, and there is a general presumption that vertical equity under the standard of ability to pay would require some degree of progression in tax burdens.

The point is that while different standards of tax fairness may give different answers about how people with different incomes should be taxed (e.g., regressively, proportionately, or progressively), in theory or in practice, they generally give a similar answer about how people with the same incomes should be taxed—namely, that tax burdens should be distributed in a manner that is horizontally equitable.

Horizontal equity and consumption versus income taxation

Several conceptual issues should be kept in mind when applying the horizontal equity principle. One has to do with the measure of income that is used to group taxpayers as equals.

The most commonly used yardstick is annual income, comprehensively measured. Many economists, however, believe that a taxpayer's lifetime income is a better measure. One's judgment about whether taxing income or consumption is consistent with horizontal equity depends on which definition of income one uses.

Consider, for example, the case of two people, taxpayer A and taxpayer B, who, for purposes of illustration, are assumed to live for only two periods of time. In the first period, both taxpayers work and earn $50,000; in the second, they retire and live from the proceeds of savings they collected in the first period. Assume that taxpayer A saves $20,000 of income earned in the first period, and invests it at a return of 10 percent, while taxpayer B saves only $10,000, also invested at 10 percent.

The question is, do taxpayers A and B have "equal incomes"? The answer depends on whether one measures income annually or over a taxpayer's lifetime. If annual income is used as the standard, then taxpayers A and B would be seen to have the same income in period one ($50,000), but taxpayer A would have a higher income in period two because of investment income of $2,000 compared with only $1,000 of income for taxpayer B. Applying the principles of horizontal and vertical equity would require taxpayers A and B to pay the same tax in period one, and taxpayer A to pay more taxes than taxpayer B in period two.

Clearly, in this case, taxing income meets the standard of horizontal equity, but taxing consumption does not. The reason is that in period one, taxpayers A and B would pay taxes only on the amount of their income that is consumed, so that taxpayer A would pay less in tax than would taxpayer B, even though they have the same amount of annual income.

If, however, one believes that lifetime income should be used to compare taxpayers, the answer changes. The reason is that from a lifetime perspective, taxpayers A and B have the same lifetime income. They each earn $50,000 of income in period one, and this means that they have the same possibilities for consumption over their lifetimes. How they decide to allocate their consumption between present and future is a matter of personal preference. Taxpayer A would rather have more consumption in period two, and so saves more than does taxpayer B. As a byproduct of these choices, the two taxpayers wind up with different amounts of *annual* income in period two, but this simply reflects the fact that taxpayer A would rather consume less in period one and more in period two than would taxpayer B. If lifetime income is the standard of comparison, it can be shown that taxing based on consumption achieves horizontal equity, while taxation of income imposes a heavier tax burden on people who have the same lifetime incomes as others, but who prefer to shift more of their lifetime consumption to later years through saving.

Horizontal equity and implicit taxes

There are also situations in which horizontal "inequities" may be more apparent than real. Income received from tax-exempt bonds is a case in point. Suppose that taxpayers A and B are identical in all respects save for the fact that taxpayer A receives $7,000 in interest from tax-exempt bonds, while taxpayer B receives $7,000 in fully taxable interest. Assume for purposes of illustration that the tax rate is 30 percent. It might seem that horizontal equity is violated because both taxpayers have the same measured income, even though taxpayer B will pay $2,100 on his or her interest income, while taxpayer A owes no tax on his or her tax-exempt interest.

But, as Bittker (1980) notes, the two taxpayers are not really in the same position. The reason is that tax-exempt bonds will pay a lower rate of interest because of their tax-free status. For example, if the interest rate on fully taxed bonds were 10 percent, and the tax rate 30 percent, the interest on tax-exempt bonds would be 7 percent. This means that in order to earn $7,000 in tax-exempt interest, taxpayer A must have bought $100,000 of tax-exempt bonds, whereas taxpayer B needed to buy only $70,000 worth of bonds to earn the same income. Many economists would say that taxpayers A and B are really in the same position, because while taxpayer B faces an explicit tax of 30 percent on interest earnings, taxpayer A faces an implicit tax, levied in the form of the lower return received on the tax-favored investment.

Cases in which horizontal equity does not apply

The standard of horizontal equity will have limited applicability when taxes are levied to account for external costs. For example, smokers and nonsmokers will face sharply different tobacco tax burdens, even when their incomes are the same. To the extent, however, that tobacco taxes are intended to force smokers to bear the external costs of smoking, the apparent violation of horizontal equity would not be seen as a problem.

Application to tax policy

The concept of horizontal equity plays an important role in the evaluation of tax policy. For example, treating taxpayers with equal incomes equally was one of the central organizing principles of the landmark reform of the federal income tax that took place in the Tax Reform Act of 1986.

ADDITIONAL READINGS

Auerbach, Alan. "A New Measure of Horizontal Equity." *American Economic Review* 92, no. 4 (2002): 1116–25.
Bittker, Boris. "Equity, Efficiency, and Income Tax Theory: Do Misallocations Drive Out Inequities?" In *The Economics of Taxation,* edited by Henry Aaron and Michael Boskin (19–31). Washington, DC: The Brookings Institution, 1980.
Kaplow, Louis. "Horizontal Equity: Measures in Search of a Principle." *National Tax Journal* 42, no. 2 (1989): 139–55.
Musgrave, Richard. "Horizontal Equity Once More." *National Tax Journal* 43, no. 2 (1990): 113–23.

Cross-references: ability to pay; benefit principle; fairness in taxation; progressivity, measures of; tax reform, federal; tax reform, state; vertical equity.

I

Implicit taxes

Harry Watson
George Washington University

Costs, in the form of lower rates of return or higher prices, that may be borne by participants in untaxed or favorably taxed markets as a result of tax shifting.

While taxpayers usually focus on the amount that they must remit to the government—their explicit tax burden—their true tax burden usually will not coincide with these payments. One reason for this discrepancy is that a tax in one market may be shifted to another market in the form of higher prices or lower rates of return. While these changes in prices or rates of return are not a direct result of explicit tax payments, they have the same economic consequences for taxpayers, and therefore can be viewed as implicit taxes.

Implicit taxes play an important role in incidence analysis—the question of who bears the economic, as opposed to statutory, burden of a tax. Measuring the incidence of a tax by looking only at explicit taxes paid will often produce a biased measure of burden in the presence of implicit taxes. The classic example of this bias is the belief that those who invest in state and municipal bonds in the United States face no tax burden; while they face no explicit tax burden, they do face a material implicit tax burden in the form of a lower no-tax rate of return. Because of the significant role played by implicit taxes in determining incidence, it is useful to understand the mechanism by which such taxes are created, the factors that influence their magnitude, and the form such taxes can take.

Implicit taxes are created when taxpayers attempt to ameliorate the impact of their explicit tax burden. In the case of income taxation, taxpayers may substitute tax-preferred investments for fully taxed ones. These tax-induced substitutions produce an increase in demand in markets that face a lower level of explicit taxation, which results in higher prices or lower rates of return in these markets. This process effectively shifts an explicit tax in one market to an implicit tax in another.

Consider, for example, the case of tax-exempt bonds. Suppose that initially the interest from all bonds is taxed fully at a rate of 30 percent, and that a decision is made to exempt the interest on bonds issued by state and local governments from taxation. Assume that before the exemption is granted, all bonds offer a rate of 10 percent. When the exemption is granted, in-

vestors presumably would flock to buy tax-exempt municipal bonds, believing that these bonds would pay a tax-free return of 10 percent, compared with the after-tax rate of only 7 percent [= 10% (10% 0.30)] that they earn on fully taxed bonds. But this would boost the demand for tax-exempt bonds, which would allow the issuers of these bonds to command a higher bond price or, equivalently, offer a lower rate of return on them. Capital markets would adjust until the last dollar invested in either a fully taxed or a tax-exempt bond earned the same after-tax return. The result would be that investors in tax-exempt bonds would receive a return on their investment that was 30 percent less than the return they could earn by investing in fully taxed bonds. Thus, if they bought a fully taxed bond at, say, 10 percent, they would pay an explicit tax of 30 percent on their return. If they bought a tax-exempt bond, they would not have to write a check to the government, but they would also earn a return of only 7 percent, whereas in a world with no taxes, they would have been able to earn 10 percent. Thus, they would face an implicit tax of 30 percent.

The magnitude of implicit taxation depends in large part on how much latitude taxpayers have in lessening their explicit tax burden. This latitude depends critically on two factors: the form of the tax system and how responsive taxpayers are to economic incentives—that is, the elasticity of their response to changes in prices and rates of return.

Tax systems characterized by broad bases and uniform treatment of all items in these bases will leave taxpayers with limited opportunities to lessen explicit tax burdens, and therefore will generate few implicit taxes. For example, taxpayers who face a flat-rate income tax that provides uniform treatment for all forms of saving will find that no amount of portfolio juggling, apart from reducing the size of their portfolio, will alter their explicit tax liability. As portfolio adjustments provide few tax benefits, asset prices and rates of return will change little, and there will be no appreciable implicit taxation. Conversely, if the income tax provides numerous tax preferences, the range of opportunities for reducing explicit tax liability may lead to substantial alterations in taxpayer portfolios and, concomitantly, substantial changes in pretax rates of return. In this situation, the explicit tax on heavily taxed forms of saving will be shifted to forms of saving that are treated preferentially.

For a given tax system, the magnitude of implicit taxes will reflect the elasticity of taxpayer response to changes in prices and rates of return. Generally, the more elastic the response, the greater is the magnitude of implicit taxation. Compare, for example, an excise tax levied on a lifesaving pharmaceutical with an excise tax levied on hardcover books. The absence of any substitutes for the lifesaving pharmaceutical means that taxpayers in need of such a product will not alter their demands for other goods or services—their response will be inelastic—and, as a result, other market prices will remain unaffected and no implicit taxes will be created. On the other hand, with an excise tax on hardcover books, one would expect taxpayers' responses to be quite elastic, resulting in a significant shift to paperbacks and a corresponding increase in paperbacks' price. The magnitude of the price increase will be directly related to the ease of substituting a paperback for a hardcover book.

Unlike explicit tax burdens, implicit tax burdens may arise before any tax statutes are enacted. As long as taxpayers anticipate new tax codes or changes in existing ones, these anticipation effects will alter market behavior and market prices. Suppose that taxpayers believe that an investment tax credit with a given structure will be enacted, but that the timing of enactment is uncertain. Because potential users of capital subject to the credit may delay investing with the expectation of receiving this credit, the market price of existing capital will fall, creating a capital loss—implicit tax—for owners of this capital. Thus, even though tax code provisions have not changed, and therefore explicit tax liabilities arising from the credit have not changed, an implicit tax will have been levied on owners of existing capital.

Although most implicit taxes are produced by tax-induced changes in prices and rates of return, such taxes can be created in other ways, a testament to their ubiquitous nature. Consider a market in which products can be distinguished on the basis of their quality (or by the level of services provided to consumers by producers). If an excise or sales tax is levied on these products, the producer of one of them can react by altering the price of the product or by altering its quality. In most cases, the imposition of the tax will lead to a higher tax-inclusive price for consumers, and the price increase represents the portion of the explicit tax paid by consumers. However, a producer may try to offset some of the decline in demand that results from the higher price by increasing product quality. This higher level of quality could reasonably be viewed as an implicit subsidy to consumers, a subsidy that lowers the true tax burden of consumers.

Cross-references: fringe benefits; incidence of taxes; marginal effective tax rate; saving, taxes and.

Imputed income

Jane G. Gravelle
Congressional Research Service, Library of Congress

Income that is not received in monetary form and therefore is not typically subject to taxation. Imputed income, in economic theory, would include income from the flow of all durable goods, including assets held by consumers, and the value of leisure and unpaid work (such as food grown for home use).

According to the reconciliation between adjusted gross income and personal income in the National Income and Product Accounts, in 2001, $364.4 billion of imputed income was excluded from the tax base. (This figure does not include employee fringe benefits). The largest item was $259.5 billion in the category of personal interest income, which includes the benefits of banking services provided free to customers in lieu of interest. The next largest item was $84.2 billion of imputed rental income on owner-occupied housing. There were also imputations for labor income and for proprietors' income.

The Treasury Department's Office of Tax Analysis prepares distributional tables using an expanded income concept that includes imputed rent on owner-occupied housing.

Cross-references: adjusted gross income; homeowner preferences, individual income tax.

Incidence of taxes

George R. Zodrow
Rice University

The analysis and measurement of who bears the final burden of a tax.

One of the most fundamental questions in public finance is who bears the final burden of a tax. Calculating tax incidence is complex because tax-induced changes in individual and firm behavior and the associated changes in commodity prices and factor returns often imply that the final burden or "economic incidence" of a tax will be different from its "statutory incidence"—that is, once markets adjust, a tax may be partially or fully "shifted" from one set of economic agents to another. Business taxes are a frequently cited example, as they may be either "shifted forward" as higher consumer prices or "shifted backward" as lower wages or land prices. The tax incidence literature provides many insights and has played a critical role in the development of tax policy (McLure and Zodrow 1994).

Public finance economists have used three basic approaches to analyze tax incidence. One method analyzes the effects of taxes in theoretical models of the economy; these analytical models differ in many dimensions, including the number of markets analyzed, the extent to which factor supplies are assumed to be fixed, the method of capital accumulation, the nature of market competition, and the extent to which transitional issues are addressed. The second closely related approach involves numerical simulations of tax incidence in computer-based models that are basically complex variants of the analytical models described above. Finally, some incidence studies estimate individual tax burdens directly using large microdata sets. All of these approaches have become increasingly sophisticated over time, and several excellent surveys of the incidence literature, which examine in detail the various types of models outlined below, have appeared over the years (Mieszkowski 1969; Break 1974; McLure 1975; Kotlikoff and Summers 1987; Atkinson 1994; Fullerton and Metcalf 2002).

Partial-equilibrium analysis

The simplest type of incidence analysis examines the impact of a tax in a "partial equilibrium" framework—that is, within the context of a single market, neglecting any tax-induced effects on other markets. Although relevant only when such effects can reasonably be assumed to be unimportant, partial-equilibrium models provide many insights. Most important, they demonstrate that incidence is determined primarily by the extent to which individuals or firms are able to change their behavior to avoid the tax. For example, the burden of an excise tax tends to be borne by consumers if demand is relatively inelastic and by producers if supply is fairly inelastic; indeed, if supply is perfectly elastic (as is the case with constant returns to scale in production) or demand is perfectly inelastic, consumers bear the entire burden of an excise tax. In addition, these same factors determine who bears the excess burden of a tax—the efficiency cost attributable to tax-induced distortions of individual and firm behavior. Finally, partial-equilibrium analysis can be used to demonstrate another basic tenet of incidence analysis—that the economic incidence of a tax in a competitive system depends solely on market conditions and is independent of its statutory incidence.

Nevertheless, partial-equilibrium analysis is limited in that most taxes have important effects on markets other than the ones in which they are assessed. Moreover, the focus in partial-equilibrium models on incidence in terms of producers and consumers is unsatisfactory, as one would like to identify explicitly the factor owners who bear the producer portion of the tax burden and the types of consumers that are affected by tax-induced commodity price changes.

Static general-equilibrium analysis

These two problems are resolved in general-equilibrium models of tax incidence. Such models account explicitly for market interactions by calculating the effects of tax-induced factor reallocations on all other markets in the economy. In addition, the effects of tax changes on individuals can be determined explicitly by specifying individual tastes and patterns of factor ownership and calculating the welfare changes (typically equivalent variations, including excess burdens) associated with various tax reforms.

The simplest general-equilibrium models are "static," in that total factor supplies are assumed to be fixed. Much of this research is based on the seminal article by Harberger (1962), which built on Musgrave (1953, 1959). The Harberger model assumes perfectly competitive markets and zero initial taxes

and has a single consumer, two production sectors, and two factors of production—capital and labor—that are perfectly mobile between the sectors, although fixed in total supply. The model is thus ideally suited to analyzing the intermediate-run effects of sector-specific taxes; it was initially used to examine the incidence of the corporate income tax, with the two production sectors representing corporate and noncorporate output.

The primary insight obtained from such models is that general-equilibrium effects in markets other than those in which a tax is introduced are often very important in determining the incidence of a tax. For example, the imposition of a partial factor tax drives the factor out of the taxed sector into the untaxed sector, tending to depress the overall return to the factor. (Note that the assumption of intersectoral mobility implies that the burden on any factor is shared among all factor owners rather than just the owners of the factor in the taxed sector.) Incidence results in such models are almost always theoretically ambiguous, but numerical calculations can shed some light on the range of reasonable outcomes. For example, Harberger argued that, for plausible parameter values, capital owners bear the full burden of the corporate income tax on equity income, a result that was generally confirmed in subsequent numerical simulation models (Shoven 1976).

The static general-equilibrium model has also been used to argue that the property tax is primarily a tax on capital, because capital owners bear the average burden of property taxation in the nation, while tax differentials across jurisdictions cause higher commodity prices and lower factor returns in relatively high tax jurisdictions and the opposite effects in relatively low tax jurisdictions (Mieszkowski 1972; Zodrow and Mieszkowski 1986). This view has been challenged, however, by those who argue that the property tax, when combined with the appropriate zoning restrictions or by perfect capitalization of fiscal differentials in land prices, is effectively a benefit tax for local public services (Hamilton 1975, 1976). This issue, critical to an understanding of state and local public finance, is still controversial (Fischel 2001; Zodrow 2001).

The two-sector static general-equilibrium model has the significant advantage of being simple enough to be solved analytically for the factors that determine incidence as well as the parameters that establish their magnitudes. For example, the effect of the corporate income tax on the return to capital in the Harberger model can be decomposed into two components (Mieszkowski 1967). The first is a "substitution effect," which reflects reduced demand for capital in the taxed corporate sector and has an unambiguously negative effect on the return to capital. The second is an "output effect," which reflects reduced demand for corporate output because of its tax-induced increase in price; the output effect has a negative (positive) effect on the return to capital if the taxed sector is capital (labor) intensive, as the reallocation of production from the taxed to the untaxed sector implies an excess supply of capital (labor), which must be eliminated by a reduction in its relative price. Such results are typical of analytical general-equilibrium models, with commodity demand elasticities, consumption shares, factor intensities, and elasticities of substitution in production among the critical factors that determine the magnitudes of general-equilibrium tax incidence effects.

The basic analytical static general-equilibrium model constructed by Harberger has been extended in a wide variety of ways. One extension allows consumers with different tastes, in which case income redistribution affects consumer demands and thus relative consumer and factor prices and net incomes (Mieszkowski 1967). The assumption of perfect factor mobility has also been relaxed, in which case the burden of taxes tends to fall on relatively immobile factors (McLure 1970, 1971). The assumption of perfect competition has been questioned, especially for analysis of the corporate tax. Although no widely accepted model of imperfect competition exists, these models tend to be characterized by more forward shifting of taxes to consumers than occurs under perfect competition (Katz and Rosen 1985; Anderson, de Palma, and Kreider 2001).

The basic static general-equilibrium model has also been used to analyze tax incidence in open economies, in which case one sector represents a small open economy and the second sector represents the rest of the world (or country, in the case of a state or regional analysis). In the simplest cases, the main result is that, although capital still tends to bear the overall burden of a tax on capital in the small taxing jurisdiction, the outflow of capital caused by the tax lowers returns to immobile factors in the jurisdiction by the sum of the tax and its excess burden (Brown 1924; Bradford 1978). The policy implication is that small open economies facing a perfectly elastic supply of a factor should not tax that factor (Gordon 1986; Slemrod 1988). More generally, increasing international mobility of capital suggests that open economy considerations should play an important role in tax incidence analyses, although the extent and implications of international capital mobility are still controversial (Harberger 1980; Feldstein and Bacchetta 1991; Gravelle and Smetters 2001; Ballard, 2002).

Finally, because the Harberger model assumes that initial taxes are zero, excess burden effects cannot be analyzed because they are second-order effects and thus do not appear in a differential analysis. The extension to an existing tax structure allows explicit analysis of the burden of the efficiency costs of taxation (Ballentine and Eris 1975; Vandendorpe and Friedlaender 1976); such models are essential for the analysis of the incidence of tax reforms (Feldstein 1976; Zodrow 1981, 1985).

A key problem associated with the analytical studies described above is that the number of markets and consumers must be severely limited to keep the models tractable. This problem has been attacked by utilizing the basic structure of the Harberger model in the construction of large-scale computable general-equilibrium models that analyze tax incidence in economies with many production sectors, types of assets, and types of consumers (Ballard et al. 1985; Jorgen-

son and Wilcoxen 2002). In addition, these numerical models have been extended to include considerations of risk and endogenous financial behavior (Slemrod 1983; Galper, Lucke, and Toder 1988).

Dynamic general-equilibrium analysis

The primary problem with the static analyses described above is that tax effects on total factor supplies are ignored; in particular, many observers have argued that this assumption is unreasonable when the incidence of a tax is borne by capital owners (although similar points could be made regarding the supply of labor and the stock of human capital). The following discussion outlines several approaches used in analyzing tax incidence from a dynamic perspective.

Early analyses of dynamic tax incidence focused on adding taxes to the neoclassical growth model. In this case, capital income taxation reduces saving, which in turn lowers the equilibrium capital-labor ratio; as a result, labor productivity falls and wages decline, implying that the tax has been at least partially shifted from capital to labor. Indeed, in the special case in which capital owners save all their income and workers save none, the burden of a capital income tax is fully shifted to labor; more generally, the extent of shifting varies from about one-third to one-half (Krzyzaniak 1967; Feldstein 1974), although reaching the new equilibrium may take considerable time (Boadway 1979).

More recent analyses of dynamic tax incidence have modeled individual saving and investment decisions explicitly, within the context of either infinite horizon models or, more commonly, overlapping-generations life-cycle models. The former approach assumes perfect foresight by one or more types of optimizing infinitely-lived individuals. These analyses stress the long-run effects of capital taxes on capital accumulation and typically calculate the incidence of reforms as the equivalent variations, expressed in present value terms, experienced by suppliers of labor and by capitalists (Judd 1985).

In contrast, overlapping-generations life-cycle models stress that the effects of taxes on capital accumulation depend on their relative effects on individuals at different stages of their life cycles, and calculate the differential incidence of tax reforms across the various generations alive at the time of reform as well as on future generations. For example, under a switch from an income tax to a cash-flow consumption tax, double taxation of existing assets results in a large welfare loss to the elderly, which in turn implies lower steady-state tax rates; by comparison, a switch to a wage tax confers a windfall gain to the elderly (who expected to be taxed on the income earned by their capital assets) and implies relatively higher steady-state tax rates (Summers 1981a; Auerbach and Kotlikoff 1987; Altig et al. 2001; Zodrow 2002).

Finally, both the static and dynamic analyses described above assume that capital reallocations are instantaneous and costless; however, in the presence of adjustment costs, tax incidence analysis must consider tax-induced changes in asset prices (Summers 1981b). Such asset price changes measure the windfall gains and losses attributable to the enactment of tax reforms and, if the adjustment period is long, may be a more important determinant of incidence than the long-run changes in factor prices stressed in most analyses. Moreover, the nature of such windfall gains and losses may be surprising. For example, the enactment of an investment incentive that applies only to a new investment is likely to result in a loss to the owners of existing capital assets; equilibrium returns, which accrue to both new and old capital, will decline because they are determined by the tax treatment of new investment, and these lower returns will be capitalized as lower values of existing assets (Auerbach and Kotlikoff 1983).

Empirical incidence analysis

Another approach to determining tax incidence uses microdata sets to estimate individual tax burdens and thus estimate their distribution across individuals. These studies draw on the theoretical and empirical literatures to make assumptions about the incidence of various taxes and typically include calculations for a variety of incidence assumptions. Such studies have generally found—depending on the incidence assumptions made, especially regarding the corporate income tax and property taxes—that the combined federal, state, and local tax structure in the United States is either modestly progressive or modestly regressive and roughly proportional over a wide income range (Pechman and Okner 1974; Pechman 1985). The aggregation of all taxes, however, masks the progressivity of the federal income tax; one recent study estimates that the average effective individual income tax rate for a married couple filing jointly with two children varies from −40 percent at an adjusted gross income (AGI) of $10,000 (due to various refundable credits), to 8.4 percent at an AGI of $100,000, to nearly 24 percent for households with an AGI of $1,000,000 (Burman and Saleem 2004).

Such studies have often played an important role in tax reform debates; for example, their basic methodology was used by the U.S. Treasury in determining whether the various reform proposals considered before passage of the Tax Reform Act of 1986 satisfied the constraint of "distributional neutrality" (McLure and Zodrow 1987). Nevertheless, they have been criticized on a number of grounds. Although many critiques focus on the specific incidence assumptions used to allocate tax burdens across income classes (Joint Committee on Taxation 1993), another critical issue is the use of annual income as a classifier. Many observers have argued that lifetime income is a better measure of ability to pay taxes, and that the distribution of tax burden should be measured by comparing lifetime income and taxes. Such calculations generally indicate that consumption taxes are less regressive and income taxes less progressive than do studies based on annual income (Davies, St-Hilaire, and Whalley 1984; Poterba 1989; Casperson and Metcalf 1994; Fullerton and Rogers 1993). The lifetime approach to tax incidence analysis is, however, by no means universally accepted (Barthold 1993; Reschovsky 1998).

ADDITIONAL READINGS

Altig, David, Alan J. Auerbach, Lawrence J. Kotlikoff, Kent A. Smetters, and Jan Walliser. "Simulating Fundamental Tax Reform in the U.S." *American Economic Review* 91 (June 2001): 574–95.

Anderson, Simon P., Andre de Palma, and Brent Kreider. "Tax Incidence in a Differentiated Product Oligopoly." *Journal of Public Economics* 81 (August 2001): 173–92.

Atkinson, Anthony B. "The Distribution of the Tax Burden." In *Modern Public Finance,* edited by John M. Quigley and Eugene Smolensky (13–49). Cambridge, MA: Harvard University Press, 1994.

Auerbach, Alan J., and James R. Hines. "Taxation and Economic Efficiency." In *Handbook of Public Economics,* vol. 3, edited by Alan J. Auerbach and Martin Feldstein (1347–1421). Amsterdam: North-Holland, 2001.

Auerbach, Alan J., and Laurence J. Kotlikoff. "Investment versus Savings Incentives: The Size of the Bang for the Buck and the Potential for Self-Financing Business Tax Cuts." In *What Determines Savings?* edited by Laurence J. Kotlikoff (264–89). Cambridge, MA: MIT Press, 1983.

———. *Dynamic Fiscal Policy.* Cambridge, U.K.: Cambridge University Press, 1987.

Ballard, Charles A. "International Aspects of Fundamental Tax Reform." In *United States Tax Reform in the 21st Century,* edited by George R. Zodrow and Peter Mieszkowski (109–39). Cambridge, U.K.: Cambridge University Press, 2002.

Ballard, Charles A., Don Fullerton, John B. Shoven, and John Whalley. *A General Equilibrium Model for Tax Policy Evaluation.* Chicago: University of Chicago Press, 1985.

Ballentine, J. Gregory, and Ibrahim Eris. "On the General Equilibrium Analysis of Tax Incidence." *Journal of Political Economy* 83 (June 1975): 633–44.

Barthold, Thomas. "How Should We Measure Distribution?" *National Tax Journal* 35 (September 1993): 291–99.

Boadway, Robin. "Long Run Tax Incidence: A Comparative Dynamic Approach." *Review of Economic Studies* 46 (1979): 505–11.

Bradford, David F. "Factor Prices May Be Constant but Factor Returns Are Not." *Economics Letters* I (November 1978): 199–203.

Break, George F. "The Incidence and Economic Effects of Taxation." In *The Economics of Public Finance,* edited by Alan S. Blinder, Robert M. Solow, George F. Break, Peter O. Steiner, and Dick Netzer. Washington, DC: The Brookings Institution, 1974.

Brown, Harry G. *The Economics of Taxation.* New York: Holt, 1924.

Burman, Leonard E., and Mohammed Adeel Saleem. "Income Tax Statistics for Sample Families, 2003." *Tax Notes* 102 (January 19, 2004): 413–18.

Casperson, Erik, and Gilbert Metcalf. 1994. "Is a Value Added Tax Progressive? Annual versus Lifetime Incidence Measures." *National Tax Journal* 47: 731–46.

Davies, James, France St-Hilaire, and John Whalley. "Some Calculations of Lifetime Tax Incidence." *American Economic Review* 74 (September 1984): 633–49.

Feldstein, Martin S. "Incidence of a Capital Income Tax in a Growing Economy with Variable Savings Rates." *Review of Economic Studies* 41 (October 1974): 505–13.

———. "On the Theory of Tax Reform." *Journal of Public Economics* 6 (July–August 1976): 77–104.

Feldstein, Martin S., and Phillipe Bacchetta. "National Saving and International Investment." In *National Saving and Economic Performance,* edited by B. Douglas Bernheim and John B. Shoven (201–20). Chicago: University of Chicago Press, 1991.

Fischel, William A. "Homevoters, Municipal Corporate Governance, and the Benefit View of the Property Tax." *National Tax Journal* 54 (March 2001): 157–82.

Fullerton, Don, and Gilbert Metcalf. "Tax Incidence." In *Handbook of Public Economics,* vol. 4, edited by Alan J. Auerbach and Martin Feldstein (1787–1872). Amsterdam: North-Holland, 2002.

Fullerton, Don, and Diane Lim Rogers. *Who Bears the Lifetime Tax Burden?* Washington, DC: Brookings Institution Press, 1993.

Galper, Harvey, Robert Lucke, and Eric Toder. "A General Equilibrium Analysis of Tax Reform." In *Uneasy Compromise: Problems of a Hybrid Income-Consumption Tax,* edited by Henry J. Aaron, Harvey Galper, and Joseph A. Pechman. Washington, DC: The Brookings Institution, 1988.

Gordon, Roger H. "Taxation of Investment and Savings in a World Economy." *American Economic Review* 76 (December 1986): 1086–1102.

Gravelle, Jane G., and Kent Smetters. "Who Bears the Burden of the Corporate Tax in the Open Economy?" National Bureau of Economic Research Working Paper 8280. Cambridge, MA: National Bureau of Economic Research, 2001.

Hamilton, Bruce W. "Zoning and Property Taxation in a System of Local Governments." *Urban Studies* 12 (June 1975): 205–11.

———. "Capitalization of Intrajurisdictional Differences in Local Tax Prices." *American Economic Review* 66 (December 1976): 743–53.

Harberger, Arnold C. "The Incidence of the Corporate Income Tax." *Journal of Political Economy* 70 (June 1962): 215–40.

———. "Vignettes on the World Capital Market." *American Economic Review* 70 (May 1980): 331–37.

Joint Committee on Taxation. "Methodology and Issues in Measuring Changes in the Distribution of Tax Burdens." Washington, DC: U.S. Congress, 1993.

Jorgenson, Dale, and Peter J. Wilcoxen. "The Economic Impact of Fundamental Tax Reform." In *United States Tax Reform in the 21st Century,* edited by George R. Zodrow and Peter Mieszkowski (55–88). Cambridge, U.K.: Cambridge University Press, 2002.

Judd, Kenneth. "Redistributive Taxation in a Simple Perfect Foresight Model." *Journal of Public Economics* 73 (October 1985): 557–72.

Katz, Michael L., and Harvey S. Rosen. "Tax Analysis in an Oligopoly Model." *Public Finance Quarterly* 13 (January 1985): 3–19.

Kotlikoff, Laurence J., and Lawrence H. Summers. "Tax Incidence." In *Handbook of Public Economics,* edited by Alan J. Auerbach and Martin Feldstein. Amsterdam: North-Holland, 1987.

Krzyzaniak, Marian. "Long-Run Burden of a General Tax on Profits in a Neoclassical World." *Public Finance* (1967): 472–91.

McLure, Charles E., Jr. "Taxation, Substitution, and Industrial Location." *Journal of Political Economy* 78 (January–February 1970): 112–32.

———. "The Theory of Tax Incidence with Imperfect Factor Mobility." *Finanzarchiv* 30 (1971): 27–48.

———. "General Equilibrium Incidence Analysis: The Harberger Model after Ten Years." *Journal of Public Economics* 4 (February 1975): 125–61.

McLure, Charles E., and George R. Zodrow. "Treasury I and the Tax Reform Act of 1986: The Economics and Politics of Tax Reform." *Journal of Economic Perspectives* 1 (Summer 1987): 37–58.

———. "The Study and Practice of Income Tax Policy." In *Modern Public Finance,* edited by John M. Quigley and Eugene Smolensky (165–209). Cambridge, MA: Harvard University Press, 1994.

Mieszkowski, Peter. "On the Theory of Tax Incidence." *Journal of Political Economy* 75 (June 1967): 250–62.

———. "Tax Incidence Analysis: The Effects of Taxes on the Distribution of Income." *Journal of Economic Literature* (December 1969): 1103–24.

———. "The Property Tax: An Excise Tax or a Profits Tax?" *Journal of Public Economics* 1 (April 1972): 73–96.

Mitrusi, Andrew, and James Poterba. "The Distribution of Payroll and Income Tax Burdens, 1979–1999." *National Tax Journal* 53, no. 3 (September 2000): 765–94.

Musgrave, Richard A. "General Equilibrium Aspects of Incidence Theory." *American Economic Review* 43 (May 1953): 504–17.

———. *The Theory of Public Finance: A Study in Political Economy.* New York: McGraw-Hill, 1959.

Pechman, Joseph A. *Who Paid the Taxes, 1966–85?* Washington, DC: The Brookings Institution, 1985.

Pechman, Joseph A., and Benjamin A. Okner. *Who Bears the Tax Burden?* Washington, DC: The Brookings Institution, 1974.

Poterba, James M. "Lifetime Incidence and the Distributional Burden of Excise Taxes." *American Economic Review* 79 (May 1989): 325–30.

Reschovsky, Andrew. "The Progressivity of State Tax Systems." In *The Future of State Taxation,* edited by David Brunori (161–90). Washington, DC: Urban Institute Press, 1998.

Shoven, John B. "The Incidence and Efficiency Effects of Taxes on Income from Capital." *Journal of Political Economy* 84 (December 1976): 1261–83.

Slemrod, Joel. "A General Equilibrium Model of Taxation with Endogenous Financial Behavior." In *Behavioral Simulation Methods in Tax Policy Analysis,* edited by Martin S. Feldstein. Chicago: University of Chicago Press, 1983.

———. "Effect of Taxation with International Capital Mobility." In *Uneasy Compromise: Problems of a Hybrid Income-Consumption Tax,* edited by Henry J. Aaron, Harvey Galper, and Joseph A. Pechman (115–48). Washington, DC: The Brookings Institution, 1988.

Summers, Lawrence H. "Capital Taxation and Capital Accumulation in a Life Cycle Growth Model." *American Economic Review* 71 (September 1981a): 533–44.

———. "Taxation and Corporate Investment: A q-Theory Approach." Brookings Papers on Economic Activity. Washington, DC: The Brookings Institution, 1981b, pp. 67–127.

Vandendorpe, Adolph L., and Ann F. Friedlaender. "Differential Incidence in the Presence of Initial Distorting Taxes." *Journal of Public Economics* 6 (October 1976): 205–29.

Zodrow, George R. "Implementing Tax Reform." *National Tax Journal* 34 (December 1981): 401–18.

———. "Optimal Tax Reform in the Presence of Adjustment Costs." *Journal of Public Economics* 27 (July 1985): 211–30.

———. "The Property Tax as a Capital Tax: A Room with Three Views." *National Tax Journal* 54 (March 2001): 139–56.

———. "Transitional Issues in the Implementation of a Flat Tax or a National Retail Sales Tax." *In United States Tax Reform in the 21st Century,* edited by George R. Zodrow and Peter Mieszkowski (245–83). Cambridge: Cambridge University Press, 2002.

Zodrow, George R., and Peter Mieszkowski. "The New View of the Property Tax: A Reformulation." *Regional Science and Urban Economics* 16 (August 1986): 309–27.

Cross-references: capital export neutrality; capital import neutrality; elasticity, demand and supply; general-equilibrium models; implicit taxes; life cycle model; lump-sum tax; tax equity analysis.

Income tax, corporate, federal

Jane G. Gravelle
Congressional Research Service, Library of Congress

A tax imposed on the profits of corporations, calculated by deducting costs—including interest payments—from gross receipts.

The corporate income tax, enacted in 1909, actually predates the individual income tax, enacted in 1913. The corporate tax comes in a distant third (after the individual income and payroll taxes) as a source of federal tax revenue.

During its history, the statutory rate has fluctuated substantially, rising as high as 52 percent; currently the top rate is 35 percent. The tax is graduated, and closely held corporations may elect to be taxed as partnerships.

Rationale for the corporate tax

A corporate tax has been justified by the special privileges the corporation receives (in terms of limited liability), the independent economic power of large corporations, the prevention of income sheltering by high-tax-rate individuals (current tax rates make sheltering less important, however), and the tax's contribution to tax progressivity and revenue.

Many economists have been critical of the corporate tax, citing uncertainty as to the burden of the tax and its creation of a variety of distortions. They view limited liability as an efficient way to organize the raising of large amounts of capital and allocating risk, which should not be discouraged.

Who bears the burden?

While the corporate tax is presumed to fall on shareholders in the short run, when the firm cannot change its capital stock, behavioral responses can alter the long-run burden. (Taxes on excess monopoly profits are not likely to be shifted, however.)

Who pays the corporate tax is relevant to issues of distribution and progressivity. Capital income is concentrated among higher-income individuals, and the tax contributes to progressivity if it falls on capital rather than labor.

Theoretical analysis indicates that corporate taxes are borne by all capital income. Harberger's (1962) landmark two-sector study shows how the reactions of investors to lower after-tax returns, following the imposition of the tax, serve to spread the tax. As the return falls in the taxed sector, investors shift their investments to the untaxed sector and its (initially) higher rates of return. This shift sets in motion a series of adjustments in prices, wages, rates of return, output, and factor allocations.

In equilibrium, the corporate sector becomes smaller, with higher relative prices and with lower ratios of capital to labor than it had before, while the noncorporate sector becomes larger, with lower relative prices and higher ratios of capital to labor than it had before. The pretax rate of return in the corporate sector rises, while the pretax return in the untaxed noncorporate sector falls, until it equals the after-tax return in the corporate sector. The effect on wages and labor shifts is indeterminate in direction. The magnitude and, for wages, the direction of these adjustments depend on how easily capital and labor can be substituted for production in each sector, how willing consumers are to substitute corporate and noncorporate products, and what the original allocations of capital and labor were. In some cases, capital can bear more than 100 percent of the tax and in some cases less than 100 percent, but overall the tax tends to fall on capital.

This finding has held up through many modifications of the model, with the exception of models that allow the capital stock to change. In a small, open economy, where capital is perfectly mobile and goods in international trade are perfect substitutes, the burden of capital income taxes imposed on capital used in a given country falls on that country's immovable factors (labor) because both worldwide prices and returns are

fixed. Gravelle and Smetters (2001) show that relaxing any of these assumptions will shift part of the tax burden away from labor and back to capital; they find that under reasonable assumptions, the burden still falls largely on capital.

Growth models of the tax introduce further complications in the form of a time dimension and uncertainty (see Fullerton and Rogers 1993). One must now distinguish between the burden on individuals living in the near-term and in the long-run equilibrium, and the incidence would then refer to lifetime incidence, rather than a cross-section in a single year. If the savings response to a tax increase is negative, the burden of the corporate tax partially falls on labor in the long run, as the contraction in the total capital stock drives down the wage. At the same time, it is not clear that the corporate tax has caused the capital stock to fall, even on a theoretical basis (that answer depends in part on the disposition of the proceeds of the tax). Empirical evidence on the response of savings to changes in the rate of return is mixed (see Gravelle 1994, ch. 2 for a summary of this evidence). At the same time, the relationships between sources of income and level of income (i.e., high-income individuals have more capital income) tend to be muted in a life cycle model, so that even if the corporate tax falls on capital (because savings do not respond to changes in the rate of return), the effect on progressivity may be lessened.

Efficiency costs of the corporate tax

The corporate tax causes resources to be misallocated in the economy: too much capital relative to labor is used in the noncorporate sector and too little is used in the corporate sector, causing inefficient production. In addition, prices are distorted, causing too little corporate production. Most models of the corporate tax have produced welfare costs equivalent to a loss of about 0.5 percent of income, a not-insignificant amount.

The following discussion elaborates on certain matters simplified by the original Harberger model.

Fundamental changes in the structure of the model

Harberger's model explores a tax imposed on capital used to produce a particular type of good, while the corporate tax is imposed on firms because they are incorporated. The Harberger model does not allow taxed and nontaxed firms to produce the same product.

Several different methods of explaining the coexistence of corporate and noncorporate sectors in an industry have now been explored, generally relating to firm size. Gravelle and Kotlikoff (1989) suggest that large corporate firms benefit from scale advantages, while small firms benefit from entrepreneurial ability; hence, each form of production can coexist, given an imperfectly elastic supply of entrepreneurial skills. Other approaches (see Gravelle 1994 for a summary) allow corporate and noncorporate firms to produce differentiated products or allow different after-tax returns. Size might also play a role in these models (e.g., corporate products may be characterized by consistency and predictability, and corporate investments by liquidity and risk-sharing; noncorporate products and assets may be characterized by flexibility and the "personal touch").

While these models do not alter the estimates of burden, they increase the cost of distortions, because they allow for intra-industry substitution. There has been little empirical research, however, to establish the degree of substitutability of corporate and noncorporate capital directly, and such research is very difficult to perform.

Marginal tax rates, personal-level taxes, and the treatment of dividends

At the personal level, taxes are imposed immediately on dividends, but retained earnings are not subject to tax until gains are realized (and never taxed if passed on at death). Capital gains have typically benefited from special rates or exclusions and in 2003 a partial integration proposal led to lower rates for dividends (15 percent for taxpayers in the higher brackets). This provision is scheduled to expire at the end of 2008 but may be extended. Effective tax rates can also be affected by various special provisions (such as accelerated depreciation) and the failure to index for inflation. Current tax models generally employ more sophisticated measures of effective tax burdens that account for these factors.

This recognition of personal taxes, and of imprecisely measured income, does have several implications for the structure of corporate tax models. First, it means that the excess corporate tax (combined corporate and personal taxes on corporate income in excess of taxes on noncorporate income) varies from one individual to the next in a progressive tax system. Thus, some sort of portfolio effect should probably be included in any model of the corporate tax.

Second, the particular nature of the tax treatment of corporate source income at the personal level has given rise to extensive debate on the effects of taxes on dividends.

Because retained earnings are taxed more lightly than dividends, why do firms pay dividends? Firms wishing to distribute profits could effectively do so by repurchasing shares (causing share prices to go up). Several theories have been advanced to explain why firms pay dividends; they can be divided into the "traditional" and the "new" view of dividends (Zodrow 1991 provides a more extensive discussion of these views).

The new view presumes that dividends and capital gains are perfect substitutes and that firms cannot repurchase shares. Under the new view, dividend taxes in excess of capital gains taxes do not affect investment when that investment is financed out of retained earnings. By choosing reinvestment, the stockholder forgoes the excess dividend tax—a saving that offsets, in present value, future excess dividend taxes.

The new view also suggests that dividend taxes in excess of capital gains taxes are capitalized in the value of stock—hence the new view is sometimes referred to as the "trapped equity" view, or the "tax capitalization" view.

In the traditional view of dividends, they have some intrinsic value. Dividends may serve a signaling function: stockholders may not have full information about the profitability of a firm, and the payment of dividends might be used as a method to make clear that the firm is doing well. Agency cost may play a role: because of the separation of ownership and control in modern corporations and limited information, stockholders may wish to limit managerial discretion by requiring payment of regular dividends. Finally, shareholders may not view dividends and capital gains as perfect substitutes (because, for example, of differences in risk and transaction costs).

Empirical evidence has been mixed, but tends to favor the traditional view (see Gravelle 1994, ch. 4, for a summary of the empirical research). There are also some more straightforward empirical problems with the new view. Share repurchases (on the open market) can and do freely occur (at least in the United States), and firms sometimes issue new shares while paying dividends, a behavior inconsistent with the new view. At the same time, it is not entirely clear how the different traditional theories of tax should be incorporated into the tax burden.

The dividend tax debate is important for assessing the costs of distortions. Under the new view, the excess corporate tax is much smaller, and the efficiency gains reduced. If dividends and capital gains are imperfect substitutes, however, there is an additional element of distortion imposed by the current tax treatment along with the lock-in effect for corporate capital gains.

The use of debt finance

Corporate firms could avoid the tax by using debt finance. Yet, U.S. corporations not only use equity capital, they use it in substantial amounts. What explains corporations' choice of taxed equity capital?

Clientele effects were initially used to explain debt/equity choices: with high individual tax rates, some individuals would face lower taxes on equity than on debt. However, this argument was inconsistent with the mixed portfolios held by individuals at different tax rates.

The increased risk of bankruptcy can explain why firms do not choose all debt finance, even though debt may be attractive because of the agency-cost issue discussed with dividends—limiting managerial discretion through requiring periodic interest payments.

A final explanation is a portfolio explanation, in which debt is seen as an imperfect substitute for equity (because of differences, for example, in risk or in transactions costs).

None of these reasons alters the incidence effects of the corporate tax, but they do have implications for efficiency.

Debt finance reduces the differential between taxes in the corporate and noncorporate sectors but causes a distortion between debt and equity finance. Little empirical research has been conducted on the magnitude of the substitutability of debt and equity, although the evidence that does exist suggests that it is small (see Gravelle 1994 for a discussion).

Policy options

The excess corporate tax can be reduced in several ways. Dividend relief, common in other countries, could be provided by exclusion at the personal level, a deduction at the firm level, or a credit imputation method under which the firm withholds dividend taxes and the individual shareholder takes a credit for these taxes. The latter two methods preserve tax progressivity, and the last method can maintain some tax on otherwise tax-exempt entities (including foreign shareholders). Full partnership taxation could be achieved by providing a credit-imputation method for both dividends and retained earnings. Overall relief from double taxation could also be provided through elimination of individual-level taxes on dividends and capital gains.

In 1992, the U.S. Treasury Department undertook an extensive study of various methods, ultimately favoring dividend exclusion at the personal level. The firm-level deduction, which was actually proposed in 1984, did not allow the flexibility of imposing some tax on tax-exempt shareholders. The other methods were viewed as undesirable because of their complexity. In 2003 temporary dividend relief was enacted in the form of a lower tax rate.

Treasury also explored a new and much more far-reaching approach—the Comprehensive Business Income Tax (CBIT). This proposal would tax all business income—from both debt and equity—at the firm level. Firms would not be able to deduct interest, but this interest would not be taxed to the recipient. This proposal would eliminate virtually all of the existing distortions, would not lose revenue (thus meeting both revenue and distributional objectives), and would be relatively simple to administer. CBIT does face some problems in transition and application to small businesses, and it might discourage foreign supplies of debt capital.

Even a partial reduction in the excess tax may be well worthwhile, because the excess burden of a tax rises with the square of the tax. The welfare gain per dollar of revenue may therefore be quite large, even with only a partial movement toward a neutral system.

ADDITIONAL READINGS

Bradford, David F. *Untangling the Income Tax.* Cambridge, MA: Harvard University Press, 1999.

Carroll, Robert, Kevin Hassett, and James B. Mackie III. "The Effect of Dividend Tax Relief on Incentives." *National Tax Journal* 56 (September 2003): 629–53.

Fullerton, Don, and Diane Lim Rogers. *Who Bears the Lifetime Tax Burden?* Washington, DC: The Brookings Institution, 1993.

Gravelle, Jane G. *The Economic Effects of Taxing Capital Income.* Cambridge, MA: MIT Press, 1994.

———. "The Corporate Tax: Where Has It Been and Where Is It Going?" *National Tax Journal* 57, no. 4 (December 2004): 903–23.

Gravelle, Jane G., and Laurence J. Kotlikoff. "The Incidence and Efficiency Costs of Corporate Taxation When Corporate and Noncorporate Firms Produce the Same Goods." *Journal of Political Economy* 97 (August 1989): 749–90.

Gravelle, Jane G., and Kent Smetters. "Who Bears the Burden of the Corporate Tax in an Open Economy?" National Bureau of Economic Research Working Paper 86280, Cambridge, MA, 2001.

Harberger, Arnold H. "The Incidence of the Corporation Income Tax." *Journal of Political Economy* 70 (June 1962): 215–40.

U.S. Department of the Treasury. *Report on Integration of the Individual and Corporate Tax Systems.* Washington, DC: U.S. Government Printing Office, January 1992.

Zodrow, George R. "On the 'Traditional' and 'New' Views of Dividend Taxation." *National Tax Journal* 45 (December 1991): 497–510.

Cross-references: cost of capital; dividends, double taxation of; foreign corporations, federal taxation of; incidence of taxes; income tax, federal; integration, corporate tax; inventory accounting; investment tax credits; marginal effective tax rate; multinational corporations, taxation; subchapter S corporation; taxable income, corporate; uniform capitalization rules.

Income tax, corporate, state and local

Robert P. Strauss
Carnegie Mellon University

April Franco
University of Iowa

A tax levied on the net income of general corporations subject to tax in 45 states and the District of Columbia.

This tax is variously defined in state tax law as a direct tax on income, or as a franchise or privilege tax measured by net income. A number of states, most notably New York and Ohio, impose the larger of a net income tax or a tax on a corporation's net worth, which in turn is limited in dollar amount. The latter is viewed as a minimum tax imposed when net income is zero or negative. In addition to these state-level levies, there are a number of municipal corporate net income taxes; the most prominent is imposed by New York City at a rate of 8.85 percent (in addition to the state corporate net income tax rate of 7.5 percent). The states collected $25.1 billion of corporate net income taxes in 2002, or 4.7 percent of state general tax revenues.

State corporate net income tax rates (as of 2004) vary among the states from as low as 1 percent, the lowest marginal corporate tax rate in Alaska and Arkansas, to as much as 10.5 percent, the highest marginal tax rate in North Dakota. Of the 45 state corporation income taxes, only 13 (Alaska, Arkansas, Hawaii, Iowa, Kentucky, Louisiana, Maine, Mississippi, Nebraska, New Mexico, Ohio, North Dakota, and Vermont) provide for a progressive rate structure; the others impose proportional tax rates. The top marginal tax rate in these 13 states' rates occur on net incomes of between $10,000 and $250,000.

The general structure of the state corporate income tax base parallels that of the federal corporate income tax base, and all states either adopt or heavily refer to the Internal Revenue Code in the definition of receipts, deductions, and net income. Virtually all state corporate net income taxes define state-taxable corporate net income with reference to federal net income as shown on line 28 of federal corporate tax Form 1120; this initial measure of net income is then adjusted for federal and state bond interest.

Net income is reduced in all but 10 states by the amount of federal bond interest received by a corporation; 40 states increase state corporate income by the amount of interest received on other states' bonds; 14 states add back interest earned on their own state and local bonds. Of the 45 states that impose a corporate net income tax, 36 allow the deduction of other states' corporate net income taxes in determining taxable income.

The states vary considerably in their treatment of intercorporate dividends received. Some states allow the federal deduction of 100 percent of dividends received by subsidiaries owned 80 percent or more by a parent taxable in their state, while others allow higher or lower percentage deductions that depend on the relationship between the payor and payee. Some states, not only California, tax all inter-corporate dividends. Among the states, all but New York and Michigan accord some variant of current federal depreciation rules, although many that follow the federal rules do not provide the bonus depreciation that was enacted in 2002 and 2003. Michigan accords an investment tax credit in lieu of depreciation, and New York allows federal depreciation rules prior to the Accelerated Cost Recovery System.

Application of state corporate net income taxes to corporations engaged in multistate business is governed by the federal Constitution through the Commerce, Equal Protection, and Due Process Clauses, U.S. Supreme Court decisions interpreting these constitutional protections, and Public Law 86-272 and its state constitutional and statutory counterparts. In 1959, the U.S. Supreme Court determined that state taxation of income earned in interstate commerce was not a violation of the Commerce Clause as long as the method of assessing the taxable income was in line with the local activities of the taxpayer in the state. The Supreme Court later provided a four-pronged test to establish the constitutionality of state taxes on interstate commerce.

The test measures whether the tax is applied to an activity with substantial nexus, fairly apportioned, nondiscriminatory against interstate commerce, and fair relative to the services provided by the state to the taxpayer. The first prong of the test is also part of Public Law 86-272. In the case of a property tax levied by a state in which the commerce involves a foreign country, two additional tests are used. If the tax is shown to subject foreign commerce to the risk of multiple taxation or to impair the federal government's ability to "speak with

one voice," then the tax will be disallowed. Further, Public Law 86-272 determines whether or not a firm engaged in the interstate sale of tangible personal property may be subject to a state's corporate net income tax. Generally, an out-of-state business must have a permanent physical presence and employees in a state in order to be taxable under a state's corporate income tax.

Geographic attribution on a state-by-state basis of a multistate corporation's overall net income is accomplished through either the use of establishment-level books and records (separate accounting) or the proportionate attribution among states of overall income based on the location of its payroll, property, and sales. In 1957, a model statute, the Uniform Division of Income for Tax Purposes Act, was developed by the states to define state-taxable net income and procedures recommended to determine in a practical manner the payroll, property, and sales of a multistate corporation. In addition, the model statute provides that investment income, defined as nonbusiness income, be entirely attributed or allocated to the commercial domicile of the corporation. Over the past 45 years, special apportionment rules have been developed for transportation, telecommunications, and financial institutions (see also *apportionment*).

State taxation of the corporate form of business dates back to the early 19th century when corporate charters were initially granted through individual acts of state legislatures, and fees were collected for the privilege of incorporating and doing business in the state. It should be noted that the corporation generally succeeded earlier colonial business forms such as trading and joint-stock companies, because the corporate form offered limited liability as well as ease of investment to shareholders and perpetuity to the business itself. Corporate registration fees were broadened in the middle of the 19th century in many states to levies on the measured capital stock (usually net worth) of the incorporated company. As incorporation became administered through state secretaries of state, and information was routinely collected on the officers and amount of capitalization of the newly formed corporation, these fees became general corporation taxes. Like the development of state personal income taxes, state adoption of the corporate income tax preceded federal enactment of the federal corporate income tax: Hawaii enacted the first corporate net income tax in 1901, eight years before Congress enacted the modern federal corporate income tax.

Unlike the corporate form in other industrialized countries, the U.S. corporation is a legal instrumentality of subnational governments. Until the turn of the 20th century, one corporation could not own shares of another. New Jersey was the first to permit, through state law, one corporation's ownership of another. Other states quickly followed as the business community pressured state legislatures for the authority to create such parent corporations or holding companies. Until the New Jersey statute was enacted, trusts were used to own corporations. Especially with the advent of the holding company, corporations enjoyed a number of distinct benefits:

perpetual life, limited liability for shareholders or investors, and ready transferability or liquidity of investment interests. Additional benefits that corporations (and unincorporated businesses) enjoy include the definition, enforcement, and protection of private property rights and contracts and various specific services provided by the state. Because of these benefits, and the legality of the corporation as a separate entity, taxation of corporate net income has been justified under both the benefit and the ability-to-pay theories of taxation.

While the corporation is a legal entity of state government, recent federal tax treatment of limited liability corporations, which are a hybrid of the corporate and partnership forms of business organizations, have led all but New Jersey and Texas to follow designations of limited liability corporations based on federal tax law. Older industrial states, primarily in the East, which began imposing capital levies in the 19th century in conjunction with the corporate registration process, have tended to treat corporations that are part of a holding company as separate entities. States that began taxing corporations after the advent of the holding company form have generally looked to the overall corporation or the unitary business as the basis of taxation. California, which adopted its first corporate net income tax statute in 1929, has been the most aggressive in employing the unitary business tax concept.

Three tests, resulting from a series of U.S. Supreme Court decisions, are used in determining whether a business is unitary: the three-unities test, the dependency/contribution test, and the factors of profitability test. The first is a three-pronged test, which holds that a business is unitary as long as any one of three tests is satisfied. They are tests of unity of ownership; unity of operation, which is linked to staff functions; and unity of use, which is linked to line functions. These tests are widely criticized for their ambiguity. The second test, dependency/contribution, establishes a business to be unitary when instate operations depend upon, or contribute to, out-of-state operations. The final test, factors of profitability, requires proof of functional integration, centralization of management, and economies of scale. It is important to notice that these tests are not discrete; there is substantial overlap because the same factors can be used as evidence in more than one test. The U.S. Supreme Court has offered no "bright line" test requiring a business to have a substantial flow of goods in order to be held to be unitary. In fact, it has declared that the prerequisite is a "flow of value, not a flow of goods."

Which of these tests is used in the state's determination of a unitary business depends primarily on the form of the business organization. Vertically integrated corporations will usually be treated as unitary, and horizontally integrated corporations will not. In the case of vertically integrated corporations, the tests of dependency/contribution and factors of profitability are used, while in the case of the horizontally integrated corporations, the three-unities test is used. In the case of vertically integrated corporations, the three-unities test does not "fit" well, and the California Supreme Court has indicated that it would apply less weight to this test. For a vertically integrated corporation, the need by one division for the raw materials or products provided by another division is viewed as proof for the dependency/contribution test. In the case of the factors of profitability test, proof is given by either centralized management or controlled interaction of the divisions. For a horizontally integrated corporation to be treated as unitary, there must be a sufficient degree of centralized management and central services. In 1982, the U.S. Supreme Court stated that the mere potential of contribution to income from functional integration, centralization of management, and economies of scale is not sufficient for a business to be held to be unitary; this contribution must actually occur. Further, the Supreme Court has noted no difference in applying the standards of central management and economies of scale to either vertically or horizontally integrated businesses.

The unitary business concept has effects in several areas of state corporate income tax. One area involves whether a business must use formula apportionment or separate accounting in determining taxable income. If a business is held to be unitary, then it must use formula apportionment. A second area is a test of whether an affiliated group of corporations must file on a combined report basis in a particular state. For instance, nearly one-quarter of the states require unitary businesses to file a combined report, and more than half have combined reporting. More than half of the states permit businesses to file on a consolidated rather than a combined basis.

While state application of the unitary business concept has been upheld by the U.S. Supreme Court, it continues to be the source of considerable friction between business taxpayers and state tax administrators. Business taxpayers often express the view that the ambiguity of the concept, especially when applied on a worldwide basis, encourages aggressive tax administration and materially increases the risk of multiple taxation. On the other hand, state tax administrators often express the view that multistate business taxpayers aggressively plan their state corporate income taxes, utilize transfer pricing and other mechanisms to overstate income in non–income tax states, and understate their income in states with corporate income taxes.

ADDITIONAL READINGS

Commerce Clearing House. *All States Tax Guide.* Chicago: Commerce Clearing House, 2004.

Fox, William F., and LeAnn Luna. "State Corporate Tax Revenue Trends: Causes and Possible Solutions." *National Tax Journal* 55, no. 3 (September 2002): 491–508.

Gellis, Ann J. "Legal and Constitutional Foundations of Taxation." In *Handbook on Taxation,* edited by W. Bartley Hildreth and James Richardson (5–20). New York: Marcel Dekker, Inc., 1999.

Gupta, Sanjay, and Lillian F. Mills. "Does Disconformity in State Corporate Income Tax Systems Affect Compliance Cost Burdens?" *National Tax Journal* 56, no. 2 (June 2003): 355–71.

Hellerstein, Jerome R., and Walter Hellerstein. *State Taxation. I. Corporate Income and Franchise Taxes,* 2nd ed. Boston: Warren, Gorham, and Lamont, 1995.

Hellerstein, Jerome R., Walter Hellerstein, and Joan Youngman. *State and Local Taxation: Cases and Materials,* 6th ed. St. Paul, MN: West Publishing Company, 1997.

McIvre, Charles E., Jr. "Defining a Unitary Business: An Economists View." In *The State Corporation Income Tax on Worldwide Unitary Combination,* edited by Charles E. McLure (89–124). Stanford, CA: Hoover Institution Press.

Multistate Tax Commission. *Multistate Tax Compact.* Washington, DC: Multistate Tax Commission. http://www.mtc.gov.

Oslund, Patricia C. "Corporate Income and Franchise Taxes." In *Handbook on Taxation,* edited by W. Bartley Hildreth and James Richardson (205–26). New York: Marcel Dekker, Inc., 1999.

Schoettle, Ferdinand P. *State and Local Taxation: The Law and Policy of Multi-Jurisdictional Taxation.* Newark, NJ: LexisNexis/Matthew Bender, 2003.

Cross-references: apportionment; income tax, corporate, federal; income tax, federal; multinational corporations, taxation of; multistate tax commission; value-added tax, state.

Income tax, federal

Emil M. Sunley
Janet G. Stotsky
International Monetary Fund

A tax levied by the federal government on the incomes of individuals and businesses.

At the federal level, the personal income tax is the most important revenue source, comprising 9.2 percent of gross domestic product in fiscal year 2002, while the corporate income tax comprised 2.0 percent of gross domestic product that year.

The income tax applies to every individual and entity having taxable income. Taxpayers are classified by the type of returns they are required to file. Individuals file the individual tax return; in 2002, 130.2 million of these forms were filed, making them the best-known and least-liked government forms. Corporate returns totaled 5.1 million in 2002. Trusts, estates, and partnerships file another form.

The base of the income tax falls far short of a comprehensive notion of income. The starting point is "gross income," defined broadly as "all income from whatever source derived." Taxable income is determined for both individuals and corporations by subtracting allowable exclusions, exemptions, and deductions from gross income.

The personal income tax

For individuals, gross income includes wages and salaries, taxable interest, dividends, capital gains, rents, royalties, pension income including distributions from Individual Retirement Accounts (IRAs), business income from sole proprietorships, income from partnerships, income from estates and trusts, farm income, refunds of state and local income taxes (if they were previously deducted), alimony received, unemployment benefits, Social Security benefits over certain dollar limits, and other income. U.S. residents are generally taxed on worldwide income, although they may receive credit for taxes paid to foreign countries. There is also an exclusion for earned income derived from a foreign source.

Gross income is a misnomer in two important ways. First, certain items are specifically excluded from gross income. These include gifts and bequests, death benefits, interest on tax-exempt state and local bonds, compensation for injuries or sickness, amounts received on accident and health plans, certain fringe benefits (the most important being pension contributions and health care benefits), and certain income transfers. Second, gross income is in some cases a net concept because certain expenses relating to earning income are netted out (e.g., from partnerships and subchapter S corporations). Individuals who derive income from sole proprietorships may claim their incomes and expenses related to their business activities on a separate schedule, which is then integrated with the rest of the personal income tax.

Taxpayers are allowed to deduct certain amounts, termed "adjustments," from gross income to arrive at adjusted gross income (AGI). The most important of these adjustments are one-half of self-employment taxes paid by the self-employed, qualified contributions to certain tax-deferred retirement accounts (IRAs and Keogh retirement plans), and alimony paid.

Taxable income is defined as AGI minus personal exemptions and either a standard deduction or allowable itemized deductions. Taxpayers could claim a personal exemption of $3,050 in 2003 for each taxpayer and dependent included on the tax return, although these exemptions are phased out for high-income taxpayers. Individuals can choose to itemize personal deductions or to claim the standard deduction—$4,750 for single individuals and $9,500 for married couples filing jointly in 2003. Itemized deductions consist of medical expenses over 7.5 percent of AGI; mortgage interest (with some restrictions); charitable contributions; state and local income and property taxes (but not sales or excise taxes or fees paid to state and local governments); casualty or theft losses over 10 percent of AGI; and unreimbursed employee business expenses, expenses incurred in earning investment income, and other miscellaneous expenses over 2 percent of AGI. Middle- and higher-income families and individuals are more likely to itemize their personal deductions because they tend to pay high state and local taxes and have larger home mortgage interest deductions. Overall, more than 32 percent of individual taxpayers itemized in 2002. Taxpayers reported taxable income of $4.1 trillion in 2002.

The U.S. personal income tax had a rate schedule in 2005 with six marginal tax rates—10, 15, 25, 28, 33, and 35 percent. In addition, various phase-out provisions for personal exemptions and itemized deductions can increase the effective marginal tax rate for many taxpayers. The combination of six brackets and phaseouts has resulted in a marginal tax rate schedule that does not vary smoothly with income. Preferential taxation of some forms of capital income and the interaction of the tax system with the earned income tax credit for low-income families and Social Security taxes, as well as with expenditure programs, results in an even more complicated marginal tax rate schedule.

Individuals may file under four different rate schedules, applying to different forms of household composition. The most widely used schedules are for married couples filing jointly and for single-income individuals. The widths of the tax brackets are wider for joint filers than for single filers. There is a rate schedule for married couples filing separately, but it is little used as it is seldom advantageous on tax grounds for married couples to file separately. The final rate schedule, which applies to heads of households, is generally used by unmarried individuals with a "qualifying dependent" (a child or parent who lives with the taxpayer; however, a dependent parent may live apart). It provides brackets that are wider than the rate schedule for single filers but narrower than the rate schedule for joint filers.

By permitting joint filing, the U.S. personal income tax imposes the same tax on married couples with the same income (regardless of how the total income is split between the spouses) but imposes a different tax on a married couple and an unmarried individual with the same income. One result of permitting joint filing is that the personal income tax results in both marriage penalties and marriage subsidies. If two individuals with about the same income marry, their tax burden under the joint rate schedule will be higher than it would be if they were both permitted to continue to file as unmarried individuals. On the other hand, if two individuals with highly uneven incomes marry, the combined tax burden will be lower under joint filing.

Realized capital gains are included in full in taxable income, but most long-term capital gains (and dividends) are subject to lower rates: a maximum rate of 15 percent (5 percent for individuals in the 10 or 15 percent tax bracket). Thus, for higher-income taxpayers, there is a significant difference between the tax rates on ordinary income and capital gains (and dividends). Capital losses may be offset against capital gains and then against ordinary income, but no more than $3,000 per year in losses may be offset against ordinary income, with the remainder carried forward indefinitely. Taxpayers may exclude $250,000 of gain ($500,000 for a joint return) on the sale of a personal residence; this exclusion is available every two years.

After computing tax on taxable income, the individual taxpayer is allowed to claim certain tax credits. The most important of these are the earned-income credit (a variable, vanishing credit targeted to low-income filers who work), the child credit, the education credit, the credit for child or dependent care, the foreign tax credit, and the retirement savings contribution credit. Of these, only the earned-income credit and child care credit are refundable (the excess of the credit over the tax liability is returned to the taxpayer). Many low-income households are not liable to tax (if their AGI is less than the total of their deductions and personal exemptions), but may still receive a tax credit refund through the earned-income credit.

The personal income tax is partly indexed to inflation. The personal exemption, the standard deduction, the maximum earned income and the phaseout base amounts of the earned-income credit, the bracket widths, the income limits for limiting itemized deductions and phaseouts of the personal exemptions, and the maximum earnings subject to self-employment tax are all indexed to overall changes in the Consumer Price Index. Indexing of fixed dollar amounts was first enacted in 1981 for tax years after 1984, but frequent changes in the tax law since then have resulted in a number of discretionary changes in the indexed parameters. There is no indexing of depreciation, capital gains, or interest income and expense.

Individuals are also subject to the alternative minimum tax. This tax is computed by taking AGI, making adjustments and additions for tax preferences, and then subtracting certain itemized deductions and the allowable exemption. The rate is 26 or 28 percent for individuals. Taxpayers pay the alternative minimum tax if it exceeds their regular tax. An increasing number of taxpayers are falling under the alternative minimum tax, as the tax brackets and the exemption are not indexed for inflation.

The main form of tax collection is based on withholding of employee earnings, instituted in 1943 with the dramatic expansion of the income tax to finance World War II. There is only very limited withholding of capital income. However, individuals with significant income outside the withholding system must estimate their tax liability and pay it in quarterly installments during the year. On their final tax return, taxpayers reconcile their final tax liability with amounts already paid.

The corporation income tax

Taxable income for corporations and other entities required to file the corporation income tax return is defined as gross income less allowable deductions. Domestic corporations are, in general, taxed on worldwide income, although they may receive credit for tax paid to foreign countries. Most businesses use the accrual method of accounting; businesses that have inventories are required to use the accrual method. Reserves typically are not allowed for tax purposes, although small banks can maintain tax-deductible reserves for bad debts and insurance companies can maintain reserves for future liabilities. Businesses may use either the last-in first-out (LIFO) or first-in first-out (FIFO) methods of inventory accounting. Business taxpayers depreciate machinery and equipment under accelerated methods and real estate using the straight-line method over lifetimes set to approximate the economic usefulness of the asset. They can also expense up to $100,000 of machinery and equipment each year. State and local taxes paid by a business are generally deductible business expenses for income tax purposes. Net operating losses can typically be carried back two years and forward 20 years.

The United States adheres to a modified classical system of a separate corporate tax, as dividends received by individuals are taxed at a maximum rate of 15 percent. Potential double taxation—one tax at the corporate level and a second tax at the shareholder level—is mitigated for subchapter S corporations (small corporations taxed like partnerships), cooperatives, regulated investment companies, real estate investment trusts, and real estate mortgage investment conduits. In addition, domestic corporations are allowed a deduction of 70, 80, or 100 percent of dividends received from taxable domestic corporations, with the amount of the deduction dependent on the degree of ownership.

The formal tax rate schedule for corporations has progressive marginal rates of 15, 25, 34, and 35 percent, with the top rate applying to corporations with taxable income in excess of $18.3 million. The benefit of the lower tax rates, however, is phased out or recaptured over certain income ranges by imposing additional taxes of 3 or 5 percent. As a result, the marginal tax rate schedule for corporations can be said to have eight marginal rates of 15, 25, 34, 39, 34, 35, 38, and 35 percent, with the 39 and 38 percent rates being the marginal rates for taxable income in the income range over which the benefits of the lower marginal rates are phased out. The taxable income of certain personal service corporations is taxed at 35 percent.

Corporations can claim certain tax credits, including the foreign tax credit and the general business credit. The latter is an umbrella covering the investment credit (made up of the energy credit, the rehabilitation credit, and the reforestation credit), the work opportunity credit, the welfare-to work credit, the alcohol fuels credit, the increased research activities credit, the low-income housing credit, and so forth. The empowerment zone and renewal communities employment credit is part of the general business credit but is calculated separately.

Corporations pay tax on income from the sale of capital assets at the same rate as other income. Certain tax benefits, such as depreciation, are subject to recapture at ordinary income tax rates. Unlike individuals, corporations can only offset capital losses against capital gains. The remaining losses may be carried back three years and carried forward five years against capital gains.

Certain nonprofit organizations, including charitable, religious, educational, and medical organizations, trade associations, labor unions, and fraternal organizations, are exempt from corporate income taxes. These organizations are, however, subject to tax on business income derived from activities unrelated to their exempt purposes.

Business income is not indexed for inflation. Depreciation allowances are based on historical cost. Accelerated depreciation is sometimes justified on the grounds that this compensates businesses for the use of historical cost basis in an inflationary environment. Though inventories are based on historical costs, businesses may choose whether to use LIFO or FIFO inventory accounting. LIFO offers some advantages in an inflationary environment. Financial assets are not indexed to inflation. There is no adjustment to the stock of debt based on changes in its value from inflation fluctuations. Nominal capital gains and nominal interest income are taxable, while nominal interest payments are deductible.

Corporations are also subject to an alternative minimum tax, which was designed to ensure that all corporations pay tax, even those benefiting from extensive tax preferences. The base of this tax is computed by recalculating taxable income, making adjustments, and adding back certain tax preference items. The rate of tax is 20 percent for corporations. In addition to the alternative minimum tax, corporations are subject to an environmental tax. The base for this tax is alternative minimum taxable income in excess of $2 million. The tax rate is 0.12 percent.

There is no withholding system for corporations. Instead, they are required to pay estimated taxes in quarterly installments based on their estimated current earnings or, in some cases, previous earnings. On their final tax return, taxpayers reconcile their final tax liability with amounts already paid.

ADDITIONAL READINGS

Auerbach, Alan J., and Joel Slemrod. "The Economic Effects of the Tax Reform Act of 1986." *Journal of Economic Literature* 35 (June 1971): 389–632.

Burman, Leonard. *The Labyrinth of Capital Gains Tax Policy.* Washington, DC: Brookings Institution, 1999.

Carasso, Adam, and C. Eugene Steuerle. "How Marriage Penalties Change under the 2001 Tax Bill." Discussion paper no. 2, Washington, DC: Urban Institute/Brookings Institution Tax Policy Center, 2002.

Gravelle, Jane G. "The Economics of Taxing Capital Income: The Twentieth Century and Beyond." In *Tax Conversations: A Guide to Key Issues in the Tax Reform Debate: Essays in Honour of John G. Head,* edited by Richard Krever (223–59). London: Kluwer Law, 1997.

Internal Revenue Service. Statistics of Income, various years.

Slemrod, Joel, and Jon Bakija. *Taxing Ourselves: A Citizens Guide to the Great Debate over Tax Reform.* Cambridge, MA: MIT Press, 1996.

Steuerle, C. Eugene. *The Tax Decade: How Taxes Came to Dominate the Public Agenda.* Washington, DC: Urban Institute Press, 1992.

U.S. Office of Management and Budget. Historical Tables: Budget of the United States Government, various years.

Wallace, Sally, and Barbara M. Edwards. "Personal Income Tax." In *Handbook on Taxation,* edited by Hildreth W. Bartley and James A. Richardson (149–90). New York: Marcel Dekker, Inc., 1999.

Cross-references: adjusted gross income; alternative minimum tax, corporate; alternative minimum tax, personal; capital cost recovery; child care credit; dividends, double taxation of; family, tax treatment of; income tax, corporate, federal; inventory accounting; itemized deductions; marriage penalty; nonprofit organizations, federal tax treatment of; taxable income, corporate; withholding of taxes.

Individual retirement accounts

Paul Burnham and Larry Ozanne
Congressional Budget Office

Savings accounts with specific income tax incentives and penalties designed to encourage working people to save for retirement.

Individual Retirement Accounts (IRAs) were first authorized in the Employee Retirement Income Security Act of 1974 (ERISA) as a means of encouraging working people to save for retirement. Recently, preretirement withdrawals from IRAs for major medical expenses, higher-education costs, and a first-time home purchase have been authorized. Unlike 401(k) and related salary reduction plans, IRAs are not run by employers. The enactment of IRAs extended to workers without pensions the same kind of tax advantages already granted to pension funds and the self-employed.

History

Starting in 1975, individuals were allowed to set up separate accounts at financial institutions and deduct the value of their contributions from their current taxable income. Only employees without pensions were eligible to contribute, and their annual contributions were limited to 15 percent of pay or a maximum of $1,500. The investment returns of these accounts were also excluded from taxable income in the year earned, but withdrawals were to be included in taxable income in the year they occurred. To encourage use of the accounts for retirement saving, ERISA set a penalty of 10 percent additional tax on withdrawals by taxpayers before age 59½.

The Economic Recovery Tax Act of 1981 expanded IRA eligibility and increased maximum contributions. Starting in 1982, all persons with earnings could contribute to IRAs, whether or not they were in a pension plan, and the maximum contribution was increased to 100 percent of earnings or $2,000. In response, tax returns with IRA contributions jumped from 4 percent of all returns with wage and salary income in 1981 to 14 percent in 1982 and 18 percent in 1986. Deductible IRA contributions were restricted by the Tax Reform Act of 1986. Starting in 1987, the act allowed deductible contributions only by an individual who was not covered by an employer pension plan (and whose spouse was not covered), and who had adjusted gross income between $25,000 and $35,000 (or, for joint returns, $40,000 to $50,000). Those not qualifying for deductible contributions could still make nondeductible contributions, thereby benefiting from the exclusion of investment returns from taxable income. The restriction caused tax returns with deductible IRA contributions to drop to 8 percent of all returns in 1987 and to decline slowly from there, reaching 4 percent in 1997.

The Taxpayer Relief Act of 1997 substantially raised the income limits applying to taxpayers covered by an employer plan. Eventually, those limits will be $50,000 to $60,000 for single taxpayers (2005 and after) and $80,000 to $100,000 for married taxpayers (2007 and after). Even higher limits ($150,000 to $160,000) were enacted for married taxpayers previously disqualified from making deductible contributions solely by virtue of a spouse being covered by an employer plan. The act also allows individuals to elect back-loaded IRAs, called "Roth" IRAs, in which contributions are not deductible but withdrawals are not taxed—a treatment similar to that of a tax-exempt bond. These IRAs are phased out between $95,000 and $110,000 of income for singles, and $150,000 to $160,000 for joint returns. All but the highest-

income taxpayers will thus be eligible for some type of fully tax-favored IRA. Regulations imposing penalties on premature withdrawals were also relaxed, so that the accounts may be used to save for higher education expenses or the first purchase of a home.

The Economic Growth and Tax Relief Reconciliation Act of 2001 (EGTRRA) increased the maximum allowable contribution to both deductible IRAs and Roth IRAs. For taxpayers under age 50, the limit will reach $5,000 in 2008 and then will be indexed for inflation. Taxpayers age 50 and above are allowed to make additional contributions up to a limit that will reach $1,000 in 2006. Like all provisions of EGTRRA, the higher limits are scheduled to expire in 2011 and revert to $2,000. EGTRRA also provides lower-income taxpayers with a nonrefundable credit of up to 50 percent of IRA contributions up to $2,000 through 2006.

Effect on saving

IRAs have been popular among taxpayers. For example, during the years in which all taxpayers were eligible to contribute to IRAs, up to $40 billion of savings was deposited into IRA accounts annually. The large volume of IRA contributions, however, does not necessarily indicate that IRAs increased saving. IRAs increased personal saving only to the extent that people funded their contributions by reducing their consumption. Contributions funded by saving less in other accounts and by paying fewer taxes do not raise saving.

In principle, the incentive structure of IRAs could increase or decrease saving. The deferral of taxation on contributions and investment earnings until withdrawal increases the rate of return to saving. Because a higher return to saving has offsetting substitution and income effects, the net effect could be to increase or decrease saving. In addition, the limit on contributions means that persons able to contribute more than the limit without increasing their saving have only an income effect, which could reduce saving. Finally, features of the IRA and its marketing by financial institutions may have increased saving by making it easier for people to save. The heavy advertising of IRAs between 1982 and 1986 may have helped people focus on the importance of saving for retirement, and the deduction on contributions and the penalty on withdrawals may have helped people make and preserve their contributions.

Empirical studies have not been able to resolve the uncertainty about how IRAs affect saving, although many attempts have been made. The evidence for the full population is contradictory, but a limited consensus suggests that IRAs increased saving for nonelderly and less-wealthy families. The range of results is indicated by three pairs of analysts who have each measured saving for samples of families, estimated models of saving behavior, and used those models to predict how IRAs affected saving between 1982 and 1986. One pair, Venti and Wise (1986, 1990, 1991), estimate in three separate studies that if the contribution limit had been raised above

$2,000, between 57 and 66 percent of additional IRA contributions would have come from reduced consumption. A second pair, Gale and Scholz (1994), estimate that the level would be at most 2 percent, and that IRAs possibly increased consumption. The third pair, Joines and Manegold (1991), find that the expansion of eligibility in 1982 had no statistically significant effect on consumption for the full population.

Although Gale and Scholz and Joines and Manegold find no increase in saving for the full population, each pair finds an increase for a subpopulation. Gale and Scholz find that people under age 60, who could not withdraw from IRAs without paying the penalty, reduced their consumption by up to 35 cents per dollar contributed. Joines and Manegold find that people who had less than $25,000 of taxable financial assets in 1982 reduced their consumption by 63 cents per dollar contributed. Because Venti and Wise find large increases in saving for the full population, all three studies present evidence that IRAs increased saving for sizable subpopulations. Studies finding an increase in saving for subpopulations but not for the full population indicate either that the increases found for some subpopulations were small relative to saving for the full population or that other subpopulations reduced their saving.

More recently, Attanasio and DeLeire (2002) found little evidence of an IRA savings effect, using a methodology similar to Joines and Manegold.

ADDITIONAL READINGS

Attanasio, Orazio P., and Thomas C. DeLeire. "The Effect of Individual Retirement Accounts on Household Consumption and National Saving." *The Economic Journal* 112 (July 2002): 504–38.

Congressional Budget Office. *The Uncertain Effect of IRAs on Saving.* Washington, DC: Congressional Budget Office, 1994.

Engen, Eric M., William G. Gale, and John Karl Scholz. "The Illusory Effects of Savings Incentives on Savings." *Journal of Economic Perspectives* 10 (Fall 1996): 113–38.

Gale, William G., and John Karl Scholz. "IRAs and Household Saving." *American Economic Review* 84, no. 5 (December 1994): 1233–60.

Gravelle, Jane G. "Do Individual Retirement Accounts Increase Saving?" *Journal of Economic Perspectives* 5, no. 2 (Spring 1991): 133–48.

Hubbard, R. Glenn, and Jonathan S. Skinner. "Assessing the Effectiveness of Savings Incentives." *Journal of Economic Perspectives* 10 (Fall 1996): 73–90.

Joines, Douglas H., and James G. Manegold. "IRAs and Saving: Evidence from a Panel of Taxpayers." Mimeograph, Table 8. University of Southern California, September 1991.

Poterba, James, Steven Venti, and David A. Wise. "How Retirement Saving Programs Increase Saving." *Journal of Economic Perspectives* 10 (Fall 1996): 91–112.

Skinner, Jonathan. "Individual Retirement Accounts: A Review of the Evidence." *Tax Notes,* January 13, 1992: 201–12.

Venti, Steven F., and David A. Wise. "Tax Deferred Accounts, Constrained Choice and Estimation of Individual Saving," *Review of Economic Studies* 53 (1986): 593–94.

———. "Have IRAs Increased U.S. Saving? Evidence from Consumer Expenditure Surveys." *Quarterly Journal of Economics* 105, no. 3 (August 1990): 691.

———. "The Saving Effect of Tax-Deferred Retirement Accounts." In *National Saving and Economic Performance,* edited by B. Douglas Bernheim and John B. Shoven (123). Chicago: University of Chicago Press, 1991.

Cross-references: deferral of tax; income tax, federal; profit-sharing plans; saving, taxes and.

Inflation indexation of income taxes

Vito Tanzi
International Monetary Fund

Measures undertaken to prevent real income tax burdens from rising with general price inflation.

When the price level increases, the real burden imposed by income taxes may also increase. Indexing income taxes for inflation prevents this by (1) adjusting tax rates, exemptions, and the standard deduction, and (2) adjusting how the base of the income tax itself is defined, to offset the effects of general increases in price level.

Adjustments in tax rates, exemptions, and the standard deductions

Table 1 shows how inflation could affect the real tax burden of a taxpayer whose only source of income was wages and salaries. The example assumes that in the absence of inflation, the taxpayer's income would be $40,000, and that the tax system would allow the taxpayer to claim a personal exemption of $4,000 and an additional standard deduction of $6,000. The example further assumes that taxable income between $0 and $30,000 is taxed at a rate of 10 percent, while each $1 of taxable income in excess of $30,000 is taxed at a rate of 20 percent.

Column (1) shows that if there were no inflation, the hypothetical taxpayer would face a tax liability of $3,000, which equals 7.5 percent of the taxpayer's total income.

Now assume that the price level increases by 10 percent, and that the taxpayer gets a cost-of-living increase of 10 percent from the employer. As can be seen from column (2), this would increase the taxpayer's income in "current dollars" from $40,000 to $44,000. If no adjustments were made in either the exemption or the standard deduction, the taxpayer's taxable income would increase from $30,000 to $34,000. If there were also no adjustments in tax rates, the "extra" $2,000 in income would also be taxed at the higher rate of 20 percent. Overall, the taxpayer would see tax liability increase from $3,000 to $3,800, which equals 8.6 percent of total income. Because the taxpayer is paying a larger percentage of income in tax than before, the real tax burden has increased.

The real tax burden goes up in this example for two reasons. One is that the exemption and the standard deduction are not increased to keep pace with inflation. In a world with no inflation, the combined effect of these two provisions was to exempt $10,000/$40,000, or 25 percent of the taxpayer's income, from tax. After inflation, if these amounts are not increased, the provisions exempt only $10,000/$44,000 (or just under 23 percent of income) from tax.

TABLE 1. **Effect of Inflation on Real Tax Burden**

Items on tax return	No inflation (1)	10% inflation with no indexing (2)	10% inflation with indexing (3)
Wages and salaries	$40,000	$44,000	$44,000
Personal exemption	$4,000	$4,000	$4,400
Standard deduction	$6,000	$6,000	$6,600
Taxable income	$30,000	$34,000	$33,000
Tax liability	$3,000	$3,800	$3,300
Tax brackets			
$0–$30,000	10%	10%	10%
Over $30,000	20%	20%	20%
Average tax rate	7.5%	8.6%	7.5%

The other reason the real tax burden increases is that the taxpayer is moved into a higher tax bracket because of the cost-of-living increase. This phenomenon has been given the name of "bracket creep" to reflect that, unless tax rates are adjusted, inflation has the effect of pushing taxpayers into higher tax brackets.

Column (3) shows what would happen if personal exemptions, the standard deduction, and tax rates were adjusted for inflation. Adjustments would take the following forms: First, the amounts of the exemption and standard deduction would need to be increased by 10 percent. Second, the 10 percent tax bracket would need to be widened by increasing the upper limit by 10 percent, so that the higher tax rate would take effect at an income of $33,000 instead of $30,000.

If these adjustments were made, the taxpayer would face a postinflation tax liability of $33,000 instead of $34,000 and pay a tax of $3,300 on this income. The inflation-adjusted tax liability would equal 7.5 percent of the taxpayer's current dollar income of $44,000, which is the same real tax burden as before inflation.

Although this illustration is hypothetical, it is not fanciful. During the postwar period, increases in the price level pushed U.S. taxpayers into higher tax brackets while at the same time eroding the value of personal exemptions and the standard deduction. These effects became especially pronounced in the 1970s and early 1980s as oil shocks accelerated the pace of general price increases.

From time to time, Congress and the president took measures to "cut taxes" by raising the amount of the personal exemption or by lowering personal income tax rates. These measures, however, only partially offset the increase in real tax burdens brought about by failing to index exemptions and the standard deduction, and by bracket creep.

The Economic Recovery Tax Act of 1981 marked a fundamental break with this pattern. The act provided, beginning in 1985, that exemptions, the standard deduction, and the width of tax brackets would be adjusted for inflation in a manner similar to that illustrated in the table. Since that time, these items have been adjusted by the Treasury Department each year, based on the Consumer Price Index. The result is that real tax burdens on wage and salary income no longer increase automatically with inflation.

Inflation and the measurement of capital income

This illustration is only one way in which inflation can affect real income tax burdens. The amount of capital income, such as interest, capital gains, and profits reported on tax returns, also rises with inflation. Much of the increase in taxable income, however, may really be a return of capital, which in principle should not be taxed, rather than a return on capital, which should be included in the base of a comprehensive income tax.

Inflation poses more complicated issues for the proper measurement and taxation of capital income. These are best illustrated using the three most important examples: the measurement of income from capital gains, the depreciation deductions, and the measurement of interest income and expense.

Capital gains

Consider first the case of income from capital gains. Suppose that if prices were stable, a real asset would have increased in value by 10 percent, from $100,000 to $110,000, over a given period. Thus, the capital gains, if realized through sale of the asset, would have been $10,000. Assume instead that over the same period the price level rises by 10 percent so that the nominal value of the asset grows at a rate of 20 percent, of which 10 percent represents inflation and 10 percent represents the real, or inflation-adjusted, return. In this latter case, the value of the asset at the time of sales is $120,000. Without an adjustment for inflation, the reported capital gain would be $20,000, which is more than twice the amount of the real or capital gain of $10,000. In extreme cases, failure to account for inflation may cause taxpayers to be taxed as if they had received a capital gain, when they had either no gain or even a capital loss. In the illustration above, if the real value of the asset appreciated at a rate of 0 percent instead of 10 percent when prices were stable, the taxpayer would have no capital gain. However, if prices rose by 10 percent its value would "increase" from $100,000 to $110,000, and without adjusting for inflation, the taxpayer would be taxed as if the capital gain had been $10,000, when in reality the gain was $0.

Depreciation

The value of tax deductions for depreciation, which represent a return of capital rather than a return on capital, is also affected by inflation. Consider a piece of equipment that is initially purchased for $60,000 and that depreciates on a straight-line basis over three years. If prices were stable, and deductions for economic depreciation were allowed, the taxpayer would take a depreciation deduction of $20,000 each year for three years.

Suppose now that prices increase at a rate of 10 percent per year. In that case, allowing the taxpayer to take depreciation deductions based on the "historical" or non-inflation-adjusted basis of the depreciable asset would not allow the investor a full return of capital; the cost of replacing the services provided by the depreciating machine would rise each year by 10 percent.

Interest income and expense

When prices are not stable and inflation is anticipated, the monetary rate of interest will tend to be higher than the rate prevailing with price stability. If investors have perfect foresight about inflation, the monetary or nominal rate of interest can be assumed to approximate the sum of the real rate and the anticipated increase in the price level. Thus, if the anticipated rate of inflation were 10 percent and the real rate of interest were 5 percent, the nominal interest rate would approximate 15 percent.

In this case, in the absence of a tax on interest income, someone who lent $1,000 would receive $1,050 after one year. If prices were unstable, the lender would receive $1,150 but would not be any better off than if he or she had received $1,050 when prices were stable. This is because $100 out of the $150 of interest income just compensates the lender for the loss caused by inflation on the original financial capital of $1,000. Taxing the full $150 thus overstates the actual interest income received by the lender and paid by the borrower by the amount of $100.

Indexing the tax base

The administrative measures that would need to be implemented in order to prevent inflation from mismeasuring capital income are more complex than those required to deal with bracket creep. In principle, capital gains can be indexed by increasing the taxable basis by the amount of inflation that has occurred since the asset was purchased. Thus, in the example above, the taxable basis of the asset at the time of sale would be multiplied by 110 percent, giving an inflation-adjusted

basis of $110,000. The taxable capital gain would then be the difference between the sales price of the asset of $120,000 and the adjusted basis of $110,000, which would yield the correct result of an inflation-adjusted capital gain of $10,000.

A similar adjustment could be made in the case of depreciable assets. In this case, the undepreciated basis of the asset would be increased each year to reflect the increase in the inflation rate, and this amount would then be divided by number of years remaining. Thus, in the above example, where prices rise at a rate of 10 percent per year, the undepreciated basis at the end of the first year would be $40,000 ($60,000 − $20,000). This amount would be multiplied by 1.10 to yield the inflation-adjusted basis of $44,000. Dividing by 2, the number of years remaining, would result in a year 2 (indexed) deduction of $22,000. Subtracting this amount from $44,000 would yield an undepreciated basis of $22,000, which when multiplied by 1.10 would yield a year 3 (indexed) depreciation deduction of $24,200.

In the case of interest income and expense, an appropriate remedy would be to subtract the inflationary component of interest payments in both interest income received by creditors and interest income paid by borrowers. Thus the borrower in the above example would be required to include $50 instead of $150 as taxable interest income, and the borrower would be allowed to deduct $50 instead of $150 as interest expense.

Both the capital gains exclusion and accelerated depreciation have been defended as crude ways to deal with the effect of inflation on the measurement of capital income. Economists agree, however, that these methods are inexact ways of dealing with the problem, and that using more exact ways of indexing the tax base (such as those summarized above) would be preferable in principle.

In the United States, proposals have been made from time to time to index capital gains and depreciation for inflation following the procedures outlined above; proposals were made to allow for partial indexing of interest payments in the Treasury Department's 1984 proposal for fundamental tax reform. Although the economic principles to be followed in indexing capital income are clear, implementing these principles in practice has proved to be administratively complex, which is one reason why these proposals have yet to be enacted.

Both the political impetus and the economic need for indexing the tax base for inflation are greatest when inflation rates are high. Thus, at the current low rates of inflation, it seems unlikely that significant efforts to index the tax base will be made.

One attractive feature of taxing individuals and business on the basis of consumption instead of income is that one does not need to index capital income for inflation. This is because a consumption tax base would include neither capital gains nor interest payments in taxable income and would not allow deductions to be taken for interest expense. Because the capital cost of assets would be deducted immediately or expensed, adjusting capital cost recovery allowance to reflect the replacement cost of depreciating assets would also not be necessary.

ADDITIONAL READINGS

Congressional Budget Office. "Indexing Capital Gains." Washington, DC: Congressional Budget Office, 1990.

Halperin, Daniel, and C. Eugene Steuerle. "Indexing the Tax System for Inflation." In *Uneasy Compromise: Problems of a Hybrid Income-Consumption Tax,* edited by Henry Aaron and Harvey Galper (347–72). Washington, DC: The Brookings Institution, 1988.

Steuerle, C. Eugene. *The Tax Decade: How Taxes Came to Dominate the Public Agenda.* Washington, DC: The Urban Institute Press, 1992.

Tanzi, Vito. "Inflation and the Indexation of Personal Income Taxes in Theory and Practice." *Banca Nazionale Del Lavoro Quarterly Review* 118 (September 1976): 241–72.

U.S. Department of the Treasury, Office of the Secretary. *Tax Reform for Fairness, Simplicity and Economic Growth,* vol. 2, ch. 9. Washington, DC: U.S. Department of the Treasury, 1984.

Cross-references: capital cost recovery; capital gains taxation; consumption taxation; expensing; inflation tax; interest deductibility; personal exemption, federal; standard deduction, federal.

Inflation tax

G. Thomas Woodward
Congressional Budget Office

A type of finance for which the government increases the supply of money and generates inflation to obtain real resources from the public.

The inflation tax is based on the power of sovereign governments to regulate the money supply. Money—a symbol of purchasing power, such as a coin, note, or book entry—is a medium between selling and buying, used to avoid cumbersome barter. While a variety of entities can function as money, the right to furnish a basic medium of exchange is typically monopolized by the government.

To perform its transactions role, money need only symbolize wealth, not embody it. Thus, it is possible to profit from supplying money. Paper money, for example, is produced at a fraction of its value in the marketplace. Commodity monies, such as precious metals, may also produce a profit for the government if the metallic value of the coin is less than the coin's face value. Consequently, a government can obtain goods and services by creating and spending money into existence, reducing the reliance on explicit taxes.

The government can generate some revenue from money creation simply by satisfying the public's growing need for exchange media. But the need for money for transactions depends largely on the level of economic activity. And the physical capacity of the economy to produce typically places limits on how much additional money is needed. Money serves few purposes other than for exchange. Consequently, infusions of money in excess of what is demanded by eco-

nomic growth result in efforts by the public to spend the excess on the limited goods and available services. This tends to bid up prices.

The revenue gained from money creation without inflation is called seigniorage. When the government goes beyond seigniorage and generates inflation to obtain resources, the additional revenue is said to result from an "inflation tax."

Classification as a tax

The term "tax" stems from two characteristics of seigniorage and inflation. First, through spending the newly created money, the government acquires command over resources. Second, through inflation, the public loses command over resources.

The first part of the process is simple. When the government spends money into existence, it acquires resources equal to the difference between the cost of producing the money and the money's purchasing power. The second part occurs because the excessive creation of money generates inflation, and inflation reduces the purchasing power of the money already in the hands of the public. The real value of all previously issued government money decreases as the prices of goods and services rise. This decrease in the value of the public's money holdings corresponds to the increase in purchasing power by the government.

Consequently, with an inflation tax, the government finances some of its activities by creating money, and the creation of money generates inflation that deprives the public of some of its purchasing power. The result is equivalent to an explicit tax imposed on the money holdings of the public.

The transfer that constitutes the inflation tax should not be confused with other wealth transfers caused by inflation. For example, when inflation is unanticipated, rising prices transfer buying power from creditors to debtors as the latter repay the former with money that is worth less than when the loan was initially extended. Although the government is typically a debtor and often gains from inflation as the real value of its outstanding debt shrinks, this transfer is not considered part of the inflation tax.

Similarly, checking accounts, because they are used as transactions media, are considered money. However, they are not government-created money. The decrease in the purchasing power of money in a checking account is not part of the inflation tax because the gain does not accrue to the government (it typically accrues to the banks' borrowers). Hence, the inflation tax label applies only to government-created money or "monetary base."

Role in government finance

The inflation tax has two unique characteristics that increase its importance as a revenue source—especially as a tax of last resort. First, the tax cannot be evaded. Like any tax, it can be avoided by reducing one's holdings of money; but if one has the money to be taxed, no amount of subterfuge can hide it. Unlike cigarettes, alcohol, income, or other items that may be concealed from taxation, wherever money balances are, inflation will tax them.

Second, the inflation tax rate rises to the level required to earn the revenue that the government decides to collect with it. In the case of any other tax, the government must set a tax rate; its receipts from that tax are then determined by the tax rate interacting with the existing tax base. The resulting receipts may or may not match the government's expectation of what the tax should yield. The inflation tax, however, is set in terms of what the government desires to collect—as much newly created money is spent as is necessary to purchase what the government wants—and for a given tax base (money balances), the tax rate needed to yield those receipts is automatically generated (through inflation).

Consequently, the inflation tax can be a buffer or slack variable in a government's budget, filling whatever gap is created when other revenues and borrowing fall short of outlays. Increasing revenues through other taxes requires explicit increases in tax rates; but the inflation tax rate automatically adjusts itself as necessary to garner a specific amount of revenue. And unless legislated constraints have been imposed on the money creation process, the tax may be imposed administratively, through treasury or central bank action. A government that is weak because it does not command a majority in the legislature or maintains tenuous control over its territory may find that the inflation tax is virtually the only levy it can implement or enforce.

But heavy reliance on the inflation tax is usually short-lived; very large sums can be collected by the government only when the public is ignorant of the rate at which it will be taxed. As with any tax, the revenue yielded depends on whether the public knows in advance what the tax rate will be, with more being collected if people do not expect the tax (or do not expect it to be so high) and fail to minimize their tax burden. In the case of inflation, they may reduce their tax obligation by using foreign currencies for transactions or by using cash management techniques that reduce the money balances they hold.

Because the inflation tax adjusts to the rate necessary to garner a given amount of revenue, it is effective in exploiting this difference between the expected and unexpected tax rate: if the public expects a given rate and reduces its money balances accordingly, the government increases the amount of money it creates to buy goods and services, and the inflation tax rises to an unexpectedly higher rate.

This automatic adjustment can create a dynamically unstable relationship that generates phenomenally high rates of inflation. If the revenue sought by the government is especially large, exceeding the maximum collectible by the tax when the public knows what the rate is, then the tax (and inflation rate) must always be higher than the public expects. And because rising inflation typically engenders expectations of more rising inflation, the inflation rate will have to accelerate to continue yielding the desired revenue. The result is a hyperinflation.

Using inflation to obtain revenues need not result in hyperinflation. It will only generate moderate inflation if the revenue aim of the government is modest. But out-of-control inflations are almost always caused by attempts to raise large amounts of revenue by the inflation tax.

Problems with terminology

A problem with the term "inflation tax" is that it suggests an equivalence between the inflation tax rate and the inflation rate. They are actually different. The tax rate is the amount of real resources obtained by the government divided by the real value of the money supply. This is less than the rate of increase in the overall price level. How much less depends on how quickly prices change in response to money creation and the pattern of government purchases with the newly created money.

Some analysts object to the use of the term inflation tax, regarding it as confusing. An alternative is to call all income from money-creation *seigniorage*. One advantage would be to avoid the confusion arising from inflation that does not derive from money creation. If, for example, the public learns to get by on less money for a given amount of economic activity, the current money supply will become too large and the price level will increase. The public experiences a loss in the value of its real money holdings, but no corresponding increase in government purchasing power occurs. Past seigniorage is transformed into inflation tax, *ex post*. This awkward result is avoided if no distinction is made between seigniorage and the inflation tax to begin with.

ADDITIONAL READINGS

Cagan, Phillip. "The Monetary Dynamics of Hyperinflation." In *Studies in the Quantity Theory of Money,* edited by Milton Friedman (129–221). Chicago: University of Chicago Press, 1999.
Keynes, John Maynard. *Treatise on Money.* New York: Harcourt Brace, 1930.
Sargent, Thomas J., and Neil Wallace. "Rational Expectations and the Dynamics of Hyperinflation." *International Economic Review* 14, no. 2 (June 1973): 328–50.

Cross-references: income tax, federal; inflation indexation of income taxes; seigniorage tax.

Infrastructure financing

Holley H. Ulbrich
Clemson University

Updated by
Steven Maguire
Congressional Research Service, Library of Congress

Methods of financing public investments in physical capital, such as roads, schools, and public works.

The term "infrastructure" carries many meanings, but it generally refers to physical capital—sometimes all capital, sometimes just public capital. The term infrastructure has even been extended to the intangible: Central European nations have been described as lacking the "social infrastructure" essential to democratic capitalism, such as a banking system, laws protecting property rights, and stock exchanges. In the narrow sense, however, infrastructure is generally understood to consist of public physical capital, such as roads, school buildings, water and sewer systems, and parks. Even with that narrower definition, the line between public and private infrastructure is fuzzy. One area may be served by a municipal water system, another by a private for-profit water supplier. Electricity is most often in the private sector, but the industry includes municipal retailers and federal wholesalers.

Public infrastructure, measured by total government fixed assets as a share of total fixed assets in the U.S., has declined from almost 28 percent in 1970 to about 21 percent in 2002 (U.S. Census Bureau, National Economic Accounts). The largest share (76 percent) of public infrastructure is in the state and local public sector—schools, roads and bridges, parks, jails, hospitals, and water and sewer systems.

Why public capital?

In a market system, private entities are the default provider of goods and services. Public provision is justified when the market fails to create the incentives for private entities to provide necessary goods and services. For infrastructure, or physical capital, several types of market failures are at work, all of which influence the method of financing.

First, much public-sector physical capital has attributes of a public or at least quasi-public good. The services of the physical capital are nonrival in consumption, because the marginal cost of an additional user of public physical services is low to nonexistent (up to some congestion level). In addition, the costs of excluding nonpayers exceed the potential benefits. These attributes characterize roads and parks.

Second, public-sector capital usually has strong positive externalities, even those kinds that create capturable private benefits. Often those externalities accrue to adjacent landowners. The value of a house adjacent to an attractive park, for example, may increase, even if the current owner has no interest in the park. These benefits can be measured and captured more effectively through ad valorem property taxes than through a private market pricing scheme. For example, the added value of being near a public park increases the assessed value of the house, thus increasing the property tax bill.

Third, public infrastructure is generally used to provide services for which a disproportionate share of the cost is the initial capital investment, with relatively low operating costs thereafter. (School buildings and education services are a notable exception.) This kind of cost structure makes it unlikely that the market would support more than one supplier in a given area, making the sole supplier a monopolist. Because monopolies usually produce less service at a higher price and are relatively unresponsive to consumer demand, many coun-

tries rely on the public sector to provide these services. Municipal water and sewer systems are a good application of this rationale for public provision.

Fourth, private financing may be difficult for new or risky ventures, or when capital is put in place in anticipation of growth that may not occur. Government backing of such projects, either directly as owner or indirectly as guarantor, can reduce the lender's risk (which is spread to all taxpayers) and induce the needed investment in public capital.

Financing infrastructure

The federal government does not have a capital budget, whereas state and local governments usually separate capital expenditures and operating expenditures. State and local governments finance most capital spending by a mix of debt and current revenue. In addition, states and, in particular, local governments operate many capital-intensive operations that sell services directly to citizens as separately accounted-for enterprise funds. The primary reason for the separate accounting is to prevent cross-subsidy between the enterprise activity and the general fund. Because the federal government does not account separately for capital expenditures and financing, state and local public capital expenditure financing is the focus here.

When the primary beneficiaries of most public capital are internal to the state, county, city, or special district, there is ample justification for the primary financing responsibility to remain at that level. In the 1960s and 1970s, however, a significant source of funding for state and local infrastructure was the federal government in the form of grants, especially for water and sewer projects and public housing. Today, that source of revenue has greatly diminished. Although federal aid for infrastructure could be defended as a form of fiscal equalization, it has not been proven as the most efficient. Fiscal equalization can be achieved by other methods that more effectively target poor states and poor individuals.

Public-sector capital is most often financed through capital markets (debt). State and local governments enjoy the advantage of offering bonds whose interest is exempt from federal income taxes. Some bonds are general obligation bonds, backed by the full faith and credit of the issuing government; others are revenue bonds, with the revenue from the sale of services pledged to service the debt. Historically, general obligation bonds have been used for public infrastructure that does not generate a revenue stream, and revenue bonds have been used for infrastructure that does. School buildings, jails, police stations, and city halls do not directly generate revenue. In contrast, college dormitories, stadiums, toll roads, water and sewer systems, and parking garages generate an identifiable revenue stream, which can be pledged to service the debt.

Recent developments in infrastructure financing

A search for new ways to finance infrastructure was driven by high interest rates in the 1980s, declining federal grants, and the pressures that population and economic growth exact on existing infrastructure. Popular techniques include so-called public-private partnerships; state guarantees, intermediation, and debt subsidies; creation of new quasi-governmental bodies for the sole purpose of developing and financing infrastructure; and shifting of the cost to identified beneficiaries and away from all taxpayers.

Public-private partnerships take many forms. Local governments may contract out a service, shifting the production of a public service to the private sector. Waste collection is often provided on this basis. It is important to note, however, that government is still providing for the public good because tax revenue (or government debt) is used to fund the expenditure.

Recently, sale-leaseback arrangements for public-sector capital have grown considerably. This growth has been stimulated by private investors seeking to exploit potential tax loopholes generated by tax-exempt municipal borrowing. That option has become less attractive because tax reforms have limited the use of such arrangements. There has also been some limited use of equity financing of public capital that generates a defined revenue steam, such as sewage treatment plants and landfills.

States have assumed some responsibility for helping local governments finance infrastructure, most often with help in borrowing rather than grants. Bond banks and revolving state loan funds are two widely used methods (Petersen et al. 1988). State guarantees can allow local governments to borrow on more favorable terms. States can pool borrowing requests from many small communities, with or without a state guarantee, generating economies of scale and reducing borrowing costs. Some states borrow on their own credit and use the proceeds to create credit banks that lend to local governments.

Recently, the use of special districts whose sole purpose is to fund (and in some cases, maintain or operate) particular kinds of infrastructure has increased. Water and sewer districts have been commonplace for many years, but more recently, other kinds have appeared on the scene. Texas has pioneered the use of road districts. Montana uses neighborhood rural special-improvement districts. Such special districts serve some combination of three purposes. They can provide residents with some of the benefits, including infrastructure, that one attains by being part of a municipality, without all the additional costs and restrictions. They can allow additional borrowing, and added tax levies to repay that borrowing, when general purpose local governments have exhausted their borrowing or taxing capabilities. And special districts can ensure that the cost falls on the primary beneficiaries. Special districts encompass a variety of entities ranging from those that are entirely tax financed (typically roads, neighborhood parks, street lights, and beautification) to those entirely financed by user fees (water and sewer). What they have in common is a need to provide infrastructure to serve a defined area.

A final notable trend in infrastructure financing is the shift from general revenue financing to exactions (fees) from those who benefit, with increased diversity in how those beneficiaries are identified and how payments are extracted. Three of the more popular methods are impact fees, special assessments, and tax-increment financing.

Impact fees on developers, special assessments for improvements, and tax-increment financing are increasingly commonplace ways to finance improvements that benefit a particular property, neighborhood, or defined area. New residents require not only the extension of water and sewer lines but also more police cars, fire substations, and public parks. Impact fees cover the additional capital costs imposed by developing vacant lots or adjacent tracts. Special assessments are more likely to pay for infrastructure improvements to serve already developed lots. Tax increment financing seeks to capture the additional property tax revenue from the increase in property value that results from infrastructure improvements and dedicates that revenue stream to paying the capital costs.

ADDITIONAL READINGS

Ostrom, Elinor, Larry Schroeder, and Susan Wynne. *Institutional Incentives and Sustainable Development.* San Francisco: Westview Press, 1993.

Petersen, John E., Susan Robinson, Percy Aguila, Joni L. Leithe, and William Graham. *Credit Pooling to Finance Infrastructure: An Examination of State Bond Banks, State Revolving Funds, and Substate Credit Pools.* Government Finance Officers Association, September 1988.

Robbins, Mark D., and Daehwan Kim. "Do State Bonds Banks Have Cost Advantages for Municipal Bond Issuance?" *Public Budgeting and Finance* 23, no. 3 (Fall 2003): 92–108.

World Bank. *World Development Report: Infrastructure for Development.* Washington, DC: World Bank, 1994.

Zimmerman, Dennis. *The Private Use of Tax-Exempt Bonds: Controlling Public Subsidy of Private Activity.* Washington, DC: Urban Institute Press, 1991.

Cross-references: benefit principle; earmarking of taxes; fiscal federalism; tax-exempt bonds.

Insurance industry, federal taxation of

Jack Taylor
Congressional Research Service, Library of Congress

Imposition of income taxes on insurance companies at corporate rates but with special accounting rules based on regulatory accounting methods, and limited taxation of beneficiaries, implying light federal taxation of life, and possibly property and casualty, insurance industries.

Insurance involves the transfer of risk of financial loss from one person (the insured) to another (the insurer) for a fee (a premium). In the modern insurance industry, insurer companies pool the risks of many insureds to diversify their own potential liabilities and pool the premiums received to earn a return while waiting to be used to pay claims. The industry thus offers two distinct but interrelated services, insurance and financial intermediation.

Insurance companies are subject to the federal corporate income tax on premium and investment income, but they are allowed to deduct additions to reserves for estimated future losses. Insurance policy owners and beneficiaries are not taxed on the investment income accumulated for them by the insurance companies, and they may also receive some distributions tax-free, especially in the case of life insurance. The net result of these special rules is to ensure that life insurance will be very lightly taxed and that other forms of insurance, notably property and casualty, will sometimes be undertaxed as well.

Because different forms of insurance are subject to different income tax rules, they will be discussed separately in later sections. They have in common, however, the continued use of reserve deductions to establish taxable income.

Reserve accounting

The first modern income tax law in 1909 provided that the accounting rules insurance companies use for regulatory and book purposes would also be used to calculate taxable income. (This was originally the case with most industries.) The purpose of the insurance accounting rules, however, was to ensure the solvency of the company and protect policyholders; they were therefore designed to prevent overstatement of income. It became obvious as time went by that deliberate overstatement of income was not the problem in tax accounting, and many of the regulatory rules have since been superseded.

The most important vestige of this regulatory accounting bias is the continued use of reserves to calculate taxable insurance income (although current tax law prescribes discount rates and other rules for reserves that are less conservative than the regulatory rules). Deductions from current income to cover future liabilities are not allowed in most tax accounting, which uses the stricter rule of allowing a deduction only when the liability is known with reasonable certainty as to both amount and time of payment. Because insurance companies are in the business of estimating such future liabilities, however, deducting additions to reserves as they are actuarially determined has seemed reasonable. Insurance company taxable income for any year, therefore, is net of that year's additions to reserves for policy obligations to be paid in future years.

Property and casualty insurance

The tax rules basically separate insurance into "life" and everything else (with noncancelable health insurance included in "life" insurance). Nonlife companies are allowed a deduction for 80 percent of unearned premiums plus additions to

loss reserves discounted over the expected payment period for the policies reserved against. The discount rate is prescribed as the federal midterm rate (the average rate on outstanding federal government securities with maturities of three to nine years). (This discount rate is intended to represent a pretax rate of return on the companies' investments.) The payment period is established by reference to the industrywide payment pattern for each line of business (although a company can establish and use its own payment pattern from its own records).

The insured parties pay companies premiums that are taxdeductible for business insurance and nondeductible for personal insurance, and, most benefits, when received, are tax-free unless they exceed the insured's basis in the lost property and create a capital gain. (Some liability insurance proceeds are taxable.)

A properly discounted reserve deduction for properly estimated losses would create no tax advantage; it would, in fact, be relatively tax-neutral. Current law, however, has several potential flaws that could undermine the assumed neutrality: (1) The prescribed discount rate may be lower than the earnings rate the company uses to set premiums and the actual earnings rate; if so, the initial deduction will be larger than required and some of the cost of the insurance will be paid with tax-sheltered dollars (or, more likely, the benefit will go to reduce premiums and thus the cost of buying insurance as opposed to self-insuring). (2) Crediting reserves at the pretax discount rate does not allow recapture of excess deductions until claims are paid. (3) The payment pattern may be manipulable by the companies, allowing systematic overstatement of deductions. (4) Contested and uncertain liabilities may be deliberately included, again allowing overstatement of deductions.

To the extent that any of these biases exist, the nonlife insurance industry would enjoy a tax advantage.

Special provisions reduce or eliminate taxes for smaller companies. Nonlife insurance companies with annual premiums of $350,000 or less are tax-exempt; those with premiums between $350,000 and $1.2 million may elect to be taxed on only their investment income, ignoring underwriting income.

Life insurance

Life insurance is essentially insurance that depends on life expectancy or mortality rates, including noncancelable accident and health insurance. A life insurance company in tax law is one in which more than half of its reserves are for life insurance. Qualifying as life insurance allows substantial tax advantages.

Life insurance policies often cover many years and are designed to accumulate large amounts of investment income ("inside buildup," in the jargon of the industry). Because this accumulating income represents the companies' obligation to pay benefits, it is deducted from the companies' taxable incomes as additions to policy reserves. The tax-free investment income, therefore, pays for a substantial part of the insurance coverage promised by the policies.

Although inside buildup is "credited" to the policies, it is not taxed to the policy owners either. It accumulates tax-free until it is paid out as death benefits, as policyholder dividends, or upon surrender of the policies. Death benefits are not taxed at all, and policyholder dividends and cash-surrender values are not taxed until they exceed the premiums paid for them.

In times past, companies used their own actuarial and interest rate assumptions in establishing reserves and funding policies, so policies could be significant tax shelters. Tightening of the law over the last decade or so has reduced the tax shelter opportunities; policies must now meet prescribed tests for actuarial and earnings assumptions to ensure that they are really insurance policies, and investing too much in a policy will now disqualify it for tax-free accumulation of inside buildup.

It remains true, however, that a substantial portion of the income generated by the industry is not taxed at either the corporate or the individual level.

Company taxation is further complicated by a peculiarity in the structure of the industry: A significant share of the business and assets of the industry derive from mutual companies, most very large, that are "owned" by their policyholders. Policyholder dividends are deductions for the companies, and stockholder dividends are not, so level taxation of the stock and mutual segments of the industry is a difficult problem.

For some time, the solution was to disallow a portion of the mutual companies' policyholder dividends by use of a rather arbitrary formula (Section 809 of the Internal Revenue Code) that is supposed to equal the share of income paid to stockholders of stock companies. The formula did not work to anyone's satisfaction, and considerable argument raged between the segments of the industry as to which is overtaxed. This provision was suspended for 2001–2003 and repealed in 2004.

"Small" life insurance companies also receive a special tax break. A company with less than $500 million in gross assets is allowed a deduction equal to 60 percent of the first $3 million of taxable income, reduced by 15 percent of the excess of taxable income over $3 million (thus phasing out the deduction at $15 million).

Health insurance

Taxation of medical insurance involves some special problems, partly because of its close relationship to national health policy. Most medical insurance is purchased as an employee fringe benefit, deductible by the employer and tax-free to the employee. It ranges from typical indemnity insurance to prepayment for medical care from health maintenance organizations, increasingly with blurred lines between the types. And the entities offering the various types are covered under at least

five tax regimes: (1) life insurance companies, (2) nonlife companies, (3) partially tax-exempt Blue Cross/Blue Shield organizations, (4) exempt HMOs and hospitals, and (5) for-profit, nonexempt hospitals or health providers taxable under the regular corporation income tax rules.

ADDITIONAL READINGS

Aaron, Henry J. *The Peculiar Problem of Taxing Life Insurance Companies.* Washington, DC: The Brookings Institution, 1983.

Graetz, Michael J., ed. *Life Insurance Company Taxation: The Mutual vs. Stock Differential.* Larchmont, NY: Rosenfeld, Emanuel, Inc., 1986.

Harmon, William B., Jr. "Two Decades of Insurance Tax Reform." *Tax Notes* 57 (November 12, 1992): 901–14.

McLure, Charles E., Jr. "The Income Tax Treatment of Interest Earned on Savings in Life Insurance." In *U.S. Congress, Joint Economic Committee, The Economics of Federal Subsidy Programs, Part 3—Tax Subsidies.* Washington, DC: U.S. Government Printing Office, 1972.

Pike, Andrew D. "Reflections on the Meaning of Life: An Analysis of Section 7702 and the Taxation of Cash Value Life Insurance." *Tax Law Review* 43 (Spring 1989): 491–587.

U.S. Congress. Joint Committee on Taxation. *Tax Reform Proposals: Taxation of Insurance Products and Companies.* Washington, DC: U.S. Government Printing Office, 1985.

Cross-references: fringe benefits; income tax, corporate, federal; income tax, federal; insurance industry, state taxation of.

Insurance industry, state taxation of

Thomas S. Neubig
Ernst & Young LLP

State-level tax treatment of insurance companies.

State taxation of insurance companies is important to the industry, to its competitors and customers, and to the states. In 2003, insurance companies paid $12.5 billion in state premium taxes. In 2001, insurance companies paid nearly as much in state premium taxes ($10.3 billion) as in federal corporate income taxes ($10.5 billion). While federal income taxation has moved toward taxing all types of financial institutions more similarly, state taxation of insurance companies differs greatly from state taxation of banks and general business corporations.

State taxation of insurance companies may appear to be simple and straightforward with its reliance on premium taxation. In actual practice, premium taxation differs by state and by line of business, interacts with state income taxes and solvency assessments, and incorporates a unique system of retaliatory taxation.

Premium taxation

All 50 states impose premium taxes on insurance companies for insuring risks or property in the state. Six states allow special municipal taxation of insurance premiums. In 2001, premium taxes were 1.7 percent of insurance premiums (excluding annuities) and accounted for 1.8 percent of total state revenues. The trend during the last ten years has been for states to reduce their premium tax rates, with several states reducing the rate to below 1.5 percent.

Premium tax rates differ according to the type of insurance product. Fire insurance premiums are often taxed at higher rates, the extra tax being earmarked to local fire departments or state fire marshals. Many states impose lower tax rates on health insurance and long-term care policies, and higher tax rates on workers' compensation policies. Seven states taxed some annuity considerations in 2003. In many states, premium taxes are "in lieu of" other taxes, such as state corporate income taxes.

A significant change in premium tax has been the removal of domestic preferences since the *Metropolitan v. Ward* Supreme Court decision in 1985. Thirty-four states had lower tax rates for domestic (in-state) insurers compared to foreign (out-of-state) insurers, but due to legislative changes almost all of those explicit domestic preferences have been removed. Some states still provide home office or rate reduction for large investments in the state to encourage insurers to locate in the state.

Premium taxes are relatively easy to administer, and they provide a relatively stable source of revenue. Premium taxation dates back to the 19th century before the federal income tax. By contrast, the income tax rules for insurance companies at the federal level have evolved over the last 70 years and are still the subject of considerable debate.

A simple comparison of premiums to net income suggests that the modal 2 percent premium tax rate is equivalent to a high effective tax rate on net income, several times higher than states' general business tax rates on net income. Although premium-tax-related price differentials may be small in percentage terms as a result of low state tax rates, the absolute tax differential can be large, since premium taxes apply to a large tax base. Even small price differences for identical products can place competitors at a significant disadvantage, especially for financial service providers where margins are often low.

Because the insurance premium tax is a destination tax, allocated completely to the state of the insured risk, and all insurance companies are generally subject to the same tax rate on similar products, companies are likely to recover most of the tax cost through higher premiums without fear of losing market share. Premium taxes therefore are likely to be borne largely by resident households and local businesses. The exception would be retaliatory taxes for which some foreign companies pay higher taxes than domestic companies on the same policies.

With the growth of self-insurance, financial securitization, and the emergence of direct competitors as the regulatory barriers between financial service providers erode, differences in state effective tax rates across providers and products can cause economic distortions and inefficiencies. Higher effective tax rates on insurance companies and their products increase the incentive to self-insure risks or to purchase comparable services from non-insurance companies.

Income taxation

Nine states impose corporate income or franchise taxes on insurance companies. In most states, the income or franchise tax is creditable against the premium tax, or the premium tax is creditable against the income tax. Given the typical relationship between gross premiums and net income, most companies are effectively subject to just the premium tax. Oregon was the first state to impose only an income tax on insurance companies, while Illinois and New York have a low rate premium tax plus a supplemental income tax.

Retaliatory taxation

Retaliatory taxation is unique to the insurance industry. Retaliatory taxes are paid by a non-domicile (foreign) company selling premiums in a state with a lower tax burden than the insurer's state of domicile. For example, a California-domiciled insurer selling insurance to Ohio residents would pay the Ohio rate of 1.4 percent plus a retaliatory tax of 0.95 percent, equal to the excess of the 2.35 percent California rate above the Ohio rate.

To determine the retaliatory tax, states increasingly include income taxes, fees, and in some cases guaranty fund assessments, in addition to premium taxes. Some also include other states' municipal taxes. A recent estimate of total retaliatory taxes totaled more than $1 billion in 2003, in excess of 10 percent of premium taxes.

Retaliatory taxes were enacted when most states had discriminatory tax rules against foreign insurers. The retaliatory tax system was designed to reduce tax barriers to interstate business activity of domestic insurers. Retaliatory taxation provides an incentive for states to keep their tax burdens on insurance companies in line with those of other states. If a state increases its tax rate or fees, its domestic insurers will pay higher retaliatory taxes to other states and the state will reduce its own retaliatory tax revenues.

Guaranty assessments

All 50 states have guaranty funds to pay claims of insolvent companies. Separate state guaranty funds are established for property and casualty companies, life insurance, annuities, and health policies. Guaranty fund assessments are levied as a percentage of premiums, when needed by a state to cover the costs of resolving an insurance company insolvency. Most states provide a credit against the premium tax for guaranty fund assessments, most commonly for 100 percent of the eligible assessments taken pro rata over the next five years. Guaranty assessments paid by insurance companies in 2002 totaled $1.3 billion.

Other taxes and burdens

States impose other taxes and burdens on insurance companies. Insurance companies pay fees and licenses generally associated with the administrative costs of the state insurance regulatory agencies. In 2000, fees and assessments on insurance companies totaled $1.1 billion, 25 percent more than the $880 million spent on state insurance department budgets.

Some states have considered extending their sales tax to services, including insurance services. A sales tax on gross insurance premiums would greatly overstate the value of insurance services, because insurance premiums generally include three elements: a pure insurance (transfer) element, a savings element, and a service (administrative, marketing, and entrepreneurial) element.

A sales tax on insurance services could further exacerbate the distortion between purchased insurance and self-insurance and between savings through life insurance companies and other financial service providers. A sales tax could also have significant retaliatory tax implications for domestic insurers.

A more appropriate measure of insurance services might be the value added by the industry. A value-added tax base would be considerably smaller than gross premiums. The New Hampshire Business Enterprise Tax uses an addition method to measure insurance companies' value added, including employee compensation, interest paid on non-policyholder reserves, and shareholder dividends.

States also impose nontax burdens on companies. In many states, insurance companies are required to provide minimum benefit levels in their health insurance policies. New Jersey prevented insurance companies selling automobile insurance in the state from pulling out of that line of business without also withdrawing from all other lines of business. Florida imposed a temporary moratorium on insurance companies' canceling or not renewing personal property lines in the wake of the large losses from a hurricane. Insurance companies are required to pay assessments in some states for assigned risk pools, which sell insurance to the otherwise uninsured, or are required to participate in coverage of individuals in the state risk pool. The additional cost associated with assigned state risk pools creates an advantage for firms that can self-insure and avoid those costs.

ADDITIONAL READINGS

American Insurance Association. *State Taxation Manual.* Washington, DC: American Insurance Association, 2004.

Neubig, Thomas S., and Harold L. Adrion. "Value Added Taxes and Other Consumption Taxes: Issues for Insurance Companies." *Insurance Tax Review,* December 1993.

Neubig, Thomas S., and Michael Vlaisavljevich. "Economic Issues in State Taxation of Insurance Companies." In *State Taxation of Business: Issues and Options,* edited by Thomas F. Pogue (217–42). Westport, CT: Praeger, 1992.

Quantitative Economics and Statistics Group of Ernst & Young LLP. "Excessive Taxation of Life Insurance Companies in the 50 States." *State Tax Notes,* August 12, 2002.

Cross-references: banks, state taxation of; income tax, corporate, state and local; insurance industry, federal taxation of.

Intangible assets, income tax treatment of

Jack Taylor
Congressional Research Service, Library of Congress

In income tax accounting, those business assets that are not accounted for after valuing all physical and financial capital of the business.

Purchasers of a business or professional practice may pay more than the market value of the firm's physical and financial assets because an ongoing business has name recognition, relationships with customers and suppliers, technical knowledge, established operations that have proven successful, rights represented by patents, copyrights, franchises, and licenses, and other such intangible factors that add to the income-earning potential of the firm. The more amorphous of these intangibles are sometimes called "goodwill" or "going-concern value." These intangible assets have proven to be a problem for income tax accounting because of uncertainties in measuring the income they generate.

An asset that declines in value as it produces income requires an offsetting deduction from that income equal to the decline in value; income from machines that wear out as they produce must be netted against the machines' depreciation. Measuring income from them requires some measure of the rates at which they decline in value. An asset that does not decline in value presents no such problem; income from land, for example, requires no periodic deductions because land retains its value from purchase to resale (barring extraneous influences).

As with any asset, the capitalized value of an intangible is equal to the present value of its expected stream of future income. For intangible assets purchased as a part of a business, however, several difficulties arise. One problem is measuring the expected future income from the asset (i.e., valuing the asset). Another is determining the expected duration of the income stream (i.e., measuring the life of the asset). Even if both are established, a determination still needs to be made whether the income stream should be offset by any decline in the value of the asset (i.e., does the asset depreciate, as a machine would, or does it maintain its value from purchase to resale, as land would?).

These difficulties arise in the case of intangible assets whose value is determined by their relationship to a specific firm. Intangible assets that are usable in many firms, such as general-purpose computer software or purchased mailing lists, or that have market value apart from the firm, such as patents or copyrights, can be valued by reference to market prices and their lives determined by reference to general business practices, much as with tangible assets. But assets whose value depends on the continuation of a specific business are a different problem; at the very least, their market value is not the same apart from the business.

Intangible assets such as knowledge or a relationship with clients can have value and increase future income for two reasons. One is that some expense may be involved in creating the asset. The firm or professional practice may have to advertise, pay for training, join country clubs, buy lunches, or incur other expenses to acquire the asset in question. But even if no expense is involved, it still often takes time for the firm to form the relationships or acquire the knowledge needed to secure the future income. Purchasing an ongoing business that has already developed the necessary relationships or knowledge saves both the expenses and the opportunity costs that would otherwise be involved.

The policy dispute

Policy arguments over whether or how intangibles should be depreciated for tax purposes have often been made by analogy to physical depreciable assets. Neutral taxation of depreciable physical capital generally requires that the amount allowed as a depreciation deduction vary with the expected life of the asset; so it was often assumed that similar treatment should apply to intangible assets.

However, there is an important difference in the tax treatment of the costs of creating and maintaining the two types of assets. The costs of creating physical assets are capitalized and deducted only as depreciation, the same treatment given the purchase price of a purchased asset. The costs of creating the types of intangible assets discussed here, however, are typically deducted as they are incurred (or are "opportunity costs" not subject to taxation). The same costs that serve to create the asset in the first place also serve to maintain its value in the hands of the purchasers; and by deducting the costs currently (or not reporting the opportunity costs), the taxpayer in effect writes off exactly the amount, other things being equal, that will maintain the value of the asset—that is, an amount equal to what the depreciation would be if the asset were depreciated. Thus the life of the asset is irrelevant; each asset is effectively a nondepreciable asset. This treatment actually gives these assets lower effective tax rates than capitalizing and depreciating them would (Gravelle and Taylor 1992). Neutral tax treatment requires that these assets be treated uniformly, not written off over estimated useful lives. In fact, a zero depreciation deduction for purchased intangibles is probably the most nearly neutral.

It should be obvious from this discussion that the correct distinction between types of assets is not physical and intangible, but capitalized and expensed, creation costs. Some intangible assets, such as over-the-counter software or motion picture films, are like physical assets in that their creation costs are fully capitalized, and neutral tax treatment requires that these assets be depreciated over their estimated useful lives.

It should also be obvious that none of these distinctions is totally clean in actual tax law. In the Internal Revenue Code, both intangible and physical capital assets are sometimes expensed. Patents, for example, may be produced by research and experimentation expenditures that are written off currently, and many of the repairs to machines and buildings that are actually capital in nature are deducted. The general principle remains in spite of the exceptions, however.

The practical dispute

Valuing intangible assets, establishing their useful lives, and determining the proper deductions, if any, for their cost have been major questions in past U.S. federal tax policy. Taxpayers had an incentive to allocate greater portions of the purchase price of a business to depreciable physical assets or to intangible assets whose depreciation could be established and so reduce their future taxes. Disputes over the allocation of purchase prices became routine between taxpayers and the Internal Revenue Service (IRS) throughout the 1980s.

Taxpayers were able to use revenue projections to establish a value for such things as customer lists, "core deposits" of banks, or "insurance in force" for insurance companies and agencies. Reasoning that these customer relationships would decline over time as customers moved, died, or went to competitors, taxpayers also made statistical projections of the rate of decline to establish useful lives. Using the analogy with depreciable physical assets, they further reasoned that an annual allowance for depreciation based on the useful lives was required to properly measure income from the assets. Some lower courts accepted these arguments and some did not, although the IRS adamantly rejected them. The Supreme Court eventually decided (Newark Morning Ledger, 113 S.Ct. 1670 [1993]) that intangible assets could be depreciated if a value and a limited useful life could be established. This left a large backlog of cases in dispute between the IRS and taxpayers, however, and provided no general principles to help determine the proper useful life.

Current tax treatment

Congress imposed a solution to the disputes, or at least to future disputes, in the Omnibus Budget Reconciliation Act of 1993 (PL 103-66). This act established a new category of amortizable asset called a "Section 197 intangible" (after the section of the Internal Revenue Code). The purchase price of these assets is to be written off by the straight-line method (equal deductions each year) over 15 years. These assets are defined as purchased (1) goodwill or going concern value; (2) information bases, know-how, and relations with customers, suppliers, and workers; (3) licenses, permits, and other government-granted rights; (4) covenants not to compete; and (5) franchises, trademarks, and trade names. Specifically excluded are self-created assets and financial assets, leases, patents and copyrights, computer software, films, sound recordings, books, sports franchises, and a few other categories. For the most part, the definitions correspond to the distinction between expensed and capitalized costs discussed earlier.

The 15-year write-off period is essentially arbitrary, chosen because it was approximately "revenue neutral," neither gaining nor losing revenue over the five-year period for which revenue estimates were made. The basis for the revenue estimate was that some intangibles were previously amortizable over periods shorter than 15 years and some would not have been amortizable at all. The average for revenue neutrality over the five years was calculated at 15 years.

ADDITIONAL READING

Gravelle, Jane G., and Jack Taylor. "Tax Neutrality and the Tax Treatment of Purchased Intangibles." *National Tax Journal* 45 (March 1992): 77–88.

Cross-references: capital cost recovery; cost of capital; depreciation recapture; uniform capitalization rules.

Integration, corporate tax

Glenn Hubbard
Columbia University

Policies for reducing or removing the double tax on returns to corporate equity that can be imposed by the existence of a separate corporate and personal income tax.

Current U.S. income tax laws treat corporations and their investors as separate entities. Under this so called "classical" system of corporate taxation, two levels of tax are levied on earnings from investments in corporate equity. First, income earned by corporations is taxed at the corporate level. Second, when the corporation distributes dividends to shareholders, the income is taxed again at the shareholder level (historically as ordinary income, though temporarily at lower rates). Undistributed earnings, which increase share values, are also double-taxed, because they are taxed at capital gains rates when shares are sold.

In contrast, investors who conduct business activity in noncorporate form, such as a sole proprietorship or partnership (or in corporate form through a subchapter S corporation), are taxed once on their earnings at their individual tax rate. Corporate earnings distributed as interest to suppliers of debt capital are generally deductible by the corporation, and thus not subject to tax at the corporate level.

Integration of the corporate and individual income taxes refers to any plan in which corporate income is taxed only once, rather than twice, both when earned and when distributed to shareholders as dividends.

The need for integration

The classical corporate tax system distorts three economic and financial decisions—whether to (1) invest in noncorporate rather than corporate form; (2) finance investments with debt rather than with equity; and (3) retain rather than distribute earnings.

Organizational form

Traditional arguments for integrating corporate and individual income taxes emphasize distortions of business organizational form. By taxing corporate equity income twice, the classical corporate tax system discourages equity-financed investments by corporate organizations. Also, the corporate sector must earn a higher pretax rate of profit to prevent capital from flowing to the corporate sector. The tax distorts the allocation of resources by discouraging the use of the corporate form even when incorporation would provide nontax benefits—such as limited liability for the owners, centralized management, free transferability of interests, and continuity. Corporations may also be better able to exploit scale economies, while noncorporate organizations may be better able to encourage entrepreneurial skill. Distorting the choice between these business forms thus means diminishing the use of scale economies, as well. While the use of an S corporation can provide nontax benefits of the corporate form while avoiding the problem of double taxation, a number of restrictions on their use limit their applicability. Nonetheless, the use of S corporations has increased significantly.

Corporate capital structure

Corporations have three alternatives for financing new investments: issuing new equity, using retained earnings, or issuing debt. The classical corporate tax system discriminates against equity financing of new corporate investment; because corporate profits are taxed twice, the cost of equity capital generally exceeds the cost of debt capital. Projects funded with new equity or retained earnings therefore require a higher pretax rate of return than projects financed with debt. The lower effective tax rate for debt-financed versus equity-financed corporate investment encourages the use of debt finance by corporations, holding nontax factors constant.

If debt issuance involved no nontax considerations, corporate borrowing would be an efficient type of "self-help" integration, because interest payments are deductible. But, while leverage has some nontax benefits, the most efficient financial arrangements will involve both debt and equity, with equity serving as a cushion against economy-wide fluctuations in profitability. Higher debt levels can also increase nontax costs of debt, including costs associated with financial distress.

One result is tax-induced distortions in corporations' comparisons of nontax advantages and disadvantages of debt entail significant efficiency costs.

Corporate dividend distributions

The current system of corporate income taxation may also distort a corporation's choice between distributing or retaining earnings and, if amounts are distributed, its choice of whether they are paid in the form of nondividend distribution, such as a share repurchase. Distributing earnings through dividends will be taxed relatively highly versus distributing earnings through capital gains generated by reinvested earnings or share repurchases.

Despite the tax disadvantage of paying dividends, corporations do so. Financial economists have offered two explanations as to why corporate dividends are paid despite the tax bias against dividend distributions. The first—known as the "traditional view"—argues that dividends offer nontax benefits to shareholders that offset their apparent tax disadvantage. For example, a high dividend payout may decrease managerial discretion over internal funds. Or dividends may provide signals to investors about a firm's prospects or relative financial strength.

The second explanation or "tax capitalization" view assumes that dividends offer no nontax benefits to shareholders relative to retained earnings. An additional assumption in this view is that corporations have no alternative to dividends (like share repurchases) for distributing funds to shareholders. As a result, investor-level taxes on dividends reduce the value of the firm as they are capitalized in share value, but would generally affect neither corporate dividend nor investment decisions. Under the assumptions of the tax capitalization view, corporate tax integration would not encourage corporations to increase dividend payouts, but would confer a windfall on holders of existing equity.

Administrative means of achieving corporate tax integration

It would be relatively easy to design an integrated tax system if all shareholders were taxed at the same rate, shareholder and corporate tax rates were the same, all corporate income were taxed in the same manner, and the United States were a closed economy. The real world is not so simple, and evaluating alternative prototypes for integrating the corporate and individual tax systems requires making judgments on four issues: the treatment of corporate-level tax preferences (e.g., accelerated depreciation or tax-exempt interest in municipal bonds); corporate income received by tax-exempt investors; corporate income received by foreign shareholders; and foreign taxes paid by U.S. corporations.

The Treasury Department's 1992 study of corporate tax integration was based on the following principles for judging different administrative prototypes for corporate tax integration: First, the benefit of corporate-level tax preferences should not be extended to shareholders. Second, corporate tax integration should not reduce taxes paid on corporate capital income by tax-exempt investors. Third, the benefits of integration should not be extended to foreign shareholders by statute, although benefits may be extended by treaty. Fourth, foreign taxes paid by U.S. corporations should not be treated identically by statute to taxes paid to the U.S. government,

although extending the benefits of integration to foreign-source income could be accomplished through bilateral treaty negotiations.

Full integration

One method of integration would treat the corporation as a conduit, taxing all corporate earnings—irrespective of whether they are distributed—once. One way to implement this would be a "shareholder allocation" prototype, in which shareholders would include their share of the corporation's income in their income subject to tax. Tax would be withheld at the corporate level, and shareholders could apply the credits for corporate taxes paid against their income tax liability. A disadvantage of this alternative is that corporate tax preferences would be passed along to shareholders, because such preferences would be included in the calculation of taxable income.

Avoiding such pass-throughs would be both inconsistent with the spirit of full integration and administratively complex. For this reason, and because of the general administrative complexity of this prototype, the Treasury report did not recommend its enactment.

Dividend relief

Most proposals for integration have focused on eliminating the double taxation of those earnings that are distributed—in short, dividend relief. A number of options are possible. In an "imputation credit" system, tax is collected at the corporate level, but shareholders receive a credit to apply against investor-level taxes. In a "dividend-deduction" system, corporations could deduct dividend payments just as they do interest payments in calculating taxable income. Or in a "dividend exclusion" system, shareholders would not be taxed on dividend income.

The imputation credit prototype might work this way: Corporations would determine their income for tax purposes, as they do now, and would pay corporate-level tax. Shareholders would include in their income the "grossed-up" amount of the dividend—that is, including both the dividend and the associated tax paid at the corporate level. They could apply toward individual tax payments a credit equal to the amount of corporate tax that would be associated with gross dividends. This system is similar to the taxation of wages and salaries for employees, in which an employee includes gross wages in taxable income and receives a credit equal to the amount of the tax withheld. In principle, an imputation system could be structured so as to conform to the Treasury's principles for integration, but doing so would be relatively complex. Nonetheless, the fact that most integrated tax systems use imputation credit prototypes suggests it will continue to be studied as a model for corporate tax integration in the United States.

A dividend-deduction system would treat dividends and interest payments symmetrically at the corporate level. Although this approach would be simple, it would violate the Treasury's recommendation that the benefits of integration not be extended to tax-exempt and foreign shareholders. Moreover, this proposal would be significantly more costly in terms of tax revenue than other alternatives.

The Treasury report recommended a dividend exclusion prototype for dividend relief as the most straightforward means of implementing the general policy recommendations requiring the least change from current law. Under this prototype, corporations would pay the corporate income tax, computing taxable income in the same way as under current law. However, dividends paid out of fully taxed corporate income would not be taxed again at the investor level.

If adopted, the Treasury proposal might work in the following manner: Fully taxed income would be tracked by corporations in an excludable dividend account (EDA) based on corporate taxes paid. For example, a corporate tax payment of $34 would permit $66 to be contributed to the EDA. That is, because the $34 of tax paid is equivalent to paying the statutory corporate tax rate on $100 of earnings, the corporation would be allowed to add $100 − $34, or $66, to its EDA, from which it could pay excludable dividends to its shareholders. Amounts of dividends distributed that are greater than the EDA balance, such as distributions from corporate tax preference income, would be taxable at the individual level.

Under the dividend exclusion prototype, tax-exempt investors would not pay tax on either "excludable" or "taxable" dividends, but would not be granted a refund of applicable corporate taxes. Essentially, those shareholders would bear the same tax burden on corporate equity income as they do now. Foreign shareholders would also be treated as they are under current law; a withholding tax of 30 percent on dividends paid by U.S. firms to foreign shareholders would remain (with lower rates available by treaty). With respect to foreign-source income earned by U.S. firms, corporations would be permitted to credit foreign taxes paid against U.S. corporate tax (as under current law). However, the EDA would not be increased by U.S. corporate tax liabilities offset by foreign tax credits.

The model recommended by the Treasury influenced strongly President George W. Bush's 2003 proposal to eliminate investor-level dividend taxes and provide a basis adjustment for retained earnings. Compromise with the Congress produced a temporary (as of this writing) reduction in income tax rates on dividends and capital gains, but the direction for reform became more established.

The Treasury report also considered, as a longer-run option, a broad extension of the dividend exclusion integration prototype to interest payments. This prototype—the Comprehensive Business Income Tax (CBIT)—would apply to all businesses, noncorporate and corporate, with the exception of very small firms. Under the CBIT prototype, neither deductions for payments to debt-holders nor those to equity-holders would be permitted, and a tax would be collected at the entity level (at a rate equal to the highest marginal individual tax rate). However, both interest and equity distributions would then be excludable from income by investors.

Economic benefits of integration

The direction of the tax biases under an unintegrated system is clear. The size of the resulting inefficiency will be determined by how much households and firms respond to these tax considerations. These responses can be studied using computational general-equilibrium models.

Removing the double tax on corporate equity reduces the amount of revenue raised. For this reason, the Treasury report examined the gains in economic efficiency that would result from integration, assuming that other taxes are changed to offset the revenue effects of integration.

Based on simulations using several different general equilibrium models, the Treasury report concluded that the economic benefits from corporate tax integration appear to be significant. Gains would be culled from improved allocation of real resources, reductions in the likelihood of a firm's experiencing financial distress, and the shift toward allowing corporations to make capital structure and dividend decisions based on nontax benefits and costs.

The Treasury report offers estimates of how much the various prototypes would increase the amount of capital in the corporate sector. Depending on the prototype, model, and financing assumptions, this increase ranges from 2 to 8 percentage points. In addition, the integration prototypes generally encourage corporations to use less debt. Estimated debt-to-asset ratios decrease by 1 to 7 percentage points. The integration prototypes encourage corporations to increase the portion of earnings distributed as dividends. Depending on the model, financing assumptions, and prototype, dividend payout ratios rise modestly by between 2 and 6 percentage points. By shifting resources into the corporate sector, reducing corporate borrowing, and encouraging dividends, the prototypes increase economic well-being by an amount that ranges from $2.5 to $26 billion per year.

ADDITIONAL READINGS

This article is based on Hubbard, R. Glenn. "Corporate Tax Integration: A View from the Treasury Department." *Journal of Economic Perspectives* 7, no. 1 (1993): 115–32. A more recent discussion can be found in the 2003 Economic Report of the President, chapter 5.

U.S. Department of the Treasury. *Integration of the Individual and Corporate Tax Systems: Taxing Business Income Once*. Washington, DC: U.S. Government Printing Office, 1992.

Cross-references: dividends, double taxation of; general-equilibrium models; income tax, corporate, federal; income tax, federal.

Interest deductibility

Michael J. McIntyre
Wayne State University

The theory and practice underlying the deduction of interest expenses under an income tax.

Most countries allow taxpayers to deduct interest payments under at least some circumstances and to prohibit or defer the deduction under other circumstances. Many individuals and most corporations claim an interest deduction, and the aggregate amounts are large. In 1986, the United States imposed significant limitations on the deductibility of interest. Nevertheless, interest remains the most important deduction allowable under the U.S. income tax. According to the Statistics of Income figures published by the Internal Revenue Service, U.S. corporations deducted well over $1.2 trillion in interest payments in 2001. Nearly 37 million individual taxpayers claimed the deduction in that year, for aggregate deductions of about $340 billion.

For U.S. individual taxpayers, interest paid on home mortgages is by far the most important category of interest. The benefits of the deduction for home mortgage interest go primarily to taxpayers with relatively high incomes, with nearly 80 percent of the benefits going to taxpayers in the top 20th percentile.

To regulate the deduction for interest payments, a country must provide a workable definition of interest that conforms, to the extent feasible, to economic realities. In general, interest may be defined as a rental payment for the use of someone else's money. A more ornate definition is needed, however, to specify what constitutes a genuine debt obligation. For example, the definition should make some attempt to distinguish debt from equity so as to prevent closely held corporations from obtaining a deduction for disguised dividends. Detailed rules must also be provided to distinguish interest on a loan from repayment of the principal amount of the loan. Those rules tend to be particularly complex when the issuer of a debt instrument receives as loan proceeds less than the face amount of the debt instrument (so-called original issue discount bonds). Under such circumstances, the difference between the face amount of the loan and the amount received by the borrower constitutes economic interest.

The rules governing interest deductibility must also specify the timing of the deduction. In principle, a tax system that taxes only realized gains should not allow interest payments made to earn unrealized income to be deductible until that income is subject to tax. How to link a present interest payment with future income, however, is often a vexing question, as the discussion below suggests. Many countries have also faced serious political obstacles in adopting appropriate timing rules, at least in part because they had adopted overly generous interest deductibility rules before the importance of time-value-of-money issues was appreciated by their policymakers.

Tax theorists disagree sharply on the proper treatment of interest payments under a personal income tax and a corporate income tax. One prominent view is that the deductibility of interest payments on a loan ought to turn on the use made of the loan proceeds. To implement that principle, a tax system needs to adopt tracing rules that link specific interest payments to particular uses.

Tracing is easily accomplished whenever the lender requires the borrower to utilize the proceeds of a loan for a particular purchase. Such loans are typically called "purchase-money loans." The most common example is a mortgage that finances the purchase of a personal residence. Indeed, most real estate construction and acquisition loans are purchase-money loans. Purchase-money nonrecourse loans are a central feature of many tax shelter schemes.

Under other circumstances, tracing may be more difficult. For example, physical tracing is clearly impossible when a taxpayer has commingled borrowed and saved funds in a common account. To deal with the difficult cases, tax analysts have proposed various presumptive tracing techniques. These techniques are analogous to the inventory accounting rules used for linking the costs incurred purchasing goods of a certain type with the proceeds derived from the sale of such goods.

One such tracing technique is called "permissive stacking." Under permissive stacking, taxpayers are presumed to have used their borrowed money in accordance with the best available tax advice. Assume, for example, that G has $1,000 in her checking account, of which $500 came from a loan and the remaining $500 from savings. She writes two checks, one of $400 to pay a business expense and the other of $600 to pay for personal consumption. The permissive stacking rule assumes that she used borrowed money to pay the $400 business expense and is entitled to a deduction for 80 percent ($400/$500) of the interest payments on her loan.

An alternative to permissive stacking is "strict stacking." A strict stacking rule makes the assumption that taxpayers have spent their borrowed money for the use that provides the least favorable tax result. In the example above, G would be assumed to have paid for $500 of her personal consumption out of her $500 loan and to have paid the business expense of $400 from her savings. Thus, G would not be entitled to any interest deduction. Strict stacking is often a favored technique for limiting the scope of various tax-expenditure programs. For example, strict stacking has been recommended as a way to prevent borrowers from obtaining the benefits of tax incentives designed to encourage taxpayers to save.

The main competition to the tracing approach is the view that interest is inherently a current expense and ought to be deductible in all cases in an ideal income tax. Some proponents of this view would favor limitations on the deductibility of interest, however, in a less-than-ideal income tax system that gives preferences to certain categories of income. For example, they might not want home mortgage interest to be deductible unless the imputed income from home ownership is taxable. Similarly, they might favor deferring the deduction for interest used to purchase appreciating property if accrued gains are not taxable until they have been realized.

Proponents of tracing claim that their favored approach is consistent with the general treatment afforded to other deductions in an ideal income tax. They note that the deductibility of a rental payment for the use of property generally depends on the use made of that property. For example, an amount paid for an apartment is deductible if the apartment is used as a business office; the payment is not deductible if the apartment is used as a personal residence. Because interest is a form of rental payment—an amount paid for the use of someone else's money—the asserted analogy between interest and rent is strong.

Opponents of tracing contend that the fungibility of money makes tracing meaningless. For example, they note that, in a tax system that made the deductibility of interest on a loan turn on the use made of the loan proceeds, a taxpayer holding $1,000 worth of stock and contemplating a $1,000 consumption expenditure would get a better tax result by selling the stock, using the proceeds to make the consumption expenditure, and then borrowing $1,000 to repurchase the stock. Proponents of tracing respond that the above example simply shows that a pure tracing system might impose some transactional costs on certain savers. To minimize those costs, they have proposed presumptive tracing ("permissive stacking") rules that would allow interest to be deductible when it is clear that the taxpayer would be able to claim the deduction through a mere rearrangement of his or her portfolio of assets.

Proponents of tracing contend that it is a fallacy to conclude that the fungibility of money supports the case for a universal deduction for interest. Their position is illustrated by the following example. F, a taxpayer, leases two identical automobiles at a monthly rental fee of $500 per car for his use and the use of his wife. F sometimes uses a car for business and sometimes for pleasure. His wife always uses a car for consumption purposes. For obvious reasons of convenience, F and his wife take whichever car is at the top of the driveway whenever they want to drive somewhere. The question arises as to how much of the automobile rental fees they should be allowed to deduct.

No one would seriously contend that the fungibility of F's cars justifies a deduction for the entire cost of renting them. F would not strengthen his claim for a full deduction, moreover, by demonstrating the administrative difficulties that he might encounter in distinguishing between the two cars. Because the cars are fungible, physical tracing of the rental fees to the business use of each car might not be necessary. The tax authorities might adopt a presumptive tracing rule for determining the portion of the rental fees attributable to business based on the ratio of business miles of use to total miles of use. The fungibility of rental cars, however, would not undermine the case for making the deductibility of rental fees turn on the use made of the rented property.

A second argument commonly made against tracing is that it would improperly advantage persons holding net assets over net borrowers. As an illustration of that argument, consider two taxpayers, both of whom have the same salary income. Mr. Ant, a thrifty person, holds a $1,000 money market certificate earning 10 percent interest; Mr. Grasshopper, who is a spendthrift, has accumulated no savings at all. Assume that Mr. Ant and Mr. Grasshopper each spend $1,000 on a personal vacation. Mr. Ant finances his vacation by cashing in his demand certificate. Mr. Grasshopper finances his by borrowing the $1,000 and paying $100 of interest. He and Mr. Ant spend all of their remaining net income on food and recreation. Both have enjoyed the benefit of a vacation worth $1,000, but Mr. Ant has $100 more than Mr. Grasshopper to spend on food and recreation. Unless permitted a deduction for his interest payment, Mr. Grasshopper will pay the same amount of tax as Mr. Ant, despite this difference in their power to buy food and recreational services.

Supporters of limitations on the interest deduction have two responses to the argument illustrated above. First, they note that the argument applies not just to interest but to all forms of rental payments, although no one is suggesting that the argument has force in these other contexts. For example, assume that Mr. Ant and Mr. Grasshopper are similarly situated except that Mr. Ant owns a vacation home. If Mr. Grasshopper wants to use an equivalent vacation home, he must pay a rental fee to the owner. That rental fee is not deductible under normative income tax principles.

The second and more fundamental response to the Ant-Grasshopper example is to point out that it merely illustrates that an income tax is not neutral in its treatment of savers and consumers. The more famous example of that non-neutrality arises when one taxpayer saves his income and the other one spends it. The saver is taxed on the income and also on the income generated by the savings, whereas the consumer is taxed on his initial income and is not subject to any further tax. Defenders of an income tax argue that this non-neutral treatment is justified because of the difference in ability to pay of savers, who are concentrated at the top of the income band, and non-savers. Whatever the merits of this differential treatment of savers and consumers, it is well understood to be a fundamental attribute of income taxation. The ant/grasshopper example simply shows that a saver who later draws down his savings enjoys the same tax benefit enjoyed by other persons who consume their income.

Normative income tax principles are not particularly relevant in determining the proper treatment of interest payments when the interest is paid on a loan that finances tax-favored activities. Many tax systems include tax incentives and other special relief measures that ought to be evaluated in terms of spending goals. Whether interest on a loan should be deductible when the loan finances an activity favored by a tax incentive depends on the goals of that incentive, not on normative income tax principles.

For example, the United States allows taxpayers to exclude the interest earned on state and local bonds from their incomes, presumably to subsidize the state and local governments that issue those bonds. Whether interest paid with respect to loans used to finance state and local bonds is deductible ought to depend on the utility of the deduction in advancing the goal of subsidizing state and local governments. Allowing the deduction will present taxpayers with arbitrage opportunities. Commentators do not agree as to whether those arbitrage opportunities are harmful or beneficial. If arbitrage is to be eliminated, however, the technique for doing so is strict stacking. Under strict stacking, a borrower holding state and local bonds will be considered to have purchased those bonds with borrowed money, up to the amount of the loan proceeds. Interest on the portion of the loan so linked with the purchase of the state and local bonds would be denied.

Most commentators agree that the deductibility of interest should be limited during periods of inflation. During such periods, a nominal interest payment typically includes not only genuine interest but also a payment to compensate the lender for the decline in the value of the principal amount of the loan. In substance, that latter portion is a prepayment of principal and should not be deductible. One way to prevent a deduction for the inflation component of nominal interest is to adopt a comprehensive indexing scheme. However, the perceived complexity of comprehensive indexing schemes has discouraged many governments from adopting them.

Some limitations on the interest deduction should be applied to taxpayers who are earning foreign income. Otherwise a country would be giving an improper incentive to invest abroad and would be ceding some of its jurisdiction to tax domestic income to foreign governments. Countries that exempt foreign income from taxation should prohibit taxpayers from deducting interest payments properly linked to the earning of foreign income.

Many countries, including the United States, impose their normal income tax on the worldwide income of resident taxpayers and then allow a foreign tax credit, subject to important limitations, for income taxes paid to foreign governments. The credit is typically limited to the amount of tax otherwise imposed on the taxpayer's foreign taxable income. Thus if a taxpayer's foreign taxable income is $100 and the tax rate is 35 percent, then the limitation on the credit would be $35. The foreign tax credit limitation cannot operate properly unless the credit country has appropriate rules for apportioning interest deductions between foreign and domestic sources.

The United States generally uses what is referred to as the asset method for linking interest payments with foreign and domestic income. Under that method, a taxpayer allocates its interest payments pro rata to its worldwide assets. Interest deductions are linked to foreign income to the extent that they have been allocated to assets that generate foreign income. Assume, for example, that a taxpayer has an asset having a value for tax purposes of $1 million that generates foreign income and also has an asset with a tax value of $4 million

that generates domestic income. In computing the limitation on its foreign tax credit, the taxpayer is required under the asset method to attribute 80 percent of its interest deduction to domestic income and the remaining 20 percent to foreign income.

The tax reforms adopted in the landmark Tax Reform Act of 1986 generally make the deductibility of interest paid with respect to a loan depend upon the use made of the loan proceeds. Current U.S. law prohibits individuals from deducting consumer interest and limits the deduction for interest traceable to tax-shelter activities to the income (usually negligible) generated by those activities. Interest traceable to traditional investment assets is also limited to the income generated by those assets. As an incentive for home ownership and a response to political pressures, Congress continues to allow interest to be deductible when it is traceable to the purchase of the taxpayer's personal residence or to one other designated residence. Under some circumstances, individuals and corporations are required to capitalize interest payments made with respect to loans used to finance capital acquisitions. The U.S. limitations on the deductibility of corporate interest payments continue to be far more generous than would be appropriate under a tracing approach.

ADDITIONAL READINGS

Abreu, Alice G. "Distinguishing Interest from Damages: A Proposal for a New Perspective." *Buffalo Law Review* 40 (1992): 373–439.

Arnold, Brian J. "Is Interest a Capital Expense?" *Canadian Tax Journal* 40 (1992): 533–53.

———. "General Report: Deductibility of Interest and Other Financing Charges in Computing Income." In *Cahiers de Droit Fiscal International* 79a (489–541). Deventer, Netherlands: Kluwer, 1994.

Auerbach, Alan J. "Should Interest Deductions Be Limited?" In *Uneasy Compromise: Problems of a Hybrid Income-Consumption Tax,* edited by Henry Aaron, Harvey Galper, and Joseph Pechman (195–221). Washington, DC: The Brookings Institution, 1988.

Block, Cheryl. "The Trouble with Interest: Reflections on Interest Deductions after the Tax Reform Act of 1986." *University of Florida Law Review* 40 (1988): 689–753.

Bossons, John. "Indexing for Inflation and the Interest Deduction." *Wayne Law Review* 30 (1984): 945–68; "Reply" 983–89.

Crane, Charlotte. "Matching and the Income Tax Base: The Special Case of Tax Exempt Income." *American Journal of Tax Policy* 5 (1986): 191–268.

Dixon, Darryl A. "A Consideration of the Theory of the Deductibility of Interest Payments from the Personal Income Tax Base." *National Tax Journal* 23 (1970): 168–76.

Dixon, Gordon D., and Brian Arnold. "Rubbing Salt into the Wound: The Denial of the Interest Deduction after the Loss of a Source of Income." *Canadian Tax Journal* 39 (1991): 1473–96.

Fleming, J. Clifton, Jr. "The Deceptively Disparate Treatment of Business and Investment Interest Expense Under a Cash-Flow Consumption Tax and a Schanz-Haig-Simons Income Tax." *Florida Tax Review* 3 (1997): 544–61.

Goode, Richard. *The Individual Income Tax.* Washington, DC: The Brookings Institution, 1976.

Gunn, Alan. "Is an Interest Deduction for Personal Debt a Tax Expenditure?" *Canadian Taxation* 1/4 (1979): 46–50.

Halperin, Daniel I. "Interest in Disguise: Taxing the 'Time Value of Money.'" *Yale Law Journal* 95 (1986): 506–52.

Hickman, Frederic W. "Interest, Depreciation, and Indexing." *Virginia Tax Review* 5 (1986): 773–806.

Hoerner, J. Andrew. "Indexing the Tax System for Inflation: Lessons from the British and Chilean Experiences." *Tax Notes International* 2 (June 1990): 552–56.

Johnson, Calvin H. "Tax Shelter Gain: The Mismatch of Debt and Supply Side Depreciation." *Texas Law Review* 61 (1983): 1013–55.

———. "Is an Interest Deduction Inevitable?" *Virginia Law Review* 6 (1986): 123–82.

Kahn, Charles H. *Personal Deductions in the Federal Income Tax.* Princeton, NJ: Princeton University Press, 1960.

Kayle, Bruce. "Where Has All the Income Gone? The Mysterious Relocation of Interest and Principal in Coupon Stripping and Related Transactions." *Virginia Tax Review* 7 (1987): 303–61.

Klein, William A. "Borrowing to Finance Tax-Favored Investments." *Wisconsin Law Review* (1962): 608–36.

Koppelman, Stanley. "Tax Arbitrage and the Interest Deduction." *Southern California Law Review* 61 (1988): 1143–1217.

Kurtz, Jerome. "Comments on 'Indexing for Inflation and the Interest Deduction.'" *Wayne Law Review* 30 (1984): 969–72.

———. "The Interest Deduction Under Our Hybrid Tax System: Muddling Toward Accommodation." *Tax Law Review* 50 (1995): 153–236.

Mann, Roberta F. "The (Not So) Little House on the Prairie: The Hidden Costs of the Home Mortgage Interest Deduction." *Arizona State Law Journal* 32 (2000): 1347–97.

Mathias, William T. "Curtailing the Economic Distortions of the Mortgage Interest Deduction." *University of Michigan Journal of Law Reform* 30 (1996): 43–76.

McIntyre, Michael J. "An Inquiry into the Special Status of Interest Payments." *Duke Law Review* (1981): 765–810.

———. "Comments on 'Indexing for Inflation and the Interest Deduction.'" *Wayne Law Review* 30 (1984): 973–82.

———. "Contributions Made by the U.S. Tax Reform Act of 1986 to Distributive Justice." In *Flattening the Tax Rate Scale: Alternative Scenarios and Methodologies,* edited by John Head and Richard Krever. Melbourne: Longman Professional, 1990.

———. "Tracing Rules and the Deduction for Interest Payments: A Justification for Tracing and a Critique of Recent U.S. Tracing Rules." *Wayne Law Review* 39 (1992): 67–120.

McMahon, Martin. "Reforming Cost Recovery Allowances for Debt Financed Depreciable Property." *St. Louis University Law Journal* 29 (1985): 1029–132.

Mundstock, George. "Accelerated Depreciation and the Interest Deduction: Can Two Rights Really Make a Wrong?" *Tax Notes* 29 (1985): 1253–60.

Oliver, Philip D. "A Counter-Productive Solution to a Nonexistent Problem." *Tax Law Review* 40 (1985): 351–410.

Shakow, David. "Confronting the Problem of Tax Arbitrage." *Tax Law Review* 43 (1987): 1–50.

Shoup, Carl S. "Deductions of Homeowners' Mortgage Interest, Interest on Other Consumer Debt, and Property Taxes, under the Individual Income Tax: The Horizontal Equity Issue." *Canadian Tax Journal* 27 (1979): 529–533.

Snoe, Joseph A. "My Home, My Debt: Remodeling the Home Mortgage Interest Deduction." *Kentucky Law Journal* 80 (1992): 431–97.

Steuerle, C. Eugene. "Tax Arbitrage, Inflation, and the Taxation of Interest Payments and Receipts." *Wayne Law Review* 30 (1983): 991–1013.

———. *Taxes, Loans, and Inflation: How the Nation's Wealth Becomes Misallocated.* Washington, DC: The Brookings Institution, 1985.

Taggart, John Y. "Denial of the Personal Interest Deduction." *Tax Lawyer* 41 (1988): 195–278.

Vann, Richard J., and Darryl A. Dixon. "Measuring Income under Inflation." Research Study no. 12. Australian Tax Research Foundation, 1990.

White, Melvin. "Proper Tax Treatment of Deductions for Personal Expense." In *House Committee on Ways and Means, 86th Cong., 1st Sess., 1959, Tax Revision Compendium 1* (365–74). Washington, DC: House Committee on Ways and Means.

White, Melvin, and Anne White. "Horizontal Equity in the Federal Income Tax Treatment of Homeowners and Tenants." *National Tax Journal* 18 (1965): 225–39.

———. "Tax Deductibility of Interest on Consumer Debt." *Public Finance Quarterly* 5 (1977): 3–7.

Whitt, Deborah. "Interest Deductions after the Tax Reform Act of 1986 and the Revenue Act of 1987." *Boston University Journal of Tax Law* 6 (1988): 85–115.

Cross-references: homeowner preferences, individual income tax; income tax, federal; itemized deductions; original issue and market discount.

Intergovernmental grants

Mark Shroder
U.S. Department of Housing and Urban Development

Payments generally made from a higher to a lower level of government to subsidize the cost of providing specific public goods or services.

In a federal system, one level of government may receive funding from another level of government, generally a higher one, either for the provision of a specific public service or for the general conduct of public business.

In the United States, the decade of the 1990s to the present witnessed a 75 percent increase in the level of federal grants relative to total federal outlays. As of 2003, total federal, state, and local government outlays in fiscal year 2003 amounted to $385.7 billion (17.9 percent total federal outlays). The largest amount was for Medicaid ($160.7 billion, 42 percent), followed by Highways ($2.6 billion, 7.4 percent), Housing Certificates ($20.9 billion, 54 percent), Temporary Assistance for Needy Families ($19.1 billion, 50 percent), and Child Nutrition ($10.4 billion, 2.7 percent). Another 712 programs account for $146.0 billion (38.6 percent) (U.S. Census Bureau 2004).

Rationale

It is almost universally believed that some public services are most efficiently delivered by subnational governments. The question is why the residents of the jurisdiction doing the spending should not pay for all such services. The scholarly literature employs four different ideas to explain the increasing transfer of resources from higher to lower levels of government:

Externalities

A particular service provided by a lower-level government may have benefits that spill over to residents of other jurisdictions. Feasible lower-level tax systems (e.g., property or sales) do not capture these external benefits. It is inequitable for residents of the provider jurisdiction to pay for nonresidents' benefits, and, in the absence of external assistance, the provider jurisdiction would choose an inefficiently low level of service. As spillovers increase, the argument for the higher level of government assuming the function entirely may grow stronger.

Vertical equity

Higher-level authorities may believe that feasible lower-level tax systems have undesirable distributional consequences. Resources for essential public services that can most efficiently be provided by the lower level of government should be obtained in part from a tax system that has more desirable distributional properties (e.g., income).

Income elasticity of demand

Demand for public services is highly income-elastic, but lower-level tax systems may not be. As society becomes richer, it demands disproportionately more public services, some of them local, and must use those tax systems most responsive to wealth and income changes to pay for them, regardless of the level of government providing them.

Fiscal illusion

When the taxing entity is not the same as the spending entity, some level of spending on the particular public service appears to the lower-level authorities as a free good. They will then spend more for that service than their own electorate would be willing to pay for it. The higher-level authority's interest in maintaining the illusion arises from the political influence of groups with special interests in raising expenditures on those services.

Locally provided elementary and secondary education can serve as an illustration for all four arguments. This service cost $365 billion in fiscal year 2000, and states provided more than half the money in an increasing departure from the tradition of dependence on the local property tax. Education exhibits interjurisdictional externalities: in an increasingly mobile society, the children educated by one jurisdiction may live and work as adults in other areas, and some of the benefits of their education are lost to the community that paid for it. Vertical equity is surely relevant: the property tax base per child is very unevenly distributed across communities, and either legislatures or courts come to believe that providing a minimum standard of education to all children is unfairly burdensome for property-poor communities. Tax elasticity comes into play: The economy demands an increasing proportion of high school graduates, and the traditional property tax base may well not expand as quickly as school enrollments. Finally, fiscal illusion might be driving the trend: the substantial growth in state aid to local schools has been an avowed goal of groups interested in higher aggregate expenditure levels, like teachers' unions.

Appropriate design of grants programs

The design of grant allocations across jurisdictions does not always reflect the intent of the legislators as well as it could. Grants may be categorical—that is, tied to a particular public

service—or untied; they may be awarded competitively or by formula. If they are awarded by formula, they may be awarded with or without a matching requirement; a matching requirement may reflect various efficiency and equity concerns.

Untied grants

An untied grant (like the former federal revenue-sharing program) invites the lower-level government to choose from a wide menu of spending increases and/or tax reductions.

Competitive grants

In the federal government, small grant programs are almost necessarily competitive. Competitive processes have both positive and negative features. The higher-level government can use the competition to reward those lower jurisdictions that have made the greatest effort to solve a problem of general concern, or to assist jurisdictions for whom the problem is particularly acute, although the latter approach can give rise to perverse incentives. It is sometimes argued that competitions stimulate lower-level jurisdictions to give greater consideration to particular problems, even if they fail to receive funding. On the other hand, competitive processes consume scarce resources at both the lower and upper levels of government; much of the time spent in grant writing and proposal evaluation is deadweight loss.

Categorical grants with no matching requirement

The higher-level authorities may award funds for some public service without requiring the lower-level jurisdiction to devote additional resources to that service. The accepted view of economists is that matching provisions will cause the lower-level government to provide greater amounts of service; the reasons are discussed below.

Open-ended or limited matching requirements

The higher-level legislators may choose not to continue to match lower-level expenditures above some threshold. An open-ended matching program could easily lead to spending levels in excess of those the legislators are committed to supporting. On the other hand, limited matching programs offer no incentives, and relatively less aid, to those jurisdictions that have high spending propensities for the service in question.

Maintenance of effort requirements

The higher-level government might condition any grant on a certain minimum contribution by the lower-level jurisdiction from its own revenues. When the minimum is set at the jurisdiction's past contribution level, this is called a "maintenance of effort" requirement. For example, the welfare reform act of 1996 replaced a system of open-ended federal matching with lump-sum block grants, but required the states to spend at least as much on welfare from their own resources as they had in past periods.

Efficiency considerations in matching formulas

When creating matching formulas, legislators typically fail to provide adjustments for the extent to which service delivery in one jurisdiction has more or less spillover externalities than in others. The predictable consequence will be inefficient under-provision of the service. For example, if differences in the level of welfare benefits motivated migration across state lines, the spillover could lead to inefficiently low levels of benefit in all states. Transparent (and therefore uncontroversial) measures of spillover propensities are seldom at hand, but the almost universal lack of interest in construction of such measures suggests that spillovers play a much smaller role in motivating grants in the real world than in the theory of fiscal federalism.

Effects of categorical grants on spending

A substantial body of scholarly literature, both theoretical and empirical, has analyzed the effects of categorical grant programs on lower-level public service expenditure. Two sorts of findings about price and income effects have arisen from it.

First, each public service is presumably a good thing that almost every citizen would like to have a little more of as the price of obtaining it falls. Categorical grants that require matching funds effectively lower the price of the public service. For example, if the federal government pays 80 percent of the cost of an interstate highway, then each state obtains the benefits of an additional mile of highway at an apparent price of 20 cents on the dollar. Economists have predicted that any given amount of funds delivered in the form of categorical matching grants would stimulate more spending on the targeted services than the same amount of money provided without matching. The matching requirement lowers the price of additional units of service, while the grant without a matching requirement leaves the price of additional units to the lower-level government unaffected.

Most empirical studies confirm this prediction, but it may be extended too far. In the 1996 welfare reform block grants replaced matching grants to the states, and some specialists incorrectly predicted that "a race to the bottom"—large reductions in the level of benefits—would result, because under block grants every additional dollar of benefit would be paid from the state's own revenues. (They failed to consider either the maintenance of effort requirement or the offsetting effect of greater state power to determine eligibility for assistance, among other factors.)

A second type of finding has been that grant money is less fungible than one might expect. Suppose that Dirty City, where the citizens have a total private income of $100 million a year, spends $400,000 a year (0.4 percent) to control water pollution. Now suppose that Dirty City receives a grant of $200,000 to increase its pollution control activity. Under a variety of economic models of political behavior, the grant is equivalent to some distribution of $200,000 to particular individuals in the community. From this one might anticipate a trivial increase in anti-pollution spending, somewhere around $800 (0.4 percent) of the grant—perhaps a little more if clean water is a luxury good. The remainder would be used for other public purposes and/or reducing community taxes.

But the prediction of trivial impact has no empirical support. Instead, it would be more typical to find Dirty City increasing its water pollution control budget from $400,000 to $480,000—less, possibly, than the higher-level authorities wanted, but an increase that is a hundred times larger than what one would expect from the simple fungibility of money. Most empirical studies have found this flypaper effect, so called because grant funding tends to "stick where it hits" (Courant, Gramlich, and Rubinfeld 1979).

The flypaper effect has provoked much controversy and inspired much creativity in the building of new behavioral models, but no consensus has emerged. If citizens are unwilling to spend a large fraction of "their own" tax money on the targeted public service, the question is why they let "their own" government spend a large fraction of grant money on that service rather than on goods and services that they care more about. Tax illusion, special interest pressure, bureaucratic power, institutional restrictions like constitutional caps on property tax rates, and the political interest in stable tax rates (rate cuts based on intergovernmental grants could be destabilizing if future grants were not forthcoming) are among the explanations in the literature.

ADDITIONAL READINGS

Ahmad, Ehtisham. *Financing Decentralized Expenditures: An International Comparison of Grants.* Cheltenham, U.K.: Edward Elgar, 1997.

Bradford, David F., and Wallace E. Oates. "The Analysis of Revenue Sharing in a New Approach to Collective Fiscal Decisions." *Quarterly Journal of Economics* (August 1971): 416–39.

Canada, Ben. "Federal Grants to State and Local Governments: A Brief History." Washington, DC: U.S. Library of Congress, Congressional Research Service, 2003.

Chubb, John E. "The Political Economy of Federalism." *American Political Science Review* (December 1985): 994–1015.

Courant, Paul N., Edward M. Gramlich, and Daniel L. Rubinfeld. "The Stimulative Effects of Intergovernmental Grants: Or Why Money Sticks Where It Hits." In *Fiscal Federalism and Grants-in-Aid,* edited by Peter Mieszkowski and William H. Oakland (127–43). Washington, DC: The Urban Institute, 1979.

Dafflon, Bernard, and François Vaillancourt. "Problems of Equalisation in Federal Systems." In *Federalism in a Changing World—Learning From Each Other,* edited by Raoule Blindenbacher and Arnold Koller (395–411). Montreal: McGill-Queen's University Press, 2002.

Fossett, James W. "On Confusing Caution and Greed: A Political Explanation of the Flypaper Effect." *Urban Affairs Quarterly* 26 (September 1990): 95–117.

Gramlich, Edward M. "Intergovernmental Grants: A Review of the Empirical Literature." In *The Political Economy of Fiscal Federalism,* edited by Wallace E. Oates (219–40). Lexington, MA: Lexington Books, 1975.

———. *Financing Federal Systems: The Selected Essays of Edward M. Gramlich.* Edward Elgar, Cheltenham, U.K., and Northampton, MA: 1997.

Inman, Robert P. "Grants in a Metropolitan Economy—A Framework for Policy." In *Financing the New Federalism: Revenue Sharing, Conditional Grants, and Taxation,* edited by Wallace E. Oates. Baltimore: Johns Hopkins University Press, 1975.

———. "The Fiscal Performance of Local Government: An Interpretive Review." In *Current Issues in Urban Economics,* edited by Peter Mieszkowski and Mahlon Straszheim. Baltimore: Johns Hopkins University Press, 1979.

———. "Federal Assistance and Local Services in the United States: The Evolution of a New Federalist Fiscal Order." In *Fiscal Federalism,* edited by Harvey Rosen (33–74). Chicago: University of Chicago Press, 1988.

Joumard, Isabelle. "Problems of Equalisation in Federal Systems—The Concept of Equalisation." In *Federalism in a Changing World—Learning From Each Other,* edited by Raoule Blindenbacher and Arnold Koller (471–80). Montreal: McGill-Queen's University Press, 2002.

Ladd, Helen F., and Fred C. Doolittle. "Which Level of Government Should Assist the Poor?" *National Tax Journal* 35 (September 1982): 323–36.

Logan, Robert R. "Fiscal Illusion and the Grantor Government." *Journal of Political Economy* 94 (December 1986): 1304–18.

Ma, Jun. "Intergovernmental Fiscal Transfers in Nine Countries." Policy Research Working Paper 1822. Washington, DC: World Bank, 1997.

Nathan, Richard P. "State and Local Government under Federal Grants: Toward a Predictive Theory." *Political Science Quarterly* 98, no. 1 (Spring 1983): 47–57.

Nathan, Richard P., and Fred Doolittle. "Federal Grants: Giving and Taking Away." *Political Science Quarterly* 100, no. 1 (Spring 1985): 53–74.

Oates, Wallace E. *Fiscal Federalism.* New York: Harcourt Brace Jovanovich, 1972.

———. "An Essay on Fiscal Federalism." *Journal of Economic Literature* 37 (September 1999): 1120–49.

Reischauer, Robert D. "General Revenue Sharing—The Program's Incentives." In *Financing the New Federalism: Revenue Sharing, Conditional Grants, and Taxation,* edited by Wallace E. Oates. Baltimore: Johns Hopkins University Press, 1975.

Shah, Anwar. "The Reform of Intergovernmental Fiscal Relations in Developing and Emerging Market Economies." Policy and Research Series 23. Washington, DC: World Bank, 1994.

Shroder, Mark. "Approximately Efficient Federal Matching Grants for Subnational Public Assistance." *National Tax Journal* 45, no. 2 (June 1992): 155–66.

Singh, Nirvikar, and Ravi Thomas. "Matching Grants versus Block Grants with Imperfect Information." *National Tax Journal* 42, no. 2 (June 1989): 191–239.

U.S. Census Bureau. "Federal Aid to the States for Fiscal Year 2003." Washington, DC: U.S. Department of Commerce, 2004.

Vaillancourt, François. "Simulating Intergovernmental Equalization Transfers with Imperfect Data." In *Proceedings of the Ninety-Fourth Annual Conference on Taxation* (57–64). Washington, DC: National Tax Association, 2001.

Wilde, J. "Grants in Aid: The Analytics of Design and Responses." *National Tax Journal* (June 1971): 573–84.

Cross-references: education financing, state and local; fiscal federalism; Tiebout model.

Inventory accounting

David W. Brazell

Department of the Treasury

Methods used to match costs incurred in producing, purchasing, transporting, or storing property against revenues received from the sale of that property; different inventory accounting rules apply for financial accounting and income tax purposes.

Under inventory accounting, the costs of acquiring, producing, and maintaining inventory property are generally capitalized and allocated to the property. These capitalized costs are deducted from the firm's gross receipts as the "cost of goods sold" when inventory property is sold to obtain the entity's gross income. The cost of goods sold during an accounting period is determined by adding total inventory costs capitalized during the period to the value of the beginning-of-period inventory, and by deducting the value of the end-of-period inventory.

The need for inventory accounting

Inventory accounting is used in the preparation of financial reports and tax returns to measure asset values and income. It ensures that inventory costs are not treated as period expenses, but are deducted only in the period in which the property is sold. Inventory costs contribute to a firm's asset value and net worth, and accounting for the creation and disposition of inventory contributes to the proper measurement of income.

Tax consequences of inventory accounting

Designation of property as inventory has tax consequences in addition to the income measurement effects described above. Inventory may be subject to state or local property taxes. Also, a taxpayer having inventories must use an accrual method of accounting with respect to their acquisition and sale. In addition, gains and losses recognized with respect to inventory are treated as items of ordinary income or loss, and are not subject to the special rules and tax rates that apply to gains and losses on capital assets. Finally, in some circumstances, inventory may be valued at the "lower of cost or market" (LCM), which allows losses to be recognized without the occurrence of an accompanying transaction.

General principles

The U.S. Internal Revenue Code imposes two general restrictions on a taxpayer's choice of inventory methods: the methods must conform as closely as possible to the best accounting practice in the trade or business of the taxpayer, and they must clearly reflect income. These requirements usually are interpreted as demanding that a taxpayer's accounting methods by and large conform to generally accepted accounting principles (GAAP) which underlie financial accounting, and that the chosen methods are used consistently from year to year.

Description of inventory accounting

Inventory accounting requires an identification of property considered to be inventory, an identification of the costs to be capitalized, an allocation of those costs to physical inventory, possible revaluation of inventory under certain circumstances, and the identification of property sold from inventory. Generally, at least two inventory accounting systems—financial and tax—must be maintained. In some cases, separate tax inventory accounting systems—for computing regular tax, alternative minimum tax, and corporate earnings and profits—are maintained.

What is inventory?

GAAP and tax rules agree that inventory must include all finished or partly finished goods acquired or produced for sale at a profit. In addition, raw materials and supplies are inventory, but only if they are acquired for sale at a profit or will physically become a part of merchandise that is held for sale at a profit. Normally, inventory is included in a taxpayer's books only if title to the property is held by the taxpayer. Property acquired with the intention of earning an investment return (including fixed tangible capital), or which is acquired with the intent to be sold at cost, is not inventory. Supplies that are to be used in manufacturing but will not be physically incorporated into products to be sold at a later date are not treated as inventory (but their costs will be incorporated into the inventory cost of the produced property). Real estate may be treated as inventory for financial reporting purposes, but never in income tax accounts. Livestock and other farm products need not be treated as inventory for tax purposes if a farmer elects not to use an inventory method. However, such an election may not be made by a corporation or other farm entity that is otherwise required to use an accrual method of accounting.

Identification of inventory costs in general

Manufacturing costs that must be inventoried under GAAP generally include those costs that can be identified specifically with the manufactured product: direct materials costs, direct labor costs, and indirect production costs (also referred to as factory "overhead" or "burden"). GAAP inventory costs for purchased merchandise include direct purchasing costs, including transportation costs. Before 1987, tax accounting generally followed GAAP in identifying inventory costs. Wholesalers and retailers were required to capitalize direct purchasing costs, while manufacturers were subject to the "full absorption" regulations. These rules specified that, while certain indirect costs had to be capitalized, other identified costs were to be capitalized for tax purposes only if they were capitalized into inventory by the taxpayer in preparing its financial statements. Thus, taxpayers were usually required to keep only one set of inventory records for both tax and financial reporting purposes.

The uniform capitalization rules (UCR)

The Tax Reform Act of 1986 added the "uniform capitalization rules" (UCR) to the Internal Revenue Code. The UCR mandate that taxpayers allocate to inventory those costs that "directly benefit or are incurred by reason of the performance of production or resale activities" [Reg. §1.263A-1(e)(3)(i)]. Consequently, certain administrative, service, and support overhead—costs for items such as insurance, data processing, legal services, merchandise purchasing and handling, and offsite storage—must be capitalized into inventory to the extent they are allocated to production or resale activities. In addition, certain costs (e.g., depreciation and depletion), previously capitalized under tax rules only to the extent they were capitalized under financial accounting rules, are fully includible under the UCR as inventory costs. Indirect costs that continue to be deductible under the UCR include selling and advertising costs, research and experimentation costs, income taxes, and most interest costs. The UCR regulations authorize a number of accounting techniques that allow firms to calculate the additional UCR inventory values and to allocate them to physical inventory using simplified methods. The statute also contains a de minimis rule that exempts small resellers (those with a three-year average of annual gross receipts of $10 million or less) from the UCR.

Additional tax accounting systems

Inventory values calculated for purposes of the alternative minimum tax (AMT), or used to compute corporate earnings and profits (E&P), may differ from those computed under the regular tax rules, because depreciation expense in these systems is calculated under different rules than for regular tax depreciation expense. However, taxpayers may elect to use their regular tax inventory values in computing income under the AMT (including the calculation of the adjusted current earnings adjustment under the AMT), thereby avoiding additional tax compliance burdens, albeit at the cost of potentially paying additional tax under the AMT.

Allocation of inventory costs

Both GAAP and tax rules authorize methods to allocate direct and indirect costs to physical inventory using predetermined unit cost ratios and measures of direct costs, hours, or similar items. These methods go under the names of *burden rate* and *standard cost methods*. The burden rate method uses predetermined ratios to allocate various indirect costs to units of inventory. The standard cost method is similar but also allocates direct costs based on predetermined standard cost ratios. If actual costs vary from costs computed using predetermined cost ratios under these methods, such "variances" are often allocated on a pro rata basis to end-of-period inventory. However, if the variances are "not significant in amount," and positive and negative variances are treated consistently, then the variances may be deducted, provided similar deductions are made for financial reporting purposes. Under GAAP, a manufacturer may use a plant's estimated "practical capacity" production level to estimate fixed overhead unit costs. This allows a lower unit cost to be used to establish inventory cost if actual production falls below the practical capacity level. However, the method—expressly allowed under the full absorption regulations—is not allowed under the UCR regulations.

Valuation of inventory

Inventory can conceivably be valued using a variety of cost concepts. The most prevalent valuation standard used in financial and tax accounting systems is historic cost, or simply "cost." Cost represents the consideration paid to acquire or otherwise bring property to its existing condition and location. Under UCR, certain post-acquisition or post-production costs must also be included in the cost of an item of inventory. Inventory could also conceivably be valued at its current replacement or reproduction cost, but current cost is not generally authorized as a stand-alone valuation method under GAAP or the tax rules. *Replacement cost* refers to the current bid prices for like goods. (For manufactured goods that are not in salable form, it refers to the current bid prices for goods in a previously salable form, plus the additional costs necessary to bring the goods to the current state of completion.) Reproduction cost is similar but represents the current cost of reproducing the inventory in the same manner as it was originally produced. Replacement/reproduction cost is used in both financial and tax accounting under the lower-of-cost-or-market (LCM) method of inventory valuation (see below), where it represents *market*. Inventory investment reported in the national income and product accounts (NIPA) is also measured using estimates of current-year replacement or reproduction cost. Net realizable value is a third valuation standard. It normally refers to the estimated selling price for inventory sold in the ordinary course of business, less the estimated costs of completing the sale, and is used under limited circumstances in applying the LCM method where replacement cost is not available. Net realizable value is also used to value "subnormal" goods, irrespective of whether cost or LCM is used as a general valuation method. Subnormal goods are those that are unsalable at normal prices or unusable in the normal way because of damage, imperfections, change of style, or other similar reasons. Finally, in some limited cases, inventory is valued at fair market value. Security dealers, for example, must value their inventories at fair market value for tax purposes. Commodity dealers can elect to do so.

The lower-of-cost-or-market (LCM) method

While cost is the usual valuation method required under GAAP and tax principles, the lower-of-cost-or-market (LCM) method is also allowed. The Internal Revenue Code, however, requires that inventories be valued only at cost if the LIFO method of identifying inventory is used (see below). Under LCM, inventory may be revalued at "market," if market is less than historical cost, and vice versa, (assuming that the goods are not subject to sale under a fixed price contract such that the taxpayer is protected against loss). In most cases, market is

the current replacement or reproduction cost of the inventory. GAAP rules limit market on the high side by net realizable value (ordinary selling price, less disposition costs) and on the low side by net realizable value reduced by an allowance for an approximately normal profit margin. Income tax regulations define market as "the aggregate of the current bid prices prevailing at the date of the inventory of the basic elements of cost" [Reg. §1.471-4(a)(1)]. The tax regulations do not contain the limits on market specified under GAAP. In two situations—when no market bid price is available, and when the merchandise has been offered for sale in the regular course of business at prices lower than the current bid price—the tax rules allow net realizable value to represent market. Once an item is valued at market, that value generally then becomes its "cost" in the following accounting period.

Criticism of LCM

The LCM method allows losses on inventory to be recognized without actual transactions taking place, while similar unrealized gains are never recognized under LCM. For this reason, proposals for its repeal under the tax rules have been frequently advanced (but never enacted). The method has been justified by the conservatism principle of GAAP. The reasoning is that a departure from the cost basis of pricing inventory is required, and a current loss should be recognized, when the realizable value of the inventory in the normal course of business is no longer as great as its cost.

Inventory investment in the national income and product accounts (NIPA)

As mentioned above, inventory investment in the NIPA is measured using estimates of current-year replacement cost. As a result, by measuring both beginning- and end-of-period inventory values at current-year cost, NIPA inventory investment differs from the change in inventory values reported in either financial or tax accounts. The NIPA estimators convert historical cost inventory values into current replacement cost estimates using available price series and estimates of inventory turnover rates. The NIPA also report an inventory valuation adjustment (IVA) that equals the difference between the change in aggregate inventory valued at current cost and the change in the aggregate book value of inventory. The IVA is subtracted from reported profits in calculating NIPA estimates of corporate profits and proprietors' income, so that the NIPA-adjusted profit measures do not reflect inflationary gains (or deflationary losses) on inventory. This is in accordance with the general exclusion of asset gains and losses from the NIPA income measures.

Identification of inventory items

Because items included in inventory are usually valued at cost, the flow of items into and out of inventory must be identified in some way. This identification could be accomplished by tracking individual items of inventory. Financial accounting also authorizes "average costing," under which end-of-period inventory is valued using weighted average costs of items in the beginning-of-period inventory and of acquisitions made during the period. More commonly, however, a flow-of-cost assumption is employed. The tax regulations specifically recognize two such assumptions. The "first in, first out" (FIFO) method assumes that the remaining items in inventory are those last purchased or last produced. The "last in, first out" (LIFO) method is also authorized. Under LIFO, it is assumed that items in the current inventory are the earliest acquired or manufactured. While a more complicated method to implement, LIFO generally yields lower inventory values, higher values for the cost of goods sold, and lower reported profits in periods of rising costs. LIFO may be viewed as delaying the recognition of inventory inflationary gains. As costs increase, these costs enter inventory only in the latest LIFO increment, so that most inventory is valued at older, lower costs. If inventory levels fall, however, profit rates tend to increase as older and lower-valued inventory layers are brought into the cost of goods sold.

LIFO requirements

If LIFO is elected for tax purposes, the identified inventory must be evaluated at cost, even if LCM had previously been used. Other restrictions are also placed on LIFO taxpayers. For example, LIFO may be used for tax purposes only if it is used for most financial reporting purposes. A corporate taxpayer must include the change in its "LIFO recapture amount" (the amount by which the corporation's FIFO-valued inventory exceeds its LIFO-valued inventory) in calculating the adjusted current earnings adjustment under the AMT rules. Accordingly, the benefits of LIFO are lessened if the corporation is subject to additional tax from the AMT. A similar adjustment must be made to calculate a corporation's E&P, which could affect the taxable character of corporate distributions. Corporations converting to FIFO accounting from LIFO and those converting to S corporation status must include their LIFO recapture amount in income over four years.

LIFO methods

LIFO inventory is valued under either the "specific goods" method (in which quantities are measured in terms of physical units) or, most often, the "dollar-value" method (in which quantities are aggregated into LIFO pools, and the pools are measured in terms of fixed dollar equivalents of base-year costs). The standard approach to implementing dollar-value LIFO is the "double-extension" method. Under this method, the items in a pool are "extended" (i.e., costed) using fixed base-year unit costs and using current-year unit costs to obtain total inventory valued at both base-year and current year costs. The ratio of these two values provides the current-year value of a LIFO cost index. Comparing the base-year value of end-

of-period inventory with the base-year value of beginning-of-period inventory provides a measure of the year's inventory increment or decrement. If a decrement has occurred, then prior increments (at base-year values) are removed or reduced in reverse chronological order to the extent of the decrement. If an increment has occurred, it is valued at current-year costs using the LIFO cost index, and is added to the prior increments to obtain end-of-period inventory valued at cost. Under the double-extension method, a new item entering the inventory must be valued at base-year cost, even if it did not exist in the base year. Such a cost must be constructed or estimated in some acceptable fashion. This method may therefore become impractical because of "technological changes, the extensive variety of items, or extreme fluctuations in the variety of the items" [Reg. §1.472-8(e)(1)]. Consequently, other variants of dollar-value LIFO are specifically authorized. The "index" method uses a representative portion of the inventory pool to estimate the LIFO cost index. The "link-chain" method allows the introduction of new items without reconstructing base-year costs. Simplified methods are also authorized, in which cost indexes are developed from price indexes published by the Bureau of Labor Statistics.

Summary

Measurement of income in a world where asset values are not, or cannot be, obtained routinely by reference to market prices is an intricate and complex undertaking. The methods used to value inventory must deal with many difficulties in attempting to assign reasonable values to items of inventory. This entry has only scratched the surface in describing the details of the subject, yet the complexity of inventory accounting is evident. Complications arise because product costs are not always immediately evident (witness the UCR), because inventory values may not always reflect current economic values even in the absence of general inflation or deflation (witness the use of LCM), because historic cost valuation cannot ensure an appropriate matching of current receipts with current production or acquisition costs when aggregate price levels are changing (witness the use of LIFO as means to counter the effects of inflation), and because of other reasons.

ADDITIONAL READINGS

American Institute of Certified Public Accountants, Inc. (AICPA). *Accounting Research Bulletin* 43, ch. 4 (1953).

Garrett, Richard, and James E. Connor. "Uniform Capitalization Rules: Inventory; Self-Constructed Assets; Real Estate." *Tax Management Portfolio No. 576-2nd.* Washington, DC: Tax Management, Inc., 2003.

Godbout, James C., Diane P. Herndon, Helen M. Hubbard, and Barry A. Tovig. "Inventories: General Principles; LIFO Method." *Tax Management Portfolio No. 578-2nd.* Washington, DC: Tax Management, Inc., 1999.

U.S. Department of Commerce, Bureau of Economic Analysis. *Readings in Concepts and Methods of National Income Statistics.* Washington, DC: National Technical Information Service, 1976.

Cross-reference: uniform capitalization rules.

Inverse elasticity rule

Harry Watson

George Washington University

A principle for choosing tax rates to minimize the excess tax burden.

The inverse elasticity rule is one of the few simple rules that derive from the optimal commodity tax literature, a literature that examines how excise taxes should be structured in order to achieve some revenue target while ensuring that the excess burden of taxation is minimized. Because most of the optimal tax rules that have been derived are not very transparent and would require a substantial amount of information were they to be used, some effort has been devoted to finding conditions under which simple rules of thumb might serve as a guide in the choice of optimal tax rates. One such guide is the inverse elasticity rule, the application of which requires that the demands and supplies of all the goods or services subject to taxation depend only on their own price.

Supposing that demands of taxed goods or services are sensitive only to their own price and assuming that production of the taxed goods or services occurs in perfectly competitive industries with constant average costs (so that producer prices are unaffected by taxation) yields the simplest variant of the inverse elasticity rule: The excise tax rates of any pair of taxed goods or services, say i and j, should be set so that $\theta_j/\theta_i, = \varepsilon_j/\varepsilon_i$, where θ is the ad valorem tax rate and ε is the elasticity of demand.

Thus, the tax rates should vary inversely with the responsiveness of consumers to price changes, a relationship that minimizes the excess burden that such taxes can create. Assuming that there are n taxed goods or services and that all their elasticities are known, the problem of selecting optimal excise tax rates is quite simple. By the inverse elasticity rule, it must be that $\theta_2 = (\varepsilon_1/\varepsilon_2)\theta_1$, $\theta_3 = (\varepsilon_1/\varepsilon_3)\theta_1$, etc. The values of all these tax rates are simply multiples of θ_1, and the value of θ_1 can be adjusted upward until the revenue target is met.

When producer prices can vary—that is, when the assumption of constant average costs is dropped—and the supplies and demands of taxed goods or services depend only on their own price, the inverse elasticity rule becomes: The ad valorem excise tax rates for any pair of goods or services, say θ_i and θ_j, should be set so that

$$\theta = 1/\varepsilon + (1 - \theta)/\eta$$

where ε is the consumer's demand elasticity and η is the producer's supply elasticity.

As in the previous case, the logic behind this rule is to shift the tax burden to the market in which price changes produce limited responses. If the supplier of good j is not price-sensitive, so η_j is small, the tax on good j should be large relative to the taxes on other goods. On the other hand, if the producers of goods i and j are very price-sensitive, so that η_i

and η_j are large, the rule above collapses to the simple variant and tax rates are inversely related to the elasticities of consumers, or $\theta_j/\theta_i = \varepsilon_j/\varepsilon_i$.

The simplicity of the inverse elasticity rule comes at the cost of assuming that the demands and supplies of taxed goods or services are insensitive to changes in all prices except their own. Generally, one would expect that the impact of a tax on one good would not be limited to the market for that good; the imposition of a tax in one market will lead to supply or demand adjustments in other markets and, concomitantly, changes in the prices of other goods. It is these intermarket effects, which the inverse elasticity rule assumes away, that complicate the search for optimal tax rules.

Thus, the appropriateness of using the inverse elasticity rule hinges on the assumption that these intermarket effects can be ignored. For example, consider levying excise taxes on two different pairs of goods, say gasoline and tobacco versus beer and wine. For most consumers, spending on gasoline is independent of spending on tobacco—one cannot be substituted for the other, nor does one complement the use of the other—so it is likely that the impact of an excise tax on either good on the market for the other good can be ignored. On the other hand, because beer and wine may be substitutes for some consumers, the impact of an excise tax on either good may alter demand for the other, so that intermarket effects cannot be ignored. Ignoring intermarket effects may lead to the inappropriate application of the inverse elasticity rule. Suppose this rule is used to determine whether labor and capital income should face different rates of income taxation. Leaving aside the more complicated features of income taxation, it is possible to interpret a capital income tax as an excise tax that raises the price of future consumption—or reduces the return to saving—and a labor income tax as an excise tax that reduces the wage so that, together, these excise taxes capture the essence of income taxation. Provided the supply of labor was unaffected by the price of future consumption and the demand for future consumption was unaffected by the after-tax wage, it would follow that optimal pattern-of-labor versus capital-income-tax rates would be inversely related to the responsiveness of labor supply to the after-tax wage relative to the responsiveness of saving to after-tax rates of return.

This result suggests that whether labor or capital income should face a higher tax rate depends on a simple comparison of elasticity values. However, even if these elasticities could be accurately measured, this outcome cannot be assured unless it is true that labor supply does not respond to after-tax rates of return and saving does not respond to after-tax wage rates. While it is possible that labor supply is not significantly affected by after-tax rates of return, theory and empirical evidence do not support the assumption that saving does not respond to tax-induced changes in labor income, a fact that would preclude the use of the inverse elasticity rule in analyzing income taxation.

Although literal application of the inverse elasticity rule may not be feasible or appropriate in the practical design of tax systems, the spirit behind the rule provides some broad guidance to policymakers—namely, that in setting tax rates one should be mindful of the potential gains in economic efficiency by imposing heavier tax burdens on goods or activities that are relatively less sensitive to the changes in market prices that typically result from the imposition of taxes.

Cross-references: elasticity, demand and supply; excess burden; optimal taxation.

Investment tax credits

Robert S. Chirinko
Emory University and CESifo

Reductions in tax liabilities determined as a percentage of the price of a purchased asset.

Starting with the Revenue Act of 1962, the investment tax credit (ITC) has been set at various rates, suspended, reinstated, repealed, resurrected, increased, and then finally completely eliminated in the Tax Reform Act of 1986. Reinstituting the ITC was part of the Clinton administration's initial economic proposal to Congress, but it was not enacted into law.

Tax credits were initially granted primarily for the purchase of business capital equipment, then extended to other assets and activities (e.g., expenditures on research and development, restoration of historic buildings, and hiring of certain classes of workers). ITCs have constituted a quantitatively important tax expenditure (e.g., $21.3 billion in 1985).

This entry is divided into three parts. Part one discusses the history, scope, and types of ITCs. The chief reason for granting these subsidies has been to stimulate economic activity, although which aspect of economic activity was the appropriate target for this stimulus has varied because of changing views about the structure of the economy and the possibilities for constructive public policies. These changes are considered in the second part. Finally, the impact of the ITC on economic activity is reviewed briefly in the third part of this entry.

History, scope, and types of ITCs

ITCs have been used frequently as an instrument of fiscal policy in the United States. Beginning in 1962, the statutory rate for the ITC was set at 7 percent for spending on business capital equipment with tax lives greater than three years and for special purpose structures replaced contemporaneously with the equipment that they house, support, or serve. The statutory rate was increased to 10 percent in 1975. The Tax Reform Act of 1986 abolished the ITC. Between 1962 and 1986, the ITC was not in force for two periods: suspended from October 1966 to March 1967 and repealed from April 1969 to August 1971. Public utility property (equipment plus structures) has also received a credit, ranging from 3 percent in 1962, to 4 percent in 1971, to 10 percent in 1975. Assets

generally become eligible for the tax credit when they are placed in service.

Several complicating factors have driven a wedge between the statutory rates of the investment credit (at times when it has existed) and its ultimate impact on businesses. Four are discussed here. First, the ITC is not refundable and hence is valuable to a taxpayer only if there is a current tax liability. (Legislation has generally exacerbated this problem by restricting the percentage of the current tax liability that can be reduced by the ITC.) This shortcoming is mitigated by carryback and carryforward provisions, but the delay in realizing the tax credit lowers its value. Problems caused by the absence of a current tax liability were overcome with the safe-harbor leasing provisions in the Economic Recovery Tax Act of 1981 that, in effect, permitted the sale of unused tax credits to firms with current tax liabilities. While such an expansion of markets is generally welcomed by economists, the realization that many large, profitable corporations were paying little or no taxes led to a public outcry, and safe-harbor leasing was eliminated at the end of 1983.

Second, the statutory impact of the ITC increases with the tax life of the asset. For example, under the 1962 legislation, eligible property with a tax life of four to six years received one-third of the ITC, and eligible property with a tax life of six to eight years received two-thirds of the ITC. The tax lives determining the percentage of the available credit, as well as the percentages themselves, have been changed periodically. A larger ITC for longer-lived assets can be an important feature in attempting to preserve neutrality of the ITC across assets (Bradford 1980).

Third, the impact of the ITC on investment incentives also depends on whether it reduces the basis used in calculating tax depreciation. The 1962 legislation that introduced the ITC subtracted its value from the basis. This basis reduction (known as the Long Amendment after the chairman of the Senate Finance Committee) was repealed in 1964. Thus, the 7 percent ITC in 1962 was not as large as the 7 percent ITC in 1964. In 1982, the tax depreciation basis was lowered by one-half of the tax credit, thus reducing the value of the ITC.

Fourth, the limited coverage of the ITC creates an incentive to reclassify assets as equipment or special-purpose structures. While the original legislation explicitly excluded any "building and its structural components," this restriction has been circumvented by creative accounting. As a result of this response to incentives, along with a slow expansion of the tax code to broaden the coverage of the ITC, more than 50 percent of the cost of the acquisitions of structures (as defined in the National Income and Product Accounts) was eligible for the ITC in 1975.

The above considerations suggest the difficulty in specifying the impact of the ITC (see Fullerton et al. 1987 for estimates).

For a given effective rate, several types of ITCs are available to policymakers. The ITC can be targeted to particular classes of capital or be uniform across all capital.

The ITC can be *permanent* or *temporary*. An ITC with a credible expiration date will induce firms to accelerate their investment spending to capture the transient tax benefits. It is unclear whether a temporary credit leads to an overall increase in investment spending or just intertemporal substitution with no increase relative to the level of investment that would have prevailed without the tax credit.

The ITC can be *unilateral* or *incremental*. A unilateral ITC applies to all investment in a category and has been the type adopted in all previous U.S. legislation for fixed capital. An incremental ITC—proposed by the Kennedy and Clinton administrations—applies to all equipment investment above a threshold, which might be specified as some average of the firm's past investment expenditures or sales, or some industrywide variables. While both types of ITCs provide an incentive to increase investment, the government would expect to lose less revenue for a given amount of investment—that is, would expect a greater "bang for the buck"—with an incremental ITC.

The threshold creates several thorny problems for the incremental ITC. The benefits of an incremental ITC would not be distributed fairly, because firms that have recently undertaken major investment programs would receive relatively less benefit from their higher threshold. Further difficulties would be faced in the long run, because incentives would exist to "reinvent" the company (in an accounting sense) every few years to lower the threshold. If the incremental ITC is in force for several years, firms would face an intertemporal trade-off that would lower the impact of this fiscal policy. A firm that invests today may raise its threshold (depending on the definition) for calculating tomorrow's tax benefit, thus lowering the overall stimulus afforded by the ITC. These last two concerns suggest that an incremental ITC would be most useful as a temporary policy providing short-term stimulus to the economy.

Reasons for adopting an ITC

The ITC is one of several fiscal policies that affect firms directly and that are available to policymakers to stimulate economic activity. Other fiscal instruments include the income tax rate, depreciation allowances, and the percentage of asset purchase price eligible for a tax or subsidy. While an ITC, the income tax rate, and depreciation allowances can be adjusted so that they all have the same present value to an investing firm (see *cost of capital*), the ITC carries some additional advantages. Decreases in the income tax rate affect the returns on both existing and new capital and hence are more costly to the government for a given amount of investment incentive. Depreciation allowances are subject to the uncertainty associated with discount rates (perhaps caused by inflation) or repeal. The immediate value imparted by the ITC makes it a more potent fiscal policy instrument than depreciation allowances.

Between 1962 and 1986, the ITC was changed several times. To understand the reasons for tax legislation changes, it is useful to remember that investment plays two pivotal roles in the macroeconomy. The considerable volatility of business investment spending is a prime contributor to short-run fluctuations in the aggregate economy. Additionally, the long-run potential of the economy is directly linked to the amount of capital available to businesses and the efficient allocation of that capital among firms. Because of changing views about the structure of the economy and the possibilities for constructive public policies, the reasons for adopting an ITC have varied between some combination of short-run stabilization and long-run allocation goals.

The Revenue Act of 1962 represented a major innovation in tax policy by introducing the ITC as a fiscal policy instrument. Many economists believe that the ITC was adopted initially to strengthen short-run economic activity in the tradition of Keynesian demand management. However, the first economic report of the Kennedy administration reveals that the 1962 act sought to meet both allocation and stabilization goals (Economic Report of the President 1978, 10; U.S. Treasury 1979, 365).

Keynesian economics had come to dominate policymaking by the mid-1960s and early 1970s. Consequently, the ITC was viewed solely as a tool for stabilization when suspended in 1966 and reinstated in 1967 (U.S. Treasury 1967, 28–31).

In 1969, the ITC was repealed, and the budget saving was used to remove the income tax surcharge then in effect. Interestingly, despite the ascendancy of Keynesian thought at this time, the repeal was based on the "consideration of the longer-range issues" because "the national priorities of the 1970s did not require or justify this special incentive" (Economic Report of the President 1970, 31).

Stabilization goals reemerged when the ITC was resurrected in 1971 (Economic Report of the President 1972, 69). Concern about a depressed level of aggregate economic activity led to an increase in the ITC in 1975. This increase was to last only two years and was intended to give businesses "an incentive to undertake some investment now that they would otherwise have undertaken only later" (Economic Report of the President 1975, 20). This temporary ITC was extended on a temporary basis in the Tax Reform Act of 1976.

During the latter part of the 1970s, questions arose as to the usefulness of fiscal policy as a stabilization tool. Lags in recognizing the need for a fiscal stimulus, passing the appropriate legislation, and obtaining the desired spending by firms undermined the usefulness of discretionary fiscal policy. Furthermore, because of deficiencies in both empirical predictions and theoretical foundations, the Keynesian model of the macroeconomy lost favor in the economics profession (see Mankiw 1990). This disenchantment led to a change in emphasis for adopting the ITC. When the ITC was made permanent (until 1986) in 1979, the goal of growth, not stabilization, was emphasized (Economic Report of the President 1978).

The demise of the stabilization goal was complete by the beginning of the 1980s with the passage of the Economic

Recovery Tax Act of 1981 (ERTA). This fundamental legislation emphasized, among other things, distortions affecting the intertemporal allocation of resources (Economic Report of the President 1982, 7). While ERTA had major effects on raising investment incentives, this legislation affected the ITC only slightly, by increasing the percentage of the credit available to shorter-lived equipment, thus creating a credit uniform across all eligible assets.

The substantial incentives in ERTA, along with ongoing academic and government research, highlighted an additional dimension to efficient resource allocation. Not only must resources be allocated efficiently between consumption and investment, there is an additional issue of allocating a given amount of aggregate investment among capital assets. Asset neutrality occurs when taxes do not affect the interasset allocation of capital, and was enshrined in the concept of the "level playing field." The uniform ITC in place in the early 1980s posed major problems for creating a level playing field for business capital assets, and was eliminated in the Tax Reform Act of 1986 (Fullerton 1994).

Reviewing tax systems in several industrialized countries, Pechman (1987b, 3) echoed the sentiments of many economists at that time in noting a "growing disenchantment almost everywhere with investment incentives. Opinion is widespread that they distort the allocation of resources and generate numerous inequities among industries and firms."

However, the case for asset nonneutrality and an equipment ITC re-emerged quickly. As has been the case with the ITC throughout its history, views about investment incentives are affected by economic events and research findings. The impressive growth of several industrializing nations called attention to the strong correlation between growth and investment spending. Influential research by DeLong and Summers (1992), combined with a large body of extant work on developing economies, highlighted the positive externalities that may be associated with equipment investment. These research findings have been disputed, however (Auerbach et al. 1994; DeLong and Summers 1994).

The Clinton administration proposed reinstituting a permanent ITC for equipment investment targeted to small businesses. Moreover, a sluggish economy prompted a call for a temporary incremental ITC. Using the ITC to address both allocation and stabilization goals is similar to the approach taken by the Kennedy administration 30 years before, although the temporary nature of the incremental ITC and the reasons for the permanent ITC differed. However, the Clinton ITCs were not enacted into law.

The impact of the ITC

The impact of the ITC can be viewed in several different ways. From an accounting perspective, profitability and cash flow are affected initially, although the ultimate effect depends on the general equilibrium response of output prices, input prices,

and final sales. Economists tend to focus on the impact of the ITC at the margin; that is, on the final (or additional) dollar of investment spending. From a marginal perspective, the ITC also has several different impacts: the intertemporal allocation of resources between consumption and investment, the interasset allocation of resources among capital assets, the overall level of economic welfare, the marginal cost of funds, and the additional investment per dollar of tax loss. Calculations of the last two effects will be reviewed here.

Assessments of the ITC at the margin cannot be undertaken in isolation; they must consider all taxes impinging on the investment decision. The analytic tool used by economists is the cost of capital, first applied to tax policy analysis by Hall and Jorgenson (1967) and used more recently by Jorgenson and Yun (1991) to study tax reforms in the United States. The cost of capital combines in a single measure several taxes affecting the decision to acquire capital (see *cost of capital*). Conceptually, the cost of capital is the price of "renting" a unit of capital for one period. The ITC effectively lowers the purchase price of the asset and hence the "rental" that is required from the firm.

In a simulation study representative of those with computational general-equilibrium models, Fullerton and Henderson (1989) calculated the marginal cost of funds—the decrement to total welfare (measured in dollars) from raising an additional dollar of tax revenue—associated with taxes on 38 different types of capital assets. The marginal cost of funds is usually greater than the dollar in new revenue because of distortions introduced by taxes. Given the tax code that existed in 1984, their simulations revealed that reducing the ITC is the most efficient way of raising revenue (with available tax instruments). Because of a reduction of distortions among assets, the marginal cost of funds is only $0.62; hence, by appropriate reductions in the ITC, collecting $1 of revenue leads to a fall in consumer welfare of only $0.62. While several important factors are not represented in this model (e.g., investment externalities and stabilization problems), these calculations suggest that investment decisions are sensitive to the ITC and that its elimination in 1986 was welfare-enhancing.

However, when assessed in terms of econometric investment equations, the ITC appears to have less impact (see Chirinko 1993 for a survey). Estimates of tax policy effects on investment vary widely, and these differences are related to some of the key assumptions and caveats used in specifying the econometric model. For example, Chirinko and Eisner (1982) analyzed the investment equations in six quarterly macroeconometric models. In one partial-equilibrium simulation, a doubling of the ITC for equipment and the institution of a 10 percent credit for structures leads to a "bang for the buck"—the additional investment per dollar of tax loss—of between $0.13 and $1.43 (five years after the ITC increases). The mean value for all six models was $0.84, corresponding to an elasticity (with respect to the cost of capital) of 0.52.

A number of these aggregate equations contain overly restrictive assumptions. When the investment equations are reestimated with more general specifications, the mean impact of tax policy is lowered ($0.47 with a corresponding elasticity of −0.29) and the range of results across models is narrowed considerably ($0.14 to $0.82).

Thus, simulation studies indicate a more substantial impact of the ITC than do econometric studies. Reconciling these differences would begin by examining the many assumptions maintained in simulation models that may not accurately describe the economy. Alternatively, econometric estimates of the potency of the ITC may be attenuated by biases arising from aggregation, simultaneity, or measurement error in the cost of capital. See Cummins, Hassett, and Hubbard (1994) and Chirinko, Fazzari, and Meyer (1999) for recent work with panel data that address some of these issues.

ADDITIONAL READINGS

Auerbach, Alan, Kevin Hassett, and Stephen Oliver. "Reassessing the Social Returns to Investment." *Quarterly Journal of Economics* 109 (August 1994): 789–802.

Ballentine, J. Gregory. "Three Failures in Economic Analysis of Tax Reform." *National Tax Association–Tax Institute of America* Proceedings (1986): 3–6.

Bradford, David F. "Tax Neutrality and the Investment Tax Credit." In *The Economics of Taxation,* edited by Henry J. Aaron and Michael J. Boskin (281–98). Washington, DC: The Brookings Institution, 1980.

Brown, E. Cary. "Business Income Taxation and Investment Incentives." In *Income, Employment, and Public Policy: Essays in Honor of Alvin H. Hansen.* New York: W. W. Norton & Company, 1948.

Chirinko, Robert S. "Business Fixed Investment Spending: Modeling Strategies, Empirical Results, and Policy Implications." *Journal of Economic Literature* 31 (December 1993): 1875–1911. An extended version of this survey has been published as "Econometric Models and Empirical Findings for Business Investment." A monograph in the Salomon Brothers Center Series Financial Markets, Institutions & Instruments. New York: Basil Blackwell, 1993.

Chirinko, Robert S., and Robert Eisner. "The Effect of Tax Parameters in the Investment Equations in Macroeconomic Econometric Models." In *Economic Activity and Finance,* edited by Marshall E. Blume, Jean Crockett, and Paul Taubman (25–84). Cambridge, MA: Ballinger, 1982.

Chirinko, Robert S., Steven M. Fazzari, and Andrew P. Meyer. "How Responsive Is Business Capital Formation to Its User Cost? An Exploration with Micro Data." *Journal of Public Economics* 74 (October 1999): 53–80.

Cummins, Jason G., Kevin A. Hassett, and R. Glenn Hubbard. "A Reconsideration of Investment Behavior Using Tax Reforms as Natural Experiments." *Brookings Papers on Economic Activity* 1994 (2): 1–60.

DeLong, J. Bradford, and Lawrence H. Summers. "Macroeconomic Policy and Long-Run Growth." In *Policies for Long-Run Growth* (93–128). Kansas City, MO: Federal Reserve Bank of Kansas City, 1992.

———. "Equipment Investment and Economic Growth: Reply." *Quarterly Journal of Economics* 109 (August 1994): 803–7.

Economic Report of the President. Washington, DC: U.S. Government Printing Office, various annual issues.

Fullerton, Don. "Tax Policy." In *American Economic Policy in the 1980s,* edited by Martin S. Feldstein (165–233). Chicago: University of Chicago Press, 1994.

Fullerton, Don, and Yolanda Kodrzycki Henderson. "The Marginal Excess Burden of Different Capital Tax Instruments." *The Review of Economics and Statistics* 71 (August 1989): 435–42.

Fullerton, Don, Robert Gillette, and James Mackie. "Investment Incentives under the Tax Reform Act of 1986." In *Compendium of Tax Research 1987* (131–72). Washington, DC: Office of Tax Analysis, U.S. Department of the Treasury, 1987.

Hall, Robert E., and Dale W. Jorgenson. "Tax Policy and Investment Behavior." *American Economic Review* 57 (June 1967): 391–414.

Jorgenson, Dale W., and Ralph Landau. *Tax Reform and the Cost of Capital: An International Comparison.* Washington, DC: The Brookings Institution, 1993.

Jorgenson, Dale W., and Kun-Young Yun. *Tax Reform and the Cost of Capital.* Oxford: Clarendon Press, 1991.

Mankiw, N. Gregory. "A Quick Refresher Course in Macroeconomics." *Journal of Economic Literature* 28 (December 1990): 1645–60.

Pechman, Joseph A. *Federal Tax Policy.* 5th ed. Washington, DC: The Brookings Institution, 1987a.

———, ed. *Comparative Tax Systems: Europe, Canada, and Japan.* Arlington, VA: Tax Analysts, 1987b.

U.S. Office of Management and Budget. *Budget of the United States Government.* Washington, DC: U.S. Government Printing Office, various annual issues. Information on tax developments can be found in the main budget document (under "Budget Receipts: Enacted Legislation" or similar titles) or the supplements entitled "Special Analyses" and "Analytical Perspectives" from 1981 onward.

U.S. Treasury. *The Annual Report of the Secretary of the Treasury on the State of the Finances.* Washington, DC: U.S. Government Printing Office, various annual issues from 1962 through 1980 inclusive.

Cross-references: capital cost recovery; cost of capital.

Itemized deductions

Sally Wallace
Georgia State University

In computing taxable income (the base on which the federal income tax falls), individuals are permitted to deduct a series of expenditures.

Itemized deductions from adjusted gross income are allowed for business expenses, catastrophic losses, interest payments, medical and dental expenses, miscellaneous expenses, or other taxes paid under the federal individual income tax system (Internal Revenue Code, Section 63). Taxpayers compute their total itemized deductions, compare this total to the standard deduction allowed for their filing status, and subtract the greater amount from adjusted gross income. While the standard deduction simply provides a threshold for taxation, itemized deductions are targeted at individual circumstances or specific policies (Goode 1976). Itemized deductions have been allowed under the federal income tax law for many years. However, they have been altered over time; some have been disallowed, some have been added, the computations have changed, and so forth.

Beginning in 1991, taxpayers with income over a threshold amount are subject to a limitation on their total itemized deductions. In 2003, the threshold was $139,500 ($69,750 for married taxpayers filing separately). For taxpayers with adjusted gross income over the threshold, allowable itemized deductions (other than medical, investment interest, casualty, theft, or wagering losses) are reduced by 3 percent of the excess, to a maximum reduction of 80 percent of total allowable deductions (excluding medical, investment interest, casualty, theft, or wagering losses) (Commerce Clearing House 1996). Taxpayers must use tax form 1040 if they itemize their deductions. In 2002, approximately 35 percent of all federal individual income tax returns filed used itemized rather than standard deductions.

Of the 43 states and the District of Columbia that have an income tax, 34 allow some itemized deductions in the calculation of taxable income (Wisconsin Legislative Fiscal Bureau 1999). The majority of these states have adopted most of the same itemized deductions allowed by the federal government.

The purpose of itemized deductions is fourfold: to ease the burden of catastrophic expenditures that affect a taxpaying unit's ability to pay tax, to encourage certain types of activities such as home ownership and charitable contributions, to ease the burden of taxes paid to state and local governments, and to allow taxpayers to deduct the cost of legitimate business expenses (Pechman 1987). Under current law, there are seven main classes of itemized deductions.

Medical and dental expenses are justified on the grounds that catastrophic medical expenses alter a taxpayer's ability to pay taxes (Pechman 1987). A taxpayer may deduct non-reimbursed medical and dental expenses that exceed 7.5 percent of adjusted gross income.

An individual may deduct payment of the following taxes: state and local government income taxes, real estate taxes, personal property taxes, income taxes paid to a foreign country, war profits or excess profits taxes, generation-skipping transfer taxes, and environmental taxes (Commerce Clearing House 1996). Previously, federal excise taxes (e.g., gasoline) and state and local sales taxes were also allowed as deductions, along with some other minor state and local taxes, but these were removed by the mid-1980s. The federal deduction of state and local government taxes effectively reduces the "price" of state and local taxes. If taxpayers itemize and deduct the allowed state and local government taxes, the federal income tax bill is reduced by taxpayers' deduction times their federal marginal tax rate. Consider the following example: A taxpayer pays $100 in state income and property taxes and faces a federal marginal tax rate of 28 percent. An itemizer would deduct the $100 of state taxes and reduce the federal tax liability bill by $28. In effect, $100 in state taxes cost only $72 ($100–$28), because of the federal income tax saving received.

There is debate about this deduction. Proponents see it as a means of aiding state and local government budgets by reducing the price of state and local government goods. Opponents argue that providing assistance directly with federal aid would be more efficient. Another argument is that the deductibility of taxes serves to level the playing field among higher and lower taxing states. Taxpayers in higher-taxing states will receive more federal tax savings through deductibility, thereby reducing their total federal, state, and local tax liability relatively more than for those taxpayers in lower-taxing states. Critics ask why the federal government should subsidize higher-taxing states and also point out that, because itemizers are higher-income individuals, deductibility will reduce the overall progressivity of the federal-state-local tax system. The taxes paid deduction is the second most popular deduction, accounting for 33 percent of itemized deductions in 2002.

Mortgage interest payments and points and investment interest expenses are deductible subject to certain limits. Mortgage interest (up to two homes), interest on home equity loans, and interest expenses incurred for investment purposes (up to a limit equal to investment income) are deductible. Before the Tax Reform Act of 1986, consumer interest was also deductible, and the rules for investment interest deductions were generally more lenient. The deduction for investment-related interest expenses is justified as a cost incurred in doing business. Mortgage interest is less easily justified as a deduction. It probably does encourage home ownership, which may help to provide stability in the economy. However, because homeowners do not report income from their owner-occupied homes, the deduction of interest expenses would not seem justified as an expense (Pechman 1987). Additionally, this deduction gives homeowners a great advantage over renters. This is the most used deduction, and interest paid accounts for 37.9 percent of all itemized deductions in 2002.

Cash and in-kind gifts to charity are another form of itemized deductions. (Between 1982 and 1986, nonitemizers were also allowed to deduct some charitable contributions.) In general, taxpayers can deduct an amount equivalent to up to 50 percent of their adjusted gross income. A limit of 30 percent of adjusted gross income applies to gifts to some foundations and organizations. Because charitable contributions are deductible, the federal government in effect pays part of the individual taxpayer's contributions. Whether or not the income tax system should support such contributions has been a matter of limited debate. Some believe that the good done by these charitable organizations is worth the federal government's support (Pechman 1987), while others believe that allowing such deductions is a violation of the separation between church and state (Rosen 1995).

The casualty and theft loss deduction applies only to nonbusiness property. The goal is to protect a taxpayer in the event of catastrophic loss. The deduction is limited to losses in excess of 10 percent of the taxpayer's adjusted gross income.

Job expenses and "miscellaneous itemized expenses" are a separate group of deductions, justified as expenses incurred in the production of income. Job expenses include job-related travel, union dues, job education, uniforms, and subscriptions to professional journals. Miscellaneous deductions include

TABLE 1. Summary of Itemized Deductions, 2002

	Number of returns	Amount ($ millions)
Total itemized deductions after limitation	45,572,589	879,237
Medical and dental expenses deduction	8,527,941	51,873
Taxes paid deduction	44,742,669	298,629
Interest paid deduction	35,509,263	343,192
Contributions deduction	40,443,074	136,356
Total returns	130,201,415	
Total adjusted gross income reported		6,039,405

Source: Internal Revenue Service (2003–2004).
Note: Total deductions are after limitation.

tax preparation fees and expenses incurred in the production or collection of taxable income such as safe deposit box rental, legal and accounting fees, and clerical help. All deductions reported in this group are subject to a 2 percent floor—the taxpayer can deduct only those expenses that exceed 2 percent of adjusted gross income.

Certain other miscellaneous deductions that may be itemized include moving expenses incurred in an earlier period, gambling losses that offset gambling winnings, federal estate tax on income in respect of a decedent (income received but which was also included in the valuation of a decedent's estate for estate tax purposes), and impairment-related work expenses of a disabled person (Commerce Clearing House 1996). These deductions are not subject to any floor.

The data in table 1 summarize the use of itemized deductions for tax year 2002. This information shows that itemized deductions have a significant impact on federal individual income tax revenue. In fact, the tax expenditure estimate of the main itemized deductions for 2004 is $133.8 billion, about

17.5 percent of expected federal individual income tax revenue for 2004.

ADDITIONAL READINGS

Advisory Commission on Intergovernmental Relations. *Significant Features of Fiscal Federalism.* Washington, DC: Advisory Commission on Intergovernmental Relations, 1994.

Commerce Clearing House. *1996 U.S. Master Tax Guide.* Chicago: Commerce Clearing House, 1996.

Goode, Richard. *Individual Income Taxation.* Washington, DC: The Brookings Institution, 1976.

Internal Revenue Service, Statistics of Income Division. *SOI Bulletin* (Winter 2003–04). Washington, DC: Internal Revenue Service. http://www.irs.gov/taxstats/article/0,id=96625,00.html.

Office of Management and Budget, *Analytical Perspectives Budget of the United States Government, FY2005.* Washington, DC: Office of Management and Budget.

Pechman, Joseph A. *Federal Tax Policy.* Washington, DC: The Brookings Institution, 1987.

Rosen, Harvey S. *Public Finance.* Chicago: Irwin, 1995.

Cross-references: adjusted gross income; income tax, federal.

J

Joint Committee on Taxation, U.S. Congress

Albert Buckberg
Joint Committee on Taxation

A well-staffed committee of members made up of the two "fiscal committees" of the Congress (House Committee on Ways and Means and Senate Finance) charged, among other things, with providing estimates of revenue provisions.

The Joint Committee on Taxation (JCT) was established in the Revenue Act of 1926. The committee is composed of 10 members, five each from the House Committee on Ways and Means and the Senate Committee on Finance (the five being the chairman and the two senior members from the majority and minority of each committee). The chairmanship rotates annually between the chairmen of the House and Senate committees. The JCT was given two assignments: (1) oversight of the administration of the tax, including income tax refunds above a specified threshold; and (2) technical assistance to the Ways and Means and Finance Committees on tax legislation, which has become the JCT's predominant responsibility.

The chairman and vice chairman appoint the chief of staff. The chief of staff selects the nonpartisan committee staff, which consists of lawyers with experience in tax law, economists with graduate degrees, certified public accountants, other accountants, technical assistants, secretaries, and clerks.

Administrative oversight

Oversight of tax administration is carried out primarily by a small staff, with an office at the Internal Revenue Service (IRS), that reviews income tax refunds and carries out assignments of administrative investigations. The Government Accountability Office also performs investigations of selected issues in tax administration at the request of the Joint Committee.

Legislative assistance

The JCT performs identical roles for the two tax committees during the legislative process. Before public hearings on proposed tax legislation, the JCT staff cooperates with the tax committee's staffs in preparing for public hearings on major legislation. The JCT and congressional tax staffs and the Treasury and IRS tax staffs often meet jointly to explore administrative compliance problems with existing law, implications of proposals for improving compliance, and other tax matters of mutual concern to Congress and the executive branch. The JCT staff prepares documents for the committees that describe present law, analyze its effects on taxpayer activities and private and public administrative problems, describe legislative proposals for changes, and present estimated revenue effects of the proposals.

During committee markup sessions, the JCT chief of staff summarizes the materials prepared by the staff and responds to inquiries for clarification and greater detail. As the committees complete their legislative decisions, the JCT staff meets with the legislative counsel of the respective chambers and appropriate committee tax staffs to translate the decisions into statutory language. Members of the tax staffs of the Treasury Department and the IRS also participate in these sessions. The JCT prepares committee reports on the bills reported by the committees to their respective chambers and statements for the bills' floor managers, which describe present law, the reasons for making the changes, and how they will be applied in practice.

Tables listing estimates of the effects of the changes on tax revenue are also prepared. Differences in the provisions of the House and Senate bills are resolved in a conference of the tax committees. Before and during the conference, JCT documentation summarizes the two bills for the conferees and highlights the differences between them. At this time, the JCT chief of staff briefs each committee on the differing bills in detail. The JCT chief of staff performs a crucial communication role between the two committees. This vital part of his job requires that he develop their confidence in him not only by demonstrating his mastery of the complex interdependencies of the Internal Revenue Code, but also by conveying to the committees that they can rely on the authenticity of the information. He must relate accurately and coherently the nuances of the political, business, and economic issues each committee considers when making its decisions. In this role as a trusted and reliable intermediary, the chief of staff smoothes the path to a successful conference agreement because the conferees understand the dimensions of the legislative matrix within which they may feel free to negotiate.

After completing the conference, the JCT prepares the report, which details present law, reasons for changes, the provisions agreed upon, and their expected effects, and summarizes the reasons for rejecting other provisions. Revenue estimates are provided for each provision approved by the conference for as many years into the future as budget procedures require.

Throughout the legislative process, the JCT staff prepares revenue estimates that measure the magnitude of each provision's effects. These are the official estimates for congressional tax legislation. Because the net revenue effect of a bill must comply with the limits established in the currently prevailing budget resolution, specific proposed tax changes often need to be offset by changes with the opposite revenue effect. As a result, controversies have arisen among proponents and opponents of proposals. Recently, JCT estimates have been criticized for not adequately measuring revenue and economic growth that would result from major tax structural changes. The JCT convened a public forum on such dynamic forecasting in January 1997 in which results of research into this subject were presented. While sanguine about the potential of dynamic forecasting, the participants indicated that the promise of practical dynamic forecasting lies in the future.

ADDITIONAL READINGS

Bennett, Rob, and R. Eliot Rosen. "An Interview with Former JCT Chief of Staff Ronald Pearlman." *Tax Notes* (January 28, 1991): 328–33.

Rosen, R. Eliot, and Lee A. Sheppard. "Estimating Process Still Evolving on Capital Gains." *Tax Notes* (February 4, 1991): 443–48.

Cross-references: Finance Committee, U.S. Senate; Office of Tax Policy; Ways and Means Committee.

Labor supply, taxes and

James P. Ziliak
University of Kentucky

Effects of income and other taxes on the number of hours worked by taxpayers.

Many taxes reduce workers' take-home pay. In some cases, the effects of taxation are obvious, as in the case of income and payroll taxes, where workers see the taxes withheld from their paychecks. The effects of sales taxes are more subtle and indirect than income and payroll taxes, but broadly similar. Although a sales tax does not directly reduce a worker's pay, it generally raises the prices of goods that people buy and lowers the purchasing power of labor income. Thus, whether income, payroll, or sales are taxed, an hour of work buys the worker less consumption than it would in the absence of taxation. This issue has been studied most intensively in the context of income taxation.

A question that has long occupied public finance economists is whether taxes reduce the amount that people are willing to work. Economic theory does not offer a definite answer. The reason is that reducing the after-tax wage is likely to pull a person in two different directions. A lower after-tax wage makes a person want to work fewer hours because it is more attractive to spend one's time in leisure pursuits, or in undertaking nonmarket labor activities (such as home production) that are not taxed. This tendency, known as the substitution effect, tends to reduce a person's work effort.

Yet, a lower after-tax wage may cause a person to work more hours because each hour of work buys less in the way of goods than if income were not taxed. This tendency, known as the income effect, has the opposite effect. When the substitution effect is stronger than the income effect, taxing income will lower work effort; but when the substitution effect is as strong as the income effect, the net effect of taxing income may be to leave the amount of work effort unchanged.

Efficiency cost of taxing labor income

Even when taxes do not change the total number of hours worked, they still drive a wedge between the wage the person earns before taxes and the wage received after taxes, causing a distortion in the person's labor supply that is a potential ex-

cess burden, or efficiency cost of taxation. This point is illustrated by the following example. Consider the case of a worker who in the absence of taxation would work 1,000 hours at a before-tax wage of $10 an hour. Now assume that income is taxed at a rate of 20 percent, so the after-tax wage falls from $10 to $8. Suppose further that the substitution effect of the drop in the after-tax wage would, other things being equal, cause the individual to want to reduce hours from 1,000 to 800, but that the fact that the tax lowers the person's income counteracts this tendency, so work effort remains unchanged at 1,000 hours. Although work effort is the same, taxing the person in a way that drives a wedge between the before- and after-tax wage reduces the well-being the person could attain, compared with a tax that did not lower the wage. To see this, assume that the same revenue ($2,000) were raised from the individual by a tax, such as a "head tax" that did not change the person's after-tax wage. Presumably in this case, because the taxpayer could earn $10 an hour instead of $8, the taxpayer would not want to substitute leisure for work; and indeed, the taxpayer might choose to increase work effort above the original 1,000 hours. Thus, the incentive to substitute leisure for work that results from the tax wedge is masked by the income effect.

The size of this distortion depends on the size of the substitution effect. Thus, if an income tax is imposed on a person who has a "small" substitution effect that is counteracted by a "small" income effect, the tax leaves labor supply unchanged and has a small efficiency cost. In contrast, a tax imposed on a person who has a "large" substitution effect that is counteracted by a "large" income effect can have a sizable efficiency cost, even though the taxpayer's observed labor supply does not change.

Policy implications

Because income taxes account for nearly 80 percent of all federal revenues collected, their effects on labor supply figure prominently in debates about tax policy. Assumptions about how people are likely to respond to changes in tax rates were, for example, necessary in order to project the effects on tax revenue of reforms such as the Tax Reform Act of 1986 and the Omnibus Budget Reconciliation Act of 1993.

In the early 1980s, advocates of supply-side tax cuts argued that lower tax rates would expand the tax base by spurring greater work, which would offset some of or all the effects on taxing income at a lower rate. Echoes of the supply-side debate in the 1990s were heard in an exchange between Martin Feldstein (1993) and the U.S. Treasury. In 1993, the Clinton administration proposed increasing marginal tax rates by more than one-third for the highest-income Americans. In estimating how much revenue the tax increase would produce, it was assumed that hours worked by American taxpayers would not change and that, hence, tax collections would rise by an amount directly proportional to the rate hike. Feldstein countered that the tax increase would lower work effort, both by encouraging primary workers to reduce their hours of work and, especially, by encouraging secondary workers in high-income households to leave the labor force altogether so that tax revenues would rise much less than predicted. Feldstein even constructed a scenario where the response would be so great that tax collections would fall after the tax increase.

The size of the work disincentive of taxes is also relevant to assessing the implications of introducing a single-rate (flat) income tax. For example, if a flat tax is adopted that lowers the marginal tax rate for the typical worker, but the typical worker's labor supply does not respond to the higher after-tax wage, then tax collections will fall. If, instead, a typical worker responds to the higher after-tax wage by supplying more hours to the labor force, then tax collections will not fall as much as the rate cut, and in extreme cases of a large response, revenues may even increase.

Empirical evidence

Labor economists have spent considerable time and effort trying to determine how sensitive hours worked are to changes in the wage. These estimates are relevant for assessing the magnitude of any work disincentive created by income taxes. Studies of labor supply behavior undertaken in the 1970s, surveyed in Killingsworth (1983) and Pencavel (1986), indicated that labor supply, especially of male heads of households, was fairly unresponsive to changes in the after-tax wage. The basic finding was that persons were found to have a relatively "small" tendency to substitute leisure hours for work when the wage falls, offset by a similarly small tendency to work more hours in response to a lower after-tax income. These findings provided the basis for a rough consensus that changes in tax rates were likely to have little or no effect on labor supply. The fact that the estimated size of the substitution effect was small also suggested that any distortion in people's labor supply decisions caused by income taxes was likely to be small, so cutting tax rates would do little to make people's labor supply decisions more efficient.

This consensus was challenged by a series of studies undertaken in the 1980s, surveyed in Hausman (1985), that found that labor supply was sensitive to changes in the wage rate. These results implied that progressive income taxes had a measurable, and negative, effect on labor supply.

These divergent results stemmed from the divergent methodologies used to estimate the effect of income taxation on labor supply. The earlier studies that found labor supply relatively unresponsive to income taxes generally treated the individual's observed marginal tax rate as a "given" and then used standard multivariate regression techniques to estimate the individual's labor supply function. Subsequent research, pioneered by Hausman (1981), attempted to account for the fact that under a progressive income tax, the individual's tax rate is not given, but is determined in part by how much labor the person decides to supply, which determines the person's income, income tax bracket, and hence observed marginal tax rate. What the individual faces as a "given" is thus not a single tax rate, but a range of after-tax wages that vary with the amount of hours that the person chooses to work.

Taking this fact into account seemed to make a difference. Hausman found significantly larger substitution and income effects than the previous literature. This had two implications. First, Hausman's methodology implied that cutting taxes would lead to some increase in labor supply. Second, his estimates implied that tax rates resulted in a measurable distortion in labor supply decision, which meant that taxing income, especially at progressive rates, imposed an efficiency cost on taxpayers.

Hausman's work was challenged, however, by MaCurdy, Green, and Paarsch (1990), who cast doubt on the statistical validity of Hausman's methodology. They argued that Hausman's statistical model rested on too many untenable assumptions. In particular, Hausman's method assumes that the individual worker has complete knowledge of all the marginal tax rates and deductions, and that the pretax wage and nonlabor income are givens and not affected by the amount of labor supplied. The gross wage or pretax wage is likely affected by the number of hours worked because the gross wage is typically measured as the ratio of annual earnings over annual hours of work. Most important though, the method used by Hausman required that a lower wage encourages a person to substitute leisure for work when income is held constant and to work more (fewer) hours when the wage rises (falls). This requirement can have the statistical effect of forcing labor supply to be more responsive to tax changes than what actually happens in the data.

Although MaCurdy and colleagues recognized the shortcomings of the 1970s vintage literature on labor supply, their research reached conclusions broadly similar to those obtained with improved statistical methods. Thus, if valid, the MaCurdy et al. critique of Hausman's findings questions the efficacy of many supply-side arguments in favor of income tax reduction that have relied on Hausman's estimates.

More recent research on the work-disincentive effects of income taxes has extended the basic model of household labor supply in several ways. One way is to better account for such factors as people's tastes for and ability to work that are likely to affect how much labor they supply. Another is to recognize the possibility that changes in wages or tax rates can affect the timing of people's labor supply over their life cycle. Last, one should also account for the fact that most Western countries tax both wage and interest income, which implies that labor supply decisions made today are based not only on today's wage but also on expected values of the future wage and marginal tax rate (Blomquist 1985).

Ziliak and Kniesner (1999) incorporate these elements into a statistical model of labor supply. Although they use the modeling approach recommended by MaCurdy et al., they find a labor supply response larger than that found by MaCurdy et al. but smaller than that found by Hausman (1981). They find, however, that incorporating lifecycle considerations into the model results in an estimated efficiency cost of income taxes larger than that found by Hausman.

The general conclusion from much of the research on labor supply done to date is that on average the total hours of work of married men is relatively unresponsive to changes in the tax code, though the efficiency cost of taxation is not. Research on the labor supply of women has produced more mixed findings. Several studies of married women have found that their total hours of work are fairly sensitive to the wage and, hence, to the tax rate (Kimmel and Kniesner 1998). This finding is of some policy importance so far as married women treat their income as "stacked" on top of their spouse's income and hence subject to high next-dollar marginal tax rates. Other studies, however, do not indicate that income taxation reduces the women's labor supply (Mroz 1987), while a recent study finds that the labor supply of married women has become more like that of men between 1980 and 2000 (Blau and Kahn 2005).

Although much of the evidence to date suggests that hours worked by households are not affected a great deal by taxation, it does not imply that how labor compensation is received is similarly unaffected. For example, workers can choose to be paid in the form of cash wages that are taxed or fringe benefits that are not, and there is evidence that the choice of how much labor income to receive in the form of fringe benefits is sensitive to changes in tax rates. In addition, workers can choose to work in activities where it is possible to evade paying some or all taxes. The decision to evade taxes may also depend on the level of tax rates.

ADDITIONAL READINGS

Blau, Francine, and Lawrence Kahn. "Changes in the Labor Supply Behavior of Married Women." Working Paper no. 11230. Cambridge, MA; National Bureau of Economic Research, 2005.

Blomquist, N. Soren. "Labor Supply in a Two-Period Model: The Effect of a Nonlinear Progressive Income Tax." *Review of Economic Studies* 70 (1985): 515–24.

Feldstein, Martin. "Tax Rates and Human Behavior." The *Wall Street Journal,* May 7, 1993.

Hausman, Jerry. "Labor Supply." In *How Taxes Affect Economic Behavior,* edited by Henry Aaron and Joseph Pechman (27–72). Washington, DC: The Brookings Institution, 1981.

———. "Taxes and Labor Supply." In *Handbook of Public Economics 1,* edited by Alan J. Auerbach and Martin Feldstein (213–63). Amsterdam: North-Holland, 1985.

Killingsworth, Mark. *Labor Supply.* Cambridge, U.K.: Cambridge University Press, 1983.

Kimmel, Jean, and Thomas J. Kniesner. "New Evidence on Labor Supply: Employment versus Hours Elasticities by Sex and Marital Status." *Journal of Monetary Economics* 42 (1998): 289–301.

MaCurdy, Thomas, David Green, and Harry Paarsch. "Assessing Empirical Approaches for Analyzing Taxes and Labor Supply." *Journal of Human Resources* 25 (1990): 415–89.

Mroz, Thomas A. "The Sensitivity of an Empirical Model of Married Women's Hours of Work to Economic and Statistical Assumptions." *Econometrica* 55 (1987): 765–99.

Pencavel, John. "Labor Supply of Men." In *Handbook of Labor Economics I,* edited by Orley Ashenfelter and Richard Layard (3–102). Amsterdam: North-Holland, 1986.

Triest, Robert K. "The Effect of Income Taxation on Labor Supply in the United States." *Journal of Human Resources* 25 (1990): 491–516.

Ziliak, James P., and Thomas J. Kniesner. "Estimating Life Cycle Labor Supply Tax Effects." *Journal of Political Economy* 107 (1999): 326–59.

Cross-reference: elasticity, demand and supply; excess burden.

Land value capture taxes

Enid Slack
Enid Slack Consulting Inc.

Taxes on the increment in land value attributable to public investment.

Land value capture taxes are levied to capture the increment in land value attributable to public investment. These taxes are also known as land value increment taxes, betterment levies, special assessments, and valorization taxes. Land value capture taxes are similar to site value taxes (see *site value taxation and single tax*) in that they both tax the unearned increment in the site value of the property. There are two main differences between land value capture taxes and site value taxes, however. First, the land value capture tax only applies to that portion of the unearned increment in land value that is a direct result of public investment. Site value taxes, on the other hand, also tax the unearned increment from other factors, such as the external economies of face-to-face interaction that arise in a highly urbanized area (Bird 1992). Second, only the land value capture tax (and not the site value tax) is designed specifically to raise revenues to provide the public investments that will lead to an increment in the land value.

Land value capture taxation has generally been proposed when the public sector is contemplating a major infrastructure investment that increases the value of adjacent land (such as a new subway, highway exchange, school, park, or other public infrastructure). An investment of this nature requires a large, immediate capital outlay but the benefits will not be enjoyed until several years later. The tax is designed so the current costs incurred are shared among future beneficiaries.

The decision of the public sector to construct major infrastructure results in a windfall gain to owners of property nearby. For example, a subway increases demand for housing and offices on properties located near it. Given normal demand and supply conditions, the increased demand results in higher prices for these properties. Moreover, zoning changes often accompany investment in infrastructure: increased densities permitted along the subway line, for example, will result in increased land values. A land value capture tax is a way for the public sector to tax some of or all the windfall gain it has created.

The land value capture tax is considered a benefit tax because taxpayers receive benefits from the public investment (access to improved services and higher property values) that are equal to or greater than the taxes they pay. This is an important advantage of the tax; taxpayers put up less resistance when they perceive they are receiving a benefit for their taxes. Since the tax is paid before the investment is made and before land values increase, however, the estimate of the increase in land value has to be equal to or greater than the amount of the tax. The predicted increase in land values is more likely to exceed the tax in areas of rapid urban growth because the increment in value from the growth provides a cushion in case the increment from the public investment turns out to be less than the taxes paid (Bird 1992).

The land value capture tax, like site value taxes but unlike property taxes (see *property tax assessment*), is a tax on pure site values. For this reason, it does not penalize the development of unimproved land. It will tend to encourage more intensive uses of land by making it less profitable for landowners to withhold land for speculative purposes. It is also likely more effective at increasing the intensity of land use than site value taxes because it is a relatively large tax assessed over a relatively short period of time.

In terms of ability to pay, the land value capture tax is likely to be a progressive tax because the tax is in proportion to property values and property ownership is more unequally distributed than income in most countries. In terms of benefits received, the tax should be neutral because it is matched by the benefits received from increased land values.

Land value capture taxes have some advantages in terms of administration but also some potential problems. Enforcement is somewhat easier than with a general property tax because the tax is collected in large amounts from a relatively small number of taxpayers. Poor administration, however, can also lead to criticisms of the tax where, for example, projects financed by tax revenues are not on schedule or the tax is calculated to be more than the resulting increase in property values (Bird 1992). There are further difficulties in isolating the change in property value arising from the public investment in infrastructure as opposed to other market forces that affect land prices.

Two variants of land value capture taxes are special assessments and tax increment financing (TIF). Special assessments (also known as local improvement charges) are compulsory charges imposed on residential, commercial, and industrial properties to pay for additions or improvements to existing capital facilities that border on those properties. They are most often used for capital expenditures to pave or repave streets, install or replace water mains or sewers, construct sidewalks, install street lighting, or other local improvements. Although the magnitude of the charge is based on a particular capital expenditure in a particular year, the costs may be spread over several years.

Special assessments do not generally contribute a large amount of money to municipal revenues in countries where they are used, such as Canada, but they are an important way to finance local improvement projects. The costs of the projects financed in this way are allocated on the basis of the benefits received from the infrastructure.

The most common base for special assessments is the front footage of those properties that abut the capital works in question, but the charges can also be levied based on size of lot, assessed value of property, or zone. Many public works increase the value of nearby land, providing a financial benefit to the owners. With a special assessment, the municipality constructs the works and then recoups the cost through a special assessment on the properties that directly benefit from the government expenditure. Because it is difficult to isolate the impact of one capital expenditure from other influences on property values, however, front footage and lot size are often used rather than assessed value.

In the United Sates, tax increment financing has become quite popular as a means to finance infrastructure investments and revitalize blighted areas. TIF legislation was first enacted in California in 1952; it now exists in 48 U.S. states.

Under a TIF, a district is defined for renewal. The annual property tax revenue accruing to all taxing authorities within the district (the municipality, the county, school districts, and other taxing authorities) is frozen at pre-revitalization levels. Once the public investment is made, it is anticipated that property values (and property taxes) will increase in the district. For a period of time, generally between 15 and 35 years, all or some portion of the incremental property tax generated above the base level accrues to the redevelopment agency to be used for the redevelopment. After the TIF period expires, tax revenues from the expanded assessment base again flow through the taxing authorities. Based on these TIFs, the local government (or the private sector) can borrow funds to pay for the infrastructure. TIF revenues are used to pay back the borrowed funds.

The idea behind a TIF is that public investment in infrastructure or redevelopment will result in an increase in land values in the TIF district. The increase in land values generates the revenues needed to pay for the debt that was used to finance the infrastructure that resulted in the increase in land values. Under a TIF, cities (or redevelopment agencies) borrow funds to pay for the investment and pay back the borrowed funds with the tax increments. Unlike most land value capture taxes where the tax increment is collected before land values increase, incremental taxes under a TIF are collected after land values increase.

Although TIFs are widely used in the United States, they have been criticized on a number of grounds. TIFs may not always be able to generate an increment large enough to cover the debt costs. TIFs may merely accelerate development that would have occurred anyway. Other taxing authorities (especially school districts) resent that their property taxes are frozen when they are experiencing growth in demand as a result of the revitalization. Finally, TIFs may target funds to a designated area at the expense of areas on the periphery of the TIF district or overall municipal growth.

ADDITIONAL READINGS

Bird, Richard M. *Tax Policy and Economic Development.* Baltimore: The Johns Hopkins University Press, 1992.

Bird, Richard M., and Enid Slack, *International Handbook of Land and Property Taxation.* Cheltenham, UK: Edward Elgar Publishing, 2004.

Chapman, Jeffrey I. "Tax Increment Financing as a Tool of Redevelopment." In *Local Government Tax and Land Use Policies in the United States: Understanding the Links,* edited by Helen F. Ladd (182–98). Cheltenham, UK: Edward Elgar Publishing Limited in association with the Lincoln Institute of Land Policy, 1998.

Life cycle model

Diane Lim Rogers
Ways and Means Committee, U.S. House of Representatives

A theory of consumer behavior that asserts a household or individual decides about the timing of consumption and saving to maximize lifetime utility subject to a lifetime budget constraint.

In the purest version of the life cycle model, capital markets are assumed to be "perfect," meaning that consumers can borrow or lend (save) against their own future income at a constant interest rate and to an unlimited extent. Assuming no transfers from parents to children or vice versa, a simple, two-period version of the pure life cycle model would state that the consumer will choose how much to consume and how much to save in the first period in a way that maximizes some function of present and future consumption (the "lifetime utility function"). The consumer's budget constraint is that the present value of the stream of consumption must equal (or be less than) the present value of the stream of labor income. Because that stream of income spans the consumer's lifetime, it is often referred to as "lifetime income." Note that no period-by-period budget constraint exists; that is, current-period consumption is not constrained to be equal to or less than current-period income.

An important implication of the pure version of the life cycle model is that consumption in any given period will be dependent only on the consumer's preferences (i.e., the form of the utility function), the rate of interest, and *lifetime* income, but will be independent of current income (controlling for lifetime income). Assuming diminishing marginal utility of consumption, a consumer will maximize utility by "smoothing" consumption between the two periods, no matter how dissimilar present and future incomes are. Thus, if labor in-

come is high during working years but low or zero in retirement, the life cycle model would predict positive amounts saved during the working years (where consumption plus saving would equal labor income) and a drawing down of savings in retirement (where consumption would equal any labor income plus interest-augmented savings from the previous period). The amount of present relative to future consumption will be higher the higher the consumer's rate of time preference (i.e., the more impatient the consumer is) and/or the lower the rate of interest, because the "price" of present consumption relative to future consumption is one plus the rate of interest.

The life cycle model has important implications for the effects of taxation, from both efficiency and distributional standpoints. First, because the model acknowledges that the timing of consumption over the life cycle is subject to consumer choice, it reveals the potential inefficiency caused by taxes that affect the net rate of return on savings. An interest income tax, for example, reduces the net rate of interest and thus the relative price of present to future consumption. Present consumption is thus encouraged by this substitution effect, and (assuming that a no-tax allocation is efficient) this results in a less-than-efficient level of saving in the economy. This inefficiency results even where the total effect of an interest income tax on saving is zero. The income effect of an interest income tax on savers is to save more because real income has fallen, but the substitution effect is to save less, and the substitution effect creates excess burden. The allocative inefficiency caused by interest income taxes will be larger the greater the size of the interest income tax and/or the greater the intertemporal elasticity of substitution (how sensitive consumers are to changes in the interest rate). Evidence on the size of the intertemporal elasticity is quite mixed, although empirical studies using aggregate consumption data typically conclude that the elasticity is close to zero (Hall 1988). Apparently, the consumption of the majority of households has little sensitivity to changes in interest rates.

On distributional concerns, the life cycle model suggests (1) the desirability of using lifetime (versus annual) incomes as a measure of *current* ability to pay, (2) the superiority of consumption-based (over income-based) taxes, and (3) the lifetime present-value equivalence of consumption and wage-income taxes.

If the pure version of the life cycle model holds, then current consumption should be proportional to lifetime income. Therefore, if current ability to pay taxes is reflected by current consumption, then lifetime income is a better measure than annual income of current ability to pay. Categorizing households based on annual incomes can give misleading pictures of the incidence of taxes, because households with the same annual income can have very different consumption possibilities and thus very different current abilities to pay taxes. If the life cycle model holds to a more limited extent, however, then current consumption will depend somewhat on both current and lifetime income, and lifetime income will be a less accurate reflection of current ability to pay taxes. [Under such circumstances, lifetime income could still be interpreted as a measure of *lifetime* ability to pay taxes (Fullerton and Rogers 1993).] Empirical research suggests that liquidity constraints *do* exist and that they are binding for many households (Zeldes 1989), so the life cycle model's assumption of unlimited abilities to borrow and lend against future income seems rather unrealistic.

Regardless of whether liquidity constraints exist, however, the general life cycle theory of consumer behavior implies that consumer well-being ultimately depends on consumption streams, not income streams. It thus suggests that consumption-based taxes are more equitable than income-based taxes. In addition, from a lifetime perspective, interest income taxes appear unfair, because under such taxes lifetime tax liabilities depend on the *timing* of consumption and not just lifetime consumption possibilities. A general consumption tax or a wage income tax, on the other hand, would impose equal lifetime taxes on two individuals with the same lifetime incomes, independent of how they chose to allocate their consumption over time.

Finally, the lifetime budget constraint in the pure life cycle model suggests that taxes on wage income are equivalent, in lifetime present-value terms, to taxes on consumption. The timing of the two taxes differs, however, because consumption tax burdens will be smoother over the life cycle, while wage-income taxes will be greater when young and smaller following retirement. The pure life cycle model would imply that because capital markets are perfect, the timing of taxes should not affect a consumer's well-being; thus, consumption taxes and wage-income taxes are equivalent for any individual alive when these taxes are fully phased in. During a transition to a new tax, however, the two types of taxes *can* have redistributive effects across generations. For example, switching from a general income tax to a consumption tax will more heavily burden older generations (who have already paid income taxes on their labor income when the switch takes place), compared with a switch to a wage-income tax (Auerbach and Kotlikoff 1987). The present-value equivalence of consumption and wage-income taxes also breaks down in the presence of intergenerational transfers, because with such transfers the present value of consumption need not equal the present value of labor income.

ADDITIONAL READINGS

Auerbach, Alan J., and Laurence J. Kotlikoff. *Dynamic Fiscal Policy.* Cambridge, U.K.: Cambridge University Press, 1987.

Fullerton, Don, and Diane Lim Rogers. *Who Bears the Lifetime Tax Burden?* Washington, DC: Brookings Institution Press, 1993.

Hall, Robert E. "Intertemporal Substitution in Consumption." *Journal of Political Economy* 96 (April 1988): 339–57.

Zeldes, Stephen P. "Consumption and Liquidity Constraints: An Empirical Investigation." *Journal of Political Economy* 97 (April 1989): 305–46.

Cross-references: ability to pay; consumption taxation; excess burden; expenditure tax; fairness in taxation; flat tax; generational accounting; incidence of taxes; income tax, federal; saving, taxes and.

Lottery tax, implicit

Charles Kurt Zorn
School of Public and Environmental Affairs, Indiana University

Although participation in state-run lotteries is voluntary, the price of participation includes an implicit tax that is economically equivalent to a sumptuary excise tax.

The modern era of state-run lotteries was ushered in when New Hampshire authorized its lottery in 1964, with New York following shortly thereafter in 1967. However, it wasn't until New Jersey started its lottery in 1971 and began marketing the games as a form of entertainment that states began to see lotteries as a lucrative source of revenue for states. The result was a rapid succession of adoptions. By the end of the 1970s, 10 additional states had begun lotteries. Another 10 states commenced lotteries by 1985, and 14 more states adopted lotteries between 1986 and 1995. In 2002, South Carolina became the most recent state to join the lottery ranks.

State policymakers favor lotteries for several reasons. Lotteries provide a good source of revenue for states and are especially attractive as states face increasing fiscal pressures. Constituents tend to find the lottery more palatable than taxes because participation in the former is voluntary. Also, a state may adopt lotteries when it sees the loss of potential revenue as its citizens travel to neighboring states to purchase lottery tickets.

Fiscal significance

During fiscal year 2002, state lottery ticket sales exceeded $39.4 billion. Net proceeds from these sales, after deducting prize payouts and administrative costs, were approximately $12.7 billion. These proceeds, while a welcome source of revenue to states, constitute a modest share of state own-source general revenue. Net lottery revenue made up 1.75 percent of total own-source revenue in the 38 states operating lotteries in 2002. Of these 38 states, 13 states realized less than 1 percent of own-source revenue from lottery proceeds, 11 states generated between 1 and 2 percent, and 14 states generated more than 2 percent of own-source general revenue from lotteries. A small subset of these states place a relatively large reliance on these revenues, with Rhode Island receiving 6.75 percent, South Dakota 7.1 percent, and Delaware 8.9 percent of their own-source general revenue from lotteries in 2002 (Bureau of the Census 2002).

Further evidence supports the conclusion that net proceeds generally constitute a modest addition to overall state revenue. Fink, Marco, and Rork determine that overall tax revenue is not affected significantly by lottery revenue on a per capita basis. However, its composition does change with sales tax revenues decreasing and personal and corporate income tax revenue increasing (Fink et al. 2002). The explanation for the decline in sales tax revenue may be the result of consumers financing their ticket purchases with a reduction in non-gambling consumption (Kearney 2002). These findings are consistent with earlier research that determined the presence of a lottery slightly decreased other state revenues (Clotfelter and Cook 1989).

The implicit lottery tax

Despite claims by proponents that lottery proceeds are a painless way for states to generate revenue because they are generated by voluntary action on behalf of participants, in essence there is no difference between the net revenues derived from lottery operations and revenues generated by sumptuary excise taxes. In both cases, voluntary activities are involved that result in compulsory payments to the state treasury (Mikesell and Zorn 1988). Therefore, it is appropriate to evaluate this mechanism for generating state revenue using conventional criteria to evaluate taxes.

Reliability and administrative cost

Lotteries do not fare well in the area of revenue adequacy as their net proceeds generally make up a relatively insignificant portion of total own-source general revenue. In addition, net lottery revenue tends not to be a stable, reliable source of revenue. It has been shown that many things affect the flow of revenue. These include the lottery activities of other states, illegal gaming activities, the phase in the lottery's life cycle, the size of lotto jackpots, changing consumer preferences, and marketing efforts (Mikesell and Zorn 1986, 1988).

Even though lotteries have minimal compliance costs associated with them, they still compare very unfavorably with other taxes in terms of administrative cost rates. The relatively high cost rates are because of the need to aggressively market and promote lotteries. Also, lottery customers have to be certain that games have not been fixed, requiring strict security to protect the integrity of the games (Mikesell and Zorn 1988).

Efficiency

Lotteries generate monopoly profits from a state-owned enterprise, inferring that the implicit tax rate is relatively high. Mikesell and Zorn demonstrate that the take-out-rate, defined as net revenue plus administrative costs plus commissions paid to sales agents, is significantly higher than those for other major games of chance and for state-operated liquor stores, another state-owned monopoly enterprise (Mikesell and Zorn 1988).

Clotfelter and Cook showed that the percentage of lottery sales going to the state treasury generally exceeds comparable tax rates on sumptuary items such as alcoholic beverages and cigarettes. High tax rates on sumptuary items can be justified because the state wants to discourage consumption. However, in the case of lotteries, states aggressively market the games, meaning the implicit tax rate on lottery items is too high, resulting in a substantial deadweight loss (Clotfelter and Cook 1990).

Equity

Numerous studies have decisively demonstrated that the implicit tax associated with state lotteries is regressive. When vertical equity is considered, state lotteries clearly place a greater burden on low-income families than on high-income families. Even when compared with other state taxes, many of which are regressive, only taxes on tobacco approach the degree of regressivity demonstrated by the implicit tax on lottery revenues (Clotfelter and Cook 1989).

The same conclusion is reached when the horizontal equity implications of the implicit lottery tax are considered. A study by Stranahan and Borg observed that "individuals who have a taste or preference for lottery tickets pay substantially more in consumption based taxes than equals without a taste for that good." They also demonstrated that African Americans and individuals with the lowest levels of educational attainment bear a much greater lottery tax burden than individuals who have identical characteristics sans a taste for lottery products (Stranahan and Borg 1998).

Notwithstanding the drawbacks associated with this type of tax, lotteries have had a robust past and promise to continue to be an integral, albeit relatively minor, source of revenue for states.

ADDITIONAL READINGS

Clotfelter, Charles T., and Philip J. Cook. *Selling Hope: State Lotteries in America.* Cambridge, MA: Harvard University Press, 1989.
———. "On the Economics of State Lotteries." *Journal of Economic Perspectives* 4, no. 4 (Fall 1990): 105–19.
Fink, Stephen C., Alan C. Marco, and Jonathan C. Rork. "The Impact of State Lotteries on State Tax Revenues." *Proceedings of the Ninety-Fifth Annual Conference of the National Tax Association, Orlando, Florida* (2002): 391–95.
Kearney, Melissa Schettini. "State Lotteries and Consumer Behavior." NBER Working Paper 9330. Cambridge, MA: National Bureau of Economic Research [NBER], 2002.
Mikesell, John L., and C. Kurt Zorn. "State Lotteries as Fiscal Savior or Fiscal Fraud: A Look at the Evidence." *Public Administration Review* 46, no. 4 (July/August 1986): 311–20.
———. "State Lotteries for Public Revenue*." Public Budgeting and Finance* 8, no. 1 (Spring 1988): 38–47.
Stranahan, Harriet, and Mary O'Malley Borg. "Horizontal Equity Implications of the Lottery Tax." *National Tax Journal* 51, no. 1 (March 1998): 71–82.
U.S. Bureau of the Census. *Census of Governments, 2002.* Washington, DC: U.S. Bureau of the Census, 2002.

Cross-references: excise tax; gaming taxation, state; sumptuary taxes.

Low-income housing credit

Leonard E. Burman
The Urban Institute, The Tax Policy Center, and Georgetown University

Alastair McFarlane
Department of Housing and Urban Development

Designed to encourage the acquisition, construction, and rehabilitation of housing for low-income families, this federal tax credit, which is criticized for its inefficiency and complexity, is a major source of low-income housing support.

Enacted as part of the Tax Reform Act of 1986, the credit replaced a variety of incentives for investment in low-income housing with a tax subsidy aimed more directly at lower-income households. The original low-income housing credit expired in 1989, but it was extended three times before the Omnibus Budget Reconciliation Act of 1993 made it permanent.

Overview

Under Section 42 of the Internal Revenue Code, qualifying individuals and corporations can claim a tax credit over a 10-year period equal to a percentage of the depreciable costs (excluding land) incurred to provide low-income housing. For new construction and costs of renovation on qualified housing that does not receive additional federal subsidies, the credits may have a present value of up to 70 percent of the depreciable basis in low-income units. A reduced credit with a present value of up to 30 percent is available for housing with other federal subsidies, such as tax-exempt bond financing, and for the cost of purchasing existing housing that is renovated. The corresponding maximum annual credit percentages were 8.07 percent and 3.46 percent, respectively, in August 2004. The Internal Revenue Service (IRS) sets these credit percentages every month based on current interest rates; they tend to remain near 8.2 percent for the larger credit and 3.5 percent for the reduced credit. The tax credit received depends on the proportion of units set aside for low-income tenants. Additionally, developers are eligible for a further 30 percent of the tax credit amount if the project is located within a low-income or high construction cost area.

To qualify for the credit, either 20 percent of units in a housing project must be rented to tenants with incomes below 50 percent of the area's median income, adjusted for family size, or 40 percent of units must be rented to tenants with incomes below 60 percent of the median income. The rent on a low-income unit is limited to 30 percent of the qualifying income level, assuming a family size equal to 1.5 times the number of bedrooms in the unit. The qualifying income level is 50 percent of the area median family income for projects that meet the "20–50" threshold or, more commonly, 60 percent for those that meet the "40–60" threshold. HUD's esti-mated median area income for a family of four in FY 2004 was $57,400. For such a family, the qualifying income limit would be either $34,450 (60 percent standard) or $28,700 (50 percent standard), and the restricted rents would be $861 or $718, respectively. The qualifying income (and thus the rent limit) is adjusted for family size.

Past tax credits are recaptured with interest if the project fails to comply with the rent limits and set-aside requirements during the first 15 years. The percentage of credits recaptured phases out in the 11th through the 15th years. In addition, project owners must agree to provide low-income units for at least 30 years, although owners may terminate this commitment after 15 years under certain conditions.

Cost and allocation of the credits

State housing authorities allocate credits for housing projects. Credit allocations for each project are supposed to be limited so that investors and project organizers do not reap excessive profits. In 2004, each state was allowed to allocate up to $1.80 per capita for projects that were not financed with tax-exempt bonds, with a minimum of slightly more than $2 million per state. The per capita limit was indexed to inflation in 2003. Total credits allocated for bond-financed projects are only limited by states' authority to issue tax-exempt bonds. For a more detailed description, see Guggenheim (2003).

The Joint Committee on Taxation projects that annual credit allocations will increase from $4.3 billion in 2004 to $5.3 billion in 2008, because of population growth and inflation. As a result, they estimate that the tax expenditure on low-income housing credits will total $23.8 billion from 2004 to 2008 (Joint Committee on Taxation 2003). Thirty percent of credits are claimed by individuals, and 70 percent by corporations. Note that credits paid in any year go to projects placed in service not just in that year, but also during the preceding 10 years.

Official estimates are not available, but Abt Associates, Inc. (2003), estimates that 1,300 projects and 90,000 units were placed in service annually from 1995 to 2001. Sixty-two percent of the projects placed in service were newly built; 37 percent of the projects were rehabs; and 1 percent of the projects were composed of both newly constructed and rehabilitated buildings. The average project size is 68 units and most (95 percent) units within a project are Low-Income Housing Tax Credit (LIHTC) program units. These tax credit units represent approximately one-fifth of all new multifamily rental unit completions from 1995 to 2001.

Cummings and DiPasquale (1999) find that tax credits cover 46 percent of the average development cost of a project; 38 percent is covered by first mortgage loans and the rest by gap financing provided primarily by local governments. They report that 78 percent of tax credit projects had positive cash flows. Moreover, the perception of risk associated with the program appears to have declined over time. Cummings and DiPasquale estimate that the internal rate of return of tax credit projects declined from 20.5 percent in 1987 to 11.8 percent in 1994. Part of the decline in the internal rate of return may also reflect better management of credit allocations by state housing authorities.

The GAO (1997) also concludes that tax credit projects became more efficient over the first 10 years of the program, for several reasons: increased participation of private banks as lenders in order to comply with the Community Reinvestment Act; equity funds developed by states that compete for tax credits and drive down the "price"; and increasing investment by corporations encouraged by tax laws that exempt them from passive loss rules that apply to individual investors.

Analysis

The question "Is the low-income housing credit an efficient way to help poor people meet their housing needs?" can be dissected into two parts. First, how efficient are government subsidies to the supply of housing compared with demand-based subsidies? Second, if supply subsidies are called for, how efficient is the low-income housing credit compared with other subsidy mechanisms? The debate on both of these questions has been lively and remains unresolved.

Efficacy of housing supply programs

If the supply of low-income housing is very elastic in the long run, then production of limited amounts of subsidized housing will simply replace other housing that would otherwise have been provided. Housing supplied or subsidized by the government might increase the average quality of housing available to low-income tenants, but it would have little lasting effect on the quantity or price of housing available to poor people. (See Weicher and Thibodeau 1988 for a discussion of the effects of subsidized housing on the housing market as a whole.) Moreover, because new and substantially rehabilitated housing is expensive to produce, it is likely to be worth far less to tenants than an equal cash supplement, such as housing vouchers. Furthermore, DiPasquale, Fricke, and Garcia-Diaz (2003) estimate that the average cost of producing a tax credit unit exceeds the cost of the average voucher unit by 19 percent. (For an early comparison of housing vouchers with low-income housing credits, see Congressional Budget Office 1992.)

Advocates of supply subsidies argue that, in certain housing markets, the supply of housing is inelastic, even in the long run. Apgar (1990) argues that shortages of decent low-rent housing have been getting worse over time. As a result, housing produced or subsidized by the government will permanently increase the stock of housing available. Moreover, because supply is inelastic, supply-based programs can be more efficient than demand subsidies because they generate pecuniary externalities. The augmented supply lowers the price of housing, generating benefits not only for the tenants in the new housing, but also for others in the market (Coate, Johnson, and Zeckhauser 1994). In contrast, a program like housing vouchers, which expands the demand for

housing without affecting the supply, raises the price, harming low-income tenants who do not have vouchers.

But supply is likely to be elastic in markets with high vacancy rates even in the short term (because there is a surplus of units available to rent). According to the U.S. Census Bureau's Annual Survey of Housing Vacancies and Homeownership, the vacancy rate for rental housing was 9.8 percent in 2003, which is relatively high by historical standards. By comparison it was 7.4 percent in 1993 and 5.7 percent in 1983. Vacancy rates have been on a steady upward trend since 1981 and reached the record level of 10.4 percent by the first quarter of 2004. National rental vacancy rates from the decennial census are 7.1 percent, 8.5 percent, and 6.8 percent for 1980, 1990, and 2000, respectively. In the 75 largest metropolitan areas, the average vacancy rate was 9.6 percent in 2003. Only four metropolitan areas had vacancy rates below 5 percent.

Examining more detailed data on housing characteristics for 2003, the vacancy rate for older housing (built before 1980, and thus more likely of lower quality) is 8.6 percent, compared with 13.3 percent for housing built during or after 1980. Although the market for older housing is relatively tight, these vacant units—especially the inadequate ones— are likely to leave the stock if better quality housing is supplied (Weicher 1990). In other words, tax credits may not increase markedly the overall supply of housing.

In the long run, the supply of unsubsidized housing is likely very elastic because housing investments have to earn rates of return competitive with other capital. Malpezzi and Vandell (2002) find a very high rate of substitution between LIHTC and unsubsidized units based on a cross-state regression. Thus, even in tight markets, subsidized housing starts are likely to displace unsubsidized housing over the long run. However, adjustment to this long-run equilibrium may be slow. Thus, targeted supply subsidies might speed adjustment to equilibrium. For this reason, some analysts advocate supply subsidies as a complement to demand subsidies in tight housing markets (Struyk 1990).

Supply subsidies might also enhance efficiency if they mitigate market failures. The market for low-income housing might fail for several reasons. Lenders might be unwilling to lend to investors in neighborhoods where many poor people live because of class or racial biases (a form of discrimination often referred to as "redlining"). To the extent that discrimination in lending occurs, a capital subsidy might improve the allocation of capital.

In addition, when an area falls into decline, decayed housing creates a negative externality that discourages investment in housing on a small scale. A significant part of property value arises from the characteristics of the neighborhood (indeed, externalities are sometimes referred to as "neighborhood effects" in the economics literature). Thus, if all or most of the housing in a neighborhood were improved, it would be worth more per unit than would one or two improved buildings. As a result, government investment, directly or indirectly, might generate social benefits by improving a neighborhood.

Indirect evidence of such market failures might be the poor quality of housing available for rent to poor families. The Joint Center for Housing Studies of Harvard University (2003) reports that 15 percent of renter households in the lowest income quintile lived in households with moderate or severe structural inadequacies in 2001, compared with 10.5 percent of the second quintile and approximately 8 percent for each one of the top three quintiles. However, a simpler competing explanation is that low-income households cannot afford decent housing, even if it is available. In 2001, 55 percent of renter households in the lowest income quintile faced a severe cost burden, compared with an average of 4 percent for the top four income quintiles. In most housing markets, the primary problem seems not to be market failure, but affordability.

Advantages and disadvantages of the low-income housing credit

Supposing policymakers decide that the government should build or subsidize the creation of affordable housing, how does the low-income housing credit compare with other available mechanisms for increasing supply? The credit has obvious political advantages. First, the private sector builds the housing, rather than state or federal governments. Second, the program devolves almost total control over allocation of the credits to state housing agencies, a sterling example of how fiscal federalism can be implemented through the tax code. Third, new spending done through the tax code (see *tax expenditures*) is viewed as a tax cut, rather than increased government spending.

These advantages come at a high price. The equity capital raised for investment generally comes from syndicates of individual investors or from corporations. Syndicating limited partnerships is technically complex, and expensive. Moreover, because the credit is very complex and risky to investors, who might become ineligible for credits and have to repay past credits with interest if their project fails to comply with the restrictions of the law, investors require high after-tax rates of return. Stegman (1991), using an estimated internal rate of return of 15 percent, estimates that housing produced by syndicates of individuals costs the government nearly twice what a direct capital grant to the project sponsor would cost.

Corporate investors do not have to form syndicates to raise capital, thereby lowering overhead costs, but this may translate into higher profits rather than smaller subsidies. Lampert (1993), who calls the low-income housing credit "perhaps, the last true tax shelter remaining—especially for the widely held corporation," claims that "lofty internal rates of return, ranging from 15 percent to 25 percent, are possible in today's market."

The costs of the low-income housing credit include the costs of administration by federal and state housing agencies and by the IRS. Adequate monitoring by state housing agencies and the IRS would be expensive, but, without such monitoring, credits might be allocated to fraudulent claimants, to those who do not comply with the income or rent restrictions

of the law, or to investors who otherwise manage to extract unwarranted economic rents. The GAO (1997) observes that the cost control measures of state agencies to ensure the reasonableness of tax credits vary by state from a limited verification of cost and financing data to frequent site visits and independent audits of developers. GAO estimates that for about 14 percent of the projects, the states lacked complete information on the uses of funds. Although the IRS has improved its oversight since 1995, the year of the study, the IRS still faces obstacles in collecting reliable data on taxpayer compliance. Both the costs of noncompliance and the costs of administration must be added to the total cost of the tax credit approach.

ADDITIONAL READINGS

Abt Associates, Inc. "Updating the Low-Income Housing Tax Credit Database: Projects Placed in Service through 2001." Paper prepared for the U.S. Department of Housing and Urban Development. Cambridge, MA: Abt Associates, Inc., 2003.

Apgar, William C., Jr. "Which Housing Policy Is Best." *Housing Policy Debate* 1 (1990): 1–32.

Coate, Stephen, Stephen Johnson, and Richard Zeckhauser. "Pecuniary Redistribution through In-Kind Programs." *Journal of Public Economics* 55 (September 1994): 19–40.

Congressional Budget Office [CBO]. "The Cost-Effectiveness of the Low-Income Housing Tax Credit Compared With Housing Vouchers." Washington, DC: CBO staff memorandum, April 1992.

Cummings, Jean L., and Denise DiPasquale. "The Low-Income Housing Tax Credit: An Analysis of the First Ten Years." *Housing Policy Debate* 10, no. 2 (1999): 251–307.

DiPasquale, Denise, Dennis Fricke, and Daniel Garcia-Diaz. "Comparing the Costs of Federal Housing Assistance Programs." *Federal Reserve Bank of New York Economic Policy Review* (June 2003): 147–66.

Guggenheim, Joseph. *Tax Credits for Low-Income Housing.* 12th ed. Glen Echo, MD: Simon Publishers, 2003.

Guttman, George. "Despite Assurances to Congress, IRS Slow to Track LIHC Compliance." *Tax Notes* 67 (June 26, 1995): 1715–17.

Joint Center for Housing Studies of Harvard University. *The State of the Nation's Housing 2003.* Cambridge, MA: President and Fellows of Harvard College, 2003.

Joint Committee on Taxation. "Estimates of Federal Tax Expenditures for Fiscal Years 2004–2008." Washington, DC: U.S. Government Printing Office, December 22, 2003.

Lampert, Peter M. "Corporate Investment in the Low-Income Housing Credit." *The Journal of Taxation* 79 (December 1993): 344–50.

Malpezzi, Stephen, and Kerry Vandell. "Does the Low-Income Housing Tax Credit Increase the Supply of Housing?" *Journal of Housing Economics* 11, no. 4 (2002): 360–80.

Stegman, Michael A. "The Excessive Costs of Creative Finance: Growing Inefficiencies in the Production of Low-Income Housing." *Housing Policy Debate* 2 (1991): 357–73.

Struyk, Raymond J. "Comment on William Apgar's 'Which Housing Policy Is Best.' " *Housing Policy Debate* 1 (1990): 41–51.

U.S. General Accounting Office [GAO]. *Tax Credits: Opportunities to Improve Oversight of the Low-Income Housing Program.* Washington, DC: GAO, 1997.

Weicher, John C. "Comment on William Apgar's 'Which Housing Policy Is Best.' " *Housing Policy Debate* 1 (1990): 33–39.

Weicher, John C., and Thomas G. Thibodeau. "Filtering and Housing Markets: An Empirical Analysis." *Journal of Urban Economics* 23 (January 1988): 21–40.

Cross-references: tax-exempt bonds; tax expenditures.

Lump-sum tax

Joseph J. Cordes
George Washington University

A tax that does not cause those affected by it to change their behavior in response to it.

In the process of extracting resources from the private sector, taxes generally affect prices faced by consumers and/or producers of the taxed activities. Thus, an income tax causes workers to receive after-tax wages below what their labor is actually worth to their employers, and savers to receive after-tax returns below the before-tax return earned on their savings. Similarly, an excise tax causes buyers to pay a higher price for the taxed good than it costs sellers to produce it. The response of buyers and sellers to these effects of taxation imposes an economic cost, in the form of reduced productivity or consumer well-being, that is referred to as the excess burden of taxation.

A lump-sum tax is levied in such a way that it does not create economic incentives for either buyers or sellers to change their behavior. The classic example of a lump-sum tax is a so-called head tax, in which every taxpayer would simply be assessed some fixed amount, which would not depend in any way on the taxpayer's economic circumstances, as, for example, measured by income or wealth, or on any other characteristics that the taxpayer could change. Because the amount of the tax could not be changed by anything that the taxpayer did, a taxpayer's economic choices would not be affected by the tax, and there would be no excess burden resulting from collecting such a tax.

The role of lump-sum taxes in tax policy is more conceptual than it is practical. Tax economists find it extremely useful to conduct the "thought experiment" of comparing the economic effects of actual taxes, such as income and excise taxes, that raise a given amount of revenue with some hypothetical lump-sum tax that would raise the same amount of money. This allows the analyst to focus on the effects of different ways of raising a given amount of revenue from the private sector.

In practice, it is difficult, if not impossible, to levy lump-sum taxes. One reason is that the distribution of tax burdens that would result under many lump-sum taxes would be widely perceived as unfair. For example, under a head tax, everyone would pay the same amount of tax, without regard to either income or the benefits received from public spending. Such a distribution of the tax burden would be seen as unfair under either the ability-to-pay or benefit principles of taxation. Similarly, it has sometimes been observed that taxes on goods that are "necessities" could be equivalent to lump-sum taxes because consumers need to buy a fixed amount of such goods, without regard to the market price. But taxing necessities is generally seen as unfair because taxpayers will pay a declining share of their income in taxes on necessities as their income rises.

Taxes levied on so-called economic rents may be lump-sum, at least in the short run, and be less likely to be criticized on ability-to-pay grounds. For example, suppose that a profit-maximizing business that holds an exclusive patent on a new technology is able to earn a return of 20 percent when the competitive return to capital is 10 percent in other lines of business. A tax on the excess return of 10 percent would be lump-sum because the owner of the business would have no reason to change behavior. If, for example, the excess profits were taxed at a rate of 50 percent, the best the owner could do would be to earn the maximum total profit of 20 percent, and pay the excess profits tax of 5 percent, leaving an after-tax excess return of 5 percent.

Taxes based on past economic behavior would also be examples of lump-sum taxes, provided that the imposition of these taxes was not anticipated by the taxpayer. If the tax is based on decisions made by the taxpayer in the past, the taxpayer cannot avoid paying tax in the present. And if the tax was unanticipated when the past decision was made, it cannot be said to have affected that decision either.

Yet, even the above examples may not be pure lump-sum taxes to the extent that they affect some margins of choice made by buyers and sellers. Taxing "necessities" at a high enough rate may eventually create economic incentives for buyers and sellers to find substitutes for the taxed goods. Taxes on economic rents will have behavioral effects when the rents represent a reward for risk-taking or entrepreneurship. In such cases, taxing excess profits would change behavior over time, by discouraging risk-taking or reducing the supply of entrepreneurs. Similarly, imposing a tax based on past behavior can change current behavior if taxpayers form expectations about future taxes.

Cross-references: ability to pay; excess burden; head tax.

Luxury taxes

Bruce Davie
Department of the Treasury

Updated by
Dennis Zimmerman
Congressional Budget Office

Excise taxes on goods or services predominantly consumed by persons with high incomes or wealth.

Luxury taxes are, for several reasons, as old as taxation itself. By taxing items uniquely or predominantly consumed by the rich, a government attempts to secure revenue from those with an ability to pay while minimizing the number of transactions subject to tax and the number of persons responsible for remitting taxes. Historically, luxuries have often been identified with foreign goods that could easily be taxed upon importation. In modern economies, luxury taxes are insignificant because income taxation and, to a much lesser extent, taxes on estates and wealth are used to satisfy distributional objectives, and broad-based taxes are used to generate most government revenue. Economists can easily demonstrate the distortionary effects of specific excise taxes that lead to deadweight losses of consumer welfare. Luxury taxes also create horizontal inequities among taxpayers in the same income (or consumption) class when taxpayers have different tastes.

Luxury excise taxes are usually imposed ad valorem at the retail level. In many cases the determination of whether an item meets the definition of a taxable luxury can only be made at the point of sale to a final consumer. Taxing at the retail level is also likely to avoid imposing the tax on an intermediate good—for example, diamonds used as an abrasive in industrial processes. But taxation at retail makes evasion more likely and is more expensive to administer than taxation at the manufacturer level.

In the United States, the federal government has a long, albeit intermittent, history of imposing luxury excise taxes. The first revenue measure enacted under the Constitution, on July 4, 1789, included high-rate tariffs on snuff and carriages, specifically because these items were identified with a luxurious lifestyle. Calling distilled spirits a luxury was one of the arguments made for imposing the first domestic excise tax, in 1791. The tariff on snuff and carriages was supplemented in 1794 with a tax on domestically manufactured snuff (at 8 cents a pound while the tariff rate was 10 cents a pound) and an annual tax on carriages ranging from $2 to $15. The tax on domestic snuff production was soon repealed because administrative costs were high relative to revenues. The annual carriage tax was repealed in 1802, along with all other domestic excises (except a tax on salt repealed in 1807), including the tax on distilled spirits. Excise taxes on liquor and carriages were reenacted in 1812 as a wartime measure, along with use taxes on household furniture and watches. All these domestic excises were repealed in 1817. No luxury taxes, or indeed any other domestic excise taxes, were imposed again until the Civil War.

In addition to incomes, the Civil War Congress taxed legacies and successions; the gross receipts of certain industries; banks; a long list of specified trades, professions, and businesses; alcohol and tobacco products; manufactured goods generally; and certain classes of sales. Stamp taxes were imposed on a wide variety of financial instruments and legal documents. A very minor part of these taxes was specifically directed against luxury consumption. At one time or another during the war, taxes were imposed on the ownership of carriages; yachts; billiard tables; gold and silver plate (with an exemption for silver plate owned by religious societies); pianos, organs, and other musical instruments; and watches. Revenue commissioners routinely recommended their repeal. As one commissioner put it, the amounts collected had paid "but indifferently for the expense of collection." Congress was unwilling to repeal these taxes while the war continued because, as one Ways and Means Committee report put it,

"the owners of carriages valued at over $300, and gold watches and silver plate, were among those persons best able to contribute something to the support of the Government under whose protection they have been able to acquire articles indicative of wealth and assured means of support."

Along with explicit luxury taxes, taxes during the Civil War were seemingly aimed at amusements and frivolity. Among the businesses subject to a gross receipts tax (at a 2 percent rate) were operas, theaters, circuses, and museums. Sales of perfume and cosmetics were taxed at a 4 percent rate, photographs and playing cards at 5 percent. Billiard rooms were subject to an annual license tax of $10 a table and bowling alleys of $10 an alley. Circuses, theaters, and museums were required to pay a license tax of $100 in addition to the receipts tax. The license tax for jugglers was $20. Between 1863 and 1871, the government collected $16,872.20 from jugglers.

By 1871, most Civil War excise taxes had been repealed. Taxes on liquor and tobacco were retained, however, and have been continuously imposed ever since. The tax on perfume and cosmetics was repealed in 1883.

Financing the Spanish American War involved increasing tobacco and fermented liquor (beer) taxes (but not taxes on distilled spirits) and bringing back some luxury taxes. In 1898, special taxes were imposed on proprietors of theaters, bowling alleys, billiard and pool rooms, and other places of amusement. Taxes, administered through the use of stamps, were also imposed on cosmetics and chewing gum. By 1902, all the wartime luxury taxes had been repealed. Alcohol and tobacco taxes, however, remained a major source of revenue.

World War I brought luxury taxes back. Bowling alleys and pool halls were again taxed annually at $10 an alley or table, and a general tax was imposed on admissions. Manufacturers' excise taxes were imposed on automobiles and major home appliances, soft drinks and candy, cameras and film, sporting goods, musical instruments, records, and long-distance telephone messages. An annual use tax was imposed on boats, graduated by size. Retail taxes were imposed on jewelry, furs, cosmetics, and luggage. Wearing apparel was taxed to the extent that its price exceeded relatively high thresholds. These taxes appear to have generated about 5 percent of the government's total revenue by the end of the war. Practically all the wartime taxes were repealed during the 1920s. At the end of the decade, the only remnant was a tax on theater admissions of more than $3.

As part of the attempt by the Revenue Act of 1932 to bring the federal budget back into balance, manufacturers' excise taxes were reimposed on automobiles, certain consumer durables, jewelry, furs, luggage, cosmetics, and sporting goods. An annual use tax ranging from $10 to $200 was imposed on pleasure boats. The base of the admissions tax was broadened by reducing the threshold level to 40 cents. Some of these taxes were repealed later in the decade.

During World War II, excise tax rates on automobiles and consumer durables were generally increased and additional items subjected to tax. Retail excise taxes were imposed on furs, jewelry, cosmetics, and luggage at a 20 percent rate. The tax rate on admissions was doubled, to 20 percent. Bowling alleys and pool tables were again subject to annual use taxes. The tax on long-distance telephone calls was extended to local telephone service. A few tax rates were reduced after the war, and Congress was considering repeal of all the World War II luxury taxes when the Korean War broke out. Instead, the luxury taxes were retained and the manufacturers' excise tax on automobiles increased from 7 to 10 percent. The World War II/Korean War luxury taxes were not generally repealed until 1965. The manufacturers' tax on automobiles was retained (at a 7 percent rate) until 1971. The tax on telephone services was still in effect (at a 3 percent rate) in 1997, even though its rationale as a wartime luxury tax had disappeared.

Excise taxes explicitly designated as luxury taxes reappeared in the United States with the Omnibus Budget Reconciliation Act of 1990. They were designed to help achieve a specified distribution, by income class, of a whole package of tax increases. Retail excise taxes were imposed at a 10 percent rate on sales of jewelry and furs (for prices over $10,000), automobiles (for prices over $30,000), airplanes (for prices over $250,000), and boats (for prices over $100,000). Complex rules were provided to exempt items used in a trade or business, to deal with leases, to tax additions or modifications made within the first six months of initial purchase, and to exempt used items. For example, limousines used in a limousine service were not taxed, but limousines used by a corporate executive were. In fiscal year 1992, these luxury taxes raised about $300 million, of which 90 percent came from the tax on automobiles.

The luxury taxes enacted in 1990 were widely unpopular, particularly the tax on boats. Boat makers complained that the tax was responsible for the demise of their industry and the unemployment of their workers. With the exception of the tax on automobiles, these taxes were repealed on August 10, 1993. The repeal was retroactive to January 1 of that year, creating the further complication of providing a refund mechanism. The tax on automobiles was modified in 1996 to be phased out by 2003.

American states use sales taxes as a major source of revenue but generally have not attempted to impose higher-than-normal rates on luxury goods. The ease with which transactions in luxury goods could move out of state undoubtedly provides the reason. The relatively few instances in which higher-than-normal rates are applied—for example, high rates on hotel and motel room rentals—are almost always explained as attempts to export taxes to nonresidents.

Many countries impose value-added taxes (VATs) at more than one rate. This practice is typically defended on distributional grounds; "necessities" are taxed at a lower rate than "luxuries." With a two-rate system, this practice is more accurately described as taxing a specifically identified list of items at a preferentially low rate and taxing everything else at a higher, regular rate. That is, the "necessities" are specifically defined rather than the "luxuries." Some countries do impose higher-than-normal VAT rates on specifically enumerated luxuries. Other than applying high VAT rates to automobiles, these higher-than-normal rates generally apply to a small portion of total consumption, generate little additional revenue, have little effect on the distribution of aggregate tax burdens, and are difficult to administer. VAT experts view the use of specific excises as a better technique for subjecting luxury goods to high tax rates for sumptuary or distributional purposes.

ADDITIONAL READINGS

Brownlee, W. Elliot. *Federal Taxation in America: A Short History.* New York: Cambridge University Press, 1996.

Davie, Bruce F. "Tax Expenditures in the Federal Excise Tax System." *National Tax Journal* 48, no. 1 (March 1944): 39–62.

Dewey, Davis Rich. *Financial History of the United States.* New York: Longmans, Green and Co., 1939.

Due, John F., and John Mikesell, eds. *Sales Taxation: State and Local Structure and Administration.* Washington, DC: Urban Institute Press, 1994.

Pechman, Joseph A. *Federal Tax Policy.* 5th ed. Washington, DC: Brookings Institution Press, 1987.

Smith, Harry Edwin. *The United States Federal Internal Tax History from 1861 to 1871.* Boston: Houghton Mifflin, 1914.

Tait, Alan A. *Value Added Tax: International Practice and Problems.* Washington, DC: International Monetary Fund, 1988.

Talley, Louis Alan, Jack Taylor, and Dennis Zimmerman. *History and Economics of U.S. Excise Taxation of Luxury Goods.* 91-306 E. Washington, DC: The Library of Congress, Congressional Research Service, April 2, 1991.

The Tax Foundation. *Federal Excise Taxes.* Project Note No. 40. New York: The Tax Foundation, 1956.

U.S. Congress, House, Committee on Ways and Means. *Excise Tax Compendium.* 88th Cong., 2d sess., 1964.

Zimmerman, Dennis. *The Effect of the Luxury Excise Tax on the Sale of Luxury Boats.* 92-149 A. Washington, DC: The Library of Congress, Congressional Research Service, February 10, 1992.

Cross-references: ability to pay; excess burden; excise taxes; fairness in taxation; horizontal equity; vertical equity.

Marginal effective tax rate

Don Fullerton
University of Texas

Designed to measure incentives for investment, a calculation that takes into account effects of measurement and timing of income in determining the impact of a tax applied to an additional dollar of capital income.

The marginal effective tax rate on capital income is the expected pretax rate of return minus the expected after-tax rate of return on a new marginal investment, divided by the pretax rate of return. It typically accounts for an investment tax credit, a statutory tax rate, accelerated depreciation allowances, and historical cost depreciation that falls in real value with inflation. It may include just corporate income taxes, or it may also include personal taxes and local property taxes. It may account for nominal interest deductions, inventory accounting, the alternative minimum tax, and other detailed provisions of the tax law. Several studies have estimated effective marginal tax rates for different assets under different laws (see Jorgenson and Yun 1991 for a time series in the United States and Jorgenson and Landau 1993 for nine different countries).

The marginal effective tax rate is a forward-looking measure that summarizes the incentives to invest in a particular asset as provided by complicated tax laws. It may bear little relation to an industry's "average effective tax rate," defined as the actual tax paid in a particular year divided by the actual capital income in that year, because that measure averages over taxes on income from all past investment (minus credits on that year's new investment).

Any particular estimate of a marginal effective tax rate will depend on particular assumptions about equilibrium in capital markets, the rate of discount, the rate of inflation, expectations of investors, churning, financing, the treatment of risk, and even the choice between the "old view" (where dividend taxes matter) and the "new view" (where they do not). For the simplest example, consider a perfectly competitive firm contemplating a new investment with outlay q that has return c in a world with no uncertainty. Assume that the firm has sufficient tax liability to take associated credits and deductions and that it does not resell the asset. An investment tax credit at rate k reduces the asset's net cost to $(1 - k)q$. The

return c grows with inflation at constant rate π, but the asset depreciates at exponential rate δ. The corporate income tax is levied at statutory rate u, and local property tax at rate w is deductible against it. Net returns are discounted at the firm's nominal after-tax discount rate r, and the present value of depreciation allowances per dollar of investment is z. The particular value for z will reflect the discount rate, the tax lifetime for the asset, the depreciation schedule, and whether allowances are based on historical or replacement cost. In equilibrium, the net outlay must be exactly matched by the present value of new returns:

$$(1) \quad (1 - k)q = \int_0^\infty (1 - u)(c - wq)e^{(\pi - \delta)t}e^{-rt}dt + uzq$$

This condition can be used to solve for the Hall and Jorgenson (1967) "cost of capital" formula providing ρ^c, the real social rate of return in the corporate sector, gross of tax but net of depreciation:

$$(2) \quad \rho^c = \frac{c}{q} - \delta = \frac{r - \pi + \delta}{1 - u}(1 - k - uz) + w - \delta$$

In calculations below, common values are used for r, π, and u, but each asset has a specific value for δ, k, z, and w. (If u and the corporate discount rate are replaced by the noncorporate entrepreneur's personal marginal tax rate and corresponding discount rate, then equation (2) gives an analogous expression for ρ^{nc}, the social rate of return in the noncorporate sector.)

The "marginal effective corporate tax rate" t can be found by setting the property tax w to zero and then taking the gross-of-tax return (ρ^c) minus the net-of-tax return ($r - \pi$), all divided by the gross-of-tax return. Simple algebra can then be used to demonstrate several important conceptual results. First, this effective rate t is equal to the statutory rate u if the investment tax credit is zero and depreciation allowances are based on replacement cost [because z is then $\delta/(\delta + r - \pi)$]. Second, this effective rate still equals the statutory rate if the investor receives only an immediate deduction equal to the purchase price times the fraction $z = \delta/(\delta + r - \pi)$, the first-year recovery proposal of Auerbach and Jorgenson (1980). Third, the effective tax rate is equal to zero with expensing of new investment (because z is then 1). Thus uniform effective taxation of all assets can be achieved either with economic depreciation (all $t = u$) or expensing (all $t = 0$). Fourth, uniform effective tax rates can be achieved at any rate between zero and *u,* if all assets receive an investment tax credit that is proportional to $(1 - z)$. That is, replace k in equation (1) with $k(1 - z)$, where z is based on economic depreciation at replacement cost, and the resulting effective tax rate is $(u - k)$ on all assets.

To account for personal taxes and deductibility of interest, assume that the firm can arbitrage between debt and real capital, as in Bradford and Fullerton (1981). If i is the nominal interest rate, then the corporation can save $i(1 - u)$ by retiring a unit of debt, so any marginal real investment must earn the same rate of return in equilibrium. All nominal net returns are then discounted at the rate $r = i(1 - u)$, whatever the source of finance.

A fraction c_d of corporate investment is financed by debt, and the personal marginal rate of debt holders is τ_d. The net return to debt holders is thus $i(1 - \tau_d)$. A fraction c_{re} of corporate investment is financed by retained earnings, and the return after corporate taxes $i(1 - u)$ results in share appreciation that is taxed at the effective accrued personal capital gains rate τ_{re}. The net return to the shareholder is then $i(1 - u)(1 - \tau_{re})$. The remaining fraction c_{ns} of corporate investment is financed by new shares, subject to personal taxes at rate τ_{ns}, so the net return is $i(1 - u)(1 - \tau_{ns})$. In combination, the real net return in the corporate sector is:

$$(3)\ s^c\ =\ c_d\left[i\left(1 - \tau_d\right)\right] + c_{re}\left[i\left(1 - u\right)\left(1 - \tau_{re}\right)\right] + $$
$$c_{ns}\left[i\left(1 - u\right)\left(1 - \tau_{ns}\right)\right] - \pi$$

The "marginal effective total tax rate" in the corporate sector, including all corporate, personal, and property taxes, is $t = (\rho^c - s^c)/\rho^c$, the tax wedge as a fraction of the pretax return. Similar expressions for the noncorporate sector and owner-occupied housing are detailed in Fullerton (1987).

This inclusion of personal taxes, and more simple algebra, can be used to demonstrate additional important conceptual results. Consider a tax-exempt investor such as a university endowment or a pension fund $(\tau^d = 0)$, and suppose that the marginal investment is entirely financed by debt $(c_d = 1)$. Then with economic depreciation at replacement cost, the marginal effective total tax rate is now zero. The corporate income tax may collect plenty of revenue on past equity-financed investment, but at the margin the corporate income tax is entirely nondistorting (Stiglitz 1973). The reason is that the normal return to the asset is paid out as interest, which is deductible against the corporate income tax. Thus we get a zero marginal effective tax rate either with expensing or with debt finance. As a consequence, we get a negative effective tax rate with expensing and debt finance. Thus, to maintain neutrality, proposals for expensing must also disallow interest deductions.

Under actual laws, the marginal effective tax rate can be large for an asset with no investment tax credit and slow depreciation allowances based on historical cost with high in-

flation, especially if the weight on debt is low and the weights on equity are high. It can be negative for an asset with an investment tax credit and accelerated depreciation allowances, especially if the weight on debt is high. Differences in effective tax rates among assets can be used to measure the welfare cost of resource misallocations.

Actual estimates of effective tax rates depend on numerical assumptions about parameters. For example, Fullerton (1987) calculates marginal effective total tax rates for 36 assets in 18 industries, using 4 percent inflation, 5 percent real net return, actual depreciation based on historical cost, one-third debt financing, and weighted-average personal tax rates on interest, dividends, and capital gains. Before the Tax Reform Act of 1986, that paper finds corporate-sector effective rates equal to 0.18 for equipment, 0.37 for structures, 0.29 for public utility assets, 0.42 for inventories, 0.45 for land, and 0.29 overall. Equipment is subsidized by the combination of investment tax credit, accelerated depreciation, and interest deductions at the high 46 percent statutory corporate tax rate. After the Tax Reform Act of 1986, these rates become 0.37, 0.44, 0.44, 0.41, 0.44, and 0.41, respectively. The overall rate rises from 0.29 to 0.41, suggesting less overall incentive to invest, but the different assets are treated much more uniformly. The subsidy to equipment is eliminated with the repeal of the investment tax credit and with the reduction of the statutory corporate tax rate to 34 percent.

We now turn to a discussion of some caveats. These calculations assume that the asset is held forever, but Gordon, Hines, and Summers (1987) show that investors could sell a building, pay the capital gains tax, increase the basis for the new owner's depreciation, and pay less total tax. Churning can reduce the effective tax rate, narrow the difference between structures and equipment, and thus decrease the efficiency gain from a more level playing field. However, Gravelle (1987) indicates that the net effects on the cost of capital are small and depend on transaction costs. Second, the model assumes that firms can use all credits and deductions. Effects of uncertainty and imperfect loss offsets are discussed in Auerbach (1986). Third, it excludes intangible capital that arises from advertising, research, and development. Summers (1987) suggests that the inclusion of these tax-favored assets would reduce the gain from removing the tax-favored status of equipment, but Fullerton and Lyon (1988) show that the 1986 act still provides efficiency gains by reducing the effective tax rate on other assets such as structures, land, and inventories.

These calculations also assume the same financing for all assets. Gordon et al. (1987) note that structures might use more debt and thus have an effective tax rate that does not exceed equipment, but they provide no evidence on actual financing. Results in Gravelle (1987) support the assumption of equal financing for all assets.

The model includes all major tax provisions as well as considerable disaggregation and detail, such as the half-year convention, the half-basis adjustment, LIFO (last in, first out) inventory accounting, and noncorporate taxes. It ignores some specific provisions, however, such as the minimum tax, passive loss rules, and accounting changes in 1986. Lyon (1990) provides a full discussion of the minimum tax, and Fullerton, Gillette, and Mackie (1987) show that some of these other provisions have a very small effect on the cost of capital even though they raised noticeable revenue in the five-year budget period.

Results from the Tax Reform Act of 1986 are particularly sensitive to the assumption about the importance of dividend taxes. Calculations reported above correspond to the "new view" because they use observed financing of new investment, where most equity is financed from retained earnings subject to the low capital gains rate, and little equity is financed by new share issues subject to the high personal tax rate on dividends. Thus, the 1986 act's reduction of personal tax rates receives low weight, and the repeal of the investment tax credit helps ensure that the overall effective tax rate rises. In contrast, the "old view" would use observed dividend payout rates of about 50 percent and thus assign a higher 50 percent share to the equity income subjected to high personal taxes on dividends. In this case, the reduction of personal income tax rates is more important, and some estimates find that the Tax Reform Act of 1986 actually lowered overall marginal effective tax rates on income from capital.

ADDITIONAL READINGS

Auerbach, Alan J. "The Dynamic Effects of Tax Law Asymmetries." *Review of Economic Studies* 53 (April 1986): 205–25.

Auerbach, Alan J., and Dale W. Jorgenson. "Inflation-Proof Depreciation of Assets." *Harvard Business Review* 58 (September–October 1980): 113–18.

Bradford, David F., and Don Fullerton. "Pitfalls in the Construction and Use of Effective Tax Rates." In *Depreciation, Inflation and the Taxation of Income from Capital,* edited by Charles R. Hulten. Washington, DC: Urban Institute Press, 1981.

Fullerton, Don. "The Indexation of Interest, Depreciation, and Capital Gains and Tax Reform in the United States." *Journal of Public Economics* 32 (February 1987): 25–51.

Fullerton, Don, and Andrew B. Lyon. "Tax Neutrality and Intangible Capital." In *Tax Policy and the Economy,* vol. 2, edited by Laurence H. Summers. Cambridge, MA: MIT Press, 1988.

Fullerton, Don, Robert Gillette, and James Mackie. "Investment Incentives under the Tax Reform Act of 1986." In *Compendium of Tax Research 1987.* Washington, DC: U.S. Treasury Department, 1987.

Gordon, Roger H., James R. Hines, and Lawrence H. Summers. "Notes on the Tax Treatment of Structures." In *The Effects of Taxation on Capital Accumulation,* edited by Martin Feldstein. Chicago: University of Chicago Press, 1987.

Gravelle, Jane G. "Tax Policy and Rental Housing: An Economic Analysis." Congressional Research Service Report No. 87-536 E. Washington, DC: Library of Congress, 1987.

———. *The Economic Effects of Taxing Capital Income.* Cambridge, MA: MIT Press, 1994.

Hall, Robert, and Dale W. Jorgenson. "Tax Policy and Investment Behavior." *American Economic Review* 57 (June 1967): 391–414.

Jorgenson, Dale W., and Ralph Landau, eds. *Tax Reform and the Cost of Capital: An International Comparison.* Washington, DC: The Brookings Institution, 1993.

Jorgenson, Dale W., and Kun-Young Yun. *Tax Reform and the Cost of Capital.* Oxford: Clarendon Press, 1991.

Lyon, Andrew B. "Investing Incentives under the Alternative Minimum Tax." *National Tax Journal* 43 (December 1990): 451–65.

Stiglitz, Joseph E. "Taxation, Corporate Financial Policy, and the Cost of Capital." *Journal of Public Economics* 2 (February 1973): 1–34.

Summers, Lawrence H. "Should Tax Reform Level the Playing Field?" *Proceedings of the National Tax Association–Tax Institute of America.* Washington, DC: National Tax Association, 1987, 119–25.

Cross-references: average effective tax rate; capital cost recovery; cross-border shopping; expensing; income tax, corporate.

Marriage penalty

Leslie A. Whittington
Georgetown University

Updated by
James Alm
Georgia State University

An increase in federal individual income tax liability solely as a result of marriage.

When two individuals marry, their income tax liability as a married couple may exceed their combined income tax liabilities as singles. This additional tax burden resulting from marriage is referred to as a "marriage penalty" (or "marriage tax"). Marriage can also reduce the federal tax liability of two people, in which case the reduction in tax is called a "marriage bonus" (or "marriage subsidy").

This concept is easily illustrated using a hypothetical couple. Assume that in 2001 two people each have an annual income of $30,000. Assume also that each uses one personal exemption of $2,900 and that each takes the standard deduction of $4,550. Each has an income tax liability of $3,383, and their combined tax liabilities as singles total $6,766. If they were to marry and use the standard deduction for married couples filing jointly ($7,600) and two personal exemptions, then their married tax liability would be $7,172. This hypothetical couple would pay $406 more in federal income taxes as a married couple than they would as two single individuals. This difference in tax liability ($406) is the so-called marriage penalty.

It is also easy to construct examples in which combined taxes fall with marriage. If one person in this couple had most of or, especially, all the family income, then the couple would experience a reduced income tax liability—a marriage bonus—as a result of marriage. For example, a single individual with income of $60,000 would have a tax liability of $11,198. If this individual were to marry someone with no income (and no income tax liability), then their taxes as a married couple would decline from $11,198 to $7,172, giving them a marriage subsidy of $4,026.

In general, the existence and magnitude of the marriage penalty depends on the distribution of income across the two partners because its calculation requires comparing taxes as single versus taxes as married. One common misconception is that married people have the choice of filing as single or married. A married couple can elect to file separate tax returns in lieu of a joint return. However, the tax rate schedule applied to married taxpayers filing separately is not the same as that used for single taxpayers, so that the total tax liability of a couple rarely differs if they file separately rather than jointly. Very few married couples file separate tax returns.

The creation of the marriage penalty

There is no explicit federal policy in the United States for penalizing or subsidizing marriage. The marriage penalty results from two general features of the federal individual income tax code: the use of the family as the taxable unit and the imposition of progressive taxation. Many features of the tax (and transfer) system create these marriage nonneutralities. According to the U.S. General Accounting Office (1996), there are 59 provisions in the individual income tax code that contribute to a marriage tax or subsidy, and over a thousand federal laws in which benefits received or taxes paid depend in some way upon marital status.

An income tax system could instead have the individual as the unit of taxation, taxing each member of the marital unit on his or her own income. Such a tax system would be "marriage-neutral," meaning that the tax liability of a couple would not change with marriage. The income tax systems in many countries exhibit marriage neutrality because the unit of taxation is the individual, not the family.

The individual income tax in the United States was largely marriage-neutral before 1948 because the tax was levied individually. However, in community property states wives had a claim to the income of their husbands, allowing the husband and wife to each report half of the joint income; with progressive marginal tax rates, this "income splitting" resulted in a marriage bonus. This treatment led to geographic inequity, which became more problematic as rates rose, and states whose property laws derived from common law began to follow suit. After World War II, Congress extended community property treatment to all married couples, and in 1948 the practice of income splitting between spouses was adopted for all couples. This allowed couples to aggregate their income on a joint tax return, and it doubled the width of each tax bracket for married couples. Each spouse was effectively assessed taxes on half of the joint income regardless of how much of the income that spouse actually earned. This was a major shift in the orientation of the federal income tax because it changed the unit of taxation from the individual to the family.

Originally, family taxation was advantageous to married couples because it lowered their average tax rate and thus commonly resulted in a marriage subsidy. However, single taxpayers were relatively disadvantaged, and this penalty on singles grew over time. Despite subsequent statutory changes designed to alleviate the burden, income splitting meant that a single taxpayer's liability could be as much as 40 percent higher than that of a married couple with equal income.

The Tax Reform Act of 1969 addressed the disparity between single and married persons by creating a new tax schedule for single taxpayers, under which the differential between the tax liability of a single person and that of an equal-income married couple could not exceed 20 percent. There was no actual change in the tax burden imposed on married persons, but the introduction of the new single schedule caused their relative position to worsen. This change created the marriage penalty: in a reversal of the previous situation, the combined tax liability of two single people often increased with marriage. Since the reforms of 1969, numerous modifications have been made to the income tax laws that have altered the magnitude of the marriage penalty. However, most recent evidence documents that many couples still face a tax penalty because they are married. (For a comprehensive review of the history of the marriage penalty in the United States, see Bittker 1975.)

The magnitude of the marriage penalty

It is straightforward to determine the marriage penalty for a particular couple in the year that they marry. The calculation becomes much more complex when it involves couples who are already married because it hinges crucially on the assumptions made about the behavior of the people were they to split up. For example, if a married couple with two children and a home that is mortgaged were not married, what would they pay in taxes? Who would claim the children as dependents and therefore have the right to use the head of household tax schedule? Would both partners purchase homes and take itemized deductions? Would one spouse make alimony payments to the other? Would the spouses change their labor decisions? These issues would all affect the tax burden of the two former partners and thus the marriage penalty. Because the marital split is hypothetical, the value of the marriage penalty cannot be unambiguously determined, and there is no one precise algorithm for determining either the average value of the marriage penalty or the precise number of married couples who pay a marriage tax. Several reasonable approaches have been employed to estimate the probable magnitude and coverage of the marriage penalty. The general conclusion is that the tax effects of marriage—both positive and negative—can be quite large.

Recent estimates suggest that the percentage of married couples incurring a marriage tax has risen fairly steadily since the Tax Reform Act of 1969. According to Alm and Whittington (1996), about 57 percent of married couples in the United States now pay a marriage penalty, almost 30 percent receive a marriage subsidy, and the remainder experience no change in tax liability as a result of marital status. They also estimate an average marriage penalty that generally ranges from about $100 to almost $400, but this average masks large variations across the population. For example, among those who paid a marriage penalty in 1994, the average penalty was at least $1,200; for those incurring a subsidy, the average subsidy was roughly $1,100. Penalties and subsidies in excess of $5,000 for some couples are common. Feenberg and Rosen (1995) generate similar estimates, while estimates by the Congressional Budget Office (1997) suggest that a higher percentage of families receives a subsidy (51 percent) and a lower percentage pays a tax (42 percent). Dickert-Conlin and Houser (1998) demonstrate that lower-income individuals are especially likely to face a marriage penalty, owing to the interaction of transfers with the individual income tax.

Dual-income couples are most likely to incur a marriage penalty, especially if their incomes are similar and large. Single-earner couples are likely to gain a tax subsidy through marriage. The large increase in female labor force participation over the past few decades has been one contributing factor to the estimated upward trend in the percentage of families experiencing a marriage penalty and the general increase in the value of that penalty.

Can the marriage penalty be eliminated?

Eliminating the marriage penalty would require a major philosophical shift in the orientation of the federal tax system, away from the family as the unit of taxation and toward the individual as the unit. An income tax structure cannot be marriage-neutral and progressive and also tax equal-income married couples equally. Contrast the hypothetical dual-earner couple discussed earlier with an equal-income couple with a single earner. Because the family is the unit of taxation under current law, the single-earner couple has the same marital tax liability as the dual-earner couple: there is equal treatment of married couples. However, suppose that the unit of taxation was the individual. The single earner in one couple would now have a tax liability of $11,198, while each individual in the dual-earner couple would have a liability of $3,383. Under a system of individual taxation, the single-earner couple would pay $4,432 more than the dual-earner couple, due largely to the progressive tax rates. This system of individual taxation would eliminate the marriage penalty or bonus and so would be marriage-neutral, but families with equal income would no longer be treated equally.

In general, a progressive tax system faces a trade-off: it cannot achieve both marriage neutrality and equal treatment of married couples. (See Alm, Dickert-Conlin, and Whittington 1999 for additional discussion.)

The marriage penalty and human behavior

Defining the taxable unit as the family rather than the individual is controversial. The principal arguments revolve around equity issues. However, there are also efficiency issues. For example, it is well recognized that the secondary earner in a couple will likely experience an increase in his or her marginal tax rate upon marriage, making market work less attractive.

Recent empirical research also provides support for anecdotal evidence that individuals consider the tax consequences of marital events in making decisions about marriage. Researchers have found that the marriage penalty negatively influences the probability (and timing) of marriage and positively affects the probability (and timing) of divorce. The marriage penalty also influences the likelihood that individuals live together as a legally married versus as a cohabiting couple. In most instances, however, the magnitude of the tax impact is small. (See Whittington and Alm 2003 for a summary of the empirical work.)

Conclusions

The appropriate tax treatment of the family is unclear and controversial. At a time when "family values" is increasingly the focus of public discussion, it is important to identify the magnitude of any impacts of income taxes on family structure, to estimate any behavioral responses to these taxes, and to design tax policies that either minimize these tax impacts or use any responses to taxes in the most appropriate manner.

ADDITIONAL READINGS

Alm, James, and Leslie A. Whittington. "The Rise and Fall and Rise . . . of the Marriage Tax." *National Tax Journal* 49, no. 4 (1996): 571–89.

Alm, James, Stacy Dickert-Conlin, and Leslie A. Whittington. "Policy Watch: The Marriage Penalty." *The Journal of Economic Perspectives* 13, no. 3 (1999): 193–204.

Bittker, Boris. "Federal Income Taxation and the Family." Stanford Law Review, 27, no. 4 (1975): 1388–1463.

Congressional Budget Office. *For Better or For Worse: Marriage and the Federal Income Tax.* Washington, DC: Congress of the United States, 1997.

Dickert-Conlin, Stacy, and Scott Houser. "Taxes and Transfers: A New Look at the Marriage Penalty." *National Tax Journal* 51, no. 2 (1998): 175–217.

Feenberg, Daniel R., and Harvey S. Rosen. "Recent Developments in the Marriage Tax." *National Tax Journal* 48, no. 1 (1995): 91–101.

U.S. General Accounting Office. *Income Tax Treatment of Married and Single Individuals.* GAO/GGD-96-175. Washington, DC: U.S. General Accounting Office, 1996.

Whittington, Leslie A., and James Alm. "The Effects of Public Policy on Marital Status in the United States." In *Marriage and the Economy: Theory and Evidence from the Advanced Industrial Societies,* edited by Shoshana Grossbard-Shechtman (75–101). New York: Cambridge University Press, 2003.

Cross-references: adjusted gross income; family, tax treatment of.

Median voter theorem

Randall G. Holcombe

Florida State University

Majority rule decisionmaking will produce the outcome most preferred by the median voter.

The median voter theorem is a prediction about how demands for public spending are expressed through majority rule voting. According to this hypothesis, the median voter's demand determines the group's demand in the political process.

Different models lead to this conclusion, but they all share two fundamental assumptions. First, the alternatives must be capable of being ranked on a single-dimension continuum. Second, when the alternatives are so ranked, each voter has single-peaked preferences—that is, voters prefer outcomes closer to their most preferred alternatives over outcomes that are farther away. A model specifying an institutional structure can then be used with these assumptions about voter preferences to yield the conclusion that majority rule decisionmaking will produce the outcome most preferred by the median voter.

The median voter theorem has been demonstrated using a number of different assumptions about the institutional structure of majority rule voting. Hotelling (1929) suggested the idea in an article on spatial competition, and his framework was developed extensively by Downs (1957) to explain how competition between political parties produces the results most preferred by the median voter. In this model, two political candidates compete for office based on their political platforms, which are located on a single-dimension continuum from political left to political right. Voters always choose the candidate closest to their own position, so both candidates have an incentive to move their platforms toward the center to compete for the median vote. The candidate who gets the median vote also will get all votes to one side of the median and so will get a majority of the votes and win the election. The process of political competition described by Hotelling and Downs causes both candidates' platforms to converge on the median, producing the outcome most preferred by the median voter.

Bowen (1943) comes up with the same conclusion with a model of referendum voting. Bowen's voters are asked to vote on the quantity of a publicly produced good with the understanding that if they vote against that quantity they will be offered an opportunity to vote on a marginally lower quantity. The process continues until voters approve a quantity, and Bowen shows that the quantity approved will be that most preferred by the median voter. The same conclusion is reached by a process in which voters are offered a small amount of the good and if they vote in favor are offered marginal increases as long as they continue to favor them. Again, the quantity produced by majority rule in a referendum setting is the quantity most preferred by the median voter.

Black (1958) describes yet another institutional arrangement in which a committee chooses an outcome by majority rule. Motions are put forward by committee members and compete against each other in pairwise elections. The winning motion remains on the floor and can face a potentially unlimited number of competing motions, but Black shows that the motion most preferred by the median voter can defeat any other motion by majority rule. Black discusses the role of single-peaked preferences in detail and shows how the possibility of cyclical majorities can arise when this assumption is not satisfied.

This overview shows that the median voter theorem can be demonstrated under different institutional arrangements, all pointing to the general conclusion that majority rule de-

cisionmaking produces the outcome most preferred by the median voter. If the median voter theorem is descriptive, it provides researchers with a good model of public-sector demand, which allows theoretical modeling of public-sector resource allocation and provides the basis for empirical models of public-sector supply and demand. Most empirical studies of the median voter theorem tend to support it. For example, Inman (1978) demonstrates that median population characteristics tend to explain public-sector output better than average data, and Holcombe (1980) uses school referendum data to conclude that the median voter theorem describes election outcomes better than other plausible alternatives.

Holcombe (1989) discusses the empirical evidence in more detail and notes that while the evidence is not unanimous, it tends to be consistent with the median voter theorem. This statement is comforting to researchers who want to apply this simple yet powerful theorem to understand how the democratic decisionmaking process allocates economic resources. It also provides a useful foundation for empirical models because it suggests that there are equilibrating forces in the political process and that the differences in the characteristics of median voters across jurisdictions can cause differences in the types of public-sector output produced by those jurisdictions.

While the empirical evidence has been generally supportive, a substantial amount of theoretical work has called the median voter theorem into question. This is partly because the theorem rests on simple assumptions that appear not to be met in the real world and partly because the model was used to draw conclusions that were well beyond what it actually implied. The theorem found its strongest acceptance in the early 1970s, and a number of empirical articles in top journals used it to justify the conclusion that the public sector produces what the median voter most prefers. This strong interpretation of the theorem leaves it vulnerable to attack on several grounds. First, some of the assumptions of the theorem may not be satisfied, but more significantly, the theorem deals only with the way majority rule voting aggregates demands, yet this strong interpretation suggests that the theorem describes both the supply and demand sides of the market for public-sector output. If this overly strong interpretation is accepted, any evidence that the public sector does not provide what the median wants can be taken as evidence against the theorem's applicability.

Niskanen's (1971) well-known economic analysis of bureaucracy illustrates this point. Niskanen develops a model of bureaucratic resource allocation that concludes that government bureaucracies produce far more output than the median voter would most prefer; critics of the theorem took the finding as evidence against the theorem's validity. Yet Niskanen clearly builds his analysis using the median voter theorem to model the demand side of the public sector and then adds a supply side to draw his conclusions. Although Niskanen accepted the median voter theorem as a model public-sector demand aggregation, others took Niskanen's model to imply that the theorem was not applicable to public-sector resource allocation.

More serious questions about the applicability of the median voter theorem arose in the late 1970s, when a group of economists, using sophisticated mathematical models, demonstrated that its conclusion is crucially dependent on the assumption that the political issue space is single-dimension. For example, using a framework similar to Black's, McKelvey (1976) shows that if the issue space is extended even to two dimensions, there is no outcome that can defeat all others by majority rule, even if all voters have single-peaked preferences. This finding suggests that a cyclical majority model would be more descriptive of democratic decisionmaking than the median voter theorem. A number of economists and political scientists responded by noting that public-sector outcomes in fact tend to be very stable, with programs, institutions, and even elected officials displaying more stability than is observed in the market sector. The evidence seems to weigh against continual voting (or policy) cycles in the public sector.

If one accepts the conclusion that the outcomes from collective choices tend to be stable over time, that still leaves open the question about what produces the stability. It could be that the median voter theorem explains the stability because public-sector demand is a reflection of the preferences of the median voter, whose characteristics do not change much over time. Another possibility is that the institutional structure of the public sector leads democratic decisionmaking to produce stable outcomes. Institutional constraints can have many effects, but two important potential effects deserve mention. First, they can limit the range of options over which groups can make collective choices, which can produce stability but also is a potential source of inefficiency in collective decisionmaking. Second, they can limit the ability of people to participate in the collective decisionmaking process because of high transaction costs. The fact that some people (such as legislators and lobbyists) face lower transaction costs in the political decisionmaking process than others (such as the general public) has given rise to special-interest models of legislation that conclude that representative government tends to favor special interests over the general public interest.

The assumptions behind the median voter model fit U.S. winner-take-all general elections very well, and the implications of the theorem also conform to the American experience. The theorem explains why candidates take similar platforms when running against each other (both are aiming their platforms at the median voter) and why candidates who take extreme positions lose badly (they are too far away from the median voter). The theorem also explains why two is the equilibrium number of political parties in this type of election system. (A third party must compete with a party on one side of the median, making two of the three parties unable to win elections and so not viable in the long run.) Note that although the United States has had only two major parties throughout its history, the Constitution says nothing about political parties, and third parties have continued to spring up, either to disappear (Progressive Party) or to replace one of the two dominant parties (Republican Party). In certain circumstances, the median voter theorem is very descriptive of real-world political processes and lends a great deal of insight into the way majority rule voting aggregates the preferences of voters.

The simple structure of the theorem that allows it to illuminate clearly the demand aggregation characteristics of majority rule voting also limits its applicability. The median voter theorem has nothing to say about the supply side of the public sector, and when its assumptions are violated, voting cycles are possible. Furthermore, the institutional environment can affect election outcomes in ways that are not reflected in the theorem. In this regard, the median voter theorem might be considered similar to the neoclassical model of purely competitive markets. Because of the simplifying assumptions underlying the models, they may be inapplicable to many situations. Still, the models lend powerful insights into the fundamental processes underlying markets and voting. Seen in this way, the median voter theorem provides a good foundation for understanding how resources are allocated when demands are aggregated through majority rule voting.

ADDITIONAL READINGS

Black, Duncan. *The Theory of Committees and Elections.* Cambridge, U.K.: Cambridge University Press, 1958.

Bowen, Howard R. "The Interpretation of Voting in the Allocation of Economic Resources." *Quarterly Journal of Economics* 58 (November 1943): 27–48.

Downs, Anthony. *An Economic Theory of Democracy.* New York: Harper and Row, 1957.

Holcombe, Randall G. "An Empirical Test of the Median Voter Model." *Economic Inquiry* 18 (April 1980): 260–74.

———. "The Median Voter Model in Public Choice Theory." *Public Choice* 61 (1989): 115–25.

Hotelling, Harold. "Stability in Competition." *Economic Journal* 29 (March 1929): 41–57.

Inman, Robert P. "Testing Political Economy's 'as if' Assumption: Is the Median Income Voter Really Decisive?" *Public Choice* 33 (1978): 45–65.

McKelvey, Richard D. "Intransitivities in Multi-Dimensional Voting Models and Some Implications for Agenda Control." *Journal of Economic Theory* 12 (June 1976): 472–82.

Niskanen, William N. *Bureaucracy and Representative Government.* Chicago: Aldine-Atherton, 1971.

Steuerle, C. Eugene. "Are Estimates for Years to Come Merely Science Fiction?" *Tax Notes* (October 25, 1999).

Cross-references: budget process, federal; budget processes, state; tax illusion; Tiebout model.

Medicare Trust Fund

Robert Friedland

Center on an Aging Society, Georgetown University

One of the component programs of the Social Security system, an arrangement for federal funding of health care for the elderly and certain people with disabilities.

Medicare was enacted in 1965 under Title XVIII of the Social Security Act to help older persons obtain and pay for medical care. Just before passage of Medicare, only about half of Americans age 65 or older had any health insurance (compared with 75 percent of those under the age of 65). Many who sought private coverage were denied on the basis of age or preexisting conditions; others could simply not afford it.

When originally enacted, Medicare had two parts, two trust funds, and two separate financing mechanisms: Hospital Insurance (Part A) and Supplementary Medical Insurance (Part B)—which represent two of the four Social Security trust funds (the others address retirement/survivors and disability income). Over the years the program has changed considerably. In 1972, the program was extended to certain people under age 65: those with end-stage renal disease (kidney failure) and people receiving Social Security Disability Insurance (DI) benefits for at least two years. In 1997, the program made a fundamental change to actively promote a wide variety of private plans, including plans that did not yet exist in the marketplace. Many of these plans, however, would be required to take on some of the health care risks of Medicare beneficiaries. Managed care plans that met Medicare's requirements were included as a new part of Medicare under Part C of Medicare, or Medicare+Choice. Health care plans providing care to Medicare beneficiaries who choose to get their coverage through Part C, however, are financed through Parts A and B.

Perhaps the most sweeping set of changes occurred in December 2003, under the Medicare Prescription Drug, Improvement, and Modernization Act. Many aspects of Medicare were altered, including the addition of drug coverage under Part D of Medicare. Some of the new provisions have gone into effect, but most have not. Most provisions will be phased in between 2004 and 2006. This write-up of the new law assumes that the provisions will be phased in as outlined in law.

Who is eligible for Medicare?

In 2003, there were about 40.6 million Medicare beneficiaries. Most were age 65 or older, but about 6 million were under the age of 65. Generally, eligibility for Medicare is based on working at least 40 quarters in Medicare-covered employment. Once that has occurred, beneficiaries and their spouses will be eligible for Medicare at age 65. Younger workers and their dependents can also qualify if they have been receiving federal Disability Insurance benefits for two years or have end-stage renal disease. Persons age 65 and older whose work histories are not sufficient to result in eligibility can also enroll in Part A of Medicare by paying a monthly premium ($343 a month in 2004 for those with less than 30 quarters and $189 a month for those with 31–39 quarters).

Medicare Part A is an earned benefit. Most people who have worked 10 or more years are entitled to coverage without having to pay a premium. In contrast, participation in Medicare Part B is voluntary for those eligible for Part A, but is heavily subsidized by taxpayers. In 2004 and earlier, the Medicare Part B premium was set at 25 percent of anticipated Part B program costs ($66.60 a month in 2004) and was the same for everyone choosing to enroll in Part B coverage. About 97 percent of Medicare Part A beneficiaries enroll in Part B.

Starting in 2007, however, beneficiaries with incomes above specific thresholds (based on the previous year's federal income taxes) will be required to pay a greater premium. The new provisions are to be phased in over five years. Once fully phased in, Part B premiums will be set at 25 percent of expected Part B costs for everyone whose individual income is below $80,000, but at different amounts among those with incomes above this threshold. For example, individuals with incomes between $100,000 and $150,000 will be required to pay 50 percent of anticipated Part B costs and individuals with incomes of $200,000 or more will be required to pay 80 percent of anticipated Part B costs. In 2003, these amounts would have been $134 a month and $214 a month, respectively.

Medicare and health care

Medicare is a major payer in the U.S. health care system, accounting for 19 percent of personal health care expenditures nationwide. For hospitals, Medicare represents 31 percent of patient revenues, while for physicians Medicare represents 21 percent of patient revenues. From the perspective of the beneficiary, Medicare, on average, covers about 58 percent of health care spending.

What does Medicare cover?

Medicare was designed to cover necessary acute care provided in hospitals and by physicians in the hospital and in their offices. Over the years, more and more preventive care has been added. Outpatient prescription drug coverage is being added to the coverage. The following provides an overview of coverage by Medicare Trust Fund.

Part A, Hospital Insurance Trust Fund, provides the following coverage:

1. Inpatient hospital care coverage for the first 60 days less a deductible ($876 in 2004) for each episode of acute illness. For days 61 to 90 in a hospital, a beneficiary must pay a daily copayment ($219 in 2004). Beyond 90 days, beneficiaries may elect to draw upon a 60-day lifetime reserve with a daily copayment ($438 in 2004).
2. Inpatient psychiatric care (190-day lifetime maximum).
3. Skilled nursing care or rehabilitation associated with recuperation for up to 100 days following a hospitalization. (There is no cost sharing for the first 20 days; the daily copayment for days 21 to 100 was $109.50 in 2004.)
4. Home health care, that is, skilled nursing or rehabilitation benefits provided in the home and prescribed by a physician. There are no deductibles, coinsurance, and limits on the number of covered days.
5. Hospice care (care for the terminally ill, ranging from home health aide services to medical supplies and limited, short-term inpatient care). Coinsurance for some services ap-

plies. Hospice care necessitates physician recognition that the patient has less than six months to live and the patient must forgo coverage other than hospice care under Part A of Medicare.

Part B, Supplementary Insurance, generally pays 80 percent of physician and outpatient services after an annual deductible, leaving a 20 percent copayment. In 2004 the deductible was $100. Starting in 2005, the Part B deductible will increase to $110. In addition, the deductible will now be indexed to annual increases in Part B expenditures. Coverage under Part B of Medicare includes the following:

1. physician services;
2. laboratory and other specific diagnostic tests;
3. X-ray and other radiation therapy;
4. outpatient services at a hospital, rehabilitation facility, or rural health clinic;
5. home dialysis supplies and equipment;
6. ambulance services;
7. physical and speech therapy;
8. mammography screening and screening pap smears;
9. outpatient mental health services (although only 50 percent of the approved amount is covered); and
10. starting in 2005, an initial routine physical examination, cardiovascular blood screening tests, and diabetes screening tests and services.

In June 2004, Medicare began offering access to *Part D,* Outpatient Prescription Drug coverage, a Medicare-endorsed prescription drug discount card. For Medicare beneficiaries with family incomes below 135 percent of the poverty level the government will provide $600 a year through those discount cards for prescription drug coverage and the annual enrollment fee. The discount cards will expire at the end of 2005. In 2006, Medicare will pay for outpatient prescription drugs though private plans. At that time, beneficiaries will be able to remain in Medicare and enroll in a separate private prescription drug plan or they can join a Medicare managed care plan under Part C of Medicare (now called Medicare Advantage plans, rather than Medicare+Choice plans) for all their Medicare-covered benefits including outpatient prescription drugs.

Part D of Medicare, like Part B, is voluntary, but instead of a legislated national premium paid to Medicare, the premium will be set and collected by privately administered drug plans or by managed care plans offering a drug benefit. The specific drugs covered and the premiums charged for each prescription drug plan are expected to vary by plan and, even within a plan, by region of the country.

Low-income Medicare beneficiaries with few financial assets can also be eligible for Medicaid. Medicaid programs, which are administered in each state, provide health care coverage to certain categories of persons with low incomes and few financial resources. Medicaid, which was enacted in 1965, has been a vital source for outpatient prescription

drugs, long-term care, health care services not covered by Medicare, as well as the Medicare copayments and deductibles. Under the new provisions, Medicare beneficiaries can still be eligible for Medicaid; however, they will no longer be able to get their drug coverage through their state Medicaid program.

The new Medicare provisions, for the first time, provide beneficiaries with different financial means different benefits. Under the new law, Medicare beneficiaries with incomes below 135 percent of the poverty level and few financial assets (less than $6,000 for individuals and $9,000 for couples) will receive substantial assistance for their Part D coverage, through Medicare and not from a program supplementing Medicare. The drug coverage, however, will probably not be the same as what is currently provided by Medicaid. Medicaid coverage is likely to be much more comprehensive and substantially less expensive to beneficiaries than the drug coverage through Part D of Medicare, even with Medicare's subsidies.

Medicare beneficiaries with family incomes above 135 percent of the poverty level or with financial resources in excess of the low-income thresholds will be able to purchase drug coverage through Medicare Part D by joining a private prescription drug plan or a Medicare Advantage managed care plan with prescription drug coverage. These Part D plans will charge a premium and will have discretion as to which drugs they cover and the premium charged. The plans must provide coverage for 75 percent of the cost of covered prescriptions for the first $2,250 in prescription drug expenses after a $250 deductible. By legislative design, the plans will be restricted from providing coverage for covered drug expenses between $2,250 and $5,100. The plans will resume coverage at 95 percent of covered prescription drug expenses above $5,100. (Note that all these amounts will be indexed to the increase in drug expenditures financed through Part D.)

Medicare does not cover

1. routine physical examinations (beyond an initial examination);
2. nonsurgical dental services;
3. hearing aids;
4. eyeglasses;
5. most long-term care in nursing facilities, in the community, or at home; and
6. until 2006, outpatient prescription drugs, or outpatient prescription drugs not included in the formularies of prescription drug plans after 2006.

Beneficiaries face cost-sharing in the form of premiums, deductibles, and coinsurance, as well as the cost of services and products not covered by Medicare. Unlike most private insurance, Medicare does not cap a beneficiary's out-of-pocket costs. In most insurance plans the deductible is annual. In Medicare, the deductible is by episode of care. Therefore, two separate hospital admissions would result in paying the hospital deductible two times. In 2002, Medicare beneficiaries spent on average $3,757 on health care, or 22 percent of their average household income. This figure includes Part B premiums as well as the premiums for supplemental insurance, the co-payments and deductibles for Medicare covered services, and the cost of health care services not covered by Medicare. This figure does not include the out-of-pocket expenditures for long-term care.

Supplemental coverage

As of 2001, most Medicare beneficiaries (89 percent) had supplemental Medicare coverage. For the most part, this coverage covers Medicare's copayments and deductibles; a few policies cover some of the services not covered by Medicare. Sources of supplemental coverage include employer-provided retiree coverage (34 percent), purchased private insurance ("Medigap," 23 percent), Medicaid (12 percent), and Medicare managed care plans (18 percent).

Medicare managed care

In 2004, about 4.6 million Medicare beneficiaries (11 percent) were enrolled in a Medicare Managed Care plan. These plans must provide all Medicare-covered services. Under this arrangement, the managed care plans receive a monthly payment from Medicare. The beneficiary becomes a member of the managed care plan and must obtain health care services through the plan.

Medicare pays health care providers when services are rendered, but must pay managed care plans, regardless of whether their members needed any services. If managed care plans serve a large number of Medicare beneficiaries that are as healthy as other Medicare beneficiaries, then reimbursements based on the average cost of care will likely be similar to the cost of caring for Medicare beneficiaries outside the managed care plan. If Medicare beneficiaries are disproportionately sicker than other Medicare beneficiaries, then payments will likely be less than they otherwise would have been. However, studies have shown that Medicare beneficiaries enrolled in managed care plans tend to be healthier than other Medicare beneficiaries and therefore Medicare reimbursement rates were costing Medicare money.

The Balanced Budget Act of 1997 expanded the role of private health plans in Medicare. Medicare Part C was created and called Medicare+Choice. Reimbursement would no longer be simply 95 percent of the average Medicare expenditure per person in the country. In fact, the reimbursement would no longer depend on what Medicare was spending for other beneficiaries. The changes in reimbursement, however, resulted in a dramatic decline in the number of Medicare+Choice plans. In 1998 there were 346 managed care plans in Medicare covering 6.1 million (17 percent) Medicare beneficiaries; by 2004 there were only 145 plans with 4.6 million Medicare beneficiaries.

The 2003 legislation changed the name of Medicare Part C from Medicare+Choice to "Medicare Advantage." More than a name change, the new legislation explicitly recognizes the need to pay managed care plans more than what Medicare pays for the services it covers for other beneficiaries in order to expand this market. The law calls upon above-average payments through 2013. Before Part C was created, managed care plans were paid 5 percent less than Medicare payments made on behalf of beneficiaries not in managed care. Yet, it was clear that Medicare was losing money because only those in above-average health were likely to be in a managed care plan. Under the new provisions of Medicare advantage, it is expected that managed care plans will be paid, on average, 8.4 percent more than Medicare payments made on behalf of beneficiaries not in managed care plans.

Medicare financing

Medicare is financed through two trust funds. Hospital Insurance (HI), or Medicare Part A, helps pay for hospital, home health, skilled nursing facility, and hospice care. Supplementary Medical Insurance (SMI) is composed of Part B and, beginning in 2004, Part D of Medicare. Part B pays for physician, outpatient hospital, home health, and some other services. Part D will initially provide access to prescription drug discount cards and transitional assistance to low-income Medicare beneficiaries. In 2006 and later, Part D will provide subsidized access to private drug insurance coverage on a voluntary basis for all beneficiaries and cost-sharing subsidies for low-income beneficiaries.

The Hospital Insurance (HI) Trust Fund is financed primarily (89 percent) by payroll taxes (1.45 percent each on employees and employers' payrolls; the self-employed pay 2.9 percent), taxes from Social Security (7 percent), and interest payments on reserves (4 percent). Most of the annual trust fund income is used to fund current-year benefits. The HI Trust Fund is essentially operating largely on a "pay-as-you-go" basis. There were, however, nearly $234.8 billion in reserves at the end of 2002. In 2003, expenditures were $21.2 billion less than income, and thus reserves increased to $256 billion.

The Supplementary Medical Insurance (SMI) Trust Fund is primarily financed (74 percent) by transfers from the general fund of the U.S. Treasury and by monthly Part B and Part D premiums paid by Medicare beneficiaries. Because of how premiums are set, the SMI Trust Fund is always "adequately financed." Although the SMI Trust Fund had $24 billion in assets at the end of 2003, these reserves are not intended to accumulate to pay for future benefits. Premiums are supposed to be adjusted so that there are few reserves.

With the creation of Part D, the SMI Trust Fund is required to maintain Part B and Part D as distinct accounts. There are no provisions that enable transfers of funds between Part B and Part D.

Medicare expenditures

In 1970, Medicare expenditures as a percentage of gross domestic product (GDP) were 0.7 percent. By 2003 Medicare expenditures had increased to 2.6 percent of GDP. By 2035, the Trustees of the Social Security trust funds project that Medicare expenditures could be 7.8 percent of GDP. If this occurs, then without any other changes in current law, the Part A Hospital Insurance trust fund will be seriously out of balance.

In 2003, program costs as a percentage of taxable income were 3.01 percent and the income or revenue received as a percentage of taxable payroll was 3.06 percent. This is the last year in which it is anticipated that program costs will be less than or equal to the program income. By 2015, the cost rate of Medicare (expenditures as a percent of taxable payroll) is projected to reach 3.49 percent, while the income rate (program revenues as a percent of taxable payroll) is 3.18 percent. By 2035, the gap between expenditures and revenue could be even larger, with the cost rate at 6.43 percent and the income rate at 3.37 percent of taxable payroll. At these rates of cost and income growth, the HI trust fund will be exhausted by 2019.

Cost containment efforts

A growing number of Medicare beneficiaries in the face of technological advancements in medical care mean more people can be diagnosed and treated. Historically, earned income has never increased as fast as the cost of health care; therefore, without ongoing changes in how the program is financed, health care expenditures will continue to increase faster than the revenues used to finance the Medicare program. The only way to avoid this is for wages to increase faster than the cost of medical care, to find dramatic new ways to attain more efficiency in medicine, or to find a way to stop the advances in medical diagnosis and treatment that occur in the market.

Past efforts to balance Medicare expenditures with program revenues have taken many forms, such as explicitly reviewing each medical procedure to be sure it was medically necessary; limiting reimbursement to providers; altering provider incentives by paying for care on a prospective basis, regardless of actual costs; and increasing the copayments and deductibles, as well as the Part B premiums, paid by beneficiaries. In 1983, for example, hospitals were no longer paid on their costs but rather were provided a fixed amount per patient depending on the medical diagnosis of the patient. In January 1992, how physicians serving Medicare beneficiaries were reimbursed changed as well. Instead of getting paid based on what they charged, physicians were paid based on a national fee schedule. The fee schedule was based on the average amount of resources used to provide specific services. The "resource-based relative value scale" included not only current resources, such as time and materials, but also the medical training necessary to perform this service. More recently (1998), prospective reimbursement systems were implemented for care provided in skilled nurs-

ing facilities as well as the care provided by home health agencies.

The Medicare Prescription Drug, Improvement, and Modernization Act of 2003 includes provisions that require the president and Congress to change the program if anticipated general revenues necessary to fund SMI (Medicare Parts B and D) exceed 45 percent of anticipated Medicare expenditures under Parts A, B, C, and D for two years in a row. In the second year in which anticipated revenues exceed 45 percent of expenditures, the president must submit to Congress a proposal to change the Medicare program. The Modernization Act directs the Social Security trustees to implement this measure of fiscal integrity and sets forth congressional procedures that bypass the usual rules of order to expedite the legislative process. Of course, future Congresses can amend the legislative rules set forth in the Modernization Act. The adaptation of legislative rules was done with the hope that the Medicare funding "crisis" will occur when the party in control of Congress and the White House is the same party most responsible for including this provision in the new law.

The future of Medicare and policy debates

Health programs, like retirement programs, are affected by the aging of our society. Unlike retirement programs, however, they are also affected by the rapid development of medical technology and rising costs of health care. Proposed short-term solutions for the Medicare funding gap include raising payroll taxes, shifting contributions from other trust funds, changing premiums and rates of copayment, expanding managed care, or reexamining cost-sharing to influence the use of certain services. Each of these options has different consequences.

More profound restructuring was initiated in the 2003 legislation and will likely be a part of the ongoing Medicare debate. Other parts of this debate will likely include combining Parts A and B and rethinking the existing trust fund financing arrangements, increasing beneficiaries' costs further, changing the benefits, increasing the age of eligibility, and fostering health plan competition to keep health care costs in check.

ADDITIONAL READINGS

Aaron, Henry J. *Serious and Unstable Condition: Financing America's Health Care.* Washington, DC: Brookings Institution Press, 1991.

Moon, Marilyn. *Medicare Now and in the Future,* 2nd ed. Washington, DC: Urban Institute Press, 1993.

Orszag, Peter. "Tax on Social Security Benefits Providing More Trust Fund Revenue." *Tax Notes* 97, no. 10 (December 9, 2002): 1359.

Steuerle, C. Eugene, Christopher Spiro, and Adam Carasso. "Social Security Benefits under Current Law: What Happens when the Trust Fund Runs Dry?" *Straight Talk on Social Security and Retirement Policy Series,* no. 17. Washington, DC: The Urban Institute, 2000.

Cross-references: health expenditures, tax treatment; payroll tax, federal; Social Security Trust Fund.

Mortgage interest deduction

Richard K. Green

George Washington University

A deduction from adjusted gross income as part of the determination of taxable income, intended to encourage home ownership and encourage spending on owner-occupied housing.

Before the Tax Reform Act of 1986, consumer interest was generally deductible from gross income. Indeed, the original Income Tax Act of 1913 allowed for the deduction of consumer interest (see Pechman 1987). But since 1986, the only interest expense that consumers have been able to completely deduct from gross income in order to calculate taxable income has been interest paid on specified home mortgages.

These mortgages include those on first and second homes with balances totaling less than $1 million. The definition of "home" is quite broad: motor homes and yachts, for example, by virtue of their indoor plumbing and kitchens, qualify as homes for tax purposes. Beyond the $1 million limit, mortgages on which interest is completely deductible may not exceed the maximum of the equity value of the house securing the loan, or, on a refinanced loan, the outstanding balance of the original mortgage plus $100,000.

According to the Joint Committee on Taxation, in 2003 the value of the mortgage interest deduction to taxpayers was roughly $70 billion.

Importance of the benefit

In the popular press, the mortgage interest deduction is often characterized as the principal tax benefit accruing to homeowners. This is certainly not correct. First, fewer than 50 percent of homeowners itemize on their tax returns; the remainder use the standard deduction. This is because the value of itemized deductions for low- to moderate-income homeowners in states with low marginal tax rates will almost certainly be less than the value of the standard deduction, which in 2003 was $9,500 for married couples filing jointly. Also, according to tabulations from the Survey of Consumer Finances, many households with elderly heads own their homes entirely with equity (i.e., do not have mortgages). For these households, the mortgage interest deduction has no value.

Second, even for those who do itemize, the mortgage interest deduction does not necessarily produce the largest tax benefit arising from owning. The imputed rent that households earn from their owner-occupied housing (i.e., the rents that households are not required to pay anyone else because they own) goes untaxed. This rent is therefore favored relative to most other types of income, including ordinary income, taxable bond income, dividend income, and capital gains income, which, while favored and deferrable, is still generally taxed. The average loan-to-value ratio in the United States is less than 50 percent. Thus, even if all owners with mortgages itemized on their tax returns, the value of the nontaxation of imputed rent would be larger than that of the mortgage interest deduction.

Effect of the benefit on choice of financing

One could argue that the effect of the mortgage interest deduction is to put debt on a level playing field with equity as a way to finance housing. This contrasts with the tax treatment of corporate income, where interest is deductible and the opportunity cost of equity capital is not. Many analysts have shown that the U.S. tax system encourages corporations to take on debt. Capozza, Green, and Hendershott (1996) have shown how the combination of nontaxation of imputed rent and the absence of a mortgage interest deduction would discourage households from financing housing with debt. In Australia, imputed rent is not taxed and mortgage interest is not deductible, and households there generally pay off their mortgages more quickly than in the United States.

Mortgage interest deduction and efficiency

For many years, the mortgage interest deduction was viewed as a mechanism that steered investment capital away from plants and equipment and toward the housing market. Laidler (1969) and Rosen (1979), among others, found that the quantity effects of the mortgage interest deduction (and nontaxation of imputed rent) were large, because they assumed that housing was supplied perfectly elastically.

Some more recent work by King (1980) and Poterba (1984) relaxed the assumption of perfect elasticity and still found large quantity effects. But the most recent work (Mayer and Somerville 1997; Skinner 1996; and Capozza et al. 1996) has found housing to be supplied very inelastically and consequently finds small quantity effects and large price effects (e.g., capitalization effects) arising from the tax preferences for owner-occupied housing. This suggests that the efficiency costs of the mortgage interest deduction are rather small.

An interesting question raised by the mortgage interest deduction is whether it causes market segmentation. Within a housing market, households with the highest marginal tax rates have an incentive to outbid everyone else for owner-occupied housing. Once these households are exhausted, the households with the second highest rates can outbid everyone else, and so on. If this were to happen, tax benefits could be entirely capitalized. If, on the other hand, market values are determined by some average marginal tax rate, households with high tax rates will consume more housing than they would in the absence of the tax preference, and households with low tax rates would consume less (or might even rent).

The mortgage interest deduction and vertical equity

The mortgage interest deduction generally reduces progressivity in the income tax system, because it gives higher-income taxpayers higher levels of benefits. On the other hand, how sharply the mortgage interest deduction reduces progressivity depends on the elasticity of housing supply. If housing were inelastically supplied (i.e., could be represented by a vertical supply curve), all tax benefits would be capitalized into prices, and owners would receive no net benefits from the mortgage interest deduction. Those benefits that are not capitalized determine the extent to which the mortgage interest deduction hampers progressivity.

ADDITIONAL READINGS

Capozza, Dennis, Richard K. Green, and Patric H. Hendershott. "Taxes, Mortgage Borrowing, and Residential Land Prices." In *Economic Effects of Fundamental Tax Reform,* edited by Henry Aaron and William Gale (chapter 5). Washington, DC: Brookings Institution Press, 1996.

Joint Committee on Taxation. *Estimates for Federal Tax Expenditures for Fiscal Years 2002–2006.* Washington, DC: U.S. Government Printing Office, 2002.

King, M. A. "An Econometric Model of Tenure Choice and the Demand for Housing as a Joint Decision." *Journal of Public Economics* 14, no. 2 (1980): 137–59.

Laidler, David. "Income Tax Incentives for Owner-Occupied Housing." In *The Taxation of Income from Capital,* edited by Arnold Harberger and Martin Bailey. Washington, DC: Brookings Institution Press, 1969.

Mayer, C., and T. Somerville. "Testing Alternative Paradigms of the Supply of Owner-Occupied Housing." Mimeograph, 1997.

Pechman, Joseph. *Federal Tax Policy,* 5th ed. Washington, DC: Brookings Institution Press, 1987.

Poterba, James. "Tax Subsidies to Owner-Occupied Housing: An Asset-Market Approach." *Quarterly Journal of Economics* 99, no. 4 (1984): 729–52.

Rosen, Harvey. "Housing Decisions and the U.S. Income Tax: An Econometric Analysis." *Journal of Public Economics* 11, no. 1 (1979): 1–23.

Skinner, Jonathan. "The Dynamic Efficiency Cost of Not Taxing Housing." *Journal of Public Economics* 59, no. 3 (1996): 397–417.

Cross-references: homeowner preferences, individual income tax; implicit taxes; progressivity, measures of; standard deduction, federal.

Multinational corporations, taxation of

Eric J. Toder
The Urban Institute

A system of taxation of large U.S. corporations that have foreign operations organized under laws of another country or operate abroad in branch form.

Global capital flows increased dramatically in the 1990s. Capital flows take many forms, including loans, cross-border equity investments, and foreign direct investment (FDI) by multinational corporations. While portfolio investments have grown in recent years, FDI continues to account for a substantial share of the net capital flows from mature to emerging markets (International Monetary Fund 2001).

Multinationals need not own overseas facilities to secure the cost and market access advantages of foreign production; they can (and sometimes do) contract out production to locally owned firms. The usual reason economists advance for direct ownership is that the high transactions costs of negotiating and enforcing rights to the returns from intangible assets (such as patents, production processes, and reputation) make internal ownership of those assets preferable (Markusen 1995).

In the domestic context, a tax on corporate retained earnings protects the income tax base by preventing individual investors from accruing untaxed income within corporations. When the same corporation receives income from production in more than one taxing jurisdiction, however, and when rights to that income accrue to shareholders of different nationalities, both domestic and foreign tax rules determine whether taxation of corporate income is achieving the goal of taxing undistributed income of shareholders at the applicable rate under domestic tax law, without imposing extra tax penalties on international investment flows.

In determining rules for taxing cross-border income flows, two principles of tax neutrality are in conflict. Locational neutrality, often called "capital-export" neutrality (Musgrave 1969), means that tax rules should not distort the location of economic activity among countries. This form of neutrality requires that (risk-adjusted) pretax returns be equalized among countries and (with perfect capital markets) would result from profit-maximization in the absence of taxes. It can be achieved if all countries taxed the worldwide income (including income accrued within foreign affiliates) on a current basis of all corporations with headquarters within their borders (resident corporations), but allowed a credit for foreign income taxes paid. This would make a corporation's tax rate on profits equal to its home country rate in all locations, without regard to the local country's tax rate. But, unless all countries have the same tax rules, residence-based corporate taxation does not ensure that any one country's multinationals face the same total tax rate on investments in any location as multinationals resident in other countries.

An alternative and related concept of locational neutrality, called "national neutrality," would be achieved by any country that taxed the worldwide income of its corporations, but with a deduction instead of a credit for foreign taxes. This rule would encourage corporations to equalize the yield before domestic taxes, but net of foreign taxes, and would therefore equalize the home country's return to investment in all locations. But it would cause international capital flows to bear higher tax rates than domestic investments, unless all countries eliminated taxation of inbound capital flows.

Producer neutrality (often called "capital import" neutrality) requires that the after-tax return to investment in any location be equalized for all corporations, without regard to their country of residence. This can be achieved if all countries taxed income from production within their borders (domestic-source income) at the same rate, regardless of the residence of the investing corporation, and imposed no taxes on foreign source income of its own resident corporations because it would make the tax rate in any location the same for all corporations. But, unless all countries imposed the same tax rate, such a rule would not produce locational neutrality; required pretax returns would be higher in high-tax than in low-tax countries and world capital stocks would be misallocated.

If all resident corporations in any country are owned exclusively by domestic residents, and domestic saving is inelastic with respect to the after-tax rate of return, the higher tax rates any country may impose on its corporations are likely to be borne by its own savers in the form of lower after-tax yields instead of raising the cost of capital on its resident corporations. For this reason, many international tax experts have favored residence-based taxation on efficiency grounds (Musgrave 1984). If, however, corporations issue equity on a world market, then higher taxes on profits on any one country's resident multinationals will not be fully shifted backward to shareholders and could, by raising their cost of capital, place resident corporations at a disadvantage relative to corporations with headquarters in other countries. Tax systems that impose higher effective tax rates on the foreign source income of one country's multinational corporations than on others can reduce global economic efficiency to the extent that corporate residence is associated with differences in productivity. (See Desai and Hines 2003, who label this efficiency property "capital ownership neutrality.")

Because policies that broaden taxation of foreign-source income of U.S. multinationals can improve locational neutrality at the expense of reducing producer neutrality, economists have actively and continually debated the relative merit of the two objectives (Altshuler 2000). Proponents of emphasizing locational neutrality cite studies and evidence showing a high and increasing sensitivity of investment location to differences in tax rates (Grubert and Mutti 1995; Altshuler, Grubert, and Newlon 2001). Those who emphasize producer neutrality argue that portfolio flows undermine the effort to achieve locational neutrality by taxing worldwide income of corporations, cite the fiscal benefit to home countries of encouraging investment by their companies in low-tax countries, and note that offsetting capital flows by foreign multinationals can render ineffective attempts to achieve locational neutrality by taxing outbound investment of domestic multinationals (Hines 1999a; Desai and Hines 2003).

While efficiency considerations arguably favor residence-based taxation, administration and compliance considerations may favor source-based taxation because countries can more easily collect taxes on income accrued within their own borders. Taxing foreign-source income as accrued is especially difficult when a resident corporation or individual has only a minority interest in a foreign entity and cannot compel the entity to report data to domestic tax authorities. The model tax treaties of the Organisation for Economic Co-operation and Development (OECD) and the United Nations both give source countries the first rights to tax income accrued by permanent establishments within their borders. The United States

and its major trading partners all tax domestic-source income of foreign-owned, as well as domestically owned, corporations.

But determining the allocation of income by country is difficult because of the large amount of cross-border trade in the form of transactions between branches and affiliated companies within multinational corporations. When a corporation purchases goods or services from a foreign branch or a wholly owned foreign subsidiary, the price it pays (called a "transfer price") has no effect on the aggregate pretax profits of the corporate group, but does affect the shares of total taxable income reported by the separate entities to different countries. Consequently, multinational corporations have an incentive to set high prices (low prices) for purchases from (sales to) subsidiaries in low-tax countries, in order to raise the amount of income reported to low-tax countries and reduce reported income in high-tax jurisdictions. How corporations allocate joint costs to the corporate group (such as research and development expenses or interest payments) also affects the allocation of net profits among jurisdictions.

Under the "arms-length" standard, transfer prices between affiliates should be set equal to the prices of sales of comparable goods and services in transactions between unrelated entities. Often, however, appropriate comparable transactions cannot be identified. The typical case is where a multinational corporation licenses the use of its unique intangibles (patents and production processes) to a foreign subsidiary that uses the intangible assets in production. The royalty charged to the subsidiary cannot be compared to any arms-length transaction if the corporation does not sell or lease its intangible assets to unrelated parties. To address this problem, the United States has developed detailed transfer pricing regulations that allow alternative methods based on comparable profit rates in cases where suitable comparable transactions do not exist. Such methods, nevertheless, attempt to establish prices or royalties that would be charged at arm's length.

In view of problems in determining appropriate transfer prices, some experts favor replacing the arm's-length system with a system of "formulary apportionment," which ignores intercompany transactions and allocates income for an entire corporate group among jurisdictions in proportion to shares of certain defined variables. Formulary apportionment is used by states within the United States to allocate domestic U.S. profits among states. States typically base their allocation formulas on a weighted average of a company's sales, assets, and payroll among jurisdictions, although some have recently moved toward a sales-only formula.

Opponents of the formulary approach point out that, to be workable, it would require a much greater degree of harmonization among countries' tax systems than exists today or is feasible in the immediate future. In this view, formulary apportionment works (though not without problems and economic distortions) for U.S. states only because states use a common accounting framework with a corporate tax base that is the same, or similar, to the base of the U.S. corporate income tax. Opponents of formulary apportionment note further that, through the efforts of the OECD, the world's major economies have reached a consensus that supports the arm's-length test and rejects formulary apportionment. (See papers collected in U.S. Department of the Treasury 1996.) Recently, however, the European Union (EU) has been considering a form of formula apportionment for companies within the EU, but views on its practicality are mixed (Hellerstein and McLure 2004; Mintz 2004).

In addition to taxing U.S.-source corporate income, the United States taxes the worldwide income of its resident corporations, with a credit for foreign income and withholding taxes paid. But, in general, the United States allows corporations to defer tax on most active business income accrued within foreign subsidiaries until that income is repatriated in the form of dividend payments to the parent U.S. multinational. Special rules (the subpart F rules) tax passive income and certain other forms of "easily shiftable" income of foreign subsidiaries on a current basis to limit the erosion of the U.S. tax base that opportunities to accrue income in low-tax jurisdictions would otherwise create.

The United States adjusts for double taxation on that portion of foreign-source income that is taxable (repatriated income and subpart F income) by allowing corporations to claim a credit for foreign taxes paid. (Some other countries exempt foreign-source business income of their resident multinationals, but do tax investment income that is generally subject to lower foreign taxes, with a credit or deduction for such taxes. Exemption of some foreign-source income reflects a "capital import neutrality" approach.) The U.S. foreign tax credit is limited to the tax liability that would otherwise be payable on the foreign-source income under U.S. tax law. Companies can, however, effectively claim credits in excess of the U.S. tax rate in a high-tax country by earning enough income in low-tax jurisdictions to soak up the excess credits. To limit such "cross-crediting," the U.S. tax law establishes separate "baskets" for different types of income and applies a separate foreign tax credit limit to each "basket."

U.S. multinationals unable to use all their foreign tax credits (owing to an average foreign tax rate for any basket that is higher than the U.S. tax rate) are said to be in an "excess credit" position. Corporations in an excess credit position have an incentive to characterize more of their income to U.S. authorities as foreign source in order to claim credits against U.S. tax for more of the income taxes they pay to foreign governments. Companies in a long-term excess credit position also face different effective tax rates on foreign investments than companies in an excess limit position. Excess credit companies effectively pay no residual U.S. tax on additional foreign-source income, while excess limit companies pay U.S. tax on additional income from low-tax jurisdictions.

In recent years, numerous studies have estimated how U.S. multinationals respond to the incentives in U.S. international rules. The research shows that differences in effec-

tive tax rates among locations affect the location of real investment and where firms report income, given the location of real investment (Hines 1999b). There is also evidence that deferral and the U.S. foreign tax credit rules affect the decision of multinationals to retain earnings overseas instead of repatriating dividends to U.S. parent companies. Although some evidence suggests that the estimated response primarily represents changes in timing in response to annual changes in foreign tax credit positions (Altshuler, Newlon, and Randolph 1995), others find that the tax rules reduce and distort repatriations and impose a significant welfare loss (Desai, Foley, and Hines 2001).

The U.S. rules for taxing foreign-source income seek to balance three sometimes contradictory goals—limiting tax preferences for U.S. firms to invest abroad (by limiting disparities in effective tax rates between domestic and foreign investments), protecting the competitiveness of U.S.-resident multinationals (by limiting disparities in effective tax rates on foreign investments of U.S. and foreign multinationals), and protecting the domestic income tax base (by preventing income-shifting to low-tax jurisdictions). Advocates of policy changes differ in the goals they emphasize. Some members of Congress have expressed concern that deferral encourages U.S. corporations to invest abroad instead of at home and have proposed measures to expand subpart F to cover "runaway" plants that produce goods for export to the United States. In contrast, others in Congress and the business community view the U.S. anti-deferral rules as too harsh, relative to tax rules imposed on foreign-source income by other capital-exporting countries, and believe they damage competitiveness of U.S. resident multinationals. Corporations also complain about the complexity of rules designed to limit tax-motivated income shifting.

One way for U.S. companies to avoid U.S. (or other residual) tax on their foreign-source income is to shift their corporate residence to a tax-haven country. Corporate residence, for example, can be moved to a tax haven by establishing a head office there, even when the bulk of the company's production facilities, employees, shareholders, and customers continue to be located elsewhere. This type of transaction, called a corporate inversion, can be economically costly if the corporation realizes a large capital gain on the sale of its shares to the new foreign-resident company, but if the company does not have significant accrued gains, the up-front tax price of an inversion would be low. Corporate inversions have drawn heavy press and congressional criticism; in one highly publicized case, a manufacturing firm withdrew plans to establish Bermuda as a corporate headquarters in response to this criticism (Johnston 2003).

Some OECD countries exempt most active foreign-source income of their multinational companies from tax, while maintaining rules to try to prevent individuals from avoiding their domestic corporate tax through investments in tax havens. Some experts argue that the current U.S. system of taxing dividend repatriations, but allowing foreign tax credits and favorable income allocation rules, may be more favorable to foreign investment of multinational companies than exemption. For example, Grubert (2001) estimates that, absent behavioral responses, exemption of repatriated dividends, combined with full taxation of sales source and royalty income and modification of expense allocation rules, would increase revenue. Similarly, Altshuler and Grubert (2001) conclude that investment location decisions would not be affected significantly by a move toward exemption. Note that this conclusion does not imply a preference for exemption over a full anti-deferral regime; rather, it suggests that the current complex rules produce a result close to exemption of active foreign-source income and that replacing these rules with an explicit territorial system could increase revenue and efficiency, depending on details of the system.

Replacing the current U.S. individual and corporate income taxes with a consumption-based tax, as some have advocated, would have a profound impact on worldwide taxation of multinationals. For example, under a consumption-based "flat tax" (as originally proposed by Hall and Rabushka 1995) or a national sales tax, multinationals would have a powerful incentive to shift both real and reported income to the United States. (For a more complete discussion, see Grubert and Newlon 1995.) Other countries are likely to respond by taking measures to protect either their domestic tax base (such as by taxing U.S.-source income on an accrual basis as "tax haven" income) or their domestic capital stock by reducing corporate income taxes. While discussion of such U.S. reforms has waned in the past decade, continued support for a consumption tax among influential academics and some politicians combined with the recent trend toward lower taxes on capital income of individuals suggests that interest in a broad-based consumption tax could be revived at some future time.

ADDITIONAL READINGS

Altshuler, Rosanne. "Recent Developments in the Debate on Deferral." Rutgers University Working Paper 200013 New Brunswick, NJ: Rutgers University, 2000.

Altshuler, Rosanne, and Harry Grubert. "Where Will They Go If We Go Territorial? Dividend Exemption and the Location Decisions of U.S. Multinational Corporations." *National Tax Journal* 54, no. 4 (December 2001): 787–809.

Altshuler, Rosanne, Harry Grubert, and T. Scott Newlon. "Has U.S. Investment Become More Sensitive to Tax Rates?" In *International Taxation and Multinational Activity,* edited by James R. Hines Jr. (9–32). Chicago: University of Chicago Press, 2001.

Altshuler, Rosanne, T. Scott Newlon, and William C. Randolph. "Do Repatriation Taxes Matter? Evidence from the Tax Returns of U.S. Multinationals." In *Studies in International Taxation,* edited by Martin Feldstein, James R. Hines, and R. Glenn Hubbard (253–72). Chicago: University of Chicago Press, 1995.

Desai, Mihir A., and James R. Hines Jr. "Evaluating International Tax Reform." *National Tax Journal* 56, no. 2 (September 2003): 487–502.

Desai, Mihir A., C. Fritz Foley, and James R. Hines Jr. "Repatriation Taxes and Dividend Distortions." *National Tax Journal* 54, no. 4 (December 2001): 829–51.

Grubert, Harry. "Enacting Dividend Exemption and Tax Revenue." *National Tax Journal* 54, no. 4 (December 2001): 811–27.

Grubert, Harry, and John Mutti. "Taxing Multinationals in a World with Portfolio Flows and R&D: Is Capital Export Neutrality Obsolete?" *International Tax and Public Finance* 2, no. 3 (November 1995): 439–57.

Grubert, Harry, and T. Scott Newlon. "The International Implications of Consumption Tax Proposals." *National Tax Journal* 48, no. 4 (December 1995): 619–47.

Hall, Robert E., and Alvin Rabushka. *The Flat Tax.* 2nd ed. Stanford, CA: Hoover Institution Press, 1995.

Hellerstein, Walter, and Charles E. McLure Jr. "The European Commission's Report on Company Income Taxation: What the EU Can Learn from the Experience of the U.S. States." *International Tax and Public Finance* 11, no. 2 (March 2004): 199–220.

Hines, James R., Jr. "The Case against Deferral: A Deferential Reconsideration." *National Tax Journal* 52, no. 3 (September 1999a): 385–404.

———. "Lessons From Behavioral Responses to International Taxation." *National Tax Journal* 52, no. 2 (June 1999b): 305–22.

International Monetary Fund. "International Capital Markets: Developments, Prospects, and Key Policy Issues." Washington, DC: International Monetary Fund, August 2001.

Johnston, David Cay. *Perfectly Legal.* New York and London: Penguin Group, 2003, 229–50.

Markusen, James R. "The Boundaries of Multinational Enterprises and the Theory of International Trade." *Journal of Economic Perspectives* 9, no. 2 (Spring 1995): 169–89.

Mintz, Jack. "Corporate Tax Harmonization in Europe: It's All About Compliance." *International Tax and Public Finance* 11, no. 2 (March 2004): 221–34.

Musgrave, Peggy B. *United States Taxation of Foreign Investment Income: Issues and Arguments.* Cambridge, MA: International Tax Program, Harvard Law School, 1969.

———. "The Taxation of International Capital Income." In *Taxation Issues of the 1980s,* edited by John G. Head. Sydney: Australian Research Foundation, 1984.

U.S. Department of the Treasury. Conference on Formula Apportionment, December 12, 1996.

Cross-references: allocation rules, multinational corporations; capital export neutrality; capital import neutrality; foreign tax credit; income tax, federal; national neutrality; taxable income, corporate.

Multistate Tax Commission

Dan R. Bucks
Montana Department of Revenue

An organization of member states that serves as an administrative, joint-auditing, and research agency for state governments.

The Multistate Tax Commission is the governing body and operating agency of the Multistate Tax Compact, an interstate compact with 21 member states, 5 sovereignty member states, 18 associate member states, and 3 project member states as of June 2004.

The states created the Multistate Tax Commission (MTC) in 1967 to preserve fiscal federalism and promote fair and effective taxation of interstate and international commerce.

The full members of the MTC (i.e., those whose legislatures enacted the compact) are Alabama, Alaska, Arkansas, California, Colorado, District of Columbia, Hawaii, Idaho, Kansas, Maine, Michigan, Minnesota, Missouri, Montana, New Mexico, North Dakota, Oregon, South Dakota, Texas, Utah, and Washington. These states govern and pay dues to support the commission and typically participate in a wide range of projects and programs. They are represented on the commission by the directors of their revenue agencies.

The sovereignty members of the MTC are Florida, Kentucky, Louisiana, New Jersey, and Wyoming. Sovereignty members have not enacted the compact. However, similar to the compact members, they support the uniformity, education, litigation support, and federal relations work of the MTC. They vote on all general MTC committees except for the executive committee and the Commission itself. They also often participate in MTC compliance programs.

The associate members of the MTC are Arizona, Connecticut, Georgia, Illinois, Maryland, Massachusetts, Mississippi, New Hampshire, New York, North Carolina, Ohio, Oklahoma, Pennsylvania, South Carolina, Tennessee, Vermont, Wisconsin, and West Virginia. Nonvoting associate members participate in committees and meetings and often join MTC projects or programs. The three project member states (Iowa, Nebraska, and Rhode Island) also participate in MTC tax compliance programs.

The Multistate Tax Compact was written in the mid-1960s, principally by representatives of the Council of State Governments and the National Association of Tax Administrators (predecessor to the Federation of Tax Administrators, the professional association of state revenue agency directors and staff). The compact was drafted as a response to the final report of the Willis Committee, a multiyear congressional investigation of state taxation of interstate commerce. In response to complaints by the American business community that nonuniform state tax methods resulted in substantial compliance burdens and double taxation of income, the Willis Committee proposed federal legislation to preempt significant features of state corporate income taxes and retail sales taxes. The compact and the MTC were developed as mechanisms to help states work voluntarily toward greater uniformity in tax policy and administration, as a substitute for federal preemption of what states perceived as their sovereign power of taxation. The compact went into effect on August 4, 1967, following its adoption by seven state legislatures. Implementation of the compact and advocacy by the states forestalled congressional adoption of the Willis Committee recommendations, which were introduced in a variety of bills throughout the 1970s.

The stated purposes of the Multistate Tax Compact are to (1) facilitate proper determination of state and local tax liability of multistate taxpayers, including the equitable apportionment of tax bases and settlement of apportionment disputes; (2) promote uniformity or compatibility in significant components of tax systems; (3) facilitate taxpayer convenience and compliance in the filing of tax returns and in other phases of tax administration; and (4) avoid duplicative taxation. Implicit in the history surrounding the development of the compact is a fifth purpose: to prevent unwarranted federal preemption of state tax practices that otherwise pass constitutional muster (e.g., that do not impermissibly discriminate against interstate commerce).

The MTC engages in various activities and programs to further these goals. Its standing Uniformity Committee develops model regulations, statutes, and policy guidelines to address areas of taxation of interstate commerce for which nonuniformity has been identified as imposing business compliance burdens and/or as providing an opportunity for business tax avoidance. The MTC has been especially active in developing detailed regulations to implement the Uniform Division of Income for Tax Purposes Act (UDITPA), a model law developed in 1957 that provides the basic set of apportionment rules for the division of the corporate income tax base in nearly all states (Multistate Tax Commission 2003a). (UDITPA is embodied in the compact itself as Article IV.) Following a public hearing process, the full commission votes on the formal endorsement of uniform regulations and laws developed by the Uniformity Committee. The MTC then seeks to persuade its member states to adopt these uniformity recommendations as their own policy, which may require action by the state legislature or implementation of formal regulation adoption procedures by the tax agency.

As a legal instrumentality of its member states, the MTC has authority to engage in tax compliance activities. The MTC's Joint Audit Program has a staff of tax auditors who conduct corporate income tax and retail sales and use tax audits of large multistate companies on behalf of a number of states simultaneously. (The validity of the Multistate Tax Commission 289 Compact and the authority of the MTC to conduct audits were upheld by the U.S. Supreme Court in *U.S. Steel Corp. et al. v. Multistate Tax Commission,* 434 US 452 [1978].) Simultaneous multistate auditing achieves economies of scale in this vital tax administration function, and it reduces the burdens and disruption imposed on businesses by the need to respond to information requests from numerous auditors. These joint audits also help achieve more uniform treatment of taxpayers amongst the various states. The MTC National Nexus Program engages in a variety of information-sharing, voluntary taxpayer negotiation, and investigation efforts, all aimed at getting on the states' tax rolls businesses that should be, but are not, paying corporate income or collecting sales and use taxes.

The commission also functions as a policy and legal development "think tank" for state tax agencies. It conducts research, it sponsors conferences, and its staff members frequently speak and publish to apprise state tax officials of how changes in the structure of the economy and business operations require changes in tax policy and tax law. In 2002 and 2003, the MTC conducted an extensive series of seminars on the status of state and local tax systems in the context of the modern economy. The conclusions from that study process were presented in a major report, *Federalism at Risk* (Multistate Tax Commission 2003b). The MTC frequently files amicus curiae briefs in U.S. Supreme Court and lower court cases involving major issues in state taxation of interstate commerce.

Finally, the commission is an organization of state government officials that seeks to protect state and local taxing prerogatives when these are threatened by proposed action by Congress or federal agencies.

As of mid-2004, the MTC had a staff of about 40 (composed of managers, auditors, attorneys, lobbyists, economists, and administrative support personnel) and an annual budget of approximately $3.5 million. It has headquarters in Washington, D.C., and field audit offices in New York City, Chicago, and Houston.

ADDITIONAL READINGS

Multistate Tax Commission. *Federalism at Risk.* Washington, DC: Multistate Tax Commission, 2003a.

———. *Model Regulations, Statutes and Guidelines: Uniformity Recommendations to the States.* Washington, DC: Multistate Tax Commission, 2003b.

Cross-references: apportionment; fiscal federalism; income tax, corporate, state and local; retail sales tax, state and local; tax administration, state, private, and public cooperation in; unitary taxation.

National neutrality

Peggy B. Musgrave
University of California–Santa Cruz

A condition in which the tax treatment of foreign investment income by the residence country ensures that its national gain from foreign investment is maximized.

The foreign corporation income tax is treated as a cost of doing business abroad and allowed as a deduction from taxable income. The purpose is to provide equal, and therefore neutral, tax treatment to domestic investment income and that part of foreign investment income which may be said to accrue to the country of residency, that is, what is left over after foreign countries of source have taken their tax share. The economic significance of national neutrality is that it promotes a nationally (as distinct from internationally) efficient allocation of investment, where national efficiency is defined as a condition that promotes maximization of the residency county's national output or income (Feldstein and Hartman 1979).

Under the foreign tax regime of residency taxation with foreign tax credit, investors will find it in their interest to invest abroad until the net after-tax returns are equalized at home and abroad. This meets the goal of international efficiency in resource allocation, but not that of national efficiency. The reason is that the foreign tax part of the return on foreign investment does not accrue to the capital-exporting country, but is lost. Foreign investment is therefore carried too far (Musgrave and Musgrave 1989). The higher the foreign tax, the larger the national loss. This conflict with national efficiency is further magnified where the foreign tax credit regime encourages the capital-importing country to raise its tax in order to soak up the tax of the crediting country.

For national efficiency to be met, and the capital-exporting country's gain from foreign investment to be maximized, foreign investment should be carried to the point at which its return net of foreign tax equals the gross (before-tax) domestic return. The foreign tax is lost to the national income of the capital-exporting country and is dropped out. By permitting the foreign tax to be deducted from the investor's taxable income, the investing entity is induced to carry foreign investment to the point at which its net return equals the gross (before-tax) return on domestic investment. The system will no longer distort investment away from the national interest.

Tax treatment is rendered neutral with regard to the treatment of national gain from foreign and domestic investment.

This goal is not met under a regime of residence taxation where the foreign tax is credited rather than deducted. Investing entities will then find it in their interests to invest abroad until the gross (before-tax) returns are equalized at home and abroad, thus achieving capital export neutrality and international efficiency in capital allocation. At the same time, and seen from the perspective of national neutrality, this leaves foreign investment to be carried too far since the loss of foreign tax is not accounted for.

The deduction approach not only ranks ahead of the foreign tax credit with respect to national efficiency, but also has the further advantage of simplifying administration and compliance compared with the complexities presented by the foreign tax credit. At the same time, deductibility does not meet the same standard of international efficiency as does the crediting of foreign tax. A choice has to be made since both goals can only be met simultaneously as the foreign tax rate approaches zero.

ADDITIONAL READINGS

Feldstein, Martin S., and David Hartman. "The Optimal Taxation of Foreign Source Investment Income." *Quarterly Journal of Economics* 93 (November 1979): 589–612.

Musgrave, Peggy B. *Taxation of Foreign Investment Income: An Economic Analysis.* Baltimore, MD: Johns Hopkins Press, 1963.

———. *United States Taxation of Foreign Investment Income: Issues and Arguments.* Cambridge, MA: International Tax Program, Harvard Law School, 1969.

Musgrave, Richard A., and Peggy B. Musgrave. *Public Finance in Theory and Practice,* 5th ed. New York: McGraw-Hill, 1989.

Cross-references: capital export neutrality; capital import neutrality; foreign tax credit.

National Tax Association

Frederick Stocker
Ohio State University

Updated by
J. Fred Giertz
Institute of Government and Public Affairs, University of Illinois at Urbana-Champaign

An organization of tax professionals that fosters the study and dissemination of work relating to tax theory, practice, and policy as well as the study of broader public finance issues.

The National Tax Association (NTA) is an organization of tax professionals from academia, government, business, and consulting organizations that focuses on the understanding of complex tax and broader public finance issues through the exchange of information and research. It is the leading such organization in the United States and, arguably, the world.

NTA is a nonpolitical, nonpartisan 501(c)(3) organization that does not promote any particular programs or policies and encourages research and discussion from members with divergent viewpoints. The topics covered span the range from local to state to national to international issues as well as intergovernmental ones.

Membership in 2004 numbered more than 1,100 individuals, with academics and representatives from government comprising the two largest groups. In addition, there were more than 1,500 subscribers to the Association's *National Tax Journal*.

Under its bylaws, NTA is governed by a board of directors, made up of 15 elected members serving three-year terms plus the two immediate past presidents of the organization. There are also up to five nonvoting advisory board members. The officers consist of the president, two vice presidents (who are in line to become president), the secretary, and the treasurer. By tradition, the NTA board members and officers are balanced among the groups (academic, government, and business and consulting) that make up the association's membership. The executive director and other professional staff oversee the day-to-day operations of the Association. The NTA office is located in Washington, D.C., on 15th Street, NW, near the U.S. Treasury building.

History

The National Tax Association was founded in Columbus, Ohio, in 1907 by a group of the nation's leading professors of public finance, tax administrators, and corporate tax representatives. Unlike the non-advocacy approach of the current NTA, the main focus in the early days was on the reform of the "general" (property) tax, under which states sought, with notable lack of success, to apply a uniform (ad valorem) levy on all classes of property.

Over the years, the topics addressed by NTA members have broadened, reflecting evolution of the tax system. Income taxation generated considerable debate before and after adoption of the federal income tax in 1913. Corporate taxation and estate and inheritance taxation also received increasing attention. In the 1930s, state sales tax issues became prominent on the conference agenda. While NTA maintains its long-standing focus on tax issues, the range of topics has expanded in recent decades to include many public expenditure issues, including Social Security.

In 1972, NTA merged with the Tax Institute of America. Since then, the official name of the organization has been National Tax Association–Tax Institute of America. Still, the name National Tax Association, or NTA for short, is universally applied to the organization.

Publications

NTA's most important publication is the *National Tax Journal* (NTJ), a refereed journal founded in 1948. More than 2,600 copies of the NTJ are distributed to NTA members and other subscribers, including most major libraries around the world. With the cooperation of Tax Analysts, the NTJ is available in electronic form on the web. Access to the last two years of the NTJ is password-protected for members, while older issues are freely available.

The *National Tax Journal* is the premier scholarly journal in the field of taxation and public finance. While tax issues are the most numerous single subject, *Journal* articles focus on a wide range of topics in public finance theory, application, and policy. While many articles are technical in nature, brief non-technical summaries make essential analysis and conclusions available to a wide audience of those concerned with taxation. By discipline, economists make up the largest single group of contributors, but there are also articles by lawyers, accountants, and tax administrators.

In addition to refereed research papers, each issue of the NTJ contains a forum section with papers on a topic of current interest chosen by the editors. Recent forum topics have included the fiscal crisis of the states, corporate tax disclosure, innovations in education policy, environmental federalism, and health insurance in the United States. The September issue each year is devoted to edited versions of the papers presented at the NTA's Spring Symposium, dealing largely with issues of federal tax policy. In recent years, a number of special issues have dealt with topics of interest. The special issue in 2000 on the taxation of electronic commerce was the culmination of an NTA project on this subject that highlighted the new challenges to state and local sales taxes resulting from the Internet.

The NTJ was edited for many years by Daniel Holland of MIT. After his death in 1991, Joel Slemrod of the University of Michigan served as editor until 1998, when he was succeeded by Douglas Holtz-Eakin of Syracuse University. When Holtz-Eakin left for service at the Council of Economic Advisers and later as director of the Congressional Budget Office, Rosanne Altshuler of Rutgers University and Therese McGuire of Northwestern University became coeditors. The editorial office is located (as of 2004) at Northwestern University in Evanston, Illinois.

In addition to the NTJ, the papers presented at the association's annual conference are published in the *Proceedings of the Annual Conference on Taxation,* a fascinating archive of almost a century of American fiscal thought. The *Pro-*

ceedings have included important and influential papers, many on applied policy issues of taxation. NTA is also a cosponsor with the Urban Institute Press of *The Encyclopedia of Taxation and Tax Policy*. The editors of the encyclopedia are longtime members of the association.

Awards and recognitions

NTA's most prestigious award is the Daniel M. Holland Medal, presented to an NTA member for distinguished lifetime contributions to the study of the theory and practice of public finance. Since the award was first presented in 1993, the winners have included (through 2004) Carl Shoup, Richard Musgrave, George Break, Richard Goode, C. Lowell Harriss, Oliver Oldman, John Due, Arnold Harberger, Wallace Oates, Martin Feldstein, and Charles McLure. Three years before he became a Nobel Prize winner, long-time NTA member William Vickrey was made an honorary member of NTA. After his untimely death, NTA member Lowell Harriss accepted the Nobel Prize for Vickrey. Since 1970, NTA has also awarded prizes for the outstanding dissertations in the area of public finance. In recent years, the Musgrave Prize has been awarded each year to the author(s) of the NTJ article judged most outstanding.

Conferences and symposia

NTA's principal meeting is the Annual Conference on Taxation, which is held in a major U.S. city each year in November. At this conference, leading experts address topics of both current and long-term significance including federal, state, local, and international tax and other public finance issues. The conference is designed to bring out differing views, reflecting the diversity within the association's membership and the best of contemporary thought. The NTA's annual business meeting is held at the Annual Conference, at which the Holland Medal is awarded. Most presentations at the Annual Conference are published in the *Proceedings*.

NTA also sponsors an annual Spring Symposium in May or June each year in Washington, D.C. The Symposium has a general theme each year related to federal tax policy issues. There is also one session that focuses on state or local issues. Papers presented at the symposium are published in the September issue of the *National Tax Journal*. Beginning in 2003, an additional, optional program following the Spring Symposium has been held on a topic of importance in the state tax area.

NTA also works with other groups in organizing meetings. Since 1971, the association, in cooperation with Wichita State University, has conducted an annual workshop on the appraisal for ad valorem taxation of communications, energy, and transportation properties. This Wichita Workshop offers professional education to corporate and state government officials responsible for valuing these specialized properties for property tax purposes.

In addition to these three regular annual conferences, the NTA cosponsors occasional seminars on special topics in public finance, often in cooperation with other organizations. Recent topics have included sales taxation, taxation of business property, taxation of financial services, the taxation of electronic commerce, the fiscal crisis of the states, interdisciplinary research in taxation, and public disclosure of corporate tax information.

In keeping with its role for providing a neutral, evenhanded forum for learned examination and policy discussion of "cutting edge" issues in public finance, in 1996 the NTA established the Communications and Electronic Commerce Tax Project. Project members represented the broad spectrum of business and government interests concerned with the application of state and local taxes and fees to electronic commerce. Within this context, the project focused on state and local sales and use taxation of communications and electronic commerce, including gross receipts taxes that are functionally equivalent to sales and use taxes. The final report may be found at the NTA's web site (http://www.ntanet.org).

Membership in NTA is valuable to all tax professionals, whether their interests are theoretical or applied, or their employment is in academic or in the public or private sectors. More information about the organization, including membership and subscription procedures, is available at http://www. ntanet.org/. The NTA e-mail address is natltax@aol.com.

Nexus

Paul Mines
Multistate Tax Commission

For a government to levy a tax on an activity or entity, the taxing jurisdiction must demonstrate that the event to be taxed has a presence or connection in the jurisdiction. The question of what constitutes a sufficient connection—or taxable nexus—has created considerable economic, legal, and political controversy. Resolving the nexus question is of increasing importance to the states in an era of sales by catalogue/direct mail and electronic commerce.

Nexus describes whether a taxpayer, property, or activity has sufficient connection with a state to be subject to that state's taxing jurisdiction. The term today principally refers to federal constitutional limitations on state taxing power that emanate from a state's territorial boundaries and the free flow of interstate commerce. The U.S. Constitution's due process clause (minimum contacts and fairness) and commerce clause (contracts that ensure there is not an unreasonable burden on multijurisdictional commerce) define the outermost limit of a state's taxing power.

The most relevant discussion of federal constitutional nexus in these evolutionary times focuses on the commerce clause. The most impartial observation one can make is that federal constitutional nexus in 1998 is a controversial concept due to its *cliff* nature (nexus exists or not) and the tax consequences of finding nexus after the fact. Nexus issues in sales and use taxes raise a special problem—the potential imposition of a tax where the seller may have previously forgone any opportunity to be made economically whole from its customer. There are numerous unresolved nexus issues under the U.S. Constitution. These issues remain because of the political unwillingness of Congress to provide a bright-line legislative solution and the judicial restraint of the U.S. Supreme Court, which requires a maturation of each category of issue before providing a judicial resolution. All these aspects of nexus create more than the usual amount of tension associated with taxation in general.

Nexus also may be used to describe limitations in legislative enactments, including federal legislation enacted under the commerce power of Article I of the U.S. Constitution. Chief among these is PL 86-272, 73 STAT 55 (1959), codified at 15 USC § 381 et seq., which restricts the application of a "net income tax" where the taxpayer's connection to the taxing state is limited to certain specified circumstances. States also define by statute the limits of their own taxing power. State-defined legislative limits may be less than what the U.S. Constitution or federal statutes permit but may never exceed these limits.

Nexus also is suggested in the territorial limitation of formula apportionment of multijurisdictional income that is embodied in the U.S. Supreme Court's unitary business rule. This rule prohibits inclusion of business income in the preapportionment tax base of the taxing state unless the income is derived from a unitary business at least part of which is in the taxing state.

Analysis of nexus

The following is a possible analytical approach for determining nexus. The approach reflects the Multistate Tax Commission's unfinished uniformity project to develop a guideline on the federal constitutional limits on nexus for sales and use taxes and some special income tax nexus issues.

Use tax collection nexus

Nexus in the sales and use tax context can arise in the imposition of a sales tax, a use tax, and a use tax collection duty on an out-of-state seller. *National Bellas Hess, Inc. v. Department of Revenue,* 386 U.S. 753 (1967), and *Quill Corporation v. North Dakota,* 504 U.S. 298 (1992), deal only with the third area, although *Quill* suggests that its nexus principle may apply to sales and use taxes in general. *Quill* also reflects a tension between the Court's technical holding

and its descriptive language. The technical holding of *Quill* is an affirmation of the safe harbor of *Bellas Hess*—the commerce clause prohibits the imposition of a use tax collection duty if the out-of-state seller's only connection to the customers in the taxing state is through a common carrier or the U.S. mail. The U.S. Supreme Court describes this holding as a "physical presence" rule. Because a connection with the taxing state that exceeds the safe harbor would not necessarily constitute physical presence in all cases, there is an unresolved question of whether the Court uses the physical presence term descriptively or substantively. There is at least one way to resolve the tension: When the taxpayer is outside the safe harbor of *Bellas Hess* but not clearly within the physical presence realm, a use tax collection duty may be imposed, provided it does not unreasonably burden interstate commerce.

Meaning of physical presence

Assuming physical presence is a substantive term, what does it mean? Many practitioners apply their own textual understanding, suggesting, for example, that intangibles could never give rise to a physical presence. A textual understanding of *Quill's* physical presence term raises conceptual difficulty, however. As Professors Richard Pomp and Michael McIntyre (1996) have observed, typically, an out-of-state seller as a judicial person is never physically present in a taxing state. Only the *relationship* of this legal fiction we call a corporation to persons, property, or activities in the taxing state supports a finding of physical presence. Therefore, the determination of physical presence should focus on the out-of-state seller's relationship with employees, independent contractors and agents, property, and activities in the taxing state. The analysis should seek to determine (1) whether the relationship has sufficient substance to conclude that the out-of-state seller is for all practical purposes in the taxing state, and (2) if some of these substantive relationships that exceed the safe harbor of *Bellas Hess* are not physical, whether the imposition of a use tax collection duty would result in an unreasonable burden on interstate commerce.

Among the relationships that support a finding of physical presence under the commerce clause is the permanent posting of an employee in the taxing state, regardless of the duties assigned. The temporary presence of an employee is more problematic. If the temporary presence is associated with market enhancement activities, the relationship suggests physical presence; if not, then at least some instances (e.g., an executive giving a speech) probably would not constitute physical presence.

Use of independent contractors and agents raises an issue similar to the temporary presence of employees. If independent contractors and agents are engaged in market enhancement activities, including performing repairs to fulfill the out-of-state seller's warranty, that relationship should be sufficient for physical presence. Some business representatives have argued that independent contractors and agents must actually solicit before physical presence occurs. That reading of the U.S. Supreme Court's holdings seems unreasonably narrow. Additionally, using an independent contractor or agent as a substitute for the permanent presence of an employee (e.g., a leased employee who works full time under the control of the out-of-state seller), even though not involved in market enhancement activities, should be treated the same as the permanent presence of an employee in the taxing state.

Bellas Hess limited its safe harbor to contact by common carriers and U.S. mail. Extensive use of contract carriers raises the issue of whether an out-of-state seller using such a carrier has a representative in the taxing state engaged in market enhancement activities. To the extent a contract for delivery can properly be characterized as creating a representational relationship, there seems to be no sound reason not to apply the independent contractor and agent rules.

Some type of minimal presence may not support a finding of nexus. This raises the issue of properly stating a de minimis rule. The U.S. Supreme Court has clearly stated that a "slightest presence" will not support the imposition of a use tax collection duty. Additionally, taking a clue from the Supreme Court's view of PL 86-272, there is a sense that an inadvertent presence that does not reflect a conscious submission to the jurisdiction of the taxing state should also be protected under de minimis. A possible conclusion is that any presence reflecting a business decision to seek the market of the taxing state through a conscious presence is not de minimis. If this is true, then nexus should flow from a physical presence in the form of a very few sales trips into the taxing state for the purpose of fulfilling the business strategy of the out-of-state seller. The commerce clause statement of nexus is "substantial nexus," not "substantial physical presence."

Sales tax nexus

Nexus to impose a sales tax is different from nexus to impose a use tax collection duty. At a minimum, a sales tax may only be imposed by a state in which the sale occurs. See *Evco v. Jones,* 409 U.S. 91 (1972). Additionally, it is difficult to question the simple declarative statement that a state may impose its sales and use tax on any sale or use that occurs within the taxing state. See *Oklahoma Tax Commission v. Jefferson Lines, Inc.,* 514 U.S. 175 (1995). Yet some argue that jurisdiction does not attach unless the seller is also physically present through means other than the activity of the sale. This counterargument raises the issue of whether a sale or use can occur in a taxing state without the taxpayer thereby having sufficient connection to the taxing state for the transaction to be taxed. It is not clear that the counterargument can rely on the physical presence rule of *Quill* because that case, involving the imposition of a use tax collection duty, assumed the out-of-state seller had not sold or used property in the taxing state.

Constitutional concept of a sale

If the state where a sale occurs may impose a sales tax, the challenge becomes knowing what constitutes a sale in constitutional terms. The best understanding is that a constitutional sale of tangible goods finally occurs after there has been both transfer of title or possession and passage of risk of loss to the purchaser. See *McGoldrick v. Berwind-White Co.,* 309 U.S. 33 (1940) and Tribe (1988). Sale of a service or intangible property probably occurs after commencement of delivery (see *Oklahoma*). Regardless of one's reaction to these definitions, it is unlikely that the U.S. Supreme Court would view the bare transfer of title as defining a constitutional sale (see *McGoldrick*).

Income tax nexus

The income tax nexus issue drawing the most attention is whether *Quill,* a use tax collection duty case, also applies to income taxes. There is significant opposition, especially from the financial institutions industry that does not generally enjoy the benefit of PL 86-272, to recognizing nexus based on something other than physical presence or perhaps something even stricter. The case most often cited in this area is *Geoffrey, Inc. v. South Carolina Tax Commission,* 437 S.E. 2d 13 (S.C. 1993), *cert. denied,* 510 U.S. 992 (1993), holding that income tax nexus exists over a company that licensed a trademark in the state and derived income therefrom. The failure to accept that income tax nexus can be based on something less than *Quill* is puzzling to some observers. *Quill* itself may suggest that income tax nexus may well be a lower threshold: "Although in our cases subsequent to *Bellas Hess* and concerning other types of taxes we have not adopted a similar bright-line, physical-presence requirement, our reasoning in those cases does not compel that we now reject the rule that *Bellas Hess* established in the area of sales and use taxes" (504 U.S. at 317).

For those who argue that a relationship with intangibles cannot establish physical presence, *International Harvester Co. v. Wisconsin Department of Taxation,* 322 U.S. 435 (1944) is disquieting. In that case, the Court upheld under a due process challenge a dividends-paid withholding tax against nonresident shareholders. See also *Whitney v. Graves,* 299 U.S. 366 (1937). While some argue that due process nexus cases are irrelevant after *Quill,* it is difficult to accept that position when the Court reviewed its earlier due process cases in *Quill* to secure an understanding of its physical presence concept. In addition, the Court in *Quill* does not suggest that it is adopting anything new. And the administrative burden issue, a strong factor in *Quill,* is quite different for income taxes than for use tax collection. The number of income taxing jurisdictions is exponentially less, and there is more uniformity in income taxes. Further, the taxpayer is paying its own tax and not acting as a collection agent for the state. Therefore, if the taxpayer is wrong in its nexus determination, it pays its own tax and not its customer's tax.

Regardless of whether an income tax nexus standard is ultimately found to be less stringent, arguments that it is more stringent than *Quill* seem misplaced. But in one sense the nexus burden of imposing an income tax is different. The difference takes the form of the unitary business principle described above. There is no unitary business connection requirement for sales and use taxes because a sale or use must occur in the taxing state in order to be taxed. A more accurate description of the nexus requirements of a sales and use tax and an income tax is that they are different, because a sales tax is a transactional tax and the income tax is an operational tax.

ADDITIONAL READINGS

McLure, Charles E., Jr. "Implementing State Corporate Income Taxes in the Digital Age." *National Tax Journal* 53, no. 4 (2000): 1287–1305.

McLure, Charles E., Jr., and Walter Hellerstein. "Congressional Intervention in State Taxation: A Normative Analysis of Three Proposals." *State Tax Notes* (March 1, 2004): 721–35.

Pomp, Richard, and Michael McIntyre. "State Taxation of Mail-Order Sales of Computers after *Quill:* An Evaluation of MTC Bulletin 95-1." *State Tax Notes* 11 (1996): 177, 181.

Swain, John A. "Cybertaxation and the Commerce Clause: Entity Isolation or Affiliate Nexus?" *Southern California Law Review* 75, no. 2 (2002): 419–74.

———. "State Income Tax Jurisdiction: A Jurisprudential and Policy Perspective." *William and Mary Law Review* 45, no. 1 (2003): 319–94.

———. "State Sales and Use Tax Jurisdiction: An Economic Nexus Standard for the Twenty-First Century." *Georgia Law Review* 38, no. 1 (2003): 343–93.

Tribe, Laurence H. *American Constitutional Law.* 2nd ed. New York: Foundation Press, 1988, 447–48.

Nonprofit organizations, federal tax treatment of

Terry Knoepfle
Karen Froelich
North Dakota State University

Organizations that engage in charitable and other activities that are deemed to be socially meritorious may be exempt from certain taxes.

Changes to the federal tax laws and related changes in the financial accounting standards applied to tax-exempt organizations have permitted greater public scrutiny of the activities of public charities, but also have given charities the opportunity to position themselves better in the public eye.

Internal Revenue Code § 501 exempts dozens of different types of organizations from federal income taxation, including those formed and operated for charitable, religious, scientific, literary, or educational purposes, and those formed to engage in testing for public safety or preventing cruelty to animals or children [IRC §501(c)(3); Treas. Reg. §§ 1.501(a)-(1), 1.501(c)(3)-1(d)(1)]. The criteria for exemption under § 501(c)(3) are that (1) the organization is organized and oper-

ated exclusively for exempt purposes as defined by the Internal Revenue Code and regulations; (2) no part of the organization's net earnings inures or will inure to the benefit of any private shareholder or individual; and (3) the organization does not engage in activities a substantial part of which consist of carrying on propaganda or otherwise attempting to influence legislation, or of participating or intervening in any candidate's political campaign for office [IRC § 501(c)(3); Treas. Reg. § 1.501(c)(3)-1].

The Internal Revenue Code authorizes deductions for contributors to most organizations that meet the criteria for exemption [IRC §§ 107(c)(2) (income tax), 2522(a)(2) (gift tax), 2055(a)(2) (estate tax)]. Unless expressly excused from making the disclosure, a tax-exempt organization must specifically disclose to contributors what part of their contributions are or are not tax-deductible [IRC § 170(c), 6113].

An organization meeting Code § 501(c)(3)'s criteria (plus specific organizations enumerated elsewhere in § 501) may be variously referred to as a "not-for-profit," "nonprofit," "exempt," "public charity," or "nonbusiness" organization. An organization seeking tax-exempt status must apply for the exemption and submit and establish proof of its exempt character [Treas. Reg. § 1.501(a)-1; Form 1023 (Application for Recognition of Exemption under § 501(c)(3))]. The application and the documents supporting it are open to public inspection [Internal Revenue Service (IRS) Notice 92-28, 1992-1 C.B. 515 (June 22, 1992)].

Once an organization has been granted exempt status, it maintains that status unless its circumstances change substantially. Many organizations establish their continuing right to exempt status by filing an annual information return, usually IRS Form 990 [IRC § 6033; Treas. Reg. §§ 1.501(a)-1(d), 1.6033-2(g)]. Only about 30 percent of exempt organizations are required to file Form 990, because religious organizations, organizations with gross receipts that normally do not exceed $25,000 in each tax year, and certain other specified organizations are excused from filing. The Form 990, as discussed below, must be made available by the exempt organization to the public upon request.

If an organization's revenues inure to or benefit private individuals or shareholders, it loses its exempt status [Treas. Reg. § 1.501(c)(3)-1(c)(2)]. To stay tax-exempt, an organization must irrevocably and consistently dedicate its earnings and profits to its exempt purpose.

The private instrument or "excess benefits transaction" rule is applicable when the economic benefit provided by an exempt organization to a key employee or other "disqualified person" exceeds ordinary and necessary expenses as determined by the general fair-market value [IRC §§ 162, 4958]. Examples of prohibited transactions include compensation to an individual that is unreasonable in relation to the services performed, the payment of most forms of revenue-based incentive compensation, the payment of rentals or interest to such individuals at higher-than-market rates, and the payment of above-market prices for assets purchased from such individuals.

"Disqualified persons" include all persons in a position to exercise substantial influence over the organization's affairs, such as officers, key employees, large donors, their relatives, and entities in which the ownership interest of one of these persons is at least 35 percent [IRC § 4958(f)]. Sanctions available against these persons were increased by the 1996 Taxpayer Bill of Rights 2, in response to highly publicized scandals involving the misuse of assets by the United Way and other well-known exempt organizations [IRC § 4958; Taxpayer Bill of Rights 2, PL 104-168 (adopted July 30, 1996, and effective for transactions on and after September 14, 1995)].

Disqualified persons who are found to improperly benefit from an excess benefits transaction with an exempt organization, and managers within the organization who have abetted them, each now must pay a heavy excise tax (25 percent for the disqualified person, 10 percent for the manager) in addition to any income tax owed on the income [IRC § 4958(a)]. The disqualified person must also return the excess benefit. If the excess benefit is not repaid within a specified time, then the disqualified person is subject to an additional excise tax of 200 percent of the benefit received. This two-tiered set of excise taxes is referred to as "intermediate sanctions," because they fall short of the severe penalty of revoking an organization's tax-exempt status.

The Commissioner of Internal Revenue may impose the heavy, two-tier excise taxes and other sanctions on both the private individuals who benefited by an improper transaction and the officers and managers who allowed the organization's assets to be misused, without having to also resort to the harsh sanction of revoking the organization's exempt status. This gives the commissioner the flexibility to correct misuse of an organization's assets by a few individuals, without having to attack the status of an organization that on the whole is properly functioning as an exempt organization. Recently promulgated final regulations clarify statutory definitions and rules relating to excess-benefit transactions [67 FR 3076 (Jan. 23, 2002)]. These final regulations provide a safe harbor for organization managers who rely on written opinions about a transaction, based on the organization's full disclosure of the relevant facts, by attorneys, certified public accountants, or accounting firms with appropriate expertise [26 C.F.R. § 53-4958-1(d)(4)(iii)]. The regulations also provide that a manager's participation in a prohibited transaction is not deemed "knowing" if the elements of a rebuttable presumption of reasonableness are satisfied [26 C.F.R. §§ 53.4958-1(d)(4)(iii), 4958-6].

The 1996 statutory changes also tightened overall reporting requirements for exempt organizations. An exempt organization that has experienced excess benefits transactions must report, on Form 990, the nature of those transactions, the names of all individuals involved, and the excise taxes. The commissioner may require further disclosures by the disqualified persons [IRC § 4958].

An organization may operate a trade or business that primarily furthers its exempt purposes and still maintain its ex-

empt status [Treas. Reg. § 1.50(c)(3)-1(e)]. It may also own a taxable subsidiary without itself becoming taxable [Priv. Ltr. Rul. 9519057 (February 16, 1995)]. However, an exempt organization may be taxed on income from business enterprises not related to the purpose that supports its tax exemption. This is the "unrelated business income tax," or "UBIT," which applies to gross income, after deductions, derived from (1) the operation of a business enterprise unrelated to the organization's exempt purpose, and (2) rentals of property leased to others if the organization is carrying any indebtedness on the property related to its purchase, acquisition, or improvement. UBIT does not include activities in which the work is performed by volunteers or for the members' convenience, sales of donated merchandise, qualified public entertainment activities, some forms of passive income, or certain other specified activities [IRC §§ 501(b), 511–515]. UBIT activities must be separately reported on Form 990-T.

Similarly, the revenues of a "feeder" organization operated by an exempt organization primarily as a trade or business are taxable even if its profits are payable to the tax-exempt organization [IRC § 502; Treas. Reg. 1.50(a)-1]. On the other hand, an exempt organization's revenues are tax-exempt if its exclusive purpose is to hold property, collect the income from it, and turn over the entire net income after expenses to another exempt organization [IRC §§ 501(c)(2), 503; Treas. Reg. §§ 1.50(a)-1, 1.50(c)(2)-1].

The Internal Revenue Code tightly restricts lobbying and political contributions by exempt organizations. The Code contains several complex definitions of lobbying activities that are subject to different regulatory schemes, making compliance difficult to maintain. A recent Revenue Ruling discusses the tax consequences when an exempt organization engages in public advocacy [Rev. Ruling 2004-6, 2004-1 C.B. 328].

Generally speaking, a Section 501(c)(3) exempt organization will lose its tax-exempt status or be subjected to an excise tax if it participates or intervenes in any individual candidate's political campaign, or if a substantial part of its activities consist of lobbying efforts to influence legislation [IRC § 501(h); Treas. Reg. 1.50(h)-1]. For example, a bar association that rated judicial candidates lost its tax-exempt status as a charitable and educational organization [*Ass'n of the Bar of the City of N.Y. v. Comm'r,* 858 F.2d 876 (2d Cir. 1988), *cert. denied,* 490 U.S. 1030, 109 S. Ct. 1768 (1989)]. An organization that engages in such activities is considered an "action organization" [IRC § 501(c)(3); Treas. Reg. 1.50(c)(3)-1(c)(3)].

However, a public charity qualifying under § 501(c)(3) may make an election that allows it to make limited and "grass roots" lobbying expenditures [Form 5768 (Election for Lobbying Expenditures)]. The election allows an organization to make expenditures for lobbying within specified dollar limits, with any excess expenditures subjected to a 25 percent excise tax [IRC §§ 501(h)(4), 491(c); Treas. Reg. § 1.50(h)-1 to -2]. If an organization consistently has excess expenditures from year to year, it can lose the protection of this election [Treas. Reg. § 1-501(h)-3].

The federal tax-exempt status enjoyed by exempt organizations has implications beyond exemption from payment of taxes. Form 990, the annual information return, is a major source of financial information about the activities of exempt organizations. Members of the public, press, and regulatory agencies scrutinize Form 990s, together with an organization's annual reports and financial statements, for purposes of analyzing the organization's use of financial resources. They may look especially hard at the information on Form 990 reporting executive compensation, and at the figures showing the percentage of expenditures used to directly promote exempt purposes of the organization compared with its administrative expenses. Because of this scrutiny, Form 990s also have become a tool for organizations to present favorable program-related information to potential donors and other interested persons.

IRS Form 990 is a public document. Changes in the tax laws were designed to make Form 990 widely available. In the past, an exempt organization was merely required to keep a copy of its Form 990 available for inspection at its main offices. Now, an exempt organization must proactively make its information returns available to the public [IRC § 6104(e)(1)A; Taxpayer Bill of Rights 2, PL 104–168]. Currently, the IRS posts on the Internet the name of political organizations that file a notice with the Treasury Secretary, the name of the organization's contact person, his or her address, and e-mail address [IRC § 6104(a)(3)]. Public access to Form 990s filed by many nonprofit organizations is available at http://www.guidestar.org.

An exempt organization must mail its three most recent Form 990s to anyone who requests them. Requests made by mail must be fulfilled within 30 days. The organization may charge reasonable copying fees and postage. Its Form 990 must also be immediately available to anyone who requests it at the organization's main business offices during regular business hours and at every office where the organization has three or more employees. "Availability" includes copying the return and providing copies of related documents, such as the organization's Form 1023, if requested.

There are penalties for providing incomplete information or failing to provide copies of Form 990 upon request, including a $20 per day fine, up to $10,000 or 5 percent of the organization's gross receipts, with higher rates imposed on organizations with gross receipts above $1 million ($100 per day and $50,000 maximum) [IRC § 6652(c)(1)]. If the failure to provide copies is willful, a fine of $5000 for each failure is assessed [IRC § 6685].

One of the most significant changes in exempt-organization law was the revision of Form 990 in 1996 to reflect changes in financial accounting standards, in particular the changes made by the new Statement of Financial Accounting Standards 116 (Accounting for Contributions Received and Contributions Made) and 117 (Financial Statements of Not-for-Profit

Organizations). These Statements resulted in changes to Part IV of Form 990 (balance sheets), and the addition of new Parts IV-A (reconciliation of revenue per audited financial statements with revenue per return) and IV-B (reconciliation of expenses per audited financial statements with expenses per return).

Balance sheets must be filed with an organization's Form 990 and reconciled with the figures contained therein. Form 990 must include a complete listing of officers, directors, managers, and other highly compensated employees and the compensation paid to each, and report excess-benefits transaction information. The coordination of Form 990 with the financial documents required by the new accounting standards is less than perfect. Form 990 distorts some financial data that may be more accurately presented on the organization's annual financial statements.

Reporting under revenue categories such as government funding and program service fees seems particularly prone to distortion. Other areas where discrepancies arise between Form 990 and audited financial statements are total revenues, gross profits from sales, unrealized gains and losses on investments, treatment of donated services and use of facilities, total program expenses, and total salaries and wages. Thus, preparation of Form 990 in light of the new financial accounting standards, so that both present a consistent and accurate picture of financial status, is likely to be an ongoing challenge for exempt organizations.

Another challenge is the increase in IRS audits of exempt organizations. Among the issues raised in these audits are lobbying and political contributions by exempt organizations, inurements and private benefits resulting from extraordinary compensation arrangements and excessive executive compensation, the relationships between exempt organizations and related for-profit entities, various unrelated business income tax issues such as failure to report advertising income and the treatment of associate member dues, and the improper structuring of mailing list rentals [addressed by the Ninth Circuit in *Sierra Club Inc. v. Comm'r,* 86 F.3d 1526 (9th Cir. 1996)].

ADDITIONAL READINGS

Craig, Caroline K. "The Internet Brings 'Cyber Accountability' to the Nonprofit Sector." *Taxation of Exempts* 13 (September/October 2001): 82.

Froelich, Karen A. "The IRS 990 Return: Beyond the Internal Revenue Service." *Nonprofit Management and Leadership* (Winter 1997): 40–52.

Froelich, Karen A., and Terry W. Knoepfle. "Internal Revenue Service 990 Data: Fact or Fiction?" *Nonprofit and Voluntary Sector Quarterly* (March 1996): 40–52.

Froelich, Karen A., Terry W. Knoepfle, and Thomas H. Pollak. "Financial Measures in Nonprofit Organization Research: Comparing IRS 990 Return and Audited Financial Statement Data." *Nonprofit and Voluntary Sector Quarterly* (June 2000): 232–54.

Gordon, T., J. Greenlee, and D. Nitterhouse. "Tax-Exempt Organization Financial Data: Availability and Limitations." *Accounting Horizons* (June 1999): 227–99.

Hodges, Charles E., II, and Edward M. Manigault. "Political Activity and Lobbying by Charities: How Far Can It Go? What Are the Risks?" *Journal of Taxation* 93 (September 2000): 177.

Hodgkinson, Virginia A., Murray S. Weitzman, Stephen M. Noga, and Heather A. Gorski. *A Portrait of the Independent Sector: The Activities and Finances of Charitable Organizations.* Washington, DC: Independent Sector, 1993.

Kaufman, Pamela S. "Designing Executive Compensation in the Era of Intermediate Sanctions." *Taxation of Exempts* 13 (March/April 2002): 203.

Klapach, Joseph S. "Thou Shalt Not Politic: A Principled Approach to § 501(c)(3)'s Prohibition of Political Campaign Activity." *Cornell Law Rev.* 84, no. 504 (1999).

Monk, Harold J., Brenda Cline, Winford Paschall, Stephen Eason, Marilyn Patterson, and Martha Benson. *Guide to Preparing Nonprofit Financial Statements.* 3rd ed., Fort Worth, TX: Practitioners Publishing Company, 1996, chs. 1, 4, 5.

New York University. "Tax Exempt Organizations." *Proceedings of the Fifty-Fourth Institute on Federal Taxation* (1996) § 25.08, 2, 25-144-15-154.

Steinberg, Richard. "Nonprofit Organizations and the Market." In *The Nonprofit Sector: A Research Handbook,* edited by Walter W. Powell. New Haven, CT: Yale University Press, 1987.

Trussel, John. "Assessing Potential Accounting Manipulation: The Financial Characteristics of Charitable Organization with Higher than Expected Program-Spending Rations." *Nonprofit and Voluntary Sector Quarterly* (December 2003): 616–34.

Cross-references: nonprofit organizations, payments in lieu of taxes; low-income housing credit; state tax treatment of.

Nonprofit organizations, payments in lieu of taxes (PILOTs)

Evelyn Brody

Chicago-Kent College of Law, Illinois Institute of Technology

Payments made voluntarily by tax-exempt nonprofits as a substitute for property taxes.

For some nonprofit organizations, lying between the haven of property-tax exemption and the pain of fully taxable status is the shadowy realm of "payments in lieu of taxes," or PILOTs. These payments do not automatically favor either the municipality or the nonprofit organization. Nor, except in the rare case when a statute or global agreement regularizes the arrangement, are PILOTs necessarily consistent among nonprofit organizations in the jurisdiction. Rather, PILOTs represent a compromise between the parties using what leverage they have available and negotiating in light of the hazards of litigation. (See the public choice analysis in Sjoquist's commentary regarding Brody 2002.) As in any negotiation, either party could make the concession: In some cases, PILOTs represent an erosion of statutory tax exemption; in other cases, they forestall the imposition of tax, and so are synonymous with giveaways. In the battles fought in this realm, it is sometimes difficult to agree even on rhetoric: Charity partisans characterize PILOTs as "extortion," while municipality supporters term them "contributions."

Three features characterize the current property-tax exemption for nonprofits (which is generally limited to churches, schools, hospitals, arts organizations, and other charities that own their own property). First, the data, while sparse, suggest that charity exemptions constitute only a small fraction of total exemptions—the largest category of exempt property belongs to governments. Second, municipal demands for "voluntary" PILOTs occur only sporadically; and even where PILOT programs exist, they raise comparatively little revenue. Third, and seemingly paradoxically, the press treats the charity exemption as front-page news. However, averages mask the widely varying impact of exemptions on particular communities and of taxes or PILOTs on particular nonprofits (see chapter 4 of Brody 2002.) Finally, as charities engage in a wider range of activities—some indistinguishable from those engaged in by taxpaying entities (see Weisbrod 1998)—public support for exemption crumbles. Much to the nonprofit sector's consternation, tax exemption has come to be viewed as a subsidy granted by government, rather than an inherent entitlement of the organizational form.

From Boston's 1925 pioneering agreement with Harvard and MIT to Providence's 2003 arrangement with four local universities, PILOTs are only one mechanism to moderate the effects of property-tax exemption. (Compare the chapters by Leland, Glancey, Gallagher, and Youngman in Brody 2002.) Of long-standing practice, municipalities commonly charge user fees for specific services. However, user fees cannot recoup the general portion of the forgone tax, notably the amount paid for public schools. A few states allow municipal veto by placing certain types of charities in "local option" exemption categories. Most extremely, as nonprofit organizations become more commercial, property-tax exemptions have begun to be denied on an ad hoc basis, either for an individual charity or for a type of charity. These challenges succeed most frequently where state law requires that charitable organizations provide benefits to the poor and relieve the burdens of government.

Currently, the practices of challenging exemption or seeking PILOTs focus on hospitals, institutions of higher education, nursing homes, and retirement homes. After all, the charities that look most attractive to local governments are those (1) that have "income" (excluding, in general, only donations), and often compete with for-profit businesses, and (2) whose income comes primarily from patrons (or third-parties, such as private health insurers and Medicare) outside the taxing jurisdiction. Accordingly, taxing the nonprofit can be viewed as a proxy for taxing the nonresident payors. Under the same theory, municipalities could extend this policy to museums and performing arts organizations—and even to break-even social service nonprofits, thus adding taxes to the costs passed on to government funders (state and federal). Such a theory might provide a non-constitutional explanation of why municipalities have not sought to tax churches, which rely primarily on donations, and whose benefits are primarily local. Under this commerciality view, the property tax becomes almost an income tax.

Finally, we find a growing trend by center-city nonprofit property owners—notably universities—to pour funds into local community development, a form of "services in lieu of taxes" (SILOTs). For universities located in undesirable neighborhoods, this represents a reversal of their traditional siege mentality, and reflects, no doubt, some self-interest in the competition for young students.

Critics of PILOTs and SILOTs contend that public finance should not rely on voluntary, negotiated agreements carried out without sunshine and without the opportunity of the public (and charities) to monitor. Occurring haphazardly, and at times opportunistically, PILOTs highlight why an ideal tax system is visible, systematic, and evenhanded. Indeed, Leland's findings reveal that even in cities where some PILOTs are made, some city officials or other charities are unaware of them. Most generally, no uniform percentage-of-tax formula applies. PILOTs seem to be most acceptable to nonprofits when they apply only to new construction or to taxable property being taken off the rolls, and are time-limited.

As a separate issue, charities often produce positive externalities that spill over municipal boundaries, arguing for a state-level solution. Carbone and Brody (in Brody 2002) describe one such intergovernmental transfer system: Connecticut makes PILOTs to municipalities hosting private hospitals and colleges. (Under such a regime, state officials might need to take a more active role in assessing nonprofit exempt properties: Where no private party makes tax "co-payments," local governments might be tempted to overvalue this base.) However, while the state payments smooth town-gown relations, this program depends on annual legislative appropriation. Connecticut's scheme has been copied only (and not to the same degree) by neighboring Rhode Island. A similar proposal introduced in Maryland in January 2003 has not been enacted.

States might prefer to adopt more systemic reform of the property-tax treatment of charities (although in many states repeal of exemptions would require a constitutional amendment). (See Pomp's proposals in Brody 2002.) So far, though, charities have succeeded in fighting fundamental change (see Salomone's chapter in Brody 2002).

ADDITIONAL READINGS

Brody, Evelyn, ed. *Property-Tax Exemption for Charities: Mapping the Battlefield.* Washington, DC: Urban Institute Press, 2002.

Ebel, Robert D., and Joan E. Towles. *Payments In Lieu of Taxes on Federal Real Property.* Washington, DC: U.S. Advisory Commission on Intergovernmental Relations, 1981.

National Council of Nonprofit Associations. "Tool Kit: Facing Challenges to Property Tax Exemptions." Washington, DC: National Council of Nonprofit Associations, 2003.

Weisbrod, Burton A., ed. *To Profit or Not to Profit: The Commercial Transformation of the Nonprofit Sector.* Cambridge, U.K.: Cambridge University Press, 1998.

Cross-references: benefit principle; business location, taxation and; fiscal equalization; homestead exemption and credit programs; nonprofit organizations, federal tax treatment of; nonprofit organizations, state tax treatment of; property tax, real property, business; property tax, real property, residential; property tax assessment; tax abatement programs; tax reform, state; Tiebout model; user charges, federal; zoning, property taxes, and exactions.

Nonprofit organizations, state tax treatment of

John Mikesell
Indiana University

Relief from sales and use, property, and corporate income taxes that state and local governments provide for private charitable, religious, and educational nonprofit organizations.

Numerous private charitable, religious, and educational organizations provide services—hospital operation and healthcare delivery, assistance for the at-risk young and old, education and training, sponsorship of cultural events, aid to the poor, and so on—that would almost certainly become a state or local responsibility if not provided by a nonprofit organization. Several states also exempt hospitals, regardless of owner. In these instances, the loss of tax revenue may be justified as a way to encourage service provision without direct government involvement. The nonprofit organization may also provide a quality standard against which for-profit providers may be tested.

Nonprofit organizations fall into two groups. The older, philanthropic sector includes entities operating on donations, either from endowments (past gifts) or current gifts; sales income contributes a minor part of their finances. Commercial nonprofit organizations, now about two-thirds of all nonprofit organizations, receive virtually all their income from sales. Despite different financing, these two types of organizations share the basic distinction from proprietary firms: "No one owns the right to share in any profit or surplus of a nonprofit" (Weisbrod 1988, 14).

State and local tax policy toward these organizations is inconsistent, partly because governments have not fully adjusted to the commercial nonprofit sector, but partly because of "a larger debate on the appropriate roles for private, nonprofit, and public organizations—a debate about privatization that affects many industries all over the world" (Herzlinger and Krasker 1987, 93). Governments often encourage nongovernmental responses to social problems because they may be less bureaucratic and more sensitive to public wants. At the same time, those governments want to avoid unfair competition between nonprofit and proprietary providers. State and local tax systems have to balance the desire to encourage the nonprofit spirit and to use these organizations to relieve governmental service demands against the concern about unfair competition, especially as higher tax rates increase the advantage from exemption. In many cities, nonprofits (hospitals or universities) are the largest single employer and are inviting targets when government finances are tight, particularly when the largest source of revenue to the nonprofit is charges for services, not contributions.

State-local tax exemption is distinct from federal exemption; receiving federal exempt status is no guarantee of state or local exemption because each establishes its own system.

Sales and use taxation

Simple generalizations about how sales and use taxes treat nonprofit organizations, as sellers or as buyers, are impossible, either across states or by type of nonprofit organization (Mikesell 1992). Many nonprofit organizations provide services that are not taxed, regardless of seller, but some services are taxed, and nonprofit organizations sell some goods. Sales may be of (1) the core good or service, such as the services of a nonprofit hospital; (2) a good or service related to the core, such as prints in an art museum shop; or (3) an unrelated good or service sold as a fundraiser, such as Girl Scout cookies. State policy has been more directed toward the third category, although the first two are more important for the commercial nonprofit sector and promise to become even more significant as states broaden sales tax coverage to include services in addition to the traditional coverage of goods.

States traditionally exempt at least some nonprofit organizations, especially charitable, religious, and educational institutions, (1) on casual sales; (2) on sales during periodic fundraising events like fish fries, bean suppers, and similar regional favorites; and (3) on sales of seasonal fundraising items. (The entity may, however, be taxed on the purchase of supplies for these sales or of merchandise sold, or may need special registration for tax-exempt purchase. Some states have experienced political grief when, as they extended sales taxes to include "snack food," they found they had taxed Girl Scout cookies.) To provide no sales exemption at all is the exception. Many states extend the normal casual sales exemption with, for instance, a maximum number of days for the sales event, a ceiling on the price of items sold, or limits on total sales. Some states, including Arizona, Nevada, Missouri, and Vermont, exempt all sales by such entities. [*Swaggart Ministries v. California Board of Equalization* (110 S. Ct. 688) removed the concern that uniform and neutral application of the tax when the seller was a religious organization and the items were religious might be constitutionally prohibited.] A few states make exemption dependent on how proceeds are used—for example, if profits benefit schools or students—or on whether the organization competes with private business.

Nonprofit organizations purchase many taxable items, and no state provides them a global exemption. However, only California, Hawaii, Louisiana, South Carolina, and Washington provide no exemption for charitable, religious, or educational institutions or hospitals, the entities most often provided preferential treatment, and some specific organizations in even these states have purchase exemptions. About 20 states exempt purchases by virtually all those nonprofit organizations, mostly through exemption certificates. The major difference among them is whether the entity determines its own eligibility or whether there is a formal application process. Somewhat more than a dozen states exempt some of

but not all the charitable-religious-educational group, either by establishing the general classification that will be exempt (e.g., youth organizations) or by identifying an extensive list of entities that will be exempt (e.g., the Arkansas Poets Roundtable). There is little uniformity in the extent to which exempt entities may pass their exemption to contractors working for them (Healy and Klemm 1990).

Property taxation

All states exempt property held by some nonprofit organizations. Governments often require assessments of these properties, but few assessment officials attempt a serious valuation, preferring to devote their resources to tax-yielding properties. These exemptions, in common with those for sales and income taxes, are virtually always provided by state action, even though any property tax lost is predominantly from local government, in contrast with the other taxes. That can be a considerable policy problem, because the fiscal impact is not equally distributed across the state (Pfister 1976). Some universities and other nonprofits make payments in lieu of taxes (PILOTs), but no uniform systems relieve local fiscal burdens, and voluntary payments are both rare and seldom seen by recipients as fully adequate. Boston and communities in Pennsylvania are particularly aggressive in seeking PILOTs, but payments are modest and nonsystematic (Gallagher 2003).

Most states require that property be used primarily for an exempt purpose and that it benefit an indefinite nonexclusive class (Wellford and Gallagher 1988). Some states permit considerable nonexempt use of the property, but most constrain commercial activities on the property. One exception is Kentucky, which exempts property owned by the nonprofit organization regardless of use. The struggle to delimit exempt from taxable use is difficult, and there are few clear standards. Tensions are particularly great in operations of auxiliary enterprises and housing by educational institutions, although exemptions provided to fraternal organizations in some states cause similar problems. Most states have specific application procedures before the exemption can be granted; about half also require regular renewal (Balk 1971). Whether fees are associated with use of the exempt property is usually not relevant, although some states do limit fees to the cost of service or require some waiver for those unable to pay. No general standard for nonprofit organization exemption extends across property, sales, and corporate income tax laws, but property tax rules are the most independent of all.

Income taxation

To receive exemption from corporate income tax, the nonprofit organization may not distribute any profits to those in control of the organization. It is not required to be zero profit, but it must devote any return to its primary exempt purpose. Other conditions are not so simple. A nonprofit organization may earn income from gifts and investment of its resources, from activities related to its primary exempt purpose, and from unrelated business activity. Following the federal system, states and their local governments do not tax qualified nonprofit organizations on their income from gifts or investment of endowment, and they do not tax income from the primary exempt purpose, assuming those incomes are used appropriately. Income from activities not related to the purpose for which the organization was granted tax-exempt status—that is, not for the charitable or mutual benefit purposes of the organization—is taxed as "unrelated business income." Many nonprofit organizations use unrelated business activity to provide resources to subsidize their charitable activities. It is the activity, however, not how the profits are used or the status of the operating organization, that determines whether the profits will be taxed. Dividing organization operations between exempt and unrelated has proven administratively difficult.

Problems

Are the services provided by the nonprofit organization worth the lost tax revenue, and does the nonprofit receive an unfair competitive advantage over proprietary firms? Several argue that the property exemption permits uneconomic holdings of real property, especially by religious and educational institutions (Balk 1971; Pfister 1976). The strongest empirical evidence comes from the hospital industry, where government, proprietary, and nonprofit firms all operate. For instance, evidence shows the state market share of nonprofit hospitals is greater where exemption from state corporate income and local property taxes is more valuable—that is, where the tax rates are higher (Gulley and Santerre 1993). This is the clearest direct evidence to date that state and local tax exemptions make a competitive difference. If the commercial nonprofit sector continues its expected growth, state and local governments will find exemption systems established for the charitable nonprofit to be ever more strained by the commercial nonprofit sector.

ADDITIONAL READINGS

Balk, Alfred. *The Free List: Property without Taxes.* New York: Russell Sage Foundation, 1971.

Bennett, James, and Gabriel Rudney. "A Commerciality Test to Resolve the Commercial Nonprofit Issue." *Tax Notes,* September 14, 1987.

Brody, Evelyn, ed. *Property-Tax Exemption for Charities: Mapping the Battlefield.* Washington, DC: Urban Institute Press, 2002.

Gallagher, Janne G. "Sales Tax Exemptions for Charitable, Educational, and Religious Nonprofit Organizations." *Exempt Organization Tax Review* 7 (March 1993): 429–36.

———. "The Legal Structure of Property Tax Exemption for Charities." *Exempt Organization Tax Review* 40 (June 2003): 285–93.

Gulley, O. David, and Rexford E. Santerre. "The Effect of Tax Exemption on the Market Share of Nonprofit Hospitals." *National Tax Journal* 46 (December 1993): 477–86.

Healy, John C., and Kenneth D. Klemm. "Sales and Use Tax Implications for Construction Contractors." *Journal of State Taxation* 8, no. 4 (1990): 315–40.

Herzlinger, Regina E., and William S. Krasker. "Who Profits from Nonprofit?" *Harvard Business Review* 87 (January–February 1987): 93–106.

McDermott, Richard E., Gary C. Cornia, and Eugene Beck. "Property Tax Exemption for Nonprofit Hospitals." *Hospital and Health Services Administration* 34 (Winter 1989): 493–506.

Mikesell, John L. "Sales Taxation of Nonprofit Organization Purchases and Sales." In *Sales Taxation, Critical Issues in Policy and Administration,* edited by William F. Fox (121–130). Westport, CT: Praeger, 1992.

Pfister, Richard L. "A Reevaluation of the Justification for the Property Tax Exemption." *Public Finance Quarterly* 4 (October 1976): 431–52.

Steinberg, Richard. " 'Unfair' Competition by Nonprofits and Tax Policy." *National Tax Journal* 44 (September 1991): 351–64.

Weisbrod, Burton A. *The Nonprofit Economy.* Cambridge, MA: Harvard University Press, 1988.

———. *To Profit or Not to Profit: The Commercial Transformation of the Nonprofit Sector.* Cambridge, U.K.: Cambridge University Press, 1998.

Wellford, W. Harrison, and Janne G. Gallagher. *Unfair Competition? The Challenge to Charitable Tax Exemption.* Washington, DC: National Assembly of National Voluntary Health and Social Welfare Organizations, 1988.

Zimmerman, Dennis. "Nonprofit Organizations, Social Benefits, and Tax Policy." *National Tax Journal* 44 (September 1991): 341–49.

Cross-references: income tax, corporate, state and local; nonprofit organizations, federal tax treatment of; property tax, real property, business; retail sales tax, state and local.

O

Office of Tax Policy

Donald W. Kiefer
Department of the Treasury

Office in the Treasury Department charged with providing advice and analysis on matters of tax policy.

The Office of Tax Policy (OTP) assists the secretary in developing and implementing tax policies and programs; provides the official estimates of all government receipts for the president's budget, fiscal policy decisions, and Treasury cash management decisions; establishes policy criteria reflected in regulations and rulings, and, with the Internal Revenue Service, guides preparation of them to implement and administer the Internal Revenue Code; negotiates tax treaties for the United States and represents the United States in meetings and work of multilateral organizations dealing with tax policy matters; and provides economic and legal policy analysis to the secretary and other senior administration officials for domestic and international tax policy decisions.

In the early 1960s, the tax policy and research functions at Treasury were brought together under an assistant secretary for tax policy. The assistant secretary for tax policy is the senior advisor to the secretary of the Treasury for analyzing, developing, and implementing federal tax policies and programs. The assistant secretary is often called upon to testify before Congress, and to respond to communications from the congressional tax-writing and budget committees, other government agencies, individual members of Congress, foreign governments, and the public.

Under the assistant secretary for tax policy are the deputy assistant secretaries for tax policy, for tax analysis, for regulatory affairs, and for tax, trade, and tariff policy. The deputy assistant secretary for tax policy is the reporting authority for OTP's legal staffs—the Office of the Benefits Tax Counsel (responsible for pensions, employee benefits, and related matters), the Office of the International Tax Counsel (responsible for international issues including tax treaties), and the Office of the Tax Legislative Counsel (responsible for all other tax issues)—and assists in establishing and implementing the legislative goals of the OTP. The deputy assistant secretary for tax analysis is the reporting authority for the Office of Tax Analysis (OTA) and, along with the OTA director, assists in establishing and implementing the analytical research of the OTA, including its studies and reports.

The deputy assistant secretary for regulatory affairs provides management and oversight of OTP's administrative guidance projects. The Office is responsible for policy oversight of IRS revenue rulings and regulations and, working with the IRS Chief Counsel, publishes a priority guidance plan. The deputy assistant secretary for tax, trade, and tariff policy provides policy oversight for the Alcohol and Tobacco Tax and Trade Bureau and for issues regarding the department's Customs revenue functions.

The Office of Tax Analysis advises and assists the assistant secretary for tax policy and the deputies in developing, analyzing, and implementing tax policies and programs. The Office provides economic and policy analyses leading to development of the administration's tax proposals and assesses major congressional tax proposals.

OTA analyzes the effects of the existing tax law and alternative tax programs and prepares a variety of background papers, position papers, policy memoranda, and analytical reports on economic aspects of domestic and international tax policy. OTA is responsible for official administration estimates of all federal receipts included in the president's budget and mid-session review, and revenue estimates for actual and proposed tax legislation, earmarked revenue allocated to various trust funds, Treasury cash management decisions, and the tax expenditure budget. OTA staff members also engage in tax treaty negotiations with foreign governments and participate in meetings of international organizations.

OTA develops and operates several major microsimulation models and maintains large statistical databases to analyze the economic, distributional, and revenue effects of alternative tax proposals and tax systems. Many of the large microdata files used in OTA's models are developed from samples of tax returns prepared by the IRS Statistics of Income Division under the Office's direction.

OTA helps implement the administration of tax provisions by assisting the IRS in developing studies of tax compliance and taxpayer compliance burdens, developing and revising tax forms and, working with the Tax Legislative Counsel, International Tax Counsel, and Benefits Tax Counsel staffs, in formulating and reviewing tax regulations.

OTA is divided into five divisions: Business Taxation, Economic Modeling and Computer Applications, Individual Taxation, International Taxation, and Revenue Estimating.

Currently, the Office of Tax Policy contains about 100 economists, attorneys, and support staff. In the past few years, the

Office has prepared major studies on a wide range of topics including return-free tax systems, the tax treatment of credit unions compared with other depository institutions, credit union member business lending, the taxation of Social Security and railroad retirement benefits, the deferral of income earned through U.S.-controlled foreign corporations, tax benefits for adoption, taxpayer confidentiality and disclosure provisions, depreciation recovery periods and methods, penalty and interest provisions, and corporate tax shelters.

Offsetting collections and receipts

Pearl Richardson
Retired, Congressional Budget Office

Funds credited against federal budget outlays (expenditures).

Apart from the proceeds of borrowing, all collections flowing from the public to the federal government are classified in the budget as either offsets against outlays or governmental receipts (also known as "budget receipts" and "federal revenues"). Offsets against outlays include loan repayments, interest, miscellaneous recoveries and refunds, and a wide variety of fees. Governmental receipts generally consist of taxes, customs duties, and miscellaneous collections, including penalties and some fees. The general guidelines for assigning collections to the revenue or spending side of the budget are relatively straightforward (see below), but the terms are confusing and likely to vary with the user.

Offsets against outlays show up in the budget as either reimbursements to expenditure accounts or offsetting receipts.

Offsetting collections to appropriations

In some cases, the law specifies that a collection be offset within an expenditure account. Such collections are "reimbursements to appropriations." Reimbursements to appropriations are deposited as credits to the expenditure accounts that they finance and, in many cases, may be spent without further action by Congress. For example, under current law, the Postal Service may use collections from the sale of stamps to finance its operations without a requirement for annual appropriations. Depending on whether the funds originate from within or outside the government, budget documents identify reimbursements to appropriations as "offsetting collections from federal sources" (which includes trust and off-budget funds) or as "offsetting collections from nonfederal sources." Reimbursements to appropriations are frequently referred to simply as "offsetting collections," thus creating a confusion of terms.

Offsetting receipts

If the law does not specify that a collection be assigned to an expenditure account, it will go into a receipt account and be classified as an offset to budget outlays, not as a governmental receipt. Such collections are entitled "offsetting receipts," and if they come from outside the government, they are called "proprietary receipts from the public." Offsetting receipts, including proprietary receipts from the public, appear in the budget as negative outlays.

In brief, where a provision of law authorizes the offset to occur within an expenditure account, the collections are reimbursements to appropriations (either to discretionary or mandatory appropriations). All other offsetting collections are called offsetting receipts. Otherwise, there is no real difference between reimbursements to appropriations and offsetting receipts.

Budget classification guidelines

In 1967, a commission appointed by President Lyndon Johnson recommended guidelines on budget concepts, including the classification for budgetary purposes of funds flowing to the federal government. Among its many other recommendations were several dealing with when to offset collections against expenditures, and when to record them as governmental or budget receipts.

At the time the commission issued its report, the classification of a collection depended entirely upon provisions of law. Over the years, the classification of items had become inconsistent. To remedy the problem, the commission suggested that the nature of a collection should determine its classification. It recommended that collections associated with activities that operated as business-type enterprises or were market-oriented should be included as offsets to related expenditures. But collections from activities that were essentially governmental, involving regulation or compulsion, should be reported as receipts.

The commission distinguished between fees imposed primarily to channel the private demand for, and use of, valuable resources or materials owned by the government and taxes designed to raise revenues for the government or charges associated with the government's regulatory activities. The basis for the distinction was the commission's conviction that budget receipts should reflect the activities in which the government engages by virtue of its powers as a sovereign state.

In examining federal collections, the commission identified the following types as basically governmental and recommended that they be treated as budget receipts: income, excise, franchise, and employment taxes; customs receipts; social insurance premiums (the commission recommended classifying those social insurance collections arising from the government's sovereign powers as budget receipts and those arising from noncompulsory insurance activities as offsetting collections); payments of excess earnings of the Federal Reserve system to the Treasury; gifts and contributions; patent and copyright fees; judiciary fees; immigration, passport, and consular fees; and registration and filing fees associated with regulatory activities.

The commission recommended that the following types of collections be treated as offsets to expenditures: repayments of loans and advances; receipts of government enterprises and enterprise funds; charges for permits; hunting and grazing licenses and fees; interest, dividends, rents, and royalties; sales of products; sales of government property; and fees and charges for services and benefits of a voluntary character.

The commission's recommendations were applied administratively (by presidential direction) beginning with the budget for 1969. Thereafter, in principle, all collections except those arising from the sovereign powers of government were offset against outlays.

In practice, the commission's recommendations have generally served as a guide—at least to the extent that business-type fees are offsets against outlays and taxes are always budget receipts. Although the commission's guidelines remain in force today, provisions of law or administrative decisions are increasingly likely to intervene and lead to budget classifications that depart from the guidelines. Provisions of law always take precedence over guidelines.

Current practice

Since the mid-1980s, the dominant trend in budget classification has been to offset as many collections as possible against outlays, regardless of their nature. Thus, many collections that, based on the recommendations of the President's Commission on Budget Concepts, would be governmental receipts are now offsets against outlays. These collections consist primarily of compulsory fees for regulatory activities (see *user charges, federal*).

In the 1990s, legislation to reduce the deficit—in particular the Budget Enforcement Act of 1990—and rules within Congress governing the budget process have provided further incentives to levy fees and offset them against outlays. Increases in offsetting receipts or collections count as reductions in spending and thus provide a means for complying with spending limits or meeting budget reconciliation targets. In consequence, user charges have grown, and the practice of levying charges that may be similar to taxes and offsetting them against outlays has become increasingly common. The only measures that are exempt are provisions that actually amend the Internal Revenue Code, levy duties, or assess fines and penalties.

The Office of Management and Budget (OMB) has acknowledged the practice by describing some collections as "offsetting governmental collections" and others as "offsetting governmental receipts." In line with the recommendations of the Commission on Budget Concepts, OMB distinguishes between governmental receipts, which are collections from the public that result from the exercise of the sovereign powers of the government, and offsetting collections, which are derived from business-type transactions.

ADDITIONAL READING

Congressional Budget Office. *The Budget and Economic Outlook: 2006–2015.* Washington, DC: Congressional Budget Office, 2005.

Cross-reference: user charges, federal.

Optimal taxation
William M. Gentry
Williams College

A set of normative prescriptions for tax policy usually based on maximizing social welfare for a given revenue requirement.

Optimal tax theory addresses such questions as: Should the government use income or commodity taxes? Within commodity taxes, how should tax rates vary across commodities? How progressive should the tax system be?

Optimal tax theory encompasses a range of models that focus on particular aspects of the tax system. These different models share three features. First, each model specifies a set of feasible taxes for the government, such as commodity taxes, and the government's revenue needs. The models typically rule out lump-sum taxes, which would cause no economic distortion. Second, each model specifies how individuals and firms respond to taxes. That is, individuals have preferences about goods and leisure; firms have a given technology for producing goods; and individuals and firms interact in a given market structure (often perfect competition). Third, the government has an objective function for evaluating different configurations of taxes. In the simplest models, the government's objective is to minimize the excess burden generated by the tax system while raising a set amount of revenue. The more complicated models balance efficiency considerations with equity concerns. The models that include equity are usually more concerned with vertical equity rather than either horizontal equity or the benefit principle.

One of the oldest strands of the optimal tax literature is the optimal configuration of commodity tax rates. The basic question is whether uniform commodity tax rates—taxing all goods and services at the same rate—are optimal. This problem is commonly referred to as the Ramsey problem after the solution proposed by Frank Ramsey in his 1927 article. The short answer is that, abstracting from the collection costs of administering differentiated tax rates, uniform commodity taxes are rarely optimal.

The simplest version of the Ramsey problem is a static model (i.e., a one-period model without saving) with a representative consumer (alternatively, the model could have many consumers with the same demand functions). The government's objective is to raise a given amount of revenue while minimizing the distortions (excess burden) created by the tax system. This formulation minimizes economic distortion without concern for the fairness of the tax system. The feasible set of taxes includes flat rate taxes on different goods and services but excludes taxes on wage income. Uniform commodity taxes have the appeal of raising all prices by the same magnitude, and thus not distorting the relative prices of different goods. This simple intuition has two problems. First, it ignores the fact that commodity taxes cannot directly tax one especially important good: leisure. Second, it implicitly assumes that supply curves are perfectly elastic so that consumers bear the entire incidence of the taxes.

By maintaining the assumption that supply of all goods is perfectly elastic, Ramsey's solution to this problem yields an elegant rule: The optimal set of commodity taxes leads to an equal percentage reduction in the compensated (Hicksian) demands for all goods. (The compensated demand for a good is derived by fixing utility and calculating how demand changes with a change in price. The compensated demand functions capture the substitution effect of price changes without measuring the income effect.) Thus, rather than having each price change by an equal percentage as would be implied by uniform taxation, the optimal tax system has an equal percentage change in the quantities of each good. Corlett and Hague (1953) proposed an alternative interpretation of the Ramsey rule. They point out that the optimal tax rates on different goods depend upon the relationship between the demand for the good and leisure. The optimal configuration of commodity taxes has higher tax rates on complements to leisure and lower tax rates on complements to working. The intuition is that, because leisure is the untaxed good, taxing goods that are complementary to leisure implicitly taxes leisure.

Some of the many extensions to the Ramsey problem provide intuition about possible policy prescriptions. In the special case that demands for different goods are unrelated (i.e., the demand for one good does not depend on the price of other goods), the Ramsey rule simplifies to the "inverse-elasticity rule." The inverse-elasticity rule states that tax rates should be inversely proportional to their elasticity of demand. Goods for which demand is inelastic should have a high tax rate since changing their prices does not create much distortion. Conversely, the government should set lower tax rates on price-elastic goods since small price changes may create large distortions in the quantity demanded.

One criticism of the Ramsey solution, especially the special case of the inverse-elasticity rule, is that the solution may require higher taxes on necessities than on luxury goods since necessities often have relatively inelastic demands. Diamond (1975) extends the Ramsey problem to allow for households with different tastes and incorporates concerns for fairness among the different types of households. In Diamond's model, the government's social welfare function is a weighted average of the utilities of individual consumers. The social welfare weights for the households could depend on the well-being of the household, with higher weights for less-advantaged households. Incorporating fairness into the Ramsey problem modifies the basic result so that the percentage reduction in goods consumed heavily by the households favored by the government (often assumed to be the poorer households) is smaller than the percentage reduction in the goods consumed by households with lower weights in the social welfare function. Thus, equity can be introduced into the optimal commodity tax system by having higher taxes on the goods consumed predominantly by the rich. This result accords with the intuition behind many state governments exempting groceries from their sales tax bases: Because poor people spend a higher fraction of their income on groceries than rich people, excluding groceries from the sales tax base adds fairness to the tax system. This exemption is counter to the basic Ramsey rule because grocery demand is relatively price-inelastic.

Another branch of the optimal taxation literature addresses the optimal design of income (direct) taxes. As with optimal commodity taxation, the basic models are static, so they focus primarily on labor income rather than saving decisions or capital income. However, more recent models have added intertemporal saving and investment decisions.

Static models of optimal income taxation are of two types: linear and nonlinear (general) income taxes. Linear income tax systems have two parameters, a demogrant and a marginal tax rate. The demogrant can either be a lump-sum grant of money to each individual, in which case it provides a guaranteed income to each individual, or a lump-sum tax. The marginal tax rate on income distorts the labor supply decision and thus has an efficiency cost. By choosing both parameters, the government can simultaneously raise revenue and redistribute income across income groups. The optimal choice of parameters depends on how much revenue the government needs to raise; society's preferences for redistribution, as summarized by a social welfare function; how responsive individuals' labor supply decisions are to changes in the after-tax wage; and the distribution of pretax wages in the economy, which determines the inequality of the pretax income distribution. Stern (1976) provides examples suggesting that the optimal linear income tax is quite sensitive to these parameters, and even if society has an extreme aversion to inequality, the marginal income tax rate is less than 100 percent.

General, nonlinear income tax systems allow the marginal tax rate to change continuously with the level of income. As with linear income tax systems, the goal of a nonlinear tax system is to raise revenue (as evidenced by positive average tax rates) equitably while minimizing economic distortions created by nonzero marginal tax rates. The problem facing the government is that people have different innate ability levels that the tax authorities cannot observe. If the government could observe these ability levels, then it could levy nondistortionary individual-specific taxes on ability. As a proxy for taxing ability, the government taxes income but must recognize that the income tax gives people incentives to change how hard they work to escape taxation.

The degree of abstraction in models of optimal nonlinear income taxes has limited the policy relevance of their results. One often-cited result is that the marginal tax rate on the highest-income person (who has, presumably, the highest ability) is zero (see Seade 1977). The intuition behind this result is that a nonzero marginal tax rate distorts the labor supply of the highest-ability person. If this tax rate were changed to zero, the highest-ability person might work more, which would make that person better off (having the choice of whether to work more). However, government revenue would not change, because with a positive tax rate, this labor is not provided, and with a zero tax rate, the extra labor supply is not taxed. The logic of this argument applies only at the top of the income distribution, because changes in marginal tax rates below this level affect the taxes paid by people with higher incomes. Unfortunately, this result does not give any information about how high marginal tax rates should be just below the top of the income distribution. Also, from a practical standpoint, it is almost impossible to determine the "top" of the ability or income distribution.

As suggested from these results, the outcomes from optimal tax models depend on the set of possible taxes the government can implement. A long-standing debate surrounds the choice between indirect (e.g., commodity) and direct (e.g., income) taxation. That is, when the government can use both direct and indirect taxes, what is the optimal mix of taxes? Atkinson and Stiglitz (1980) show that commodity taxes are a relatively inefficient way of increasing the equity of a tax system that includes an optimally designed income tax. However, there may be administrative reasons for using indirect taxes.

One major consideration in designing an optimal tax system is how taxes interact with market imperfections. Externalities, such as pollution, are one example of a market imperfection that can affect optimal tax policy. Taxes on activities that create externalities can be one mechanism to reduce the economic inefficiency caused by externalities. For example, a tax on polluting may have the social benefit of reducing the level of pollution. Optimal tax models aimed at correcting externalities suggest that the optimal tax balances the marginal social damage from the externality with the marginal social benefit of the activity that generates the externality. The optimal tax does not necessarily eliminate the activity that generates the externality; for example, even with an optimal tax there may still be some pollution. For more on the corrective role of taxes in the case of externalities, see Baumol and Oates (1988).

While the optimal taxation literature is large and complex, there are several helpful reviews of the material. Rosen (2002) provides a useful introduction to the issues. Auerbach and Hines (2002), Stern (1987), and Stiglitz (1987) offer more technical summaries of optimal commodity and income taxation. Slemrod (1990) presents a critical review of the modern optimal tax literature and argues for including issues of administrative costs and compliance to the models.

ADDITIONAL READINGS

Atkinson, Anthony B., and Joseph E. Stiglitz. *Lectures on Public Economics.* New York: McGraw-Hill, 1980.
Auerbach, Alan J., and James R. Hines Jr. "Taxation and Economic Efficiency." In *Handbook of Public Economics,* vol. 3, edited by Alan Auerbach and Martin Feldstein (1347–1422). Amsterdam: North-Holland, 2002.
Baumol, William J., and Wallace E. Oates. *The Theory of Environmental Policy.* 2nd ed. New York: Cambridge University Press, 1988.

Corlett, W. J., and D. C. Hague. "Complementarity and the Excess Burden of Taxation." *Review of Economic Studies* 21 (1953): 21–30.
Diamond, Peter A. "A Many-Person Ramsey Rule." *Journal of Public Economics* 4 (1975): 335–42.
Mirlees, James A. "An Exploration in the Theory of Optimum Income Taxation." *Review of Economic Studies* 38 (1971): 175–208.
Ramsey, Frank P. "A Contribution to the Theory of Taxation." *Economic Journal* 37 (1927): 47–61.
Rosen, Harvey S. *Public Finance.* 6th ed. New York: McGraw-Hill Irwin, 2002.
Seade, Jesus K. "On the Shape of Optimal Tax Schedules." *Journal of Public Economics* 7 (1977): 203–36.
Slemrod, Joel. "Optimal Taxation and Optimal Tax Systems." *Journal of Economic Perspectives* 4 (Winter 1990): 157–78.
Stern, Nicholas H. "On the Specification of Models of Optimum Income Taxation." *Journal of Public Economics* 6 (July–August 1976): 123–62.
———. "The Theory of Optimal Commodity and Income Taxation: An Introduction." In *The Theory of Taxation for Developing Countries,* edited by David Newbery and Nicholas Stern (22–59). Oxford, U.K.: Oxford University Press, 1987.
Stiglitz, Joseph E. "Pareto Efficient and Optimal Taxation and the New Welfare Economics." In *Handbook of Public Economics 2,* edited by Alan Auerbach and Martin Feldstein (991–1042). Amsterdam: North-Holland, 1987.

Cross-references: elasticity, demand and supply; excess burden; labor supply, taxes and; saving, taxes and.

Origin principle

George Carlson
Deloitte & Touche LLP

A principle for taxing goods based on where they are produced rather than on where they are sold.

Under the origin principle of taxation, goods and services are taxed where they are produced or originate, rather than where they are purchased or consumed. Origin-basis treatment can be contrasted with the destination principle, under which goods and services are taxed where they are consumed. The term "origin principle" typically applies to taxes on goods and services such as sales, excise, or value-added taxes, rather than those on income. (A tax on income is normally levied under either the source or residence principle. The term "source principle" refers to the site of the activity generating the income, and "residence principle" to the residence or location of the recipient of the income.)

Consider the case of a sales or value-added tax in Country A. If goods and services are produced in Jurisdiction A (the origin) but sold in Jurisdiction B (the destination), the origin principle is implemented if Jurisdiction A applies no border tax adjustments to either imports or exports. Specifically, Jurisdiction A should not apply the tax to imports and should not rebate or "forgive" the tax on exports to Jurisdiction B. The effect of these so-called origin principle border tax adjustments is to ensure that all goods produced in Jurisdiction A (the origin jurisdiction) are taxed in Jurisdiction A regardless of where they are consumed. Thus, goods or services produced in Jurisdiction A but exported to Jurisdiction B are taxed by Jurisdiction A under the origin principle. (Jurisdiction B, of course, could decide to treat the product under either the origin principle [no tax] or the destination principle [impose tax].)

International tax and trading rules, established by the General Agreement on Tariffs and Trade (GATT), provide that the origin, but not the destination, principle can be applied to income or social insurance taxes. Thus, a direct tax (income, social insurance, etc.) cannot be applied to imports or rebated on exports under these international rules. Under the origin principle, direct taxes apply to all domestic production, regardless of where the good or service is sold or consumed. No adjustment is made, under the origin principle, for applying the tax to imports or relieving it on exports.

In countries with federal systems of government, such as the United States and Canada, subnational governmental entities may also be able to levy taxes. If so, the movement of goods and services among these subnational units of government requires choosing between the destination and origin principle. In the United States, for example, states tend to follow a destination principle method of taxation. Within a common market or economic union, however, the origin principle could be readily applied. Use of the origin principle, however, would require tax rates to be roughly similar across jurisdictions. Otherwise, the origin principle would tend to discourage economic activity in the high-tax locations or origins of production relative to low-tax jurisdictions.

The primary effect of the origin principle is to tax production, rather than consumption. All goods and services produced in the origin jurisdiction are taxed, provided they are not specifically exempted from the tax base. Many jurisdictions, for example, choose to exempt food, medicine, and other "necessities" from taxation for reasons of fairness and equity. These exemptions or preferences reflect policy judgments distinct from choice of applying the origin or destination principle. But provided a good or service is generally subject to taxation, the origin principle demands that the tax be levied only if the good or service was produced in the origin jurisdiction. Only the origin of the good or service is relevant in determining tax liability. Because the origin of a service (e.g., financial advice) can be less certain than that of a good (e.g., an automobile), it may be more difficult to apply the origin principle to some services than to goods.

A completely general tax applied uniformly to either the consumption or the production of all goods in an economy will not affect the allocation of resources. In an open economy, this implies that the choice of either origin or destination principle border tax adjustments is irrelevant to resource allocation. This result is explained in the Tinbergen Report, which was authorized by the European Coal and Steel Community, the forerunner of the European Economic Community. In particular, assuming a comprehensive tax applying to all products, the choice of either the destination or the origin principle will not affect the distribution of resources or the direction or extent of trade between the countries.

There is a monetary difference between the two principles in that a general tax imposed under the origin principle will initially worsen the country's trade balance, causing an offsetting devaluation in its currency, whereas a general tax imposed under the destination principle will have no trade balance repercussions. This is another way of saying that currency depreciation and destination principle border tax adjustments produce the same results. There is, however, a fiscal difference in that taxes are collected by the exporting country under the origin principle; no taxes are collected on imports by the jurisdiction following the origin principle.

The choice between the destination and origin principle, however, will have resource allocation and trade balance effects for a tax that does not apply uniformly to all commodities. Since a tax treated under the origin principle taxes goods (or services) where they are produced, a non-uniform tax imposed on the origin basis will alter production patterns. In particular, application of the origin principle will reduce production (and net exports) of any commodity that is taxed more heavily than average. Application of the origin principle, however, serves to increase production (and net exports) of any commodity taxed more lightly than average.

Cross-references: apportionment; border tax adjustments; destination principle; multinational corporations, taxation of; residence principle; value-added tax, state; value-added tax, federal.

Original issue and market discount
Ted Sims
Boston University

Since interest received is a form of taxable income, special tax issues arise when the nominal interest rate on an obligation differs from that of the market rate.

Between 1954 and 1984, income taxation of taxable debt underwent a transformation that acknowledged the importance of "discounted" or "present" values to income measurement. (See generally Canellos and Kleinbard 1983; Halperin 1986; and Sims 1992.) As a result, the U.S. income tax more consistently takes interest into account as it accrues. One major stimulus for these changes was the set of issues that arise when the interest rate explicitly provided for in a debt obligation differs from the prevailing market rate, referred to as "original issue discount" and "market" premium or discount. (Closely related problems involve the issuance of debt for property, now dealt with largely by Internal Revenue Code [IRC] § 1274, and the disassembly of debt into its constituent elements in so-called "coupon stripping" transactions, dealt with by IRC § 1286. See Canellos and Kleinbard 1983 and Kayle 1987.)

Debt

A debt obligation issued for money or property consists of a sequence of discrete (re)payments. Conventional debt, most typically a "coupon" bond, is usually issued for a specified "face" (or "stated principal") amount, with a "stated interest rate" and a finite maturity date. If the periodic (coupon) payments before maturity are at the prevailing rate of interest for obligations of comparable risk and maturity, the instrument's value will equal its stated principal amount. But there are other possibilities, of which two extreme versions are of interest. At one extreme, the "consol" (common in the United Kingdom but not the United States) has no maturity date but calls for an infinite stream of periodic payments. At the other, "pure discount" (or "zero-coupon") debt provides for a single repayment at maturity and no periodic payments before then. Between the extremes lies a continuum of types, including instruments whose payments before maturity, while greater than zero, are less than the interest that periodically accrues, and instruments that call for periodic payments in excess of the interest that accrues, with the excess applied to the amortization (reduction) of "principal." Whenever an instrument prescribes periodic payments that are less than accrued interest, the instrument will be valued at a discount to its stated principal amount. Conversely, when the prevailing market rate falls below the coupon interest rate, an instrument will typically be valued at a premium.

Income ("accretion") taxation of debt

Theoretically, proper income taxation of all these variants flows directly from Samuelson (1964), extended to uncertainty by Fane (1987). The value of debt will be invariant to the tax rates of its holder (issuer) if, and only if, in each period the holder includes in gross income (the issuer deducts in determining taxable income) the accrued change during that period in the instrument's value. The accrued change in value is given by exponential growth. (Samuelson 1964 dealt explicitly with "economic" depreciation, but it is easy to show that allowing economic depreciation is equivalent to taxing exponential accrual of value.) Proper taxation of debt that provides for current payment of interest accrued at a market rate has never been especially controversial. Since the amount accrued has also been paid, the issuer is simply allowed to deduct under IRC § 163(a) and the holder required to include under IRC § 61(a)(3) the interest "paid or incurred" in each period.

The rate of interest stated on a debt instrument may differ for any of several reasons from the prevailing market rate, however, and proper taxation then becomes more complex.

Original issue discount (IRC §§ 1271–73)

When such a discrepancy exists at the time of issue, it usually takes the form of a stated interest rate that is less than the prevailing market rate, and periodic payments of "stated interest" that are less than what would have been called for by a market rate (the extreme instance being the pure discount bond). Under such circumstances, the instrument's market value at issue will be less than its "stated principal amount."

The difference is denoted "original issue discount" (OID) by IRC § 1273(a).

As an economic matter, a discount bond changes value as interest accrues over time. Nevertheless, pre-1954 decisions like *Commissioner v. Caulkins* (1944) suggested that the holder should not be taxed until any accrued gain was technically "realized" under the predecessor of IRC § 1001(a) through either a sale in the market or surrender at maturity; and also that such gain, when realized, might be treated as favorably taxed long-term capital gain under IRC § 1222. (The history is recounted in more detail in several places, including Canellos and Kleinbard 1983, Garlock 2001, Lokken 1986, and Sims 1992.) In 1954, Congress provided that realized gain on debt was to be treated as ordinary income to the extent of any original issue discount [IRC § 1271(c)(2)(A)]. [The same treatment was subsequently applied to instruments issued before 1954 by the decision of the Supreme Court in *United States v. Midland-Ross Corporation* (1965).] Revisions in 1969 required that OID be periodically accrued, and included in the income of the holder and deducted by the issuer, using a ratable (or linear) methodology to determine how much was to be included each year [IRC § 1272(b); Income Tax Regs. § 1.163-4]. The 1969 revisions thus recognized that interest was accruing over time, but ignored the fact that it was accruing exponentially. In 1982, Congress finally amended the statute to require, as it now does, that OID be taken into account by holders and issuers using a discrete approximation of exponential accrual [IRC §§ 1272(a), 163(e)].

Specifically, for a debt instrument whose "stated redemption price at maturity" exceeds by more than a de minimis amount its actual "issue price," the statute requires a determination of the "yield to maturity," assuming at least annual compounding, that sets the "issue price" equal to the contractually prescribed subsequent payments. A portion of the aggregate OID is then required to be accrued for tax purposes in each "accrual period," which is typically six months but may be as long as one year, by both the holder and issuer. The portion taken into account is determined for the first period after issue as the product of the instrument's yield-to-maturity and its issue price. The issue price is then adjusted upward by the accrued OID, and the portion of the aggregate OID taken into account in the next accrual period is the product of the yield-to-maturity and the resulting "adjusted" issue price. (In each period, the accrued OID taken into account is reduced by any amount actually payable as interest, which is separately treated under IRC §§ 61 and 163.) This procedure is iterated to the point of surrender [IRC §§ 1273, 1272(a)(3)–(5), 163(e); Garlock 2001; Lokken 1986]. At the close of each accrual period, the holder's basis for determining gain or loss on any subsequent disposition is also adjusted upward by the amount of OID included in gross income during that period [IRC § 1272(d)(2)]. If an instrument subject to the OID rules changes hands in the midst of an accrual period, the OID accrued in that period is prorated on a daily basis between the transferor and transferee [IRC § 1272(a)(1) and (3)]. The procedures prescribed by IRC § 1272, consistently applied, set an instrument's adjusted issue price (and adjusted basis) equal to its stated redemption price by its stipulated maturity date.

While the incorporation of exponential accrual into the taxation of debt seems widely regarded as a salutary, if somewhat complex, development, these provisions have not been free of criticism. In particular, Bankman and Klein (1989) have pointed out that IRC § 1272(a) ignores the impact of the interest rate term structure, although it remains unclear how serious a set of distortions this deficiency produces (see Sims 1992 and Strnad 1995).

Market premium and discount

The market value of a debt instrument may vary from its unrepaid principal balance because of events that occur after issue, including changes in the creditworthiness of the issuer. More commonly, the value of debt will fluctuate with changes in the market rate of interest, declining with rises in the interest rate and conversely rising with declines. Consequently, when debt changes hands in a taxable transfer after issue but before surrender at maturity, it will usually be acquired at "market premium" to or a "market discount" from its unrepaid balance. Such premiums or discounts have the effect of adjusting the instrument's (market) yield-to-maturity to set it equal to the prevailing market interest rate. Theoretically, pure accrual taxation would appear to require exponential accrual of the premium or discount to the holder. The statute does not, however, generally so require.

Premium (IRC § 171)

In particular, the statute allows market premium to be ignored. IRC § 171(a) allows holders of debt acquired in the market at a price that exceeds the aggregate amounts (other than interest) repayable on the bond to amortize (deduct) the resulting premium over time, but only if the holder elects to do so under IRC § 171(c)(1). [The election, once made, applies to all bonds then held and subsequently acquired by the electing taxpayer, unless and until revoked with the consent of the authorities, IRC § 171(c)(2).] Until 1986, regulations under IRC § 171 generally provided for ratable amortization of the premium [Income Tax Regs. § 1.171-2(f)(2)(i)]. In 1986, however, in the wake of the general shift to compound interest methodologies legislated in 1982 and 1984, IRC § 171 was amended to require the use of a bond's market yield-to-maturity in the hands of its holder to determine the amount of premium to be amortized each year.

Discount (IRC §§ 1276–1278)

Even though original issue discount was required to be currently included in gross income as early as 1969, and determined using compound interest as of 1982, so-called "market" discount remained essentially untouched. Although market discount operates to increase the holder's yield, and is therefore essentially "interest," gain from the sale of an instrument

acquired in the market at a discount was not taxed until "realized" by sale or other disposition; and, if the instrument qualified under IRC § 1221 as a "capital asset" in the hands of its holder, it was eligible for preferential capital gains taxation.

In 1984, Congress acted to require that, on disposition at a gain of any debt instrument previously acquired in the market at a discount, to the extent it does not exceed the increase in the instrument's value over time resulting from the variable accrual of market discount, the gain be treated as ordinary income. The holder may, however, elect with respect to any market discount bond to treat the discount as accruing exponentially on the basis of the instrument's market yield-to-maturity as of the time it was acquired [IRC § 1276(b)(2)]. In addition, a separate election is available pursuant to which market discount on all market discount debt held by the electing taxpayer may be currently included in income using either of the methods prescribed by IRC § 1276(b).

Borrowing to buy market discount bonds

One way in which the pre-1984 treatment of market discount was exploited was by borrowing to purchase market discount bonds. The interest paid on the borrowing was deducted currently, while the return attributable to the accrual of the discount over time was taxed later, often as long-term capital gain. The recharacterization rule of IRC § 1276(a) forestalled the "conversion" of ordinary income into long-term capital gain using such arrangements, but it would have remained possible, despite IRC § 1276, to achieve deferral through approximately riskless debt-financed investments in market discount bonds. To curtail that remaining possibility, Congress simultaneously enacted IRC § 1277, which defers interest deductions in any year on debt (borrowing the formulation of IRC § 265) "incurred or continued" to "purchase or carry" market discount bonds, to the extent of any untaxed market discount that accrues during that year.

Interactions between original issue discount and market premium or discount

Instruments acquired at a market premium or discount may obviously include those originally issued at a discount. The 1982 and 1984 enactments deal specifically with these possibilities. If, for example, an OID instrument is subsequently acquired in the market at a premium to its "adjusted issue price," the statute, consistent with IRC § 171, permits the resulting "acquisition premium" to be deducted against the accruing OID [IRC § 1272(a)(7)]. Conversely, if such an instrument is subsequently acquired at a discount from the adjusted issue price, the amount of market discount subject to IRC § 1276(a) is limited to the difference between the adjusted issue price (rather than the redemption price at maturity) and the holder's acquisition cost [IRC § 1278(b)(2)(B) and (4)].

The principles outlined above were fashioned with the taxation of conventional debt in mind. Often, however, instruments are issued in a form that incorporates payments that are more contingent (as to the amount or timing) than the formally unqualified payments characteristic of conventional debt. The Treasury has addressed the problem of specializing the rules for the taxation of debt (including the OID rules) to "contingent" debt instruments in Income Tax Regs. § 1.1275-4. A principal feature of those regulations is the treatment of debt instruments with contingent payments issued for cash, using what the regulations denote a "non-contingent bond method" of taxation. Under that method a "comparable" yield to maturity is approximated and a "projected payment schedule" is constructed for a debt instrument with contingent payments. The holder and issuer are then taxed using the comparable yield-to-maturity according to the projected payment schedule, with subsequent adjustments to income as the contingencies are resolved.

ADDITIONAL READINGS

Bankman, Joseph, and William A. Klein. "Accurate Taxation of Long-Term Debt: Taking Into Account the Term Structure of Interest." *Tax Law Review* 44 (1989): 335.

Canellos, Peter C., and Edward D. Kleinbard. "The Miracle of Compound Interest: Interest Deferral and Discount after 1982." *Tax Law Review* 38 (1983): 565.

Fane, George. "Neutral Taxation under Uncertainty." *Journal of Public Economics* 33 (1987): 95–105.

Garlock, David C. *The Federal Income Taxation of Debt Instruments.* Englewood Cliffs, NJ: Prentice Hall Law and Business, 2001.

Halperin, Daniel I. "Interest in Disguise: Taxing the 'Time Value of Money.' " *Yale Law Journal* 95 (1986): 506.

Kayle, Bruce. "Where Has All the Income Gone? The Mysterious Relocation of Interest and Principal in Coupon Stripping and Related Transactions." *Virginia Tax Review* 7 (1987): 303.

Lokken, Lawrence. "The Time Value of Money Rules." *Tax Law Review* 42 (1986): 1.

Samuelson, Paul. "Tax Deductibility of Economic Depreciation to Insure Invariant Valuations." *Journal of Political Economy* 72 (December 1964): 604–6.

Sims, Theodore S. "Long Term Debt, the Term Structure of Interest and the Case for Accrual Taxation." *Tax Law Review* 47 (1992): 313.

Strnad, Jeff. "Taxation of Bonds: The Tax Trading Dimension." *Virginia Law Review* 81 (1995): 47.

Cross-references: interest deductibility; tax arbitrage; tax shelters.

Partnerships

George Mundstock

University of Miami School of Law

Taxation of an unincorporated association (but not a trust or estate) of individuals requiring a set of decision rules for assigning tax obligations of the owner or partner individuals.

The income tax policy issues presented by the partnership can be traced to the basic decision to respect the character of partnerships under nontax substantive partnership law. Historically, this law treated partnerships as complicated arrangements between partners, and not as legal entities. For example, partnerships could not own real property because only legal persons could own property, and a partnership was not a legal person. The modern trend in this law, however, has been toward reification. Partnerships now own all property in their own name. U.S. tax law had developed similarly, historically treating partnerships as merely a bundle of relationships (usually referred to as an "aggregate" approach) but increasingly treating partnerships as entities separate from their owners.

Current tax law's provisions for partnerships date back to 1954. At the time, most partnerships were service or family businesses with a small group of partners. The tax provisions were directed toward these types of partnership. Today, there are capital intensive partnerships with numerous partners. As articulated below, the current rules work particularly badly with these large partnerships. Even small partnerships can present difficult policy issues, however.

A partnership generally determines its taxable income (or loss) and credits as an entity, as if it were an individual. The partnership entity is not a taxpayer, however. The aggregate view results in a partnership's tax items flowing through to the partners as if earned directly by them. In other words, for purposes of determining and taxing most tax items, a partnership is a hybrid, pass-through entity. This presents two initial concerns. First, because corporations are generally taxed along with their shareholders, pass-through treatment subjects partnerships to only one level of taxation, whereas corporate income is taxed twice. It is difficult to justify this preference for the partnership form. Some argue, however, that the partnership regime, because it does not involve the double taxation of the corporate regime, is the more attractive

of the two (see *integration, corporate tax*). Second, pass-through treatment facilitates the use of partnerships as a vehicle for tax shelters (see *tax shelters*). Shelter promoters form a partnership and sell partnership interests to the investors seeking shelter. The partnership is particularly attractive for leveraged tax shelters, as a partner is allowed losses attributable to partnership borrowing, even nonrecourse borrowing. This means that a partner can receive losses as a consequence of the partnership investment that are well in excess of the partner's out-of-pocket investment (see *passive activity losses*).

The question arises as to what types of business organizations should qualify for this pass-through treatment. Limited partnerships (partnerships with one class of partners that are not liable for partnership debts) generally are taxed as partnerships. Limited partnerships (with active businesses) whose interests are traded in public markets are treated like corporations, however. Some believe that all limited partnerships resemble corporations and should be taxed accordingly. Limited partnerships historically were the preferred vehicle for tax shelters. Thus, taxable entity treatment of limited partnerships would restrict tax shelters as well. Recently, states have been enacting new vehicles called "limited liability companies." Limited liability companies resemble partnerships except that all shareholders (not just a limited class) are shielded from liability. These generally also are treated as partnerships for income tax purposes, presenting concerns analogous to those presented by limited partnerships.

Classifying a business entity as a corporation or partnership for tax purposes has been particularly troublesome for foreign entities. Current U.S. law makes it easy to create business organizations that are classified differently under U.S. and foreign tax law, facilitating tax-avoidance planning.

A difficult issue associated with pass-through treatment is how tax items are allocated among the partners. These problems build a case against pass-through treatment, because they do not arise if all income or loss is taxed to the partnership. This case is strongest with respect to partnerships with large numbers of partners or with complicated economic arrangements among the partners, because these partnerships present the most involved allocation difficulties.

Allocation problems arise in two situations. First, problems arise with tax items, such as accelerated depreciation and tax credits, for which there is no corresponding identifiable economic item treated separately for nontax purposes. In this case, there is no nontax point of reference from which the tax law can view an item. This makes allocation difficult. For example, consider a two-person services partnership, where one partner is a non–U.S. person who works primarily offshore. The partnership pays foreign taxes that would be fully creditable to the other, U.S. partner (so as to have no net cost after the U.S. foreign tax credit) but would be of limited tax benefit to the foreign partner. Should these taxes be allocated pro-rata or primarily to the foreign partner (who earns most of the foreign income)?

Second, even when a tax item corresponds to an economic item, allocation problems arise under some of the varied and complex economic arrangements allowed by flexible nontax partnership law. It can be quite difficult to determine the real present economic consequences of a current economic item. This can be seen in an example: Assume that two women form a partnership to acquire an office building and operate it for 15 years. They share revenues 50–50. The first partner puts up the cash used to purchase the building. The second partner agrees to pay all operating expenses (out of her pocket or out of her share of the revenues). How should (economic) depreciation on the building be allocated? At first glance, it would seem that the depreciation should go to the first partner, as she provided the cash for the building. On the other hand, the first partner has more than a building. The first partner has rights against the other partner for 15 years of operating expenses. In effect, the second partner is making a deferred capital contribution. So viewed, the second partner might be allocated some depreciation. In short, allocating even economic items can be quite difficult because the complex relationships involved in many partnerships make it difficult in a given year to measure how much a partner gets richer or poorer as a consequence of the partnership.

One solution to the allocation problem is to allow the partners to allocate tax items (benefits and burdens) as they see fit. Under such a regime, one can expect partners to allocate items to minimize their total tax. For example, the partners would allocate taxable income to low-bracket partners (such as partners with excess net operating losses) and allocate tax-free income, deductions, and credits to high-bracket partners. Such a regime is a form of free transferability of tax benefits. Congress generally rejects transferability, as in safe-harbor leasing and in acquisitions of corporations with net operating losses. This rejection prevents unintended tax benefits. With partnerships, however, tax benefit transfers are possible under current law.

The sale of a partnership interest by a partner presents two policy issues. First, the character (capital or ordinary) of any gain (or loss) must be determined (see *capital gains taxation*). An entity view suggests that the gain should be capital. If the partnership owns property whose sale would result in ordinary income, an aggregate approach concludes that the selling partner is selling his share of the ordinary income asset and should be taxed on his share of the underlying ordinary income. Current law strikes an awkward compromise. Second, the consequences of the sale of a partnership interest on

the future taxation of partnership income must be determined. An entity perspective shows no consequences, as the partnership itself is not a party to the sale of the partnership interest. An aggregate view sees a sale of a pro-rata share of the partnership's assets by the selling partner to the buyer, so that the buyer gets a new cost basis in her share of the partnership's assets. Current law allows the partnership to elect aggregate treatment. However, aggregate treatment is unwieldy when applied to a partnership where numerous partnership interests change hands frequently.

The difference between aggregate and entity approaches here can be illustrated with an example: A partnership's principal asset when a partnership interest is sold is appreciated land. Later, the partnership sells the property. Under an entity approach, the amount of gain to the partnership upon the later sale is the difference between the amount realized by and the cost to the partnership. This gain is allocated among the partners. If the property had been owned directly by the partners (the aggregate view), the total gain would be smaller. Each co-owner (partner) would determine gain by comparing his share of the sale price to his cost. In the case of the new co-owner, her cost would be higher than that of the former owner from whom she bought her interest, because the partnership's property appreciated from when it was acquired by the partnership to when the selling partner sold his interest. This results in less gain than if the new co-owner's gain was measured using the old cost. Yet, in the partnership entity regime, the old low cost, not the real high cost of the new co-owner, is used in determining the partnership's gain. In other words, the selling partner paid tax on gain in an amount equal to the difference between his cost and the new cost paid by the new partner. The aggregate approach prevents taxing this gain again when the underlying property is sold.

In many important situations, current law is more generous than either entity or aggregate treatment. The clearest example is a partner transferring property to her partnership. Under the entity approach, this is a taxable exchange of property for a partnership interest. The entity approach views the contribution as the contributing partner exchanging most of her transferred property for interests in the other partners' partnership assets. Current law adopts a hybrid approach that views the transfer as a nontaxable mere change in form. Under this hybrid approach, to prevent tax avoidance, unrealized gain or loss in the contributed property must be taxed later. Because this gain or loss actually occurred while the property was owned by the contributing partner, these items should be allocated to the contributing partner (to prevent tax benefit transfers). Current law goes partly toward this result. Similar problems are presented whenever the partners' rights to specific partnership assets shift, including as a consequence of a non-pro-rata distribution.

In conclusion, the evolution of tax policy thinking and in the use of entities classified as partnerships for U.S. tax purposes has rendered current law rules inadequate. Wholesale reform is badly needed.

ADDITIONAL READINGS

McKee, William S., William F. Nelson, and Robert L. Whitmire. *Federal Taxation of Partnerships and Partners.* 2nd ed. 2 vols. Boston: Warren, Gorham, & Lamont, 1990.

Mundstock, George. *A Unified Approach to Subchapters K and S.* St. Paul, MN: West Group, 2002.

Willis, Arthur B., John S. Pennell, and Philip F. Postlewaite. *Partnership Taxation.* 2 vols. Colorado Springs: Shepards/McGraw-Hill, Inc., 1989.

Cross-references: capital gains taxation; passive activity losses; proprietorships; tax shelters.

Passive activity losses

Bradford L. Ferguson
Retired; former partner, Sidley and Austin, Chicago, and previously with the Treasury Department

Frederick W. Hickman
Retired; former partner, Hopkins and Sutter, Chicago, and previously with the Treasury Department

A defined term in Section 469 of the Internal Revenue Code of 1986, introduced by the Tax Reform Act of 1986 for the purpose of limiting "tax shelter" activity and raising revenue.

The statutory term "passive activity" was intended to encompass investments generally regarded as "tax shelters"—that is, investments in business assets by an investor with little or no personal participation in the business—designed to initially generate tax losses or tax credits that can be used to reduce tax liabilities on the investor's income from other sources.

The passive activity loss (PAL) provisions apply to taxpayers other than broadly held corporations. They identify a "basket" consisting of items of income from "passive activities" (excluding portfolio income—i.e., interest, dividends, and other investment income not derived in the ordinary course of a trade or business) and items of deduction and credit deemed to relate to that income. If there is net income in the basket, it is added to the taxpayer's other income. But if there is net loss in the basket, it is "disallowed": It may not be used to reduce the taxpayer's other income, except to the extent attributable to final dispositions of property accounted for within the basket. Disallowed PALs may be carried forward to offset any net income in the basket in future years. Tax credits, if any, that relate to income in the basket may be used only to offset tax liability deemed attributable to income from the basket.

The loss limitation turns neither on the nature of the activity nor on the loss-creating deductions or credits, but on whether the taxpayer is "passive" with the "activity." If the taxpayer is deemed sufficiently engaged in the activity, the net losses or credits from it are unaffected by the limitations, although they reduce (i.e., "shelter") tax on the taxpayer's income from other sources.

To understand the design of the PAL provisions, it is necessary to understand the principal loss-producing deductions and credits involved in tax shelters.

One or more of the deductions for interest, for depreciation, and for the current expensing of costs that relate to future income are likely to be involved in an investment in business assets. Those deductions are likely to produce a net loss for a given investment project in its early years, either because the deductions are skewed toward the front end of the project life, or because the natural pattern of project revenue is skewed toward the back end, or both. The net loss shelters other income from tax, producing positive cash flow in the form of a reduction in the taxes that would otherwise be paid. The benefit is a "timing" benefit: The deducted costs are legitimate, deductible costs, and the "shelter" is a function of the timing of the deduction. While that tax reduction attributable to taking larger deductions in early years is offset by a corresponding increase in tax from taking smaller deductions in later years, the net result is equivalent to a non-interest-bearing loan from the Treasury. It reduces the private financing required and confers an economic benefit that reduces the taxpayer's project cost.

The principal tax credits affected are the credits for rehabilitation of buildings, low-income housing, and research and development. (The larger investment tax credit was repealed in 1986.) Because a credit produces a permanent tax reduction, and not just a timing reduction accompanied by a corresponding tax increase later, each dollar of credit produces a larger reduction in project cost than a dollar of tax reduction, which is equivalent to a non-interest-bearing loan. The tax credits and many of the depreciation and expensing provisions involved were intended by Congress to produce the described tax shelter benefits and thus to be an "incentive" for businesses to invest. The interest deduction is an exception: it does not provide an overall incentive to investment because, unlike the depreciation and expensing deductions, it does not reduce the total amount of income in the tax base, either temporarily or permanently. Every deducted interest payment creates an equal and offsetting item of income for the recipient. But the interest deduction may nonetheless create a net loss from the project for the investing taxpayer in periods when the project's gross income is small.

In the 1970s and 1980s, financing business assets by syndicating tax shelters was widespread. Investors were offered the opportunity to acquire ownership of all or a portion of the asset (directly or through partnerships), receive income from the business that used it, and become entitled to the interest, depreciation, expensing deductions, and tax credits that accrue to "owners" of business assets, without participating personally in the operation of the business using the asset. The tax shelter vehicle permitted full use of the deductions and credits attributable to the investment in instances where the business-user, if also the owner, could not have fully used them. Further, as long as the marginal tax rate of the owner-investor was higher than that of the business-user (before 1982 the top individual rate was 70 percent and the top corporate rate less than 50 percent), the arrangement permitted a shift of deductions to a higher-rate bracket without an offsetting shift of income. After the top rate for individuals dropped to 50 percent in 1982, the potential for significant "bracket shifting" disappeared, except in those situations where the business-user has net losses and thus a marginal rate of zero.

There is no persuasive evidence that the tax incentives described produce higher returns on investment, either for user-investors or for tax shelter investors, because the tax reductions represent reductions in investment cost and, like other generally applicable reductions in investment cost, translate into lower output prices. The hoped-for increase in investment and business activity created by tax "incentives," whether or not in tax shelters, occurs if lower output prices elicit larger demand. Nonetheless, unsophisticated tax shelter investors often believed there was an advantage in taking investment return in the form of reductions in tax on their other income, notwithstanding that investments that reduced taxable income in early years produced commensurately higher taxable income in later years, that many such investments were ultimately unsuccessful, and that virtually all were illiquid. The real advantage to the tax shelter investor—if any—was in the opportunity to make higher-risk, illiquid, business investments that produced commensurately higher returns if successful, and to finance a portion of the investment "automatically" with reductions in tax on other income.

The growth of a market that enables individuals to participate in an expanded variety of business investments and that indirectly makes existing tax incentives more universally available to all operating businesses (rather than only to those businesses that can use them directly and immediately) seems generally desirable. On the other hand, extending investment opportunities heavily laden with tax incentives to less sophisticated investors had some undesirable side effects. There were inevitably abuses that required audit surveillance (as where inflated asset values or essentially nonexistent assets were used to produce inflated depreciation deductions). There were also instances in which the illusory lure of "tax advantage" and the lessened financing requirements permitted promoters to raise financing from unsophisticated tax shelter investors for projects that non–tax shelter owner-investors using the same tax deductions and credits would not find economic.

However, the chief problem with tax shelters—the problem that most concerned Congress and gave rise to the PAL provisions—was the "appearance" problem. Tax shelter investment packages very visibly produced, in some periods, deductions and credits that individual taxpayers used to reduce their tax on other income. A large segment of the public had been educated to an awareness of that fact and had been exhorted to view it as favoritism to high-income taxpayers. This public perception, justified or not, was seen as corroding public trust in the fairness of the tax system.

The PAL provisions were accordingly tailored to address only taxpayers who visibly used loss deductions and credits

from particular investments to shelter "other" income. But if an investment asset is part of a larger activity in which the investor is sufficiently active, the same deductions and credits can continue to shelter not only the investor's income from that activity but any other income.

The aim of the 1986 Tax Reform Act was to broaden the income tax base, use the revenues generated to reduce tax rates, and keep the act "revenue neutral." If the PAL provisions had been limited to property involved in tax shelter transactions entered into after 1986, the revenue gain would have been modest. The PAL provisions were accordingly made applicable—with some transitional relief—to preexisting investments, rendering many of them uneconomic but allowing the official revenue estimates to show a large revenue gain that could be "spent" on tax rate reductions. Investors reacted by restructuring their investments to generate "passive activity income" in the basket sufficient to absorb the disallowed PALs.

Tax shelter transactions dried up after 1986. The 1982 and 1986 reductions in tax rates, the repeal of the investment tax credit, and the revised limitations on deductions for depreciation, expensing, and interest all lessened the degree of "shelter" provided by such transactions and may have dried them up in any event. However, the PAL rules are widely credited with administering the coup de grace.

While the PAL provisions appear simple conceptually, they are extraordinarily complex in application. Taxpayers plan, primarily, to avoid having PALs, and, secondarily, if PALs cannot be avoided, to have sufficient passive activity gross income to absorb them. There is no simple test for what is deemed "passive." Characterization depends on the nature of the activity and the hours spent by the taxpayer, with different requirements in different contexts. The degree of investor participation is largely irrelevant in a few cases: Virtually all ordinary rental activities are deemed passive, and virtually all "working interests" in oil and gas investments are deemed not passive.

Elaborate regulations contain numerous exceptions and "recharacterization" rules intended to prevent taxpayers' burying inappropriate nonpassive items in passive activities, or inappropriate passive activity items in nonpassive activities. Perhaps the critical regulations are those relating to the definition of an "activity," for items may be "passive" if included in one activity but "active" if included in another, or activities may be converted from active to passive, or vice versa, if specific activities or functions are included or excluded. By paring or adding, aggregating or disaggregating specific activities or functions—all in a context in which the potential permutations are legion—passive items can be converted from passive to active or vice versa. While the taxpayer is given much flexibility, detailed planning and analysis is typically required.

The extraordinary complexity of the PAL rules does, ironically, achieve a kind of simplification. The difficulties in planning for investments that will fall under the rules is so great that taxpayers simply avoid them.

The PAL provisions stand as still another example of how the income tax system becomes barnacled with complexity (and is seldom scraped clean) as political goals are compromised, ad hoc, in the legislative process.

ADDITIONAL READINGS

Auerbach, Alan J., William G. Gale, and Peter Orszag. "The Budget Outlook and Options for Fiscal Policy." Washington, DC: Brookings Institution, 2002.

Burman, Leonard E., Alan J. Auerbach, and Jonathan M. Siegel. "Capital Gains Taxation and Tax Avoidance: New Evidence from Panel Data." In *Does Atlas Shrug? The Economic Consequences of Taxing the Rich,* edited by Joel B. Slemrod. Cambridge, MA: Harvard University Press, 1997.

Carasso, Adam, and C. Eugene Steuerle. "Tax Expenditures: Revenue Loss Versus Outlay Equivalents." *Tax Notes* 30, no. 2 (October 13, 2003): 287.

Cross-references: partnerships; tax shelters.

Payroll tax, federal

Edward W. Harris
Congressional Budget Office

A group of taxes levied on the earnings of employees and self-employed persons.

Payroll taxes have grown substantially in past decades and are now the second largest source of federal revenues. As a share of total receipts, payroll taxes increased from 10 percent in 1937 to 40 percent in 2003. Over the same period, payroll taxes grew from 1 percent to almost 7 percent of gross domestic product.

Components of federal payroll taxes

Federal payroll taxes, or social insurance contributions, consist of tax revenues from Social Security, Medicare hospital insurance, unemployment insurance, railroad retirement, and other retirements. Social Security makes up the lion's share of federal payroll taxes—73 percent of the $713 billion collected in 2003. Medicare, the second largest component, makes up 21 percent of payroll tax revenues. The remaining revenue is divided between unemployment insurance (5 percent), railroad retirement (less than 1 percent), and other retirements (less than 1 percent).

Social Security

Social Security (OASDI, or Old Age, Survivors, and Disability Insurance) began in the late 1930s as a mandatory old-age insurance program for most employees in the private sector. Over time, the program was expanded to include disability insurance and mandatory coverage for almost all workers.

The Social Security Act of 1935 provided monthly benefits to retired workers covered by Social Security. In 1939, benefits were extended to the dependents and survivors of covered workers. The program was further expanded to provide disability insurance to covered workers and their dependents in 1956 and 1958, respectively.

Even in its infancy, coverage under Social Security was broad. All workers in commerce and industry—except railroad workers, who had their own retirement plan—were originally covered under Social Security. Beginning in the 1950s, coverage was expanded to include most workers in the private sector not originally covered. Participation was mandatory for some, such as farm and domestic workers and self-employed persons, and elective for others, such as nonprofit workers, state and local government workers, and employees of religious bodies. Additional legislation in the mid-1980s expanded coverage to federal workers hired after 1983 and mandated coverage for employees of nonprofit organizations. In 2002, about 96 percent of all jobs in the United States were covered by Social Security. Workers excluded from coverage fall into four major categories: federal civilian employees hired before 1984, railroad workers, certain state and local government workers covered under a retirement system, and workers whose earnings do not meet minimum earnings requirements.

Benefits earned by covered workers are financed primarily by a payroll tax on a worker's wages. Both the employee and the employer pay taxes based on the worker's earnings up to a maximum amount or taxable maximum earnings base. In 1937, both employee and employer each paid a 1 percent tax, levied on all covered earnings up to $3,000. This captured the full earnings of about 97 percent of all covered workers. Since then, both the tax rate and the maximum taxable earnings base have been increased by myriad legislative measures. The most recent increase in the OASDI tax rate occurred in 1990, when the rate was increased from 6.06 percent to 6.2 percent. The tax rate applicable to self-employed persons has varied over the years; since 1990, self-employed persons have been subject to a tax rate of 12.4 percent, which is equal to the combined employee and employer tax rates. The taxable maximum was increased by a series of ad hoc legislative changes until 1975, when Congress tied the maximum earnings base to changes in the national average wage. Since then, the taxable maximum earnings base has been automatically indexed each year. In 2004, the taxable maximum earnings base was $87,900, which is expected to capture the full earnings of around 94 percent of the workforce.

Medicare hospital insurance

The Social Security Act was amended in 1965 to include Medicare hospital insurance (HI). This program, which is financed primarily through payroll taxes, provides hospitalization benefits to eligible persons age 65 or older. Generally, eligible persons have paid HI taxes based on their covered earnings.

For many years, the pool of workers paying HI taxes and the taxable maximum earnings base were identical to those under Social Security. In the mid-1980s, however, the HI pool was expanded to include all federal workers and all state and local workers hired after March 31, 1986. In 1991, the HI taxable maximum earnings base was raised from $53,400 to $125,000, and in 1994 it was eliminated entirely, thereby decoupling it from the Social Security base and making all covered earnings subject to the tax.

The HI tax rate is 1.45 percent on all covered earnings. Both the employee and the employer pay this tax rate, and self-employed persons pay the combined tax rate. While the original tax rate was 0.35 percent in 1966 and increased steadily over the next three decades, no further increases are currently scheduled.

All revenue generated from the HI payroll tax is deposited in the Hospital Insurance Trust Fund. Revenues in that trust fund are used to finance inpatient hospital, skilled nursing facility, home health, and other institutional services.

Unemployment insurance

Unemployment insurance (UI) payroll taxes began in the 1930s; the taxes are used to finance unemployment benefits for workers involuntarily unemployed.

Basically, the UI payroll tax has two parts: the Federal Unemployment Tax Act (FUTA) tax and the state tax. FUTA taxes finance the administrative expenses of the program, the federal account for state loans, and half the expense of extended benefits. State taxes, which are deposited in the U.S. Treasury, finance regular UI benefits and half the expense of extended benefits.

The FUTA program is designed to induce state participation by granting a credit against the federal tax if the state program conforms to federal standards. FUTA generally determines which workers are covered by UI. Originally, coverage was limited to industrial and commercial workers in the private sector. Currently, the vast majority of workers, with the exception of self-employed persons, are eligible for UI benefits. FUTA imposes some other guidelines on state programs, but states are generally free to determine the amount and duration of benefits, the tax rate, and eligibility requirements.

FUTA currently imposes a 6.2 percent gross tax rate on the first $7,000 paid annually by covered employers to each employee. Employers in states with programs approved by the federal government and with no delinquent federal loans may credit 5.4 percentage points against the 6.2 percent tax rate, making the minimum, net federal tax rate 0.8 percent. Currently, all states have approved programs, so the relevant rate is 0.8 percent. Included in these rates is a 0.2 percent surtax, which was originally enacted in 1976 and extended several times since then. The surtax is currently set to expire at the end of 2007.

Originally, the FUTA tax applied to total annual wages. In 1939, however, a $3,000 taxable wage base was established that exceeded the annual wages of 98 percent of the workers subject to the tax. The taxable wage base was increased three

times: to $4,200 in 1972, to $6,000 in 1978, and to $7,000 in 1983.

States must impose a payroll tax on employers for at least the first $7,000 paid annually to each employee to be eligible for the 5.4 percentage point FUTA credit. In 2003, 42 states had taxable wage bases greater than $7,000; Hawaii has the highest base, at $30,200. All state laws have experience ratings that vary individual employers' tax based on their previous unemployment experience. In 2003, the national average of state tax rates was 0.6 percent of total wages, or 2.1 percent of taxable wages.

Railroad retirement

Federal involvement in providing and financing railroad retirement began in the mid-1930s, when declines in the railroad industry imposed tremendous financial hardships on the railroads. The current system was established in 1974, and substantial modifications were made to the program in 2001.

The retirement system has two tiers that are financed by federal payroll taxes on the wages of railroad employees. The tier 1 tax rate is equivalent to the combined Social Security and Medicare HI tax rate. Under tier 1, both employee and employer pay taxes on covered wages up to the applicable maximum taxable earnings base for Social Security and all covered wages for HI. Under tier 2, the wage base is equal to what the Social Security tax base would have been without the ad hoc increases in the taxable wage base provided by the Social Security amendments of 1977. In 2004, the tier 2 taxable wage base was $65,100. Unlike tier 1 and Social Security, where both the employer and employee tax rates are 7.65 percent, tier 2 employers' contributions are much greater; in 2004, the tier 2 employer and employee tax rates were 13.1 percent and 4.9 percent, respectively. Under the 2001 legislation, the tier 2 rates automatically adjust, beginning in 2004, based on the financial status of the retirement system. The employer rate varies from 8.2 percent to 22.1 percent, and the employee rate ranges from 0.0 percent to 4.9 percent.

Other retirements

Basically, revenues classified as "other retirements" in the federal budget are the retirement contributions of federal government workers. [Employer and employee payroll taxes for District of Columbia government employees are also included as other retirement revenues in the federal budget.] Federal government workers are covered under one of two retirement programs. For decades, all workers were covered under the Civil Service Retirement System (CSRS). Under this program, most employees contribute 7 percent of wages to finance retirement benefits. (A higher tax rate is levied on workers in special groups, such as law enforcement officers and congressional staff.) CSRS employees are not covered by the Social Security system. In 1984, a new retirement program for federal workers, the Federal Employees' Retirement System

(FERS), was introduced. FERS is mandatory for workers hired in 1984 and later. FERS replaced the defined benefit program under CSRS with a smaller defined benefit program, but added Social Security coverage for FERS employees. The defined benefit portion is financed by employee contributions of 0.8 percent of wages. Under both programs, the federal government also makes an employer contribution based on the workers' wages; this, however, is considered an intergovernmental transfer and not included in the revenue totals.

Incidence of federal payroll taxes

Unemployment taxes are statutorily levied on employers only, while Social Security and Medicare taxes are levied on both the employer and the employee. Economists generally believe that the burden of payroll taxes is borne by workers in the form of lower wages, regardless of whether the tax is levied on the employer or the employee.

Payroll taxes are less progressive than individual income taxes because payroll taxes tax only earned income, and most payroll taxes include a maximum taxable earnings base. Effective or average federal payroll taxes rates increase across the bottom of the income distribution, since the lowest-income people generally have little income from wages. Average rates are virtually flat across the broad middle of the income distribution, and decline at the top of the income scale, where people often have earnings above the taxable level. (Including both payroll taxes and the benefits financed by those taxes would show a more progressive system.) In an effort to increase the progressivity of payroll taxes and to create incentive to entering the labor force, the earned income tax credit (EITC) was introduced in 1975 to lighten the burden on working people below certain incomes. Since then, the EITC has been expanded several times, including the Omnibus Budget Reconciliation Acts in 1990 and 1993.

ADDITIONAL READINGS

Burman, Leonard E. "Is the Tax Expenditure Concept Still Relevant?" *National Tax Journal* 56 (September 2003): 613–27.

Musgrave, Richard A., and Peggy B. Musgrave. *Public Finance in Theory and Practice.* 5th ed. New York: McGraw-Hill, 1989.

Pechman, Joseph A. *Federal Tax Policy.* 5th ed. Washington, DC: Brookings Institution Press, 1987.

Rosen, Harvey S. *Public Finance.* 6th ed. New York: McGraw-Hill/Irwin, 2002.

Sammartino, Frank, Eric Toder, and Elaine Maag. "Providing Federal Assistance for Low-Income Families through the Tax System: A Primer." Tax Policy Center Discussion Paper no. 4. Washington, DC: The Urban Institute, 2002.

U.S. Congress, Congressional Budget Office. *The Economic and Budget Outlook: Fiscal Years 2005–2014.* 108th Cong., 2d sess., 2004.

U.S. Congress, House of Representatives, Committee on Ways and Means. *2004 Green Book: Background material and Data on the Programs within the Jurisdiction of the Committee on Ways and Means.* 108th Cong., 2d sess., 1996.

Cross-references: earned income credit; fairness in taxation; Medicare trust fund; Social Security benefits; Social Security Trust Fund.

Pensions, tax treatment of

John A. Turner

AARP Public Policy Institute, Washington, D.C.

To encourage saving for retirement, tax policy generally accords favorable treatment toward contributions, investment income, and benefits related to assets accumulated in pension plans for retirement.

Private pensions receive favorable tax treatment in the United States and in all developed countries with well-developed pension systems, though the particularities of the tax treatment differ (Rein and Turner 2004). In the United States, an employer's pension contribution is deductible in computing corporate income taxes, the investment earnings on plan assets are not taxed, and neither the contribution nor investment earnings are treated as taxable income to the worker at the time those monies are received by the pension plan. The employee is taxed once—personal income tax liability is deferred until the employee receives a distribution from the plan. In comparison, for savings through wage payments, the employee is taxed twice—when wages are received and when investment earnings are received on the subsequent savings.

Policy aspects of the tax treatment of pension plans

The U.S. tax code requirements to qualify for favorable tax treatment are used to regulate pension plans. To be tax-qualified, a plan must meet minimum standards regarding worker participation and vesting, and nondiscrimination against lower-paid workers (McGill et al. 1996). For plans not meeting these standards, the employer's contribution must be included in the employee's taxable income if it is to be tax-deductible to the employer.

Favorable tax treatment is justified by the argument that without a tax subsidy, many families would save too little for retirement. A key issue, however, is do the tax exemptions increase pension coverage and individual savings or do they merely substitute pensions for other forms of saving? As well as the possible effect on workers' savings, the tax treatment of pensions may affect other microeconomic decisions of workers and employers: wages versus pensions, deferred wages versus pensions, other fringe benefits (such as employer-provided health insurance) versus pensions, Social Security versus pensions, defined benefit versus defined contribution plans, individual plans versus employer-provided plans, self-employment versus corporate employment, lump-sum benefits versus annuities, and pension investments in some types of assets versus others.

Calculating the tax liability

Private pension plans involve three transactions that are possible occasions for taxation—contributions, investment earnings and assets, and benefits payments.

Contributions

Because employer pension contributions and wages are both deductible business expenses under the corporate income tax, from a tax perspective employers are indifferent between paying wages and contributing to pension plans. However, they are not indifferent between making pension contributions and paying deferred wages. Because employers cannot shelter money set aside to pay deferred wages from the corporate income tax, employers prefer to defer compensation using pensions instead of deferred wages.

To protect the Treasury against excessive tax deductions, limits are placed on pension contributions. Maximum contributions to a pension plan depend on plan type (e.g., defined benefit, profit sharing), whether the employee is covered by more than one plan, and whether the plan is top-heavy, which refers to plans (mainly for small firms) where a disproportionate amount of the benefits accrues to the owners of the firm and key employees. Limits are also placed on the maximum employee earnings that can be used to determine benefits or contributions. There are also contribution limits for employers in defined benefit plans based on how far pension assets exceed or fall short of liabilities.

Employer and employee contributions are treated differently by the U.S. tax code. Employer contributions are not taxed as income to the employee, avoiding personal income and Social Security payroll taxation when the contributions are made.

Employee contributions are generally taxable under the personal income tax and the Social Security payroll tax. Employee contributions to salary reduction plans are an exception, being exempt from taxation.

The most common type of salary reduction plan is the 401(k) plan, named after the Internal Revenue Code section enabling it. In salary reduction plans, employee contributions are deductible from before-tax wage earnings, a feature that may explain much of their popularity. Presumably as a result of the disparate tax treatment, while salary reduction plans generally require employee contributions, other pension plans rarely do.

Investment earnings and assets

Once an employer or employee has contributed to a pension plan, the investment earnings on those funds are not taxed. This exemption from tax results in what is called the "inside buildup." Pension assets maintained in the pension plan are also not taxable. However, when an employer terminates an overfunded defined benefit plan and surplus plan assets revert to the employer, those assets are taxed at the corporate income tax rate plus an excise tax of 20 percent. The excise tax rate is increased to 50 percent unless the employer transfers part of the excess assets to a replacement plan or provides a benefit increase under the terminating plan. This tax discourages firms from terminating overfunded defined benefit plans.

Benefits payments

Pension benefits received at retirement or earlier are taxed under the federal and state personal income taxes, but are not subject to the Social Security payroll tax. Participants generally recover tax-free the amounts, if any, that have been included previously in their taxable income. These tax-free amounts are called "basis," and generally consist of the employee's after-tax contributions to 401(k) plans. Because of the progressivity of the income tax system and the reduced income most people receive in retirement, workers frequently have lower marginal income tax rates in retirement than while working. Lump-sum distributions received before retirement are subject to an excise tax as well as the personal income tax. In addition to income taxes, a tax of 10 percent is levied on lump-sum distributions before age $59\frac{1}{2}$ unless the worker has separated from service and is at least age 55. The excise tax is designed to discourage those distributions under the theory that pension plan assets should be used exclusively for financing retirement consumption. Retired workers wishing to postpone benefit receipt are required to begin receiving their pension benefits by age $70\frac{1}{2}$ or pay an excise tax of 50 percent on the amount that was required to be distributed. With increases in life expectancy, there has been some discussion of raising this age.

Implications of the tax treatment of pensions

The tax treatment of pensions moves the United States toward a consumption tax system. Earnings saved through a pension are not taxed until received and presumably consumed in retirement. A consumption tax avoids the double taxation of savings that occurs under the current income tax system.

The two aspects of the tax advantage of pensions are income smoothing and the tax-exempt status of pension plan earnings. When income is taxed according to a progressive tax scale, workers can avoid paying high marginal tax rates on pension contributions during their working lives and instead can pay lower inframarginal tax rates when they receive their pension during retirement.

Even if the marginal tax rates the worker paid were the same in retirement as when working, with a progressive tax scale the worker can gain because the first pension dollars are taxed at lower inframarginal rates. The first dollar received in retirement is taxed at the lowest tax rate, and subsequent dollars are taxed at progressively higher marginal rates. Because of the tax advantages of income smoothing, workers will want larger pensions under a progressive tax system than a flat tax system (Ippolito 1990).

Changes in the tax system have reduced the desirability of defined benefit plans relative to defined contribution plans. Since the early 1980s, employees have been able to make tax-deductible contributions to defined contribution (401(k)) plans but not to defined benefit plans. Also, the Omnibus Budget Reconciliation Act of 1987 reduced the amount of funding that could be put into an overfunded pension plan. This reduced the amount that could accumulate in a defined benefit plan earning the tax-free rate of return, reducing the tax advantage of defined benefit plans relative to defined contribution plans.

Pension tax expenditures

Offsetting the advantages provided by the favorable tax treatment of pensions is the loss in tax revenue that results. The tax expenditure figures indicate the amount of federal income tax revenue lost in a tax year as a result of private pensions. Tax expenditures for pensions are measured relative to a comprehensive income tax under which the increase in the present value of expected retirement benefits (roughly equal to the employer contribution plus investment earnings on pension assets) is included in the employee's taxable income. Pension benefits are not taxed. Thus, the Treasury Department's estimate of tax expenditures consists of the revenue loss from exempting employer contributions and investment earnings, offset by the revenue gain from currently taxing private pension benefits. Most of the tax benefits of pensions accrue to middle-income families. The tax expenditure for pensions is the largest tax expenditure for individuals.

The tax expenditure figures overstate, however, the long-term loss of revenue. A worker's lifetime loss measure would calculate the amount of revenue lost this year as a result of pension accruals for workers and subtract the expected present value of taxes paid on those currently accruing benefits. Unlike health insurance premiums, which are never subject to federal taxation, retirement fund contributions and investment earnings eventually face the individual income tax when paid out to retired workers.

ADDITIONAL READINGS

Ippolito, Richard A. *An Economic Appraisal of Pension Tax Policy in the United States*. Homewood, IL: Irwin, 1990.

McGill, Dan M., Kyle N. Brown, John J. Haley, and Sylvester J. Schieber. *Fundamentals of Private Pensions*. 7th ed. Philadelphia: University of Pennsylvania Press, 1996.

Rein, Martin, and John Turner. "Pathways to Pension Coverage." In *Reforming Pensions in Europe: Evolution of Pension Financing and Sources of Retirement Income,* edited by Gerard Hughes and James Stewart (285–300). Cheltenham, UK: Edward Elgar Publishing, 2004.

Cross-references: consumption taxation; fringe benefits; individual retirement accounts; profit-sharing plans; saving, taxes and; Social Security, federal taxation of.

Personal exemption, federal

Joseph J. Cordes
George Washington University

The amount of money that a taxpayer can deduct from federal adjustable gross income, based on the number of dependents claimed on the tax return.

In arriving at taxable income, taxpayers are allowed to deduct a certain amount based on the number of dependents claimed on the tax return. People who are claimed as dependents on another taxpayer's tax return cannot claim themselves as dependents on their own tax returns.

In 2004, the amount of the federal personal exemption equaled $3,100 per dependent. Thus, a single taxpayer would be entitled to claim a single personal exemption of $3,100, a married couple could claim two personal exemptions worth $6,200, a married couple with two children would have four personal exemptions worth $12,400, and so on. For many families, the personal exemption, together with the standard deduction, defines a threshold level of income below which no tax is due. Table 1 shows the levels of this threshold in 2004 for families of different types. (These families may receive a tax benefit through the earned income credit or the child credit; these provisions raise further the exempt threshold for eligible families.)

Failing to index the personal exemption for inflation reduces the real value of the threshold level of nontaxable income and raises the average effective tax rate. For example, in 1950, the personal exemption was $600. In 1986, the personal exemption was $1,080, even though over the same period the cost of living had risen by more than 350 percent. Thus, over 36 years, the real value of the exemption had fallen by almost half, to $304 in 1950 dollars. Put somewhat differently, had the 1950-level personal exemption been increased for inflation over the same 36-year period, it would have equaled $2,129 in 1986.

The steady erosion in the real value of the personal exemption was halted by the Tax Reform Act of 1986, which raised it to $2,000 by 1989 and which provided that the personal exemption, along with the standard deduction, was to be adjusted annually for inflation beginning in 1990. (Personal exemptions and the standard deduction were also indexed in 1985 and 1986.)

Although the personal exemption is available to most taxpayers, higher-income taxpayers are subject to a phaseout of their personal exemption after their income reaches a certain level. In 2004, the phaseout began at $142,700 for a single taxpayer and at $214,050 for married taxpayers filing jointly. This provision increases the effective marginal tax rate of taxpayers subject to the exemption phaseout.

TABLE 1. Federal Personal Exemption and Taxable Income Thresholds

Family type	Value of personal exemptions ($)	Standard deduction ($)	Taxable income threshold ($)
Single	3,100	4,850	7,950
Husband and wife	6,200	9,700	15,900
Single head of household and two children	9,300	7,150	16,450
Husband, wife, and two children	12,400	9,700	22,100

ADDITIONAL READING

Pechman, Joseph. *Federal Tax Policy.* 5th ed. Washington, DC: The Brookings Institution Press, 1987.

Cross-references: adjusted gross income; inflation indexation of income taxes; marginal effective tax rate; standard deduction, federal.

Portfolio choice

James Poterba

Massachusetts Institute of Technology and National Bureau of Economic Research

Differing tax treatments on portfolio income (the name for the group of various types of investments not related to income earned from trade or business) will affect investors' decisions on which investments to hold.

The personal income tax in the United States levies different tax burdens on different types of capital income. Interest and dividend income in excess of low thresholds has been included in taxable income, although since 2003 dividends have been taxed at preferential lower rates. Capital gains are only taxed upon realization, and then at a preferential rate. Interest paid on state and local government bonds is tax-exempt. As a result of these tax provisions, individual investors in different tax circumstances may choose to hold different portfolios.

This entry begins by summarizing existing theoretical models of individual portfolio choice in the presence of taxation. It then describes the empirical evidence on how asset choice, and in particular the dividend yield on common stock held by different investors, is affected by taxation. The final section describes the rise of targeted retirement saving accounts, such as individual retirement accounts (IRAs) and 401(k) plans, that permit households to defer taxes on capital income.

Models of portfolio choice with differential taxation

If investors face different marginal tax rates on different assets, if there is heterogeneity in these tax rates in the investor population, and if all assets are riskless, then investors should segregate into asset clienteles. This can be illustrated in a simple model, based on Miller (1977), in which there are only two portfolio assets: corporate debt and corporate equity.

Assume that corporate equity is untaxed at the investor level. Investors facing high tax rates should therefore specialize in equity, while investors in lower tax brackets should hold only corporate debt. Assume further that there are fixed supplies of corporate debt and equity, and that corporate capital earns a fixed pretax rate of return, f. Corporate interest payments are deductible from corporate income tax, but corporate profits net of interest rate are taxed at the corporate income tax rate, τ_C. In this setting, the returns that investors receive from holding bonds and stocks will adjust to clear the stock and bond markets. This requires equality between the return after investor taxes on debt and equity for the lowest-tax-rate investor holding equity. If the pretax rates of return on debt and equity are r_D and r_E, respectively, and the tax rate of this marginal investor is τ^*, the after-tax returns received by the marginal investor must satisfy $(1 - \tau^*)r_D = r_E$. Normalizing the price of equity to equal unity, $r_E = (1 - \tau_C)f$, and $r_D = [(1 - \tau_C)/(1 - \tau^*)]f$. The value of τ^* depends on the supply of equity, the distribution of wealth across taxpayers with different marginal tax rates, and the marginal tax rate schedule.

The pretax return on debt exceeds that on equity by just enough to compensate the marginal investor for the higher taxes on debt than equity. For an investor with a tax rate (τ) above that of the marginal investor, the incremental after-tax return from holding equity rather than debt is $r_E - (1 - \tau)r_D = (1 - \tau_C)f - (1 - \tau)[(1 - \tau_C)/(1 - \tau^*)]f = [(\tau - \tau^*)/(1 - \tau^*)] (1 - \tau_C)f$. If the pretax returns on debt and equity were equal, the corresponding incremental return would be $\tau(1 - \tau_C)f$. The higher pretax return on debt than equity illustrates the notion of an implicit tax: Although equity investors are not taxed on their returns, the relative pretax returns on equity are reduced by the heavier taxation of bonds. This is a pervasive effect of taxes specific to particular assets or types of capital income. Scholes and colleagues (2005) present examples of implicit taxes that arise with respect to both portfolio and real investments.

This simple model illustrates the importance of general equilibrium considerations in analyzing financial markets in the presence of taxes. Asset supplies are not fixed in Miller's model; they respond to taxes and other market factors. Under the strong assumptions of the model, the tax rate of the marginal investor must equal the corporate tax rate ($\tau = \tau_C$). Any individual firm should therefore be indifferent between issuing debt and equity. The model also shows how investors might segment into different clienteles, with different types of investors holding different types of securities.

The Miller model nevertheless neglects important aspects of actual financial markets. Perhaps most important, the returns on most assets are uncertain. In this case, a key determinant of portfolio patterns is whether investors can obtain all possible pretax return streams from assets with their own most-preferred tax treatment. For example, if both debt and equity in the earlier model had risky but identical returns, then the clientele results of the type described above would still be obtained. If investors cannot span the set of pretax returns with tax-preferred assets, however, Auerbach and King (1983) show that simple portfolio clientele results break down. Investors will hold portfolios determined in part by their tax preferences and in part by their risk preferences. More realistic models generally do not yield stark predictions on clientele formation.

Empirical evidence on taxes and portfolio behavior

Whether taxes affect portfolio decisions can be tested in many ways. One strategy is to test whether investors segment into tax-based clienteles. King and Leape (1998) explored this issue using data from a 1978 survey conducted by SRI International. They found that most investors held incomplete portfolios—that is, they had zero holdings in many broad asset categories such as corporate stock, corporate bonds, and tax-exempt bonds. Leape (1987) tries to model such incompleteness as the optimal response to information and transaction costs; he also surveys much of the previous literature on this issue. King and Leape (1998) also found that most investors with relatively tax-favored assets also held more heavily taxed assets, contrary to the prediction of the simple clientele models described above.

Table 1 presents current evidence on this question, drawn from the 2001 Survey of Consumer Finances (SCF). The entries report the probabilities of holding corporate stock (Stocks); stock mutual funds (StockMF); corporate bonds or corporate bond mutual funds (Bonds); and tax-exempt debt or tax-exempt mutual funds (Tax-Exempt), conditional on positive holdings of the other asset categories. These tabulations exclude holdings in targeted retirement accounts, such as IRAs and Keoghs.

The data do not suggest the presence of sharp asset-holding clienteles. For example, two-thirds of households holding tax-exempt bonds also own taxable government or corporate bonds. More than one-third of those who own stock directly also own stock through an equity mutual fund, and nearly half of those who own an equity mutual fund also own corporate stock directly, even though stock held through a mutual fund often faces a higher effective tax burden than stock held directly. The table also underscores the small number of households that make investments in taxable bonds and tax-exempt bonds.

A second strategy for testing portfolio models moves beyond summary information on portfolio holdings and tests for a link between a household's marginal tax rate and its investment choices, after controlling for other factors. Feldstein (1976), King and Leape (1998), and Poterba and Samwick (2003) are examples of studies in this tradition.

Feldstein (1976) analyzes portfolio data from the 1962 SCF, when the top marginal federal tax rate was 91 percent.

He finds that a household's income has a substantial effect on the mix of assets it holds, conditional on net worth. He interprets this evidence as showing that marginal tax rates affect portfolio composition, although the perennial problem in cross-sectional analysis of tax effects, separating tax rate effects from income effects, complicates this conclusion.

King and Leape (1998) present similar evidence, although their findings imply a weaker relationship between marginal tax rates and portfolio choice. They find some evidence that tax variables affect the set of assets that investors decide to hold, but much weaker evidence on the link between tax rates and the level of asset holdings, or the fraction of the portfolio held in different assets.

Poterba and Samwick (2003) analyze cross-sectional patterns of asset holding in the SCFs conducted between 1983 and 1992, and they introduce a richer set of controls for income-related differences in tax rates than earlier studies. They continue to find substantial effects of marginal tax rates on the set of assets that households hold. The ownership effects are again more pronounced than the effects of taxation on the portfolio shares in different assets. While it would seem natural to exploit panel data to investigate how portfolio structure has changed in response to tax reform, theory often provides stronger predictions regarding cross-sectional asset holding patterns. When both corporate and personal tax rates change, as they often do in major tax reforms, the general equilibrium effects of tax reform can make it difficult to derive clear and testable empirical predictions.

A stark example of an asset that should exhibit a tax-rate-sensitive demand is tax-exempt debt. All three empirical studies described above find that higher income households are more likely to hold tax-exempt debt. Only the last of these studies finds an effect for marginal tax rates after controlling for household income. Feenberg and Poterba (1991) consider the inverse problem, studying the distribution of marginal tax rates among individuals who hold tax-exempt debt. In 1988, a year when the top stated bracket in the federal income tax schedule was 33 percent, less than one-fifth of outstanding tax-exempt debt was held by taxpayers in the 33 percent bracket. Taxpayers with marginal tax rates between 28 and 33 percent held an additional two-thirds of the tax-exempt debt held by individuals. Slightly less than 10 percent of individual holdings of tax-exempt debt were reported by taxpayers with marginal rates of less than 20 percent. The explanation for the nontrivial holdings among low marginal tax rate households

TABLE 1. Probability of Owning Assets in One Class, Conditional on Ownership of Another Asset Category

Conditional on holding	Probability of holding			
	Stocks	Stock MF	Bonds	Tax-exempt
Stocks (22%)	1.00	0.37	0.10	0.15
Stock MF (17%)	0.48	1.00	0.13	0.20
Bonds (3%)	0.69	0.70	1.00	0.32
Tax-exempt (5%)	0.61	0.81	0.65	1.00

may be inertia in portfolio choice, inheritance, or transitory fluctuations in marginal tax rates.

One aspect of taxation and portfolio choice that has been an active subject of empirical research is the relationship between marginal dividend tax rates and the dividend yield on common stock held by different households. Low-yield stocks are assumed to deliver most of their return in the form of lightly taxed capital gains rather than as taxable dividends. The tax rate differential between dividends and capital gains has varied over time, for most of the post-war period dividends have been taxed more heavily than long-term capital gains. The 2003 tax reform changed this pattern, and equated the statutory tax rate on dividends and long-term capital gains on corporate stock.

Most empirical studies on portfolio structure, which were carried out when dividends were taxed more heavily than capital gains, suggest that taxpayers facing higher dividend tax burdens hold lower-yield stocks, although this effect is substantively small. Blume, Crockett, and Friend (1974) study a unique sample of tax returns from 1971 and find that the ratio of dividends to market value of equity varies by approximately 75 basis points between investors facing the lowest and highest marginal tax rates. Petit (1977) estimates that a 10 point increase in an investor's marginal tax burden on dividend income would reduce his portfolio's dividend yield by approximately 35 basis points. Chaplinsky and Seyhun (1990) analyze tax return data, rather than brokerage firm records, and they show that the ratio of dividends to realized capital gains varies as a function of an investor's tax position. This is not direct evidence of dividend-yield clienteles, because it could also reflect tax effects on decisions to realize capital gains. Scholz (1992) studies data from the SCF and estimates a larger tax effect than earlier studies. His results suggest that a 10 percentage point increase in an investor's marginal dividend tax rate would reduce his portfolio's dividend yield by between 100 and 150 basis points.

Graham and Kumar (2004) offer related evidence on the presence of dividend clienteles. They study a more recent data set of holdings and transactions by households that invest through a large retail brokerage. They find evidence that low-income, and presumptively low-tax, investors are more likely to hold high-dividend stocks. They also observe some evidence of tax-cognizant trading around ex-dividend days. High tax investors appear more likely to purchase a dividend-paying stock after the ex-dividend day, thereby avoiding the receipt of highly-taxed dividend income. Allen and Michaely (2003) survey the voluminous literature on share pricing and investor trading patterns around ex-dividend days.

The foregoing studies on taxation and equity portfolio choice focused on the choice of individual equity securities, ignoring open-end mutual funds. These funds are a significant and rapidly growing part of individual portfolios. Because investors do not control the timing of asset sales for the securities owned by mutual funds, as they do for securities held on their own account, mutual funds present individual investors with different tax minimization problems. Dickson and Shoven (1995) discuss the effects of a fund's gain and loss realization strategies on the after-tax return earned by investors. They show that the after-tax return differential between a fund that is managed in a tax-efficient way and a fund that is not can be substantial. Bergstresser and Poterba (2002) study inflows to mutual funds and find that funds with lower tax burdens attract greater inflows, all else equal, than funds with higher tax burdens.

Investing through tax-deferred saving vehicles

The preceding discussion concentrated on investors that hold securities in currently taxable form. Yet during the 1980s, many investors took advantage of new tax provisions that created opportunities for tax-deferred saving. IRAs, described in more detail in Venti and Wise (1992), were a popular saving vehicle from their introduction in 1981 until eligibility restrictions were imposed in the Tax Reform Act of 1986. A second type of tax-deferred saving vehicle, the 401(k) plan, grew rapidly throughout the 1980s and early 1990s. By the late 1990s, Poterba, Venti, and Wise (2000) report that more than 35 million workers participated in 401(k) plans. Participation rates for eligible workers often exceed 70 percent. Poterba, Venti, and Wise (2004) report that contributions to IRAs and 401(k) plans exceeded the reported flow of personal saving in the national income and product accounts for some years in the late 1990s.

IRAs as offered in the early 1980s, and 401(k) plans, allow investors the opportunity to defer taxes on current income saved through these accounts. Moreover, taxes on the income from assets held in these accounts are deferred until the accounts are drawn down. Withdrawals from these accounts are taxed as ordinary income, and they are subject to an additional 10 percent penalty tax if they are made before age $59\frac{1}{2}$. And 401(k) plans frequently offer an additional attraction: employers may match worker contributions to these plans and often do so at substantial rates.

One of the key questions associated with the increasing importance in household portfolios of assets held in IRAs and 401(k) plans is whether these assets replace those that would otherwise have been held in traditional taxable accounts. This issue has attracted some controversy, illustrated in the debate between Engen, Gale, and Scholz (1996) and Poterba, Venti, and Wise (1996, 1998). The balance of evidence suggests that contributions to tax-deferred accounts, particularly 401(k) type plans, raise personal and national saving, although the net effect is smaller than the gross contribution and it is likely to be smaller at high than at low income levels.

Both 401(k) plans and IRAs are saving vehicles with attractive tax features, not assets with attractive tax characteristics. Investors therefore have some discretion in selecting the assets held in these accounts. If an investor holds both highly taxed bonds and less-heavily taxed equity in a portfolio, current taxes could be reduced by placing the bonds in the tax-deferred saving vehicle and the stocks in the taxable account. The choice of which assets to hold in a taxable account and which ones to hold in a tax-deferred account is labeled the "asset location" problem by Shoven (1998). Barber and Odean (2004) and Bergstresser and Poterba (2004) present empirical evidence on the asset location choice of households. The former study employs data from accounts at brokerage firms, while the later analyzes the 2001 SCF. Barber and Odean (2004) find that most households locate bonds in their tax-deferred account and stocks in their taxable account, but they find evidence of higher trading rates in taxable than tax-deferred accounts. This pattern could raise the household's taxes. Bergstresser and Poterba (2004) find that a substantial group of households make asset location choices that result in higher tax burdens, and lower after-tax returns, than they could otherwise achieve, but that reallocating only a few thousand dollars of portfolio assets would move the majority of these households to a tax-efficient location.

Taxation and portfolio adjustment

This discussion focuses on how taxes affect the composition of household portfolios, neglecting the important related question of how taxation, particularly capital gains taxation, affects decisions to sell assets and adjust portfolios. Numerous empirical studies, starting with Feldstein, Slemrod, and Yitzhaki (1980) and surveyed in Poterba (2002), have shown that capital gains realization behavior is affected by the level, and expected change, in capital gains tax rates. The general effect of realization-based capital gains taxation is to encourage investors to defer sale of appreciated assets, but because this applies to all assets that may generate capital gains, the overall effect of such "lock-in" on the mix of assets held in investor portfolios is difficult to assess.

ADDITIONAL READINGS

Allen, Franklin, and Roni Michaely. "Payout Policy." In *Handbook of Economics and Finance,* vol. 1A, edited by G. Constantinides, M. Harris, and R. Stulz. Amsterdam: North-Holland, 2003.

Auerbach, Alan J., and Mervyn A. King. "Taxation, Portfolio Choice, and Debt-Equity Ratios: A General Equilibrium Model." *Quarterly Journal of Economics* 98 (1983): 587–609.

Barber, Brad, and Terrence Odean. "Are Individual Investors Tax Savvy? Evidence from Retail and Discount Brokerage Accounts." *Journal of Public Economics* 88 (January 2004): 419–42.

Bergstresser, Daniel, and James Poterba. "Do After-Tax Returns Affect Mutual Fund Inflows?" *Journal of Financial Economics* 63 (March 2002): 381–414.

———. "Asset Allocation and Asset Location: Household Evidence from the Survey of Consumer Finances." *Journal of Public Economics* 88 (September/October 2004): 1893–1915.

Blume, Marshall E., Jean Crockett, and Irwin Friend. "Stockholders in the United States: Characteristics and Trends." *Survey of Current Business* 64 (November 1974):16–40.

Chaplinsky, Susan, and H. Nejat Seyhun. "Dividends and Taxes: Evidence on Tax Reduction Strategies." *Journal of Business* 63 (1990): 239–60.

Dickson, Joel, and John B. Shoven. "Taxation and Mutual Funds: An Investor Perspective." In *Tax Policy and the Economy,* vol. 9, edited by James Poterba (151–80). Cambridge, MA: MIT Press, 1995.

Engen, Eric, William Gale, and J. Karl Scholz. "The Illusory Effects of Savings Incentives on Saving." *Journal of Economic Perspectives* 10 (Fall 1996): 113–38.

Feenberg, Daniel R., and James M. Poterba. "Which Households Own Municipal Bonds? Evidence from Tax Returns." *National Tax Journal* 44 (December 1991): 93–103.

Feldstein, Martin S. "Personal Taxation and Portfolio Composition: An Econometric Analysis." *Econometrica* 44 (July 1976): 631–49.

Feldstein, Martin S., Joel B. Slemrod, and Shlomo Yitzhaki. "The Effects of Taxation on the Selling of Corporate Stock and the Realization of Capital Gains." *Quarterly Journal of Economics* 94 (1980): 777–91.

Graham, John, and Alok Kumar. "Do Dividend Clienteles Exist? Evidence on Dividend Preferences of Retail Investors." Mimeo, Duke University Fuqua School of Business, 2004.

King, Mervyn A., and Jonathan I. Leape. "Wealth and Portfolio Composition: Theory and Evidence." *Journal of Public Economics* 69 (August 1998): 155–93.

Leape, Jonathan I. "Taxes and Transaction Costs in Asset Market Equilibrium." *Journal of Public Economics* 33 (1987): 1–20.

Lewellen, Wilbur G., Kenneth L. Stanley, Ronald C. Lease, and Gary G. Schlarbaum. "Some Direct Evidence on the Dividend Clientele Phenomenon." *Journal of Finance* 33 (December 1978): 1385–99.

Miller, Merton. "Debt and Taxes." *Journal of Finance* 32 (May 1977): 261–75.

Petit, R. Richardson. "Taxes, Transaction Costs, and the Clientele Effect of Dividends." *Journal of Financial Economics* 5 (1977): 419–36.

Poterba, James M. "Taxation, Risk-Taking, and Household Portfolio Behavior." In *Handbook of Public Economics 3,* edited by Alan J. Auerbach and Martin S. Feldstein (1109–71). Amsterdam: North-Holland, 2002.

Poterba, James M., and Andrew Samwick. "Taxation and Household Portfolio Composition: Evidence from the Tax Reforms in the 1980s and 1990s." *Journal of Public Economics* 87 (January 2003): 5–39.

Poterba, James M., Steven F. Venti, and David A. Wise. "How Retirement Saving Programs Increase Private Saving." *Journal of Economic Perspectives* 10 (Fall 1996): 91–112.

———. "Personal Retirement Saving Programs and Asset Accumulation: Reconciling the Evidence." In *Frontiers of the Economics of Aging,* edited by David Wise (23–106). Chicago: University of Chicago Press, 1998.

———. "Saver Behavior and 401(k) Retirement Wealth." *American Economic Review* 90 (May 2000): 297–302.

———. "The Transition to Personal Accounts and Increasing Retirement Wealth: Macro and Micro Evidence." In *Perspectives on the Economics of Aging,* edited by David Wise (17–71). Chicago: University of Chicago Press, 2004.

Scholes, Myron S., Mark A. Wolfson, Merle M. Erickson, Edward L. Maydew, and Terrence J. Shevlin. *Taxes and Business Strategy: A Planning Approach.* 3rd ed. Englewood Cliffs, NJ: Prentice Hall, 2005.

Scholz, John Karl. "A Direct Examination of the Dividend Clientele Hypothesis." *Journal of Public Economics* 49 (1992): 261–85.

Shoven, John. "The Location and Allocation of Assets in Pensions and Conventional Savings Accounts." NBER Working Paper 7007. Cambridge, MA: National Bureau of Economic Research [NBER], 1998.

Venti, Steven F., and David A. Wise. "Government Policy and Personal Retirement Saving." In *Tax Policy and the Economy 6,* edited by James M. Poterba. Cambridge, MA: MIT Press, 1992.

Cross-references: capital gains taxation; dividends, double taxation of; implicit taxes; individual retirement accounts; saving, taxes and; tax-exempt bonds.

Presumptive taxation

Victor Thuronyi

International Monetary Fund

Taxation according to indicators in lieu of actual measurement of the tax base.

Presumptive taxation is commonly employed when taxpayers cannot be relied on to measure their income or expenses using proper accounts. Small businesses and agriculture are often taxed under presumptive methods in developing countries, and even in a few developed ones. Presumptive taxation is rarely used in the United States, although techniques such as the standard deduction can be said to embody a presumptive approach.

Presumptive taxation is commonly used for the so-called "hard to tax," who might be defined as taxpayers that are administratively impossible to tax under the normal rules because revenues would be so small compared with administrative costs.

Presumptive taxation can be exclusive or can take the form of a minimum tax. In the latter case, tax liability is the greater of that measured according to the normal rules and that resulting from the presumption.

Where presumptive taxation is exclusive, actual income is irrelevant. Instead of being taxed on income, the taxpayer is taxed on land ownership or on other factors used for the particular presumptive scheme. The incentive effects of such a tax accordingly may be quite different from those of an income tax. The marginal tax rate on income may be zero if the tax is based, for example, on land area and quality alone.

The most common presumptive methods of the minimum tax type are based on gross receipts or on assets. For example, income tax liability may be fixed as no less than 3 percent of gross receipts or 1 percent of assets. The specified percentage of gross receipts may be the same for all taxpayers, or it may vary depending on industry. Gross receipts may also be the exclusive method of taxation for smaller businesses. In this case, businesses subject to this regime would be required to report for tax purposes only their receipts, not their expenses. Minimum assets taxes have become quite widespread in Latin America—not just for small business but for large companies as well, generating design flaws in the interaction between the minimum and the regular taxes.

Individuals conducting business on their own might be taxed a fixed amount depending on the nature of the activity. Activities such as gambling machines may be taxed in the same way (i.e., a flat amount per machine).

A more sophisticated approach takes into account a number of factors. The taxpayer may furnish information about these factors to the tax inspector, who calculates the estimated income and tax for a two- or three-year period. The taxpayer then pays tax on this basis, rather than on actual income. This method (known as the *forfait*) was used in France until fairly recently, and similar methods are used in some developing countries.

For individuals, another method pioneered in France is taxation based on outward signs of lifestyle. This calculates a presumed income based on the value of the taxpayer's home and automobile(s), and expenditures on various luxuries.

Presumptive taxation of agriculture is based on land area and quality. Tables are prepared based on studies of expected yields. For small farmers, this approach can be more reliable than reported receipts from crop sales. Developing countries that do not simply exempt agriculture from income tax often use the presumptive approach, because normal bookkeeping is impractical for small farmers.

Tonnage taxes, under which profits from shipping activities are taxed on the basis of tonnage of the ships rather than on the basis of actual accounts of income and expenses, are another commonly used form of presumptive taxation.

Taxation of insurance companies on the basis of a percentage of insurance premiums can also be considered presumptive. Indeed, any withholding taxes applied to the gross amount of specified payments to nonresidents in lieu of an income tax on actual profit can be said to take a presumptive approach.

Typically, presumptive taxation replaces or (in the case of minimum-tax-type presumptions) bolsters income or profit taxation. It may dispense with the need to keep account of income and/or expenses. Indirect taxes based on books of account (for example, sales taxes) can also be replaced by presumptive taxation. Although not common, excise taxation could also be presumptive: if the taxpayer's capacity to produce alcoholic beverages is measured, for example, the tax could simply be imposed on the basis of this capacity rather than on actual production. This may make sense for very small producers, particularly when the excise rate is not too high.

Of course, there are many instances in which legal presumptions are used in taxation (for example, the tax administrations assessment may be presumed correct, or two persons may be presumed to be associated if related in a specified manner unless the taxpayer proves otherwise) but "presumptive taxation" is usually used in the sense identified above, rather than as including all presumptions that apply in taxation.

ADDITIONAL READINGS

Rajaraman, Indira. *A Fiscal Domain for Panchayats.* Oxford, U.K.: Oxford University Press, 2003.

Taube, Gunther, and Helaway Tadesse. *Presumptive Taxation in Sub-Saharan Africa: Experiences and Prospects,* IMF Working Paper 96/5. Washington, DC: International Monetary Fund, 1996.

Thuronyi, Victor. "Presumptive Taxation." In *Tax Law Design and Drafting.* 1st ed., edited by Victor Thuronyi (1–32). Washington, DC: International Monetary Fund, 1996.

———. "Presumptive Taxation of the Hard-to-Tax." In *Taxing the Hard-to-Tax,* edited by James Alm, Jeoges Martinez-Vazquez, and Sally Wallace. St. Louis, MO: Elsevier Science, 2005.

Cross-references: excise taxes; income tax, corporate, federal; income tax, corporate, state and local; income tax, federal; insurance industry, federal taxation of; insurance industry, state taxation of; luxury taxes; standard deduction, federal; tax; withholding of taxes.

Profit-sharing plans

Dallas Salisbury

Employee Benefit Research Institute

A type of defined contribution plan in which the employer's only financial obligation is the contribution made.

Profit-sharing plans are sometimes structured in such a way that employees share in their company's profits and potentially gain a greater interest in their firm's success.

In 1939, legislation clarified the tax status of deferred plans. This legislation and the World War II wage freeze resulted in the rapid growth of profit-sharing plans in the 1940s. The Employee Retirement Income Security Act of 1974 (ERISA) furthered this growth by imposing less burdensome regulations on profit-sharing plans than on defined benefit pension plans, thus increasing their attractiveness. The Revenue Act of 1978 created Section 401(k) of the Internal Revenue Code (IRC), which provided for employee pretax contributions to profit-sharing plans.

Types of plans

There are three basic types of profit-sharing plans.

Under a cash plan, at the time profits are determined, contributions are paid directly to employees in the form of cash, checks, or stock. The amount is taxed as ordinary income when distributed.

Under a deferred plan, profit-sharing contributions are not paid out currently but rather are deferred to individual accounts set up for each employee. Benefits—and any investment earnings accrued—are distributed at retirement, death, or disability, and sometimes at separation from service or other events, at which point they are taxable.

Under a combination plan, the participant has the option of deferring all or part of the profit-sharing allocation. That portion taken as a deferral is placed into the participant's account, where it and investment earnings accrue tax-free until withdrawal. Any amount taken in cash is taxed currently. For tax purposes, Internal Revenue Service (IRS) qualification of profit-sharing plans is restricted to deferred or combination plans, which may be 401(k) arrangements. According to more recent tabulations of data from the 5500 series of tax forms, 95.7 percent of all 401(k) plans in 1992 were profit-sharing and thrift saving plans.

Plan qualification rules

Profit-sharing plans, like other retirement plans, must meet a variety of requirements to qualify for preferential tax treatment. These rules, created under ERISA, are designed to protect employee rights and to guarantee that pension benefits will be available for employees at retirement. The rules govern requirements for reporting and disclosing plan information, fiduciary responsibilities, employee eligibility for plan participation, vesting of benefits, form of benefit payment, and funding. In addition, qualified plans must satisfy a set of IRS nondiscrimination rules [under IRC Sections 401(a)(4), 410(b), and, in some cases, 401(a)(26)] designed to ensure that a plan does not discriminate in favor of highly compensated employees.

Contributions

Employer contributions

Plans must define how employer contributions will be allocated to employee accounts. The allocation formula is generally based on compensation. Sometimes the allocation is a flat percentage of pay, or it may be determined by calculating the proportion of each employee's compensation relative to the total compensation of all plan participants. For example, if the employee earns $15,000 annually and total annual compensation for all participants is $300,000, the employee would receive 5 percent of the employer's annual contribution. With the advent of Section 401(k), many employers now offer a matching contribution that is tied to contributions made by the employee.

Some plans base their allocations on compensation and service credits. These plans must be careful to ensure that the wage/service formula meets the regulatory scheme for demonstrating that the formula does not discriminate in favor of highly compensated employees. Allocation formulas may be integrated with Social Security within prescribed limits. Maximum annual contributions (employer and employee, if any) on behalf of each plan participant are limited by the defined contribution limits under Section 415 of the IRC. But the total amount of contributions for all employees that an employer may deduct for federal tax purposes is limited to 15 percent of all covered employees' compensation.

Until recently, an employer's contribution to a profit-sharing plan was limited to the extent of an employer's current or accumulated profits. Currently, an employer does not have to have profits to establish a profit-sharing plan, and total contributions are not restricted to total profits. Plan documents, however, must specify that the plan is a profit-sharing plan.

If an employer's contribution for a particular year is less than the maximum amount for which a deduction is allowed, the unused limit may not be carried forward to subsequent years unless the carryforward exists as of December 31, 1986. These limit carryforwards may be used to increase the general deduction limit to 25 percent until the carryforwards are exhausted.

A deduction carryforward of contributions in excess of the deduction limit for a particular year may be deductible in succeeding taxable years to the extent allowed. Such contributions, however, may be subject to a 10 percent nondeductible excise tax. Excess contributions are defined as the sum of total amounts contributed for the taxable year over the amount allowable as a deduction for that year plus the amount of excess contributions for the preceding year, reduced by amounts returned to the employer during the year, if any, and the portion of the prior excess contribution that is deductible in the current year. In other words, if an excess contribution is made during a taxable year, the excise tax would apply for that year and for each succeeding year until the excess is eliminated. Excess contributions for a year are determined at the close of the employer's taxable year, and the tax is imposed on the employer.

Employee contributions

Pure profit-sharing plans do not require employee contributions, but some may permit voluntary employee contributions up to certain limits. Employee contributions in the form of a salary reduction are becoming increasingly popular. When pretax salary reduction is allowed, the plan must follow rules for 401(k) arrangements.

Distributions

Retirement, disability, and death benefits

The law requires that participants' account balances fully vest at retirement. In addition, plans generally provide for benefits upon death or disability. A plan's vesting provisions determine whether an employee will receive full or partial benefits upon other types of employment termination. However, if the plan is contributory (that is, if employees make contributions), the employee will always receive the benefits that are attributable to "I" or the employee's own contributions.

Profit-sharing plans typically give retiring participants and beneficiaries of deceased participants a choice between a lump-sum payment and installments. Usually, those who terminate employment for reasons other than retirement, death, or disability receive lump-sum distributions, although if the benefit exceeds $5,000, the participant cannot be forced to take an immediate benefit. Distributions from profit-sharing accounts must follow the general distribution rules for all qualified retirement plans. Distributions must begin by the year following the attainment of age $70\frac{1}{2}$ even if the individual has not retired. There are minimum and maximum limits on the amount of annual distribution, both subject to penalty taxes if not followed.

In-service withdrawals

Some profit-sharing plans provide for partial account withdrawals during active employment. Plans allowing participants to elect account withdrawals impose certain conditions, which vary widely. But generally, the funds must be held in the plan for two years before a withdrawal is allowed. A 10 percent additional income tax applies to most early distributions made before age $59\frac{1}{2}$. The 10 percent additional tax does not apply to distributions that are (1) a result of the participant's death or disability; (2) in the form of an annuity or installments payable over the life or life expectancy of the participant (or joint lives or life expectancies of the participant and the participant's beneficiary); (3) made after the participant has separated from service on or after age 55; (4) used for payment of medical expenses deductible under federal income tax rules; (5) made to or on behalf of an alternate payee pursuant to a qualified domestic relations order; or (6) rolled over to an individual retirement account or other qualified plan within 60 days.

Conclusion

Profit-sharing offers employees a chance to share in their company's success. The level of company success is directly related to profits, which often define the amount of profit-sharing allocation. So the greater the profits of the company, the larger the potential allocation. However, profit-sharing plans can serve several goals. If the plan is cash-only, it is generally viewed as a form of bonus. If profits are good, benefits are paid. Deferred plans are usually intended to supplement other pension plans and thus are generally more appropriate for retirement purposes. With a 401(k) feature, the plan serves as a vehicle for employees to save for their retirement on a pretax basis.

ADDITIONAL READINGS

Allen, Everett T., Jr., Joseph Melone, Jerry Rosenbloom, and Jack L. VanDerhei. *Pension Planning.* 7th ed. Homewood, IL: Richard Irwing, 1992.

Employee Benefit Research Institute. *Fundamentals of Employee Benefit Plans.* 5th ed. Washington, DC: Employee Benefit Research Institute, 1996.

U.S. Department of Labor, Bureau of Labor Statistics. *Employee Benefits in Medium and Large Firms, 1993.* Washington, DC: U.S. Government Printing Office, 1995.

Watson Wyatt Worldwide. *Top 50: A Survey of Retirement, Thrift and Profit Sharing Plans Covering Salaried Employees at 50 Large U.S. Industrial Companies as of January 1, 1995.* Washington, DC: Wyatt Research and Information Center, 1996.

Cross-references: employee stock ownership plan; fringe benefits; pensions, tax treatment of; saving, taxes and.

Progressivity, measures of
Donald W. Kiefer
Office of Tax Analysis, U.S. Department of the Treasury

Although there is wide agreement on the definition of progressivity—the ratio of tax payment to income rises as income rises—there are variants regarding the measurement and valuation of the numerator and denominator.

A tax is progressive if the ratio of taxes to income rises as income increases, proportional if the ratio is constant for all incomes, and regressive if the ratio falls as income increases. Progressivity measures describe the degree of progressivity (or regressivity) in a tax system and assess whether a tax revision has made a tax more or less progressive.

Types of progressivity indexes

While the definition of tax progressivity is generally agreed upon, the way to measure it is not. Over the years, a wide variety of indexes of tax progressivity has been suggested and used. These tax progressivity indexes may be categorized in at least two ways: first, by what they measure, and second, by what affects their numerical value.

Some progressivity indexes measure the distribution of the tax burden, whereas others measure the effect of the tax system on the distribution of income. There is no universal agreement that the latter type of index should be regarded as a measure of "progressivity," and not all writers who have used indexes of income redistribution have referred to them as measuring progressivity. Both types of measures will be discussed here.

The numerical value of one group of indexes, which might be called "structural indexes," is a function of the relationship between the amount of income and the amount of tax imposed on that income. The numerical value of the second group of indexes, which might be called "distributional indexes," is a function of the tax structure but also of the distribution of income.

Structural progressivity indexes

Three commonly used structural progressivity indexes are average-rate progression, liability progression, and residual income progression (see Musgrave and Thin 1948).

Average-rate progression is the ratio of the change in effective tax rate to the change in income over some income interval. The value is positive when the tax is progressive, zero when the tax is proportional, and negative when the tax is regressive.

Liability progression is the ratio of the percentage change in tax liability to the percentage change in income. This index has a value greater than 1 when the tax is progressive, equal to 1 when the tax is proportional, and less than 1 when the tax is regressive.

Residual income progression is the ratio of the percentage change in after-tax income to the percentage change in before-tax income. The index is less than 1 when the tax is progressive, equal to 1 when the tax is proportional, and greater than 1 when the tax is regressive. A related measure, relative share adjustment (RSA), which for each income group equals the after-tax income share divided by the pretax income share, was introduced by Baum (1987). Values of RSA greater than or less than 1 have the opposite meaning as those for residual income progression.

These measures will differ in what is characterized as a progressivity-neutral tax change. In a progressive tax system, an equal percentage point change in average tax rates will preserve average-rate progression, and proportionate changes in average tax rates will preserve liability progression. A tax change resulting in proportionate changes in after-tax incomes is neutral in terms of residual income progression.

Residual income progression is perhaps the most interesting of these measures from a welfare perspective because it relates to the effects of taxes on the distribution of disposable income.

Distributional progressivity indexes

The distributional progressivity indexes are grouped here according to the measure of dispersion on which they are based: the concentration index, an index based on the concept of equally distributed equivalent level of income, or generalized entropy measures.

Indexes based on a concentration index

A concentration index is based on a concentration curve. The best known of these measures are the Gini index and the Lorenz curve. With population members ordered from lowest to highest income, the Lorenz curve relates the cumulative share of population (on the horizontal axis) to the cumulative share of income (on the vertical axis). If income is equally distributed, the Lorenz curve lies on a 45 line, because each given fraction of the population has that same fraction of the total income. If income is not equally distributed, a given fraction of the population will have less than the same fraction of the aggregate income, and the Lorenz curve will lie beneath the 45 line, coinciding only at the 100 percent and 0 percent points. The Gini index is the ratio of the area between the Lorenz curve and the 45 line to the entire area under the 45 line. The Gini index is 0 when income is equally distributed and rises toward 1 as income becomes more unequally distributed.

The following distributional progressivity indexes are based on the concentration index:

1. Musgrave and Thin (1948) introduced an index they labeled "effective progression," defined as

$$EP = \frac{(1 - G_a)}{(1 - G_b)}$$

where G refers to the Gini index, and the a and b subscripts refer to after-tax and before-tax income, respectively. For $EP > 1$, the tax is progressive; for $EP = 1$, the tax is proportional; for $EP < 1$, the tax is regressive.

2. The progressivity index used by Pechman and Okner (1974) is

$$PO = \frac{(G_a - G_b)}{G_b}$$

If $PO < 0$, the tax is progressive; if $PO = 0$, the tax is proportional; if $PO > 0$, the tax is regressive.

3. A related index was used by Reynolds and Smolensky (1977):

$$RS = G_a - G_b$$

If $RS < 0$, the tax is progressive; if $RS = 0$, the tax is proportional; if $RS > 0$, the tax is regressive.

4. The index used by Khetan and Poddar (1976) is

$$KP = \frac{(1 - G_b)}{(1 - C_t)}$$

where C_t is the concentration index of taxes; that is, it is calculated like the Gini index with tax liability substituted for income. For $KP > 1$, the tax is progressive; for $KP = 1$, the tax is proportional; for $KP < 1$, the tax is regressive.

5. The index used by Kakwani (1977), which he labeled P, is

$$P = C_t - G_b$$

If $P > 0$, the tax is progressive; if $P = 0$, the tax is proportional; if $P < 0$, the tax is regressive.

6. Khetan and Poddar (1976) and Suits (1977) developed two closely related indexes. The Suits index, S, which is the better known of the two, is the relative concentration index of taxes with respect to income; that is, it is calculated like the Gini index with tax liability substituted for income and income substituted for population. If $S > 0$, the tax is progressive; if $S = 0$, the tax is proportional; if $S < 0$, the tax is regressive. The Khetan-Poddar version is $1/(1 - S)$.

Indexes based on the concept of equally distributed equivalent level of income

From a social welfare perspective, the Gini index and related concentration indexes suffer from well-known deficiencies. Atkinson (1970) emphasized that underlying any summary statistic of inequality "is some concept of social welfare and it is with this concept that we should be concerned." Atkinson and several other authors—including Dasgupta, Sen, and Starrett (1973); Sen (1973); and Blackorby and Donaldson (1978)—examined the social welfare concept underlying the Gini index and found it wanting. For brevity, the specific criticisms of the Gini index will not be detailed here, but an overview is provided in Kiefer (1984).

Kolm (1969), Atkinson (1970), and Sen (1973) developed an alternative inequality index based on the concept of equally distributed equivalent level of income, designated by Y_{ede}. Given a social welfare function, Y_{ede} is that level of per capita income which, if equally distributed, would produce the same level of social welfare as the current income distribution. The

inequality index, I, is equal to 1 minus the ratio of Y_{ede} to mean income. Blackorby and Donaldson (1983) proposed a tax progressivity index based on this inequality index:

$$BD = \frac{(1 - I_a)}{(1 - I_b)} - 1$$

If $BD > 0$, the tax is progressive; if $BD = 0$, the tax is proportional; if $BD < 0$, the tax is regressive.

Kiefer (1984) proposed an alternative tax progressivity index of the form

$$K = I_b - I_a$$

If $K > 0$, the tax is progressive; if $K = 0$, the tax is proportional; if $K < 0$, the tax is regressive. This tax progressivity index shows tax changes that make equal improvements in social welfare to be equally progressive regardless of the initial income distribution. The BD index does not have this property.

Indexes based on a generalized entropy measure

More recently, progressivity measures based on a generalized entropy measure have been proposed. Zandvakili (1995), for example, proposed such a measure using the same general form as the Kiefer index. While these measures lack a direct welfare interpretation, they are decomposable, a property that is useful in some applications. That is, a change in progressivity from one tax structure to another can be expressed as the weighted sum of the change affecting each of several population subgroups (e.g., marrieds, singles, and heads of households) and a term measuring the change in between-group equalization.

Inconsistencies

Kiefer (1984) and Greene and Balkan (1987) demonstrated that the various tax progressivity indexes may give inconsistent results in comparisons of tax systems and income distributions. Each progressivity index is, in effect, associated with a unique definition of progressivity. Hence, a conclusion about which of two tax systems is more progressive may be dependent on which tax progressivity measure is used for the evaluation. It is, therefore, incumbent upon the researcher to choose among the tax progressivity indexes based on an understanding of their characteristics and implications.

ADDITIONAL READINGS

Atkinson, Anthony B. "On the Measurement of Inequality." *Journal of Economic Theory* 2 (September 1970): 244–63.

Baum, Sandra R. "On the Measurement of Tax Progressivity: Relative Share Adjustment." *Public Finance Quarterly* 15 (April 1987): 166–87.

Blackorby, Charles, and David Donaldson. "Measures of Relative Equality and Their Meaning in Terms of Social Welfare." *Journal of Economic Theory* 18 (June 1978): 59–80.

———. "Ethical Social Index Numbers and the Measurement of Effective Tax/Benefit Progressivity." Mimeograph, University of British Columbia, May 1983.

Dasgupta, Partha, Amartya Sen, and David Starrett. "Notes on Measurement of Inequality." *Journal of Economic Theory* 6 (April 1973): 180–87.

Greene, Kenneth V., and Erol M. Balkan. "A Comparative Analysis of Tax Progressivity in the United States." *Public Finance Quarterly* 15 (October 1987): 397–416.

Kakwani, Nanak C. "Applications of Lorenz Curves in Economic Analysis." *Econometrica* 45 (April 1977): 719–27.

Khetan, C. P., and S. N. Poddar. "Measurement of Income Tax Progression in a Growing Economy: The Canadian Experience." *Canadian Journal of Economics* 9 (November 1976): 613–29.

Kiefer, Donald W. "Distributional Tax Progressivity Indexes." *National Tax Journal* 37 (December 1984): 497–513.

Kolm, S. C. "The Optimal Production of Social Justice." In *Public Economics,* edited by J. Margolis and H. Guitton (145–200). London: MacMillan, 1969.

Musgrave, Richard A., and Tun Thin. "Income Tax Progression, 1929–48." *Journal of Political Economy* 56 (December 1948): 498–514.

Pechman, Joseph A., and Benjamin A. Okner. *Who Bears the Tax Burden?* Washington, DC: The Brookings Institution, 1974.

Reynolds, Morgan, and Eugene Smolensky. "Post Fisc Distributions of Income in 1950, 1961, and 1970." *Public Finance Quarterly* 5 (October 1977): 419–38.

Sen, Amartya. *On Economic Inequality.* Oxford, U.K.: Clarendon Press, 1973.

Suits, Daniel B. "Measurement of Tax Progressivity." *American Economic Review* 67 (September 1977): 747–52.

Zandvakili, Sourushe. "Decomposable Measures of Income Tax Progressivity." *Applied Economics* 27 (1995) 657–60.

Cross-references: ability to pay; fairness in taxation.

Property tax assessment

Michael E. Bell
George Washington University and MEB Associates, Inc.

Determining the base of the property tax.

The property tax is unique among state and local revenue sources. It is the largest single source of state and local revenues, it is the only major tax applied in all 50 states, and it is the only major revenue source with a tax base estimated by a government official. Both consumption and income taxes are based on current flows or transactions, the values of which are relatively clear. The property tax, however, is based on a stock of wealth that does not change hands every year. Therefore, the value of property, which is the base of the tax, must be estimated annually. This process of property tax assessment is inherently subjective and requires the talents of highly trained and experienced personnel—generally referred to as assessors, valuers, property appraisers, or property valuation administrators. These officials typically work for local governments responsible for determining property values. They are appointed in 10 states and elected in 22 states, and in 14 states the assessing jurisdiction has the option of appointing or electing the assessor.

The definition of the property tax base varies across states. Locally assessed property includes both real property (land and improvements) and personal property (machinery, household goods, automobiles, business inventories, and so forth). The trend in the United States has been to deemphasize the contribution of personal property to the tax base. As a result of these trends, real property accounts for more than 90 percent of total locally assessed taxable property, and personal property accounts for just 9 percent of the taxable base. (The most recent data on property taxation come from the 1992 Census of Governments [the Census Bureau discontinued this series in subsequent censuses]. Based on these data, real property is taxed in all 50 states, but motor vehicles are subject to some form of personal property tax in 18 states, household property in 17 states, and business inventories in 18 states; commercial and industrial personal property are taxed in 42 states, and agricultural property in 32 states.)

In addition to this locally assessed property, the tax base includes state-assessed property, which includes large, complex properties whose values are determined at the state level, such as utilities, railroads, oil and gas production properties, and mining properties. In 1991, state-assessed taxable property had an estimated value of $286 million, compared with locally assessed taxable property, which had an assessed value of $6.4 trillion.

Each state, in its constitution or statutes, defines one legal standard for all assessed values. While all standards have a basis in or a relationship to market value, market value and assessed value are not synonymous. Market value is the estimated selling price that a willing buyer would pay to a willing seller in a transaction where neither party is under duress—this is called an arm's length transaction. Assessed value is the value assigned to each property to determine its property tax liability.

All but five states require every assessing unit to maintain the same assessment level and definition of value—that is, they require uniformity of assessment. For real property, the 1992 Census of Governments (the most recent data available) indicates that 20 states and the District of Columbia require assessed values to equal market values (or fair cash value, or true value). An additional 15 states specify a single percentage of market value, or a way of calculating a single percentage annually, to determine assessed value. For 14 states, the single assessment level for real property has disappeared and has been replaced by a "classified property tax," which assesses different types of property (classified by ownership or use characteristics) at different percentages of market value. California is unique because it adjusts the prior year's assessment, but the annual increase is limited to 2 percent unless the property is sold.

The assessing function—the process of determining assessed values—involves three specific activities: the discovery, listing, and valuation of each parcel of land. Discovery requires the identification of each parcel of real property (or each taxable unit of personal property). This activity is typically manifested in a tax, or cadastral, map that displays parcels of real property, showing for each the boundaries, size, location, parcel identification number, ownership, value, and other spatially oriented details such as easements, rights-of-way, soil types, and flood plains. As a result of this activity, the assessor is custodian of the largest public database on property parcels. Listing underlies the preparation of a permanent record of each taxable property. Valuation is the most complicated component of the process.

The ultimate goal of the assessor during valuation is to provide the most accurate estimate of what an individual property would sell for on the open market at a given time. Written procedures, establishing the parameters or rules governing subjective judgments that an individual assessor must make, help reduce the variation in estimated market value between different assessors. These standard procedures result in less variation in property assessments, thereby minimizing some of the confusion on the part of both practitioners and the general public.

Whatever the exact provisions of a state's assessment law, assessors employ three common approaches to the valuation of property that are endorsed by the American Institute of Real Estate Appraisers:

1. Cost approach—the current cost of reproducing a property minus depreciation from deterioration or functional and economic obsolescence.
2. Income approach—the value that the property's potential net earning power will support, based on a capitalization of net income.
3. Market data approach—the value indicated by recent sales of comparable properties in the marketplace.

Typically, each approach to valuing property is applied to a specific subset of property uses. For example, market data are more commonly used in valuing single-family residences than in valuing commercial or industrial properties, because the latter are relatively heterogeneous and sell relatively infrequently. However, each approach to value, if accurately carried out, should produce approximately the same estimate of market value—in the absence of serious market disequilibrium. These individual approaches should not be considered mutually exclusive, but rather as alternatives that may be used to verify the results of the "traditional" approach to valuing each property type.

Because the actual market value for an individual parcel is observed only when a sale takes place, local officials and property owners are concerned about how well assessors estimate the value of property that does not sell. How accurately does the assessor's estimated market value—which is the product of the assessment process described above—reflect the "true" market value as indicated by actual sales data? In addition, are properties assessed uniformly? Such uniformity among local property owners and between taxing districts is important because property valuations serve as a basis for

- tax levies by overlapping governmental units—for example, counties, school districts, and special districts;

- determinations of net bonded indebtedness, which often is restricted to a percentage of either the local assessed value or market value of property in a jurisdiction;
- determinations of authorized levies restricted by tax-rate limits; and
- apportionment of state assistance to local governmental units—for example, school aid formula, local government aid formula.

The consequence of nonuniform assessment is an unwarranted shift in the tax burden to the benefit of some property owners but to the detriment of others. An equitable distribution of the tax burden is achieved only if built upon uniform assessment. With uniform assessment, property owners with properties of equal value pay the same tax—this is horizontal equity. Similarly, those with more valuable property pay a higher tax—this is vertical equity. Achievement of both types of equity requires uniform assessments.

To evaluate the degree of uniformity across properties and jurisdictions, reasonably accurate and acceptable statistical techniques are used. Assessment/sales ratio studies are used in approximately 40 states to measure the degree of assessment inequality in and across jurisdictions. The assessment/sales ratio for an individual parcel is simply the relationship between the assessor's estimated market value and the actual sales price, expressed as a ratio. If perfect assessment uniformity existed in an area, the assessor's estimated market value for a property that sold would be 100 percent of the actual sales price and no ratio would deviate from that level. In practice, however, actual assessment/sales ratios vary substantially.

The uniformity of a group of assessment/sales ratios is initially described by various measures of central tendency. For example, the mean ratio, or arithmetic average, of a group of assessment/sales ratios is derived by computing the ratios for individual properties, adding the ratios together, and dividing the total by the number of parcels. For the sample properties in table 1, the mean is 87.0 (435/5). Alternatively, the individual ratios can be arranged from the highest to lowest values and the middle ratio in the series can be selected; this is the median ratio. In table 1, the median ratio is 90.0. Another common method of describing the degree of uniformity among a group of assessment/sales ratios is to calculate the aggregate average, or the weighted mean. This measure is computed by dividing the assessor's total estimated market value for all properties sold by the total sales prices of those properties. In table 1, the aggregate, or weighted, average ratio is 81.4 ($136,750/$168,000). Thus, the measure of central tendency used to describe a series of individual assessment/sales ratios can influence the perception of how well property is being assessed in an area. The International Association of Assessing Officers (IAAO) has established standards for median assessment/sales ratios of 90 to 110 percent of actual sales price.

A second dimension of assessment quality that needs monitoring is the dispersal of actual assessment ratios around

TABLE 1. Assessment/Sales Ratios

Property	Assessed value (A)	Sales price (S)	A/S ratio	Absolute deviation
1	$20,900	$19,000	110.0%	20
2	$28,500	$30,000	95.0%	5
3	$22,950	$25,500	90.0%	0
4	$33,200	$41,500	80.0%	10
5	$31,200	$52,000	60.0%	30
Total	$136,750	$168,000	81.4%	65

the measure of central tendency. For example, for any particular taxing jurisdiction, the median assessment ratio may equal 1.0, indicating that the estimated value of the median property exactly equaled its actual selling price. However, this provides no information about the variation in the individual ratios in the jurisdiction—that is, how closely clustered around the median those other ratios are.

The coefficient of dispersion is the most common measure of the variability of individual assessment/sales ratios—used in 19 states. It measures the deviation of individual parcel ratios from the average ratio as a percentage of the average ratio—in other words, it is a measure of horizontal equity. The higher the coefficient, the less uniform the assessments. In table 1, individual assessment/sales ratios are subtracted from the median ratio, and the difference is recorded in the last column without regard to its sign (absolute deviation from the median). Next, these absolute deviations are summed and divided by the number of homes in the sample (65/5 = 13). This average absolute deviation is expressed as a percentage of the median ratio [(13/90) 100 = 14.4 percent]. The International Association of Assessing Officers (IAAO) has established a standard for the coefficient of dispersion of under 10 percent for new and/or homogeneous areas and under 15 percent for older or otherwise heterogeneous areas.

A final measure of assessment quality is the price-related differential. While the coefficient of dispersion is a measure of horizontal equity in assessment, the price-related differential is a measure of vertical equity. It measures the inequality that exists in the assessment between high- and low-value properties. The price-related differential is calculated by dividing the mean (or median) assessment ratio by the weighted mean (discussed above). Assessments are considered regressive if high-value properties are systematically valued at a lower share of market value than low-value properties resulting in a value for the price-related differential greater than 1. Alternatively, assessments are considered progressive if high-value properties are systematically valued at a higher share of market value than low-value properties resulting in a value for the price-related differential of less than 1. As a generally accepted rule, the IAAO suggests that the price-related differential should fall between 0.98 and 1.03. Using the median ratio of 90.0 and the weighted mean of 81.4 we see that the properties in table 1 have a price-related differential of 1.11—in other words, the assessments are regressive.

Finally, the assessment process has been revolutionized with the advent and application of computers. Computer-assisted mass appraisal (CAMA) models analyze extensive real estate market data and/or housing characteristic and sales data to estimate market values of properties not recently sold. CAMA allows frequent reassessment of residential properties. The improved quality of assessments obtained with CAMA models makes it possible to monitor and reassess property annually to ensure equitable assessment. According to a 1990 Survey of State and Provincial Assessment Administration Practices undertaken by the IAAO and the Lincoln Institute of Land Policy, 16 states monitor computer use by the primary assessing units. State programs are of several kinds: (1) maintaining a centralized computer system that generates values and tax lists or processes locally developed values; (2) providing software, usually with technical assistance and training, to local units; and (3) reviewing and approving contracts for computer-assisted valuation services provided by private firms.

Mapping for assessors is emerging as an integral element of a local geographic information system (GIS). GIS is essentially a multipurpose assemblage of computer capability designed to receive, display, manipulate, or otherwise process digital data with a spatial dimension. All these new technologies, however, require a commitment of funds on the part of the local jurisdiction for the hardware and software necessary to implement them, in addition to the highly trained (and paid) professional staff necessary to operate them. The cost of these new technologies must be weighed against the improved quality of assessment, and their impact on the coordination of information across governmental functions must be measured.

ADDITIONAL READINGS

Bell, Michael, and John Bowman. "Property Taxes." In *Local Government Finance: Concepts and Practices,* edited by John Petersen and Dennis Strachota (85–111). Chicago: Government Finance Officers Association, 1991.

Bowman, John H. "Real Property Taxation." In *Taxing Simply, Taxing Fairly,* edited by the District of Columbia Tax Revision Commission (119–97). Washington, DC: District of Columbia Tax Revision Commission, 1998. http://www.ntanet.org.

Bureau of the Census, Governments Division. *1992 Census of Governments. Vol. 2: Taxable Property Values, No. 1: Assessed Valuations for Local General Property Taxation.* GC92(2)-1. Washington, DC: Bureau of the Census, 1994.

Eckert, Joseph K., with Robert J. Gloudemans and Richard R. Almy. *Property Appraisal and Assessment Administration.* Chicago: The International Association of Assessing Officers, 1990.

Malme, Jane. "Property Tax Administration in North America." *Property Tax Journal* 9, no. 4 (December 1990): 235–47.

Cross-references: property tax, farm; Proposition 13/property tax caps; property tax, real property, business; property tax, real property, residential.

Property tax, farm

Donald F. Vitaliano

Rensselaer Polytechnic Institute

Updated by

Jennifer Gravelle

U.S. Government Accountability Office

Property used in connection with farming frequently receives special treatment under state and local property taxes.

Virtually every state in the Union has some sort of program designed to confer special property tax treatment upon farms. Although such plans were originally conceived as a way to preserve family farming, supporters of preferential treatment of farmland now include environmentalists who see it as way of preserving open spaces from encroaching suburban development. However, the weight of professional judgment and empirical evidence appears not to support such programs, whether judged on their own terms or by the conventional public finance criteria of equity, economic efficiency, and ease of administration.

The impetus to grant relief to farm real estate derives from a (correct) perception by the general public and policymakers that the property tax is regressive in relation to income, rather than a type of wealth tax. This attitude is reinforced by pressure for full-value assessment as communities undergo the transition from rural to suburban, a movement that particularly burdens farm real estate because it is typically assessed at the lowest fraction of market value among the several types of real property. A legitimate case for relief is conceivable if present owners reasonably anticipated continuation of these assessment practices at the time of purchase.

Preservation of family farming may be viewed as a form of income redistribution, whereas open-space preservation has to do with possible market failure. In the absence of market failure, economic efficiency favors full-value taxation because it is neutral in its impact on land-use decisions: the tax burden is unaffected by the use of the land.

Farm property is accorded special treatment in several different ways: preferential assessment at current use value instead of market value, deferred taxation of land kept in farming, credits against state income taxes, purchase of development rights, and land-use zoning. Zoning tends to impose the cost

of farm preservation on landowners, and their resistance to it can be expected. But land not subject to significant development pressure may actually increase in value when subjected to strict agricultural zoning resulting from, say, reduced uncertainty and limits on nearby incompatible activities.

Forty-five states rely primarily upon some variant of use-value assessment. The popularity of this type of assessment may be attributed to the fact that it benefits farmers and investors who receive significant amounts of nonfarm income and who would not qualify for much, if any, relief under a tax credit scheme.

The impact of use-value taxation on the rate of conversion of farmland has been found to be negligible by Gloudemans (1974), Gustafson and Wallace (1975), Conklin and Lesher (1977), and Blewett and Lane (1988). Ladd (1980) and Kashian and Skidmore (2002) suggest that use-value assessment may have questionable distributional consequences.

The existence of external benefits of open space not reflected in the pecuniary and psychic returns to the farm operator is one type of market failure that may justify a farm tax subsidy. In addition, because automobile drivers do not bear the full social cost of commuting to work, inefficient overexpansion of suburbs may occur. One study suggests that the private supply of open space was 20 percent less than the socially optimal amount in densely populated, higher-income areas of Massachusetts (Lopez, Shah, and Altobello 1994). However, the effectiveness of preferential farm property taxation in slowing conversion is likely to be least in just such areas because the value of property tax abatements is usually small relative to potential development profit.

To slow the pace of development, preferential taxation must push forward the date at which the landowner chooses to sell out for development. In the simplest case where development income does not grow, the decision to sell merely involves comparison of the present discounted value of net farm income versus the discounted value of the potential net income from the most profitable development option. Thus, development must be able to absorb the opportunity cost of sacrificed farm output plus the capital cost of conversion, such as new structures. This illustrates how shaky is the argument for special property tax treatment of farmland based on running out of land used to grow food and other useful crops. Present and expected future returns from farming clearly incorporate estimates of future food prices. Unless it can be shown that systematic myopia exists, anticipated food scarcity automatically rations land to farming uses by raising the opportunity cost of development.

In the situation where expected development revenues grow through time as land ripens, the timing of the development act is dependent on the gain to the landowner from postponement of development (appropriately discounted to reflect the time value of money) compared with the forgone development profit during the period of postponement (say, one year). The more rapid the rate of ripening, the sooner the parcel will be developed because of the higher cost of postponement.

Credits against state income tax (often labeled circuit breaker programs) can, at least in principle, better focus the redistribution of income by explicitly taking into account the overall economic circumstances of the farmer. However, the typical tax credit program omits the increased value of the land as a component of income, a serious deficiency when judged by the widely accepted Haig-Simons definition of income for tax purposes: consumption plus changes in net worth. Wisconsin (which also values farmland according to use) and Michigan use credits against income tax to grant relief to low-income farmers.

Tax relief, whether via credits or preferential assessment, assumes that the true burden of the property tax is measured by actual tax payments by current landowners. However, if property taxes are capitalized into a decreased market price of the property, as is usually assumed by economists, the current owner bears only that part of the tax that was increased or not anticipated to increase during his ownership tenure. The relief granted may therefore not be justified.

Empirical evidence

The emphasis of empirical studies relating to farmland taxation has been on the degree of capitalization of the various property tax preferences into the market price of the land. This effort is complicated by the typically weak administration of the property tax. Fractional assessments and lags in updating assessment rolls in many communities mean that farm property is rarely taxed at current market value. This is especially so in rural communities where farming interests effectively control the local government apparatus.

One study used regression analysis to examine 458 sales of arable farmland and pastures, without structures, between 1982 and 1985 in New York state (vineyards and tree croplands were excluded) (Vitaliano and Hill 1994). New York employs use-value assessment of farms voluntarily enrolled in agricultural districts for an eight-year period, which is renewable. No statistically significant effect of the use-value program on the sale price of farmland was detected. The authors suggested that this finding was likely a result of widespread de facto use-value assessment in rural areas, as well as the voluntary nature of the tax abatement program in New York. Another possible reason is that locally financed tax abatement is partly offset by a higher tax rate as the tax base shrinks from assessment erosion; this effect can be significant in communities where farm property constitutes the bulk of the base and much of it is granted relief, de jure or de facto. Parcels located near strong nonfarm influences (e.g., shopping centers) sold for an average 45 percent more than otherwise similar parcels. Farmers are not likely to forgo these potential gains voluntarily when they are likely to realize many of the tax abatement benefits without participating in the Agricultural District Program.

Michigan's program of credits against state income tax relieved enrolled properties of 80 to 90 percent of annual property taxes, which were capitalized into an average 10 percent higher property value (Anderson and Bunch 1989). These numbers indicate how difficult it is to materially affect the pattern of land use by means of locally financed tax concessions. Few communities could afford to grant widespread abatement of 80 percent or more of farm property taxes. And even in this situation, property values rise by only 10 percent, which is significantly less than the prospective gain from a typical development sale.

While much of the empirical work has centered on farmland prices, a recent study examined the tax distributional effects of the 1995 change from market value to use-value assessment in Wisconsin (Kashian and Skidmore 2002). The authors based their analysis on data from Muskego, an agricultural town with recent exposure to urban sprawl. They conclude that use-valuation essentially subsidizes suburban fringe communities and is a questionable policy for farmland preservation.

Another study estimated the value of the tax expenditures from use assessment (Anderson and Griffing 2000). The study, which looked at the difference between market value and use value of agricultural land in the Omaha and Lincoln urban areas of Nebraska, found that the amount of tax expenditures associated with use assessment ranged from $6.42 per acre ($3 million total) in Lancaster County to $59.75 ($6 million total) per acre in Sarpy County. The paper also found that, as urban land value models predict, the difference between market value and use value declines with distance from the central business district.

Tax relief for farm property, whether justified as income redistribution or correction of market failure, should probably be financed by higher levels of government, either because the sources of these higher-level tax subsidies are more equitable or because the locus of external benefits from open-space preservation is more widespread than the local taxing jurisdiction. Administration of tax concessions to farmland causes problems because use value is difficult to determine. Capitalization of existing net income flows assumes present crops and farm management are optimal. Comparable sales are unhelpful because they will incorporate anticipated development value. Further, tax credits require a more comprehensive measure of economic capacity than current definitions.

Overall, the typical use-value farm tax abatement program seems to get low marks in preserving open spaces, either because abatement is not worth as much as development or because de facto abatement accomplishes the same thing. As a method of income redistribution, the programs are too blunt, granting aid without properly measuring need. An alternative might be a phase-in of full-market assessment or loans at market interest payable upon sale to finance current tax payments. Both these measures would discourage forced sales, which are often used as a justification of existing abatement programs, even though their extent is largely undocumented. Despite their shortcomings, current programs appear to be politically popular and are likely to be continued.

ADDITIONAL READINGS

Anderson, John E. "Use-Value Property Tax Assessment: Effects on Land Development." *Land Economics* 69 (August 1993): 263–69.

Anderson, John E., and Howard C. Bunch. "Agricultural Property Tax Relief." *Land Economics* 65 (February 1989): 13–22.

Anderson, John E., and Marlon F. Griffing. "Use-Value Assessment Tax Expenditures in Urban Areas." *Journal of Urban Economics* 48 (November 2000): 443–52.

Bentick, Brian L., and Thomas F. Pogue. "Development Timing and Property Taxes." *Land Economics* 64 (November 1988): 317–24.

Blewett, Robert A., and Julia I. Lane. "Development Rights and Differential Assessment of Agricultural Land: Fractional Valuation of Farmland Is Ineffective for Preserving Open Space and Subsidizes Speculation." *American Journal of Economics and Sociology* 47 (April 1988): 195–205.

Conklin, Howard E., and William G. Lesher. "Farm Value Assessment as a Means for Reducing Premature and Excessive Agricultural Disinvestment in Urban Fringes." *American Journal of Agricultural Economics* 59 (November 1977): 755–59.

Gloudemans, Robert J. *Use-Value Farmland Assessments: Theory, Practice and Impact.* Chicago: International Association of Assessing Officers, 1974.

Gustafson, Gregory C., and L. T. Wallace. "Differential Assessment as Land Use Policy: The California Case." *Journal of the American Institute of Planners* 41 (September 1975): 379–84.

Henneberry, David M., and Richard I. Barrows. "Capitalization of Agricultural Zoning." *Land Economics* 66 (August 1990): 249–58.

Kashian, Russ, and Mark Skidmore. "Preserving Agricultural Land via Property Assessment Policy and the Willingness to Pay for Land Preservation." *Economic Development Quarterly* 16 (February 2002): 75–87.

Ladd, Helen F. "The Considerations Underlying Preferential Tax Treatment of Open Space and Agricultural Land." In *Property Tax Preferences for Agricultural Land,* edited by Neal A. Roberts and H. James Brown (15–42). New York: Lincoln Institute of Land Policy and Universe Books, Inc., 1980.

———. *Local Government Tax and Land Use Policies in the United States.* Northampton, MA: Edward Elgar Publishing, 1998.

Lopez, Rigoberto A., Farhed A. Shah, and Marilyn A. Altobello. "Optimal Allocation of Land." *Land Economics* 70 (February 1994): 53–62.

Vitaliano, Donald F., and Constance Hill. "Agricultural Districts and Farmland Prices." *The Journal of Real Estate Finance and Economics* 8 (May 1994): 213–23.

Cross-reference: property tax assessment.

Property tax, motor vehicle taxes

Maxim A. Shvedov
Congressional Research Service, Library of Congress

Taxes levied on motor vehicles according to value.

In the United States, personal property taxes on noncommercial motor vehicles are levied by states and localities. Currently, local governments in 12 states impose value-based (ad valorem) tax on motor vehicles at locally determined rates. Sixteen more states have a state value-based tax "in lieu" of property tax on vehicles. Three more have some hybrid structure. In addition, states and localities also impose a variety of flat registration fees, weight-based taxes, and sales taxes on vehicles. The distinction between ad valorem and other types of levies is important, because only regular ad valorem taxes and fees are deductible for federal individual income tax purposes. Finally, vehicles used for business purposes are often subject to business personal property taxes.

Property taxes are an important source of state and especially local government financing. In 2000, states received about $11.0 billion (less than 1 percent of the total revenues) and localities about $238.2 billion (over 23 percent) in total property tax revenues, but most was generated by real property taxes. Personal property taxes represented a small, though significant, portion. Beyond noncommercial use motor vehicles, personal property includes other household property, intangible property, business inventory, and depreciable assets.

Historically, personal property was an important part of the tax base in the early 19th century, but after peaking during the Civil War period, property taxation shifted toward real property. The trend continued throughout the 20th century. Personal property represented 16.0 percent of the net taxable property assessed value in 1961, but just 8.8 percent in 1991, the latest year the U.S. Census compiled the data.

The primary reason for the decline has been the increasing administrative complexity of the tax as the economy has diversified and taxpayers and property have become increasingly mobile. For example, inventorying and assessing household property became impractical, essentially exempting most of it from taxation. Motor vehicles, along with boats, aircraft, and similar items, are the few remaining types of household property still taxable. The high value, relative homogeneity, and registration requirements make taxing these types of property administratively feasible and cost-effective.

Tax administrators use several techniques to determine the value of the motor vehicles: National Automobile Dealers' Association's (N.A.D.A.) Official Used Car Guide (the "blue book") values, depreciated manufacturer suggested retail price, or depreciated purchase price. The choice of technique varies by jurisdiction, which often leads to disparities among localities. The valuation technique, the assessment ratio, and the nominal tax rate determine the effective tax rate. In 1998, the effective rates varied from 0.3 percent to 5.4 percent for localities imposing the tax. These were extreme values, each one found in just one locality. The median personal property tax rate was 1.9 percent, and the median state in lieu of rate, 1.8 percent.

Personal property taxes on motor vehicles have many of the features of other property taxes. It is an easy-to-administer and stable revenue source. There is a strong link between the tax and public services it funds. Thus, the tax serves as a fee for local services. Most administrative problems relate to the vehicle situs (physical location for tax purposes) and the determination of the purpose of its use.

The tax's structure and rates determine its degree of progressivity. The tax is likely to be fairly consistent with taxpayers' ability to pay principal within a given locality, due to the fact that higher-income individuals tend to buy more expensive vehicles and do so more frequently. At the same time, critics of the tax often point to the large disparities among localities. Furthermore, the tax is imposed on a relatively illiquid property and does not take into account taxpayers' current income, which may pose a problem in certain instances. By using various exemptions, deferrals, and other "circuit breaker" mechanisms it is possible to adjust the burden distribution to meet the desired parameters. State "in lieu" taxes alleviate the disparities among jurisdictions within a state and simplify situs determination.

In terms of behavioral responses, Ott and Andrus (2000) found that the tax has a weak effect on vehicle-buying decisions, even though their study participants believed the taxes were too high. Mikesell (1992) found that a lower personal property share in the property tax base leads to a higher total property tax per dollar of personal income.

Property taxes on vehicles are highly visible, making their reduction politically attractive. In the past decade, they were a key local political issue in a number of states, most notably in California and Virginia. Other states where related proposals were floated include Missouri and South Carolina.

ADDITIONAL READINGS

Brunori, David. *Local Tax Policy: A Federalist Perspective.* Washington, DC: Urban Institute Press, 2003.

Mikesell, John L. "Patterns of Exclusion of Personal Property from American Property Tax System." *Public Finance Quarterly* 20, no. 4 (October 1992): 528–42.

National Conference of State Legislatures. "State and Local Value-Based Taxes on Motor Vehicles," Jan. 28, 1998. http://www.ncsl.org/programs/fiscal/autotaxs.htm.

Ott, Richard L., and David M. Andrus. "The Effects of Personal Property Taxes on Consumer Vehicle-Purchasing Decisions: A Partitioned Price/Mental Accounting Theory Analysis." *Public Finance Review* 28, no. 2 (March 2000): 134–52.

U.S. Bureau of the Census. *1992 Census of Governments. Volume 2: Taxable Property Values, Number 1, Assessed Valuations for Local General Property Taxation.* GC92(2)-1. Washington, DC: GPO, 1994.

———. *Statistical Abstract of the United States: 2003.* Washington, DC: U.S. Department of Commerce, 2003.

Wheeler, Laura A. "Reducing the Property Tax on Motor Vehicles in Georgia." Atlanta: Georgia Public Policy Foundation, 1998.

Property tax, real property, business

Marion S. Beaumont
California State University–Long Beach

Since business is an organizational form of individuals acting collectively, the (usually local) taxation of the business entity is often the most efficient and fair way to assess individuals for public services that accrue to them indirectly; however, the form of the tax may vary depending on policy objectives.

The business real property tax is a component of the property tax base in the United States (all 50 states and the District of Columbia) and in numerous countries worldwide. It is conditioned on the ownership, and measured by the value, of business real property: land and improvements that are permanently attached to the land (structures and other immovables including mines, minerals in place, oil and gas wells). In the United States, the business real property tax is primarily an own-source of tax revenue for local governments. The tax is also a feasible own–local revenue source for new democracies (e.g., in Central and Eastern Europe) and developing countries that are hard-pressed to finance their local service requirements (Bird, Ebel, and Wallich 1998; World Bank 1988; Almy 2003).

Tax base, valuation, revenue

No single, nationwide business real property tax exists in the United States. Instead, each state's property tax law, often with individual jurisdictional variations, defines the tax base, rates, valuation system, and administration. The Bureau of the Census's quinquennial Census of Governments, in which the locally assessed value of taxable real property is listed by use category—residential (single-family, multifamily), commercial, industrial, acreage, and vacant platted lots—is the best source of aggregate business real property tax data. In this taxonomy, commercial (retail stores, restaurants, office buildings, hotels) and industrial (manufacturing plants, warehouses) parcels of locally assessed real property are the core components of the business real property tax. In 1986, the last year census data are available by use category, commercial and industrial property accounted for only 4 percent of the 108 million locally assessed parcels, but 21 percent of total gross assessed value. In practice, the business real property tax base may also include other locally assessed realty (e.g., multifamily farm acreage) and state-assessed real property. Although some states (e.g., Minnesota) publish property tax data by use category, lack of aggregate use-category data since the 1987 Census of Governments is an unfortunate obstacle to understanding the current status and role of the business real property tax in the information age. Devolution of responsibility from the federal to the state-local sector for important services and the complexities of deregulation (e.g., utilities), environmental concerns (e.g., pollution control, valuation of environmentally sensitive land), public education funding priorities, economic development pressures, and homeland security readiness) all affect the business real property tax and require informed policymaking.

In addition to taxes on real property (defined as rights, protected by law, to land and improvements to the land), firms pay taxes on some personal property. Defined as all property (tangible or intangible) other than real property (realty), personal property (personalty) is movable—not permanently attached to real estate. Whether a particular item is real or personal property—computer hardware and components, for example—can be controversial and may be specified by statute or litigation. The number of states that assessed certain types of personal property in 1999 were as follows: inventories, 15 states; machinery and equipment, 43; tangible business personal property, 35; and intangible personal property, 10 (see Almy 2000). Business inventories are wholly exempt in 18 states and exempt partially or by local option in three states (Sexton 2003). The trend to exempt intangible personal property (equities, bonds, copyrights, patents, franchises, deposits, and other financial assets) is likely to continue for several reasons: litigation, preference of states to tax the income flow from intangibles under a broad-based income tax, the ease of moving and hiding intangibles to evade taxation, and the widespread use of economic development incentives to businesses for which intangible assets are an increasingly important part of production. Numerous other exemptions and exclusions further narrow the business real property tax base (see Tannenwald 2002 and Netzer 2003).

A glimpse of the potential business real property tax base in 1986 is provided by computing the ratio of the gross assessed value of nonresidential realty, $1,880.9 billion (U.S. Department of Commerce 1998), to the Department of Commerce's estimated value of the net stock of nonresidential Fixed Reproducible Tangible Wealth in the United States in 1986, $5,211.5 billion (Katz and Herman 1997). Dividing the numerator ($1,880.9 billion) by the denominator ($5,211.5 billion) and multiplying the result by 100 indicates that in 1986 an estimated 36 percent of the potential real property tax base (Department of Commerce data) was included in the gross assessed value of business property (U.S. Department of Commerce 1998).

The Department of Commerce, Bureau of Economic Analysis (BEA), introduced new wealth estimates and new methodology (e.g., business and government expenditures for software are considered investment, a new pattern of depreciation of personal computers is employed, and new terminology is used: fixed assets instead of fixed reproducible tangible wealth) (see Herman 2000). Updated wealth estimates, from 1925 to the latest data year, are available in interactive tables at BEA's web site, http://www.bea.gov/ (click Fixed Assets). BEA defines fixed assets as "produced assets that are used repeatedly, or continuously, in processes of production for more than one year." Produced assets are "nonfinancial assets that have come into existence as outputs from a production process" (BEA 2003). For the 11-year period 1992–2002, a portion of the potential business real property tax base can be estimated. The current-cost net stock of private nonresidential fixed assets (PNFA), consisting of equipment, software, and structures, increased 64.7 percent, from $6,936.3 billion in 1992 to $11,424.7 billion in 2002. As a percent of PNFA in 1992, equipment and software declined from 39.4 in 1992 to 38.6 in 2002; structures increased from 60.6 percent of PNFA in 1992 to 61.4 percent in 2002. By industry group, PNFA values are the sum of information processing equipment and software, industrial equipment, transportation equipment, other equipment, and structures. Information processing equipment increased from 10.6 percent of PNFA in 1992 to 11.4 percent in 2002; industrial equipment declined from 13.5 percent to 11.7 percent in 2002; transportation equipment increased from

7.8 percent to 8.7 percent; and other equipment declined from 7.5 percent to 6.8 percent.

The new wealth estimates confirm macroeconomic structural change, from industrial to services production in the United States, and suggest a widening gap between the actual (taxable) and the potential business real property tax base. Equipment and software used by businesses may be assessed as real property, or quite likely, as personal property that many states choose to exempt, fully or partially.

In a 50-state study of business taxes, the Council On State Taxation (COST), a nonprofit trade association, used a comprehensive business property tax base (including commercial and industrial property taxes; residential rental property taxes; the taxable portion of educational, farm, and not-for-profit-entity property taxes; and state-level intangible property taxes) to determine for each state the property taxes paid by business entities (corporations; noncorporate businesses, including sole proprietorships, partnerships, and not-for-profit entities; and rental property held by individuals) (Cline et al. 2004). In fiscal year 2003, property taxes paid by business accounted for the largest share, 38.6 percent ($156.1 billion), of total state and local business taxes ($404.1 billion). For the 2000–03 period, property taxes increased $14.9 billion (11.4 percent) and represented the largest dollar increase of any of the state and local business taxes included in the study. Findings of the COST study illustrate the relative stability of state and local business property tax revenue in a period of structural change in the macroeconomy and of cyclical change (the 2000–03 period included the March–November 2001 recession in the United States).

Each item in the business real property tax base is appraised to determine its market value, and the assessed (taxable) value is computed as a certain percentage of market value. Market value is usually defined by statute (for example, "full value" in California, "fair and reasonable market value" in Alabama), and the assessment procedure is prescribed by law and/or traditional practice. Of the three major approaches to estimating market value—sales comparison, income (or capitalization), and cost—the income and cost approaches, or a combination of value indicators, are preferred to the sales comparison approach alone in commercial/industrial appraisals; comparable sales data are often scarce or nonexistent (see International Association of Assessing Officers 1996).

Appraisals are performed by the local assessor, subject to the supervision of a state agency (tax commission, department of revenue, board of equalization). Properties that cross the boundaries of a single local taxing jurisdiction are generally state-assessed. In California the State Board of Equalization assesses annually the property of these types of companies: telephone and telegraph; railroads; gas, electric, and water; and intercounty pipelines, flumes, canals, ditches, and aqueducts. The assessed value of these properties is allocated among the counties where the properties are physically located and is subject to local taxation. Revenue from California's only state property tax, the private railroad cars tax, is deposited in the state's General Fund (California State Board of Equalization 2003). Almy noted a trend of state governments outpacing local governments in collecting property tax revenues (Almy 2000). Reasons include states' need to comply with court-ordered changes in funding public schools and diversion of property tax revenue from local to state governments during fiscal crises, as noted in California's 2004–05 state budget. Computer and information management systems, statistical modeling, computer assisted mass appraisal, and geographic information systems facilitate updating assessments and improving property tax administration in large and small jurisdictions (see Ireland and O'Connor 2002).

Myriad legal assessment standards (such as Proposition 13's 1975 base or acquisition-year methodology in California), differential assessment rules to promote or retain certain uses of property (farm, scenic, and recreational uses; historic preservation; energy conservation; environmental protection), and classified property taxation are among the many legal variations that complicate property valuation. Structural changes and cyclical effects are additional complexities. Twenty-four states and the District of Columbia employ a legal assessment ratio for more than one class of property (Sexton 2003). The assessment ratio (assessment level as a percentage of market value) for classified commercial/industrial property is generally the same or higher than for residential property.

Business real property tax revenues are the product of the net (of exemptions) assessed value of business realty and the nominal property tax rate. Increasingly, nominal tax rates are specified by tax rate or expenditure limits rather than by computing the ratio of a jurisdiction's levy to its net assessed value. The Advisory Commission on Intergovernmental Relations (ACIR) estimated business real property tax revenue in 1991 at $44.1 billion, or approximately 8 percent of state and local government tax revenue (ACIR 1993).

The COST study's estimate of business real property tax revenue in fiscal year 2003 ($156.1 billion) is 3½-fold higher than ACIR's 1991 estimate ($44.1 billion) and is 16.5 percent of total state and local tax revenue ($948.1 billion) in 2003. (See Cline et al. 2004).

Economic effects

Owners of business realty bear the legal responsibility (statutory incidence), but not necessarily the final burden (economic incidence), of the business real property tax. Property tax incidence, the study of the changes in the distribution of economic welfare resulting from imposition of the tax, has an extensive literature (R. Zodrow 2001; Fischel 2001; Fullerton and Metcalf 2002). Two major theories that are especially relevant to business real property tax incidence are the "new view" introduced by Mieszkowski (1972) and the "benefit" approach (Hamilton 1975).

According to the "new view," the local general property tax has two (analytic) parts. One is the "average" nationwide effective property tax rate, borne by all owners of capital.

The second part, the local differential tax rate, has excise tax effects because mobile capital can leave localities with above the (national) average tax rates. In the "new view," if the quantity of capital (property) is fixed in the short run, and if local tax differentials are relatively small, the property tax is a distortionary tax on all capital. Assuming capital ownership rises with income, the property tax burden is distributed progressively.

In biennial empirical studies that conceptualize the "new view," the incidence of the Minnesota business real property tax (the state does not tax personalty) is analyzed in three steps: (1) Impact, the initial imposition of the tax; (2) Incidence, after shifting, the actual burden of the tax on Minnesota consumers, capital, and labor and on nonresidents; and (3) Allocation, the actual burden of the tax on specific Minnesota households. Results indicate that in 2000, 32 percent of the business real property tax was distributed to consumers, 2 percent to labor, 24 percent to capital, and 42 percent was exported to nonresidents (see Minnesota Department of Revenue 2003). Minnesota's tax incidence studies include estimates of tax incidence in the current data year (2000) and five years hence (2005). The forecasting feature of the incidence studies is intended to provide policymakers insight into Minnesota's state and local tax system under current law and what it would be with changes in the law.

According to the "benefit" approach, the property tax is a nondistortionary payment for local public services, similar to a user fee. This view is accommodated by extending, through zoning and other land use restrictions, the all-consumer Tiebout model of efficient provision of local public goods to include commercial/industrial property (see Fischel 1992 and 2001). A suggested implementation of the benefit approach is to levy uniform tax rates on value added (Oakland and Testa 1996).

Each theory—new view or benefit—can be shown to be consistent with the other theory; depending on assumptions made, time period (long-term, short-term) and behavioral responses expected (G. Zodrow 2001; Fischel 2001; Nechyba 2001). The benefit theory assumes the mobility of households (business firms) and the immobility of housing (capital); the new view assumes the mobility of housing (capital) and a fixed national capital stock. Because of its assumption of capital mobility, the new view seems more applicable to business taxation than the benefit view (see Nechyba 2001).

Among the many implications of the benefit theory are these: Is the present assignment of fiscal instruments and functions in multilevel government efficient (does it minimize deadweight loss) when domestic and global mobility of nonland production factors is possible? What are the economic effects of federal government subsidization of local public services through permitting income tax deductibility of property taxes? Do homeowners who itemize income tax deductions have an incentive to encourage local governments to provide additional services that are paid for by property taxes? Are economic development incentives by subnational governments—property tax exemptions, abatements, tax increment financing—effective or desirable? Is a winner's curse a likely outcome?

Some old questions in the vast property tax literature are inspiring new approaches and exciting prospects for more definitive answers. While the significance of property taxes in business location decisions remains an unsettled issue (see Carroll and Wasylenko 1994 and Luce 1994), Ladd reports a changing consensus—from thinking taxes do not matter in locational decisions to the new consensus that taxes may have some effects (Ladd 1998). Proposals to pool the business portion of the property tax base statewide and redistribute the proceeds to local jurisdictions appear to be gaining acceptance as an alternative to intergovernmental aid as a fiscal equalization measure in the United States. Instead of partitioning the tax base, taxing land at a higher rate than improvements is often suggested. Both theoretical analysis (George 1956) and empirical evidence support, on efficiency grounds, adopting site value taxation, particularly in urban areas. Equity aspects are less convincing (see Bowman and Metcalf 2004; DiMasi 1987; and Beaumont 1992). With new computational capabilities, improved statistical models, and data that are timely, relevant, and consistently reliable and accessible, the long-sought empirical research—to better understand the effect of taxes on locational decisions, how best to encourage effective fiscal equalization, whether land value taxation's time has come, and which incidence theory is most relevant to the taxation of business real property—will be forthcoming.

ADDITIONAL READINGS

Advisory Commission on Intergovernmental Relations [ACIR]. *Significant Features of Fiscal Federalism 1992,* vol. 2. Report M-180. Washington, DC: ACIR, 1993.

Almy, Richard R. "Property Tax Policies and Administrative Practices in Canada and the United States: Executive Summary." *Assessment Journal* 7 (July/August 2000): 41–57.

———. "Modernizing Property Taxes: The Case Study of Lithuania." *Fair and Equitable* (Magazine of the International Association of Assessing Officers) 1 (December 2003): 7–10.

Beaumont, Marion S. "Optimal Property Taxation in California: Is Greater Reliance on Land Values Feasible and Desirable?" *Review of Urban and Regional Development Studies* 4 (1992): 162–78.

Bird, Richard M., Robert D. Ebel, and Christine I. Wallich. "Fiscal Decentralization: From Command to Market." In *The Economics of Fiscal Federalism and Local Finance,* edited by Wallace E. Oates (646–717). Cheltenham, U.K., and Northampton, MA: Edward Elgar Publishing, 1998.

Bowman, John H., and Gilbert E. Metcalf. "Implications of a Split-Rate Real Property Tax: An Initial Look at Three Virginia Counties." *State Tax Notes* (April 26, 2004): 261–91.

Brunori, David. *Local Tax Policy: A Federalist Perspective.* Washington DC: Urban Institute Press, 2003.

California State Board of Equalization. "2002–03 Annual Report, Table A-15, 2003." http://www.boe.ca.gov.

Carroll, Robert, and Michael Wasylenko. "Do State Business Climates Still Matter? Evidence of a Structural Change." *National Tax Journal* 47 (1994): 19–33.

Cline, Robert, William Fox, Tom Neubig, and Andrew Phillips. "Total State and Local Business Taxes: A 50-State Study of the Taxes Paid by Business in Fiscal 2003." *State Tax Notes* (March 1, 2004): 737–50.

Colker, David. "Property Taxation of Telecommunications Companies in California." *Assessment Journal* 4 (May/June 1997): 47–52.

DiMasi, Joseph A. "The Effects of Site Value Taxation in an Urban Area: A General Equilibrium Computational Approach." *National Tax Journal* 40 (1987): 577–90.

Fischel, William A. "Property Taxation and the Tiebout Model: Evidence for the Benefit View from Zoning and Voting." *Journal of Economic Literature* 30 (1992): 171–77.

———. "Municipal Corporations, Homeowners and the Benefit View of the Property Tax." In *Property Taxation and Local Government Finance,* edited by Wallace E. Oates (33–77). Cambridge, MA: Lincoln Institute of Land Policy, 2001.

Fisher, Ronald C. *State and Local Public Finance.* 2nd ed. Chicago: Irwin, 1996, 324–54.

Fullerton, Don, and Gilbert E. Metcalf. "Tax Incidence." In *Handbook of Public Economics 4,* edited by Alan Auerbach and Martin Feldstein (1787–1872). New York and Amsterdam: Elsevier, 2002.

George, Henry. *Progress and Poverty.* New York: Robert Schalkenbach Foundation, 1956 (first published 1879).

Hamilton, Bruce W. "Zoning and Property Taxation in a System of Local Governments." *Urban Studies* 12 (1975): 205–11.

Herman, Shelby W. "Fixed Assets and Consumer Durable Goods." Survey of Current Business 80 (April 2000): 17–30.

International Association of Assessing Officers [IAAO]. *Property Assessment Valuation.* 2nd ed. Chicago: IAAO, 1996.

Ireland, Michael W., and Patrick O'Connor. "Location Analysis for Commercial Properties." *Assessment Journal* 9 (November/December 2002): 21–26.

Katz, Arnold J., and Shelby W. Herman. "Improved Estimates of Fixed Reproducible Tangible Wealth, 1929–95." *Survey of Current Business* 77 (May 1997): 169–92.

Ladd, Helen F. "Effects of Taxes on Economic Activity." In *Local Government Tax and Land Use Policies in the United States, Understanding the Links,* edited by Helen F. Ladd (82–101). Cheltenham, U.K., and Northampton, MA: Edward Elgar, in association with the Lincoln Institute of Land Policy, 1998.

Luce, Thomas F., Jr. "Local Taxes, Public Services, and the Intrametropolitan Location of Firms and Households." *Public Finance Quarterly* 22 (April 1994): 139–67.

Mieszkowski, Peter. "The Property Tax: An Excise Tax or a Profits Tax?" *Journal of Public Economics* 1 (1972): 73–96.

Mieszkowski, Peter, and George R. Zodrow. "Taxation and the Tiebout Model: The Differential Effects of Head Taxes, Taxes on Land Rents, and Property Taxes." *Journal of Economic Literature* 27 (1989): 1098–1146.

Mikesell, John L. "Selected Business Property Taxation Issues: Personal Property." In *Taxation of Business Property,* edited by John H. Bowman (161–70). Westport, CT: Praeger, 1995.

Minnesota Department of Revenue, Tax Research Division. *2003 Minnesota Tax Incidence Study: An Analysis of Minnesota's Household and Business Taxes.* St. Paul: Minnesota Department of Revenue, Tax Research Division, 2003. http://www.taxes.state.mn.us/reports/reports.html.

Nechyba, Thomas J. "The Benefit View and the New View: Where Do We Stand Twenty-Five Years into the Debate?" In *Property Taxation and Local Government Finance,* edited by Wallace E. Oates (113–21). Cambridge, MA: Lincoln Institute of Land Policy, 2001.

Netzer, Dick. "The Relevance and Feasibility of Land Value Taxation in the Rich Countries." In *Land Value Taxation: Can It and Will It Work Today?* edited by Wallace E. Oates (109–40). Cambridge, MA: Lincoln Institute of Land Policy, 1998.

———. "Local Government Finance and the Economics of Property Tax Exemptions." *State Tax Notes* (June 23, 2003): 1053–69.

Oakland, William, and William A. Testa. "State-Local Business Taxation and the Benefit Principle." *Federal Reserve Bank of Chicago Economic Perspectives* 21 (January/February 1996): 2–19.

Sexton, Terri A. "The Property Tax Base in the United States: Exemptions, Incentives, and Relief." *Assessment Journal* 10 (Fall 2003): 5–33.

Tannenwald, Robert. "Are State and Local Revenue Systems Becoming Obsolete?" *National Tax Journal* 55 (September 2002): 467–89.

Tiebout, Charles M. "A Pure Theory of Local Expenditures." *Journal of Political Economy* 64 (1956): 416–24.

U.S. Department of Commerce, Bureau of the Census. *Taxable Property Values. 1987 Census of Governments 2.* Washington, DC: U.S. Government Printing Office, 1988.

U.S. Department of Commerce, Bureau of Economic Analysis. *Fixed Assets and Consumer Durable Goods in the United States.* Washington DC: U.S. Government Printing Office, 2003.

World Bank. *World Development Report 1988.* New York: Oxford University Press, 1988, 43–185.

Youngman, Joan M., and Jane H. Malme. *An International Survey of Taxes on Land and Buildings.* Boston: Kluwer Law and Taxation Publishers, 1993.

Zodrow, George R. "The Property Tax as a Capital Tax: A Room with Three Views." *National Tax Journal* 54 (March 2001): 139–56.

Zodrow, Robert R. "Reflections on the New View and the Benefit View of the Property Tax." In *Property Taxation and Local Government Finance,* edited by Wallace E. Oates (79–111). Cambridge, MA: Lincoln Institute of Land Policy, 2001.

Cross-references: fiscal federalism; incidence of taxes; property tax assessment; property tax, farm.

Property tax, real property, residential

Steven M. Sheffrin

University of California–Davis

Taxes levied on the value of residential property.

The residential real property tax is a tax levied on the value of residential structures, both owner-occupied and rented. It is part of the entire system of property taxation that includes taxation on real business property and personal property (see *property tax, real property, business* and *property tax, motor vehicle taxes*). The residential real property tax accounts for over 56 percent of total real property tax revenues nationwide (Fisher 1988).

Today, the property tax is primarily a local government revenue source, and local governments receive more than 96 percent of property tax revenues. This stands in contrast to the early 1900s, when the property tax provided more than half of state government revenues in the United States. Increased demands placed on state governments led them to seek additional revenue sources and, as a consequence, the share of tax revenue from property taxes declined. The Great Depression of the 1930s accelerated this decline, so that by 1940 the property tax provided less than 8 percent of state tax revenue. The share had fallen to 2 percent by 1980 and remained virtually unchanged throughout the 1980s (Advisory Commission on Intergovernmental Relations 1992, vol. 2, table 65).

Although the property tax still dominates local revenue structures, there is a substantial degree of variation in reliance on the property tax by type of local government (counties, cities, school districts, and special districts). Throughout the past twenty years, the distribution of the property tax pie remained fairly stable, with school districts receiving the largest piece, 44 percent in 2000–01 (U.S. Census Bureau 2004). Traditionally, the property tax had been the major source of school finance. However, as a result of lawsuits throughout the country attacking inequalities in school finance, state governments are playing an increasing role in financing local education.

The property tax is intended to be a tax on wealth. Initially, the property tax in the United States was an in rem tax—so many dollars per unit—applied to ownership of very specific types of property such as cattle, land, and improvements. However, as new forms of wealth, both tangible and intangible, began to appear in the early 19th century, the structure of the property tax was altered. The base was expanded to include most varieties of property, which necessitated a switch from in rem to ad valorem percentages of value taxation. The past several decades have reversed this trend toward a more general tax, back to a more specific tax. The emphasis today is clearly on real property, land, and improvements.

Unlike several other taxes levied against property owners, such as property transfer taxes, real estate and gift taxes, and capital gains taxes, the property tax is a recurrent tax that must be paid annually. The taxability of a property owner is determined by the product of the tax base—a measure of the property's value—and the tax rate expressed as a percentage of value. The property tax in the United States is far from uniform. There is significant variation in the definition and scope of the tax base and in the magnitude of tax rates across states, and even within states across local taxing jurisdictions.

The base for the residential property tax is typically calculated using an estimate of the market value of the property. The assessed value (taxable value of a property) is often just a fraction (the assessment ratio) of the true market value of the property. The assessment ratio is typically governed by law. For example, in 2004 in Colorado, residential properties are assessed by law at only 7.96 percent of market value, whereas all other properties are assessed at 29 percent. If all types of properties were assessed at the same ratio within a jurisdiction, the actual assessment ratio would not really matter; for example, a 50 percent assessment ratio with a 2 percent rate is equivalent to a 100 percent assessment at a 1 percent rate. However, many jurisdictions (such as Colorado) assess different types of properties at different rates. In that case, the assessment ratio is a tool used to distribute the tax burden across different types of properties.

Estimates of market value are provided by the local assessor (see *property tax assessment*). The assessor's primary task is to provide estimates of the market value of all taxable properties. For residential property, assessors typically use a method known as the comparable sales approach. This approach involves comparing the property being appraised with similar properties that have recently been sold. Statistical analysis of sales prices and property characteristics can identify hedonic prices or implicit values for each characteristic, including locational attributes. These prices can then be applied to the specific characteristics of the property in question. The success of this approach requires data on a substantial number of recent sales of similarly situated properties. For larger rental properties, assessors use the income capitalization method. This approach requires information on income and operating expenses for the property, which may be available from the property owner or can be determined from standardized tables available to assessors. The net income stream generated by the property is discounted (capitalized) at an appropriate rate to determine the property's value.

Property tax rates are typically set by local jurisdictions. Local governments have fiscal authority to set or change tax rates in 41 states. Most taxing jurisdictions set rates based on budgetary needs and the available tax base as measured by the assessed valuation in the jurisdiction. In general, the tax rate necessary to support a given budget is the budget divided by assessed valuations.

Because assessment ratios differ across localities, the most informative way to compare the burden of taxation is through effective tax rates, which are defined as the ratio of property taxes to market value. The most comprehensive data on effective tax rates for single-family homes across jurisdictions are from the Advisory Commission on Intergovernmental Relations, or ACIR (1989, vol. 1, table 33). Overall, the effective tax rate for the United States as a whole fell from 1.67 percent in 1977 to 1.15 percent in 1987. This decrease occurred in large part because of the tax revolts in the late 1970s and early 1980s, particularly in California and Massachusetts. There is substantial variation in effective tax rates across states. In 1987, New York, Oregon, South Dakota, New Jersey, Nebraska, and Michigan all had effective tax rates exceeding 2 percent. In the same year, seven states had effective tax rates less than 0.75 percent. In a more recent study, the median nominal residential property tax rate for the largest city in each state was 1.55 percent in 1999; however, this study did not take into account systematic underassessment of property relative to market value (Lorelli 2001, table 5).

The final component of the structure of the property tax is relief provisions. Property tax relief refers to any measure that reduces property taxes below what they otherwise would be. Relief has taken many forms, including homestead exemptions or credits, classification, deferral programs, preferential assessment of farmland, and tax breaks for business, but the most widely employed method for residential property consists of tax credits, or "circuit breakers," to offset property tax liabilities. Used in many states, circuit breakers are typically targeted to low-income and elderly homeowners.

While in the United States residential property taxes are based on the assessed value of property, different systems are used in other parts of the world. Two of these are annual-value and site-value systems.

An annual-value-based system taxes the yearly rental income of properties and hence is more of an income than a wealth tax. Most of such systems in use today are derived from the pre-1989 British property tax system known as "rates." In this system, the tax base is defined as the annual rent that a property could be expected to earn on the market. Ideally, the annual value base and the capital value base would be essentially equal because capital value is equivalent to the discounted stream of net rental income. However, a number of factors cause the two to differ. Deductions are often allowed to cover the costs of repairs, insurance, taxes, and other expenses. In some cases, the legally allowed deduction is as high as 50 percent of the rent and clearly exceeds actual costs. Moreover, rent controls can cause actual rental payments to differ from market rent.

Site-value taxation is a form of capital value taxation in which improvements are exempt. Site- or land-value systems differ as to whether improvements such as clearing, leveling, drainage, and surrounding infrastructure are included or ignored. Differences also arise concerning the standard of valuation—highest and best use or current use. This approach has several advantages, among which are lower assessment costs because reassessment is not needed to capture the value of new buildings.

Virtually all jurisdictions that have property taxes have some form of accompanying tax limitations. As of 1991, only six states were free of limitations on property taxes (ACIR 1992, vol. 1, table 7). Property tax limitations take on a variety of forms. There can be limitations on the growth of the property tax base for individual properties or for a given jurisdiction; there can be limitations on rates; and there can be limitations on the growth of property tax revenues. Overall, limits in assessed value are in place in 10 states, rate limits are in effect in 30 states, and a large number of other states have limits on total property tax revenues.

One of the most dramatic limitations on the property tax base came into effect with the passage of Proposition 13 in California. There, the assessed value of a property can only be increased by a maximum of 2 percent a year until the property is sold, at which point it is assessed at market value. If inflation in housing prices exceeds 2 percent a year, then newly purchased properties will be assessed at substantially higher rates than properties that have not been sold.

Studies have revealed that these limitations on assessed value growth have dramatically affected effective tax rates. (See O'Sullivan, Sexton, and Sheffrin 1995, ch. 4, for an analysis of effective tax rates.) For example, in Los Angeles County in 1992, 43 percent of homeowners had been in their homes since 1975. On average, the effective tax rate for those homeowners was 0.2 percent, compared with 1 percent for newly purchased homes. In California, the average effective tax rate was 0.55 percent and the statutory rate was 1 percent. These disparities in effective tax rates were challenged in the Supreme Court on grounds that they violated the equal protection clause of the Constitution. However, the Court has generally given wide discretion to states in the design of their fiscal systems, and it upheld Proposition 13 on these grounds.

(See O'Sullivan et al. 1995, ch. 1, for an analysis of the legal arguments.)

Who bears the property tax? The economic incidence of the property tax has been the subject of considerable dispute. (A good reference on this topic is Aaron 1975.) According to the traditional or "old view" of property taxation, the land component of property was borne by the landowner, but the part of the tax levied on structures was borne by the inhabitant of the property. The rationale for this view was that land is supplied inelastically while capital, used in structures, was supplied elastically to any jurisdiction. According to the old view, homeowners would therefore bear the full burden of the tax, while renters would bear all the tax except for the part levied on land.

The "new view" of the property tax takes the position that property taxes are levied nationwide. Thus, capital used in structures is taxed throughout the United States, and capital cannot escape the tax. According to this view, owners, not renters, would bear the burden of the tax. Many economists believe that, while the new view may describe the burden of an average national tax, differences from this average should be allocated according to the old view.

ADDITIONAL READINGS

Aaron, Henry J. *Who Pays the Property Tax?* Washington, DC: The Brookings Institution, 1975.

Advisory Commission on Intergovernmental Relations [ACIR]. *Significant Features of Fiscal Federalism.* Vol. 1. Washington, DC: U.S. Government Printing Office, 1989.

———. *Significant Features of Fiscal Federalism,* vols. 1 and 2. Washington, DC: U.S. Government Printing Office, 1992.

Fisher, Glenn W. "Real Property Tax." In *Handbook on Taxation,* edited by W. Bartley Hildreth and James A. Richardson (91–118). New York: Marcel Dekker, 1999.

Fisher, Ronald C. *State and Local Public Finance.* Glenview, IL: Scott, Foresman, and Company, 1988.

Lorelli, Michael F. "State and Local Property Taxes." Special Report no. 106. Washington, DC: Tax Foundation, August 2001.

Malme, Jane H., and Joan M. Youngman, eds. *The Development of Property Taxation in Economics in Transition: Case Studies for Central and Eastern Europe.* Washington, DC: The World Bank, 2001.

Oates, Wallace E., ed. *Property Taxation and Local Government Finance.* Cambridge, MA: Lincoln Institute of Land Policy, 2001.

O'Sullivan, Arthur, Terri A. Sexton, and Steven M. Sheffrin. *Property Taxes and Tax Revolts: 77th Legacy of Proposition 13.* New York: Cambridge University Press, 1995.

Plummer, Elizabeth. "Evidence on the Incidence of Residential Property Taxes across Households." *National Tax Journal* 56, no. 4 (December 2003): 739–53.

U.S. Census Bureau. "Summary of State and Local Government Finances by Level of Government, 2000–2001." Washington, DC: U.S. Census Bureau, 2004. http://www.census.gov/govs/estimate/01sp00us.html and http://www.census.gov/govs/estimate/01sl00us.html

Wallis, John Joseph. "A History of the Property Tax in America." In *Property Taxation and Local Government Finance,* edited by Wallace E. Oates (123–47). Cambridge, MA: Lincoln Institute of Land Policy, 2001.

Zodrow, George R. "The Property Tax as a Capital Tax: A Room with Three Views." *National Tax Journal* 54, no. 1 (March 2001): 139–56.

Cross-references: circuit breaker; incidence of taxes; property tax assessment; Proposition 13/property tax caps; wealth taxation.

Property value banding

William J. McCluskey
University of Ulster, United Kingdom

Dividing properties into different categories according to an estimate of their capital or rental value to determine property tax.

In a property value banding system, properties are divided into categories according to an estimate of their capital or rental value to determine a property tax bill. Rather than valuing the properties to a discrete figure and assigning them to a band, the property values are estimated according to a range of values or bands. It is, of course, possible to value to a discrete figure and then to place the property into the appropriate value band. Banding is used predominantly in the United Kingdom and while few other countries use banding, interest does appear to be growing internationally, particularly for developing countries (Plimmer, McCluskey, and Connellan 2000). The banding approach can also be used as an integrated tax system, because built into the system is the tax liability on a per property basis.

Property value banding: the theory

There are essentially three key elements of banded systems: the number of value bands, the band widths, and the tax multiplier (or tax ratio) per band. The final element is essentially the tax liability for each owner or occupier of taxable property. These elements can be modified in different ways to examine whether a banding system is adequately progressive, a key factor in assessing the fairness of a tax. Progressivity is of particular importance, as any change to the tax basis is likely to have a considerable redistributive effect.

The property value banding system as used in Great Britain

A banded property value/tax system (known as the Council Tax) for domestic property was introduced in Great Britain in 1993 (DoE 1991). The Council Tax came into force in April 1993 and was based on property values as of April 1, 1991. The Department of the Environment green paper (1991) laid out the basic underpinnings of the banded system:

- There were to be eight valuation bands (categorized as A through H).
- There would be a 3:1 tax ratio between the bill paid by owners of property in the highest value band (H) and the bill paid by owners of property in the lowest (A); in other words, if a taxpayer owned a property in band A and paid US$1,000, then the owner of a property in band H would have to pay US$3,000.
- Band D would represent the reference band from which the tax paid for the other bands is mathematically related.

TABLE 1. Banding Structure

Band	Tax ratio (based on "ninths")	Tax liability (US$)	Tax to be paid (US$)
A	6/9	500 × 6/9	333
B	7/9	500 × 7/9	389
C	8/9	500 × 8/9	444
D	9/9	500 × 9/9	500
E	11/9	500 × 11/9	611
F	13/9	500 × 13/9	722
G	15/9	500 × 15/9	833
H	18/9	500 × 18/9	1,000

- A system of "ninths" would determine the relevant tax multipliers per band, with band D representing "nine ninths," or 1 (see table 1).
- The starting point for Band A would be "six-ninths," or 0.66.

Table 1 provides an example of the tax liabilities for properties in each value band based on eight bands and a tax ratio of 3:1 on ninths. Band D is taken as the reference band with a liability of, for example, US$500. The overall tax ratio is 3:1; the band A property pays one-third (US$333) of property in band H (US$1,000). The tax to be paid for property in the other bands is also shown in the table.

Remember that the number of bands, their value widths, and their tax ratios are variables. They can be changed to fit in with the property market of the jurisdiction or to meet other requirements of tax progressivity. The banding system finally adopted in Great Britain is depicted in table 2. Tax is payable in the proportions on the eight bands (A to H).

Under a banding system, the amount of tax payable will vary according to the value of the property but only within a limited range. Taxpayers in the lowest band will pay about two-thirds what those in the middle bands will; those in the highest band will pay three times more than those in the lowest band (see figure 1).

Figure 1 illustrates the tax bill progressivity, in that the bills increase as the value of property increases; in this case, the tax ratio of 3:1 applies.

To the British government, the key attraction of property value banding was establishing bands based on the average value of dwellings in different regions; therefore, bands are distinct for England, Scotland, and Wales (see table 2).

Advantages of a property value banding system

The strength of a banding system rests on the robustness of the valuation of the property on which it is levied. The banding system is designed to place properties into wide valuation bands so that major changes in relative property prices would have to occur before significant numbers of properties were unfairly treated. A large part of the appeal of banding lies in the simplicity of its structure and the low cost and relative ease of valuation. In the long run this is undoubtedly true; properties, as opposed to people, are relatively immobile, and the problem of evasion is therefore diminished. Banding at least partly mitigates the need for the individual valuation of every property. A further advantage of banding is that property improvements and small changes in capital values resulting from the vagaries of the property market need not lead to changes in a property's valuation band and thus unpalatable increases in yearly tax bills. Revaluations, therefore, become much less of an administrative and financial burden, as the period between revaluations can be as much as ten years. The challenge for many jurisdictions will be justifying fully discriminating capital value property tax systems by cost of introduction, annual maintenance, human resource capacity, and expertise.

Plimmer et al. (2000) highlight the advantages of banding as follows:

- Banding is a quicker process, when timing is important.
- Banding is a cheaper process, when cost is important.
- Banding makes valuation easier.
- Banding requires less accuracy in valuation.
- Banding is a robust system designed to contain value movements within its broad framework.
- Banding affords a less precise area of valuation dispute, reducing the number of appeals.
- Banding allows for a process of competitive tendering by using the expertise of the private sector.

TABLE 2. Valuation Bands in Great Britain

Valuation band	Range of values			Proportion of band D bill payable
	Scotland (£)	England (£)	Wales (£)	
A	Up to 27,000	Up to 40,000	Up to 30,000	6/9
B	27,001–35,000	40,001–52,000	30,001–39,000	7/9
C	35,001–45,000	52,001–68,000	39,001–51,000	8/9
D	45,001–58,000	68,001–88,000	51,001–66,000	9/9
E	58,001–80,000	88,001–120,000	66,001–90,000	11/9
F	80,001–106,000	120,001–160,000	90,001–120,000	13/9
G	106,001–212,000	160,001–320,000	120,001–240,000	15/9
H	Over 212,000	Over 320,000	Over 240,000	18/9

FIGURE 1. Tax Bills as a Percentage of Band D

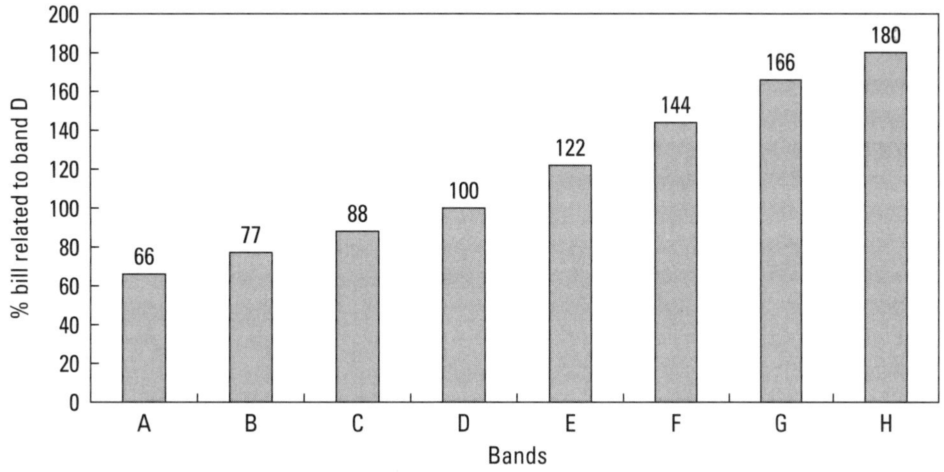

The Department of the Environment in its white paper *Modern Local Government: In Touch with the People* (1998) stated that the Council Tax was working well as a local tax, as it had been widely accepted and was generally well understood.

Disadvantages

Weighted against these attractions is that, as with any system of banded rather than continuous taxation, decisions at the margin become more contentious. For example, some taxpayers on band boundaries may face a substantial difference in payments, depending on the band their properties fall into. In addition banding may result in a regressive tax system, which could well lead to costly and time-consuming appeals. A further disadvantage is that you cannot apply a flat tax rate to arrive at a tax bill.

ADDITIONAL READINGS

Department of the Environment (DoE). *The New Tax for Local Government: A Consultation Paper.* London: Department of the Environment, 1991.

———. *Modern Local Government: In Touch with the People.* London: Department of the Environment, Transport and the Regions, 1998.

Her Majesty's Stationery Office (HMSO). *A New Tax For Local Government.* London: HMSO, 1991.

Hills, John, and Holly Sutherland. "The Proposed Council Tax." *Fiscal Studies* 12, no. 4 (1991): 1–21.

McCluskey, William J., Frances Plimmer, and Owen Connellan. "Reform of U.K. Local Government Domestic Property Taxes." *Property Management* 17, no. 4 (1999): 336–52.

———. "Valuation Banding—An International Property Tax Solution." *Journal of Property Investment & Finance* 20, no. 1 (2002): 68–83.

———. "Property Tax Banding: A Solution for Developing Countries." *Assessment Journal* 9 (March/April 2002): 37–47.

McCluskey, William J., Peadar Davis, and Lay Cheng Lim. "Residential Property Taxation: A Capital Value Banding Approach." *Journal of Property Tax Assessment & Administration* 1, no. 3 (2004): 51–64.

Plimmer, Frances, William J. McCluskey, and Owen Connellan. *Equity and Fairness within Ad Valorem Real Property Taxes,* Lincoln Institute of Land Policy Working Paper (WP00FP1). Cambridge, MA: Lincoln Institute of Land Policy, 2000.

Smith, Stephen, and Duncan Squire. *Local Taxes and Local Government,* Institute for Fiscal Studies, Report Series No. 25. London: Institute for Fiscal Studies, 1987.

Cross-references: flat tax; progressivity, measures of; property tax assessment; property tax, farm; property tax, real property, business; property tax, real property, residential; tax.

Proposition 13/property tax caps
Steven M. Sheffrin
University of California–Davis

State limits on property tax rates or increases, with the most well-known instance being Proposition 13 in California.

In June 1978 the voters in California enacted Proposition 13, the first major property tax limitation measure in the post–World War II era. Following the passage of Proposition 13, other states, including Massachusetts, passed related property tax limitation measures. These modern-day tax revolt measures had antecedents during the 1930s, which featured tax revolts and even an extended tax strike in Chicago. During the Great Depression, the voters and public reacted to increasing property tax burdens stemming from falling incomes and deflation; in the late 1970s, the culprit was property inflation.

Property tax limitations are a form of tax and expenditure limitations. At the state and local levels, tax and expenditure measures are ubiquitous. By 1994, all but four states had passed some form of tax or expenditure limitation measures (see O'Sullivan, Sexton, and Sheffrin 1995). The passage of Proposition 13 accelerated this movement. Six months after the passage of Proposition 13, tax limitation measures appeared on 17 ballots and all but 5 were approved.

Property tax limitation measures can take a number of forms. Some of these limitations focus either on the property tax rate or on the percentage increase in property tax revenue that can be collected in a jurisdiction. Proposition 2½ in Massachusetts was a combination of both limitations on the property tax rate and limitations on the percentage increase in revenue (for an analysis of the effects of Proposition 2½ see Bradbury, Mayer, and Case 2001).

Proposition 13 is the most famous and most complex of all property tax limitation measures. It also included a limit on the property tax rate. But instead of limiting the percentage increase in property tax revenue in an individual jurisdiction, it imposed limitations on individual properties. Specifically, Proposition 13 had the following key provisions: it limited the property tax rate to 1 percent; it initially rolled back assessments on existing properties to their 1975 values; it limited increases in property tax assessments to 2 percent a year until a property was sold, at which time it would be assessed at market value; and it required the state to devise a scheme to divide existing property tax revenues among tax jurisdictions within a county.

Each provision of Proposition 13 had important consequences. Before the passage of Proposition 13, the average property tax rate in California was approximately 2½ percent. Thus, reducing the rate to 1 percent dramatically reduced property tax revenues and required the state to formulate a method to divide the reduced property tax collections among competing jurisdictions. As a consequence, the state became more directly involved in local government and school finance than ever before. The state shifted property tax revenues from the schools to cities, counties, and special districts and then "backfilled" the schools with revenue from the state general fund. Later in the 1990s during periods of tight budgets, it partially reversed this process.

Before Proposition 13, cities, counties, school districts, and special districts all levied their property tax rates separately on a parcel and the taxpayer paid the sum of these rates. Since Proposition 13 limited the total rate to 1 percent, the state legislature had to develop a formula to allocate both the existing revenues and the future growth in revenues across these jurisdictions. This resulting system is very complex (see McCarty et al. 2002) and creates inequities across jurisdictions.

Perhaps the most well-known aspect of Proposition 13 is its "acquisition tax" feature, which places a differential tax burden on new versus existing property owners. As long as inflation in property values exceeds 2 percent, there will be a gap between the amount of tax paid by existing owners of property and new purchasers. In addition, since property tax assessments were rolled back to 1975 values during a period of double-digit property inflation, the system quickly generated substantial inequities in assessments for virtually identical properties. As an example, in 1991, 43 percent of all homeowner properties in Los Angeles County had been held since 1975; on average, these properties were assessed at only 20 percent of market value. That means that a new purchaser

of a home would pay an average of 5 times as much in the basic property tax as a neighbor who had resided in his or her home since 1975. The U.S. Supreme Court reviewed this aspect of Proposition 13 in *Nordlinger v. Hahn* (505, U.S. 1992) and ruled that the inequities did not violate the Equal Protection Clause of the U.S. Constitution.

Over time, several factors affect these horizontal inequities. As properties turn over, they are assessed at market value, thereby reducing inequities; on the other hand, property inflation in excess of 2 percent exacerbates these inequalities. During sluggish real estate markets (such as occurred in the middle 1990s in California), the inequities across taxpayers were partially reduced. As an example, in 1996, the percentage of homeowner properties in Los Angeles held since 1975 fell to approximately 33 percent and these properties were assessed at 26 percent of market value. Moreover, home prices in more affluent areas of Los Angeles fell more than prices in the less affluent areas (Sexton and Sheffrin 1998).

Acquisition value property tax systems will pose a penalty on mobility because the owner will sacrifice a lower assessed value when the property is sold. O'Sullivan, Sexton, and Sheffrin (1995) analyzed this excess burden through a calibrated simulation model. They found that this burden was relatively small for the 1 percent tax rate that prevails in California, but would substantially increase at higher tax rates.

In designing property tax limitation measures, a number of key issues must be addressed. First, what happens during downturns when property tax values fall? California requires the assessor to lower the assessment on properties to the lesser of market value or the original purchase price plus 2 percent per year since acquisition. Thus, during a severe deflation in property values, assessments can be decreased, but they will subsequently increase when the property market recovers. Second, should property tax limitation measures apply just to homeowners or to all properties? Florida passed an acquisition value tax measure, similar to Proposition 13, limiting assessment growth in individual properties to 3 percent a year, but limited it to homeowners. Massachusetts allowed communities to classify properties and allow, within limits, higher rates on non-homeowner property.

Proposition 13 applies to all property—not just owner-occupied housing. Most observers recognize that the rationale for providing Proposition 13 taxpayer protection to commercial and industrial property owners is not as strong as it is for homeowners. Studies have documented that substantial revenue would be available from changing Proposition 13 to tax commercial and industrial property at market value (Sexton and Sheffrin 2003). Since Proposition 13 is enshrined in the state constitution, it would require a vote of the electorate to change any of its provisions.

The school finance equalization movement has spurred limitations on property taxation. Systems of school finance have been challenged in virtually every state on the grounds of either equal protection or adequacy of educational funding. As a result, many states have enacted measures to redistribute an increasing amount of revenue (often from the property tax) to abide by court decisions or avoid litigation. However, as William Fischel (1989) observed, state or judicial actions to limit the spending of local jurisdictions on their own schools undercut the political rationale for a local, discretionary tax like the property tax. Communities have little incentive to raise their local property tax rate if the funds they collect are simply redistributed throughout the state. While property taxes fund other local services besides schools, good schools are the principal preoccupation of homeowners and potential home purchasers. In Fischel's view, redistributing local property tax revenues will lead to a sharp diminution in political support for the property tax. If states do not make up for the reduction in property tax funding, schools will ultimately suffer.

It is important to recognize that property tax limitations do not necessarily reduce the growth of state and local government. In the face of tax limitation measures, state and local governments typically rely on other sources of funds, including increased fees and charges particularly associated with growth and infrastructure. Although state and local government revenues and expenditures slowed directly after the tax revolts in the late 1970s and early 1980s, state and local government revenue and expenditure growth soon returned to its trend levels (Sexton and Sheffrin 1998). Sheffrin (1998) argued that, over the long term, the growth of alternative revenue sources in the face of tax limitations may reduce the transparency of local taxation and lead to further direct voter involvement in local public affairs.

ADDITIONAL READINGS

Bradbury, Katharine A., Christopher J. Mayer, and Karl E. Case. "Property Tax Limits, Local Fiscal Behavior, and Property Values: Evidence from Massachusetts under Proposition 2½," *Journal of Public Economics* 80, no. 2 (May 2001): 287–311.

Fischel, William. "Did Serrano Cause Proposition 13?" *National Tax Journal* 42 (1989): 465–74.

McCarty Therese A., Terri A. Sexton, Steven M. Sheffrin, and Stephen D. Shelby. "Allocating Property Tax Revenue in California: Living with Proposition 13." In *94th Annual Conference Proceedings of the National Tax Association* (71–80). Washington, DC: National Tax Association, 2002.

O'Sullivan Arthur, Terri A. Sexton, and Steven M. Sheffrin. *Property Taxes and Tax Revolts: The Legacy of Proposition 13.* New York: Cambridge University Press, 1995.

Sexton Terri A., and Steven M. Sheffrin. *Proposition 13 in Recession and Recovery.* San Francisco: Public Policy Institute of California, 1998.

———. "The Market Value of Commercial Real Property in Los Angeles County in 2002." *State Tax Notes* (April 7, 2003).

Sheffrin, Steven M. "The Future of the Property Tax: A Political Economy Perspective." In *The Future of State Taxation,* edited by David Brunori (129–45). Washington, DC: Urban Institute Press, 1998.

Cross-reference: tax limitations.

Proprietorships

James E. Long
Auburn University

Issues arise as to whether taxation will affect an individual's decision to go into business for him- or herself (but not in partnership with others).

Proprietorships are one of the three primary forms of business organization in the United States, the other forms being partnerships and corporations. A proprietorship is a firm owned and operated by a single individual or family. The sole proprietor or self-employed individual has total control over his or her business, receives all the firm's profits, and is responsible for all its liabilities. About 70 percent of the businesses in the United States are proprietorships, operating primarily in the professional services, retail trade, construction, and agriculture sectors. For example, the hometown hardware store, the local drug store, the family-owned restaurant, and the neighborhood gas station and auto repair shop are likely to be proprietorships. While extremely numerous in the economy (more than 20 million, according to tax return data), proprietorships are usually very small in terms of number of employees and size of sales and profits. In 2001, the average nonfarm proprietorship had annual revenues of about $55,000, compared with $1 million for the typical partnership and $3.4 million for the average corporation.

The popularity of proprietorships can be traced to several advantages of this type of business organization. The ease of establishing and dissolving a proprietorship is probably its major advantage. After satisfying a few legal formalities (such as obtaining appropriate licenses), the owner-operator commences operations by announcing that goods and services are available for sale to consumers. When the owner decides to end the proprietorship, he or she simply stops doing business with customers. Another advantage is that the owner directly receives all the proprietorship's profits, which are taxed as self-employment income under the individual income tax, as opposed to being taxed under a separate business income tax such as the corporate income tax. A final advantage of self-employment is that the sole proprietor exerts total control over the business. The opportunity to make business decisions independently of other owners or employers, including the decisions of when to work and how much time to spend working, is surely a major reason some individuals choose self-employment rather than salaried jobs that may provide higher monetary compensation.

As might be expected, the sole proprietorship also has some disadvantages that limit its effectiveness as a business structure, especially when large, complex, or capital-intensive undertakings are involved. First, the owner-operator personally bears all the losses of the business and is responsible for all the firm's liabilities, so the proprietor's personal assets and income are at risk. Second, because of this unlimited financial liability and the absence of a legal life for the business independent of the owner's life, a proprietorship has difficulty attracting the outside capital funds necessary for business expansion.

In terms of their representation in the U.S. labor force, proprietors or self-employed workers steadily declined for roughly a century after the Civil War. In more recent decades, the proportion of civilian employees who are self-employed has fallen, from 22 percent in 1940 to less than 9 percent in 1970. Not surprisingly, this decline in overall self-employment coincides with the shift of the American economy away from agriculture, an industry of historically high proprietorship activity. The long-running decline in self-employment ceased in the early 1970s, however, and the proportion of self-employed workers in nonagricultural sectors rose over the next two decades before falling slightly since the mid-1990s. Today, about 10 percent of the entire labor force is self-employed, with the self-employment rate substantially higher among men than women and higher among older (age 50 and above) than younger workers.

The reversal of such a pronounced trend as the decline in self-employment is a significant phenomenon and, understandably, has attracted interest in the determinants of self-employment and proprietorship activity. The possible influence of the tax system on the self-employment choice has received considerable attention in recent years, especially because of relatively large legislated and inflation-driven changes in income tax rates during the 1970s, 1980s, and 1990s. The traditional analysis of how income taxation influences the amount of work effort, by affecting the choice between labor (money income) and leisure, has been expanded to consider the potential impact of taxation on the allocation of working time across different employments.

In a modern economy, individuals can work for business firms or governmental agencies as wage or salaried employees, or they can supply labor to their own enterprise or proprietorship. In theory, the individual income tax is general in the sense that its impact is the same on returns from all types of labor market activity. For example, under a proportional income tax of 30 percent, an additional dollar of salary or business income will yield 70 cents of disposable (after-tax) income for both the corporate accountant and the self-employed one. In this case, the income tax will not influence the choice between self-employment and salaried work.

In practice, however, the income tax is not perfectly general and thus may influence an individual's choice of employment. The returns from self-employment or proprietorship activity are thought to be less heavily taxed than wages or salaries, and this tax advantage might lead individuals to prefer self-employment over salaried jobs. First, wages and salaries are subject to both tax withholding by employers and return filing requirements, whereas taxation of the self-employed depends primarily on voluntary compliance. Studies have found that a larger percentage of proprietorship and self-employment income goes unreported to the Internal Revenue Service and other tax authorities, which implies

that effective or actual tax burdens are relatively lower for the self-employed than for salaried employees. Second, proprietors can lower their taxable incomes, and hence their tax liabilities, through deductions for expenses incurred in earning income from their business or trade. To the extent that some deductible "business" expenses (e.g., for travel, entertainment, office furnishings) also yield personal (consumption) benefits, the proprietor effectively earns tax-free income. Contributions to individual retirement saving plans represent another tax-deductible expenditure that, as a result of the Tax Reform Act of 1986, has been made more accessible to self-employed persons than to wage or salaried workers. In recent years, Keogh retirement saving plans for proprietors have expanded steadily in terms of both number and annual volume of deposits.

The findings of several empirical studies suggest that rising income tax rates do in fact induce workers to choose self-employment rather than wage or salaried jobs although other research has found a negative (albeit small) impact of the income tax rate on the propensity to become self-employed. The individual need not make an all-or-nothing choice, however, because wage and salaried workers can also operate their own business on the side (the number of proprietorship tax returns filed far exceeds the number of individuals reporting their main activity as self-employment). There is also some evidence that high-salaried (and high tax bracket) individuals establish proprietorships in addition to their full-time jobs for tax-avoidance purposes. For instance, many high-income employees reporting Schedule F (farm) losses on their individual tax returns are quite possibly "farming the tax code" rather than the soil.

Proprietorship activity may be affected by other fiscal and governmental policies besides the general taxation influences described above. For example, entrepreneurial investment may be influenced by a specific and controversial feature of the income tax structure, its treatment of capital gains income. Advocates of preferential (lower) tax rates on capital gains maintain that full taxation of nominal realized capital gains combined with limited loss offsets deters would-be proprietors from starting new firms.

In contrast, self-employment among older Americans has probably been encouraged by the disincentive for full-time salaried employment inherent in the Social Security earnings test. Government regulations and required paperwork are thought to disproportionately burden proprietorships because of their small size relative to partnership and corporate enterprises, which often employ persons specifically to assist in compliance with government mandates. Had governmental information, environmental, safety, and other requirements on firms not increased so sharply over the past two or three decades, the recent reversal of the decline in proprietorship activity in the United States might have been more dramatic.

One potential new government mandate facing American businesses, employer-provided health insurance for all employees, could have an extremely large impact on small business and has attracted much interest in the discussion of health care reform in the United States. Employer-provided health insurance and other fringe benefits are generally paid for by employees through reduced wages. But many small firms and proprietorships pay wages that are already close to the legal minimum and cannot be significantly reduced. Consequently, some analysts believe that mandated insurance coverage is likely to produce labor cost increases large enough to devastate many small businesses.

It is unlikely that proprietorship activity in the United States will ever again reach the scale it once exhibited when the nation was largely rural and agricultural. However, as long as individuals value the flexibility afforded by self-employment, and the desire to be one's own boss exists, proprietorships can be expected to remain a popular form of business organization.

ADDITIONAL READINGS

Blau, David M. "A Time-Series Analysis of Self-Employment in the United States." *Journal of Political Economy* 95 (June 1987): 445–67.

Bruce, Donald. "Taxes and Entrepreneurial Endurance: Evidence from the Self-Employed." *National Tax Journal* 55 (March 2002): 5–24.

Kahn, C. Harry. *Business and Professional Income under the Personal Income Tax.* Princeton: Princeton University Press (for National Bureau of Economic Research), 1964.

Long, James E. "The Income Tax and Self-Employment." *National Tax Journal* 35 (March 1982): 31–42.

———. "Income Taxation and the Allocation of Market Labor." *Journal of Labor Research* 3 (Summer 1982): 259–76.

———. "Farming the Tax Code: The Impact of High Marginal Tax Rates on Agricultural Tax Shelters." *American Journal of Agricultural Economics* (February 1990): 1–12.

———. "Estimates of Tax-Favored Retirement Saving Behavior of the Self-Employed." *Public Finance Quarterly* 21 (April 1993): 163–77.

Moore, Kevin B. "The Effects of the 1986 and 1993 Tax Reforms on Self-Employment." Finance and Economics Discussion Series 2004–05. Washington, DC: Board of Governors of the Federal Reserve System, 2004.

Park, Thae S. "Comparison of BEA Estimates of Personal Income and IRS Estimates of Adjusted Gross Income." *Survey of Current Business* (November 2002): 13–20.

Public utilities, taxation of

Gary Cornia
Brigham Young University

Unique or heavier taxes imposed on utilities as regulated industries.

Public utilities, most notably energy, transportation, and communication, face economic regulation in terms of the geographic areas they service, their allowed rate of growth or investment, the tariffs they may charge for their goods and services, and the quality of services they provide. The practice of regulation is most common in energy and communication. One alternative to regulation has been outright public ownership. Regulation in the United States was validated in the landmark case of *Munn v. Illinois* in 1877, and the prac-

tice began to dominate many markets during the 1930s and 1940s. In the United States, regulation is imposed by multiple levels of government. Interstate regulation is generally the responsibility of federal regulatory bodies, most notably the Federal Energy Regulatory Commission, and intrastate regulation is the responsibility of state public service commissions or state public utility commissions. In limited situations, local governments may also play a role in regulation.

The justification for the economic regulation of some industries was initially based on the assertion that the production technology in specific industries could create situations in which the marginal cost of providing an output would decline as firms within the industry increased in size. Also, in some industries the cost function is subadditive, suggesting that one firm would have lower costs than multiple firms. The result of these arguments was the belief that a single firm, if allowed to operate without direct competition, could provide lower-cost services than multiple smaller firms. It was assumed that economies of scale were relevant in the major aspects of production, including exploration, transportation, and distribution. An outcome of regulation was that large, vertically integrated firms emerged and were granted exclusive franchise rights to provide service to a specific geographic area. The explicit role of regulation was to control tariffs and prevent firms from achieving outcomes that reflected monopoly pricing practices. Many of the assumptions underlying the need for regulation have since been challenged, and the result has been a recent reduction in the explicit regulation for many industries. In the United States, for example, regulation has been substantially reduced for interstate trucking, railroads, and air transportation. There has also been a worldwide movement to privatize previously publicly owned monopolies.

Regulation has also had an extensive effect on the policies surrounding the taxation of goods and services sold by public utilities. For the most part, regulated firms have traditionally been attractive entities to tax because taxing the utility simplifies both the compliance and administrative challenges of taxation. Utilities have developed efficient billing and collection schemes for their own charges, and piggybacking the collection of taxes and fees on such processes is readily accomplished. Perhaps the main reason utilities have been heavily taxed has been the fact that regulated utilities do not face direct competition, and the opportunity to pass a tax forward to ratepayers is constrained only by the price elasticity of the service being sold. The opportunity to avoid direct political responsibility for a tax because it was collected as part of the billing cycle is not lost on public officials. For example, public utilities have traditionally faced higher effective property tax rates than nonregulated industries. Public utilities are also commonly burdened with a gross receipts tax, which may have been intended to tax business activities but in practice is likely passed forward to consumers with all the unfavorable characteristics of a turnover tax. In addition to gross receipt taxes, many states—and, where possible, local governments—have imposed a retail sales tax on the services of utilities, although frequently at a lower rate than the general retail sales tax.

In addition to using broad-based taxes, state and local policymakers in the United States have traditionally imposed a series of excise taxes on public utilities. The excise tax has been based on either a flat charge on the quantity of the service sold, such as a fee per kilowatt hour of electricity consumed, or as a percentage charge against the billed charges. Excise fees on utilities' transactions have been used by both state and local governments, but the majority of such taxes have been used by local governments, specifically cities. In general, the ability of a local government to impose an excise tax must be granted by the state government. The policy justification for excise fees at the local level has been developed on the assumption that local governments have the right to grant the privilege to conduct business within their boundaries, so in such cases, excise taxes are considered compensation for the right to use the public right-of-ways. Such excise taxes are often imposed on gas distribution firms, electric firms, and local transportation firms such as taxi operators. Excise taxes are also imposed by some states in the form of special fees to fund the operations of the public service commission and, in some cases, the operation of consumer advocacy groups.

The current pattern of deregulating industries or portions of industries has dramatically altered the past practices of heavily taxing utilities. Many utilities that did not face competition in the past are now sensitive to the price of the services they sell. The ability to transport such services as natural gas and electric power has increased because of changing federal regulatory practices and changing technology. Deregulation has created opportunities and incentives to disinvest some portions of the industries that were formerly vertically integrated. The electric utility industry has rapidly moved toward the generation of electric power by nonregulated merchant power firms, and gas distribution firms have been broken up into local distribution firms and interstate transportation firms. Where these practices have developed, the ability of utilities to pass taxes forward to consumers has been limited, a limitation that has been especially notable in sales to industrial and commercial firms that are able to purchase services from nonregulated suppliers. A common source of nontaxed or lighter taxed services is municipally owned distribution companies that, under deregulation, can function as a conduit of lower-priced services to such firms.

Deregulation has had two notable consequences on tax practices. First, the lower prices associated with deregulation have reduced the amount of revenue that is based on ad valorem taxes. Second, regulated utilities have directly responded to the pricing threat of nonregulated providers by seeking a reduction in their existing taxes and fees. Few would dispute that deregulation has changed the historical patterns of utility taxation in the United States. Policymakers concerned about deregulation must consider the potential reduction of utility taxes in the long term.

ADDITIONAL READINGS

Bland, Robert L. "Franchise Fees and Telecommunications Services: Is a New Paradigm Needed?" *State Tax Notes* (February 10, 1997): 437–43.

Kahn, Alfred E. *The Economics of Regulation: Principles and Institutions,* vol. 1. New York: John Wiley & Son, 1971.

Phillips, Charles F., Jr. *The Regulation of Public Utilities: Theory and Practice,* Arlington, VA: Public Utilities Reports, Inc., 1993.

Viscusi, W. Kip, John M. Vernon, and Joseph E. Harrington Jr. *Economics of Regulation and Antitrust.* 2nd ed. Cambridge, MA: MIT Press, 1997.

Walters, Lawrence C., and Gary C. Cornia. "The Implications of Utility and Telecommunications Deregulation for Local Public Finance." *State and Local Government Review* 29, no. 3 (1997): 172–87.

Woolery, Arlo. *Valuation of Railroad and Utility Property,* Cambridge, MA: Lincoln Institute of Land Policy, 1992.

Cross-references: elasticity, demand and supply; excise taxes; retail sales tax, state and local; telecommunications and electronic commerce, state taxation of.

Rainy day funds (budget stabilization, budget reserve funds)

Corina Eckl
National Conference of State Legislatures

Jed Kee
George Washington University

A hedge against the unpredictability of the revenue stream and forecasting errors.

Budget stabilization funds, often called "rainy day funds," have been established in 46 states and the District of Columbia. Five jurisdictions have more than one such fund (Alaska, Florida, Iowa, South Carolina, and the District of Columbia, which is conventionally treated as a state for purposes of fiscal analysis). The states without rainy day funds are Arkansas, Colorado, Kansas, Montana, and Oregon (NCSL 2005). Florida established the first rainy day fund, the Working Capital Fund, in 1959.

The initial concept of a budget stabilization fund is straightforward: funds are set aside when times are good for use when state finances take a downturn. Deposits typically take the form of a line-item appropriation in an annual or biennial budget or are designated portions of an operating budget surplus. In some cases, deposits are made from revenue windfalls, such as the 1998 Master Settlement Agreement between states and tobacco companies. These reserve funds then can be used when the state faces an unexpected revenue shortfall or budget deficit due to errors in revenue forecasting or a downturn in the economy (thus the term "rainy day fund").

Over time, the rationale for a stabilization fund has been expanded to encompass other budgetary concerns. Although a "revenue shortfall" or "budget deficit" still remains the most common condition for tapping the rainy day fund (35 states), withdrawals also are permitted to address a natural disaster or other declared emergency (e.g., in Iowa, Massachusetts, Nevada, Oklahoma, West Virginia, and the District of Columbia). In some cases, the fund can be accessed for whatever purpose the governor (upon notifying the legislature) or legislature deem appropriate (e.g., in Georgia, Maine, Maryland, North Carolina, Texas, Wisconsin, and Wyoming). In 12 states, a withdrawal requires a supermajority vote of the legislature.

It is useful to note that rainy day funds are distinct from "contingency" or "emergency" funds (in all 50 states and Puerto Rico) that are established to address events such as natural disasters, public safety, and unexpected expenditures (e.g., the Massachusetts Welfare Caseload Mitigation Fund). This latter category of funds generally can be authorized by an administrative authority—for example, by the governor (21 states), state budget director (three states), or some specially appointed board (e.g., the Emergency Council of the Wild Land Fire Emergency Fund) (NASBO 2004).

Fund sources (deposits) and uses (withdrawals)

Most states authorize rainy day funds by statute, although seven states do so in their constitutions (Alaska, Delaware, Louisiana, Oklahoma, South Carolina, Texas, and Virginia). There also is diversity in the source of fund deposits. While most states link the deposits to line-item appropriations or year-end budget surpluses, others tie deposits to specific revenue sources. Examples include mineral revenues in Louisiana, a portion of lottery funds in Oregon, and a percentage of general fund revenues in Maryland, North Dakota, and Rhode Island. In some states (e.g., Arizona, Idaho, Tennessee, and Virginia), a deposit is triggered when revenues or state economic growth exceed certain levels. Other states mix it up with guidelines for minimums or maximums (e.g., Minnesota and New Hampshire). In the District of Columbia, complex federal laws and regulations constrain the government's fiscal autonomy (Lazere 2003).

While there is no "ideal" amount that should be accumulated in rainy day funds, a rule of thumb recommended by the National Conference of State Legislatures' Fiscal Affairs and Oversight Committee (and informally used by municipal bond rating agencies) is that the combination of general fund surpluses and rainy day funds should equal at least 5 percent of total state expenditures. This suggested level varies according to individual state circumstances, economic conditions, and access to atypical revenue sources (such as vast mineral resources). States with highly elastic revenue sources, such as progressive income taxes, might opt for a larger balance because their revenues may fluctuate more during economic swings. Most states limit the size of the reserves to a range of 3 to 10 percent of appropriations.

At the end of FY 2004, aggregate state ending balances totaled $26.5 billion, with budget stabilization funds accounting for almost half ($13 billion) of this total. The combined reserves equaled approximately 5.3 percent of projected general fund expenditures ($502.2 billion). By comparison, state ending balances were $47.3 billion, or 10.4 percent of general fund expenditures, at the end of FY 2000 (NCSL 2005).

The amounts that states held solely in their rainy day funds at the end of FY 2004 varied substantially. At the high end were Alaska (78.8 percent) and Wyoming (53.9 percent), where taxes on natural resources tend to bolster rainy day fund balances. At the other end of the spectrum were the 11 states whose funds were empty. Withdrawals from these funds during the state fiscal crisis that began in FY 2001 partially explain these zero balances. Nationally, the amount states held in their rainy day funds represented 2.6 percent of general fund spending.

There are three closely related arguments in favor of rainy day funds. The first is that they provide the legislature with flexibility to deal with inevitable errors in budget forecasting. This was the rationale Minnesota used when setting up a "budget reserve" fund in the mid-1980s to manage up to a 5 percent variance in revenue forecasts (Ebel and McGuire 1986). The second argument is to provide a fiscal cushion to mitigate the fiscal stress of an economic downturn, an outcome that some evidence shows occurs (Sobel and Holcombe 1996). The third argument is that for some states, the rainy day fund serves as a vehicle for real savings (Gonzalez and Levinson 2003).

Arguments against rainy day funds include the view that surplus state revenues should fund needed state projects (generally capital spending) or reduce accumulated debt. Some also argue that surplus revenues should finance incremental changes in tax policy through tax reductions. A related critique is that if states are accumulating surplus revenues in rainy day funds, then tax rates must be too high and should be cut, thereby returning unneeded revenue to taxpayers. As a practical response to these concerns, most states hold modest balances in their funds.

Although rainy day funds are a permanent feature of nearly every state's budget, they serve as a short-term strategy to address budget difficulties. They tend to work best when used primarily as a hedge against an economic downturn and when they are sufficiently funded to cushion what otherwise might be difficult spending cuts and tax increases. They are not useful, however, in dealing with long-term structural deficits. Based on the evidence of recent recessions, a 5 to 10 percent state revenue shortfall is typical. Because it is politically difficult to accumulate a rainy day fund that equals 10 percent of expenditures, some combination of approaches including rainy day fund withdrawals, expenditure reductions, and tax increases may be necessary to deal with severe economic downturns, especially those that last longer than one year.

ADDITIONAL READINGS

Braun, Bradley M., L. E. Johnson, and Robert D. Ley. "State Revenue Shortfalls: Budget Restraints and Policy Alternatives." *The American Journal of Economics and Sociology* 52, no. 4 (October 1993): 385–97.

Ebel, Robert D., and Therese J. McGuire. "Minnesota's Budget and Budget Process." In *Final Report of the Minnesota Tax Study Commission* (33–42). St. Paul, MN: Butterworths, 1986.

Eckl, Corina L. "States Broaden the Scope of Rainy Day Funds." *The Fiscal Letter* 17, no. 2 (March/April 1995).

Gold, Steven D. "Preparing for the Next Recession: Rainy Day Funds and Other Tools for States." Legislative Finance Paper no. 41. Denver: National Conference of State Legislatures, 1983.

Gonzalez, Christian, and Arik Levinson. "State Rainy Day Funds and the State Budget Crisis of 2002–?" *State Tax Notes* 30, no. 5 (November 2003): 405–15.

Lazere, Ed. "Fixing DC's Rainy Day Fund." Washington, DC: D.C. Fiscal Policy Institute, 2003.

National Association of State Budget Officers (NASBO). *Budget Processes in the States,* Washington, DC: NASBO, 2004.

National Conference of State Legislatures (NCSL). *State Budget Actions: FY 2004 & FY 2005.* Denver: NCSL, 2005.

Sobel, Russell S., and Randall G. Holcombe. "The Impact of State Rainy Day Funds in Easing State Fiscal Crises during the 1990–1991 Recession." *Public Budgeting and Finance* 16, no. 23 (1996): 28–38.

Vasche, Jon David, and Brad Williams. "Optimal Governmental Budgeting Contingency Reserve Funds." *Public Budgeting and Finance* 7, no. 1 (Spring 1987): 66–82.

Wagner, Gary A. "The Bond Market and Fiscal Institutions: Have Budget Stabilization Funds Reduced State Borrowing Costs?" *National Tax Journal* 57, no. 4 (December 2004): 785–804.

Cross-references: automatic stabilizers; revenue elasticity (tax elasticity); revenue estimation, state.

Rehabilitation tax credit

Louis Alan Talley and Pamela J. Jackson
Congressional Research Service, Library of Congress

A credit allowed for capital expenditures incurred in rehabilitating either nonresidential real property (commercial property) or qualified residential rental property. No federal tax incentives exist for the rehabilitation of an individual's private residence. A 10 percent tax credit is allowed for rehabilitation of buildings constructed before 1936 and a 20 percent credit is allowed for certified historic structures.

Defining historic structures

Certified historic structures are either individually registered in the National Register of Historic Places or certified by the Secretary of the Interior as having historic significance and being located in a registered historic district. In either case, an application form must be filed with the respective state's historic preservation office, which reviews the certification application and either recommends or denies designation of historic significance. The state office forwards the information and recommendation to the Secretary of the Interior, who certifies that the preservation preserves the historic character of the building or integrates with the historic district.

Rehabilitation standards

The Secretary of the Interior has 10 standards for rehabilitation of historic structures, to ensure that the historic character of the building is preserved. There are other important provisions such as the substantial rehabilitation test, the types of expenditures qualifying for the credit, provisions for tax-exempt use property, and recapture rules. Projects eligible for the 10 percent credit are also restricted; in particular, at least 75 percent of the external walls must be retained (50 percent as external walls), and 75 percent of the internal structure must be retained.

Legislative history

The Tax Reform Act of 1976 first provided for a historic preservation tax incentive, allowing a five-year write-off for rehabilitation expenditures for business and residential rental property. Historic structures were those individually registered in the National Register of Historic Places or certified by the Secretary of the Interior as having historic significance and located in a registered historic district. Structures located in a historic district under state or local statute and certified by the Department of the Interior were also eligible. Penalties imposed for tearing down certified historic structures disallowed the deduction of demolition costs and reduced depreciation for new structures built on sites of previous historic structures.

The Revenue Act of 1978 extended the 10 percent investment tax credit to qualified rehabilitation expenditures for nonresidential buildings. Expenditures had to begin at least 20 years after the building was first placed in service and have a useful life of five years or more. If the investment tax credit was claimed, the five-year write-off could not be used. Costs for acquisition, replacement, or enlargement of the building did not qualify, nor was the credit available if more than 25 percent of the exterior walls were replaced. Work on certified historic structures had to be certified by the Secretary of the Interior to qualify for the credit.

The Economic Recovery Tax Act of 1981 changed the depreciation benefit to a tax credit. This was done partly as a simplification and partly to add counterbalance to new provisions of the 1981 tax law that provided for accelerated cost recovery. The credit was three-tiered: a 15 percent credit for nonresidential buildings at least 30 years old, a 20 percent rate for nonresidential structures at least 40 years old, and a 25 percent credit reserved for certified historic structures. The building's basis for depreciation purposes was reduced by one-half of the credit.

The Tax Reform Act of 1986 changed the three-tier credit to the current two-tier one and reduced the basis by the full credit, rather than half of it. Many of the prior law's provisions were retained, such as the substantial rehabilitation test, the types of expenditures qualifying for the credit, provisions for tax-exempt use property, and recapture rules. The old rules for how much of the structure must be retained to receive the non-historic structure credit were replaced by more stringent rules that required retention of at least 75 percent of the external walls (with at least 50 percent remaining as external walls) and 75 percent of internal structural framework. External wall requirements were deleted from the rules for certified historic structures because those restorations are supervised by the Secretary of the Interior.

To restrict tax shelter investing, Congress in 1986 prohibited the deduction of losses from a business activity in which the taxpayer does not "materially participate" from any other kind of income (or in this case using tax credits generated in such a business to offset taxes on other income) until the investment is sold. Ownership of a limited partnership interest and rental of property were both defined as passive activities. There were, however, two exceptions for those engaged in rehabilitation activity. First, those investors did not have to "actively participate" in managing the property to be allowed the credit, so a limited partner could take the credit. Second, taxpayers with higher incomes than those eligible for other "passive losses" were eligible for the credit.

The Revenue Reconciliation Act of 1989 eliminated the income limitation on taking the credit, and all individuals were permitted a $25,000 deduction equivalent regardless of income. A provision enacted as part of the Revenue Reconciliation Act of 1993 eased restrictions on passive activity losses from rental real estate in general for "eligible" taxpayers.

Rationale

Rapid depreciation of these investments was adopted as an incentive in response to declining usefulness of older buildings and was designed to promote stability and economic vitality to deteriorating areas through the rehabilitation and preservation of historic structures and neighborhoods. Achievement of this goal was thought to depend upon enlistment of private funds in the preservation movement.

Partly as a simplification and partly to counterbalance the new accelerated cost recovery rules, the tax incentives were changed to a tax credit in 1981 and made part of a set of credits for rehabilitating older buildings (varying by type or age). Congress hoped to help revitalize the economic prospects of aging areas and preclude the decay and deterioration of distressed economic localities.

The credit amount was reduced in 1986 because the rate was deemed too high relative to the new lower tax rates, and a reduction from a three- to a two-tiered rehabilitation rate credit was adopted. The credit was retained because Congress was concerned that social and aesthetic values were not necessarily taken into account in project profit projections. A higher credit rate was allowed for preservation of historic structures than for rehabilitations of older qualified buildings first placed in service before 1936. This differential was provided to ensure that the credits would be focused on historic and older buildings.

Impact and assessment

The credit reduces the taxpayer's cost of preservation projects, which can turn unprofitable rehabilitation into profitable rehabilitation and in some cases make rehabilitation more profitable than new construction. Thus, owners of historic buildings and older commercial structures may be encouraged to renovate them through the use of the tax credit available for substantial rehabilitation expenditures.

It is argued that to the extent that businesses renovate rather than relocate, inner-city jobs can be saved with less relocation of workers and changes in commuter patterns. To the extent commuter patterns are changed, governments may be required to make additional investments in transportation modes (roads, commuter rail, and so forth). Before the tax reform in 1986, historic preservation projects had become a popular tax shelter with rapid growth. The limits on credits under the passive loss restrictions limit the use of this investment as a tax shelter for those taxpayers not engaged in the business of real estate.

Some have questioned why the credit is allowed only for business property. Individual homeowners are precluded from use of the credit but find that many of the reasons stated for the credit would apply equally to the preservation of owner-occupied homes.

Opponents of the credit note that investments are allocated to historic buildings that would not be profitable projects without the credit, resulting in economic inefficiency. Proponents argue that investors fail to consider external benefits (preservation of social and aesthetic values) that are desirable for society at large. Thus, this allocation may be desirable if there are external benefits to society that the investors would not take into account.

It has also been argued that the credit has an adverse effect on administration of the tax law. The Internal Revenue Service finds the present system difficult to administer with approval made by a different department of the government. Elimination of the credit would simplify the tax code.

ADDITIONAL READINGS

Brody, Evelyn, and Joseph J. Cordes. "The Unrelated Business Income Tax: All Bark and No Bite?" *Emerging Issues in Philanthropy* no. 3. Washington, DC: The Urban Institute and Harvard University Hauser Center, 2001.

Cheverine, Carolyn Ells, and Charlotte Mariah Hayes. "Rehabilitation Tax Credit: Does it Still Provide Incentives?" *Virginia Tax Review* 10 (Summer 1990): 167–214.

Fein, David B. "Historic Districts: Preserving City Neighborhoods for the Privileged." *New York University Law Review* 60 (April 1985): 64–103.

Lipton, Richard M. "TRA '93 Eases Rules Affecting Debt-Financed Property and Passive Losses from Realty." *Journal of Taxation* 80 (May 1994): 260–65.

Mann, Roberta F. "Tax Incentives for Historic Preservation: An Antidote to Sprawl?" *Widener Law Symposium* 8 (2002): 207–36.

Sage, Judith A., Sonia Elias Gorgy, and Lloyd G. Sage. "The Effect of the Revenue Reconciliation Act of 1993 on Real Estate Owners." *Tax Adviser* 25 (August 1994): 491–97.

Schneider, Todd. "From Monuments to Urban Renewal: How Different Philosophies of Historic Preservation Impact the Poor." *Georgetown Journal on Poverty Law and Policy* 8 (Winter 2001): 257–81.

U.S. Congress, Joint Committee on Taxation. *General Explanation of the Revenue Act of 1978 (H.R. 13511, 95th Congress; Public Law 95-600).* Washington, DC: U.S. Government Printing Office, March 12, 1977, 155–58.

———. *General Explanation of the Economic Recovery Tax Act of 1981 (H.R.4242, 97th Congress; Public Law 97-34).* Washington, DC: U.S. Government Printing Office, December 31, 1981, 111–16.

———. *General Explanation of the Tax Reform Act of 1986 (H.R. 3838, 99th Congress; Public Law 99-514).* Washington, DC: U.S. Government Printing Office, May 4, 1987, 148–52.

———. *Description of Selected Federal Tax Provisions That Impact Land Use.* Washington, DC: U.S. Government Printing Office, July 11, 1996.

U.S. General Accounting Office. *Historic Preservation Tax Incentives.* Washington, D.C.:U.S. General Accounting Office, 1986.

Cross-references: business location, taxation and; enterprise zones; low-income housing credit; passive activity losses.

Research and experimentation tax credit

Joseph J. Cordes
George Washington University

Tax credit provided to companies based on qualified expenditures on research and development.

The U.S. tax code provides special treatment of business investments in research and development (R&D) in the form of two provisions: an option to expense R&D expenditures and an incremental tax credit for qualified expenditures on research and experimentation (R&E).

History of the research and experimentation credit

A tax credit for R&D was first introduced in the Economic Recovery Tax Act of 1981 and has been extended with several modifications since then. When it was first enacted, businesses could claim a 25 percent tax credit on eligible spending on R&E that exceeded a base amount. The base amount was originally defined as the average of the three prior years' spending on R&E with an additional limitation that the amount of the base used to determine the credit could not be less than one-half of the taxpayer's qualified expenditures during the taxable year. In effect, this "base period limitation" reduced the effective statutory rate of incremental credit for firms with R&D growing at more than twice the level of base spending from 25 percent to 12.5 percent. Expenses that qualified for the original credit were salaries of R&D personnel, expenses of materials used in R&D, and 65 percent of the cost of R&D services purchased from other providers.

The Tax Reform Act of 1986 reduced the R&E credit from 25 to 20 percent and tightened some definitions of the type of R&E spending eligible to receive the credit. These changes in the definition of qualifying R&D were made in response to criticisms that the 1981 enactment of the R&E credit created incentives for firms to redefine activities as R&D in order to qualify for the credit. A tax credit also was provided for company-funded basic research conducted at universities. Under the original tax credit enacted in 1981, 65 percent of company-funded university research was eligible for the incremental credit. Under the 1986 tax law, company-funded university basic research was given separate treatment. The subsidy provided by the credit was further reduced in 1988 by making half of the credit claimed taxable income by requiring businesses to deduct the tax credit from their expensing deduction.

In 1989, the amount of credit claimed was made 100 percent taxable, and the method of determining the base for calculating the amount of R&E eligible for the credit was changed. Instead of using the average of three prior years' R&E spending, the base became the product of a fixed ratio of R&E spending to sales (referred to as the "fixed base percentage") times average gross sales of the business for the preceding four years. As in the earlier version of the credit, the base period limitation was maintained so that the base used to determine the credit could not be less than one-half of the taxpayer's qualified expenditures during the taxable year. To avoid unduly penalizing businesses with unusually high R&D-to-sales ratios, the fixed ratio used to determine the base was defined to be the lesser of 0.16 or the actual ratio of R&E to sales for at least three years between 1984 and 1988. Businesses without the requisite number of taxable years between 1984 and 1988 were assigned a fixed ratio of 0.03. Beginning in 1994, businesses without the requisite number of taxable years were allowed to retain the fixed base of 0.03 for only the first five years after 1993; additional calculations of the fixed base percentage were then required in the 6th through 10th years so that by the 11th year the firm's fixed base percentage reflected its actual ratio of qualified R&E spending to sales in five of the previous six tax years. In 1996, firms that were unable to claim the regular credit were allowed to claim an alternative credit that applied a lower credit rate to a smaller fixed base.

Since its initial enactment in 1981, the R&E tax credit has never been a permanent provision in the federal tax code. It has, however, been extended 11 times since it was originally scheduled to expire in 1985. The R&E credit will expire on December 31, 2005, unless it is extended.

Policy issues

Since its enactment, the R&E tax credit has provided tax subsidies to industrial spending on R&E in excess of $1 billion a year. The rationale for the subsidy is that investments in in-

dustrial R&D often have social returns above the private return captured by the business that makes the investment. The existence of such external benefits from R&D spending means that private investments in R&D may be less than would be socially optimal.

Economists generally agree that certain types of spending on industrial research can generate sizable external benefits and that, for this reason, some form of government subsidy for R&E may be justified. As with other tax expenditures, however, the broad issue of whether the R&E tax credit has subsidized spending on industrial research that otherwise would not have been undertaken has surfaced at several points in the credit's history.

One noteworthy feature of the R&E credit is that from its inception, attempts have been made to avoid crediting R&E spending that businesses would have undertaken in the absence of the credit. Allowing businesses to claim a tax credit only on the amount by which current spending exceeded some predetermined base was intended to make the R&E tax credit an incremental subsidy for spending on R&E that the business would not otherwise have undertaken.

Economists who have studied the credit agree that the initial attempt to define the base was seriously flawed. By defining the base as the average of the firm's qualified R&D spending in the past three years, an additional $1 of R&D spending in the present allowed a business to claim a tax credit, but at a cost of not being able to claim a comparable tax credit in future years. The reason was that the additional $1 spent in the present reduced the amount of future R&D eligible for the credit by $0.33 in each of the subsequent three years.

This feature of the current credit had two effects. One was that the effective rate of subsidy provided by the credit was significantly reduced from its statutory level of 20 percent to something closer to 3 percent. Another effect was that businesses faced incentives to change the timing of their R&D spending to maximize the amount of credits that could be claimed. Firms with declining R&D spending in a given year faced an incentive to defer R&D spending to subsequent years, while other firms faced incentives to vary or to "cycle" R&D spending over several years to be able to claim more R&D credits.

This shortcoming was addressed by the change in defining the base enacted in 1990. As a result of this change, a firm's base depends on two factors—the fixed base percentage, and the average of three prior years' sales—that are not directly affected by how much the business spends on R&E. Thus, increased spending on R&E today does not automatically make it harder for a business to claim the credit in the future, which had the effect of diluting the effective rate of subsidy provided by the credit.

Even though the base has been defined more satisfactorily, there is still an issue of whether the credit truly encourages a significant amount of R&E spending that otherwise would not have taken place. Two factors determine the size of the credit's impact on new R&D spending. One is the effective reduction in the after-tax cost of R&E as a result of the credit. Although the statutory tax credit on eligible R&E is 20 percent, the effective rate of subsidy has been estimated at between 3 and 5 percent.

The other important factor is the price sensitivity (elasticity) of spending on R&D. If, for example, decisions about spending on R&D depend on considerations other than cost, then reducing the after-tax cost of R&D will be a relatively ineffective stimulus to R&D spending, and much of the tax subsidy would reward businesses for doing what they would have done in any case. If, however, cost is a consideration, the tax subsidy is more likely to encourage "new" spending on R&D.

Economists who study the behavior of businesses that conduct R&D generally agree that the amount of R&D spending is sensitive to its cost, so that the R&E tax credit has stimulated some additional industrial R&D. Empirical studies have reported estimates of the price elasticity of R&D that range from −0.2 to −2.0, which means that a 1 percent reduction in the cost of R&D would increase R&D spending by between 0.2 and 2 percent.

An analysis by the Joint Committee on Taxation (2003) concludes that there is general agreement that the price elasticity of R&D is less than −1.0 and may be less than −0.5. If these estimates are applied to the estimated 3 percent effective reduction in the cost of R&D, the implication is that the percentage increase in R&D spending resulting from the credit would be on the order of 1.5 to 3 percent.

Concerns have also been raised about the R&E credit's lack of permanence. Although congressional support for the credit has generally been broad, the credit has not been made permanent, largely for budgetary reasons: by keeping the credit as a temporary provision, its revenue cost only has needed to be scored for the years in which it is officially in effect. Some have argued that the lack of permanence has reduced the incentive effect of the credit; businesses cannot factor the credit into their longer-range spending plans for R&D as long it remains a temporary tax provision that must periodically be reenacted.

ADDITIONAL READINGS

Cordes, Joseph J. "Tax Incentives and R&D Spending: A Review of the Evidence." *Research Policy* 18 (1989): 119–33.

Cordes, Joseph J., Harry S. Watson, and J. Scott Hauger. "The Effects of Tax Reform on High Technology Firms." *National Tax Journal* 40, no. 3 (1987): 373–91.

Guenther, Gary. *Research and Experimentation Tax Credit: Current State and Policy Issues for the 108th Congress.* U.S. Library of Congress, Congressional Research Service Report RL31131, updated June 24, 2004.

Hall, Bronwyn. "R&D Tax Policy during the 1980s: Success or Failure." In *Tax Policy and the Economy,* vol. 7, edited by James Poterba (1–35). Cambridge, MA: MIT Press, 1993.

———. "The Private and Social Returns to Research and Development." In *Technology, R&D, and the Economy,* edited by Bruce L. Smith and Claude E. Barfield (140–183). Washington, DC: Brookings Institution Press, 1996.

U.S. Congress, Joint Committee on Taxation. *Description of Revenue Provisions Contained in the President's Fiscal Year 2004 Budget Proposal.* Joint Committee print, JCS-7-03 108th Cong., 1st sess. Washington, DC: Joint Committee on Taxation, March 2003), 520.

Cross-references: basis adjustment; expensing; investment tax credits; tax expenditures.

Residence principle

Joseph J. Cordes
George Washington University

A basis for assigning tax liabilities to individuals and businesses located in one jurisdiction and earning income in another.

Taxation on the basis of residence, rather than at the source, means that the amount a person pays in taxes depends on where the person lives, rather than on where the income is earned. Consider the case of a resident of the United States who earns interest from a bank account located in another country. If the United States and that country agree, typically through a tax treaty, to tax each other's citizens on the basis of residence, the investor would be required to report and pay taxes on the interest income to the United States instead of to the country where the interest income is earned.

In the United States, individual states often agree to tax citizens of other states on the basis of residence to ease the compliance burden of taxpayers. This can be especially important in border areas where residents of one state may work and earn income in another. For example, in the Washington, D.C., metropolitan area, a resident of the Virginia suburbs who works in Maryland files in, and pays taxes to, Virginia rather than Maryland.

Taxation on the basis of residence means that taxes will be neutral with respect to where taxpayers decide to invest and earn their money. For example, if a U.S. resident faces a choice between investing money in the United States and earning a return of R_{US} and investing the money abroad and earning a return of R_F, the portfolio decision should depend only on which of these two returns is the greater if the taxpayer is taxed on the basis of residence. If she invests in the United States, she would be taxed on the investment at her U.S. tax rate of T_{US} percent and after paying taxes would earn an after-tax return of $R_{US}(1 - T_{US})$. If instead she invests abroad and is taxed on the basis of residence, she would also be taxed at the U.S. rate, so her after-tax return would be $R_F(1 - T_{US})$. If the decision about where to invest is based on the after-tax return, it will depend on which investment pays the highest pretax return, because that investment will result in the highest after-tax return. For this reason, taxation on the basis of residence is seen as facilitating an economically efficient flow of resources among different taxing jurisdictions.

Cross-references: capital export neutrality; capital import neutrality; national neutrality; origin principle; source principle; telecommunications and electronic commerce, state taxation of.

Retail sales tax, national

William G. Gale

Brookings Institution

A proposal for fundamental tax reform that would replace the income tax system with a consumption tax, to be collected by levying a flat-rate tax on all sales from businesses to households.

Background

One proposal for fundamental tax reform is to replace part or all of the current tax system with a national retail sales tax (NRST). The NRST is one form of a consumption tax.

Retail sales occur when businesses sell goods or services to households. Neither business-to-business nor household-to-household transactions are retail sales. For example, the sale of a newly constructed home to a family that will occupy it is a retail sale. But the sale of that same newly constructed home to a business that is planning on renting it to others is not a retail sale. Nor is a sale of an already existing home from one occupant to another.

Typically, proposed NRSTs would aim to tax all goods or services purchased or used in the United States. Exemptions would be provided for business purchases and education (both considered investments). Domestic purchases by foreigners would be taxed; foreign purchases by domestic buyers would not. To ensure that no family in poverty has to pay the sales tax, the sales tax proposals typically also offer equal per-household payments called "demogrants" that are equal to the sales tax rate times the poverty level.

A national retail sales tax structured along these lines would represent a sharp break from the current tax system. The tax base would shift to consumption. Rates would be flat. All exemptions, deductions, and preferences would be eliminated. Tax administration, enforcement, and point of collection would be altered radically.

What rate?

A key issue is the required tax rate in a sales tax. The first issue is how to define a tax rate. Suppose a good costs $100 and has a $30 sales tax. The tax-exclusive tax rate would be 30 percent, since the tax is 30 percent of the pretax selling price ($100). The tax-inclusive rate would be 23 percent, which is obtained by dividing the $30 tax by the total consumer cost ($100 + $30). Sales taxes are typically quoted in tax-exclusive terms, but income taxes are typically quoted as tax-inclusive rates. For example, a household that earns $130 and pays $30 in taxes would normally think of itself as facing about a 23 percent (30/130) income tax rate. Although there is no single correct way to report the sales tax rate, it is crucial to understand which approach is being used. The tax-inclusive rate will always be lower than the tax-exclusive rate and the difference grows as the rates rise. At a rate of 1 percent the difference is negligible, but a 50 percent tax-exclusive rate corresponds to a 33 percent tax-inclusive rate.

To determine the revenue- and budget-neutral tax rate in a national sales tax requires estimating the rates of evasion and avoidance; the extent to which deductions, exemptions, and credits would be re-introduced; and the impact on economic growth. With extremely conservative assumptions about the magnitude of evasion, avoidance, and statutory base erosion, it would require a 60 percent tax-exclusive (38 percent tax-inclusive) tax rate to replace existing federal taxes, and a 26 percent tax-exclusive (21 percent tax-inclusive) tax rate to replace the existing personal income tax. These estimates do not include any allowance for economic growth, but even if the economy grew by 5 percent, which would be an enormous effect relative to existing estimates, the tax-exclusive tax rates would only come down to 57 percent and 19 percent to replace all federal taxes, or the income tax, respectively.

Note that the eventual sales tax rate that households would face would likely be significantly higher because existing state sales tax would be added. In addition, most or all state income taxes would probably be abolished in the absence of a federal income tax system (since the states depend on the federal income tax system for reporting purposes) and converted to sales taxes. These would add considerably to the combined sales tax rate. Any transition relief provided to households would reduce the tax base and raise the required rate further. And if major consumption items like food, housing, or health care were exempted from the base (the assumption above does not allow for such large exemptions), the tax-exclusive rate could rise to over 100 percent. In short, any realistic plan for a national retail sales tax that replaced the bulk of the federal tax system would require extremely high tax rates. Sales taxes at such high rates raise crucial questions about enforceability.

Advocates and sponsors of sales tax proposals have suggested that much lower rates, on the order of 23–30 percent, would be sufficient to replace the entire federal system. These estimates are lower than the ones above for three reasons. First, they are quoted in tax-inclusive terms. Second, they assume that there is no evasion, no avoidance, and no statutory base erosion due to political pressures or hard-to-tax items.

Third, quite simply, the advocates made a mathematical mistake in calculating their required tax rate. An analysis of the required rate in a sales tax requires some assumption about what happens to the level of (the prices that consumers see before sales taxes are imposed) in the transition to a sales tax. Producer prices could (a) remain constant in nominal terms,

(b) fall by the entire amount of the previously embedded taxes, or (c) fall by an amount between the first two benchmarks. In calculating their required rate, the NRST advocates assumed that producer prices would remain constant when they calculated the amount of revenue the government would obtain from a sales tax, but assumed that producer prices would fall when calculating the amount of spending the government would have to do to maintain current programs. These assumptions are obviously inconsistent, and they either understate government spending needs, overstate the revenue likely to be obtained, or both. Making a consistent assumption about producer prices—regardless of whether the assumption is (a), (b), or (c)—leads to a higher rate than the advocates have assumed.

Enforceability and avoidance

The results above suggest that even with rates of evasion much lower than in the existing income tax system, the required national retail sales tax would be well into the 30s and possibly even higher (on a tax-inclusive basis). Governments have gone on record noting that at rates of more than 12 percent, sales taxes are too easy to evade. Thus, the most optimistic assessment would be that there is no historical precedent for a country to enact a high-rate, enforceable, national sales tax. That does not mean it is impossible, but extreme caution would be appropriate.

Sales tax advocates admit that evasion would be a certainty, yet make no account for it in their estimates and hope that sentiments of fairness will induce taxpayers not to cheat. They also point to low marginal tax rates as an inducement not to cheat, but as shown above, the tax rate would not likely be low. Another claim is that detection of cheating would rise dramatically since only retailers would have to be audited, but this is misleading. Under the sales tax, businesses that make retail sales would be responsible for sending tax payments to the government, unless the buyer used a business exemption certificate, in which case no tax would be due. But the buyer would have the legal responsibility for determining whether the good is used as a business input or a consumption item. This means that auditing and enforcement would have to focus not just on retailers, but also on all businesses that purchase from retailers, to ensure that business exemption certificates were used appropriately.

Most importantly, the sales tax would generate tremendous opportunities for evasion. For example, in the income tax, the rate of evasion is around 15 percent. But income where taxes are withheld and reported to government by a third party has evasion rates of around 5 percent. For income where taxes are not withheld and there is no cross-reporting, evasion is around 50 percent. Since the sales tax would feature no withholding and no cross-reporting, the possibility of high evasion rates needs to be taken quite seriously.

Advocates also assert that the sales tax would be more effective than the current system at raising revenue from the underground economy. The classic example is that of a drug dealer who currently does not pay income tax on the money he earns, but would be forced to pay taxes under a sales tax if he took the drug money and bought, for example, a Mercedes. The problem with this argument is laid out best by former Rep. Richard Armey (R-TX) (1995): "If there is an income tax in place, he [the drug dealer] won't report his income. If there is a sales tax in place, he won't collect taxes from his customers" and send the taxes to the government. In the end, neither system taxes the drug trade. Many other countries have attempted to implement a retail sales tax, or variants, and almost all have abandoned the tax and moved to a value-added tax.

Finally, some sales tax advocates would eliminate the IRS and have the states administer the tax. Even though the states would keep 1 percent of the revenue they collect, they would have poor incentive to collect federal taxes adequately.

The tax base

The broader the base, the lower the rate can be, but taxing a broad base will be hard. Some items are quite difficult to tax, such as imputed financial services. Other items may not be taxed for reasons of social policy, like child care, rent, and food. Some sectors might not be taxed because of strong political influences—housing and health, for instance, though exemptions here may also be related to social policy. These issues create serious trade-offs. For example, taxing health insurance under a NRST would raise the number of uninsured by an estimated 6 million to 14 million people.

But health, food, and housing make up about half of all personal consumption, so exempting even one of these sectors would cut deeply into the sales tax base and raise the rates even further.

Economic growth

Estimates suggest that a well-functioning, broad-based consumption tax with limited personal exemptions, limited transition relief, and moderate rates could raise income per person by up to 2 percent over 10 years. But more generous transition relief or erosion of the tax base would drive the growth effects to zero quickly.

Would a sales tax be fair?

Taxing consumption instead of income is often justified on grounds that consumption may be a better indicator of long-run ability to pay taxes, since income varies significantly from year to year. But for people who face constraints on what they can borrow, the long run may not be the most relevant time period. Clearly, there is nothing inherently fair (or unfair) about having a single rate. If households are classified by annual income, the sales tax is sharply regressive. Under the Americans for Fair Taxation proposal, which provides the baseline discussion for the NRST, taxes would rise for households in the bottom 90 percent of the income distribution, while households in the top 1 percent would receive an average tax cut of over $75,000. If households are classified by consumption level, a somewhat different pattern emerges. Households in the bottom two-thirds of the distribution would pay less than currently, while households in the top third would pay more. Still, households at the very top would pay much less, again receiving a tax cut of about $75,000. There appears to be little sound motivation for heaping huge tax cuts on precisely the groups whose income and wealth have benefited the most from recent events, and raising burdens significantly on others.

Advocates like to assert that sales taxes are pro-family relative to the income tax. But children and families benefit disproportionately from numerous features of the current system, including dependent exemptions, child credits, child care credits, earned income credits, and education credits. And the preferential treatment of housing, health insurance, and state and local tax payments also plausibly helps families, since they consume relatively more housing, medical services, and government-provided services such as education. All these preferences would be eliminated under a sales tax. Moreover, compared to childless couples, families with kids generally have high consumption relative to income, so switching from income tax to a consumption tax would further raise tax burdens during years when family needs were highest. Based on 1996 data, a recent study found that enactment of a broad-based, flat-rate consumption tax like the sales tax or flat tax would hurt families with incomes less than $200,000 because of the loss of tax preferences, but would help families with income above $200,000 because of the dramatic reduction in the top tax rate. Incorporating the 1997 and 2001 tax changes—especially the child and education credits—would only exacerbate these results.

Lessons from the states

Sales taxes already exist in 45 states, the District of Columbia, and over 6,000 localities. State tax rates range from 3 to 7 percent. While state sales taxes are widely viewed as successful in certain ways, they are very poor models for federal reform. States only tax about half of private consumption of goods and services. Many states exempt goods such as food, electricity, telephone service, prescription medicine, and so on. Most states do not tax services very well, if at all. In addition, between 20 and 40 percent of state sales tax revenue stems from business purchases, which are not retail sales. This causes cascading of the sales tax, which distorts relative prices in capricious ways and gives firms incentives to merge with other firms in order to avoid the tax. States often do not require their own government to pay sales taxes. And states do not provide demogrants; instead they help the poor by exempting specific items, such as food. These findings suggest that running a pure,

broad-based sales tax as envisioned by federal proposals noted above could be quite difficult in practice.

Conclusion

As a replacement for the existing federal tax system, a national retail sales tax is a nonstarter. The required rate would be sufficiently high to make enforcement too difficult and evasion too tempting. The historical record should suggest great caution in this regard. Even if the tax were enforceable at these rates, the implied effects on economic growth would be small at best, and certain sectors of the economy, such as employer-provided health insurance, could be affected significantly. The sales tax would raise burdens on low- and middle-income households and sharply cut taxes on the top 1 percent.

ADDITIONAL READINGS

Armey, Richard. "Caveat Emptor: The Case Against the National Sales Tax." *Policy Review* (Summer 1995): 31–5.

Bartlett, Bruce. "Replacing Federal Taxes with a Sales Tax." *Tax Notes* 68 (August 21, 1995): 997–1003.

Cnossen, Sijbren. "VAT and RST: A Comparison." *Canadian Tax Journal* 35, no. 3 (1987): 559–615.

Feenberg, Daniel R., Andrew W. Mitrusi, and James M. Poterba. "Distributional Effects of Adopting a National Retail Sales Tax." *Tax Policy and the Economy* 11 (1997): 49–89.

Fox, William F., and Matthew N. Murray. "A National Retail Sales Tax." *State Tax Notes* (September 2005).

Gale, William G. "The Required Tax Rate in a National Retail Sales Tax." *National Tax Journal* 52, no. 3 (September 1999): 443–57.

———. "A Note on the Required Tax Rate in a National Retail Sales Tax: Preliminary Estimates for 2005–2014." Washington, DC: Brookings Institution, 2004.

Gale, William G., and Janet Holtzblatt. "The Role of Administrative Factors in Tax Reform: Simplicity, Compliance, and Administration." In *United States Tax Reform in the Twenty-First Century,* edited by George R. Zodrow and Peter Mieszkowski (179–214). New York: Cambridge University Press, 2002.

Linbeck, Leo, Jr. "Submission of Americans for Fair Taxation on the Fair-Tax Comprehensive Tax Reform Proposal to the President's Advisory Panel on Federal Tax Reform, April 29, 2005." Washington, DC: Americans for Fair Taxation, 2005.

Metcalf, Gilbert E. "The National Sales Tax: Who Bears the Burden?" Policy Analysis no. 289. Washington, DC: The Cato Institute, 1997.

Mikesell, John L. 1997. "The American Retail Sales Tax: Considerations on their Structure, Operations, and Potential as a Foundation for a Federal Sales Tax." *National Tax Journal* 50, no. 1 (March 1997): 149–65.

Murray, Matthew N. "Would Tax Evasion and Tax Avoidance Undermine a National Retail Sales Tax?" *National Tax Journal* 50, no. 1 (March 1997): 167–82.

Slemrod, Joel. "Which Is the Simplest Tax System of Them All?" In *Economic Effects of Fundamental Tax Reform,* edited by Henry J. Aaron and William G. Gale (355–91). Washington, DC: Brookings Institution Press, 1996.

Wall Street Journal. "VAT in Drag." July 19, 1996.

Zodrow, George R. "The Sales Tax, the VAT, and Taxes in Between—Or, Is the Only Good NRST a 'VAT in Drag?' " *National Tax Journal* 52, no. 3 (September 1999): 429–42.

Cross-references: consumption taxation; expenditure tax; value-added tax, national.

Retail sales tax, state and local

John F. Due
University of Illinois

Updated by
John L. Mikesell
Indiana University

A retail sales tax is a form of sales tax that is levied on the final sale through which a commodity (or service) passes on the path to the final purchaser.

Technically, a retail sales tax is defined as a tax on sales for use or consumption and not for resale. It is not a tax solely on retailers in the usual distribution sense of that term, but on any firm making final sales as defined. Nor is it a tax confined to sales to final household consumers, because in practice the tax applies to a number of purchases for use in further production, such as machinery and equipment. It is not, therefore, a pure consumption tax related directly to household personal consumption.

Development

Until the 1930s, retail sales taxation was considered beyond the capacity of effective administration, although its use had been suggested on a few occasions—for example, in France during World War I. Use of the tax began in the United States in the early 1930s as an outgrowth of low-rate business occupation taxes. In 1932, Mississippi, desperate for additional revenue, converted its business occupation levy into a 2 percent tax on retail sales (Wheeless 1966). Despite strong protests, the tax proved productive of revenue and capable of adequate administrative effectiveness. This success led other states to follow—10 in 1933 alone and 29 by 1938 (Due and Mikesell 1994). Introduction then slowed, but it sped up after the end of World War II. By 1969, only five states did not use the tax. None has added it since then, despite many proposals, but none has repealed it either.

In parallel to the U.S. experience, the tax was introduced in Canada starting with the city of Montreal in 1935 and the province of Alberta in 1936, although Alberta later repealed the tax (Due 1964). Quebec imposed the tax in 1940, and others followed, until by 1967 all the provinces employed the tax except Alberta—as is still true. No territories levy the tax.

Elsewhere in the world, while sales taxation spread rapidly, typically other forms were used. The retail tax was used in relatively few countries. These included Zimbabwe, which imposed the tax in 1963 and continued to use it until replacing it with a value-added tax (VAT) in 2004. This is one of the very few cases in which a retail sales tax has been used successfully by a developing country, but Zimbabwe has a highly commercialized retail sector (Due 1983). South Africa imposed a retail sales tax in the 1970s, but replaced it with a

VAT in 1990. Retail sales taxes in Namibia and Lesotho have also been replaced with value-added taxes.

Other uses can be noted briefly. The tax was imposed in Iceland in 1960, used successfully at high rates—up to 20 percent—and replaced by a VAT in 1989. Norway (1940–70) and Sweden (1940–48 and 1960–69) used retail sales taxes until they replaced them with VATs. Barbados imposed a retail tax in 1975 but repealed it a year later.

The tax had limited use in Latin America, first in Honduras (1964) and then in Costa Rica (1967), Nicaragua (1968), and Paraguay (1968–92) (Birch and Due 1985). All were ultimately replaced by VATs. The retail tax has been used in several states in India, and the Swiss wholesale sales tax was in fact collected primarily at the retail level; it was replaced by a VAT in 1995. Many Russian regions levied a retail sales tax from 1999 through 2003 (Mikesell 1999).

In the United States and Canada, the sales taxes were introduced primarily to meet the need for additional revenue, not to replace other taxes. They were chosen over income tax increases primarily because of the fear of loss of business investment to other states, the height of federal income taxes, and the greater cyclical stability of revenue relative to income taxes.

The retail sales taxes in the United States have yielded from 30 to 34 percent of state tax revenue in recent years, although they range from less than 25 percent in Vermont, New York, and Massachusetts to a high of 61 percent in Tennessee and more than 50 percent in Nevada, Florida, and Texas, all states without a broad-based individual income tax (Mikesell 2004). In Canada, the tax yields an overall 21 percent of provincial and territory tax revenue, ranging from 18 to 31 percent among adopting provinces.

The remainder of this entry concentrates on the experience in the United States and Canada, given the tax's current limited use elsewhere.

Coverage—commodities

The typical retail sales tax applies to all commodities—that is, tangible personal property—other than ones specifically exempted, but only to their final sales; as noted, purchase must be for use or consumption and not for resale. All purchases for resale are therefore free of tax; universally, purchases of materials to be physically incorporated into products are included in the category of sales for resale. Sales for delivery outside the state are exempt; purchases from out of state are subject to levies called use taxes, imposed at the same rate as the sales tax.

Exemptions of commodities fall into two general classes. First, certain production inputs, particularly those used in manufacturing and agriculture, are specifically exempted (Due and Mikesell 1994; Hellerstein and Hellerstein 1992, ch. 14; Ring 1999). Following the rationale for its use, a retail sales tax should apply only to purchases for household consumption expenditures and thus logically should not apply to any purchases acquired for business use. But in practice, the taxes were not designed in this fashion; use or consumption has been interpreted to mean use by business firms as well as final consumers. This rule, of course, results in multiple applications of the tax to final consumption goods, contrary to the consumption principle. In addition, it may lead to pyramiding—that is, price increases in excess of the tax by applying percentage markups to prices, including tax. It may deter real investment by making investment more costly, and by encouraging firms to reduce the amount of tax by producing goods for use in further production instead of purchasing them.

Accordingly, almost all states and provinces have gradually added various categories of production inputs to the exempt list. About half of the states and several Canadian provinces, for example, exempt machinery and equipment used in manufacturing, and agricultural feed, seed, and fertilizer are universally excluded, as is farm machinery and equipment in a number of states. One result is to complicate somewhat the operation of the taxes and pave the way for evasion. Determination by the seller of the ultimate use of many goods is difficult.

The second group of exemptions is designed to bring about a distribution of the tax burden that is less regressive and thus more acceptable (Due and Mikesell 1994, ch. 4; Hellerstein and Hellerstein 1992, ch. 3). On this issue, state practice varies substantially. Some states provide virtually no exemptions of this type, others a wide range. Food is the most significant exemption in terms of revenue. Only 13 states tax food at the full standard rate in 2004, and all Canadian provinces exempt food. It has been a common exemption in other countries as well. Medicines and related items, especially those on prescription, are now exempt in virtually all states and provinces, although the specific coverage differs.

States provide a variety of other exemptions—books in some, for example, and clothing in a few states. The exemptions, particularly food, have drastic effects on revenue, the food exemption alone reducing revenue by as much as 20 percent. The exemptions inevitably complicate compliance, audit, and control, because of interpretative problems relating to the coverage of the category and misapplication of the tax at point of sale. Food exemption does significantly reduce the regressivity of the tax and the absolute burden on the poor.

There are other exemptions of varying significance, such as sales to government and various charitable and educational institutions, and commodities, such as motor fuel, subject to excises. A number of states also offer sales tax holidays, usually on clothing and a few other items, for a week or so, in an effort to stimulate sales or provide limited relief on particular purchases, like supplies for the new school year.

This section is concerned with commodities—that is, tangible personal property. Sale of real property is generally never taxed, nor is intangible property, including securities and various credit instruments—basically because purchase is not considered consumption.

Services

The treatment of services varies substantially among the states and has gradually changed over the years (Due and Mikesell 1994, ch. 5; Hellerstein and Hellerstein 1992, ch. 15; Federation of Tax Administrators 1996). The original taxes applied solely to tangible personal property, thus excluding all services, and in a few states—California, for example—the taxes are still primarily of this nature. Many states do not even tax repair or installation of tangible personal property, which would be taxable when purchased. Only two states, Hawaii and New Mexico, initially followed the opposite taxation pattern: In addition to commodities, virtually all services rendered to customers, but not services of employees, were taxed. South Dakota's treatment later moved relatively close to these. Gradually, other states have added services—some only a few, such as transient accommodations and utilities, others a hundred or so.

The result is to increase revenues, but rarely by a high percentage, because the states are reluctant as a matter of principle and politics to include some of the most productive services from a revenue standpoint, such as medical care and legal services. It is not at all clear that including services brings the pattern of distribution more in line with accepted standards (Fox and Murray 1988; Siegfried and Smith 1991). One major sector, real property contract work, receives special treatment. Typically, the tax applies to materials purchased for this work, rather than the full contract price including labor.

Rate structures

Unlike some other forms of sales tax, retail sales taxes typically have uniform rates, in part because of the difficulty for retailers in keeping adequate records of sales at various rates. In the United States, the principal exceptions are the application of lower rates to industrial equipment and machinery, used in lieu of exemption. Rarely is a higher than basic rate applied. Paraguay was an exception, and a few U.S. states tax motel and hotel services, car rental, and alcoholic beverages more heavily than the basic figure; outside the United States, rates have typically been under 10 percent, although Iceland used a 20 percent rate. The initial rates for United States state taxes were typically 2 percent, but they have gradually increased until by 2004 the median rate is 5.4 percent, with actual rates ranging from 2.9 to 7 percent. Concurrently, in a number of states, various local governments (primarily cities and counties) levy the tax, with most rates ranging from 2 to 3 percent. Combined state-local rates reach 7 to 10 percent. In Canada, the rates have typically been higher than in the United States, but the exemptions are broader. In 2004, the median rate among the nine adopting provinces was 8 percent, with a range from 7 percent (Saskatchewan and Manitoba) to 10 percent (Prince Edward Island). Alberta and the territories levy no tax. The provincial tax applies to selling price including the federal goods and services tax in Quebec and Prince Edward Island and selling price before that tax in the other provinces.

Distribution of burden of a retail sales tax

The traditional view of the distributional effects of a retail sales tax is that the tax will be reflected in higher prices to consumers, and thus the burden will be distributed in relation to consumption expenditures. Empirical evidence was provided by Poterba (1996) and Besley and Rosen (1999). It is also widely believed that quoting the tax separately from the prices for goods or services, an almost universal practice in the United States and Canada but not in many other countries, facilitates forward shifting by encouraging competing firms to follow the same pricing policies.

It has long been recognized, however, that there are certain exceptions. Demand elasticities for various goods will differ, even with a uniform tax rate, and firms may readjust prices to push more of the burden onto the goods with inelastic demands. As noted, a portion of the tax rests on goods purchased for use in production; the distribution of this portion of the burden is by no means clear. Finally, it has long been argued that the overall higher prices will result in reduced demand for factor units and thus reduce their prices, some of the burden being borne in relation to factor income. But if fiscal policy seeks to maintain the same overall level of demand for factors, factor prices will not fall.

In summary, while the assumption of exact forward shifting is an oversimplification, it is still generally accepted as the basis for legislative action and analyses of burden distribution. Many studies have been made of the distribution of burden by income class, on the assumption of forward shifting. In general, these studies concluded that the tax, without exemptions, will be regressive relative to incomes and place considerable absolute burden on the lowest income groups. If food is exempt, then regressivity is greatly reduced. Adding services to the coverage does not much lessen regressivity.

An alternative to food exemption is to provide for credit against state income tax with a refund, or a direct cash payment, to compensate for the tax on the lower-income groups (Case and Ebel 1989). Such programs that provide payment explicitly identified as sales tax rebates are used in Idaho, Oklahoma, Kansas, and South Dakota; the number of such programs has been falling as states adopt food exemptions or seek additional revenue by abandoning the credit. The credit approach is used by the Canadian government on its value-added tax and in several provinces (including British Columbia, Ontario, Newfoundland and Labrador, and Saskatchewan).

This general view of regressivity has been criticized on two grounds. First, it is argued that distributional effects should be considered in terms of lifetime income, not annual income; many of the low-income groups are not really poor, but drawing on previously accumulated funds. On a lifetime basis, recent studies have shown the tax to still be regressive, but much less so (Fullerton and Rogers 1993; Caspersen and

Metcalf 1994). The second objection is that many people in the lowest income groups are receiving incomes (e.g., welfare) that are indexed to the general price level; if the sales tax rises, the transfer payments will also rise (Browning 1985). But many lower-income groups do not benefit from such indexing.

The other problem with studies of sales tax incidence is that they basically employ a partial equilibrium analysis, when a general-equilibrium analysis would be more suitable because all or most prices are changing. But obtaining adequate data poses serious problems.

Administration of the taxes

When retail sales taxes have been introduced by national governments, administration has typically been assigned to Customs and Excise along with other indirect taxes. Individual states in the United States have followed various routes. In earlier years, sales tax administration was typically placed as a separate division in the general revenue agency. In recent years, the trend has been toward functional organization, in which each activity involved in sales tax administration has been entrusted to the division performing similar functions for other taxes, including income tax as well, although in practice some specialization of personnel takes place.

In addition to routine registration of firms and handling incoming returns and payments, there are two major aspects of administration. First is control of delinquency—checking on firms not filing returns or paying on time. Second is auditing—inspecting firms' records to ensure that correct amounts are paid (Due and Mikesell 1994, ch. 6). Operations are now highly computerized, so ascertainment of delinquents—those not filing or paying—is relatively easy, with contact then made by letter, phone call, and, if necessary, a visit.

Initial delinquency rates as a percentage of registered firms continue to be relatively high, with a median for all states of about 10 percent, concentrated in smaller firms. But the final action—such as seizure of property—involves no more than 0.1 percent of the firms. Audits are performed by a relatively well-trained staff, and a variety of techniques are used to establish priorities for audit. But the coverage is very limited—overall, no more than 1.2 percent of registered firms a year in recent years. There are about 7.4 million firms in the United States registered for sales tax purposes (Due and Mikesell 1994).

Overall effectiveness of the state retail sales taxes

It is very difficult to measure the exact degree of the taxes' operational effectiveness. From all indications, the intrastate operation is relatively effective, with no mass escape of taxable firms and transactions, although some revenue is lost via the underground economy (Due 1974). A recent study finds a noncompliance rate of 1.3 percent in Washington State, for instance (Washington Department of Revenue 2003). With interstate transactions, however, there is a substantial loss—as is true with interprovincial sales in Canada as well. A state cannot apply an "export" tax on buyers in other states for constitutional reasons and likely would not wish to do so anyway. Under the use tax sections of the state sales tax legislation, states can tax purchases coming from out of state, and they do reach such purchases from large traditional mail-order houses as well as the purchases of motor vehicles and other items that must be registered. But they cannot reach many smaller transactions and firms selling into a large number of states with small amounts in each, as well as many of the large mail-order vendors. Such firms could be forced, at considerable cost and nuisance, to conform with the sales-use tax laws of a number of states. These states have sought to lessen the escape, but with only limited effect (Trandel 1992; Walsh and Jones 1988; Fisher 1980; Fox 1986; Washington Department of Revenue 1990). Under current federal law, only firms with physical presence in a state may be required to register as collectors for that state's use tax. Many states have worked together to simplify compliance cost so that collection would not be an undue burden, in the hope that Congress will change the registration requirement standard, thereby allowing the use tax to be effectively enforced on purchases from firms lacking physical presence in a state, including vendors via catalog or the Internet. Congressional action has not yet been forthcoming.

The cost of administering state sales taxes ranges at around 1 percent of the revenues; exact figures are difficult to obtain because of joint administration of sales and other taxes in many states. Estimates of compliance costs for the vendors vary widely; one study suggests an overall figure of about 3 percent—but this figure ranges widely with the type of business ("Vendor Collection of State Sales and Use Tax" 1993; Peat et al. 1982) and may be extremely high for multistate retailers (Cline and Neubig 2000).

The worldwide trend

In general, national governments have moved away from retail sales taxes to VATs, basically for two reasons: to free all purchases used for business from the tax (important for a country's foreign trade position and domestic efficiency in production), and to improve administration because of the superior audit trail. The European Community's adoption of the VAT stimulated this shift. In federal countries, however, the retail sales tax remains supreme at the state level, although in the United States and Canada limited attention has been given to its possible replacement with VATs. The main reason this does not occur is the interstate problem; the interstate sales give rise to serious questions about credit for other states' taxes and engender much greater enforcement problems than does the retail tax. There are serious conflict-of-interest issues among the various states regarding allocation of the share of the total sales (value added) tax revenue between the states in which the retail sale occurs (with credit for tax

paid at pre-retail sales) and the states of origin. Sales taxes in three Canadian provinces—Nova Scotia, New Brunswick, and Newfoundland and Labrador—are harmonized in structure with the federal VAT and are federally administered, and Quebec province administers the federal tax with its sales tax. The process was complex (Hill and Rushton 1993). Should a proposed federal retail sales tax be adopted in the United States, administration and structure of state sales taxes would become substantially more complicated.

ADDITIONAL READINGS

Baum, Donald. "Economic Effects of Including Services in the Sales Tax Base: An Applied General Equilibrium Approach." *Public Finance Quarterly* 19 (April 1992): 166–92.

Besley, Timothy J., and Harvey S. Rosen. "Sales Taxes and Prices." *National Tax Journal* 52 (June 1999): 157–58.

Birch, Melissa H., and John F. Due. "Paraguay: The Retail Sales Tax." *Bulletin for International Fiscal Documentation* 39, no. 3 (1985): 103–7.

Boucher, Karen J. "Sales Tax on Services: The New Source of State Revenues." *Journal of State Taxation* 7, no. 3 (Fall 1988): 273–86.

Browning, Edgar K. "Tax Incidence, Indirect Taxes, and Transfers." *National Tax Journal* 38 (December 1985): 525–34.

Bruce, Donald, and William F. Fox. "E-Commerce in the Context of Declining State Sales Tax Bases." *National Tax Journal* 53 (December 2000): 1373–90.

Case, Bradford, and Robert Ebel. "Using State Consumer Tax Credits for Achieving Equity." *National Tax Journal* 42 (September 1989): 323–38.

Caspersen, Erik, and Gilbert Metcalf. "Is a Value Added Tax Regressive? Annual vs. Lifetime Incidence Measures." *National Tax Journal* 47 (December 1994): 731–46.

Cline, Robert J., and Thomas S. Neubig. "Masters of Complexity and Bearers of Great Burden: The Sales Tax System and Compliance Costs for Multistate Retailers." *State Tax Notes* 18 (January 24, 2000): 297–314.

Derrick, Frederick W., and Charles E. Scott. "Business and the Incidence of Sales and Use Tax." *Public Finance Quarterly* 21 (April 2, 1993): 210–26.

Due, John F. *Provincial Sales Taxes.* Rev. ed. Toronto: Canadian Tax Foundation, 1964.

———. "Evaluation of the Effectiveness of State Sales Tax Administration." *National Tax Journal* 27 (June 1974): 197–219.

———. "The Experience of Zimbabwe with a Retail Sales Tax." *Bulletin for International Fiscal Documentation* 37 (February 1983): 51–58.

———. "The Implications for Australia of the Experience of the United States, Canada, and Other Countries with Retail Sales Tax." In *Changing the Tax Mix,* edited by John G. Head (225–46). Melbourne: Australian Tax Research Foundation, 1986.

Due, John F., and John L. Mikesell. *Sales Taxation.* 2nd ed. Washington, DC: Urban Institute Press, 1994.

Duncombe, William. "Economic Change and the Evolving State Tax Structure: The Case of the Sales Tax." *National Tax Journal* 45 (September 1992): 299–313.

Dye, Richard, and Therese McGuire. "Growth and Variability of State Individual Income and General Sales Taxes." *National Tax Journal* 44 (March 1991): 55–65.

Federation of Tax Administrators. *Sales Taxation of Services: Who Taxes What?* Washington, DC: Federation of Tax Administrators, 1991.

———. "Survey on State Taxation of Services." *Tax Administrators News* 60 (December 1996): 109, 112–8.

Fisher, Ronald C. "Local Sales Taxes: Tax Rate Differentials, Sales Loss, and Revenue Estimation." *Public Finance Quarterly* 8 (April 1980): 171–88.

Fox, William F. "Tax Structure and the Location of Economic Activity along State Borders." *National Tax Journal* 39 (December 1986): 387–402.

———, ed. *Sales Taxation: Critical Issues in Policy and Administration.* Westport, CT: Praeger Publishers, 1992.

Fox, William F., and Charles Campbell. "Stability of the State Sales Tax Income Elasticity." *National Tax Journal* 37 (June 1984): 201–12.

Fox, William F., and Matthew Murray. "Economic Aspects of Taxing Services." *National Tax Journal* 41 (March 1988): 19–36.

Fullerton, Don, and Diane Lim Rogers. *Who Bears the Lifetime Tax Burden?* Washington, DC: Brookings Institution Press, 1993.

Gold, Steven D. "Simplifying the Sales Tax: Credits or Exemptions?" In *Sales Taxation: Critical Issues in Policy and Administration,* edited by William F. Fox (157–68). Westport, CT: Praeger Publishers, 1992.

Hamilton, Billy, and John L. Mikesell. "Sales Tax Policy during the Next Decade." In *Sales Taxation: Critical Issues in Policy and Administration,* edited by William F. Fox (27–40). Westport, CT: Praeger Publishers, 1992.

Healy, John C., and Kenneth D. Klemm. "Sales and Use Tax Implications for Construction Contractors." *Journal of State Taxation* 8 (1990): 315–40.

Hellerstein, Jerome R., and Walter Hellerstein. *State Taxation.* Vol. 2, part S. Boston: Warren, Gorham & Lamont, 1992.

Hellerstein, Walter. "Florida's Sales Tax on Services." *National Tax Journal* 41 (March 1988): 1–18.

———. "Sales Taxation of Services." In *Sales Taxation: Critical Issues in Policy and Administration,* edited by William F. Fox (41–50). Westport, CT: Praeger Publishers, 1992.

Hill, Roderick, and Michael Rushton. "Harmonizing Provincial Sales Taxation with the GST." *Canadian Tax Journal* 41 (April 1993): 101–22.

Mikesell, John L. "Sales Taxation and the Border County Problem." *Quarterly Review of Economics and Business* 11 (Spring 1971): 23–9.

———. "Fiscal Effects of Differences in Sales Tax Coverage: Revenue Elasticity, Stability, and Reliance." *Proceedings of the Eighty-Fourth Annual Conference on Taxation of the National Tax Association–Tax Institute of America* 84 (1991): 50–7.

———. "Sales Taxation of Services: Economic Logic versus Fiscal Politics." *State Tax Notes* 5 (August 19, 1993): 361–2.

———. "Decentralizing Government Finances in the Russian Federation: The Regional Sales and Imputed Income Taxes." *Proceedings of the Ninety-Second Annual Conference on Taxation of the National Tax Association–Tax Institute of America* 92 (1999): 15–21.

———. "Sales Tax Incentives for Economic Development: Why Shouldn't Production Exemptions Be General?" *National Tax Journal* 54 (September 2001): 557–67.

———. "State Retail Sales Tax Burdens, Reliance, and Breadth in Fiscal 2003." *State Tax Notes* 33 (July 12, 2004): 125–31.

Mikesell, John L., and Mark Brown. "How Big Is the Local Use Tax Problem for Mail-Order Vendors?" *State Tax Notes* 3 (August 31, 1992): 309–13.

Minnesota Department of Revenue, Tax Research Division. *Minnesota Tax Incidence Study.* St. Paul: Minnesota Department of Revenue, Tax Research Division, November 1993.

Peat, Marwick, Mitchell, & Co. *Report to The American Retail Federation on Costs to Retailers of Sales and Use Tax Compliance.* Washington, DC: American Retail Federation, 1982.

Pomp, Richard D., and Oliver Oldman. "A Normative Enquiry into the Base of a Retail Sales Tax: Casual Sales, Used Goods, and Trade-Ins." *National Tax Journal* 43 (December 1990): 427–38.

Poterba, James M. "Retail Price Reactions to Changes in State and Local Sales Taxes." *National Tax Journal* 49 (June 1996): 165–75.

Quick, Perry D., and Michael J. McKee. "Sales Tax on Services: Revenue or Reform?" *National Tax Journal* 41 (September 1988): 395–410.

Ring, Raymond. "Consumer's Share and Producer's Share of the General Sales Tax." *National Tax Journal* 52 (March 1999): 79–90.

Rock, Steven M. "The Impact of Deductibility on the Incidence of a General Sales Tax." *National Tax Journal* 37 (March 1984): 105–12.

Siegfried, John J., and Paul A. Smith. "The Distributional Effects of a Sales Tax on Services." *National Tax Journal* 44 (March 1991): 41–53.

Trandel, Gregory A. "Evading the Use Tax on Cross-Border Sales: Pricing and Welfare Effects." *Journal of Public Economics* 49 (December 1992): 313–32.

"Vendor Collection of State Sales and Use Tax." *Tax Administrators News* 57, no. 1 (August 1993): 88.

Walsh, Michael J., and Jonathan D. Jones. "More Evidence on the 'Border Tax' Effect." *National Tax Journal* 41 (June 1988): 261–5.

Washington Department of Revenue. *The Effect of Tax Rate Differences on Retail Trade in Washington Border Counties.* Olympia, WA: Washington Department of Revenue, 1990.

———. *Department of Revenue Compliance Study, 2002.* No. 2003-1. Olympia, WA: Washington Department of Revenue, 2003.

Wheeless, V. B. *The Sales and Use Tax: Its Origin and Background in Mississippi.* Jackson, MS: State Tax Commission, 1966.

Cross-references: consumption taxation; elasticity, demand and supply; excise taxes; fairness in taxation; incidence of taxes; life cycle model; value-added tax, state.

Revenue elasticity (tax elasticity)

Joseph J. Cordes
George Washington University

Measures the sensitivity of the tax base to changing economic conditions.

The revenue elasticity of a tax is calculated by dividing the percentage change in revenue by the percentage change in income. For example, if income increased by 100 percent and the revenue raised by a tax on widgets increased by 50 percent, the revenue elasticity of the tax on widgets would equal 0.5 = 50 percent / 100 percent. If, instead, income increased by 100 percent and the revenue raised from taxing widgets increased by 200 percent, the revenue elasticity of the widget tax would be calculated to be 2.0 = 200 percent / 100 percent.

When tax revenues grow (decline) less rapidly than income grows (declines), the calculated revenue elasticity of a tax will be less than one and the tax is said to be inelastic. Conversely, when the tax revenues grow (decline) more rapidly than income grows (declines), the calculated value of the revenue elasticity is greater than 1 and the tax is said to be elastic. (This definition is similar to that of *price elasticity of demand,* discussed elsewhere in this volume.)

Two factors come into play in determining a tax's elasticity. One is how responsive or elastic the base of the tax is to income. The other is the structure of the tax rates applied to the base.

The role of these factors can be illustrated by considering the revenue elasticity of general sales, income, and property taxes. General sales taxes are typically levied at a single rate, and to a large extent, movements in sales track movements in income very closely, so that, for example, if personal income doubles, spending (which is the base of the sales tax) also doubles. For this reason, the percentage change in sales tax revenues is apt to be virtually the same as the percentage change in income, and the revenue elasticity of a general sales tax is widely taken to be 1.0. In contrast, although specific excise taxes on goods such as motor fuels, tobacco, and alcohol are also generally taxed at a single rate, the change in spending on these goods is less than proportionate to the change in income—that is, when incomes double, we expect spending on such goods to increase less than twofold. Hence, the calculated revenue elasticity of excise taxes is generally less than 1.0. Similarly, property tax revenues are fairly inelastic because assessed property values often increase (decrease) less rapidly than does income.

Income taxes illustrate the role of the tax rate structure in determining revenue elasticity. When income rises, it is taxed at higher rates; hence, income tax revenue grows (declines) more than proportionately relative to income, making the revenue elasticity of a graduated, or progressive, income tax greater than 1. By comparison, a flat-rate income tax that taxes the first dollar of income would have a revenue elasticity of 1. These examples indicate a close connection between revenue elasticity and the progressivity of a tax. By definition, a progressive tax will have a revenue elasticity greater than 1 and be an elastic source of revenue, while regressive taxes will have elasticities that are less than 1.

Tax elasticity is a two-edged sword. On the one hand, taxes that are elastic act as automatic stabilizers by causing taxes to increase more than income does when times are good and to fall more than income falls when times are bad. On the other hand, taxes that are elastic are generally less stable sources of public revenue precisely because of their tendency to fluctuate with economic conditions. Taxes that are inelastic provide greater revenue stability but, conversely, do not act as automatic stabilizers.

Cross-references: automatic stabilizers; elasticity, demand and supply; progressivity, measures of; rainy day funds; revenue-maximizing tax rates.

Revenue estimating, federal

G. Thomas Woodward
Congressional Budget Office

The process of quantifying the revenue lost or gained from a proposed change in taxation—usually for a legislative proposal—by determining how much would be collected relative to the amount that would have been collected in the absence of that change.

Revenue estimates are part of a budgetary process involving both the executive and legislative branches of government. In making its spending and taxing decisions, the government needs to project outlays and receipts based on current policy, and to estimate the effects of proposed changes in policy. The first part of this process is commonly called revenue forecasting. The second part is typically referred to as revenue estimating.

This process is part of a greater goal of government budgeting: to impose discipline on spending and taxes. Many law changes proposed by the president or considered in Congress would affect revenues and outlays if enacted. A budget process has been established to permit the consideration of these proposals in the context of the entire budget. Estimating the effects of each bill on the budget is a critical part of this process.

Role of revenue estimates in the budget process

Each year in early February, the president proposes a budget for the forthcoming budget year, which begins on October 1, and for subsequent years. The revenue portion of that budget (the same applies for the spending portion, but is not discussed here) has two elements: revenues that would be generated under current tax law (assuming that the economy performs as forecasted) and any changes in those revenues resulting from changes in law proposed by the president.

Congress prepares its own estimates of revenues and outlays under current law, and estimates of the budgetary effects of the president's proposed legislation, based on its assumptions about economic performance. In the spring, Congress adopts a Concurrent Budget Resolution for the coming fiscal year that stipulates Congress's budget goals, including total federal revenues and the amount, if any, by which the aggregate level of federal revenues should be increased or decreased by bills and resolutions reported by the appropriate committees. Targets for total revenues and revenue changes for several years beyond the budget year are also included in the Concurrent Budget Resolution.

Under the Congressional Budget and Impoundment Control Act of 1974, which put in place the present congressional federal budget process, it is not in order for the Senate or the House of Representatives to consider any bill that would cause revenues to be less than the revenues set forth in that concurrent resolution for the first fiscal year or, in general, for the total of all fiscal years covered by the resolution.

To make this assessment possible, the Act requires that any bill reported by a congressional committee must be accompanied by an estimate of that bill's effect on federal spending and receipts. In the House of Representatives, the committee report accompanying any bill that affects federal budget revenues or expenditures must include an estimate of the budgetary effect of that bill if an estimate is "timely available." In the Senate, a committee issuing a bill for congressional consideration is not required to issue a report, although most bills in fact are accompanied by reports containing estimates of budgetary effects.

The process of generating estimates of the revenue effects of the president's tax proposals and for the reports that must accompany congressional bills is generally referred to as revenue estimating.

Federal agencies estimating revenue effects

In both the executive and legislative branches, responsibility for revenue estimation is shared among agencies. In the executive branch, the Office of Management and Budget (OMB) has nominal responsibility for producing the estimates of the president's legislative proposals. However, most of the actual estimation of revenue proposals lies with the Office of Tax Analysis (OTA) in the Department of the Treasury. Its estimates begin from a projection of receipts under current law. That projection, too, is produced by OTA, based on macroeconomic projections developed by the "troika" group whose staff reports to the secretary of the Treasury, the chairman of the President's Council of Economic Advisers, and the director of the Office of Management and Budget. For each proposed change, OTA estimates the change in revenue relative to this initial projection. OMB then reports these estimates as part of the president's proposed budget.

In Congress, responsibilities are divided between the Congressional Budget Office (CBO) and the Joint Committee on Taxation (JCT). In this case, the initial projection, or budget baseline, is developed by CBO based on its own macroeconomic projection. Estimates of the effects of legislation are divided between CBO and JCT. JCT is responsible for revenue estimates of any proposed change to the Internal Revenue Code. These constitute the overwhelming majority of proposals, as well as the most significant proposals in terms of revenues collected. CBO is responsible for estimates of those revenue bills that change other parts of the U.S. code (such as customs and Federal Reserve Receipts), as well as revenue effects of nonrevenue bills (such as mandated changes in employer-provided health insurance that affect the ratio of taxable to nontaxable compensation).

What is contained in revenue estimates

Every revenue estimate starts with a baseline projection of revenues—the revenues that would be expected given a continuation of current policy. In principle, an estimate of the effects of proposed legislation would be the change from that baseline to a new one that reflects the proposal. In practice, revenue estimates do not embody all these effects.

Virtually all taxes can be thought of as consisting of a tax rate and a tax base on which that rate is applied. Yet, the two are not independent of each other; taxpayers typically react to changes in legislated tax rates by changing the amount of the taxed activity that they engage in. Consequently, changing the rate means changing the base and affecting revenue through a second, indirect effect. For example, if gasoline excise tax rates are increased, drivers cut back on consumption of gasoline. Likewise, if the tax rate on capital gains is reduced, sales of gains-bearing assets increase, so more capital gains are realized. In each of these examples, therefore, the proposed tax rate change yields a revenue change through a primary channel (the rate change) and a secondary channel (the base change in response to the changed rate). In addition, a change in one tax can affect the base of another. For example, an increase in excise taxes is likely to either decrease corporate profits or compensation to other productive inputs, resulting in a decrease in payroll or income taxes. The effect on other tax sources constitutes yet another indirect means of transmitting an effect on receipts.

Simply multiplying the projected base by the rate change ignores the secondary routes through which legislation affects receipts. Revenue estimates that do not take into account any of these feedbacks on projected tax bases are called "static," in that they implicitly assume no behavioral change. In general, the budgetary process does not rely on static revenue estimates. The one exception is in calculating "tax expenditures." A tax expenditure—the measure of how much an activity is subsidized through the tax system—assumes no behavioral response because it measures the size of the preference, not the effect on revenues if the preference were removed. Consequently, the size of a tax expenditure and the fiscal effect of eliminating it would differ.

Revenue estimates used for legislative purposes incorporate some—but not all—behavioral responses. It is the inclusion of these responses that make revenue estimating so difficult. In general, four kinds of behavioral responses are regularly included in revenue estimates. First, the estimates include changes related to the timing of economic activity. For example, a cost estimate of an increase in capital gains taxes takes into account the fact that taxpayers will advance their realizations of gains to beat the effective date of the new, higher tax rate. Second, the estimates include shifts in the tax base between taxable and nontaxable categories. As a result, a cost estimate of a cut in marginal income tax rates includes the recharacterization of compensation from nontaxable fringe benefits to taxable wages. Third, estimates include the legislation's effects on supply and demand. Hence, a cost estimate of an increase in gasoline taxes reflects decreased gasoline consumption as consumers react to the higher price. Last, estimates include interactions with other taxes. Consequently, cost estimates of more rapid depreciation allowances for capital take into account not only the lower income tax receipts that result, but also how the reduction in taxable proprietorship income decreases the payroll tax liabilities of the self-employed.

These four categories of behavioral responses are microeconomic. What are not included in revenue estimates are macroeconomic responses. Revenue estimates do not incorporate the effects of tax changes on overall gross domestic product or its aggregate income components that are part of the baseline macroeconomic projection. That means estimates do not include the effects of a tax on the supply of labor or on saving (and hence on overall economic growth), effects on income that might result from the taxes' influence on entrepreneurship, the increases or decreases in output caused by how subsidies or taxes reallocate resources among various activities, the effects on national saving and other incentive effects that result from the government's financing of the tax change, or the income and employment effects that arise from the impact of fiscal policy on aggregate spending in the economy in a recession.

These effects are excluded by virtue of using the same baseline macroeconomic projection for all cost estimates (this is true of spending as well). Any such effects associated with legislation that is subsequently enacted is ultimately incorporated in the macroeconomic projection underlying future baselines. Also, the macroeconomic effects of administration tax proposals are commonly built into the administration's revenue projection, so that it is a post-policy baseline that has the macroeconomic effects incorporated in advance.

ADDITIONAL READINGS

Auerbach, Alan J. "On the Performance and Use of Government Revenue Forecasts." *National Tax Journal* 52, no. 4 (December 1999): 767–82.

Congressional Budget Office. *Budget Estimates: Current Practice and Alternative Approaches.* Washington, DC: Congressional Budget Office, January 1995.

———. *Projecting Federal Tax Revenues and the Effect of Changes in Tax Law.* Washington, DC: Congressional Budget Office, December 1998.

———. *An Analysis of the President's Budget Proposals for Fiscal Year 2005.* Washington, DC: Congressional Budget Office, March 2004.

U.S. Congress, Joint Committee on Taxation. *Methodology and Issues in the Revenue Estimation Process.* JCX-2-95. Washington, DC: U.S. Government Printing Office, January 1995.

———. *Overview of Revenue Estimating Procedures and Methodologies Used by the Staff of the Joint Committee on Taxation.* JCX-1-05. Washington, DC: U.S. Government Printing Office, February 2005.

Cross-references: Congressional Budget Office; dynamic scoring; Joint Committee on Taxation; Office of Tax Policy; revenue elasticity (tax elasticity); revenue estimating, state; revenue forecasting, federal; sumptuary taxes; tax expenditures.

Revenue estimating, state

Yeang-Eng Braun
Wisconsin Department of Revenue

As with the federal process, estimating state revenues is, or ought to be, subject to a systematic set of statistical practices and guidelines; however, states differ in the assignment of which agency is responsible for the process and the methodology.

The term "revenue estimating" can refer to one of two processes: the process of forecasting state tax revenue for the current and future fiscal years, also referred to as "state-revenue forecasting," or the process of estimating the impact of a change in the tax law on tax receipts, also referred to as the "fiscal note process."

State revenue forecasting

A state generally forecasts its revenue at the start of a budget cycle, with revisions made as warranted by actual tax collections and economic conditions. Most states forecast tax revenues one to two years into the future. The forecast horizon largely depends on whether the budget cycle is annual or biennial. States with biennial budgets typically forecast to the end of the current or next biennium, depending on whether they are in the first or second year of their budget.

A state's revenue-estimating process typically involves four steps:

First, a forecast of the national economy is needed to determine national economic trends and estimates of such economic variables as gross domestic product, personal income, consumption, employment, interest rates, and inflation. Most states do not produce their own national economic forecast. Instead, they subscribe to national economic forecasting services offered by private firms and universities.

Second, a state-specific economic forecast is developed from the national economic forecast adjusted to reflect the specific economic mix of the state. Some states develop their own state econometric model, while others purchase their state economic forecast from economic forecasting services. The state economic forecast provides information pertaining to the state's economic variables.

Third, the relevant state economic variables are used to make predictions about each revenue source. For example, the individual income tax forecast is based on the forecasted level and composition of personal income, the forecasted tax base, and the forecasted level of employment; the sales tax forecast is based on forecasted disposable income and the relative prices of items subject to the sales tax.

Fourth, recent tax collection data are incorporated into the estimation process, but they have to be carefully analyzed and frequently monitored because they can easily be misinterpreted—year-over-year changes in monthly collections are often affected by factors other than underlying economic trends. These factors include law changes, large refunds and audit activity, timing changes in employer payroll periods, changes in tax filing methods (paper returns versus electronic filing), and differences in the number of workdays for tax processing in each month.

Revenue estimates are never going to be exact, and some errors are inevitable. Some sources of revenue-estimating errors are the following:

1. Errors in measurement that are reflected in data revisions. Current period estimates of income and employment are often treated as "actual data" even though they may be revised several years later. Thus, if the best estimate of current (and past) income is off, for example, by 1 percent, it is not surprising that forecasts of income, and in turn tax revenues, one or two years from now will be off by 1 or 2 percent.
2. Errors in the economic forecast. The national economic forecast can be wrong because of incorrect assumptions regarding monetary and fiscal policies or consumer and investor confidence. Even if the national economic forecast is correct, the state forecast may be wrong. This error could be the result of misspecification of the revenue-estimating equations because of changes in behavior or localized action, such as large layoffs by a major employer.
3. Behavioral changes. A key ingredient to any revenue forecast is time series data. However, the benefit of the historical data is reduced when the tax law is significantly modified. This problem is compounded if tax laws are changed frequently. Under such circumstances, past activity no longer provides a good predictor of future behavior, be-

cause new tax systems mean new behavior that can have significant consequences. Forecasters do not have good estimates of the degree of behavioral response. For example, capital gains are especially difficult to predict. An increase in the federal taxes on capital gains in 1986 caused some state revenue estimators to overestimate the extent to which taxpayers would sell their assets to avoid the larger federal tax payments. These states were caught off guard by their multimillion-dollar shortfalls.

4. Unanticipated external shocks. Disasters such as the September 11, 2001, attacks have an impact at the state and national levels, as well as on international events. Other less dramatic external shocks, such as court decisions affecting tax refunds or tax assessments, or the death of a wealthy individual, are isolated events that may have an insignificant effect on federal revenues but have a noticeable impact on state tax collections.

Under fortunate circumstances, these errors may offset one another, producing an accurate forecast. Under unfortunate circumstances, these errors may compound each other and produce a very poor forecast. A good revenue estimate is one in which the error is within some reasonable range. While there is no universal measure, an acceptable margin of error (from a statistical point of view) is plus or minus 1 to 3 percent of the estimate.

The organization of the revenue-estimating function varies among states. In some states, that function is performed by the tax collection agency; in others, it is performed by the budget or finance agency. While the forecasting function is primarily the responsibility of the executive branch, some state legislatures access a legislative fiscal agency for an independent forecast of revenue.

To keep the revenue forecast from being mired in politics, some states rely on "consensus estimating" or "consensus forecasting." Consensus revenue estimating requires representatives from the executive and legislative branches of government, as well as from the business and academic communities, to reach unanimous agreement on the economic forecast as well as the revenue forecasts.

In a 1991 survey of state-revenue forecasting practices, the Federation of Tax Administrators (1993) found that out of the 45 states that responded, 23 had a single executive agency forecasting state revenue—8 of them the department of taxation or revenue and 15 the finance or budget office. Eighteen states used consensus forecasting. Four states used a hybrid procedure in which the executive and legislative agencies prepare independent forecasts and attempt to reconcile their differences. If an agreement is not reached, the legislature can adopt one as the official forecast, or combine parts of each.

The fiscal note process

"Revenue estimating" can also refer to the process of estimating the impact of a change in the tax law on tax receipts.

This is also referred to as the "fiscal note process" because these estimates are usually reported in a fiscal note accompanying the proposed change.

To prepare such an estimate, the projected revenue under current law is compared with the projected revenue under the proposal, and the difference between the two numbers is the fiscal estimate of the proposed law change. In addition, any administrative costs associated with the proposal (e.g., personnel costs, programming costs, or costs for adding lines to a tax form) have to be included in the fiscal estimate of the legislation.

One major issue is whether the fiscal estimate should be static (i.e., ignoring the economic impact of the law change) or dynamic (where economic impacts are taken into account). It is argued that if the economic impacts are taken into account, the net revenue loss associated with tax incentive legislation is reduced or transformed into revenue gains.

Even when revenue estimates do not take economic impacts into account, estimators try to take into account taxpayer behavioral response whenever possible. For example, in estimating the revenue impact of a cigarette tax increase, it is assumed that the increase would be fully passed through to the consumer, resulting in decreased tobacco consumption. In some cases, a change in a particular section of the tax code may affect other tax provisions as well, and these effects must be accounted for in the fiscal estimate. Consider, for example, a decrease in the standard deduction. This would increase tax revenue, causing some taxpayers to switch from standardized tax forms to itemized returns, and the revenue loss from switching to itemized deductions would have to be subtracted from the initial fiscal effect.

ADDITIONAL READING

Federation of Tax Administrators. *State Revenue Forecasting and Estimation Practices.* Research Report No. 139. Washington, DC: Federation of Tax Administrators, March 1993.

Rubin, Marilyn Marks, J. L. Peters, and Nancy Mantell. "Revenue Forecasting and Estimation." In *Revenue Forecasting and Estimation,* edited by W. Bartley Hildreth and James A. Richardson (769–800). New York: Marcel Dekker, 1999.

Cross-references: rainy day funds; revenue estimating, federal; revenue forecasting, federal.

Revenue forecasting, federal

G. Thomas Woodward
Congressional Budget Office

The process of projecting federal revenues, generally in connection with making a budget, and usually under the assumption that current laws and policies remain unchanged.

Revenue forecasts are part of a budgetary process involving both the executive and legislative branches of government. In making its spending and taxing decisions, the government needs to project outlays and receipts based on current policy, and to estimate the effects of changes in policy. The latter part is typically referred to as revenue estimating. The first part is commonly called revenue forecasting.

Revenue forecasts also play a role in nonbudgetary areas. In particular, they are useful in financial management. The Treasury needs to make projections of revenues over the current fiscal year in order to plan the orderly issuance, rollover, and retirement of federal debt.

Federal revenues

Federal revenues are the receipts of the government that stem from its exercise of sovereign power to exact resources from the individuals, institutions, and activities within its borders. Receipts from businesslike transactions of the government, in which the counterparty participates voluntarily, are called offsetting collections and appear as negative outlays in federal budget accounting.

In recent decades, individual income taxes have typically produced nearly half of all revenues. Social insurance taxes imposed on payrolls have generated more than a third of federal revenues, most of which financed the Social Security retirement income system. Corporate income taxes have contributed a bit less than a tenth of overall revenues. Excise taxes, mostly on transportation-related goods and services and alcohol and tobacco products, made up 4 percent of revenues. Payments from the Federal Reserve System, customs duties, estate and gift taxes, and fees, fines, and penalties accounted for the remainder.

For the most part, tax liability is defined in the Internal Revenue Code of 1986, as amended. Customs duties, fees, fines, penalties, and Federal Reserve payments are established either in laws other than the Internal Revenue Code or by administrative action. Income and payroll tax liabilities are imposed on annual flows of payments. Most other federal tax liabilities—excise taxes, customs duties, and fees, for the most part—are imposed per transaction.

The federal budget, of which revenues are a part, is primarily a "cash" budget. Federal receipts are counted when they are paid into the Treasury, not when they accrue. While the lag between accrual and payment is often short, such as for payroll and withheld income taxes, other payments may occur outside the year in which liability accrues, such as the final settlements of individual income tax that occur in the weeks approaching April 15. In addition, back taxes appear in the budget in whatever year they are collected, regardless of the tax year to which they apply. The annual time period upon which revenue measures and forecasts are based is a fiscal year that runs from October 1 through September 30.

These "unified budget" revenues differ from the revenues depicted by the federal government sector of the National Income and Product Accounts (NIPA). The NIPA measure of revenues is used for macroeconomic analysis rather than for budget formulation. NIPA measures of federal government activity calculate revenues on a mixture of payment and liability bases in order to approximate more closely the effects of taxes on economic activity. The annual time period of the NIPA is the calendar year.

The role of revenue forecasts

The primary purpose of forecasting revenues is to aid federal budgeting. Projections of baseline revenues, together with those of outlays, indicate whether current tax policies will generate resources sufficient to finance federal activities. From these projections, policymakers are able to address issues such as whether additional taxes must be imposed to finance ongoing spending or whether sufficient revenues exist to cover new spending programs.

Each year in early February, the president proposes a budget for the forthcoming budget year, which begins on October 1, and for subsequent years. The revenue portion of that budget (the same applies for the spending portion, but is not discussed here) has two elements: revenues that would be generated under current tax law (assuming that the economy performs as forecasted) and any changes in those revenues resulting from changes in law proposed by the president.

Congress prepares its own estimates of revenues and outlays under current law, and estimates of the budgetary effects of the president's proposed legislation, based on its assumptions about economic performance. In the spring, Congress adopts a Concurrent Budget Resolution for the coming fiscal year that stipulates Congress's budget goals, including total federal revenues and the amount, if any, by which the aggregate level of federal revenues should be increased or decreased by bills and resolutions reported by the appropriate committees. Targets for total revenues and revenue changes for several years beyond the budget year are also included in the Concurrent Budget Resolution.

In the executive branch, the responsibility for projecting federal revenues under current tax law for the president's budget resides with the Department of the Treasury, which shares budget forecasting responsibility with the Office of Management and Budget. The responsibility for such projections for Congress resides with the Congressional Budget Office (CBO). (The responsibility for estimating the effects on revenue flows of legislated changes in tax law resides with the congressional Joint Committee on Taxation.)

How revenues are projected

The process of projecting federal revenues combines numerical tax calculators that reproduce the stipulations of the Internal Revenue Code with approximations of the historical relationships between federal revenue flows and summary measures of their underlying economic determinants, such as the total U.S. sales of goods and services and the aggregate levels of personal and business incomes. Those calculators and approximations of historical relationships constitute statistical models that produce estimates of aggregate tax liabilities by type of tax. Those estimates of liabilities—typically calculated on the basis of calendar years—are then transformed into fiscal year receipts.

Given the composition of federal revenues, the federal budget is very sensitive to overall economic performance. The economic aggregates most important for determining revenues are wages, salaries, and other types of personal income; corporation income; sales of taxed goods; and the amount of imported goods and services. All revenue forecasts, therefore, begin with forecasts of such macroeconomic variables as employment, income, interest rates, and prices. The CBO employs its own macroeconomic forecast in its budget forecast. The president's budget usually uses a macroeconomic forecast of the "troika" group whose staff reports to the secretary of the Treasury, the chairman of the President's Council of Economic Advisers, and the director of the Office of Management and Budget. Both projections are heavily informed by those of private forecasting firms and others who make projections of economic performance.

Both the Office of Tax Analysis (OTA) and CBO use similar approaches to turning these macroeconomic projections into revenue forecasts. They both project each component of revenue separately. And they employ different types of models for the different tax sources. Model outputs are calibrated to recent levels of receipts. And judgment must be applied with respect to how these calibrating factors are carried out over the future years of the projection. The projections of the individual sources are added together to yield a projection of total revenue.

Revenues from the individual income tax are estimated using a type of statistical estimation technique called microsimulation. The technique begins with a statistical sample of approximately 0.1 percent of tax returns compiled by the Internal Revenue Service (IRS) from the most recent year for which those data are available (usually two years before the year analyzed), with weights assigned to those sample returns that, combined with the per return data, reproduce population totals of the number of tax returns, the amount of income subject to tax, deductions, and other tax-payment characteristics for the year of the sample.

To produce an estimate of total revenue for the current and future tax years, the tax return data from the sample year are "aged" with projections of the number of tax returns, personal income, and other components of tax liability, all based on the macroeconomic projection. Additional income information not generated by macroeconomic forecasts—such as capital gains realizations and pension distributions—are developed from separate models and included. A calculator that uses legislated tax law computes the tax liability for each sample return for each year of the projection. The liabilities estimated in that process are weighted up to a measure of total tax liability for the estimation year. Those liabilities by tax year are then converted to fiscal year receipts based on models of how liabilities

stemming from particular sources of income are paid in withholding, estimated payments, and final settlements.

OTA and CBO employ different approaches for the largest components of payroll taxes: Old-Age, Survivors, and Disability Insurance (OASDI, or Social Security) and Hospital Insurance (HI, or Medicare). OTA provides its macroeconomic assumptions to the Social Security Administration, which produces estimates based on its sample of wage and salary records for every worker and calculator that computes the employer and employee contribution for each worker. CBO employs its own microsimulation model based on the sample of income tax returns, with nonfilers imputed and noncovered workers removed based on information from other data sources. Projections of the remaining payroll tax revenues, including unemployment insurance contributions and pension contributions of federal and railroad workers, are based on relatively simple models.

Corporation income taxes are estimated statistically, using an equation in which corporate tax liabilities are typically a function of (along with other less important determinants) the top statutory corporation income tax rate, corporate profits and losses, and adjustments for recent changes in tax law. The profits input to the model, and measures closely related to it, come from the macroeconomic forecast. Depreciation deductions taken for tax purposes by corporations that invest in plant and equipment are computed using a calculator based on Internal Revenue Code depreciation rules, combined with estimates of investment.

The bulk of federal excise tax revenues (motor fuels, alcohol, and tobacco products) are also projected using statistical models (e.g., an estimation equation for motor fuel excise tax liabilities would typically cast liabilities as a function of variables such as the statutory tax rate, the relative price of gasoline, a measure of overall economic activity, and average mileage per vehicle). Most of the rest of excise taxes are projected to grow with nominal or real GDP depending on whether they are ad valorem or specific levies.

For the estate tax, a microsimulation model is used. The value of taxable estates is projected using data from the Survey of Consumer Finances and flow-of-funds accounts (in the case of CBO) or estate tax returns (in the case of OTA), combined with demographic projections of wealth imputed from the macroeconomic forecast. Using mortality tables and a random number generator, the model selects estates from the sample. It then applies the tax rate schedule and credits to determine the amount of tax generated, if any.

Federal Reserve receipts are projected based on a model of the Fed's portfolio and interest rates. The value of the Federal Reserve's portfolio is derived from macroeconomic projections of monetary components. Projected Treasury interest rates are applied to that portfolio to determine Federal Reserve earnings. Customs duties are projected to grow largely with the nominal value of nonoil imports, as projected in macroeconomic projection. (Oil imports are subject to a specific tariff.) That growth is adjusted for the effects of trade legislation. Receipts from the remaining, smaller revenue sources are estimated statistically when feasible or by using simple trends extrapolated from historical revenue data.

In all cases, model projections of current year receipts based on the macroeconomic forecasts are compared with receipts data from the Treasury. These latter measures, while accurate of the current revenue flow into the Treasury, are not return-based. Hence, while the receipts can be attributed to general categories such as excise or corporate income taxes, they cannot yet be matched with the detailed sources of income used in the projection models. Therefore, differences between the model estimates and the current receipts cannot be reconciled in time for the projection. Any differences require calibration of the models to bring current year projections in line with observable receipts. Judgment must then be applied to determine how this current year calibration is to be carried out into future years.

Other uses of forecasts

Forecasts of revenue play a less important role in federal fiscal affairs than they do for most states or for many other countries. The balanced-budget requirements in many states, and the difficulties inherent in borrowing in economies with less fully developed capital markets mean that errors in budget projections have greater consequences for these other entities. Overestimates of revenues in those instances may require lawmakers to cut planned spending or immediately move to raise more revenue. Forecasting errors in U.S. budgeting are not so critical because the federal government can generally borrow large amounts of money at any time, giving it years to adjust its budget balance.

Nonetheless, revenue forecasts are desirable as a part of the cash and debt management responsibilities of the Treasury. The flows of receipts and outlays of the federal government are not steady throughout the year. Moreover, the difference between the two may change from year to year. To ensure an optimal level of balances for the purposes of making its required payments, the Treasury's Office of Financial Management needs to make its own forecasts of revenue.

These projections are true forecasts and not baseline projections. The Treasury needs to know as best as it can what will as opposed to what would flow into the government's coffers. Doing so permits the Treasury to plan for issuance of debt when cash is needed; to help determine to best maturity composition of that debt, depending on how long the funds will be needed; and to plan retirement of debt should expected cash flows obviate the need to roll it over. Projections for these purposes use different techniques: they are for shorter horizons, they are not liability-based, and they typically use time-series statistical procedures for their extrapolations.

ADDITIONAL READINGS

Congressional Budget Office. *Description of Economic Models.* Washington, DC: Congressional Budget Office, November 1998.

———. *Description of CBO's Models and Methods for Projecting Federal Revenues.* Washington, DC: Congressional Budget Office, May 2001.

———. *The Budget and Economic Outlook, Fiscal Years 2005–2015.* Washington, DC: Congressional Budget Office, January 2005.

Cross-references: Congressional Budget Office; Joint Committee on Taxation; revenue elasticity (tax elasticity); revenue estimating, federal; revenue estimating, state.

Revenue-maximizing tax rates

Richard Bird
University of Toronto

Sally Wallace
Georgia State University

The tax rate that results in the largest revenue yield, taking into account behavioral responses to taxation.

The complex relationships between tax rates and the behavior of individuals and firms leads to a natural tension between raising tax rates and raising revenue. As tax rates rise, economic agents (individuals and companies) seek to lower their tax liability through legal means (tax avoidance) or illegal means (tax evasion). Because of these relationships, there is, theoretically, a tax rate that maximizes government revenue. This tax rate is known as the revenue-maximizing tax rate, or RMTR. At rates lower than the RMTR, the government could increase the tax rate and achieve a higher level of revenue; at rates higher than the RMTR, the government could lower the rate and achieve a higher level of revenue. These relationships are depicted graphically in a curve showing the relationship between tax revenues (on the vertical axis) and tax rates (on the horizontal axis) (figure 1). Long a staple of economics principles texts, this depiction was popularized by economist Arthur Laffer in the 1970s, who argued that the United States was operating to the right of the curve (Laffer 1979). The implication of that view was that cutting taxes would raise revenue. This "upside down" U-shaped curve suggests that there is a revenue-maximizing tax rate for any particular tax, holding all other aspects of the economy and tax system constant. The example below demonstrates a RMTR of between 50 and 55 percent. Fullerton (1982) analyzed a variety of empirical issues associated with measuring RMTRs and finds that in the case of U.S. labor taxes, the U.S. system was to the left of the RMTR under generally accepted assumptions regarding the behavior of labor.

RMTRs exist because individuals and firms alter their behavior as tax rates change, if they can do so. For example, as the tax rate on beer increases, all else constant, consumers may shift to consumption of wine. This reduces the tax base for a beer tax and for every 1 percent increase in the tax rate, may reduce the tax base more than 1 percent. This behavior may eventually lead to a reduction in revenue as tax rates increase.

This same type of behavior is possible for income taxes. If individuals have the means to do so, they will substitute lower-taxed compensation for higher-taxed compensation,

FIGURE 1. Laffer Curve example

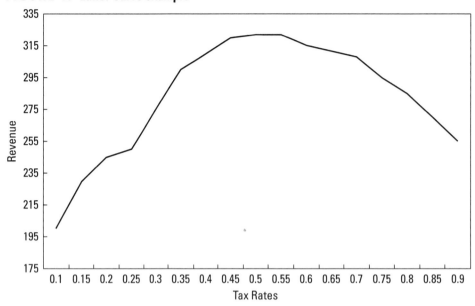

such as substituting fringe benefits for wages. The more flexibility in substitution of consumption or among types of income, the lower the RMTR.

The basic economic relationship between taxes and revenues is determined by the price elasticity of the taxed good—the higher the price elasticity of demand, the lower the RMTR. This applies to goods that are consumed, such as food, beverages and cars, and to goods used in production, such as labor and capital. A simple analytic relationship for measuring the RMTR is the following: if there is only one good to consider, the RMTR, t^*, is equal to $-\frac{1}{2}\varepsilon$, where ε is the own price elasticity of demand for the taxed good. More generally, the revenue maximizing rate is a more complicated function of demand and supply elasticities. Of course, taxes are not costless, and both the administrative and compliance costs associated with particular tax rates should also be taken into account when computing the RMTR.

There is a very practical reason for analyzing RMTR. Policy decisions often hinge on the revenue cost associated with changes in the tax law. A move to increase the progressivity of the tax system, for example, would have to be considered along with the associated revenue implications. In the case of many "sin" taxes, the RMTR may differ from the tax rate needed to accomplish some other goal, such as significantly reducing the consumption of a particular item, and these two policy goals would have to somehow be balanced.

TABLE 1. Revenue-Maximizing Tax Rates (RMTRs) on Beer

	Long-run own-price elasticity assumptions		Current tax rates		Long-run RMTR	
Country	Traditional or other brew	Market brew	Traditional brew	Market brew (assuming imports)	Traditional brew	Market brew
Kenya	−1.11	−5.49	1.03	1.33	0.45	0.091
Tanzania	−0.44	−0.312	0.5	0.75	1.136	1.603
South Africa		−0.53		0.57		0.94
Uganda	−1.11	−5.49	0.77	0.92	0.45	0.091
	−0.44	−0.312	0.77	0.92	1.136	1.603
Rwanda	−1.11	−5.49	0.40	1.05	0.45	0.091
	−0.44	−0.312	0.40	1.05	1.136	1.603
Mauritius	−1.11	−5.49	0.45	1.55	0.45	0.091
	−0.44	−0.312	0.45	1.55	1.166	1.603

Source: Bird and Wallace (2003).
Notes: The current tax rate on traditional brew is the sum of the statutory excise tax rate on beer and VAT rate. The RMTR is calculated as $\frac{1}{2}\varepsilon$, where ε is the price elasticity of demand for brew. The current tax rate on market brew is the sum of the statutory excise tax rate on beer, the VAT rate, and the import duty. This exercise assumes that market brew is imported, which is a simplification since most countries also have domestic production of market brews, and in some countries, like South Africa, consumption of domestic production of market brews dominates consumption of imports.

There has been much debate over the calculation of RMTR, particularly in the case of the taxation of capital gains. If higher tax rates on realized capital gains encourage individuals and companies to hold onto their stocks, versus sell their stocks and realize a capital gain, then, as the tax rate increases, the amount of taxable capital gains may decrease. This debate is summarized in a number of books and articles including Burman (1999), Gravelle (1994), and Zodrow (1993).

In simpler cases, such as excise taxes, estimates of RMTR for alcohol taxes suggest a wide range of rates, based on the exact type of alcoholic beverages. A specific example from a sample of African countries may highlight the difficulties with measuring the RMTR (Bird and Wallace 2003). Using a simple analytic model that assumes one good, linear demand, and infinitely elastic supply, an estimate of the long-run RMTR for both "traditional brew" and for "market brew" is provided in table 1. This analysis gives some idea of the possible magnitude of the revenue-maximizing tax rates, assuming that consumers in each country respond similarly to price increases. The ratio of these RMTRs to the actual tax rates may indicate how close actual policy is to revenue-maximizing tax rate policy. In the case of those countries in the table, the estimates suggest that current direct taxes on alcohol are too high in Kenya but too low in Tanzania.

The analysis of RMTR is therefore very important in the policy debate, but it is also a difficult methodology to execute in practice. Much detailed information is needed about behavioral responses to tax changes. However, simpler analysis of RMTR, especially in the case of excise taxes, can be an important input into the policy debate.

ADDITIONAL READINGS

Bird, Richard, and Sally Wallace. "Taxing Alcohol in Africa: Reflections from International Experience," Paper prepared for Southern African Conference on Excise Taxation, Centurion Lake Hotel, Gauteng Province, South Africa, June 11–13, 2003.

Burman, Leonard. *The Labyrinth of Capital Gains Tax Policy: A Guide for the Perplexed.* Washington, DC: Brookings Institution Press, 1999.

Fullerton, Don. "On the Possibility of an Inverse Relationship between Tax Rates and Government Revenues." *Journal of Public Economics* 19, no. 1 (October 1982): 3–22.

Gravelle, Jane. *The Economic Effects of Taxing Capital Income.* Cambridge, MA: MIT Press, 1994.

Haughton, Jonathan. "Calculating the Revenue-Maximizing Excise Tax." African Economic Policy Discussion Paper no 13. Washington, DC: USAID Equity and Growth through Economic Research [EAGER] project, December 1998.

Laffer, Arthur B. "Statement Prepared for the Joint Economic Committee, May 20, 1979." Reprinted in *The Economics of the Tax Revolt: A Reader,* edited by Arthur B. Laffer and Jan P. Seymour. New York: Harcourt Brace Jovanovich, 1979.

Okello, Andrew Kazora. "An Analysis of Excise Taxation in Kenya." African Economic Policy Discussion Paper no. 73. Washington, DC: USAID EAGER project, June 2001.

Osoro, Nehemiah, Philip Mpango, and Hamisi Mwinyimvua. "An Analysis of Excise Taxation in Tanzania." African Economic Policy Discussion Paper no. 72. Washington, DC: USAID EAGER project, September 2001.

Pogue, Thomas F., and Larry G. Sgontz. "Taxing to Control Social Costs: The Case of Alcohol." *American Economic Review* 79, no. 1 (1989): 235–43.

Scully, Gerald. "Tax Rates, Tax Revenues, and Economic Growth." Policy Report no. 98. Dallas, TX: National Center for Policy Analysis, 1991.

Zodrow, George. "Economic Analyses of Capital Gains Taxation: Realizations, Revenues, Efficiency and Equity." *Tax Law Review* 48, no. 3 (1993): 419–527.

Cross-references: revenue elasticity (tax elasticity); revenue estimating, federal; revenue estimating, state; revenue forecasting, federal.

Ricardian equivalence

Angelo R. Mascaro
Congressional Budget Office

The proposition, stated by 19th-century British economist David Ricardo, that a given path of government expenditures could, under certain conditions, have the same effects on the economy irrespective of how the expenditures are financed.

For Ricardo, the proposition of Ricardian equivalence was intended to establish the important principle that the economic cost of government expenditures could not be lessened if, instead of financing the full amount of the expenditure with taxes, government issued debt and levied taxes to finance the payment of interest and the retirement of principal. For modern scholars and policy analysts, the proposition yields a set of conditions for determining how government spending and the method of financing that spending may influence aggregate demand and employment, interest rates, national saving, and capital accumulation.

Ricardo was apparently the first to recognize the theoretical possibility of equivalence if individuals realized that government bonds issued to finance an expenditure could be used to pay taxes levied to retire the debt and that interest income from the bonds could also be used to pay taxes levied to service the debt. By increasing savings to purchase the bonds, and by saving the interest income from the bonds as well, individuals could insulate themselves from all future taxes associated with debt finance. Consequently, if individuals behaved this way, any effects on the economy would arise only from government expenditure itself and not from the method of financing the expenditure. However, Ricardo doubted individuals would behave in the required way. He believed they would underestimate future tax liabilities and not save to the same extent under debt finance as they would under full and immediate tax finance. Therefore, he gave little weight to the equivalence proposition and regarded debt finance disfavorably because of its likely adverse effects on national saving and investment.

Contemporary analysis of the equivalence proposition, motivated in response to Barro's (1974) analysis of when tax or debt finance would have equivalent effects on interest rates and aggregate demand, has refined the theoretical conditions required for equivalence. In addition to Ricardo's requirement that individuals see through the veil of government debt to the future taxes that must be levied, at least three additional requirements seem necessary for equivalence to hold. (These and other requirements are evaluated in Smetters 1999.) First, individuals of one generation must be concerned about the welfare of the next. Such concern, or altruism, requires that if the tax liability from debt finance extends into the next generation, enough wealth will have been bequeathed to discharge the future liability and leave the next generation positioned as if the expenditure had been financed entirely by current taxes. Second, institutional imperfections must not exist that would inhibit individuals from sharing their resources between current and future dates through borrowing and lending, or between one generation and the next through gifts and bequests. If imperfections exist, the timing of the taxes could affect aggregate demand, interest rates, savings, and investment and nullify the equivalence proposition. For example, one imperfection emerges when borrowers face liquidity constraints. Such constraints can exist when borrowers and lenders do not have identical information, so that capital markets are unable to function efficiently and borrowing is inhibited. Third, the taxes levied under debt finance must not introduce any new distortions relative to the taxes levied under full and immediate tax finance. Lump-sum taxes that do not distort the choice between work and leisure, between current and future consumption, or between consumption and investment provide a case in which equivalence will hold. However, any tax that distorts such choices, as most taxes do, will nullify Ricardian equivalence.

Although most economists agree that the conditions required for exact equivalence do not hold in reality, many disagree strongly as to whether the conditions might hold approximately and, consequently, whether the predictions of Ricardian equivalence might also hold approximately. If approximate equivalence prevails, then the choice of taxes or debt to finance government spending would not matter much, because it would have only small additional effects on aggregate demand, interest rates, saving, and capital accumulation, compared with the effects of the spending itself. If approximate equivalence does not prevail, however, the choice will be important, because the financing method will have additional effects that could be exploited. For example, the potentially adverse effects of increased government spending on private capital accumulation could be offset by increased taxes that reduced private spending on consumption.

The issue of the approximate validity of Ricardian equivalence is an empirical one, and economists have tried to resolve it in two basic ways. Some have tried to determine how closely reality conforms to the theory's assumptions and others have tried to determine how closely reality conforms to the theory's predictions. Because the approximate validity of a theory is often more difficult to test than its exact validity, however, empirical research has yielded ambiguous evidence on approximate equivalence. Some research on the assumptions of Ricardian equivalence has found that bequests from one generation to the next do reflect, in part, the altruistic motive needed for equivalence, but other research finds that bequests reflect unrelated motives as well, including uncertainty about life span, that could nullify equivalence. Analogous ambiguity surrounds the interpretation of evidence of whether liquidity constraints and distortionary taxes support or reject approximate equivalence. Some evidence on the predictions of Ricardian equivalence shows no strong, statistically significant relationship between deficits (or debt) and interest rates, apparently supporting approximate equivalence. Similarly, some evidence on the relationship between taxes and private spending that takes government spending into account finds no strong relationship in the data, also giving apparent support to approximate equivalence. In both cases, however, the interpretation of the evidence has been challenged and confronted with other evidence that apparently rejects approximate equivalence. (The extensive research is surveyed in Bernheim 1988; Seater 1993; and Elmendorf and Mankiw 1999.)

Obviously, the issue of approximate equivalence remains unresolved. Nevertheless, the research on Ricardian equivalence has deepened our understanding of the many channels through which government spending, taxes, deficits, and debt influence the economy.

ADDITIONAL READINGS

Barro, Robert J. "Are Government Bonds Net Wealth?" *Journal of Political Economy* 82, no. 6 (November/December 1974): 1095–1117.

Bernheim, B. Douglas. "Ricardian Equivalence: An Evaluation of Theory and Evidence." In *NBER Macroeconomics Annual 1987,* vol. 2, edited by Stanley Fischer (263–315). Cambridge, MA: MIT Press, 1988.

Elmendorf, Douglas W., and N. Gregory Mankiw. "Government Debt." In *Handbook of Macroeconomics,* vol. 1c, edited by J. B. Taylor and M. Woodford (1619–99). New York: Elsevier Science, 1999.

Ricardo, David. *The Principles of Political Economy and Taxation.* Original work 1817. Reprinted in *The Works and Correspondence of David Ricardo,* vol. 1, edited by Piero Sraffa. Cambridge: Cambridge University Press, 1951.

———. "Funding System." Original work 1820. Reprinted in *The Works and Correspondence of David Ricardo,* vol. 4, edited by Piero Sraffa. Cambridge: Cambridge University Press, 1951.

Seater, John J. "Ricardian Equivalence." *Journal of Economic Literature* 31, no. 1 (March 1993): 142–90.

Smetters, Kent. "Ricardian Equivalence: Long-run Leviathan." *Journal of Public* Economics 73, no. 3 (September 1999) 395–421.

Cross-references: lump-sum tax; saving, taxes and; tax-exempt bonds; tax illusion.

S

Sales tax relief programs, state

Corina Eckl and Arturo Pérez

National Conference of State Legislatures

State governments employ a variety of programs to reduce the tax burden (tax regressivity) on low-income families.

The sales tax is a very important source of revenue for most states. In fiscal year 2004, sales tax revenues accounted for 33.4 percent of total state own-source revenues and exceeded 50 percent of total state revenues in six states. However, despite its important role in state finances, the sales tax is often criticized because it is regressive: Poor people pay a higher percentage of their income in sales taxes than people with higher incomes. Regressivity increases when necessities, such as food, are included in the taxable base.

This entry reviews state sales tax relief programs. The states have followed two approaches to reduce the regressivity of the sales tax: exemptions of certain purchases—usually food and other necessities—or credits representing a portion of the sales tax paid for these necessities. Because sales tax relief is most often discussed in the context of food purchases, this discussion uses food as the basis for its analysis. The analysis may also apply to purchases of other necessities.

Forty-five states levy a sales tax. In January 2004, 28 of these exempted food purchases from the sales tax and eight provided a sales tax credit or rebate. (Some states also provide relief for other necessities. For example, 44 states provide sales tax exemptions for prescription drugs, 11 for nonprescription drugs, 29 for consumer electric and gas utilities, and 8 for clothing, usually up to a specified dollar limit. In some states, these items remain taxable but at a lower rate.) There are benefits and drawbacks to each form of sales tax relief, making the decision of which form to use—an exemption or a credit—difficult. Policymakers are faced with issues of forgone revenue, targeting, and administrative concerns, just to name a few. The following sections examine the two forms of sales tax relief and identify their advantages and disadvantages using four important tax relief goals: targeting efficiency, certainty of relief, cost containment, and stability of revenue and permanence.

Targeting efficiency

If the goal of tax relief programs is to target the relief to low-income households, tax credits are better than exemptions.

Credits typically target needy recipients because they specify eligibility, usually limiting relief to households below certain income levels. Some states have selected different eligibility requirements and target their programs to senior citizens or disabled persons. Sales tax exemptions are inadequate in their targeting efficiency because they are available to everyone, regardless of their income. In fact, exemptions provide larger amounts of tax relief to middle- and high-income households because these families spend more (in dollar terms) on food than low-income families (who spend a greater proportion of their income on food). Some states have attempted to improve the targeting efficiency of the sales tax exemption by limiting the exemption to certain types of purchases. For example, certain "luxury" foods, such as caviar, or "luxury" clothing, such as formal wear, may be ineligible for the sales tax exemption.

Certainty of tax relief

Another goal of tax relief programs is to ensure that poor individuals and households actually receive relief. Certainty of sales tax relief is best achieved by a sales tax exemption because relief occurs automatically at the point of purchase. Households are guaranteed relief as long as they are making qualified food purchases. (Depending on a state's definition of food, some purchases—such as food items for immediate consumption—may not qualify for the sales tax exemption.)

Certainty of tax relief also improves if administrative burdens are minimized or eliminated. Because tax exemptions are automatic, no administrative tasks are associated with receiving tax relief. Tax credits, on the other hand, require applications for relief that often must be accompanied by documentation, such as proof of age for programs that are limited to senior citizens or household income for programs that tie the credit to income level. Such requirements may actually undermine the goals of tax relief if they discourage qualified individuals or households from applying for the relief. This has been a serious concern in some states where participation rates have been low. One way to combat low participation rates is through aggressive education and outreach programs.

Although sales tax exemptions relieve the administrative burden for recipients, they impose burdens on sellers of food products who must be careful to apply the exemption to qualified food items yet tax nonqualified food items. The widespread use of Universal Product Code (UPC) scanners has

351

eased this burden considerably, although the burden remains for small or locally owned and operated stores that have not acquired UPC scanner technology.

Another factor related to certainty of tax relief is timing. Timing is improved with an exemption because it occurs immediately—at the time of purchase. As noted above, with a tax credit, relief occurs only after a claim has been made. This imposes a delay between when the tax is paid and when the relief is provided. This delay can be considerable, especially in states where credit programs are tied to personal income tax.

Cost containment

Exempting food purchases from the sales tax is an expensive way of providing sales tax relief in terms of state revenue collections. According to information provided by state departments of revenue, sales tax exemptions for food cost states anywhere from 6 percent to 29 percent of total sales tax revenues (Pérez 1992). As a result, states with a food exemption lose substantial amounts of revenue, and the bulk of the exemption's benefits go to higher income families. In order to minimize the revenue loss, some states continue to tax food, but at a lower rate (which can pose an administrative burden for retailers). Others replace the lost revenue by imposing a higher overall sales tax rate on items that remain taxable. In 2005, for example, the statutory sales tax rate in states fully exempting food purchases averaged 5.5 percent. The rate was 4.7 percent in those states fully taxing food.

Because credit programs limit eligibility to certain households, credits are less costly to states than broad exemptions. Costs can increase slightly if states undertake programs to notify eligible households of the tax relief program.

Stability of revenue

Because the consumption of goods is closely tied to economic conditions, consumer purchases tend to decline when the nation enters a recession. Local or regional fiscal problems can lead to the same effect. This consumption pattern makes the sales tax generally unstable as a source of revenue. This instability increases when food is exempt from the sales tax, for two main reasons: (1) While purchases for some items, such as new cars, furniture, or appliances, may be reduced or eliminated during a recession, food purchases remain fairly constant: and (2) as noted above, the revenue derived from sales taxes on food can be substantial. If an important goal of a sales tax relief program is to preserve the stability of the sales tax as much as possible, credits are preferable to exemptions.

Summary of state credit programs

Five states currently offer a credit program to offset some regressivity of the state sales tax on food and other essentials. Idaho, Kansas, Oklahoma, South Dakota, and Wyoming each provide some level of tax relief through a credit program aimed at low-income individuals and families, the elderly, the disabled, or taxpayers in general. Income restrictions are placed on applicants for the sales tax credit programs in Kansas, South Dakota, Oklahoma, and Wyoming. Idaho, Kansas, South Dakota, and Wyoming also use age as an eligibility factor in determining who can receive a tax credit.

Eligible individuals need to file a state income tax return to receive the tax credit in Idaho and Oklahoma. Kansas's credit program is tied to the homestead exemption under the property tax. Because they do not levy a state personal income tax, South Dakota and Wyoming provide direct payments to eligible applicants.

In addition to the tax relief goals discussed above, there may be other broad issues associated with state sales tax relief programs. For instance, state policymakers may want to consider whether and how local governments would be affected by state changes. Another broad issue is the overall regressivity or progressivity of the state's tax system.

The sales tax is just one piece of the overall revenue picture, so its regressivity should be examined in the context of the overall tax structure.

There are strong arguments for and against each form of state sales tax relief. It is likely that the states that already exempt food purchases will continue their exemption, barring any disastrous events in state finances. The debate on which form of relief is preferable, therefore, will occur in those states that continue to tax food or those that offer credits but may be rethinking them.

ADDITIONAL READINGS

Case, Bradford, and Robert D. Ebel. "Using State Consumer Tax Credits for Achieving Equity." *National Tax Journal* 42, no. 3 (1989): 323–37.

Due, John F., and John L. Mikesell. *Sales Taxation: State and Local Structure and Administration.* Washington, DC: Urban Institute Press, 1994.

Federation of Tax Administrators. *2005 State Tax Collections.* Washington, DC: Federation of Tax Administrators, 2005.

Fox, William F., and Matthew N. Murray, eds. *The Sales Tax in the 21st Century.* Westport, CT: Praeger Publishers, 1997.

Gold, Steven D. "Simplifying the Sales Tax: Credits or Exemptions?" In *Sales Taxation: Critical Issues in Policy and Administration,* edited by William F. Fox (157–68). Westport, CT: Praeger Publishers, 1991.

Mikesell, John L. "Should Grocery Food Purchases Bear a Sales Tax Burden?" *State Tax Notes* 11 (September 9, 1996): 753.

Pérez, Arturo. "Food Purchases Add Weight to State Sales Tax Collections." *The Fiscal Letter* 14, no. 3 (May/June 1992): 4.

U.S. Bureau of the Census. *State Tax Collections, 2005.* Washington, DC: U.S. Bureau of the Census.

Cross-references: fairness in taxation; progressivity, measures of; retail sales tax, state and local; tax equity analysis.

Saving, taxes and

B. Douglas Bernheim
Stanford University

John Karl Scholz
University of Wisconsin–Madison

The "right" amount of saving, the decision to allocate income to future rather than current consumption, is important to a nation's economic growth. Tax policy can, and often does, affect the saving decision through a variety of channels.

The tax treatment of capital income is a potentially important determinant of national saving. It affects private saving by altering the economic benefits associated with thrift, and it affects public saving by altering the balance between government revenues and expenditures. Those who favor tax incentives for saving argue that these incentives would reduce the excess burden associated with the tax system, and that this would stimulate capital accumulation. Policy initiatives to encourage saving include broad-based measures (such as consumption or wage taxation), as well as more narrowly targeted measures (such as individual retirement accounts and other tax-favored vehicles for saving).

The components of national saving

National saving has two components: private saving and public saving. Private saving takes place in the personal and corporate sectors of the economy. Public saving is the sum of budget surpluses (deficits) for federal, state, and local governments. For the United States, the National Income and Product Accounts (NIPA), published by the Commerce Department, provide extensive data on each of these sectors. Net national saving fell sharply from 8.3 percent of net national product in 1980 to 1.8 percent in 2003. Net national product is equal to the more familiar concept of gross domestic product (GDP) minus depreciation on existing plant and equipment, while net national saving also measures private and public saving net of depreciation. There is some disagreement over the specific causes of this decline, but factors that play a role include reductions in the rate of private saving, large government budget deficits, and substantial increases in the value of existing housing and stock market wealth.

Some economists contend that it is meaningless to decompose national saving into public, corporate, and private components. They point out that all economic assets and liabilities ultimately belong to households. Consequently, saving is saving, regardless of where it occurs. If this is correct, then the allocation of national saving among sectors is merely an exercise in accounting and has no behavioral significance (see *Ricardian equivalence*).

Other economists believe that it is possible to obtain a better understanding of national saving by decomposing it into personal, corporate, and public saving. They argue that, for various reasons, households do not regard an additional dollar of corporate or public saving as equivalent to a dollar of personal saving. This is sometimes referred to as the hypothesis that households do not perfectly pierce either the "corporate veil" or the "government veil."

This issue is of great practical importance. If one accepts the premise that households regard all forms of national saving as equivalent, then it is impossible to influence the level of national saving by adjusting government budget deficits, or by influencing corporate saving, because households simply adjust their behavior to offset these effects. Conversely, if one rejects this premise, then policies that affect government budget deficits and corporate saving will—all else remaining the same—alter national saving.

How do taxes affect saving?

Tax policy can, in principle, affect saving through a variety of channels. Economists have traditionally emphasized the fact that capital income taxation reduces the after-tax rate of return available on investments, thereby diminishing the rewards associated with thrift. The interest elasticity of saving is a common quantitative measure of how saving changes in response to movements in the real after-tax rate of return (see the related discussion under *elasticity, demand and supply*). The real after-tax rate of return is defined as the difference between the after-tax rate of return and the rate of inflation. If the interest elasticity of saving is positive, then saving rises with the real after-tax rate of return, and falls with the rate of taxation applicable to capital income.

Many economists believe that the interest elasticity of saving is positive. They assert that households will save more when saving is more rewarding economically. As a matter of theory, this issue is far from clear. An increase in the real after-tax rate of return effectively reduces the price of future consumption, in the sense that households do not need to sacrifice as much current consumption to achieve a given level of future consumption. Therefore, even if future consumption rises in response to a higher real after-tax rate of return, saving may fall.

A simple calculation illustrates this point. Suppose that a household wishes to accumulate $100,000 over the next 10 years to send a child to college. Suppose also that this household expects to earn 8 percent on its investments, and to pay 25 percent of capital income as taxes. Finally, suppose that the household expects an annual inflation rate of 4 percent. Then the real after-tax rate of return is 2 percent (75 percent of 8 percent, minus 4 percent), and the household can achieve its target by saving roughly $7,160 a year. Now suppose that the government permits this same household to accumulate these resources in a special account, and exempts all associated capital income from taxation. Then the real after-tax rate of return is 4 percent, and the household can achieve its target by saving roughly $6,390 a year.

This example illustrates an important point: If households save for fixed targets, then saving must fall in response to an increase in the real after-tax rate of return, and must rise in response to higher capital income taxation. Of course, asset targets are not usually fixed. With higher real after-tax rates of return, households may set higher targets, particularly for objectives that do not require fixed expenditures, such as retirement. However, even if asset targets rise in response to increases in the real after-tax rate of return, saving may still fall. The interest elasticity of saving will be positive only if saving targets are sufficiently responsive to the real after-tax rate of return.

Much controversy surrounds the empirical measurement of the interest elasticity of saving. Although the evidence is mixed, most studies that have relied on macroeconomic data conclude that saving is not very responsive to the after-tax rate of return. These studies are, however, vulnerable to a variety of criticisms that call the reliability of macroeconomic estimates into serious question. Some analysts have also attempted to infer the interest elasticity of saving from simulation models. Simulation studies have identified some important factors that should make saving more sensitive to the real after-tax rate of return. For example, simulations have shown that an increase in the after-tax rate of return significantly decreases the value of "human wealth" by reducing the present discounted value of all future earnings and pension income. In response to this reduction in wealth, households should consume less and save more. Unfortunately, the simulation methodology cannot reliably establish the interest elasticity of saving. Simulated values of this parameter are highly sensitive to the assumptions on which the simulations are based.

Even if the interest elasticity of saving is small, personal saving may still be sensitive to tax policy. Psychological theories of saving suggest that certain institutional arrangements may increase thrift by promoting self-discipline. For example, an individual might choose to place funds in a tax-favored retirement account, rather than in a more flexible savings vehicle, knowing full well that early withdrawals from the retirement account will be subject to heavy penalties, in part because the existence of these penalties helps to enforce self-discipline. Tax-favored retirement accounts may ultimately stimulate greater total personal saving precisely because households are less likely to invade these accounts prematurely. But there is little solid empirical evidence for or against these considerations.

Tax policy can also affect corporate saving. The taxation of dividends may discourage cash distributions to shareholders, and encourage the retention of earnings (see *dividends, double taxation of*), thereby increasing net saving in the corporate sector. Similarly, high rates of corporate taxation can reduce corporate saving by siphoning off earnings that might otherwise have been reinvested. Of course, these are valid concerns only if households do not perfectly pierce the corporate veil.

Finally, tax policy can affect government saving. Tax reforms that increase revenues without associated increases in spending reduce deficits, or increase surpluses. While this is true of all taxes, the issue deserves special emphasis in the context of capital income taxes. Efforts to stimulate private saving through tax incentives generally require reductions in capital income tax rates, which tend to reduce revenue and increase government deficits. Thus, unless these measures significantly stimulate private saving, they may actually reduce national saving. Of course, effects on government saving are of concern only if households do not perfectly pierce the government veil.

Possible justifications for favorable tax treatment of capital income

One potential justification for reducing or eliminating capital income taxes is that this might reduce the excess burden associated with taxation (see *excess burden*). Capital income taxes distort households' intertemporal choices by, in effect, raising the price of future consumption relative to current consumption. The elimination of capital income taxes would remove this source of excess burden. However, a revenue-neutral reduction in capital income tax revenues would necessitate an increase in other tax rates, which would in turn create other distortions. For example, an increase in the tax burden on labor income would further distort the choice of labor versus leisure. Thus, revenue-neutral cuts in capital income tax will reduce the excess burden associated with taxation only if, on the margin, capital income taxes create more excess burden per dollar of revenue than other taxes (see *optimal taxation* and *inverse elasticity rule*).

Another potential justification for reducing or eliminating capital income taxes is that it might stimulate domestic capital formation. Capital formation is important because it fuels the growth of employment, wages, and income. Historically, domestic saving has been the most important source of funds for domestic investment, so policies that stimulated saving also promoted investment. In recent years, the progressive integration of international capital markets has permitted saving and investment to diverge. Thus, although domestic investment declined significantly during the 1980s and 1990s, it did not fall as far as national saving. The impact of lower saving on investment was cushioned to some extent by inflows of foreign capital. Conversely, if the rate of domestic saving were to increase, it is likely that a significant fraction of the incremental funds would be invested abroad, rather than domestically. Nevertheless, many economists believe that domestic saving continues to constrain domestic investment over long periods.

Finally, some economists believe that an alarming number of Americans have been doing little to prepare themselves financially for economic adversity or retirement, perhaps reflecting poor planning and limited financial sophistication on the part of low-saving households, rather than deliberate choice. This view leads to a paternalistic justification for encouraging saving by reducing or eliminating capital income taxes.

Tax provisions and saving

Tax provisions for private and public pensions attempt to increase household and national saving. The tax expenditure for employer-provided pensions is estimated by the Joint Committee on Taxation to cost $522.1 billion from 2004 to 2008 (see *tax expenditures* and *pensions, tax treatment of*). It is justified in part as a way of promoting household saving and ensuring adequate retirement income security for the elderly. Social Security, a publicly provided pension system, provides income to elderly households (see *Social Security benefits, federal taxation of*).

The effect of private and public pensions on national saving is the sum of their effect on public, business, and household saving. Because Social Security benefits for current retirees are largely funded by the taxes paid by today's workers, only a small fraction of Social Security taxes go toward increasing public saving (see *Social Security Trust Fund*). In contrast, employer pension obligations are generally fully funded and hence increase business saving. Thus, private pensions have a larger positive effect on the sum of public and business saving than does Social Security. These programs will have an ambiguous effect on household saving. To the extent that pensions raise lifetime wealth, current consumption would be expected to increase and household saving would decline. If, however, pensions allow people to retire earlier than otherwise, private saving may increase in order to maintain living standards during a longer retirement period.

The crucial empirical issue when thinking about the effects of private and public pensions on saving is, to what extent do people "undo" the effect of pensions by altering private saving? If people reduce private nonpension wealth dollar for dollar in relation to private pension wealth, national saving will fall by roughly the amount of the tax expenditure associated with private pensions. If people respond in a similar way to Social Security wealth, national saving will fall by nearly the full amount of Social Security expenditures. These outcomes would be dramatically different from those intended by these programs.

Empirical studies of pensions are hampered by the difficult task of accurately calculating lifetime resources for households. This issue is important, because policies that increase the use of pensions would undoubtedly be accompanied by reductions in other forms of employee compensation. Thus, the effect of increased pension wealth for a household is to reallocate resources toward retirement, holding the present discounted value of lifetime resources constant. Studies that have most carefully addressed the effect of private pensions and Social Security on household saving find that for every dollar of pension and Social Security wealth, private wealth falls by 10 to 50 cents, depending on the study. These estimates suggest that Social Security may have an important depressing effect on national saving. In contrast, private pensions, because they are fully funded, increase national saving. The empirical literature on the effects of Social Security and pri-

vate pensions on household and national saving is far from definitive, however.

Given the low rates of household saving in the United States and the concern that Social Security depresses national saving, the country has experimented, particularly since 1981, with narrowly targeted personal saving incentives. These voluntary accounts—individual retirement accounts (IRAs), 401(k) plans, and Keogh accounts—feature preferential tax treatment of contributions and investment earnings, annual contribution limits, and penalties for early withdrawals (see *individual retirement accounts*). Since 1986, contributions to IRAs, Keoghs, and defined contribution pensions have amounted to about one-half of personal saving as measured by the NIPA.

There are sound conceptual reasons to doubt the effectiveness of voluntary saving incentives. First, contributions are capped. A single taxpayer under age 50, for example, can make no more than $3,000 in tax-deductible IRA contributions in 2004. For any taxpayer in these circumstances who would have saved more than $3,000 in the absence of IRAs, the availability of an IRA does not affect the costs or benefits to be had from an additional dollar of saving and therefore provides no incentive on the margin for the taxpayer to increase saving. Yet the IRA will reduce federal tax receipts. In addition, the IRA may actually induce the taxpayer to consume more, because it increases his or her total after-tax resources. For both these reasons, the IRA would contribute to a lower rate of national saving. 401(k) and Keogh plans have higher contribution limits (the 401(k) limit was $13,000 in 2004) and hence are more likely than IRAs to provide marginal incentives.

Second, even if a taxpayer would not (in the absence of a saving incentive) have saved more than the contribution limit in a given year, he or she could take full advantage of the saving incentive deduction either by drawing down previously accumulated assets or by borrowing. Contributions funded either by shifting existing assets or by borrowing do not increase household saving. Instead, they depress national saving by reducing federal tax receipts, thereby adding to the federal budget deficit.

Determining the effectiveness of these narrowly targeted saving incentives is difficult, given currently existing data. First, saving at the household level is very difficult to measure. Second, households with similar characteristics may save vastly different amounts, which complicates estimation of empirical models. Third, households may have different motives for saving. Some may save primarily for retirement, others may save to meet unexpected expenses, and others may follow simple rules of thumb or not save at all. If underlying motives to save are not well understood, it is difficult to predict the effects of policies that alter the incentives to save. These pitfalls contribute to widely different estimates of the effects of IRAs and 401(k) plans in the empirical literature.

Because it is difficult to design narrowly targeted saving incentives that do not reward taxpayers for borrowing, reshuffling existing assets, or redirecting saving from conventional instruments into tax-favored accounts, many economists believe a consumption-based tax system would more successfully promote household saving (see *consumption taxation*). Under the income tax, a dollar of income saved and consumed 10 years from now yields a considerably smaller amount of after-tax consumption in constant dollars than it would if it were consumed immediately. This is because income is taxed as it is earned, and again as it is saved. With an interest rate of 5 percent and a marginal tax rate of 28 percent, for example, the tax system imposes a greater than 12 percent penalty on saving after 10 years. Because of the bias toward current consumption in the tax system, many proposals to stimulate saving are designed to make the tax system more neutral toward intertemporal consumption decisions.

The present tax system could be changed to an expenditure-based system by, among other changes, eliminating contribution limits and early withdrawal penalties on IRA-type saving plans and phasing out taxation of capital income. By removing saving from the tax base, an expenditure tax eliminates distortions in intertemporal consumption decisions. Many economists believe a switch from a progressive income tax to a progressive expenditure tax would significantly increase economic efficiency. Expenditure tax advocates also argue that the tax system would be administratively simpler. Expenditure tax critics, however, argue that income is a more appropriate basis for taxation, that the difficulties in making the transition to an expenditure tax are formidable, and that absent effective end-of-life wealth transfer taxes, an expenditure tax could lead to inappropriate concentrations of wealth.

ADDITIONAL READINGS

Bernheim, B. Douglas. "The Economic Effects of Social Security: Towards a Reconciliation of Theory and Measurement." *Journal of Public Economics* 33 (1987): 273–304.

———. *The Vanishing Nestegg: Reflections on Saving in America.* New York: Priority Press Publications, 1991.

———. "Taxation and Saving." In *Handbook of Public Economics,* edited by A. J. Auerbach and M. Feldstein, vol. 3, ch. 18 (1173–1249). Amsterdam: Elsevier Science Publishers, 2002.

Bradford, David F. *Untangling the Income Tax.* Cambridge, MA: Harvard University Press, 1986.

Burman, Leonard E., Richard W. Johnson, and Deborah Kobes. "Pensions, Health Insurance, and Tax Incentives." *Tax Policy Center Discussion Paper* no. 14. Washington, DC: Tax Policy Center, December 2003.

Campbell, John, and N. Gregory Mankiw. "Consumption, Income, and Interest Rates: Reinterpreting the Time Series Evidence." *NBER Macroeconomics Annual,* 1989.

Dicks-Mireaux, Louis, and Mervyn King. "Pension Wealth and Household Savings: Tests of Robustness." *Journal of Public Economics* 23 (1984): 115–39.

Engen, Eric M., William G. Gale, and John Karl Scholz. "Do Saving Incentives Work?" *Brookings Papers on Economic Activity* 1 (1994): 85–180.

Feldstein, Martin. "The Welfare Cost of Capital Income Taxation." *Journal of Political Economy* 86, no. 2 (April 1978): 29–51.

Gale, William G. "The Effects of Pensions on Household Wealth: A Reevaluation of Theory and Evidence." *Journal of Political Economy* 106, no. 4 (August 1998): 706–23.

Gale, William G., and John Karl Scholz. "IRAs and Household Saving." *American Economic Review* 84, no. 5 (December 1994): 1233–41.

Gale, William G., J. Mark Iwry, and Peter Orszag. "The Saver's Credit: Issues and Options." *Tax Notes* 103, no. 53 (May 3, 2004): 597–612.

Graetz, Michael J. "Expenditure Tax Design." In *What Should Be Taxed—Income or Expenditure?* edited by Joseph Pechman (161–276). Washington, DC: The Brookings Institution, 1980.

Kotlikoff, Laurence J. "Taxation and Savings: A Neoclassical Perspective." *Journal of Economic Literature* (22 December 1984): 1576–1629.

Madrian, Bridget, and Dennis Shea. "The Power of Suggestion: Inertia in 401(k) Participation and Saving Behavior." *Quarterly Journal of Economics* 116 (November 2001): 1149–87.

Poterba, James M., Steven F. Venti, and David A. Wise. "Do 401(k) Contributions Crowd Out Other Personal Saving?" *Journal of Public Economics* 58 (September 1995): 1–32.

Scholz, John Karl, Ananth Seshadri, and Surachai Khitatrkun. "Are Americans Saving 'Optimally' for Retirement?" Mimeo, University of Wisconsin–Madison, 2004.

Shefrin, Hersh, and Richard Thaler. "The Behavioral Life-Cycle Hypothesis." *Economic Inquiry* 26 (1988): 609–43.

Summers, Lawrence H. "Capital Taxation and Accumulation in a Life Cycle Growth Model." *American Economic Review* 71, no. 4 (September 1981): 533–44.

Venti, Steven, and David Wise. "Have IRAs Increased U.S. Saving? Evidence from Consumer Expenditure Surveys." *Quarterly Journal of Economics* 105 (1990): 661–98.

Cross-references: consumption taxation; dividends, double taxation of; elasticity, demand and supply; individual retirement accounts; inverse elasticity rule; optimal taxation; pensions, tax treatment of; Ricardian equivalence; tax illusion.

Seigniorage

Gail E. Makinen
Congressional Research Service

A source of government revenue that comes from money creation.

Given that money is socially useful and, hence, that a demand for it exists, it is possible for the supplier of money to derive some revenue or profit from providing it. Seigniorage (and brassage, a related term) was originally applied to mean a charge imposed by a mint when bullion was converted into coins (money). As such, it represented the difference between the face and the bullion value of the coin. Seigniorage later became synonymous with the real revenue or profit government derives from creating money. Although this is often omitted from discussions of seigniorage, the word applies to the net revenue or net profit from supplying money because the maintenance of the existing money stock is not costless (even when full-bodied coins are used).

As monetary systems evolved, their ability to produce seigniorage changed, the nature of seigniorage became less obvious, and the initial collector of this revenue also changed.

When fiat paper money supplied by government came to be substituted for full-bodied coins, the potential for seigniorage rose dramatically, because the same amount of money could be supplied at a much lower resource cost to the government. Seigniorage continued to be measured as the difference between the face value of the notes and the cost to produce and maintain them in circulation.

The introduction of commercial banking and deposit money not only made the form of seigniorage less obvious, but also potentially reduced the amount that could be extracted from the monetary system. To see this, suppose that only deposit money is used and that its supply is controlled by an asset called reserves (or high-powered money), which is supplied by the central bank (it could also be supplied by the treasury). Further, assume that the relationship between reserves and deposit money is one to five. If the central bank wants the commercial banks to supply more deposit money, it can do so by supplying more reserves. One way to supply these reserves is through buying government securities in the market. The acquisition of additional securities by the central bank will reduce the government's net payment of interest, because central bank profits are remitted to the treasury. This interest "saving" is then a measure of gross seigniorage. However, because the interest is saved year after year, the present value of these "savings" is the appropriate measure of gross seigniorage. On an annual basis, this present value is equal to the amount of reserves or high-powered money created in any year.

The ability of a deposit-only money system to reduce seigniorage can be seen when it is compared to an all-currency system. Given that the same amount of money is used in both systems, in the deposit-only system, seigniorage is earned only on the system's reserves or high-powered money. And these reserves are equal in value, in the example above, to only one-fifth of the currency that would exist in an all-currency system.

A major way of earning additional seigniorage in the deposit-only system is to raise the reserve requirement. When it is raised to 100 percent, the two systems will yield the same gross seigniorage (given that the central bank will supply the reserves necessary for the money stock to remain the same in both systems). However, because 100 percent reserve banking is not common, actual seigniorage will be less in a deposit-only system or in a mixed deposit–currency system relative to a currency-only system.

When central banks replace treasuries as suppliers of paper money, the major change is in the institution that initially collects the seigniorage. In the United States, the Federal Reserve supplies currency largely through buying federal government securities in the market. Because the net earnings or profits of the Federal Reserve are remitted to the Treasury, the Fed holdings of government securities are, in effect, an interest-free loan to the government. The present value of the reduced-interest bill of the federal government, then, measures the amount of gross seigniorage. Not all of the Fed's holdings of government securities, however, are acquired through supplying paper money. Some are acquired through supplying reserves to depository institutions. Thus, on a present-value basis, it is the change in the sum of currency in circulation and the reserves of depository institutions, called high-powered money, that represents the gross seigniorage earned per year.

When the expenses of the Federal Reserve are subtracted from this total, a measure of net seigniorage results. (The Federal Reserve has additional sources of revenue, such as interest earned on its holdings of nongovernment securities and discounts, and other costs such as capital gains or losses on its holdings of foreign exchange and on the sale of government securities, that can alter the total amount of net seigniorage.)

Because the federal budget is prepared on a cash-flow basis, the amount listed per year in the budget document as seigniorage is different from the seigniorage computed on a present-value basis. Most of seigniorage in the budget represents the sum paid per year by the Federal Reserve to the Treasury, representing the net earnings from its entire portfolio of assets. In the budget document, this measure of net seigniorage is recorded as a part of "Other Receipts" subtitled "Miscellaneous Receipts." During the 1950s, '60s, '70s, '80s, and '90s, it averaged, as a percent of total federal receipts, 0.5, 1.1, 1.8, 2.7, and 1.6 percent, respectively. In addition, the Treasury itself earns a small amount of seigniorage on coinage, representing the difference between the face value of the coins and the operating costs of the U.S. Mint.

ADDITIONAL READINGS

Cukierman, Alex, Sebastian Edwards, and Guido Tabellini. "Seigniorage and Political Stability." Discussion paper 381. London: Centre for Economic Policy Research, March 1990.

Haslag, Joseph H. "Seigniorage Revenue and Monetary Policy: Some Preliminary Evidence." *Economic Review* 3rd Quarter (1998): 10–20.

Obstfeld, Maurice. "Dynamic Seigniorage Theory: An Exploration." Discussion paper 519. London: Centre for Economic Policy Research, March 1991.

Cross-reference: inflation tax.

Severance tax, state

James A. Richardson
Louisiana State University

State governments employ special taxes on the severing of nonrenewable resources from the land.

Thirty-six states raise revenues or regulate behavior by taxing the severing of renewable and nonrenewable resources from land or water within the taxing jurisdiction of the state. The severance tax is levied on a variety of resources, with 18 states taxing timber products, 26 states taxing oil and gas, 12 states taxing coal, 2 states taxing fish, and 25 states taxing a variety of minerals ranging from iron ore and phosphates to sand and gravel.

Revenues from the severance tax to all states amounted to $5.5 billion, or 1.0 percent of total state tax collections, in 2003. Ten states, having significant endowments of oil and gas or coal, collected 89 percent of total severance tax collections. These states—with their percent of the U.S. oil, gas, and coal production; their severance tax rates on oil, gas, and coal; and the significance of severance taxes—are shown in table 1. Texas and Alaska dominate oil production. Texas, Louisiana, New Mexico, Oklahoma, and Wyoming dominate natural gas production if the focus is just on production within the taxing jurisdiction of the states. U.S. production is also concentrated on the federal outer continental shelf for both oil and natural gas, with most of the oil and gas produced off the coast of Louisiana and Texas. The federal oil and gas is not subject to state severance taxes. Wyoming, West Virginia, and Kentucky dominate coal production in the United States.

Oil and gas states receive the overwhelming majority of the severance tax. Texas, Alaska, Louisiana, Oklahoma, and New Mexico claimed 69 percent of all severance taxes collected, and Wyoming, West Virginia, and Kentucky received just over 15 percent. Alaska and Wyoming are the states most dependent on severance tax collections.

Oil severance tax rates vary across the states, from 3.75 percent in New Mexico to 15.0 percent in Alaska. The New Mexico tax rates are only severance tax rates, but New Mexico also has a conservation tax rate and an ad valorem tax rate on oil and gas.

The tax base is typically the value of the oil at the wellhead. The natural gas severance tax is levied either on the value of natural gas at the wellhead or on a thousand cubic feet (MCF) basis. In some states natural gas is taxed per MCF but the rate is indexed to the price of natural gas. These states do not have

to write detailed rules about determining the value of natural gas at the wellhead, but still collect additional tax dollars as the price of natural gas rises. The complication of administering the oil and gas severance tax is that, while the tax is levied at the wellhead, typically no market transaction occurs at that point; the value of oil and natural gas at the wellhead is, therefore, a computation based on the price the oil or gas is sold for at the first market transaction less any transportation and processing expenses incurred between the wellhead and the first market transaction. This complication does not occur if the severance tax is levied on a per volume basis.

Coal is taxed on a cents per ton basis or as a percent of market value. The three prime coal-producing states use percent of value as the tax base, although the rates vary from 4.5 percent in Kentucky to 7.0 percent for surface-mined coal in Wyoming. The coal in the western states of Wyoming and Montana has less sulfur content than the coal in Kentucky and West Virginia, creating an environmental advantage for the western coal. State severance taxes had national implications in the 1970s because of rising energy prices, federal controls on domestic oil and natural gas prices, and several severance tax increases. Nonproducing states feared that producing states were shifting their tax burden to consumers in nonproducing states. However, the fears of tax exportation failed to materialize.

First, only three states increased their severance taxes after January 1974, the time of the initial oil embargo. Alaska in-

TABLE 1. Resource Production, Severance Tax Rates, and Significance of Severance Tax Collections, 2003

Top 10 severance tax–collecting states	Severance tax rates			Percent of U.S. production			Tax as % of total state collections
	Oil	Gas	Coal	Oil	Gas	Coal	
Alaska	15.0%[a]	10.0%[a]		17.1	2.3	0.1	55.2
Kentucky	4.5%[a]	4.5%[a]	4.5%[a]	0.1	0.4	12.2	2.1
Louisiana	12.5%[a]	17.1¢/MCF[b]	10¢/ton	4.3[c]	6.8[c]	2.4	6.5
Montana	9.26–15.06%[d]	9.26–15.06%[d]					
Surface			10–15%[e]	1.0	0.4	3.5	7.5
Underground			3–4%[e]				
New Mexico	3.75%[f]	3.75%[f]	55–57¢/ton[g]	3.2	8.2	2.5	13.4
North Dakota	11.5%[a]	Determined annually by State Tax Commissioner	39.5¢/ton	1.4	0.3	2.9	5.4
Oklahoma	7.085%[a]	7.085%[a]		3.1	7.8	0.1	9.3
Texas	4.6%[a]	7.5%[a]		19.5[c]	25.8[c]	4.6	5.2
West Virginia	5.0%[a]	5.0%[a]	5.0%[a]	0.04	0.9	14.7	5.4
Wyoming	6.0%[a]	6.0%[a]					
Surface			7.0%[a]	2.5	7.3	31.6	36.2
Underground			3.75%[a]				

a. Percent of value at wellhead.

b. Rate indexed to price of natural gas. MCF = 1,000 cubic feet.

c. These estimates do not include federal offshore production, which is primarily off the coast of Louisiana and Texas. Federal offshore oil production is 27.4 percent of U.S. oil production, and federal offshore gas production is 23.5 percent of U.S. natural gas production.

d. Rate varies based on date of well drilled, working or nonworking interest in well, and well productivity.

e. Rate varies on btu rating per pound.

f. Other taxes are levied on oil and gas such as conservation fee, ad valorem production tax, and oil and gas privilege tax.

g. Rate varies on surface versus underground mining.

creased the tax rate on oil from 12.5 to 15.0 percent, and Montana and Wyoming increased their severance taxes on coal. Louisiana had increased its severance tax on oil from 26 cents per barrel to 12.5 percent of value in 1973. Second, the ability to export any severance tax through price increases was facilitated more by federal price controls than by states having a disproportionate share of these energy resources. Third, in a free market, increases in severance taxes are more likely to be exported, if at all, through effects on wages, royalties, lease payments, and other input payments than via consumer prices. The elimination of the federal price controls and the general availability of energy resources in the 1980s and 1990s have substantially reduced the tax-exporting opportunities of producing states. Oil and gas prices are rising in the 2003–04 period. Producing states have tax laws that may increase the tax rate if prices (especially oil prices) reach a certain amount. States are extracting some of the rent from the oil and gas producers.

State policies relating to severance taxes focus on the choice of the tax base, the predictability and stability of the revenue stream, the long-term depletion of the resource, and the impact at the margin on resource development and production. As illustrated in table 1, states have chosen value over volume as the appropriate tax base for energy resources. The only major gas producer with a volume tax is Louisiana, but this 17.2 cents per MCF is indexed to increases or decreases in the price of natural gas. The severance tax base for other minerals, timber products, and fish varies, from gross proceeds to tons, stump value, and cords.

Severance tax revenues are related to long-term production prospects and price conditions. Oil and gas production has been declining in the United States since 1970. Oil production declined by about 12 percent from the beginning of 1996 through the last quarter of 2003. Oil and gas activity in the federal OCS has moderated the decline in U.S. oil and gas production.

The fiscal advantage of having oil and gas resources is not permanent, but states have ample time to plan for the replacement of this tax base because the production declines are gradual and predictable. The long-term depletion of the energy reserves can be accommodated for current and future citizens by a permanent trust fund that converts the depletable oil and gas or coal resource into a nondepletable financial asset. A permanent trust fund preserves the use of the natural wealth of a state for future generations.

Price variation is another matter. In 1981, oil prices had moved close to $40 per barrel, but by early 1987, they were closer to $10 per barrel. Severance tax collections, or the lack thereof, forced the major oil- and gas-producing states to raise other taxes or curtail state programs. These states faced budgetary turmoil throughout the 1980s and even into the 1990s. In the 1990s, oil prices gyrated with swings in the global economy, supply disturbances, and international tensions. The swings in oil prices were moderate. From 1999 through 2004, oil prices have climbed to record nominal highs—above $40

per barrel. States with oil resources benefit, but oil revenues as part of their state budget have diminished in importance.

Price variation is unpredictable and is created by short-run disturbances, not long-run trends. Hence, states that use severance taxes to fund key state programs have to be aware of the "boom and bust" cycle associated with such revenues. Price variation in energy resources can be accommodated by "rainy day funds" that grow when energy prices are high and then are used when energy prices fall.

Energy-producing states became accustomed to the industrial development that accompanied the discovery of oil, natural gas, or coal, just as they became accustomed to the severance taxes as a way to finance public programs. Any impediment to the exploration, development, or production of the energy resources adversely affects employment and economic activity within the energy-producing states. High severance taxes could be one such impediment.

Severance taxes postpone the depletion of energy reserves. The degree of economic distortion caused by the severance tax depends on who in the production line actually pays the taxes. The ultimate incidence of the severance tax becomes the critical issue. Participants in the development/consumption process are listed in table 2. The severance tax is imposed on those severing the resource. Severance taxes are almost always levied at the point of severance from the ground. The economic incidence of the tax does not necessarily coincide with the legal incidence of the tax.

Contractual relationships link the suppliers of energy resources. The principal features of the contract with the owners of the mineral rights are royalty rates, bonus payments, and rental fees. The explorer/developer/producer shares the risk with the landowner by paying upon production, as opposed to a strictly up-front purchase of the resource rights. The royalty rate is the percentage of production value that accrues to the landowner. Higher severance taxes may lead to lower royalty rates as the tax is shifted back to the landowner. Bonuses represent cash payments made at the initiation of the contract. Higher severance tax rates reduce bonus payments if royalty rates are not reduced. Rental payments are penalty payments for not drilling within a specified amount of time and are usually related to bonus payments. Rental payments may be reduced by higher severance taxes. Transactions between the person who originally owned the mineral rights

TABLE 2. Resource Development and Resource Consumption Process

Owners of mineral rights	Resource Development
Exploration/development	↑
Drilling activity	
Production	Tax Levied
Transportation	↓
Refiner/processor	
Industrial users	
Retailer	
Final consumer	Resource Consumption

and the person who eventually drills can become even more complicated. For example, a person purchasing the right to drill can farm out the drilling to another operator in exchange for a share of the production.

In the long run, severance taxes can be shifted back to the owners of the mineral rights. In the short run, however, contractual obligations between mineral owners and producers will prevent an increase in the severance tax from being shifted immediately back to the landowner unless the original contract between the landowner and the operator allows such a shift in severance taxes.

Higher severance tax rates raise the operating costs leading to earlier abandonment of existing fields for a given price projection. Higher severance tax rates can also neutralize new technology. In particular, enhanced recovery methods will not be as profitable if severance tax rates are raised. Secondary recovery methods, including water flooding and internal combustion, are commonly used in mature producing states. Tertiary recovery methods, such as chemically induced pressurization, are much more expensive and sensitive to higher severance tax rates.

Energy states are concerned with employment policies. Higher severance taxes are weighed against any possible employment loss, and severance tax reductions are weighed against possible employment gains. In fact, many states made changes in the severance tax laws to allow severance tax rates to decline if oil and gas prices dropped and then to rise again if oil and gas prices rose. States were "encouraging" oil and gas activities within their boundaries if the price incentives were not very high. Studies are still to be done verifying if these tax incentives really worked in terms of encouraging further oil and gas activity.

ADDITIONAL READINGS

Ahmad, Ehtisham, and Eric Mottu. "Oil Revenue Assignments: Country Experiences and Issues." IMF working paper no. 02/203. Washington, DC: International Monetary Fund, 2002.

Burness, Stuart. "On the Taxation of Nonreplenishable Natural Resources." *Journal of Environmental Economics and Management* 3, no. 4 (March 1976): 289–311.

Cuciti, Peggy, Harvey Galper, and Robert Lucke. "State Energy Revenues." In *Fiscal Federalism and the Taxation of Natural Resources,* edited by Charles McClure Jr. and Peter Mieszkowski (11–60). Lexington, MA: D.C. Heath, 1983.

Deacon, Robert J. "Taxation, Depletion, and Welfare: A Simulation Study of the U.S. Petroleum Resource." *Journal of Environmental Economics and Management* 24 (March 1993): 159–87.

English, Jeffrey E., and Mark S. Klan. "Optimal Taxation: Timber and Externalities." *Journal of Environmental Economics and Management* 18 (May 1990): 263–75.

Friedman, Julia Mason. "Taxation of Timber." In *Final Report of the Minnesota Tax Study Commission,* edited by Robert D. Ebel and Therese J. McGuire (399–410). Boston, MA: Butterworths, 1986.

McKenzie, Kenneth J. "Fiscal Federalism and the Taxation of Non-Renewable Resources." In *Fiscal Federalism in Russia,* edited by Richard M. Bird and Francois Vaillancourt. New York: World Bank Institute, forthcoming.

Olson, Kent W., and James W. Kleckley. "Severance Tax Stability." *National Tax Journal* 42 (March 1989): 69–78.

Richardson, James A. "Severance Tax Reform." In *Reforming State Tax Systems,* edited by Steven D. Gold (277–90). Denver, CO: National Conference of State Legislatures, 1986.

Richardson, James A., and Loren C. Scott. "Resource Location Patterns and State Severance Taxes: Some Empirical Evidence." *Natural Resources Journal* (Winter 1983): 352–64.

Ward, Frank A., and Joe Kerkvliet. "Quantifying Exhaustible Resource Theory: An Application to Mineral Taxation Policy." *Resources and Energy Economics* 15 (June 1993): 203–41.

Cross-references: energy taxes; environmental taxes, state; site value taxation and single tax; tax exportation.

Site value taxation and single tax

Joan M. Youngman
Lincoln Institute of Land Policy

Site value taxes—Taxes on the value of land in its original, unimproved state.

Single tax—A site value tax proposed to replace all other taxes as the sole source of government revenue.

The unusual economic characteristics of land, particularly its nearly inelastic supply and its growth in value with community development, have long supported special approaches to its taxation. Because real property taxes generally combine land and building values in a single tax base, those interested in distinct taxes on land itself have focused on various alternatives: graded property taxes at higher rates on land than buildings; land value taxes limited to land value rather than land and buildings; site value taxes, reaching land in its original state before private capital improvements; and the single tax, a site value tax serving as the sole source of government tax revenue. Graded taxes have been used in several U.S. states and Canadian provinces, and land value taxes have been imposed in Jamaica and individual cities in Australia and New Zealand.

"Site value" denotes that portion of land wealth not attributable to private investment: land alone, without consideration of privately financed improvements to its original state. The "single tax" that would replace all other forms of taxation with a site value tax was brought to greatest popular attention by Henry George (1839–97), a 19th-century social reformer and author of the 1879 work *Progress and Poverty*. This product of George's long self-education, even typeset by the author himself, garnered enormous attention. It drew the support of admirers as diverse as Tolstoy, George Bernard Shaw, and Sun Yat-sen, and it inspired reform efforts ranging from land tax legislation to the formation of utopian communities. *Progress and Poverty* deals with many issues, but the single tax is its central prescription for redress of the inequities it passionately assails. It constitutes a compelling work of literature, as well as a political and economic tract.

The case for site value taxation is based on both efficiency and equity. The existence of a tax base in nearly inelastic supply offers the possibility of collecting revenue without distorting prices and economic incentives. Similarly, taxation of a form of wealth not due to individual human effort does not claim the product of the taxpayer's own labor. By excluding value resulting from private investments, such as grading and planting, site value taxation is designed to reach only the "unearned increment," the value resulting from community development and thus properly claimed by the community itself. While a tax on site value could be set at any rate, Henry George advocated a confiscatory tax equal to the full annual rental value of the unimproved land. He wrote: "What I, therefore, propose, as the simple yet sovereign remedy, which will raise wages, increase the earnings of capital, extirpate pauperism, abolish poverty, give remunerative employment to whoever wishes it, afford free scope to human powers, lessen crime, elevate morals, and taste, and intelligence, purify government and carry civilization to yet nobler heights, is—*to appropriate rent by taxation*" (George 1979, 405–6).

The greatest difficulties facing such a policy concern treatment of land claims established under a previously settled regime of property rights. A confiscatory tax would not reach only future unearned increments; it would also abolish property values held by investors who recently purchased land in reliance on past tax practices. William Vickery included as a "basic desiderata in a land tax base" the principle of legitimacy: "Expectations legitimately developed in the past must be sufficiently honored to create confidence in the expectations intended to be generated by the new tax regime" (Holland 1970, 26). Henry George considered such claims spurious when land title could be undermined by legal technicalities, pointing out that "if Quirk, Gammon & Snap can mouse out a technical flaw in your parchments or hunt up some forgotten heir who never dreamed of his rights, not merely the land, but all your improvements, may be taken away from you" (George 1979, 366–67). George had little use for compromise, such as John Stuart Mill's proposal that legislation provide for confiscating value increments realized after its implementation. George replied, "Because I was robbed yesterday, and the day before, and the day before that, is it any reason that I should suffer myself to be robbed today and tomorrow?" (George 1979, 365). The political problems raised by such an approach have generally left land value taxes well below the level of full annual rental value. Conversely, special opportunities exist for introducing land taxes in economies in transition from state ownership to private rights in property, because equitable issues concerning settled expectations are obviated if new owners take title with full understanding of their future tax liabilities.

Many important issues in site value taxation, as in land value taxation generally, concern assessment, administration, and implementation. For example, market value is often equated with value at "highest and best use," the most profitable use that is legal and feasible, and a heavy or even confiscatory tax on land value would be intended in part as an incentive to development. Yet no consensus exists today that development uniformly constitutes the "highest and best use" of land in a social sense. In all 50 U.S. states and in many other nations, property tax benefits for farmland, forests, and open space explicitly seek to counteract the economic incentive for con-

version of such land to other uses. George considered taxation at highest and best use a central advantage of his proposal: "The monopolist of agricultural land would be taxed as much as though his land were covered with houses and barns, with crops and with stock. The owner of a vacant city lot would have to pay as much for the privilege of keeping other people off of it until he wanted to use it, as his neighbor who has a fine house upon his lot" (George 1979, 437–38). The burden of any annual wealth tax on cash-poor property owners generates intense political pressure for relief. This is dramatized by the reluctance of elderly homeowners to take advantage of mitigation provisions, such as tax deferral and reverse-annuity programs, that would encumber their property, seeking a reduction in the tax itself instead.

Much research on land taxation and site value taxation has focused on their effects on land prices and development decisions. The nondistortionary aspects of a tax on a commodity in inelastic supply contrast with the development incentive exerted by a tax based not on current rental income but on potential sale value. That incentive varies with the tax rate. Under a confiscatory tax equal to the rental value of the unimproved site, development to full economic potential would be imperative. At the tax rates commonly found in contemporary property tax systems, the role of the property tax in development decisions is less clear. The difficulty of taxing land at its highest and best use, even at the generally low rates currently prevailing, indicates the problems that would confront a tax patterned on George's model.

Studies on the influence of land taxes on development use differing assumptions of whether the tax would reach the full potential land value or only value at current use (e.g., Mills 1981; Tideman 1982). As noted earlier, general reliance on highest and best use valuation means that, in the absence of special statutory exceptions, land value for tax purposes should reflect the most profitable use that is feasible and legal (although the value of buildings and other improvements not suited to that use may be reduced to reflect this obsolescence or depreciation). The fact that such explicit valuation provisions coexist with genuine uncertainty as to actual assessment practices illustrates the need to further study the administration of the tax in order to gauge its effects.

Problems of this type already arise under the land tax component of current real property taxes. A tax on the value of the original and unimproved site would raise many additional valuation and assessment challenges. For example, in suggesting use of a legally defined "standard state" as the basis for assessment, Vickery wrote: "To value land in an original substandard state requires an even greater feat of the imagination than the valuation of the land in a standard state: how, for example, would one value the site of the World Trade Center on the assumption that it was still a part of the bed of the North River? What is substandard for one purpose might be superior for another. The fill that is an advantage for the construction of a four-story walk-up may simply have to be removed for the skyscraper; it might be much easier to dredge mud and pump water" (Holland 1970, 28). Site value taxation could also require legal innovations, such as an appeals process protecting taxpayers' rights to contest their individual assessments while preserving the integrity of a mapping system under which taxable values of neighboring parcels stand in predictable relationship to one another.

ADDITIONAL READINGS

Baird, Richard M., and Enid Slack, eds. *International Handbook on Land and Property Taxation.* Cheltenham, U.K.: Edward Elgar, 2004.

Bell, Michael E., and John H. Bourman. "Factions Influencing the Choice of Site Value Taxation among Local Governments." In *Property Taxes in South Africa,* edited by Michael E. Bell and John H. Bowman (97–112). Cambridge, MA: Lincoln Institute of Land Policy, 2002.

Bentick, Brian L. "The Impact of Taxation and Valuation Practices on the Timing and Efficiency of Land Use." *Journal of Political Economy* 87 (1979): 859–68.

———. "A Tax on Land Value May Not Be Neutral." *National Tax Journal* 35 (1982): 113.

Brueckner, Jan K. "A Modern Analysis of the Effects of Site Value Taxation." *National Tax Journal* 39 (1986): 49–58.

Calvo, Guillermo A., Laurence J. Kotlikoff, and Carlos Alfredo Rodriguez. "The Incidence of a Tax on Pure Rent: A New (?) Reason for an Old Answer." *Journal of Political Economy* 87 (1979): 869–74.

George, Henry. *Progress and Poverty.* New York: Robert Schalkenback Foundation, centenary ed. of original 1879 work, 1979.

Holland, Daniel M., ed. *The Assessment of Land Value.* Madison: The University of Wisconsin Press, for the Committee on Taxation, Resources, and Economic Development, 1970.

Ladd, Helen F., and Katharine L. Bradbury. "City Taxes and Property Tax Bases." *National Tax Journal* 41 (1988): 503–23.

Lindholm, Richard W., and Arthur D. Lynn Jr. *Land Value Taxation: The Progress and Poverty Centenary.* Madison: The University of Wisconsin Press, for the Committee on Taxation, Resources, and Economic Development, 1982.

Mills, David E. "The Non-Neutrality of Land Value Taxation." *National Tax Journal* 34 (1981): 125–29.

———. "Reply to Tideman." *National Tax Journal* 35 (1982): 115.

Netzer, Dick, ed. *Land Value Taxation: Can It and Will It Work Today?* Cambridge, MA: Lincoln Institute of Land Policy, 1998.

Oates, Wallace E., and Robert M. Schwab. "The Impact of Urban Land Taxation: The Pittsburgh Experience." *National Tax Journal* 50, no. 1 (March 1997): 1–21.

Tideman, T. Nicolaus. "A Tax on Land Value Is Neutral." *National Tax Journal* 35 (1982): 109–11.

Cross-reference: lump-sum tax.

Social Security benefits, federal taxation of

David Weiner
Congressional Budget Office

A portion of Social Security benefits counted as taxable income for taxpayers with incomes above specified thresholds.

In the years following the original enactment of the Social Security system, administrative rulings by the Treasury Department, in 1938 and 1941, excluded Social Security benefits from the income tax base. At that time, incomes were low enough that even if benefits had been included there would have been little effect on taxes collected. From that time until 1983, several proposals were made to subject benefits to taxation, but nothing was implemented until the Social Security Amendments of 1983.

The Social Security Amendments of 1983 required that taxpayers with incomes above specified levels include up to 50 percent of their Social Security benefits in their adjusted gross income (AGI). This change was effective beginning in tax year 1984. The amendments, which followed the recommendations of the National Commission on Social Security Reform, credited the additional revenue raised from benefit taxation to the Social Security Trust Fund (see table 1). The Social Security Amendments of 1983 were in response to a projected shortfall in the Social Security Trust Funds and included other provisions to strengthen the long-term actuarial balance of the funds such as phased-in increases in the payroll tax rate and the retirement age. Not all taxpayers must include a portion of benefits as income when calculating income taxes. The 1983 amendments set a threshold below which benefits were totally excluded from income. Individuals with incomes below $25,000 and couples with incomes below $32,000 included no benefits when calculating their taxable income. A special definition of income was used to test whether an individual was below the threshold. It included three items:

1. AGI (without regard to Social Security benefits)
2. Half of Social Security benefits
3. Tax-exempt interest income

The threshold was designed to alleviate the effect of benefit taxation on lower-income families. Although tax-exempt interest is excluded from AGI, it was included in this special income definition so that a family with high total income would not be excluded from benefit taxation if a large fraction of its income was in the form of tax-exempt interest. The 1983 amendments did not index the thresholds for inflation, so as incomes increase over time, a greater fraction of the beneficiaries are over the threshold and must include a portion of their benefits in income for tax purposes. This feature of the amendments was deliberate and was designed to gradually extend the inclusion of benefits in AGI to all beneficiaries. (Not all beneficiaries would pay tax on their benefits, even if they all included benefits in the calculation of AGI, because other aspects of the tax system—the personal exemption and standard deduction, for example—would reduce the taxable income of many beneficiaries to zero.)

The 1983 amendments phased in the taxation of benefits. A family whose income increased from the threshold to one dollar over the threshold did not have to include half its benefits in AGI. For each dollar a family's income was over the threshold, it was required to include 50 cents of benefits in AGI, up to a maximum of half of its benefits. This phasein avoided problems of a "notch," but it did increase implicit marginal tax rates for those in the phasein range. These higher implicit marginal rates reduced the incentives to work and

TABLE 1. Number of Returns Reporting Taxable Benefits and Revenues Collected and Revenues as a Share of Total Benefits, Selected Years

Year	Number of Returns Including Benefits in AGI (millions)	Revenues Credited to Trust Fund (billions of dollars)		Revenues Credited to Trust Fund as a Share of Total Benefits (percent)	
		OASDI	HI	OASDI	HI
1984	2.6	2.3	—	1.3	—
1990	5.1	3.1	—	1.3	—
1994	5.9	5.7	1.6	1.8	0.5
2000	10.6	13.2	8.7	3.3	2.2

Sources: Department of the Treasury, Internal Revenue Service, *Statistics of Income* 1984, 1990, 1994, 2000; Social Security Administration, *Annual Supplement to the Social Security Bulletin,* 2003.
Notes: — = not applicable; OASDI = Old-Age, Survivors, and Disability Insurance; HI = Hospital Insurance;

save. The formula for taxing benefits was changed as part of the Omnibus Budget Reconciliation Act of 1993 (OBRA93). As a result of this act, taxpayers with incomes over a second set of thresholds, $34,000 for individuals and $44,000 for couples, must include up to 85 percent of their benefits. The act had no effect on taxpayers with incomes below these thresholds. Under the 1993 act, taxpayers first calculate the taxable portion of benefits according to the formula established in the 1983 amendments, and then perform a second calculation if their incomes are above the 1993 act's higher thresholds. Like the 1983 amendments, the additional taxation of benefits is phased in. The phasein rate is 85 percent (as opposed to the 50 percent phasein under the 1983 amendments) and raises implicit marginal tax rates for those in the new phasein range.

The 1993 changes in benefit taxation were part of a general effort to reduce the deficit. The increase in the inclusion percentage was justified in part as making the taxable portion of Social Security benefits parallel to private contributory pension plans. The additional revenue from this change was not to be transferred to the Old-Age and Survivors Insurance Trust Fund from which the benefits were paid. Instead, it was dedicated to the Hospital Insurance Trust Fund.

The proper tax treatment of Social Security depends in part on whether Social Security is viewed as a pension program or a tax-transfer program. If benefit payments are unrelated to payroll taxes, then full taxation of benefits would be justified. If, on the other hand, benefit payments are directly related to payroll taxes in the same way that pension benefits are related to pension contributions, then only a portion of the benefits should be subject to tax.

The Social Security program has elements of both a tax-transfer program and a pension program. Benefits are related to payroll taxes, but the benefit formula has a redistributive element. Lower-wage earners get a higher fraction of their wages in benefits than do those with higher wages. This suggests that only a fraction of benefits should be subject to taxation, but the exact percentage would differ among beneficiaries because the benefit formula is not uniform.

The 85 percent inclusion percentage enacted in OBRA93 is based on a hypothetical individual earning at the maximum earnings level over the course of his or her lifetime, retiring around 1993, and earning benefits over an average expected lifetime. For that individual, total payroll taxes paid divided by total benefits paid is approximately 15 percent. Because income taxes were already paid on that 15 percent, only 85 percent of the benefits should be subject to tax.

While the 85 percent inclusion formula approximates the proper tax treatment for a hypothetical case, the current law (as of 2005) rules still understate the fraction of benefits that might be included. Most beneficiaries earn below the maximum earnings level and receive benefits that are more than 85/15 of their payroll taxes. (This discussion assumes that the proper tax treatment of Social Security parallels that of private contributory pension plans. However, most private plans are noncontributory or do not tax pension plan contributions— a significant tax preference. If Social Security benefits were treated in the same way, a smaller percentage of benefits would be subject to tax.) Also, the current taxation rules exclude many beneficiaries from taxation at 85 percent since the 85 percent inclusion rate is phased in.

ADDITIONAL READINGS

Diamond, Peter A., and Peter R. Orszag. "Saving Social Security." *Journal of Economic Perspectives* 19, no. 2 (Spring 2005): 11–32.

Gale, William G., and Peter Orszag. "Private Pensions: Issues and Options." Tax Policy Center Discussion Paper no. 9. Washington, DC: Tax Policy Center, 2003.

Ippolito, Richard A. "Book Review: Privatizing Social Security." *National Tax Journal* 52, no. 1 (March 1999): 139–44.

Lyon, Andrew B., and John L. Stell. "Analysis of Current Social Security Reform Proposals." *National Tax Journal* 53, no. 3 (September 2000): 459–72.

National Commission on Social Security Reform. *Report of the National Commission on Social Security Reform.* Washington, DC: National Commission on Social Security Reform, 1983.

Pattison, David. "Taxation of Social Security Benefits under the New Income Tax Provisions: Distributional Estimates for 1994." *Social Security Bulletin* (Summer 1994): 44–50.

Sammartino, Frank J., and Richard Kasten. "The Distributional Consequences of Taxing Social Security Benefits: Current Law and Alternative Schemes." *Journal of Post-Keynesian Economics* (Fall 1985): 28–46.

Smith, Karen E., Eric Toder, and Howard Iams. "Lifetime Distributional Effects of Social Security Retirement Benefits." Prepared for the Third Annual Joint Conference for the Retirement Research Consortium, *Making Hard Choices About Retirement,* May 17–18, 2001. Washington, DC: The Urban Institute.

Steuerle, C. Eugene, and Adam Carasso. "Lifetime Social Security and Medicare Benefits." *Straight Talk on Social Security and Retirement* Policy Brief no. 36. Washington, DC: The Urban Institute, 2003.

U.S. Congress, House of Representatives. *Social Security Amendments of 1983: Conference Report.* 98th Cong., 2nd session. Washington, DC: U.S. Congress, House of Representatives, 1983.

Cross-references: income tax, federal; payroll tax, federal; Social Security Trust Fund.

Social Security Trust Fund

Robert B. Friedland

Center on an Aging Society, Georgetown University

Social Security is a broad term for a variety of programs intended to soften the financial impact of change in employment status, health, and family status.

Social Security is a national, federally administered program that covers almost all workers. The primary exception is 20 percent of state and local employees and some federal employees hired before 1984. For all other workers, the program is compulsory, requiring that workers contribute based on their earnings and entitling them to a benefit, after working a sufficient number of quarters. While benefits are a statutory right, the provisions of the program—such as payroll contributions or amount of benefits—can be modified through federal legislation, and indeed have been several times in the past six decades.

Social Security consists of four trust funds. The four trust funds, listed in order of their relative size, are (1) Old-Age and Survivors Insurance (OASI), (2) Hospital Insurance (HI, or Medicare Part A), (3) Supplementary Medical Insurance (SMI, or Medicare Part B and Part D), and (4) Disability Insurance (DI). While the OASI and DI trust funds are often reported together, this entry focuses primarily on the OASI program and its trust fund.

Each trust fund and the program it reflects is quite different. What all four share, however, is the political logic for establishing a trust fund. Social Security's financial structure is based on the principle of employees making contributions and earning, through employment, the right to protection for themselves and their families against the risk of reduced income and economic uncertainty. This underlying principle led to the use of payroll taxes as the primary source of financing.

The Social Security Act was passed in 1935. President Roosevelt was adamant that Social Security be financed by workers and that their "contributions" go into a trust fund. This mode of financing was intended to underscore the notion of an earned right to benefits and to give workers the sense that their "contributions" were safe but transferred—unlike private pensions, however, contributions are not saved, but for the most part merely pass through the "trust fund" on their way to retirees. Because contributions paid into the fund were paid to current beneficiaries, the political message was not consistent with the financing that would actually take place. However, Roosevelt's political instinct was to ensure that the program would be popular and hence politically secure.

In 1965, Medicare was added to the Social Security Act. The political success of OASI was the basis for proposing a similar mechanism for what is now known as Part A of Medicare. The fact that Medicare has two distinct trust funds with very different financing is, in part, a reflection of the nature of the legislative process that combined three distinct proposals into what is now Medicare.

Under the Federal Insurance Contributions Act (FICA), each worker covered by Social Security pays a payroll tax of 5.30 percent of earnings for OASI (retirement and survivor's coverage) and 0.90 percent for DI (disability coverage), up to the maximum taxable earnings. Indexed to wage growth, maximum taxable earnings were $87,900 in 2004. (Employees also pay 1.45 percent of all earnings for HI, or Medicare Part A.) Employers are responsible for paying the same percentage of an employee's payroll as the employee pays. And most economists believe that employees bear the burden of that tax as well. Self-employed workers pay the 15.2 percent of their payroll for OASI, DI, and HI. However, to maintain horizontal equity vis-à-vis corporate businesses, which treat Social Security contributions as a deduction in computing taxable business net income (profits), the unincorporated self-employed person may deduct half of this (7.65 percent) in computing his or her personal income tax liability. These payroll taxes are the primary source of financing.

In 2003, total income flowing into the OASI trust fund was $543.8 billion. Most of the OASI income (84 percent) was from payroll taxes on covered employees and their employers. However, the OASI trust fund also earned interest on trust funds and received part of the income taxes paid by higher-income Social Security beneficiaries. In 2003, interest earned on the OASI trust fund reserves accounted for 13.8 percent of the trust fund's income that year.

Another 2.3 percent of OASI trust fund income was from the income taxes on Social Security benefits. Most Social Security benefit payments are free from income taxes; however, individuals with a combined income of over $25,000 ($32,000 if married) pay income taxes on up to half of their Social Security benefits, and individuals with combined income over $34,000 ($44,000 if married) pay tax on up to 85 percent of their Social Security benefits.

Who receives benefits from OASI?

After 40 quarters (10 years) of employment in a position covered by Social Security, claims may be made upon the death of the worker or for retirement income anytime after age 62. For persons attaining age 62 after 1991, benefits are calculated based on their highest average indexed taxable earnings over 35 years. Like contributions, earnings are subject to tax only up to a maximum under OASDI, but not AI. Full retirement benefits are calculated based on retirement at age 65 (increasing to age 67 for workers born after 1959). Retirees can claim benefits at age 62, but those benefits are permanently reduced to reflect the actuarial equivalent of retiring at age 65 (increasing to age 67 by 2027).

In December 2003, approximately 39.4 million retired workers or their survivors were receiving OASI benefits (29.5 million retired workers, 2.6 million children of workers, and 7.3 million spouses of workers). Total benefit payments were $406 billion and the average monthly benefit at the end of 2003 was $903 for a retired worker. For a widow with two children, the average monthly benefit was $1,865. For a couple retiring in 2005, average-income lifetime benefits are expected to be about $400,000.

Social Security's achievements

Social Security is a major source of income for the elderly, providing 36 percent of total incomes and helping to ensure that older persons have an income that will keep them from being destitute. Social Security, however, was never intended to be the only source of retirement income. However, for 65 percent of persons age 65 or older, Social Security constitutes 50 percent of more of their income. Because the program is not means-tested, workers and employers can plan private pension and personal savings strategies around Social Security benefits. The popularity of Social Security (supported by more than 80 percent of the population for more than 50 years) stems from the underlying concept of an earned right to benefits, as well as its record of enhancing dignity and stabilizing families. Social Security allows the elderly to live independently for more time. By the same token, so far no generation has paid for its Social Security and Medicare benefits but passed on much of the costs to the next generations.

Adequacy versus individual equity

Social Security attempts to balance two goals: assuring that beneficiaries have an adequate retirement income and that those who pay more receive more than those who pay less. The program attempts to achieve adequacy by having a benefit formula that provides proportionately larger benefits to workers with lower incomes and increasing benefits with increases in the cost of living. At the same time, those whose earnings over their working years were greater, and hence paid more in FICA contributions, receive a higher benefit amount. Progressivity, however, is significantly attenuated by the higher nontaxability rates of lower-income groups.

How OASI differs from private pensions

Unlike employer-provided pension plans (defined benefit or defined contribution), Social Security participation is compulsory. Social Security is completely portable. Benefits do not require long-term employment with one employer. Survivor benefits are paid to each child, regardless of how many children, and Social Security benefits are taxed somewhat less than income from an employer pension plan. And, as noted, there is little real saving in Social Security since it operates like a transfer program.

OASI Trust Fund outlook

Social Security was initially designed to be funded on a "pay-as-you-go" basis. That is, current-year benefits would primarily be financed by current-year taxes. Since 1983, Social Security has operated on a "partially prefunded" basis, meaning a small portion of anticipated future benefits are partially funded in advance. Contributions now flowing into the trust fund exceed benefits paid out and are projected to continue to do so until about 2018. Trust fund assets are then projected to decline, and to be exhausted by 2045, under what is deemed the intermediate or more likely set of economic and demographic assumptions. Under more pessimistic assumptions, which yield higher trust fund costs and lower trust fund income, the OASI trust fund is projected to be exhausted by 2030. More optimistic assumptions suggest that through the end of the projection period (2080) the OASI Trust Fund will never be exhausted. The pressures from elderly programs, however, intensify long before trust fund calculations show shortfalls. After all, the money to pay interest on trust fund bonds or to purchase back bonds comes from the taxpayer. As Social Security benefits take an increasing share of national income, a decreasing share is left for everything else.

Retirement of the baby boomers

Changes in demographics resulting from the retirement of the "baby boom" generations have received a lot of attention. When the baby boomers start making claims for Social Security benefits (from about 2010 to 2030), their benefits will be supported by a relatively smaller taxpaying work force.

Analysts have shown that baby boomers as a group will pay in taxes about what they receive back in benefits, adjusted for inflation, plus a real rate of return of 2 percent. (Lower-wage workers and workers with families will get back more, however; higher-paid workers and single workers will receive a lower rate of return.) When today's younger workers retire, Social Security will have an even lower (but still positive) rate of return than for previous retirees. Even these returns are overstated, since reform is inevitable. Many have focused on this rate of return to suggest that future beneficiaries will not be getting their money's worth.

There is little question that, historically, the rate of return on equities has been greater than the anticipated rate of return on Social Security in the future. For this reason some have argued that a part or all of Social Security contributions should be invested, on behalf of each worker (or directly by each worker) in the equity market to prefund more of their retirement income.

This argument, however, tends to suppose that future rates of return in the equity markets would reflect historical rates. Investing Social Security contributions in the equity market is likely to have a tremendous effect on the supply of capital in the private equity market. Unless the demand for capital increases by as much as the increase in supply, it is unlikely that future rates of return in the equity markets would be as large once Social Security contributions were also being invested in the equity markets.

There are, however, other reasons besides the future value of contributions to argue for a change in how Social Security is financed. Some believe that the government has no role in insuring life's contingencies, especially those that can be insured in the private market, while others see the trust fund structure as an inefficient way of encouraging national savings, particularly since the surplus in the Social Security trust funds masks how much government spending exceeds tax revenues raised to finance the rest of the government.

Proponents of the current structure, however, highlight the effective and efficient way the program has redistributed income. It has enabled many more older persons to remain financially independent far longer than might otherwise have occurred in the absence of Social Security. The transfers are countercyclical and the pooling of the risks against which the program insures is far more efficient and effective than simply relying on private insurance.

Whatever the reason for a call for reform, the problem that most reform proposals must grapple with is that at any point in time current and future beneficiaries have already spent considerable time working (and therefore paying benefits) in covered employment. Changing the program necessitates deciding how persons in each of these groups would be treated. Moreover, assuming current beneficiaries and others will be a part of the old program, taxpayers will have to finance the benefits in the old program while also financing the benefits in the new program. These transition costs are likely to be as large as the cost of eliminating the currently projected trust fund shortfall.

ADDITIONAL READINGS

Burtless, Gary. "Social Security's Long-Term Budget Outlook." *National Tax Journal* 50, no. 3 (September 1997): 399–412.

Hines, James R., and Timothy Taylor. "Shortfalls in the Long Run: Predictions about the Social Security Trust Fund." *Journal of Economic Perspectives* 19, no. 2 (Spring 2005): 3–10.

Mariger, Randall P. "Social Security Privatization: What Are the Issues?" *National Tax Journal* 52, no. 4 (December 1999): 783–802.

Steuerle, C. Eugene, and Jon M. Bakija. *Retooling Social Security for the 21st Century: Right and Wrong Approaches to Reform.* Washington, DC: Urban Institute Press, 1994.

Cross-references: income tax, federal; Medicare trust fund; payroll tax, federal; Social Security benefits, federal taxation of.

Source principle

Joseph J. Cordes
George Washington University

A basis for assigning tax liabilities to individuals and businesses who are located in one jurisdiction while earning income in another.

Taxation at the source, rather than on the basis of residence, means that the amount that a taxpayer pays in taxes depends on where the income is earned rather than on where the taxpayer resides. Consider the case of a multinational company with headquarters in the United States that earns income from an affiliate located in another country. Income taxation at the source means that the company would be required to report and pay taxes on the income to the foreign country. Typically, to prevent taxing the income twice, the company would then be allowed to claim a credit, based on taxes paid to the foreign government, against taxes owed to the United States on the foreign-source income.

Tax scholars broadly agree that jurisdictions have the right to tax income and production that occurs within their boundaries. But, to avoid double-taxation of individuals and businesses that are located in one jurisdiction and earn income in another, the taxpayer's home jurisdiction needs to forgo taxing the income of residents that is earned elsewhere. Administratively, this is usually accomplished, as in the example above, by allowing residents who are taxed at the source to take a credit for taxes paid to other jurisdictions against taxes they would otherwise owe to their home jurisdiction.

In the United States, the issue of whether to tax income at the source or on the basis of residence comes up in many metropolitan areas because people live in the suburbs but work in the city.

Commuter taxes are an example of attempts to tax people living in urban areas at the source.

Cross-references: commuter taxes; destination principle; multinational corporations, taxation of; origin principle; residence principle.

Standard deduction, federal

Joseph J. Cordes
George Washington University

The fixed amount of money that taxpayers who do not itemize deductions can deduct from federal adjustable gross income, based on the taxpayer's filing status.

In arriving at taxable income, taxpayers who do not itemize deductions are allowed to subtract a fixed sum, which varies with their filing status, from adjusted gross income. In 2004, the standard deduction for nonelderly, nonblind taxpayers equaled $4,850 for single filers, $9,700 for a married couple filing jointly, and $7,150 for a head of household. Taxpayers who are 65 or older and/or blind were allowed to take larger standard deductions, ranging from $6,050 for a single filer who is either blind or elderly to $13,500 for a married couple who file jointly and who are both elderly and blind. Along with personal exemptions, the standard deduction has been indexed for inflation, beginning first in 1985–86, and then starting again in 1990. Increases in the standard deduction for joint returns to make them twice the single amount were phased in by the 2001 tax cut and the phasein was eliminated to achieve this effect immediately, but temporarily, for 2003 and 2004 (although these provisions are not permanent). This change was part of provisions adopted to eliminate the marriage penalty for most taxpayers.

Together with the personal exemption, the standard deduction defines a threshold level of income below which no tax is due (see *personal exemption, federal*). In addition, the more generous the amount of the standard deduction, the fewer the number of taxpayers who will itemize deductions. Historically, between 6 and 7 out of 10 taxpayers have claimed the standard deduction instead of itemizing deductions on their federal tax returns.

Cross-references: adjusted gross income; income tax, federal; inflation indexation of income taxes; marriage penalty; personal exemption, federal.

State and local tax deductibility

Steven Maguire
Congressional Research Service

The interplay of the federal and state/local tax systems as a result of the deductibility of income, sales, and property taxes for those who itemize for federal personal income tax purposes.

In calculating federal taxable income, taxpayers who itemize are permitted to deduct payments for (1) state and local real and personal property taxes and (2) either income or general retail sales taxes. As a result, the federal government offsets (indirectly pays) part of the state and local bill in the form of lower federal tax collections. The initial value of the deduction is equal to the amount of total tax deducted multiplied by the taxpayer's marginal federal tax rate. However, for those taxpayers subject to the individual alternative minimum tax (AMT), the federal tax-offset is partially recaptured for the federal Treasury. The significance of this recapture is growing as middle-income taxpayers become increasingly subject to the AMT.

Theory suggests that taxpayers are willing to accept higher state and local tax rates, and thus, a higher level of state and local public spending because they pay less federal income tax as the net "tax price" of federally deductible state and local

taxes falls. It follows that repeal of the federal deductibility provision would cause a rise in the "tax price" of state and local government spending, particularly for states that rely heavily on income, property, and sales taxes. More than a fifth of returns and 29 percent of deductions are in just two states—California and New York; ten states account for 60 percent of total deductions (Rueben and Burman 2005).

The deduction for state and local taxes paid dates from the inception of the federal income tax in 1913, under which all taxes, including federal, state, and local taxes not directly tied to a benefit, were deductible. However, over time, the scope of federal deductibility changed. Thus, broad-based state sales taxes that were first introduced in the Depression of the 1930s were not deductible until the Revenue Act of 1942 (PL 77-753). The U.S. Treasury Department's initial *Blueprints for Tax Reform* (1997) proposed several tax base broadening initiatives, including entirely eliminating federal deductibility. Congress partly repealed deductibility with the Tax Reform Act (TRA) of 1986 by eliminating the sales tax deduction. However, with the American Jobs Creation Act of 2004 (AJCA), Congress reinstated the sales tax deduction, but only if taken *in lieu of* income taxes. Here the clear "winners" are the states with general sales taxes but no income taxes: Florida, Nevada, South Dakota, Texas, Washington, and Wyoming. The AJCA 2004 sales tax deductibility provision is set to expire after the 2005 tax year. The itemized deduction phases out for wealthy taxpayers, limiting the benefit at the highest end of the income distribution. Taxpayers may also choose between reporting actual sales tax paid, verified with saved receipts indicating sales taxes paid, and an estimated amount found in tables provided by the IRS (this was also true prior to TRA 1986).

Deductible state and local taxes

Federal deductibility arises only for those taxpayers who itemize rather than use the standard deduction. Business taxpayers, in contrast, may continue to deduct state/local taxes as a cost of doing business. The value of the personal income tax deduction increases with income under the rate structure of the federal personal progressive income tax; this favors taxpayers in higher income tax brackets. Table 1 reports the number and percentage of returns with itemized deductions for the four deductible state and local taxes. The 1986 tax year is included in table 1 to show the deduction for sales taxes paid, which was repealed by TRA 1986.

General sales tax

As of 1986, the sales tax deduction was the most common itemized deduction for taxes paid. Many taxpayers would claim a sales tax deduction not only because all but five states imposed a sales tax, but also due to the fact that the property tax deduction was conditioned on owning property, real or personal.

TABLE 1. Number and Percentage of State and Local Taxes Paid Itemizers, 1986 and 1995–2002

	1986	1995	1996	1997	1998	1999	2000	2001	2002
	Number of returns (in millions)								
All returns	103.0	118.2	120.4	122.4	124.8	127.1	129.4	130.3	130.1
Itemized deductions	40.7	34.0	35.4	36.6	38.2	40.2	42.5	44.6	45.6
Income taxes	33.2	28.6	29.7	30.8	31.9	33.6	35.4	37.0	37.6
Sales taxes	39.0	n.a.	n.a.	n.a.	n.a.	n.a.	n.a.	n.a.	n.a.
Real estate taxes	32.9	30.1	31.3	32.3	33.6	35.4	37.1	38.7	39.7
Personal property taxes	11.5	15.6	16.7	17.4	18.2	19.0	19.6	20.0	20.6
Other taxes	9.1	3.9	3.6	3.5	3.4	3.4	3.3	3.7	3.4
	Percentage of returns								
All returns	100.0	100.0	100.0	100.0	100.0	100.0	100.0	100.0	100.0
Itemized deductions	39.5	28.8	29.4	29.9	30.6	31.7	32.9	34.2	35.1
Income taxes	32.2	24.2	24.7	25.2	25.6	26.4	27.4	28.4	28.9
Sales taxes	37.8	n.a.	n.a.	n.a.	n.a.	n.a.	n.a.	n.a.	n.a.
Real estate taxes	32.0	25.5	26.0	26.3	27.0	27.9	28.7	29.7	30.5
Personal property taxes	11.1	13.2	13.8	14.2	14.6	15.0	15.2	15.3	15.8
Other taxes	8.8	3.3	3.0	2.9	2.7	2.6	2.6	2.8	2.6

Source: U.S. Department of Treasury, Internal Revenue Service, Statistics of Income Division, *Individual Income Tax Returns, various years,* Publication 1304.
Note: n.a. = not applicable

There is little disagreement that if no other direct changes are made to the system, state and local governments will rely more heavily on a tax that is subject to federal deductibility, although there are differing views on the magnitude of this effect. (See Gramlich 1985, Lindsey 1988, and Feenburg and Rosen 1986.)

However, other policy factors are rarely constant. Thus, due to a convergence of intergovernmental policy factors, the expected post–TRA 1986 shift away from sales taxes did not occur. At first glance, this outcome seems counterintuitive: after all, it was only the sales tax that lost its deductible status. However, as a result of the intergovernmental interplay, the post–TRA 1986 net "tax price" of state income taxes exceeded the sales "tax price." Three factors converged to explain this result (Ebel and Zimmerman 1992; Tannenwald 1997). First, because businesses pay as much as 45 percent of the "typical" state sales tax, legislators understood that much of the sales tax was still exportable to the federal government as a business cost under federal income tax law. Second, pre–TRA 1986, individual taxpayers' ability to shift large amounts of sales taxes through federal deductibility was dampened because rather than keep track of their sales taxes paid during the year, taxpayers who itemized turned to IRS-provided optional sales tax tables—but these tables were capped for taxpayers with incomes above $100,000. Third, TRA did more than eliminate sales tax deductibility: it also dropped the top marginal tax rate from 50 to 33 percent and reduced the propensity to itemize, as a relatively large standard deduction and personal income exemption replaced the old federal zero bracket system and a wide array of deductions and exclusions were eliminated (e.g., consumer interest, medical expenses, employee expenses). As a result, TRA 1986 effectively increased the net tax price of the income tax by nearly 15 percent versus an 8 percent tax-price increase for the sales tax (Pollock 1991).

Property tax

The property tax deduction is claimed on approximately 30 percent of all tax returns. However, almost twice as many homeowners pay property taxes on owner-occupied housing (U.S. Census Bureau 2002). In short, not all homeowners itemize, and only those who do can take the property tax deduction.

Property taxes are a major source of local government revenue, and thus the federal transfer through deductibility is also quite large. State governments, in contrast, are less dependent upon property tax revenue and instead rely more upon income and sales taxes. Nationally, property taxes make up 45.1 percent ($269.4 billion in FY2002) of all local government tax general revenue and 1.3 percent ($9.7 billion in FY2002) of all state government tax revenue (U.S. Census Bureau 2004). The federal tax expenditure is estimated to be approximately $19.6 billion in 2005 (see table 2).

If the property tax deduction were eliminated, taxpayers would gradually reduce their housing consumption and thus the size of their property tax bill. Though this shift would be gradual (housing consumption choices are not as responsive to changes in after-tax price as other expenditures, given the relative illiquidity of housing assets), the government's incentive is to reduce property tax reliance and, for a given total revenue flow, shift to other revenue sources. Local governments would have more at stake than state governments because the real property tax is primarily a local source of revenue.

Income taxes

The income tax is primarily a state revenue; however, some permit local income taxation. In FY2002, state governments collected $185.7 billion in individual income taxes and local governments collected $17.2 billion ($202.9 billion com-

TABLE 2. Estimated Federal Tax Expenditure on the State and Local Tax Deduction ($ billions)

	2004	2005	2006	2007	2008	2009	Total
Deduction for property taxes on owner-occupied housing	n.a.	19.6	15.0	13.4	13.0	13.2	74.1
Pre-AJCA estimate							
Deduction for state and local income and personal property taxes	44.3	40.9	37.9	36.7	35.4	n.a.	195.2
Post-AJCA estimate							
Deduction for state and local income, sales, and personal property taxes	n.a.	46.2	36.8	33.9	33.7	35.2	185.8

Source: Maguire 2005, 12.
Note: AJCA = American Jobs Creation Act of 2004; n.a. = not applicable.

bined). Federal deductions claimed on federal income tax forms for both state and local income taxes in the 2002 tax year totaled $182.0 billion. The difference between what was collected and what was claimed on federal returns stems from taxpayers who did not itemize or individuals who were not required to file federal returns. Both groups are significantly more likely to be relatively low income.

Two estimates of the tax expenditure for the deduction of income, personal property, and sales taxes are included in table 2. One estimate was calculated before the AJCA of 2004 was enacted and the second after the AJCA had been enacted. Both estimates include the personal property tax deduction, but it is a small fraction of the federal tax expenditure.

As noted, the deduction for state and local income taxes affects the distributional burden of both state and federal taxes. First, the deduction could increase the progressivity of state taxes if it causes states to rely more on progressive taxes, such as the income tax. Part of the cost of the deduction for high-rate taxpayers is effectively "exported" to all federal taxpayers. A state that collects a larger share of income taxes from taxpayers in high federal income tax brackets is, therefore, more effective at exporting some of its state tax burden to all federal taxpayers.

The federal tax burden, however, could be shifted to the majority of taxpayers who do not itemize deductions. Before the AJCA provided the alternative sales tax deduction, taxpayers in states without an income tax were more likely to be non-itemizers; thus, taxpayers in these states bore a relatively higher federal tax burden than taxpayers in states with an income tax. The AJCA has partially muted that burden with the two-year sales tax deductibility provision in lieu of income taxes.

Federal tax base broadening: eliminate deductibility of state and local taxes

If deductibility were eliminated and state and local governments were policy neutral (that is, would do nothing in response to the federal changes), then the initial impact on the distributional tax burden among the states would remain essentially unchanged (although the in-state taxpayer distribution can be expected to become more regressive). The federal tax burden, however, would shift from low-tax states to high-tax states.

More generally, if state and local tax deductibility were eliminated, the federal tax burden would shift from all federal taxpayers to itemizers. As noted earlier, itemizers tend to be higher income, thus, federal income taxes would become more progressive if the deduction for state and local taxes paid were eliminated (Rueben 2005).

Just as was true post–TRA 1986, some secondary effects (though of a different nature) can be anticipated. First, if deductibility were eliminated, state and local governments might be less willing to finance projects that generate benefits that extend beyond the taxing jurisdiction. The tax price to a community of these projects would increase as the federal "contribution" through deductibility is lost. Projects and initiatives whose benefits extend beyond the local jurisdiction would likely be the most sensitive to changes in the tax price as the benefits are more widely dispersed.

The second is the interplay between federal deductibility and the alternative minimum income tax (AMT). While, as noted, taxpayers in all 50 states now claim some amount of deduction, the benefits of the deductions are concentrated in a relatively few states and accrue to high-income taxpayers. But these are the same taxpayers who are more likely to be subject to the AMT (Burman et al. 2003). Indeed, federal deductibility of state and local taxes often triggers the AMT. Assuming no change in federal law, the more taxpayers become subject to the AMT, the more federal deductibility is "recaptured." In short, for many households, elimination of the deductibility of state and local taxes is already built into the system (Rueben 2005).

ADDITIONAL READINGS

Bradford, David F. *Blueprints for Basic Tax Reform.* Arlington, VA: Tax Analysts, 1984.

Burman, Leonard E., William G. Gale, and Jeffrey Rohaly. "Policy Watch: The Expanding Reach of the Individual Alternative Minimum Tax." *Journal of Economic Perspectives* 17, no. 2 (2003): 173–86.

Ebel, Robert D., and Christopher Zimmerman. "Sales Tax Trends and Issues." In *Sales Taxation: Critical Issues in Policy and Administration,* edited by William Fox. Westport, CT: Praeger, 1992.

Feenberg, Daniel R., and Harvey S. Rosen. "The Interaction of State and Federal Tax Systems: The Impact of State and Local Tax Deductibility." *American Economic Review* 76, no. 2 (May 1986): 126–31.

Gramlich, Edward M. "The Deductibility of State and Local Taxes." *National Tax Journal* 38, no. 4 (Dec. 1985): 462.

Lindsey, Lawrence B. "Federal Deductibility of State and Local Taxes: A Test of Public Choice by Representative Government." In *Fiscal Federalism: Quantitative Studies,* edited by Harvey Rosen (137–76). Chicago: University of Chicago Press, 1988.

Maguire, Steven B. "Federal Deductibility of State and Local Taxes." Washington, DC: Congressional Research Service, 2005.

Pollock, Stephen H. "Mechanisms for Exporting the State Sales Tax Burden in the Absence of Federal Deductibility." *State Tax Notes* 1, no. 14 (December 1991): 483–93.

Rueben, Kim. "The Repeal of the Deductibility of State and Local Taxes and the Impact on State and Local Governments." Conference on Federal Tax Reform and the States, Washington, DC, May 18, 2005. http://www.taxpolicycenter.org.

Simons, Henry Calvert. *Personal Income Taxation: The Definition of Income as a Problem of Fiscal Policy.* Chicago: University of Chicago Press, 1938.

Tannenwald, Robert. "The Subsidy from State and Local Deductibility: Trends, Methodological Issues, and Its Value after Tax Reform." Working Paper 97-9-1997. Boston: Federal Reserve Bank of Boston, 1997.

U.S. Census Bureau. *Current Housing Reports, Series H15/01, American Housing Survey for the United States: 2001.* Washington, DC: GPO, 2002.

U.S. Census Bureau, Governments Division. *State and Local Government Finance Estimates, by State: various years.* Washington, DC: U.S. Bureau of the Census. http://www.census.gov/govs/.

U.S. Congress, Joint Committee on Taxation. "General Explanation of the Tax Reform Act of 1986 (H.R. 3838, 99th Congress, PL 99-514)." JCS-10-87. Washington, DC: GPO, 1987.

———. "Estimates of Federal Tax Expenditures for Fiscal Years 2004–2008." JCS-08-03. Washington, DC: GPO, 2003.

———. "Estimates of Federal Tax Expenditures for Fiscal Years 2005–2009." JCS-01-05. Washington, DC: GPO, 2005.

Cross-references: alternative minimum tax; fairness in taxation; itemized deductions; retail sales tax, state and local; property tax, real property, residential; tax exportation; tax reform, federal; tax reform, state.

State formula apportionment

Kelly Edmiston
Federal Reserve Bank of Kansas City

Empirical evidence suggests that changes in apportionment weights (sales, property, payroll) for the state corporate income taxes affect firms' choices of employment and investment and other state revenue sources.

U.S. states and most Canadian provinces use a formulary method to apportion the total taxable income of multistate corporations that is not otherwise specifically allocated to the domicile state—for example, as in the case of income from investments and some other sources that do not arise in "ordinary business"—among the different jurisdictions (e.g., states) in which a firm operates (has nexus). In the United States, three factors are used to make this allocation, with the attribution of income to each state based on the relative distribution of the firm's gross receipts (sales), employee compensation (payroll), and property in that state (see *apportionment*). In adopting this formula apportionment method, the three "apportionment factors" may be weighted either equally or differentially. With equal weighting, each factor has a 33⅓ degree of "importance" in the apportionment of the firm's total multistate income. Differential weights may assign greater or lesser weight to one or more of the three factors (including assigning a zero weight).

Economic implications

To the extent that tax rates and/or apportionment factor weights vary across jurisdictions, formula-apportioned corporate income taxes (or as in the case of Michigan, formula-apportioned taxes on value-added) are similar in their incidence to a set of implicit excise taxes on the apportionment factors. That is, they mimic the effects of sales taxes, payroll taxes, and property taxes. Thus, placing a relatively greater weight on the sales factor (with commensurate reductions in property and payroll factor weights) would diminish the excise tax effect on in-state land and labor. The argument thus goes that firms with a large share of productive activity in the state relative to sales activity would see their tax liabilities diminish relative to sales-intensive firms, and hence, corporate income taxes would in some sense be exported to out-of-state enterprises. Beginning in the late 1970s, but increasingly since the early 1990s, several states have amended three-factor formulas to place a disproportionately heavy weight on the sales factor in hopes of reaping economic development gains and exporting more of the tax burden. At present, the most common formula places a double-weight on the sales factor, although several states now employ a single-factor sales formula (100 percent weight on sales).

These recent policy changes have generated an increasing amount of research designed to test whether heavier sales factor weights in corporate income tax apportionment formulas do indeed have a stimulative impact on payroll and property. The answer appears to be that there is some such effect. One study, for example, suggests that for the average state, reducing the payroll factor weight from one-third to one-fourth (double-weighted sales) results in a 1.1 percent increase in manufacturing employment (Goolsbee and Maydew 2000). Another shows that the elasticity of new capital expenditures with respect to the property burden (defined as the product of the property factor weight and the top statutory tax rate) to range between 0.05 and 0.35 (Gupta and Hoffman 2003). This means that a move from an equally weighted formula to a double-weighted sales formula (a 25 percent reduction in the burden) would be expected to increase new capital expenditures by 1.25 to 8.75 percent.

Other research suggests that while moving to a heavier sales factor weight is production-enhancing for any state in isolation, and was production-enhancing for the average state over the time periods covered in the previously noted studies, the economic development effects may be markedly dampened as more states move to heavier sales factor weights, and there is a clear first-mover advantage (Edmiston 2002). For some states, the stimulative impact is moderated by changes in other states but remains positive, while other states would be better off if all states maintained a uniform three-factor formula. The stimulative impact also varies substantially across states, depending on the statutory corporate income tax rate, industrial structure, and the size of the state.

Revenue implications

The corporate income tax revenue impact of apportionment policies can be either positive or negative, depending on the sales or production intensity of corporations in the state and on the relative strengths of static and dynamic revenue effects.

The immediate or static effect of placing a greater weight on the sales factor depends on whether multistate corporations in the state are relatively sales- or production-intensive. If they are relatively sales-intensive, meaning that the state accounts for relatively more of the national sales of multistate corporations than of their national production, weighted by profits, the immediate effect will be to increase corporate income tax collections, because the share of national income apportioned to the state will be higher under the new formula. Likewise, if multistate corporations are relatively production-intensive in the state, the share of national income apportioned to the state will decrease, and thus the immediate revenue effect will be negative. This effect is complicated by nexus rules. Under PL 86-272, states are not allowed to tax the income of multistate corporations for which the only activity in the state is sales, or activities ancillary to sales. This law makes a negative immediate revenue impact more likely.

Once the change in the apportionment formula is made, dynamic revenue effects come into play. These effects arise because a greater weight on the sales factor vis-à-vis productive factors encourages the location of payroll and property in the state and discourages sales in the state. Additional payroll and property will increase the share of multistate corporate income apportioned to the state, while decreases in sales will have the opposite effect. In the case of double-weighted sales, this dynamic effect will be revenue positive only if the resulting average increase in state payroll and property shares outweighs the decrease in the state's share of national sales. In the case of single-factor sales formulas, this dynamic effect will always be revenue negative because payroll and property factors are assigned zero weight in the formula. Simulations suggest that the one-time static effect on revenues tends to outweigh the dynamic effects of increased payroll and property and decreased sales (Edmiston 2002). The overall revenue effect thus may be positive or negative, depending on the specific state undertaking the policy change and its relative sales and production intensities.

Revenue impacts on other tax bases are also likely, and over the long term, may be more significant than the impact on corporate income tax collections. Increased payroll directly expands the base of the individual income tax and indirectly expands the sales tax base, while increased property in the state expands the property tax base and may modestly expand the individual income tax and sales tax bases, depending on the location of property owners. Finally, decreased sales would likely diminish the sales tax base. A study for the state of Georgia suggests that the revenue gained from increased individual income tax collections would more than offset negative consequences on the corporate income tax base there (Edmiston, 2004).

ADDITIONAL READINGS

Edmiston, Kelly D. "Strategic Apportionment of the State Corporate Income Tax." *National Tax Journal* 55 (June 2002): 239–62.

———. "Single Factor Sales Apportionment in Georgia: What Is the Net Revenue Effect?" *State Tax Notes* 31 (January 12, 2004): 107–11.

Federation of Tax Administrators. "State Apportionment of Corporate Income." http://www.taxadmin.org/fta/rate/corp_app.html.

Goolsbee, Austan, and Edward L. Maydew. "Coveting Thy Neighbor's Manufacturing: The Dilemma of State Income Apportionment." *Journal of Public Economics* 75 (January 2000): 125–43.

Gupta, Sanjay, and Mary Ann Hofmann. "The Effect of State Income Tax Apportionment and Tax Incentives on New Capital Expenditures." *Journal of the American Taxation Association* 25 (2003 Supplement): 1–26.

Cross-references: apportionment; income tax, corporate, state and local; nexus; throwback rules, multistate corporations; value-added tax, state; unitary taxation.

Subchapter S corporation

George A. Plesko
MIT Sloan School of Management

An incorporated business that, having met certain eligibility requirements and made an effective federal tax election, is generally not subject to the federal corporate-level income tax.

The income (and losses) of a Subchapter S corporation flow through to shareholders as they are realized by the entity, much like a partnership rather than a corporation. As a general principle, actual distributions of dividends to shareholders are received free of tax up to the basis of each shareholder in his or her shares. These corporations continue to share all other attributes of incorporated entities (e.g., separate legal entity, limited liability, unlimited life).

Subchapter S of the Internal Revenue Code (§ 1361 through § 1379), for and by which these corporations are named and governed, was enacted in 1958 and substantially revised in 1982 and 1996. The basic eligibility requirements to be met by a Subchapter S corporation are (1) that it be a U.S. corporation with no more than 75 shareholders, with married couples counting as a single shareholder, (2) that only individuals may be shareholders, with the exception of some estates and trusts, (3) that it may not have a nonresident alien as a shareholder, (4) that it may have only one class of stock, and (5) that it may not be a bank that uses the reserve method of accounting for bad debts; an insurance company or a member of an affiliated group; or any of certain other types of corporations. Individual states set their own rules for the state income tax treatment of S corporations, which range from full conformability to federal rules to the non-recognition of

S corporations, which subjects all of the entity's income to the state corporate income tax.

An S election requires the unanimous consent of shareholders. Unlike C corporations, S corporations must generally use a calendar-year tax year, but may choose either the cash or the accrual method of accounting. Unlike C corporation shareholders, an S corporation employee who owns more than 2 percent of the corporation's stock will face partnership treatment of fringe benefits.

Additional taxes may apply to C corporations converting to S corporations. A C corporation that used last in, first out in its inventory accounting will have to pay a recapture tax. If the corporation has carryovers of net operating losses or tax credits, they cannot be used by the S corporation. An S corporation that was a C corporation may also be taxed on its passive income (e.g., interest, dividends, rents, and royalties) if it has Subchapter C earnings and profits at the time of conversion. A final issue in the conversion decision is the "built-in gains" tax of IRC § 1374, enacted in 1986. This provision requires an S corporation to pay a corporate level tax on any pre-conversion Subchapter C "built-in" gains if they are realized within 10 years of the conversion. (Conversions that took place before 1987 remain subject to an earlier form of the rule that contained a three-year recognition period.)

While an S corporation can voluntarily revoke its status at any time, care must be exercised to ensure that S treatment is not involuntarily terminated. Involuntary termination can take place if the corporation fails to continuously meet the eligibility requirements listed above. A voluntary revocation during the first two and one-half months of a tax year is effective for that year; otherwise it will take effect at the beginning of the next taxable year. A termination becomes effective on the date the firm violates any of the eligibility requirements. A firm that either revokes or terminates its S status cannot elect to become an S corporation again for five years (although relief can be granted for accidental termination). This prohibits firms from making frequent changes to take advantage of the differing tax treatments accorded S and C corporations.

Subchapter S is an attractive option for startup firms that are able to meet the eligibility requirements. In the early years of operation, when firms are likely to have negative income, the losses would flow through to shareholders and be deducted against their individual income. Losses passed through to shareholders are deductible up to each individual's basis in the corporation's stock and debt. Losses in excess of basis can be carried forward to offset future Subchapter S income. The S corporation's income is taxable to the individual shareholder as it is received or accrued, regardless of whether the income is distributed (as in a partnership). The amount of income recognized by each shareholder increases his or her basis in the corporation. This basis affects the amount of distributions receivable tax-free. Unlike a partnership, all gains and losses must be allocated pro rata to each share.

For closely held corporations, S and C status can be used as part of a tax-minimizing strategy. In the case of loss cor-

porations, S is preferred because the losses can be immediately deducted at the individual level. For profitable corporations, election of S status would eliminate the corporate-level tax. However, in some cases (particularly before the Tax Reform Act of 1986), an S election may subject the income to an individual tax rate that is higher than the corporate rate. In 1986, the maximum tax rates were 46 percent for corporations and 50 percent for individuals (as recently as 1981 individual tax rates were 70 percent). When shareholder rates are higher than the corporate rate, a strategy of paying the corporate tax as a C corporation and not distributing income to shareholders may result in less tax paid in the current year, and a deferral of the individual tax. If capital gains are more favorably taxed than ordinary income, the deferral of income also benefits from lower tax rates if it is ultimately recognized through a sale of the stock in the corporation. There are various strategies to remove income from the taxable corporate sector without paying two levels of tax. Because these are closely held corporations, managers and employees of the firm may also be shareholders. Thus, payments of wages and salaries, deductible at the corporate level, will be taxed only once when received by individuals (and not at all in the case of some benefits). In addition, subject to some constraints, the corporation could reduce its exposure to the corporate tax by borrowing from its shareholders because interest payments (and rents and royalties) are deductible at the corporate level (Plesko 1994; Cloyd, Limberg, and Robinson 1997; Ayers, Cloyd, and Robinson 2001).

After the Tax Reform Act of 1986, the maximum individual and corporate marginal tax rates were reduced, with the maximum corporate rate (34 percent) higher than that for individuals (28 percent). This made C corporations less attractive as a means of minimizing taxes. Since 1986, the use of S corporations has expanded dramatically, even though in 1993 the maximum individual federal income tax rates were raised above the maximum corporate rate. An S election eliminates one of the two taxes, amounting to integration of the corporate and shareholder taxes by election.

S corporations grew from 6.2 percent of corporate returns in 1960 to 20.1 percent in 1980 and 24.1 percent in 1986. After the Tax Reform Act of 1986, the growth in S corporations was dramatic, increasing to 1,575,092 of the 3,716,650 corporate returns filed in 1990 (42.4 percent). This growth continued to the end of the decade, with S corporations representing 55.2 percent of all corporate returns filed in 1999. Accompanying the growth in the number of S corporations is their share of corporate economic activity. Before 1986, S corporations were responsible for less than 6 percent of business receipts, increasing to 10.1 percent in 1987. In 1999, S corporations were responsible for 17.5 percent of total receipts. Despite these increases in returns, S corporations remain a small proportion of corporate assets: in 1999, 3.9 percent of corporate assets were in S corporations.

While 35 was, until the 1996 legislation, the maximum number of shareholders allowed under federal law, the constraint seemed to affect only a small percentage of firms; the typical firm had fewer than three shareholders and more than 90 percent of firms had 10 or fewer (Nelson 1992; Plesko 1994). In 1999, the average S corporation had $597,515 in assets, compared with an average of approximately $18.0 million for non-S corporations. Eighteen percent of S corporations are in wholesale and retail trade, and 14.6 percent in professional, scientific, and technical services. Nelson (1993) and Plesko (1995) provide data on the characteristics of business corporations after the Tax Reform Act of 1986.

Limited liability corporations (LLCs) and limited liability partnerships (LLPs) have become popular alternatives to S corporations. Recognized in nearly all 50 states, these entities offer the same benefits of limited liability and pass-through tax treatment as S corporations but have fewer operational restrictions. For example, LLCs have no limits on the number of shareholders or classes of stocks.

ADDITIONAL READINGS

Ayers, Benjamin C., C. Bryan Cloyd, and John R. Robinson. "Organizational Form and Taxes: An Empirical Analysis of Small Businesses." *Journal of the American Taxation Association* 18 (Supplement, 1996): 49–67.

———. "The Influence of Income Taxes on the Use of Inside and Outside Debt By Small Businesses." *National Tax Journal* 54 (March 2001): 27–56.

Cloyd, C. Bryan, Stephen T. Limberg, and John R. Robinson. "The Impact of Federal Taxes on the Use of Debt by Closely Held Corporations." *National Tax Journal* 50 (June 1997): 261–77.

Hodder, Leslie D., Mary Lea McAnally, and Connie D. Weaver. "The Influence of Tax and Non-Tax Factors on Banks' Choice of Organizational Form." *The Accounting Review* 78, no. 1 (January 2003): 297–325.

Internal Revenue Service. *Corporation Income Tax Returns*. Publication 16. Washington, DC: U.S. Government Printing Office, various years.

McNulty, J. K. *Federal Income Taxation of S Corporations*. Westbury, NY: Foundation Press, 1992.

Nelson, Susan C. "S Corporations since the Tax Reform Act of 1986." *Proceedings of the Eighty-Fourth Annual Conference, Williamsburg, 1991* (18–24). Columbus, OH: NTA-TIA, 1992.

———. "S Corporations: The Record of Growth after Tax Reform." *Journal of S Corporation Taxation* 5 (Fall 1993): 138–61.

Omer, Thomas C., George A. Plesko, and Marjorie K. Shelley. "The Influence of Tax Costs on Organizational Choice in the Natural Resource Industry." *The Journal of the American Taxation Association* 22, no. 1 (2000): 38–55.

Petska, T. B., and R. A. Wilson. "Trends in Business Structure and Activity, 1980–1990." *SOI Bulletin* 13 (Spring 1994): 27–72.

Plesko, George A. "Corporate Taxation and the Financial Characteristics of Firms." *Public Finance Quarterly* (July 1994): 311–34.

———. "Gimme Shelter? Closely Held Corporations since Tax Reform." *National Tax Journal* 48 (September 1995): 409–16.

Cross-references: dividends, double taxation of; income tax, corporate, federal; income tax, federal; integration, corporate tax; partnerships; proprietorships.

Sumptuary taxes

Bruce F. Davie
Department of the Treasury

Updated by
Dennis Zimmerman
Congressional Budget Office

Excise taxes intended to discourage the consumption of specific commodities or services.

The term sumptuary taxation has gone out of fashion. An earlier generation of writers used the term to categorize taxes imposed for moral or religious reasons. Contemporary economists would describe a tax intended to discourage consumption of a specific commodity as adjusting for a negative externality. Politicians and journalists might use the term "sin taxes."

Excise taxes have been and are widely used by governments to discourage consumption of specific commodities; taxes on alcoholic beverages and tobacco products are the obvious examples. Using the old-fashioned term "sumptuary tax" helps to clarify thinking about excise taxes of this sort. The need for clarity is illustrated by the literature regarding cigarette taxes and smoking. Those who view tobacco taxes as instruments for adjusting for externalities are interested in measuring the negative externalities and reaching a conclusion about whether the tax, as a policy instrument for increasing the price by an amount that corresponds to the measured externalities, is too high, too low, or about right. Those who view cigarette taxes from a sumptuary stance argue for taxes above the externality-adjusting level because they regard protection of every individual's health a public policy obligation. In this view, it is a moral imperative to reduce consumption below what would occur when consumers are fully aware of the risks of smoking and cigarette prices include measured externalities.

Both advocates of externality-adjusting excise taxes and advocates of sumptuary taxes would agree that the revenue generated by the tax is not a primary objective. Similarly, they would agree that the distribution of either tax among taxpayers classified by income or consumption levels is largely irrelevant. For both, the object of the tax is to get the gross-of-tax price "right."

Sumptuary taxes set "too high" verge upon prohibition through the tax system rather than by regulation. Because the social costs of prohibition can be significant—for example, the costs of controlling smuggling and illicit domestic production and distribution—a sumptuary tax rate that is in some sense optimal is not a rate that minimizes consumption. Clearly, sumptuary taxation involves issues that go well beyond traditional tax analysis.

The United States has a long history of sumptuary taxation of alcoholic beverages and tobacco products mixed with revenue-raising objectives. The first domestic tax, enacted by the United States in 1791, was on distilled spirits at rates ranging from 7 to 18 cents per gallon depending on the alcohol content, or proof, of the liquor, and was imposed on the distiller. The first secretary of the Treasury, Alexander Hamilton, sought a revenue source not dependent on foreign trade. Sumptuary motives were also involved. As Hamilton put it, "The consumption of ardent spirits particularly, no doubt very much on account of their cheapness, is carried on to an extreme, which is truely to be regretted, as well in regard to the health and morals, as to the economy of the community (quoted in Forsythe 1977, 40). The tax was resisted in western Pennsylvania and other areas where whiskey was used as a medium of exchange. In 1794, troops had to be called out to put down the "Whiskey Rebellion." The military operation was successful in establishing the power of the new government to collect taxes, but the tax continued to be unpopular. Soon after the Jeffersonians took power, the whiskey tax was repealed. It was reenacted briefly during the War of 1812 and then not again until the Civil War, primarily as a revenue-raising measure. At the time, only a few members of Congress argued for the tax on sumptuary grounds. During the 1860s taxes were also imposed on beer, tobacco products, and wine, but again, sumptuary objectives were secondary to revenue. Taxes on alcoholic beverages and tobacco products have been part of the federal taxes ever since the Civil War. The sumptuary character of these taxes, and of similar state and local taxes, seems to form a substantial part of their continuing public acceptance.

The 10 percent tax on wagers on sporting events, elections, and contests enacted in 1951 might be regarded as a sumptuary tax. Its intent was to aid law enforcement efforts aimed at illegal bookmaking. The rate was reduced to 2 percent in 1974 and, in the case of legal wagers such as sports betting in Nevada, to 0.25 percent in 1982. Exemptions are provided for state lotteries, state-sanctioned horse races, and similar events. Given the low rate on legal wagers and the broad exemptions, the tax on wagers seems to have a role only in enforcement of laws against illegal bookmaking and thus is not truly sumptuary.

Sumptuary taxes present special administrative problems because they are typically high relative to the value of the product, increasing the payoff for successful tax evasion. The enforcement problem is further complicated by the typical rules allowing the product to be exported or used for a purpose other than human consumption on a tax-free basis. For these reasons, sumptuary taxes involve systems of inspection and control not typical of other excise taxes.

Structuring a tax to accomplish a sumptuary objective also presents difficulties. Instead of an ad valorem tax, taxes on liquor and tobacco are usually in rem taxes based on volume and weight, respectively. For example, the U.S. tax on distilled spirits applicable in 2004 was $13.50 per proof gallon; wine was taxed at rates ranging from $1.07 to $3.15 per gallon, depending on alcohol content, with wines having an alcohol content of more than 24 percent taxed like distilled spirits; beer was taxed at a rate of $18 per 31-gallon barrel; and champagne at $3.40 per gallon. In terms of alcohol content, the distilled spirits tax results in a tax of about 21 cents per ounce, the beer tax about 10 cents per ounce, and the wine tax about 8 cents per ounce. These differences seem to reflect political judgments about the relative degree to which sumptuary taxes should be imposed on different classes of alcoholic beverages. Because these taxes are not structured solely on alcohol content, definitional problems continually emerge as new products come on the market. Inflation has the effect of eroding the real value of in rem taxes. Despite ad hoc increases in tax rates on alcohol and tobacco, in real terms U.S. rates were generally lower in 2004 than in 1951.

ADDITIONAL READINGS

Congressional Budget Office. *Federal Taxation of Tobacco, Alcoholic Beverages, and Motor Fuels.* Washington, D.C.: Congressional Budget Office, June 1990.

Cook, Phillip J., and Michael Moore. "This Tax's for You: The Case for Higher Beer Taxes." *National Tax Journal* 47, no. 3 (September 1994): 559–74.

DeCicca, Philip, Donald Kenkel, and Alan Mathios. "Putting Out the Fires: Will Higher Taxes Reduce the Onset of Youth Smoking?" *Journal of Political Economy* 110, no. 1 (February 2002): 144–69.

Forsythe, Dall W. *Taxation and Political Change in the Young Nation, 1781–1833.* New York: Columbia University Press, 1977.

Gravelle, Jane, and Dennis Zimmerman. "Cigarette Taxes to Fund Health Care Reform." *National Tax Journal* 47, no. 3 (September 1994): 575–90.

Smith, Harry Edwin. *The United States Federal Internal Tax History from 1861 to 1871.* Boston: Houghton Mifflin, 1914.

Viscusi, W. Kip. *Smoking: Making the Risky Decision.* New York: Oxford University Press, 1992.

Cross-references: elasticity, demand and supply; excess burden; luxury taxes; retail sales tax, state; revenue elasticity (tax elasticity); severance tax, state; tobacco taxes.

T

Tax

Victor Thuronyi
International Monetary Fund

A compulsory contribution to government imposed in order to raise revenue.

It can be difficult to pin down in specific cases what is and what is not a "tax." Classification can be attempted from a legal or an economic point of view. The legal definition of tax depends on the context and the legal system. Typical elements that define a tax are that it is compulsory (in distinction to voluntary payments, particularly for a service provided by government), required by law (although sometimes the issue is whether a particular charge is in the nature of a tax and hence illegal because it is not imposed by a law as required), made to the government for revenue purposes (thus distinguishing it from "nontax revenues" such as fines, penalties, and regulatory charges) and not made in return for a service or other benefit (thus distinguishing it from fees).

In economic terms, any appropriation of resources from individuals or firms by the government can be considered a tax. For example, economists frequently talk about the inflation tax, since inflation appropriates resources to the government. Legally, though, it is clear that inflation is not a tax since it does not involve a payment by the taxpayer to the government. Similarly, regulatory requirements can have the same economic consequence as taxes. For example, a legal requirement for employers to provide health insurance to their employees may have the same economic effect as a tax imposed on the employer; the revenues from this requirement are used to provide health benefits to employees. For purposes of economic analysis, the two are equivalent, but from a legal point of view they are not. Public finance economists therefore do not spend much time discussing whether a particular levy is a "tax" or not (for example, the question is addressed only tangentially in Musgrave and Musgrave [1989]).

From a budgeting point of view, revenues must be classified as taxes or as either a tax or nontax revenue (IMF 2001). Perhaps more problematic is budgeting for tax expenditures. While tax revenues are conventionally recorded in the budget, net of tax expenditures, this is conceptually arbitrary and causes the apparent size of government to differ depending on whether certain programs are carried out as expenditure programs or by tax expenditures.

Depending on the context, form may not be decisive for classification. A fine or other regulatory measure may take the form of a tax, yet not satisfy the above definition of a tax (e.g., the tax on self-dealing for private foundations in Internal Revenue Code section 4941). On the other hand, the fine may legally be a tax, at least as far as applying the rules of tax procedure is concerned. Names of taxes also vary. Customs duties are taxes, although they are not called taxes. Other names for taxes are excise, impost, levy, cess, and rate.

Some fees (or taxes) are hybrids, in that the amount of the fee is disproportionate to the cost of the benefit provided—for example, a registration fee for transferring real property. Economically, this might be viewed as part tax and part charge for a service.

As an abstract concept, "tax" is somewhat malleable. This may not be troubling but for the fact that in different legal contexts (e.g., the Constitution, trade law, the foreign tax credit provisions, or contracts) it may be critical whether a particular payment is considered a tax. The answer may differ according to the context and the country in which the question is asked. In many civil law countries, tax is a subset of a broader category of required contributions that include fees and special contributions. While the United States considers Social Security contributions taxes, many countries do not because they entitle the payer to a benefit.

ADDITIONAL READINGS

International Monetary Fund [IMF]. *Government Finance Statistics Manual.* Washington, DC: IMF, 2001.

Musgrave, Richard A., and Peggy B. Musgrave. *Public Finance in Theory and Practice.* New York: McGraw-Hill Education, 1989.

Westin, Richard A. *Lexicon of Tax Terminology.* Arlington, VA: Tax Analysts, 1989.

Cross-references: inflation tax; tax and revenue effort; tax illusion; tax price; user charges, federal; zakat.

Tax abatement programs

Dick Netzer
Urban Research Center

Most states and many local governments offer some type of business tax reduction to selectively promote an economic activity. These incentives come in various forms, such as income tax credits, sales tax exemptions or rate reductions, and, most commonly, full or partial forgiveness of the local property tax for some period of years on real estate that is being rehabilitated or developed. The efficiency benefits of such abatements are the topic of considerable debate and empirical examination.

Tax incentives to foster the economic behavior preferred by legislative bodies take on a variety of forms and names—exemptions, deductions, credits, and abatements. The last ordinarily refer to time-limited reductions, possibly to zero, in the increase in tax liability that would otherwise be triggered by the economic action being encouraged. However, state and local government policymakers are not rigid in their nomenclature, and the term "abatement" is frequently used to describe tax incentive programs that are called by other names in most places. Moreover, time-limited reductions in tax liability may be made permanent by changes in the law or by repeated extensions of the original period.

The great majority of states have programs for the abatement of some state or local taxes. Usually, but not invariably, it is local—rather than state—taxes that are abated, and for the most part, the programs concern local property taxes. The typical form of the abatement—say, to encourage new office building construction in an older central business district—is the following: the assessed value of the land underlying the new building is frozen at the time the abatement is requested (the almost universal undervaluation of sites by American local assessors ensures that this value will be a low one) for a specified number of years, and the taxes on the new building are abated at a declining rate over that period. At the end of the period, the property becomes fully taxpaying.

Some programs are highly automatic, or "as-of-right." Once an official agency determines that the action of the taxpayer (construction of a new building or purchase of equipment ordinarily subject to the state sales tax, for example) qualifies, both the amount of the tax reductions and their timing are set, with no administrative discretion. Other programs involve considerable negotiation about the specific expenditures that are eligible, the size of the tax reduction, and even the schedule. In some cases, a state government agency must approve local government actions. "As-of-right" provisions tend to be more common for programs designed to encourage housing investment than for those concerned with business investment decisions, and more common for investments located in specific places, such as old industrial sections of large cities, that are the objects of local economic development policy (see *enterprise zones*).

Informal tax abatement by local assessors—by simply neglecting to list new buildings on the tax rolls for a year or two, or more—is as old as the American property tax. Indeed, that, along with systematic undervaluation, was the predominant instrument of economic development policy in smaller cities and towns for many decades. The first major formal tax abate-

ment programs appear to have developed in New York State in the 1920s, to encourage the construction of new housing. One program, confined to New York City, provided for an abatement schedule that began at 100 percent for new owner-occupied housing; another was the first in a long series of tax abatement programs for new construction and major rehabilitation of multifamily housing.

More than 30 states authorize property tax abatements for new business investment, in most cases focusing on the manufacturing industry (National Association of State Development Agencies 2002). Smaller numbers authorize abatements for investment in specified types of housing—in either residential or nonresidential urban renewal areas—and in the preservation of historic properties. A few abate sales tax on purchases of specific business equipment or other intermediate business purchases. Also, there are numerous abatements specific to a single industry, like shipbuilding or railroads (in New York State, the abatement is termed an "exemption," but the size of the exemption is inversely related to the railroad's net operating income, and it changes each year).

In most places, the revenue losses associated with tax abatements are quite small relative to total tax revenue (the costs are usually estimated on the assumption that economic behavior is unaffected by the tax incentive, which, of course, is not the intent of the program [see *tax expenditures*]). For example, revenue losses in the state of Washington from time-limited economic development property tax abatements in the 1991–93 biennium were estimated at less than 0.05 percent of total property tax levies (Washington State Department of Revenue 1992a, 1992b). At the other extreme, time-limited property tax abatements in New York City were valued at roughly 7.1 percent of the total tax levy; three-quarters of the abatements were for housing and the rest for commercial and industrial property (New York City Department of Finance 1993). Economists generally have been skeptical about the efficacy of tax abatement programs in achieving policy goals. For housing tax abatements, the goal is to expand the supply of housing services, that being a final, rather than intermediate, product. For tax abatements designed to promote local economic development, the intermediate product is increased business investment in a community and the final product is increased local employment, income, and—ultimately—tax revenue. The key empirical questions are (1) how much of the tax abatements are captured by investments and other economic actions that are truly induced by the program, rather than actions that would have occurred in its absence; (2) whether, in the case of economic development incentives, there really are those final products in the form of increased income; and (3) whether the tax-favored investments impose large external costs, such as new infrastructure requirements, within the local jurisdiction.

The most important question is the first one; the answer largely determines both the benefits and costs of a tax abatement program. Most of the program costs are likely to consist of the taxes forgone on the investment that would have occurred in any case; the taxes forgone on the induced investment are not costs in any economic sense.

The empirical evidence is sketchy (Wolkoff 1985; Netzer 1991; Wassmer 1992; Coffman 1993; Anderson and Wassmer 2000; Buss 2001). This is not surprising, in view of the difficulty of specifying the independent policy variable for use in multivariate analysis across taxing jurisdictions and finding enough observations. It is hard enough to estimate the locational effects of differentials and changes in the level and nature of general state–local taxes (see *business location, taxation and*), but a typical state tax policy regression study will use straightforward tax policy variables like effective rates of the major taxes, top marginal rates, and measures of the total tax burden and can rely on the fact that the major taxes apply more or less uniformly to a vast number of firms. In contrast, with regard to economic development tax abatements, there is considerable interstate variation in the specific provisions of similar-sounding measures, and rates of participation in similar programs differ greatly over time and place, with resulting variation in the composition of those firms that do participate.

In rare instances, such as projects in the form of real estate developments, separately incorporated with sale of the equity interest fairly soon after the physical investment has been put in place, rates of return with and without the tax abatement subsidy can be calculated, yielding reliable conclusions about the causal role of the subsidy (White 1983).

Another approach has been used in some studies: calculating the break-even point—that is, the proportion of the increase in investment or employment experienced (or promised) by the firms receiving the subsidy that must be induced by the subsidy if the benefits are to equal the costs of the subsidy. If the break-even point is very low, then it really is not important to worry about the other causes for the new investment; if the break-even point is very high, then the assumption must be that the program will not be cost-effective.

One consideration in measuring cost-effectiveness of tax abatement policy is the level of government from whose perspective the analysis is performed. In one study, the break-even point for the local government was an encouraging 8.8 percent, but that included substantial increases in state school aid to offset the local tax losses. When that possibility was excluded, the break-even point rose to a very discouraging 41.7 percent (Morse and Farmer 1986).

In general, the empirical analyses of tax abatement programs for economic development purposes show negative results: most tax abatements do accrue to investments that would have been made in the absence of the tax incentives. The empirical evidence on housing tax abatements is more ambiguous, and there do seem to be strong effects on the timing of housing investments for those programs that are expected to be temporary.

There is, nonetheless, an economic logic to property tax abatements for new investment: Local property taxes at a given rate will have a far stronger negative effect on new investment than on old investment. This is a point of special importance for those jurisdictions that habitually impose differentially high effective tax rates on investment in new commercial and multifamily residential structures, a practice that continues in a number of states.

ADDITIONAL READINGS

Anderson, John E., and Robert W. Wassmer. *Bidding for Business: The Efficacy of Local Economic Development Incentives in a Metropolitan Area.* Kalamazoo, MI: W.E. Upjohn Institute, 2000.

Burman, Leonard, Elaine Maag, and Jeff Rohaly. "The Effect of the 2001 Tax Cut on Low- and Middle-Income Families and Children." Washington, DC: The Urban Institute, 2002.

Buss, Terry. "The Effect of State Tax Incentives on Economic Growth and Firm Location Decisions: An Overview of the Literature." *Economic Development Quarterly* 30 (February 2001): 90–105.

Coffman, Richard B. "Tax Abatements and Rent-Seeking." *Urban Studies* 30 (April 1993): 593–98.

Durchslag, Melvyn R. "Property Tax Abatement for Low-Income Housing: An Idea Whose Time May Never Arrive." *Harvard Journal on Legislation* 30 (Summer 1993): 367–82.

McDonald, J. F. "An Economic Analysis of Local Inducements for Business." *Journal of Urban Economics* 13 (November 1983): 322–33.

Menezes, Marco, and Lawrence W. Morgan. "P.A. 198: Michigan's Industrial Property Tax Abatement Law: Fortuity or Futility?" *Cooley Law Review* 7 (1990): 139–77.

Morgan, W. E., and M. M. Hackbart. "An Analysis of State and Local Industrial Tax Exemption Programs." *Southern Economic Journal* 41 (October 1974): 200–5.

Morse, G. W., and M. C. Farmer. "Location and Investment Effects of a Tax Abatement Program." *National Tax Journal* 39 (June 1986): 229–36.

National Association of State Development Agencies. *Directory of Incentives for Business Investment and Development in the United States: A State by State Guide.* Woodbridge, VA: National Association of State Development Agencies, 2002.

Netzer, Dick. "An Evaluation of Interjurisdictional Competition through Economic Development Incentives." In *Competition among States and Local Governments: Efficiency and Equity in American Federalism,* edited by Daphne A. Kenyon and John Kincaid (221–45). Washington, DC: Urban Institute Press, 1991.

New York City Department of Finance. *Annual Report on Tax Expenditures, Fiscal Year 1993.* November 1993.

Reese, Laura A. "Municipal Fiscal Health and Tax Abatement Policy." *Economic Development Quarterly* 5 (February 1991): 23–32.

Washington State Department of Revenue. *Tax Exemptions—1992.* Olympia: Washington State Department of Revenue, January 1992 (1992a).

———. *Tax Statistics 1991.* Olympia: Washington State Department of Revenue, March 1992 (1992b).

Wassmer, Robert W. "Property Tax Abatement and the Simultaneous Determination of Local Fiscal Variables in a Metropolitan Area." *Land Economics* 68 (August 1992): 263–82.

White, Michelle J. "J51: Incentive, Subsidy, or Windfall?" *New York Affairs* 7, no. 4 (Winter/Spring 1983): 112–25.

Wolkoff, Michael J. "Chasing a Dream: The Use of Tax Abatements to Spur Urban Economic Development." *Urban Studies* 22 (August 1985): 305–15.

Zoeckler, Robert L. "The Tax Abatement Program for Historic Properties in Georgia." *Georgia State Bar Journal* 28 (February 1992): 129–33.

Cross-references: enterprise zones; property tax, real property, business; tax competition.

Taxable income, corporate

Michael McDonald
U.S. Treasury

Matthew Knittel
U.S. Treasury

The computed base of gross income less allowable deductions on which the federal (and state, for certain states that conform to federal statute) income tax rates are applied.

Corporations have been subject to income tax since 1913. Although the tax code has changed extensively in the past 90 years, the "classical" system of separate, and substantially unintegrated, individual and corporate income taxes has remained unchanged. This entry describes the tax-based measure of corporate profits, corporate taxable income. It defines the base of the corporate income tax, identifies its components, compares this profits measure to similar measures in financial accounting and national income accounts, and discusses recent historical trends.

Since 1987, corporations have computed two separate measures of taxable income—"regular" taxable income and taxable income under the corporate alternative minimum tax (AMT). This entry discusses regular taxable income.

Computing taxable income

To determine taxable income, corporations use Form 1120, the Corporate Income Tax Return. Income and deductions are reported separately, and many items require supporting forms and schedules.

Income

The corporate income tax classifies income into two broad categories: ordinary and capital gains. Ordinary income includes gross operating profit (gross sales less cost of goods sold), dividends, interest (except interest on certain municipal bonds), rents, royalties, and other miscellaneous income (e.g., fees). Most corporations must use accrual accounting for tax purposes and therefore recognize income when it is earned. To calculate cost of goods sold, corporations have some flexibility to choose the valuation of end-of-year inventory (at historical cost, market value or the lower of cost or market value), and the assumed flow of cost—last in, first out (LIFO); first in, first out (FIFO); or specific identification—to minimize tax liability.

Corporate capital gains are taxed when they are realized, not as they accrue. This is similar to the treatment of capital gains under the individual income tax. Also similar to individual tax treatment, capital gains may be netted against capital losses. Unlike the individual tax, however, capital losses cannot offset ordinary income, nor do they enjoy a preferential tax rate.

Deductions

Corporations are allowed deductions for the ordinary and necessary costs of doing business. The major components of these costs are salaries and wages, pension contributions, employee benefits, interest expenses, state and local taxes, rents, charitable contributions, bad debt losses, advertising expenses, tangible capital asset depreciation, and intangible asset amortization. For all but the last two deductions, corporations generally deduct these costs in the year the liability is incurred, as required under accrual accounting. When corporations purchase tangible capital assets (i.e., investment in plants, equipment, or structures), they are not allowed to deduct the full cost in the year of the acquisition. Instead, they use a permitted depreciation method (usually more accelerated than straight-line depreciation) over each asset's determined cost-recovery period to calculate the deduction. Corporations may generally amortize intangible assets, including goodwill, over 15 years.

Total income less total deductions

If total deductions exceed total income, then a corporation has negative net income, or a loss. This outcome has two implications. First, the corporation has no taxable income for the year. Second, the corporation may carry back the loss to offset any taxable income reported during the previous two years, and claim a refund for any taxes paid. If the corporation is unable to use the entire loss by this carryback, it may carry the remaining loss forward for up to 20 years to offset future taxable income. Losses that are carried forward to offset future taxable income are referred to as "net operating loss deductions."

If total income exceeds total deductions, then a corporation has positive net income and may take two additional deductions, called the special statutory deductions, to derive its taxable income. The first deduction is the intercorporate dividends received deduction (DRD). The DRD is equal to 70 percent for dividends attributable to "portfolio stock" (stock for which the corporation owns less than 20 percent), 100 percent for wholly-owned subsidiaries, and 80 percent for most other stock. The DRD is designed to limit the tax burden on corporate income. If corporations paid tax on dividends received from other corporations, that income would be taxed more than once at the corporate level. A 100 percent intercorporate DRD helps ensure that income is taxed only once at the corporate level.

The second deduction is the net operating loss deduction. Corporations may offset income with unused (i.e., carried forward) losses from previous years. The residual income after a corporation takes these two deductions is equal to taxable income.

Corporate taxable income versus other profit measures

Corporate taxable income is a measure of profits consistent with corporate tax law. Two other popular measures of corporate profits differ conceptually in certain ways from taxable income. These are "pretax book income," used in financial statements, and "corporate profits," used in the National Income and Product Accounts (NIPA).

Pretax book income

Corporations that publish financial statements for shareholders use generally accepted accounting principle (GAAP) rules to measure profits. Although pretax book income is similar to taxable income, they differ in some important ways. Unlike taxable income, pretax book income (1) includes certain unrealized capital gains and losses in income; (2) excludes the DRD and net operating loss deduction; (3) uses straight-line, rather than accelerated, depreciation for tangible assets; (4) includes certain tax-exempt income, such as interest from municipal bonds; and (5) allows a deduction for contributions to a bad debt reserve account, rather than a specific charge off. In addition, GAAP's rules for consolidating affiliated corporations differ from the tax law.

NIPA corporate profits

The NIPA seeks to measure the value of national output, called gross domestic product (GDP). One way to calculate GDP is by summing all income earned by various entities for a given calendar year. NIPA corporate profits is one the income component. Other income components include wages and salaries, supplements to wages and salaries, rental income, net interest income, and sole proprietor income.

Although NIPA corporate profits relate to, and can be reconciled with, corporate taxable income, the two profit measures are quite different. Unlike taxable income, NIPA corporate profits (1) values all depreciation and inventory at replacement cost, which prevents inflationary gains from being counted as income; (2) excludes capital gains income and intercorporate dividends; (3) includes income earned by certain federal agencies, primarily the Federal Reserve; (4) includes income earned by pass-through entities, primarily subchapter S corporations and real estate investment trusts, which are generally not subject to the corporate income tax; (5) includes an adjustment for the underreporting of corporate taxable income; and (6) includes state and local taxes, which corporations may deduct to determine taxable income. (Besides these six, there are about a dozen other comparatively minor differences between taxable income and NIPA corporate profits.)

Recent historical trends in taxable income

The Tax Reform Act of 1986 instituted significant changes to the corporate income tax base and rate. Since that Act, the corporate tax base has not changed appreciably. (Notable exceptions are the temporary changes to depreciation schedules allowed by the Job Creation and Worker Assistance Act of 2002 and the Jobs and Growth Tax Relief Reconciliation Act of 2003.) Between tax years 1988 and 2000, corporate taxable income (excluding negative income and pass-through entity income) increased 92 percent, from $448 billion to $859 billion. Although the average annual growth rate was 5.6 percent, growth rates varied considerably during this 13-year span. For tax years 1988–91, taxable income decreased 11 percent (average annual growth rate of −4 percent). For tax years 1991–2000, taxable income increased 114 percent (average annual growth rate of 9 percent). Because of the 2001 recession, corporate taxable income declined to $714 billion (−17 percent) for tax year 2001.

In addition to the inherent volatility of corporate taxable income, another notable trend during tax years 1988–2001 has been the relative popularity of pass-through entities: subchapter S corporations and real estate investment trusts. Although these entities file a corporate tax return, they generally do not remit corporate income taxes. Any income earned by these entities is passed through to shareholders who then remit any individual income tax that is due. From 1988 to 2001, taxable income of these pass-through entities increased at an average annual rate of 11.4 percent, from $59 billion to $240 billion. By comparison, the taxable income of C corporations that are taxable under the corporate income tax increased at an average annual rate of 3.6 percent. In general, the relative popularity of pass-through entity status has reduced the long-run growth of corporate taxable income below the growth rate of the economy as a whole, as measured by GDP (5.4 percent average annual growth rate).

ADDITIONAL READINGS

Steuerle, C. Eugene. *The Tax Decade.* Washington DC: Urban Institute Press, 1992.

———. *Contemporary U.S. Tax Policy.* Washington, DC: Urban Institute Press, 2004.

U.S. Department of Commerce, Bureau of Economic Analysis. *Corporate Profits: Profits before Tax, Profit Tax Liability, and Dividends.* Washington, DC: U.S. Department of Commerce, May 1985.

U.S. Department of the Treasury, Internal Revenue Service. *Source Book: Corporation Income Tax Returns.* Publication 1053. Various years.

Cross-references: alternative minimum tax, corporate; capital cost recovery; dividends, double taxation of; income tax, federal; inventory accounting; subchapter S corporation; state formula apportionment.

Tax administration mechanisms for intergovernmental cooperation

Harley T. Duncan
Federation of Tax Administrators

Charles E. McLure Jr.
Hoover Institution, Stanford University

Several cooperative agreements between state tax administrators and the Internal Revenue Service are designed to improve tax compliance and enforcement.

Despite the highly independent system of tax administration resulting from the sovereignty accorded the states by the U.S. Constitution, there are a number of cooperative arrangements between state and federal tax authorities and among various groups of states. These arrangements are aimed primarily at improving tax compliance and enforcement; relatively few address the administrative and compliance burdens faced by multistate taxpayers—a lacuna that has been the focus of recent criticism.

Each state has its own tax administration agency (commonly known as the department of revenue) that is responsible for collecting the taxes imposed by that state. State tax agencies are generally headed by individuals appointed by the governor, the elected chief executive of the state. In three states, the head of the tax agency is a statewide elected official, and several state revenue agencies are governed by a multimember commission appointed by the state's governor.

State tax agencies are usually organized around the core functions of tax administration rather than by type of tax. A revenue department has major organizational subunits devoted to identification and registration of taxpayers, processing of returns and remittances, taxpayer accounting, audit and enforcement, and taxpayer education and assistance, as well as various organizational support functions such as legal services, personnel, facilities, and information systems. For taxpayers desiring to adjudicate actions of the tax authority, there is at least one level of administrative appeal within the revenue agency, with rights of subsequent appeal to other administrative tribunals and the state judicial system.

Federal-state exchanges of information

The cornerstone of cooperative tax administration in the United States is an active exchange of information between federal and state tax authorities to support enforcement of the personal and corporation income tax. Federal law authorizes the U.S. Internal Revenue Service (IRS) to provide federal tax return information to state tax agencies, provided it is used solely for tax administration purposes and is properly safeguarded against unauthorized disclosure or release. (State tax statutes likewise authorize the exchange of return information with other states and with the federal government under appropriate

safeguards.) All states have entered into an exchange-of-information agreement with the IRS, through which they receive an abundance of tax information. Information exchanged includes copies of all federal audits or other adjustments to a taxpayer's return, identification of taxpayers filing a federal income tax return with an address in the receiving state, extracts of items of income and expense reported on the federal tax return, and information reports filed by third-party payers (e.g., banks, brokerage firms, and employers) with respect to taxpayers in a particular state.

Given the basic level of conformity between state and federal income tax bases, the information is often used to assess additional state tax directly. For example, one of the most effective information exchanges is an IRS program that matches third-party reports of income to entries on taxpayer returns. The IRS assesses additional federal tax where income has been omitted and provides information on the adjustment to the state tax authority where the taxpayer resides. The state customarily issues an automated assessment of additional state tax unless the income is exempted by the state. States also compare the exchanged data with state files to ensure consistency in amounts reported to federal and state tax authorities and to identify nonfiling taxpayers. With the massive amounts of information involved, nearly all information is exchanged on computer-readable or electronic media instead of paper.

Federal data and federal audit reports are the only, or at least the predominant, way to independently audit state individual income tax returns in many states. The rates of state individual income taxes (generally 5–8 percent of taxable income) are such that it is not cost-effective (particularly compared with the yield on audits of state corporation income taxes and retail sales taxes) to maintain a substantial cadre of state revenue agents to conduct on-site audits of individual income tax returns.

States also use the results of federal corporation tax audits for enforcement. Because the computation of state tax generally begins with federal taxable income, states rely extensively on federal examination activities for verification of the tax base and the proper treatment of various transactions, particularly those involving international operations. State agencies devote their audit activities primarily to verifying the apportionment of income across states, examining the taxpayer's treatment of certain types of transactions, and determining the membership of the unitary group if the state employs combined reporting.

In addition, states have recently gained access to data from other federal agencies to aid in tax enforcement activities. They receive regular reports from the U.S. Customs Service on imported goods that they use to identify goods to which the retail sales and use tax may apply or to identify potential taxpayers who may not be registered.

Historically, information flowed mostly from the federal government to the states. In recent years, however, states have begun providing more information to federal tax administrators. In particular, federal administrators use state lists of registered sales-tax payers to identify nonfilers of federal employment and corporation taxes and to cross-check reported receipts. Administrators also use files maintained by other state agencies that license individuals engaged in various trades and professions as a source of leads (e.g., on nonfilers). Finally, state driver's license files provide a good source of address information and potential assets in seizure situations. Here again, the data are exchanged under legal agreements regarding the use and safeguarding of the data, and most information is exchanged in computer-usable form.

There are relatively few instances in which the states and federal government conduct joint audits of individual taxpayers, except in the motor fuel excise tax area if earlier investigative work by either the federal or the state tax authority has revealed evidence of criminal tax evasion.

Cooperative efforts between state and federal agencies in the administration of excise taxes on alcoholic beverages or tobacco products are few, except for occasional working arrangements between individual agencies and local governments. Federal law, however, does require that manufacturers of tobacco products and alcoholic beverages provide reports to state tax authorities on all products shipped to wholesalers in the state. This practice helps ensure that tax is paid on all products entering the distribution chain in a particular state.

Likewise, little cooperation exists in the collection of delinquent tax obligations, even though a delinquent taxpayer may owe money to both state and federal authorities. This situation is often a source of friction between tax authorities, with one level attempting to assert priority over the other where resources are not sufficient to satisfy both obligations.

Since 2000, however, states have been able to participate in the federal Treasury Offset Program in which certain state individual income tax debts may be offset against (i.e., recovered from) federal income tax refunds that would otherwise be paid to the taxpayer. Nearly every income tax state participates in this program, which generates about $200 million in debt recoveries for the states each year. In addition, about 30 states provide a reciprocal service that allows the IRS to recover individual tax debts from state income tax refunds.

Cooperative taxpayer assistance

Beyond audit and enforcement efforts, state and federal tax authorities have undertaken a wide range of cooperative taxpayer service and education activities. Of particular note are cooperative or joint programs for providing training and education to tax practitioners and preparers as well as providing cooperative registration and filing assistance to new businesses. State and federal authorities often offer on-site taxpayer assistance at a single site.

The most ambitious effort builds on a computerized or electronic filing program begun by the IRS in the early 1990s. States were, at the same time, beginning to enter the electronic filing arena. To avoid duplicative efforts and simplify matters

for taxpayers, most states decided to enter into a cooperative filing effort with the IRS rather than develop their own individual filing program. At present, 38 states are participating in the joint Fed-State electronic filing program. Under the program, the federal and state individual income tax returns for persons using a participating tax preparer or approved tax preparation software can be filed in a single electronic transmission with the IRS, which in turn provides the state return to the appropriate state tax authority. In 2004, more than 30 million returns will be filed under this program.

Collaborative training efforts

A final area of collaboration between state and federal tax authorities is in training personnel. This cooperation takes three forms:

1. State tax agency personnel can take part in all IRS-sponsored training sessions if space is available. Personnel have access to a wide range of courses from short-term, specialized courses to more basic courses lasting several weeks (e.g., basic criminal investigation). This cooperation enables states to leverage the resources of the IRS to meet certain training needs when it would be impractical to develop state-level offerings.
2. State and federal tax authorities have sometimes jointly developed specialized training programs. Most recently, they cooperated in developing basic and advanced courses in motor fuel audit and investigation; more than 2,000 state and federal agents have attended the course since it was developed.
3. IRS personnel regularly participate, both as instructors and students, in training sessions conducted by state agencies or their representatives. For example, the Federation of Tax Administrators (FTA) sponsors training workshops and conferences on current tax administration topics and techniques for state agency personnel.

Procedures for cooperation

The way these cooperative tax administration activities are initiated, developed, and implemented is diverse and somewhat dependent on the nature of the initiative. Outside the information and data exchange area, cooperative efforts are often generated by individual state tax authorities working with IRS personnel in the same geographic or subject matter area. Representatives from the IRS and state tax agency regularly meet to examine ways to cooperate, and many individual initiatives grow out of such liaisons. Once developed and tested, these initiatives are likely to be replicated in other states. But the implementation of many efforts may not occur in all areas of the country.

A similar coordinative mechanism exists at the national level for efforts affecting all states. The FTA holds regular liaison sessions with the executive leadership of the IRS to discuss and coordinate cooperative activities. The IRS maintains a small national office staff (about 15 people) dedicated to assisting states in working with the IRS and in providing information on the types of cooperative activities conducted across the country. Numerous IRS staff throughout the country and in various functions devote at least part of their time to working with states. Leadership and staff of the IRS and FTA play a lead role in designing and implementing such nationwide efforts as the joint electronic filing program and the information exchange program.

ADDITIONAL READINGS

Duncan, Harley T., and Charles E. McLure Jr. "Tax Administration in the United States of America: A Decentralized System." *Bulletin of the International Bureau of Fiscal Documentation* 51 (February 1997): 74–85.

Peha, Jon M., and Robert P. Strauss. "A Primer on Changing Information Technology and the Fisc." *National Tax Journal* 50, no. 3 (September 1997): 607–21.

Cross-references: budget processes, state; budget process, federal.

Tax administration, federal

Ed Nannenhorn
U.S. Government Accountability Office

A general overview of the Internal Revenue Service, the federal agency that has primary responsibility for tax administration.

The federal government levies individual and corporate income taxes, social insurance taxes, excise taxes, estate and gift taxes, custom duties, and other miscellaneous taxes and fees. In order to transfer resources from the private sector to the public sector, individual and business taxpayers spend time and employ others to calculate the tax they owe, prepare tax returns and other documents, and send appropriate documents and payments to the government. The government employs resources to provide services to taxpayers and to check compliance with the law. These compliance and administration costs, along with the economic efficiency losses created by taxes, represent the social costs of the tax system.

The Internal Revenue Service (IRS) is the federal agency with primary responsibility for tax administration. The IRS receives and processes tax returns and other documents, enforces compliance through audits and other programs, collects delinquent taxes, and provides a number of services to help taxpayers understand their responsibilities. The mission of the IRS is to "provide America's taxpayers with top quality service by helping them to understand and meet their tax responsibilities and by applying the tax law with integrity and fairness to all." The strategic goals the IRS has set to achieve this mission are to improve taxpayer service, enhance enforcement of the tax law, and modernize the IRS through its people, processes, and technology.

The IRS has a budget of approximately $10 billion and employs about 99,000 people. The IRS Restructuring and Reform Act of 1998 (RRA) made significant changes to IRS management and operations. The law created the IRS Oversight Board, expanded taxpayers' rights, established a Taxpayer Advocate Service, and established the Treasury Inspector General for Tax Administration (TIGTA). The Act also prompted the IRS to reorganize many activities along four taxpayer segments. The Wage and Investment Division serves approximately 116 million taxpayers who file individual and joint tax returns. The Small Business/Self-Employed Division serves approximately 45 million small businesses and self-employed taxpayers. The Large and Mid-Size Business Division serves businesses with assets of more than $10 million. The Tax-Exempt and Government Entities Division serves employee benefit plans, tax-exempt organizations, and governmental entities. Other divisions include Appeals, Communications and Liaison, and Criminal Investigation. The Office of Chief Counsel provides legal services to the agency.

A GAO (2003a) analysis of how IRS allocated staff in 2003 found that about 46 percent of staff years were spent ensuring compliance with tax laws, 21 percent were spent assisting taxpayers, about 19 percent were used to supply program support, and about 14 percent were spent processing tax returns. About 70 percent of IRS costs are for labor; other expenditures are used for contracts, rent, equipment, and communications and utilities.

Tax return processing and taxpayer services

The administration of the federal tax system relies on large numbers of tax returns and information returns. While some low-income taxpayers are not required to file a return, most households and businesses are required to file an income tax return. Businesses with employees are required to withhold income tax from wages and salaries and make periodic income tax payments for their employees, file employment tax returns and make payments, and provide the information returns to the IRS and employees. Self-employed individuals must periodically report and pay income and self-employment tax liability. Table 1 shows the number and type of returns filed in 1996 and 2003.

In addition to these returns, the IRS received more than 1.3 billion information returns in 2003, an increase of about 23 percent since 1996.

The RRA set a goal that 80 percent of individual income tax returns would be filed electronically by 2007. The IRS has taken steps to reduce the cost to taxpayers of electronic filing by forming a partnership with private-sector tax preparation firms and allowing the use of a personal identification number, which eliminated the need for taxpayers to file a paper document with a signature. Electronic filing is thought to reduce administrative costs by eliminating the need for the IRS to keypunch return information, a costly process that can introduce additional errors that taxpayers and IRS subsequently

TABLE 1. **Number of Returns Filed, by Type** (thousands)

Type of return	Fiscal year 1996	Fiscal year 2003
Income tax (total)	165,297	171,909
Individual	118,833	130,728
Estimated individual tax	36,044	28,588
Estate and trust	3,923	4,321
Partnership	1,623	2,381
Corporation income tax	4,874	5,891
Employment taxes	28,562	29,916
Estate and gift taxes	312	379
Excise taxes	765	812
Employee plans/exempt organizations	855	789
Supplemental documents	12,573	18,465
Total	208,938	222,271

Sources: IRS Data Book, 1996 and 2003.
Note: Figures may not add to totals shown due to rounding.

have to resolve. In 1998, approximately 20 percent of individual taxpayers filed electronically. This percentage increased to almost 50 percent in 2004.

The IRS provides several services to taxpayers to help them meet their responsibilities and resolve problems. The IRS provides forms, publications, and answers to frequently asked questions via telephone, walk-in assistance sites, and the IRS web site. IRS telephone service, heavily criticized in the mid-1990s, has improved in recent years as taxpayers have had an easier time reaching assistors and have been getting accurate answers more frequently. The IRS web site has been an effective tool for distributing forms and other information. Because taxpayers can obtain this information without speaking to IRS personnel, telephone assistance can be geared toward answering more difficult or more taxpayer-specific questions.

Enforcement activity

The IRS identifies three aspects of compliance: (1) filing compliance (whether required returns have been filed in a timely manner); (2) reporting compliance (whether forms contain complete and accurate information); and (3) payment compliance (whether amounts owed have been paid in a timely man-

ner). The IRS has produced estimates of the "tax gap," or the difference between the amount that should have been paid and was paid on a timely basis. The most recent estimate is for tax year 2001. Of an estimated total tax liability of about $2 trillion, it was estimated that 85 percent was voluntarily paid on a timely basis. IRS estimated that of a gross tax gap of about $310 billion, $30 billion resulted from nonfiling, about $32 billion represents underpayment, and about $250 billion in tax liability is underreported (table 2). Of these totals, IRS considers only the underpayment data reliable because the nonfiling and underreporting estimates are based in part on data gathered in the 1980s. Of the $310 billion, IRS estimates that about $55 billion will ultimately be collected either through enforcement action or voluntary late payment by taxpayers.

The IRS has begun a new research effort to measure noncompliance. The IRS believes that this study—the National Research Program—will provide reliable updated data on the level of tax compliance and the reasons for noncompliance. The current estimates of compliance are based on the results of Taxpayer Compliance Measurement Program (TCMP) studies in the 1980s, under which extensive line-by-line audits of randomly selected taxpayers were conducted to find patterns of noncompliance. These studies found that voluntary compliance with the individual income tax was much higher for

TABLE 2. **Components of the Tax Gap, Tax Year 2001** ($ billions)

Tax	Nonfiling gap	Underreporting gap	Underpayment gap
Individual income tax	28.1	148.8	19.4
Corporation income tax	—	29.9	2.3
Employment tax	—	66.1	7.2
Estate tax	2.0	4.0	2.3
Excise tax	—	—	0.5
Total	30.1	248.8	31.7

Source: IRS Office of Research.
Note: — = not available.

income and deductions subject to information reporting than for other types of income, such as business income, that are not subject to reporting by third parties.

The IRS has four major enforcement programs to address noncompliance. Under the audit program, an IRS auditor checks compliance either through a face-to-face meeting with a taxpayer or through correspondence. The other three enforcement programs—the math error, document matching, and nonfiler programs—check tax returns for accuracy and compare the amounts reported to amounts on information returns and tax returns from prior years to identify potential compliance issues. Through the document matching and nonfiler programs, data from information returns are used to both check the accuracy of reported tax liability and identify taxpayers who failed to file a required return.

Individual income tax returns are selected for audit largely on the basis of the amount of additional taxes likely to result. The IRS has used a discriminant function methodology to rank returns by their likelihood that an audit will result in additional taxes. This scoring methodology has been based on findings from the TCMP. However, these formulas may have become less useful over time in identifying returns where audits are likely to result in additional taxes. If the National Research Program studies of compliance are successful, the IRS should be able to better focus compliance efforts on noncompliant taxpayers and reduce the burden of audits for taxpayers who are found to be already in compliance.

Table 3 shows examination rates for fiscal years 1996 through 2003. The decline in audit rates has been substantial for all types of individuals and corporations over the period. One reason for the decline in examination rates may be a decline in staffing; the number of revenue agents fell by 27 percent and the number of tax compliance officers fell by about 50 percent from 1996 to 2003. Also during this period, examination and collection staff were reassigned to provide taxpayer assistance. The scope of the math error program was

also expanded in 1996 to include some Taxpayer Identification Number checks that had been classified as audits, thereby lowering audit rates. In general, many compliance problems that in the past would have required an audit to resolve can now be addressed through other compliance programs.

After reviewing a return and a taxpayer's support for the return, IRS agents or auditors decide whether to recommend changes to tax liability. If a change is recommended, the taxpayer can agree with the change or appeal the decision through the IRS Office of Appeals or the Tax Court. After determining that a taxpayer has not paid the full tax owed, the IRS will request that the taxpayer make the appropriate payment. If payment is not received, the IRS will send a series of collection notices demanding payment. If payments are again not received, the taxpayer becomes delinquent and the IRS will begin collection actions through its telephone and field collection programs. Subject to rules protecting taxpayer rights, the IRS has the authority to use liens, levies, and seizures to settle delinquent cases.

By most measures, IRS collection activity declined significantly from 1996 to 2001. GAO reported that cases closed in the telephone and field collection programs declined by 36 and 45 percent, respectively, and dollars of unpaid taxes collected fell by 15 and 7 percent. Recent data compiled by TIGTA (2004) shows some increases in collection activity in the past few fiscal years.

Systems modernization

Despite several attempts to modernize basic information infrastructure, the IRS relies on technology systems that date back to the 1960s and 1970s. In contrast, while not operating on the scale that the IRS does, businesses that use new technology can process account transactions much more quickly and accurately and identify and resolve customer problems more effectively. The current Business System Modernization

TABLE 3. Compliance Program Coverage Rates by Fiscal Year (percent), 1996–2003

	1996	1997	1998	1999	2000	2001	2002	2003
Examinations								
Individuals	1.67	1.28	0.99	0.90	0.49	0.58	0.57	0.65
Corporations (assets < $10m)	1.88	2.22	1.67	1.16	0.77	0.60	0.63	0.58
Corporations (assets ≥ $10m)	25.33	24.29	21.43	19.05	16.30	15.08	14.17	12.08
S corporations	0.92	1.04	1.04	0.81	0.55	0.43	0.39	0.30
Partnerships	0.49	0.59	0.58	0.43	0.33	0.25	0.26	0.35
Employment tax	0.20	0.21	0.14	0.10	0.07	0.06	0.06	0.06
Excise tax	4.17	3.14	2.48	1.53	1.25	0.96	1.03	1.05
Estate tax	14.47	12.90	10.22	8.46	6.89	6.24	5.84	6.38
Math error	4.01	4.97	4.63	5.25	4.53	4.70	10.22	3.80
Document matching	1.66	0.79	1.43	1.44	1.08	0.91	1.15	1.20
Nonfiler	0.62	0.33	0.35	0.48	0.27	0.26	0.19	0.36

Sources: GAO, TIGTA.

Note: The large increase in math error cases in FY 2002 was because of confusion over the rate reduction credit.

TABLE 4. Collection Sanctions

	FY 1996	FY 1997	FY 1998	FY 1999	FY 2000	FY 2001	FY 2002	FY 2003
Levies	3,108,926	3,659,417	2,503,409	504,403	219,778	674,080	1,283,742	1,680,844
Liens	750,225	543,613	382,755	167,867	287,517	426,166	482,509	548,683
Seizures	10,449	10,090	2,307	161	74	234	296	399

Source: TIGTA.

effort has made progress in several areas. However, implementation of several modernization projects, including the key effort to replace the tape-based IRS Master Files—the Customer Account Data Engine—have been subject to cost overruns and delays. The IRS and its stakeholders believe that successful modernization of IRS computer systems must be accomplished so the IRS can resolve taxpayer account problems more efficiently and identify and resolve compliance problems more effectively, reducing taxpayer compliance and administrative costs.

ADDITIONAL READINGS

Aaron, Henry J., and Joel Slemrod, eds. *The Crisis in Tax Administration.* Washington, DC: Brookings Institution Press, 2004.

Internal Revenue Service [IRS]. *Data Book 2003.* Publication 55B. Washington, DC: IRS, 2004.

IRS Oversight Board. *Annual Report 2004.* http://www.treas.gov/irsob/index.html.

Joint Committee on Taxation. *Report of the Joint Committee on Taxation Relating to the Internal Revenue Service as Required by the IRS Reform and Restructuring Act of 1998.* JCX-53-03. Washington, DC: U.S. Government Printing Office, 2003.

Slemrod, Joel, and Shlomo Yitzaki. "Tax Avoidance, Evasion, and Administration." In *Handbook of Public Economics,* vol. 3, edited by Alan J. Auerbach and Martin Feldstein (1423–65). New York: North-Holland, 2002.

U.S. Department of the Treasury, Internal Revenue Service. *Report to Congress: IRS Tax Compliance Activities.* Washington, DC: U.S. Government Printing Office, 2003.

U.S. General Accounting Office [GAO]. *IRS Modernization: Continued Progress Necessary for Improving Service to Taxpayers and Ensuring Compliance.* GAO-03-796T. Washington, DC: GAO, May 20, 2003a.

———. *Tax Administration: IRS Should Continue to Expand Reporting on Its Enforcement Efforts.* GAO-03-378. Washington, DC: GAO, January 31, 2003b.

———. *Internal Revenue Service: Assessment of Fiscal Year 2005 Budget Request and 2004 Filing Season Performance.* GAO-04-560T. March 30, 2004.

U.S. Treasury Inspector General for Tax Administration. *Trends in Compliance Activities Through Fiscal Year 2003.* Reference number 2004-30-083. Washington, DC: U.S. Treasury Inspector General for Tax Administration, 2004. http://www.ustreas.gov/tigta/index.html.

Cross-references: adjusted gross income; income tax, federal; tax administration, state, private, and public cooperation in.

Tax administration, state, private, and public cooperation in

Harley T. Duncan
Federation of Tax Administrators

Charles E. McLure Jr.
Hoover Institution, Stanford University

Several organizations, public and private, cooperate both informally and by law in the administration of state and local taxes.

Several multistate organizations, private and public, contribute to coordination and collaboration for the purpose of (a) improving state tax compliance through information sharing; (b) improving the uniformity of state tax laws and practices to increase compliance and reduce complexity for taxpayers; (c) conducting administrative operations in combination to reduce administrative costs and the complexity of operating in multiple states; and (d) educating the public and their clientele on recent developments in taxation, tax policy, and best practices.

The private organizations include the Council on State Taxation (COST), an adjunct of the Council of State Chambers of Commerce, which consists of roughly 500 multistate companies. The primary purpose of COST is to advocate for multistate taxpayers before state and federal legislative and judicial bodies and to provide training to member companies. Similarly, the Tax Executives Institute is an organization of tax professionals from major multistate and international corporations domiciled in the United States and Canada. Its mission includes professional development and advocacy before state and federal policymakers. The Institute for Professionals in Taxation consists of tax professionals and representatives in the property, sales, and use tax areas. Its mission is limited to professional development for its members and working with appropriate state and local tax authorities on matters of mutual interest. The Institute also administers a program for certification of tax professionals in the property tax and sales/use tax areas.

There are five key public vehicles for cooperation. The two most prominent—the Federation of Tax Administrators (FTA) and the Multistate Tax Commission—are discussed in separate entries in this encyclopedia. The three other cooperative arrangements are discussed below.

Regional cooperative agreements

In several areas of the country, state tax agencies have joined together to adopt regional agreements to encourage information sharing among the states as a way to improve tax compliance on interstate sales. These regional agreements provide that information gathered on transactions meeting specified criteria will be shared among the states. In practice, however, these regional information exchanges fall far short of providing information on all interstate sales. The following two political realities force tax administrators to pay particular attention to the political interests in their state to avoid losing the support of elected officials: (1) providing information to other states may lead to increased taxation of companies (or their products) operating in the state providing the information and (2) substantial portions of their economy may benefit from compliance difficulties currently faced by other states.

Certain agreements (primarily in the Great Lakes, Midwest, and Southeast regions) call for actively encouraging retailers to register in all states into which they ship goods. New York, New Jersey, and Connecticut have extended this type of agreement to include a mechanism under which a retailer can file a single return with one state to satisfy its sales tax obligations for all three states. The Southeast also includes procedures for routinely sharing certain corporation income tax information.

Bilateral exchanges

Each state has entered into agreements to exchange tax return information with nearly all other states. This exchange may be accomplished either through the Uniform Exchange of Information Agreement, developed by the FTA and executed by about 45 states, or through separate bilateral exchange agreements. Under these bilateral arrangements, states routinely share compliance information with other states on a taxpayer-by-taxpayer and state-by-state basis. The exchanges may be more comprehensive. Thus, New York, New Jersey, and Connecticut routinely exchange information on individual taxpayers in the New York City metropolitan area who work in one state but reside in another to ensure consistent sourcing of the income and proper computation of credits for taxes paid in another state. Recently, about 45 states have used the Uniform Exchange of Information Agreement as a framework for a separate agreement calling for the exchange of certain information as well as certain cooperative activities to combat potentially abusive tax avoidance transactions (tax shelters).

International Fuel Tax Agreement

Since the mid-1990s, states have been required by federal law to join the International Fuel Tax Agreement (IFTA) as a way to reduce the administrative burden on taxpayers through participation in a joint tax administration project. All states (and some Canadian provinces) are now members of IFTA, which provides a mechanism for apportioning the motor fuel excise tax liability of an interstate or multijurisdictional motor carrier among the states in which it operates.

In the United States, a carrier pays tax at the time fuel is purchased or "at the pump" but is then responsible for apportioning the tax paid on its entire fleet based on the miles traveled in each jurisdiction. Before the adoption of IFTA, a carrier was responsible for filing quarterly returns in each jurisdiction in which it operated, detailing its mileage, purchases, consumption, and any tax or refund owed.

Under IFTA, the carrier files a single tax return with the state in which it is domiciled or based, together with information on its operations (purchases, mileage, etc.) in all jurisdictions for the reporting period. The "base state" provides information to other jurisdictions, reconciling the tax owed by the carrier in all jurisdictions and otherwise providing for the administration of the other jurisdictions' taxes on behalf of the carrier. The base state also audits carriers on behalf of all other jurisdictions. In short, the interstate carrier deals only with the tax authority in its base state, which is responsible for all contacts on behalf of the carrier with other jurisdictions.

New York State has taken the joint administration of IFTA one step further. It has developed a data processing facility that provides tax return and remittance processing services for IFTA jurisdictions, including two Canadian provinces. The processing center captures all data from returns filed with it and handles all financial transactions among the states and other IFTA jurisdictions involved. The states are individually responsible for registering and auditing carriers and dealing with delinquent carriers. IFTA began as a voluntary cooperative effort among a relatively small number of states—three at the outset. However, because of the perceived benefits, the interstate trucking industry pushed hard for further participation and eventually secured enactment of a federal law requiring states to participate in IFTA if they wished to continue imposing the apportioned fuel use tax beyond September 30, 1996. Although some states initially resisted enactment of the requirement, all complied with its provisions by the deadline.

ADDITIONAL READINGS

Auerbach, Alan J., William G. Gale, and Peter R. Orszag. 2004. "Bush Administration Tax Policy: Introduction and Background." *Tax Notes* 104, no. 12. (September 13, 2004): 1291–1300.

Duncan, Harley T. "Interstate Cooperative Efforts to Enforce State Sales and Use Taxes." *Proceedings of the 81st Annual Conference on Taxation.* Columbus, OH: National Tax Association–Tax Institute of America, 1989.

Duncan, Harley T., and Charles E. McLure Jr. "Tax Administration in the United States of America: A Decentralized System." *Bulletin of the International Bureau of Fiscal Documentation* 51 (February 1997): 74–85.

Gale, William, and Peter Orszag. "Bush Administration Tax Policy: Short-Term Stimulus." *Tax Notes* 105, no. 6 (November 1, 2004): 747–55.

Special Committee on State Taxation of Interstate Commerce, Committee on the Judiciary, U.S. House of Representatives, pursuant to Public Law 86-272. (The special committee operated from 1962 to 1966. These hearings were generally known as the "Willis Committee" hearings, named after the committee chairman, Rep. Edwin E. Willis of Louisiana.)

Cross-references: Multistate Tax Commission; tax administration, federal.

Tax amnesty

Ronald C. Fisher

Michigan State University

A program offering reduced financial and/or legal penalties to taxpayers who voluntarily agree to pay outstanding past tax liabilities.

Programs that might be called "formal tax amnesties" usually are intended to be unique, one-time opportunities that typically apply for a very limited period and usually occur just before an increase in tax enforcement and penalties. These formal amnesties should be distinguished from the more common practice by many tax authorities of negotiating payments and penalties if taxpayers offer to settle past disputes or liabilities, which might be called "informal amnesties."

Amnesty practice and experience

Forty state governments in the United States plus the District of Columbia held more than 75 formal tax amnesties between 1982 and 2004, with the first substantial amnesties occurring in 1984 in Illinois and Massachusetts. Because these state amnesties differed widely in their coverage and characteristics, collections varied from as little as $200,000 (North Dakota in 1983) to as much as $532 million (Illinois, 2003) and $583 million (New York, 2003). Even the largest programs were relatively small, however, as most amnesty collections were less than $30 per capita, or 2 percent of annual state revenue. Tax amnesties also have been used by many local governments in the United States and by other nations, although the focus of most research has been on these state programs.

Although the original amnesty concept emphasized that amnesties were to be "one-time" opportunities, in fact a substantial number of states have repeated them. Of the 40 states and the District that have held amnesties, 26 states and D.C. have done so more than once, often for the same taxes. The use of amnesties by states has in fact been concentrated in two periods, with 29 amnesties occurring between 1982 and 1987 and between 2000 and 2004. Both periods were times of serious fiscal difficulty for states and localities. Thus, states seem to have seen and used amnesties as sources of short-term revenue gain.

Amnesties can be distinguished by the number of eligible taxes, whether they apply to both underreporting and nonfiling, whether taxpayers with previously identified liabilities (accounts receivable) are eligible, the nature and magnitude of the reduced penalties, and whether they preceded enhanced enforcement and stricter penalties. Three-quarters of state amnesty programs applied to all taxes (or all administered by the state revenue department); except for a few specialized amnesties limited to minor taxes, most included the general sales and personal income taxes. Participants included both individuals and firms—taxes collected from business, including corporate income taxes, have been part of many amnesties.

Most tax amnesties applied to both underreporting of transactions or tax base and failure to file, although the statute of limitations typically is shorter for underreporting. Of more importance is whether delinquent taxpayers who have been identified by tax authorities or who have had outstanding liabilities assessed before the amnesty are allowed to participate. About 55 to 60 percent of state amnesties included these taxpayers (often identified as accounts receivable), a share that seems to have been increasing over time. But these cases were included in nearly all the state amnesties that generated substantial revenue. Thus, in those cases, amnesty can be thought of as a convenient, low-cost method of collecting known, outstanding debts.

All amnesties waived any potential criminal penalties, and most eliminated or substantially reduced the financial penalties that applied to underpayment. In most states, amnesty participants did have to pay interest on the outstanding liabilities, although about a third of state amnesties also reduced or eliminated interest charges. Perhaps surprisingly, Alm and Beck (1991) reported evidence that reducing interest charges tended to increase the revenue generated by the amnesty (increased revenue from more participation offsetting the loss of interest payments).

Finally, many states used amnesties to smooth the transition to a regime of stricter enforcement (about 60 percent of amnesties) and higher penalties (75 percent). Typical amnesty advertising focused on such slogans as "Don't Say We Didn't Warn You" (Colorado) and "Get to Us Before We Get to You" (Michigan). Amnesties and enhanced enforcement seem complementary in two ways—the new enforcement and penalties in the future create an incentive for taxpayers to participate in an amnesty, and the amnesty may make the change to a new tax collection regime seem fairer by providing taxpayers an opportunity to avoid what might be perceived as an arbitrary or unannounced change in policy. As expected, amnesties that were to be followed by enhanced enforcement seemed to have more participation and generate larger amounts of collections (Alm and Beck 1991).

Success of tax amnesty

Tax amnesties have three main objectives. The first is to generate revenue in the short run. As noted, states that offered the broadest programs with the greatest incentives to participate were most successful in achieving this objective. Second, governments want to increase revenue in the long run by changing the behavior of some taxpayers, inducing taxpayers who had been evaders to comply fully in the future. Third, governments hope to generate information both about amnesty participants, which could be used to enforce compliance by those individuals in the future, and about tax compliance and evasion in general, which could be used to improve tax collection and enforcement programs.

It is evident, however, that the long-run implications of amnesties are ambiguous. The potential gain from identifying past evaders and improving their compliance in the long run must be weighed against three factors that might reduce compliance of others in the long run. First, some complying taxpayers might decide to not pay taxes fully in the future and to wait for an amnesty. To mitigate against this potential problem, states holding amnesties have often emphasized the unique, one-time aspect of the opportunity, promising not to hold another amnesty (for the same tax) soon. (But, as previously noted, the facts suggest that such promises are often hollow.) Second, there is concern that some compliers might become disillusioned by the perceived unfairness of offering relief to past noncompliers, leading to less compliance overall. And third, some worry that the amnesty experience and attention might provide information about the ease of and opportunities for evasion.

In fact, state amnesties attracted a variety of taxpayers but not necessarily the most serious evaders (Fisher, Goddeeris, and Young 1989; Joulfaian 1989). Among the large multitax amnesties, the individual income tax accounted for the majority of tax cases resolved but a smaller share of collections, because many of these participants used the amnesty to pay very small amounts (in many instances less than $100). In addition, not having filed (rather than having filed incorrectly) was the most common form of evasion among participants, and most of these nonfilers used amnesty to file for one or two years. In many cases, participating nonfilers had paid most tax due through withholding or quarterly payments but had not filed a return to settle their accounts. In Michigan, for instance, 60 percent of the taxpayers using amnesty to file individual income tax returns had already paid at least 80 percent of the total tax owed (Fisher et al. 1989). Some had even filed federal returns.

Businesses participated in amnesties mostly to resolve corporate income and sales tax matters (Fisher and Goddeeris 1989). Corporate income tax cases were particularly important, accounting for a larger share of amnesty collections than did sales tax cases. Many of the income tax cases, as with the individual cases, involved small amounts, with a few firms in each case paying large amounts that represented a substantial percentage of amnesty collections. In those states that allowed taxpayers with known outstanding liabilities or audits in progress to participate, collections from accounts receivable often represented at least half of amnesty collections for corporate income and sales taxes. In at least one state, however, many business participants used amnesty to file for several years, including a large number who had never filed returns.

It seems, then, that relatively few individual taxpayers who participated in amnesties were "hardcore evaders," having evaded larger amounts of taxes over long periods of time,

and that a larger number of chronic business tax evaders may have been detected by amnesties. Certainly some individual and business taxpayers who had a serious past history of evasion or who were completely outside the tax system were uncovered. Still, most participants might be called "marginal tax evaders"—taxpayers who received only a small gain or who found themselves in the situation reluctantly or by accident. Not surprisingly, therefore, examination of tax enforcement had no long-run effect on revenue collections (Alm and Beck 1993). Possibly, any long-run gains from returning or adding taxpayers to the rolls were offset by new evasions.

Recent research about the long-run effects of the 1986 Michigan amnesty (Christian, Gupta, and Young 2002) confirms the result that amnesties seem to have had a negligible long-term effect on revenue, although a positive effect on tax compliance. They reported that two-thirds of new income tax filers in the state amnesty and nine-tenths of past filers who used the amnesty to file amended returns continued to file subsequent income tax returns. But the gross revenue gain was only about 0.1 percent of state individual income tax revenue and the net gain even less.

Future for tax amnesties

Tax amnesties seem to have been most successful in generating immediate revenue, part of which represented known liabilities that were collected sooner or at lower cost than from enhanced enforcement alone. Amnesties also have provided states useful information about taxpayers, tax compliance problems, and tax collection and enforcement policies. But it seems that amnesties generally did not succeed in generating substantial long-term additions to revenue as a result of additional taxpayers and improved compliance. Neither, however, did amnesties seem to hurt revenue collection.

A federal tax amnesty for the United States has been discussed, but the state results coupled with the substantially different nature of federal tax evasion have generated little momentum for a federal tax amnesty. Tax amnesties for local governments and other nations are likely to continue, however.

ADDITIONAL READINGS

Alm, James, and William Beck. "Tax Amnesties and Tax Revenue." *Public Finance Quarterly* 18 (October 1990): 433–53.

———. "Wiping the Slate Clean: Individual Response to State Amnesties." *Southern Economic Journal* 57 (April 1991): 1043–53.

———. "Tax Amnesties and Compliance in the Long Run: A Time Series Analysis." *National Tax Journal* 46 (March 1993): 53–60.

Alm, James, Michael McKee, and William Beck. "Amazing Grace: Tax Amnesties and Compliance." *National Tax Journal* 43 (March 1990): 23–37.

"Amnesties." Washington, DC: The World Bank Group, 2002. http://www1.worldbank.org/publicsector/tax/amnesties.html.

Andreoni, James. "The Desirability of a Permanent Tax Amnesty." *Journal of Public Economics* 45 (July 1991): 1435–59.

Cassone, Alberto, and Carla Marchese. "Tax Amnesties as Special Sales Offers: The Italian Experience." *Public Finance* 50 (1995): 51–66.

Christian, Charles, Sanjay Gupta, and James Young. "Evidence on Subsequent Filing from the State of Michigan's Income Tax Amnesty." *National Tax Journal* 55, no. 4 (December 2002): 703–21.

Crane, Steven E., and Farrokh Nourzad. "Amnesty for State Tax Evaders: Lessons from the California Experience." In *Proceedings of the 81st Annual Conference, 1988,* edited by Frederick D. Stocker (133–39). Columbus, OH: National Tax Association–Tax Institute of America, 1989.

———. "Tax Rates and Tax Evasion: Evidence from California Amnesty Data." *National Tax Journal* 43 (June 1990): 189–99.

Dubin, Jeffrey, Michael Graetz, and Louis Wilde. "State Income Tax Amnesties: Causes." *Quarterly Journal of Economics* 107 (August 1992): 1057–70.

Ehrenhalt, Alan. "Beware the Amnesty Binge." *Governing Magazine* (January 2003).

Fisher, Ronald C., and John H. Goddeeris. "Participation in Tax Amnesties: The Case of Business Taxes." In *Proceedings of the 81st Annual Conference, 1988,* edited by Frederick D. Stocker (139–45). Columbus, OH: National Tax Association–Tax Institute of America, 1989.

Fisher, Ronald C., John H. Goddeeris, and James C. Young. "Participation in Tax Amnesties: The Individual Income Tax." *National Tax Journal* 42 (March 1989): 15–27.

Goddeeris, John H., Susan W. Martin, and James C. Young. "Tax Amnesty in Michigan: Characteristics of Individual Income Tax Participants." *Journal of State Taxation* 7 (Winter 1989): 373–95.

Graetz, Michael, and Louis Wilde. "The Decision by Strategic Nonfilers to Participate in Income Tax Amnesties." *International Review of Law and Economics* 13 (September 1993): 271–83.

Hasseldine, John. "Tax Amnesties: An International Review." *Bulletin for International Fiscal Documentation* 52 (July 1998): 303–10.

Joulfaian, David. "Participation in Tax Amnesties: Evidence from a State." In *Proceedings of the 81st Annual Conference, 1988,* edited by Frederick D. Stocker (128–33). Columbus, OH: National Tax Association–Tax Institute of America, 1989.

Leonard, Herman B., and Richard J. Zeckhauser. "Amnesty, Enforcement, and Tax Policy." In *Tax Policy and the Economy,* edited by Lawrence Summers (55–86). Cambridge, MA: MIT Press, 1986.

Lerman, Allen. "Issues in Amnesty from the Federal Viewpoint." *National Tax Journal* 39 (September 1986): 325–32.

Malik, Arun, and Robert Schwab. "The Economics of Tax Amnesty." *Journal of Public Economics* 46 (October 1991): 29–49.

Mikesell, John L. "Amnesties for State Tax Evaders: The Nature of and Response to Recent Programs." *National Tax Journal* 39 (December 1986): 507–25.

Parle, William M., and Mike W. Hirlinger. "Evaluating the Use of Tax Amnesty by State Governments." *Public Administration Review* (May/June 1986): 246–55.

Spencer, Linda. "More States Conduct Tax Amnesty Programs." *Journal of State Taxation* 7 (Winter 1989): 361–71.

"State Tax Amnesty Programs." Washington, DC: Federation of Tax Administrators, March 2004. http://www.taxadmin.org/fta/rate/amnesty1.html.

Stella, Peter. "An Economic Analysis of Tax Amnesties." *Journal of Public Economics* 46 (1991): 383–400.

Cross-references: tax administration mechanisms for intergovernmental cooperation; tax evasion.

Tax and revenue capacity

Daphne A. Kenyon

D. A. Kenyon & Associates

A measure that compares the relative potential tax and revenue bases ("representative capacity") of similar jurisdictions, such as the U.S. states. Tax and revenue capacity show how much revenue would be raised in each

state if all states (and their local governments) applied uniform rates to a uniform set of bases.

Tax and revenue capacity describes a government's ability to generate receipts from its own sources (i.e., exclusive of intergovernmental transfers) in order to fund public services. Tax capacity refers to the potential ability (the capacity) of a government to generate receipts from taxes—compulsory payments to governments for which there is no direct quid pro quo consequent to the payment. The government essentially considers its flow of receipts independent from expenditures for any specific service. Revenue capacity measures, in addition to taxes, potential "nontax" governmental receipts derived from such sources as user charges and fees, interest earnings, net lottery receipts, special assessments, and property sales. It is important to note that tax and revenue capacity are not synonymous with fiscal capacity or adequacy, which incorporate an expenditure dimension into the measurement. In this entry, the term tax capacity will be used to refer to both tax and revenue capacity, except where explicit distinctions are drawn.

Tax capacity is an idea that derives from applied public finance rather than economic theory. One controversy in the capacity literature involves whether various measures of capacity have sound theoretical foundations (Fastrup 1986; Barro 1986). To the extent that tax capacity links to a theoretical construct, it can be thought of as determined by the budget constraints facing a government or group of governments in a particular geographic area.

Several measures of capacity exist, all in the form of index numbers that compare the tax capacity of one state to a national or regional average or one local government to other local governments in the same state. Tax capacity measures are used to compare and monitor trends in the fiscal health of states and local governments, target grants to those governments with less ability to raise revenue, or evaluate the distribution of intergovernmental grants.

Four common indices of the capacity of state and local governments to mobilize revenues, by state, are per capita personal income (PCI), the representative tax system (RTS), the representative revenue system (RRS), and total taxable resources (TTR). Measures and rankings for 1997 for PCI, TTR, and RTS are shown in table 1. The 1997 data are presented because this is the latest year for which all three measures have been estimated. The last year for which RTS data alone (see next essay) are available is 1999 (Tannenwald 2004).

PCI, which is readily available by state from the Department of Commerce, includes labor compensation; proprietors' income; net rent, interest, and dividends; and transfer payments. PCI is the measure of capacity most used in federal grant formulas; indeed, it was the only capacity measure used until 1987. (For example, the federal matching rate for Medicaid funding is inversely related to state PCI.) Despite its widespread use, PCI has been roundly criticized as a measure of governmental receipts-generating capacity. The two major

TABLE 1.   Alternative Indices of 1997 State Tax Capacity (100 = U.S. Average)

State	PCI Index	PCI Rank	TTR Index	TTR Rank	RTS Index	RTS Rank
Alabama	82	41	78	46	81	48
Alaska	106	11	122	6	133	1
Arizona	86	37	89	36	100	21
Arkansas	77	48	76	48	80	49
California	104	14	104	15	116	8
Colorado	107	10	105	14	115	9
Connecticut	137	1	145	2	129	3
Delaware	105	13	144	3	120	7
District of Columbia	133	2	159	1	123	6
Florida	98	21	94	27	98	22
Georgia	94	27	97	22	98	23
Hawaii	101	17	101	18	130	2
Idaho	81	45	80	45	87	44
Illinois	110	7	109	12	103	16
Indiana	92	32	90	34	95	28
Iowa	92	30	93	29	94	29
Kansas	95	25	95	25	94	32
Kentucky	83	40	83	41	86	45
Louisiana	82	42	91	32	89	43
Maine	87	36	82	42	95	27
Maryland	114	6	110	11	106	14
Massachusetts	121	4	121	7	112	11
Michigan	100	20	91	33	96	26
Minnesota	107	9	102	16	103	17
Mississippi	73	51	70	51	71	51
Missouri	94	28	93	30	93	33
Montana	78	47	74	49	92	36
Nebraska	95	26	95	24	98	24
Nevada	106	12	114	10	129	4
New Hampshire	107	8	120	8	110	12
New Jersey	125	3	129	4	114	10
New Mexico	77	49	85	40	90	41
New York	117	5	120	9	106	13
North Carolina	92	31	93	31	93	35
North Dakota	81	46	81	44	96	25
Ohio	97	22	94	28	94	31
Oklahoma	82	43	76	47	83	47
Oregon	96	24	100	19	103	15
Pennsylvania	101	19	96	23	92	39
Rhode Island	101	18	100	20	92	38
South Carolina	83	39	81	43	84	46
South Dakota	86	38	90	35	94	30
Tennessee	90	35	88	38	90	42
Texas	94	29	98	21	91	40
Utah	81	44	85	39	92	37
Vermont	91	34	89	37	101	19
Virginia	104	16	106	13	101	20
Washington	104	15	102	17	101	18
West Virginia	76	50	73	50	77	50
Wisconsin	96	23	94	26	93	34
Wyoming	92	33	123	5	125	5

Source: Tannenwald (2002), appendix table 1.
Note: PCI = per capita personal income; TTR = total taxable resources; RTS = representative tax system.

criticisms are that it does not measure income comprehensively (e.g., it omits corporate income other than dividends) and that it does not take into account a government's potential to expand its capacities by exporting taxes.

The RTS was developed for the U.S. Advisory Commission on Intergovernmental Relations (ACIR) in 1962 by Selma Mushkin and Alice Rivlin and has been refined since then, with new state estimates published every few years. The RTS index is constructed by estimating the national average effective tax rates that apply to a large number of different tax bases (e.g., personal income, corporation income, severance), applying those representative rates to each state's actual tax bases, and computing the relative per capita revenue each state would raise if it levied those tax rates. The RTS has never been used to help determine the distribution of federal grants in the United States, but Canada has used an RTS method for distributing grants under its federal-provincial equalization program since 1967. Many European countries also employ some form of RTS in their intergovernmental transfer arrangements (Bird and Wallich 1995).

The RTS has an advantage over PCI in that the RTS implicitly takes some tax-exporting opportunities into account by including severance taxes and selective sales taxes related to tourist activity among its tax bases. The primary criticism of the RTS is that it cannot be derived from the theory of government budget constraint. For example, the RTS adds sales tax capacity to income tax capacity in computing total tax capacity. The theorist would argue that tax capacity depends primarily on resident income and that there is no independent sales tax capacity. Another criticism of the RTS is that it does not take into account tax exporting through federal deductibility of state and local taxes.

The RRS, which is very similar to the RTS, was developed by the ACIR in 1986. The ACIR RRS includes the tax bases used in the RTS plus the revenue bases of rents and royalties, lotteries, and user charges. In 1994, the latest year for which both RTS and RRS rankings were estimated, most states had nearly identical rankings under the RTS and the RRS.

TTR is defined as the unduplicated sum of income produced within a state and income received by its residents that a state can tax. As the concept is currently implemented, TTR is calculated by assigning a share of the nation's gross domestic product (GDP) to each state. A state's share is equal to the state's average share of the nation's personal income and GDP. TTR was used as a measure of receipts-generating capacity for the Community Mental Health Services and Substance Abuse Prevention and Treatment block grants (Compson and Navratil 1997). TTR is more comprehensive than PCI and may be considered more theoretically consistent than either the RTS or the RRS, but TTR does not account for tax exporting through federal tax deductibility.

Table 1 shows the alternative measures of tax capacity among the states (although the relative values of the indices are likely to change over time). For 10 states (Alaska, Connecticut, Delaware, District of Columbia, Hawaii, Montana,

Nevada, New Jersey, North Dakota, and Wyoming), there is at least a 15 point difference in index numbers among the three alternative measures of tax capacity.

Measures of tax or revenue capacity can also be generated for local governments within states or for cities across the United States, but such research is more preliminary than that for the state capacity measures described here (Ferguson and Ladd 1986; Texas Advisory Commission on Intergovernmental Relations 1986). Current efforts to advise developing countries or transition economies use capacity measures as guides for grant programs (Bahl 1994; Ma 1997).

ADDITIONAL READINGS

Advisory Commission on Intergovernmental Relations. *RTS 1991: State Revenue Capacity and Effort.* Washington, DC: U.S. Government Printing Office, 1993.

Bahl, Roy. "Revenues and Revenue Assignment: Intergovernmental Fiscal Relations in the Russian Federation." In *Russia and the Challenge of Fiscal Federalism,* edited by Christine I. Wallich (129–80). Washington, DC: The World Bank, 1994.

Barro, Stephen M. "State Fiscal Capacity Measures: A Theoretical Critique." In *Measuring Fiscal Capacity,* edited by H. Clyde Reeves. Boston, MA: Oelgeschlager, Gunn & Hain, 1986.

Bird, Richard, and Christine Wallich. "Financing Local Government in Hungary." In *Decentralization of the Socialist State,* edited by Richard Bird, Robert Ebel, and Christine Wallich (68–116). Washington, DC: The World Bank, 1995.

Cohen, Carol, Robert Lucke, and John Shannon. "The ACIR Representative Tax System for Estimating the Fiscal Capacity of the Fifty State-Local Systems." In *Measuring Fiscal Capacity,* edited by H. Clyde Reeves. Boston, MA: Oelgeschlager, Gunn & Hain, 1986.

Compson, Michael, and John Navratil. "An Improved Method for Estimating the Total Taxable Resources of the States." Research Paper No. 9702, Office of the Assistant Secretary for Economic Policy, U.S. Department of the Treasury. Washington, DC: U.S. Government Printing Office, 1997.

Fastrup, Jerry C. "Fiscal Capacity, Fiscal Equalization, and Federal Grant Formulas." *In Federal-State-Local Fiscal Relations: Technical Papers, Vol. I,* Office of State and Local Finance, U.S. Department of the Treasury). Washington, DC: U.S. Government Printing Office, 1986.

Ferguson, Ronald F., and Helen F. Ladd. "Measuring the Fiscal Capacity of U.S. Cities." In *Measuring Fiscal Capacity,* edited by H. Clyde Reeves. Boston, MA: Oelgeschlager, Gunn & Hain, 1986.

Ma, Jun. "Intergovernmental Fiscal Transfers in Nine Countries: Lessons for Developing Countries." Policy Research Working Paper 1822. Washington, DC: The World Bank, 1997.

Rafuse, Robert. *Representative Expenditures: Addressing the Neglected Dimension of Fiscal Capacity.* Washington, DC: Advisory Commission on Intergovernmental Relations, 1990.

Sawicky, Max B. "The 'Total Taxable Resources' Definition of State Revenue-Raising Ability." In *Federal-State-Local Fiscal Relations: Technical Papers, Vol. 1,* Office of State and Local Finance, U.S. Department of the Treasury. Washington, DC: U.S. Government Printing Office, 1985.

Tannenwald, Robert. "Interstate Fiscal Disparity in 1997." *New England Economic Review* Third Quarter 2002.

———. "Interstate Fiscal Disparity in State Fiscal Year 1999." *Discussion Paper No. 04-9,* Federal Reserve Bank of Boston, December 2004.

Texas Advisory Commission on Intergovernmental Relations. "Local Government Fiscal Capacity Measures: A Profile of State Studies." In *Federal-State-Local Fiscal Relations: Technical Papers, Vol. I,* Office of State and Local Finance, U.S. Department of the Treasury. Washington, DC: U.S. Government Printing Office, 1986.

Cross-references: tax and revenue effort; tax competition; tax exportation.

Tax and revenue effort

Daphne A. Kenyon

D. A. Kenyon & Associates

*Tax and revenue effort refers to the extent to which a
government uses the potential receipts-generating capacity
(tax or revenue bases) available to it.*

Tax and revenue effort is measured as a ratio of revenues collected to capacity, so there are potentially as many effort indices as there are indices of capacity.

As with the term *capacity,* tax or revenue *effort* refers to
comparisons among governments and not to the fiscal well-
being of taxpayers (individuals or businesses). This distinction
between a government's fiscal status and that of its taxpayers
may be significant if some governments are able to generate
large amounts of revenues from nonresidents through tax exporting. Thus, a government may have a high tax or revenue
effort that places a low burden on its taxpayers if it can take
advantage of opportunities for tax exporting.

Effort measures can be used to monitor the fiscal health of
state or local governments. Effort can be an indicator of fiscal
stress, because attempts to collect more revenues on a given
base or shrinkage of the revenue base can be considered fiscally stressful events (Benson, Marks, and Raman 1988).
Measures of effort have also been used in grant formulas to
reward those governments raising a higher level of revenues.
For example, the General Revenue Sharing program (1972–86)
allocated greater funds to those states with higher tax effort,
measured as the ratio of state and local tax revenue to aggregate state personal income.

Beginning in 1962, the U.S. Advisory Commission on Intergovernmental Relations (ACIR) published periodic estimates of state and local tax or revenue effort together with its
state capacity estimates. The most recent estimates of capacity
and effort using the representative tax system (RTS), developed by Tannenwald (2004), are shown in table 1. The RTS
measures effort as the ratio of actual taxes collected to estimated tax capacity.

Those states whose collections exceed their estimated capacity have an effort index greater than 100. States that rank
in the top five in tax effort are the District of Columbia, New
York, Minnesota, Wisconsin, and Connecticut. States that rank
in the bottom five for tax effort are Nevada, Wyoming, New
Hampshire, South Dakota, and Tennessee.

Some states have computed receipts-generating effort indices for their local governments. For example, the University of Kentucky has published estimates of tax effort by
county using a methodology like the ACIR (Hoyt 2001).
Maine's Margaret Chase Smith Center for Public Policy presents a simpler measure of property tax effort for Maine
towns and cities—property taxes per household as a percentage of median household income (Allen 2002). In addition,
several states use some measure of revenue effort as a factor

TABLE 1. Index of 1999 State Tax Capacity and Effort
(100 = U.S. Average)

State	RTS Capacity	RTS Effort
Alabama	82	82
Alaska	109	87
Arizona	98	87
Arkansas	81	91
California	111	96
Colorado	105	95
Connecticut	127	119
Delaware	123	89
District of Columbia	127	151
Florida	103	86
Georgia	98	94
Hawaii	116	95
Idaho	84	97
Illinois	104	101
Indiana	94	93
Iowa	96	93
Kansas	92	99
Kentucky	85	97
Louisiana	83	98
Maine	92	118
Maryland	104	103
Massachusetts	114	106
Michigan	99	103
Minnesota	108	113
Mississippi	74	99
Missouri	93	92
Montana	94	82
Nebraska	98	94
Nevada	129	76
New Hampshire	114	76
New Jersey	114	113
New Mexico	87	99
New York	106	143
North Carolina	97	92
North Dakota	96	92
Ohio	94	103
Oklahoma	79	98
Oregon	108	80
Pennsylvania	92	107
Rhode Island	91	119
South Carolina	86	90
South Dakota	96	79
Tennessee	92	78
Texas	90	91
Utah	90	95
Vermont	99	102
Virginia	102	94
Washington	110	96
West Virginia	72	110
Wisconsin	96	115
Wyoming	111	86

Source: Tannenwald (2004), tables 2 and 5.
Note: RTS = representative tax system.

in allocating grant funds to local governments (Texas Advisory Commission on Intergovernmental Relations 1986).

There are important limits in the information that can be gleaned from fiscal effort measures, however. High fiscal effort may be an indication of many different phenomena: above-average expenditure needs, voter tastes for above-average government spending, waste in government spending, successful efforts by interest groups pressing for more government spending, or below-average tax or revenue capacity. Further, because effort is a ratio of revenues to capacity, effort indices will rise either when revenues are raised or when capacity falls. Both changes would lead to fiscal stress, but each has very different policy implications for relieving that stress.

ADDITIONAL READINGS

Advisory Commission on Intergovernmental Relations. *RTS 1991: State Revenue Capacity and Effort.* Washington, DC: U.S. Government Printing Office, 1993.

Allen, Thomas G. "An Overview of the Demographic and Economic Conditions in Maine: A Background for Workforce and Tax Policy Considerations." Orono, ME: Margaret Chase Smith Center for Public Policy, 2002. http://www.umaine.edu/mcsc/Research/EcoDev/Allen_EDA2.htm.

Benson, Earl D., Barry R. Marks, and K. K. Raman. "Tax Effort as an Indicator of Fiscal Stress." *Public Finance Quarterly* 16 (April 1988): 203–17.

Gold, Steven D. "Measuring Fiscal Effort and Fiscal Capacity: Sorting Out Some of the Controversies." In *Measuring Fiscal Capacity,* edited by H. Clyde Reeves. Boston, MA: Oelgeschlager, Gunn & Hain, 1986.

Hoyt, William A. "Differences in Tax Bases and Tax Effort across Kentucky Counties." Kentucky Annual Economic Report, Center for Business and Economic Research, Gatton College of Business and Economics, University of Kentucky, 2001. http://gatton.uky.edu/CBER/Downloads/annrpt01.pdf.

Tannenwald, Robert. "Interstate Fiscal Disparity in State Fiscal Year 1999." Discussion Paper No. 04-09, Federal Reserve Bank of Boston, December 2004.

Texas Advisory Commission on Intergovernmental Relations. "Local Government Fiscal Capacity Measures: A Profile of State Studies." In *Federal-State-Local Fiscal Relations: Technical Papers, Vol. I,* Office of State and Local Finance, U.S. Department of the Treasury. Washington, DC: U.S. Government Printing Office, 1986.

Cross-reference: tax and revenue capacity.

Tax arbitrage

Andrew A. Samwick
Dartmouth College

Profit opportunities created by differential taxation of gains and losses.

An arbitrage is the opportunity to buy and sell the same asset in two different markets in order to profit from a price differential. By purchasing the asset in the market where it is cheaper and selling it in the market where it is more expensive, the investor can earn the difference in prices without incurring any risk. In a tax arbitrage, the price differential is the result of a feature of the tax code that treats gains and losses generated by an asset asymmetrically.

The assets that form the basis of tax arbitrages are typically financial rather than real. Consequently, buying and selling an asset at different prices is equivalent to lending and borrowing the same cash flows at different after-tax interest rates. Under a pure income tax system, interest paid on borrowed funds is deductible from taxable income, and interest received on loaned funds is included in taxable income. Tax arbitrage occurs whenever it is possible to use borrowed funds whose interest expenses are fully deductible to lend in the same market at an interest rate that is not fully taxed. The size of the deductions will exceed that of the receipts, and the investor's tax burden on income from other sources will be reduced.

Under the current tax code, the primary source of deductible interest payments for households is home mortgages or other home equity loans. A household can engage in a "debt" tax arbitrage by taking out a home equity loan and investing the proceeds in municipal bonds, the interest on which is untaxed. Alternatively, the household could use the loan to buy taxable bonds and hold them in an individual retirement account (IRA) or make larger contributions to a pension plan that invests in taxable bonds. Investment income on assets in these retirement accounts is tax-deferred until retirement. An additional tax advantage may exist if the household's marginal tax rate is lower in retirement than during its working years. (A similar tax arbitrage is also available to a corporation that sponsors a pension plan in which a fund is established to provide for promised future benefits. No income tax is paid on contributions to the pension fund or the income earned on the fund until the fund is distributed to pensioners. The corporation could simultaneously issue a bond, on which interest is fully deductible, make a larger contribution to its pension fund, and invest the contribution in a taxable bond of similar duration and risk to the one it issued.)

Households can also engage in "equity" tax arbitrages. The asymmetry in the tax treatment of equities is that capital gains and losses are taxed only when they are realized, not when they are accrued. Because the household determines when to buy or sell its stock, losses can be taken immediately while gains are postponed. A tax arbitrage can therefore be constructed simply by simultaneously buying and short-selling two highly correlated portfolios of stocks. At the end of a year, one of the positions will have increased in value and the other will have decreased. The latter can be liquidated to generate a loss for tax purposes. The investor can then maintain the tax arbitrage by taking an offsetting position in a new portfolio of stocks that is highly correlated with the position that has increased in value. The effective tax rate on the gains when all positions are liquidated is further reduced by either a preferential statutory tax rate of 28 percent on capital gains (for high-income investors) or the step-up of basis of the value of capital gains at death. (This example is based on Stiglitz 1985, who shows how strategies of this sort can be used to eliminate an investor's tax liability on all capital income and, in some cases, on all ordinary income.)

Provisions in the tax code and other capital market imperfections prevent households from fully exploiting either of these tax arbitrages. In the debt tax arbitrage, the government allows interest deductions primarily in conjunction with real estate holdings. The size of the debt that can be issued to finance the purchase of tax-preferred assets is therefore limited by the size of the real estate. There are also fairly low limits on the amounts that can be contributed to IRAs and other tax-preferred accounts. It is also important to note that the mortgage borrowing, the real estate on which it is based, and the tax-preferred assets that are purchased are not without risk. Banks will charge a premium over the risk-free rate for the mortgage that may exceed the tax advantages to the municipal bond or retirement account.

These obstacles are even more pronounced for the equity arbitrage. Transaction costs associated with trading stocks are not negligible, particularly when short-sales are involved. There are also fairly low limits on how much of a net capital loss can be used to offset noncapital income in a given year rather than being carried forward. Households without substantial other capital income will find the tax arbitrage strategy less profitable. More important, the equity tax arbitrage cannot be constructed simply by buying and selling two different shares of the same security. The investor must find two different portfolios that are highly correlated. Because this correlation will in practice be less than perfect, the investor will be exposed to risk. (Standard portfolio theory has strong conclusions regarding the optimality of holding well-diversified portfolios of risky assets. Asset pricing models typically imply that idiosyncratic risk that could have been diversified away is not reflected in the price of securities. Tax arbitrage using different portfolios implies an exposure to some idiosyncratic risk.) An investor's willingness to exploit a potential tax arbitrage may be limited by aversion to this risk.

A corporate tax arbitrage that has been of interest to policymakers is that of accelerated depreciation. The reduction in the present value of an asset over time is called its economic depreciation. Under an income tax, this depreciation should be deducted from the firm's taxable income each year. Historically, the federal tax code has allowed firms to claim depreciation expenses in a fashion that is accelerated relative to the asset's economic depreciation. In the period before the Tax Reform Act of 1986 (TRA86), two common forms of accelerated depreciation were the accelerated cost recovery system and the investment tax credit (ITC). When the asset is sold, the gain is taken with respect to the depreciated basis, but the gain may be treated preferentially. A corporation that borrows to purchase an asset that is eligible for accelerated depreciation is engaging in a tax arbitrage similar to the debt tax arbitrage described above. (See Warren 1985 for a thorough discussion of depreciation and tax arbitrage.) As in the debt tax arbitrage, an investor's risk aversion will limit how this arbitrage is exploited. Additionally, because the asset involved is real rather than financial, diminishing marginal returns to investment may limit the amount of funds that can be arbitraged in this way.

In the years before TRA86, there was a thriving tax shelter industry that was based on extending this corporate tax arbitrage to individual investors. Tax shelters were typically packaged as limited partnerships, which combined the advantages of limited liability found in corporations with the pass-through of profits and losses to the taxable incomes of the partners. Before TRA86, the top marginal tax rate for individual investors exceeded that of corporations, so the ability to deduct interest payments suggested that noncorporate entities should borrow to purchase depreciable assets and then lease them to corporations. (An obvious tax arbitrage would be for a corporation to sell its asset to a limited partnership and then agree to lease it back in perpetuity. Such sale-leaseback arrangements are prohibited by law.) TRA86 contained a number of provisions that were targeted at tax shelters, including the repeal of the ITC, the lengthening of depreciation schedules, the lowering of top marginal tax rates, and the passive activity loss limitations (PALLs). The PALLs limited the extent to which losses from activities in which the investor did not materially participate (i.e., limited partnerships) could offset gains from other sources. (Cordes and Galper 1985 discuss tax shelters before TRA86. Samwick 1996 analyzes the impact of TRA86's several anti–tax shelter provisions on their subsequent decline.)

Tax arbitrages can be understood as unintended consequences of government tax policy. Because home ownership, retirement security, investment, and the like are viewed as desirable social objectives, the federal government has attempted to promote them through the tax code. But the government cannot, for example, require that households use their IRAs only for retirement. Each special provision permits the possibility that it will be used only to lower households' tax liabilities and not to further the government's objective. Tax policy has been modified to strike a balance between promoting the objective and limiting abuse. In the case of IRAs and pensions, there are ceilings on contributions for both individuals and corporations. The size of the tax preference on particular assets may be tied to the investor's willingness to bear risk, such as the limited offset of capital losses against contemporaneous noncapital income and the PALLs. The most obvious abuses are simply prohibited directly by law, such as the buying and selling of the same security in the equity tax arbitrage or sale-leaseback arrangements between corporate and noncorporate entities.

These restrictions also play a role in establishing equilibrium asset prices. Asset markets cannot be in equilibrium if there are exploitable arbitrage opportunities. The price of each asset must be such that no investor has an opportunity to profit by tax arbitrage. This implies that the risk-adjusted after-tax return on all investments must be equal at the margin or that the marginal investment is prohibited by a legal or institutional constraint. Tax policy will therefore have an impact on the rates of return of all assets and the distribution of asset holdings in the population, but in equilibrium, no investor will be able to profit by engaging in another tax arbitrage. Cordes and Galper (1985) discuss tax shelters before TRA86. Samwick (1996) analyzes the impact of TRA86's several anti–tax shelter provisions on their subsequent decline.

ADDITIONAL READINGS

Cordes, Joseph J., and Harvey Galper. "Tax Shelter Activity: Lessons from Twenty Years of Experience." *National Tax Journal* 8 (September 1985): 305–24.

Miller, Merton H. "Debt and Taxes." *Journal of Finance* 32 (May 1977): 261–76.

Ross, Stephen A. "Arbitrage and Martingales with Taxation." *Journal of Political Economy* 95 (April 1987): 371–93.

Samwick, Andrew A. "Tax Shelters and Passive Losses after the Tax Reform Act of 1986." In *Empirical Foundations of Household Taxation,* edited by Martin Feldstein and James M. Poterba (193–226). Chicago: University of Chicago Press, 1996.

Stiglitz, Joseph E. "The General Theory of Tax Avoidance." *National Tax Journal* 38 (September 1985): 325–37.

Warren, Alvin C., Jr. "Accelerated Capital Recovery, Debt, and Tax Arbitrage." *Tax Lawyer* 38, no. 3 (1985): 549–74.

Cross-references: capital cost recovery; capital gains taxation; depreciation recapture; expensing; individual retirement accounts; interest deductibility; investment tax credits; partnerships; passive activity losses; tax shelters.

Tax competition

Robert Tannenwald
Federal Reserve Bank of Boston

The design of tax policy to attract and to retain geographically mobile capital, labor, and consumption.

Always a contentious issue, tax competition is more salient and more controversial today than ever before. Over the past 25 years, profound technological and political changes have enhanced the geographic mobility of capital, extended firms' geographic range, and therefore heightened economic competition in the United States and throughout the world. These developments have stimulated interest in tax competition at all levels of government, from the municipal to the supranational.

Forms of tax competition

Tax competition can be explicit or implicit (Kenyon 1991). Governments engage in explicit tax competition when they enact tax laws and regulations expressly designed to enhance the attractiveness of their jurisdiction to businesses, residents, employees, or consumers. The purest form of such competition is "smokestack chasing," offers of tax benefits to a specific company on condition that it locate facilities within a particular jurisdiction. For example, in 1993 the city of Tuscaloosa and the state of Alabama offered Daimler-Benz, Inc., an estimated $150 million in tax incentives to build a new Mercedes-Benz plant in Tuscaloosa.

Governments engage in implicit tax competition when they modify their pursuit of other tax policy goals—such as equity, neutrality, simplicity, revenue adequacy, or tax exporting—to mitigate anticompetitive consequences. An example was Florida's decision in December 1987 to abandon its attempt to tax services under its sales tax. Earlier that year, Florida had incorporated a wide array of services into its sales tax base in order to enhance the tax's lucrativeness, equity, and neutrality. After several interest groups, especially those representing advertisers and the media, claimed that taxing them would drive businesses out of the state, the state reversed itself.

Effectiveness of tax-competitive strategies

Hundreds of empirical studies have investigated how a jurisdiction's tax characteristics influence its attractiveness to businesses, employees, residents, and consumers (literature surveys can be found in Bartik 1991, Wasylenko 1997, and Lynch 2004). Most studies conclude that (1) taxes are a less powerful determinant of business location and expansion than centrality of location, wage rates, regulatory burden, and the availability of appropriately skilled labor and (2) because sites within a metropolitan area tend to be similar with respect to these prime locational determinants, taxes are a more effective instrument of intrametropolitan competition than of intermetropolitan or interstate competition.

Evidence concerning the effectiveness of tax policy as an instrument of interstate and intermetropolitan economic competition is inconclusive, however. Until about 25 years ago, most academic studies found very little connection between interstate tax differences and interstate differences in economic performance. Since about 1980, empirical studies have produced mixed results. While many studies still conclude that taxes "don't matter," several others have found that differences among states in tax characteristics do affect economic growth and site selection by firms. Moreover, there is still little agreement among academic studies about which interstate tax differences are the most significant locational determinants. Evidence tends to be "fragile." Some studies find significant tax effects in some decades, but other studies using a similar methodology find that the tax effects disappear in other decades (see, e.g., McGuire and Wasylenko 1987 and Wasylenko and Carroll 1994). (See *business location, taxation and.*)

The difficulty of evaluating a jurisdiction's tax competitiveness

No statistics are widely recognized as superior indicators of tax competitiveness. This is not surprising, given the absence of conclusive empirical evidence on which tax characteristics, if any, most heavily influence location.

Neoclassical economic theory, however, provides some insight into the characteristics of a good indicator of tax competitiveness. The prototypical neoclassical firm should be most concerned about how taxes imposed at a given site affect the long-run rate of return on its investments. Consequently, it should be most sensitive to interjurisdictional differences in the burden of those taxes that most directly affect its profitability, such as taxes on corporate profits, industrial and commercial property, and the purchase of intermediate goods.

The neoclassical firm should also be concerned about the burden of state and local taxes paid by individuals, such as the personal income tax, the residential property tax, and the retail sales tax. Such taxes can indirectly affect a firm's bottom line by inducing workers to demand higher pretax compensation. Highly compensated managers and professionals are more likely than other workers to make their wage demands stick because they are well informed and possess scarce, valuable skills. Consequently, a jurisdiction's tax competitiveness theoretically should be affected by how heavily it taxes its high-income households.

Estimating how the burden of business taxes and taxes on high-income households varies across subnational jurisdictions is hindered by (1) the absence of subnational data on business profits, (2) the tendency of state and municipal governments not to report the division of their property tax and sales receipts between residential and nonresidential taxpayers, and (3) differences across jurisdictions in the ability of firms to export the burden of their taxes to taxpayers in other jurisdictions (see *incidence of taxes* and *tax exportation*).

Despite these empirical difficulties, many states and municipalities closely monitor their tax competitiveness with whatever imperfect statistics are available. Four of the most widely monitored and publicized indicators of state tax competitiveness are (1) total receipts from taxes levied by all state and municipal jurisdictions within the state's boundaries divided by the total personal income of its residents, (2) total state and municipal taxes per capita, (3) total receipts from all own-source revenues (fees and charges as well as taxes) as a percentage of statewide personal income, and (4) total receipts from all own-source revenues per capita. None of these indicators focuses on those taxes that theoretically should concern businesses the most. As table 1 shows, the ranking of many states varies dramatically from measure to measure.

Perhaps the most misleading, widely cited indicator of a state's tax competitiveness is "business's share": the percentage of all state and local taxes imposed within a state for which businesses, as opposed to households, are liable. In constructing this measure, analysts classify each state and local tax according to whether it is paid by businesses or households. For each state, taxes paid by both types of taxpayers, such as the property tax and sales tax, are decomposed into their business and household components. The statistic was first constructed by the U.S. Advisory Commission on Intergovernmental Relations (1981). The tax system of a state collecting a relatively large share of its taxes from businesses, as opposed to households, is sometimes criticized as "uncompetitive" and "unfair" to business. Estimates of business's share in fiscal year 2003 for the 50 states (Cline et al. 2003) are presented in the fifth column of table 1.

Unlike the indicators shown in the first four columns of the table, business's share focuses on those state and local taxes that should concern businesses the most. Nevertheless, the share of a state's taxes collected from businesses has little to do with how heavily or fairly its businesses are taxed. Business's share is influenced primarily by two characteristics of a state's economy: its capital intensity and the importance of extractive industries in its industrial mix (Tannenwald 1994). In states with capital-intensive economies, the bases of major business taxes, such as profits (the return to capital) and nonresidential property, are large relative to the bases of major household taxes, such as personal income. Business taxes as a percentage of profits, however, are not necessarily high. States rich in extractable resources, such as Alaska, Wyoming, and Montana, generate a large fraction of their revenues from severance taxes and property taxes on natural resources. The burden of these taxes is borne by energy consumers throughout the world, companies engaged in mineral extraction, or owners of mineral rights, not by business as a whole. In these states, business's share bears little relationship to how heavily the typical business is taxed.

In recent years, economists have experimented with the representative firm approach to evaluating a jurisdiction's tax competitiveness. Businesses representative of selected industries are assumed to invest in a new facility at various sites. All nontax costs are assumed to be constant across sites. Each firm's liability for taxes levied by all levels of government is computed at each site before and after the investment is undertaken. The more taxes levied at a given site depress the rate of return on the new facility, the less competitive is the site (see Papke and Papke 1981; Tannenwald 1996). A similar approach has been tried with representative households (see, for example, Government of the District of Columbia 2003 and Tannenwald 1994).

Costs and benefits of interjurisdictional tax competition

Critics of interjurisdictional tax competition contend that (1) state and local tax incentives generally produce little "bang for the buck," rewarding firms for behavior that they would have exhibited anyway; (2) tax competition ultimately lowers the revenues of all competing jurisdictions without enhancing the competitive standing of any, thereby resulting in insufficient spending for needed state and local public services; (3) tax incentives confer windfalls capriciously, favoring firms in some industries but not others, and therefore distort the nation's interindustry allocation of resources; and (4) tax competition discourages subnational governments from progressive taxation (see *ability to pay*). They fear that highly skilled managers and professional workers, who tend to earn high incomes, will respond to heavy tax burdens by migrating to other jurisdictions.

Proponents of interjurisdictional competition make four arguments in its favor. One is that it curbs governments'

TABLE 1. Selected Frequently Cited Indicators of State Tax Competitiveness

	2000 state and local taxes as a percentage of personal income	Rank	2000 state and local taxes per capita ($)	Rank	2000 state and local own-source general revenue as a percentage of personal income	Rank	2000 state and local own-source general revenue per capita ($)	Rank	Ernst & Young 2000 estimate of business share of state and local taxes	Rank
AL	9.1	49	2,117.2	51	15.4	27	3,581.1	47	41.6	26
AK	12.7	4	3,687.1	7	42.1	1	12,171.2	1	81.0	1
AZ	10.5	31	2,598.6	37	14.5	38	3,583.7	46	46.2	16
AR	10.4	34	2,230.2	48	15.3	31	3,276.8	50	39.9	29
CA	11.4	12	3,544.7	8	16.2	19	5,015.9	10	37.3	40
CO	9.7	44	3,072.8	19	14.5	39	4,585.9	17	39.4	30
CT	11.5	9	4,595.1	2	14.3	41	5,706.0	4	37.0	42
DE	11.2	16	3,340.1	13	18.8	4	5,577.5	5	53.6	10
DC	14.6	1	5,622.0	1	18.1	5	6,965.9	2	NA	NA
FL	9.5	46	2,624.0	36	14.6	37	4,013.6	33	47.5	13
GA	10.5	30	2,840.6	26	14.7	36	3,984.9	35	37.9	38
HI	12.2	7	3,384.2	11	17.3	11	4,783.5	11	38.4	35
ID	10.9	20	2,545.8	39	16.3	18	3,807.2	39	37.6	39
IL	10.4	33	3,241.5	15	13.9	46	4,318.3	21	46.3	15
IN	10.2	38	2,691.4	31	15.3	30	4,042.8	32	35.8	44
IA	10.7	24	2,765.0	28	16.2	20	4,186.2	28	42.0	25
KS	10.5	29	2,833.5	27	15.1	33	4,058.3	30	42.8	24
KY	10.7	25	2,516.7	40	15.5	25	3,668.4	42	39.2	32
LA	10.8	21	2,436.2	42	17.1	14	3,864.9	37	56.5	5
ME	13.2	3	3,342.9	12	18.0	6	4,556.5	18	45.0	19
MD	10.5	32	3,453.5	10	14.0	44	4,619.8	15	30.7	50
MA	10.5	28	3,786.7	5	13.9	45	5,017.5	9	35.5	45
MI	11.0	18	3,167.1	17	16.0	22	4,637.2	14	39.2	33
MN	11.9	8	3,694.4	6	17.2	12	5,323.8	7	37.1	41
MS	10.8	22	2,214.2	49	17.2	13	3,536.7	48	44.0	22
MO	9.7	45	2,558.3	38	13.7	48	3,624.1	45	38.0	37
MT	10.6	27	2,363.5	46	17.7	9	3,936.3	36	54.4	8
NE	10.7	23	2,906.5	25	15.8	24	4,272.5	23	43.6	23
NV	9.9	43	2,915.3	24	14.2	43	4,183.8	29	46.0	17
NH	8.3	51	2,652.4	33	11.9	51	3,796.5	40	62.7	3
NJ	10.7	26	3,902.8	4	14.2	42	5,184.4	8	39.0	34
NM	12.3	6	2,639.1	34	19.6	3	4,213.0	27	50.2	12
NY	13.6	2	4,577.8	3	18.0	7	6,042.0	3	40.4	28
NC	10.2	39	2,663.7	32	15.2	32	3,985.6	34	34.9	46
ND	11.4	14	2,754.1	29	17.9	8	4,343.2	19	54.6	7
OH	10.9	19	3,015.8	21	15.3	29	4,235.4	26	38.4	36
OK	10.2	36	2,391.0	44	15.5	26	3,627.1	44	44.1	21
OR	10.1	40	2,751.2	30	16.8	17	4,599.8	16	33.8	48
PA	10.3	35	2,978.7	22	14.7	35	4,243.7	25	41.1	27
RI	11.5	10	3,256.1	14	15.4	28	4,342.8	20	45.7	18
SC	10.0	41	2,378.6	45	16.1	21	3,826.2	38	39.3	31
SD	9.1	48	2,298.8	47	13.8	47	3,471.9	49	57.4	4
TN	8.6	50	2,185.1	50	12.8	50	3,252.4	51	50.6	11
TX	9.2	47	2,504.6	41	13.6	49	3,690.9	41	56.3	6
UT	11.4	13	2,630.2	35	17.5	10	4,046.5	31	32.9	49
VT	11.5	11	3,079.7	18	15.9	23	4,259.0	24	44.3	20
VA	9.9	42	2,978.2	23	14.3	40	4,297.8	22	35.9	43
WA	10.2	37	3,178.5	16	15.0	34	4,682.5	13	54.2	9
WV	11.3	15	2,412.8	43	17.0	16	3,631.3	43	47.3	14
WI	12.4	5	3,457.6	9	17.1	15	4,756.3	12	33.8	47
WY	11.1	17	3,045.9	20	19.7	2	5,391.8	6	66.4	2

Sources: U.S. Census Bureau, U.S. Bureau of Economic Analysis, and Cline et al. (2003).
Note: NA = not applicable

inherent tendency to maximize revenues and exploit tax-payers (the "Leviathan principle"). A second is that such competition encourages states and municipalities to tax their constituents according to the "benefit principle"—that is, in proportion to the benefits they receive from state and municipal services. Departure from this principle will cause some of those paying taxes in excess of benefits received to move to another jurisdiction. Distributing tax burdens in proportion to benefits received is a second normative principle of tax fairness that complements the principle of ability to pay (see *benefit principle*). The third argument is that, much as free-market pricing leads to efficient resource allocation in the private sector, so benefit taxation maximizes allocative efficiency within the public sector and promotes an optimal public/private mix of goods and services (see *Tiebout model*). Fourth, proponents argue that while interjurisdictional competition encourages regressive taxation, progressive taxation at the federal level can offset the resulting inequities without the attendant distortions in location.

Proponents of interjurisdictional tax competition generally acknowledge that its benefits can be fully realized only when fiscal disparities across competing jurisdictions are small (see *fiscal disparities*). Otherwise, jurisdictions with low fiscal capacity and/or high fiscal need will be at an inherent competitive disadvantage no matter what competitive tactics they pursue. Fiscally comfortable jurisdictions will be able to provide a given level of services at a lower average tax burden than their more fiscally stressed competitors. For this reason, tax competition is most beneficial when pursued within a federal context, in which higher levels of government redistribute resources across jurisdictions to maintain a level interjurisdictional "playing field."

Alternatives to explicit tax competition in economic development policy

The high costs of explicit interjurisdictional tax competition, as well as persistent doubts about its effectiveness, have spurred states and municipalities to pursue economic development strategies designed to foster business creation and expansion rather than to attract and to retain existing firms. For example, the National Governors Association argued in a formal policy statement adopted in 1993 that "state competition [for business investments] should not be characterized by how much direct assistance a state can provide to individual companies . . . [but] on how each state attempts to provide a business climate in which existing businesses can operate profitably and expand and new businesses can be established and survive" (Kayne and Shonka 1994, 25).

Some groups and individuals have urged the federal government to regulate the use of tax incentives at the subnational level and to renew revenue sharing arrangements in order to curb incentives for explicit tax competition (see, e.g., Rivlin 1991; Enrich 1996; Burstein and Rolnick 1996).

ADDITIONAL READINGS

Bartik, Timothy J. *Who Benefits from State and Local Economic Development Policies?* Kalamazoo, MI: W.E. Upjohn Institute for Employment Research, 1991.

———. "Federal Policy toward State and Local Economic Development in the 1900s." In *The Millenial City: Classic Readings on U.S. Urban Policy,* edited by R. D. Norton (235–52). Stamford, CT: JAI Press, 1993.

Burstein, Melvin L., and Arthur J. Rolnick. "Congress Should End the Economic War for Sports and Other Businesses." *The Region.* Special Issue, *The Economic War among the States* (35–36). Minneapolis, MN: The Federal Reserve Bank of Minneapolis, June 1996.

Cline, Robert J., William F. Fox, Thomas S. Neubig, and Andrew Phillips. "Total State and Local Business Taxes: Fiscal 2003 Update." *State Tax Notes* 30 (October 20, 2003): 205–8.

Enrich, Peter D. "Saving the States from Themselves: Commerce Clause Constraints on State Tax Incentives for Business." *Harvard Law Review* 110, no. 2 (December 1996): 377–468.

Harden, J. William, and William H. Hoyt. "Do States Choose Their Mix of Taxes to Minimize Employment Losses?" *National Tax Journal* 56, no. 1 (March 2003): 7–26.

Government of the District of Columbia. *Tax Rates and Tax Burdens in the District of Columbia: A Nationwide Comparison.* Washington, DC: Government of the District of Columbia, 2003.

Kayne, Jay, and Molly Shonka. *Rethinking State Development Policies and Programs.* Washington, DC: National Governors Association, 1994.

Kenyon, Daphne A. *Interjurisdictional Tax and Policy Competition: Good or Bad for the Federal System?* Washington, DC: U.S. Advisory Commission on Intergovernmental Relations, 1991.

Lynch, Robert G. *Rethinking Growth Strategies: How State and Local Taxes Affect Economic Development.* Washington, DC: Economic Policy Institute, 2004.

Mark, Stephen T., Therese J. McGuire, and Leslie E. Papke. "The Influence of Taxes on Employment and Population Growth: Evidence from the Washington, D.C. Metropolitan Area." *National Tax Journal* 53, no. 1 (March 2000): 105–23.

McGuire, Therese, and Michael Wasylenko. *Employment Growth and State Government Fiscal Behavior: A Report on Economic Development for States from 1973 to 1984.* Trenton: New Jersey State and Local Expenditure and Revenue Policy Commission, 1987.

Mead, Charles Ian. "State User Costs of Capital." Working Paper 01-3. Boston: Federal Reserve Bank of Boston, 2001.

Mills, Edwin S. "Toward the Next Massachusetts Miracle: The Limits of Economic Development Programs." In *The Millenial City: Classic Readings on U.S. Urban Policy,* edited by R. D. Norton. Stamford, CT: JAI Press, 1997.

Oates, Wallace E. "Economic Competition versus Harmonization among Jurisdictions: An Overview." *National Tax Journal* 54, no. 3 (September 2001): 507–12.

Papke, James A., and Leslie E. Papke. "Microanalytic Simulation for Analyses of Intersite Business Tax Differentials." In *Proceedings of the Seventy-Fourth Annual Conference* (78–85). Columbus, OH: National Tax Association–Tax Institute of America, 1981.

Rivlin, Alice M. "Distinguished Lecture on Economics in Government: Strengthening the Economy by Rethinking the Role of Federal and State Governments." *Journal of Economic Perspectives* 5 (Spring 1991): 3–14.

Tannenwald, Robert. "Massachusetts Tax Competitiveness." *New England Economic Review* (January/February 1994): 31–49.

———. "State Business Tax Climate: How Should It Be Measured and How Important Is It?" *New England Economic Review* (January/February 1996): 21–39.

U.S. Advisory Commission on Intergovernmental Relations. *Regional Growth: Interstate Tax Competition.* Washington, DC: U.S. Government Printing Office, 1981.

U.S. Department of Commerce, Bureau of the Census. *Governmental Finances 1990–91.* Washington, DC: U.S. Government Printing Office, 1993.

Wasylenko, Michael. "Taxation and Economic Development: The State of the Literature." *New England Economic Review* (May/June 1997): 37–52.

Wasylenko, Michael, and Robert Carroll. "Do State Business Climates Still Matter? Evidence of a Structural Change." *National Tax Journal* 47 (March 1994): 19–38.

Cross-references: benefit principle; business location, taxation and; enterprise zones; tax abatement programs; tax and revenue capacity.

Tax equity analysis

Donald Phares
University of Missouri–St. Louis

A review of the concept and process for understanding the distribution of the tax burden among people (individuals, families, households).

A tax system is a complex set of instruments employed to accomplish varied public purposes. Evaluation of such a system could use many criteria such as adequacy, efficiency, or responsiveness, but a factor that receives considerable taxpayer and legislative attention is "equity." Who pays and how much? What impact does taxation have on taxpayers with different economic status? Is it "fair"?

Why is equity of concern? A broad response is "fairness." But the core is more complex. How is the cost of public programs apportioned? Who bears the burden and how much is it? What are the impacts of changes in a tax system and how should they be apportioned? How do equity concerns weigh against other evaluation criteria? How focal should equity be as a determinant of tax policy? The real answers are far more involved than simply to "be fair."

Looking back at the seeds of Proposition 13 in California, Proposition 2 ½ in Massachusetts, or their myriad progeny, many fiscal limitations over the past few decades had equity, de facto, as a focal issue. Taxpayers felt that they were paying too much and that the cost was not fairly distributed. Such concern continues in 2005.

Key issues

In considering equity, several points are pivotal. First, a revenue system's overall impact should be considered, not just the marginal effect of one component. During legislative deliberations, attention necessarily might be on a specific item, but the marginal change should be factored into overall impact. Second, nontax sources, such as fees and charges, play an increasingly important role in public finances; their impact, often ignored, needs to be considered also. Third, equity is traditionally evaluated in the context of ability to pay. This is complicated by varying interpretations of what defines ability to pay, who should pay, and how much. Fourth, revenue systems are economically open.

Taxes are not contained by jurisdictional boundaries. A relatively large percentage of tax burdens may be "exported."

Taxes may also be "imported" from other jurisdictions. To the extent that exporting and importing occur, burden and equity for a given revenue system are affected.

Gauging the equity of tax systems

Equity for a tax system cannot be established a priori. Determination is a function of rather complex theoretical and empirical analysis. The following sections will sketch this out.

What is equity?

Equity (vertical) analysis most commonly examines the pattern of tax burdens across an income spectrum from low to high. It reflects how effective tax rates vary with income.

Estimating tax burdens and then equity is an exercise in applied economic analysis. It involves the use of economic theory and various quantitative techniques. The lexicon of equity analysis tends to become "application-specific" and needs to be set out clearly in order for discussion to be interpreted properly. The most commonly encountered terms are the following:

Burden: The claim on economic status, usually income, resulting from the imposition of a tax.

Effective rate: A measure of tax burden that relates taxes paid to ability to pay.

Nominal rate: The statutory rate.

Equity: The pattern of the tax burdens' effective rate across the income spectrum. Equity patterns are usually classified as regressive—burden declines as income rises; proportional—burden is invariant with income; or progressive—burden increases as income increases.

Impact: The impact on those legally required to pay.

Incidence: Contrasted with impact, the actual economic impact on those who must ultimately bear the burden.

Shifting: The movement (shifting) of the burden from its point of legal impact to its final economic resting place (incidence).

Exporting: The geographical movement of taxes from where legally imposed to residents of another jurisdiction(s) or, with state/local taxes, also to the federal tax system.

Importing: The movement of taxes into one jurisdiction from another.

How is equity determined?

Determination of equity involves blending economic theory on shifting/incidence, the interjurisdictional movement of revenues, and the application of quantitative techniques to summarize the resultant information. Stated in its simplest terms, divide the income spectrum into groupings that are appropriate to policy and then determine the taxes that are paid by each group as a percentage of income. This gives an effective rate. Then examine the pattern of effective rates across the income spectrum. This pattern reflects the equity of specific taxes or sets of taxes.

Several steps are entailed. First, determine payments for each income group by applying shifting/incidence theory. A tax on business provides a good illustration. Businesses do not bear the burden of tax payments. Rather, they are shifted to consumers as higher prices, workers as lower compensation, owners as reduced returns, or some combination. Applying shifting/incidence theory permits estimation of actual tax burdens.

Second, revenues are not constrained by boundaries. They move because of the openness of our economic system. A tax imposed in one area can exert its economic incidence on residents elsewhere. Estimation of effective rates, and therefore the pattern of burden, must account for such tax movement to accurately reflect the actual burden and equity within the area of concern. Also, part of the state/local tax burden may be shifted to the federal revenue structure through IRS deductibility provisions.

A final consideration is measurement of ability to pay, the denominator of an effective rate. Measures vary from very narrow ones such as adjusted gross income to much more sophisticated ones such as "permanent income," a lifetime income flow. A key issue for tax policy is the current tax burden and the current income to pay it. This focuses more on the immediacy of tax policy to fund public programs. While AGI is generally considered too narrow a definition of ability to pay, a broader measure such as money income is closer to measuring ability to pay in an immediate policy-relevant context—that is, to pay current taxes out of current income.

With payments of taxes measured for the numerator and ability to pay for the denominator of an effective rate, burden across income groups can be estimated. Determination of equity then entails an examination of the pattern of these burdens across the income spectrum. The following summarizes the components that make up effective rates:

$$ER_{ij} = \frac{T_{ij}}{Y_{ij}}$$

   ER = effective rate (burden)
    Y = ability to pay
    T = $(C - E - F + I)$
     i = income group
     j = specific tax or set of taxes

where
C = revenue
E = exported taxes
F = exporting due to IRS provisions (state/local only)
I = imported taxes

Measures of equity

The final task in equity analysis is to examine the pattern of effective rates as it varies with income. The expression above

defines the level of effective rates for income classes but does not portray the pattern of burden. Equity is concerned with this pattern. To reflect this, an index is needed to depict the magnitude of variation and allow a general classification (regressive, proportional, progressive). Such an index greatly facilitates comparisons for policy options.

One widely used equity measure employs a simple regression analysis using data on the effective rate and income by income class. The index is taken from the coefficient in the regression equation and reflects the change in burden as income changes; it is usually estimated in percentage terms. If this index is negative (burden falls as income rises), equity is regressive; if it is positive (burden increases with income), it is progressive; if there is no statistical association between burden and income, equity is proportional. Quantitative comparisons can be made by examining the magnitude of the indices.

A second equity index, the Suits index, has been used quite widely. It examines the concentration of tax payments by income class. It ranges in value from +1.0 where all payment is made by the highest class (extreme progressivity), through 0.0 where the burden is evenly spread across classes (proportionality), to –1.0 where the lowest class makes all payment (extreme regressivity).

The clear advantage of such indices is the ability to make comparisons. Is one tax more equitable than another? How regressive/progressive is a tax system? What impact do policy changes have? How do jurisdictions compare? What change has occurred over time?

Limitations of equity analysis

Equity analysis does have limitations. One relates to applying theoretical information on shifting/incidence to make quantitative estimates of effective rates. Economic theory is used to reflect how a tax shifts from point of legal impact to economic incidence. This relates to shifting not only among economic groups but also geographically. Sales taxes may be shifted to consumers; a residential property tax may be shifted to renters; business taxes may affect owners. Each, in turn, may be exported geographically. The primary objective is to determine who pays, how much they pay, and where they reside.

A difficulty is that there is not universal agreement about shifting/incidence. As an example, debate continues over who pays the corporation income tax and, more recently, who pays the property tax. Both instances focus on burden being shifted to consumers or being borne by owners. Needless to say, equity is sensitive to the assumptions. Frequently this is resolved by relying on professional judgment, selecting assumptions that are reasonable, and setting them as "benchmarks." Sensitivity analysis can then be used with alternative assumptions to determine a range.

A second limitation is that equity tends to focus on taxes. Clearly, taxes affect private economic status. However, expenditures also affect economic status. An above-average burden may be offset by above-average spending on public programs; the revenue burden is accompanied by an expenditure benefit. An apparently regressive tax system may be mitigated by increased spending benefits for lower-income households.

It should also be noted that the type of equity study discussed here does not examine what the situation is within any given income group, which also may be of interest for certain policy issues.

Finally, a tax's equity must be weighted against the magnitude of the burden the tax imposes. A highly regressive tax on a necessity and large budget item, such as food, is very different from a highly regressive tax on an item of choice (and low budget item), such as tobacco.

Policy relevance of equity analysis

What is the relevance of equity for revenue policy? Consider the following questions: Who bears the burden of public programs—who pays? How redistributive is a tax system; what is its impact on different economic groups? How do taxes vary in equity? How does tax policy affect burden / equity for different economic groups? What changes have occurred over time? Are they consistent with policy intent? How do specific changes affect a revenue system? How do jurisdictions compare? How does equity, as one goal, relate to other goals, such as revenue efficiency, responsiveness, and adequacy or public acceptance?

Although this entry focuses on tax equity, it should be noted that equity analysis can also deal with public expenditures, other revenue sources such as fees and charges, and the total budgetary impact of the government budget on private well-being. Also, the level of analysis can vary from a very specific change in policy (i.e., a tax credit or exemption) to the broad impact of any "collection" of public revenues or expenditures to entire government sectors (federal, state, local).

ADDITIONAL READINGS

Institute on Taxation and Economic Policy [ITEP]. *Who Pays? A Distributional Analysis of the Tax Systems in All 50 States.* 2nd ed. Washington, DC: ITEP, June 1996 and January 2003.

Musgrave, Richard A., and Peggy B. Musgrave. *Public Finance in Theory and Practice.* 5th ed. New York: McGraw-Hill, 1989.

Phares, Donald. *State-Local Tax Equity: An Empirical Analysis of the Fifty States.* Lexington, MA: Lexington Books, 1973.

———. *Who Pays State and Local Taxes?* Cambridge, MA: Oelgeschlager, Gunn & Hain, 1980.

Phares, Donald. "The Role of Tax Burden Studies in State Tax Policy." In *Reforming State Tax Systems,* edited by Steven D. Gold (67–88). Denver: National Conference of State Legislatures, 1987.

Slemrod, Joel B., ed. *Tax Progressivity and Income Inequality.* New York: Cambridge University Press, 1994.

———. *Does Atlas Shrug?* Cambridge, MA: Harvard University Press, 2000.

Cross-references: ability to pay; benefit principle; fairness in taxation; horizontal equity; incidence of taxes; progressivity, measures of; revenue elasticity (tax elasticity); tax exportation; vertical equity.

Tax evasion

James Alm
Andrew Young School of Policy Studies, Georgia State University

Illegal and intentional actions taken by individuals or firms to reduce their tax payments.

Tax evasion is one of the most common economic crimes and has been present since the introduction of taxes. People do not like paying taxes, and they pursue many avenues to reduce their payments. Legal methods known as "tax avoidance" take full advantage of the tax code. "Tax evasion" represents illegal and intentional actions by which evaders fail to pay legally due obligations. Individuals and firms evade taxes by underreporting incomes, sales, or wealth; by overstating deductions, exemptions, or credits; or by failing to file appropriate tax returns.

Tax evasion is important for many reasons. It reduces tax collections, thereby affecting taxes that compliant taxpayers face and public services that citizens receive. Evasion creates misallocations in resource use when individuals and firms alter their behavior to cheat on their taxes. Its presence requires that government expend resources to deter noncompliance, to detect its magnitude, and to penalize its practitioners. Tax evasion alters the distribution of income unpredictably; unless tax evaders are caught, they pay fewer taxes than honest taxpayers. Evasion may contribute to feelings of unfair treatment and disrespect for the law, creating a self-generating cycle that feeds upon itself and leads to even more evasion. It affects the accuracy of macroeconomic statistics. More broadly, it is not possible to understand the true impact of taxation without recognizing the existence of evasion.

Tax evasion raises many issues. How extensive is it? What leads individuals and firms to cheat on their taxes? What is the evidence on behavioral responses? What are appropriate government policies toward evasion? Each issue is considered. (For comprehensive surveys on various aspects of tax evasion, see Roth, Scholz, and Witte 1989; Cowell 1990; Elffers 1991; Andreoni, Erard, and Feinstein 1998; Alm 2000; and Slemrod and Yitzhaki 2002.)

Measurement of tax evasion

A major difficulty in analyzing evasion is in its measurement (Schneider and Enste 2002). After all, individuals have incentives to conceal their cheating. Several direct and indirect methods have been developed to measure evasion, all subject to imprecision and controversy.

One direct method relies on information generated by the tax authority as part of its audit process. For example, from 1965 to 1988 the United States Internal Revenue Service (IRS) conducted line-by-line audits of individual tax returns for its taxpayer compliance measurement program (TCMP) on a roughly three-year cycle. These audits yielded an estimate of the taxpayer's "true" income, allowing measures of individual and aggregate tax evasion to be calculated. However, TCMP data had some serious deficiencies. The audits did not detect all underreported income (especially income arising from the "underground economy"), nonfilers were not often captured, honest errors were not identified, and final audit adjustments were not included. TCMP information is now quite outdated.

Another direct method involves surveys. These surveys are typically designed to elicit taxpayers' attitudes about their reporting, but such surveys can also be used to estimate noncompliance. However, the accuracy of surveys is uncertain. Individuals may not remember their reporting decisions, they may not respond truthfully or at all, and the respondents may not be representative.

Indirect methods attempt to infer the magnitude of unreported income from its traces in other, observable areas. One approach looks at discrepancies between income and expenditures in budget surveys or in national income accounts. Another looks at discrepancies between "official" labor force participation rates and estimates of "true" participation rates. A third approach looks for traces of unreported income in monetary aggregates. All these methods are subject to serious criticisms. They may simply compound measurement errors, they attribute all discrepancies to unreported income, and often they are able to estimate only the change in unreported income over some period, not its absolute level.

Despite these measurement difficulties, it appears that tax evasion is a widespread and growing problem in the United States. The most reliable estimates project the amount of the federal "tax gap"—or the amount of federal income taxes due but not collected—at $127 billion for 1992 and suggest an annual growth rate of roughly 10 percent since 1973 (Internal Revenue Service 1996). More recent IRS estimates put the 2002 tax gap at $311 billion. State and local governments also report problems with noncompliance and evasion. Evidence suggests that tax evasion is even more widespread in other countries than in the United States.

Theories of tax evasion behavior

The basic theory used in nearly all compliance research builds on the economics-of-crime model, in which an individual maximizes the expected utility of the tax evasion gamble, balancing the benefits of successful cheating against the risky prospect of detection and punishment. This approach concludes that compliance depends largely upon audit and fine rates. Indeed, its central conclusion is that an individual pays taxes only because of the fear of detection and punishment, and will pay more taxes with an increase in the fine or audit rate. Surprisingly, an increase in the tax rate generally has an ambiguous effect on reported income; under plausible assumptions, compliance actually rises with higher tax rates.

However, it is clear to many observers that compliance cannot be explained entirely by the level of enforcement. The levels of audit and penalty rates are set at such low levels that most individuals would evade if they are rational because it is unlikely that cheaters will be caught and penalized.

This observation suggests that the compliance decision must be affected by factors not mentioned in the basic model, or must be affected in ways not captured appropriately by the theory. Many attempts have been made to expand the basic model to include other factors, such as

- government services,
- uncertainty enforcement,
- tax complexity,
- endogenous audit rules,
- use of paid preparers,
- labor supply and occupational choice,
- tax avoidance,
- structure of taxation,
- overweighting of low probabilities, and
- tax amnesties (see *tax amnesty*).

Other factors may well be relevant. In particular, there is increasing evidence that societal institutions, including the existence of a "social norm" of compliance and the presence of an effective but service-oriented tax administration, are crucial and influence the magnitude of tax evasion; indeed, these institutions are closely linked and work together to help determine the extent of tax evasion. However, no single theory has been able to incorporate more than a few of these factors in a meaningful way.

Evidence on tax evasion behavior

There is a growing body of empirical literature on the responses of individuals in their tax evasion behavior, largely focusing on the United States. As emphasized above, availability of data is a major difficulty, and the evidence is drawn creatively from many sources. The most extensively used source is TCMP data. Others include taxpayer returns, survey data, national income accounts, and laboratory experiments.

In its entirety, the literature suggests the following patterns of evasion:

- Tax evasion varies greatly across types of income. The percentage of wage income that is voluntarily reported is much higher than that for self-employed income.
- Unreported income increases (but less than proportionately) with income.
- A higher audit rate leads to more compliance, at least to a point, with an estimated reported income-audit rate elasticity ranging from 0.1 to 0.2.
- A higher fine rate leads to marginally more compliance, with an estimated reported income-fine rate elasticity less than 0.1.
- A higher tax rate leads to less compliance, with an estimated reported income-tax rate elasticity of −0.5 to −3.0.
- There is strong evidence that audit rates are endogenous and that this endogeneity increases the efficiency of the tax agency.

- An increase in tax complexity leads to greater use of a tax practitioner, and the average level of noncompliance is higher for returns prepared with paid assistance.
- Prior audit experience has an uncertain impact on subsequent compliance. Experimental studies suggest that post-audit compliance increases, while empirical evidence indicates little if any effect on future reporting behavior.
- The audit selection criteria of state and federal enforcement agencies are somewhat different, suggesting that sharing information could increase agency revenues.
- Rewards can provide a significant positive inducement for greater compliance. More broadly, the provision of taxpayer services can increase compliance.
- Many individuals substantially overweight the probability of an audit.
- Individuals pay more in taxes when faced with a public program that they have selected, that they value, and that they know enjoys widespread support.
- The social norm of compliance can be affected by the institutions that face individuals and by individual participation in the selection of those institutions.
- Demographic variables are important determinants of behavior. For example, at an individual level, compliance tends to be higher for individuals over the age of 65, for females, and for households in which the household head is married. When the voluntary compliance rate is examined at the ZIP Code level, compliance is higher when the non-white proportion of the population is lower, among other things.

Given the underlying data problems, these patterns need to be viewed cautiously. Still, these results indicate that the enforcement agency can increase compliance by changing its enforcement strategy, but that there are limits to strategies based only on greater enforcement.

Government policies

Governments everywhere wish to increase tax compliance. The standard policy prescription has long been an increase in penalty and audit rates. Both theoretical and empirical work indicates that greater enforcement can increase compliance. Sufficient—and draconian—increases in penalties and audit rates could substantially eliminate evasion. Conversely, lower enforcement is predicted to generate greater levels of noncompliance.

Indeed, one explanation for the increase in the United States tax gap over time is the secular decline in IRS enforcement activities. The percentage of individual returns that are audited has fallen from 6 percent in the 1960s to a current level of roughly 0.5 percent. More recently, the IRS staff, including field compliance personnel, has declined significantly. At the same time, the opportunities for evasion have increased, as reflected in a large increase in the number of tax returns (especially those of individuals with "large" incomes) and in the increased use of illegal tax shelters or questionable individual and corporate tax practices.

Nevertheless, it is unlikely that extreme enforcement measures will be implemented. There is a widespread belief that "the punishment should fit the crime." Moreover, higher penalty and audit rates entail costs, both to the government that must use real resources in its efforts and to the individuals who suffer a loss in utility from greater enforcement. Finally, it may be inappropriate to increase the IRS budget, even if a dollar spent on more enforcement increases collections by more than one dollar. The additional budget allocation represents a real resource cost, while the additional revenues are simply a transfer from the private to the public sector. Instead, the optimal amount of government enforcement must equate its marginal costs and benefits, where the benefits should include added revenues but also should reflect the impacts of government-induced honesty and the loss in individual expected utility.

It may well be that the best government policy is a pragmatic one that recognizes that evasion cannot—and should not—be completely eliminated. Such a policy should include greater enforcement but should also emphasize the use of source withholding, a reliance on computers, social obligations of compliance, positive rewards, the wise use of taxpayer dollars, and individual participation in the decision process. Until more is known about evasion, this strategy may well be the best.

In this regard, it should be remembered that people exhibit remarkable diversity in their behavior. There are individuals who always cheat and those who always comply, some who behave as if they maximize the expected utility of the tax evasion gamble, others who seem to overweight low probabilities, individuals who respond in different ways to changes in their tax burden, and many who seem to be guided by such things as a social norm of compliance. Any government approach toward tax compliance must address this "full house" of behaviors in devising policies to ensure compliance. Consequently, a government compliance strategy based only on detection and punishment may well be a reasonable starting point for a strategy but not a good ending point. Instead, what is needed is a multifaceted approach that emphasizes enforcement, but that also emphasizes the much broader range of actual motivations that explain why people pay taxes.

There is much that we do not know about tax evasion. We are constantly struggling to measure its extent, to discover its motivations, to estimate individual responses, and to implement appropriate policies. As long as there are taxes, this struggle will continue.

ADDITIONAL READINGS

Alm, J. "Tax Compliance and Administration." In *Handbook on Taxation*, edited by W. B. Hildreth and J. A. Richardson (741–68). New York: Marcel Dekker, Inc., 2000.

Andreoni, James, Brian Erard, and Jonathan Feinstein. "Tax Compliance." *The Journal of Economic Literature* 36, no. 2 (1998): 818–60.

Cowell, Frank A. *Cheating the Government: The Economics of Tax Evasion.* Cambridge, MA: MIT Press, 1990.

Elffers, Henk. *Income Tax Evasion: Theory and Measurement.* Deventer: Kluwer, 1991.

Internal Revenue Service. *Federal Tax Compliance Research: Individual Income Tax Gap Estimates for 1985, 1988, and 1992.* Publication 7285. Washington, DC: U.S. Department of the Treasury, 1996.

Roth, Jeffrey A., John T. Scholz, and Ann Dryden Witte, eds. *Taxpayer Compliance. Vol. 1, An Agenda for Research* and *Vol. 2, Social Science Perspectives.* Philadelphia: University of Pennsylvania Press, 1989.

Schneider, Friedrich, and Dominik H. Enste. *The Shadow Economy—An International Survey.* Cambridge, MA: Cambridge University Press, 2002.

Slemrod, Joel, and Shlomo Yitzhaki. "Tax Avoidance, Evasion, and Administration." In *Handbook of Public Economics,* edited by Alan J. Auerbach and Martin Feldstein (1423–70). Amsterdam, The Netherlands: Elsevier Science Publishers B.V., 2002.

Cross-references: income tax, federal; tax administration, federal; tax amnesty; taxpayer compliance measurement program.

Tax-exempt bonds

Dennis Zimmerman
Congressional Budget Office

A bond, issued by a state or local government, the interest on which is exempt from federal taxation.

State and local governments issue debt ($454 billion in 2003) in exchange for the use of the savings of individuals and corporations. This debt obligates state and local governments to make interest payments for the use of these savings and to repay, some time in the future, the amount borrowed (the bond proceeds).

The income tax adopted in the United States in 1913 excluded from taxable income the interest income earned by holders of the debt obligations of states and their political subdivisions. In 1988 the U.S. Supreme Court in *South Carolina v. Baker* (485 U.S. 505 [1988]) rejected the assertion that any federal taxation of interest income derived from this debt is unconstitutional because the exemption is protected by the Tenth Amendment and the doctrine of intergovernmental tax immunity. The Court denied the claim of constitutional protection and found tax exemption to be dependent upon statute and regulation. In short, Congress has the right to tax this interest income if it chooses—which it has not done.

Because the interest income on most state and local debt (all but $42 billion in 2003) is excluded from federal income taxation, the interest rate on this "tax-exempt" debt is lower than the interest rate on taxable debt. In effect, the federal government pays a share of state and local interest costs by foregoing the tax revenue it would receive if taxable debt had been issued. Tax-exempt debt has its own "market" and is an important factor in several economic policy issues.

Characteristics of tax-exempt bonds

Maturity

State and local governments must borrow money for long periods and for short periods. Long-term tax-exempt debt in-

struments are usually referred to as bonds and carry maturities in excess of one year ($343 billion in 2003). Because public capital facilities provide services over a long period, it makes sense to pay for these facilities over a long period. Thus, long-term bonds are an effort to match the timing of the payments for the capital facilities (taxes raised to fund interest and principal payments) to the flow of services from the capital facilities. An attempt to pay for capital facilities "up front" is likely to result in a less-than-optimal rate of public capital formation, as current taxpayers vote against paying taxes now for benefits provided to future citizens.

Short-term tax-exempt debt instruments are usually referred to as notes and carry maturities of 12 months or less ($68 billion in 2003). Notes usually are paid from specific taxes due in the near future or from anticipated intergovernmental revenue and are often referred to as tax and revenue anticipation notes. These short-term notes are issued because governments are faced with the necessity of planning a budget for the year (or in some cases for two years). This requires a balancing of revenue forecasts (see *revenue forecasting, federal*) against forecasts of the demand for services and spending. Not infrequently, the inevitable unforeseen circumstances that undermine any forecast cause a revenue shortfall that must be financed with short-term borrowing. In addition, even when the forecasts are met, the timing of expenditures may precede the arrival of revenues, creating the necessity to borrow within an otherwise balanced fiscal year. Finally, temporarily high interest rates that prevail at the time bonds are issued to finance a capital project may induce short-term borrowing in anticipation of a drop in rates.

Security

General obligation debt, which is the sum of short-term notes plus long-term bonds, pledges the "full faith and credit" of the issuing government, an unconditional pledge of its powers of taxation to guarantee its liability for interest and principal repayment ($202 billion in 2003). Revenue notes and bonds, or nonguaranteed debt ($252 billion in 2003), pledge only the earnings from revenue-producing activities, most often the earnings from the facilities being built with the debt proceeds. Should these earnings prove inadequate to repay interest and principal, the issuing government is under no obligation to utilize its taxing powers to finance the shortfall.

New issue versus refunding

New-issue debt ($334 billion in 2003) finances new capital facilities. Refunding-issue debt ($95 billion in 2003) replaces outstanding debt issues with debt that carries more favorable terms, such as lower interest rates. The refunding issue usually does not add to the stock of outstanding debt or the stock of capital facilities; its proceeds are used to pay off (retire) the remaining principal of the original debt issue. Advance refunding debt is issued before the date on which the original debt is refunded and adds to the outstanding stock of debt without adding to the stock of capital facilities. Another $25 billion of debt combined new and refunding issues.

Arbitrage

State and local governments do not pay federal income tax, and absent federal constraint they have unlimited capacity to issue debt at low interest rates and reinvest the bond proceeds in higher-yielding taxable debt instruments, thereby earning arbitrage profits (see *tax arbitrage*). Unchecked, state and local governments could substitute arbitrage earnings for a substantial portion of their own citizens' tax effort.

Such activity lies outside the purpose of tax exemption, and the federal tax law requires that tax-exempt bond proceeds be used as quickly as possible to pay contractors for the construction of capital facilities. Because it is impossible for bonds to be issued on the day every contractor must be paid for expenses incurred in building public capital facilities, a two-year spend-down period is granted to disburse the bond proceeds. Bond issues whose disbursements fall short of this two-year spend-down schedule must rebate any arbitrage earnings to the U.S. Treasury. Bond issues are considered taxable arbitrage bonds if a governmental unit, in violation of the arbitrage restriction in the tax code, purposely invests a substantial portion of the proceeds in assets that earn interest rates that exceed the tax-exempt interest rate by more than one-eighth of a percentage point.

Public purpose versus private purpose

Before the late 1960s, nothing in the tax law prevented state and local officials from issuing bonds and using the proceeds to finance investments for private individuals and businesses. This "conduit" financing became an increasingly larger share of the total volume of bonds from the early 1970s through the early 1980s. Unfortunately, these bonds generated no public capital facilities (the reason for having tax-exempt bonds).

Most of the legislation pertaining to tax-exempt bonds over the 30 years from 1968 to 1998 represents an effort to reduce this "conduit" financing. The legislation restricted tax exemption to bonds issued for activities that satisfy some broadly defined "public" purpose, that is, for which federal taxpayers are likely to receive substantial benefits. Bonds used in business activities are considered to satisfy a public purpose if they meet either of two criteria: no more than 10 percent of the proceeds are used directly or indirectly in a trade or business; and no more than 10 percent of the proceeds are secured directly or indirectly by property used in a trade or business. Bonds that satisfy either of these tests are termed "governmental" bonds and can be issued without limit. Bonds that fail both these tests are considered to primarily benefit private businesses, are termed "private-activity" bonds, and are ineligible for tax-exempt financing. In addition, bonds for which more than 5 percent of the proceeds are used to finance loans to individuals are considered to primarily benefit individuals, are private-activity bonds, and are ineligible for tax exemption.

Some activities that fail the two business tests or the private loan test are considered to provide some public benefits in addition to private benefits. These activities, termed qualified private activities, can be financed with tax-exempt bonds. The annual volume of bonds issued within a state for all qualified private activities is restricted to the greater of $75 per state resident or $225 million. The majority of bonds issued for these qualified private activities finance mortgages for owner-occupied housing, student loans for postsecondary education, and loans for private manufacturing facilities. By 1990, legislative changes had succeeded in reducing private-activity bonds to 20 percent of total bond volume. As of 2000, new issue private-activity bond volume was $41 billion.

Tax-exempt bonds and economic issues

The lower interest rate of tax-exempt bonds relative to taxable bonds makes these bonds an important factor in four economic policy issues.

Intergovernmental fiscal relations

In the context of the U.S. system of fiscal federalism (see *fiscal federalism*), federal taxpayers have decided that it makes economic sense to subsidize (reduce the cost of) state and local services. The lower interest rate of tax-exempt bonds is one form of subsidy; two others are grants-in-aid (which increase the income of the governmental unit) and the deduction of state and local income and property taxes from federal taxable income (which reduces the tax price [see *tax price*] of state and local government services). During the 1980s, the real value of intergovernmental aid provided via tax-exempt bonds grew dramatically, while the real value of grants-in-aid and tax deductibility declined. Providing aid via tax-exempt bonds rather than grants-in-aid allows state and local governments to determine the total cost to the federal government (bond issuance is unconstrained except for private-activity bonds); costs more than a dollar to provide a dollar of aid; allows state and local taxpayers to decide which goods and services should be subsidized; and keeps administrative costs relatively low.

Federal budget deficit

The desire to control the deficit was an important factor in legislative efforts in the 1980s to restrict state and local use of private-activity bonds. The exclusion of interest income from federal income taxation imposes a revenue loss on the federal government and contributes to the federal deficit; in fact, this revenue loss is among the largest of all preferential tax provisions listed in the federal government's tax expenditure budget. The revenue loss is calculated as the taxes that would have been collected if tax-exempt bond purchasers had instead purchased taxable debt and received taxable interest income. The revenue loss from the outstanding stock of tax-exempt debt in 2004 is estimated to be $32.19 billion.

Resource allocation

The exclusion of interest income lowers the cost of capital for facilities that can be financed with tax-exempt bonds, thereby raising their after-tax rate of return and reallocating resources (savings) away from ineligible facilities. This absence of neutral taxation occurs in three areas. First, because almost all public investment is eligible for tax-exempt financing and most private investment is not eligible, it increases public investment relative to private investment. Second, it increases private investment in the subset of private activities that are eligible for tax-exempt financing and decreases investment in nonqualifying private activities. And third, it changes state and local production processes toward more use of capital, which is subsidized, and away from labor, which is not subsidized.

All these changes impose losses of national income on society, because the pretax rate of return on most of these subsidized investments is lower than the pretax rate of return on the unsubsidized investments that are displaced. The welfare of federal taxpayers is enhanced only if taxpayers value the social benefits produced by the subsidized investments more than the lost national income.

Tax equity

Tax-exempt bonds present an opportunity for individuals and corporations to shelter their income from federal income taxation. Because the bonds are most valuable to taxpayers with relatively high marginal tax rates, the reduced tax liability tends to reduce the progressivity of the distribution of the tax burden by income class and raises concerns about high-income taxpayers' use of tax-exempt bonds to escape their social duty as taxpayers.

If one ignores or dismisses as of little value the social objectives of the interest income exclusion that is used to justify resource reallocation, one is left with the conclusion that tax-exempt bonds are, from the federal perspective, little more than a vehicle for investors to shelter a portion of their income from federal taxation. This is not, however, a balanced view. It is true that one can use tax-exempt bonds to reduce one's marginal tax rate to zero, but this is accompanied by an implicit tax in the form of a lower pretax rate of return that generates a positive marginal effective tax rate. Furthermore, society's vertical equity objectives are not expressed by the statutory rate structure, but by the effective rate structure that results from each income class's access to the numerous exemptions, deductions, exclusions, credits, deferrals, and so forth. This suggests that any effort to alter tax-exempt bonds on equity grounds is likely to be countered by adjustments in other tax preferences that leave the overall pattern of marginal effective tax rates by income class relatively unchanged.

ADDITIONAL READINGS

Fortune, Peter. "The Municipal Bond Market, Part I: Politics, Taxes and Yields." *New England Economic Review* (September/October 1991): 13–36.

———. "The Municipal Bond Market, Part II: Problems and Policies." *New England Economic Review* (May/June 1992):47–64.

———. "Tax-Exempt Bonds Really Do Subsidize Municipal Capital!" *National Tax Journal* 51, no. 1 (1998).

Hilhouse, Albert M. *Municipal Bonds: A Century of Experience.* New York: Prentice Hall, 1936.

Ott, David J., and Allan H. Meltzer. *Federal Tax Treatment of State and Local Securities.* Washington, DC: The Brookings Institution, 1963.

Petersen, John E., and Ronald Forbes. *Innovative Capital Financing.* Chicago: American Planning Association, 1985.

Zimmerman, Dennis. *The Private Use of Tax-Exempt Bonds: Controlling Public Subsidy of Private Activity.* Washington, DC: Urban Institute Press, 1991.

Cross-references: cost of capital; fairness in taxation; implicit taxes; marginal effective tax rate; progressivity, measures of; tax arbitrage; tax expenditures; tax increment financing; vertical equity.

Tax expenditures
Jane G. Gravelle
Congressional Research Service, Library of Congress

Revenue losses resulting from federal tax provisions that grant special tax relief designed to encourage certain kinds of taxpayer behavior or to aid taxpayers in special circumstances.

Tax expenditures may, in effect, be viewed as spending programs channeled through the tax system. They are classified in the same functional categories as the federal budget. Section 3(3) of the Congressional Budget and Impoundment Control Act of 1974 specifically defines tax expenditures as

> those revenue losses attributable to provisions of the Federal tax laws which allow a special exclusion, exemption, or deduction from gross income or which provide a special credit, a preferential rate of tax, or a deferral of tax liability.

In the legislative history of the Congressional Budget Act, provisions classified as tax expenditures are contrasted with those provisions that are part of the "normal structure" of the individual and corporate income tax necessary to collect government revenues. Tax expenditures, therefore, do not cover all departures from the economist's concept of income. In particular, they do not include imputed and unrealized income (such as capital gains accruals and imputed rent on owner-occupied housing). Nor do they measure tax penalties (such as the failure to index for inflation).

The measurement of tax expenditures is sometimes arbitrary. For example, the single largest business tax expenditure, for depreciation, is based simply on differences between regular tax depreciation and depreciation used in the alternative minimum tax. Tax expenditures represent cash flow measures of benefits, as would be the case in a budget document, rather than the economic value of a subsidy. Thus, the depreciation tax expenditure reflects the difference in current depreciation deductions and not the timing value of accelerated depreciation.

Tax expenditure budget

The listing of tax expenditures, taken in conjunction with the listing of direct spending programs, is intended to allow Congress to scrutinize all federal programs relating to the same goals—both nontax and tax—when developing its annual budget. Only when tax expenditures are considered will congressional budget decisions take into account the full spectrum of federal programs. The tax expenditure budget also identifies provisions that could be considered in any base-broadening tax reform program.

Because any qualified taxpayer may reduce tax liability through use of a tax expenditure, such provisions are comparable to entitlement programs under which benefits are paid to all eligible persons. Because tax expenditures are generally enacted as permanent legislation, they are not renewed each year and thus are not subject to automatic review. Indeed, the original rationale for some tax expenditures may no longer be relevant.

Tax expenditure budgets that list the estimated annual revenue losses associated with each tax expenditure have to be published in the administration's budget (since 1975) and by the Budget Committees (since 1976). The congressional Joint Committee on Taxation has also published estimates. The tax expenditure concept is still being refined; therefore, the classification of certain provisions as tax expenditures continues to be discussed.

As defined in the 1974 act, the concept of tax expenditure refers to corporation and individual income taxes. Other parts of the Internal Revenue Code—excise taxes, employment taxes, estate and gift taxes—also have exceptions, exclusions, refunds, and credits (such as a gasoline tax exemption for nonhighway uses) that are not included in the formal tax expenditure budget.

Major forms of tax expenditures

Tax expenditures may take any of the following forms:

1. Exclusions, exemptions, and deductions, which reduce taxable income;
2. Preferential tax rates, which apply lower rates to part or all of a taxpayer's income;
3. Credits, which are subtracted from taxes as ordinarily computed;
4. Deferrals of tax, which result from delayed recognition of income or from allowing in the current year deductions that are properly attributable to a future year.

The amount of tax relief per dollar of each exclusion, exemption, and deduction increases with the taxpayer's tax rate. A tax credit is subtracted directly from the tax liability that would otherwise be due; thus, the amount of tax reduction is the amount of the credit—which does not depend on the marginal tax rate.

Order of presentation

The tax expenditures are presented in an order that generally parallels the budget functional categories used in the congressional budget; tax expenditures related to "national defense" are listed first, those related to "international affairs" are listed next, and so on. This parallel format is consistent with the requirement of section 301(d)(6) of the act, which requires that the Budget Committees present the estimated levels of tax expenditures "by major functional categories" in the tax expenditure budgets that they publish in their April 15 reports.

Although it is not strictly correct to add tax expenditure items, a sum of tax expenditures provides some information on their size and importance. Data from the Joint Committee on Taxation show $903 billion in tax expenditures in fiscal year 2004—$790 billion in the individual income tax and $113 billion in the corporate tax. In both cases, the largest major budget function was commerce and housing, reflecting, in the individual tax case, tax benefits for owner-occupied housing and capital income, and, in the corporate tax case, depreciation and industry-specific tax provisions. The second largest category for individuals was income security, with pension benefits the largest single tax expenditure in that area.

If tax expenditures are viewed in terms familiar to tax practitioners rather than budget analysts, the largest category of benefits for individuals was investment income subsidies ($204 billion), with about 60 percent resulting from capital gains and dividend subsidies, and the remainder largely from life insurance, tax-exempt bonds, and individual retirement accounts (IRAs). Itemized deductions accounted for $167 billion. Employer fringe benefits were also large ($101 billion for pensions, $96 billion for health, and $35 billion for other fringe benefits). Retirement income exclusions and other benefits for the elderly were also substantial at $52 billion. Business-related provisions for individuals were relatively small ($24 billion). For corporate tax expenditures, depreciation accounted for $55 billion, industry-specific provisions for $13 billion, tax-exempt bonds for $9 billion, and small business benefits for $3 billion.

Distributional issues

Tax expenditures tend to benefit higher-income individuals compared with many other spending programs, which has caused some observers to refer to them as "upside-down" subsidies. Not only are higher-income individuals likely to be subject to higher tax rates, but they are also more likely to itemize deductions, to have significant capital investments, and to own their homes—all characteristics associated with tax expenditures. Of course, if we were to adopt a broader-based tax system, we might also adopt flatter tax rates, so that eliminating tax expenditures need not necessarily lead to a more progressive tax system.

ADDITIONAL READINGS

Brannon, Gerard M. "Tax Expenditures and Income Distribution: A Theoretical Analysis of the Upside-Down Subsidy Argument." In *The Economics of Taxation,* edited by Henry J. Aaron and Michael J. Boskin (87–98). Washington, DC: Brookings Institution Press, 1980.

Burman, Leonard E. "Is the Tax Expenditure Concept Still Relevant?" *National Tax Journal* 56, no. 3 (September 2003): 613–28.

The Century Foundation. *Bad Breaks All Around: The Report of The Century Foundation Working Group on Tax Expenditures.* New York: The Century Foundation Press, 2002.

Ladd, Helen. "The Tax Expenditure Concept after 25 Years." Presidential address to the National Tax Association 86th Annual Conference on Taxation, Charleston, Nov. 1994.

Mikesell, John L. "The Tax Expenditure Concept at the State Level: Conflict between Fiscal Control and Sound Tax Policy." In *National Tax Association Proceedings of the Ninety-Fourth Annual Conference on Taxation* (265–72). Washington, DC: National Tax Association, 2001.

Polackova, Hana Brixi, Christian M.A. Valendue, and Zhicheng Swift, eds. *Tax Expenditure: Shedding Light on Government Spending through Taxation.* Washington, DC: World Bank, 2004.

Surrey, Stanley S., and Paul R. McDaniel. "The Tax Expenditure Concept and the Legislative Process." In *The Economics of Taxation,* edited by Henry J. Aaron and Michael J. Boskin (123–44). Washington, DC: Brookings Institution Press, 1980.

U.S. Congress, Joint Committee on Taxation. *Estimates of Federal Tax Expenditures for Fiscal Years 2004–2008.* Prepared for the Committee on Ways and Means and the Committee on Finance. Committee Print, 108th Cong., 1st sess. Washington, DC: U.S. Government Printing Office, December 22, 2003.

U.S. Congress, Senate Committee on the Budget. 107th Cong., 2nd sess. *Tax Expenditures: Compendium of Background Material on Individual Provisions.* Washington, DC: U.S. Government Printing Office, December 2002.

U.S. General Accounting Office. *Tax Expenditures: A Primer.* PAD 80-26. Washington, DC: U.S. Government Printing Office, 1979.

U.S. Office of Management and Budget. "Tax Expenditures." *Budget of the United States Government Fiscal Year 2005, Analytical Perspectives.* Washington, DC: U.S. Government Printing Office, 2004.

Cross-references: alternative minimum tax; capital gains taxation; fringe benefits; individual retirement accounts; mortgage interest deduction; tax-exempt bonds.

Tax exportation
Donald Phares
University of Missouri–St. Louis

The process by which a tax levied by one jurisdiction is shifted ("exported") to a taxpayer of another jurisdiction.

Having "someone else" help pay the bill for public services is obviously less painful for governments. Accordingly, states have grown more sensitive to opportunities for export-

ing tax burdens to nonresidents. While a great deal of attention has focused on the examples of tourism- or energy-rich states, the issue is much broader. Other states, because of fiscal and economic circumstance, can also shift some of their tax burden onto nonresidents. Tax exporting is not an isolated phenomenon affecting only states such as Alaska, Florida, Nevada, or Texas. To some degree it influences the fiscal environment in every state. In addition, the same process applies from a cross-national to a cross-locality perspective.

How are taxes exported?

Taxes can be exported in two general ways. In the United States, the first derives from Internal Revenue Service provisions that allow itemization of state and local taxes on income and property. In 1970, all property, income, general sales, and gasoline taxes were allowed; in 1980, gasoline taxes were eliminated; and by 1995 so were general sales taxes.

The second mechanism relates to the open movement of goods and services, capital, and people across state borders. This economic flow, combined with ownership, migration, and journey-to-work patterns, means that taxes flow out of (and then, of course, into) each state. This entry discusses each general type of exporting. Tax importing, the flip side of this issue, has received far less scrutiny but must be recognized to get a complete picture of interjurisdictional tax flows.

Federal offset exporting

For those who itemize for federal tax purposes, each dollar deducted shifts part of the tax burden onto the federal revenue structure. Its impact then is in accordance with the incidence characteristics of this system and into the future through deficit financing. Because two major state and local taxes (income and property) can still be itemized, the impact is, de facto, a subsidy through the federal tax system. The more a state relies on deductible taxes, the larger the potential exporting and, therefore, de facto subsidy. The subsidy amount is not dollar for dollar, however. It is a function of how many taxpayers use deductible taxes, the income level of the taxpayers, and the taxpayers' federal marginal tax rate: $1,000 itemized in the 35 percent tax bracket reduces federal taxes by $350.

It needs to be emphasized that these tax burdens do not disappear; they are shifted from state and local to federal taxpayers, and then their impact is felt through the federal tax system. The net effect state by state, however, does vary considerably.

Although recent studies exist of the importance of the tax offset for individual states, no examination of its aggregate importance for all states has been made since 1980 (Phares).

Almost $21 billion in state and local taxes was shifted to the federal revenue structure as a result of IRS provisions in 1980, up from $8.8 billion in 1970. The figure for 2004 would be even greater. The largest contributor is the individual income tax, for two reasons. Almost all states use this tax and rely on it heavily as a revenue source. Second, this state tax liability rises with an individual's income, and thus this deduction is worth more on the federal return. The next largest contributor is real property taxes, followed by personal property taxes. Past estimates showed that just shy of 50 percent of total exporting derived from IRS provisions.

Price/migration exporting

The second type of exporting results from the openness of state economies and the ease with which economic activity flows among states; while boundaries represent legal or political definitions, they do not constrain taxes. Taxes move freely with goods and services, people, and capital flows. The more "open" a state's economy, the greater the possibility for shifting part of its tax burden elsewhere.

Price/migration exporting is similar in focus to the concerns of tax shifting and incidence—that is, to trace the movement (shifting) of a tax from its point of legal impact to its final economic resting place (incidence). A tax on gaming, for example, is legally imposed on the provider (as seller) but is shifted to the final consumer. Price/migration exporting uses this input but must go one step further. Not only must the "interpersonal" movement of a tax be traced, from gaming seller to gaming consumer, but the spatial location of the burden also must be determined. Casinos in Nevada pay gaming taxes. This burden, however, largely falls not on the casino, but on gamblers. The task is to determine in what state a gambler resides. While the tax has been legally imposed by Nevada, most of the burden falls on nonresidents who have visited the state. Thus, the tax is shifted in two distinct senses—first, from a business, the casino, to a consumer, the gambler; and second, geographically from Nevada to residents elsewhere.

Table 1 shows some states that exemplify this type of spatial tax movement. While these are blatant cases, all states export to some extent.

The full theoretical and empirical model estimating this exporting is presented elsewhere (see McLure 1966, 1967, or Phares 1980). Again, recent data on the price-migration effect are not available but, as with the federal offset, the amount is quite large (far more than the $22 billion in 1980).

The dominant category is income taxes. Some income tax is derived from individuals, but most is corporate-related. Corporate ownership is not confined to state of location, and price/migration exporting reflects movement of the burden to the owner's state of residence. The second-largest category is

severance taxes, which grew dramatically during the 1970s as a result of the rising price of oil and gas, and the yield from taxing resource extraction. Most of this tax burden falls on residents outside the levying state. Overall, price/migration exporting rose 125 percent during the 1970s and 1980s, slightly less than the 135 percent for federal offset exporting.

Policy implications

Tax exporting is a significant factor affecting the fiscal environment among states. The amounts involved are substantial and probably accounted for about one-fifth of all state and local taxes for 1980.

Contained within aggregate numbers, however, is detail on each state. It is in this context that relative fiscal and economic behavior is influenced and policies altered. While the U.S. average for exported taxes was 18 percent, there is considerable variance around this mean. Although Tennessee exported only 11 percent of its taxes, Delaware was able to shift 33 percent of its burden onto out-of-state residents or the federal tax system. Such differentials might influence policy in several areas.

Interstate competition

To the extent its taxes can be shifted to nonresidents or the federal revenue system, a state enjoys, de facto, a lower tax status. To the extent that low taxes favorably influence business and residential location decisions, a comparative advantage exists. Considering taxation in the context of all other factors affecting location decisions, high-export states such as Nevada or Delaware might gain an advantage.

Fiscal capacity

Formulas have been an important and integral part of allocating revenues to public programs. The oldest and most complex are the state school aid formulas. General revenue-sharing, housing and community development, and the Comprehensive Employment and Training Act were three more notable examples of formula-driven aid programs. Elements of many distribution schemes have included tax effort and capacity. Both can be affected by tax exportation.

Implicit federal aid

The implicit subsidy (tax expenditure) to state and local taxpayers, through IRS provisions for the deduction of state and local taxes, amounts to tens of billions of dollars. This form of aid, albeit implicit, has become a major component in the overall system of intergovernmental transfers and has grown. The federal tax system has been used to subsidize a vast array of activities and to encourage certain types of "socially beneficial" behavior. This tax break for state and local operations has grown large but is also less visible.

TABLE 1. High Tax Export States

State	Type of exported tax	Reason
Nevada	Selective sales	Gambling activity
Delaware	Corporation taxes	Corporate headquarters
Alaska, Texas	Severance taxes	Natural resources
Hawaii	General excise tax	Tourism
Florida	Specific tourism taxes	Tourism

Federal tax reform proposals

Reform proposals from Washington have focused on eliminating (limiting) deductibility for state and local taxes. No doubt the sheer cost to the U.S. Treasury weighs heavily. Eliminating these provisions, however, could have dramatic implications for the fiscal operations of states and localities. An additional tax burden would be shifted from the federal revenue system onto state and local taxpayers. This would undoubtedly affect the array of public goods and services provided. It would affect the real cost of these public operations, it could increase taxpayer resistance to new or increased taxes, and it conceivably might even lead to a new round of "taxpayer revolt" activity.

Tax-adjusted price of state-local goods

Individual economic decisions respond to the price of factors, goods, and services. State and local public goods are similar in terms of taxpayer (qua consumer) response. When part of the cost of these public operations is shifted to residents of other states or the federal tax structure, the net cost of public goods is lowered. A state such as Delaware that exports perhaps one-third of its taxes can, de facto, provide public goods for a lower tax cost to its residents. Examined in a relative context across states, this can lead to differential responses to the provision of public goods, depending upon exportability.

Conclusion

This entry has outlined how taxes levied at the state and local levels can be rearranged within the federal system, with about half related to IRS provisions and the rest to the flow of economic activity among states. This rearrangement has a potential impact on fiscal decision making in the American federal system. While the impact is somewhat hidden, it certainly should not escape attention.

ADDITIONAL READINGS

Gade, Mary N., and Lee C. Adkins. "Tax Exporting and State Revenue Structures." *National Tax Journal* 43 (March 1990): 39–52.

McLure, Charles. "An Analysis of Regional Tax Incidence, with Estimation of Interstate Incidence of State and Local Taxes." Ph.D. dissertation, Department of Economics, Princeton University, 1966.

———. "Tax Exporting in the United States: Estimates for 1962." *National Tax Journal* 20 (March 1967): 49–77.

Mak, James. "Taxing Travel and Tourism." In *International Handbook of Tourism*, edited by Peter Forsyth and Larry Dwyer. London: Edward Elgar Publishing,

Metcalf, Gilbert E. "Tax Exporting, Federal Deductibility, and State Tax Structure." *Journal of Policy Analysis and Management* 12 (1993): 109–26.

Phares, Donald. *Who Pays State and Local Taxes?* Cambridge, MA: Oelgeschlager, Gunn & Hain, 1980.

———. "Missourians and the Taxes They Pay." St. Louis: University of Missouri–St. Louis, Public Policy Research Centers, March 1996.

Rueben, Kim. "The Repeal of Deductibility of State and Local Taxes and the Impact on State and Local Governments." Conference on Federal Tax Reform and the States, Washington, DC, May 18, 2005.

Cross-references: fairness in taxation; incidence of taxes; itemized deductions; severance tax, state; state and local tax deductibility; tax and revenue capacity; tax equity analysis; tax expenditures; tourist tax.

Tax illusion
Michael L. Marlow
California Polytechnic State University

Even the rational fiscal voter who looks at the benefits and costs of public programs may lack adequate information (perhaps because of the complexity of the tax code itself), thereby underestimating the true costs of public activities.

Voters base their demand for public programs on expected costs and benefits. A long-standing issue in public finance concerns the ability of demanders to understand the true nature of costs and benefits of programs because, without perfect information, demands must be based on perceived, as opposed to actual, costs and benefits. The tax illusion hypothesis proposes that voters base their demands on an illusion that the costs of public programs are lower than true costs (Puviani 1903). An important implication of the tax illusion hypothesis is that, because the net benefit for any public program is measured as the difference between benefits and costs, net benefits are overestimated whenever costs are underestimated. This hypothesis therefore predicts that the public sector overexpands whenever net benefits are overestimated by misinformed voters.

One reason voters may underestimate costs of public programs is the complexity of the tax system. Consider, for example, that until 1942 the Internal Revenue Service collected income tax after the year was over; now, these taxes are withheld from each paycheck received. Taxes are also collected at grocery stores, gasoline stations, bars, sporting events, and department stores, and are attached to utility bills and interest income earned on savings. There is little question that tax sources are plentiful. Moreover, if voters feel they have little recourse about changing their tax burdens, they may be even less inclined to calculate the true costs than if they feel that knowing the true costs might allow them to lower their tax burdens.

A related hypothesis is that voters underestimate costs of public programs when governments operate budget deficits (Buchanan and Wagner 1977). This implies, for example, that voters perceive that $100 billion of public spending costs less when financed through public debt than through taxation. This would represent just another form of tax illusion, or what might be referred to as deficit illusion, because budget deficits reflect taxes that are deferred to the future. Underestimation occurs when voters believe that taxes paid today cost more than the present value of taxes paid tomorrow that are required to pay off today's deficit.

The implication of the deficit illusion hypothesis is the same as before: when voters underestimate future tax burdens associated with deficit finance, public programs appear cheaper than they really are. Consequently, these voters overestimate the net benefits of public programs, which results in higher demand for programs than if current spending were financed entirely by current taxes. An important implication of the deficit illusion hypothesis is that some portion of federal spending expansion during years in which budgets are in deficit reflects overexpansion. This implication follows from the prediction that deficit illusion causes voters to approve more spending than if expansion of public debt had not caused them to underestimate the full costs of public programs.

Two possible remedies for removing tax and deficit illusions are simplification of tax policies and constitutional limitations on budget deficits. While most states have some constitutional or legislative limitations on taxes and deficits, the federal government does not operate under any such rule. Proponents of adopting these rules at the federal level predict that these changes would allow voters to approve public spending on the basis of true costs and, possibly, lead to lower funding of public programs as well.

Critics of the deficit illusion hypothesis argue that voters are not likely to systematically underestimate financing burdens and that therefore overexpansion of the public sector is unlikely (Barro 1978). This view is consistent with the Ricardian equivalence proposition, which hypothesizes that voters recognize, for given levels of public spending, the equivalence between taxes and public debt. Voters therefore do not operate under an illusion that public debt offers a cheaper alternative to taxation. Unlike the tax and benefit illusion hypotheses, this hypothesis predicts that the public sector neither overexpands nor underexpands as a result of deficit finance.

There is also a long-standing counterhypothesis that, while voter illusion exists, it arises over the benefits, not the costs, of public programs (Downs 1960). This hypothesis proposes that, because voters underestimate the benefits of programs, underexpansion of public programs occurs from the resulting underestimation of net benefits. Other than policies that attempt to inform voters about the true nature of benefits, it is unclear what remedies would dispel benefit illusion and promote government programs more in line with their true costs and benefits. Of course, it could also be argued that underestimation of benefits may fully or partially counter underestimation of tax or deficit burdens thus leading to further complications in determining whether or not there is overexpansion or underexpansion of the public sector.

There is mixed empirical support for the hypothesis that voters underestimate tax bills of public programs (e.g., for support see Wagner 1976, and for rejection see Greene and Munley 1979). However, a survey of the empirical evidence finds little overall support for the hypothesis (Oates 1988). While the deficit illusion hypothesis is especially interesting in light of the record string of federal deficits for 1970–97 (which was followed by four consecutive years of surplus, before returning to consecutive deficits once again), little empirical research has been conducted on its influence on public-sector expansion, and therefore testing of this hypothesis is likely to be the subject of expanded interest in the future.

ADDITIONAL READINGS

Barro, Robert J. "Comments from an Unreconstructed Ricardian." *Journal of Monetary Economics* (August 1978): 569–81.

Buchanan, James M., and Richard E. Wagner. *Democracy in Deficit. The Political Legacy of Lord Keynes.* New York: Academic Press, 1977.

Calomiris, Charles W., and Kevin A. Hassett. "Marginal Tax Rate Cuts and the Public Tax Debate." *National Tax Journal* 55, no. 1 (March 2002): 119–31.

Downs, Anthony. "Why the Government Budget Is Too Small in a Democracy." *World Politics* (July 1960): 541–63.

Greene, Kevin V., and Vincent G. Munley. "Generating Growth in Public Expenditures: The Role of Employee and Constituent Demand." *Public Finance Quarterly* (January 1979): 82–109.

Oates, Wallace E. "On the Nature and Measurement of Fiscal Illusion: A Survey." In *Taxation and Fiscal Federalism: Essays in Honour of Russell Mathews,* edited by Geoffrey Brennan, Bhajan S. Grewel, and Peter D. Groenewegen (65–82). Canberra: Australian National University Press, 1988.

Puviani, Amilcare. *Teoria della illusione finanziaria,* edited by Remo Sandron. Palermo, Italy, 1903.

Wagner, Richard E. "Revenue Structure, Fiscal Illusion, and Budgetary Choice." *Public Choice* (1976): 45–61.

Cross-references: budget process, federal; budget processes, state; median voter theorem; Ricardian equivalence; saving, taxes and; Tiebout model; withholding of taxes.

Tax increment financing

Joel Michael

Research Department, Minnesota House of Representatives

A financing mechanism that temporarily dedicates the increased tax revenue from a new development to pay real estate development or infrastructure costs.

Nearly all states authorize local government units to use tax increment financing, or TIF. Most state TIF laws allow the municipality (typically the city, but sometimes a county) to capture the increased property taxes from a new development and to use the revenues to assist the development. A handful of states also allow capturing of non–property tax revenues (typically sales tax revenues) under TIF. The captured revenues ("tax increments") may be used to pay for private development costs (e.g., land assembly and preparation costs) or public costs (e.g., installing public infrastructure, such as sewer, water, roads, and parking, that serve the site or the area). Debt is often issued to capitalize the tax increments, to pay up-front development costs, or to provide the equivalent of lump-sum property tax abatements to developers.

History and purposes of TIF

States initially enacted TIF laws as a way to pay the state and local match for federal urban renewal funds in the 1950s and 1960s. However, more widespread adoption of state TIF laws and use of TIF did not occur until the 1970s and 1980s, when state and local governments looked for ways to replace reductions in federal urban renewal funding. Forty-eight states and the District of Columbia now authorize some type of TIF use.

TIF use initially focused on urban redevelopment—replacing or rehabilitating slums, deteriorating commercial properties, and other "blighted" areas of cities. But there is a great deal of variation in state laws, and authorized TIF uses now extend well beyond urban redevelopment. TIF is often used for general "economic development"—i.e., to provide incentives to firms to make capital investments—and to fund public infrastructure, such as streets, parking, and sewer and water improvements. These uses often are unrelated to urban redevelopment or renewal and may be used by developing suburbs or for non-blighted areas. Some states also allow TIF to be used to help construct housing, typically for units to be occupied by low- and moderate-income individuals and families. In housing uses, TIF is often combined with federal housing programs, such as the low-income housing credit or tax-exempt bonding.

Basic mechanics of TIF

State TIF laws commonly provide for certification of a base or original assessed value for the geographic area of the TIF district. Increases in the district's assessed value are then separately accounted for or "captured." Note that these increases may result from new development (e.g., construction of a new building), general inflation in property values, and changes in assessment practices or the tax status of properties. A few state laws attempt to limit captured assessed value to amounts mainly attributable to new development.

Taxpayers in the TIF district pay their regular property taxes, but the taxes are divided into two accounts—those attributable to the base assessed value are paid to the regular taxing districts for general government purposes, and those attributable to the captured value (the "tax increment") are diverted to a special account for the municipality or development authority. These tax increments are then used to assist the development, finance public infrastructure, or other permitted costs under the TIF law. This apparent "self-financing" nature of TIF through the recycling of the development's property taxes is one element that makes TIF more politically popular than straightforward property tax abatements. In some instances, the actual economic effect may be little different, though.

Most TIF laws limit how long the incremental taxes can be diverted to these special purposes. The time limits vary from state to state and sometimes within states by the type or purpose of the district. Duration limits can be as short as 8 years and as long as 50 years. The mode is likely 20 years.

TIF debt and financing mechanisms

TIF costs are generally incurred up front, such as to pay for preparation of an urban redevelopment site (e.g., land acquisition and clearance) or construction of public infrastructure.

However, tax increments are received as a stream of increased property or other taxes only after construction of the new development. To overcome this mismatch between expenditures and revenues, municipalities have traditionally incurred debt in anticipation of the increments.

Under many state laws, TIF debt is exempt from statutory or constitutional limits on the amount of debt, often called net debt limits, and/or from requirements that the voters approve issuance of municipal bonds. These exemptions likely encourage municipalities to use TIF.

TIF debt most often is incurred with municipal revenue bonds, that is, debt payable only from the project's stream of increments or other revenues. The holders of revenue bonds bear the risk of shortfalls if the increased property taxes or other revenues prove insufficient. Some state laws also allow the municipality to back the bonds with its general obligation, that is, a pledge of its general taxing authority, providing additional security and another public subsidy for the development.

Since the issuer is a local government unit, TIF bonds' interest payments traditionally were exempt from federal income taxation. However, the Tax Reform Act of 1986 made it more difficult to use tax-exempt TIF bonds. In response, local governments have turned to using taxable bonds for all or parts of many TIF projects. (Tax-exempt TIF bonds still tend to be used to finance general infrastructure improvements.) In some states, local governments have shifted to pure developer financing—often called "pay as you go" financing—where the developer is expected to arrange its own financing and is reimbursed as increments are received. This approach eliminates two traditional components of TIF debt subsidies: the federal income tax exemption of state and local interest and credit enhancements provided by the municipality.

Intergovernmental relations aspects of TIF

The financial structure of TIF creates the potential for implicit economic transfers across different units and levels of governments. Most states authorize municipalities unilaterally to make TIF decisions, but tax increments are derived from the tax rates imposed by all property taxing entities (e.g., counties and school districts). In addition, state intergovernmental aid programs may contribute to the fiscal equation through need or capacity to pay measures of the property tax base that exclude amounts "captured" by TIF. A state foundation aid-type program for K–12 education would be a common example of such an aid program. Since aid is typically inversely related to local property tax wealth, capturing tax base in TIF that otherwise would be used in aid calculation will increase state aid. For an aid program with a fixed appropriation, TIF use may shift the distribution of aid among recipients, rather than increasing total state outlays.

The financial structure of TIF can be justified on the theory that the municipality should not bear the full burden of undertaking redevelopment and economic development activities that benefit all of the overlapping taxing districts. On the other hand, the structure creates a misalignment between decisionmaking and the responsibility for bearing the costs. This seems especially the case because a prime effect of TIF is to redistribute the location of private development and investment. State laws attempt to address this issue in a variety of ways. Often states require municipal findings that the development wouldn't occur "but-for" TIF (cold comfort, perhaps, if the main effect is to divert development from elsewhere in the overlapping taxing districts). A few states give overlapping taxing districts a role in making TIF decisions. A very small number of states prohibit capturing school district taxes with TIF.

The basic financial structure of TIF creates an incentive and potential for budget manipulation or gaming by municipalities with TIF authority. For example, from a municipal perspective, the least cost financing mechanism for new infrastructure often would be to use TIF to capture taxes from expected growth. Such TIF use will export some or all of the municipal costs to taxpayers in these jurisdictions, but outside the municipality; TIF use may also maximize state intergovernmental aid to the apparent benefit of local taxpayers. There is anecdotal evidence that some municipalities engage in these types of budget manipulations using TIF; the empirical evidence is mixed. Researchers have found correlations between higher predicted tax base growth and the use of TIF, which may be consistent with using TIF for budget manipulation. However, researchers have not found a statistically significant relationship between a city's proportionate ability to export or shift its costs using TIF and municipal use of TIF.

Economic theory predicts that competitive pressures to attract a tax base may be a factor in stimulating use of TIF, as well as use of other economic development tools and tax incentives for investment. As one local unit in a metropolitan area uses TIF to attract investment, surrounding units may feel they need to do so as well to remain competitive. Some empirical research tends to confirm that this is a factor in municipal TIF adoption decisions.

Evidence on the effectiveness of TIF

Municipal officials often view TIF as a useful way to finance urban redevelopment or to stimulate real estate development generally. The typical goals are to expand the tax base (on the assumption that the revenue yield from the development exceeds the cost of services) or to provide other, perhaps more intangible, benefits associated with urban redevelopment, such as reduction of crime or other social costs associated with substandard housing and deteriorating commercial areas. This view may be supported by economic theory if TIF subsidies help to correct market failures, such as conditions in local real estate markets that create externalities or private redevelopments that provide public benefits. However, it may be that TIF subsidies tend to be market distorting and actually relocate investment to less productive locations.

A few empirical studies have investigated whether TIF is effective in stimulating tax base increases in municipalities or districts. These studies have reached mixed results from which it is difficult to draw any firm conclusions beyond the need for further, more sophisticated research. Moreover, the studies focus on the first order question of whether there is a statistical relationship between TIF use and increases in property values (or other measures of economic activity), rather than the second order question of whether the public benefits of TIF exceed its costs.

ADDITIONAL READINGS

Anderson, John E. "Tax Increment Financing: Municipal Adoption and Growth." *National Tax Journal* 43, no. 2 (June 1990): 155–63.

Dye, Richard F., and David F. Merriman. "The Effects of Tax Increment Financing on Economic Development." *Journal of Urban Economics* 47, no. 2 (March 2000): 306–28.

Johnson, Craig L., and Kenneth A. Kriz. "A Review of State Tax Incremental Financing Laws." In *Tax Increment Financing and Economic Development,* edited by Craig L. Johnson and Joyce Y. Man (31–56). Albany, NY: SUNY Press, 2001.

Kriz, Kenneth A. "The Effect of Tax Increment Finance on Local Government Financial Condition." *Municipal Finance Journal* 22 (2001): 41–64.

Man, Joyce Y. "Effects of Tax Increment Financing on Economic Development." In *Tax Increment Financing and Economic Development,* edited by Craig L. Johnson and Joyce Y. Man (101–09). Albany, NY: SUNY Press, 2001.

———. "Fiscal Pressure, Tax Competition and the Adoption of Tax Increment Financing." *Fiscal Studies* 36 (1999): 1151–67.

Man, Joyce Y., and Mark S. Rosentraub. "Tax Increment Financing: Municipal Adoption and Effects on Property Tax Growth." *Public Finance Review* 26 (1998): 417–30.

Merriman, David. "Book Review: Tax Increment Financing and Economic Development: Uses, Structures, and Impact." *National Tax Journal* 55, no. 4 (December 2002): 839–43.

Mikesell, John L. "Nonproperty Tax Increment Programs for Economic Development: A Review of the Alternative Programs." In *Tax Increment Financing and Economic Development,* edited by Craig L. Johnson and Joyce Y. Man (67–69). Albany, NY: SUNY Press, 2001.

Cross-references: property tax, real property, business; site value taxation and single tax; tax-exempt bonds; tax exportation; zoning, property taxes, and exactions.

Tax limitations

Perry Shapiro
University of California–Santa Barbara

Updated by
Steven Maguire
Congressional Research Service, Library of Congress

Using a combination of constitutional and/or statutory approaches, some state and local governments place an overall cap on tax proceeds. Often accomplished by initiative, the "tax revolt" was primarily a late 1970s–1980s phenomenon. More recent data and research, when available, are included.

All 50 states in the country limit taxes and expenditures in some way. The most prevalent limitation is the requirement of a balanced state budget; in fact, all states but Vermont have one. Other common restrictions include supermajority vote requirements for passage of tax increases, line-item gubernatorial vetoes, bond limitations, and indexation of income taxes. Tax limitations, however, generally refer instead to legislation that constrains specific sources and uses of tax revenue. The 1970s and 1980s witnessed an explosion of tax limitations in the United States, highlighted by such well-known political struggles as California's Proposition 13.

The tax rebellion of the 1970s and 1980s was billed by advocates as a popular revolt against governments that were unresponsive to popular will. They cast government as a leviathan, the monopoly supplier of public services with an unbridled ability to finance its provision of public goods through taxation and inflation. Tax and expenditure limitations were advocated as a means for taming the public sector.

This interpretation poses an interesting question, however. Why, in a stable democracy, should fiscal policy diverge so far from the collective will? Economists have long theorized that the mix of goods and services provided by the government in any jurisdiction is the mix and quantity demanded by the median voter. While there are always voters that desire more than the amount provided and voters that desire less, the voter with the median preference in a majority-rule society should be satisfied. Tax limitation bills cannot capture a majority vote in such a world, so the median voter model cannot adequately explain the popularity of the tax limitation movement.

New Jersey passed the first limitation of state fiscal authority in 1976 and was followed, in one form or another, by 20 states over the next 10 years. While these state laws differ widely, several regularities can be observed. A vast majority of states with active legislation restrict expenditures rather than tax revenues. Many of these states tie spending growth directly to the growth in state personal income; several also adjust for inflation. Almost all states retain the option to override the terms of the limitation with a simple two-thirds majority vote of the legislature during emergencies, although several require voter or governor approval. A more detailed description of state-by-state tax and expenditure limitation laws can be found in the National Association of State Budget Officers (NASBO) publication.

The tax revolt was a citizen effort. Not surprisingly, tax and expenditure limitation measures are more common in states that have citizen initiative laws. Of the 26 states that have those laws, nearly half have passed tax and expenditure limitation bills. Only one state in four that lacked popular access to state government passed a tax and expenditure limitation bill. It must be noted, however, that in only five states was passage of a limitation measure accomplished by citizen initiative. Thus, it is unclear whether the differential is because states with citizen initiative laws have an a priori greater proclivity to bind government or whether the presence of the initiative induces elected officials to comply with popular will.

While legislation that constrains state fiscal authority is a relatively recent phenomenon, local government has a long history with tax limitations. The first property tax limitation was enacted by Rhode Island in 1870 (ACIR 1977). However, the number of states with limitations on municipal taxation and spending almost doubled—from 14 to 26—between 1976 and 1987 (Preston and Ichniowski 1991). Among the statutes passed in the 1970s and 1980s, California's Proposition 13 and Massachusetts's Proposition 2 ½ were unique. Both directly reduced taxes. Other limitations laws merely constrained the rate of future tax growth.

Because local governments derive most of their revenues from property taxes, the traditional form of tax limitation has been control of property tax rates. A shift toward limiting the growth of property tax levies has occurred, however. In 1987, 19 states limited the total property tax burden that could be levied on property owners, compared with 9 in 1976. Levy limits frequently stipulate a maximum permissible rate of growth in property tax collections, although most allow for population growth and inflation. Between 1976 and 1987, allowable growth rates ranged from 0 percent in Kansas to 10 percent in Mississippi. Arizona, California, and Idaho have coupled tax rate limitations with limits on assessment increases, which, in effect, indirectly constrains the growth in property tax levies (Preston and Ichniowski 1991). A smaller number of states restrict own-source municipal expenditures or revenues directly, although few rely exclusively on this mechanism.

The presence of popular referenda is equally important as a determinant of local-level tax limitations. In fact, more than three-quarters of states with citizen initiative laws had local tax limitations during the peak reform years, 1976 to 1987, whereas only 42 percent of the states without such provisions had limitations during the same period. As with state-level limitations, however, a causal chain between referenda and tax limitation cannot be inferred.

Economists have proposed numerous explanations of the tax limitation movement and potential failure of the median voter model. Many postulate the existence of a leviathan government, unresponsive to popular will. For example, one compelling version theorizes that government has grown too large because of imperfections in the agenda formation process that favor high demanders of public goods and services. An alternative theory suggests that limitation measures might reflect discontent with the method of finance rather than the level of service, particularly at the local level. In this view limitations might reflect the desire to shift the burden from local property taxes to more progressive state income taxes. Yet another idea suggests that voters might be expecting something for nothing.

Denzau, MacKay, and Weaver (1979) motivate Leviathan by suggesting that ballot initiatives are a public good, available to all, irrespective of whether one contributes. Because participation in the political process is costly and because the tax burden is generally more widely dispersed than are benefits, Denzau et al. model a government that becomes effectively controlled by a dominant coalition of high demanders. It is conceivable, however, that low demanders could also form such a special interest group. As a result, the outcome of democratic voting reflects only voter demand along a narrow array of predetermined alternatives, and a constitutional spending limit provides one way to widen the array.

Table 1 presents the historical trend of the public sector. There was clear growth in the relative size of government for the nation as a whole from 1959 to 2002. Federal, state, and local government own-source revenues constituted 23.3, 28.1, and 30.3 percent of gross domestic product (GDP), and direct

TABLE 1. Government Own-Source Revenues and Direct Expenditures, Relative to GDP

Year	Revenue as a percentage of GDP				Direct expenditures as a percentage of GDP			
	Federal	State and local	State	Local	Federal	State and local	State	Local
1959	15.63	7.68	3.59	4.09	18.18	11.56	4.43	7.13
1960	17.57	8.27	3.92	4.35	17.52	11.59	4.21	7.38
1961	17.33	8.61	4.02	4.59	17.94	12.30	4.51	7.79
1962	17.03	8.60	4.04	4.56	18.24	12.05	4.35	7.69
1963	17.26	8.77	4.15	4.62	18.02	12.26	4.48	7.78
1964	16.97	8.81	4.25	4.56	17.86	12.14	4.46	7.68
1965	16.24	8.76	4.26	4.50	16.44	12.05	4.38	7.68
1966	16.60	8.86	4.38	4.48	17.07	12.05	4.34	7.71
1967	17.87	9.11	4.54	4.57	18.92	12.73	4.77	7.96
1968	16.81	9.24	4.75	4.49	19.57	12.77	4.87	7.90
1969	18.98	9.69	5.03	4.66	18.65	13.37	5.02	8.34
1970	18.57	10.49	5.54	4.95	18.83	14.26	5.41	8.85
1971	16.60	10.54	5.44	5.10	18.65	15.15	5.87	9.28
1972	16.74	11.00	5.71	5.29	18.63	15.38	5.85	9.53
1973	16.69	10.92	5.82	5.10	17.77	14.86	5.64	9.22
1974	17.55	11.06	5.94	5.11	17.96	15.05	5.75	9.30
1975	17.04	11.06	5.91	5.15	20.28	16.37	6.53	9.85
1976	16.33	10.99	5.88	5.11	20.37	16.60	6.74	9.86
1977	17.51	10.97	5.93	5.03	20.15	15.91	6.34	9.57
1978	17.41	10.74	5.91	4.83	19.99	15.05	5.95	9.10
1979	18.07	10.46	5.89	4.57	19.66	14.84	5.80	9.04
1980	18.54	10.73	6.07	4.66	21.18	15.50	6.21	9.29
1981	19.16	10.65	5.99	4.66	21.68	15.51	6.34	9.17
1982	18.98	11.38	6.33	5.05	22.91	16.06	6.49	9.57
1983	16.98	11.22	6.16	5.06	22.86	15.97	6.58	9.39
1984	16.95	11.33	6.34	5.00	21.66	15.22	6.17	9.04
1985	17.39	11.66	6.54	5.12	22.42	15.54	6.38	9.16
1986	17.24	11.84	6.61	5.23	22.19	16.03	6.55	9.48
1987	18.03	12.07	6.68	5.39	21.19	16.34	6.63	9.71
1988	17.82	11.94	6.62	5.31	20.86	16.15	6.52	9.62
1989	18.07	12.04	6.69	5.35	20.85	16.19	6.56	9.63
1990	17.78	12.28	6.74	5.54	21.60	16.76	6.85	9.92
1991	17.60	12.48	6.81	5.67	22.09	17.68	7.38	10.30
1992	17.22	12.56	6.92	5.64	21.80	18.10	7.88	10.22
1993	17.34	12.66	6.99	5.67	21.17	18.18	7.95	10.23
1994	17.80	12.51	6.90	5.62	20.67	17.83	7.78	10.04
1995	18.27	12.72	7.08	5.64	20.49	18.22	8.06	10.16
1996	18.59	12.64	7.03	5.61	19.96	17.83	7.77	10.06
1997	19.02	12.58	7.04	5.54	19.28	17.54	7.57	9.97
1998	19.68	12.70	7.12	5.58	18.89	17.44	7.44	10.00
1999	19.72	12.55	7.04	5.51	18.36	17.50	7.48	10.02
2000	20.63	12.73	7.24	5.49	18.22	17.75	7.71	10.04
2001	19.71	13.10	7.36	5.74	18.45	18.76	8.27	10.48
2002	17.68	12.63	6.94	5.70	19.19	19.50	8.74	10.76

Sources: U.S. Census Bureau, *Annual Survey of State and Local Government Finances and Census of Governments* (1959–2002) and *Economic Report of the President,* 2004, table B-80.
Note: GDP = gross domestic product.

expenditures 29.7, 36.7, and 38.7 percent, in 1959, 1975, and 2002, respectively. However, the majority of the increase took place well before the beginning of the tax revolt in the mid-1970s.

Analysis at the national level, however, may conceal important state and local patterns. For instance, excessive public welfare is a common focal point for pro-limitation arguments. State and local public welfare expenditures increased steadily from 0.78 percent of GNP in 1955 to 1.76 percent of GNP in 1975, the eve of the rebellion. However, state and local public welfare did not decline after passage of so many limitation measures (ACIR 1989b). Additionally, local government is heavily reliant on property taxes, though property taxes as a percentage of local revenues decreased steadily from 92.4 percent in 1942 to 73.7 percent in 1987 (ACIR 1989b). This trend, however, disguises an increasing burden on property owners in the years before the tax revolt. Local property taxes increased from 2.4 percent of GNP in 1948 to 3.7 percent of GNP in 1972, the eve of the tax rebellion, before returning to 2.5 percent of GNP in the 1980s (ACIR 1989b).

Many explanations center on state-specific events. Take California; its fiscal history has been well documented. Oakland (1981) found that state and local taxes as a percentage of personal income were higher and increased faster than the national average over the 20 years preceding Proposition 13. By 1977, they were almost 4 percentage points higher than the national average. California's budget may have gotten out of line, and Proposition 13 may have been the voters' way of reasserting control. Oakland, Shapiro, and Sonstelie (1982) used the passage of Proposition 13 as a natural experiment to test whether California's municipal governments were behaving according to the median voter or the Leviathan model. They found evidence for the latter.

Proposition 13 primarily affected property taxes, however. Shapiro (1981) proposed another explanation based on a public opinion survey, conducted just before the election, which suggested that expenditure levels for most public services, except for administrative costs and welfare, were not perceived as too high. Because the share of property taxes paid by citizens had risen from 45 to 53 percent between 1973 and 1978, and because the state had a $7 billion surplus, Shapiro suggests that Proposition 13 might have reflected a desire to shift financial responsibility from local to state government. The desirability of state financing, however, was inversely related to income because California income taxes were progressive; low-income groups were the primary beneficiaries. Shapiro found no support for the hypothesis empirically, though, because, in the survey, support for Proposition 13 did not differ systematically across incomes. He did, however, find support for Leviathan because estimated demand for school and county expenditures was between 7 and 8 percent too high. Oakland was critical of the methodology employed and unwilling to dismiss the hypothesis.

Fischel (1989) has advanced the role played by the California Supreme Court in precipitating Proposition 13.

Tiebout (1956) argued that the free rider problem could be overcome for local public goods because communities could offer different mixes and levels of local services and like-minded individuals would choose to settle together. In this way, property taxes behaved like user costs. In attempting to equalize educational opportunity statewide, the court ruled in the second *Serrano v. Priest* decision (1976) that all California school districts must equate, within $100, expenditures per student. This restriction meant that public school expenditures could no longer signal community demand for education, and thus most property taxes were a deadweight loss. The block of voters in communities with greater-than-average demand for education, who generally reside in affluent areas, and who ordinarily would have opposed the proposition, were silent.

A final argument is more cynical. Citrin (1979, 13) recognizes that "the public's readiness to demand and consume government programs is understandably greater than its willingness to pay for them." It is unclear whether support for tax limitation measures reflects a belief about the proper size of government or antagonism toward particular programs, welfare in particular. Considering California, Citrin concluded that, while Proposition 13 certainly expressed a collective preference for lower taxes, maintaining the status quo was a prominent, and in some areas a majority, view.

Tax limitations are an important component of state and local fiscal policy in the United States. The tax limitation movement reached its peak during the frenzied 1970s and 1980s with the adoption, in one form or another, of legislation in a majority of states. The causes appear to be numerous, although it is clear that state and local government did grow faster than the willingness of the electorate to finance it. Furthermore, citizen access to referenda is strongly correlated with the passage of tax limitation legislation.

ADDITIONAL READINGS

Advisory Commission on Intergovernmental Relations [ACIR]. *State Limitations on Local Taxes and Expenditures.* Washington, DC: U.S. Government Printing Office, 1977.

———. *Significant Features of Fiscal Federalism 1989. Vol. 1.* Washington, DC: U.S. Government Printing Office, January 1989a.

———. *Significant Features of Fiscal Federalism 1989. Vol. 2.* Washington, DC: U.S. Government Printing Office, August 1989b.

Bails, Dale G. "The Effectiveness of Tax-Expenditure Limitations: A Reevaluation." *American Journal of Economics and Sociology* 49 (April 1990): 223–38.

Baker, Samuel H. "The Tax Revolt and Electoral Competition." *Public Choice* 115 (2003): 333–45.

Blankenau, William F., and Mark Skidmore. "School Finance Litigation, Tax and Expenditure Limitations, and Education Spending." *Contemporary Economic Policy* 22 (January 2004): 127–43.

Citrin, Jack. "Do People Want Something for Nothing: Public Opinion on Taxes and Government Spending." *National Tax Journal* 32 (June 1979): 113–30.

Courant, Paul N., Edward M. Gramlich, and Daniel L. Rubinfeld. "Why Voters Support Tax Limitation Amendments: The Michigan Case." *Tax and Expenditure Limitations,* COUPE Papers on Public Economics. Washington, DC: Urban Institute Press, 1981.

Denzau, Arthur, Robert MacKay, and Carolyn Weaver. "Spending Limitations, Agenda Control, and Voters' Expectations." *National Tax Journal* 32 (June 1979): 189–200.

Economic Report of the President. Washington, DC: U.S. Government Printing Office, February 2004.

Elder, Harold W. "Exploring the Tax Revolt: An Analysis of the Effects of State Tax and Expenditure Limitations Laws." *Public Finance Quarterly* 20 (January 1992): 47–63.

Fischel, William A. "Did Serrano Cause Proposition 13?" *National Tax Journal* 42 (December 1989): 465–73.

Ladd, Helen F., and Julie Boatright Wilson. "Why Voters Support Tax Limitations: Evidence from Massachusetts' Proposition 2-1/2." *National Tax Journal* 35 (June 1982): 121–47.

Magleby, David B. *Direct Legislation: Voting on Ballot Propositions in the United States.* Baltimore: The Johns Hopkins University Press, 1984.

McGuire, Therese J. "Proposition 13 and Its Offspring: For Good or for Evil?" *National Tax Journal* 52, no. 1 (March 1999): 129–38.

Oakland, William H. "Discussion of Perry Shapiro, 'Popular Response to Public Spending Disequilibrium: An Analysis of the 1978 California Property Tax Limitation Initiative.'" *Tax and Expenditure Limitations,* COUPE Papers on Public Economics. Washington, DC: Urban Institute Press, 1981.

Oakland, William H., Perry Shapiro, and Jon Sonstelie. "Did Proposition 13 Slay Leviathan?" *The American Economic Review* 72 (May 1982): 184–90.

Preston, Anne E., and Casey Ichniowski. "A National Perspective on the Nature and Effects of the Local Property Tax Revolt, 1976–1986." *National Tax Journal* 44 (June 1991): 123–45.

Sexton, Terri A., Steven M. Sheffrin, and Arthur O'Sullivan. "Proposition 13: Unintended Effects and Feasible Reforms." *National Tax Journal* 52, no. 1 (March 1999): 99–112.

Shadbegian, Ronald J. "The Effect of Tax and Expenditure Limitations on the Revenue Structure of Local Governments, 1962–87." *National Tax Journal* 52 (June 1999): 221–37.

Shapiro, Perry. "Popular Response to Public Spending Disequilibrium: An Analysis of the 1978 California Property Tax Limitation Initiative." *Tax and Expenditure Limitations,* COUPE Papers on Public Economics. Washington, DC: Urban Institute Press, 1981.

Shapiro, Perry, David Puryear, and John Ross. "Tax and Expenditure Limitation in Retrospect and in Prospect." *National Tax Journal* 32 (June 1979): 1–10.

Skidmore, Mark. "Tax and Expenditure Limitations and the Fiscal Relationships between State and Local Governments." *Public Choice* 99 (April 1999): 77–102.

Tiebout, Charles. "A Pure Theory of Local Expenditures." *Journal of Political Economy* 64 (October 1956): 416–24.

U.S. Bureau of the Census. *Historical Statistics of the United States: Colonial Times to 1957.* Library of Congress Card No. A 60-9150. Washington, D.C.: U.S. Bureau of the Census, 1960.

Cross-references: education financing, state and local; Proposition 13/property tax caps; tax price; Tiebout model.

Taxpayer Compliance Measurement Program (TCMP)

William Lefbom

Internal Revenue Service (Emeritus)

An IRS program designed to assess the degree of noncompliance with law and regulation.

The taxpayer compliance measurement program (TCMP) was designed by the Internal Revenue Service (IRS) in the early 1960s to measure the extent to which taxpayers voluntarily comply with tax laws. TCMP is designed to measure how many taxpayers file an accurate return and pay on a timely basis before any direct enforcement actions. The purpose was to define the extent and characteristics of noncompliance so that optimal solutions could be initiated to improve compliance. These solutions have included recommendations for changing the laws, improved IRS workload (audit) selection systems, changed emphasis in enforcement programs, tax form design, and educational efforts.

To achieve the desired compliance measurement objectives, the IRS randomly selects a sample of accounts, potential nonfilers, or returns; conducts a thorough investigation or audit; and captures the results on a database. The term "investigation" is used in this entry to describe the techniques used by the IRS collection function to determine if a potential nonfiler has already filed, is not required to file, or has not filed a required tax return. The IRS uses the term "examination" instead of "audit." The term "audit" is used in this entry because it is the more commonly understood word used to describe an IRS examination of books, records, financial transactions, and so forth to determine the accuracy of the tax return submitted by the taxpayer.

Scope of TCMP surveys

The IRS developed terms to define the many different surveys conducted since 1963. The term "phase" is used to designate what compliance aspect is being measured, and the IRS uses roman numerals to designate a phase. A "cycle" is used to designate the specific period the survey measures. Eleven phases and 35 cycles were completed from 1963 through 1996. Surveys designated Phase I are designed to measure timely payment, Phase II and IX surveys measure compliance in filing of returns, and Phase III, IV, V, VI, VII, VIII, X, and XI surveys measure the accuracy of a filed return. The following surveys have been completed: Phase I (Surveys of Delinquent Accounts)—7 cycles, last survey 1984; Phase II (Delinquent Returns Non-Farm Business Surveys)—3 cycles, last survey 1969; Phase III (Surveys to Measure Accuracy of Individual Income Tax Returns)—10 cycles, last survey 1988; Phase IV (Surveys to Measure Accuracy of Corporation Income Tax Returns)—5 cycles, last survey 1988; Phase V (Survey to Measure Accuracy of Estate Tax Returns)—1 cycle, only survey 1971; Phase VI (Surveys to Measure Accuracy of Exempt Organization Returns)—3 cycles, last survey 1988; Phase VII (Survey to Measure Accuracy of Fiduciary Income Returns)—1 cycle, only survey 1975; Phase VIII (Survey to Measure Accuracy of Employee Plans Returns)—1 cycle, only survey 1980; Phase IX (Delinquent Returns Individual Income Tax)—2 cycles, last survey 1988; Phase X (Survey to Measure Accuracy of Partnership Returns)—1 cycle, only survey 1982; Phase XI (Survey to Measure Accuracy of S Corporation Returns)—1 cycle, only survey 1985.

TCMP process

The TCMP process from initial planning to beginning to analyze results takes five years, and the IRS has generally followed these steps:

Preliminary planning

This step determines the overall scope and objectives of the survey—for example, what type of return, the period of sample selection, whether results are to be used for workload selection formulas, preliminary sample design, approval to commit resources, and development of a detailed action plan. A memorandum on the "scope and objectives" of a specific survey summarizes these tasks.

Sample design and computer programming

All TCMP surveys are based on audits or investigations of a random stratified sample. Income levels (individual income taxes), asset size (corporations), and availability of information returns (delinquent return surveys) are some of the criteria that determine the strata. The selection of potential nonfilers or returns within a sample stratum is entirely random, but the sample rate varies greatly by stratum. The size of the sample, within a stratum, is determined by the survey scope and objectives, which are normally the measurement of compliance and the development of workload selection formulas. One way the IRS has identified which returns to audit is a mathematical technique known as discriminant function (DIF). DIF formulas are developed for each audit class, based on TCMP. Samples are normally designed to be large enough to measure compliance and develop DIF formulas for each audit class. DIF requirements greatly increase the sample size that would be required if compliance measurement were the only objective. Data from tax returns and information returns submitted by taxpayers or third parties are transcribed (or electronically transmitted to the IRS) and retained on a master file. The master file is programmed to identify selected returns when they post to the system based on the strata criteria and sample selection rate. For delinquent return surveys, the master file is programmed to stratify potential nonfilers, for a specific year, based primarily on information returns and prior tax year return information. (The most recent TCMP survey of potential nonfilers also sampled individuals who are not on the master file system and for whom no information return data were available to the IRS.)

Selection of returns or potential nonfilers

The sampling of filed returns normally takes place weekly for an entire year—for example, sampling of tax year 1988 individual income tax returns would start in January 1989 and continue through the end of December 1989. The sampling of potential nonfilers, however, occurs once, after information returns have been received, processed, and correlated. The sampling of potential nonfilers of tax year 1988 individual income tax returns took place in April 1990, for instance. The sampled returns or investigations of potential nonfilers are controlled so that every sampled case is included in the survey unless there is a legitimate reason for excluding it— for example, if a taxpayer died after filing and there is no executor that can provide any type of information for use in an audit.

Development of a questionnaire

An instrument is used to collect the data necessary to meet the scope and objectives of the survey. (The IRS uses the term "check sheet" to describe this instrument.) The IRS tries to obtain only data that can be obtained by a thorough audit or investigation. The only information sought from the taxpayer during the audit or investigation is what is necessary to determine the accuracy of the return, or determine if the taxpayer meets tax return filing requirements in case of delinquent return surveys. Generally, a check sheet designed to measure the accuracy of a return will contain most of the line items on the tax return as reported by the taxpayer and determined by the examiner to be the correct amount— for example, interest income reported and the amount the examiner determines is correct, which may be the same, higher, or lower.

Training and audits or investigations

The employees assigned to conduct TCMP audits or investigations are not trained in survey methodology or research, but they do understand tax law, so their training emphasizes the importance of an in-depth audit or investigation and the accurate completion of the check sheet. The taxpayer selected for the audit or investigation is entitled to all the normal appeals processes. The taxpayer may receive a "no change" report, receive a refund, be required to pay additional taxes, or even be the subject of a criminal referral if fraud is uncovered. IRS examiners are required to review all potential issues to determine if the return is correct as filed. The IRS relies on the professional judgment of its employees to ensure that all potential issues that would affect the reported tax liability are explored. All TCMP audits or investigations are subject to a separate technical review. Particular emphasis is placed on use of proper auditing techniques to detect unreported income. Normally, at least 18 months are allowed for the audit portion of a TCMP survey. The most complex returns, which take the longest time to audit, are normally the last to be filed and, therefore, sampled. The taxpayer may not agree with the examiner's recommendations and may request an appeal. The results of the audit are normally set forth on the check sheet before any appeals organization or tax court decisions that could increase or decrease the tax changes recommended by the examiner or investigator.

Datafile creation

The check sheets are designed so that numerous validity or consistency tests can be applied to ensure data integrity. In earlier surveys, the check sheets were sent to a central processing center where they were key entered and subject to testing. In more recent surveys, the check sheets are entered in field offices, to move the timing and placement of error correction closer to the source. The datafile would include all items from the check sheet and other items from the IRS master file.

Output tables and preliminary analysis

Diagnostic tables, which provide frequency counts and values for check sheet line items, serve as another check to ensure data integrity. The TCMP database is then available for analysis of compliance and the development of DIF formulas for workload selection. A public use file like that developed by the Statistics of Income program is not developed for TCMP because availability of a micro-level file could enable someone to determine tax return line item variables and relative weights associated with high tax change returns—the same general means the IRS uses to develop scoring formulas (DIF) for workload (audit) selection. The IRS believes the formulas might be approximated and individuals might improperly manipulate their tax returns to avoid the possibility of being audited.

An example of a tabulation is "Table 10," frequently used within the IRS. This table contains, for each line item on the tax return, the amount reported, the amount increased, decreased, not reported but established (by the examination), and reported and changed to zero. This table is aggregated by audit class. While the IRS produces the table for internal use, it has occasionally provided the table to academics and others with an interest in overall tax compliance and the components of compliance such as proper reporting of income, deductions, and credits.

Voluntary compliance level

An aggregate measure that has been used since the first TCMP cycles is the voluntary compliance level (VCL). The IRS wanted one simple measure that depicted overall compliance for a year and for each audit class. The VCL is calculated by dividing the tax reported on the return by the tax reported plus the tax increase determined by the examiner. The result is multiplied by 100. The IRS also develops "tax gap" estimates—the amount of "true" tax liability for a particular tax year that is not paid voluntarily and timely—primarily from TCMP data. Tax gap estimates include compliance percentages in addition to amounts. The tax gap compliance percentages (or the inverse noncompliance percentages) are much broader than the VCL measures, and the two measures are not comparable. (Some media articles compared the VCL to tax gap percentages and incorrectly implied a major decline in voluntary compliance.)

Published results from TCMP surveys

The primary focus of TCMP is to improve tax administration. Measurements of voluntary compliance that result from TCMP are provided to congressional tax-writing committees and the Government Accountability Office. These results may only reflect a specific aspect of tax compliance, which may be the subject of a hearing. The IRS makes publicly available two documents that may contain summary measures from completed TCMP surveys.

The IRS Research Bulletin, Publication 1500, formerly known as the *Trend Analysis and Related Statistics,* is generally published once a year. The 1993/1994 *Bulletin* includes articles and tables on the accuracy of the latest survey to measure accuracy of filed 1988 individual income tax returns and to compare them with secured delinquent returns. Earlier issues include articles on compliance levels from the most recently completed TCMP survey and compliance trends from prior surveys.

The *Statistics of Income (SOI) Bulletin, Publication 1136,* published quarterly, occasionally includes compliance measures from TCMP surveys. The summer 1993 and fall 1994 issues contain articles and tables on tax year 1988 individual income tax return filing compliance.

ADDITIONAL READINGS

Internal Revenue Service. *The IRS Research Bulletin.* Washington, DC: U.S. Government Printing Office, various years.

———. *Statistics of Income (SOI) Bulletin.* Pittsburgh: Government Printing Office, various years. Superintendent of Documents, P.O. Box 371954, Pittsburgh PA 15250-7954.

Cross-references: income tax, federal; tax administration, federal; tax administration, state, public, and private cooperation in; tax evasion.

Tax price

Walter Hettich
California State University

A concept developed in analogy to price as observed in private markets.

The tax price is usually defined as the payment required of a consumer for an extra unit of a public good (Stiglitz 1988). The term may also be used more broadly to indicate the marginal or average unit cost of public services to a particular taxpayer or group of taxpayers.

Tax price differs from tax rate by making an explicit connection between tax payments and the consumption of public services. While it is related to the term user fees, its meaning is more general, because an implicit tax price exists in all cases regardless of whether consumers are being charged for the good or service.

Tax price is most often used in theoretical discussions of how to equate the demand and supply of public services. In the private economy, market prices play an important function in establishing such equality by serving as crucial signals to buyers and sellers. Under competitive conditions, price adjustments in response to shortages or surpluses lead to market equilibrium and to an efficient use of resources in production and consumption. Economists have asked whether there are charges or payments that can serve a similar role in the public sector.

The main conceptual difficulty arises from the special nature of public goods. It is often pointed out that public services such as defense do not diminish in availability when one more consumer is added; those already living in the community continue to enjoy the same level of protection as before. Furthermore, it is not feasible to exclude anyone residing in the country from benefiting from expenditures on national defense. These characteristics make it impossible to use private-market institutions and market prices to match demand and supply in the case of public goods and to allocate such goods among consumers efficiently.

Theorists have proposed various mechanisms to determine tax prices that would provide appropriate signals to the consumers of public goods. The most famous contribution was made in 1919 by Lindahl (1958), who suggested a mechanism to let consumers react to individually differentiated tax prices. Price ratios for public and private goods were to be adjusted separately for each consumer until everyone demanded the same amount of the public good, an equilibrium situation having efficiency properties similar to a private market solution. Lindahl's work implies that consumers pay differing unit prices for the same amount of public good in equilibrium, reflecting variations in their demand for the good. This outcome is necessary because quantity cannot be adjusted separately by each individual, as is possible for goods sold in private markets.

While Lindahl's work provides a conceptual solution for determining equilibrium tax prices, it has a theoretical shortcoming. Participants in the scheme who understand its functioning can reduce their payments by misrepresenting their true demand in response to announced price ratios, leading to free riding on their part. If such actions are prevalent, the mechanism no longer yields efficient tax prices. Economists have attempted to devise other approaches that would force participants to reveal their true demands (Clarke 1971; Feldman 1980), but as yet no mechanism with broad applicability in practice has been discovered.

Lindahl's model is a simplified and highly stylized representation of public goods provision. While it clears up important theoretical issues, it does not describe how decisions are made. In democratic societies, taxpayers express their demands for public goods and services primarily by voting. This has led to analyses of voting mechanisms and their role in the determination of public-sector output.

An approach frequently used in research on the public sector is the median voter model. Under the conditions specified in this framework, the voter with the median demand for a public good determines the equilibrium level of output. In making choices, this voter relates his or her tax price to the benefit from additional units of public output until tax price equals the value of the last unit of the good provided. Researchers who use this model attempt to determine tax prices faced by the median voter in particular political decision contexts, such as referenda on bond issues, in order to test the model against actual data.

Outcomes in a median voter framework generally differ from those in Lindahl equilibrium. Depending on the conditions facing the median or decisive voter, budgets may be higher or lower than with efficient pricing. This is not surprising, because results hinge on the tax price of a particular voter and do not represent the marginal responses of all participants. While tax price remains important, it no longer simulates the role played by prices in efficient private markets. The necessity of using a collective choice process exacts a cost if market efficiency is taken as a standard of comparison.

While the median voter model links budgetary choices to voting, it is based on rather strict assumptions concerning the nature of preferences and the number of dimensions in which decisions are made. In situations where choices are complex, with several issues decided simultaneously, the model no longer yields predictable, stable outcomes. In alternative frameworks more suited for analyzing complex tax and expenditure situations, such as expected vote maximization, the links between tax prices for particular public goods and budget size are less direct, even though voters still relate the overall benefits from increased public output to the cost of paying additional taxes.

As mentioned, the difficulties of appropriate pricing arise primarily from the nature of public goods. However, not all goods or services provided by governments are "public" in the full sense of the term because they are subject to not being diminishable in consumption and to not being excludable. Some are closer in nature to private goods, although they may have a public aspect or component. An example is provided by higher education, where students capture a large proportion of benefits from the activity privately in the form of increased earnings after completion of studies, and where exclusion by price can readily be practiced. In such a context, user fees (i.e., tuition) can be applied. If their level were determined by considerations of economic efficiency alone, such fees would represent prices similar to those observed in private markets, although they would contain an element of subsidy to reflect any public component or externality attached to the good. In practice, determination of such charges or fees represents additional factors reflecting the political mechanism through which decisions are made and distributional considerations that may be important in public policy.

Because of the size and complexity of the modern public sector, it is hard for the average voter to link changes in his or her tax burden directly to changes in specific public benefits. The individual pays a multitude of taxes, each of which may be subject to special provisions, such as exemptions, deductions, and credits, making it difficult to calculate marginal tax payments. One should also note that some taxes can be shifted, giving rise to complex questions of incidence. As a result, it may be next to impossible to know how an individual's tax liability will be affected by a small increase in public expenditures and thus to estimate an appropriate marginal tax price. Similar problems will also arise if we attempt to determine actual average tax prices.

Although economists are aware of the difficulties of implementation, they continue to employ the concept in theoretical discussions. Analysis based on tax price clarifies important issues about the similarities and differences of the public and private sectors and yields general conclusions that are useful in policymaking. It strongly suggests that efficiency in public resource use will be improved by mechanisms establishing a closer link between the consumption of publicly provided goods and the cost to those who benefit from these goods.

ADDITIONAL READINGS

Clarke, Edward H. "Multipart Pricing of Public Goods." *Public Choice* (Fall 1971): 17–33.

Feldman, Alan M. *Welfare Economics and Social Choice Theory.* Boston: Kluwer Nijhoff Publishing, 1980.

Lindahl, Erik. "Just Taxation—A Positive Solution" (translated). In *Classics in the Theory of Public Finance,* edited by Richard A. Musgrave and Alan T. Peacock (167–178). New York: St. Martin's Press, 1958.

Stiglitz, Joseph. *Economics of the Public Sector.* 2nd ed. New York: Norton, 1988.

Cross-references: benefit principle; median voter theorem; tax.

Tax reform, federal

C. Eugene Steuerle
The Urban Institute

A review of the federal government experience in adjusting its revenue system to changes in the national economy, demography, and its institutional and political arrangements. The term usually refers to broad rather than piecemeal change in law.

Changes to the tax laws are almost always labeled reforms, but reform as improvement, not merely amendment, generally is based upon bringing the law into closer adherence to certain principles or goals. The public finance principles of efficiency, growth, equal treatment of those in equal situations (horizontal equity or fairness), progressivity, and simplicity provide a useful listing around which tax changes can be analyzed.

Although tax changes are put forward for many reasons, the fundamental purpose of taxation is to raise revenues. Taxes generally are not good in and of themselves. They pro-

vide the means by which government programs are financed; hence, their benefits cannot be separated from the expenditure side of the budget. By themselves, taxes nearly always distort behavior, add complications to the lives of at least some taxpayers, and, in practice, create problems of equity between some who pay and some who are equally capable of paying, but from whom payment is more difficult to extract for administrative or political reasons. Much of traditional tax reform, therefore, is aimed at minimizing the costs of taxation—reducing the inefficiencies of taxation—more than at maximizing some efficiencies it somehow adds to society.

Historical context

At the end of the 19th century and the beginning of the 20th, many federal reform efforts were aimed at displacing or replacing old taxes with new taxes. During the 19th century, government was financed primarily through tariffs. Today large tariffs are generally viewed as both unfair and inefficient, but in the earlier period they could be assessed conveniently at the time that goods were transferred from sellers to buyers, and an accounting was engaged at the port or dock. With the rise of the corporation and the large organization, however, more elaborate accounting systems allowed better assessment of returns to factors of production such as labor and capital. It was this development, more than any other, that allowed replacement of tariffs by income and wage taxes as the primary sources of revenues to the federal government. At the same time, the growth of government was also made possible in part by the ability of business to manage larger scale tax systems, whether based on income or some other measure such as value added (see *value-added tax, national*).

As income taxes grew in size and importance, more and more attention was paid to their design, rather than their adoption, expansion, or contraction, as a major reform option. Many fights, of course, also ensued over the size of the tax system, but the revenue goal here was closely related to how large government expenditures should be, an issue that extends far beyond tax reform. Still, budget, expenditure, and tax issues were often combined and confused. Major changes to the tax system were often the consequence of budgetary rather than tax pressures. In some periods, such as wartime, consensus on the need for expenditures left as a remaining debate only the issue of who should pay. In other periods, many policymakers argued for higher or lower taxes primarily on the basis of what expenditures could be financed. In these cases, the tax debate often could not be separated from the issue of size of government.

Another confusion in the tax reform debate often arises from considerations of the design of the tax base and its interaction with the progressivity of the system itself. While tax progressivity generally can be determined by the setting of tax rates, reform often began with statutory rates considered fixed. Hence, when the base changed, the reform often had distributional consequences across income classes even if the initial goals of reform were unrelated to redistribution. For instance, barring offsetting changes in the tax rate structure, cutting back on a particular tax preference might be favored or opposed primarily on the grounds of what it did to the relative tax burdens of the rich or poor. If rates could be adjusted, however, then the distributional issue likely can be removed, and the issue is whether the particular preference for recipient groups is better than simply lowering their taxes by the same amount.

Still another source of confusion arose over use of the tax system for growth or macroeconomic purposes versus other improvements in well-being, such as might be achieved through more standard improvements in efficiency. In the United States, these issues arose particularly in tax reform debates in the post–World War II era. In tax reform options put forward in the early 1960s, for instance, President Kennedy made a strong pitch that tax reductions would help spur the economy and produce economic growth by expanding demand. At the same time, he proposed a number of changes to the tax base to make it more inclusive of different sources of income. The macroeconomic goal at the time was associated closely with Keynesian economics, and the argument put forward was that the additional money circulating in the economy would spur demand. In 1981, President Reagan put forward a tax reform proposal that also used macroeconomic arguments. Indeed, its primary features were very similar to those adopted during the Kennedy round of tax reform in the early 1960s: rate reduction and expansion of incentives for investment in physical capital, particularly equipment. In the 1981 round, however, the justification put forward was that lower tax rates would spur suppliers of labor and capital to work harder and save more; the term "supply side" was applied to this macroeconomic argument. Thus, a similarly designed tax change was justified in both cases by an appeal to macroeconomics, yet the theory or apologetics used were very different. In 2001, President George W. Bush argued for a tax cut emphasizing rate reduction. In this case, the argument initially was supply-side in nature and involved the spending of some temporary budgetary surpluses. As recession hit, the arguments for acceleration and expansion of those cuts became increasingly centered on Keynesian notions of stimulus.

Thus, whenever the macroeconomic justification was used, as it was for many other tax reductions, it often tended to dominate not only the debate, but the outcome. The goals—an expansion of the economy, a higher rate of growth, or a quicker turn out of recession—were given priority over such issues as defining the tax base properly. The last was a longer-term objective that could always be put off until another day. Thus, in the 1960s round the question of base definition was essentially abandoned and the macroeconomic goal given preference, while in 1981 and 2001 to 2003 almost no base broadening was proposed and new preferences were added.

For many tax reformers, the issues of defining the tax base in a way that would promote efficiency, fairness, and simplicity often have been given far too little weight because of the greater attention focused on size of revenues, progressivity of the system, and macroeconomic incentives to spur either supply or demand. To these reformers, the issues could and should be separated. Given a tax base, the level of revenues and degree of progressivity could be determined by adjusting the tax rate schedule, including allowances for low-income individuals. Hence, the issue of what would be included in the base for the most part was a separable issue. If a given deduction was eliminated, for instance, any revenue raised could be offset by a reduction in rates, and any effect on progressivity could be offset by a change in the rate schedule itself.

Base broadening to include more items of income, better compliance with respect to items that were reported poorly, and reductions in preferences did receive significant attention between 1982 and 1986. At the beginning of that brief reform period, the issue was again driven by a concern that went beyond tax reform: large levels of government deficit. Several base-broadening reforms in the 1980s were enacted as part of deficit reduction bills. President Reagan's strong antipathy to raising tax rates, coupled with Congress's reluctance or inability to deal with entitlement types of spending, left base broadening not so much a popular option as a less unpopular choice for reducing the deficit.

Between 1984 and 1986, the nation engaged in an extensive debate over a tax reform that would center almost entirely on the tax base itself and the lower rates that might be possible if that base were appropriately expanded. The effort for the most part attempted to put aside the issues of total revenues, progressivity, and short-term macroeconomic incentives for growth. Thus, the reform was designed approximately to be "revenue neutral" and "distributionally neutral." A large number of deductions, exclusions, credits, and other preferences were either pared or eliminated. Rates were reduced significantly, but unlike the Kennedy, Reagan, or George W. Bush rounds of rate reductions, they were paid for through other tax changes. Like all reforms, the Tax Reform Act of 1986 was made possible by a combination of opportunities: a president who especially disliked high tax rates, the rapid expansion of tax shelters, the increased income taxation of the poor, and growing concerns over taxation of the family.

By the time the 1986 act was signed into law, it involved the most comprehensive reform of this type ever achieved for the income tax. According to Witte (1991), "Of the 72 provisions which tightened tax expenditures, 14 tax expenditures were eventually repealed, a figure approximately equal to the total that had been repealed from 1913 to 1985." Treasury had advocated repeal of 38 tax expenditures.

Another detailed analysis, by Neubig and Joulfaian (1988), indicated that under some simplifying assumptions, this tax reform produced the equivalent of $193 billion in tax expenditure reduction for the year 1988 alone. Base broadening was directly responsible for $77 billion of this total, and the rate reduction it made possible indirectly reduced the value of tax expenditures by the remainder.

Further reform options

Debate over federal tax reform will continue as long as there is a tax system. Many discussions in the modern era combine different reform options into a single package. Among the principal reforms suggested are the following:

Conversion of income tax to a consumption tax

Should the tax base be reduced to exclude all purchases of capital equipment and net saving? Many current proposals would begin, as a base, with a subtraction method value-added tax applied to business—that is, by taking current income and subtracting net purchases of assets (Bradford 1996). To this system could be added an individual tax—either on wages at the individual level, or a complementary consumption tax at the individual level—which essentially would attempt to allow subtraction of savings from income. Some versions of these more elaborate reforms would maintain or expand an estate tax (Aaron and Galper 1985), and, thus, could be considered more as extending the accounting period for the income tax from a year to a lifetime, rather than excluding from taxation any income that was not consumed by the person who earned it.

Value-added taxes

More narrow reforms would simply add a value-added tax (VAT) to the existing tax system. In many cases, the VAT would follow more traditional types of consumption taxes adopted in other countries. The motives are diverse—increasing revenues to support some expenditure like health care, increasing the share of government burden paid by the elderly, who now receive a substantial share of government expenditures, financing the reduction in taxes on labor or on capital, adopting a tax with a border tax adjustment (rebate of taxes) for exports, or replacing a large portion (but not all) of the income tax and moving many people off the income tax rolls (Graetz 1997).

Flat rate taxes

Still other reforms would convert the tax system into one with a single rate of tax applying to most of the tax base. Strictly speaking, most of these proposals allow some income to be taxed at a zero rate, so they are not flat. Most current proposals also are consumption tax proposals in that they allow the cost of capital equipment to be written off (expensed) right away rather than depreciated over time (Hall and Rabushka 1985); many merge into one of the consumption tax type proposals noted above. If carried out throughout the tax structure, flat taxes have the advantage of dramatically reducing the requirements for individual filing. That is, if the same rate applies to all income, it is not necessary to know to whom the income accrues. A payer—employer, bank, corporation—could sim-

ply pay over a flat rate tax on the tax base, and the amount paid over or withheld on behalf of eventual recipients would be exactly equal to the final tax owed. No filing or reconciliation would be required. This goal might also be achieved in part through essentially flat taxes on particular items of income—a schedular approach more popular in many other industrialized countries. Generally speaking, a flat rate tax would also reduce taxes for those with the highest incomes and increase the share of the tax burden borne by those with incomes in the middle range.

Income tax reform

Many reforms would expand the efforts symbolized by the 1986 tax reform and other base broadening efforts between 1982 and 1986. A primary goal would be to define the tax base in a manner considered appropriate. Often such proposals involve eliminating social preferences, cutting back on the value of various exclusions or deductions, and eliminating the taxation of items that would not legitimately be included in a system that more purely taxed income once and only once. There might be a reduction in the special preferences applied to health insurance purchased by employers, for example. Or integration of corporate and personal income taxes would eliminate the double taxation of capital income earned and paid out to equity owners of corporations.

Integration of tax and transfer systems

In recent years, there has been increased realization not only that expenditures are hidden in the tax system, but that taxes are hidden in the expenditure system. Most transfers from the government involve some sort of implicit tax. The Social Security benefit formula, for instance, provides for lower returns on taxes of higher-income individuals. Welfare systems typically phase out benefits as income rises. Means testing may be applied to a variety of health benefits. Each of these tax systems tends to develop independently, leading to a combined tax system that is little understood or appreciated. Some reforms would aim themselves more directly at determining an integrated rate structure for the systems as a whole. Here, of course, tax and expenditure reform become inseparable.

Tax simplification

Seldom, if ever, has tax reform focused primarily upon simplification. Although it was one of the goals of the 1986 reform, it was achieved only in part for moderate-income taxpayers, while filing became more complex for many businesses or individuals with significant capital income. Simplification might be sought through one of the broader reforms listed above, or it could be pursued step by step within the existing income tax framework. The large potential growth in number of taxpayers paying the alternative minimum tax

(AMT) in the first part of the 21st century has spurred simplification efforts, as well.

ADDITIONAL READINGS

Aaron, Henry A., and Harvey Galper. *Assessing Tax Reform.* Washington, DC: Brookings Institution Press, 1985.

Adams, Thomas S. "Fundamental Problems of Federal Income Taxation." *Quarterly Journal of Economics* 35, no. 4 (1921): 527–56.

Bradford, David F. *Fundamental Issues in Consumption Taxation.* Washington, DC: AEI Press, 1996.

Brownlee, W. Elliot. *Federal Taxation in America: A Short History.* 2nd ed. Cambridge, U.K.: Cambridge University Press, 2004.

Fullerton, Don, and Diane Lim Rogers. *Who Bears the Lifetime Tax Burden?* Washington, DC: The Brookings Institution.

Graetz, Michael J. *The Decline [and Fall?] of the Income Tax.* New York: W. W. Norton and Company, 1997.

Hall, Robert E., and Alvin Rabushka. *The Flat Tax.* Stanford, CA: Hoover Institution Press, 1985.

Neubig, Thomas, and David Joulfaian. "The Tax Expenditure Budget before and after the Tax Reform Act of 1986." Office of Tax Analysis Paper 60. Washington, DC: U.S. Department of the Treasury, 1988.

Slemrod, Joel, and Jon Bakija. *Taxing Ourselves: A Citizen's Guide to the Great Debate Over Tax Reform.* 3rd ed. Cambridge, MA: MIT Press, 2004.

Steuerle, C. Eugene. *Contemporary U.S. Tax Policy.* Washington, DC: Urban Institute Press, 2004.

Witte, John F. "The Tax Reform Act of 1986: A New Era in Tax Policy?" *American Politics Quarterly* 19 (October 1991): 438–57.

Cross-references: consumption taxation; excess burden; fairness in taxation; flat tax; integration, corporate tax; payroll tax, federal; pensions, tax treatment of; retail sales tax, national; tax administration, federal; tax equity analysis; value-added tax, national.

Tax reform, state

Steven D. Gold
National Conference of State Legislatures

Updated by
Robert D. Ebel
The Urban Institute

A review of the periods in which there have been broad changes made in the way U.S. state government tax systems work.

One strength of United States federalism is the flexibility it provides to the public sector to adjust the nation's changing economic, demographic, and institutional trends. A key element of this fiscal flexibility is the ability of the state and local sector to reform its revenue systems.

The record of state tax reform can be divided into six phases.

1789–1911

Since the nation was formed, intergovernmental relations can be characterized as a dynamic tension in the sorting out of roles and responsibilities among federal, state, and local governments. Under the Articles of Confederation (1781), the states were so strong they threatened the survival of the national government. Congress had limited power to either administer or finance its functions, and attempts to strengthen the national government often failed because changes to the Articles required state unanimity. The framework changed in 1789 when the new Constitution gave the federal government to power to "lay and collect taxes, duties, and imposts and excises and to pay the debts and to provide for the common defense and general welfare of the United States" (Article 1, Sec. 8).

Despite this dramatic change, state governments maintained their predominance; but the results were divisive and the nation drifted to Civil War. One effect of the War was to diminish the prestige of the states by state enactment of constitutions limiting state legislative and executive powers. By the turn of the century the federal government was beginning to fiscally assert itself largely through a variety of selective consumption taxes (37 percent of total general revenues), compared to an 11 percent state share (mix of excises, fees, and property taxes). Local governments still dominated (51 percent of total general government revenue, 95 percent of which was property-based).

1911–29

With the federal government burdened with paying for WWI, the responsibility for civil functions grew for the state and local sector. And with that came the beginning of the modern state tax system: (1) Wisconsin established the first broad-based personal income tax in 1911, and by 1929 another 13 states had followed suit. (The territory of Hawaii adopted an income tax in 1901, but it was not to become a state until 1959); (2) sixteen states imposed corporate income taxes, again following Wisconsin's precedent; (3) every state enacted a gasoline tax between 1919 and 1929; and (4) after Iowa created the first state cigarette tax in 1921, five states followed by 1929. Most other states followed with cigarette taxes in the 1930s and early 1940s with tobacco states Virginia (1960), and North Carolina (1969) the longest holdouts (Sagoo 2004).

The Great Depression and expansion of the sales and income tax

The Great Depression provided a tremendous impetus to state tax reform, particularly since the property tax, which had been the bulwark of state-local fiscal systems, was viewed as onerous in a period of widespread unemployment, low income, and declining property values. Many states relieved some of the pressure on the property tax by adopting new broad-based taxes. A major innovation occurred when Mississippi pioneered the general sales tax in 1932, and by 1939 half of the 48 states had adopted one. Like the sales tax, use of the income tax spread rapidly during the 1930s, with 16 states adopting an income tax. Not much happened for the next two decades, but during the 1960s and 1970s 11 states adopted the income tax, while one, Alaska, repealed it. Several states also turned to local option sales taxes (from 12 state authorizations in 1963 to 34 today). The 11 local option income tax states saw a rapid growth of local income tax adoptions between 1970 and the mid-1990s, with Pennsylvania accounting for more than two-thirds of the now approximately 4,100 local income tax jurisdictions in the United States (Sjoquist 2003).

Baby boom reform

State tax reform resumed after World War II. One driving force was demographic—the tremendous costs of educating the baby boom generation. In the early 1960s, more than half of state-local spending was for elementary and secondary education. In addition, state government began a transformation in the 1960s, modernizing its institutions and greatly expanding systems of higher education, health, and social services. From 1947 to 1960, 11 more states adopted sales taxes, and 3 added corporate income taxes, but no new personal income taxes were established. Reform accelerated between 1961 and 1971, with 9 new broad-based personal income taxes, 9 corporate income taxes, and 10 sales taxes. State-local tax revenue increased from 9.2 percent of personal income in 1960 to a 1970s' peak of 12.3 percent in 1973. The ratio declined slightly in the 1970s and then in the '80s and '90s trended to 15.2 percent by 2002 (http://www.census.org).

1973–81

Demographic pressures abated after 1973 as public school enrollment decreased. The nature of reform changed in this period, focusing more on relieving and limiting taxes than on raising them. New Jersey's personal income tax, adopted in 1976, was the only new broad-based levy. Important developments focused on the property tax, the personal income tax, and formal tax limitations:

- Property tax relief was a high priority, and property tax collections fell from 4.6 percent of personal income in 1973 to 3.3 percent in 1982. The most important factor was increased state aid, especially for schools, but many states also relieved localities of responsibility for functions like welfare and Medicaid. There was also increased reliance on local sales and income taxes and user charges, expanded credits and exemptions for homeowners and other property owners, and new state imposed limitations on property taxes or spending.
- Circuit breakers—state-financed tax credits whose value depends on both household income and property tax liability—spread rapidly, with their number growing from 5 in 1970 to 29 in 1979. Thirty-four states now have some form of property tax circuit breaker.

- Personal income tax revenue continued to grow faster than personal income, but its increase was slowed by two developments—the adoption of indexation by numerous states, and rate reductions in states where (in some cases) empirical research demonstrated the personal income tax had a negative effect on the job growth in employment in some key sectors (Ebel and McGuire 1986).
- Limitations on the growth of state taxes or spending proliferated. New Jersey adopted the first one in 1976, restricting the growth of state appropriations to the rate of increase of personal income. By 1982, 19 states had similar measures, in some cases tying growth to the inflation rate and population increases.
- Limitations also spread to property taxes and local spending. The most well-known were Proposition 13 in California (1978), which limits the effective property tax rate to 1 percent of market value and also restricts assessment increases, and Proposition $2\frac{1}{2}$ in Massachusetts (1980), which permits property tax revenue to grow only 2.5 percent per year and places a 2.5 percent ceiling on the effective tax rate. Many other states imposed limitations on annual revenue increases in 1971 and later years. The proliferation of tax and spending limitations was one aspect of the so-called tax revolt that was signaled by Proposition 13.
- Other changes led to wider use of indexation, permanent tax reductions and one-time rebates, and reluctance to raise taxes.

These changes had led to a trend toward centralizing the state/local relationship as the share of state/local revenue collected by states rose from 55.3 percent in 1970 to 61.3 percent in 1980. The number is much more balanced today (2002) at 55 percent state, 45 percent local (though of course with wide variation among the states: from the Hawaii and Vermont nearly 80 percent state share to Colorado and New York both 54 percent local).

The 1980s and '90s

Back-to-back recessions in the early 1980s resulted in widespread state fiscal distress, and most states responded with substantial tax increases in 1982 and 1983. Although tax reform was not a prominent feature of these tax increases, many governors and legislators recognized that serious problems existed in their tax policies. More than half the states responded by establishing tax studies to analyze the deficiencies of their state tax systems, several of which still serve as models for current reform discussions. A key impetus for these studies was to prepare states to respond to federal tax reform.

The Tax Reform Act of 1986 offered most states substantial potential windfalls because it broadened the federal definition of income subject to taxation and curtailed numerous itemized deductions; these provisions are normally used (with minor modifications) in determining state taxable income.

Unless they lowered tax rates or took other actions, states would have received substantial increases in tax revenue. In fact, most states responded to federal tax reform by mimicking it—cutting and flattening tax rates, raising standard deductions and personal exemptions, and targeting relief to low-income households. States generally conformed to the federal base-broadening changes (except for taxation of Social Security benefits) and in fact repealed many of their own provisions that did not conform to the federal tax code. The majority of states avoided most, if not all, of the potential revenue windfall.

The early 1990s witnessed a considerable amount of state tax reform. The most important accomplishments were the following:

- Connecticut enacted a new personal income tax; 12 other states restructured income tax rates, in nearly all cases increasing progressivity (although four of these changes were temporary); and 12 others broadened the tax base by reducing deductions.
- Twenty-eight states broadened the sales tax base (although two of these expansions were subsequently repealed).
- Most states that enacted large tax increases made their tax systems more balanced in the sense that they increased reliance on a major tax that was previously underused.

Although this list is impressive, much of the base broadening and tax relief for the poor was relatively modest in scope. Only Connecticut and New Jersey instituted sweeping reforms, and many reforms in New Jersey were subsequently repealed. When state fiscal conditions improved in 1994 and 1995, reform focused primarily on income tax relief, increasing personal exemptions or credits, and reducing tax rates.

Two other important areas of reform in the first half of the 1990s involved school property taxes and tax limitations. Seven states raised state taxes to substantially increase the state share of school costs, and five states enacted stringent new tax limitations or required extraordinary legislative majorities or popular votes to increase state taxes.

The 2000s agenda

The state (and local) tax reform agenda is always unfinished, for two reasons. The first is the political reality that over time as laws are enacted to address specific short-run consideration, the tax system can become an overlapping and unwieldy whole, unnecessarily complex, and patchworked in a manner that thwarts the accomplishment of the tax system's originally intended objectives. Accordingly, periodic review and reform is required. Second, economic, demographic, institutional, and technical changes are occurring in the nation and the world; and although these changes are largely beyond the control of any state, policymakers cannot ignore the need to adjust and to capture the fiscal benefits of these changes.

That over time the buildup of patchworking and/or external trends occur is not a cause for alarm; indeed, as this entry makes clear, state and local systems are remarkably adaptable to external change in an (often) fair, effective, and efficient manner. As the nation enters the 21st century, once again the "big-picture" is rapidly evolving; and the manner in which state and local fiscal systems adjust can become the key—or a constraint—to achievement of the broader national objectives of intentional competitiveness, and economic growth and stability. Yet numerous scholarly and practitioner analyses warn that state tax systems in use today still reflect the reforms that are now a quarter- to a half-century old.

There are several concerns:

- State (and local) tax systems have remained essentially unchanged despite the fact that the tax base has moved from heavy manufacturing to one dominated by services and intellectual property.
- Electronic commerce has revolutionized how people earn and spend. Under current (federal) law, avoiding (and, some argue, evading) state sales taxes is just a couple keystrokes away (Brunori 2001). Under current institutional arrangements, the trend—and tax base erosion—will grow, especially as consumerism turns increasingly global.
- If, as is now projected, the federal budget deficit remains near historic highs over at least the short run, pressures will further increase on state and local systems to deliver an increasing share of public goods. In the recent past the states have been asked (and in many cases, been mandated) to administer and pay for once largely federally funded programs in welfare, health care, highway maintenance, and low-income housing. In some cases this expenditure sorting out has been meritorious; but whatever the expenditure assignment, the fact remains that responsibilities, old and new, must be financed from a system that is not only still largely mid- to late 20th century–based, but also prone to eroding.
- With respect to the federal fiscal squeeze, most discussions of federal tax reform turn to the possible enactment of some form of broad-based national consumption levy. If such a development does occur, the pressure will be on for states to adjust to protect their general sales taxes (still important at 25 percent of total state local tax collections) Dual (national-subnational) consumption tax systems are feasible, but to make it work will require a major rethinking of state tax structures.
- And then there is changing fiscal architecture. Consider the interplay of the nation's demographics and the personal income tax. Under current state tax law nearly all pension (and other fringe benefit) income is tax-exempt. But in just five years (2010) the baby boom generation—the one that led to the reforms in the 1960s (above)—will begin to reach retirement age, and the percentage of the retirement population that is over 65 will increase rapidly. Whereas 12.3 percent for the 2010 population will be over 65 in 2010 (it was 12.8 percent in 1995), in just 10 more years (2025) the over-65 population will be 28.2 percent of the total (http://www.census.gov).

It can be expected that the states will (and should) respond as they often have: designing a system that fits their own fiscal architecture. Nine states still do not impose a broad-based personal income tax (Alaska, Florida, Nevada, New Hampshire, South Dakota, Tennessee, Texas, Washington, and Wyoming), and five states have no general sales tax (Alaska, Delaware, Montana, New Hampshire, and Oregon). Whether the numbers will change is not at all clear since some of these states have compensated by either levying high tax rates on other bases, such as property or specialized sources (oil production in Alaska, gaming in Nevada), or opting for a smaller public sector.

As citizens continue to demand public services, state governments will, as they have throughout history, need to find a way to pay for these programs. Throughout U.S. state tax reform history, political leaders have proved resourceful in financing services despite often significant political and economic challenges. For the past quarter-century, the demand for reform has been emerging, but not urgent. That lack of urgency is about to change.

ADDITIONAL READINGS

Alm, James, and Sally Wallace. "State and Local Governments' Susceptibility to Globalization." In *Proceedings of the 95th Annual Conference on Taxation* (155–64). Washington, DC: National Tax Association, 2002.

Aronson, J. Richard, and John L. Hilley. *Financing State and Local Governments.* 4th ed. Washington, DC: Brookings Institution Press, 1986.

Bahl, Roy, ed. *Taxation and Economic Development: Blueprint for Ohio Tax Reform.* Columbus, OH: Battelle Press, 1996.

Brunori, David. *State Tax Policy: A Political Perspective.* Washington, DC: Urban Institute Press, 2001.

———, ed. *The Future of State Taxation.* Washington, DC: Urban Institute Press, 1998.

Ebel, Robert, ed. *A Fiscal Agenda for Nevada.* Reno: University of Nevada Press, 1990.

Ebel, Robert, and Therese McGuire, ed. *Final Report of the Minnesota Tax Study Commission. Volume 2, Technical Papers.* Boston: Butterworth, 1986.

Fox, William. "The Ongoing Evolution of State Revenue Systems." *Marquette Law Review* 88 (October 2004): 19–44.

Gold, Steven D., ed. *The State Fiscal Agenda for the 1990s.* Denver: National Conference of State Legislatures, 1990.

Gold, Steven D., and Jennifer McConnick. "State Tax Reform in the Early 1990s." *State Tax Notes* (May 2, 1994): 1146–61.

Hovey, Hal. "State and Local Tax Reform." In *Handbook on Taxation,* edited by W. Bartley Hildreth and James A. Richardson (283–308). New York: Marcel Dekker, 1999.

McGuire, Therese J., and Eugene Steuerle. "State Fiscal Crises: Causes, Consequences." *State Tax Notes* 30, no. 5 (2003): 363–448.

Murray, Matthew. "Competition, Complexity and Constraints: The Evolving Nature of State and Local Tax Systems." In *Proceedings of the 95th Annual Conference on Taxation* (27–33). Washington, DC: National Tax Association, 2002.

Sagoo, Sumeet, ed. *Facts and Figures on Government Finance.* Washington, DC: Tax Foundation, 2004.

Schwartz, Amy Ellen, ed. *City Taxes, City Spending: Essays in Honor of Dick Netzer.* Northampton, MA: Edgar Elgar, 2004.

Sjoquist, David L, ed. *State and Local Finances under Pressure.* Northampton, MA: Edward Elgar, 2003.

Snell, Ronald K., ed. *New Realities in State Finance.* Denver: National Conference of State Legislatures, 2004.

Tannenwald, Robert. "Are State and Local Revenue Systems Becoming Obsolete?" *National Tax Journal* 55, no. 3 (September 2002): 467–89.

The World Bank. *Entering the 21st Century.* Oxford, UK: Oxford University Press, 2000

Cross-references: circuit breaker; fairness in taxation; fiscal architecture; income tax, corporate, state and local; property tax, real property, business; property tax, real property, residential; retail sales tax, state and local; tax limitations; tax reform, federal; telecommunications and electronic commerce, state taxation of.

Tax shelters

Jack Taylor
Congressional Research Service, Library of Congress

Popularly, investments that take such advantage of preferential tax provisions that they reduce taxes on other activities; more generally, any arrangements undertaken to minimize taxes.

The opportunity to "shelter" income from taxation arises because different sources of income are taxed at different rates. Moving income from higher-tax sources to lower-tax sources reduces the total tax bill and "shelters" income from tax, whether the move involves investing in tax-favored activities such as oil and gas exploration or contracting with one's employer to receive some of one's compensation in the form of tax-free health insurance rather than taxable wages. Both of these would be, in the broad meaning of the term, "tax shelters."

However, the term is more often heard in a narrower meaning. Popular usage pictures an investment or enterprise designed to take extraordinary advantage of provisions that reduce taxes, so that the investment or enterprise not only bears no current tax, but also generates losses or credits that can be used to reduce taxes on other income. In this usage, the investment shelters both its own income and income from other sources.

It is this popular definition that has had the important impact on tax policy, and public perceptions of the rich "sheltering" their income from tax have littered the Internal Revenue Code with restrictions on tax shelters and penalties for "abusive" ones. This perception of tax shelters has even been credited with helping to bring about the Tax Reform Act of 1986 (Steuerle 1992; Shaviro 1993). There are at least three explicit definitions of a "tax shelter" in the code, and several more by implication, and all relate more closely to the popular definition than to the more general definition.

The popular definition might also be thought of as the "commercial" definition. In the 1970s and early 1980s, tax shelter investments were aggressively marketed on the promise that they would generate no current tax themselves and would reduce taxes on other income.

Many of the restrictions currently placed on tax shelter investing are aimed at these promotions of tax shelters rather than the investments themselves. This reflects another aspect of the tax shelter phenomenon: The tax differentials introduced to encourage activities deemed socially desirable or to assist groups deemed socially worthy are the differentials that make tax shelters possible. Any restrictions placed on tax shelters necessarily also restrict the incentives for the desirable activity. Reform of tax shelter provisions has been constantly inhibited by this dilemma.

Tax shelters, past

Classic tax shelters ended (for the moment) with the Tax Reform Act of 1986 (TRA86), which not only restricted them directly but also reduced overall tax rates (so sheltering was no longer as lucrative) and differences in tax rates (so finding worthwhile shelters was harder). Before TRA86, however, high marginal tax rates and large differences in rates for different income sources created an ideal climate for tax shelters.

The classic tax shelter consisted of combining several tax code provisions that allowed reduced or deferred taxes. Deductions greater than economic costs, such as percentage depletion of minerals or accelerated depreciation of buildings, were an essential element; the tax shelter investor did not want real economic losses. This element alone provided a tax shelter; excess deductions taken against otherwise taxable income at least postponed taxes until the property was sold.

But the reduced tax rate on capital gains gave an added benefit. The deductions could be taken against income otherwise taxed at rates of up to 70 percent (the maximum rate on ordinary income at one time), and the deferred tax, when finally paid upon the sale of the investment, could be calculated at the capital gains rate, which was 50 or 60 percent less. (This did not work for equipment, because all gain due to depreciation was taxed at ordinary rates at sale.)

A third important element could also be added: leverage. If the investment generated enough income to pay actual economic expenses and interest, as was common in real estate investments, for example, it could be largely financed by borrowed funds and the investor's return on his own invested capital greatly enhanced.

Because transaction costs and risk in such investments tend to be high, they were originally restricted mostly to the rich. In the 1960s and 1970s, however, there was a growing trend toward packaging and marketing tax shelters for the middle class. Limited partnerships were a particularly favored vehicle; they allowed participation of many smaller investors, allocation of losses and credits to the limited partners, and strict limits on risk.

Aggressively marketed tax shelters became notorious. "Rent-a-cow" shelters advertised in *The Wall Street Journal:* Cattle breeders sold their herds to investors and leased them back, giving the investors the deductions for raising calves and capital gains tax rates when the herd was sold. Motion picture film syndicates made films for the sole purpose of generating large artificial losses; the films might never even be shown. The investors often risked no money, because nonrecourse financing was part of the deal.

The elements of these classic tax shelters can be summarized as: (1) deferral or elimination of tax through deductions in excess of current economic costs; (2) conversion of income taxed at ordinary rates into income taxed at reduced rates; and (3) leverage. To market tax shelter investments to smaller investors, syndication or some other form of packaging was required. The tax reform efforts from 1969 to 1986 attacked each of these elements on a multitude of fronts.

Tax shelters, present

The tax code in the late 1990s honors tax shelters mostly by the effort it makes to prevent them (although it still allows quite a few).

Many of the basic rules that created tax shelter opportunities, particularly excessive depreciation deductions, investment credits, and large rate differentials for capital gains, no longer exist. In addition, however, a number of explicit provisions undermine tax shelters. It is no longer possible to take deductions larger than one's investment (at-risk rules, Internal Revenue Code Section 465), to deduct investment interest in excess of investment income (Section 163(d)), or to deduct losses and credits from a business in which one is not an active participant from other income sources (the "passive activity" rules, Section 469). Finally, if one slips through these and several other restrictive provisions, a second tax computation, required of anyone with extraordinary tax preference items, may result in the payment of an "alternative minimum tax" (Sections 55–59).

Certain defined tax shelters are required to be registered (Section 6111) and to provide IRS with a list of their investors (Section 6112). For these purposes, tax shelters are defined as investments that offer an investor deductions and credits greater than twice his investment and are either registered syndications, or that involve five or more investors or total investment of $250,000 or more. There are penalties for "abusive" tax shelters, defined as partnerships or other entities offering fraudulent deductions or credits (Section 6700). There are special rules (and yet more definitions) for economic performance (Section 461(i)(3)) and for substantial understatement of tax (Section 6662(d)(2)(C)). Special hedging transaction rules are provided for "syndicates," defined as partnerships or similar entities allocating more than 35 percent of their losses to limited partners (Section 1256(e)(3)(B)).

As the underlying philosophy of TRA86 was abandoned, the basic changes that made tax shelters uneconomic began to erode. Rate differentials between ordinary income and capital gains have been reintroduced (and extended to dividends). Incentives to encourage investment and other activities have expanded. But tax rates have remained relatively low, and today's tax shelters are rather anemic compared with the robust ones of the past. To date, the tax shelter industry (for individual taxpayers) has not recovered from the effects of TRA86.

Corporate tax shelters

Growing activity has been occurring in corporate tax shelters, which are more complex and varied than the traditional individual tax shelters. Often, corporate tax shelters do not involve investments in real assets but rather in financial instruments that are highly liquid, held for a short time, and structured to avoid risk. They typically involve transactions between taxable U.S. firms and "tax indifferent" parties (such as foreign corporations or tax-exempt entities such as state, local, and foreign governments), designed to shift income to the tax-indifferent party and deductions to the taxable firm. Examples include leasing operations, partnership arrangements that assign basis or losses to the taxable firm, corporate "inversions" that reorganize a firm as a foreign parent, and securities transactions. As of this writing, Congress is considering legislation that would address some of these sheltering issues.

ADDITIONAL READINGS

Cordes, Joseph J., and Harvey Galper. "Tax Shelter Activity: Lessons from Twenty Years of Evidence." *National Tax Journal* 38 (September 1985): 305–24.

Desai, Mehir. "The Corporate Profit Base, Tax Sheltering Activity and the Changing Nature of Employee Compensation." Working Paper 8866. Cambridge, MA: National Bureau of Economic Research, April 2002.

Nelson, Susan. "Taxes Paid by High-Income Taxpayers and the Growth of Partnerships." *SOI Bulletin* 5 (Fall 1985): 55–60.

Shaviro, Daniel N. "Rethinking Anti-Tax Shelter Rules: Protecting the Earned Income Base." *Taxes* 71 (December 1993): 859–81.

Steuerle, C. Eugene. *The Tax Decade.* Washington, DC: Urban Institute Press, 1992.

Stiglitz, Joseph E. "The General Theory of Tax Avoidance." *National Tax Journal* 38 (September 1985): 325–37.

U.S. Congress, Joint Committee on Internal Revenue Taxation. *Tax Shelter Investments.* JCS-8-76. Washington, DC: U.S. Government Printing Office, 1976.

U.S. Congress, Joint Committee on Taxation. *Tax Reform Proposals: Tax Shelters and Minimum Tax.* JCS-34-85. Washington, DC: U.S. Government Printing Office, 1985.

———. *General Explanation of the Tax Reform Act of 1986.* JCS-10-87. Washington, DC: U.S. Government Printing Office, 1987, pp. 209–61.

Whitmire, James, and Bruce Lemons. "Putting Tax Shelters at Risk—Discussion and Proposal for Change." *Tax Notes* (January 27, 2003): 585–96.

Cross-references: alternative minimum tax, corporate; alternative minimum tax, personal; capital cost recovery; deferral of tax; depreciation recapture; partnerships; passive activity losses; tax arbitrage; tax evasion tax expenditures; tax reform, federal.

Tax transparency

W. Bartley Hildreth
Wichita State University

Symmetry of information between tax authorities and the taxpayer.

Tax transparency refers to the symmetry of information between tax authorities and taxpayers. The economics of information affects markets and accountability (Hayek 1945; Stiglitz 1999). In the context of taxation, transparency is important from the first day a tax structure is introduced in the policy arena to the last day of its economic impact. Information relevance depends on the needs of taxpayers, not just what the tax authority provides.

Adam Smith's (1776) second maxim of tax policy calls for a tax to be "certain, and not arbitrary. . . . clear and plain to the contributor, and to every other person." Smith adds, "The uncertainty of taxation encourages the insolence and favours the corruption of an order of men who are naturally unpopular, even where they are neither insolent nor corrupt." By this logic, a clear and plain tax, instead of an uncertain and complex one, helps avoid corruption. Tax transparency, therefore, promotes good governance.

Tax transparency is a responsibility equally shared by the tax authority and the taxpayer and includes an open and participatory policy process and clear and tractable tax rules. As the traditional target of transparency initiatives, the tax authority refers to the aggregate institution represented by a diverse group of policymakers, officials, and administrators of the tax system. Tax authorities typically enjoy discretion in their openness during tax policymaking and in their provision of information later during tax administration. Usually, taxpayers are on the receiving end of this information flow, but understanding a tax begins with a degree of participation.

Tax transparency entails an open policymaking process. The goal is to minimize the secrecy of decisionmaking. Occasionally, the need to prevent premature disclosure is necessary to avoid tax-induced transactions. Frequently, however, this surprise is a political strategy. Regardless, tax transparency calls for the initiator of tax proposals to make timely disclosure of all tax details to allow inquiry and debate during the remainder of the tax policy process. Disclosure includes the release of the data and tax incidence models upon which the proposed policies are premised. Only by having access to the equal information can the assumptions, methods, and results be contested by others (Burton 2002).

Transparency further requires accurate and rational justifications for tax proposals including how the tax fits into an integrated, comprehensive revenue and expenditure policy package, so that the merits of the proposal can be evaluated in full context. In contrast, transparency is reduced when the tax change occurs without public debate or legislative action (Vetter and Gallaway 1998). Two notable non-transparent actions regarding the treatment of exemptions and deductions to the personal income tax include the phase-out of these provisions at specific income levels and any failure to index for inflation (AICPA 2003). Tax expenditure budgets expose the cost of tax preferences (Stiglitz 1998).

Expanding the "circle" of involved participants in policy-making strengthens transparency and improves decisionmaking quality by providing tax authorities different perspectives (Stiglitz 1999; Everson 2004). Passive taxpayer behavior during the policy process is contrary to the contest of ideas expected by a transparent policy process. Taxpayers have an incentive to take advantage of an open policy process that could impose a tax burden. Public choice theory suggests that if only elites exercise the option to participate, then the self-interest of those participants can accentuate the propensity of policymakers to follow incentives other than welfare maximization. The cost of participation, however, may outweigh individual benefits. Taxpayers may respond to opacity by using the ballot to impose tax limits and transparency institutions.

Tax transparency demands the tax authority to provide clear tax rules. Imprecision and vagueness are not only contrary to transparency, but can make it difficult to assess and collect taxes (Burgess and Stern 1993). While taxpayer ignorance of the law is no excuse, the tax authority has the burden to make clear tax rules. Obscurity in tax rates and base violate transparency (Mikesell 1998; AICPA 2003). Hiding a tax in prices is an example of non-transparency, as with the taxing of business inputs in a retail sales tax. Moreover, transparency is violated when the application of tax rules is subject to negotiation for particular taxpayers (International Monetary Fund 2001). Clarity also requires precise rules on taxpayer rights and responsibilities.

Transparency fundamentally rests on the taxpayer being able to understand and meet tax responsibilities by predicting the consequences of taxable characteristics. Tractable tax policy leaves few borderline cases in the application of tax rules (Paul 1997). In all but objectively observable, direct tax structures (e.g., the poll tax), individuals differ in their taxable characteristics (Atkinson and Stiglitz 1976). Tax systems, therefore, emphasize voluntary compliance to elicit the needed tax-relevant information. Taxpayers must know how to meet tax rules and to calculate their respective tax burdens. Retroactive taxes are contrary to predictable taxes. There are problems with "unduly complex rules," as there are with "uncertain but less complex standards" (Weisbach 1999). The use of anti-abuse rules as a bridge between complexity and uncertainty introduces its own transparency problem. By definition, an anti-abuse rule prevents literal compliance with a tax rule from overruling the purpose of the tax law (Weisbach 1999). In another example, partnerships offer tax transparency, in that the tax burden resides with the partners instead of the pass-through partnership entity (Seevers 2001/2002). Additional transparency initiatives include the call for disclosure of corporate tax returns for comparison to corporate financial statements and the pressure on "tax haven" countries to increase the flow of information to other members of the international community (Makhlouf 2000).

In summary, uncertainty and complexity promote tax illusion and tax evasion. Transparency reduces principal-agent problems and minimizes transaction costs in the economy. However, tax transparency is not costless and the benefits may be hard to prove.

ADDITIONAL READINGS

American Institute of Certified Public Accountants [AICPA]. *Guiding Principles for Tax Law Transparency.* New York: Tax Division, AICPA, Inc., 2003.

Atkinson, Anthony B. and Joseph E. Stiglitz. "The Design of Tax Structures: Direct versus Indirect Taxation." *Journal of Public Economics* 6 (1976): 55–75.

Burgess, Robin, and Nicholas Stern. "Taxation and Development." *Journal of Economic Literature* 31 (June 1993): 762–830.

Burton, David R. "Reforming the Federal Tax Policy Process." *Cato Institute Policy Analysis* No. 463. Washington, DC: Cato Institute, 2002.

Everson, Mark W. Remarks of Mark W. Everson, Commissioner of Internal Revenue, before the National Press Club, Washington D.C., on March 15, 2004. http://www.irs.gov/newsroom/article/0,id=121226,00.html.

Hayek, F. A. "The Use of Knowledge in Society" *American Economic Review* 35 (September 1945): 519–30.

International Monetary Fund. "Manual on Fiscal Transparency." Washington, DC: International Monetary Fund, 2001. http://www.imf.org/external/np/fad/trans/manual/sec01b.htm

Makhlouf, Gabriel. "Transparency in Tax Systems: Keeping Pace with the Information Age." *INTERTAX: European Tax Review* 28 (February 2000): 64–66.

Mikesell, John. "Changing the Federal Tax Philosophy: A National Value-Added Tax or Retail Sales Tax?" *Public Budgeting & Finance* 18 (Summer 1998): 53–68.

Paul, Deborah L. "The Sources of Tax Complexity: How Much Simplicity Can Fundamental Tax Reform Achieve?" *North Carolina Law Review* 76 (November 1997): 151–221.

Seevers, Martin H. "Taxation of Partnerships and Partners Engaged in International Transactions: Issues in Cross-Border Transactions in Germany and the U.S." *Houston Business & Tax Law Journal* 2 (2001/2002): 143–73.

Smith, Adam. *An Inquiry into the Nature and Causes of the Wealth of Nations.* London: Methuen and Co., 1776.

Stiglitz, Joseph E. "Distinguished Lecture on Economics in Government: The Private Uses of Public Interests: Incentives and Institutions." *Journal of Economic Perspectives* 12 (Spring 1998): 3–22.

———. "On Liberty, the Right to Know, and Public Discourse: The Role of Transparency in Public Life." Oxford Amnesty Lecture, Oxford, U.K., January 27, 1999.

Vetter, Richard K., and Lowell E. Gallaway. *Underlying Principles of Tax Policy.* Washington, DC: Joint Economic Committee, August 1998.

Weisbach, David A. "Costs of Departures from Formalism: Formalism in the Tax Law." *University of Chicago Law Review* (Summer 1999): 860–86.

Cross-references: partnerships; tax administration, federal; tax evasion; tax expenditures; tax illusion.

Tax versus book accounting

Lillian F. Mills

University of Arizona

Differences between income reported for financial statement purposes and income reported to tax authorities are called book–tax differences.

Corporate income tax laws define taxable ("Tax") income. Primarily, tax laws raise tax revenues. Secondarily, the tax system contains various economic and social incentives. Examples include accelerated depreciation deductions to spur investment in equipment and pension plan deductions to encourage corporations to provide retirement plans for workers.

Corporations report their accounting ("Book") income to owners and creditors using Generally Accepted Accounting Principles (GAAP). Accounting principles are designed to provide relevant and reliable information to financial statement users. In the United States, the Financial Accounting Standards Board provides authority for GAAP. The specific authority for accounting for income taxes is found in Statement of Financial Accounting Standards (SFAS) No. 109, and, for publicly traded corporations, in Securities and Exchange Commission Regulation S-X, Rule 4-08(h).

Although both book and tax rules address the same economic transactions, they define income differently. What types of income or expense are reported in different periods? What types of income or expense are measured completely differently? Where are book–tax differences reported? What factors complicate comparing financial statements to tax returns? What do book–tax differences imply about tax compliance or financial reporting? This entry considers each issue.

Temporary differences

Many items of income and expense are recognized in different periods for book income than for taxable income. A temporary difference is said to be "reversing," because book and tax income will equalize over time.

A common temporary difference arises from depreciation. Depreciation is the allocation of the cost of an asset as an expense over time. GAAP allocates the cost over the asset's useful life. However, the tax law often provides shorter periods as an incentive for capital investment. Thus, early in an asset's life, tax depreciation exceeds the book depreciation. Later, book depreciation will exceed tax depreciation, so the difference reverses. Over time, total book depreciation equals total tax depreciation.

Another example of temporary differences arises from estimated expenses. Under GAAP, corporations record an expense as soon as an obligation has probably occurred and they can estimate the amount. For example, suppose a corporation sells cars with a five-year, 50,000 mile warranty. In the year it sells the car, the corporation records an expense

for the estimated future cost of repairs under the warranty. However, the tax law does not permit deductions for estimated expenses. When the warranty service is performed, the tax deduction reverses the book expense from the prior period.

Accelerated tax deductions like depreciation cause taxable income to be less than book income initially. Thus, corporations pay less tax now and more tax in the future. The future tax cost is called a deferred tax liability. In contrast, delayed deductions for estimated expenses like warranties cause taxable income to exceed book income initially. The expected tax refund for the future deduction is called a deferred tax asset.

Permanent differences

Some types of income or expense recognized under one reporting system are never recognized under the other reporting system.

Examples include the following:

- Book income for municipal bond interest income and key person life insurance proceeds is never taxable.
- Book expenses for fines and penalties are never deductible.
- Tax deductions for dividends received from other corporations do not generate book expenses.

Although SFAS 109 specifically defines temporary differences, it does not define permanent differences. However, because the predecessor authority (Accounting Principles Board Opinion No. 11) defined permanent differences, accounting practitioners still commonly use this term.

Where are book–tax differences reported?

Financial statements

Corporations disclose details about income taxes in financial statement tax footnotes. These disclosures include components of deferred tax assets and liabilities. Disclosures do not directly reveal the amounts of gross temporary differences between book and tax income, because they are the tax amounts rather than income amounts.

The income tax footnote also explains why total tax expense does not equal pretax book income multiplied by the U.S. statutory tax rate (35 percent in 2004). Reconciling items include the effects of state income taxes, foreign taxes at higher or lower rates than the United States, and the tax effects of permanent differences.

For example, consider a corporation that records a book expense for a nondeductible penalty. The penalty creates a permanent difference and is its only book–tax difference. Suppose the corporation earned $10,000,000 after expensing a $1,000,000 penalty. It must record tax of 35 percent on $11,000,000 of taxable income. Tax expense of $3,850,000 represents a 38.5 percent effective tax rate on book income of

$10,000,000. The tax footnote would explain the difference between 35 percent and 38.5 percent.

Although financial statement users can use the tax footnote information on deferred tax assets and liabilities and the effective tax rate reconciliation to construct estimates of book–tax differences, these estimates are imprecise. Hanlon (2003b) discusses the limitations of using financial statement data to estimate taxable income for a corporation. In particular, accounting for stock options complicates these estimates.

Tax returns

On the tax return, corporations must reconcile net income per books with taxable income. This reconciliation is reported on Form 1120, Schedule M-1. Until 2004, Schedule M-1 was unchanged for 40 years.

The Schedule M-1 provides few discrete items of difference. Discrete items include federal income tax, the excess of capital losses over capital gains, depreciation, travel and entertainment, and tax-free income.

All other book–tax differences are aggregated into four general categories:

1. "income subject to tax not recorded on books this year,"
2. "expenses recorded on books not deducted on the return,"
3. "income recorded on books this year not included on this return," and
4. "deductions on this return not charged against book income."

The IRS's *Internal Revenue Manual* (IRM) describes the role of the Schedule M-1 in the audit process. IRM §4.10.3.6.1 notes, "Schedule M-1 is a critical schedule for identifying potential tax issues resulting from both temporary and permanent differences between financial and tax accounting." Consistent with the IRS audit motive, Mills (1998) finds IRS tax deficiencies are larger when book–tax differences are more positive.

Mills and Plesko (2003) discuss limitations in Schedule M-1. One limitation is uncertainty about how taxpayers report related corporations. Parent and subsidiary corporations are combined as a single reporting entity through a process called consolidation, in which transactions between related corporations are eliminated to prevent double-counting. The book and tax rules differ concerning which entities are included in the consolidated group. Generally, a consolidated financial statement includes all controlled corporations. GAAP generally assumes a parent has control when it owns more than 50 percent of a subsidiary. However, a consolidated tax return only includes domestic (not foreign) subsidiaries owned at least 80 percent by the parent corporation. These entity differences make it difficult to compare a financial statement to a tax return.

Mills and Plesko (2003) also recommend that the Schedule M-1 be revised to require separate reporting of permanent and temporary differences and to include more standard categories of disclosure.

On July 7, 2004, the Internal Revenue Service issued Schedule M-3, Net Income (Loss) Reconciliation for Corporations with Total Assets of $10 Million or More. The U.S. Treasury issued a new Schedule M-3 to increase the transparency of corporate tax returns. The new form provides specific entity reconciliation to address the consolidation problems identified above, requires disclosure of temporary and permanent differences, and provides more standard descriptive lines of difference. This new reconciliation is effective for any taxable year ending on or after December 31, 2004.

Implications for tax compliance

Book–tax differences have traditionally been associated with aggressive tax reporting or generous tax subsidies. The Citizens for Tax Justice (1985) reported that half of America's largest and most profitable corporations were frequently able to avoid paying any income tax at all, in part because of super-accelerated tax depreciation. More recently, the U.S. Treasury (1999) has charted the large increase in book–tax differences in the 1990s as consistent with the increase in abusive corporate tax shelters.

Implications for financial reporting

Large book–tax differences could also indicate that managers use discretion in financial reporting rules to report higher book income, indicating lower earnings quality. Hanlon (2003a) and other recent researchers find evidence that firms with higher book–tax differences have less persistent earnings patterns, consistent with lower quality.

Conclusions

Differences between financial reporting rules (book) and tax laws (tax) result in differences between income reported on financial statements and on tax returns (book–tax differences). Although many such differences arise through the different purposes of financial reporting standards and tax laws, large differences can also indicate either tax avoidance (or evasion) or lower-quality accounting earnings in the eyes of different researchers and administrators. More research is needed to fully understand the implications of book–tax differences for financial and tax reporting.

ADDITIONAL READINGS

Accounting Principles Board. *Accounting for Income Taxes.* New York: American Institute of Certified Public Accountants, 1967.

Center for International Tax Education. "Presentation on Special Tax Accounting Issues and Accounting for Income Taxes by Pricewaterhouse/Coopers for the 5th Annual Conference on 'Managing the Global Corporate Effective Tax Rate.'" New York: Center for International Tax Education, 2002.

Citizens for Tax Justice. *Corporate Taxpayers and Corporate Freeloaders.* Washington, DC: Citizens for Tax Justice, 1985.

Hanlon, Michelle. "The Persistence and Pricing of Earnings, Accruals and Cash Flows when Firms Have Large Book-Tax Differences." Working paper. Ann Arbor: University of Michigan, 2003a.

———. "What Can We Infer about a Firm's Taxable Income from Its Financial Statements?" *National Tax Journal* 56, no. 4 (December 2003b): 831–64.

Hanlon, Michelle, Stacie Kelley, and Terry Shevlin. "Evidence on the Possible Information Loss of Conforming Book Income and Taxable Income." Working paper. Seattle: University of Washington, 2003.

Mills, Lilian. "Book-Tax Differences and Internal Revenue Service Adjustments." *Journal of Accounting Research* 36, no. 2 (Autumn 1998): 343–56.

———. "The Influence of Tax and No Tax Costs on Book-Tax Reporting Differences: Public and Private Firms." *Journal of the American Taxation Association* 23, no. 1 (Spring 2001): 1–19.

Mills, Lillian F., and George A. Plesko. "Bridging the Reporting Gap: A Proposal for More Informative Reconciling of Book and Tax Income." *National Tax Journal* 56, no. 4 (2003): 865–93.

Plesko, George. "Book-Tax Differences and the Measurement of Corporate Income." In *Proceedings of the Ninety-Second Annual Conference on Taxation, 1999* (171–6). Washington DC: National Tax Association, 2000.

U.S. Department of the Treasury. *The Problem of Corporate Tax Shelters: Discussion, Analysis and Legislative Proposals.* Washington DC: Government Printing Office, 1999.

Cross-references: cost of capital; depreciation recapture; earnings and profits; inventory accounting; tax; tax-exempt bonds; throwback rules, multistate corporations.

Telecommunications and electronic commerce, state taxation of

Matthew N. Murray
University of Tennessee

The ongoing deregulation of the telecommunications industry, coupled with the rapid development of new technologies and the emergence of new competitors, has created an intricate web of state taxes on telecommunications and electronic commerce. The resulting uneven structure of taxation imparts both inefficiencies and inequities and entails potentially high costs of administration and compliance. Tax policy issues are often complicated by the unique ways in which some communications activities have been treated historically for tax purposes.

The telecommunications industry, including both providers and consumers, has been subjected to a unique structure of taxation by the states since the inception of telegraphy services in the 1800s. Providers of electronic commerce and services other than traditional telecommunications firms have been taxed largely as ordinary business entities that provide intangible services; consumers of electronic commerce may confront general or specific transactions taxes depending on the location and nature of their purchases.

Industry definitions

Telecommunications is defined here as an electronic mode of transmitting data, information, and audio/video signals. This includes both one-way and two-way signals using traditional landline phones, cellular phones, paging devices, satellites, microwave systems, and so on. Telecommunications is best viewed as a medium or mode of delivery, not the actual content of the information transmitted over the medium. By analogy, it is similar to a common carrier delivery truck that provides transportation or a natural gas pipeline that provides transmission services. The common carrier analogy is useful because telecommunications firms have little or no control over the content provided over the medium by others.

The intent here is to provide a distinction between economic activities, rather than to develop a definition tied to specific technologies or industry practices that are fluid over the course of time. This approach is not, however, free of problems. Services and content are often bundled, and it is not always possible to observe explicit prices for transmission and other components of the bundle.

In practice, states differ in how they define telecommunication services, although generally the definition goes beyond simply transmission. A broader definition of telecommunications might include, in addition to basic services such as local and long-distance calling, enhanced services such as call forwarding and voice mail, and perhaps even Internet access. A common feature of enhanced services is that there is additional value added beyond simply transmission. But including enhanced services, or going the next step to include content, can lead to administrative and compliance problems. Generally, this clouds the distinction between transmission, often used as a distinct productive input by business establishments, and services or content, which often reflect final consumption by individuals and households. This in turn makes it difficult to discern exempt from taxable sales, leads to tax pyramiding, and complicates efforts to assign tax collection and remittance responsibilities under transaction taxes.

Electronic commerce includes services and content provided or accessed by telecommunications media. Examples include voice mail, online banking, music services, the acquisition of computer software, and the purchase of tangible property through a site on the World Wide Web. Two important categories of electronic service are Internet service providers, firms that provide access to the Internet, and online service providers, firms that provide access to proprietary subscriber networks or independent services. The services and content available directly via electronic commerce are inherently intangible. Accordingly, tax policy toward electronic commerce will hinge largely on how states treat service providers as opposed to providers of tangible products.

Tax treatment of telecommunications

The historical roots of the taxation of telecommunications begin with the telegraph companies that were granted the privilege of conducting business and stringing wires on public rights-of-way by states and their constituent local governments in the 1800s. The initial privilege (franchise) taxes were generally flat-rate levies applied to miles of wire, numbers of poles, or receipts. These taxes were productive revenue sources with low administration and compliance costs.

By the mid-1930s, telecommunications firms had fallen under the regulatory auspices of both federal and state governments. This regulated environment allowed firms to shift taxes forward to consumers so that taxes would not burden the telecommunications providers.

The modern telecommunications firm confronts many different taxes at the state and local levels, depending on where business is conducted. Most states impose a corporate income tax on the activities of telecommunications firms. This corporate tax structure often entails unique formulary apportionment of multijurisdictional earnings, as opposed to the traditional three-factor formula that includes sales, property, and payroll. The situs of the sales component of the corporate apportionment formula is typically determined on an origin basis—that is, where the activity is produced rather than where it is consumed. This differs from the treatment of sales of tangible goods, where sales are distributed on a destination basis. The state-level corporate franchise tax also would generally apply to telecommunications firms, unless specifically exempted.

Sales and specific transactions taxes may fall on transmission activities, services, content, or some combination thereof, depending on the jurisdiction. Most states tax landline transmission of interstate or intrastate calls under the general sales tax. Following *Goldberg v. Sweet,* 488 U.S. 252, 1989, states can tax interstate calls if they are billed in the state, and if the call either originates in the state or has an in-state destination. No apportionment is required of these taxes. Cellular calls, on the other hand, are sitused based on "place of primary use," per the Mobile Telecommunications Sourcing Act signed into law in 2000. Additional telecommunications service or transaction taxes may apply to specifically enumerated services (beyond simply transmission). Sales tax is paid on most input purchases; exemptions are less generous than for manufacturing. With few exceptions (for example, 900 calls), transmission companies have been spared the responsibility of tax collection on sales made by providers of services and content. Some states have assigned collection responsibilities to transmission companies (using the concept of attributional nexus) because they cannot impose collection obligations on service/content providers directly for lack of nexus.

A minority of states apply gross receipts taxation to telecommunications firms. Local gross receipts (or explicit privilege/franchise) taxes also are common, and the ability of local governments to impose such taxes was sustained by the Telecommunications Act of 1996. The lack of uniformity in tax structure across jurisdictions raises compliance costs substantially for multijurisdictional firms. In addition, a wedge can be created between firms traditionally obligated to pay such taxes (including telecommunications firms and cable operators) and their modern competitors (such as the Internet) that escape gross receipts taxation.

Finally, telecommunication firms are exposed to a unique system of property taxation. This includes the unit (as opposed to summation) method of assessment, relatively higher assessment ratios, assessments applied to both real and personal property, and often central state (versus local) assessment.

The trend toward deregulation, especially the breakup of AT&T in 1982 and the Telecommunications Act of 1996, coupled with the rapid development of new technologies and new competitors, is placing pressures on this historical system of taxation. Competition, in lieu of the old monopoly structure, means that firms confront a more level playing field in the market. But if tax structure differs for functionally equivalent media (services), which is often the case, tax-induced advantages and disadvantages will surface for different firms (and consumers). For example, an Internet service provider that offered long-distance calling might escape gross receipts and transaction taxation, giving it a tax advantage over the traditional telecommunications provider.

Taxation of electronic commerce

The tax structure confronting providers of electronic services and content (which may include traditional telecommunications providers) is similar to the structure that would confront any firm selling intangibles and services. Under most state corporate income tax systems, some variant of the three-factor apportionment formula will distribute sales to where they are produced rather than to where services are sold. A small number of states (market states) assign the sale of intangibles on a destination basis. This approach can reduce the incentives to relocate the firm to a state with a low corporate income tax rate.

In general, nexus is not as easily established for sellers of intangible property relative to sellers of tangible products, as physical presence in the taxing jurisdiction can easily be avoided. One consequence is that a firm could penetrate the markets of many states through electronic contacts, but pay apportioned corporate income tax solely in the domiciled jurisdiction. Incorporated electronic marketers will generally confront the same state-level franchise taxes that other corporations confront. Gross receipts taxes on electronic commerce are uncommon. The reason is that such taxes often have their roots in the privilege or franchise tax. And because electronic marketers are not franchise monopolies and generally do not use public rights-of-way, they typically are not exposed to such taxes. Exceptions can exist for public utilities (e.g., telecommunications companies) and monopoly franchises (e.g., cable operators) that provide services in addition to transmission.

A controversial tax issue is the transactions tax treatment of electronic commerce. The Internet Tax Freedom Act, originally passed by Congress in 1998, has been extended. The Act prohibits taxes on Internet access and any multiple or discriminatory taxes; the Act does not preclude application of existing taxes, including the sales tax. Special transaction or excise taxes for specific services (e.g., 900 calls) may apply at the state and local levels. Inconsistency in structure is a burden to compliance and is inequitable and distortionary. At best, industry views these taxes as a nuisance.

Under the general sales tax, states tax services primarily on an enumerative basis, meaning that each component or category of the base must be identified explicitly through statutory language or administrative rulings. An extensive array of services and intangibles escape taxation, although it is common state practice to apply tax if the service is bundled with a tangible product. (An example is repair services and parts.) This means that absent statutory intent or administrative interpretation, most electronic commerce will escape sales taxation as well. There are numerous efforts to place certain forms of electronic commerce (such as Internet access charges) under the definition of telecommunications services, which are taxed to varying degrees by the states. This leads to considerable uncertainty about the taxable status of specific transactions and to significant differences in tax structure across jurisdictions. Moreover, the general enumerative approach will not keep up with rapid changes in technology, and continual revisions to the sales tax structure will impart significant burdens on taxpayers and tax administrators alike.

Balance is needed as the sales tax is applied to electronic commerce to ensure a level playing field. Currently, one can purchase computer software from electronic vendors in many states without paying tax on it, but the same purchase would be taxable if delivered on disk. In other cases, states may seek to impose tax on information services such as electronic newspapers that would be exempt if sold in traditional tangible form. While the issue is balance, balance can be achieved in two ways. The first entails leveling up, or imposing sales tax on electronic services that would have been taxed if delivered in nonelectronic form. The second is leveling down, or removing tax from currently sales-taxable activities so that they are on a par with electronically provided services.

Collection of the sales tax on electronic commerce is complicated by the electronic nature of transactions and constitutional nexus constraints. Because tax administrators have little or no hope of directly observing electronic transactions, they must turn to buyers or sellers, as happens with sales of tangible property. But the buyer generally is not known to tax authorities, and voluntary compliance with use tax requirements on electronic commerce will likely be worse than with tangible goods. Sellers with nexus would argue that they do not know the situs of delivery (consumption) and therefore they cannot charge and remit tax. This is a serious problem that will ultimately be resolved through development of practical, workable rules for determining situs.

More problematic is the firm without nexus. Electronic commerce severs the direct link between buyer and seller, analogous to the situation for catalog sales, tangible commodities, and common carriers. But the substantial nexus requirements of the Commerce Clause for electronic commerce may be more difficult to establish than for marketers of tangible goods. Hence, it is more difficult to assign tax collection obligations to marketers of electronic services and content. Some well-known brick-and-mortar retailers have established separate click-and-order subsidiaries that do not have nexus

and thus can avoid sales tax collection and remittance obligations. As states attempt to redefine nexus to bring electronic commerce into the sales tax net, they are being met by court challenges throughout the United States. Perhaps the best remedy from a tax policy perspective is congressional action that would define nexus based on economic contacts with a state. Sales tax and business activity nexus continues to be a hotly debated topic among policy analysts, tax administrators, businesspeople, and members of Congress.

Finally, sales tax will apply to most tangible inputs and specifically enumerated and taxed services that go into the production of electronically provided services and content. While industry would like broader resale exemptions, these are uncommon outside the manufacturing sector (where final sales are generally subject to sales tax). The disparate taxation of inputs, coupled with uncertainty regarding tax status, raises compliance costs, is inefficient, and results in tax pyramiding.

ADDITIONAL READING

Advisory Commission on Intergovernmental Relations [ACIR]. "Taxation of Out-of-State Mail-Order Sales." Washington, DC: ACIR, 1986.

Bruce, Donald, William Fox, and Matthew Murray. "To Tax or Not to Tax? The Case of Electronic Commerce." *Contemporary Economic Policy* 21, no. 1 (2003): 25–40.

Cline, Robert J., and Thomas Neubig. "Masters of Complexity and Bearers of Great Burden: The Sales Tax System and Compliance Costs for Multistate Retailers." Washington, DC: Ernst & Young, September 1999.

Cordes, Joseph J., Charlene Kalenkoski, and Harry S. Watson. "The Tangled Web of Taxing Talk: Telecommunication Taxes in the New Millennium." *National Tax Journal* 53, no. 3 (September 2000): 563–88.

Fox, William F., and Matthew N. Murray. "The Sales Tax and Electronic Commerce: So What's New?" *National Tax Journal* 50, no. 3 (September 1997): 573–92.

Frieden, Karl. *Cybertaxation: The Taxation of E-commerce.* Chicago: CCH, Inc., 2000.

Hellerstein, Walter. "Transaction Taxes and Electronic Commerce: Designing State Taxes That Work in an Interstate Environment." *National Tax Journal* 50, no. 3 (September 1997): 593–606.

McLure, Charles E., Jr. "Electronic Commerce and the State Retail Sales Tax: A Challenge to American Federalism." *International Tax and Public Finance* 6 (1999): 193–224.

Mines, Paul. "Conversing with Professor Hellerstein: Electronic Commerce and Nexus Propel Sales and Use Tax Reform." *Tax Law Review* 52, no. 4 (1997).

National Tax Association. *Electronic Commerce Tax Project.* http://www.ntanet.org.

Zimmerman, Dennis. *Economic Issues in Taxing Internet and Mail Order Sales.* Washington, DC: U.S. Congress, Congressional, Budget Office, 2003.

Cross-references: income tax, corporate, state and local; National Tax Association; nexus; retail sales tax, state and local; tax reform, state.

Throwback rules, multistate corporations

LeAnn Luna

University of Tennessee

A rule that allows income not taxable in the destination state to be taxed in the state where the sale originates.

Background

A taxpayer is subject to taxation in states where the taxpayer has nexus (a sufficient connection to be taxed). Through Public Law (PL) 86-272, Congress has precluded states from asserting nexus over corporations that do not have physical presence in a state and limit their activities to solicitation of sales of tangible personal property. States normally apportion corporate income using a three-factor formula (with various weightings) based on property, payroll, and sales, where the situsing of sales of tangible personal property is typically on a destination basis. The interplay of PL 86-272 and destination situsing of sales causes corporations without state nexus to often have "nowhere" income that without special rules is untaxed by any state. States have responded to this situation in two ways—imposing either a "throwback" or "throwout" rule or leaving the income untaxed.

Under the throwback rule, sales into a state where the taxpayer is not taxable are "thrown back" from the destination state to the origin state by adding the nontaxable sales to the numerator in the apportionment factor. The effect is to make those otherwise nontaxable sales subject to tax in the home (origin) state. Currently, 23 U.S. states have adopted the throwback rule (Commerce Clearing House State Tax Guide, Charts 600–810). Alternatively, the throwout rule, adopted by only a few states, eliminates or "throws out" sales from the denominator of the apportionment factor when sales are not taxable in the destination state.

The throwback (and throwout) rules attempt to capture the nontaxable income and tax it in the state where the sale originates. In addition, all sales to the U.S. government are subject to the throwback rule, generally taxing the sales in the origin state.

UDITPA's "subject to taxation" tests

The Uniform Division of Income for Tax Purposes Act (UDITPA) imposes the throwback rule if the corporation "is not subject to taxation in the destination state." UDITPA provides two mutually exclusive rules when a taxpayer is considered subject to taxation and therefore assigns the sales to the destination state. Two state supreme courts have held this standard applicable to the throwback rule. (See *Scott and Williams Inc. v. Board of Taxation* [NH SCt 1977] 117 NH 189, 400 A2d 786 and *Goldberg v. State Tax Commission*

and A.P Green Refractories Co. [MO SCt 1981] 618 SW2d 635.) First, a taxpayer is "taxable in another jurisdiction" if he is subject to a net income tax, a franchise tax measured by net income, a franchise tax for the privilege of doing business, or a corporate stock tax in the destination jurisdiction. For example, in *Morton International Inc. v. Illinois Department of Revenue,* the taxpayer paid income tax in six foreign countries on other income, but did not pay tax on its sales of tangible personal property. The court held that the Illinois statute did not require the taxpayer to be taxable on *particular* receipts. Therefore, since the taxpayer had paid income tax on other income, the court held the taxpayer was subject to tax in the foreign jurisdictions and therefore not subject to the throwback rule. However, the Multistate Tax Commission regulations state that payment of a minimum tax will not make the taxpayer "subject to taxation" if the activity is not sufficient for nexus.

Second, a taxpayer is considered subject to taxation if the destination state has jurisdiction to tax, regardless of whether it does or does not in fact levy a tax. This provision is designed to prevent the operation of the throwback rule on sales to market states that impose no income tax when the taxpayer's presence in the market state would allow imposition of a tax. Therefore, sales protected under PL 86-272 can generally be thrown back to the origin state only because the destination state does not have the right to tax the income (because the entity lacks nexus in the market state). However, several states (e.g., California) violate the general rule and require all nontaxable sales to be thrown back, even if the destination state did have the right to tax the income but has no income tax.

Policy implications and empirical research

Throwback rules can be good policy when all states impose the corporate income tax at the same rate, since the firm is taxable at the destination state rate (though the revenue would go to the origin state). Throwback rules are also defensible if the goal is simply to raise tax revenues in the throwback state (though there is no obvious reason why the throwback rule is the best means to generate additional revenue). The rule further helps ensure that all revenues get taxed somewhere (Mazerov 2002), even if the revenues go to the origin state rather than the destination state. In addition, the throwback rule is intended to discourage tax planning strategies that arise because of PL 86-272 protection (such as intentionally avoiding nexus in higher-tax states).

However, there are some policy shortcomings. First, the imposition of the throwback rule by only a few states will limit tax planning only in those states and arguably has little effect on flexible multistate businesses. Thus, the existence of any no-tax or non-throwback state will allow PL 86-272 planning to continue. Since corporations can easily plan to avoid the tax burden, increased tax revenues from thrown back sales may be offset by tax revenue decreases from firms that choose to limit their activity in throwback states.

The throwback rule has two additional policy shortfalls (Fox, Luna, and Murray 2004). First, the throwback rule will not achieve neutral taxation because it imposes additional taxes on the taxpayers producing in the home state but selling out of the state. The resulting tax base is no longer a good proxy for the income earned in the origin state, since the base now includes the destination component of sales. In addition, throwback rules encourage firms to move (e.g., reduce their rate of capital investment or organizationally restructure) to minimize the increased degree of origin taxation. Klassen and Shackelford (1998) find that firms are discouraged from locating sales activity in the throwback state because doing so raises the extent of origin-based taxation. Gupta and Hofmann (2003) find that throwback requirements are one of the most significant factors that influence the location of capital investment.

ADDITIONAL READINGS

Fox, William F., LeAnn Luna, and Matthew N. Murray. "How Should a Tax on Multistate Business Be Structured?" Presentation at the National Tax Association's 34th Spring Symposium, Washington D.C., May 21, 2004.

Gupta, Sanjay, and Mary Ann Hofmann. "The Effect of State Income Tax Apportionment and Tax Incentives on New Capital Expenditures." *Journal of the American Taxation Association* 25 (2003 Supplement): 1–25.

Klassen, Kenneth, and Douglass Shackelford. "State and Provincial Corporate Tax Planning: Income Shifting and Sales Apportionment Factor Management." *Journal of Accounting and Economics* 25 (1998): 385–406.

Lightner, Teresa. "The Effect of the Formulary Apportionment System on State-Level Economic Development and Multijurisdictional Tax Planning." *Journal of the American Taxation Association* 21 (1999 Supplement): 42–57.

Mazerov, Michael. "Closing Three Common Corporate Income Tax Loopholes Could Raise Additional Revenue For Many States." *State Tax Notes* 24 (April 29, 2002): 421–34.

Multistate Tax Commission. "Factor Presence Nexus Standard." *State Tax Notes* 25 (September 30, 2002): 1035–36.

Smith, J. "Guide to State Corporate Income Tax Apportionment—Part II." *Journal of State Taxation* 19 (2000): 26–46.

Cross-references: destination principle; income tax, corporate, state and local; Multistate Tax Commission; origin principle; retail sales tax, state and local; state formula apportionment; tax competition; tax versus book accounting.

Tiebout model

Wallace E. Oates
University of Maryland and University Fellow, Resources for the Future

Robert M. Schwab
University of Maryland

A classic statement of why people may move across jurisdictional boundaries—"vote with their feet"—as a way to live in a jurisdiction that best fits their (tax and spending) preferences.

In the field of public finance, the Tiebout model has come to serve as the cornerstone or organizing principle for the theory of local finance. The model provides a market-like conception of the working of the local public sector that generates outcomes with efficiency properties much like those of competitive markets. In the Tiebout model, mobile households choose a community of residence from a broad menu of alternatives on the basis of the levels of public services offered and the associated tax liability. Local tax bills function much like prices in a market, so that individuals make location choices that reflect their preferences for public services and the cost of services they consume.

The origins and intent of the model are instructive, if somewhat curious. Charles Tiebout, in a terse and informal paper of only 8½ pages in the *Journal of Political Economy* in 1956, outlined his conception of the local public sector not so much to set forth a theory of local finance as to contest a central proposition in public expenditure theory. As explicated by Paul Samuelson, Richard Musgrave, and others, this proposition maintains that public goods cannot be provided by a decentralized pricing system. It was Tiebout's intent to show that this contention is not universally true—that a class of public goods ("local public goods") exists for which there is, in principle at least, such a decentralized pricing mechanism.

The original paper envisions a world in which a large number of local governments offer a wide variety of levels of local services for which they charge a "tax-price" equal to the marginal cost of servicing an additional household. In this setting, Tiebout notes, "Spatial mobility provides the local public-goods counterpart to the private market's shopping trip. . . . Just as the consumer may be visualized as walking to a private market place to buy his goods, the prices of which are set, we place him in the position of walking to a community where the prices (taxes) of communities are set" (422). This is a world in which consumer-voters, instead of voting for public outputs at the ballot box, vote "with their feet." In so doing, they both reveal their preferences for local public goods and consume efficient levels of these goods. The model produces an equilibrium in which we have perfectly homogeneous communities in terms of individual household demands for local public goods; people who have high levels of demand join with others who have similarly high levels of demand, and the converse is also true.

On first glance, the stark simplicity of the model involving a set of seemingly unrealistic assumptions raises serious questions about its application to understanding the real worlds of local finance. In particular, Tiebout assumed a world of footloose consumers who move costlessly among local jurisdictions solely in response to fiscal considerations; the Tiebout household is unconstrained by travel costs to a location of employment or by any other nonfiscal ties to a particular locality. Moreover, Tiebout's original paper is disturbingly silent on a number of key issues. There is little explicit discussion of where the "supply" of communities comes from or how each determines its fiscal package. There is virtually no treatment of the form of local taxes; the reader is left with the vague sense that each community somehow charges its residents some kind of price for the public services they consume, but the form this "tax" takes is unspecified. The article thus leaves us with the tantalizing and perplexing question of the potential of the Tiebout model for understanding, predicting, and prescribing fiscal behavior in the local public sector.

Much of the later work on both the theory and empirical study of local finance has been devoted to answering these questions. For example, in the United States (and a number of other countries), local governments rely primarily on property taxation. Such taxes on the value of local residences (land and structures) seem to bear little resemblance to a Tiebout "price" for local services. But, as Hamilton (1975) showed, if communities use local zoning ordinances that effectively set lower limits on consumption of housing (an ordinance that specifies a minimum lot size may be a reasonable approximation), the property tax becomes a perfect benefit tax; it is transformed into a price for the consumption of local public services, just as envisioned in the Tiebout model.

Moreover, a large body of empirical work confirms the pervasiveness of certain kinds of Tiebout behavior. It comes as no surprise, for example, to find that people are willing to pay more to live in communities that have superior schools and are relatively safe from crime. In an early paper, Oates (1969) found that after controlling for other factors, the value of local houses is positively correlated with measures of outputs of local public services. He found, in addition, that higher rates of local property taxation resulted, other things equal, in lower house values. There is now a large body of empirical literature that finds fiscal differentials across communities in the form of both variations in outputs of local services and differences in local tax burdens largely capitalized into local property values. This evidence is consistent with the view that people do, in fact, "shop" among communities in their selection of a locality in which to live; in so doing, they bid up the prices of houses in fiscally favored jurisdictions. This literature, interestingly, has provided an empirical handle on the important issues of people's valuation of local services. By measuring the differences in the selling prices of houses in different jurisdictions, we can obtain estimates of what people are willing to pay for higher levels of local services, including things like better schools, lower crime rates, and higher levels of environmental quality. In addition, Fischel (1975) and others have shown how the model can be extended to encompass mobile business property within local jurisdictions.

The Tiebout model, in its extended form, has thus gained considerable currency as a useful way to characterize the operation of the local public sector. Notably, in large metropolitan areas, households and business firms have a large number of jurisdictions from which to choose. For example, an individual who works in the central city typically has a diverse menu of suburban communities as potential places to reside (Fischel 1981). And the evidence suggests that local public services and taxes play an important role in determining the choice of a community of residence.

The Tiebout vision of local finance has some important implications for fiscal outcomes. From a perspective solely of economic efficiency, a Tiebout equilibrium has the same attractive properties as a competitive market. Individuals survey alternative levels of local public policy outputs and, facing tax prices equal to marginal cost, they select their desired level of consumption of these services in much the same way that they choose their preferred levels of consumption of private goods. The result is an efficient allocation of resources of the local public sector.

Such an outcome, however, is less satisfying on equity grounds. Because people's demands for local public services (as measured by what they are willing to pay) are highly correlated with income, a Tiebout model can be expected to exhibit a high degree of segregation by income. We would expect, in a Tiebout world, to find communities composed of high-income households that consume high levels of public services in sharp contrast with communities of lower-income households with inferior levels of public services. This, of course, is simply a manifestation of the high demand for goods (private or public) that accompanies higher levels of income. This prediction of the Tiebout model concerning economic segregation, incidentally, also finds considerable empirical support: There is typically much less inequality in the distribution of income within a local municipality in a metropolitan area than across the metropolitan area as a whole (Hamilton, Mills, and Puryear 1975).

The nature of many local public goods is likely to reinforce this pattern of segregation by income. For many goods, the level of public services depends not only on expenditures by local governments but also on the characteristics of the population. Consider education, for example. A student's achievement depends in part on the textbooks and teachers the school provides. But it also depends on the characteristics of the student's family and classmates. The empirical evidence suggests that peer group effects are significant and often quite large (see, for example, Henderson, Mieszkowski, and Sauvageau 1978; Summers and Wolfe 1997).

Suppose low-income children reduce the academic performance of children from high-income families. As argued by Schwab and Oates (1991), high-income families would then be willing to live in mixed-income communities only if low-income families compensated them for this negative externality by paying higher taxes. Such "superregressive taxes" are implausible and, on equity grounds, very unattractive. Thus, the mixing of families with different incomes may be even less likely than the original version of the Tiebout model would suggest.

The wide variation in the quality of local public services, especially public schools, that results from such residential segregation by income has caused much concern. Through the 1960s, local governments provided the majority of funds for primary and secondary public education in the United States. Because property taxes traditionally have been the primary source of local tax revenue, the resources devoted to education were to a large extent a function of the local property tax base. Critics argued that this system of finance was inherently unfair and, beginning with *Serrano v. Priest* (1971) in California, they challenged the constitutionality of local education funding.

By 1996, the supreme courts in 43 states had heard cases on the constitutionality of school finance systems. The courts have overturned systems in 16 states and upheld them in 20; seven cases are pending. In addition, further litigation has been filed in a number of states where the state supreme court had ruled. In California, for example, there have been three separate decisions in the Serrano case; New Jersey has six versions of *Robinson v. Cahill,* and there are indications that its current active challenge, *Abbott v. Burke,* may surpass the Robinson record of repeated litigation.

Most states where the courts have overturned school financing plans have responded either by shifting the financing of public schools explicitly to the state level or by introducing equalizing state grants that redistribute funds to poorer districts. And, as Murray, Evans, and Schwab (1997) show, these new measures significantly reduced the inequality in school spending. It is noteworthy that the real culprit here is not local property taxation per se; the reliance on practically any local tax base is bound to involve large differentials in tax bases across local jurisdictions that give rise to substantial variations in levels of spending on local public services.

In spite of its extreme simplification, the Tiebout model thus provides a number of important insights into the workings of the local public sector. We see, in particular, the role that locational choice plays in the local fiscal system and the kinds of constraints that the mobility of households imposes on local fiscal decisions. From an efficiency perspective, a Tiebout world has much appeal. A large number of small competing local communities provides powerful incentives for the efficient provision of local public services while offering consumer households a wide variety of fiscal packages from which to choose. The local public sector, in short, provides a close analogue in its operation to the functioning of a competitive market. But such a world, in which communities are characterized by a high degree of segregation by income, implies very limited scope for redistributive activities within communities and large potential differentials in levels of local public services across these communities. This situation places the major responsibility for socially desired income redistributions for the support of low-income households and poorer local jurisdictions with higher levels of government. However we may feel about this tension between efficiency and our various equity objectives, the Tiebout model focuses our attention on some powerful economic and social forces that must be addressed in the design of public policy (see Hamilton 1987 for a more technical treatment of the Tiebout model).

There are some interesting parallels between Tiebout's paper and Coase's classic 1960 paper on externalities. Both were written four decades ago. Research in economics has a notoriously short half-life, yet both remain seminal contributions to public economics literature today. As one small indicator, Tiebout's paper was cited in economics journals roughly

300 times over the past four years. Both papers are deceptively simple, and neither is filled with the pages and pages of equations we now expect to find in journal articles. Both offered new, fundamental insights that set the field off in important new directions. Perhaps the most important lesson we can learn from Tiebout and Coase is that mathematical elegance is rarely a substitute for important ideas.

ADDITIONAL READINGS

Coase, Ronald. "The Problem of Social Cost." *Journal of Law and Economics* 3 (October 1960): 1–44.

Fischel, William A. "Fiscal and Environmental Considerations in the Location of Firms in Suburban Communities." In *Fiscal Zoning and Land Use Controls,* edited by Edwin S. Mills and Wallace E. Oates (119–73). Lexington, MA: D.C. Heath, 1975.

———. "Is Local Government Structure in Large Urbanized Areas Monopolistic or Competitive?" *National Tax Journal* 34 (March 1981): 95–104.

Hamilton, Bruce W. "Zoning and Property Taxation in a System of Local Governments." *Urban Studies* 12 (June 1975): 205–11.

———. "Tiebout Hypothesis." In *The New Palgrave: A Dictionary of Economics 4,* edited by John Eatwell, Murray Milgate, and Peter Newman (640–42). London: Macmillan & Co., 1987.

Hamilton, Bruce W., Edwin S. Mills, and David Puryear. "The Tiebout Hypothesis and Residential Income Segregation." In *Fiscal Zoning and Land Use Controls,* edited by Edwin S. Mills and Wallace E. Oates (101–18). Lexington, MA: D.C. Heath, 1975.

Henderson, Vernon, Peter Mieszkowski, and Yvon Sauvageau. "Peer Group Effects and Educational Production Functions." *Journal of Public Economics* 10 (August 1978): 97–106.

Murray, Sheila E., William N. Evans, and Robert M. Schwab. "Education Finance Reform and the Distribution of Education Resources." Working paper. College Park: University of Maryland, January 1997.

Oates, Wallace E. "The Effects of Property Taxes and Local Public Spending on Property Values: An Empirical Test of Tax Capitalization and the Tiebout Hypothesis." *Journal of Political Economy* 77 (November/December 1969): 344–58.

Schwab, Robert M., and Wallace E. Oates. "Community Composition and the Provision of Local Public Goods: A Normative Analysis." *Journal of Public Economics* 44 (March 1991): 217–37.

Summers, Anita A., and Barbara L. Wolfe. "Do Schools Make a Difference?" *American Economic Review* 67 (September 1977): 639–52.

Tiebout, Charles M. "A Pure Theory of Local Expenditures." *Journal of Political Economy* 64 (October 1956): 416–24.

Cross-references: education financing, state and local; tax competition; tax price; zoning, property taxes, and exactions.

Tobacco taxes

W. Kip Viscusi
Harvard University

Tobacco products are subject to a variety of special federal, state, and local taxes.

Tobacco products such as cigarettes, like other consumer products, are subject to sales taxes. However, they are also subject to excise taxes at the federal, state, and local levels. These taxes have been of substantial economic interest both because of the economic functions the taxes serve and because of the moneys raised through these taxes.

Economic rationales for tobacco taxes

In addition to raising money, cigarette taxes may serve other economic functions. Cigarette taxes and alcohol taxes are the two most prominent "sin" taxes now imposed on consumer goods. (See *alcoholic beverage taxes, federal.*) The rationale for tobacco taxes, though, stems not necessarily from religious or ethical beliefs but rather from economic aspects of smoking behavior, including the social costs. Excise taxes will raise the price of smoking to consumers, thus potentially discouraging smoking. Deterring smoking in this manner may be viewed as socially desirable if cigarette smokers are making mistaken consumption decisions. For example, if cigarette smokers underestimate the risks associated with smoking or do not fully internalize the costs imposed on society, there would be a rationale for discouraging this behavior through a tax.

Much of the recent impetus for cigarette taxes has stemmed from a concern with the social costs associated with smoking. If smoking cigarettes and other tobacco consumption activities generate social costs, such as higher medical care expenditures, then cigarette taxes can serve as a mechanism for recouping this social cost. In effect, cigarette smokers will pay with each purchase for the cost inflicted by their smoking activity.

Evidence regarding the rationality of smoking decisions for the smoker remains much debated. Several decades of government warnings and annual reports by the surgeon general have publicized the risks associated with smoking. Survey evidence suggests that smokers are now not only aware of the risk, but may in fact overestimate the hazards. Evidence regarding habituation or addiction problems associated with smoking remains controversial as well. Quitting smoking is clearly difficult, but some economists have hypothesized that addictions of this type may be the result of rational individual choices. Other researchers hypothesize that smokers are victims of time inconsistency so that the addictive properties of cigarettes lock smokers into decisions that are not efficient.

The potential role for government intervention is greater with respect to societal costs if net damages are inflicted. There are, however, many conflicting aspects of net damages. Smoking shortens life, which reduces retirement benefit costs, but it leads to ill health, which increases medical care costs. The overall effect on society hinges on the net influence of these and other competing factors.

Profile of tobacco taxes

Tobacco taxes are among the most prominent excise taxes levied on consumer products. Estimates by Fullerton and Rogers (1993) suggest that as a percentage of the purchase price, the implied tax rate on tobacco products is higher than it is for alcoholic beverages, gasoline, automobiles, or utilities.

The federal government and the states tax cigarettes roughly equally. For fiscal year 2001, federal cigarette taxes were $0.34 per pack and state taxes averaged $0.408 per pack.

These values ranged from a low tax of $0.025 per pack from the tobacco-producing state of Virginia to a high of $1.11 per pack in New York. Municipalities in eight states have imposed taxes as well, ranging from $0.01 to $0.35 per pack. (The federal tax was increased in 2002 to $0.39 per pack.)

The dollar magnitude of these tobacco taxes is substantial. In fiscal year 2001, federal tobacco tax revenues were $7.1 billion and state tax revenues were $8.4 billion. The total value of all excise taxes on cigarettes was $15.6 billion.

In 1998, the U.S. tobacco companies settled a series of lawsuits filed by the state attorneys general, who sought to recoup the state Medicaid costs of smoking. The settlement of the suits was not a conventional damages payment but rather took the form of a per pack levy on cigarettes that was tantamount to an excise tax of about $0.40 per pack.

Tobacco taxes are generally set at tax rates per package, which are revised periodically through legislation. The incidence of tobacco taxes is highly regressive. Smoking rates increase as the income level of the group declines, so that the poor segment of the population tends to be hit particularly hard by cigarette taxes. The population group whose annual earnings are below $10,000 pay cigarette taxes of 1.5 percent more per person than the group with incomes of $50,000 or more. The average taxes paid per person in 1990 were $81 for this poorest group and $49 for the most affluent group. Thus, cigarette taxes are regressive in absolute terms and even more regressive as a percentage of income.

Cigarette taxes and smoking behavior

Like raising the price of any good, raising cigarette taxes reduces consumer demand for the product. What this effect on demand will be depends on the estimated elasticity of demand with respect to the total price of cigarettes.

Dozens of studies have estimated cigarette demand functions. Most of the demand elasticities are clustered in the range from −0.4 to −1.0, meaning that for every cigarette tax that raises the price of smoking by 10 percent there should be a 4 to 10 percent decrease in the consumption of cigarettes. Women increasingly have begun smoking as well, and the demand elasticities for women are comparable to those for men.

This price responsiveness will not be uniform for all population segments. Some estimates suggest that teenagers are particularly price-sensitive, with a demand elasticity that is perhaps as high as −1.4. If so, a 10 percent increase in the purchase price would consequently reduce teenage smoking by 14 percent.

Cigarette taxes also reduce cigarette consumption in much the same way that heightened perceptions of the risk would. Estimates presented in Viscusi (1992) indicate that the average national excise tax for cigarettes has the same effect in discouraging smoking behavior as would a belief that there was a 27 percent chance that smoking would cause lung cancer, assuming a price elasticity of demand of −0.7.

Estimates of the social costs of smoking

Most of the economic analyses of tobacco taxes have been concerned with how these taxes relate to the financial costs associated with smoking. The justification for such taxes hinges, however, on the presence of net positive social costs.

The empirical evidence suggests that the net effects may be surprising. The study by Shoven, Sundberg, and Bunker (1989) found that smoking leads to a reduction in Social Security costs through the premature mortality of smokers. This analysis was extended by Manning et al. (1991) to consider not only pension effects but also the effects on medical insurance, nursing home expenditures, and related financial costs. Their study found that at low discount rates of about 3 percent or less, cigarette smoking generated net financial savings, even excluding the role of excise taxes, and that at very high discount rates, there would be a net social cost of smoking. Gravelle and Zimmerman (1994) extended this analysis both to update it and to include a sensitivity analysis with respect to the role of environmental tobacco smoke (ETS), or secondhand smoke. The basic conclusions regarding the self-financing aspect of cigarette smoking remained unchanged.

The most recent extension is that by Viscusi (2002), who updated the earlier results and also recognized the influence of the changing risk of cigarettes. This analysis, using a 3 percent discount rate, suggested that cigarette smoking imposed a medical care cost per pack of $0.58, a sick leave cost per pack of $0.01, a group life insurance cost per pack of $0.14, and a cost per pack of fires of $0.02. The offsetting savings were nursing home care cost savings of −$0.24 and retirement pension savings of −$1.26. On balance, then, cigarette smoking saves society −$0.32 per pack, even excluding the role of excise taxes.

Although the scale of the costs is much less for particular states than for the nation as a whole, cigarettes are self-financing for every state. In every instance, the combined value of excise taxes and savings in pension costs and nursing home costs offsets any increased medical costs due to smoking.

These cost figures, however, exclude the potential societal costs associated with ETS. Depending on the risk assumptions that are employed and the lag time between smoking and the health effects, these much-debated ETS risks can alter the desirability of an offsetting excise tax. For all but the most extreme risk assumptions, however, the current level of excise tax is sufficient to offset the total value of the health risks to society, where these calculations assume an implicit value of statistical life of $5 million. Whether excise taxes are needed to offset the financial costs on society will hinge in large part on how the assessment of ETS risks is resolved.

ADDITIONAL READINGS

Cnossen, Sijbren, and Michael Smart. "Taxation of Tobacco." In *Theory and Practice of Excise Taxation,* edited by Sijbren Cnossen (20–55). Oxford, U.K.: Oxford University Press, 2004.

Fullerton, Don, and Diane Lim Rogers. *Who Bears the Lifetime Tax Burden?* Washington, DC: Brookings Institution Press, 1993.
Gravelle, Jane, and Dennis Zimmerman. "Cigarette Taxes to Fund Health Care Reform: An Economic Analysis." Washington, DC: Congressional Research Service, 1994.
Hersch, Joni. "Gender, Income Levels, and the Demand for Cigarettes." *Journal of Risk and Uncertainty* 21, no. 2/3 (November 2000): 263–82.
Manning, Willard G., Emmet B. Keeler, Joseph P. Newhouse, Elizabeth M. Sloss, and Jeffrey Wasserman. *The Costs of Poor Health Habits.* Cambridge, MA: Harvard University Press, 1991.
Shoven, John B., Jeffrey O. Sundberg, and John P. Bunker. "The Social Security Costs of Smoking." In *The Economics of Aging,* edited by David A. Wise (231–351). Chicago: University of Chicago Press, 1989.
Tobacco Institute. *The Tax Burden on Tobacco: Historical Compilation 1996,* vol. 36. Washington, DC: Tobacco Institute, 2001.
Viscusi, W. Kip. *Smoking: Making the Risky Decision.* New York: Oxford University Press, 1992.
———. *Smoke-Filled Rooms: A Postmortem on the Tobacco Deal.* Chicago: University of Chicago Press, 2002.

Cross-references: alcoholic beverage taxes, federal; excise taxes; retail sales tax, state and local; sumptuary taxes.

Tourist taxes

James Mak
University of Hawaii

Taxes that largely fall on tourists (and tourism businesses) are often referred to as tourist or tourism taxes; only a few taxes qualify under such a restrictive definition.

Tourists encounter a wide variety of indirect taxes when they travel. They include excise and sales taxes levied on lodging accommodations, automobile rentals, admissions to visitor attractions, restaurant meals, purchases of gifts and souvenirs, and so on. When traveling internationally, visitors may also have to pay an entry or departure tax (though not in the United States). Moreover, embedded in the price of an airline ticket may be additional taxes for airplane noise pollution and carbon dioxide emissions. While most of these taxes are nondiscriminatory in that residents of tourist destinations must also pay them when they make the same purchases, some that largely fall on tourists or tourist businesses are often referred to as tourist taxes. Only a few taxes qualify under such a restrictive definition.

In the United States, the most commonly encountered tourist tax is the hotel occupancy tax, a selective sales or excise tax levied by state and/or local governments on occupied hotel rooms. Another widely levied tourist tax is the daily car rental tax.

The hotel room tax is typically an ad valorem tax expressed as a percentage of the rental price of an occupied room, although a few cities such as New York City and Washington, D.C., also levy an additional per diem tax. The median hotel room tax rate among America's largest cities exceeds 12 percent. The effective hotel room tax rates tend to be higher in cities that piggyback a special room tax on top of existing general excise or sales taxes; rates also tend to be higher in cities that cater largely to less–price sensitive business travelers than pleasure travelers.

In most states, tourist taxes generate only a modest percentage of total tax revenues; moreover, the revenues generated are often earmarked for specific uses such as tourism promotion and convention center financing. In the two most tourism dependent states of Hawaii and Nevada, tourist taxes play a much larger fiscal role. In Hawaii, the combined general excise and hotel occupancy taxes (11.416 percent) levied on tourist lodgings generate about 7 percent of total state (but excluding local) tax revenues. Adding the $3 per diem car rental and the monthly tour vehicle surcharge taxes increases the percentage to slightly over 8 percent. In Nevada, gaming taxes account for a much higher share of total state tax revenues (Mak 1990).

Rationale

State and local governments levy tourist taxes to diversify and expand their tax base, pay for visitor-induced increases in public service costs, extract economic rents from tourism to benefit residents, and correct for market failure.

Revenue diversification

Taxing travel and tourism allows a destination to diversify and expand its tax base. As demand for tourism tends to be income-elastic, taxing tourism builds in buoyancy in the destination's revenue system. The downside of this is that the industry is also highly sensitive to economic recessions, and a revenue system highly dependent on tourist taxes can also be highly volatile.

Paying for benefits received

Tourists benefit directly from publicly provided services such as lifeguard services, visitor information services, and police protection. Tourism can also impose indirect costs on destination governments. For example, if an increasing number of tourists leads to labor in-migration, destination governments may have to provide more public services, schools, roads, public transportation, and so on to meet the additional demands of a growing resident population. By the benefits principle of taxation, it is appropriate to require tourists to help pay for the cost of providing additional public services that stem directly and indirectly from their presence (Mathematica, Inc. 1970).

However, only a few tax handles effectively target tourists for taxation. To illustrate, among Hawaii's major taxes, 22 percent of the state's broad-based general excise tax, 16 percent of the taxes levied on corporate income, banks, and other financial institutions, 9 percent of the real property tax, and none of the state's personal income tax are shifts to nonresident tourists. The tax that works "best" in "exporting" taxes to tourists is the hotel occupancy tax, which is almost entirely borne by nonresident tourists (Miklius, Moncur, and Leung 1989; see also Fujii, Khaled, and Mak 1985).

It is not uncommon for states to design their tax systems to export taxes to nonresidents (Gade and Adkins 1990), although some controversy prevails over the issue of exporting taxes to tourists. Some argue that revenues collected in excess of the cost of service provision to tourists and tourism suppliers violate economic efficiency, equity, and accountability because residents are then led to miscalculate the true cost of public services they consume and end up overconsuming some public services (Forsyth and Dwyer 2002). That argument is weakened where there are scarcity rents to be extracted (Gray 1974) or negative environmental externalities stemming from tourism development (Mathematica, Inc. 1970).

Extract economic rents

Because every tourist destination has distinctive attributes as a result of its location, natural amenities, or unique man-made attractions, tourism gives rise to economic rents. Destinations have an incentive to extract these rents to benefit residents before they are dissipated (e.g., duty-free shops, fees to environmentally fragile bays). Generally there are two types of taxes to appropriate rents from tourism: entry (e.g., Chile, Bulgaria) and exit (e.g., Caribbean, Middle East, and North Africa) taxes and the hotel occupancy tax (Tisdell 1983; Bird 1992). In practice it is difficult to fine-tune tax rates to extract only the scarcity rents. It has been argued that an additional 5 percent room tax levied in 1990 by the New York state legislature on hotel rooms priced at $100 or more per night lost more tax revenues than it collected, persuading the state to rescind the tax in 1994 (Mak forthcoming).

Correct for market failure

Taxes levied to correct for the negative environmental externalities stemming from tourism is becoming more prevalent. For example, Norway imposes a carbon dioxide tax on domestic flights. Australia imposes a noise tax of $3.58 on airline tickets between Sydney and London. Venice imposes a "coach tax" on motor coaches, and the amount depends on where the vehicle is parked in the city. The hotel occupancy tax is widely used to finance destination tourism promotion and convention centers. As destination tourism promotion is a public good that gives rise to free-rider problems, taxing tourism to finance tourism promotion enhances economic efficiency and equity. As stand-alone facilities, convention centers are generally money losers, and in the absence of public financing, convention centers are unlikely to be built by profit-maximizing firms.

Incidence and impacts

Empirical studies on the incidence of tourist taxes have focused mostly on the hotel occupancy tax. Some studies have used time series data and others have used cross-section data. Most of them estimate only the demand elasticities for lodging; supply elasticities are rarely estimated. Ex ante studies suggest that demand for lodging is generally price inelastic while the supply of lodging is price-elastic, implying that hotel room taxes are largely passed on to hotel guests as higher prices. By contrast, Bonham et al. (1992) employed interrupted time series analysis to evaluate, ex post, the impact of a newly imposed 5 percent hotel room tax in Hawaii and found that the new tax had no statistically significant negative impact on hotel room rental revenues, implying that the room tax was fully passed on to hotel guests. However, they cautioned that their findings may not be surprising since a 5 percent increase in lodging expenditures represented less than 1.5 percent of the total cost of a typical vacation to Hawaii inclusive of round-trip airfare. That may not be true of travel to other destinations.

There is a dearth of rigorous analyses of the impacts of destination taxes on travel demand and on the economies of tourist destinations. Data compiled by the World Travel and Tourism Council of the amount of taxes paid as a percent of the total bill (i.e., the average tax rate or the tax effort) for four nights of lodging, five days' car rental, 12 meals, and one set of international arrival and departure airport charges at 52 leading tourist destinations around the world reveal huge differences among countries in efforts to tax tourism. In 2002, the destination with the highest tax effort was Copenhagen at 24.25 percent and the average tax effort among the 52 destinations was around 14 percent (Mumbai and Sao Paulo), while Asian destinations like Tokyo (6.27), Taipei (5.54), and Hong Kong (2.18) were at the tail end. Whether such differences in average tax rates have a significant influence on travel demand has yet to be rigorously studied. To date, evidence on the negative impact of taxes on travel demand remains largely anecdotal.

ADDITIONAL READINGS

Bird, Richard. "Taxing Tourism in Developing Countries." *World Development* 20, no. 8 (1992): 1145–58.

Bonham, Carl, and Byron Gangnes. "Intervention Analysis with Cointegrated Time Series: The Case of the Hawaii Hotel Room Tax." *Applied Economics* 28, no. 10 (October 1996): 1281–93.

Bonham, Carl, Edwin Fujii, Eric Im, and James Mak. "The Impact of the Hotel Room Tax: An Interrupted Time Series Approach." *National Tax Journal* 45, no. 4 (December 1992): 433–42.

Forsyth, Peter, and Larry Dwyer. "Market Power and the Taxation of Domestic and International Tourism." *Tourism Economics* 8, no. 4 (2002): 377–99.

Fujii, Edwin, Mohammed Khaled, and James Mak. "The Exportability of Hotel Occupancy and Other Tourist Taxes." *National Tax Journal* 38, no. 2 (June 1985): 169–78.

Gade, Mary, and Lee C. Adkins. "Tax Exporting and State Revenue Structures." *National Tax Journal* 43 (March 1990): 39–52.

Gray, H. Peter. "Towards an Economic Analysis of Tourism Policy." *Social and Economic Studies* 23, no. 3 (September 1974): 386–97.

Mak, James. "The Tourist Industry." In *A Fiscal Agenda for Nevada,* edited by Robert D. Ebel (167–94). Reno: University of Nevada Press, 1990.

———. *Tourism and the Economy: Understanding the Economics of Tourism.* Honolulu: University of Hawaii Press, 2004.

———. "Taxing Travel and Tourism." In *International Handbook of Tourism Economics,* edited by Peter Forsyth and Larry Dwyer. London: Edward Elgar Publishers, forthcoming.

Mak, James, and Edward Nishimura. "The Economics of a Hotel Room Tax." *Journal of Travel Research* 17, no. 4 (1979): 2–6.

Mathematica, Inc. *The Visitor Industry and Hawaii's Economy: A Cost-Benefit Analysis.* Princeton, NJ: Mathematica, Inc., 1970.

Miklius, Walter, James Moncur, and Ping Sun Leung. "Distribution of State and Local Tax Burdens by Income Class." In *Hawaii Tax Review Commission, Working Papers and Consultant Studies,* vol. 2 (7–19). Honolulu: State of Hawaii Department of Taxation, 1989.

Tisdell, Clem A. "Public Finance and the Appropriation of Gains from International Tourism: Some Theory with ASEAN and Australian Illustrations." *Singapore Economic Review* 28 (1983): 3–20.

Wanhill, Stephen. "VAT Rates and the U.K. Tourism and Leisure Industry." *Tourism Economics* 1, no. 3 (1995): 211–24.

For listing by country of entry and departure taxes and fees see http://travel.state.gov/visa/americans1.html.

Cross-references: benefit principle; consumption taxation; destination principle; excise taxes; retail sales tax, state and local; tax exportation.

Trade taxes

John H. Mutti
Grinnell College

Taxes imposed on imports or exports of goods and services, when no comparable tax is imposed on domestic production or sales.

Import tariffs may be a fixed amount per unit of imports (a specific tariff) or a percentage of the value of imports (an ad valorem tariff). For a small country that cannot affect international prices, either type of tariff raises the relative price of imported goods. In a world with no other distortions, the tariff causes two losses in economic efficiency: it encourages greater production of a good where the importing country is less efficient than producers in the rest of the world; and it discourages consumption of a good that purchasers value more highly than the alternatives they otherwise buy. A country large enough to affect international prices nevertheless may experience a gain at the expense of foreign exporters, if the tariff causes a sufficient reduction in the net-of-tariff price at which exporters sell to the importing country. World efficiency declines because the loss to the exporter exceeds any gain to the importer, and the world allocation of resources is less efficient. Even the country that imposes the tariff may become worse off if its trade partners retaliate.

Import tariffs and export taxes often are an important source of revenue in countries where the costs of administering other tax systems are high. That is likely to be the case where literacy rates are low and most transactions are carried out by cash or barter. Regulating transactions at a few major ports may be a less costly procedure. At the outset of the U.S. Civil War, import duties accounted for 95 percent of federal government revenues. Although export taxes are prohibited by the U.S. Constitution, many developing countries rely upon them. For low-income countries, trade taxes accounted for nearly 40 percent of tax revenue in 1988.

The efficiency cost of relying on trade taxes may be low when tariffs act as excise taxes on inelastically demanded consumer goods not produced in the country. At the end of the 19th century, the British tariff schedule was limited to such cases or simply matched domestic production taxes. Computable general-equilibrium models have been used to analyze the efficiency costs of current regimes of trade taxes in developing countries. While replacing existing trade taxes with general consumption or production taxes does not raise welfare in all cases, it generally tends to do so because tariffs on intermediate inputs create a significant production distortion. Tariffs were exceptionally high at the time of the Great Depression in the 1930s, and in the United States the average rate exceeded 50 percent. Rates have fallen since then, in part a result of inflation that has reduced the protective effect of specific tariffs. Countries have engaged in multilateral negotiations to reduce tariffs under the auspices of the General Agreement on Tariffs and Trade (GATT), and some countries have unilaterally reduced tariffs to pursue more open trading policies.

The World Trade Organization (WTO) has not paid comparable attention to export taxes, although economic theory indicates that when prices are flexible, import tariffs and export taxes have symmetric effects in reducing international trade and protecting domestic producers of import-competing goods. WTO negotiations in the Doha Development Round begun in 2001 have dealt with export taxes and prohibitions on agricultural goods. Importing countries have sought to convert prohibitions into exports taxes, which will be bound and negotiated downward in a way similar to tariffs. Some developing countries have sought exemptions from such a standard, in order to allow them to prohibit the export of raw materials and to develop domestic processing industries. Those countries are particularly concerned over escalating tariff structures elsewhere, which impose higher tariffs on more highly processed products and thereby discourage industrialization by suppliers of raw materials. A more direct solution would be to eliminate the escalating tariff structures.

ADDITIONAL READINGS

Ebrill, Can. *Trade Taxes Are Better?* Ph.D. dissertation, Boston College, 2003.

Irwin, Douglas. "Free Trade and Protection in Nineteenth-Century Britain and France Revisited: A Comment on Nye." *The Journal of Economic History* 53, no. 1 (March 1993): 146–52.

Lerner, Abba. "The Symmetry between Import and Export Taxes." *Economica* 3, no. 11 (August 1936): 306–13.

Cross-references: excise taxes; GATT.

Transfer pricing, federal

T. Scott Newlon
Department of the Treasury

Taxes are often measured by the price attached to the transfer of goods, foods, services, and/or funds across national borders; however, when multinationals make transfers "within company," prices must be estimated.

Transfer prices are the prices established for transfers of goods or intangibles, the lending of money, or the provision of services from one company to a related company or from one part of a company to another part located in a different tax jurisdiction. Transfer prices are used by the U.S. government and by most other countries in determining the income, for tax purposes, of companies engaging in such transfers.

Role of transfer prices in the firm

Transfer pricing is most relevant in the context of the transfer within a multinational firm of goods, intangibles, services, or funds across national borders. Such transactions may occur between a parent company and a foreign subsidiary, between two subsidiary companies that have a common parent, or between a branch office of a company and another part of the company. The prices established for such transactions are important for tax purposes because they affect the amount of taxable income reported in each country in which the multinational firm operates. For example, a higher price on a sale of goods from a parent company to a foreign subsidiary generally means that more revenue is reported in the tax jurisdiction of the parent and greater deductions are reported in the tax jurisdiction of the subsidiary. Where tax rates differ across countries, an incentive exists for multinational firms to set their transfer prices to shift income from high-tax jurisdictions to low-tax jurisdictions.

An incentive to use transfer prices to shift income between related companies can exist even when both companies are located in the same tax jurisdiction. If the companies do not consolidate for tax purposes, and one company is reporting income while the other is reporting losses, then the overall tax liability of the two companies can be reduced by shifting income from the income-reporting to the loss-reporting company.

Transfer prices can also serve a role in promoting the efficient operation of a firm. Where management is decentralized, transfer prices may serve as shadow prices on which the firm's managers may base their decisions. This role may place some limitations on the flexibility of the firm to optimize the setting of transfer prices for tax purposes, particularly in jurisdictions where it is illegal to keep two sets of books.

The separate entity approach and the arm's-length standard

Transfer prices are relevant for the determination of the taxable income of a multinational firm in each country in which it operates because most countries adopt the separate entity approach to the taxation of multinational firms. Under this approach, a multinational firm's operations in a country are treated as if they were an entity distinct from the multinational firm's operations in other countries, so only the income accruing from the activities and transactions of the operations in that country is taxable there.

Countries that impose substantial taxes on company income and adopt the separate entity approach need to set and enforce some standard for setting transfer prices in order to limit tax base erosion brought about by the manipulation of transfer prices on cross-border transactions. The standard generally adopted is the arm's-length standard, which dictates that transfer prices should be set at the level that would have prevailed had the transactions taken place between unrelated parties under the same circumstances. The arm's-length standard is the international norm for determining transfer prices for tax purposes. In the United States, the Income Tax Regulations under Section 482 of the Internal Revenue Code require the use of the arm's-length standard in determining transfer prices for federal tax purposes.

The arm's-length standard is also enshrined in nearly all the bilateral tax treaties the United States has entered into, as well as the model income tax treaties of the Organisation for Economic Co-operation and Development (OECD) and the United Nations. The arm's-length standard was also affirmed as the international norm for transfer pricing in the OECD's 1979 report *Transfer Pricing and Multinational Enterprises* and its 1995 revision of that report, *Transfer Pricing Guidelines for Multinational Enterprises and Tax Administrations.*

Two features of the arm's-length standard may account for its broad international acceptance. First, the arm's-length standard treats vertically or horizontally integrated firms the same for tax purposes as firms that are not integrated. In principle, the same tax liability should accrue from a given business, whether that business is carried out by a company acquiring inputs and selling its outputs to unrelated parties or by a company that has integrated across borders and acquires inputs or sells its outputs to related parties within a multinational firm (unless the total amount of income is different in the two cases as a result of integration economies). Second, the arm's-length standard provides a clear principle for determining transfer prices that all countries can understand and accept, thereby providing a basis for agreement among countries about the appropriate division of a multinational firm's income among them. Such an agreement avoids subjecting the income of multinational firms to taxation by multiple jurisdictions, a result that would inhibit and distort cross-border investment.

The U.S. states generally use formulary apportionment rather than the separate entity approach and the arm's-length standard to determine how the income from a business operating in more than one state should be allocated among those states. Under formulary apportionment, each state typically allocates to itself a portion of the total U.S. income of such a business, using a formula based on some measure of the size of the business's activities in the state relative to the size of the total business. Typical formulas use one or more of property, payroll, and sales as the apportionment factors. The Canadian provinces and Swiss cantons follow a similar approach.

Application of the arm's-length standard

The arm's-length standard is generally applied by comparing the results of a transaction between related parties (called a controlled transaction to denote that it is between parties under a certain degree of common control) to the actual results, or the results that would be anticipated, from transactions between unrelated parties (called uncontrolled transactions). Various transfer pricing methods are used in practice. The methods differ in the type of transaction results they compare: prices, gross profit margins, net profit measures, or profit splits.

The most important factor affecting the reliability of the results of a transfer pricing method is generally considered the comparability of the controlled transaction to the transactions and activities of unrelated parties used as a basis for comparison. Comparability is determined based on those factors in the open market that could be expected to affect the particular result (price or profit measure) being compared. For example, the price or profit margin for a sale of goods might be affected by the characteristics of the product, the contractual terms of the transaction, and the market conditions. The importance of specific comparability criteria may vary depending upon the result being compared. For example, the characteristics of a product conveyed in a transaction would be expected to have a greater impact on the price in the transaction than on the profit margin realized from the transaction, while the vintage of plant and equipment used in producing a product might affect a measure of the profit margin on sales of the product, but would be unlikely to affect the sales price for the product.

Five principal transfer pricing methods are provided in the Section 482 regulations and in the OECD's 1995 *Transfer Pricing Guidelines:*

Comparable uncontrolled price method

The appropriate transfer price is determined based on the price established in uncontrolled transactions involving similar goods or services conveyed under similar terms and conditions. In the Section 482 regulations, this method is labeled the comparable uncontrolled transaction method when it is applied to transfers of intangibles. This method is considered the most accurate way to determine transfer prices when closely similar transactions between unrelated parties can be found, because it is based directly on a market price.

Cost-plus method

This method is often applied in situations in which the buyer receives a product manufactured by the seller or services provided by the seller. The appropriate transfer price is determined by applying a markup to the production cost of the good or service. The markup is derived from the gross profit margin realized by sellers in similar sales to unrelated parties under similar circumstances.

Resale price method

This method is frequently applied in situations in which a product is purchased from a related party and resold to an unrelated party. The appropriate transfer price is determined by deducting an appropriate markup from the resale price. The markup is derived from the gross profit margin obtained by resellers in similar purchases and resales of goods involving unrelated parties. This method is also sometimes referred to as the resale minus method.

Comparable profits method or transactional margin method

The appropriate transfer price is determined based on some measure of the profit rate or profit margin derived by one of the parties to the controlled transactions from its business activities associated with those transactions. The appropriate transfer price is the price that results in that party earning the same profit rate or profit margin as is earned by independent parties engaged in similar activities under similar circumstances. The profit rate measure is generally based on operating profit—that is, revenue after deduction for all nonfinancial costs.

Profit-split method

This method explicitly measures and divides the joint profit from controlled transactions. Most profit-split applications divide the joint profit based on the relative value of the factors of production each party contributes to the earning of the joint profit.

Conceptual and practical problem

Several problems that arise in applying the arm's-length standard can lead to opportunities for income shifting by multinational firms, disputes between taxpayers and tax authorities, substantial compliance burdens and uncertainty for taxpayers, and substantial enforcement burdens for tax authorities.

One of the most important problems is that it is often difficult to identify uncontrolled transactions that can be used in establishing appropriate transfer prices for controlled transactions. A principal reason for a firm to become multinational is that it possesses valuable intangible assets such as unique skills, know-how, and technology, and there is an economic advantage to the firm in exploiting those assets itself in other markets rather than attempting to transfer them to an independent company over which it has limited control. Where such valuable intangible assets are present, the transactions and activities of the multinational firm may be unique in important respects.

Even if closely comparable transactions exist, it may be impossible for taxpayers or tax authorities to identify them, because that information may not be public. Tax authorities are often at a particular disadvantage in this regard because they may have much less information about the taxpayer's business and industry than does the taxpayer.

When potentially comparable uncontrolled transactions are identified, it can be difficult to make adjustments to reflect differences from the controlled transaction in question. Transactions frequently have a complex set of attributes in terms of the characteristics of the property conveyed, the contractual terms, and the market conditions.

The large number of related-party transactions within multinational firms also represents a problem. It can place a significant compliance burden on firms wishing to ensure that all their controlled transactions satisfy the arm's-length standard. Tax authorities can incur significant enforcement costs in attempting to identify and evaluate such transactions.

Fundamental differences in relationships between related and unrelated parties can also complicate application of transfer pricing methods. For example, if integration economies are present, then related parties dealing with each other have lower costs, and therefore higher profits, than unrelated parties would have under similar circumstances. Determining how such cost savings should be reflected in transfer prices (that is, how integration benefits should be divided between the parties) is problematic.

Cross-references: allocation rules, multinational corporations; foreign tax credit; multinational corporations, taxation of.

Transfer taxes, real estate

John O. Behrens

Updated by
Jennifer Gravelle
Government Accountability Office (GAO)

State and local government–imposed taxes at the time of transfer or recording of residential real estate transactions.

The real estate transfer tax (one of the so-called documentary taxes) is imposed at the time of transfer or recordation and is nonrecurring. It is a levy on the transfer of real property, usually measured by the sales price or the price exclusive of mortgages or other liens. Transfer taxes usually make up a minor share of state or local revenue. The exact annual yield nationwide is difficult to identify because in some states the total constitutes part of revenue from all documentary taxes (such as transfer of stocks, bonds, debentures, and certificates of indebtedness). Documentary taxes as a group constituted less than 2 percent of total state tax revenue in 2003. Documentary revenue ranged from less than 1 percent (for most states) to between 5 and 10 percent (two states) of total tax revenue for the 35 states reporting such revenue.

Virginia imposed the first transfer tax in 1922, followed by South Carolina in 1923 and Florida in 1931. By 1940, Alabama, Maryland, Tennessee, and Washington also had transfer taxes. Now, they exist in 37 states and the District of Columbia. Arizona also has a flat fee of $2 per real estate transfer.

From 1932 until its repeal in 1968, the federal Stamp Tax on Conveyance of Realty Sold covered state real estate taxes. The documentary stamps affixed to the deed of conveyance on payment were perceived to be indicative of the sale price, data essential for professional assessors. The federal government urged the states to adopt transfer taxes when the federal levy was repealed.

Three recent court cases, taken together, test but in the end leave intact the conventional wisdom that market value, or a reasonable proxy, remains the most accepted basis for transfer tax liability, even though adjustments may be necessary in particular legal or economic situations—*A. Bradley Askin v. District of Columbia* (DC Superior Court, Tax Division, N. 5572-93, April 1991, 1995); *Gottfried, Inc. v. Wisconsin Department of Revenue* (429 NW 2d 508, 1988); and *Wisconsin Department of Revenue v. Mark* (483 NW 2d 168, 1992).

Rate patterns and varieties

Rates (usually a percentage of taxable consideration) range from 0.01 percent in Colorado to 2 percent in Delaware. Transfers under $100 are exempt in 14 states; Colorado, Iowa, and New York exempt transfers under $500; and Connecticut exempts transfers under $2,000. Each state has several other exemptions, including transfers in which a federal, state, or local government is a party; any tax deed; deeds without consideration between husband and wife; and instruments intended only to secure a debt.

Transfer tax procedures for property tax benefits

There is a connection between real estate transfer tax administrators and local property tax assessors and recording officials. In many areas, county registrars of deeds or treasurers collect the taxes for the states. Many states use stamps as evidence of payment, along with documentation requirements that are comprehensive enough to be of value to local tax assessors, such as the address and legal description, use of the property, and conditions of the sale or other transfer. Some states require more extensive information, including considerable detail about location and property use, sale price, and conditions of sale.

Local real estate transfer taxes

Local real estate transfer taxes may be levied in the following states: California—counties (0.11 percent) and cities at one-half the county rate; Delaware—state (2 percent) and counties (no more than 1.5 percent of property value, first-time homeowners exempt); Florida—counties (surtax not to exceed 0.45 percent, except single-family residences), collected by the state; Illinois—state (0.1 percent transfer tax), Chicago (0.75 percent transfer tax), and Cook County (0.05 percent transfer); Maryland—home-rule counties (0.5 percent, 0.25 percent for first-time buyers); Michigan—county trans-

fer tax of 0.11 percent to 0.15 percent, depending on population; Nevada—0.13 percent for counties up to 400,000 population and 0.25 percent for counties with population over 400,000; New Jersey—up to 0.1 percent additional tax (as of 2003); New York—New York City (1 percent up to $500,000, 1.425 percent up to $500,000); Pennsylvania—county rates vary, for example, Philadelphia imposes a 3 percent tax and Pittsburgh imposes 1.5 percent tax; Ohio—counties (not to exceed 0.30 percent); South Carolina—counties, mandated (0.11 percent of value over $100); and Virginia—cities and counties (one-third of state recordation tax).

Selected other levies

Some states levy other taxes that are sometimes included within the realty transfer category: Alabama—leasehold interest in nonproducing oil, gas, and other minerals, in lieu of all ad valorem taxes (5 cents per acre up to 10 years, 10 cents per acre for 10 to 20 years, 15 cents per acre for more than 20 years, minimum $1); Connecticut—(1) farm and forest land conveyance tax applicable to sales of designated "open space" if conveyed or changed in classification within 10 years (10 percent of sale price or market value in the first year, down 1 percent each year to 1 percent for the 10th year), and (2) controlling interest in an entity having an interest in Connecticut realty over $2,000 value (1.11 percent except in an enterprise zone); Mississippi—leasehold interest in nonproducing oil, gas, or other minerals (3 cents per mineral or royalty acre up to 10 years, 6 cents for 10 to 20 years, and 8 cents for more than 20 years, minimum $1); and Vermont—gains from land sale or exchange of land (amount realized minus the basis as determined by the Internal Revenue Code—from 80 percent for less than four months to 5 percent for more than five but less than six years).

Other issues of real property transfer taxes

Despite their relatively modest revenue potential, transfer taxes are helpful as documentation and as information sources for property tax assessors.

However, transfer taxes can be volatile, being sensitive to changes in economic conditions such as interest rates, mortgage rates, and employment rates. For example, low employment rates may reduce the number of transactions on the market and thus the amount of tax revenue. Volatility in high-value transactions also affects the tax revenue, with drops in economic downturns when the potential asking price of big-ticket property may decline and the selling of these properties is delayed. Property transfer taxes are apt to be regressive, as high-income individuals have more investment options than housing alone and lower-income individuals are more likely to rent and find housing a higher proportion of their consumption.

A study of a 1988 increase in Philadelphia real estate transfer taxes (Benjamin, Coulson, and Yang 1993) showed some evidence that the increase led to lower house sale prices and that sales prices increased prior to the implementation of the tax increase. The study used sale prices of houses over a 30-month period, with a sample of 157 sales from Philadelphia and 195 sales from neighboring Montgomery County. The decrease in sales price was more than would be expected with perfect capital markets, which the authors attribute to imperfect mortgage markets or the news effect of the tax increase.

ADDITIONAL READINGS

Advisory Commission on Intergovernmental Relations [ACIR]. *Intergovernmental Aspects of Documentary Taxes.* Washington, DC: ACIR, 1964.

———. *State and Local Taxes.* ACIR Legislative Program, vol. 3. Washington, DC: ACIR, 1975.

Benjamin, John D., Edward N. Coulson, and Shiawee X. Yang. "Real Estate Transfer Taxes and Property Values: The Philadelphia Story." *Journal of Real Estate Finance and Economics* 2, no. 1 (September 1993): 151–57.

Cordero, Michael. *Field Guide to Real Estate Transfer Taxes.* Chicago: National Association of Realtors, 2003.

International Association of Assessing Officers. *Standard on Ratio Studies.* Chicago: International Association of Assessing Officers, 1990.

Rifkin, Bernard. "Transfer Taxes: A National Survey." *Real Property, Probate and Trust Journal* 19 (Winter 1984): 1035–97.

State Tax Reporter. Chicago: Commerce Clearing House, various dates.

U.S. Department of Commerce, Bureau of the Census. *State Government Tax Collections.* Washington, DC, selected annual issues.

———. *State and Local Ratio Studies, Property Tax Assessment, and Transfer Taxes.* State and Local Government Special Studies, no. 99. Washington, DC, October 1980.

———. *Taxable Property Values and Assessment–Sales Price Ratios.* 1982 Census of Governments, vol. 2 (Washington, DC, February 1984). (*Taxable Property Values,* 1987 Census of Governments, vol. 2; and *Assessed Values for Local General Property Taxation,* 1992 Census of Governments, vol. 2, no. 1, do not contain any de facto levels of assessment [ratios of assessed value to sales price] because no ratio studies were completed for those years.)

Cross-references: excise taxes; property tax, real property, residential; zoning, property taxes and exactions.

Treaties, income tax

Henry J. Louie
U.S. Department of the Treasury

Bilateral agreements to reduce tax-related barriers to cross-border investment.

National economies around the globe are becoming increasingly intertwined as corporations, with growing frequency, expand operations beyond their country of residence. The reasons that companies seek opportunities across national borders are self-evident; vast new markets of consumers and pools of labor and other inputs may await. Rapid advances in technology have also greatly enhanced a company's ability to reach consumers and earn profits in other countries even without engaging in direct investment. In the case of the United States, in 2000 almost a quarter of business receipts of U.S. corporations involved cross-border transactions, up from 15 percent in 1980 (IRS, Statistics of Income Division).

The increasingly global nature of corporate activity presents many challenges to public policies that were designed largely in the context of a more closed economy. This is especially true in the realm of taxation. For instance, when an investor earns income internationally, he becomes subject to the taxation laws of two countries, the country in which the income is earned (the "source state") and his country of residence (the "residence state"). The burden of this double layer of source- and residence-based taxation has the undesired potential to drive the after-tax rate of return of some cross-border activities so low as to render them unprofitable. While domestic law commonly provides relief from international double taxation (an example of this is the U.S. foreign tax credit), statutory remedies may not always sufficiently mitigate excessive taxation that could result from high rates, conflicting definitions of terms, or incompatible transfer pricing principles applied by the source and residence states.

To supplement their unilateral measures and avoid double taxation, countries enter into bilateral income tax treaties that allocate taxing rights on cross-border income between the source and residence state, thus avoiding excessive taxation that could otherwise result if both countries applied the full force of domestic law. Although each agreement is unique, income tax treaties between industrialized countries generally allocate most taxing rights to the residence state, whereas greater taxing rights are commonly allocated to the source state in tax treaties with developing countries. In addition to allocating taxing rights, tax treaties mitigate differences between two tax systems by coordinating definitions and practices of taxation, and establishing avenues through which governments can cooperate in tax administration.

U.S. income tax treaties—background

Each country's tax treaty network varies in size and coverage. In terms of numbers of agreements concluded, the United Kingdom and France are among the world leaders, each with over one hundred tax treaties in force. In contrast, many developing countries have few or no income tax treaties. The 56 income tax treaties of the United States are modest in number compared with the networks of other large economies. However, this belies the effective coverage of the U.S. network; almost 90 percent of all cross-border direct investment involving the United States falls within the ambit of a tax treaty (U.S. Department of Commerce 2002). The United States has an income tax treaty in force with every member country of the Organisation for Economic Co-operation and Development. The first income tax treaties entered into by the United States were with France and Sweden in 1939 (both have since been revised). The oldest U.S. tax treaty currently in force is a 1953 agreement with Greece. In 2004, the U.S. Senate approved treaties with Japan (replacing an existing agreement from 1970) and Sri Lanka.

Main components of income tax treaties

Income tax treaties aim to remove tax-related barriers to nascent cross-border investment by prescribing a level of preliminary economic activity that a company from one country may carry on in the other country without being subject to tax in that country. This is intended to make it easier for companies to explore new markets and business opportunities in the other country. When its economic activity surpasses the prescribed threshold, the company is deemed to have a taxable presence in the source country known as a "permanent establishment" (customarily this is a fixed place of business) and will be taxed by the source state on a net basis on business profits attributable to the permanent establishment.

Another primary feature of income tax treaties is the reduction or elimination of withholding taxes (which are levied on a gross basis) on payments of dividends, interest, and royalties arising in one country to residents of the other country. A treaty also sets forth agreed definitions of dividends, interest, and royalties that both countries must apply. Payments attributable to a permanent establishment in the source state shall be taxed by that state on a net basis.

Beyond providing certainty regarding the extent and level of source-state taxation, tax treaties create a more stable investment climate in other important ways. For example, they confirm that both countries will use transfer pricing methods based on the internationally accepted arm's-length standard when allocating income between the two jurisdictions. They protect nonresident investors from discriminatory tax treatment and establish avenues through which taxpayers who feel they have been wrongly taxed can seek recourse from tax authorities. In addition, tax treaties provide mechanisms through which tax authorities assist each other in tax administration. An example of this are rules that permit authorities to exchange taxpayer information for use in tax assessments and audits (generally, such exchange of information between two countries is prohibited unless sanctioned through a tax treaty or other agreement).

A comprehensive income tax treaty also seeks to remove tax-related impediments to the mobility of labor by providing benefits to individuals who work and live across national borders. Most significant of these are rules which protect service providers from taxation in the source state unless they are deemed to have a "fixed base" (a concept similar to the permanent establishment concept for companies) in the source state, or if their employer has a permanent establishment in the source state that bears the cost of the employee's salary. Also in this vein, tax treaties contain rules that govern the taxation of cross-border pension payments, and in some cases provide rules that recognize (for purposes of deductibility in the host state) contributions to retirement plans in the individual's home state when that individual is temporarily in the host state.

All modern U.S. income tax treaties contain comprehensive provisions intended to prevent residents of third states from obtaining the benefits of a tax treaty (commonly referred to as "treaty shopping"). The United States combats treaty shopping by using a series of objective tests to determine if a resident of a treaty country has a business and economic connection to that country, or simply established legal residence in order to obtain treaty benefits. These "limitation on benefits" provisions have become increasingly popular internationally as countries strive to control treaty shopping.

Economic effects of income tax treaties on investment

While countries have engaged in tax treaties for decades, little empirical research has been done to measure the impact tax treaties have on foreign direct investment (FDI). This may in part reflect the inherent difficulties of the task. Blonigen and Davies (2000) were the first to offer empirical evidence aimed specifically at measuring the effects of income tax treaties on investment. Based on a regression study, they determined that U.S. FDI in a host country was positively correlated with the age of the country's U.S. tax treaty. The study, however, was based on cross-country comparisons, and their conclusions may therefore have suffered from reverse causality; that is, tax treaties were concluded earlier with some countries because bilateral investment levels were already higher than in other countries. In later research, Blonigen and Davies (2001) attempt to address the causality issue by focusing their analysis on tax treaties concluded during the 1970s and 1980s with countries that the authors demonstrate were not leaders in FDI activity with the United States during their sample period (1970–90). To avoid the problems inherent in making cross-country comparisons, they measure how the new treaties affected changes in the levels of investment in those same countries relative to investment levels before each treaty was concluded. In this newer study, Blonigen and Davies are unable to find evidence that those U.S. income tax treaties increased U.S. FDI in the treaty partner. Although before-and-after comparisons may eliminate the causality problem present in the earlier study, the period covered by their data may have been too short to demonstrate the effects of the treaties on cross-border investment.

Louie and Rousslang (2004) use company-level data from U.S. tax returns to measure the effects of both income tax treaties as well as the quality of host-country governance on U.S. FDI in the treaty partner. They are unable to find empirical evidence that the presumably enhanced and more stable investment environment created by income tax treaties leads investors to forego the premium they would otherwise require as compensation for greater investment risk in the absence of an income tax treaty (this finding is generally consistent with Blonigen and Davies 2001). They do find empirical evidence showing that U.S. companies will require a higher rate of return on their investments in countries afflicted by high levels of corruption and political instability because of the relatively uncertain nature of the investment climate. However, because such countries also may make less attractive treaty partners, it is difficult to separate the effects on investment of political stability and corruption from the effects of tax treaties.

ADDITIONAL READINGS

Blonigen, Bruce A., and Ronald B. Davies. "The Effects of Bilateral Tax Treaties on U.S. FDI Activity." NBER Working Paper 7929. Cambridge, MA: National Bureau of Economic Research [NBER], October 2000.

——. "The Effects of Bilateral Tax Treaties on U.S. FDI Activity." Mimeo, University of Oregon, 2001.

Hartman, David. "Tax Policy and Foreign Direct Investment." *Journal of Public Economics* 26 (February 1985): 107–21.

Louie, Henry, and Donald J. Rousslang. "Host-Country Governance, Tax Treaties and U.S. Direct Investment Abroad." Mimeo, U.S. Treasury Department, 2004.

Organisation for Economic Co-operation and Development [OECD] Committee on Fiscal Affairs. *Model Tax Convention on Income and on Capital.* Paris: OECD, January 2003.

U.S. Department of Commerce. *Survey of Current Business.* Washington, DC: U.S. Department of Commerce, 2002.

U.S. Treasury Department. Testimony of Barbara M. Angus, International Tax Counsel, U.S. Treasury Department before the Senate Committee on Foreign Relations on Pending Income Tax Agreements, Washington, D.C., February 2004.

——. *Technical Explanation of New Model Income Tax Convention.* Washington, DC: U.S. Treasury Department, 1996.

——. *United States Model Income Tax Convention.* Washington, DC: U.S. Treasury Department, 1996.

Cross-references: border tax adjustments; income tax, corporate, federal; income tax, corporate, state and local; GATT; unitary taxation.

Tribal taxation, state

Judy Zelio
National Conference of State Legislatures

Because of Indian tribes' legal status, determined by federal-Indian agreements and congressional and presidential action, states and tribes often enter cooperative agreements to resolve issues of levying and collecting taxes within the state whose boundaries surround the tribal government boundaries.

Because of historical treaty and trust responsibilities, the federal government provides funds to Indian tribal governments. But under growing pressure to cut spending, the federal government has appeared increasingly eager for tribal governments to assume a greater share of the costs of reservation services as well as administrative responsibilities. Federal agencies have been directed to treat tribal governments like state governments for funding purposes. Tribal governments traditionally have been reluctant to levy taxes on their members because of general hostility to taxation and the extensive poverty that exists on many Indian reservations. But some tribes are assuming heavier burdens of social and educational services. They also are making greater efforts to raise revenues through operation of various tribal businesses and through

tax collection. This entry discusses state-tribal cooperation on tax issues.

Tribes are governmental entities and retain limited sovereignty under federal law, including the right to make their own laws and be governed by them. Outside the boundaries of a reservation, Indian people are subject to the same state tax laws that apply to everyone else, unless a federal law or treaty confers a special immunity, or unless a state grants exemptions. States have some powers to tax on reservations, but these powers are limited by congressional authority over Indian matters, particularly when Indian economic interests are affected.

Beyond those guidelines, there are three sets of conditions under which states generally may and may not impose taxes on tribal members or on tribal lands.

One is state income taxes. States may tax the income of tribal members who live and work off the reservation, but they may not tax the income of tribal members who live and work on their tribe's reservation. In addition, states may impose taxes on income and nontrust property of Indian individuals who are not members of the tribe on whose reservation they work and reside. States also may tax non-Indians' income earned on a reservation.

A second set is property taxes. State and local governments have the power to levy taxes on most real property owned by non-Indians within reservation boundaries. Similarly, land owned by individual Indian people may be subject to property taxation. Most land owned by tribes and land held in trust by the federal government is not taxable.

The third set is state sales and use taxes. Indian people are liable for state sales taxes on transactions conducted off reservation lands, unless a state chooses to exempt tribal members from this obligation. States may not tax sales to and by tribal members when the transactions occur on tribal or trust lands. However, states may tax sales to and by non-Indians on tribal lands. Non-Indians are liable for state taxes on purchases they make on Indian lands, and tribes are obligated to help collect validly imposed state taxes on such sales.

The Indian Gaming Regulatory Act of 1988 specifies that tribal gambling revenues are not taxable by states. However, at least seven states—Arizona, California, Connecticut, Michigan, New Mexico, New York, and Wisconsin—have reached revenue-sharing agreements with tribes that provide for a portion of tribal gambling revenues to be paid to the state, usually in exchange for economic benefit to the tribe.

Even though states may have the right to impose taxes on Indian lands under certain conditions, the collection of those taxes may be problematic. Retail outlets located on Indian lands and operated by tribes (or in some cases Indian individuals) sometimes offer products—especially gasoline and cigarettes, whose price elsewhere includes state excise taxes—at lower prices than non-Indian businesses can set, creating a competitive advantage for Indian retailers. Sales of this nature can mean tax revenue losses for states. Although in most states non-Indian buyers are obligated to pay state taxes on these retail purchases, they often do not do so unless the Indian retailers agree to cooperate with state officials. Some states and tribes have agreements in place to work on these issues. States and tribes that together examine tax issues as an economic question rather than a purely legal one sometimes find their overall interests served by a tax-sharing arrangement reached through a negotiated agreement.

A state-tribal tax agreement is an arrangement between two governments that addresses specific jurisdictional issues in taxation. State-tribal agreements require government-to-government discussion between tribal and state officials. Such discussions allow tribal and state leaders to talk directly and specifically about revenue needs, economic development objectives, and the practical, political, and economic concerns that arise from tax conflicts. This approach—unlike litigation—enables the tribe and the state, not a court, to decide whether results are satisfactory.

States must negotiate a separate agreement with each tribal government. If a tax conflict is to be resolved, both the tribe and the state must assent to the terms of any agreements. Agreements may not be possible with all tribes within a state's borders. Each state also must consider whether it is necessary to enact an enabling statute before creating such agreements.

Several states have addressed state-tribal tax issues through legislation and regulations: Florida (1977), Mississippi (1986), Montana (1993), Nevada (1991), New Mexico (1992), Oklahoma (1992), Washington (1985), and Wisconsin (1987). Minnesota has tax agreements with 10 different tribes. These agreements, which use formulas to determine refunds to tribes from sales and motor vehicle excise taxes, cigarette taxes, alcoholic beverage taxes, and petroleum taxes, attempt to preserve the tribes' and tribal members' immunity while collecting the state tax legally owed by nonmembers of the tribe.

Other states and tribes also have reached agreements that illustrate a variety of approaches: Louisiana and the Chitimacha Tribe (1990); Nevada and the Reno Sparks Tribe (1991); Montana and the Fort Peck and Assiniboine Sioux Tribes (1992); Oklahoma and the Cherokee Nation and four other tribes (1992); Oregon and the Warm Springs Confederated Tribes (1979); South Dakota and the Standing Rock Sioux, Rosebud Sioux, Cheyenne River Sioux, and Oglala Sioux Tribes (beginning in 1971); and Wisconsin and seven different tribes (agreements were updated in 1996). New Mexico and some Pueblos have explored the development of a unified tax collection system that would allow shared revenues. New York has explored such agreements in the past and may continue to do so because of a 1994 U.S. Supreme Court decision (*New York v. Milhelm Attea and Bros., Inc.*) that upheld a state law imposing certain restrictions on wholesalers' cigarette sales on reservations.

Tax revenues are essential to the operation of government, the delivery of services, and the development of infrastructure. Rather than compete for revenue from the same sources—either non-Indian businesses operating on a reservation or transactions between tribal businesses and non-Indians—a number of states and tribes are choosing to negotiate tax-sharing agreements and forgo expensive and time-consuming litigation. In the negotiation process, both sides can discuss, in a nonadversarial environment, revenue needs and economic concerns.

ADDITIONAL READINGS

Ahene, Rexford A. "Local Government versus Traditional Authority in Sub-Saharan Africa." In *Property Taxes in South Africa: Challenges in the Post-Apartheid Era,* edited by Michael E. Bell and John H. Bowman (177–95). Cambridge, MA: Lincoln Institute of Land Policy, 2002.

Canby, William C., Jr. *American Indian Law in a Nutshell.* 2d end. St. Paul, MN: West Publishing Co., 1988.

Cohen, Felix S. *Handbook of Federal Indian Law, with Reference Tables and Index.* Washington, DC: U.S. Government Printing Office, 1942. Reprinted, Albuquerque: University of New Mexico Press, 1972.

Duncan, Harley. "Issues in State-Tribal Taxation." Bulletin B-232. Washington, DC: Federation of Tax Administrators, 1991.

Endreson, Douglas B. L. *Resolving Tribal-State Tax Conflicts.* Washington, DC: National Indian Policy Center, 1991.

Getches, David H., and Charles F. Wilkinson. *Federal Indian Law: Cases and Materials.* 2d ed. St. Paul, MN: West Publishing Co., 1986.

Michael, Joel. "Taxation in Indian Country." In *Indians, Indian Tribes, and State Government* (57–74). St. Paul: Minnesota House of Representatives, Research Department, 1993.

Montana Committee on Indian Affairs (Eddye McClure, Connie Erickson, Stephen Maly, and Susan Byorth Fox, staff). *The Tribal Nations of Montana: A Handbook for Legislators.* Helena: Montana Legislative Council, 1995.

Pevar, Stephen L. *The Rights of Indians and Tribes: The Basic ACLU Guide to Indian and Tribal Rights.* 2nd ed. Carbondale: Southern Illinois University Press, 1992.

Reed, James A., and Judy A. Zelio. *States and Tribes: Building New Traditions.* Denver: National Conference of State Legislatures, 1995.

Solomon, David, Ndumiso Gola, Mbulelo Ngxesha, and Wycliffe Ndela. "Tribal Land and the Property Tax." In *Property Taxes in South Africa: Challenges in the Post-Apartheid Era,* edited by Michael E. Bell and John H. Bowman (195–214). Cambridge, MA: Lincoln Institute of Land Policy, 2002.

Steinman, Erich. "American Federalism and Intergovernmental Innovation in State-Tribal Relations." *Publius: The Journal of Federalism* 34, no. 2 (Spring 2004): 95–114.

Cross-references: gaming taxation, state; income tax, corporate, state and local; property tax (all topics); retail sales tax, state; tobacco taxes.

Uniform capitalization rules

Gerard M. Brannon

Consultant

When the law requires that an expenditure be treated as a capital rather than a current expense, special rules are promulgated for how this transaction is valued for income tax purposes.

When to expense or capitalize business costs is an aspect of a serious problem in a Haig-Simons income tax—namely, that the requirement for taking account of changes in wealth calls for annual valuations of assets, which in many cases are not provided by market institutions.

Income tax laws in all countries contain compromises with the theoretical demands of annual valuations. For most investment assets, appreciation is ignored until realization. Fixed business assets not sold are presumed to decline in value according to an arbitrary depreciation schedule. In addition, there are many rules, such as those relating to the cost of goods sold and the basis of inventory, distinguishing deductible current expenses, which presumably create no increased value (beyond cash receipts), and capitalizable outlays, which presumably create increased unrealized value equal to the expenditure thereon and therefore are not to be deducted.

If a business cost is incurred to increase future income, the assumption of business rationality suggests that the future income should exceed the current cost by the normal rate of return compounded. The time value of money suggests that a current deduction for the cost and deferral of the related income is equivalent to making the return on the cost tax-free (Johnson 1994; Mundstock 1990).

The policy issue in many of these compromises involves balancing accuracy against complexity in income measurement. Moreover, in some situations better income measurement is sacrificed for an expected incentive effect, which is the case with accelerated depreciation and research and development outlays. A number of cases in which current deduction is allowed, despite related future value, are listed in Section 263 of the Internal Revenue Code.

That partial deductibility of capital expenditures in the U.S. tax law has been characterized as an "uneasy compromise" (Aaron, Pechman, and Galper 1988). Some commentators see the unsatisfactory state of these compromises as the

strongest case for a consumption, or cash flow, tax. Such a tax is equivalent to allowing a deduction for all capital expenditures or an exemption for investment income (Bradford 1986).

Much of the tax reform effort in the United States in the past decade has been toward purifying the income concept by eliminating several accounting compromises that allowed expensing of capital investments. These accounting changes were attractive to Congress, in part because they provided politically acceptable revenue increases. They generally involved short-run "transitional" revenues that appeared larger in the five-year revenue window used in congressional committee reports than their actual steady-state effect. These changes generally reduced currently deductible business costs, leaving higher year-end capital accounts. The changes ranged from tightening of depreciation rules to statutory changes in long-term contract accounting and formulaic deferral of long-term insurance acquisition costs.

One such change was the 1986 enactment of Section 263, which authorized the Treasury to issue detailed regulations to require that certain current outlays be capitalized—that is, included in the basis of property held for sale or use. These rules are commonly referred to as the uniform capitalization or Unicap rules.

Historically, for business taxpayers in wholesale and retail trade, direct costs—the costs of raw materials and wages of workers in production—were not deducted but were allocated as cost of goods. As these goods were sold, the allowable business deduction was for cost of goods sold. Costs allocated to goods not (yet) sold became the basis of inventory. Indirect costs such as taxes and interest were simply deductible.

Manufactured inventories were, by regulation, subject to rules requiring that some indirect costs be capitalized by adding them to the cost of goods sold, the "full absorption" rules. Congress applied similar rules to accounting for long-term contracts in 1982. The Treasury tax reform proposals in 1985 recommended unifying the rules for including indirect costs in costs of goods produced. Congress carried the proposal further by applying it to costs of goods purchased for resale as well as costs of goods produced for either sale or use.

Section 263A broadly requires that nearly all indirect costs be allocated to the cost of goods and thus be deductible only in proportion to the goods sold. Broadly, the indirect costs covered included the allocable portion of the costs that benefit assets produced or acquired for resale, among them general, administrative, and overhead costs; depreciation; fringe benefits; and interest allocable to the goods involved. The regulations allow various simplifications. In certain circumstances, for instance, the taxpayer may establish a historical ratio of indirect to direct inventory costs and use that ratio to comply with the new rules. (Details of this legislation as elaborated by regulations are provided in Garrett and Connor 1992.)

The transition rule provided that the basis of inventories on hand be immediately written up (and be available for deduction again), but the write-up is treated as a change in accounting and thus has to be added to income over a four-year period. Effectively, any extra deductions the taxpayer obtained from the old rule, based on how many related goods were still on hand, were returned to income over a four-year period. Enactment of the Unicap rules was credited with a revenue gain of $35 billion over five years. About 70 percent of this was a result of the transition effect.

Despite the lofty name of "uniform" rules, the new section comes with exceptions. Separate rules provided under the code continue generous deductibility for research and development expenses, for intangible expenses of oil and gas wells, for certain mineral development costs, and for the developmental outlays of tree growers, and these expenses are not allocated to the costs of goods. Some small businesses that are required to do inventory accounting are still exempt from the Section 263A refinements. Farmers who generally are excused from the rigors of accrual accounting will continue to be exempt from any inventory accounting. In addition, many costs in a business, such as advertising aimed at name recognition, are still deductible, thus increasing the business's year-end value. The effect of these outlays is commonly recognized in the sale of a business as "goodwill." (For a discussion of the implication of deducting expenses that give rise to goodwill, see Gravelle and Taylor 1992 and *expensing*.)

Legislative activity requiring more capitalization continued after 1986. The Omnibus Budget Reconciliation Act of 1990 (OBRA90) provided that the acquisition costs for long-term insurance policies should be capitalized and deducted over an arbitrary period. Similarly, three years later, OBRA93 conformed accounting required for dealers in securities more closely to the Haig-Simons concept by requiring that inventories be "marked-to-market"—that is, that unrealized appreciation in inventory securities be included in income.

The Internal Revenue Service has indicated an intention to require capitalization of a number of environmental costs that increase the value of property (Technical Advice Memorandum 920004).

The courts have also been concerned with issues of deductibility versus capitalization. The Supreme Court, in *INDOPCO v. Commissioner* (112 Sup. Ct. 1039 (1992)), held that professional fees incurred in a tax-free acquisition produced significant future benefits and were thus capitalizable, not deductible, even though the fees produced no separate and distinct asset. This decision was seen by some as presaging other situations where historically deductible costs might come

under a capitalization rule (Johnson 1994). The Treasury is concerned that a significant future benefit rule is excessively complicated and prefers to rely on the test that an item should be capitalized if it generates a separate asset of measurable and transferable value. This position has been criticized as excessively favorable to business interests (Sheppard 2002).

ADDITIONAL READINGS

Aaron, Henry, Joseph Pechman, and Harvey Galper, eds. *Uneasy Compromise: Problems of a Hybrid Income–Consumption Tax.* Washington, DC: The Brookings Institution, 1988.

Bradford, David. *Untangling the Income Tax.* Cambridge, MA: Harvard University Press, 1986.

Garrett, Richard, and James Connor. *Unified Capitalization Rules.* Washington, DC: Tax Management Portfolio Series, Tax Management Inc., 1992.

Gravelle, Jane, and Jack Taylor. "Tax Neutrality and the Tax Treatment of Purchased Intangibles." *National Tax Journal* 45 (March 1992): 77.

Johnson, Calvin. "Capitalization after the Government's Big Win in INDOPCO: The Saga Continues." *Tax Notes* 63 (June 6, 1994): 1323.

Mundstock, George. "Franchises, Intangible Capital and Assets." *National Tax Journal* 43 (September 1990): 299.

Sheppard, Lee. "Bringing the Separate Asset Test Back from the Dead." *Tax Notes* 97 (December 20, 2002): 1655.

U.S. Congress, Joint Committee on Taxation. *General Explanation of the Tax Reform Act of 1986.* Washington, DC: Government Printing Office, 1986.

Cross-references: adjusted gross income; inventory accounting; tax versus book accounting.

Unitary taxation

Walter Hellerstein
University of Georgia Law School

Use of the unit rule to determine a multijurisdictional taxpayer's tax base.

Unitary taxation is a methodology for determining a multijurisdictional taxpayer's tax base. It is commonly associated with the taxing methodology employed by U.S. states to determine the portion of a multijurisdictional corporation's income that may be attributed to and taxed by the state. The underlying principle, however, has its roots in property taxation.

The unitary business principle derives from the "unit rule" developed in the late 19th century for apportioning property values of railroad, telegraph, and express companies to state or local taxing jurisdictions. To ascertain the value of a company's property that was properly attributable to the taxing jurisdiction, states and localities would determine the value of the entire operating system and then assign to the state or locality a proportion of the system value based on the ratio of the amount of some identifiable factor within the state to the amount of such factor in the entire system. For example, a railroad's property would typically be apportioned to the state by reference to the ratio of the miles of track within the state to the total miles of track in the system.

When taxpayers complained that taxing jurisdictions were exceeding their power by taking account of extraterritorial values to determine the proper value of the taxpayer's property attributable to the taxing state or locality, the U.S. Supreme Court responded that a railroad must be regarded for most purposes "as a unit"; that the "track of the road is but one track from one end of it to the other and, except in its use as one track, is of little value"; that each taxing jurisdiction through which the railroad passes has "an interest much more important than it has in the limited part of it lying within its boundary"; and that it doubted there was any better mode of determining the value of that portion of the track within the taxing jurisdiction than to ascertain the value of the whole road and apportion the value within the jurisdiction by its relative length to the whole (State Railroad Tax Cases, 92 U.S. 575, 608 (1875)).

The U.S. Supreme Court subsequently expanded the concept of the "unit rule" beyond cases in which there was a contiguous physical unity to cases in which there was operational—but no physical—unity. Thus it sustained the power of a state to consider the value of all of an express company's horses, wagons, and furniture in determining the value of such property that ought to be attributed to the state, even though there was no physical link, such as a railroad track or telephone line, between the taxpayer's in-state and out-of-state property.

When the U.S. Supreme Court began to confront constitutional challenges to apportioned corporate net income taxes in the 1920s, it applied the same "unit rule" or unitary taxation principles it had developed in adjudicating the constitutionality of apportioned property taxes. The Court recognized that when corporate income was "largely earned by a series of transactions beginning with manufacture in [one state] and ending with sales in other states," apportionment was a reasonable method for assigning the taxpayer's income to each of the various states in light of the "impossibility of allocating the profits earned by the processes conducted within its borders" (Underwood Typewriter Co. v. Chamberlain, 254 U.S. 113, 120–21 (1920)).

The existence of a unitary business thus became the critical factor in determining whether a state could consider income earned outside its borders in ascertaining by an apportionment formula the portion of the taxpayer's income that the state could tax. Under the unitary business principle, if the taxpayer was carrying on a single unitary business within and without the state, the state had the requisite connection to the out-of-state activities of the business to justify including in the taxpayer's apportionable tax base all the income generated by the combined effect of the out-of-state and in-state activities. By the same token, if the taxpayer's income-producing activities carried on within the state were not unitary with its income-producing activities carried on elsewhere, the state was constitutionally constrained from including the income arising from those out-of-state activities in the taxpayer's apportionable tax base. In short, as the U.S. Supreme Court

declared, "the linchpin of apportionability in the field of state income taxation is the unitary business principle" (Mobil Oil Corp. v. Commissioner of Taxes, 445 U.S. 425, 439 (1980)).

In delineating the contours of a unitary business, the U.S. Supreme Court focused on the underlying factors that created an organic connection between the corporation's activities within and without the state and that warranted the state's consideration of the corporation's out-of-state activities in determining the income derived from its in-state activities. Thus the Court observed that it was "unity of use and management of a business" (Butler Bros. v. McColgan, 315 U.S. 501, 508 (1942)) that justified the state's including income generated by out-of-state activities in the apportionable tax base. The Court described a unitary business as one characterized by "functional integration, centralization of management, and economies of scale" (Mobil Oil Corp. v. Commissioner of Taxes, 445 U.S. 425, 438 (1980)). It emphasized the fundamental notion that, for a business to be unitary, "the out-of-state activities of the purported 'unitary business' must be related in some concrete way to the in-state activities" (Container Corp. of America v. Franchise Tax Bd., 463 U.S. 159, 166 (1983)), and there must be "some sharing or exchange of value not capable of precise identification—beyond the mere flow of funds arising out of a passive investment or a distinct business operation."

The Court also made clear that everything a taxpayer happened to own did not necessarily constitute part of its unitary business. For example, when North Dakota sought to include the value of interstate railroads' stocks and bonds in its apportionable property tax base, the Court observed that "the only reason for allowing a state to look beyond its borders when it taxes the property of foreign corporations is that it may get the true value of the things within it, when they are part of an organic system of wide extent, that gives them a value above what they would otherwise possess" (Wallace v. Hines, 253 U.S. 66, 69 (1920)). The purpose is not, the Court continued, "to expose the heel of the system to a mortal dart—not, in other words, to open to taxation what is not within the State." Consequently, the bonds secured by mortgage of lands in other states and other property that "adds to the riches of the corporation but does not affect the North Dakota part of the road" could not be included in the apportionable tax base.

The Court applied the same principle when dealing with the question whether items of income could be included in the taxpayer's apportionable tax base. It concluded that a state in which a taxpayer was not domiciled could not require the taxpayer to include income from investments that did not serve an "operational function" in the taxpayer's business (Allied-Signal, Inc. v. Director, Division of Taxation, 504 U.S. 768 (1992)). Consequently, the state could not tax an apportioned share of the gain that the taxpayer derived from its investment in another corporation, when the investment did not serve as working capital for the taxpayer and when the other corporation's activities were unrelated to those carried on by the taxpayer in the taxing state.

In recent years, the most controversial aspect of the unitary business principle has been in its application to multicorporate enterprises. Once formulary apportionment is accepted as a way to divide the income of a single corporation that conducts a unitary business in more than one state, there is no justification, in principle at least, for failing to apply formulary apportionment to the income of a group of controlled corporations that compose a unitary business. The only difference between the two cases lies in the form of business organization—that is, the organization of a business enterprise through subsidiaries, as distinguished from branches, a factor that should not affect a state's power to determine the portion of the income of a unitary business that is fairly attributable to the state.

The pioneer case extending the unitary business principle to the income of a multicorporate enterprise involved a Delaware corporation that owned a chain of retail stores selling shoes and accessories. Each store was organized as a separate subsidiary corporation in the state in which it did business. The parent corporation manufactured no goods but conducted its central management, purchasing, distributing, advertising, and administrative activities in St. Louis. The California subsidiary, which carried on a purely intrastate business, paid for the goods and services it received from the parent at the parent company's cost, plus overhead charges.

The taxpayer sought to have its California net income tax determined solely on the basis of that separate corporation's activities in California. The tax commissioner rejected this approach and instead applied an apportionment formula to the income of the entire chain of stores to determine the net income of the taxpayer that was apportionable to California. The taxpayer contended that the statute did not authorize the extension of the apportionment formula to the income and factors of out-of-state corporations that were not taxable in the state. The court rejected the contention, observing that "no difference in principle is discernible" whether the business is carried on by a single corporation or a group of related corporations. The income of the individual corporate taxpayer could be determined by reference to the combined income of the group of related corporations so long as the individual corporate taxpayer's business "is an integral part of a larger and unitary system" (*Edison California Stores, Inc. v. McColgan,* 176 P.2d 697 (Cal. 1947), on rehearing, 183 P.2d 16, 21 (Cal. 1947)).

The furthest extension of the unitary business principle has occurred in the context of multinational multicorporate enterprises. The U.S. Supreme Court first addressed the constitutionality of the application of the unitary business principle to a multinational multicorporate enterprise in 1983, when California sought to determine the income of a corporation doing business in California by reference to worldwide combined income of all the affiliated corporations that were conducting a unitary business. The Court sustained California's application of the unitary business principle on a worldwide basis to a group of affiliated corporations with a U.S. parent, despite the taxpayer's contention that applying the unitary method led to international multiple taxation and prevented the U.S. government from speaking with one voice in foreign policy.

In 1994, the U.S. Supreme Court reaffirmed the constitutionality of the application of the unitary business principle as a basis for taxing the income of a corporation on a worldwide unitary basis when it sustained the application of the method to a multinational multicorporate group with a foreign parent (*Barclays Bank PLC v. Franchise Tax Board,* 512 U.S. 298 (1994)). The Court reiterated the position it had taken a decade earlier, and it found no significant distinction between the application of the unitary method to a foreign-based, as distinguished from a United States–based, multinational multicorporate group.

The executive branch of the U.S. government, foreign governments, and the international business community have expressed their strong opposition to the states' application of the unitary method in the context of international commerce because it is contrary to the accepted international norm for taxation of related corporations. The international norm strictly respects the separate corporate entity and adjusts the income separately reported by such entities only when transfers between the related corporations do not reflect arm's-length pricing. Even though opponents of worldwide unitary taxation have been unsuccessful in challenging it in court, the states have responded to this opposition legislatively. With a few narrow exceptions, states limit the application of the unitary business principle to U.S. "water's edge" income.

ADDITIONAL READINGS

Hellerstein, Jerome R., and Walter Hellerstein. *State Taxation.* 2 vols., 3rd ed. Boston: Warren, Gorham, Lamont, 1998.

———. *State and Local Taxation.* 7th ed. St. Paul, MN: West Publishing Company, 2001.

Hellerstein, Walter. "State Taxation of Corporate Income from Intangibles: Allied-Signal and Beyond." *Tax Law Review* 48 (Fall 1993): 739–878.

Cross-references: apportionment; income tax, corporate, state and local; nexus.

User charges, federal
Pearl Richardson
Retired, Congressional Budget Office

Charges representing an attempt to match those who pay for federal services with those who receive them.

Although seemingly straightforward, the terms "user charge" and "user fee" have no set meaning. Federal agencies have defined user fees broadly, as prices that the government charges identifiable individuals or entities for a service or good that it controls, and, more narrowly, as prices the government charges to recover its costs of providing special benefits to an identifiable recipient beyond those that accrue to the general public.

The narrower definition rests on a distinction between special benefits to individuals and businesses and general benefits to the public—a distinction that is often clearer in theory than in practice. The leasing of government-owned land to private firms, for example, clearly confers a special benefit; providing for the national defense is obviously a general benefit. But between these extremes lie a wide variety of services that may provide both special benefits to particular individuals or businesses and general benefits to the public.

User charges may take the form of fees or dedicated excise taxes and may include not only payments for benefits but also assessments to lessen a burden that individuals or businesses impose (or might impose) on third parties. Liability-based charges are the mirror image of beneficiary-based charges and are an attempt to match those who pay for corrective actions with those who might cause the conditions requiring them.

There are four distinct types of federal user charges: user fees, regulatory fees, benefit-based taxes, and liability-based taxes.

User fees are payments made by individuals or businesses for goods or services provided by the government, consumed voluntarily, and not generally shared by other members of society. User fees are levied for goods and services that are beneficiary-based. Apart from being charged by the government, user fees are similar in kind, although not necessarily in amount, to payments made in ordinary business transactions in the private sector and often may be for the kinds of goods and services that the private sector also provides.

User fees include royalties on natural resources; canal, bridge, and highway tolls; insurance premiums; and lease and rental payments. They also include charges for the use of federal land, such as for grazing livestock; the use of federal facilities, such as campsites in national parks; services, such as mail delivery, waste disposal, and enrichment of uranium; permits and licenses not associated with regulatory programs; and recurring sales of products, such as power, or resources, such as water, minerals, and timber.

Regulatory fees are charges based on the government's power to regulate particular businesses or activities. These charges include fees for regulatory and judicial services; immigration, passport, and consular fees; Customs Service user fees; fees for testing, inspection, and grading services; patent, trademark, and copyright fees; and registration, filing, permit, and license fees associated with regulatory programs. In general, these charges, which may be beneficiary-based, liability-based, or both, are for functions that are traditionally performed by government and only rarely by the private sector.

Regulatory fees stem from the powers that the government exercises as a sovereign state, such as the powers to levy taxes and duties and to regulate commerce. Regulatory fees include charges for licenses, which the government may require as a condition for permitting a commercial activity, and charges for such services as inspections, which may benefit the fee payer, lessen the fee payer's imposition of costs or risks on others or on society as a whole, or both. Frequently, such charges are for activities undertaken to ensure that a firm has followed prescribed measures to avert environmental or other damage to public health and safety.

The government often sets safety standards for certain industrial activities and charges firms for the cost of inspecting their plants to ensure compliance. From the standpoint of the regulated party, such services seem to benefit the payer little, and thus the charges seem to be more like taxes than fees for service. From the standpoint of the federal government, however, such charges compensate for—and the final prices of goods and services should reflect—the costs that a business imposes or might impose on society when it pollutes or otherwise damages a public resource. Regulatory services thus may be for either direct benefits (such as passports or patents) to identifiable private individuals or measures that safeguard public health and safety. Although all regulatory fees stem from the sovereign power of government, the issue of who benefits from certain types of regulatory activity has been controversial at times.

Benefit-based taxes are charges levied on bases correlated in varying degrees with the use of a publicly provided good or service. Benefit taxes may be proxies for user fees and are usually dedicated to trust or special funds.

Most benefit taxes are related to transportation and nature conservation. More frequently than not, they are excises. Excise and other taxes are user charges when the law creates a relationship between the collection of a tax on a product and the provision of a good or service. Generally, the relationship involves dedicating the tax to a trust or special fund for a purpose that directly or indirectly benefits the payer. For example, taxes on air passenger tickets, air cargo, noncommercial jet fuel, and aviation gasoline, and a head tax on international departures and arrivals, are dedicated to the Airport and Airways Trust Fund, which finances airport construction and improvements, development of the airway system, and a portion of Federal Aviation Administration operations.

Similarly, taxes on gasoline, diesel fuel, gasohol, tires and inner tubes, truck and trailer sales, and highway vehicles weighing more than 55,000 pounds are dedicated to the Highway Trust Fund, which finances the maintenance and improvement of roads and bridges and supports highway safety and traffic control projects within the federal highway system. The taxes on trucks and trailers, highway vehicles, and tires for heavy vehicles are intended to approximate charges for highway wear and tear. (A more exact relationship between charges and use of the highways would also take distance into account.)

Beneficiary-based taxes differ from fees not only in the structure of the charge but also in the degree of connection between the payers of the charge and the benefits or services financed with the proceeds. Taxes are more likely than fees to be levied at uniform rates with less regard for differences in cost for facilities within a system or for differences in the use of the system. For example, nearly all purchasers of gasoline pay the motor fuels excise tax, even though individuals vary widely in their use of interstate highways. The charge is thus more loosely related to the benefit it provides than is, say, a highway toll. But it is more closely related to a benefit than, for example, the income tax.

Benefit taxes frequently involve some amount of cross-subsidy, which occurs when one group pays fees that reflect more than its share of costs, while another group pays fees that reflect less than its share. In these cases, the higher-paying group is subsidizing the lower-paying group. Although typically rarer with fees, cross-subsidies may occur with either fees or benefit taxes.

Liability-based taxes are excises levied for the purpose of abating hazards or compensating for injuries. Where possible, the government collects damages from responsible parties. But at times, taxes on products that might have some connection with the cause of damages serve as a proxy for recovering damages from responsible parties. Thus, for example, certain taxes on gasoline, diesel and other motor fuels, methanol and ethanol fuels, aviation fuels, and fuels used by vessels in inland waterways are dedicated to the Leaking Underground Storage Tank Trust Fund, which covers cleanup costs when damage has occurred and the party responsible is insolvent or fails to deal with the problem. Taxes on domestically mined coal finance the Black Lung Disability Trust Fund, which was set up to compensate miners disabled by pneumoconiosis (black lung disease) or to recompense their survivors. Taxes on vaccines are dedicated to the Vaccine Injury Compensation Trust Fund, which provides funds to compensate people for injuries resulting from prescribed diphtheria, pertussis, tetanus, measles, mumps, rubella, and polio vaccines administered after October 1, 1988.

These charges illustrate a trend toward using dedicated taxes to pay for environmental and other damage imposed on third parties. Liability-based taxes are likely to be reflected in consumer prices and may be said to represent an attempt—however imprecise—to include within the final prices of certain goods the costs imposed on society of producing or consuming them. In this respect, they are analogous to certain liability-based regulatory fees, just as benefit-based taxes are analogous to user fees. Taxes levied on the source of an environmental danger may reduce the activity that causes the danger.

Taxes levied on the sources of health or environmental hazards also may substitute for insurance programs. How much they do depends on the strength of the relationships between the taxes and the potential liabilities they finance. The more direct the relationship, the more effective the tax will be in averting or compensating for actual damage.

The strength of the relationships between current excise taxes and the liabilities they finance varies. For example, the excise taxes dedicated to the Leaking Underground Storage Tank Trust Fund finance control and cleanup once damage has occurred but do nothing directly to reduce or prevent it. These taxes also fall short of functioning as insurance charges because they finance cleanup of damages that occurred before the taxes were enacted. The taxes levied for the Vaccine Injury Compensation Trust Fund, in contrast, cover prospective damages, and thus more closely approximate insurance payments.

ADDITIONAL READINGS

Bird, Richard M. "User Charges: An Old Idea Revisited." In *Tax Conversations: A Guide to the Key Issues in the Tax Reform Debate,* edited by Richard Krever (513–48). Boston: Kluwer Law International, 1997.

Downing, Paul B. "User Charges, Impact Fees, and Service Charges." In *Handbook on Taxation,* edited by W. Bartley Hildreth and James A. Richardson (239–62). New York: Marcel Dekker, 1999.

Hopkins, Thomas D., ed. *Federal User Fees, Proceedings of a Symposium.* Washington, DC: Administrative Conference of the United States, 1987.

U.S. Congress, Congressional Budget Office. *The Growth of Federal User Charges.* Washington, DC: U.S. Government Printing Office, 1993.

"User Charges." U.S. Government, Executive Office of the President, Office of Management and Budget, Circular A-25, *Federal Register,* vol. 52, no. 126, July 1, 1987, pp. 24890–92.

Cross-references: Airport and Airway Trust Fund; benefit principle; environmental taxes, federal; environmental taxes, state; fuel taxes, federal; state formula apportionment; tax price.

Value-added tax and federalism

Michael Keen
International Monetary Fund

The value-added tax (VAT) has proven to be a robust revenue-raiser for national governments around the world; however, a variety of federal contexts have raised the question as to whether subnational governments might strengthen their finances by deploying their own VATs.

It is easy to share the revenues a national VAT raises with subnational governments (e.g., states), either by an explicit formula (as in Germany, for instance, and the maritime provinces in Canada) or by using VAT revenues as simply one source of transfer-financing revenues. The greater challenge is to design a subnational VAT over which each state enjoys some autonomy in setting the rates and base.

Here the difficulties concern implementing an invoice-credit, destination-based VAT as, at present, is invariably applied nationally. Implementing such a tax at a subnational level within a federation raises two problems.

The first is that of cross-border shopping and smuggling, as consumers (and exempt traders) have an incentive to purchase goods or services in whichever state charges the lower tax rate. But this problem is not unique to the VAT (arising, for instance, with state sales taxes) and is typically most severe for highly taxed and easily transportable goods, notably tobacco and alcohol.

The second problem is that the destination principle is typically implemented by zero-rating exports (that is, refunding taxes paid on their inputs by exporters), while bringing imports fully into tax. This has proven to be one of the weakest points of the VAT, as governments (often in developing countries) struggle to balance the need to pay refunds promptly (to prevent the VAT becoming an export tax), the risk of fraud, and the temptation to bolster revenues by delaying refund payments (Ebrill et al. 2001). Dealing with these problems in a federal context, with no border controls between the states— and hence no direct way of verifying claims that goods were exported to another state—is even more problematic.

The latter problem is a profound obstacle to the development of subnational VATs. While Brazil has long had a state VAT, it is of the origin type (the rate is set by the state in which goods are produced), with interstate trade subject to special rates differentiated to shift revenue to the poorer states. Subnational origin-based VATs also exist in New Hampshire, Michigan, and, as a more systematic source of local finance, in the Italian IRAP (Imposta Regionala Sulle Activita Produttive). But the only example of a subnational invoice-credit destination VAT is in Quebec, and it increasingly resembles the federal VAT. It is especially notable that the only two major countries that have not yet adopted a VAT—India and the United States—are federations in which substantial powers in respect of commodity taxation are vested in the state and local governments. (India plans to introduce a state level VAT in April 2005; several previous deadlines have been missed.) They face, in stark form, the fundamental difficulty in designing a state-level VAT that implements the destination principle: can this be done without zero-rating interstate exports?

Proposals

One simple way of avoiding all these difficulties is by implementing subnational VATs on the origin basis combined with redistributing revenue on the basis of aggregate consumption, which is the most recent proposal of the European Commission for the European Union (EC 1996). But such a system taxes production in different EU countries at different rates, and thus not only violates the idea of a neutral EC tax vis-à-vis production efficiency, but also creates incentives to transfer price-value-added into low-tax jurisdictions.

The literature has thus focused on the following proposals that implement the destination principle.

Origin taxation plus clearinghouse

Faced with the problem of protecting national VATs when internal fiscal border controls in the EU were removed in the early 1990s, the European Commission (1985) proposed that each country charge tax at its own domestic rate on exports to other member states, and the importing member then give full credit for that tax against its own VAT (as under the clearinghouse). Under a *clearinghouse* arrangement, the importing country would then reimburse the exporting country for that credit, leaving revenue in each exactly as under zero-rating exports.

The initial proposal was to exactly monitor all border-crossing transactions. One difficulty with this, stressed by Lee, Pearson, and Smith (1988), is that countries would have little incentive to properly monitor claims by their own traders for reimbursement for VAT paid on imports from other member states. Faced also with fears of creating a large bureaucracy, the Commission later suggested that reimbursement instead be on the basis of estimated aggregate consumption or trade flows. An invoice-based clearinghouse arrangement is currently in place, however—and appears to work well—between Israel and the West Bank–Gaza.

Compensating VAT

Under the compensating VAT (CVAT) proposed by Varsano (1999) and analyzed further by McLure (2000), states would zero-rate exports to other states but interstate sales would be subject to a "compensating" tax that would be fully creditable for the importing firm. In this way, interstate sales bear some tax, but the need to reallocate revenue that the clearinghouse deals with simply does not arise. To the extent that interstate purchases are by consumers or other exempt persons, net revenue raised by the compensating VAT would be positive, and the sole question would be how to allocate this between the states. Varsano envisages such a scheme being operated together with a federal VAT (against which CVAT payments could be credited), though logically it might stand alone.

Dual VAT

This is a system comprising both a national VAT and subnational VATs implemented by zero-rating interstate sales, preferably levied on a common base. This does not deal directly with the zero-rating issue, but enables synergies in the administration of the two taxes: an overarching federal administration, for instance, would be well placed to verify claims regarding interstate sales (Mikesell 2003).

Viable Integrated VAT

The viable integrated VAT (VIVAT) of Keen and Smith (1996, 2000) combines a common rate (or rates), throughout the federation, on sales to registered traders with rates on final sales determined by the states themselves. A key difference between this and the other proposals is that, under VIVAT, traders treat sales throughout the federation in the same way, but must identify whether their customers are registered traders (to be charged the rate applied to intermediate purchases) or not (charged the rate applied to final sales in their own state). Keen and Smith argue that the uniform treatment of sales throughout the federation sits well with the notion of a single federal market, and that the distinction between registered traders and others is one which traders may increasingly be required to make (in relation to taxing sales over the internet,

for example). The scheme also has some flexibility in relation to allocating revenues. It might, for instance, be operated together with a clearinghouse (or aggregate statistics used) to allocate revenue across states according to their consumption, or revenue from the intermediate rate could be allocated to the center and the rest to the states. Keen (2001) discusses various possibilities in examining how a VIVAT might be applied in the United States.

Prepaid VAT

The prepaid VAT (PVAT) scheme of Poddar and Hutton (2001) preserves the zero-rating of interstate exports but safeguards revenue by allowing input tax refunds only if the buyer proves that VAT has been paid to the destination state. For those trading routinely, this could be done easily by setting up a PVAT account in the states from which they make purchases. As with customs duties, quick informational flows are needed to prevent goods being held up.

Assessment

With the exception of the dual VAT in Quebec and the clearinghouse in Israel–West Bank/Gaza, none of these schemes has been implemented in practice. Since they are different ways of implementing the same thing, the comparison hinges on the related issues of administrability and the provision of adequate incentives for collection and information sharing between subnational tax authorities. To varying degrees, all require strong interstate cooperation and, ideally, an overarching federal administration, though not necessarily a federal VAT (except in the case of the dual VAT). Detailed discussions of their relative merits are in Bird (2001), Bird and Gendron (2000), Keen (2000), Keen and Smith (2000), and McLure (2000). Little creative thought has been given to the design of supporting incentive systems.

ADDITIONAL READINGS

Bird, Richard. "Subnational VATs: Experience and Prospects." In *Proceedings of the Ninety-Third Annual Conference on Taxation,* edited by James R. Hines Jr. Washington, DC: National Tax Association, 2001.

Bird, Richard M., and Pierre Pascal Gendron. "CVAT, VIVAT, and Dual VAT: Vertical 'Sharing' and Interstate Trade." *International Tax and Public Finance* 7 (2000): 753–61.

Ebrill, Liam, Michael Keen, Jean-Paul Bodin, and Victoria Summers. *The Modern VAT,* Washington, DC: International Monetary Fund, 2001.

European Commission. *Completing the Internal Market.* Luxembourg: Office for Official Publications of the European Communities, 1985.

———. *A Common System of VAT: A Programme for the Single Market.* Luxembourg: Office for Official Publications of the European Communities, 1996.

Keen, Michael. "CVAT, VIVAT, and All That: New Forms of VAT for Federal Systems" *Canadian Tax Journal* 48, no. 2 (2000): 409–24.

———. "States' Rights and the Value-Added Tax: How a VIVAT Would Work in the U.S." In *Proceedings of the National Tax Association,* 195–200. Washington, DC: National Tax Association, 2001.

Keen, Michael, and Stephen Smith. "The Future of Value Added Tax in the European Union." *Economic Policy* 23 (October 1996): 375–411 and 419–420.

———. "Viva VIVAT!" *International Tax and Public Finance* 6 (2000): 741–51.

Lee, Catherine, Mark Pearson, and Stephen Smith. *Fiscal Harmonization: An Analysis of the Commission's Proposals.* Report Series no. 28. London: Institute for Fiscal Studies, 1988.

McLure, Charles E., Jr. "Implementing Subnational Value Added Taxes on Internal Trade: The Compensating VAT (CVAT)." *International Tax and Public Finance* 7 (2000): 723–40.

Mikesell, John. L, "International Experiences with Administration of Local Taxes: A Review of Practices and Issues." Washington, DC: World Bank, 2003.

Poddar, Satya, and Eric Hutton. "Zero-Rating of Interstate Sales under a Subnational VAT: A New Approach." Mimeo. Toronto: Ernst & Young LLP, 2001.

Varsano, Ricardo. "Subnational Taxation and the Treatment of Interstate Trade in Brazil: Problems and a Proposed Solution." In *Decentralization and Accountability of the Public Sector,* edited by Shahid Javed Burki and Guillermo E. Perry. Washington, DC: World Bank, 1999.

Cross-references: apportionment; consumption taxation; destination principle; origin principle; retail sales tax, national; retail sales tax, state and local; tax reform, federal; value-added tax, federalism; value-added tax, national; value-added tax, state.

Value-added tax, national

Alan Tait
International Monetary Fund

Updated by
Robert Ebel
The Urban Institute and World Bank

Tuan Minh Le
World Bank

A broad-based business tax imposed at each stage of the production and distribution process that, when applied nationally, is typically designed to tax final household consumption

The value-added tax (VAT) is a general sales tax on all goods and services. It is levied on the business at each stage of the production and distribution process and is applied on the sale price of goods and services by the taxpayer net of the cost of all purchases from other firms, including previous value-added tax paid on those purchases. The sum of all such VAT payments is equivalent to a tax on final household consumption.

The VAT is therefore distinct from broader-based "gross receipts" or "turnover levy," which is also applied at each stage of the extractive, production, and distribution process, but for which no provision is made for taxpayers to deduct purchases from other firms, including taxes embedded in the cost of those purchases.

Similarly, the VAT is broader than a conventional corporate net income (profits) tax since taxpayers' payments for labor (payroll), land (rents), and capital (interest and net profits) are excluded from the "interfirm purchases" calculation (and thus included in the firm's value-added tax base).

A modern tax

Before its introduction, domestic indirect taxes were typically levied either on a narrow base (excises on various consumer items) or as broad-based turnover taxes. The distortions the turnover tax creates, such as the incentive for vertical integration and tax cascading, provided the case for a less distortionary but still highly revenue-productive tax (Ebrill et al. 2001).

The first VAT proposals were introduced in France in the 1920s and by the Shoup Mission to Japan in 1949. In 1948 France enacted a manufacturers' excise tax that some argue looked like a VAT, but it gave no allowance for capital goods. This was transformed into consumption variant (expensing of capital goods) in 1954; so arguably, this is the date of the first modern VAT.

Beginning in the late 1960s, VAT adoptions accelerated. Today, it is a key source of revenue in 125 countries (and the number is growing), with the United States as one of the few non-VAT countries. The International Monetary Fund (IMF) estimates that about 4 billion people—70 percent of the world's population—live in counties with a VAT. Today worldwide VAT revenue is estimated at $18 trillion. On average, it accounts for 25 percent of national governments' revenues (Ebrill et al. 2001).

Tax base

Value added can be measured either by subtracting from the taxpayer's gross business receipts (sales) the purchases from other firms, or by adding the sum of the payments to the factors of production (land, labor, capital, and entrepreneurship).

Nearly all countries use the subtractive type destination-based VAT pioneered by France. This variant does not actually require the trader to calculate value added by subtracting inputs from outputs, but rather, taxes every sale and purchase and then nets out the difference in tax liabilities for each trader. In this way, a trader registered for the VAT applies the tax rate on all sales. Likewise, the taxpayer pays a VAT charged on his purchases by his suppliers. Then, each taxable period (e.g., a month), the trader credits the tax paid on purchases against the tax liability on sales, and the difference is the net VAT liability to be paid to the authorities. Note that under this method of tax base computation, actual value added is never calculated; it is only the difference between two tax liabilities on outputs and inputs from other firms that is computed. The emphasis placed on each transaction means that the evidence for each sale or purchase, the invoice, becomes a crucial document to monitor and administer the VAT. For this reason, this type of VAT computation is termed a "credit-invoice VAT." The process does not always go smoothly. Delayed VAT refunds can become a problem in developed and developing countries alike. To address this for their clients, the IMF promotes a model for refund processing that includes randomized sampling for auditing high refund-risk claimants.

An alternative subtractive method is to use company accounts to deduct purchases from sales and apply the tax rate to the value added derived from these accounts. This requires calculating value added. This "accounts method" is used in Japan and administered by the income tax administration. The tax base should be the same as that when the credit-invoice method is used, but only a single VAT rate is applied (Japan applies a standard 5 percent rate). Companies make provisional tax payments through the year, and reconciliation is performed when the accounts are closed at the end of the year.

Applied nationally, the sum of all value added at each stage of production equivalent to—but not the same form of tax as—a national retail sales tax (NRST). Unlike a VAT, an NRST is applied only at the final sale to a consumer. At a glance, this may sound like the simpler of the two systems, but as a national tax vis-à-vis the VAT, the NRST creates two problems:

First, the sale at retail is frequently the easiest transaction to misrepresent and the most difficult for the tax administrators to check. This is in contrast to the VAT, in which the taxpayer must record the invoices for each transaction at each stage of production. Thus the VAT provides the better audit trail as well as incorporates a "self-enforcing" element since the taxpayers have the incentive to record all receipts for credits against taxes levied on their sales.

A second key difference between the VAT and NRST is that under the VAT, capital goods can be exempted entirely from the tax. This can be accomplished either through scheduler depreciation (the income variant) or immediate, full expensing (consumption variant). In theory, a tax that solely falls on retail sales would exclude capital goods, which are intermediate in the extraction, production, and distribution process. But the reality is that defining what is and what is not an intermediate or retail sale is such an unwieldy problem that the typical "retail sales tax" may include many intermediate goods (in some U.S. states, as much as 40 to 50 percent of the tax base).

Border tax adjustments and international trade

The VAT has another feature: it is a type of sales tax that can be identified on exports and imports. Under a credit-invoice approach, an exporting business can receive credit for the tax it paid as part of the invoice on an interfirm purchase and yet not be required to levy the tax on the value of its sale for export. That is, the export sale is zero-rated ("VAT free"). Note that this is not the same as being exempt from the tax, since, in this zero-rating case, the business firm (exporter) is a registered taxpayer.

Similarly, the VAT becomes a de facto customs levy for imported products that can be levied at the country's border at a rate identical to that used for domestic production. Thus, imports are taxed, exports are not. Note that zero rating exports and taxing imports works "both ways" among trading countries. Thus, for example, if the export leaves a country at a zero tax rate, it faces a VAT tax at its destination country's domestic VAT rate. Thus, one cannot argue—as one often hears—that the VAT promotes a nation's favorable international trade advantage. Rather, it avoids a trade-tax disadvantage. Note further that the way this border-tax adjustment works gives countries as a group the incentive to adopt the credit-invoice tax calculation.

"Fairness"

Consumption vs. income. A broadly levied VAT is often argued to be the fairest tax. There are two aspects to this argument. The first is that since an individual's consumption is one of the best indicators of living standards, consumption is therefore a fair tax base. The political "catch" to this view is that to the extent the tax is shifted to the final consumer, it will be regressive. This makes the argument for a consumption base a lot more difficult to make in a developed country that also utilizes a broad-based income tax than in a developing country, where establishing an income tax is a challenging administrative task. Recognizing both perspectives, Ebrill et al. (2001) conclude that since (1) very few taxes (including VAT) are well suited to the pursuit of vertical equity and (2) the "first duty" of taxation is to raise revenue with as little distortion of economic activity as possible, for poverty alleviation the focus should be on the expenditure side of the budget. If the tax system is to be used for low-income relief, that relief should be well targeted.

Neutrality. The second argument deals with the question of tax neutrality. This is the clearer and more conventional of the two VAT "fairness" issues. The "best practice" VAT base will be one that includes all goods and services, and that is levied on all business firms regardless of legal organization or industrial structure. As such, it includes proportionally in its base all production factors and thus neither favors or discriminates against one type of input (e.g., capital vs. labor) or organizational structure (e.g., corporate vs. noncorporate).

Thus, to the extent that special provisions and exemptions erode the VAT base, these exemptions also erode its neutrality. Typically exempt sectors include the public sector (even though it may provide services in competition with private firms), basic education and health services (inter alia, the rationale is that it competes with the tax-exempt public sector), and finance and real estate.

From a conceptual perspective, the *finance and real estate* sector is the most problematic. Identifying the tax base for financial services is particularly difficult because the charge for financial services is often a spread that may be only a few basis points. Moreover, only part of this charge is for the service of financial intermediation, and it is impossible to unbundle it from the other fees. This means that banks and insurance companies may pay a VAT on their purchases, which can be substantial (e.g., computers, buildings), and yet cannot readily determine the value added and thereby claim any credit for their payment. As a result, financial services are often exempt, but then subject to in lieu taxation.

Second-hand goods are taxed only on their markup (e.g., the added value of seller fees). However, because there is no VAT on the purchase, no credit is available if a VAT is applied to the value of the final sale. For casual sales this is a straight-forward matter—they are tax-free. The problem arises most prominently with the largest category of second-hand goods: residential houses. The usual treatment is to tax new houses fully, including the builder's profit, but tax only the real estate broker–agents' margins on sales of old houses.

The practice of applying a rule that a minimum *threshold dollar amount* of receipts (or other measure) must be exceeded before the trader or firm becomes subject to tax has merit as a strategy to eliminate from the tax base taxpayers whose administration and compliance costs are greater than their benefit (revenue) generated. Thus, all VAT countries establish some threshold below which a firm is exempt. These thresholds vary greatly. Denmark, for example, taxes all traders with an annual turnover of $1,600. Latvia's threshold is $18,000; Poland, $23,000; Spain, $341,000; Italy, $587,200; and Gabon, $1,742,000 (2001 or most recent year available, Ebrill et al. 2004).

The use of the threshold serves to make a final point regarding efficiency. Although in theory the most neutral (efficient, horizontally equitable) VAT is one that is broadly based and applied, some adjustments to (erosions of) the tax base will enhance, not diminish, economic efficiency. This is the case when the costs of not making the adjustment outweigh the benefits. Again, the obvious case is a threshold in which the revenues generated fall below the administration and compliance costs. A similar case can be made for in lieu taxation of some financial services.

Rates and revenue

The VAT is capable of generating large amounts of revenue (on average, typically equivalent to 5 to 10 percent of GDP worldwide). In practice, many countries use multiple rates that erode the neutrality of the VAT because of political pressures to correct social inequities. Such complications make the VAT more complex and expensive to administer and increase opportunities for evasion.

However, the multirate approach is beginning to lose favor. Before 1990, only one-quarter (12) of the 48 VAT countries employed a single rate. As of 2001, the number had risen to 68 of 125 countries (54 percent). Although there are some equity arguments for differential rates, the argument for the single rate is persuasive: simplifying taxpayer compliance,

facilitating audits, and reducing incentives for misclassification of transactions. In contrast, multiple rates tend to jeopardize revenue by weakening enforcement (Agha and Haughton 1960). However, some evidence exists that a targeted rate reduction and introducing a second VAT rate may produce an equity gain for the poor. But this can be a slippery slide; the more rates proliferate, the more cumbersome the equity-targeting problem becomes, and with a third, fourth, or fifth rate, the offsetting costs of administration and compliance outweigh the tax-rate subsidy benefit (Ebrill et al. 2004).

Who pays?

The conventional assumption is that the VAT is passed forward fully in prices and therefore is regressive in effect. This is an oversimplification. Depending on the elasticities of demand and supply, taxes may be shifted to individuals in one or more roles as consumers or factory suppliers. Nonetheless, that the VAT is an imbedded, broad-based tax on sales certainly gives the tax a regressive character. (Even if it is shifted backward, the burden may fall on suppliers of labor rather than of capital.)

With respect to vertical equity, governments frequently exempt items that feature prominently in low-income household budgets, such as food. Whether all food (e.g., in the United Kingdom) or only "essential" food is zero-rated, this favored treatment erodes revenue, creates definition problems, and can lead to costly settling disputes on what is and what is not a taxable item. Moreover, this approach uses the VAT to try to attain distributional ends for which it is ill suited. The VAT is levied primarily for revenue. There are more appropriate strategies for providing budget relief for the poor.

Inflation?

Because the VAT is an additional tax on household consumption, it may be reflected in higher prices in the form of a once-and-for-all jump in the price level. Whether this will, in turn, lead to an accelerated rise in prices depends on the wage-price nexus and whether the money supply is expanded to accommodate the rising prices. The evidence is that in most countries the introduction of a VAT led to a once-and-for-all shift in the price level, but not to a change in the rate of inflation. Note that this is not to say the overall national tax burden rises. If the VAT replaces other existing taxes in a revenue-neutral shift, the net burden will likely remain unchanged, but the distribution of that burden will change.

Administration

The VAT is not a cheap tax to administer. For the revenue raised to be equivalent to an NRST, more taxpayers must be registered and more tax returns made. Much money is collected only to be returned, and fraud is possible through suppression of sales figures, barter transactions, understated debtors, false invoices, misdescriptions, multiple claims, and fictitious businesses. The costs of VAT administration will vary depending on the exemptions, thresholds, number of zero-ratings, number of tax rates, frequency of audits, and the role played by other collection agencies (e.g., customs).

Cnossen (1994) reports administration costs for a "best practice" VAT for countries in the Organisation for Economic Co-operation and Development (OECD) is estimated at approximately $100 per year, but the range is wide depending on tax complexity (e.g., New Zealand has a VAT of $50 a year in New Zealand with a single rate of 12.5 percent and a simplified tax form that limits the exception to certain types of financial services, residential rental, and supply of donated goods by nonprofits; the United Kingdom, on the other hand, has a VAT of $200 a year with a standard 17.5 percent combined with reduced rates for certain items, such as a zero rate on children's clothing and the standard rate for adult clothing).

Compliance costs are estimated at $500 to $700 a year, and because compliance costs tend to be fixed regardless of business size, the burden disproportionately falls on small traders. This result, plus the fact that small traders often have relatively little market power to forward shift the tax to consumers, further stresses the case for a minimum threshold as well as provides an explanation why small firms are typically the most vigorous VAT opponents.

A United States VAT?

The United States has debated the possibility of adopting a VAT on numerous occasions. It has been seen as a way to reduce the budget deficit, finance Social Security, replace the corporate and personal income tax, and finance new programs. In the United States, a 1 percent broad-based VAT would yield approximately $37.8 billion for each percentage point levied (Bickley 2003). Recognizing that this estimated rate of revenue productivity per percentage point assumes a tax free of likely sectoral and institutional exemptions, the potential productivity of a U.S. VAT is above that of most other VAT-levying countries (e.g., about twice that of Belgium, Denmark, and the United Kingdom; 70 percent higher than Germany; and 30 percent higher than Switzerland).

At what rate shall a U.S. tax be applied? The typical VAT rate worldwide is between 15 and 20 percent. The European Union (EU) standard is 15 percent, although different rates apply in the various member countries, including some as high as 25 percent (Sweden) and as low as 5 percent on certain products in other countries (e.g., domestic fuel in the United Kingdom).

If the United States were to adopt the 15 percent EU standard rate and enact a broad-based tax, the yield would allow, on a revenue-neutral basis, a total reduction of 30 percent of other federal taxes. There is a caution here, however: such a federally administered VAT would be supplemental to existing state and local sales taxes, the combined rates for which range from 4 percent (Hawaii, Guam, and the Virgin Islands)

and 5 percent (Maine, Maryland, and Massachusetts) to 9.4 percent (Tennessee). Thus, with an EU standard rate plus a state and local sales tax, Tennessee would look, tax-wise, something like Sweden.

ADDITIONAL READINGS

Agha, Ali, and Johnathan Haughton. "Designing VAT Systems: Some Efficiency Considerations." *Review of Economics and Statistics* 78 (1960): 303–8.

Bickley, James M. "A Value-Added Tax Contrasted with a National Sales Tax." *Issue Brief for the United States Congress.* Washington, DC: Library of Congress, Congressional Research Service, 2003.

Bird, Richard M. "Review of 'Principles and Practice of Value Added Taxation: Lessons for Developing Countries.' " *Canadian Tax Journal* 41, no. 6 (1993): 1222–25.

Cnossen, Sijbren. "Administrative and Compliance Costs of the VAT: A Review of the Evidence." *Tax Notes* 63 (1994): 1609–26.

Ebrill, Liam, Michael Keen, Jean Paul Bodin, and Victoria Summers. *The Modern VAT.* Washington, DC: International Monetary Fund, 2001.

Georgakopoulos, Theodore. *Harmonization in the European Union: The Destination Principle, Transitional and Definitive VAT Systems, and the Origin Principle.* Athens, Greece: Athens University of Economics and Business, 1997.

Howell, H. "Value-Added Tax." In *Tax Policy Handbook,* edited by Parthasarathi Shome. Washington, DC: International Monetary Fund, 1955.

Le, Tuan Minh. "Making a Value-Added Tax Work: Principles and Practice." Washington, DC, and New Delhi: World Bank Public Sector Group, March 2004.

Organisation for Economic Co-operation and Development [OECD]. *Consumption Tax Trends: VAT/GST, Excise and Environmental Taxes.* Paris and Washington, DC: OECD, 2001.

Tait, Alan A., ed. *Value-Added Tax: Administrative and Policy Issues.* Washington, DC: International Monetary Fund, 1991.

U.S. Department of the Treasury. *Tax Reform for Fairness, Simplicity, and Growth. Vol. 3. Value-Added Tax.* Washington, DC: U.S. Department of the Treasury, 1984.

U.S. General Accounting Office. "Tax Policy: Value-Added Tax: Administrative Costs." Report to the Joint Committee on Taxation, U.S. Congress. Washington, DC: U.S. General Accounting Office, 1993.

Williams, David. "Value-Added Tax." In *Tax Law Design and Drafting,* edited by Victor Thuronyi (164–230). Washington, DC: International Monetary Fund, 1996.

Cross-references: border tax adjustments; consumption taxation; destination principle; flat tax; incidence of taxes; origin principle; retail sales tax, national; retail sales tax, state; tax reform, federal; tax reform, state; value-added tax, state; X-tax; zero rating.

Value-added tax, state

Robert D. Ebel
The Urban Institute

Laura Kalambokidis
University of Minnesota

A broad-based tax on businesses that is designed to measure the net dollar value contributed to the output and income generated in a state.

The bulk of attention regarding the value-added tax (VAT) has been national rather than state. Nevertheless, the idea of a VAT as a broad-based state business tax is not new. The Brookings Institution in separate studies advanced the earliest recommendations for a state VAT for Iowa (1930) and Alabama (1932). In 1932, Hawaii became the first governmental unit in the United States to employ the value-added concept with its business excise tax.

In 1953, with strong support from the automobile sector, Michigan became the first state to adopt a valued-added tax—the business activities tax (BAT)—as a replacement for the corporate net income (profits) tax. While it was adopted as a reasonably pure origin tax, over the years, the BAT became eroded with numerous special provisions, and in 1968 Michigan returned to conventional corporate profits taxation (Ebel 1972; Hines 2003). However, by 1975, legislators determined that the Michigan business tax system had again become unstable and overly complex, and replaced the corporate profits tax (plus several "nuisance" taxes) with its current VAT, the single business tax (SBT). In 1993, New Hampshire became the second state to enact a state value-added tax, the business enterprise tax (BET) (Kenyon 1996).

The tax base

A value-added tax is levied on corporate and noncorporate businesses alike, and at all stages of production and distribution. The taxpayer calculates value added either by subtracting from gross receipts all purchases from other firms (subtraction approach) or by summing up payments to production factors for labor, land, capital, and entrepreneurship—that is, the sum of payrolls, rent, interest, and profits (addition approach). Either way, the size of the tax base is the same. The choice is largely one of administrative convenience and ease of taxpayer compliance. A multistate or multinational business allocates its share of total value added to the taxing state using the same type of apportionment method the states now require for corporate income tax purposes. The firm then determines tax due by applying the tax rate to the apportioned value added attributable to the state. In some cases, the revenue administration may allow separate accounting.

In addition to choosing between adding or subtracting, the policymaker must choose between two variants of the tax base: income and consumption. (A third option, the gross product variant, is rarely given serious consideration because it disallows any deduction for capital.) Here, the issue is how to structure the taxpayer's treatment of capital expenditures. The choice focuses on the period over which the deduction will be allowed. The *income variant* (IVA) includes in its tax base net inventory accumulation and investment on taxpayers' own force account, but then allows for scheduler depreciation of all capital. With the BAT, the "income" label had important administrative and legal implications. Had the Michigan Supreme Court not agreed that the BAT was a variant of an income tax, the application of previous tax court decisions, especially those upholding the right to tax interstate business, would have led to a deluge of litigation.

Under a *consumption variant* (CVA), there is not only no addition to the tax base for investment on own force account, but capital purchases are treated as any other interfirm purchase and are fully expensed (instantaneous depreciation). As originally designed in 1975, the SBT closely approximated a classic CVA (Hines 2003). However, after many years of litigation over the constitutionality of the SBT's site-specific capital acquisition deduction, the capital acquisition deduction gave way to an investment tax credit starting in tax year 2000. Under these arrangements, capital investment is now taxed more heavily than it would be under immediate expensing (Hines 2003).

Like the now-amended SBT, the New Hampshire BET provides an investment tax credit. The SBT is still a CVA, while the New Hampshire BET is like a CVA except that it excludes from its tax base retained earnings and rent paid (which are separately treated under the complementary business profits tax).

Rationale

The rationale for a value-added tax focuses on its merits vis-à-vis its alternatives, the corporate profits and gross receipts taxes, and largely stems from the broad-based nature of the tax.

- *Revenue productivity.* A key attraction of a broad-based tax is that it can generate prodigious amounts of revenue at low statutory rates. This was the case for both Michigan taxes, each of which was enacted during a budget crisis (shortfall).
- *Benefits received, tax base accessibility.* Under a VAT, a business can be seen as a tool for taxing individuals, wherever they reside, for the benefits of public services initially accruing to the enterprise. While this broad-based character often leads to proposals that a VAT replace one or more existing business taxes, New Hampshire determined that the tax could complement a business profits tax, particularly when the competing supplements are a corporate franchise tax and an arbitrary minimum alternative tax (Kenyon 1996).
- *Efficiency.* Because a state VAT is levied on all types of businesses, regardless of organizational form, it can replace taxes that add to administration and compliance costs, thereby reducing those costs. Thus, the SBT replaced the state corporate income tax and six other taxes, including various industry-specific "privilege fees" and local taxes on business property (for which a replacement grant of about 15 percent of SBT revenues was provided). This case for eased administration and compliance is strengthened by the argument that taxpayers can take many entries on the VAT form directly from their financial statements and federal income tax returns.
- *New economy.* Here there are two important arguments. First, because a VAT includes compensation in the tax base, it can better capture total income originating in the

service and trade sectors with low profit margins but high growth than can a net income (profits) tax. The second argument goes to the current debate regarding the taxation of products sold by mail order and via electronic means. At present, Congress, through Public Law (PL) 86-272, bars a state from taxing the income of an out-of-state business when the business activities within the state are limited to soliciting sales and delivering products to in-state customers from an out-of-state distribution point. This rule is often interpreted as meaning that in order to be subject to a state corporate income tax, a firm must have a physical presence in the state. However, a physical presence has not been a requirement for the imposition of state value-added taxes. Thus, legislation is currently under consideration by the Congress that would extend PL 86-272 from income taxes to all business-activity taxes. Its enactment would subject the VAT to PL 86-272, thereby limiting the reach of state VATs (Mazerov 2001).

- *Countercyclical.* Because a large share of the tax base is labor compensation, the VAT can be a tool for decreasing volatility of state tax revenues. In Michigan, where labor compensation is approximately 70 percent of the SBT base (as it also was for the BAT), the SBT has proven to be significantly more stable than a corporate income tax (Michigan Department of Treasury, April 2003). Indeed, the SBT is strikingly countercyclical. Hines (2003) finds that whereas an increase in unemployment by 1 percent in "typical" corporate tax collections leads to a reduction in corporate tax collections of 3.5 percent, the effect of a 1 percentage point increase in the Michigan SBT increases corporate tax yields by 3.0 percent. This countercyclical nature is explained not only by the large compensation component of the tax base, but also by an inverse relationship between the capital acquisition deduction and the robustness of the state economy. In prosperous times, the capital acquisition deduction rises. Conversely, when the state's economy slows, so do capital deductions. Kenyon (1996) finds a similar evidence of stability for the BET.

Why only two states?

Taxation is at least as much a political as an economic phenomenon, and embedded in its merits are the elements of its political weakness (Ebel 1972; Kleine 1978; Bird and McKenzie 2001; Hines 2003). Primary among these is the argument that because the VAT taxes all firms that receive government benefits, a firm with zero or negative profits has a tax obligation. While this makes economic sense (even the zero-profit firm benefits from government services), the "no profit, no tax" argument has political impact. Also politically problematic is that what levels the competitive playing field for all the factors of production, most notably capital, is a loss of an indirect hidden subsidy to another factor—labor—and this can incite political opposition. And third, as discussed in this volume's essay on national VAT, unless there is an appro-

priate threshold for small businesses, the burden to the small business is disproportionately large.

Moreover, in the United States, part of the problem with a state VAT is its lack of familiarity to state policymakers and taxpayers. Although both Michigan taxes started out in relatively "pure" forms, over time they were modified to look more and more like conventional net income (profits) and sales taxes. Consider two illustrations. First, the practice of eroding the VAT base makes it look increasingly like a net income tax. Thus, both Michigan taxes built in credits for "low-profit" firms and adjustments for "excess compensation" (a credit under BAT, an exclusion under SBT).

The second illustration goes to the heart of the conceptual basis for promoting a state VAT. If a state VAT is to achieve its promised merits of a tax based on benefits received, it should be an origin tax. This, in turn, suggests that in its pure form (IVA and CVA alike), the multistate unitary tax base should be apportioned by origin factors. The problem arises when one tries to turn the VAT into a destination-based tax, that is, one that looks more like a destination retail sales tax. The SBT started out with two apportionment formulas: a two-factor formula on payroll and property (both origin) to determine the portion of personal property expenditures, and a formula for other income and expenses of unitary businesses that was equally weighted on total in-state payroll, property, and sales (Hines 2003). Had this two-formula approach stood—and in the end the courts did let it stand—the origin principle would have been adequately preserved. However, over time, the two-factor formula was repealed, and in the three-factor approach the sales tax factor grew from 33.3 to 40 percent (1991–92), 50 percent (1993), 80 percent (1995), and 90 percent (1999 to the present). This converts the initially origin SBT to very nearly a destination tax.

Finally, implementation issues create an obstacle to enacting a VAT. For example, the treatment of rent and interest poses problems. The issue is not whether to include rent in the tax bases, but rather to whom the items should be assigned: the payee or the payer. With respect to rent, the payee approach regards the unit that supplies the land as engaged in a leasing business, and value added is considered as having been created by the supplier and not the user of the resource. Thus, rent received is included as part of taxable receipts and rent paid is excluded from the tax base. The alternative is to disallow a deduction for rent paid and exclude it as a receipt. Interest payments present a similar problem, especially with respect to the unique role of financial institutions. Thus, a bank's net interest may be interpreted as the cost of acquiring funds to loan rather than payments to a factor. The practical solution is often to exempt financial institutions and subject them to in lieu taxation.

Provincial taxation: the dual VAT

The above discussion adopts the view that a state VAT is an origin-based tax. However, if the United States were to move to a broad-based national VAT, then a state-level destination VAT would not only be feasible, but potentially attractive. The example of a successful "dual VAT" (one of several dual VAT variants) is provided by Canada (Mikesell 2003; Bird and Gendron 1998; Fox and Luna 2002). All provinces other than oil-rich Alberta levy a general sales tax, the provincial sales tax (PST), alongside a federal government VAT, the goods and services tax (GST). The GST, adopted in 1991, is levied at 7 percent, and the effective provincial rates range from 0 to 10.7 percent. In five cases, the provinces levy their own PST with tax bases, rules, and regulations different from those of the GST, much like the U.S. system. However, in 1996, New Brunswick, Newfoundland, Labrador, and Nova Scotia agreed to conform fully and combine the GST and the PST into a harmonized sales tax (HST). The HST rate is 15 percent— 7 percent federal and 8 percent provincial. Each business thus collects and remits a 15 percent tax to the Canadian Customs and Revenue Agency, which returns the revenues back to the provinces based on consumption patterns. To preserve a degree of fiscal autonomy, changes in the tax rate or base require agreement of the provinces (Mikesell 2003).

That leaves Quebec, which administers the GST (in accord with federal rules) as well as it is own provincial sales tax (QST). Quebec retains autonomy over tax base and rate and receives a federal payment for collection of the tax.

Concluding comment

The VAT has fared better with tax study commissions than with legislatures. Other than Michigan and New Hampshire, the most serious consideration has been in West Virginia, where in 1977, the legislature narrowly defeated a proposal to replace the state's gross receipts tax (business and occupation tax) with an IVA. Then, in 1970, both West Virginia houses approved an IVA, but the governor vetoed the proposal. And, if Michigan maintains its present legislation to repeal the SBT in 2009, the political record for state value-added taxes will become even more dismal.

Despite this record, it would be unwise to dismiss the VAT. Many argue that in the next decade the states will have to take a new look at the revenue systems to determine if they adequately capture the fiscal flows of a changing economic, demographic, and institutional structure (Steuerle 1998). It will be a new era in state and local reform, and value-added tax will have a place in the dialogue, perhaps even as part of a dual VAT.

ADDITIONAL READINGS

Berghaus, V. Hummell, IV, and William F. J. Ardinger. "The Policy and Structure of the Business Enterprise Tax." *New Hampshire Bar Journal* 34 (December 1993): 5–18, 128–29.

Bird, Richard M., and Pierre Pascal Gendron. "Dual VATs and Cross-Border Trace: Two Problems, One Solution?" *International Tax and Public Finance* 5 (July 1998): 429–42.

Bird, Richard M., and Kenneth J. McKenzie. *Taxing Business: A Provincial Affair?* Ottawa: C.D. Howe Institute, 2001.

Capehart, Robin, and Cal Kent. "Restructuring the West Virginia Revenue System: The Potential for an SBT." In *Proceedings of the Ninety-First Annual Conference on Taxation.* Denver: National Tax Association, 1998.

Cordes, Joseph J., and Harry S. Watson. "Business Franchise and Insurance Taxes in the D.C. Tax System." Paper prepared for the District of Columbia Tax Revision Commission. Washington, DC: National Tax Association, 1998.

Ebel, Robert D. *Michigan Business Activities Tax.* East Lansing: Michigan State University, 1972.

Fox, William F., and LeAnn Luna. "State Corporate Tax Revenue Trends: Causes and Possible Solutions." *National Tax Journal* 55 (September 2002):

———. "Subnational Taxing Options: Which Is Preferred, a Retail Sales Tax or a VAT?" *Journal of State Taxation* (Winter 2003).

Fox, William F., LeAnn Luna, and Matthew N. Murray. "Issues in the Design and Implementation of Production and Consumption VATs for the American States." In *Proceedings of the Ninety-Fourth Annual Conference on Taxation* (188–99). Washington, DC: National Tax Association, 2001.

Hines, James R., Jr. "Michigan's Flirtation with the Single Business Tax." In *Michigan at the Millennium,* edited by Charles L. Ballard, Douglas C. Drake, Paul N. Courant, Ronald Fisher, and Elisabeth R. Gerber (603–28). East Lansing: Michigan State University Press, 2003.

Keen, Michael. "CVAT, VIVAT, and All That: New Forms of VAT for Federal Systems." *Canadian Tax Journal* 48, no. 2 (2000): 409–24.

———. "States' Rights and the Value Added Tax: How a VIVAT Would Work in the United States." In *Proceedings of the Ninety-Fourth Annual Conference on Taxation* (195–99). Washington, DC: National Tax Association, 2001.

Kenyon, Daphne A. "A New State VAT?" *National Tax Journal* 49 (September 1996): 381–409.

Kleine, Robert J. *The Michigan Single Business Tax.* Washington, DC: U.S. Advisory Commission on Intergovernmental Relations, 1978.

Mazerov, Michael. " 'The Business Activity Tax Nexus' Issue." Washington, DC: Center on Budget and Policy Priorities, 2001.

Mikesell, John L. "International Experiences with Administration of Local Taxes: A Review of Practices and Issues." Paper prepared for the World Bank Thematic Group on Taxation and Tax Policy. Washington, DC: World Bank, 2003.

Steuerle, C. Eugene. "Will the Single Business Tax Catch On?" Washington, DC: The Urban Institute, 1998.

Cross-references: apportionment; consumption taxation; destination principle; origin principle; tax reform, state; value-added tax and federalism; value-added tax, national.

Vertical equity

Joseph J. Cordes
George Washington University

A principle used to judge the fairness of taxes, which holds that taxpayers with different incomes should pay different amounts of tax.

Along with horizontal equity, vertical equity is a basic yardstick that is used to gauge whether tax burdens are fairly distributed. The application of the concept of vertical equity differs depending on whether taxes are judged according to the benefit principle or the ability-to-pay principle.

If judgments about tax fairness are based on the benefit principle, and one assumes that the benefits that taxpayers receive from government spending vary with their income, taxation according to the benefit principle would require that taxpayers with different incomes pay different amounts of tax. Depending on how benefits varied with income, however, vertical equity could require that benefit tax burdens be distributed regressively, proportionately, or progressively, depending on whether benefits from public goods and services rose less than proportionately, proportionately, or more than proportionately as income increased.

In contrast to the benefit principle, regressive taxes would not be seen as vertically equitable under the principle of ability to pay. But whether vertical equity under the ability-to-pay standard requires that taxes be proportional or progressive depends on one's views about the distribution of income. Those who believe that the after-tax distribution of income should be the same as the pretax distribution would favor proportional taxes; those who believe that taxes should help to equalize the distribution of income favor progressive taxes, which narrow the dispersion in the distribution of after-tax incomes. In policy debates about the distribution of the tax burden, there has traditionally been a general, though not universal, presumption that vertical equity requires that tax burdens be distributed at least somewhat progressively.

Vertical equity and consumption income taxation

As in the case of horizontal equity, one issue that arises in applying the concept of vertical equity has to do with the measure of income used to group taxpayers into different income groups. The most common yardstick is annual income, comprehensively measured. Many economists, however, believe that a taxpayer's lifetime income is a better measure. One's judgment about whether taxing consumption is inconsistent with vertical equity depends on which definition of income one uses. If the pure version of the life cycle model holds, taxes on consumption will be proportional for lifetime income because current consumption is proportional to lifetime income. The same taxes, however, will generally be regressive for annual income. The reason is that over a taxpayer's lifetime, consumption tends to be a larger share of income in years when the taxpayer's annual income is low, and a smaller share in years when income is high.

Application to tax policy

The concept of vertical equity plays an important role in ongoing evaluation of tax policy. Distributional tables, which describe how the benefits of tax cuts or the burdens of tax increases are distributed by income, play an important role in debates about changes in tax law at both the federal and the state levels.

ADDITIONAL READINGS

Kaplow, Louis. "Horizontal Equity: Measures in Search of a Principle." *National Tax Journal* 42, no. 2 (1989): 139–55.

Kiefer, Donald. "Distributional Tax Progressivity Indexes." *National Tax Journal* 37 (December 1984): 494–513.

Musgrave, Richard. "Horizontal Equity Once More." *National Tax Journal* 43, no. 2 (1990): 113–23.

Cross-references: ability to pay; benefit principle; consumption taxation; fairness in taxation; horizontal equity; life cycle model; progressivity, measures of; tax reform, federal; tax reform, state; value-added tax, national.

Ways and Means Committee

Albert Buckberg

Joint Committee on Taxation

The committee in the House of Representatives that originates tax and other revenue legislation.

The Committee on Ways and Means of the House of Representatives originates legislation to raise the revenues that are deposited in the Treasury to the general fund or to dedicated trust funds, all of which finance the federal government's expenditures.

Its purview includes the individual and corporation income taxes, payroll taxes, and excise taxes that finance spending from the general fund and the trust funds, as well as other taxes—estate and gift taxes, tariffs, and miscellaneous receipts—that are credited to the general fund. Matters relating to the issue of debt to finance budget deficits also fall within the jurisdiction of the committee. Ways and Means also authorizes all spending for several social programs and from certain trust funds.

Financing government

Ways and Means initiates legislation to provide revenues for the federal budget that are grouped under the general fund and the various trust funds. Spending from the general fund is financed by general revenues, which include the individual and corporation income taxes, some excise taxes, estate and gift taxes, tariffs, and miscellaneous receipts. Trust fund outlays are financed directly from revenues dedicated specifically to each trust fund—primarily payroll taxes on wages and salaries and excise taxes. Public debt is issued for two purposes: to finance budget deficits, and as an investment medium for surplus reserves of trust funds.

Individual and corporation income taxes in 1996 accounted for 57 percent of budget receipts, with individual income taxes providing 79 percent of that revenue. Social insurance payroll taxes and contributions—equal amounts contributed by employee and employer—constituted 35 percent of budget receipts. The remaining 8 percent consisted primarily of excise taxes—mostly dedicated to trust funds, estate and gift taxes, tariffs, and miscellaneous receipts.

Ways and Means has initiated all major legislation relating to income taxes since the 16th Amendment to the Constitution authorized such taxation, including major revisions in 1942, 1948, 1962, 1969, 1971, 1978, 1981, 1986, and the more recent changes in 2001–2004. Social insurance tax rates have been changed as needed to finance current trust fund outlays and maintain adequate trust fund reserves. Other trust fund financing has been adjusted for the same purposes, usually in response to revised spending authorizations.

The committee retains jurisdiction over the limit on outstanding federal debt and generally the terms and conditions of the several types and maturities of debt issue. It is conceivable that the debt limit would be increased solely to provide the investment medium for trust fund reserves when the general fund is in balance.

The committee's spending responsibilities vary between setting criteria for distributing benefits from federally administered social programs to establishing guidelines for state administration of some federal social programs. These programs relate to (1) loss of earnings because of retirement, disability, survivorship (widows and orphans), and cyclical unemployment, and trade assistance encompassing unemployment compensation and retraining benefits; (2) protection of retirement pension benefits by regulation of private pension funds; (3) supplemental benefits for needy and disabled elderly; (4) hospital and medical care insurance, primarily for senior citizens, and some medical care for the needy; (5) child welfare and child care; and (6) assorted social service and social welfare programs. The committee originates tax provisions to supplement and facilitate realization of these social objectives.

Committee history

The Committee was established as the Select Committee on Ways and Means on July 24, 1789. It was discharged less than two months later as Alexander Hamilton asserted the suzerainty of the Treasury Department over the fiscal affairs of the new republic. The committee was reestablished as a select committee after Hamilton left office and has operated continuously since the first session of the Fourth Congress. It was designated formally as a standing committee on January 7, 1802.

Until 1865, the committee's jurisdiction included raising revenues, appropriations, and banking. After the Civil War, separate committees were created to deal with appropriations and Ways and Means Committee 501 banking, and until the 1930s the jurisdiction of Ways and Means was limited to (1) revenue measures generally and related to insular possessions, (2) tariffs, (3) reciprocal trade agreements, (4) the bonded debt of the United States, (5) tax-exempt foundations and charitable trusts, and (6) national social security, except health care supported from general revenues. Social programs were added to its jurisdiction beginning with the Social Security Act of 1935, and the scope of such programs has expanded since then.

The committee has 36 members and a sizable professional, technical, and clerical staff. For additional staff resources, the committee relies on the staff of the Joint Committee on Taxation and may request added technical assistance from the Congressional Budget Office, the Congressional Research Service in the Library of Congress, and the Government Accountability Office.

Cross-references: Finance Committee, U.S. Senate; Joint Committee on Taxation, U.S. Congress.

Wealth taxation

Gregg A. Esenwein

Congressional Research Service, Library of Congress

Taxation of the wealth or net worth (assets less liabilities) of an individual.

Although the idea of a national wealth tax is not in vogue, it was once seriously considered by the Treasury Department as a way to retire the national debt incurred during World War I. On the other hand, several European nations currently use and have a long history of using national wealth taxes as a source of revenue. The three main arguments usually advanced in support of wealth taxation are that public services increase the value of property and, hence, should be paid for by property owners; that wealth is the best barometer of ability to pay; and that wealth taxes can be used to help prevent the concentration of wealth among a few individuals or families (Musgrave and Musgrave 1976).

From a theoretical perspective, a tax on lifetime wealth (net worth) is identical to a tax on lifetime net capital income. However, if these taxes are levied annually, their equivalence erodes and they have different incidence and efficiency effects.

The tax base

In theory, a tax on net worth or wealth would be based on a valuation of all of the assets owned by a taxpayer less all of his liabilities on a given date. In other words, an inventory of all assets would be taken and a market value established for each asset. The taxpayer's debts would be subtracted from this aggregation of gross wealth, leaving the taxpayer's net worth as the tax base.

Wealth can take a variety of forms. It can consist of financial assets, land, housing, consumer durables, jewelry, and future earning potential. It is important to note that, in theory, a full accounting of a taxpayer's assets would require including the capitalized value of a taxpayer's future earning potential. For example, at a given point the value of an animal, say a horse, represents the capitalized value of its potential future services. Because the value of the horse would be included in a wealth tax, so too should the capitalized value of the potential future services of the taxpayer himself (Rolph and Break 1961).

As a practical matter, however, it would be virtually impossible to measure accurately the value of an individual's potential future services. As a result, in practice, a wealth tax would be assessed only on physical capital.

At any given point, this stock of assets represents a taxpayer's claim to resources in the economy. These assets also yield a return that can take various forms—of money income, capital appreciation, enjoyment, or satisfaction (Organisation for Economic Co-operation and Development 1988). This relationship between wealth and the return to wealth offers a convenient way to understand the linkage between wealth and income taxation.

Wealth represents a stock, whereas income represents a flow from that stock. Wealth is measured at a point in time, while income is measured over a period of time. Hence, when measured correctly over the lifetime of the taxpayer, taxing wealth is equivalent to taxing net capital income. For example, consider the situation where the average asset yield (the return to wealth including both money and nonmoney yields) is 5 percent. In this situation, a 1 percent tax on wealth would be equivalent to a 20 percent tax on income. The tax owed for every $100 of wealth would be $1, which is the same as taxing the $5 flow (income) from the stock (wealth) at 20 percent.

Equity

It has been argued that wealth would make a more equitable tax base than income. One reason is that wealth gives the holder advantages that can exceed the income derived from it—independence, security, power, and prestige to its owner, for instance. Furthermore, the consumption of wealth requires no sacrifice of current leisure. These advantages mean that the owner of wealth has extra taxpaying capacity that is not fully reflected in the flow of income (OECD 1988). Hence, it is argued that wealth provides a superior measure of ability to pay and as such is better suited than income as a means of distributing the tax burden across the income spectrum.

It has also been argued that wealth is superior to income as a tax base from the perspective of horizontal equity. This line of reasoning suggests that, over a given period, taxpayers with identical incomes do not necessarily have identical command over resources. However, at a given point in time, taxpayers with identical net worth do have the same command over resources. As a result, horizontal equity is best satisfied by assessing the tax on the basis of wealth, not income (Rolph and Break 1961).

These arguments, however, are predicated on the assumption that a wealth tax would be assessed on individuals based on their global holdings of wealth. In practical terms, given the international legal and administrative difficulties of such a procedure, it is highly doubtful that such an assessment could be made. In a second-best world, the validity of the arguments that wealth is a more equitable tax base than income is not as clear.

Efficiency

Some have speculated that because wealth taxation is related to past rather than present or future activities, it might prove to be an efficient tax. It would introduce fewer distortions in labor/leisure choices and savings/consumption choices than would an income- or consumption-based tax. This argument, however, is valid only if the wealth tax is assessed once, and then on the basis of lifetime wealth. An annual wealth tax, on the other hand, would probably have much the same effects on economic efficiency as would an annual income tax.

From a practical perspective, some circumstance is conceivable in which an annual wealth tax used to partially substitute for an income tax might result in some efficiency gains relative to the situation under the annual income tax. These would occur if the wealth tax encouraged investment to move from low-yield to high-yield assets. For example, idle land might be brought into production because under a wealth tax an assessment would be made on the value of the land whether or not it was producing income.

At the same time, however, a wealth tax with high tax rates might increase the distortion in saving-consumption choices. Indeed, at high enough rates, a wealth tax could even produce dissaving (consumption of capital) in the economy.

Many efficiency gains commonly attributed to a wealth tax could be achieved by broadening the base of the income tax through inclusion of imputed and noncash income.

Simplicity/administration

For developing nations, a wealth tax may have some simplicity and administrative advantages over other forms of taxes. These derive primarily from the visibility of the tax base when the majority of assets consists of immovable property. In these situations, it is much easier to value assets such as cattle rather than the income they produce (Musgrave and Musgrave 1976).

In developed nations, however, wealth taxes tend to be rather complex and difficult to administer. This stems from the fact that many assets can be hidden—for instance, jewelry and collectibles—and others are difficult to value. In addition, because net worth is the tax base, liabilities also have to be valued, a task that can be difficult in a sophisticated and mature economy. It does appear that in developed nations with a wealth tax, the wealth tax provides some administrative advantages by serving as a cross-check for income tax returns.

ADDITIONAL READINGS

Dugger, William M. "The Wealth Tax: A Policy Proposal." *Journal of Economic Issues* 24 (March 1990): 133–44.

Musgrave, Richard A., and Peggy B. Musgrave. *Public Finance in Theory and Practice.* Boston: McGraw-Hill, 1976, 342–66.

Organisation for Economic Co-operation and Development [OECD]. *Taxation of Net Wealth, Capital Transfers and Capital Gains of Individuals.* Paris: OECD, 1988.

Rolph, Earl R., and George F. Break. *Public Finance.* New York: Ronald Press Company, 1961, 194–209.

Shoup, Carl S. *Public Finance.* Chicago: Aldine Publishing Company, 1969, 357–81.

Thurow, Lester C. "Net Worth Taxes." *National Tax Journal* 25 (September 1972): 417–23.

Cross-references: fairness in taxation; property tax, real property, business; property tax, real property, residential; zakat.

Willingness to pay for public services

Sumila Gulyani
Columbia University

A concept that can be used to ascertain how much consumers value a particular service and to decide on service options, levels, and prices.

A central tenet of local public finance literature is that government should "provide services that people want and for which they are willing to pay" (Milliman 1972; Gramlich 1994). In its simplest form, an individual's willingness to pay for a good or service reflects her or his preferences and demand function for that good or service. In the case of public and quasi-public goods, estimates of willingness to pay can provide useful information for planning and policymaking—they are being used to, for example, guide decisions regarding the type and quantity of public services to provide, determine the efficient price of a given service, and estimate the economic benefits generated.

Techniques for estimating willingness to pay

There are two approaches to estimating consumers' willingness to pay (WTP) for a public service. The indirect (revealed preferences) approach involves observing actual behavior and modeling this behavior to ascertain willingness to pay. The direct (stated preferences or contingent valuation) approach entails asking people how much they would pay for a hypothetical service or whether they would sign up for a hypothetical service at a specified price. The revealed preferences method can be used, for example, in a situation where a new service has been offered and some but not all households have decided to switch to this service.

The contingent valuation method can be used before the introduction of a new service to test the types of service options and features that users would prefer and, thereby, prevent costly mistakes on the part of the provider. Technically, the revealed preferences method is preferable to the contingent valuation method because what people actually do is a better guide than what they say they will do. When introducing a totally new or unfamiliar product, however, the only option may be to use the contingent valuation method.

The contingent valuation method is prone to three potential types of biases—hypothetical, strategic, and compliance biases (Griffin et al. 1995). The question of whether these methodological issues can be successfully overcome has been the subject of much debate among economists (e.g., Diamond 1996; Diamond and Hausman 1994; Portney 1994). Much of the initial application and testing of contingent valuation techniques occurred in the field of environmental and resource economics, especially in advanced industrialized countries. It is being increasingly applied in developing countries in areas as diverse as water supply and sanitation, health, surface water quality, biodiversity conservation, and recreation, tourism, and national parks (Whittington 1998). Even proponents who claim to have successfully tested this approach and demonstrated its validity, however, emphasize the need for caution; they note that methodological issues in contingent valuation surveys need to be treated with extreme care and that "quick and dirty" surveys are likely to be useless (e.g., Griffin et al. 1995; Choe et al. 1996).

WTP studies as a design and planning tool

Traditionally, decisions related to service types and quantity have been taken by governments and providers based on supply-side factors such as input costs, technology, and standards. Critics argue that these supply-side approaches are highly prone to errors and that a shift to demand-oriented planning can lead to significant improvements in service delivery. Willingness-to-pay studies can provide some of the insights required for demand-oriented planning. This set of arguments is evident, for example, in some of the literature on water supply in developing countries (Gulyani 2001). For instance, studies on willingness to pay for water have shown that, contrary to expectations, poor households in countries such as Kenya, Brazil, and India often want and are willing to pay for seemingly expensive options such as yard taps and private piped connections, rather than staying with theoretically more affordable options such as kiosks and handpumps (e.g., Briscoe et al. 1990; World Bank Water Demand Research Team 1993; Gulyani et al. forthcoming).

Such literature suggests that service providers can use willingness-to-pay studies to test the demand for different services options at specific prices and determine which menu

of options (or levels of service) to develop and offer. They can also use such studies to test explicitly the feasibility of different tariff and financing options, such as the acceptable level of an up-front connection charge and size of monthly payments, for a service and for different segments of service users. Service providers can, thereby, use the willingness-to-pay concept to improve both their planning and service delivery performance.

ADDITIONAL READINGS

Briscoe, John, Paulo Furtado de Castro, Charles Griffin, James North, and Orjan Olsen. "Toward Equitable and Sustainable Rural Water Supplies: A Contingent Valuation Study in Brazil." *The World Bank Economic Review* 4, no. 2 (1990): 115–34.

Choe, KyeongAe, Dale Whittington, and Donald T. Lauria. "The Economic Benefits of Surface Water Quality Improvements in Developing Countries: A Case Study of Davao, Philippines." *Land Economics* 72, no. 4 (1996): 519–49.

Diamond, Peter. "Testing the Internal Consistency of Contingent Valuation Surveys." *Journal of Environmental Economics and Management* 30 (1996): 337–47.

Diamond, Peter A., and Jerry A. Hausman. "Contingent Valuation: Is Some Number Better Than No Number?" *Journal of Economic Perspectives* 8, no. 4 (1994): 45–64.

Gramlich, E. M. "Infrastructure Investment: A Review Essay." *Journal of Economic Literature* 32 (September 1994): 1176–96.

Griffin, Charles C., John Briscoe, Bhanwar Singh, Radhika Ramasubban, and Ramesh Bhatia. "Contingent Valuation and Actual Behavior: Predicting Connections to New Water Systems in the State of Kerela, India." *The World Bank Economic Review* 9, no. 3 (1995): 373–95.

Gulyani, Sumila. "The Demand-Side Approach to Planning Water Supply." In *The Challenge of Urban Government: A Book of Readings,* edited by Maria Emilia Freire and Richard Stren. Washington, DC: The World Bank, 2001.

Gulyani, Sumila, Debabrata Talukdar, and R. Mukami Kariuki. "Universal (Non) Service? Water Markets, Household Demand and the Poor in Urban Kenya." *Urban Studies,* 42, no. 8 (July 2005): 1247–74.

Milliman, Jerome M. "Beneficiary Charges: Towards a Unified Theory." Chapter 2 in *Public Prices for Public Product,* edited by Selma Mushkin. Washington, DC: The Urban Institute, 1972.

Portney, Paul R. "The Contingent Valuation Debate: Why Economists Should Care." *Journal of Economic Perspectives* 8, no. 4 (1994): 3–17.

Whittington, Dale. "Administering Contingent Valuation Surveys in Developing Countries." *World Development* 26, no. 1 (1998): 21–30.

World Bank Water Demand Research Team. "The Demand for Water in Rural Areas: Determinants and Policy Implications." *The World Bank Research Observer* 8, no. 1 (January 1993): 47–70.

Cross-references: fairness in taxation; user charges, federal.

Withholding of taxes
Allen H. Lerman
Department of the Treasury

Deduction of taxes by a payor of wages or other income for direct payment to the taxing authority.

Withholding is a method of tax collection under which a payor of wages or other income deducts (i.e., withholds) the tax from the gross payment due to a worker or other payee. The payor submits the deducted tax to the taxing authority for credit to the account of the payee. Amounts "withheld" may constitute full payment of the tax obligation, or may be credited toward the payment of a tax liability that is determined separately, often after the end of the calendar year. Withholding is an important method of collecting various wage and income taxes from employees. It may also be used to collect taxes on other payments, such as pensions, interest, and dividends, as well as income taxes on payments made to recipients who reside outside the jurisdiction of the taxing authority. Typically, the payor who withholds the tax is treated as an agent of the taxing authority, and the payee receives credit for the tax payment based on the withholding, whether or not the amount withheld is paid to the taxing authority.

Major portions of the federal individual income tax and of the Social Security and Medicare taxes imposed on employees are paid through withholding. Withheld taxes represent just over 50 percent of total gross federal tax receipts. Most states and localities use withholding as the main means of collecting income and wage taxes.

Periodically, employers and other withholding agents pay the aggregate amount of withheld taxes to the taxing authority. Withheld federal income, Social Security, and Medicare taxes (together with the employers' matching Social Security and Medicare taxes) are paid to the Internal Revenue Service (IRS), generally through electronic funds transfers or deposits at local banking institutions which accept the deposits for the Treasury Department. The frequency of required deposits ranges from quarterly to daily, and depends on the amounts withheld but undeposited, or the amounts withheld during previous periods. At the end of each calendar year, employers report each worker's earnings and the amounts withheld from each worker's pay to the IRS. The amounts so reported are reconciled to the aggregate amounts of withheld taxes previously paid by each employer.

Social Security and Medicare taxes

Employees pay a Social Security tax for old age, survivors, and disability insurance (OASDI) of 6.2 percent of earnings up to an annual ceiling ($87,900 for 2004 and indexed annually). Employees are also taxed 1.45 percent of wages, with no annual limit, for the hospital insurance portion (Part A) of Medicare. These taxes are collected via withholding from wage payments. Social Security taxes have been imposed since 1937 and Medicare taxes since 1966, although wage bases and rates have varied.

Because the Social Security and Medicare taxes are imposed at a uniform percentage of covered wages and the amount of wages is known by the employer, the amount of tax withheld generally matches the employee's tax liability. However, because each employer must withhold OASDI on wages up to the annual ceiling, workers who have two or more employers during a year and whose total annual wages exceed the ceiling may have too much OASDI withheld. Workers may treat such excesses as withheld federal individual income tax and may claim credit for the excess on their individual income tax returns.

In fiscal year 2003, about $320 billion was withheld from employee wages for Social Security and Medicare taxes. That represented more than 47 percent of total Social Security and Medicare taxes; another 47 percent came from the employers' matching shares, and the remainder from taxes on self-employment income.

Federal individual income taxes

Federal income tax withholding is required for wages and salaries, which represented over 70 percent of all income reported on income tax returns for 2001. There is mandatory or optional withholding on certain other types of payments, including pensions and lump sum distributions from Individual Retirement Accounts (IRAs), and certain payments to persons living outside the United States. "Backup withholding" may be required for such items as interest, dividends, and proceeds from the sale of certain securities, if the payee does not provide a valid taxpayer identification number to the payor. Unless withholding (or a taxpayer's quarterly payments of estimated taxes) covers either 90 percent (66 $\frac{2}{3}$ percent for farmers and fishermen) of the current year's tax liability as shown on the tax return or 100 percent of the prior year's tax liability, the taxpayer is generally subject to penalties, which are calculated as if they were interest on the underpayment. (Beginning in 1999, to avoid penalties, taxpayers with incomes over $150,000 must have paid, depending on the year, 105 percent to 112 percent of the prior year's tax liability. For 2003 and later years, the required level is 110 percent of the prior year's tax liability.) There are no penalties if the unpaid balance is less than $1,000 ($500 for years prior to 1998).

Withholding was introduced in 1943, when personal exemptions were reduced and typical wage earners, rather than just a small portion of the population, began to have federal income tax liability. Withholding assured that taxpayers would be able to pay their newly imposed tax liabilities even if they became unemployed, incurred other financial crises, or failed to set aside some of their wages for taxes.

For 2001, $773 billion of withheld income tax was shown on 115 million of the 130 million federal individual income tax returns filed (of which 123 million showed some tax payments). Withholding represented 66 percent of the gross income tax payments; the other major forms of payments were estimated tax payments and payments made with tax returns. Overpayments were shown on 79 percent of all tax returns, and refunds were made to 76 percent of tax filers. A total of $237 billion was either refunded to taxpayers or credited to their estimated tax payments for 2002. For returns with overpayments, the average overpayment was $2,316, and the average refund was $2,042.

Since the 1970s, about three-quarters of each year's income tax returns have been overpaid, with aggregate overpayments averaging 15 to 20 percent of tax liability. For 2001, perhaps because taxpayers had not adjusted their tax payments to reflect large declines in dividend income and capital gains realizations compared with the previous year and tax reductions that occurred in mid-2001, nearly 79 percent of tax returns showed overpayments, and aggregate overpayments were more than 25 percent of tax liability. Taxpayers tend to have reasonably similar refunds from year to year. Part-year employment and head of household filing status may lead to overwithholding; workers with two jobs concurrently and two-earner married couples tend to be underwithheld. In the aggregate, the withholding provisions do not have a significant bias toward either over- or underwithholding, although the lack of an automatic, explicit, and precise withholding adjustment for increasingly important personal tax credits may be producing a shift toward overwithholding, especially for taxpayers with children. (In 1992, in an attempt to provide economic stimulus by reducing the aggregate amount of overwithholding, a slight bias toward underwithholding for most workers was incorporated into the withholding rate schedules. Although the underwithholding bias began to be phased out in 1995, as of 2004 a large portion of the bias remains.) Thus, the reasons for persistent aggregate overpayments are not clear. Anecdotal evidence suggests three possibilities, but the relative importance of each is not known: (1) overwithholding may be an intentional form of forced savings; (2) taxpayers may be unable or unwilling to use the withholding system's provisions to match their withholding to their tax liability; or (3) taxpayers may tolerate overwithholding to avoid having unexpected balances due.

Structure of wage and salary withholding

The withholding system for wages and salaries is a simplified analogue of the income tax system. Withholding under graduated rate schedules, which mirror the income tax rate schedules, applies to gross wages less exclusions, which reflect personal exemptions, standard deductions, and, optionally, itemized deductions, tax credits, and other common provisions that affect tax liability.

The assumptions underlying the system are that each worker is employed at only one job at a time, works for the entire year at a constant salary, has no nonwage income, and does not itemize deductions or have any tax credits. When these assumptions hold, withholding for workers who use the "single" or "married filing jointly" filing statuses closely approximates actual tax liability. Workers may have their withholding adjusted to reflect itemized deductions, certain "statutory adjustments to income," tax credits, income not subject to tax, and potential underwithholding from two-job or two-earner situations. Although withholding is designed to cover only the tax liability attributable to wages and salaries, many workers cover their liability on nonwage income via withholding

instead of making quarterly estimated tax payments directly to the IRS.

An Employee's Withholding Allowance Certificate (IRS Form W-4) is used by a worker to provide information to the employer for use in determining the amount of income tax to be withheld from the worker's wages. Every employer is supposed to provide each new employee with a Form W-4, and workers may also complete Forms W-4 at other times to change their withholding. The worker uses the Form W-4's instructions and worksheets along with information about the number of the worker's dependents, other income, tax credits, itemized deductions, and other jobs to determine the number of "withholding allowances" that generally will result in withholding closely approximating tax liability. If the number of allowances calculated is negative, the employee is instructed to claim zero allowances, and further instructions help the employee determine the additional dollar amount of withholding required to minimize or prevent underwithholding. On Form W-4, the worker also indicates whether withholding is to be at the tax rates for single taxpayers or for married taxpayers filing joint tax returns.

Originally, withholding allowances were equivalent to personal exemptions, and the size of a withholding allowance remains the same as the size of an exemption. Currently, all withholding adjustments for a worker are translated into withholding allowances on the Form W-4 worksheets. This method reduces the amount of information the employer needs to handle and permits workers to adjust their withholding without giving employers confidential personal and financial information. (Unless an employee claims an unusually large number of allowances, Form W-4 is not sent to the Internal Revenue Service, and the federal government never knows the number of withholding allowances claimed by specific workers.)

The withholding system includes a little-understood and widely ignored provision, called the special withholding allowance (SWA), which ensures that workers receive the proper amount of the standard deduction for withholding regardless of whether the worker or the married couple have one job or two jobs concurrently. One-job workers and one-earner families who fail to claim the SWA tend to be overwithheld. Failure to understand and claim the SWA may account for a significant portion of aggregate overwithholding. There is an optional adjustment for the potential underwithholding that may occur in a progressive tax system when income is earned from two or more jobs or both spouses have earnings.

All of a worker's allowances may be claimed on one job of the employee (or the employee and spouse), or the allowances may be divided among several jobs. Workers risk being underwithheld and incurring penalties for underwithholding if the total number of allowances claimed on all jobs exceeds the number resulting from the worksheet computations. Employees may claim fewer than the suggested number of allowances, and it appears that many do. The aggregate levels of overwithholding since the mid-1980s and the size of the average tax overpayments might be explained by workers claiming fewer withholding allowances than suggested by the Form W-4 worksheets. Through the mid-1990s, overwithholding was equivalent to workers claiming about two fewer withholding allowances than permitted. Thereafter, workers would have had to underclaim three to four withholding allowances to generate the average overwithholding that occurred.

For each wage payment, the employer uses the information on Form W-4 with the amount of earnings to determine the amount of income tax withheld. Net wages are calculated as gross wages less the value of the withholding allowances claimed by the worker. Withholding is determined from the net wages and the withholding rate schedules, but is increased by any extra dollar amount of withholding requested by the worker. The resulting amount is deducted or "withheld" from the worker's gross wage.

ADDITIONAL READINGS

Lerman, Allen H. "Measuring the Accuracy of Federal Income Tax Withholding." Presentation at the 1988 Annual Meeting of the National Association of Tax Administrators. Mimeograph.

Pechman, Joseph A. *Federal Tax Policy.* 5th ed. Washington, DC: Brookings Institution Press, 1987.

U.S. Internal Revenue Service. *Statistics of Income, Individual Income Tax Returns, 2001.* Washington, DC: U.S. Government Printing Office, 2004.

Cross-reference: tax; tax administration, federal; tax illusion.

X-tax

Jane G. Gravelle

Congressional Research Service, Library of Congress

A simplified consumption tax with a graduated rate structure.

One of the obstacles to shifting to indirect consumption taxes, such as value-added taxes or retail sales taxes, as a substitute for U.S. individual and corporate income taxes, is the regressive nature of these taxes. Direct taxation of consumption rather than income at the individual level, which would permit graduation, would add considerable complexity.

An alternative to these approaches is the Hall-Rabushka "flat tax," where the tax base is the same as a value-added tax base, but firms deduct wages, which are then taxed at the individual level. It is then possible to permit progressivity with respect to the wage portion; indeed, most flat tax proposals allow an individual exemption from the wage tax portion that varies with family characteristics.

The X-tax, proposed by David Bradford, adds a progressive rate structure to the flat tax approach, which allows more flexibility in the distribution of the tax burden across individuals. The tax continues to impose a flat rate on the cash flow of businesses; this cash flow tax is equivalent to a lump sum tax on wealth at the time the tax is imposed. To the extent that lower- and moderate-income individuals do not hold assets or do not hold assets in the form of equity claims or direct holdings, they would not pay the tax on this portion of the consumption base.

ADDITIONAL READINGS

Bradford, David F. "Transition to and Tax Rate Flexibility in a Cash-Flow Type Tax." In *Tax Policy and the Economy,* vol. 12, edited by James Poterba (151–72). Cambridge, MA: MIT Press, 1998.

———. *The X-Tax in the World Economy.* Washington, DC: American Enterprise Institute, 2004.

Cross-references: consumption taxation; flat tax; value-added tax, national.

Z

Zakat (Islamic almsgiving)

Medani Ahmed
University of Khartoum

Sebastiana Gianci
World Bank

An Islamic "voluntary" yet obligatory payment in which a donor self-assesses and customarily has substantial choice selecting the beneficiaries among broadly defined groups of eligible recipients.

Zakat is the amount of money that every adult, mentally stable, free, and financially able Muslim, male and female, is to pay to benefit the poor, new converts to Islam, those in bondage or debt in the service of Allah, and those who administer and collect it.

The base

As one of the Islam's five Akran, or pillars, zakat becomes an obligation (payment) due when, over a lunar year, one controls a combination of income and wealth equal to or above a minimum monetary value, called the Nisaab. Nisaab is calculated by adding the cash value of a zakatable mix of income and assets such as gold and silver, cash, bank notes, stocks and bonds, income derived from rental business, merchandise for business, and livestock. Allowable exclusions from the Nisaab calculation include items for personal needs such as clothing, household furniture, utensils and automobiles, one residence, and equipment and materials for running a business. Other than gold or silver, other metals and precious and semi-precious stones for personal use are also exempt. Allowable deductions include money owed that was borrowed from others for Islamic purpose (e.g., one cannot have borrowed for alcohol consumption or payment to infidels).

There is a Nisaab level for different commodities and rules governing jointly possessed zakatable property (Khultah) such as livestock and crops. Thus, the Nisaab of gold (and other kinds of money and currency) is equal to 85 grams of gold at current market prices; the Nisaab for silver is 595 grams of pure silver. There are web-based and other calculators for converting current gold and silver prices to local currency. Thus, at 2004 rates, the gold Nisaab is approximately US$1,200 and the silver US$150.

Rate

Zakat is a multi-rate system. Thus, the zakat rate for capital assets is often based on a traditional Qur'anic rate of taxing 2.5 percent (1/40) of the value in excess of the Nisaab(s). It is further widely accepted that zakat is payable, at different rates, on crops, harvests, herds, gold and silver, and merchandise. Five to 10 percent of agricultural produce is often also considered "zakatable."

The zakat is not a charitable contribution, nor does it supplant conventional taxes. One may sometimes deduct the amount of the zakat payment from the calculation of certain conventional tax bases, but it is not available as a credit against taxes paid. It is paid at the end of each full Islamic year (lunar 354 days as distinct from the solar 365 days), with collection or payment typically made during Ramadan. If one uses the solar year for accounting, 1.03 multiplies the lunar zakat rate.

Distribution

The Qur'an identifies groups of people eligible to receive zakat. Eight traditional definitions exist and are often interpreted quite differently across the wide range of Islamic jurists opinions and zakat-practicing governments. However, the categories largely focus on providing assistance to those whose material possessions or means of livelihood do not meet basic needs (fakir and miskin), those in debt (gharmin), refugees (ibnus sabil), and orphans. Categories such as those who make efforts to propagate Islam and the fee collector (amil) may also be eligible recipients.

Economics

For many Islamic countries, particularly those with large majority Muslim populations, the zakat is considered both an antipoverty tool and a basis for achieving social solidarity. It is, however, difficult to quantify the revenue impacts since in all but four countries (Malaysia, Pakistan, Saudi Arabia, and Sudan) the payments are often made directly by individuals who self-assess and are not required to report the zakat-base calculation. And, in the case of the state-run operations, the funds are non-transparently off-budget. In Sudan, for example, there is a presidentially appointed Zakat Chamber, but it is not accountable to the Federal Ministry of Finance.

In quantitative importance, the evidence is mixed and uncertain. A recent survey from a study of four Gulf countries finds that of those respondents holding significant investments, the overwhelming majority of them paid zakat on their investments (Guermat et al. 2003). However, research also finds that zakat evasion remains a common problem in Saudi Arabia and Malaysia (Kuran 1992), and anecdotal evidence from some countries (Egypt, Lebanon, and Turkey) suggests a low compliance rate. In the Sudan, zakat contribution relative to total federal tax collections is equivalent to 4.2 percent and 3.1 percent of total federal government revenues (2001 and 2002, respectively). To put this in perspective, in 2002 U.S. state and local corporate income taxes amounted to 3.1 percent of total state and local tax collections.

Finally, there is the question of whether zakat is an effective antipoverty tool. Available (but dated) research on the Malaysian system concludes that the unregulated, traditional system of zakat actually accentuates inequality because the burden falls on the paddy-producing agricultural households, since no explicit allowance is made for them in the traditional sources of Islam (Salleh and Ngah 1981). Conversely, a regulated system of zakat that adopts a more cost-effective system of management and transparent administration has the potential to improve income equality and help alleviate the problem of poverty.

ADDITIONAL READINGS

Guermat, C., A. T. Al-Utaibi, and J. P. Tucker. "The Practice of Zakat: An Empirical Examination of Four Gulf Countries." November 2003.

Kuran, T. "The Economic System in Contemporary Islamic Thought." In *Islamic Economic Alternatives,* edited by K. S. Jomo. London: Macmillan Academic and Professional Ltd., 1992.

Medani, Ahmed, M. Bell, and R. Ali Babiker. "Analysis of Fiscal Policies in the Sudan: A Pro-poor Perspective." UNDP, University of Khartoum, July 2004.

Salleh, I. M., and R. Ngah. "Distribution of Zakat Burden on Padi Producers in Malaysia." In *Some Aspects of the Economics of Zakah,* edited by M. R. Zaman. Gary, IN: Association of Muslim Social Scientists, 1981.

Cross references: charitable deductions; fairness in taxation; wealth taxation.

Zero rating

Joseph J. Cordes

George Washington University

A means of exempting goods from taxation under a value-added tax.

One way of making a consumption-based value-added tax (VAT) less regressive is to tax certain goods, often regarded as necessities, at lower rates at one or more stages of the distribution process. Zero rating is the most common form of reduced rating. How zero rating would work under the credit invoice method of collecting a value-added tax is illustrated in table 1.

The example assumes that the VAT rate for non-zero-rated sales is 5 percent. As may be seen, a $50 tax is initially remitted on value added at the manufacturing stage, but is then effectively forgiven in subsequent stages of production. Wholesalers receive a $50 credit for the VAT that they pay on purchases from manufacturers, but they are not themselves required to pay a VAT on their sales to retailers because the good is zero-rated.

Zero rating of goods under a credit invoice VAT needs to be distinguished from exempting businesses from taxation under a VAT. VAT exemptions are granted, usually to small businesses, as a matter of administrative convenience. When transactions are exempt from a VAT, the business does not remit any VAT on sales, but it also is not allowed to claim a credit for VAT paid on purchases from other producers. Thus, exempting transactions breaks the chain of VAT credits and does not reduce the rate at which goods are taxed.

Zero rating of goods, such as necessities, is often seen as a way of reducing the regressivity of a VAT. But studies have found that zero rating is a fairly ineffective way to reduce the burden of a VAT on low-income consumers. A main reason is that when some goods are zero-rated, the tax rate must be increased on other goods to raise a given amount of revenue.

ADDITIONAL READING

Congressional Budget Office. *Effects of Adopting a Value-Added Tax.* Washington, DC: Congressional Budget Office, 1992.

Cross references: progressivity, measures of; value-added tax, national; value-added tax, state; vertical equity.

TABLE 1. **Zero Rating under the Credit Invoice Method**

	Manufacturing	Wholesale	Retail	Total tax
Sales	1,000	2,000	2,500	
Purchases (excluding VAT)	0	1,000	2,000	
Tax on non-zero-rated sales	50	n.a.	n.a.	
Tax on zero-rated sales	n.a.	0	0	
VAT credit on purchases	0	50	0	
VAT owed	50	0	0	0

Note: n.a. = not applicable

Zoning, property taxes, and exactions

William A. Fischel

Dartmouth College

The division of a municipality into areas in which some land uses are allowed and others are not is often accompanied by fees and taxes that recognize the fiscal impact (costs and benefits) of development and changes in land use.

The fiscal powers of zoning

Zoning is the division of a municipality into contiguous areas (zones) in which some land uses are allowed and others are forbidden. Zoning exists in almost all American urban and suburban areas and, increasingly, in many rural areas. The only large city not to have zoning is Houston, Texas, whose citizens persistently vote against its adoption. Only Hawaii has statewide zoning, but a few states, such as Vermont, Oregon, and Florida, supervise and coordinate local decisions more closely than others. Even in active states, however, it is rare for a statewide body to tell a local government that it must accept a proposed land use that it does not want.

The 1928 Standard State Zoning Enabling Act was one of the most successful model acts to have been promulgated by the federal government. Its influence is still evident. The words of the original model offer a useful summary of the enormous grant of authority to the municipality over the private use of land:

Section 1: Grant of Power.—For the purpose of promoting health, safety, morals, or general welfare of the community, the legislative body of cities and incorporated villages is hereby empowered to regulate and restrict the height, number of stories, and size of buildings and other structures, the percentage of a lot that may be occupied, the size of yards, courts, and other open spaces, the density of population, and the location and use of buildings, structures, and land for trade, industry, or other purpose.

This grant of power allows communities to regulate in great detail the capital-to-land ratio. It is not merely use and lot size that are regulated; the height and bulk of buildings and their placement on the lot are clearly subject to the collective will.

Section 2: Districts.—For any or all of said purposes the local legislative body may divide the municipality into districts of such number, shape, and area as may be deemed best suited to carry out the purposes of this act; and within such districts it may regulate and restrict the erection, construction, reconstruction, alteration, repair, or use of buildings, structures, or land. All such regulations shall be uniform for each class or kind of buildings throughout each district, but the regulations in one district may differ from those in other districts.

The police power, of which zoning is an example, does not require the community to compensate owners of private property for adverse effects of regulations. The uniformity of regulations within zones mentioned above is scant protection for landowners because the community can determine the borders of the zones. These borders and permissible uses within each zone may be changed by the vote of municipal authorities. Modern ordinances also often make many of the uses subject to discretionary review by a zoning board or planning commission whose members are elected or appointed by elected officials.

Section 3: Purposes in View.—Such regulations shall be made in accordance with a comprehensive plan and designed to lessen congestion in the streets; to secure safety from fire, panic, and other dangers; to promote health and the general welfare; to provide adequate light and air; to prevent overcrowding of land; to avoid undue concentration of population; to facilitate adequate provision of transportation, water, sewerage, schools, parks, and other public requirements. Such regulations shall be made with reasonable consideration, among other things, to the character of the district and its peculiar suitability for particular uses, and with a view to conserving the value of buildings and encouraging the most appropriate use of land throughout such municipality.

The comprehensive plan mentioned above is seldom a binding document, but it sometimes has been invoked by courts as a reason to overturn ad hoc rezonings. Like zoning rules and boundaries, however, comprehensive plans can be changed when the community desires. They are not a major constraint on a municipality's ability to determine what it will become.

Section 3 also clearly indicates the fiscal basis for zoning. The possibility of substitution of regulation (which does not require much public expenditure) for taxation and spending is evident in zoning's earliest documents. A community that limits the number of new houses to avoid school costs is not doing something that is prohibited by most zoning enabling acts.

Economists sometimes regard "fiscal zoning" as different from "externality zoning," but the law makes no such distinction. Many state statutes and state courts nowadays are hostile to the more blatant forms of fiscal zoning. As a result, modern planning documents hide such intentions in more acceptable language (Bogart 1993). Expressions of the need to preserve farmland, wetlands, open space, and historic sites in areas that might otherwise be developed are usually all that are necessary to preserve the ordinance from attack as fiscally motivated "exclusionary" zoning.

Commonplace in zoning is that no landowner has a vested right to any particular zoning law. Changes that are adverse to a landowner's prospective use of the land occur often. Established uses and buildings, however, are seldom required to be discontinued or reconfigured when zoning laws are changed. Existing homeowners, who are most influential in suburban zoning politics, can thus impose higher standards for development for prospective residents without cost to themselves. Either their own homes are in an already developed zone separate from developable space in the rest of the community, or their homes are grandfathered under the newly restrictive law.

Recently, a few development-minded landowners have persuaded courts to order government agencies to pay for the consequences of downzonings (that is, more restrictive regulations) under the constitutional rubric of "regulatory takings." This doctrine poses some financial threat to local government discretion, but it is typically successful only when the landowner can claim that there is no economically viable use under the new law, a condition easily avoided by most governments.

Fiscal zoning and property taxes

Zoning permits municipalities to shape their property tax bases without having to compensate disappointed landowners. The newer (less developed) the town, the more power it typically has, but even older communities can govern their tax base extensively through controls on redevelopment. The controls are typically negative; communities cannot force landowners to build things they do not want. But given the comprehensiveness of zoning regulation, private developers must be willing to accommodate community concerns before that can proceed.

The community's fiscal concerns have several dimensions. The simplest to describe is that communities want new development to "pay its own way" in property taxes. If it is assumed that an additional residence will cause, on average, an expenditure of $5,000 a year in municipal services (schools, roads, police), and that local property taxes average 2.5 percent of value per year, the community will "break even" if the new residence is assessed for tax purposes at $200,000.

Zoning cannot declare what the minimum housing value must be. However, as the foregoing list of powers indicated, quality constraints that accomplish the same outcome (a $200,000 house) are within both the authority and the ability of the local government. Even unsophisticated governments can hire consultants who have access to published rules of thumb for what each type of development costs the town.

Hamilton (1975) showed that if there is a large number of communities free to tailor the level of services to the tastes of households (and there are scores in most large metropolitan areas), the property tax will have no deadweight loss under fiscal zoning. People will shop around—vote with their feet—for the community that best fits their demands in the manner proposed by Tiebout (1956).

Hamilton showed that in these circumstances residents will get exactly what they pay for in local taxes. The property tax becomes a fee for local services, and there is no misallocation in those local government services that are limited to the borders of the community. Shirking payment is impossible because zoning makes it impossible to build a house that confers a fiscal benefit on the occupant. The property tax has no deadweight loss in this system because it is not really a tax at all.

The Tiebout-Hamilton system is criticized often as being unrealistic. But that is only because it is an elegant model. In reality, local officials do not simply aim for a single minimum-

value house. They are able to discriminate among land uses and put them in a limited zone even if they cannot ban them altogether. Thus, condominiums and apartments, which may seem a fiscal burden to a community, may be allowed, but only in such a small area that their prices will be quite high, reflecting the fiscal benefit of owning or renting them (Hamilton 1975). In other cases, community authorities may require that developers of housing also come up with projects whose fiscal payoffs cover the burdens of more schoolchildren. More subtle applications of zoning regulation can control the population of the community (Ellickson 1977; Oates 1977), although explicit racial zoning was banned long ago.

Exaction, property taxes, and municipal corporations

Zoning allows community authorities to demand that developers pay monetary exactions to offset their fiscal or environmental costs. Exactions are essentially payments in exchange for discretionary zoning permits or rezonings. Exactions were traditionally used to pay for public infrastructure that was added to accommodate new development. Even this limited range of exactions suggests that the property tax "subsidy" to suburban sprawl or new development is a dubious claim. To look only at the average property taxes paid by a new development overlooks the exactions and payments in kind (developer-built sidewalks and sewers) that were very likely required as a condition of zoning approval and that offset the higher costs.

Since 1970, exactions have become so expansive that the developer can be required to pay for community services that have only the most tangential relationship to the project (Altshuler and Gómez-Ibáñez 1993). Courts that are protective of property rights have attempted to limit the extent of exactions, but economists should not be fooled into believing that this makes much difference. The reason exactions are paid at all is that the community's regulatory powers are so great. Developers who do not respond to community concerns simply do not get permits.

A more general theory, one that goes beyond the Tiebout-Hamilton model, sees zoning as the means by which municipal corporations establish and protect their collective property rights (Nelson 1977; Fischel 1985). These corporations are run for the benefit of those who control the political power in the community. In the suburbs, where politics is reasonably transparent, the median voter gets his or her way, and the median voter is a homeowner. Social scientists would profitably view suburban zoning and, for that matter, all municipal activity, as being managed to maximize the net worth of homeowners (Sonstelie and Portney 1978).

The homeowner, not being irrational, does not want to "minimize taxes," because minimization could be achieved by providing no local services, which would reduce the value of the home. The homeowner does not want to maximize the nonresidential tax base because the hazardous waste processor that is willing to pay 90 percent of the local taxes may nonetheless reduce home values. Nor does the homeowner want to exclude all commercial activity in order to maximize the local quality of the environment. That would mean forgoing other good things like convenience to commercial activities and, in more rural places, nearness to jobs.

The model that both fits the facts and is consistent with economic theory is that the homeowner is interested in maximizing net worth (Brueckner 1983). That usually (although not always) means maximizing the value of the homeowner's major asset, the home. (The exception occurs when a homeowner can be bought out by a developer with a lump sum payment that offsets the reduction in the home's value.) The approach nevertheless recognizes that transaction costs and agency problems may forestall value-enhancing deals among homeowners, land developers, and political authorities.

In bigger cities, such problems may sometimes result in zoning that serves interests other than those of the voters. But this is no different in principle from the agency problems that affect private corporations, in which managers sometimes govern in ways that are not in the best interest of stockholders. Zoning is a critical part of a municipality's corporate charter, and public finance would be richer if it recognized this fact.

ADDITIONAL READINGS

Altshuler, Alan A., and Jose A. Gómez-Ibáñez, with Arnold M. Howitt. *Regulation for Revenue: The Political Economy of Land Use Exactions.* Cambridge, MA: Lincoln Institute of Land Policy, 1993.

Bogart, William T. " 'What Big Teeth You Have!' Identifying the Motivations for Exclusionary Zoning." *Urban Studies* (December 1993): 1669–81.

Brueckner, Jan K. "Property Value Maximization and Public Sector Efficiency." *Journal of Urban Economics* 14 (July 1983): 1–15.

Ellickson, Robert C. "Suburban Growth Controls: An Economic and Legal Analysis." *Yale Law Journal* 86 (January 1977): 385–511.

Fischel, William A. *The Economics of Zoning Laws: A Property Rights Approach to American Land Use Controls.* Baltimore, MD: Johns Hopkins University Press, 1985.

Hamilton, Bruce W. "Capitalization of Intrajurisdictional Differences in Local Tax Process." *American Economic Review* 66 (December 1966): 743–53.

———. "Zoning and Property Taxation in a System of Local Governments." *Urban Studies* 12 (June 1975): 205–11.

Ladd, Helen F. *Local Government Tax and Land Use Policies in the United States.* Northampton, MA: Edward Elger, 1998, chapter 2.

Nelson, Robert H. *Zoning and Property Rights.* Cambridge, MA: MIT Press, 1977.

Oates, Wallace E. "The Use of Local Zoning Ordinances to Regulate Population Flows and the Quality of Local Services." In *Essays in Labor Market Analysis,* edited by Orley Ashenfelter and Wallace Oates. New York: John Wiley, 1977.

Sonstelie, Jon C., and Paul R. Portney. "Profit Maximizing Communities and the Theory of Local Public Expenditures." *Journal of Urban Economics* 5 (April 1978): 263–77.

Tiebout, Charles M. "A Pure Theory of Local Expenditures." *Journal of Political Economy* 64 (October 1956): 416–24.

Cross references: infrastructure financing; property tax, real property, business; property tax, real property, residential; Tiebout model; transfer taxes, real estate.

About the Editors

Joseph J. Cordes is a professor of economics and public policy, public administration, and international affairs at George Washington University. Previously, he was a Brookings economic policy fellow in the Office of Tax Policy in the U.S. Department of the Treasury and served as a senior economist on the Treasury's tax reform project in 1984. He was also deputy assistant director for tax analysis at the Congressional Budget Office, a visiting fellow at the Urban Institute, and a member of the research advisory council at the National Center on Nonprofit Enterprise. His current research focuses on state and local tax policy, the economics of nonprofit organizations, how public policies intended to mitigate the effects of natural hazards affect economic development, and various aspects of state and federal tax policy.

Robert D. Ebel is a senior fellow at the Urban Institute in the Urban-Brookings Tax Policy Center. Prior to joining the Urban Institute, he served as lead economist for the World Bank Institute's program on public finance, intergovernmental relations, and local financial management. He has also been the World Bank's technical representative to the Sudan peace consultations, chair of the District of Columbia Tax Revision Commission, executive director of the National Tax Association, executive director/director of special (ad hoc) state revenue study commissions, and director of finance research for the U.S. Advisory Commission on Intergovernmental Relations. He has published widely and been a regular columnist for two major U.S. newspapers. Dr. Ebel received the Steven D. Gold Award and, as a member of the West Bank/Gaza team, received the World Bank President's Award for Excellence.

Jane G. Gravelle is currently a senior specialist in economic policy in the Government and Finance Division of the Congressional Research Service (CRS). She specializes in the economics of taxation, particularly the effects of tax policies on economic growth and resource allocation. Recent papers have addressed consumption taxes, dynamic revenue estimating, investment subsidies, capital gains taxes, individual retirement accounts, estate and gift taxes, family tax issues, charitable contributions, and corporate taxation. In addition to her work at CRS, she has written numerous articles in books and professional journals, including recent papers on the behavioral responses to consumption taxes and tax depreciation. She is the author of *The Economic Effects of Taxing Capital Income* and the editor of the *Tax Expenditure Compendium*, published every two years by the Senate Budget Committee. She is also president of the National Tax Association.

Index